Generalist Practice with Organizations and Communities

Generalist Practice with Organizations and Communities

Brooks/Cole Empowerment Series

FIFTH EDITION

KAREN K. KIRST-ASHMAN
University of Wisconsin–Whitewater

GRAFTON H. HULL, JR.
University of Utah

BROOKS/COLE
CENGAGE Learning

Australia • Brazil • Japan • Korea • Mexico • Singapore • Spain • United Kingdom • United States

BROOKS/COLE
CENGAGE Learning™

**Brooks/Cole Empowerment Series:
Generalist Practice with Organizations
and Communities, Fifth Edition**
Karen K. Kirst-Ashman
Grafton H. Hull, Jr.

Executive Editor: Linda Schreiber-Ganster

Acquisitions Editor: Seth Dobrin

Developmental Editor: Robert Jucha

Assistant Editor: Alicia McLaughlin

Editorial Assistant: Suzanna Kincaid

Media Editor: Elizabeth Momb

Marketing Coordinator: Gurpreet Saran

Marketing Communications Manager:
Tami Strang

Content Project Manager: Michelle Clark

Design Director: Rob Hugel

Art Director: Caryl Gorska

Print Buyer: Judy Inouye

Rights Acquisitions Specialist: Dean
Dauphinais

Production Service: Christian Holdener,
S4Carlisle Publishing Services

Photo Researcher: Bill Smith Group

Text Researcher: Sue Howard

Copy Editor: Kirsten Balayti

Cover Designer: Lisa Langhoff

Cover Image:
Christopher Chan/Getty Images

Compositor: S4Carlisle Publishing Services

For product information and technology assistance, contact us at
Cengage Learning Customer & Sales Support, 1-800-354-9706.
For permission to use material from this text or product, submit all requests online at **www.cengage.com/permissions**.
Further permissions questions can be e-mailed to
permissionrequest@cengage.com.

Library of Congress Control Number: 2010933991

ISBN-13: 978-0-8400-3374-1
ISBN-10: 0-8400-3374-5

Brooks/Cole

20 Davis Drive

Belmont, CA 94002-3098

USA

Cengage Learning is a leading provider of customized learning solutions with office locations around the globe, including Singapore, the United Kingdom, Australia, Mexico, Brazil, and Japan. Locate your local office at **www.cengage.com/global.**

Cengage Learning products are represented in Canada by Nelson Education, Ltd.

To learn more about Brooks/Cole, visit
www.cengage.com/brookscole

Purchase any of our products at your local college store or at our preferred online store **www.CengageBrain.com.**

Printed in the United States of America
1 2 3 4 5 6 7 14 13 12 11 10

To Gary A. Kirst, Ruth Kirst, Michael Hull, and Patrick Hull

Brief Contents

Table of Contents

Council on Social Work Education Educational Policy and Accreditation Standards by Chapter

Generalist Practice with Organizations and Communities, Fifth Edition now includes explicit references to the Educational Policy and Accreditation Standards' (EPAS) ten core competencies and 41 recommended practice behaviors. The column on the right informs the reader in which chapters the icons appear.

The 10 Competencies and 41 Recommended Practice Behaviors (EPAS 2008):	Chapter(s) Where Referenced:
2.1.1 Identify as a professional social worker and conduct oneself accordingly	1 and 12
a. Advocate for client access to the services of social work	
b. Practice personal reflection and self-correction to assure continual professional development	2, 3, 5, 9, 11, and 15
c. Attend to professional roles and boundaries	1, 3, and 11
d. Demonstrate professional demeanor in behavior, appearance, and communication	13
e. Engage in career-long learning	12, 13, and 14
f. Use supervision and consultation	2 and 12
2.1.2 Apply social work ethical principles to guide professional practice	1, 4, 9, 10, and 12
a. Recognize and manage personal values in a way that allows professional values to guide practice	1, 4, and 12
b. Make ethical decisions by applying standards of the National Association of Social Workers Code of Ethics and, as applicable, of the International Federation of Social Workers/International Association of Schools of Social Work Ethics in Social Work, Statement of Principles	1, 12, 13, and 14
c. Tolerate ambiguity in resolving ethical conflicts	1 and 12
d. Apply strategies of ethical reasoning to arrive at principled decisions	1 and 12

The 10 Competencies and 41 Recommended Practice Behaviors (EPAS 2008):	Chapter(s) Where Referenced:
2.1.3 Apply critical thinking to inform and communicate professional judgments	1, 3, and 14
a. Distinguish, appraise, and integrate multiple sources of knowledge, including research-based knowledge and practice wisdom	10 and 14
b. Analyze models of assessment, prevention, intervention, and evaluation	
c. Demonstrate effective oral and written communication in working with individuals, families, groups, organizations, communities, and colleagues	2, 3, 6, 7, 10, and 14
2.1.4 Engage diversity and difference in practice	1, 2, 4, 6, 7, and 12
a. Recognize the extent to which a culture's structures and values may oppress, marginalize, alienate, or create or enhance privilege and power	1, 4, and 11
b. Gain sufficient self-awareness to eliminate the influence of personal biases and values in working with diverse groups	
c. Recognize and communicate their understanding of the importance of difference in shaping life experiences	
d. View themselves as learners and engage those with whom they work as informants	
2.1.5 Advance human rights and social and economic justice	4
a. Understand forms and mechanisms of oppression and discrimination	7 and 11
b. Advocate for human rights and social and economic justice	1, 3, 4, and 8
c. Engage in practices that advance social and economic justice	7 and 9
2.1.6 Engage in research-informed practice and practice-informed research	1, 9, 10, and 14
a. Use practice experience to inform scientific inquiry	
b. Use research evidence to inform practice	1, 7, and 11
2.1.7 Apply knowledge of human behavior and the social environment	1 and 9
a. Utilize conceptual frameworks to guide the process of assessment, intervention, and evaluation	1, 4, 8, 10, 11, and 13
b. Critique and apply knowledge to understand person and environment	8
2.1.8 Engage in policy practice to advance social and economic well-being and to deliver effective social work services	1, 11, and 12
a. Analyze, formulate, and advocate for policies that advance social well-being	5, 6, 7, and 8
b. Collaborate with colleagues and clients for effective policy action	3, 6, 9, and 11

The 10 Competencies and 41 Recommended Practice Behaviors (EPAS 2008):	Chapter(s) Where Referenced:
2.1.9 Respond to contexts that shape practice	
a. Continuously discover, appraise, and attend to changing locales, populations, scientific and technological developments, and emerging societal trends to provide relevant services	4, 8, 13, and 14
b. Provide leadership in promoting sustainable changes in service delivery and practice to improve the quality of social services	3, 5, 6, and 7
2.1.10 Engage, assess, intervene, and evaluate with individuals, families, groups, organizations and communities	1, 6, 7, and 9
a. Substantively and affectively prepare for action with individuals, families, groups, organizations, and communities	5, 9, 13, and 14
b. Use empathy and other interpersonal skills	2 and 13
c. Develop a mutually agreed-on focus of work and desired outcomes	3
d. Collect, organize, and interpret client data	1, 5, and 8
e. Assess client strengths and limitations	1, 5, 6, 7, 9, and 11
f. Develop mutually agreed-on intervention goals and objectives	4, 6, 7, and 9
g. Select appropriate intervention strategies	2, 5, 6, 7, 9, and 12
h. Initiate actions to achieve organizational goals	4 and 5
i. Implement prevention interventions that enhance client capacities	7
j. Help clients resolve problems	
k. Negotiate, mediate, and advocate for clients	3 and 11
l. Facilitate transitions and endings	12
m. Critically analyze, monitor, and evaluate interventions	6, 7, 9, and 10

Preface

This book is a guide to generalist social work practice with organizations and communities. The three adjectives that best describe this text are *relevant, practical, and readable.* Here generalist practice is clearly defined. Specific macro practice skills are presented in a straightforward and interesting manner. Applications to actual macro practice situations are emphasized throughout, as is the importance of client system strengths. The content is geared to both the undergraduate and graduate generalist practice sequences.

This text aims to fulfill five major goals. First, it provides a *readable* and *practical guide* to working in and with organizations and communities (macro practice). Numerous real-world situations and case examples are presented to make the material interesting and relevant. Organizational and community theories are examined and linked to practice applications.

Second, the text proposes a *generalist perspective* to emphasize how micro, mezzo, and macro skills are interlinked. This generalist approach assumes that group (mezzo) skills are built on a firm foundation of individual (micro) skills. Likewise, skills involved in working with organizations and communities (i.e., macro skills) rest on a solid base of both micro and mezzo skills. This text links the three levels of practice—micro, mezzo, and macro—so that students can clearly see how all three skill levels are used in everyday practice situations. Whole chapters and numerous examples throughout illustrate how micro and mezzo skills can be applied to macro practice situations. The text also aims to structure how students think about clients and clients' problems so that, as practitioners, they will automatically explore alternatives beyond the individual and small-group levels.

The text's third basic goal is to provide clearly defined, *step-by-step frameworks* for thinking about and initiating macro change in organizations and communities. A model to decide whether to pursue macro intervention is proposed. Additionally, a procedure for pursuing the macro intervention process is described.

The text's fourth goal is to identify, explain, and examine *specific skills* useful in macro practice and address significant issues relevant to this practice. Skills include working with the media, using new technological advances, fundraising, grant writing, working within court settings, evaluating macro practice effectiveness, resolving ethical dilemmas in macro contexts, and advocating for diverse populations-at-risk.

The fifth basic goal is to present material that is not only relevant and interesting but also *inclusive of major concepts currently considered critically important by the social work profession and social work educators. New material and concepts from the recently revised accreditation standards have been included.* (Please see the subsequent section on new content.) Enhanced emphasis is placed on critical thinking, empowerment and resiliency, and the global context of social work practice. The text adopts a generalist perspective, emphasizes evaluation of practice and research-informed practice, focuses on the use of various communication skills with colleagues and community members, demonstrates the appropriate use of supervision, and examines practitioner functioning within organizational structures and communities.

The Empowerment Series: Relationship with the Educational Policy Statement and Accreditation Standards(EPAS), and Professional Competencies

This book is part of the Brooks/Cole, Cengage Learning Empowerment Series and addresses accreditation standards established by the Council on Social Work Education (CSWE).[1] Our intent is to facilitate programs' ability to link content provided in this textbook with expectations for student learning and accomplishment. As is true in almost all learning, students must acquire knowledge before they are expected to apply it to practice situations.

CSWE has identified 41 practice behaviors that operationalize ten core competencies which are critical for professional practice (CSWE, 2008). For clarity, we have alphabetized in lower case the practice behaviors under each competency. **"Helping Hands" Icons** located within paragraphs clearly show the linkage between content in the textbook and specific practice behaviors and competencies. Each icon is labeled with the specific practice behavior or competency that relates directly to the content conveyed in the paragraph. For example, an icon might be labeled EP [Educational Policy] 2.1.2, which is the competency, "apply social work ethical principles to guide professional practice" (CSWE, 2008). Accredited social work programs are required to prove that students have mastered all practice behaviors for competence as specified in the EPAS. (Please refer to www.cswe.org for the EPAS document.)

For all icons, **"Competency Notes"** are provided at the end of each chapter. These "Competency Notes" explain the relationship between chapter content and CSWE's competencies and practice behaviors. They also list page numbers where icons are located and this content is discussed. A summary chart of the icons' locations in all chapters and their respective competency or practice behavior is placed in the front matter of the book.

A new **Practice Behaviors Workbook** has replaced the Student Manual for this edition, A range of experiential exercises provide students with opportunities to develop the practice behaviors in class or as part of their homework, facilitating their mastery over practical aspects of social work and minimizing the need for programs to develop additional assessments.

New Content

New content includes:

Chapter 1

- *a modified definition of generalist practice that reflects newly revised accreditation standards*
- *updating of the three models of community organization*
- *introduction of the International Federation of Social Workers (IFSW)/International Association of Schools of Social Work (IASSW) Ethics in Social Work, Statement of Principles*
- *advocacy for human rights and the pursuit of social and economic justice*
- *concepts of diversity, including gender identity and expression, immigration status, and political ideology*
- *practice-informed research and research-informed practice*
- *identification as a professional social worker.*

Chapter 2

- *consultation.*

Chapter 3

- *more globalization examples*
- *more critical thinking examples.*

Chapter 4

- *political-economy theory and the institutional perspective of organizations.*

Chapter 6

- *the appropriate use of memos and e-mails.*

Chapter 8

- *more information on globalization*
- *examples using refugees and immigrants*
- *increased content on rural communities.*

Chapter 9

- *more content on rural social work*
- *more critical thinking questions regarding ethics.*

Chapter 10

- *updated resources for social workers.*

---

1. Please note that this content addresses standards posed in EPAS. In no way does it claim to verify compliance with standards. Only the Council on Social Work Education Commission on Accreditation can make those determinations.

Chapter 11

- *more content on immigrants and refugees–global issues*
- *more content on advocacy organizations*
- *brief description of early Obama actions.*

Chapter 12

- *updated discussion of the National Association of Social Workers Code of Ethics*
- *discussion regarding the International Federation of Social Workers (IFSW)/International Association of Schools of Social Work (IASSW) Ethics in Social Work, Statement of Principles used for ethical decision making at the global level.*

Chapter 13

- *updating of resources for social workers.*

Chapter 14

- *elimination of redundant content on computer hardware*
- *use of technology in Obama and other political campaigns*
- *updating of resources for social workers*
- *global use of technology*
- *more content on unsuccessful grants*
- *example of grant application to serve rural areas.*

Student Ancillaries

Developed to accompany the Fifth Edition of *Generalist Practice with Organizations and Communities* is the new *Practice Behaviors Workbook*. This includes practice exercises that teach and assess EPAS-recommended practice behaviors to help better prepare students for competent social work practice. In addition, a robust student companion Web site includes study quizzes, weblinks, and materials to help prepare students for interviews and develop effective resumés prior to graduating from their programs. Please work with your local Brooks/Cole, Cengage Learning representative to receive a sample copy of the *Practice Behaviors Workbook*, or to request a bundle ISBN so that the text and workbook come packaged together at the bookstore.

Many generalist curricula developers structure their practice sequences so that courses oriented toward practice with organizations and communities follow practice courses concerned with smaller systems. An assumption is that students will use the content of this book close to the point at which they seek employment. Therefore, a chapter on constructing resumés and finding jobs is available online at the Book Companion Site at www.cengagebrain.com. This content is provided because it is vital to students, yet it is not necessarily incorporated elsewhere in the curriculum.

Instructor's Ancillaries

A suite of instructor's resources makes teaching with the Fifth Edition of *Generalist Practice with Organizations and Communities* easier. An online Instructor's Manual provides useful information for faculty, and an electronic Test Bank includes chapter-specific test questions that can be used immediately or adapted as needed. A complete set of PowerPoint lecture slides is also available for download. Finally, as with every text in the Brooks/Cole Empowerment Series, a *Curriculum Quick Guide: A Resource for Program Accreditation* is available in print and online. The "quick guide" provides a chapter-by-chapter overview of textbook and supplementary resources correlated to the EPAS recommended Competencies and Practice Behaviors to help programs prepare self-study materials more efficiently. Visit the companion Web site at www.cengagebrain.com or work with your local Brooks/Cole, Cengage Learning representative to have sample copies sent to you.

This text is one of two for generalist practice, the other being *Understanding Generalist Practice,* Sixth Edition (Kirst-Ashman & Hull, 2012), which focuses on micro skills within a generalist context. Both stress the links across all practice levels necessary to maintain the generalist perspective. The texts can be used in sequence because one builds on the other, or each can be used independently in conjunction with other practice texts. Either can be used to integrate a generalist perspective at some point during the practice sequence. Similar supplementary materials are also available for *Understanding Generalist Practice.*

Acknowledgments

We wish to express our sincere gratitude to Vicki Vogel for her exceptional professionalism, technical assistance, and support, and Karen Thomson for her excellent assistance. Our heartfelt appreciation goes to Gary A. Kirst, who provided steadfast consultation and expert feedback during our initial conceptualization of the book. We would like to thank Robert Jucha, Developmental Editor; Seth Dobrin, Acquisitions Editor; Arwen Petty, Assistant Editor; Rachel McDonald, Editorial

Assistant; and the other staff at Brooks/Cole who enthusiastically encouraged us to pursue this endeavor and provided ongoing help and support. Many thanks to Trent Whatcott, Senior Marketing Manager, for his admirable marketing skills and backing and also Michelle Clark, Content Project Manager, who has done an excellent job of guiding us through the production process. We extend our earnest thanks to Nick Ashman, who provided support, encouragement, and patience in addition to many hours of cooking and other domestic sustenance while Karen wrote. Appreciation is also due to Dr. Jannah Mather for her intellectual and emotional support for Grafton's work on this edition.

We would especially like to thank our reviewers who provided us with expert and excellent feedback to improve our work. They include: LaTra Tracy Rogers, Metropolitan State College of Denver; Sandra Shelly, Ball State University; Lorri Glass, Governors State University; and Marilynne Ramsey, Indiana University South Bend.

CHAPTER 1

Introduction to Generalist Practice with Organizations and Communities

- *What is **generalist practice** anyway?*
- ***Why** do you need to know what generalist practice is? Social work is social work, isn't it?*
- *Why do you need to understand **organizations and communities** if you will be working primarily with individual clients and families?*
- *Aren't **supervisors and administrators** supposed to take care of all those agency and policy matters?*
- *What is **agency life** like?*

Why Do You Need the Content in This Book?

Social workers practice with and within organizations and communities. In order to understand your agency, work effectively within it, advocate for resources on your clients' behalf, and improve service delivery for them, you must learn skills to use in the agency and community contexts.

Most social workers first entering professional practice view their jobs as work that deals mostly with individuals and families. Obviously, work takes place within an agency and community context. You usually need an agency to employ you in order to have an arena in which to practice your social work skills. Practice takes place within an agency environment. Similarly, the agency functions within a community milieu. Agencies provide resources and services to communities through their workers' performance. The point is that both agencies and communities are extremely significant factors in your ability to practice social work. However, it is probably easier for you to

focus on the individual clients sitting right in front of you and give little if any thought to the larger picture of the agency and the community. It is tempting to think in terms of administrators and politicians assuming responsibility for any administrative and political matters that arise within agencies and communities.

Yet, a much broader approach to social work practice exists, one that emphasizes the importance of the many systems engulfing and affecting large numbers of individual clients. Inevitably, you will work within some agency or organization context. Therefore, the agency's rules and policies will have a monumental impact on what you can and cannot do for your clients.

For example, your agency policy might limit the hours you can see your clients to a traditional 8-to-5 workday. What if most of your clients are readily available only during evening hours? What if you decide that your agency should be more responsive to meeting clients' real needs? Your job description will probably have *nothing* to do with changing agency policy, but what if you feel the most ethical thing to do is to implement an agency policy change on your clients' behalf? How would you go about planning such an endeavor? What specific skills would you need to pull it off? That is what this book is all about.

Consider another example. Suppose you discover that many of your clients, suffering from severe poverty, have little money to buy their children food, let alone gifts, during the upcoming holiday season. You feel this is sad and unfair. Getting additional resources for clients may have nothing to do with your job description. However, you feel that pursuing such a goal would mean very much to them. How might you go about raising the funds or getting the resources? Whom would you go to for help? What skills might be useful in this project? How might you establish a plan for accomplishing this goal? Later chapters will propose approaches to answer these questions.

Think about still another instance in which you might be working in an agency serving survivors of domestic violence. The agency supports a shelter for temporary residential respite and provides financial and emotional counseling for survivors. The agency also uses an extensive referral network for services ranging from vocational testing to day care services. Suppose, after careful thought, you determine that the agency really needs to start providing help for abusers, too. You become fully convinced of this necessity when you begin seeing second and third spouses of the same abuser visit the agency because of the abuser's continued battering. You think that an educational, self-awareness group for batterers would substantially affect the violence problem. How might you go about initiating and developing such a program? Whom would you talk to about it? Where might you get the required resources?

The three preceding examples concern internal agency issues that affect clients. Community issues also have major impacts upon your and the agency's ability to perform. Just as you function professionally within an agency context, you, your clients, and your agency function within a community context.

First, virtually every community is subject to social, economic, and political forces. For example, a community's social conditions might include extreme racial segregation accompanied by serious racist activity. Skinheads and neo-Nazis frequently burn crosses on the lawns of African-American residents. Racial slurs are commonly hurled back and forth between white and African-American groups. Race-related gang activity is prevalent. Under such social conditions, how well do you think you would be able to function as a social worker? How could you effectively practice with your clients? How could you simply ignore these conditions and go about your business? What is the ethical thing to do? Could you try to implement changes within your community that would, in turn, profoundly affect your clients' quality of life?

Likewise, a community may experience extreme economic hardships when a large corporation, the community's primary employer, moves to another country where wages are a fraction of the cost. Unemployment climbs sky-high. Subsequently, smaller businesses close because people have no money for purchases. Along with others in the community, your clients may lose their jobs. You may even lose your job if public funding or private purchasing power can no longer support social services. (*Social services* include the tasks that social workers and other helping professionals perform to help people solve problems, increase independence, sustain families, improve personal well-being, and enhance functioning in the social environment.) What kinds of things could you do in response to such economic pressure? What social work skills might help you address such a serious community problem?

Political forces also drastically affect community functioning. Suppose the state legislature or Congress decides to discontinue subsidizing public transportation in your state's major urban areas. Without such subsidies, public transportation can no longer operate. What if most of your clients depend on this transportation in order to get to work, shopping areas, and school? Essentially, most clients use public transportation to satisfy many of their travel needs. Your agency job description will probably not include anything about mobilizing support to try to change political forces. However, regardless of what specific social service you provide to your clients (for example, counseling or financial assistance), what if an issue like transportation suddenly supersedes all these other problems? What if you can't effectively do your own job because you can't see your clients when they don't have any transportation? Can you ethically just sit back and ignore the political decision to cease subsidizing public transportation?

One of this text's major assumptions is that generalist practitioners require a wide range of skills for helping individuals, groups, families, organizations, and communities in a wide variety of situations. Generalists thus require a sound understanding of the organizational environments in which they practice. They need to know what goes on in organizations and how such organizations function within the community and within larger environments, including towns, cities, counties, and states in addition to the national and international arenas.

The intent of this book is to explore the larger systems, such as organizations and communities, within which you will strive to provide services and resources to your clients. We will examine numerous approaches to intervention on the macro (that is, organizational and community) level. Our assumption is that you will probably begin your professional life providing some form of direct service or, perhaps, even serving in a lower-level administrative position. However, we also assume that you will probably have chances to effect much broader changes on your clients' behalf by seeking and implementing changes in your clients' larger (macro) environments.

You might now be asking yourself the questions, "What about agency administration? Isn't it supposed to be responsible for such macro problems and issues?" Usually, agency administrators implement changes as part of their administrative responsibility, or agency authority figures solicit help and advice from outside consultants. In both instances, formal authority figures (such as an agency director, unit service director, chief executive officer, or board of directors) initiate and control the change process. In an ideal world, administrators would automatically initiate and implement all the changes necessary for the most effective and efficient service provision to clients. However, in the real world, people in power often have multiple pressures and distractions. In reality, they either choose not to make macro changes or fail to see a valid need for such changes.

As a social work practitioner, you will likely have to face community problems and gaps in services. As a generalist practitioner, you will probably encounter times when your agency is accomplishing tasks ineffectively, is not doing something it should do, or is simply doing the wrong thing. Some problems facing human service organizations are extreme, whereas others are much more subtle. Specific problems include inefficient provision of services, ineffective outreach to clients in need, inattentiveness to clients' opinions about their needs and service requirements, sluggishness in making necessary referrals to other agencies, and lack of service differentiation to meet clients' diverse needs. When such problems exist, it is the practitioner's professional and ethical responsibility to consider helping the agency improve its service provision to clients.

Learning Objectives

This chapter will provide content concerning how social workers:

A. *Recognize the Generalist Intervention Model as a means of promoting human and social well-being in macro practice settings.*

B. *Define generalist practice and explain each component of this definition, including professional knowledge, skills, and values.*

C. *Identify personal values, and define and apply professional standards.*

D. *Describe the traditional three models of community organization and suggest an updated approach.*

E. *Examine the importance of client empowerment, the strengths perspective, and resiliency.*

F. *Recognize the importance of understanding human diversity as it shapes the human experience and its implications for practice.*

G. *Examine advocacy for human rights and the pursuit of social and economic justice as a major facet of generalist practice.*

H. *Describe the importance of working within an organizational structure as the context for generalist practice.*

I. *Identify a wide range of professional roles practitioners may assume in macro practice.*

J. *Describe critical thinking and its relevance to generalist practice.*

K. *Recognize the usefulness of research-informed practice.*

L. *Explain the planned change process within the macro practice context.*

M. *Review a brief history of practice with organizations and communities within a professional context.*

The Generalist Intervention Model

Social workers are generalists (Council on Social Work Education [CSWE], 2008) who require a wide array of skills. Social workers don't pick and choose what problems and issues they would like to address. They see a problem, even a very difficult problem, and try to help solve it. They must prepare themselves to help people with individualized personal problems on the one hand and to address very wide-ranging problems that affect whole organizations and communities on the other.

They perform their work in a broad assortment of settings that can focus on children and families, health, justice, education, economic status, and many more issues too numerous to list.

The social work profession has been struggling with the concept of generalist practice for many years. Historically, accepted practice was to educate new practitioners for only one area of skills (for example, work with individuals, groups, or communities) or one area of practice (for instance, children and families, or administration). (A subsequent section of this chapter explains this in greater depth.) Much the opposite, a generalist practitioner needs competency in many areas instead of being limited to such a single track.

Generalist practice as described here is based upon a Generalist Intervention Model (GIM)[1] characterized by at least three major features.

First, this generalist perspective is founded on a definition of generalist practice that is supported by the knowledge, skills, and values characterizing the unique nature of the social work profession. This definition is reviewed and explained more thoroughly later in the chapter.

Second, this generalist perspective uses a specific, seven-step planned change (or problem-solving) method that is infinitely flexible in its application. As illustrated in Figure 1.1, the seven steps include engagement, assessment, planning, implementation, evaluation, termination, and follow-up. Each step will be addressed in this chapter.

Third, the generalist perspective proposed here is oriented toward solving problems at multiple levels of intervention. That is, such problems may involve individuals, families, groups, organizations, and communities. In other words, the model involves micro, mezzo, and macro systems as targets of change. *Micro systems* are individuals. *Mezzo systems* are small groups. *Macro systems* are any large systems, including organizations and communities. Families, because of their intimate nature, arbitrarily lie somewhere between micro and mezzo systems.

Figure 1.2 illustrates how you as a generalist practitioner might choose any of the three levels of intervention to address a particular problem. First, you must use micro skills to engage (that is, establish a relationship and begin effective communication with) the individual or individuals with whom you are talking about the problem. Second, you assess the problem,

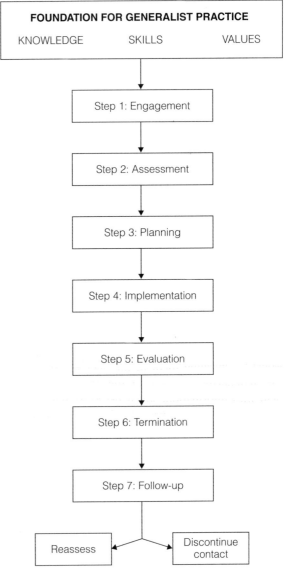

FIGURE 1.1 Planned Change Steps in the Generalist Intervention Model

which entails seeking information about various aspects of the problem. After Step 2, you might choose to pursue a micro, mezzo, or macro approach—or a combination—to solve the problem. Figure 1.2 depicts how you might progress through the planning, implementation, evaluation, termination, and follow-up process, regardless of the level of intervention you pursue.

For example, suppose you are a generalist practitioner for a rural Midwest county. Your job entails receiving referrals from your supervisor (who has received them from an intake worker). You then establish initial connections with clients and other referral

1. The Generalist Intervention Model was first proposed in *Understanding Generalist Practice* (Kirst-Ashman & Hull, 1993, 1999, 2002, 2006, 2009).

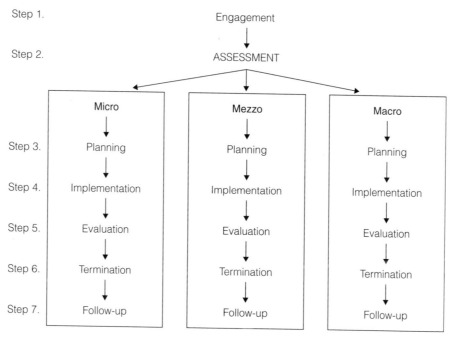

FIGURE 1.2 Steps in the Planned Change Process—Initiating Macro Change

people by engaging them in the planned change process, familiarize clients with the agency and supply them with information, solicit necessary data to assist in service provision, provide short-term counseling when needed, and make appropriate referrals to agency units and other community resources.

You receive a referral involving an older adult, Murray Strewynskowski. The person who calls, Duke Earl, is one of Mr. Strewynskowski's concerned neighbors. Mr. Earl expresses concern because Mr. Strewynskowski has twice fallen down on his icy sidewalk and been unable to get back up and into the house. Both times, Mr. Earl happened to notice the fall and was able to assist Mr. Strewynskowski into the house. While inside, Mr. Earl noticed extremely chaotic conditions: Rotting garbage was strewn all around the kitchen, and about a dozen cats leisurely wandered around. Mr. Earl noticed that a black cat with a white patch over the left eye was eating what seemed to be canned creamed corn mixed with ketchup from a plate on the table that looked as if it might have been Mr. Strewynskowski's lunch. Mr. Earl also expresses concerns about Mr. Strewynskowski's diet in a general sense and wonders whether Mr. Strewynskowski is able to shop or cook adequately, because he looks unhealthily thin.

Initially, you call Mr. Earl to clarify any questions you might have and to thank him for his interest and help. This means that you have engaged Mr. Earl in the problem-defining process. Engagement is the initial period when a practitioner becomes oriented to the problem at hand and begins to establish communication and a relationship with any other individuals addressing the problem. Subsequently, you figure out what to do about Mr. Strewynskowski. You must also engage him as the client in the planned change process. Of course, as a generalist practitioner, you must work with the client to establish what he needs and wants.

During the assessment phase, you may decide to pursue planning and implementation at the micro, mezzo, or macro level. You might also decide that intervention at more than one level would be appropriate.

A Micro Approach

A micro level plan might be to refer Mr. Strewynskowski to the appropriate services and oversee service provision. You might then continue Mr. Strewynskowski's assessment and arrange for additional services such as a traveling homemaker and daily hot meal delivery. You might also arrange for supportive services as needed, such as assisting Mr. Strewynskowski with paying his bills, obtaining medical assistance, or making arrangements to get groceries and other needed items.

A Mezzo Approach

Assuming another perspective, however, you might choose to focus on a mezzo or group/family-oriented approach. Suppose that there are no services for traveling homemakers or hot meal delivery in Mr. Strewynskowski's immediate area. Perhaps the county in which you work is neither very populated nor very wealthy. In fact, suppose that the county is downright poor. Without all the services and resources you would like to have, what would you do?

For one thing, you might decide to research whether help and support could be provided by Mr. Strewynskowski's family. Upon further investigation, you find out that Mr. Strewynskowski has two sons and a daughter living in the county. You decide to explore the extent to which they are aware of their father's situation and can provide some of the help he needs. This would involve engaging his relatives in the helping process. Additionally, you decide to look into whether Mr. Strewynskowski has any friends or neighbors who might be willing to help him out. You already know that Mr. Earl is concerned about Mr. Strewynskowski's well-being.

Using a mezzo perspective therefore involves people and family who are close to Mr. Strewynskowski. You might also pursue the mezzo approach of getting Mr. Strewynskowski into some type of social or support group to minimize his isolation. Perhaps Mr. Strewynskowski belongs to a church that could serve some of his needs, such as having volunteers take him shopping or involving him in both religious and social activities.

A Macro Approach

Finally, in addition to thinking purely in micro or mezzo terms, you might decide to pursue a macro approach. Once again, suppose that there are no services that offer traveling homemakers, meal delivery, older adult protection, or supportive workers in your area. Perhaps you discover that you have a number of older adult clients who are struggling to maintain themselves in their own homes. You find that, on a regular basis, you are having difficulty helping such clients—that this issue extends beyond the simple provision of help to an individual client. You decide that the solution will require more than the solicitation of family or group involvement at the mezzo level.

Rather, you determine that services are needed at the macro level. Perhaps your county agency should develop a new program to serve these clients. Maybe you should approach agency administrators to explore the possibility of funneling funds and resources away from other less-critical needs to these older adult clients who are in what you consider grave need. Possibly your own agency's policy should be changed. Services and resources might already be available in the agency, but are accessible only to other client populations (for example, people who have specific types of physical or developmental disabilities). Agency policy change could extend eligibility for resources to the older adult population. Such changes in agency service provision, policy, or distribution of resources is what macro practice—and this book—are all about.

What Does Generalist Practice Mean?

Generalist social work practice may involve almost any helping process. A generalist practitioner may be called upon to help a homeless family, a sexually abused child, a pregnant teenager, an older adult who is sick and unable to care for herself any longer, an alcoholic parent, a community that's trying to address its drug abuse problem, or a public assistance agency that's struggling to amend its policies to conform to new federal regulations. Therefore, generalist practitioners must be well prepared to address many kinds of difficult situations.

For our purposes, we will define generalist practice as follows: Generalist practice is the application of an *eclectic knowledge base, professional values, and ethics* and a *wide range of skills* to *target any size system* for change within the context of three primary principles, a context, and four major processes (CSWE, 2008, Educational Policy [EP] 2.1).[2] They are identified here and each is described more thoroughly later in this and subsequent chapters.

(Note that "helping hands" icons of two hands embracing a sun and illustrated in this paragraph are located throughout the book. Accredited social work programs must demonstrate that

EP 2.1

---

2. Most of these concepts are taken directly from the *Educational Policy and Accreditation Standards* (EPAS) developed by the Council on Social Work Education (CSWE) (CSWE, 2008). One major goal of social work education is to facilitate students' attainment of the EPAS-designated ten core competencies and their forty-one related practice behaviors so that students develop into competent practitioners. Students require knowledge in order to develop skills and become competent. Our intent here is to specify what chapter content and knowledge coincides with the development of specific competencies and practice behaviors. (This ultimately is intended to assist in a social work program's accreditation process.) Throughout the chapter, icons such as that located in this paragraph call attention to the location of EPAS-related content. Each icon identifies what competency or practice behavior is relevant by specifying the designated Educational Policy (EP) reference number. "Competency Notes" are provided at the end of each chapter that relate EPAS competencies and practice behaviors to content in the chapter. A summary chart of the icons' locations in all chapters and their respective competency or practice behavior is placed in the inside cover of the book.

they're teaching students to be proficient in a range of areas called competencies and practice behaviors. These are listed inside the front cover of the book. The occurrence of an icon with a numerical reference beneath it means that the corresponding content in the paragraph relates directly to the referenced competency or practice behavior. "Competency Notes" listed at the end of the chapter further clarify these relationships. The intent is to help in the accreditation process.)

The three primary principles characterizing generalist practice all involve values. The first of these principles entails an emphasis on client *empowerment, strengths,* and *resiliency. Empowerment* is "the process of increasing personal, interpersonal, or political power so that individuals can take action to improve their life situations" (Gutierrez, 2001, p. 210). It involves ensuring that others have the right to power, ability, and authority to achieve *self-determination* (each individual's right to make his or her own decisions). *Strengths* include any "capacities, resources, and assets" that can be accessed to increase empowerment (Saleebey, 2009, p. 99). *Resiliency* (discussed further in Highlight 1.4) is the ability of an individual, family, group, community, or organization to recover from adversity and resume functioning even when suffering serious trouble, confusion, or hardship (Glicken, 2006).

The second principle emphasized in generalist practice is the importance of "understand[ing] how *[human] diversity* characterizes and shapes the human experience and is critical to the formation of identity" (emphasis added) (CSWE, 2008, Educational Policy [EP] 2.1.4). The third principle accentuated in generalist practice concerns *advocacy for human rights, and the pursuit of social and economic justice.* Subsequent sections discuss these concepts in greater detail.

Social workers, employed by an organization, practice within the context of an *organizational structure.* Four processes then characterize generalist practice. First, generalist practice requires the assumption of a wide range of *professional roles.* Second, it requires the application of *critical thinking* skills throughout the course of intervention. Third, generalist practice incorporates *research-informed practice* to determine the most effective ways to help people and serve clients. Fourth, practitioners follow a seven-step *planned change* process to achieve intervention goals.

This chapter will address the 12 key dimensions inherent in that definition. The order in which they are presented does not imply that one dimension is more important than another. Each is significant. Highlight 1.1 summarizes these concepts in outline

form. Subsequent discussion of each is introduced with the headings numbered 1 through 12. The intent here is to present a definition of generalist practice that you can remember.

Figure 1.3 illustrates how the various concepts fit together. The large square labeled *Organizational Structure* represents the organization (or agency) that employs you to do a social work job. Organizational structure involves the operation of lines of authority and communication within an agency, how the administration runs the organization, and what the agency environment is like (Chapter 4, "Understanding Organizations," will discuss this in detail). As a generalist practitioner, you will work in this environment with all its constraints, requirements, and rules. Thus, Figure 1.3 pictures you, the generalist practitioner, as a rectangle within this large square. In that same square you see the terms *Knowledge, Values,* and *Skills.* These illustrate that you bring to your job a broad knowledge base, professional values, and a wide range of skills.

The concentric circles at the bottom of Figure 1.3 illustrate your potential *target systems.* As we have established, generalist practitioners may choose to work with a micro, mezzo, or macro system as the target of their change efforts. These three systems are positioned in concentric circles according to their respective sizes.

An arrow flows from the Organizational Structure square down to the Target System circles. This indicates that you, as a generalist practitioner, will apply your knowledge, skills, and values to help change a micro, mezzo, or macro system.

Other arrows point from concepts on the right and left to the central "application" arrow. This means that generalist practitioners apply the concepts the arrows represent as they undertake generalist practice. "Principles/values" concepts, portrayed on the left, include empowerment, human diversity, and advocacy for human rights and social and economic justice. Social workers also apply the "processes" inherent in generalist practice. These, depicted on the right, consist of the assumption of various professional roles, use of critical thinking skills, employment of research-informed practice, and the undertaking of the planned change process.

Note that each concept portrayed in Figure 1.3 will subsequently be addressed in greater detail.

Note that terms can sometimes be confusing. This book focuses on generalist practice and assumes that social workers are generalists. Therefore, the terms *generalist social worker, worker, generalist practitioner,* and *practitioner* will be used interchangeably throughout

HIGHLIGHT 1.1

Dimensions in the Definition of Generalist Practice

1. Acquisition of an eclectic knowledge base
   A. Theoretical foundation: Systems theories
   B. Human behavior and the social environment
   C. Social welfare policy and policy practice
   D. Social work practice
   E. Research-informed practice and practice-informed research
   F. Values and principles that guide practice
2. Acquisition of professional values and application of professional ethics
   A. National Association of Social Workers *Code of Ethics*
   B. International Federation of Social Workers/International Association of Schools of Social Work Ethics in Social Work, *Statement of Principles*
   C. Awareness of personal values
   D. Management of ethical dilemmas
3. Use of a wide range of practice skills
   A. Micro
   B. Mezzo
   C. Macro
4. Orientation to target any size system
   A. Micro

B. Mezzo
C. Macro
5. Emphasis on client empowerment, strengths, and resiliency
6. The importance of human diversity
7. Advocacy for human rights and the pursuit of social and economic justice
8. Effective work within an organizational structure
9. Assumption of a wide range of professional roles
   A. Enabler
   B. Mediator
   C. Integrator/coordinator
   D. Manager
   E. Educator
   F. Analyst/evaluator
   G. Broker
   H. Facilitator
   I. Initiator
   J. Negotiator
   K. Mobilizer
   L. Advocate
10. Employment of critical thinking skills
11. Research-informed practice
12. Use of the planned change process

this book to refer to professionals undertaking generalist social work practice.

Defining Generalist Practice: 1. Acquisition of an Eclectic Knowledge Base

Acquiring an eclectic knowledge base requires selection "of what appears to be best in various doctrines, methods, or styles," deriving this selection "from various sources" (Mish, 2008 *[Webster's Dictionary]*, p. 394). Knowledge entails understanding the dynamics of people's situations and determining what skills work best under particular circumstances.

Social work has a growing and progressive groundwork of knowledge about how social workers can become more effective in helping people solve problems. Additionally, the field has borrowed from other fields such as psychology, political science, and sociology. Social work then applies this knowledge to practice situations.

Therefore, generalist practitioners must know much about many things. Look at the vagueness inherent in

that last sentence. What does it mean? It's difficult to be specific about how much you need to know. The point is that your knowledge base must be broad so that you can select from a wide range of theoretical approaches and skills in order to apply them to your own practice. We will introduce one significant perspective—systems theories—for you to adopt as part of your knowledge base. Systems theories provide a strong part of the theoretical foundation upon which this book is based.

In addition (as shown in Highlight 1.1), the social work profession considers it necessary that you assimilate knowledge and develop competencies related to: human behavior and the social environment; social welfare policy and policy practice; social work practice; research—informed practice and practice—informed research; and values and principles guiding generalist practice (CSWE, 2008, EP 2.1). A *competency* is the proven ability to demonstrate the acquisition of sufficient knowledge, skills, and values in a designated area in order to practice effective social work. After explaining the conceptual framework of systems theories and their application to generalist practice, we will briefly address the other content areas.

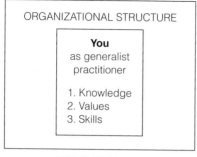

ORGANIZATIONAL STRUCTURE

You
as generalist
practitioner

1. Knowledge
2. Values
3. Skills

APPLICATION (of):

Principles/Values   *Processes*

Empowerment   Professional Roles

Human Diversity   Critical Thinking

Advocacy/Social &   Research-Informed
Economic Justice   Practice

                           Planned Change

TARGET SYSTEM

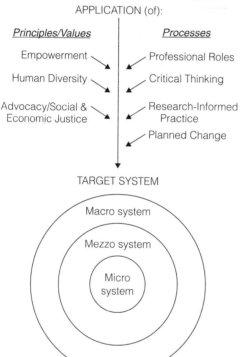

Macro system

Mezzo system

Micro
system

FIGURE 1.3 Definition of Generalist Practice

Systems Theories

EP 2.1.7a

Social work focuses on the interactions between individuals and various systems in the environment. A *system* is a set of elements that are orderly and interrelated to make a functional whole. You, your class, your family, and your college or university are all systems. Each involves many components that work together in order to function.

Systems theories provide social workers with a conceptual perspective that emphasizes interactions among various systems. They stress the relationships and interactions among individuals, families, groups, organizations, and communities as they function together in the environment. Systems theories provide a very broad approach for understanding the world that can be applied to a multitude of settings.

Understanding systems theories is especially important because generalist practice may target virtually any size system for change. As a generalist, you will evaluate any confronting problem from multiple perspectives. You will determine whether change is best pursued by individual, family, group, organizational, or community avenues. You might determine that any of these systems should be the target of your planned change efforts. We will now focus on the application to macro practice.

Conceptualizing Systems in Macro Practice

The term *macro practice,* used throughout the book, is the application of generalist practice skills in a macro (organizational or community) context to pursue planned change on behalf of a macro client system.

To better understand the macro change process, it is helpful to conceptualize a number of systems interacting within the environment. As we discussed previously, systems theories imply dynamic, connected interactions among any number of systems and subsystems. These systems are of various sizes. Within the broader context of generalist practice, we will discuss four types of systems critical to the change process: the macro client, target, change agent, and action systems (Compton, Galaway, & Cournoyer, 2005; Pincus & Minahan, 1973). (Chapter 6, "IMAGINE—How to Implement Macro Intervention: Changing Agency Policy," reviews these four concepts within an organizational context.)

The Macro Client System

A *client system* is any individual, family, group, organization, or community that will ultimately benefit from generalist social work intervention. A *macro client system* involves larger numbers of clients, families, or groups of clients with similar characteristics or qualifications for receiving resources or services, or an agency or community that will be the beneficiary of the macro intervention process. For example, as a generalist practitioner you may work to develop and implement a job placement program that will eventually affect dozens or perhaps even thousands of unemployed people. Likewise, developing an internal agency training program on new treatment techniques is intended to benefit the agency by improving its service provision.

Macro social work practice is concerned with many problems, including homelessness and unemployment. Generalist social workers can target community conditions that contribute to these problems and support social programs that aid people needing shelter and employment.

The difference is that macro change benefits larger groups of people, whether the group involves a particular client population, agency personnel, or community residents. In a different way, micro and mezzo changes benefit a *single* individual, family, or group.

The Target System

The *target system* is the system that social workers must modify or influence in order to reach their goals and have clients benefit from the planned change process (Compton et al., 2005; Pincus & Minahan, 1973; Sheafor & Horejsi, 2006). In macro practice, this usually involves an organization or community. It might be that the agency in which you work needs to improve some of its policies or services. Likewise, your community may need to provide some new service that citizens really need (for example, a drug rehabilitation program or a crime prevention effort). Consider Mr. Strewynskowski's case discussed earlier. Suppose supportive services such as hot meal delivery, part-time homemaker services, or community support groups do not exist, not for only Mr. Strewynskowski

but for numerous other senior residents. In that case you might decide to target "the system," either agency or community, to develop such resources.

The concepts of organization and community are broad. They can refer to very small organizations or communities (such as small field offices, isolated church groups, or villages) or to systems that are huge entities (such as city, county, state, or federal government units). Similarly, a community in its broad sense might be the citizens of an entire state. Systems can be of virtually any size. Therefore, the target system is any system that macro intervention intends to change.

The Change Agent System

Within a macro practice perspective, the *change agent* is the individual who initiates the macro change process. In our context, *you* are the change agent because this book intends to teach you how to implement macro level change. You might seek changes such as improving agency effectiveness or enhancing a community's quality of life. Later on, you might gain the support of, and join in coalitions with, others who also believe in the proposed macro change. Then you, as a single change agent, might become part of a larger system. Whether you undertake macro change by yourself or join with others, you are part of the action system described next.

The Action System

The *action system* includes those people who agree and are committed to working together in order to attain the proposed macro change. We have established that sometimes you alone will be the action system for the change effort. Other times you will find it more useful to join with others to help implement a macro change.

Human Behavior and the Social Environment (HBSE)

EP 2.1.7

One way of classifying the bodies of knowledge generalist social workers must have involves the educational content provided in social work education programs. The Council on Social Work Education (CSWE) is the organization that accredits social work programs throughout the country and specifies the dimensions in which social workers should establish competency. One such area is Human Behavior and the Social Environment (HBSE) (CSWE, 2008, EP 2.1.7).

Knowledge about HBSE is essential as a foundation on which to build practice skills. After engagement, the second step in the planned change process is accurate assessment of the person, problem, and situation within the context of the social environment. The environment is vitally important in the analysis and understanding of human behavior. Because social work has a person and environment focus (CSWE, 2008), the interactions among individuals, systems, and the environment are critical. Such a conceptual perspective provides social workers with a symbolic representation of how to view the world. It provides ideas for how to assess clients' situations and identify alternative solutions involving various levels of practice.

Social workers should have knowledge about biological, social, psychological, cultural, and spiritual dimensions of human functioning (CSWE, 2008). Throughout their life spans, individuals are integral members of variously sized systems including families, groups, organizations, and communities. Social workers must understand how all these dimensions of

human behavior affect people and their interactions. Social work's goal is to apply such knowledge to enhance people's functioning and involvement with a range of systems in their environment (CSWE, 2008).

Social Welfare Policy and Policy Practice

Social welfare policy is another dimension about which social workers must be knowledgeable in order to be competent practitioners (CSWE, 2008, EP 2.1.8). Policy, in its simplest portrayal, might be thought of as rules. Our lives and those of our cli-

EP 2.1.8

ents are governed by rules: rules about how we're supposed to drive our cars, about when we're supposed to go to school, and about how we're supposed to talk or write.

Policies are rules that tell us which actions we may take and which we may not. Policies guide our actions and our decisions.

Policy most relevant to social work practice might be divided into two major categories: social welfare policy and agency policy guiding what's done in social welfare agencies. *Social welfare policy* includes the laws and regulations that determine which social programs exist, what categories of clients are served, and who qualifies for a given program. It also set standards regarding the type of services to be provided, the qualifications of the service provider, and many other aspects of service provision. Social welfare policy involves "the actions of government that have a direct impact on the welfare of people by providing services and income. As principles of action, policies translate our government's sense of responsibility to us, its citizens. Thus, [social welfare] policy reflects societal values, ideals, and a vision of what the world should look like" (Tice & Perkins, 2002, p. 2). It comprises the rules for how money can be spent to help people and how these people will be treated. Social welfare policies determine who is eligible for public assistance and who is not. For example, specific policies designate what social workers can and cannot do for sexually abused children.

In addition to social welfare policies, there are *agency policies* that include those standards adopted by the individual organizations and programs that provide services (for example, a family service agency, a department of human services, or a nursing home). Such standards may specify how the agency is structured, what qualifications supervisors and workers are required to have, which rules govern what a worker may or may not do, and what the proper procedures are for completing a family assessment. These are only a few of the many aspects of agency life.

Knowledge about policy at all levels is vitally important. An organization's policy can dictate how much vacation an employee can have and how she can earn raises in salary. An adoption agency's policy can determine who is eligible to adopt a child and who isn't. A social program's policies determine who is able to get needed services and resources and who will be left without them.

Sometimes, for whatever reasons, social welfare or agency policies appear to be unfair or oppressive to clients. (Note that from here on the terms "social welfare policy" and "social policy" will be used interchangeably.) A social worker may conclude that a policy is ethically or morally intolerable. In such a case, the worker may decide to advocate on the behalf of clients to try to change the policy. Generalist practitioners require the ability to analyze policy and undertake change when it is needed. In other words, they have responsibility for undertaking policy practice. *Policy practice* involves "efforts to change policies in legislative, agency, and community settings, by establishing new policies, improving existing ones, or defeating the policy initiatives of other people" (Jansson, 2011, p. 15). Policy practice may also involve advocacy on behalf of "relatively powerless groups, such as women, children, poor people, African Americans, Asian Americans, Latinos, gay men and lesbians, and people with disabilities, [to] improve their resources and opportunities" (Jansson, 2011, p. 15). Later chapters will say much more about making changes in larger systems and their policies.

Additionally, generalist practitioners need a sound foundation of knowledge concerning social services. This includes a historical perspective about how services have been developed and an analytical perspective concerning how well services "advance social well-being" for those in need (CSWE, 2008, EP 2.1.8a).

Social Work Practice

If knowledge is the *what* of social work, then practice is the *how*. Social work practice is the *doing* of social work. It involves identifying and choosing among a range of intervention alternatives and undertaking the planned change process to achieve the intervention's goals. (The planned change process will be described in greater detail later in this chapter.)

The social work practice knowledge base includes the ability to determine what skills will be most effective in a given situation.

For example, Norman, age 14, approaches his school social worker Melba and states softly, "I think I'm going to kill myself." Melba then must determine what is the best practice alternative to pursue in order to help Norman. What counseling approach would be most effective? What crisis intervention skills would best apply? Does the problem extend even beyond Norman? Is Melba seeing many students expressing similar thoughts? Should she initiate and develop new preventive programs within the school context in order to combat this larger problem? Must Melba pursue agency and political policy changes in order to provide funding to more effectively help Norman and other students in similar situations?

Research-Informed Practice and Practice-Informed Research

Knowledge about social work research is important for at least three basic reasons (CSWE, 2008, EP 2.1.6; Tripodi & Lalayants, 2008). First, it provides a scientific orientation to identifying, evaluating, and choosing intervention approaches that are effective.

EP 2.1.6

Research-informed practice is social work practice based on empirical evidence. Framing social work interventions so that they can be evaluated through research provides information about which specific techniques work best with which specific problems. *Practice-informed research* refers to scientific investigation designed to attain results related to successful social work practice.

Second, with this scientific perspective, research can guide social workers to become more effective in their practice. It can help them get better and clearer results. When work with a client is clearly evaluated, social workers can determine whether they are really helping a client with his or her problem. Additionally, practitioners can monitor their progress during the actual implementation process. Similarly, whole agencies can use research to evaluate their programs' effectiveness.

The third reason is that accumulated research helps to build an effective knowledge base for the social work profession. This helps to define social work practice, increase the effectiveness of interventions, and enhance the profession's accountability.

Rubin and Babbie (2010) describe how social work research has at least four major approaches:

1. **Exploration:** "Much of social work research is conducted to explore a topic—to provide a begging familiarity with it. This purpose is typical when a researcher is examining a new interest, when the subject of study is relatively new or unstudied, or when a researcher seeks to test the feasibility of undertaking a more careful study. For example, suppose your first job as a social worker is to develop services for the frail [older adults] … in a predominantly ethnic minority community about which you know very little. You want to conduct a community-wide survey to assess the precise extent of the need for and likely utilization of alternative services that you are contemplating developing. Before mounting a large-scale study geared to producing conclusive findings, you'd be well advised to begin with a smaller, more flexible exploratory study that will help you plan a larger and more careful study in a culturally sensitive manner."

2. **Description:** Much social work research adopts a second approach, namely, "to describe situations and events. The researcher observes and then describes what was observed. Because scientific observation is careful and deliberate, scientific descriptions are typically more accurate and precise than casual descriptions." For example, a researcher might assess the needs of a community by conducting a survey of community residents.

3. **Explanation:** A third common approach to "social work research is to explain things. Reporting why some cities have higher child abuse rates than others is a case of explanation, but simply reporting the different child abuse rates is description. A researcher has an explanatory purpose if he or she wishes to know why battered women repeatedly return to live with their batterers, rather than simply describing how often they do."

4. **Evaluation:** A fourth approach to research in social work "is to evaluate social policies, programs, and interventions. The evaluative purpose of social work research actually encompasses all three of the preceding purposes: exploration, description, and explanation" (2010, pp. 41–42). A number of questions might be asked in order to understand whether a social policy, program, or intervention is effective or not. For example, in order to evaluate service provision in a community, one might *explore* what services are needed by administering a survey to a sample of community citizens. Similarly, research could be conducted to *describe* the services that are already available. Research might investigate variables related to service provision such as ethnicity, income level, or educational level to *explain* why services are provided to some groups more than others. Finally, *evaluation* of service provision effectiveness might focus on how services affect clients or the extent to which goals are achieved. Thus, evaluation requires a depth of understanding concerning many dimensions involved in service provision.

Note that research does not always fall neatly into one of the four categories. Many studies use more than one approach and involve a range of components.

Thus, research is important to generalist practice. Research informs and supports intervention approaches. It identifies theories and programs that are more likely to be effective. Finally, it helps the worker to ensure that the client system is being helped, rather than hurt, by what workers do.

Values and Principles That Guide Generalist Practice

Knowledge, skills, and values in social work have many overlaps. For example, consider the values and principles that guide generalist practice. These include the broad category of professional values and ethics in addition to the principles of client empowerment, understanding and appreciation of human diversity, and advocacy for human rights along with the pursuit of social and economic justice. There is much vital *knowledge* in the eclectic knowledge base concerning each of these areas that is necessary for competent social work practice. Such knowledge should be applied via *skills* during implementation of planned change. However, each concept is an important component in the definition of generalist practice. Therefore, subsequent sections involving primary *values* and principles in generalist social work will address each dimension more thoroughly in its own right.

2. Acquisition of Professional Values and Application of Professional Ethics

Not only must generalist practitioners have substantial and diverse knowledge at their disposal, but they must also have assimilated professional values (CSWE, 2008,

EP 2.1.2

EP 2.1.2). *Values* are principles, qualities, and practices that a designated group, individual, or culture deems inherently desirable. Values, then, give direction concerning what is considered right and wrong. Subsequently, values provide guidelines for behavior. Ideally, one should behave in accordance with the values one holds.

Ethics are principles based on a set of values that serve to guide one's behavior. Values reflect what you consider to be right and wrong; ethics involve how you behave based on these values. Generalist practitioners must have a sound basis for making ethical decisions that are in accord with social work values. Aspects of professional values and ethics we will discuss here (shown in Highlight 1.1) include the National Association of Social Workers (NASW) *Code of Ethics*; the International Federation of Social Workers/International Association of Schools of Social Work *Ethics in Social Work, Statement of Principles*; awareness of personal values; and management of ethical dilemmas.

National Association of Social Workers (NASW) *Code of Ethics*

Social work has a clearly delineated set of professional values reflected in the National Association of Social Workers *Code of Ethics* (NASW, 2008). The *Code*'s mission "is to enhance human well-being and help meet the basic human needs of all people, with particular attention to the needs and empowerment of people who are vulnerable, oppressed, and living in poverty" (NASW, 2008, Preamble). Highlight 1.2 cites the *Code*'s six core values.

Related to the core values recognized in Highlight 1.2, the *Code* encompasses 155 specific standards clustered under six major categories. These categories include social workers' ethical responsibilities to clients, to colleagues, in practice settings, as professionals, to the social work profession, and to the broader society. Chapter 12 of this text explores the NASW *Code of Ethics* and its application to macro practice in greater detail.

International Federation of Social Workers/International Association of Schools of Social Work *Ethics in Social Work, Statement of Principles*

Although the NASW *Code of Ethics* is the primary code followed by social workers in the United States, note that other ethical codes also are available in other nations and on an international basis. The International Federation of Social Workers (IFSW) and the International Association of Schools of Social Work (IASSW) have developed an *Ethics in Social Work, Statement of Principles*. The IFSW "is a global organization striving for social justice, human rights and social development" through the support of effective social work practice and "international cooperation between social workers and their professional organisations" (IFSW, 2009). The IASSW is a "worldwide association of schools of social work," "related educational programmes, and social work educators"; it "promotes the development of social work education throughout the world, develops standards to enhance [the] quality of social work education, encourages international exchange, provides forums for sharing social work

HIGHLIGHT 1.2

Core Values of the NASW *Code of Ethics*

The NASW *Code of Ethics* identifies the following six core values that serve as the foundation for ethical behavior:

1. *Service:* The provision of help, resources, and benefits so that people may achieve their maximum potential.
2. *Social justice:* "An ideal condition in which all members of society have the same basic rights, protection, opportunities, obligations, and social benefits" (Barker, 2003, pp. 404–405).
3. *Dignity and worth of the person:* Holding in high esteem and appreciating individual value.

4. *Importance of human relationships:* Valuing the dynamic interpersonal connections between two or more persons or systems that involve how they think about, feel about, and behave toward each other.
5. *Integrity:* Maintaining trustworthiness and sound adherence to moral ideals.
6. *Competence:* Having the necessary skills and abilities to perform work with clients effectively (NASW, 2008, Preamble).

research and scholarship, and promotes human rights and social development through policy and advocacy activities" (IASSW, 2009). Chapter 4 discusses these organizations in more detail.

The IFSW/IASSW *Ethics in Social Work, Statement of Principles* focuses on international and global issues concerning human rights. Major principles include the importance of human dignity, social justice, recognition of human diversity, and the equitable distribution of resources. It also calls for social workers to challenge discrimination and injustice by demonstrating solidarity and working together on a global basis.

Awareness of Personal Values

EP 2.1.2a

Before you are able to prevent personal values from interfering with ethical professional practice, you must clearly identify those personal values. This proposition stems directly from the fourth NASW *Code of Ethics* core value cited earlier concerning "valuing human relationships" (NASW, 2008, Preamble). Valuing the client–worker relationship means keeping it clear of personal opinions. You certainly have the right to maintain personal values and opinions. However, a generalist practitioner is professionally obligated to prevent personal values that conflict with professional values from interfering with practice (CSWE, 2008, EP 2.1.2a).

The abortion controversy provides an excellent example of the potential clash of personal and professional values. Professional values emphasize an individual's right to self-determination. Additionally, NASW's policy statement concerning abortion states that each person has the right to make her own decision concerning whether to pursue the abortion alternative (NASW, 2009). This may seriously conflict with a worker's personal values. For instance, you may feel that you would never consider an abortion for yourself under any circumstances. However, this position is totally distinct from how you should ethically behave in your professional practice. You would be ethically obligated to help a client pursue an abortion if she'd made that decision. On the other hand, your personal values may be clearly pro-choice. You may feel that women have an absolute right to abortion. Indeed, you may feel that abortion is definitely the route of choice in certain circumstances. These conditions might include when the pregnancy results from rape or incest; when carrying the pregnancy to term would endanger the mother's life; when it has been established that the

fetus is abnormal or seriously damaged; or when the pregnant woman simply does not want to have a baby. In these instances, you may find it very difficult when a client decides to have the baby anyway. You may personally feel this decision is a big mistake. However, you are professionally obligated not only to abide by your client's decision, but also to assist her to the best of your ability in attaining her goal. Sometimes, separating personal and professional values is very difficult.

Management of Ethical Dilemmas

EP 2.1.2d

An *ethical dilemma* is a problematic situation in which ethical standards are in conflict. In other words, sometimes it is not possible to make a perfect choice and abide by all ethical guidelines. For example, consider a client who tells you he plans to murder his girlfriend, yet forbids you to tell anybody. You cannot maintain the primary ethical standard of protecting human life (namely, your client's girlfriend) and confidentiality at the same time. (*Confidentiality* is the ethical principle that workers should not share information provided by or about a client unless that worker has the client's explicit permission to do so.) You are in the midst of an ethical quandary. Generalist practitioners must be vigilant and prepared to address such ethical dilemmas, because they occur regularly. Often, potential answers are unclear, confusing, and ambiguous. Each dilemma is unique. Social workers must be able to work through such situations and "apply strategies of ethical reasoning to arrive at principled decisions" (CSWE, 2008, EP 2.1.2d). Chapter 12 addresses a wide range of ethical dilemmas occurring within organizational and community settings and discusses how practitioners might make strategic decisions about what to do.

3. and 4. Mastery of a Wide Range of Practice Skills to Target Any Size System

The next two major dimensions involved in generalist practice concern a mastery of a wide range of practice skills, and targeting any size system for change. Because these two aspects are so closely intertwined, we will address them here together. Different and specific skills are used respectively with micro, mezzo, and macro systems.

Historically, social work skills were clustered into three major categories:

1. *Casework* involved working primarily on a direct level with individual clients and their families. This resembles in some ways the micro level of practice.
2. *Group work* involved organizing and running a wide variety of groups (for example, therapeutic groups or support groups). The mezzo level of practice might be said to correspond to this skill cluster.
3. *Community organization* involved working with organizations and communities. This is similar in some ways to the macro level of social work practice. A subsequent section reflects upon three models of community organization that historically preceded the concept of macro practice.

Under this old model of practice, social workers usually concentrated on developing expertise in one particular approach. They were caseworkers, group workers, or community organizers. They did not necessarily see themselves as having a sound basis of skills in more than one arena.

In contrast, the generalist perspective assumes a multiple-level approach to intervention. That is, for any particular problem or situation, a generalist practi-

EP 2.1.10

tioner might have to intervene with individuals, families, groups, organizations, or communities (CSWE, 2008, EP 2.1.10). Therefore, social workers must master and have readily available skills involved in working with any of these entities.

Micro practice is generalist social work practice focusing on planned change with and for individuals. The context is usually "intervention on a case-by-case basis or in a clinical setting" (Barker, 2003, p. 272). The focus of attention is on the individual and how to communicate and work with him or her on a one-to-one basis.

Mezzo practice is generalist social work practice with small groups. In macro settings, this primarily involves task groups, where understanding group dynamics and communication patterns among several people is important. Working with families lies somewhere between micro and mezzo practice. Because of the intimacy and intensity of family relationships and the importance of the family context to individuals, families deserve special status and attention.

Finally, we have established that *macro practice* is generalist social work practice intending to affect change in large systems, including organizations and communities. Skills involved include changing agency

and social policies, planning and implementing programs, and initiating and conducting projects within agency and community contexts. As we will see, mezzo skills (discussed in Chapter 3) are based to a great extent on micro level skills (explained in Chapter 2). In order to work with small groups of people, practitioners must thoroughly understand the communication and interaction occurring between individuals. They must know how to listen effectively, provide information, make plans, and follow through on these plans.

Likewise, macro level skills have a basis both in mezzo and micro skills. Macro interventions can involve working both with individuals within a macro context (for example, a colleague, an administrator, or a resident representing her community) and with small groups of people (for instance, a community group trying to abolish neighborhood drug houses or a group of agency staff charged with evaluating program effectiveness). Later chapters will explore a range of macro skills for you to use in practice.

Before Macro Practice: Three Models of Community Organization

Since this is a book about macro practice, we will spend a bit more time explaining it here. Historically, *community organization* was the term used to refer to macro practice in social work. The methods and directions of social work practice have changed and evolved, just as the economic and social realities of the times have drastically changed. However, reviewing the historical perspective on macro practice helps us to understand the significance of macro assessment and work today. Community organization was traditionally divided into three dimensions—social action, social planning, and locality development (Rothman, 2001; Rothman & Tropman, 1987). Note that goals for any of them may be similar because they involve improvement in specific groups' or the entire community's quality of life. All three approaches may even address the same or similar social problems. However, major differences include how citizen involvement and the professionals' roles are viewed as well as the tactics used to achieve goals.

Locality development is "community change … pursued through broad participation of a wide spectrum of people at the local community level" (Rothman, 2001, p. 29). The idea is to involve as many people as possible within the community to define their goals and help themselves in a democratic manner. The social worker was viewed as one who facilitated or coordinated the change process, working together with both citizens and people in power toward mutual community improvement goals (e.g., improving crime prevention, recreational areas and facilities, or program opportunities for youth or older adults). Today, locality development can be initiated "by a variety of organizations, including local government, private social-welfare organizations, churches," and other local groups (Cnaan & Rothman, 2001, p. 262); for example, "churches and synagogues have taken an active role in locality development in a variety of ways. ... Currently, in emerging ethnic neighborhoods containing new immigrants from Southeast Asia, Latin America, and the Caribbean, churches are often the first community institution to take steps to unite these people and work with them to obtain the resources needed to improve their life conditions" (p. 263).

Social planning is "a technical process of problem-solving regarding ... basic social problems, such as delinquency, housing, and mental health" (Rothman, 2001, p. 31). The emphasis here is reliance on outside experts or consultants to work with designated community leaders to solve specific problems. "The approach ... [assumes] that change in a complex modern environment requires expert planners who, through the exercise of technical competencies—including the ability to gather and analyze quantitative data and to maneuver large bureaucratic organizations—are needed to improve social conditions" (Rothman, 2001, p. 31). People in the general community would have little, if any, participation or input into the planning and change process. Rather, they would be considered consumers or recipients of improvements.

The following are examples of social planning (Rothman & Zald, 2001):

- *A state prison system faced with developing appropriate facilities must assess future population and needs by reviewing such variables as crime rates and sentencing policies.*
- *Forest product companies must appraise potential product demand 20 years hence because trees must be planted and allowed time to grow.*
- *"The Social Security Administration projects revenue needs, given demographic trends, eligibility rules, and benefit formulas"* (p. 299).
- *"Local councils develop plans for hospital facilities"* (p. 299), *based on projections of such elements as future needs and costs.*
- *"Universities attempt to develop models or projected enrollments and ... strategies for growth or retrenchment of faculty"* (p. 299).

- *A city might call in an urban renewal expert to recommend what should be done with a deteriorating area in the community.*

Social action is a coordinated effort to advocate for change in established laws, customs, or patterns of behavior to benefit a specific population (e.g., homeless people), solve a social problem (e.g., illicit drug use), correct unfairness (e.g., racism), or enhance people's well-being (e.g., improve access to health care). It assumes that inequities or injustices exist for designated groups in the population who are considered victims. Social action's purpose is to make basic "changes in the community including the redistribution of power and resources and gaining access to decision-making for marginal groups. ... Practitioners in the social action area generally aim to empower and benefit the poor, the disenfranchised, the oppressed" (Rothman, 2001, p. 33).

Highlight 1.3 describes a proposed update on these traditional three models.

5. Emphasis on Client Empowerment, Strengths, and Resiliency

An emphasis on empowerment, strengths, and diversity entails the fifth aspect of generalist practice. We have established that *empowerment* is the "process of increasing personal, interpersonal, or political power so that individuals can take action to improve their life situations" (Gutierrez, 2001, p. 210). We have also determined that some groups of people suffer from stereotypes, discrimination, and oppression. It is social work's task to empower clients in general and members of oppressed groups in particular. Empowerment means emphasizing, developing, and nurturing strengths and positive attributes. It aims at enhancing individuals', groups', families', and communities' power and control over their destinies.

Cowger and Snively (2002) explain:

Promoting empowerment means believing that people are capable of making their own choices and decisions. It means not only that human beings possess the strengths and potential to resolve their own difficult life situations, but also that they increase their strength and contribute to the well-being of society by doing so. The role of the social worker is to nourish, encourage, assist, enable, support, stimulate, and

HIGHLIGHT 1.3

Updating Traditional Models of Community Organization

Current macro practice in communities reflects two trends (Rothman, 2007; Rothman & Zald, 2008). First, traditional models of community organization should be updated to reflect a modification in focus. Second, practitioners should be more flexible in mixing various aspects of these three approaches to get things done.

New terms characterize these revised community organization models. First, "social advocacy" should replace social action; "*social advocacy* deems the application of pressure as the best course of action to take against people or institutions that may have [brought about] ... the problem or that stand in the way of its solution—which frequently involves promoting equity or social justice. When interests clash in this way, conflict is a given" (Rothman, 2007, p. 12). Advocacy, a concept receiving greater prominence than in the traditional models, becomes the focus of attention.

"Planning and policy practice" then replace the traditional social planning approach; planning continues to involve "proposing and enacting particular solutions" (Rothman, 2007, p. 12). We've established that *policy practice,* a newly emphasized concept, entails "efforts to change policies in legislative, agency, and community settings, whether by establishing new policies, improving existing ones, or defeating the policy initiatives of other people" (Jansson, 2008, p. 14). Changing existing policy or aggressively addressing issues in a new way often becomes an objective. This contrasts with the prior concept of social planning where experts were hired by "the establishment" to initiate and formulate policy.

"Community capacity development" is substituted for community development (Rothman, 2007, p. 12). "*Community capacity development* assumes that change is best accomplished when the people affected by problems are empowered with the knowledge and skills needed to understand their problems, and then work cooperatively together to overcome them. Thus there is a premium on consensus as a tactic and on *social solidarity* [unity including diverse community groups that is based on mutual interests, support, and goals] as [a means] ... and outcome" (italics added) (Rothman, 2007, p. 12). Here *community capacity* (the potential use of the community's inherent strengths, resources, citizen participation, and leadership) is stressed.

More globally, community capacity development can also take "place through several arms of the United Nations, including the World Health Organization [WHO], the World Bank, and others. In the United States, the Peace Corps, AID (Agency for International Development), and Agricultural Extension have conducted governmentally sponsored programs" (Cnaan & Rothman, 2001, p. 263). Such development fits extremely well with social work values. Individual dignity, strengths, participation, and free choice are emphasized.

---

unleash the strengths within people; to illuminate the strengths available to people in their own environments; and to promote equity and justice at all levels of society. To do that, the social worker helps clients articulate the nature of their situations, identify what they want, explore alternatives for achieving those desires and then achieve them. (p. 110)

EP 2.1.10e

Focusing on strengths can provide a sound basis for empowerment. Sometimes referred to as the *strengths perspective,* this orientation focuses on client system resources, capabilities, knowledge, abilities, motivations, experience, intelligence, and other positive qualities that can be put to use to solve problems and pursue positive changes (CSWE, 2008, EP 2.1.10e Saleebey, 2009; Sheafor & Horejsi, 2009).

For example, Kretzmann and McKnight (1993) suggest a strengths perspective for enhancing communities. They stress using potential community assets, including: citizens' "religious, cultural, athletic, [and] recreational" associations; "private businesses; public institutions such as schools, libraries, parks, police and fire stations; [and] nonprofit institutions such as hospitals and social service agencies" to improve a community's functioning and quality of life (pp. 6–8). They provide the following examples:

- *"A group of African-American men of middle age and older created an association to work with young men in order to help them to come of age in constructive, historically rooted and community-supported ways. The association has created workshops, presentations, classes and a network of ready and willing mentors"* (p. 134).

- *"Six local [church] congregations work together to provide a community meal on separate days during the week"* (p. 149).
- *"A group of seniors that forms the East Side Historical Society works with a local high school in space provided by the park system, to develop a museum which documents the history of four Chicago neighborhoods"* (p. 163).
- *"The Hispanic Club at an urban high school brings a sense of the importance of Latino culture to the community by hosting a Latino Cultural Week and organizing a food festival"* (p. 166).
- *"A representative from the local police precinct comes to the library to give workshops on crime prevention"* (p. 199).
- *"A hospital forms a partnership with a chain of department stores to open neighborhood health clinics in two of its branches. The same hospital already runs many other health centers including three in high schools and two at public housing developments"* (p. 266).
- *"A Washington human services agency purchased a 20-unit apartment building which was falling to pieces. With multilayered financing, volunteer support from a coalition of urban and suburban churches and donated materials, the complex was completely renovated into long-term transitional housing for homeless families. The basement of the complex is a restaurant which acts as an income-generating source and as a training ground for the unemployed"* (p. 321).

Chapter 8 will more thoroughly discuss communities and how they function.

Highlight 1.4 discusses a concept related to the strengths perspective—resiliency.

6. The Importance of Human Diversity

EP 2.1.4

Human diversity entails the vast range of differences among individuals and groups involving a wide range of variables (CSWE, 2008, EP 2.1.4). Any time a person can be identified as belonging to a group that differs in some respect from the majority of others in society, that person is subject to the effects of human diversity. Understanding and appreciating people's diverse qualities is the sixth dimension of generalist

practice. People meriting special attention include, at the very least, groups distinguished by "age, class, color, culture, disability, ethnicity, gender, gender identity and expression, immigration status, political ideology, race, religion, sex, and sexual orientation" (CSWE, 2008, p. 5). Highlight 1.5 defines each of these concepts.

EP 2.1.4a

Membership in groups that differ from the young heterosexual mainstream can place people at increased risk of discrimination, oppression, and economic deprivation (CSWE, 2008, EP 2.1.4a). *Discrimination* is the act of treating people differently because they belong to a particular group rather than on their own merit. *Oppression* involves putting extreme limitations and constraints on some person, group, or larger system. *Economic deprivation* is the condition of having inadequate or unjust access to financial resources. The latter can result from a number of circumstances, including unemployment, job discrimination, insufficient work benefits, and unsatisfactory public policies (e.g., unfair tax rates or eligibility standards for financial benefits and services that make them inaccessible to those in need).

Discrimination and oppression often result from stereotypes. A *stereotype* is a fixed mental picture of members of some specified group based on some attribute or attributes that reflect an overly simplified view of that group, without consideration or appreciation for individual differences. One might envision a number of relevant scenarios. For instance, picture being a woman in an all-male business establishment. Think of a 62-year-old person applying for a sales job in a department store where everyone else is under 30. Or consider an African-American person applying for membership in an all-white country club.

Membership in any diverse group provides a different set of environmental circumstances. A Chicano adolescent from a Mexican-American inner-city neighborhood has a different social environment than an upper-middle-class adolescent of Jewish descent living in the well-to-do suburbs of the same city. The critical thing is for social workers to be integrally aware of the awesome variety of human diversity. In order to work effectively with various groups, social workers must constantly strive to gain understanding about cultural and situational differences. Such understanding is necessary for effective communication that, in turn, is a requirement for effective generalist practice. As an example, Highlight 1.6 provides suggestions for empowering lesbian and gay people at the macro level.

HIGHLIGHT 1.4

Resiliency: Seeking Strength amid Adversity

Resiliency is the ability of an individual, family, group, community, or organization to recover from adversity and resume functioning even when suffering serious trouble, confusion, or hardship (Glicken, 2006). Norman (2000) provides an illustration of this concept:

> When a pitched baseball hits a window, the glass usually shatters. When that same ball meets a baseball bat, the bat is rarely damaged. When a hammer strikes a ceramic vase, it too usually shatters. But when that same hammer hits a rubber automobile tire, the tire quickly returns to its original shape. The baseball bat and the automobile tire both demonstrate resiliency. (p. 3)

Resiliency involves two dimensions–risk and protection (Norman, 2000). In this context *risk* involves "stressful life events or adverse environmental conditions that increase the *vulnerability* [defenselessness or helplessness] of individuals" or other systems (p. 3). *Protection,* on the other hand, concerns those factors that "buffer, moderate, and protect against those vulnerabilities" (p. 3).

On the individual level, an example of a resilient child is one who, despite being shifted from one foster home to another during childhood, still completes high school, enters college, and later begins a healthy family of her own. Regardless of the risks to which she's been exposed, she uses her strengths to protect herself and struggle through her adversity. Such strengths might include positive self-esteem and self-worth, good problem-solving abilities to address the difficulties confronting her, a positive sense of direction, the ability to empathize with others' situations, use of humor, high expectations for personal performance, and the ability to distance herself from the dysfunctional people and

negative events around her (Norman, 2000). A key to enabling resiliency is the identification and use of clients' strengths to overcome problems.

An example of resiliency at the organizational level is a public university experiencing budget cuts of several million dollars. That university is resilient to the extent that it responds to the risk of loss by protecting its most important functions, making plans to adapt to the shortfall of resources, and continuing to provide students with a quality education. Again, resiliency involves focusing on strengths to maintain basic functioning.

Resiliency in a community is illustrated by a group of urban neighborhoods that address an increasing crime and drug-use problem. These troubles put the community at risk for disorganization and destruction. Community strengths include availability of organizations that provide resources, residents' expectations for appropriate, positive behavior, and opportunities for "neighborhood youths to constructively participate in the community" (Greene & Livingston, 2002, p. 78). A resilient community might use its concerned citizens to form neighborhood organizations that oversee community conditions and upkeep, work with public services to improve conditions, and advocate for increased resources (Homan, 2008). Neighborhood Watch programs may be formed in which neighborhood residents volunteer to keep careful watch upon each other's premises to prevent and combat crime. Community residents might work with local police and schools to establish drug education and prevention programs for young people. They might also advocate for more police to increase surveillance and apprehension of drug dealers. A resilient community uses its strengths to address the risks threatening it and protect its residents.

Subsequently, wide-ranging issues concerning human diversity are addressed throughout the book.

7. Advocacy for Human Rights and the Pursuit of Social and Economic Justice

Advocacy for human rights and the pursuit of social and economic justice is the seventh concept inherent

in generalist practice (CSWE, 2008, EP 2.1.5b). A number of related terms are integrated under this general heading. *Advocacy* is the act of representing, championing, or defending the rights of others. *Human rights* involve the premise that all people, regardless of characteristics or circumstances (including those of race, culture, nationality, class, orientation, age, gender, ability, religion, or beliefs) are entitled to

EP 2.1.5b

HIGHLIGHT 1.5

Variables of Human Diversity

Age: Some period of time during a person's life span. Age is often considered an important aspect of human diversity for older adults as they experience *ageism,* discrimination based preconceived notions about older people, regardless of their individual qualities and capabilities.

Class (or social class): People's status or ranking in society with respect to such standards as "relative wealth, power, prestige, educational level, or family background" (Barker, 2003, p. 402).

Race: The category of people who share a common descent and genetic origin that may be distinguished by "certain physical traits," or "interests, habits, or characteristics" (Mish, 2008, p. 1024).

Ethnicity: The affiliation with a large group of people who have "common racial, national, tribal, religious, linguistic, or cultural origin or background" (Mish, 1995, p. 398).

(People of) color: "A collective term that refers to the major groups of African, Latino and Asian Americans, and First Nations People [Native Americans] who have been distinguished from the dominant society by color" (Lum, 2007, p. 117).

Culture: "A way of life including widespread values (about what is good and bad), beliefs (about what is true), and behavior (what people do every day)" (italics deleted) (Macionis, 2008, p. 2).

Disability: "Any physical or mental impairment [or ongoing health or mental health condition] that substantially limits one or more major life activities"; these activities include "seeing, hearing, speaking, walking, breathing, performing manual tasks, learn-

ing, caring for oneself, and working" (Equal Employment Opportunity Commission, 1997, p. 1).

Gender: "The social and psychological characteristics associated with being female or male" (McCammon & Knox, 2007, p. 112).

Gender identity: A person's internal psychological self-concept of being either a male or a female, or, possibly, some combination of both (Gilbert, 2008).

Gender expression: The manner in which we express ourselves to others in ways related to gender that include both behavior and personality.

Sex: "The biological distinction between being female and being male, usually categorized on the basis of the reproductive organs and genetic makeup" (McCammon & Knox, 2007, p. 606).

Sexual orientation: Sexual and romantic attraction to persons of one or both genders.

Immigration status: A person's position in terms of legal rights and residency when entering and residing in a country that is not that person's legal country of origin.

Political ideology: The "relatively coherent system of ideas (beliefs, traditions, principles, and myths) about human nature, institutional arrangements, and social processes" that indicate how a government should be run and what principles that government should support (Abramovitz, 2007, p. 126).

Religion: People's spiritual beliefs concerning the origin, character, and reason for being, usually based on the existence of some higher power or powers, that often involves designated rituals and provides direction for what is considered moral or right.

---

basic rights and fair, humane treatment. We have established that *social justice* is "an ideal condition in which all members of society have "the same basic rights, protection, opportunities, obligations, and social benefits" (Barker, 2003, pp. 404–405). Similarly, *economic justice* concerns the distribution of resources in a fair and equitable manner.

Conditions in the world are not necessarily benevolent or fair. People may be victimized by denial of human rights, such as in human trafficking for the purposes of sex or labor. They may be oppressed by social and economic injustices, such as poverty and

discrimination. Social work education seeks to teach students how to promote social and economic justice, fight discrimination, and advocate for improvements in the social and economic systems affecting people; the end result should involve more effective service provision and improvement in people's quality of life (CSWE, 2008).

In real life, social and economic justice is a hard goal to attain. Rarely are rights and resources fairly and equitably distributed. Even the definitions of "fair" and "equitable" are widely debated. Does "fair" mean that all people should receive the same income

HIGHLIGHT 1.6

Empowerment of Lesbian and Gay People at the Macro Level

EP 2.1.4

Tully (2000) explains that one facet of macro practice on a conceptual level intends to transform basic cultural traditions and behavioral expectations to make them less rigid and more compatible with current or evolving human need. Such practice would include political advocacy; development, implementation, and evaluation of public policy; and administration aimed at social change.... [The key] to macro-level intervention is to know what political and social issues are facing the lesbian and gay community at any point in time.... [One major concern today involves] same-sex marriage. Other current issues include hate crimes legislation, whether or not content related to gay and lesbian issues should be in the secondary school curriculum, and the status of gay clergy in the church.

Once familiar with the topics, the social worker needs to become an expert so as to be able to lobby, testify, and be prepared to ward off the assault of homophobia. So, too, does the social work practitioner need to build constituent groups and allies

that will become a coalition to fight for pro-gay legislation and defeat legislation that is homophobic. (pp. 110–111)

The following are recommendations for you to seek the empowerment of lesbian and gay people at the macro level:

Understand the many legal issues associated with lesbians and gays; Confront institutional homophobia [as manifested by unfair policies and legislation] at the state and federal levels; Become an expert in the field of gay and lesbian issues; Join and support pro-lesbian and gay organizations; ... [Seek access to legislators and lobby for legislation supporting lesbian and gay rights;] Prepare gay friendly testimony ... [if called upon to testify at] congressional hearings; ... Construct coalitions that support the gay and lesbian agenda; Create constituencies and make allies that are pro-gay; Be dignified and polite in legislative defeat; Learn to negotiate for an agreeable outcome; Be gracious, even in the face of homophobia. (Elze, 2006; Tully, 2000, p. 111)

---

regardless of what work they do or even whether they have jobs at all? The point is that social workers must be vigilantly aware of the existence of injustice. It is our ethical responsibility to combat injustice whenever it is necessary and possible to do so. Chapter 11 explores this dimension of generalist practice in much greater depth.

8. Effective Work within an Organizational Structure

Social workers practice within the context of organizations, the eighth dimension of generalist practice. *Organizational structure* is the formal and informal manner in which tasks and responsibilities, lines of authority, channels of communication, and dimensions of power are established and coordinated within an organization.

Tasks and responsibilities, of course, involve what you and other staff are supposed to accomplish during your workday. Lines of authority concern who supervises whom. You might think of them as the chain of command. For example, who has the responsibility for overseeing your work performance? Channels of communication entail who communicates with whom and how. Dimensions of power delineate whose opinions carry the most weight in agency decision making. Who captivates other staff members' attention during meetings and who bores them to tears? Who has the most control over agency policy?

Agency structure may be formal (that is, by the book and according to the rules), informal (that is, based on the more flexible way the agency really works), or some combination of the two. Consider channels of communication, for example. They may follow formal lines of authority or very informal routes.

How information really gets circulated within an agency may be very different from what the formal hierarchy indicates.

The following is an example of an informal agency structure. The agency director's brother-in-law is a direct service worker within an organization that has several levels of authority. That is, designated supervisors oversee direct worker supervisees (such as the director's brother-in-law), managers are responsible for supervisors, assistant directors supervise managers, and the agency director oversees the assistant directors. Each level is responsible for the employees on the level below.

In our example, the agency director's brother-in-law has the agency director's ear whenever he wants it. Thus, the channel of communication flows directly from the bottom level to the very top. This informal reality does not coincide with the formal structure. The brother-in-law also has greater power than other staff at his level and at higher levels because of his access to the agency director. Therefore, the dimensions of real power vary dramatically from those portrayed by the formal lines of authority.

It is very important for generalist practitioners to examine, evaluate, and understand their agency's formal and informal structure in order to do their jobs effectively. Chapter 4 will address these and other similar issues much more thoroughly.

In addition to understanding formal and informal agency operations, there are other aspects of agency life about which you should be heedfully aware. One involves the importance of developing and demonstrating a professional identity and demeanor (CSWE, 2008, EP 2.1.1). How should a "professional" act? What does a "professional" look like?

Another important facet of effective work within an organizational structure concerns using supervision appropriately (CSWE, 2008, EP 2.1.1f). What does this mean? We propose that the appropriate use of professional supervision involves all of the following: knowing practitioners' general expectations of supervisors; understanding the administrative, educational, and other functions of supervisors; using supervision as effectively as possible; addressing problems commonly occurring in supervisory relationships; and adapting specific techniques to assist supervisors in the supervisory process. Chapter 2, "Using Micro Skills in the Macro Environment," discusses professional identity, use of supervision, and other important factors concerning interpersonal agency activity in depth.

9. A Wide Range of Roles

EP 2.1.1c

The ninth dimension of generalist practice involves the assumption of professional roles (CSWE, 2008, EP 2.1.1c). *A role* is a culturally expected behavior pattern for a person having a specified status or being involved in a designated social relationship. For example, people have certain expectations regarding how social workers are supposed to act. Social workers are expected to participate in certain activities.

In order to best understand the various roles generalist practitioners play, it is useful to recall the four types of systems involved in generalist practice (illustrated in Figure 1.4). As we discussed, the *client system* includes those people who will ultimately benefit from the change process. The *change agent system* is the individual who initiates the macro change process. Where the diagrams in Figures 1.4 through 1.15 refer to the worker, they mean the change agent system—you. The *action system* includes those people who agree to and will work together to attain the proposed macro change. Finally, the *target system* is the system that social workers must "change or influence in order to accomplish (their) goals" (Pincus & Minahan, 1973, p. 58). In macro practice, our own agency, some subsystem within our agency, or the community may become the system at which we direct our intervention efforts.

Figures 1.4 through 1.15 illustrate a variety of possible social work roles characteristic of macro generalist

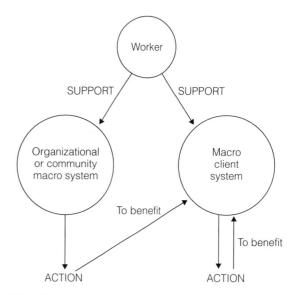

FIGURE 1.4 The Enabler Role in Macro Practice

practice. They include enabler, mediator, integrator/coordinator, manager, educator, analyst/evaluator, broker, facilitator, initiator, negotiator, mobilizer, and advocate. Although these figures represent macro practice roles, remember that many of the roles can also characterize interventions in micro or mezzo practice.

These figures will use circles to represent the worker, macro client systems, and organizational or community macro systems. Lines and arrows depict how systems relate to each other. Note that, unless specified otherwise, a macro system can illustrate interaction with either an organization or a community.

Enabler

An *enabler* provides support, encouragement, and suggestions to members of a macro client system so that the system may complete tasks or solve problems more easily and successfully. In the enabler role, a worker helps a client system cope with various stresses, ranging from crisis situations such as divorce or job loss to community issues such as inadequate housing or day care. Skills used in the enabler role include "conveying hope, reducing resistance and ambivalence, recognizing and managing feelings, identifying and supporting personal strengths and social assets," breaking down problems into more manageable parts, emphasizing goals, and identifying ways to attain them (Barker, 2003, p. 143). Enablers, then, are helpers. Practitioners can function in the role of enabler for micro, mezzo, or macro systems.

Note that this definition of *enabler* is very different from that used in the topic area of substance abuse. There, the term refers to a family member or friend who facilitates the substance abuser in continuing to use and abuse the drug of his or her choice.

Figure 1.4 illustrates the enabler role in macro practice. Arrows point from the worker system (you) to both the organizational or community macro system circle and to the macro client system. These portray the support provided by the worker that assists either macro system in undertaking some action. The latter is depicted by arrows leading from both macro systems to the word *Action*. This action, in turn, is intended to result in some benefit for the macro client system. Thus, arrows also lead from the word *Action* back to the macro client system.

Mediator

A *mediator* resolves arguments or disagreements among micro, mezzo, or macro systems in disagreement

(Toseland & Rivas, 2009; Yessian & Broskowsky, 1983). At the macro level, mediation involves helping various factions (subsystems) within a community—or helping a community system and some other system (such as another community)—work out their differences. For example, a community (or neighborhood) and a social services organization may require mediation over the location of a substance abuse treatment center. In this case, the social services organization might have selected a prime spot, but the community might balk at having such a center within its boundaries. The mediator role may involve improving communication among dissident individuals or groups or otherwise helping those involved come to a compromise. A mediator remains neutral, not siding with either party in the dispute. Mediators make sure they understand the positions of both parties. They may help to clarify positions, recognize miscommunication about differences, and help those involved present their cases clearly.

Figure 1.5 illustrates the mediator role. The worker circle is placed between the organizational or community macro system circle and the macro client system circle. This reflects the worker's neutral stance, requiring that she or he take neither of the involved parties' sides. The broken line beneath the worker circle depicts the two parties' conflicting communication and their inability to settle differences. This particular diagram depicts a worker mediating between an organizational or community macro system (on the left) and a macro client system (on the right). However, mediation can occur between or among virtually any size systems.

Integrator/Coordinator

Integration is the process of assembling different elements to form a cohesive whole. *Coordination* involves bringing components together in some kind of organized manner. An *integrator/coordinator,* therefore, brings people involved in various systems together and organizes their performance (Hardcastle & Powers, 2004;

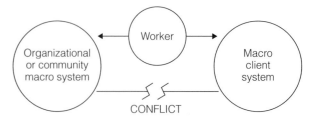

FIGURE 1.5 The Mediator Role in Macro Practice

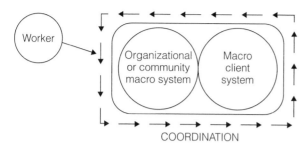

FIGURE 1.6 The Integrator/Coordinator Role in Macro Practice

FIGURE 1.7 The Manager Role in Macro Practice

Yessian & Broskowsky, 1983). A generalist social worker can function as an integrator/coordinator "in many ways, ranging from … advocacy and identification of coordination opportunities, to provision of technical assistance, to direct involvement in the development and implementation of service linkages" (Yessian & Broskowsky, 1983, p. 184).

Figure 1.6 depicts an organizational or community macro system and a macro client system located next to each other within a box to illustrate that they are working together. The arrow pointing from the worker to the box portrays the worker's active leadership in bringing together and coordinating the two systems' performances. The arrows circulating around the box reflect the coordination process.

Manager

A *manager* in social work is one who assumes some level of administrative responsibility for a social services agency or other organizational system (Brody, 2005; Yessian & Broskowsky, 1983). Administrators utilize three levels of skills—technical, people, and conceptual (Lewis, Lewis, Packard, & Souflee, 2001, p. 8). *Technical skills* include those used to direct an agency's basic activities such as overseeing counseling techniques, developing programs, or evaluating the agency's effectiveness. *People skills* concern "interpersonal effectiveness such as oral communication, listening, conflict management, leading, and motivating" (p. 8). *Conceptual skills* are those oriented toward assessing and understanding the overall operation of the agency and how it fits into its larger macro environment. These also concern being able to solve complex problems and develop creative solutions. The term *management* refers to all "the tasks and activities involved in directing an organization or one of its units: planning, organizing, leading, and controlling" (Hellriegel, Jackson, & Slocum, 2002, p. 7).

Figure 1.7 portrays the manager role. We assume that the organization employs both social workers and various staff members, including other social workers, other professionals, and support staff. The worker circle is located above two staff circles with arrows directed down from the worker circle to both staff circles. This diagram indicates that the worker, having administrative status, has authority over the staff. All three circles are located within the larger organizational environment circle to indicate that the manager role usually occurs within an organizational context.

Educator

An *educator* gives information and teaches skills to other systems (Yessian & Broskowsky, 1983, pp. 183–84). To be an effective educator, the worker must first be knowledgeable about the topics being taught. Additionally, the worker must be a good communicator so that information is conveyed clearly and is readily understood by the receivers.

In Figure 1.8, arrows run from the worker circle both to the organizational or community macro system

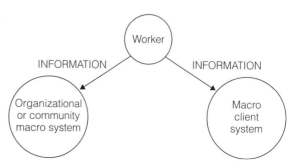

FIGURE 1.8 The Educator Role in Macro Practice

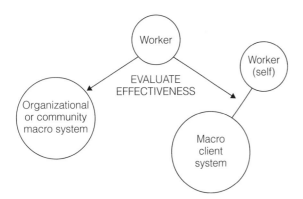

FIGURE 1.9 The Analyst/Evaluator Role in Macro Practice

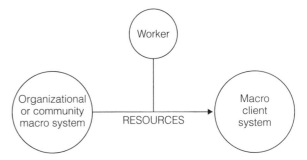

FIGURE 1.10 The Broker Role in Macro Practice

circle and to the macro system circle. This depicts that a worker conveys information to these other systems.

Analyst/Evaluator

An *analyst/evaluator* determines whether a program or agency is effective (Brody, 2005; Yessian & Broskowsky, 1983). This can occur in an organizational or community context. Generalist social workers with a broad knowledge base of how various-sized systems function can analyze or evaluate how well programs and systems work. Likewise, they can evaluate the effectiveness of their own interventions.

Figure 1.9 reflects how an analyst/evaluator functions. One arrow points from the worker (you) to an organizational or community macro system to illustrate how a worker in an analyst/evaluator role can evaluate a program's or an agency's effectiveness. A second arrow points from the worker to a line that joins another worker to a macro client system. This connecting line illustrates the worker's professional planned change relationship with his or her clients. The arrow illustrates how workers can and indeed should evaluate their own practice with clients.

Broker

A *broker* links any size system (individuals, groups, organizations, or communities) with community resources and services. Such resources might be financial, legal, educational, psychological, recreational, or health-oriented.

In Figure 1.10, the line from the worker circle to the arrow leading from the macro system to the macro client system illustrates the worker's active involvement in obtaining resources for the macro client system. The arrow points from the organizational or community macro system circle that provides resources to the client system circle that receives these resources.

Facilitator

A *facilitator* is one who guides a group experience. Although the facilitator role is very common in mezzo practice, workers also frequently lead groups in macro practice. In the macro context, a facilitator brings participants together to promote the change process by improving communication, helping direct their efforts and resources, and linking them with needed information and expert help.

Figure 1.11 depicts three circles labeled "Colleague" that are connected with each other by lines representing group interaction and communication. Additionally, the linking lines illustrate how colleagues working together form a mezzo system. These three colleague circles are enclosed by a larger circle, a mezzo system, that could be a task or planning group within an organization or a community. The arrow pointing from the worker to the mezzo system depicts the worker's leadership of the mezzo system. Hence, the rounded square entitled "Organizational or Community Macro System" encompasses all of the interaction.

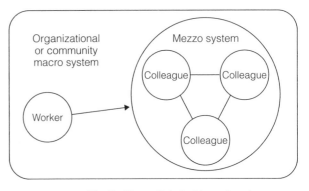

FIGURE 1.11 The Facilitator Role in Macro Practice

The worker facilitates whatever interaction occurs within the mezzo system that, in turn, occurs within the macro context. Note that, although Figure 1.11 arbitrarily depicts three colleagues, any number of colleagues, clients, community residents, administrators, or politicians could be involved in reality.

Initiator

An *initiator* is the person or persons who call attention to an issue (Hardcastle & Powers, 2004). The issue in the community may be a problem, a need, or simply a situation that can be improved. It is important to recognize that a problem does not have to exist before a situation can be dealt with. Often, preventing future problems or enhancing existing services is a satisfactory reason for creating a change effort. Thus, a social worker may recognize that a policy has the potential to create problems for particular clients and bring this to the attention of her supervisor. Likewise, a client may identify ways that service could be improved. In each case, the worker is playing the role of initiator in terms of beginning the actual change process. Usually, this role must be followed up by other kinds of work, because merely pointing out problems does not guarantee they will be solved.

In Figure 1.12, an arrow leading from the worker on the far left to the macro system circle in the middle represents the worker's activities directed at improving service provision. Another arrow, which leads from the macro system to the macro client system on the far right, reflects the benefits that the macro system provides for the macro client system as the ultimate result of the initiator's efforts.

Negotiator

A *negotiator* is an intermediary who acts to settle disputes and/or resolve disagreements. However, unlike mediators, negotiators clearly take the side of one of the parties involved.

In Figure 1.13, the macro client system and the worker are located together on the left side of the figure. This indicates that the worker is negotiating on behalf of the macro client system. Two jagged lines with arrows pointing away from them in opposing directions characterize the conflict that has arisen. The macro system on the right side of the figure represents an organization or community engulfed in conflict with the macro client system and the worker/negotiator on the left. The worker/negotiator seeks to resolve the conflict, but does so on behalf of one side of the conflict, namely, the macro client system.

Mobilizer

A *mobilizer* identifies and convenes community people and resources and makes them responsive to unmet community needs (Halley, Kopp, & Austin, 1998). The mobilizer's purpose is to match resources to needs within the community context. Sometimes a mobilizer's goal involves making services more accessible to citizens who need them. Other times a goal is initiating and developing services to meet needs that heretofore were unmet.

In Figure 1.14, the worker on the left is assuming a mobilizer role in a macro practice context. The large central circle is labeled "Community Macro System." The citizens within the community macro system circle represent an arbitrary number of community residents. (Fewer citizens may be involved, or perhaps thousands of community residents are part of the mobilization process. Ideally, an entire community with virtually all of its residents would participate in the macro intervention process.) The arrow leading from the worker (mobilizer) to the community macro system represents the worker's efforts directed toward the mobilization process. The arrows inside the community macro system leading from the citizens toward "Action" represent the resultant efforts of citizens as they participate in the process of meeting the community's unmet needs. The larger arrow leading from the community macro system circle to "Action" represents the process of pooling all the citizens' efforts into some coordinated action.

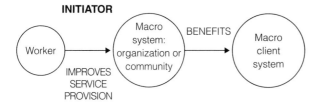

FIGURE 1.12 The Initiator Role in Macro Practice

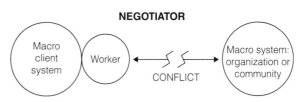

FIGURE 1.13 The Negotiator Role in Macro Practice

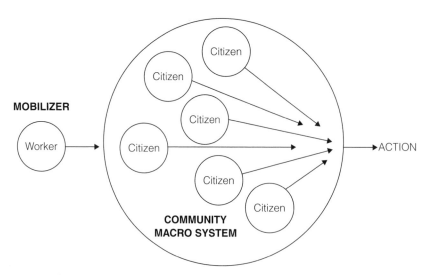

FIGURE 1.14 The Mobilizer Role in Macro Practice

Note that, unlike most of the other roles illustrated in these figures, the mobilizer role occurs *only* in the context of a community. By our definition, it does not apply to organizations.

Advocate

Advocacy is active intervention on a client system's behalf to get needed resources that are currently unavailable, or to change regulations or policies that negatively affect that client system. An *advocate* is one who steps forward and speaks out on behalf of the client system in order to promote fair and equitable treatment or gain needed resources. In macro practice, of course, it would be on behalf of some macro client system. This may be especially appropriate when a macro client system has little power to get what it needs. Advocacy often involves expending more effort than is necessary to simply accomplish your job. It also often involves taking risks, especially when advocating on a client's behalf in the face of a larger, more powerful system. Chapter 11 explores advocacy at length.

The advocate role is one of the most important roles a generalist social worker can assume, despite its potential difficulties. To emphasize its importance, it is the last macro practice role to be discussed here. It is one of the practice dimensions that makes generalist social work practice unique (Kirst-Ashman & Hull, 2009). It is part of a generalist social worker's ethical responsibility to go beyond the minimum requirements of his or her job on behalf of a client system when that client system is in desperate need of help or resources.

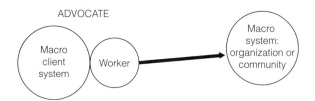

FIGURE 1.15 The Advocate Role in Macro Practice

Figure 1.15 depicts a macro client system and a worker standing together to reflect the worker's alliance with the macro client system during the advocacy process. The bold arrow leading from the worker to the macro system at the right is exceptionally thick, to represent the significant amount of energy it often takes to have an impact on a larger, more powerful system. The elevated location of the macro system above the worker and macro client system illustrates the former's greater power.

Professional Identity and Professional Roles

Regardless of what roles social workers assume while working within an organization, generalist practitioners should maintain and demonstrate a professional identity. *Identification with the social work profession* means that "social workers [should] serve as representatives of the profession, its mission, and its core values" (CSWE, 2008, EP 2.1.1). Such identification

EP 2.1.1

includes a commitment to "the profession's enhancement and to their own professional conduct and growth" in addition to knowledge of the profession's history (CSWE, 2008, EP 2.1.1). Professional identification, then, involves adherence to professional ethics, demonstration of professional roles (discussed here), and participation in lifelong learning to enhance knowledge and skills (CSWE, 2008, EP 2.1.1).

10. Use of Critical Thinking Skills

EP 2.1.3

Critical thinking is the tenth major concept inherent in the definition of generalist practice (CSWE, 2008, EP 2.1.3). It is (1) the careful scrutiny of what is stated as true or what appears to be true and the resulting expression of an opinion or conclusion based on that scrutiny, and (2) the creative formulation of an opinion or conclusion when presented with a question, problem, or issue (Kirst-Ashman, 2010). Critical thinking concentrates on "the process of reasoning" (Gambrill & Gibbs, 2009, p. 4). It stresses *how* individuals think about the truth inherent in a situation or statement, or *how* they analyze an issue to formulate their own conclusions. As Gibbs and Gambrill (1999) so aptly state, "Critical thinkers question what others take for granted" (p. 13). In generalist macro practice, critical thinking may involve seriously scrutinizing the functioning of organizations and communities in the macro environment. It also may concern analysis of the client system's problems and issues in order to determine how to proceed in the helping process.

Two dimensions included in the definition of critical thinking are significant. First, critical thinking focuses on the questioning of beliefs, statements, assumptions, lines of reasoning, actions, and experiences. This means that social workers must be able to critique arguments, statements, and experiences for inconsistencies. They must also be able to distinguish between assertion and fact, observation, and impression. When social workers meet with clients, colleagues, agency administrators, or politicians, what thoughts go through their heads? What assumptions do they automatically make? How valid are these thoughts and assumptions? Another component of critical thinking is recognizing what one does not know. In other words, what information is missing?

The second facet of the definition of critical thinking is the creative formulation of an opinion or conclusion

when presented with a question, problem, or issue. What do *you* think is the answer to a question or solution to a problem? For example, as a generalist practitioner, you would use critical thinking to determine what is the most effective approach to help solve a particular client's problem. You would choose techniques not on hearsay, but rather on such variables as their track record of effectiveness with that specific client population. Workers should carefully examine any statements or claims made as facts by evaluating arguments on both sides of an issue.

An example concerns a colleague who tells you that bubble-blowing therapy is the best thing since 40-calorie-per-slice bread (compared to the usual 70-to-80-calorie kind), and your agency should adopt this as its primary treatment modality. As a critical thinker, you would critically evaluate the validity of that statement. What research does the colleague have to back up the remark? What are the theoretical underpinnings of bubble-blowing therapy? Of course, we are being facetious about bubble blowing—but the point is that critical thinking means not necessarily accepting situations or stories at face value. Rather, it entails using your own judgment to seriously consider their worth and relevance.

A Formula for Critical Thinking

In generalist practice the goal of critical thinking is to evaluate the accuracy of impressions, assess diverse aspects of a situation, and develop creative approaches to finding solutions and making plans. One basic method for critical thinking involves the following Triple A approach (Kirst-Ashman, 2010):

1. *Ask questions.*
2. *Assess the established facts and issues involved.*
3. *Assert a concluding opinion.*

For instance, a client states, "This is a terrible community! I hate living here!" As a critical thinker, you would not take these statements at face value. Rather, you would think about what further information you would need to determine whether you agree with the statement. What questions would you *ask?* What are the reasons that the community is "terrible"? How is "terrible" being defined? What specific conditions contribute to this negative view of the community? These are just some of numerous questions that you could ask to solicit information.

Next, a critical thinker would *assess* the facts. Consider the reasons that might relate to the community being "terrible." To what extent does the word "terrible" reflect the actual conditions in the community? What facts support the accusation that the community is "terrible" and what information maintains that there are also positive dimensions inherent there?

Finally, a critical thinker would *assert* a concluding opinion. After gathering data and evaluating its accuracy and value, to what extent would you agree with the client's opinion and statement?

Fallacies to Avoid

There are a number of practice fallacies that can trick practitioners into false beliefs (Gambrill & Gibbs, 2009). A *fallacy* is a false or erroneous idea, often hidden behind what appears to be a sound argument or presentation. A fallacy or mistaken assumption can trick you into believing what is not true. Fallacies often appear to be true, but really are not.

One fallacy involves charisma, charm, and possibly even glamour (Gibbs & Gambrill, 1996). For example, a new agency director of a private family services agency assumes his post. He is a charming, charismatic character who has lots of new and exciting ideas for massive changes within the agency. Staff members are taken by his striking presence and awed by his massive accumulation of experience. However, they are just as stupefied when he loses one-third of the agency's funding because of an arrogant personal dispute with the administrators of one of the agency's primary funding sources. Likewise, they are shocked when his wife accuses him of adultery for having an affair with the agency's public relations director. Agency staff, other administrators, and board members are mortified at the negative publicity this brings to the agency. The director abruptly leaves the agency after a devastating 18 months to manifest his charisma at some other eager organization. Critical thinking would encourage the staff to review performance before forming an opinion of the director. They would scrutinize the apparently wonderful exterior appearance and wait to see what characteristics and qualities really lie underneath.

Two other fallacies involved in this particular example include those of "newness" and of "unfounded authority" based on experience (Gambrill & Gibbs, 2009, pp. 113, 115). The director came to the agency with bright new ideas. A person using critical thinking would not assume that, because these ideas are new and popular elsewhere, they must be good. The other fallacy involves the director's supposed extensive experience and his resulting authority supposedly anchored in experience. Was his experience really good? Was it relevant to what this particular agency needed? Were his interpersonal skills really effective or were they based on his pumped-up ego?

Still another fallacy concerns the "fact" that if something is written down (for example, in a book like this), then it must be true. Beware. One of the reasons that you are required to take a research course is so you can evaluate for yourself the quality of the research, backing up any "facts" you read in books and journals. Critical thinking requires that you consider the rationale and proof of anything you read.

Highlight 1.7 identifies a range of other fallacies and pitfalls to avoid when using critical thinking.

A Final Note on Critical Thinking and Generalist Practice

You can use critical thinking throughout generalist practice. This includes the evaluation of client records, agency policy, administrators' directives, the effectiveness of treatment modalities, or recommendations for planned change with clients. It is not that you should distrust everything you see or hear, but rather that you be on constant lookout for possible fallacies.

11. Incorporation of Research-Informed Practice

The eleventh important dimension of generalist practice involves the use of research. We have established that social work students must be knowledgeable about various approaches to research for a number of reasons. Subsequently, as generalist practitioners, they must demonstrate competency in *research-informed practice.* We described this as the use of approaches and interventions in practice that research has determined are effective. Social workers should employ "research findings to improve practice, policy, and social service delivery" (CSWE, 2008, EP 2.1.6).

EP 2.1.6b

Another term frequently used in social work, which has a meaning similar to research-informed practice, is *evidence-based practice.* This is the careful, thoughtful, and conscientious use of the best evidence available to implement interventions that have been proven effective in specific practice situations (Gambrill, 2005; Rubin & Babbie, 2010). Rubin and Babbie explain:

Practitioners engaged in evidence-based practice will be critical thinkers [described earlier]. Rather than automatically accepting everything others with more experience or authority tell them about practice, they will question things. They will recognize unfounded

HIGHLIGHT 1.7

More Fallacies to Avoid When Using Critical Thinking

Gambrill (2005) cites the following fallacies to avoid when using critical thinking:

1. *"Irrelevant conclusion:* A conclusion is irrelevant to the reasoning that led to it.

   I don't think Mr. Jones abused his child. He acts like a normal father; he even spends time on the weekends repairing his car" (p. 162).

2. *"Hasty generalization:* Considering only exceptional cases and generalizing from those cases to a rule that fits only those exceptions.

   Bill and a friend were discussing the director of their agency. Bill said, 'He is a total failure because he has not increased funding for our agency'" (p. 162).

3. *"Overlooking the role of chance:* Assuming that an outcome due to chance is related to past occurrences.

   My next baby must be a boy. We've had five girls" (p. 162).

4. *"Personalization:* Assuming you are the cause of some event for which you were not primarily responsible, or taking personally a statement that is not directed toward you" (p. 162).

   My supervisor didn't come to our supervisory meeting. I must have done something he didn't like. I must be to blame.

5. *"Invalid disjunction (either/or-ing):* Considering only two options when more than two should be considered" (p. 163).

   We should either get big raises or none at all.

6. *"Fallacies based on availability:* Accepting the first explanation for an event that occurs to you without considering other, less obvious, or readily available explanations.

   I can see he is an angry man by how he acts in the office. I think he is guilty of abusing his wife" (p. 163).

7. *"Argument from ignorance:* Assuming that something is true simply because it has not been shown to be false, or that it is false simply because it has not been shown to be true.

   You don't have any proof that your method works. Therefore, I don't think it does" (p. 163).

8. *"Mental filter:* Picking out some small aspect of a situation (often a negative one) and focusing on this so that the 'bigger picture' is ignored. All events are viewed through the filter of one aspect of the situation.

   I just don't like the way my director dresses" (p. 163).

9. *"Emotional reasoning:* Using our emotions or feelings as evidence of a truth.

   This is true because I feel it is true" (p. 163).

10. *"Appeal to authority:* Arguing that a claim is true based purely on an authority's status with no reference to evidence" (p. 163).

    The President of the United States said…

11. *"Argumentation ad populum:* Assuming that 'if everyone else thinks this way, it must be right.' Appeal to popularity.

    Everyone is using this new method. I think we should use it, too" (p. 163).

12. *"Appeal to tradition:* That's the way we have always done it. We should continue to use these methods" (p. 164).

13. *"Influence by testimonials:* I believe it works because Mrs. Rivera said she tried it and it helped" (p. 164).

14. *"Assume that good intentions result in good services* (e.g., protect clients from harm): In response to a question from a client about an agency's effectiveness, you say, "We really care about our clients'" (p. 164).

beliefs and assumptions and think for themselves as to the logic and evidence supporting what others may convey as practice wisdom. Rather than just conform blindly to tradition or authority, they will take into account the best scientific evidence available in deciding how to intervene at micro or macro levels of practice. (2010, p. 20)

Chapter 10 discusses the evaluation of macro practice in much greater depth.

12. Use of a Planned Change Process

The final component of generalist practice is use of a planned change process (CSWE, 2008, 2.1.10).

As you saw in Figure 1.1, this process entails seven basic steps: engagement, assessment, planning,

EP 2.1.10

implementation, evaluation, termination, and follow-up. Because of the significance of this process in generalist practice, we will spend some time discussing each step.

Note that another term often used to describe what generalist practitioners do is *problem solving,* which refers to the same thing as planned change, although many debate the nuances of difference. Social work's recent emphasis on client strengths may be at odds with the more negative connotations of the word "problem." The term "change" may have more positive connotations, despite the fact that most social work intervention deals with problem situations. Another concept similar to planned change is *intervention,* a summary term for all the "activities [required] to solve or prevent problems or achieve" practice goals (Barker, 2003, p. 227).

The planned change procedures introduced in this and subsequent chapters are intended to provide basic guidelines for how to think about and pursue the macro change process. They are meant to be easily remembered and to provide you with a clear focus concerning macro change. They are not intended to be the precisely perfect formula for achieving change in every circumstance. Other techniques and approaches may also be effectively integrated into practice with organizations and communities.

Engagement

Engagement is the initial period in which practitioners orient themselves to the problem at hand and begin to establish communication and a relationship with the individual or individuals also addressing the problem. During the engagement process, practitioners should pursue the following four tasks: "(1) to involve themselves in the situation, (2) to establish communication with everyone concerned, (3) to begin to define the parameters within which the worker and the client(s) will work, and (4) to create an initial working structure" (Brill, 2005, p. 132).

Engagement "may be as simple as walking into a crowded waiting room, or receiving a letter, a card, or a phone call, or as complicated as attending a board meeting involving differences about a major company decision, or going into a neighborhood that is in a state of crisis over some loaded issue such as school busing" (Brill, 2005, p. 132).

The outcomes of engagement should be fourfold (Brill, 2005). First, the practitioner should become an *integral* facet of the problematic situation. Thus, the worker becomes successfully engaged in the planned change process. Second, those involved in the engagement process should establish effective communication among themselves. Third, the practitioner and the client system should establish some agreement concerning the problematic issue and how to go about addressing it. Fourth, they should develop an understanding about what to do next.

In a macro practice context, engagement of others is not only limited to the first step in planned change. It may occur repeatedly throughout the planned change process. You may need to engage new individuals, contacts, resources, decision makers, or groups, depending upon how the process is proceeding. Any time you must contact a new person or nurture new relationships, engagement should occur.

Assessment: Identifying Issues and Collecting Information

Blythe and Reithoffer (2000) offer the following description of assessment:

EP 2.1.10d

> *Assessment is a cornerstone of effective practice. It involves identifying the nature and extent of client needs and concerns, as well as critical information about client resources and supports and other environmental factors. The results of assessment activities form the basis for developing, implementing, and modifying [an intervention] … plan.* (p. 551)

Several aspects of assessment are important (CSWE, 2008, 2.1.10d; Sheafor & Horejsi, 2009). First, it involves soliciting information, interpreting it, and making judgments about its usefulness. Second, practitioners initiate assessment in the early stages of the planned change process but continue it throughout. Workers must respond to environmental and client system changes and adapt intervention plans to meet newly developed needs. Third, the information collected must be organized so that the worker and client system together can formulate a plan of action to solve the problem or make the change.

We have emphasized the importance of assessing client systems from the micro, mezzo, and macro perspectives. Generalist practice means that at any time in the intervention process, you might choose either a micro, mezzo, or macro approach. One dimension of such assessment is the identification of your client system.

Identifying Your Client System

Who exactly makes up your client system? On whose behalf are you working? This may not be as easy as it sounds. It seems logical to say your clients are those people who are cited on your client list (or, you might say, your caseload). However, people, their lives, and their problems are often very complex. The designation of who is really your client and who is not may become blurred and vague. Even assuming a micro perspective in a direct service position, the issue may be complicated.

For example, you may be a social worker at a group home for delinquent female adolescents. Your pre-scribed job role might involve individual, group, and family counseling. So who is in your client system? Is it each individual female resident? Is it the entire group of eight residents? Is it each resident within her family system? Or is it all the residents and all their family systems?

In this example, your client system will sometimes be an individual teen. At other times, the client system may be a teen and her family as part of one mezzo client system. Still other times, your client system may be the mezzo system of all eight residents as you run group counseling. Finally, your client system may be a macro client system, namely, the agency or the community, depending on who is supposed to benefit from the intervention process.

Assessing the Client System's Problems and Needs from a Macro Perspective

Consider an agency serving homeless men. Many of the male clients also have substance abuse problems. However, agency staff really are not trained or prepared to deal with these issues. Suppose you are a social worker for this agency.

You think about the clients' situations. Most clients currently involved with the agency temporarily live in the homeless shelter. They are served by social work and other staff providing various types of counseling.

Likewise, you think about clients' problems and needs. Common problems involve unemployment, lack of self-esteem, poor planning skills, and substance addiction. Subsequently, typical needs include planning for vocational training or job placement, gaining self-confidence, learning planning and planned change skills, and, as it turns out, controlling addiction.

Clients are already involved with the agency at the micro level. Many also participate in group counseling at the mezzo level. You cannot think of specific ways to address substance abuse further at either the micro or

mezzo levels. The macro level—this text's focus—is the next approach to consider.

You know that the clients are readily accessible, because most live in the shelter. Additionally, most are already involved in counseling with the agency's staff. You continue to work with clients concerning their perceptions of problems and needs. Finally, you decide that the agency itself is the logical target of intervention. You begin to define the need for personnel more adequately trained in dealing with substance abuse problems.

You start thinking about the need to establish an in-service training program where the agency brings in experts to train staff concerning this issue.[3] We have established that the client system in this case would be all agency clients with substance abuse problems who would eventually benefit from this training. The client system is made up of these *agency clients* despite the fact that *agency staff* would participate in and hopefully benefit from the training.

You have come up with an idea for a macro intervention. You would like to establish a time-limited training program for agency staff on substance abuse. (This is one type of macro intervention, namely, project implementation, within an agency setting that Chapter 7 will address in much greater detail.)

Diversity. Along with assessing the client system's situation from micro, mezzo, and macro perspectives, you also must assess aspects of diversity. Suppose that many clients are Hispanic. Therefore, you consider including trainers with expertise in the area of Hispanic clients with substance abuse problems.

Identifying Client Strengths

Finally, it is critically important to incorporate client strengths into your assessment (CSWE, 2008, EP 2.1.10e). From a micro perspective, many individual clients are highly motivated to improve their life conditions. Most are penniless and feel

EP 2.1.10e

hopeless. They have "hit bottom" and sincerely desire positive change for themselves. In our example, these

---

3. *In-service training* is a program provided by an employing agency (usually conducted by a supervisor or an outside expert) designed to help agency staff improve their effectiveness (e.g., providing education about specific treatment techniques) or better understand agency functioning (e.g., educating staff about new legal issues or policy changes).

clients are readily available, because they reside in the agency's shelter.

Strengths from a mezzo perspective are a bit more difficult to pinpoint. Because most clients are severed from close family relationships, potential goals for these clients might include rebuilding some of their family relationships. Thus, perhaps some clients may be able to establish familial support at this mezzo level. Additionally, clients frequently participate in support and educational groups run by the agency, thereby establishing an additional strength at the mezzo level.

Finally, you examine strengths at the macro level. First, you verify that the agency probably has adequate resources to provide the required in-service training. Second, you think that you very likely could convince the agency administration to support the proposed project on the basis of its benefits. Third, you feel that staff would be very receptive to participation in the project because it would enhance their skills in an area of need.

Planning in Macro Practice

Planning in generalist practice is the process of identifying goals, rationally considering various ways to implement them, and establishing specific steps to achieve them. Because macro practice involves many more people, variables, contexts, and circumstances than micro and mezzo practice usually do, the planning process, too, is much more complicated. Many more variables merit consideration. At the micro and mezzo levels of intervention, the possibility of macro-level change must always be considered a possibility. Yet in most cases, generalist practitioners will address their clients' problems only from the micro and mezzo perspectives, as these workers' job descriptions probably dictate.

Once you seriously consider the possibility of pursuing macro level change, you have a number of additional issues to think about and steps to follow. Because macro practice assessment and planning are so complicated, the inherent assessment and planning steps often blend to some degree. Possible macro level alternatives usually stretch even farther beyond the worker's control than when that worker is assessing micro or mezzo problems and planning their solutions.

Implementation and Evaluation in Macro Practice

Just as assessment and planning processes for macro changes are more complex, so are the implementation and evaluation phases. *Implementation* is the actual undertaking of the plan. *Evaluation* is the process of determining whether a given change effort was worthwhile.

Termination in Macro Practice

Termination is the ending of a designated macro practice process. After an intervention has been evaluated, one of two things usually occurs. On the one hand, the planned change process in the macro context can simply be terminated. In this case, either goals and objectives have been achieved to an adequate extent or the worker determines that continuation of the macro pursuit is pointless. On the other hand, a practitioner may decide that goals and objectives have not been adequately achieved and problems still exist. In this case, the worker may decide to continue the planned change process, beginning once again with assessment.

Follow-Up in Macro Practice

Follow-up is the last step in the generalist intervention model's planned change process. After formal termination, *follow-up* involves checking on whether the macro intervention process has, indeed, succeeded or whether the same old problems have resurfaced in another form. Many times, this is the most difficult step to follow. Caseloads may be too heavy and filled with crises. The worker may be distracted by other issues and demands. Follow-up information might be hard to get. However, most often, substantial effort must be expended to pursue a macro change effort. Follow-up can establish whether the entire process produced lasting, effective changes, or whether problems have surfaced again and merit renewed attention.

Specific Steps for Pursuing Planned Change in Macro Practice

Later chapters in this book will introduce you to detailed steps that guide you through most of the planned change process. The first process model, PREPARE (an acronym for the steps involved), will lead you through assessment and planning in macro practice. The second process model, IMAGINE (also an acronym), will guide you through the implementation and evaluation steps in planned change. Figure 1.16 illustrates how PREPARE and IMAGINE synchronize with planned change in macro practice.

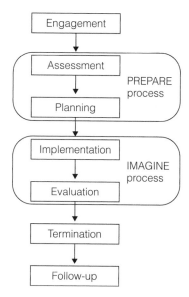

FIGURE 1.16 Macro Practice Planned Change

We will briefly introduce you to PREPARE and IMAGINE here. Later chapters will discuss each model in great detail, define the concepts involved, and elaborate upon each step. You will also be given various case examples of the models' application to macro practice.

The PREPARE model's steps (that focus on assessment and planning in planned change) are as follows:

P: Identify **Problems** to address.
R: Review your macro and personal **Reality.**
E: **Establish** primary goals.
P: Identify relevant **People** of influence.
A: **Assess** potential financial costs and benefits to clients and agency.
R: Review professional and personal **Risk.**
E: **Evaluate** the potential success of a macro change process.

The following are steps identified by the IMAGINE model (that focuses on intervention and evaluation in planned change):

I: Start with an innovative **Idea.**
M: **Muster** support and formulate an action system.
A: Identify **Assets.**
G: Specify **Goals,** objectives, and action steps to attain them.
I: **Implement** the plan.
N: **Neutralize** opposition.
E: **Evaluate** progress.

The applications of PREPARE and IMAGINE will concentrate on three major types of organizational and community change: undertaking specific projects, developing programs, and changing policies.

The Importance of Historical Perspectives

The prior sections of this chapter have reviewed the essence of generalist practice by reviewing its definition concept by concept. To grasp its significance and depth, it is also important to understand the context in which generalist practice and our focus on macro practice has developed. Highlight 1.8 discusses the history of generalist practice with organizations and communities and the development of professional social work within this macro context (CSWE, 2008, EP 2.1.1).

Chapter Summary

The following summarizes this chapter's content as it relates to the learning objectives presented at the beginning of the chapter. Chapter content prepares social workers to:

A. *Recognize the Generalist Intervention Model as a means of promoting human and social well-being in macro practice settings.*

The Generalist Intervention Model is founded on a definition of generalist practice that is supported by the knowledge, skills, and values characterizing the unique nature of the social work profession. It is based on a seven-step planned change process and is oriented toward solving problems at multiple levels of intervention (micro, mezzo, and macro).

B. *Define generalist practice and explain each component of this definition, including professional knowledge, skills, and values.*

Generalist practice is the application of an eclectic knowledge base, professional values and ethics, and a wide range of skills to target any size system for change within the context of three primary value principles, a context, and four major processes. Principles include: emphasis on empowerment, strengths, and resiliency; understanding of human diversity; and the importance of advocacy for human rights, and the pursuit of social and economic justice. The context is work within an organizational structure. Processes include: the assumption of

HIGHLIGHT 1.8

The History of Generalist Practice with Organizations and Communities in the Professional Context

EP 2.1.1

Social work practice has evolved significantly over the past 130 years. It has responded to vast social changes. It has struggled with the concept of generalist practice and with ways to integrate micro, mezzo, and macro levels of practice. The following paragraphs will review some of the major facets of the evolution of generalist practice with organizations and communities.

Between the Civil War and World War I, three major economic and social changes occurred in the United States (Day, 2006; Garvin & Cox, 1995). The first was industrialization. Mammoth growth in manufacturing and technology brought with it numerous social problems related to work, including long hours, horrendous conditions, safety risks, and child labor (Garvin & Cox, 1995).

The second primary change was urbanization. Concurrent with the centralization of industry in urban settings came the tremendous growth of urban populations. Masses of people moved from rural to urban areas on a quest for work and prosperity. Unfortunately, most were forced into the oldest, most crowded, and least sanitary sections of the cities.

The third major change during this period was explosive immigration, primarily from Europe. Immigrants brought with them their own problems. Many came from poor rural environments and had little with which to start their lives in this country. Many became ill during the immigration process. As a result, most immigrants lived in very poor conditions and accepted whatever work they could find. In response to these rapidly expanding social problems, two social and ideological movements became the foundation for social work practice in the 1880s (Hopps & Lowe, 2008; Stuart, 2008): the settlement house movement and Charity Organization Societies.

Settlement houses were "places where ministers, students, or humanitarians 'settled' (hence the name) to interact with poor slum dwellers" with the goal of improving community residents' lives and conditions" (Smith, 1995, p. 2130). For example, immigrants required education and help with obtaining citizenship; workers needed day care for their children (Popple, 1995). Day (2006) explains:

Settlement houses were run in part by client groups, and they emphasized social reform rather than relief

or assistance. Three-fourths of settlement workers were women, and most were well-educated and dedicated to working on problems or urban poverty.... Settlement workers tried to improve housing conditions, organized protests, offered job training and labor searches, supported organized labor, worked against child labor, and fought against corrupt politicians. Over time settlement houses became centers of social reform. (pp. 230–231)

Settlement houses emphasized community residents' empowerment. At its most basic level, empowerment involves providing people with authority or power. Settlements focused on social issues and improving living conditions, especially for those who were poorer or less fortunate than others. They provided the background for generalist practice within communities. People were viewed not as helpless victims, but as capable people who could gain power to improve the conditions in which they lived. The concept of community organization and group work developed within the settlement house context. Jane Addams and Ellen Gates Starr began perhaps the most famous settlement house, Hull House, in Chicago in 1889.

The settlement perspective contrasted strikingly with that of the *Charity Organization Societies (COS)*. Instead of emphasizing community strengths and capacity, Axinn and Stern (2005) explain:

Charity Organization Societies had come into being for the express purpose of reorganizing voluntary and public charities to direct toward worthy families the relief-giving of others. Their particular concern was with the poor, and especially with those individuals whose flawed character permitted them to sup at the public trough while contributing nothing to the public larder. Their investigations of applicants for relief ... were meant to individualize each poor family so that particular flaws could be detected and overcome and independence could be regained. (p. 112)

Initially, the COS used "friendly visitors" who tried to help people figure out how to solve their problems (Axinn & Stern, 2005, p. 103). As time passed, the COS sought to establish a base of scientific knowledge and apply it to the helping process. The scientific emphasis in fields such as medicine and engineering inspired this process. The COS "wanted to study the problem of dependence, gather data, test theories, systematize

© Hulton Archive/Stringer/Getty Images

Social worker Jane Addams, along with Ellen Gates Star, began perhaps the most famous settlement house, Hull House, in Chicago in 1889.

administration, and develop techniques that would lead to a cure" (Popple, 1995, p. 2283). The beginning struggle toward social work professionalism began when the COS recognized that friendly visitors needed more education and training to perform their tasks effectively (Axinn & Stern, 2005; Brieland, 1995; Popple, 1995).

The COS focused on curing individuals rather than on empowering communities. Traditional social casework developed from this approach. Additionally, because of the emphasis on expert knowledge, the significance of administration and supervised practice was incorporated into the casework concept. This emphasis on expertise contrasted sharply with the settlement approach that emphasized the empowerment and self-sufficiency of all.

Despite the different paths taken by the settlement house movement and the COS, social work pioneers were clearly devoted to helping the most impoverished and oppressed people in society (Landon, 1995). In the early 20th century, social work continued to seek a professional identity. The emphasis on scientific advances and the new, enticing therapeutic approaches being introduced during the first half of the 20th century (such

as psychodynamic and social learning theories) strengthened the profession's commitment to social casework (Day, 2006; Landon, 1995). Social casework stressed therapeutically helping individuals and families solve their particular problems. Thus, the target of change was the individual or the family.

The divergence between the settlement orientation (emphasizing group and community work) and the COS approach (oriented to individuals) remained strong. Thus, three method tracks (casework, group work, and community organization) characterized social work through the 1950s. Casework was further fortified by the developing fields of practice, or specializations, that were generally incorporated under its umbrella. These included medical social work, psychiatric social work, child welfare, and school social work (Brieland, 1995).

The Great Depression of the 1930s and the Social Security Act switched many aspects of service provision from the private to the public sector. Thus, the type of social work jobs available and the characteristics of people getting them shifted. Prior to the Depression, social work was close to becoming a profession strictly for those with graduate degrees because casework focused on the importance of psychotherapy (Popple, 1995). Many clients were not poor but suffered from other problems, such as mental health issues. Working to change communities and social policies was most often overlooked.

The Depression changed all this, however, with the massive growth of new social work jobs created by the Social Security Act. The majority of newly developed jobs addressed the needs of otherwise relatively stable people who now suddenly experienced the problems related to unemployment (Popple, 1995). Essentially, these jobs required skills other than the ability to facilitate therapy—as many master's degree social workers (MSWs) were doing. Thus, numerous baccalaureate degree social workers (BSWs) were hired for these jobs because of the different skills required. However, MSWs refused to accept BSWs as professional social workers, even prohibiting BSWs from joining professional social work organizations (Popple, 1995).

The economy saw rapid growth during and after World War II with the increased demand for production of needed goods. The resulting relative affluence of the 1940s and 1950s once again encouraged social workers to turn to psychotherapy and casework (Popple, 1995). During the 1950s, 85 percent of social work students selected casework as their orientation of choice (Popple, 1995). MSWs dominated the scene.

The 1960s produced a new focus on social change versus individual pathology. Many began to realize that poverty and other vast social problems still existed

HIGHLIGHT 1.8 *(continued)*

in the United States. A series of federal administrations began implementing anti-poverty programs. At first, these programs generally disregarded social workers because their intent was to empower the poor themselves (Popple, 1995). However, it soon became clear that expertise was needed in community organization, social service administration, and policy development (Popple, 1995). As a result, most social work schools added policy, planning, and administration specialties to their curricula (Stuart, 2008). This probably initiated the move toward working with and within organizations as a major facet of generalist practice. *Accountability* (a profession's responsibility to clients and the community that workers are effectively doing what they say they are going to do) became a key word when talking about social service provision (Popple, 1995). Taxpayers and government officials did not want to waste their money. They demanded to see results.

At this point, the social work professional faced a serious problem. More than three-quarters of all people holding social work jobs were not considered professional social workers by major social work organizations. That is, most workers did not hold an MSW degree (Popple, 1995). Needless to say, this did not enhance the profession's accountability—the vast majority of the people doing social work were not considered social workers. The logical move was to recognize the BSW as the practical requirement for an entry-level job in the social work profession. People performing social work jobs should be social workers.

In 1955, seven separate professional organizations came together to form the National Association of Social Workers (Brieland, 1995). The need for a unifying generalist approach motivated this union. Many social work leaders and educators became increasingly concerned about the profession's commitment to rectifying social injustice and advocating for positive social change.

The Council on Social Work Education (CSWE), the field's accrediting body, was born in 1952 when several predecessor organizations merged; at this time the first curriculum policy statement and accreditation standards were issued (Brieland, 1995). Such a statement and standards guided curriculum content and structure. Additionally, this initial statement required that students "develop a social philosophy rooted in an appreciation of the essential dignity of human beings" (Brieland, 1995, p. 2255). Such a broad goal implied that social work should seek to benefit society generally and oppressed populations specifically. Many social work leaders began calling for a unified foundation for social work practice (Bartlett, 1970; Boehm, 1959) and referring to levels of social work practice among various-sized systems (Pincus & Minahan, 1973; Schwartz, 1961; Siporin, 1975). Social workers needed a broad base of skills to work with individuals, families, groups, organizations, and communities. The prolific development of BSW programs in the late 1960s and early 1970s emphasized the need for a generalist foundation for social work practice (Landon, 1995). Baccalaureate and master's programs required differentiation of purpose. In 1974, CSWE "stipulated generalist education as appropriate for the baccalaureate level of practice" and in 1984 "declared that the required foundation material on both undergraduate and graduate levels should consist of the knowledge, values, and skills essential to generalist practice" (Landon, 1995, p. 1102).

Current thinking is that the foundation of social work for both BSW and MSW practice is competency in generalist practice; a BSW degree provides the foundation and an MSW offers advanced competency in some area of specialization or concentration (CSWE, 2008). Generalist practice, then, is the cornerstone of professional social work practice.

---

a wide range of professional roles; application of critical thinking skills; the incorporation of research-informed practice; and use of planned change.

The eclectic knowledge base for generalist practice comprises content involving systems theories, human behavior and the social environment, social welfare policy and policy practice, social work practice, research, and content concerning values and principles that guide practice. Generalist practice skills include those used in micro (individuals), mezzo (groups),

and macro (organizations and communities) practice.

C. *Identify personal values, and define and apply professional standards.*

Values are principles, qualities, and practices that a designated group, individual, or culture deems inherently desirable. Ethics are principles based on a set of values that serve to guide one's behavior.

Social workers must identify personal values and manage them so that they do not interfere with the use of professional values to guide practice decisions. Professional standards include the National Association of Social Workers *Code of Ethics,* and the International Federation of Social Workers/International Association of Schools of Social Work Ethics in Social Work *Statement of Principles.* Social workers must apply ethics to resolve ethical dilemmas occurring in practice.

D. *Describe the traditional three models of community organization and suggest an updated approach.*

Traditionally, "community organization" was the term used to refer to macro practice in social work. The three models included social action, social planning, and locality development. Revised, updated concepts include social advocacy, planning and policy practice, and community capacity development.

E. *Examine the importance of client empowerment, the strengths perspective, and resiliency.*

Social workers must assess client strengths and limitations to develop appropriate intervention strategies seeking client empowerment. Empowerment is "the process of increasing personal, interpersonal, or political power so that individuals can take action to improve their life situations" (Gutierrez, 2001, p. 210). Strengths include any resources, capabilities, knowledge, and other positive qualities that can be put to use to solve problems. Resiliency is the ability of an individual, family, group, community, or organization to recover from adversity and resume functioning even when suffering serious trouble, confusion, or hardship (Glicken, 2006).

F. *Recognize the importance of understanding human diversity and its implications for practice.*

Social workers must understand the significance of how diverse factors influence clients' lives. Factors include "age, class, color, culture, disability, ethnicity, gender, gender identity and expression, immigration status, political ideology, race, religion, sex, and sexual orientation" (CSWE, 2008, EP 2.1.4). Discrimination is the act of treating people differently because they belong to a particular group rather than on their own merit. Oppression involves putting extreme limitations and constraints on some person, group, or larger system.

G. *Examine advocacy for human rights and the pursuit of social and economic justice as a major facet of generalist practice.*

It is social workers' responsibility to advocate for human rights and to pursue social and economic justice. Advocacy is the act of representing, championing, or defending the rights of others. Human rights involve the premise that all people, regardless of race, culture, or national origin, are entitled to basic rights and treatment.

Social justice entails upholding the condition that in a perfect world, all citizens would have identical "rights, protection, opportunities, obligations, and social benefits" regardless of their backgrounds and membership in diverse groups (Barker, 2003, pp. 404–405). Economic justice concerns the distribution of resources in a fair and equitable manner.

H. *Describe the importance of working within an organizational structure as the context for generalist practice.*

Organizational structure is the formal and informal manner in which tasks and responsibilities, lines of authority, channels of communication, and dimensions of power are established and coordinated within an organization. Effective practice includes understanding the formal and informal structure of the agency, demonstrating a professional identity, and using supervision appropriately.

I. *Identify a wide range of professional roles practitioners may assume in macro practice.*

A role is a culturally expected behavior pattern for a person having a specified status or being involved in a designated social relationship. Professional roles in generalist practice include enabler, mediator, integrator/coordinator, manager, educator, analyst/evaluator, broker, facilitator, initiator, negotiator, mobilizer, and advocate.

J. *Describe critical thinking and its relevance to generalist practice.*

Critical thinking is (1) the careful scrutiny of what is stated as true or what appears to be true and the resulting expression of an opinion or conclusion based on that scrutiny, and (2) the creative formulation of an opinion or conclusion when presented with a question, problem, or issue (Kirst-Ashman, 2010). A straightforward formula for critical thinking entails: (1) ask questions, (2) assess the established facts and issues involved, and (3) assert a concluding opinion. It is important for generalist practitioners to avoid fallacies, that is, false or erroneous ideas, often hidden behind what appears to be a sound argument or presentation.

K. *Recognize the usefulness of research-informed practice.*

Generalist practitioners must incorporate research-informed practice by using the approaches and interventions in their practice that research has determined are effective. Social workers should employ "research findings to improve practice, policy, and social service delivery" (CSWE, 2008, EP 2.1.6).

L. *Explain the planned change process within the macro practice context.*

The planned change process includes seven steps: engagement, assessment, planning, implementation, evaluation, termination, and follow-up.

M. *Review a brief history of practice with organizations and communities within a professional context.*

Between the Civil War and World War I, three major economic and social changes occurred in the United States: industrialization, urbanization, and immigration. Within this context, settlement houses and charity organization societies developed. Settlement houses were places where educated people worked together with the poor to focus on social issues and improve living conditions. They provided the background for generalist practice within communities by emphasizing group and community work. Charity Organization Societies organized various charitable sources to provide help and relief to the worthy poor. Traditional casework developed from this approach.

The Great Depression of the 1930s and the Social Security Act switched many aspects of service provision from the private to the public sector, resulting in a massive growth of new social work jobs. Social workers provided casework and psychotherapy during the relative affluence of the 1940s and 1950s. The 1960s produced a new focus on social change versus individual pathology.

Seven separate professional social work organizations came together to form the National Association of Social Workers in 1955. The Council on Social Work Education, the field's accrediting body, was born in 1952. MSWs predominated until the 1960s and 1970s when BSW programs rapidly increased in number, reflecting the need for a generalist foundation for social work practice. Current thinking and accreditation requirements call for a generalist foundation for both BSW and MSW levels of practice.

Competency Notes

This section relates chapter content to the Council on Social Work Education's (CSWE) *Educational Policy and Accreditation Standards* (EPAS) (CSWE, 2008). One major goal of social work education is to facilitate students' attainment of the EPAS-designated 10 core competencies and their 41 related practice behaviors so that students develop into competent practitioners.

Students require knowledge in order to develop skills and become competent. Our intent here is to specify what chapter content and knowledge coincides with the development of specific competencies and practice behaviors. (This ultimately is intended to assist in the accreditation process.) Therefore, the listing presented below first cites the various Educational Policy (EP) core competencies and their related practice behaviors that are relevant to chapter content. Note that the listing follows the order that competencies and practice behaviors are cited in the EPAS.

We have established that "helping hands" icons are interspersed throughout the chapter to indicate where relevant accompanying content is located. Page numbers noted below indicate where icons are placed in the chapter. Following the icon's page number is a brief explanation of how the content accompanying the icon relates to the specified competency or practice behavior.

The following identifies where Educational Policy (EP) competencies and practice behaviors are discussed in the chapter.

EP 2.1 Core Competencies. *(P. 6):* The definition of generalist practice proposed here takes most of its concepts directly from the Educational Policy and Accreditation Standards (EPAS), including the concepts of strengths; diversity; advocacy for human rights and the pursuit of social and economic justice; ethical principles; professional roles; critical thinking; research-informed practice; and engagement, assessment, intervention, and evaluation with individuals, families, groups, organizations, and communities, among other generalist practice concepts.

EP 2.1.1 Identify as a professional social worker and conduct oneself accordingly. *(P. 28):* Practitioners should serve as representatives of the profession, its mission, and its core values. *(P. 36)*: Social workers should know the profession's history.

EP 2.1.1c Attend to professional roles and boundaries. *(P. 23)*: Social workers must be knowledgeable about and prepared to assume a wide range of professional roles.

EP 2.1.2 Apply social work ethical principles to guide professional practice. *(P. 14)*: Ethics are standards that guide behavior. The NASW *Code of Ethics* (**EP 2.1.2a**), the international Statement of Principles (**EP 2.1.2b**), awareness of personal values (**EP 2.1.2c**), and the management of ethical dilemmas (**EP 2.1.2d**) are introduced here and in subsequent pages as significant foundations of ethical practice.

EP 2.1.3 Apply critical thinking to inform and communicate professional judgments. *(P. 29)*: Critical thinking involves careful thinking about what is truth and what is assumption. It requires formulating thoughtful conclusions about how to proceed in practice. A formula for critical thinking is provided and fallacies to avoid are discussed.

EP 2.1.4 Engage diversity and difference in practice. *(P. 19)*: Human diversity refers to many differences among people, including those identified in Highlight 1.5. *(P. 22)*: Practitioners must understand how sexual orientation, a dimension of diversity, characterizes and shapes the human experience.

EP 2.1.4a Recognize the extent to which culture's structures and values may oppress, marginalize, alienate, or create or enhance privilege or power. *(P. 19)*: Practitioners must realize how cultural values can negatively affect diverse groups of people.

EP 2.1.5b Advocate for human rights and social and economic justice. *(P. 20)*: Practitioners should advocate for social and economic justice.

EP 2.1.6 Engage in research-informed practice and practice-informed research. *(P. 12)*: Empirical evidence should guide the intervention process to maximize effectiveness.

EP 2.1.6b Use research evidence to inform practice. *(P. 30)*: Social workers should use the approaches and interventions in their practice that research has determined are effective.

EP 2.1.7 Apply knowledge of human behavior and the social environment. *(P. 11)*: A person-in-environment perspective is essential for understanding human behavior.

EP 2.1.7a Utilize conceptual frameworks to guide the processes of assessment, intervention, and evaluation. *(P. 9)*: Systems theories provide a useful theoretical framework for understanding human behavior and guiding the intervention process.

EP 2.1.8 Engage in policy practice to advance social and economic well-being and to deliver effective social work services. *(P. 11)*: Understanding social welfare policy is essential before undertaking policy practice and advocating for policy change.

EP 2.1.10 Engage, assess, intervene, and evaluate with individuals, families, groups, organizations, and communities. *(P. 16)*: Practitioners must possess a wide range of skills to work with systems of all sizes. *(P. 31)*: Planned change includes engagement, assessment, intervention (implementation), and evaluation.

EP 2.1.10d Collect, organize, and interpret client data. *(P. 32)*: Assessment involves collecting, organizing, and interpreting client system data.

EP 2.1.10e Assess clients' strengths and limitations. *(P. 18)*: Practitioners should build on clients' strengths and emphasize their resiliency in the intervention process: *(P. 33)*: Identifying clients' strengths is critically important in assessment.

On the Internet

Visit the *Generalist Practice with Organizations and Communities* Web site at *www.cengage.com/social_work/kirst-ashman* for learning tools such as PowerPoint® slides, tutorial quizzing, Web links, and final exams.

CHAPTER **2**

Using Micro Skills in the Macro Environment

A colleague approaches you and says, "You know, you're really intimidating." How do you respond?

Your supervisor asks you, "Have you finished your special assignment yet?" You think, "Special assignment? What the heck is she talking about?" What should you say to your supervisor at this point?

You work for a private agency that runs a dozen homes throughout your state for adults with cognitive disabilities. The agency's board of directors (the body responsible for establishing basic agency policy) suddenly decides to combine the homes into two campuses instead of 12 individual homes. You think this would be a terrible mistake. Most clients would be moved far from their family support systems. Maintaining such familial contact was a major reason for selection of the 12 homes' location in the first place. How do you approach the board's chairperson about your concerns?

You think your agency needs to establish a personnel and policy committee to review and revise the agency's policy manual, which is 20 years out of date. Sick leave, vacation time, procedures for admitting clients, and an almost endless array of other matters need clarification and definition. What should you say when you approach the appropriate supervisors and administrators?

You applied for a grant to develop a series of training sessions for your agency's workers. The grant is not actually denied, but the grant review committee raises a variety of serious concerns. The committee encourages you to contact its members to address the issues. How do you approach these people?

A legislative committee abruptly cuts off your agency's funding. That means your job. What do you say when you contact the relevant legislators?

A worker from another social service agency in the community walks into your office and confidently says, "Hi! I thought I'd stop by and tell you to complete the summary of our meeting last week. Send me a copy when you're finished. Take it easy. See you later." He catches you off guard. You don't know what to say. You think to yourself, "What does he mean by ordering me to do some totally pointless summary report? He's not my boss. Who does he think he is? Why didn't I think faster and tell him what he can do with his report?" Okay, you weren't fast enough on your feet. What do you do now?

These are among the vast range of interpersonal scenarios you may encounter in the macro environment. We assume that you have acquired an assortment of skills for working with clients in micro and mezzo practice. However, how do you apply these skills in macro practice contexts? How can you use them to interact effectively with colleagues, supervisors, other staff, high-ranking administrators, community leaders, and politicians? How do you resolve conflicts and maintain pleasant relationships with such people? How do you gauge how assertive, nonassertive, or aggressive you should be? Such issues are what this chapter is all about.

Introduction

The concept of doing macro practice can be threatening. You might think, "What in the world can I do, in my lowly direct-service position, to influence what goes on in a whole agency, let alone a large bureaucracy, let alone a state government?"

The answer arises from the fact that agencies, mammoth bureaucracies, state governments, and even national arenas are made up of individuals, all operating within their own unique contexts. Each powerful decision maker, including prestigious politicians and directors of large agencies, is a human being just like you. Although their behavior and decisions affect many layers of people beneath them in whatever power structure they oversee, they may have direct contact with relatively few others. These few, in turn, influence the people below them in the hierarchy, and so on. The point is that each person, no matter how theoretically important he or she is, interacts and communicates in order to get things done. They do this in much the same way you will interact and communicate in your own work setting.

This chapter focuses on the techniques necessary for communicating with other people in macro practice contexts. It first reviews basic communication techniques that are similar to those used in direct practice

with clients. However, they are presented in the context of communication with colleagues, supervisors, other agency staff, community leaders, and government representatives. We have established that such basic micro techniques form the foundation for learning and applying mezzo and macro skills and that these are an absolute necessity for any type of generalist social work practice. Subsequently, this chapter explores assertiveness and conflict resolution—two common interactional issues in the macro environment.

Assertiveness

At times, you will need to become more assertive within your work setting. A supervisor may ask you to complete some work on unpaid overtime on the weekend you're planning to have a big birthday party or romantic weekend retreat. A colleague may borrow your files without asking and simply forget to return them. You may need to urge a local politician to support the building of new public housing your clients desperately need. You may feel a strong need to initiate a sex education program for your teenage clients in view of soaring pregnancy rates, even though scarce resources plague your agency. In any of these cases, and in an infinite number of other instances, you will require well-developed assertiveness skills.

Conflict

Likewise, you may often encounter conflict in your work environment. Conflicts are differences of ideas, opinions, and goals. For example, you may think that your agency should adopt a policy of enhanced worker discretion, because encouraging practitioners to make their own practice decisions would allow them to respond more effectively to each client. A colleague, on the other hand, might think that your agency should establish stronger centralized control. This colleague feels that specific regulations and procedures for handling various client-related issues make decisions easier. Likewise, this colleague believes such structure helps workers avoid making mistakes. Which policy should the agency adopt?

In another example, you may feel it is extremely important to initiate a clothing drive for your poor clients as winter approaches in your cold northern climate. Your agency's assistant director, on the other hand, may consider such an endeavor frivolous and beneath a professional social worker's role. How will you resolve these differences?

Any kind of conflict resolution requires, first, that you thoroughly understand the dynamics of conflict and, second, that you can implement conflict resolution techniques. Hence, this chapter addresses both of these needs within the macro practice context. Note that conflict is such an important aspect of interpersonal dynamics in virtually any practice setting that Chapter 3 ("Group Skills for Organizational and Community Change") examines its impacts in mezzo contexts.

Working with Supervisors

Finally, this chapter explains how you can facilitate the supervisory process. The supervisory relationship can significantly benefit from use of your micro skills. Because of the importance of supervision and of your relationship with your supervisor, we will examine the issues involved in supervision and potential problems that can arise. Ultimately, we will propose suggestions for how to use supervision most effectively.

Learning Objectives

This chapter will provide content concerning how social workers:

    A. *Use empathy and other interpersonal skills to work effectively within organizations and communities.*

    B. *Recognize how diversity shapes life experiences and employ some approaches for improving communication with people who have physical disabilities.*

    C. *Describe a variety of interviewing techniques and apply them to macro practice situations.*

    D. *Examine assertiveness and propose means for its application in macro contexts.*

    E. *Utilize critical thinking skills to investigate the pros and cons of conflict and propose procedures for conflict resolution.*

    F. *Examine the supervisory relationship, some of its inherent problems, and the concept of consultation.*

    G. *Formulate suggestions for using supervision, improving supervisory relationships, and enhancing the communication process.*

Beginning Relationships in Macro Practice

Communication with other people in macro practice is obviously necessary to get anything done. We assume here that you have already had the opportunity to learn and practice some interviewing skills within micro and mezzo practice contexts. That is, you have learned some basic skills for working with individual clients and groups. As we have discussed, you need to know how to work with people as individuals in order to work with them in groups. Likewise, you need both of these skill levels to work with people as members of organizations, communities, and political decision-making bodies.

Interviewing, of course, is considered one of the core skills for micro practice. An interview involves "interpersonal verbal and nonverbal communications" and is characterized by three attributes (Kadushin, 1995, p. 1527; Kadushin & Kadushin, 1997). First, it includes a structured purpose and goal. Second, an interview is conducted in a context where the participants have certain roles (such as practitioner and client). The interview's context also includes prescribed time limits and an assigned location. The interview's third characteristic is that it follows a number of sequential steps, including "a beginning, a middle, and a termination" (Kadushin, 1995, pp. 1527–1528). In micro practice, the interview is more than having a pleasant conversation with a client; its purpose is "to exchange information systematically with a view toward illuminating and solving problems, promoting growth, or planning strategies or actions aimed at improving the quality of life for people" (Hepworth, Rooney, Rooney, Strom-Gottfried, & Larsen, 2010, pp. 43–44).

The interview in macro practice is very similar, in that your intent usually includes communicating and problem solving. However, instead of working with individual clients, you are communicating and problem solving with groups of clients, agency administrators, your colleagues, politicians, community residents, and professionals from various other community agencies. Figure 2.1 conceptualizes macro systems as consisting of *individuals* who all are, in effect, potential targets of change or helpers in the change process. The macro environments in which you work—including agency, community, and political entities—all consist of people with individual personalities, qualities, and quirks.

In learning how to communicate and work with other people, it's wise to start by examining how to establish good relationships in general. Some people

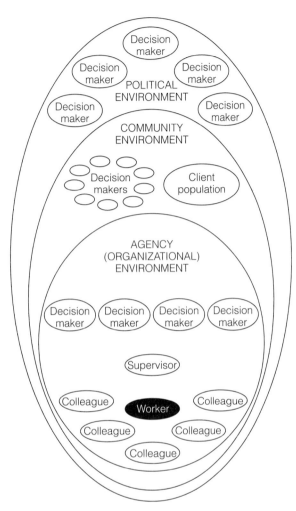

FIGURE 2.1 The Worker in the Organizational, Community, and Political Macro Environments

are naturally popular. Others are not. Certain basic behaviors and characteristics usually make a person more appealing to others. Likewise, in interpersonal dynamics, certain behaviors and personal qualities tend to nurture relationships. Exhibiting these traits and behaviors tends to put others at ease. This chapter will discuss how verbal and nonverbal behavior, in addition to certain other human characteristics demonstrated through such behavior, can enhance relationships within macro practice contexts.

We assume that your thinking about micro skills has thus far focused primarily on their application to client situations. Therefore, this chapter addresses the wider range of situations that can occur in macro settings, including those involving your initiation and

pursuit of a macro change process. For example, you might want to fight for the rights of a group of your clients, change an agency policy, help start a community program, or implement a special project. We also examine everyday interactions with colleagues and administrators in macro environments. Our assumption is that part of understanding macro practice involves cooperating with colleagues and supervisors in agency settings. Such interactions may not be addressed elsewhere in the practice curriculum. Everyday activities might include responding to a colleague's criticism of your work or making an effective request to a supervisor for help with an exceptionally difficult client. We consider any type of interaction in the macro environment where micro skills are used to be an aspect of macro practice.

A Review of Basic Micro Skills

Macro practice always involves human interaction, and any interpersonal interaction involves an intricate web of communication and interpersonal skills (CSWE, 2008, EP 2.1.10b). Many of the same skills you use to communicate with and **EP 2.1.10b**

help clients can be applied directly to macro situations. For example, you might be initiating the development of a needle exchange program for drug addicts in a deteriorating urban neighborhood to prevent the spread of HIV through contaminated needles. You would first need to establish rapport and positive relationships with community residents and decision makers (involving micro and mezzo aspects of practice) in order to get such a program (an aspect of macro practice) off the ground.

Or, suppose you work in a protective services agency and want to initiate an in-service training program focusing on new child abuse assessment techniques. You would need the help of your immediate supervisor or other agency administrators to get the project off the ground.

In either case, how likely would you be to receive assistance from someone you had already antagonized? Not very likely. Instead, you would need to have established open, positive relationships with the people who can help you. You might also need to display appropriate assertiveness when approaching those who could help you and proposing your idea to them. If an interpersonal conflict should arise, you should know how to handle and resolve it. The following sections will review verbal and nonverbal behavior, significant personal qualities involved in communication, and types of verbal responses.

Verbal and Nonverbal Behavior

As we know, the most basic level of human communication involves both verbal and nonverbal behavior. Verbal behavior is what is said. Nonverbal behavior is what is communicated without spoken words. People communicate by the expressions on their faces, the movements of their hands, the relaxed or tense manner in which they sit, the amount of eye contact they maintain, and by how close they stand to you. Any aspect of a person's presence that conveys unspoken ideas or information is an element of nonverbal communication.

For example, Monica, a county social services worker, initiates a meeting with a variety of community residents to help them talk about starting a crime prevention program. She is concerned about one resident, Jorgé Cordoba, 41. Jorgé has agreed that the program is important, yet during each of the meetings, he sits in the back of the room and closes his eyes, almost as if he is asleep. Monica happens to know that Jorgé has a 16-year-old son whom she thinks may be a member of a local gang, the Toros Machos. This gang is particularly renowned for its drug trafficking and gun sales. Monica's hunch is that Mr. Cordoba is very ambivalent regarding the crime prevention program. He wants to curb crime in his neighborhood and community, but he wants to protect his son. How might Monica approach Mr. Cordoba? What might she say? How should she act toward him? The answer is that she must master relevant micro practice skills and apply them to this particular macro practice situation.

A large body of research focuses on the importance of nonverbal behavior (Murphy & Dillon, 2008). Research reveals that about 65 percent of all face-to-face communication is nonverbal (Sheafor & Horejsi, 2009). Although there are many aspects of nonverbal behavior, here we will focus on four of them—eye contact, attentive listening, facial expressions, and body positioning.

Eye Contact

It is important to look another person directly in the eye as you communicate. This establishes a rapport between you and conveys that you are attending to what the other is saying.

You must know people who have difficulty "looking you in the eye." This can convey that they are afraid or insecure. Appearing afraid is not advantageous. For example, consider a colleague who confronts you by telling you that your writing style is exceedingly dull and overly complicated. Surprised, you feel this criticism is unwarranted and unfair. Which would be more effective—to look sheepishly down at your feet and mumble a response? Or to hold your head high, look him in the eye, and state, "I'm surprised at that feedback. I don't agree with you, but I wonder what your reasons are for saying that"? In the first instance, probably no matter what words you used, your lack of eye contact would make you appear afraid or timid. Your critic wouldn't take your response seriously—whatever it was. On the other hand, providing appropriate eye contact in addition to a straightforward response would probably convey your intent much more clearly.

Of course, this example shows that appropriate eye contact is only one channel of communication. Facial expressions, content clarity, tone of voice, and a range of other behaviors contribute to the effectiveness or lack of effectiveness of your message.

Failing to look people directly in the eye may also imply disinterest or dishonesty. A cartoon of a "guy with shifty eyes" comes to mind. On the other hand, maintaining continuous eye contact may make the other person uncomfortable. Additionally, it can be tedious—as if you were in a who-can-stare-the-longest-without-blinking contest. Eye contact is a complex nonverbal behavior. Moderate eye contact that is somewhere between no eye contact and constant eye contact seems to put people in Western societies, such as those in North America and Europe, the most at ease (Egan, 2010; Sheafor & Horejsi, 2009; Ting-Toomey & Chung, 2005). Thus, direct eye contact with an occasional glance away—at your hands, at a bookcase, or simply at nothing—is probably most appropriate.

It should be noted, however, that you must maintain a sensitivity to cultural differences concerning any aspect of nonverbal behavior, including eye contact. People with different cultural backgrounds may have different expectations in terms of appropriate nonverbal behaviors. For example, "direct eye contact can signify disrespect in Thai culture" (Ting-Toomey & Chung, 2005, p. 47). Another difference involves persons "from Asian, Latin American, Caribbean, and American Indian backgrounds [who] may offer respect by avoiding eye contact" (Jandt, 2007, p. 108).

Having good micro skills in the macro environment is critical. The professionals pictured here have established good eye contact to enhance communication.

Attentive Listening

You always listen carefully to a person who is talking to you, right? Or might you drift off for just a moment to think about whether to change the oil in your car or what to wear on Friday night? Just as in micro practice, listening in macro practice settings is not as simple as it sounds. First, the distinction needs to be made between *hearing* and *listening*. Hearing is the audio perception of spoken words. Listening means more—that you try both to hear and to understand most of what another person is saying. It focuses on comprehending the meaning of what is said.

Three barriers to attentive listening involve three aspects of communication. First, the person sends a message with some *intent,* some meaning he or she wishes to convey. Second, the receiver of the message tries to decipher the meaning of what has been said. Thus, the message has some *impact* on the receiver. This impact arises from what the receiver thinks the sender said. What the receiver actually hears may or may not be what the sender intended the receiver to hear. Third, there may be *environmental*

barriers that impede communication of the message (see Figure 2.2).

The first cluster of communication barriers involves the sender, in this case the person who is talking to you. This individual might be using words, phrases, or concepts that are unclear to you. The person may say something very vague or may wrongly assume that you already know something basic to understanding the message. The sender's *intent,* then, may not be the same as the *impact* on you—the receiver.

For example, consider a situation where you are working for a YMCA Center for Youth Alternatives.[1] You are developing a crisis intervention program that involves a telephone crisis hotline, a series of temporary placements, and referral services. Clients include "runaways, homeless youths, and troubled youths, all of whom are vulnerable to injury and exploitation in the

---

1. This example is based on a description of Project "Safe Place," Louisville, KY, in C. A. Morrow, "Child and Family Homelessness," in *Children, Families and Cities: Programs That Work at the Local Level,* J. E. Kyle (Ed.) (Washington DC: National League of Cities, 1987), pp. 137–140.

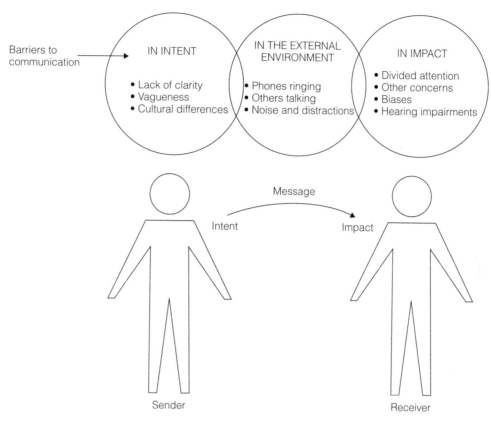

FIGURE 2.2 Barriers to Attentive Listening

streets" (Morrow, 1987, p. 138). Setting up a new program is difficult, but in the long run you feel it will be much more effective than working with clients referred in the more traditional way by other community agencies.

You are embroiled in getting the project going and have been working closely with your supervisor. As you busily pass each other in the hallway, she asks you, "Can you get it done by Monday?" Your supervisor here has a specified *intent.* You interpret "it" to mean finishing your list of temporary placements for clients, along with addresses, phone numbers, and contact persons. This, then, is the *impact* of her statement.

However, what if this is not what your supervisor really means by "it"? Suppose her real intent is to ask you if you can get the plan for publicizing the crisis hotline to her by Monday. If people don't know that the hotline exists, it will be useless. Your supervisor's intent (what she wants you to do) is very different from what you think she means. In essence, "it" is vague. You hear that you need to get your list of temporary placements completed (impact). Her intent, on the other hand, is

that you are supposed to submit your plan for publicizing the hotline to her (intent). With such a misunderstanding, you would complete the wrong thing and find yourself up a creek without a paddle.

The second type of communication barrier involves the receiver, in this case, you as the social worker. Your attention may be divided between what the other person is saying and what you want to say next. You might be preoccupied. You might be focusing on what direction the interaction should take in the future. Thus, you may not pay full attention to the sender and listen to all that is said, thereby assuming the incorrect impact. Refer to the earlier example of misunderstanding between you and your supervisor. The list of temporary placements was the last thing you remember talking to your supervisor about. Additionally, it was the primary thing on your mind when you passed each other in the hall and she made her comment.

The third cluster of communication barriers to attentive listening involves the external environment and its potential noise and distractions. For example, a telephone might ring, another staff member might approach you and start talking, a group might arrive early, or somebody might have turned the air conditioning up to frigid levels.

In summary, listening is not always easy. It demands concentration, perceptiveness, and the use of a range of interpersonal and communication skills. This chapter will describe a number of these skills.

Facial Expressions

Facial movements and expressions provide an excellent means of communicating. A furrowed brow may convey intense concentration, uncertainty, or concern. A casual smile can indicate pleasure and, many times, warmth. Raising the eyebrows may portray surprise or sudden interest. In contrast, a blank, deadpan expression usually conveys little or no information about what you mean or what you think. Note that in some instances it might also convey hostility—such as in response to someone telling a joke or bubbling with enthusiasm.

Facial expressions can be used to reinforce what is said verbally and the fact that you mean what you say. However, two aspects about using facial expressions should be noted. First, be aware of your facial responses so that you know how you are communicating. Second, make certain that your facial expressions correspond with both your other nonverbal and your verbal behavior. It is not helpful to give others mixed messages. That is, to say one thing and look as if you mean another only confuses people. It can generate doubt that you're being truthful.

For instance, you might be a practitioner working for a large public social services agency. You have been laboring on the behalf of agency employees who desperately need good child care. Specifically, you have been working with a child care committee of other interested employees to propose changing agency policy so that employees can redirect up to $5,000 of their annual salary to cover child care expenses.[2] There are a number of advantages to this plan:

Since the earned salary has been redirected before the employee receives it, employees do not have to pay taxes on the part of their incomes that [is] redirected to child care. Therefore, child care purchased in this fashion is more affordable. The city also saves dollars through this plan because it does not pay social security or withholding taxes on the money which is redirected for child care expenses. (Smith, 1987, p. 54)

You and the others on the child care committee decide that the easiest way to implement this policy would be to gain the support of the agency's assistant director. The committee designates you to meet with her and propose the change.

During the meeting, you make your proposal. In response, she states simply that it is a terrible plan. She questions why you would waste your paid work time pursuing something that she considers the employees', not the agency's, business. Subsequently, with a huge, Cheshire-cat grin reaching from ear to ear, the assistant director says, "Of course, I'm terribly sorry that your plan is unworkable." Obviously, this administrator is anything but sorry. Her facial expression clearly indicates her personal satisfaction about trashing your idea. She may have made the "I'm sorry" comment to try to terminate your generally negative meeting with her on a more positive note. Or perhaps she always says she's sorry when she disagrees with employees. Nonetheless, the lack of consistency between her verbal and nonverbal behavior clearly indicates that she does not mean what she is saying.

The postscript is that you return to the child care committee and the drawing board concerning your plan. The assistant director is obviously not going to provide any support. The committee needs to propose an alternative tactic to pursue its policy change. Perhaps going directly to the agency's executive director is now in order.

Body Positioning

The way people position their bodies and move their extremities also provides information to others. Two continuums are especially important: the tense/relaxed and formal/informal. The amount of space you allow between you and others is another aspect of body positioning.

Tense/Relaxed Continuum

Body tension is how rigid or tense your muscles appear as you position yourself. Such tension most often coincides with emotional tension. If you look uptight, you probably feel uptight inside. Such tension can be demonstrated by sitting rigidly straight and restricting movement of extremities. Tension is also apparent when you make quick, nervous movements, such as

---

2. This example is based on a description of the Office of Child Care Initiatives, Denver, CO, in *Children, Families and Cities: Programs That Work at the Local Level*, J. E. Kyle (Ed.) (Washington, DC: National League of Cities, 1987), pp. 53–55.

continuously tapping a foot or finger or jingling loose change in your pocket.

The opposite of a tense stance is a relaxed one. Relaxation can be portrayed by slow, loose movements and a decidedly casual, informal presentation of self. The most extreme relaxed stance is probably lying down. The term "laid back" describes such a relaxed approach.

When trying to communicate with another person, it is important to be aware of how you present yourself nonverbally. Extreme tension may convey a lack of confidence in yourself or excessive nervousness. It may put distance between yourself and others or make it difficult for others to feel comfortable with and trust you.

On the other hand, an extremely relaxed stance may convey to the other person that you do not care very much about what happens. It may also eat away at your credibility as a professional if you appear too lax, disinterested, and informal.

Ideally, it's best to present yourself somewhere between the two extremes. To some extent it is a matter of personal style. You need to be genuine (that is, reflecting to the other person aspects of your true individual personality). The important thing is to be aware of your body positioning and how it affects your interaction with others in the macro environment.

Formal/Informal Continuum

The second continuum, formal/informal, relates, to some extent, to the tense/relaxed continuum. Being more rigid and tense suggests formality, whereas being relaxed is associated with informality. Formality implies greater structure. It also implies less warmth. To the extent that you are more formal with someone, you are less personal. You allow less of your true personality to show through the professional façade. On the other hand, complete informality or relaxed lack of structure impedes getting anything done. Relationships with others in the macro practice context are not usually friendships. The interpersonal relationship exists for the purpose of solving a problem, initiating a plan, or attaining a goal. This requires some degree of formality and structure.

As with the tense/relaxed continuum, the extent of formality often relates to personal style. The best approach lies somewhere between the extremes. The important thing is to be aware of how you're presenting yourself, how you feel most comfortable, and how others react and relate to you. Ask questions in the way and in the tone of voice you feel at ease with. Smile when you feel like smiling. Use the gestures and personal presentation that reflect your true personality.

Personal Space

One other part of body positioning involves the use of personal space. This is the actual space or distance between you and other people as you interact. There are four distances or zones that we set in our daily interactions (Hall, 1969; Shebib, 2003). These include the intimate zone, the personal zone, the social zone, and the public zone. Each zone respectively demonstrates more formal and less intimate relationships. The *intimate zone* is just that. It ranges from skin contact to about 18 inches. It obviously is reserved for very close personal relationships. The *personal zone* ranges from about 18 inches to approximately 4 feet, the *social zone* from 4 to 12 feet, and the *public zone* outward from 12 feet. Contact with other people in a macro context should generally occur in the closer half of the social zone—that is, 4 to 8 feet. This allows for comfortable discussion, but it provides an adequate degree of personal space so that other people do not feel restricted or pressured.

However, note that there are exceptions to this rule. For example, during intense negotiations, it might be advantageous to place yourself either closer to or farther from the recommended 4 to 8 feet from your colleague. Positioning yourself closer may emphasize your strong interest in and commitment to the issues at hand. You may also need to be closer when sharing documents that are at issue. On the other hand, you may choose to position yourself farther away during times of intense conflict. This could emphasize the fact that conflict is occurring.

Multicultural Sensitivity and Nonverbal Behavior

Just as with clients, it is important to be sensitive to possible cultural differences in nonverbal behavior when communicating with others in the macro environment. When working with colleagues and decision makers, you want to get your points across effectively, understand accurately their communications, and avoid offending them. This is true whenever you work with people who have diverse cultural values in communities, agencies, or small task groups.

Ivey and Ivey (2007, pp. 131–132) provide several examples of how people from different cultures apply nonverbal behavior in very different ways. For instance, "Russians say yes by shaking the head from side to side and no by moving the head up and down. Most Europeans do exactly the opposite." People from certain Arabic cultures "prefer to be only 18 inches apart when they talk, a most uncomfortable distance for many Europeans." Arabs experiencing interaction in the 4- to 8-foot zone may interpret European behavior as exceptionally cold and aloof. Although most North American people consider smiling a gesture of warmth, "in some situations in Japan, smiling may indicate discomfort." Finally, one study explores touching among friends spending an hour together in a coffee shop (Asbell & Wynn, 1991; Ivey & Ivey, 2007). French friends touched each other 110 times, Puerto Rican friends 180 times, and English friends not at all.

Highlight 2.1 addresses some of the special issues concerning nonverbal behavior with people who have physical disabilities.

Warmth, Empathy, and Genuineness

In generalist social work practice, a variety of relationship-enhancing characteristics can be defined and learned. Using these characteristics requires the appropriate corresponding verbal and nonverbal behavior. Three specific such relationship-enhancing traits are warmth, empathy, and genuineness—attributes characterized in the social work literature as among the most basic and important in developing relationships (Hepworth et al., 2010; Ivey, Ivey, & Zalaquett, 2010; Murphy & Dillon, 2008). This is true for relationships with clients, colleagues, administrators, and anyone else with whom you interact.

Warmth

Displaying *warmth* involves conveying a feeling of interest, concern, well-being, and liking to another individual. It is often difficult to find specific, accurate English words for feelings. For example, *Merriam Webster's Collegiate Dictionary* (Mish, 2008, p. 1410) defines warmth as "the quality or state of being warm in feeling" such as "a child needing human warmth and family life." We tend to define a word by using the same word in the definition (referred to as a tautology). There's often no exact synonym available. Conveying warmth, however, does involve enhancing the positive feelings of one person toward another. Warmth promotes a sense of comfort and well-being in that other person.

Warmth can be communicated to another person verbally and nonverbally. Such behaviors can be defined, practiced, and learned. The following are examples of verbally communicating warmth:

"Hello. It's good to meet you."
"I'm glad we have the chance to talk about this."

"It's pleasant talking with you."
"It's good to see you again."
"Please sit down. Can I get you a cup of coffee?"
"You are really a good listener."
"I really appreciate your efforts and your help."

These are just a few of the many statements you can make to convey the feeling that you respect the individual with whom you are talking. Such statements help to convey a sense of concern for others and for others' well-being. There are also many ways to communicate warmth nonverbally. We've discussed how eye contact, attentive listening, and body positioning can all be used to a worker's advantage.

Empathy

Empathy is a second basic worker characteristic that enhances relationships (CSWE, 2008, EP 2.1.10b). *Empathy* is not only being in tune with how the other people feel, but also conveying to people both verbally and nonverbally that you understand how they feel. It does not necessarily mean that you think another individual's feelings are positive or negative, nor does empathy mean that you are having the same feelings yourself. It simply means that you acknowledge and understand the other person's situation.

EP 2.1.10b

For instance, Sly is a social worker for a private,[3] nonprofit[4] agency called Jobs for Youth (JFY) in a large midwestern city.[5] JFY helps impoverished youth ages 16 to 20 who are not currently in school "become self-reliant, independent, and self-supporting adults … by helping them prepare for, find, and keep jobs in local businesses and industry" (Cohen, 1987, p. 83). JFY emphasizes remedial education and job readiness skills in addition to actual initial job placement. The intent is to prepare young people for a lifetime of

---

3. *Private* social agencies are privately owned, are run by people not employed by government, and provide some specific services such as counseling or services for older adults. This is in contrast to *public* agencies that are run by a designated unit of government and are usually regulated by laws that directly affect their policies.

4. *Nonprofit* agencies and organizations are established for motives other than profit; they are generally run by a board of directors and receive funding from a variety of sources, including client fees, donations, public contributions, and grants (Barker, 2003).

5. This example is based on a description of the Chicago program Jobs for Youth, in M. I. Cohen, "Youth Employment," in *Children, Families and Cities: Programs That Work at the Local Level*, J. E. Kyle (Ed.) (Washington, DC: National League of Cities, 1987), pp. 83–86.

HIGHLIGHT 2.1

Nonverbal Behavior, Communication, Empowerment, and People Who Have Physical Disabilities

EP 2.1.4

Just as multicultural sensitivity is vital, so is sensitivity to the special issues experienced by people who have physical disabilities (CSWE, 2008, EP 2.1.4). Verbal and nonverbal behavior should be modified to empower persons with disabilities and improve your relationships with them. The following are some suggestions to enhance respect for and communication with people with visual impairments, hearing impairments, and mobility disabilities.

People with Visual Impairments. Visual impairment is difficulty in perception that is experienced through sight compared to the norm. Difficulties range from mild impairment correctable by glasses or contact lenses to total blindness. Ivey and his colleagues (2010) reflect that some people who are blind may not look you directly in the eye when they speak to you; they also suggest that you anticipate people "with limited vision to be more aware of your vocal tone" (p. 66). When people who have serious visual impairments are unfamiliar with the environment they're in, they may need information regarding the floor plan or obstacles in order to maneuver about (Sheafor & Horejsi, 2006).

For people who have partial sight be conscious of potential glare, especially sunlight (Mackelprang & Salsgiver, 1999). Close blinds or curtains where brightness is a problem, and avoid positioning yourself in front of a light source.

People with Hearing Impairments. Hearing impairment is a general concept indicating a hearing loss, which can range from mild to total deafness. Ivey and his colleagues (2010) note that "some people who are deaf do not consider themselves impaired in any way. Many of this group were born deaf and have their own language (signing) and their own culture, a culture that often excludes those who hear" (p. 66).

Arrange for a signing interpreter to be present when speaking to people who are deaf; however, make certain to speak directly to the person who is deaf and not to the interpreter (Ivey et al., 2010). Remember that maintaining "eye contact [with that person] is vital" (Ivey et al., 2010, p. 66).

For people having moderate to severe hearing loss, avoid communicating in areas with a lot of background noise, as this may aggravate the problem (Sheafor & Horejsi, 2006). Note that speaking exceptionally loudly is not necessarily helpful, as hearing aids amplify all sounds, including those in the background (Ivey et al., 2010; Sheafor & Horejsi, 2006). Sheafor and Horejsi (2006) reflect that if a person

> appears to be having difficulty hearing, ask what you can do to minimize the client's difficulty. You may need to slow down your pace slightly, speak as clearly as possible, and check often to see if the client is able to follow the conversation. Do not mistake nodding and smiling as a sign of comprehension, for that may be the client's response to being embarrassed.
>
> If your client uses speech reading (lip reading), be sure to position yourself so he or she can see your face. In addition, do not speak while looking away or down at the papers, and do not position yourself in front of a window or bright light... Do not exaggerate your words, since this will make speech reading more difficult. (pp. 209–210)

People with Mobility Disabilities. People who have mobility disabilities "are those whose physical differences compel them to achieve physical activities in a variety of alternate ways" (Mackelprang & Salsgiver, 2009, p. 177). For people using wheelchairs, do not stand so that you're looking down at them, as this implies psychological superiority and may make them strain themselves to look up at you; rather, make sure you position yourself at their eye level (Sheafor & Horejsi, 2006). For people using wheelchairs, canes, or crutches, respect their independence and avoid offering help unless it's necessary; don't provide assistance if the person refuses your offer (Sheafor & Horejsi, 2006). Finally, don't give undue attention to medical and other equipment or unique physical qualities (Sheafor & Horejsi, 2006). As Ivey and his colleagues (2010) aptly state, "focus on the person, not the disability" (p. 66).

self-reliance through work productivity. Sly functions both as a counselor and as an employer services representative. The latter role involves seeking appropriate jobs for clients and working with employers to place clients in suitable positions.

Sly likes and respects his supervisor, Rhonda, who is also JFY's director. Sly approaches Rhonda with a problem. Recently, he has been experiencing difficulty with the personnel director, Barry Helafonte, in one of the local industrial plants where JFY places some clients. Sly explains the situation to Rhonda "Okay, here's the problem. On a number of occasions, I contacted Barry about a potential job placement candidate. He tells me, 'Oh, sure, there's a great job available.' Then he stalls for weeks, sometimes even months. You know how that kind of behavior eats away at our clients' motivation and commitment to our program. I am just about at my wit's end. Barry's driving me nuts. I know we need to keep up good relationships with employing organizations, but I just do not like this guy."

Rhonda, using her nonverbal empathic skills, leans toward Sly and looks at him seriously. She then responds, "Sly, I know how hard it can be to work with some employers day after day. You're trying to do your very best, and they just don't seem to be cooperating. Why don't you avoid him for a few days and let your feelings settle down? Sometimes, it helps just to let it go for a while. I'll take up the slack temporarily."

This response conveys that Rhonda understands the situation and Sly's feelings. However, it does not condone Sly's desire to stop working with Barry. Rhonda empathizes with Sly, thereby communicating that she is on his side. She understands. Once Sly feels that she listens to how he feels and that she's not against him, he will more likely work with her toward a solution. Additionally, Rhonda proposes a solution that is satisfactory to Sly in view of Rhonda's understanding attitude.

On the other hand, Rhonda could have jumped at Sly in an abrupt, tense manner with a scowl on her face. She could have responded by saying something like, "How unprofessional! Get your act together! You are responsible for doing the job you're getting paid for. I do not want to hear another thing about it!" This reaction would blame Sly for doing something wrong. It would clearly communicate to him that Rhonda did not understand his feelings or his situation. It totally lacks empathy. Sly could easily view Rhonda as the enemy, someone to be fought with and avoided.

By taking the pressure off Sly for a few days and by empathizing with him, Rhonda significantly improved

the situation. Sly was able to think about the situation more objectively. He continued to talk about the problem with Rhonda. She encouraged him to empathize with Barry's situation. Because of the huge size of Barry's organization, Barry had many irons in the fire. Barry's heart was probably in the right place; that is, he probably wanted to help JFY's clients, all of whom really needed a job. However, Barry had many other onerous responsibilities in his own job as well. Sometimes, Barry was just overwhelmed and unable "to get his act together."

Together, Sly and Rhonda decided on a new approach to Barry. It was critical for JFY to maintain good relationships with community employers. However, Barry's behavior was not helpful to clients. Sly dealt with his own anger toward Barry and decided he needed to get control of the situation. He decided to continue referring clients when appropriate. He also would continue being courteous to Barry. However, Sly established a two-week deadline. If Barry failed to come through with a specific job possibility within two weeks of being contacted, Sly would simply look elsewhere for his client's employment. Sly would also thank Barry for his efforts and explain that he needed to move on in his client's best interests. Sly maintained his contact with Barry so that he did not alienate Barry and thus totally cut off this potential job source.

As a worker, you can use empathy to help establish an initial rapport. You can also use it to elicit feelings and begin talking about issues that might never be broached had feelings not been mentioned. Thus, empathy can provide you with a means of getting at other people's feelings that are not expressed out loud.

For example, Chung is a social worker at a health care center for older adults. He notices that Brenda, a new colleague, avoided having eye contact with him throughout the monthly staff meeting in which they both participated. After the meeting, Chung says, "Brenda, I noticed you were sort of avoiding me during our meeting. That bothers me. Is something wrong? Let's talk about it." In this way, Chung empathetically provides an opportunity for Brenda to talk to him about what was bothering her, if anything. As it turns out, in this particular instance, Brenda is furious. During the meeting she thought she heard Chung say he had completed one of her job responsibilities for a particular case. She took this as a total put-down. Chung's subsequent empathic comments to Brenda give her the opportunity to confront him with her anger. After Chung approaches her about it, they work it out. Chung apologizes and convinces Brenda that it certainly was not his intent to take credit for her work.

Yet another use of empathy involves enhancing the effectiveness of interpersonal interactions during confrontations. Empathy can be used to disperse hostility. For example, Halima, a protective services worker, is helping neighborhood residents at a fundraiser for school recreation equipment. The old equipment is rusty and decrepit, but there is no money for new things in the available budget. A community resident, Lucky, is also volunteering at the fundraiser. He stomps up to Halima, breathing shallowly and rapidly. His face is red, and his vocal tone is loud, gruff, and hostile. He states, "I'm sick of you taking over this whole shebang! All you ever do is tell other people what to do. I've had it. Go to blazes!"

Halima chooses not to respond to what Lucky has said. She does not react with something lacking in empathy like, "You have some nerve talking to me like that. If you can't talk to me courteously, don't talk to me at all!"

Rather, Halima uses empathy by stating, "You sound like you're really angry at me. I'm sorry you feel like that. Please tell me your reasons. I apologize for giving you the wrong impression." This latter response is much more likely to help Lucky calm down and talk about what's wrong. Halima's response diffuses his anger momentarily so that they are able to sit down and work out what Lucky sees as problems.

Nonverbal communication can also be used to enhance empathy. A worker's gestures can mirror how another person is feeling. For instance, furrowing the brow can convey a serious focusing of attention and reflect another person's grave concerns over some issue. Nonverbal communication can emphasize or enhance verbal empathic responses. For example, consider a coworker who appears exceptionally happy one day. Smiling broadly, you empathetically state, "You look simply radiant when you're so happy. What's up?" In this example, smiling while making an empathic verbal response may indicate more convincingly to the coworker that you really understand how she feels. However, be careful. Sometimes, smiling when addressing a serious issue may imply a lack of sincerity or sarcasm. The important thing is to attend to your own nonverbal communication and be sensitive to others' reactions.

Concerning empathy in general, we have established that using it can be a significant tool. However, as with most other techniques and approaches, it does not always work. Highlight 2.2 provides some opportunities for practicing empathic responses.

Genuineness

The third relationship-enhancing quality is *genuineness* or *authenticity*. This is the "sharing of self by relating in a natural, sincere, spontaneous, open and genuine manner" (Hepworth et al., 2010, p. 107). Genuineness simply means that you continue to be yourself, despite the fact that you are working to accomplish goals in your professional role.

Personality refers to the unique configuration of qualities and attributes that make you an individual. Some people have effervescent, bubbly, and outgoing personalities. Others have more subdued, quiet temperaments. Some people relate to others by using their sense of humor. Others prefer to relate more seriously. The point is that there is no one type of personality that is best in a professional role. Rather, it is important that you be yourself. Don't pretend to be something or someone that you're not. Genuineness conveys a sense of honesty to others and generally makes them feel that you're someone they can trust.

Communicating with Other People in Macro Contexts

EP 2.1.3c

Here we will define and explain a number of verbal responses to initiate communication, solicit information, encourage responses, and respond appropriately to something some other individual says. They include simple encouragement, sensitivity to cultural differences, paraphrasing, reflective responding, clarification, interpretation, providing information, emphasizing other people's strengths, summarization, and eliciting information. Some hesitations about using the word "why" are also examined.

Simple Encouragement

Many times a simple one-word response or nonverbal head nod while maintaining eye contact is enough to encourage the other person to continue. Verbal clues such as mm-hmm, "I see," and "uh-huh" help convey that the communication's receiver really is listening and following what the sender is saying. For example, a worker at another agency might say to you, "I've been meaning to talk to you about your agency's policy

HIGHLIGHT 2.2

Practicing Empathic Responses in Macro Practice Contexts

You can use several leading phrases to begin an empathic statement. Following are some examples:

- "My impression is that..."
- "It appears to me that..."
- "Is what you're saying that... ?"
- "Do I understand you correctly that... ?"
- "I'm hearing you say that..."
- "Do you mean that... ?"
- "Do you feel that... ?"
- "I feel that you..."
- "I'm getting the message that..."
- "You seem to be..."
- "When you said that I think you..."
- "You look like you..."
- "You sound so ___. Can we talk more about it?"
- "You look ___. What's been happening?"

EP 2.1.10b

Following are several vignettes illustrating macro situations. For each one, formulate empathetic responses in your own words and practice them. The first vignette offers an example.

Example

You are a school social worker in an urban neighborhood. Residents find out that a vacant lot near the school was used to dump dangerous chemicals between 10 and 20 years ago. One dozen children attending the neighborhood school have gotten cancer within the past 15 years.

It is not part of your job description to address this issue. However, you feel it is your professional and ethical responsibility to help the neighborhood residents formulate a plan concerning what to do. One potential idea is a class action lawsuit against the companies that dumped chemicals. The intent would be to prove that the companies are at fault and hold them responsible for their actions.

The mother of one child, Eric, who is 14 and has leukemia, makes an appointment to see you. When she enters your office, she breaks down in tears. She states, "I'm so angry! How could people do this to little children? They must have known that dumping those wastes so close to children was dangerous."

Possible empathetic responses include:

- "You sound really angry. I don't blame you. What are your thoughts about what to do?"

- "I'm hearing you say that you are furious about this situation. I'm also very upset. What can I do to help you?"
- "It appears that this whole situation has been a horror story for you. I, too, feel terrible about it. Where do you think we can go from here?"

Vignette 1

You are a social worker in a health care facility for older adults. You are very interested in starting a program for middle-school children to visit your older adult clients. You feel that such interactions between the two age groups would be beneficial for both your clients and the children. Kimberly is the other social worker in the facility. You have approached her with this idea. She has responded only hesitantly and, in your opinion, negatively. You think that she is worried that this proposed project would result in a lot more work for her than she is ready or willing to undertake.

However, you feel you have pretty much paved the way for the plan already. You have contacted school administrators and teachers to obtain their permission and support. You have established a transportation plan and created a permission form for students' parents to sign. Before you have the chance to approach Kimberly one more time, she initiates a conversation with you. She states, "I know you're trying to do the right thing with this student visitation project *[which is an empathic response on Kimberly's part]*. However, you're pushing me into it. I don't have enough time to do my own work, let alone get involved in some petty little program you propose."

You empathically respond... (Remember that you *do not* have to solve the problem right now. You only need to let Kimberly know that you understand how she feels.)

Vignette 2

You are a social worker at a diagnostic and treatment center for children with multiple disabilities. Your primary function is to work with parents, helping them to cope with the pressures they are under and connecting them with resources they need. The center's staff includes a wide range of disciplines such as occupational therapy,[a] physical therapy,[b] speech therapy, psychology, and nursing. A problem you sometimes encounter involves professionals from other disciplines asking you to keep parents from asking them questions. This is true especially when children have conditions that are sadly getting worse. One day a physical therapist approaches you and asks, "Do you think you could talk to Mrs. Harris? She keeps asking me these uncomfortable questions about Sally [Mrs. Harris's daughter]. Sally's condition is deteriorating. I don't know what to say."

You empathically respond...

Vignette 3

You are an intake worker at a social services agency in a rural area. Your job is to take telephone calls, assess problems, and refer clients to the most appropriate services. You identify a gap in service for people who have cognitive disabilities. You think that development of a social activities center is a wonderful idea. You talk with administrators in your agency who, you determine, generally support the idea but don't know where the funding will come from. They suggest you talk with

some of the local politicians to get their reactions. You make an appointment to share your suggestion and get feedback about possible funding for such a center. The chairperson responds, "Yeah, it sounds good, but who's going to pay for it and run it?"

You empathically respond...

Notes

a. *Occupational therapy* is "therapy that utilizes useful and creative activities to facilitate psychological or physical rehabilitation" (Nichols, 1999, p. 914).

b. *Physical therapy* is "the treatment or management of physical disability, malfunction, or pain by physical techniques, such as exercise, massage, hydrotherapy, etc." (Nichols, 1999, p. 996).

concerning the treatment of clients who are poor." You might simply encourage the worker to continue by saying, "I see. Please go on" or "Mm-hmm, tell me more."

Sensitivity to Cultural Differences

Again, be cautious about the indiscriminate use of any of the verbal and nonverbal techniques described here. Sensitivity to cultural differences must be ongoing. For example, Ivey and his colleagues (2010) describe a situation in which a North American discusses an issue with a woman from China. He utters "uh-huh" several times when she pauses briefly between sentences during her description of an event. However, whereas "'uh-huh' is a good minimal encouragement in North America, it happens to convey a kind of arrogance in China. A self-respecting Chinese would say *er* (oh), or *shi* (yes) to show he or she is listening. How could the woman feel comfortable when she thought she was being slighted?" (p. 76).

Paraphrasing

Paraphrasing is restating what the other person is saying, but using different words. Paraphrasing has a variety of purposes: It can communicate to another person that you are really trying to listen to what she's saying, and it can let her know you did not understand her real intent so she can clarify her meaning. Paraphrasing can also help the other person take time out and reflect on what she has just said.

Paraphrasing does not mean interpreting what the other person has said. It simply repeats a statement

using other words. For example, a colleague might state, "I'm so furious with my supervisor. He never gives me any credit for anything!" You might then reply by paraphrasing his statement: "You're mad at your boss because you don't think he appreciates all the work you do."

Reflective Responding

Reflective responding is translating into words what you think the other person is feeling. It is a verbal means of displaying empathy that conveys that you understand both what others are going through and how they feel about it. A typical scenario involves a person who *talks* about her problems, but doesn't really articulate how she *feels* about her problems. In this situation, you might help her identify and express her feelings. Only then is she likely to do something about them. Both verbal and nonverbal behavior can be used as cues for reflective responding. For example, a colleague approaches you and says, "I can't seem to keep up with all that *%#&*#! paperwork!" A reflective response might be, "Wow, you really sound mad. I guess this load of paperwork is getting to you."

Clarification

Clarification is making certain that what another person says is understood. Its intent is to make the communication's meaning more readily apparent. Clarification is typically used in one of two ways. First, you can help another person say more clearly what he really means by providing the words for it. This is clarification for the other person's benefit. A second reason for using a clarifying statement is to explain what the other person is saying for your own benefit. Many times, clarification will serve to benefit both sender and receiver. For example, the director of another agency's vocational rehabilitation unit might say to you, "I think your agency should maintain more involvement with my program."[6]

To clarify what the director said, you might respond, "You mean that you would like to have representatives from my agency visit your staff." In this situation you are attempting to clarify for both yourself and the director exactly what "more involvement" means.

In summary, clarification, paraphrasing, and reflective responding have a number of differences. Clarification is used when there is a question about what another person means. Paraphrasing, on the other hand, tries to restate exactly what the other person has said. This paraphrasing assumes that you already understand the communication. Finally, reflective responding expands on another person's statements to include the dimension of emotion.

Interpretation

Interpretation is seeking meaning beyond that of clarification. To interpret means to help bring to a conclusion, to enlighten, or to seek a meaning of greater depth than what has been stated. Interpretation helps lead another person to look deeper into the meaning of what she said. The intent is to enhance another person's perception of the meaning of her own words.

For instance, one colleague might state to another, "I like Samson, but he always seems to get the most interesting cases. It's just not fair, that's all there is to it." The second colleague might respond by interpreting this statement, "It seems you have some conflicting feelings toward Samson. On the one hand, you like him. On the other, you seem to resent the fact he's getting more challenging cases than you are."

To interpret means to take a statement a step beyond its basic meaning. In the previous example, the second colleague went beyond the first colleague's feelings of anger and resentment. He focused on the motivations behind the first colleague's feelings by trying to provide some insight into the source of such feelings.

---

6. *Vocational rehabilitation* involves teaching people with physical or mental disabilities necessary skills for employment, so that they might become more independent and rely less on public support (Barker, 2003).

Providing Information

Many times it is appropriate to provide information to another person. That person may ask you a direct question, such as what he should do in a specific situation, or where in the agency policy manual sick leave is explained. Sometimes another person is misinformed or has inaccurate information. You might then need to identify the inaccuracy and provide accurate information. The circumstances for providing information are infinite. The important thing is to give information straightforwardly and humbly. Other people will likely bristle at being told what to do in a condescending manner.

Emphasizing People's Strengths

Your instructors have probably drilled into you the importance of emphasizing your clients' strengths. It is also important to emphasize the strengths of colleagues, administrators, and others. Each individual in the macro environment has personal strengths, weaknesses, concerns, and defenses. It is critically important to tune in to these dimensions throughout your interactions and communication with others.

Even when you feel you must give another a constructive suggestion or criticism, a strengths perspective implies that it is still important to carefully support that person's ego. You want to convey to that person that you are on her side. By emphasizing that person's strengths, you can try to get the point across that you are not the enemy. You value that person's opinions and respect her right to make her own decisions. Two ways to do this include emphasizing accomplishments and stressing personal qualities. Often, prefacing a communication—even one that involves criticism—with positive feedback helps to provide a *constructive* versus *destructive* context for that communication.

An example of emphasizing accomplishments is to say, "I know you have worked with in-service training programs like this numerous times in the past. Would you mind if I made a minor suggestion concerning potential resources?"

An example of emphasizing personal qualities might be, "I appreciate how easy you are to talk to. You're a good listener. I feel comfortable talking over issues with you. However, I have some concerns about the policy you've implemented. Might you have some time to talk to me about it?"

Summarization

Summarization involves briefly covering the main points of a discussion or series of communications.

Summarizing information can be done periodically throughout a discussion. This helps the other person focus on the main points covered during a portion of the interaction. It also helps to keep communication on track. It can be used to shift to a new subject or help clarify complex concerns. Summarization is difficult in that you must carefully select only the most important facts, issues, and themes. Exclude less essential details. Condense and emphasize only the most salient points.

You can also use summarization to bring a discussion to a close. Emphasizing the major points made during a discussion can send a cue to the other discussant that the communication is ending. Summarization focuses on what has already been said. Summarizing what has been accomplished during communication or discussion allows participants to leave on a positive note. For example, at the end of a staff meeting, summarizing recommendations about who is to do what before the next meeting crystallizes the plans that have been made in all participants' minds.

Eliciting Information

Just as sometimes you will be in the position of providing information, at other times you will need to elicit information. One way of doing this is simply to ask questions. There are two basic types of questions: closed-ended and open-ended. Closed-ended questions seek simple yes or no answers, such as the following:

"Are you coming to tomorrow's boring staff
   meeting?"
"Did you have a nice time in Cudahy?"
"Do you want to run for the NASW state president?"
"Has the attorney seen the grievance yet?"
"Do you have a bachelor's degree in social work
   from an accredited program?"

Closed-ended questions may also be asked when there are a number of clearly defined answers to choose from. Such questions do not encourage or even allow an explanation of why the answer was chosen, or an elaboration of thoughts or feelings about the answer. For example, consider these questions:

"Do you prefer orange or chartreuse name tags for
   the conference?"
"What time does our policy committee meet?"
"What color tie are you going to wear to the
   hearing?"
"When do you expect the Senator to return?"
"How old are you?"

In each of the above instances, a simple response is required. The choices for the response are established ahead of time and have a closed number of options. Your job is simply to choose one. For example, your age is probably between 19 and 90 years.

In contrast, open-ended questions seek more extensive thoughts, ideas, and explanations for answers. They encourage elaboration and specifics about answers unique to the person answering them. For instance, the following are open-ended questions:

"How do you think our country should go about
   solving the homelessness problem?"
"What are your feelings and opinions about affirmative action?"
"What changes would you most like to see in the
   social work program at your school?"
"What qualities do you value most in your relationships with people?"
"What would make you more comfortable with this
   bill, Representative Schlenekinsy?"
"How would you define macro practice?"

Each of these questions allows for a more detailed explanation as an answer. Any individual in any particular situation would provide a unique answer. For example, how you would describe what you like about your favorite activity would be a unique response, unlike anyone else's.

The Use of "Why?"

It is easy and common to use the word *why* when asking questions. However, it is important to remember that "Why?" can be threatening. It can put people on the spot. In other words, it often implies that the person to whom it's directed is at fault.

For example, a practitioner enters a staff meeting three minutes late. The supervisor asks in front of all the worker's colleagues, "Why are you late?" This question places a demand on the worker to explain his reasons for doing something wrong by not being on time.

The following are other examples:

"Why did you skip out of that meeting?"
"Why are you always complaining about that
   policy?"
"Why are you so bossy?"
"Why aren't you married yet?"

The question "Why?" also can put the burden of seeking a solution on the individual to whom it is directed. The solution often involves recalling facts, organizing your thoughts and ideas, and presenting them in an understandable form right then and there. The following questions illustrate this:

"Why did the director reject our petition?"
"Why are public assistance and social security so complicated?"
"Why did you vote as you did in the last national election?"
"Why did you choose social work as your profession?"

In summary, it's best to be cautious in using "Why?"

Overlap of Techniques

Sometimes it's difficult to label a technique as undiluted "clarification" or "interpretation." Some responses fulfill only one purpose and thus will obviously fit into one of the categories. Others will combine two or more techniques as they fulfill two or more functions, because there is an endless variety of words, expressed emotions, ideas, and any combination thereof. The important thing is to master a variety of techniques and thereby become more flexible and more effective in your communication with others.

Appropriate Assertiveness in the Macro Environment: Empowering Yourself and Others

Most people sometimes wish they had been more assertive. Yet, at those moments, they feel very uncomfortable doing so. At other times they feel they were caught off guard.

For example, Caitlin works as a foster-care placement specialist for a public social services agency in a major metropolitan area on the East Coast. She has also been appointed by her agency's administration as a member of the city's Interagency Council on Adolescent Pregnancy.[7] This council, strongly supported by city government, has representatives from a dozen major social service agencies within the city. Each participating agency provides one or two council members, depending on the agency's size.

The council's task is to undertake a major assessment of the city's adolescent pregnancy problem, recommend solutions, and develop a coordinated strategy for the recommendations' implementation. Thus far, the council has gathered facts and examined the issues. It has also established a strategy that "emphasizes efforts to reduce the incidence of first pregnancies, early and continuing services to help teen parents become independent adults and enhance their children's growth and development, and special efforts to prevent repeat pregnancies and births to teens" (Pittman, Adams-Taylor, & Morich, 1987, p. 167). The council continues to work on the task of specifying its strategy to implement the plan.

Caitlin is getting out of her car, about to attend one of the council's biweekly meetings. Suddenly, Harvey, one of her colleagues and her agency's other council representative, drives up and parks next to her. He says, "Oh, hi. Would you mind writing out that announcement we talked about and circulating it to the other council members?" The announcement involves a fundraising dinner that a council subcommittee, including both Caitlin and Harvey, has planned. He continues, "I have a court appearance scheduled downtown today, so I can't make the council meeting. I'm glad I caught you because I have to get going."

He catches Caitlin off guard. Then he jumps in his car and drives away. Harvey typically "leeches" time, energy, and money from people he works with, including other council members. It may entail just asking for a cigarette from the few remaining colleagues who smoke. Or it might be a request that someone else write up the results of one of the meetings because he doesn't have time (even though it was his turn to function as the meeting's secretary). Sometimes, he asks Caitlin to pick him up the next morning because his son needs the car (even though he lives 25 miles out of her way). Another of his favorite ploys is to sheepishly request that Caitlin or some other colleague "catch the check" for lunch because he forgot his checkbook and doesn't have any cash (he typically says he will pay the lender back later, but never does—at least, not without being badgered a half-dozen times). In other words, Harvey is fairly inconsiderate about others' rights. In essence, he is downright self-centered.

When he asks Caitlin to do this favor, she doesn't have much time to think and almost automatically says, "Oh, yeah, sure." Then, 30 seconds after he's disappeared and it's too late, she thinks, "What did I do

---

7. This example is based on a description of Adolescent Pregnancy and Parenting Services, New York City, in *Children, Families, and Cities: Programs That Work at the Local Level*, by J. E. Kyle (Ed.) (Washington, DC: National League of Cities, 1987), pp. 157–194.

that for? I know better than to get sucked in by his requests. Rats!"

The problem is that he surprises Caitlin when she least expects it. She has other things on her mind. For one thing, she's thinking about the idea she wants to present at today's council meeting about developing a program for providing "vocational/ employment training and parent responsibility counseling for 18- to 25-year-old fathers who are currently neither working nor supporting their children" (Pittman et al., 1987, p. 169). Caitlin has also been wondering whether the meeting will be over in time for her to make her appointment to change her car's oil.

Caitlin would never impose upon people as Harvey does. In his view, not only should she automatically agree to circulate the dinner announcement, but she should also *write* it! She thinks, "Oh, come on. That is his responsibility." She's not certain about all the details for the dinner. She wonders why he didn't call her earlier about the announcement or drop off a note. Not expecting his sudden request, she is unprepared to respond. She never really thought about such a situation before.

Over the next half-hour Caitlin remains preoccupied about what she *should* have said. For example, "No." Or, maybe she should have compromised and replied, "Sure. You write the announcement, and I'll be happy to circulate it to the council." She continues to stew about her mistake and Harvey's inconsiderate behavior for quite a while.

But it's too late to do anything about it after the fact. Now Caitlin has already agreed to do it. She's stuck. She has simply been too unassertive in response to Harvey's request.

In other situations, people allow their frustration at their own nonassertiveness to build until they can't stand it anymore and subsequently "lose it." All their emotions explode in a burst of anger. This can readily happen to nonassertive people who allow their discomfort to build until they erupt in rage. This display of temper and anger reflects one aspect of the other end of the continuum—aggressiveness.

For example, three months ago Meena got her first social work position in a sheltered workshop[8] for adults

with cognitive disabilities. One of her male colleagues, a speech therapist also employed by the agency, regularly makes what Meena considers extremely rude, sexist comments about his female colleagues and even some of the female clients. She feels his behavior has made others so uncomfortable that they find it difficult to work effectively with him in the macro environment.

Meena considers herself a fairly confident, straightforward person. Yet she just started this job and does not want to "make any waves" or be labeled a troublemaker or a complainer. Meena knows that this man's behavior is inappropriate, derogatory, and simply wrong. Every time she runs into him at work, he makes one off-color comment or another. Meanwhile, her feelings continue to simmer… and simmer… and simmer. Finally, something snaps and she screams, "I can't stand it anymore! I think you're a disgusting sexist! Just shut up!" This outburst does little to improve their relationship or his behavior.

Appropriate assertiveness is a necessity in micro, mezzo, and macro practice. Assertiveness involves expressing yourself without hurting others or stepping on their rights. Being assertive means considering both *your own rights* and *the rights of others*. Highlight 2.3 reviews your assertive rights. When interacting with colleagues, supervisors, administrators, staff from other agencies, politicians, or community residents, it is critical to use your assertiveness skills. The following sections will discuss the assertiveness continuum, the advantages of assertiveness, and assertiveness training.

EP 2.1.1b

Nonassertive, Assertive, and Aggressive Communication

On an assertiveness continuum, communication can be rated as nonassertive, assertive, or aggressive. *Assertive* communication includes verbal and nonverbal behavior that permits a speaker to get her points across clearly and straightforwardly. A speaker who is assertive takes into consideration both her own value and the values of whomever is receiving her message. She considers her own points important, but she also considers the points and reactions of the receiver important.

Nonassertive communication comes from a speaker who devalues herself completely. She feels the other person and what that person thinks are much more important than her own thoughts. People who have difficulty being assertive can experience a range of problems.

---

8. A *sheltered workshop* is an organization that provides a range of services to people who have physical or cognitive disabilities. Programs include job skill evaluation, job training, *sheltered employment* (a program involving work in a safe, closely supervised environment for people who have trouble functioning more independently), counseling, and help in finding employment (Barker, 2003).

HIGHLIGHT 2.3

Each of Us Has Certain Assertive Rights

Part of becoming assertive requires figuring out and believing that we are valuable and worthwhile people. It's easy to criticize ourselves for our mistakes and imperfections. It's easy to hold our feelings in because we're afraid that we will hurt someone else's feelings or that someone will reject us. Sometimes feelings that are held in too long will burst in an aggressive tirade. This occurs in micro, mezzo, and macro contexts.

A basic principle in social work is that each individual is a valuable human being. Everyone, therefore, has certain basic rights. The following are eight of your assertive rights:

1. *You have the right to express your ideas and opinions openly and honestly.* For example, Manuela, a nursing-home social worker, attends a meeting at another agency also attended by workers from a range of community social service agencies. The meeting's purpose is to discuss the possibility of conducting a fundraiser to acquire Christmas presents for the poverty-stricken children in the community. Each other participant has already stated a preference for collecting money from community residents, businesses, schools, and social service agencies. Manuela, however, feels that they would get more if the group asked for donations of *toys* and *clothing* instead of *money*. Even though Manuela is going against the flow, so to speak, she still has the right to voice her opinion straightforwardly and honestly. The final consensus regarding strategy may or may not agree with her proposal. However, she has the right to be heard.

2. *You have the right to be wrong. Everyone makes mistakes.* For example, Mohammed is a school social worker who applies for a state grant to start a summer neighborhood activity program for adolescents in an urban neighborhood. He works on the grant every night for two weeks, thinking that such an activity program will keep scores of children off the streets and out of trouble for at least part of the time the following summer. His writing task is like trying to compose three 20-page research papers that you've put off until the final two weeks of the semester. This work is *tedious.* Mohammed finally gets the document off and postmarked on the day he thinks it is due. The key word in the previous sentence, of course, is "thinks." Unfortunately, he has read the due date as December 8 instead of December 5. He has probably read that grant application form 30 times. Each time, his mind saw 8 instead of 5.

Unfortunately, the state grant evaluators are strict regarding the timeliness of grant applications. Any submitted even one day late are immediately returned to the sender. (This is similar to the practice of most graduate schools concerning application dates: One day late and you're out of luck.) Mohammed is, of course, disappointed and disgusted with himself. He has bragged about his plan to his supervisor and fellow workers. Now he has to face the music. What a bummer.

However, Mohammed has the right to make a mistake, even an apparently careless one like this. The cliché that we all make mistakes is exactly right. We all have the right to make mistakes, because even when we try our best we *do* make mistakes.

It is in Mohammed's best assertive interest to chalk his endeavor up as an "experience" and learn from it. On the brighter side, first he has his proposal written up and ready for the next grant opportunity, so all his work has not really been wasted. Second, there may be other opportunities for adolescents' summer activities. He can look into other programs and other possibilities. Third, he can learn a specific axiom from the experience: *Always* make certain you know what the deadline is for *any* application. (Chapter 14, "Developing and Managing Agency Resources," will discuss grant writing in substantial detail.)

3. *You have the right to direct and govern your own life. In other words, you have the right to be responsible for yourself.* For example, Audrey directs a group home for adults with physical disabilities, run by a conservative religious organization. This organization has publicly declared its anti-abortion stance. Her direct supervisor, the organization's director, is also personally strongly anti-abortion. Audrey, however, maintains a solid pro-choice stance on the issue.

A pro-choice rally is being held on an upcoming weekend. Audrey plans to attend and participate. She even expects to hold a pro-choice banner and march in a procession through the main area of town. Audrey knows that such behavior will annoy her supervisor and the agency. However, she feels she has the right to participate in the activity on her own time. This option *is* her right. She is prepared to take responsibility for her behavior and deal assertively with any potential consequences. (Chapter 12, "Ethics and Ethical Dilemmas in Macro Practice," will discuss a range of ethical issues in greater depth.)

These women and men participating in a pro-choice rally in Washington, DC, are demonstrating a basic right—the right to behave assertively.

4. *You have the right to stand up for yourself without unwarranted anxiety and make choices that are good for you.* For example, Helena works for a child abuse and protection unit with three other workers in a rural social services agency serving several counties. The agency, like many others, is tormented by serious financial problems. Staffing is short. Funding is severely limited. Therefore, worker activities outside essential job duties are extremely restricted.

A friend and fellow social worker at an agency in another county calls Helena and excitedly describes an upcoming workshop on new identification techniques for child neglect. Helena thinks it sounds wonderful. She knows that the agency's money is tight but thinks what a beneficial investment it would be if she and her three unit colleagues could attend the workshop. The workshop would cost the agency $800 at $200 per attendant.

Helena talks to the other workers, who agree that the conference is a great idea. They tell Helena if she can muster agency support, they would love to go. Helena decides to request support from the agency, despite the fact she knows her own supervisor will bristle at the thought of spending a penny more on anything than the agency absolutely has to. Helena determines that she has the right to stand up for herself, and, in effect for her unit colleagues and ask to attend this workshop. She develops a detailed rationale concerning why and how the workshop will benefit workers and enhance agency effectiveness.

Additionally, Helena prioritizes what the agency can potentially do for her and her colleagues. She starts with her first priority and then works down to her last. First, the agency can pick up the entire workshop cost and give her and her colleagues the two days off with pay. Second, the agency can pick up part of the cost for each worker and allow them all to take the two days off without pay. (In this case, Helena and the others will have to pay the remaining costs themselves.) Third, the agency can allow Helena and her colleagues to

(continued)

HIGHLIGHT 2.3 *(continued)*

attend with pay, but require them to cover the entire workshop cost themselves. Finally, Helena decides that if she has to, she will take the two days off without pay and also pay the entire workshop fee herself. She is uncertain what her colleagues will choose to do in this instance of last resort. Helena assertively proceeds with her request. What do you think will happen?

5. *You have the right not to be liked by everyone. (Do you like everyone you know?)* For example, Hiroko is a public assistance worker for a large county bureaucracy. She is very dedicated to her job and often works overtime with clients to make certain that they receive all the benefits possible. Her colleague, Michael, holding the same job title, thinks this is utterly stupid. He resents that she seems to stand out as a star worker. Michael is not all that much into work himself. He feels he is "tenured," meaning permanently implanted in his position. He is not interested in doing any more work than he has to. He often refers to Hiroko as a "drudge."

   Hiroko really doesn't care. She knows that effective performance of her job on the behalf of clients is important to her. Frankly (she asserts), it really doesn't matter to Hiroko whether Michael likes her or not. She has the right not to be liked by everybody.

6. *You have the right, on the one hand, to make requests and, on the other, to refuse them without feeling guilty.* For example. Merle is a case manager for veterans who suffer from post-traumatic stress disorder.[a] Part of the job requires that he take turns with four other staff members to have his cell phone with him and be on call in case of an emergency for one week out of every month.

   Merle's large family is staging a reunion at a ranch resort in Colorado. It happens to be set for a week when Merle is supposed to be on call and would not ordinarily take his vacation time. Merle has the right to assertively ask one of the other three staff members on call to switch weeks (assuming that agency policy allows this practice). His colleagues, on the other hand, also have the right to refuse. From another perspective, consider what would happen if the situation were reversed. Merle then would have the right either to accept or to refuse a request to switch on-call weeks in a similar manner.

7. *You have the right to ask for information if you need it.* For example, Louise is a financial counselor at a private mental health agency. She is aware that the agency has access to special funding for persons "with exceptional needs." She knows this only informally via the agency grapevine. Therefore, she is not certain that the term "exceptional needs" means the same to her as it does to agency administrators. Because the agency is privately run, it is not subject to the same requirements to reveal funding sources as are similar public agencies. (The public, who pays for public agencies, has the right to scrutinize budgets and spending.)

   Louise is working with several families whom she feels are in dire need of special help. Problems in the families include unemployment, depression, mental illness, poverty, unwanted pregnancy, and truancy. Louise knows that her agency administrator discourages workers from seeking this relatively secret special funding. Available amounts are probably very limited, so the administration must disperse these funds with discretion. Although Louise knows that the administration will not look kindly on her request she decides to approach the agency's executive director to seek funding for the families in need and find out what requirements make clients eligible for this special funding. She feels she has the right to ask for this information, even though the agency administration would rather she did not.

8. *You have the right to decide not to exercise your assertive rights.* In other words, you have the right to choose not to be assertive if you don't want to. For example, Horace, a state probation and parole agent is a member of a task force to curb substance abuse in his state.[b] He attends the last of a series of meetings aimed at facilitating a range of educational prevention and treatment thrusts to obliterate substance abuse among youth, especially delinquents. Horace feels that the task force has made great strides. It established goals, developed plans, carried out initiatives, and evaluated its results. Throughout the process, however, he felt that the task force chairperson, Tobin, who happens to be an administrator in Horace's own state Division of Probation and Parole, was being much too pushy. Horace thinks Tobin frequently tried to coerce the group into following Tobin's own agenda.

Although the group frequently ignored Tobin's ploys, Horace thinks Tobin's actions were inappropriate and perhaps even unethical.

After careful deliberation, Horace decides that it is not worth it to assertively confront Tobin about his behavior. Horace decides not to be assertive. After all, Tobin, as task force chairperson, has led the group to achieve great things. The moral here is that you don't have to be assertive every single time the opportunity presents itself.

Notes

Most of these rights have been adapted from those identified in *The New Assertive Woman* by Lynn Z. Bloom, Karen Coburn, and Joan Perlman (New York: Dell, 1976) and in *Four One-Day Workshops* by Kathryn Apgar and Betsy Nicholson Callaghan (Boston: Resource Communications Inc. and Family Service Association of Greater Boston, 1980).

a. *Post-traumatic stress disorder* (PTSD) is a condition involving a psychological and emotional reaction in which a person continues to reexperience some traumatic event such as a bloody battle, rape, fire, or earthquake. Symptoms can include poor concentration, nightmares, emotional numbness, extreme nervousness, or sleeping problems (Barker, 2003).

b. A *task force* is a group of people, often representatives from different units within an organizational or community context, who come together on a temporary basis to serve some designated purpose or achieve a particular goal (Daft, 2004).

They can be very shy and withdrawn or afraid to express their real feelings. Although they may become increasingly uncomfortable about their failure to be assertive and protect their rights, they rarely can respond assertively.

For example, Pete has a problem. Part of his job involves collecting information about the amount of client contact from practitioners in his social work department and summarizing this data in a monthly report.

Pete's problem is that Gerri, one of the workers, typically fails to respond to his e-mails and handwritten requests for data until she is at least two weeks late. Gerri's behavior reflects negatively upon Pete's job performance. He is unable to submit the data until he gets all of it. To agency administration, Gerri's tardiness makes Pete look like he's the one who's not punctual in doing this part of his job. This infuriates Pete. However, Pete considers himself a relatively shy person. He hates to confront other people, especially people like Gerri, who have exceptionally outgoing and vibrant personalities. Thus, Pete leaves the situation as it is. He maintains his nonassertive position and allows his underlying anger to seethe.

We have indicated that *aggressiveness* lies on the opposite end of the assertiveness continuum from nonassertiveness. It engenders bold and dominating verbal and nonverbal behavior whereby a speaker presses her point of view as taking precedence above all other perspectives. An aggressive speaker considers only her views important and devalues what the receiver has to say. Aggressive behaviors are demanding and often annoying. Figure 2.3 depicts the assertiveness continuum.

One example of aggressive behavior would be a fellow worker who consistently talks and occasionally raises his voice during staff meetings so that other staff members have little or no opportunity to "get their two cents in." This worker pays attention only to his own needs with no consideration for the needs and wants of others. Another instance of aggressive behavior is the employee who consistently makes it a point to get the agency's best vehicle to make home visits. She not only feels it is supremely important for her to get the best available, she also blocks any comments about how consistently getting the best means that other workers are left with the worst on a regular basis.

Another form of aggressiveness is passive-aggressiveness. Here, an individual is really aggressive, but secretly or covertly so. Often, such a person dislikes confrontation and tries to avoid it at all costs. However, to get his own way, a passive-aggressive individual will go behind others' backs to get what he really wants. For example, Donald, a chemical dependency counselor, thinks Herschel, a colleague with the same job status, is lazy. Donald would like Herschel to be reprimanded by their supervisor Maria and, thereby, be forced to assume more of the workload. Donald does not want

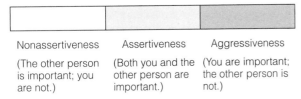

Nonassertiveness	Assertiveness	Aggressiveness
(The other person is important; you are not.)	(Both you and the other person are important.)	(You are important; the other person is not.)

FIGURE 2.3 The Assertiveness Continuum

to confront Herschel himself. Therefore, Donald passive-aggressively meets with Maria behind closed doors (literally) to complain about Herschel's laziness and work performance. He encourages Maria to reprimand Herschel. Donald is being passive in that he doesn't confront Herschel. However, Donald is also being aggressive in that he tries to manipulate the situation so that Herschel receives his reprimand. Donald, however, appears (on the outside) to remain uninvolved and blameless.

There's no perfect recipe for what to say when you are trying to be assertive. The important thing is to take into consideration both your own rights and the rights of the person with whom you are interacting. Following are a few examples.

Situation 1

Amorette is a social worker at a residential treatment center for adolescents with severe emotional and behavioral problems. She completes the draft of a grant application for funds to start a sex education program in the center. The proposal includes the sponsorship of experts to provide both educational programming and contraceptives. Agency policy requires that all grant proposal drafts be reviewed by an agency grants committee before being submitted outside the agency. Prunella, one of the center's teachers, is a member of the grants committee.

When Prunella sees the proposal, she flies through the roof. She feels that for this population, talking about sex in such explicit terms will only encourage them to engage in it. She cannot believe that the proposal also includes providing contraceptives directly to the girls. "Why not show them pornographic movies, too?" she thinks to herself.

Prunella approaches Amorette and declares, "That grant proposal you wrote is totally inappropriate. Under no circumstances will I condone it!" How should Amorette reply?

Nonassertive response: "You're probably right. I'll just forget about it."

Aggressive response: "What's wrong with you? Are you still living in the dark ages or something? Maybe what you need is a little action yourself."

Assertive response: "I understand your concerns. However, I still think this is an important issue to address. Let's talk more about it."

Situation 2

Gigette is a social worker for a public agency providing supportive home-based services for older adults. The agency's intent is to help people maintain their independence and reside in their own homes as long as possible. A county policy states that clients may receive a maximum of eight service hours from Gigette's agency or others like it each month. Gigette works with numerous clients who require more help than this. She understands that the rationale for the policy is to cut costs. However, she feels that changing the policy to increase potential service to a maximum of 16 instead of 8 hours would allow many clients to remain in their own homes much longer. Providing or subsidizing the nursing-home care clients subsequently need is monstrously expensive.

Gigette works through her agency's administration and gains its support. With the agency's sanction, she approaches Biff Bunslinger, the county board chairperson, and shares with him her proposal and its rationale. She has determined that his support would be the most beneficial in changing the county's restrictive policy. Biff responds, "It's a good idea, but where will you get the money for it? What else do you want to cut? Do you have any idea what repercussions such a major policy change would have?" How can Gigette respond?

Nonassertive response: "I don't know. I'm sorry. Let's forget it."

Aggressive response: "You haven't heard a word I've said. Get off your butt, Biff, and start thinking about those people out there who really need help!"

Assertive response: "I know funding is tight and that you have many financial needs you're trying to balance right now. Let me show you why I think this plan will both save the county money and help your older adult constituents in the long run."

Situation 3

Bo, an outreach worker for urban homeless people, is on the board of directors of another agency called the AIDS Support Network. A *board of directors* is a group of people designated to oversee the broad operations of an organization, including determination of its mission and long-range goals, establishment of personnel and operating policies, monitoring and auditing the budget, and providing direction to the chief executive officer, public relations, and fundraising (Toseland & Rivas, 2009). Another board member, Eleni, a local lawyer, bluntly states to Bo, "I wish you would be more specific when you make your comments during meetings. I can never understand what you're talking about." What can Bo reply?

Nonassertive response: "Yes, you're right. I'll try to speak more clearly in the future."

Aggressive response: "I'm not nearly as unclear as you are, nor, by the way, as arrogant!"

Assertive response: "I'm sorry you feel that way. Perhaps, you could speak up when you don't understand something during a board meeting. Your feedback will help us communicate better." (Highlight 2.4 provides a few practice examples.)

The Advantages of Assertiveness

There are many benefits to developing assertiveness skills (Egan, 2010; Ivey & Ivey, 2007, 2008). For one thing, you can gain more control over your work and other interpersonal environments. Assertiveness may help you avoid uncomfortable or hostile interactions with colleagues, administrators, other agency personnel, politicians, and community residents. You will probably feel that other people understand you better than they did before. You can enhance your self-concept and interpersonal effectiveness as the result of this increased control. In the past, bottled-up feelings may have resulted in psychosomatic problems like piercing headaches or painful stomach upsets. Appropriate assertiveness helps to alleviate the buildup of undue tension and stress. As a result, such psychosomatic reactions will probably subside and eventually cease.

Finally, other people may gain respect for you, your strength, and your own demonstration of respect for others. People may even begin to use you as a role model for their own development of assertive behavior.

Assertiveness Training

Assertiveness training leads people to realize and act on the assumption that they have the right to be

---

HIGHLIGHT 2.4

What Would You Do?

How would you respond assertively to each of the following scenarios?

Scenario A

You are a social worker for Heterogeneous County Department of Social Services. Paperwork recording your activities with clients is due promptly the Monday following the last day of each month. For whatever reason, you simply forget to get it in by 5:00 P.M. Monday, the day it's due. Your supervisor, Enrique, calls you at noon the next day. He raises his voice and reprimands, "You know that reports are due promptly so that funding is not jeopardized! How many times do I have to tell you that?" You assertively respond ...

Scenario B

You work with a colleague who consistently comes late to your social work unit's biweekly meetings. He typically saunters leisurely into the meeting room with a cup of decaf in hand, noisily situates himself in a chair at the rectangular meeting table, and casually interrupts whomever is speaking, asking for a brief review of what he missed. You are sick and tired of such rude, time-wasting behavior. Finally, after the last meeting, you pull this colleague aside and assertively state...

Scenario C

You represent your social services agency at a community meeting where 12 community residents and five workers from other agencies are discussing what additional social services the community needs. Some possible grant funding has become available to develop services. The person chairing the meeting asks for input from each person present except you. Apparently, she simply overlooked that you had not gotten an opportunity to speak. You assertively state...

themselves and express their feelings freely. They also learn the critical difference between assertive and aggressive behaviors—an important distinction. For example, consider a woman who has an excessively critical colleague. She can intentionally and aggressively do things that will bother him (bringing up topics that she knows will upset him, such as the lack of support for his pet project, reminding him that some uncomfortable deadline is fast approaching, or criticizing his behavior). She can purposely goad him into arguments with her. This would be considered aggressive behavior.

On the other hand, she can respond more assertively and counter his criticism by saying, "When you offer such excessive criticism, I think you lose some of the value of your points. Perhaps making positive suggestions for changing the system would be more useful."

As we know, social work is practical. Therefore, you can use the suggestions provided to enhance your own assertiveness in a wide range of macro settings. Alberti and Emmons (2008) suggest following a number of steps to help establish assertive behavior:

1. Scrutinize your own actions and evaluate how effective you are according to the assertiveness continuum.
2. Make a record of situations in which you feel you could have been more effective (either more assertive or less aggressive).
3. Select and focus on some specific instance when you felt you could have been more appropriately assertive.
4. Analyze how you reacted in this situation. Critically examine your verbal and nonverbal behavior.
5. Select a role model and examine how she handled a similar situation requiring assertiveness.
6. Identify a range of other new assertive verbal and nonverbal responses that could address the original problem situation you targeted.
7. Picture yourself in the identified problematic situation.
8. Practice the way you've envisioned yourself being more assertive.
9. Once again, review your new assertive responses. Emphasize your strong points and try to remedy your flaws.
10. Continue practicing Steps 7, 8, and 9 until your newly developed assertive approach feels comfortable and natural to you.
11. Try out your assertiveness in a real-life situation.

12. Continue to expand your assertive behavior repertoire until assertiveness becomes a part of your personal interactive style.
13. Give yourself a pat on the back when you succeed in becoming more assertive. It's not easy changing long-standing patterns of behavior.

A Final Note on Assertiveness Training

Remember that you choose whether to be assertive in any given situation. You always have a choice. Making an assertive response to a boss who fires people for speaking up may not be the best plan. You must make a decision about how to respond. No one else can make it for you. Also, recognize that, like any other solution to human problems, being assertive may not always work: Some people don't respond to assertiveness. They may get angry or continue to make inappropriate requests. When assertiveness does not work for you, accept this fact, praise yourself for your progress, and identify areas where you can still improve.

Conflict and Its Resolution

An *interpersonal conflict* occurs "any time people involved in relationships, such as friends, family members, coworkers, or neighbors, have differing needs, wants, desires, expectations, goals, or means of achieving certain ends" (Nugent, 2001, p. 304). According to *Webster's Dictionary,* words commonly associated with conflict include fighting, competition, incompatibility, open warfare, antagonism, "divergent ideas," opposition, and "mental struggle" (Mish, 2008, p. 261).

Conflict can occur in an infinite number of ways in an unending array of contexts in micro, mezzo, and macro situations. This chapter focuses on conflict between individuals in macro contexts. Chapter 3 ("Group Skills for Organizational and Community Change") will address specific types of conflict and conflict management guidelines for group (mezzo) situations in macro environments.

EP 2.1.10g

The Pros of Conflict

Conflicts in macro situations are difficult for many people. It is easy to view conflict and confrontation as being very negative, something to avoid at all costs. This is not necessarily the case. Conflict has some positive aspects, including the following (Johnson, 2009):

1. *Conflict can help us explore a situation more thoroughly.* It can force us to more extensively evaluate

issues and problems involved in interpersonal communication, such as identification of what problems are, who participants in the conflict are, and what can be done to achieve resolution.

2. *Conflict can cause us to make improvements in our behavior and communication.* Change is frequently avoided because it requires some energy to accomplish. When a conflict arises, you may be forced to address an issue and make changes—whether you like them or not.

3. *Conflict can generate new energy to solve a problem.* Conflict increases our awareness of issues and thus may motivate us to make changes in our behavior.

4. *Conflict can make daily routines more exciting.* Disagreements can stimulate creative thinking to develop new solutions. Argument and debate can spawn new, sometimes exciting ideas that we might never have thought of had the conflict not occurred.

5. *Conflict can improve the quality of problem resolution and decision making.* Conflict encourages exploration of ideas and options as well as more critical evaluation of these options.

6. *Conflict can release emotional "steam."* Pent-up feelings simmer and build. Release and resolution through conflict can be constructive in maintaining interpersonal relationships.

7. *Conflict can enhance our own self-awareness.* What issues bother us the most? How do we respond to conflict? Can we identify what "buttons" people can press in us to get us going?

8. *Conflict can be fun when it is not taken too seriously.* Many people enjoy hearty discussion and debate. Games are often based on conflict that is supposed to be fun. The game of "Risk" comes to mind. It is a board game in which the world is divided up into 42 countries or regions. To win, one player must conquer all the others. Explaining the details would take too much space here. However, even though no actual blood is spilled, emotions are heightened as one player "slaughters" another. This author has been known to violently hurl the board in the air when feeling betrayed by another player who has methodically and unemotionally triumphed. Yet such conflict is *fun* (although it tends to be more fun when you win).

9. *Conflict can actually facilitate the development and depth of relationships.* Working through conflicts provides opportunities to get to know another person in a deeper, sometimes very meaningful way. What things are the most important to the other person? How does that person feel about and react to these important issues? What is that person really like in situations that are not entirely positive? Additionally, conflict can dispel negative feelings when conflict resolution is achieved.

The Cons of Conflict

On the other hand, when considering confrontation as a response to some conflict, it is important to weigh at least three potential losses in the context of macro practice (Daft, 2010b). First, conflict takes energy. Energy and resources are always limited. You have just so much time, enthusiasm, effort, and initiative. What you expend in one endeavor, you will not have available to use for some other task. Therefore, you must make certain that the targeted conflict is significant enough to merit your efforts.

Second, conflict may result in winners and losers. Adequate compromise might not be possible or realistic. One opponent in the conflict may feel downtrodden and unfairly treated by the resolution.

Third, conflict may result in decreased collaboration and teamwork. Losers of conflicts often become uncooperative and cease to concern themselves with colleagues' rights and wants. Extreme conflict may end in almost total lack of communication. Concern for the opponent's welfare may vanish. When a worker is totally immersed in intense conflict, her anger might prevent her from working toward compromise. Preoccupation with conflict can even obstruct her ability to do her job.

In summary, it is very important to consider both the potential positive and negative consequences of conflict. Results can range from extraordinarily positive to absolutely destructive.

Personal Styles for Addressing Conflict

Just as each of us has a unique personality, each has an individualized style for approaching conflict. Johnson (2009, p. 253) describes at least four personal styles for managing conflict: "the turtle," "the shark," "the teddy bear," and "the fox." Of course, these are relatively simplistic categories. However, they graphically reflect the general types of behaviors people display when conflict occurs.

The turtle describes the style of people who *withdraw* into their shells to avoid or postpone conflicts. For them it is easier to avoid conflict than to muster up the initiative and energy to address it. Turtles typically have relatively poor self-concepts. They do not have faith in their ability to resolve a conflict. They are nonassertive, valuing the views and needs of others above their own.

The shark is an *aggressor*. The shark moves into a conflict boldly, pushing opponents aside. Sharks are bullies. The shark wants to win and has little interest in nurturing a relationship with an opponent. A shark approaches any situation from a win/lose perspective and won't consider negotiation or compromise. Sharks like power. To get it and win, they will do just about anything, including threatening, intimidating, and attacking opponents.

The teddy bear's style is the direct opposite of the shark's. The teddy bear *values the relationship* with the opponent much more than the achievement of his own goals. The teddy bear is a bit more assertive than the turtle because he does value his own ideas. However, teddy bears will put their own goals aside in deference to their opponent's whenever they feel their relations might be threatened.

The fox is a *compromiser*. The fox uses confrontation to reach some agreement acceptable to both herself and her opponent. The fox's orientation dictates that both parties should voice their opinions, use problem-solving techniques, and relinquish some of their demands to come to a reasonable compromise. Foxes are adept at figuring a way to work things out to the satisfaction of most.

We stress again the importance of getting to know yourself and your own reactions better. How do you address conflict? How will you react to conflict in macro situations? Are you a turtle, shrinking into your shell for safety? Or are you a shark, savagely eager to devour your opponents? Or do you tend to approach conflict somewhere in between, like the teddy bear or the fox? Identifying both your own style of conflict and that of your opponents is important in planning the most effective approach to conflict and confrontation. Generally, it is more effective to take both your needs and those of your opponents into consideration. In addition, both your goals and your relationships with your opponents merit your attention.

Steps in Conflict Resolution

Seven steps are involved in conflict resolution (Ivey & Ivey, 2008; Ivey et al., 2010; Johnson, 2009). Although it is not always possible to go through each one, it is important to keep them in mind. Emphases are on both communication and coordination with the opponent. It should be noted that Chapter 3, "Group Skills for Organizational and Community Change," will also discuss conflict management guidelines, especially in mezzo situations. The steps presented here are among the many approaches to dealing with conflict.

For the purposes of illustration, a case involving the process of conflict resolution will be presented and discussed.

Step 1: The Confrontation

The first step in resolving any kind of conflict is to confront the opponent. A *confrontation* is a face-to-face encounter where people come together with opposing opinions, perspectives, or ideas in order to scrutinize or compare them. Confrontation, intended to resolve or combat some conflictual situation, means to disagree with another person and make a point of stating that disagreement. This, of course, may inspire a negative or hostile reaction by the person you're confronting.

People handle conflict and confrontation very differently. They have widely varied interpersonal styles and skills. Usually, when engaging in a confrontation, it is wise to keep two major issues in mind. First, clearly identify and examine your personal goals. Conflicts can arise because of differences, often concerning goals or perceptions of goals. How important to you are these goals? Are they very important or only minimally so?

The second major issue to keep in mind when beginning a confrontation is the nurturance of your interpersonal relationship with the other person. Clearly showing respect for the other person's feelings, beliefs, and needs helps to sustain the ongoing relationship. Yes, you have a disagreement and you feel some degree of intensity about your position. However, to what extent are you willing to jeopardize your relationship with this person in order to win the conflict? To what extent will you be able to compromise? How can you balance conflict resolution with maintaining a positive a relationship with your opponent? You do not need any more enemies than you absolutely have to have. A major tenet in macro practice is the need to muster support from others in order to achieve your specified goals. Therefore, the more strongly you can sustain your various relationships with others in the macro environment, the better you will perform your job and achieve your intervention goals.

CASE EXAMPLE

Step 1: Setting the Stage for a Confrontation

Brainard supervises a 10-person unit that serves clients receiving public assistance in an urban county's social services department. Brainard's problem is Cheryl, one of his 10 supervisees. Essentially, Cheryl is incompetent. She consistently makes decisions that negatively affect clients, fails to complete her paperwork, and effectively disrupts any unit meetings and projects in which she participates. Scores of clients have complained pointedly about her work and her treatment of them.

Brainard, who is newly hired as unit supervisor, inherited Cheryl from the unit's former supervisor, Charlie, who had originally hired her. Cheryl is not only incompetent, she is also a bitter fighter. Two years earlier when Charlie began to notice Cheryl's difficulties in completing her work adequately, he tried to help Cheryl solve her problems and improve her performance. However, she bristled defensively and fought him every step of the way. The agency has a strong union of which Cheryl, of course, is a member. Once employees pass their probationary period of one year, they essentially gain tenure, after which it is extremely difficult, if not impossible, to terminate their employment. During Cheryl's probationary period, she accused Charlie of harassment and hired legal counsel to represent her. At the time, the agency was suffering some severe public criticism and resulting budget cuts. Therefore, higher administration commanded Charlie to leave Cheryl alone and not cause any trouble. Charlie, who was not renowned for his strength of character or ability to pursue open conflict anyway, backed down and soon thereafter transferred to another agency unit.

Now Brainard, stuck with Cheryl, continues to see the problem more clearly as the months pass. Brainard prides himself on his commitment to advocate on the behalf of clients and consistently work in their best interest. He feels it is his responsibility to do something about Cheryl and her incompetence. He, too, initially tried to help her through her difficulties, making numerous specific recommendations for how she might improve her job performance.

Every one of the other nine unit members has similar concerns about Cheryl. They all feel that Cheryl is a blight on their unit. However, she is tenured and hostile. Colleagues are at a loss about what to do.

Brainard, a competent supervisor, begins to clearly document his efforts at helping Cheryl and her failures to perform her job adequately. After several dozen incidents are noted, Brainard brings the situation to the attention of higher administration. The agency administration has a history of disagreement and conflict with the agency's union. Therefore, the administration feels their wisest alternative is to bring in a neutral

trained mediator from outside the agency to help both parties settle their differences. Obviously, there is quite a dispute between Cheryl and Brainard.

Step 2: Establish Common Ground

Establish an acceptable common definition of the problem (Johnson, 2009). Such a definition should make neither you nor your opponent defensive or resistant to working out a mutually agreeable compromise. Emphasize how important the conflictual issue is to both of you. Be as clear and specific about your concerns as possible. Express and clarify your own feelings, while drawing out those of your opponent. Most importantly, keep trying to empathize with your opponent's position.

CASE EXAMPLE

Step 2: Establish Common Ground

The mediator, Jimmy Hoffa, interviews each of the 10 unit personnel, including Cheryl. He also talks extensively to Brainard. He carefully scrutinizes and begins to bring together the evidence. Jimmy is able to establish a common ground between Cheryl and the rest of the unit. All involved staff, including Cheryl, are unhappy with the conflictual situation. They all feel both their individual performance and that of the unit in general suffers significantly because of it.

Step 3: Emphasize the Importance of Communication

When pursuing conflict resolution, it is crucial for you to establish and nurture communication channels between you and the person(s) with whom you are in conflict. Many of the communication techniques already discussed can be put to excellent use in communicating with an opponent throughout the conflict resolution process. Additionally, Sheafor and Horejsi (2009, pp. 382–383) propose the following seven general communication guidelines to keep in mind:

EP 2.1.3c

1. *Do not begin a confrontation when you are angry.* Anger makes you lose your objectivity. You may lose sight of both your goals and the welfare of your opponent and focus instead on punishing or beating your opponent.

2. *Do not enter into a conflict unless you have a clearly established reason for doing so.* Unless you are willing to try to resolve the conflict, do not bother

confronting your opponent. Such confrontation will only waste both your and your opponent's time and energy.

3. *If you absolutely despise your opponent or have immense difficulty reaching for any positive, empathic feelings about him, do not confront him.* If you do not respect your opponent, a confrontation will only waste your and your opponent's time and energy. Rather, explore other ways of addressing the conflict (such as calling upon the support of others) or drop the matter completely.

4. *Include positive statements and feedback along with the negative aspects of confrontation.* For example, you might emphasize your opponent's strengths before beginning the confrontation, thereby minimizing her perception of being attacked. You might say, "I know you are very knowledgeable and have strong ideas on this subject. I would like to discuss with you some alternative thoughts I've had about it. I know you're busy, but might you have some time to talk?"

This particular example first gives the opponent a compliment. ("I know you are very knowledgeable and have strong ideas on this subject.") Compliments, by the way, should be honest, believable ones so that you do not sound insincere. Next, the preceding example introduces the issue in a general way. ("I would like to discuss with you some alternative thoughts I've had about it.") Finally, it implies respect for the opponent's time and work efforts. ("I know you're busy, but might you have some time to talk?")

In some ways, giving your opponent positive feedback or complimenting her is similar to confrontation (Nunnally & Moy, 1989). Both complimenting and confrontation provide people with feedback or information about their behavior.

Confrontation, of course, incorporates negative feedback, while compliments involve positive feedback. It makes sense to provide some of both during the conflict resolution process.

5. *Be certain to explain your concerns regarding the conflict in a "descriptive and nonjudgmental" manner* (Sheafor & Horejsi, 2009, p. 383). Prepare details in your head beforehand in order to explain and clarify the issues and behaviors involved. In the same way, try to present your stance objectively and factually. Avoid overly emotional appeals. If your opponent hears your emotions talking instead of you, he may react to your emotions instead of to what you are intending to say.

6. *Supply relevant data in support of your stance.* Articulate your position clearly. Describe the issue straightforwardly. In other words, make sure you know what you're talking about. Have your facts straight. Have both your ideal solution and some potential compromises clearly established in your mind.

7. *An additional suggestion is to use "I-messages" frequently.* Simply rephrasing your thoughts to include the word "I" enhances the quality of personal caring and empathy. This technique can emphasize the fact that you are trying to address a conflictual issue and are seeking a mutually agreeable solution, instead of criticizing or blaming. For example, you might say, "*I* would like to share with you some inconsistencies in my perception of what you've been saying and what you've actually been doing." This is far more personal and far less blaming than a statement such as, "*You* have been saying one thing and doing another."

CASE EXAMPLE

Step 3: Emphasize the Importance of Communication

Jimmy helps people on both sides of the conflict begin to talk about their feelings and think about suggestions for improvement. By the time Jimmy arrives, the situation is so tense and threatening that communication between Cheryl and Brainard has stopped. Cheryl has also ceased to communicate with her other unit colleagues. A typical comment by other workers at unit meetings reveals that they hesitate to say anything because of Cheryl's threats to sue them. It has been very difficult to get anything accomplished in the unit for a long time.

Jimmy's approach is to use positive feedback as much as possible. He talks of how committed Cheryl is to maintaining her job at the agency. Likewise, he emphasizes that Brainard and the other workers want to function as well as they can in providing services to clients.

What about when someone confronts you? Much of this discussion involves initiating a confrontation with a colleague, supervisor, agency, administrator, some other agency representative, community leader, or the like. What about your own feelings, communication, and behavior when someone confronts you? Your opponent may or may not have well-developed conflict resolution skills. There are at least five suggestions for how to respond (Nunnally & Moy, 1989, pp. 135–136):

1. *Pay very close attention to what the confronter is telling you.* Make certain you understand exactly what the confronter intends to say. Concentrating on the specifics helps you listen to and comprehend what is being said. Is it clear or vague?

   For example, suppose a colleague approaches you and flatly states, "You really are pretty intimidating." Focusing on the specific words being said can improve your understanding. Likewise, if the statement is vague, you can ask for clarification. To "intimidate" means either "to make timid or fearful," or "to deter by or as if by threats" (Mish, 2008, p. 656). The confronter's accusation is pretty imprecise. By listening, you can clarify the negative feedback while the confrontation is occurring. Exactly whom do you intimidate? This person who is confronting you? Other agency staff? Agency administration? Everybody? Similarly, do you make some unidentified other(s) fearful or are you making threats? In either case, in what way? What verbal and/or nonverbal behaviors does your confronter feel elicit an intimidating reaction? In what contexts does intimidation occur?

   Another reason for paying close attention to the words involves your own emotional reactions to the negative feedback. Paying attention to exactly what the confronter says can divert your attention from your own reactions of anger or resentment. Becoming overly emotional and losing track of your objectivity does not help you evaluate the situation or help resolve the conflict.

2. *Explain to the confronter exactly how you will respond to his feedback.* In the first example, you might tell the confronter that you will approach the people who feel intimidated and help resolve their negative feelings. You can elaborate upon what you will do to correct the problem. Think about what else you will say and do. In what contexts will you make the changes? Staff meetings? Interviews with community leaders? Casual lunchtime interactions with colleagues?

   Sometimes, you can be caught off guard when someone confronts you. Under these circumstances, you might not be able to think quickly enough to respond immediately. Then it's no problem simply to say something like, "Oh, that surprises me. Give me some time to think about it, and I'll give you a call later."

3. *Tell your confronter that you appreciate his effort and his feedback.* This is not an easy suggestion to follow. Being criticized can be hard to take. It's really easy to get defensive: "What do you mean I'm intimidating? You have some nerve! You have a pretty noxious personality yourself!"

   In reality, feedback can almost always be helpful. Even if you don't agree with what the confronter says, at least you know how he feels. In the worst case, the interaction gives you some information concerning how to operate with the confronter in the future. In the best case, you can receive some constructive feedback that may help in your future communications and interactions.

4. *Approach your confronter later, and tell him how you have responded to his feedback.* Explain how you have changed your behavior or attitude. You might thank him once again for his effort.

   Most people are hesitant about this particular suggestion. It is important to consider and evaluate the confronter's feedback as carefully and objectively as possible. However, if you decide in good conscience that he is inaccurate, you obviously will not alter your behavior in future situations. In effect, you will not believe your behavior requires change (at least not the behavior he criticized). In that case, you can choose either to confront him about the inappropriateness of his remarks or simply let the matter drop. It might not be worth your effort to extend the confrontation.

   Also, be careful of the multi-confronter, the person who regularly tells you all the things that are wrong with you. He might do this only in his interactions with you, or he might interact in this manner with almost everyone. In any case, depending on your own motivation, you may decide to confront him about his own overly confrontational behavior. As our discussion illustrates, the possibilities for confrontation are endless.

5. *At the time of the confrontation, do not reproach the confronter with a criticism of your own.* That type of response is usually petty and inappropriate. Address the issue at hand first. Settle that. Then, as we discussed in suggestion number four, you might decide to confront the person about his own behavior at another time.

Step 4: Emphasize Your Willingness to Cooperate

Emphasize your willingness to work with your opponent to find some mutually satisfactory solution. By definition, conflict is staged in the context of disagreement. In order to minimize the disagreement or, at least, to develop a viable, agreeable plan of action, stress the commonalities you have with your opponent.

CASE EXAMPLE

Step 4: Emphasize Your Willingness to Cooperate

Jimmy encourages Cheryl and the rest of the staff to work toward some solution. He has already established the common ground of a miserable working environment. This motivates participants to cooperate and work toward a mutually satisfying decision about what to do.

Step 5: Empathize with Your Opponent's Perspective

Work to understand why your opponent feels the way she does. What is her motivation for taking the stand she does? How does the conflict affect her feelings and her work? How can you express to her that you are sincerely trying to understand her side of the conflictual issue?

CASE EXAMPLE

Step 5: Empathize with Your Opponent's Perspective

As participants become motivated to cooperate and begin to discuss their feelings, Jimmy helps each side see the other's point of view. He holds several meetings with all unit staff present and gives every one the opportunity to air their views. On the one hand, Brainard and the unit staff are terribly frustrated with Cheryl's inability to work up to the unit's standards. On the other hand, Cheryl has become so ostracized that Jimmy has some concern that she might jump off the eight-story building in which the agency is housed. Cheryl is isolated, lonely, and unhappy.

Step 6: Evaluate Both Your Own and Your Opponent's Motivation to Address the Conflict

You and your opponent may view a conflict very differently. For instance, you may feel the conflict is of extraordinary importance. Your opponent, on the other hand, may think that it's silly to even bring up the issue because it's so minor. Essentially, you need to evaluate whether it is worthwhile to expend the energy to resolve the conflict. Maybe it would simply be easier to maintain the status quo and leave the whole thing alone.

For example, the chairperson of a social work department in an undergraduate program felt it was infinitely important to emphasize that each of the six faculty members should be able to teach any course in the program. This chairperson typically spent 15 minutes to an hour at each faculty meeting chit-chatting about how important such flexibility was. One faculty member in particular thought the whole issue was blatantly absurd. Different faculty had specified areas of interest in which they both studied and published. Why should faculty be forced to teach in areas they knew very little about instead of in areas in which they had established some degree of expertise? Would it be good for students to be taught by people who knew little of what they were talking about? Of course not. However, the faculty member chose to let the entire issue rest. In reality, all the faculty taught the same classes each semester anyway, so the point was moot. The faculty member acknowledged the chairperson's strong feelings and decided that confronting the chairperson on this issue would simply not be worth the effort. The faculty member didn't think he could win anyway. Besides, the worst thing that actually occurred was wasted time at faculty meetings.

Note that in many situations it is possible to change the degree of motivation on you or your opponent's part. In this situation, the department chairperson might have begun to implement what the faculty member termed the "absurd idea" of forcing faculty to teach outside their respective areas. Subsequently, the concerned faculty members might be extremely motivated to address the conflict and pursue some resolution.

CASE EXAMPLE

Step 6: Evaluate Both Your Own and Your Opponent's Motivation to Address the Conflict

As both sides air their feelings and frustrations, Jimmy helps them verbalize their motivation for change. Both express sincere interest in halting the conflict. All unit members are getting tired. Therefore, Jimmy determines that both parties are eager to pursue a viable alternative if the group can come up with one.

Step 7: Come to Some Mutually Satisfactory Agreement

The final step in conflict resolution is to come to some mutually satisfactory agreement. To do this, follow these five suggestions (Johnson, 2009). First, articulate exactly what your agreement entails. Second, indicate how you will behave toward the other person in the future as compared with the past. Third, specify how the other person will behave toward you. Fourth, agree on ways to address any future mistakes (that is, if you or the other behaves differently than you have agreed to). Fifth, establish how and when you and the other person will meet in the future to continue your cooperative behavior and minimization of conflict.

CASE EXAMPLE

Step 7: Come to Some Mutually Satisfactory Agreement

It looks to Jimmy as if no agreement can be reached to resolve the situation if Cheryl remains in the unit. Feelings are so strongly directed against her that it is unlikely they would change. Major supervisory efforts to help Cheryl improve her work performance have hopelessly failed. Therefore, it does not look as if a change in Cheryl's behavior is a viable alternative.

Cheryl has the equivalent of tenure and refuses to leave the agency without a major battle. Thus, the only remaining alternative is to transfer her to another position. Cheryl, Brainard, and the other unit workers first breathe a sigh of relief and then are ready to cheer when they examine this alternative. Jimmy works with Brainard and the agency's administration to implement this plan. The administration arranges for the necessary retraining Cheryl needs to assume her new position.

Cheryl happily transfers to another unit. She retains a job in the agency and no longer has to deal with colleagues whom she considers irascible, irritable, faultfinding, and backbiting. Likewise, relative peace descends upon the public assistance unit, and workers can once again focus their energies on their jobs.

Cheryl is not heard from by anyone in the unit again except when her name occasionally appears in an agency newsletter, as all agency staff names do at one time or another. Brainard, despite his immense relief at Cheryl's departure, soon becomes bored at the lack of challenge and leaves the agency for a higher paying, more demanding job.

As we stated at the beginning of this section, conflict is natural and predictable. Anticipating it, learning about the various types of conflict, and considering ahead of time the possible approaches to conflict management can only increase your effectiveness as a generalist social worker.

Working under Supervisors

Your interpersonal relationship with your agency supervisor will always have special significance in the macro environment (CSWE, 2008, EP 2.1.1f). Because of the importance of this relationship, we discuss how you can best put your micro skills to use within this special context.

EP 2.1.1f

The social work profession has heavily embraced the value and use of supervision. *Supervision* is the process of overseeing, directing, coordinating, enhancing, and evaluating the "on-the-job performance" of workers for whom the supervisor is responsible (Kadushin & Harkness, 2002, p. 23). In the social services context, the intent is to provide clients with "the best possible service … in accordance with agency policy and procedures. Supervisors do not directly offer service to the client, but they do indirectly affect the level of service offered through their impact on the direct service supervisees" (p. 23).

Highlight 2.5 summarizes some general expectations workers have for supervisors. Note, however, that supervisors also have responsibilities to their agencies and to other administrative personnel. Moreover, many of their roles are complex. The following sections will describe the administrative and educational functions of supervisors, supervisors' other functions, how to use supervision most effectively, and potential problems that may arise in supervision.

Administrative Functions of Supervisors

In their administrative function, supervisors do such things as assign cases to workers, review case plans, and discuss progress on individual cases. Accomplishing these functions helps ensure that the agency's work is being completed in a proper and timely manner. Supervisors thus monitor the agency's direct service provision to clients. Supervisors also help workers stay in touch with changes in the agency. In a sense, supervisors occupy a middle ground between the worker and the agency administration. In this role they serve as a two-way communication link.

We have established that supervisors convey to higher administration how well agency services are being administered. They also convey information from agency administration to workers who provide services directly to clients. Sometimes the information conveyed from the administration is positive. For example, it might be announced that the agency received an award

HIGHLIGHT 2.5

Workers' General Expectations of Supervisors: Keys to Empowerment

Supervisors can empower supervisees to become more effective in their practice with clients by providing help, information, and encouragement. The following are some general expectations workers frequently have of their supervisors (Cassidy & Kreitner, 2010; Dolgoff, 2005; Halley, Kopp, & Austen, 1998; Kadushin & Harkness, 2002; Leonard, 2010):

1. *Be readily available to provide suggestions or assistance concerning difficult cases.* A worker expects his supervisor to help him out when he is confronted with a problem or an exceptionally difficult case. Hopefully, the supervisor will use her own well-developed micro skills to assist in the communication process.

2. *Make certain that workers are knowledgeable about agency policy.* Agency policy tells workers which actions among a multitude of actions they may take and which they may not. Additionally, the policy may specify how an agency is structured, the qualifications of supervisors and workers, and the proper procedures agency staff should follow as they go about their daily work routines. Workers depend on immediate supervisors to keep them abreast of changes in agency policy and to continue monitoring their work to make sure they remain in compliance with policy.

3. *Provide input to higher levels of administration regarding line workers' needs.* Workers rarely have direct lines of communication with high-level agency decision makers. Thus, workers must depend on their own supervisors to communicate workers' needs upward so that this information reaches people in power who can make changes and meet needs. Chapter 4,

"Understanding Organizations," will discuss formal and informal communication channels in much greater depth.

4. *Facilitate cooperation among staff.* Workers expect their supervisors to coordinate all staff work so that together they can accomplish what they're supposed to do. In the event that workers disagree with each other or enter into some conflict supervisors will step in and mediate. Workers depend on supervisors to help attain some resolution on any number of problematic issues.

5. *Nurture workers and give them support when needed.* Workers depend on supervisors to encourage them to perform well. Workers hope that supervisors will praise them when they do their work well. Often, workers look to supervisors when they need to vent feelings or discuss issues.

6. *Evaluate workers' job performance.* Workers expect supervisors to evaluate the strengths and weaknesses they demonstrate while doing their jobs. Workers depend on supervisors to get them back on track when they do something wrong or ineffectively. Workers often need constructive criticism. Frequently, supervisors have direct input in the matter of performance-based raises.

7. *Facilitate workers' development of new skills.* Supervisors by definition assume positions superior to those of workers. Workers depend on their supervisors to be more knowledgeable than they are. Thus, workers look to supervisors to help them develop new skills and improve their expertise.

for excellence or that the staff's annual vacation time will be increased. Once, I worked for a private agency whose administration decided to give all staff an extra day off on their respective birthdays. The staff applauded.

Other times, however, the administration will convey information through supervisors that will not be positive. For instance, you might be told that your caseload will be increased significantly. Or you might be instructed that you will have to remain on call and

keep your cell phone with you every other Saturday night.

In these latter cases, it is helpful to be sensitive to a supervisor and her position. Supervisors can be placed in very precarious positions: They may be given directives to convey information to you that they know you will not like. Yet they may have had little or no input into the content of such directives. It's easy for you as a worker to become angry or disgusted at hearing bad tidings and direct your negative feelings toward your supervisor. Supervisors won't always be able to quell external demands or help you as much as you need, despite their good intentions. They will have their own job constraints and demands with which to contend.

Supervisors can also assist workers to become more effective in their assigned roles. If a worker is having difficulty, the supervisor should determine the reason. For example, is the problem a lack of knowledge or skill? If so, what can the supervisor do to assist the worker in gaining what he needs?

Perhaps there is no reward system for good job performance. Consider a social worker whose program is repeatedly over budget. Rarely is anything said about this. When the worker finally ends a year within budget, no recognition or acknowledgment is forthcoming. The worker ends up asking herself, "Should I work so hard at cutting costs and keeping within my budget when no one cares anyway?" The following year, she is once again over budget. A supervisor should know what workers find rewarding and try to build in some type of reward structure.

Consider another issue. Is the worker somehow being punished for doing a good job? This can happen easily with workers who have been staying on top of the workload, getting paperwork completed on time, and otherwise performing in an exemplary fashion. A common reaction is to give this person more to do because "she can obviously handle it." Simultaneously, other workers who are less successful at balancing the job's demands are excused from additional assignments. In effect, such behavior serves to punish the good worker and reward the poor one.

Educational Functions of Supervisors

Supervisors have a multifaceted educational role. They can aid workers by helping them improve their knowledge and skills, establish priorities among work tasks, and develop increased self-awareness. They also orient workers to both agency policy and social work values.

Supervision versus Consultation

EP 2.1.1f

Consultation is the act of seeking help from someone with expertise in a subject to devise a plan or solve a problem (CSWE, 2008, EP 2.1.1f). Communication and positive interpersonal dynamics are important in order for issues to be addressed and problems solved. Unlike supervision, which is ongoing and provided by people designated as "supervisors" or "managers" in the organizational hierarchy,

consultation is usually time-limited and oriented toward some specific issue (Harkness, 2008). Consultation may be provided informally among colleagues when help is needed and sought out. It may also be imparted on a formal contractual basis when one party seeks out the established expertise of another. Consultation can occur internally within an agency or expert help can be sought outside of the agency, depending on the assistance needed. It is a generalist practitioner's professional responsibility to use both supervision and consultation appropriately (CSWE, 2008, EP 2.1.1f). Social workers have established themselves as consultants in a range of areas; they can assist other professionals in their work or be called upon to provide testimony in court as expert witnesses (Harkness, 2008).

Other Functions of Supervisors

Like many middle-management roles, the supervisor's job is not easy. Supervisors are caught between higher-level administration and their own supervisees, who operate at lower levels in the agency's structure of authority. Yet, workers expect a supervisor's assistance in negotiating the very system that pulls supervisors in opposite directions. A case in point involves a field-placement student in a hospital setting who angers a physician by writing something in a patient's chart the physician does not like. The physician misunderstands the student and is going to have the student reprimanded. The student's field instructor (her supervisor) intercedes to clarify the situation. Thus, the matter is resolved to everyone's satisfaction. The student truly needs such supervisory assistance. This illustrates how workers often depend on supervisors to help them deal with real everyday problems.

Workers also expect support from a supervisor. Unfortunately, supervisors must play a combined role as teacher-administrator-supporter. Sometimes the roles of supporter and teacher clash with the supervisor's administrative role. For example, supervisors might be called upon to reprimand or discipline supervisees. Likewise, supervisors might be asked to follow a specific course of action that is inconsistent with workers' needs or wishes.

For example, the upper-level administration of a social service organization abruptly decides to require that workers work an extra day on every other weekend in addition to their regular 40-hour Monday-through-Friday workweek. Or, administrators might instruct supervisors to inform their supervisees that annual raises will be minimal or even nonexistent due to external funding cuts.

Using Supervision Effectively

Effective use of supervision hinges partly on your own behavior and characteristics as a worker. Communicating clearly and regularly with your supervisor can get you the help you need to work through exceptionally difficult situations and find resources you would not otherwise know about. The following are some helpful suggestions for maximizing your use of supervision (Halley et al., 1998; Kadushin & Harkness, 2002; Sheafor & Horejsi, 2006; Wallace & Masters, 2006):

Use Your Communication Skills with Your Supervisor

Use the micro skills discussed at the beginning of this chapter with your supervisor just as you do with clients and other colleagues. Check to be certain that the messages you hear are clear. Ask questions. Rephrase a question if you don't think your supervisor understands what you mean. Paraphrase your supervisor's answer to ensure you understand what was said. Monitor your nonverbal behavior.

When your supervisor uses a word you don't understand or one that does not make sense, ask what he means. Sometimes people will use letters or acronyms (for example, NASW, CSWE, OSHA, KUMQUAT, or PIGWART). If you don't know what it means, *ask.*

Plan your messages to your supervisor carefully ahead of time, especially e-mail or written ones. Keep in mind the following questions:

What am I trying to get across?
Who will receive my communication?
When is the best time to communicate?
Where is the best place to communicate?
How should I communicate?
Why am I communicating? (Halley et al., 1998)

Written communication is important. Decisions that require a supervisor's agreement should often be put in writing. One way you might do this is by sending an e-mail to your supervisor, summarizing her instructions or your mutual decisions regarding some plan of action. This documents the fact that you have your supervisor's support.

Keep Your Records Up-to-Date

Agencies run on records. A common source of irritation between coworkers and supervisors concerns recordkeeping. Keeping up-to-date records is frequently difficult. The pressure of ordinary business makes it hard to take time away from serving clients to maintain case records. However, recordkeeping is essential for accountability. You are accountable to your supervisor, and he or she, in turn, is accountable to higher levels of administration. If you fail to keep up with required recordkeeping, it will reflect badly on your supervisor. Additionally, your successor will have a tough time figuring out your cases if you haven't kept records.

Plan Your Supervisory Agenda Ahead of Time

Many workers have a set time to talk with their supervisor. Use this time to the fullest. Think about the topics and ideas you want to discuss. List the questions you have. Make sure you cover the items on your list before you leave the session. If sufficient time is available, you might even e-mail or give your supervisor a copy of your agenda beforehand so that he can think about the topics prior to the meeting. However, be sensitive to your supervisor's reactions to this structured approach. Be careful not to be too aggressive or pushy. Coming on too strong is threatening to some supervisors.

Put Yourself in Your Supervisor's Shoes

Use empathy with your supervisor. She is an individual with her own feelings, interests, biases, and opinions. Think about both what she needs to know and what she needs to communicate to you. It is helpful to get to know your supervisor as well as possible. How might you best respond to her own needs and issues?

Display an Openness to Learning and to Improving Yourself

Displaying an openness to learning means that you should be willing to accept criticism and to use it to improve your work. It also means you must be able to admit when you don't know something or even when you have made a mistake. This is often hard to do. It is difficult to admit to one's lacks or failings. However, the willingness to seek help is basic to learning. Consider your supervisor a resource that you should be willing to use (that is, of course, if your supervisor is competent).

Demonstrate a Liking for Your Work

Major complainers and whiners are usually very unappealing to both supervisors and others. It is better to emphasize the positive aspects of your work, including those facets you especially like. Generally speaking, if you do not like your work, you should quit and pursue other opportunities. Continuing to hold a position that you find unsatisfying can lead to burnout and a diminished interest in fulfilling your helping role. (Chapter 15 discusses stress and time management techniques.)

An illustration of this point comes to mind. Several years ago, two probation and parole agents came to address an Introduction to Social Work class. Both had been in the corrections field for many years and had talked to other classes several years earlier. During the current talk they referred to their clients in derogatory terms, criticized their agency and agency colleagues, and displayed a high level of dislike for their work responsibilities in general.

By the end of the class, it was evident that both agents had become burned out from their jobs. They were no longer operating within a social work value system. Following their departure, the instructor had to spend some time undoing the negative impressions the speakers had left regarding what social work was all about. Of course, the instructor never again invited them back to the university, although they might have served as good examples for a class on stress and burnout.

Work Cooperatively with Other Staff

Much of social work requires teamwork. (Later chapters will further address the concept of teamwork.) Your supervisor will expect you to work well with other social workers and with professionals from other disciplines. Be sensitive to how your behavior affects others. Show respect for the competence and talents of your peers and coworkers. Be tolerant of what you see as their shortcomings. Try to see the world from their perspective and understand why they feel and act the way they do.

Give Your Supervisor Feedback

Supervisors can benefit from feedback as much as workers. Tactfully let your supervisor know what you like and dislike. If you have specific needs that your supervisor can appropriately fulfill, share them. Use the suggestions for giving feedback found earlier in the chapter in the section "Use Your Communication Skills with Your Supervisor."

Forewarn Your Supervisor about Problematic Situations

Supervisors should be alerted anytime a case becomes especially problematic. When you don't know about the implications of a particular course of action or how it might affect the agency, share this information

with your supervisor. Get help. Don't wait until things have developed to crisis proportions before talking to your supervisor.

Learn Your Supervisor's Evaluation System

Ask your supervisor for the basis upon which you will be evaluated. It might be an evaluation form or a description of the evaluation process in the agency's policy manual. Your job description can also help orient you to what you're supposed to be doing and accomplishing. Regardless, you should know far in advance what criteria your supervisor and agency will use to evaluate you. Hopefully, there will be no, or few, surprises during an evaluation meeting.

Evaluation systems may be *formative,* that is, ongoing. Such evaluations provide regular feedback, thereby allowing workers to make corrections as the need arises. *Summative* evaluations are scheduled to occur periodically. These evaluations tend to be more general in that they summarize progress and accomplishments over a longer, designated period of time, such as a year or six months. Some agencies and supervisors use both formative and summative approaches in conjunction with each other.

Problems in Supervision

Just as there is no perfect world, there is no perfect work environment. Likewise, there are no perfect supervisors. Complaints about supervisors are common. Sometimes they are valid; other times they are not.

There will be times when, despite how hard you try, you will be unable to get formal, quality supervision. Highlight 2.6 illustrates a number of unproductive games that can be played in supervisor/supervisee relationships. Other problems may also occur, including simple misunderstandings, supervisors taking credit for your achievements, supervisory incompetence, problems with delegation, laziness, and inability to deal with conflict, among many others. Highlight 2.7 addresses a variety of such scenarios.

Simple Misunderstandings between Supervisor and Supervisee

Because it is a communication-based process, supervision is subject to simple misunderstandings. For example, we've all probably had the experience of saying something to somebody and later that person insists he never heard what we know we said. Hearing without listening is amazingly common. We often use it to

Games Supervisors and Supervisees Sometimes Play

The supervisory relationship can be a complex one. In any supervisory dyad, both people are unique individuals with distinctly different personalities. Communication is rife with the potential for misunderstandings, conflicts, and manipulation. Power, of course, is also involved. As a result, there are a number of games workers and supervisors play. Because they are games, they prevent real issues from being addressed out in the open. Games can also corrode relationships.

Kadushin (1968; Kadushin & Harkness, 2002) has cited a number of games about which it is good to be aware:

1. *I'll Be Nice to You If You'll Be Nice to Me.* This game involves a supervisory relationship in which both parties are afraid to give any negative or constructive feedback. They avoid real issues by complimenting each other. This is fake interaction. Remarks are rarely genuine. The purposes of supervision are not fulfilled because of the participants' hesitation to assertively confront each other and the issues.

2. *Therapize Me.* This game involves the supervisor delving into the worker's personal life and issues. This is inappropriate. If workers need counseling —as many of us do at various times during our lives—they should receive it outside their agency setting from another professional whom they pay. It is also inappropriate for workers to use their supervisors' time in this manner and for supervisors to pry into their workers' personal lives. The purpose of maintaining a working environment is to get the necessary work done, nothing else. In the event that a worker is experiencing personal crises or emotional problems, it is appropriate for a supervisor to provide that worker with feedback. The feedback should focus on the worker's job performance and how personal issues might be affecting that performance. It is also appropriate for a supervisor to suggest that the worker get some counseling to resolve the problems that are affecting his behavior at work.

3. *Good Buddies Don't Evaluate.* This game usually entails a supervisor who feels uncomfortable holding a superior position over workers. In order to avoid having to sit down and evaluate workers' performances, the supervisor becomes friends, and, in effect, personal equals with workers. Once again, this game interferes with the purposes of supervision. Workers and supervisors fail to get constructive feedback from each other. Workers are cut off from having access to the supervisor's expertise and assumption of responsibility over them. A worker needs a supervisor, not a friend, to keep her on track.

4. *Of Course, I Know Much More than You Do.* This is a game of one-upmanship. Either the supervisor or the worker consistently reveals that he knows much more than the other. You might meet people like this in your classes: you know, someone who sits in the front row and, with an exceptionally condescending tone, corrects the instructor at least twice each week.

5. *Poor, Helpless, Little Old Me.* In this game the employee dependently leans on the supervisor for almost everything. In essence, the worker "plays dumb." She asks the supervisor to validate almost everything she does. In this way she doesn't have to do much thinking. She manipulates the supervisor into doing all of her thinking for her. She can also avoid responsibility for mistakes. In the event that she makes one, she can blame her supervisor because he "said it was OK" or "told [me] to do it that way."

6. *"Information Is Power.* This game occurs when one or the other in the supervisory relationship withholds information. A worker can withhold information from a supervisor in order to avoid the supervisor's scrutiny. For example, a worker seriously edits the facts about a particular case. He does so because he feels he should be doing more with the case. Omitting information keeps the supervisor in the dark concerning what the worker is not doing.

   Likewise, a supervisor can keep information from an employee in order to maintain greater control over that employee. Consider a supervisor who keeps one worker from knowing that her colleagues have a considerably smaller caseload than she does. In effect, not telling her that she's doing more than her share keeps her doing it and getting things done for the supervisor.

7. *Avoiding the Issue.* This game requires a supervisor or worker who avoids salient issues by using criticism or changing the subject. For example, a worker says, "I am very concerned about my client's alcohol problem. How do you think I should proceed?"

   The supervisor responds, "It sounds as if you don't feel very confident in that area." In this way the supervisor both blames the worker for ignorance and avoids providing any concrete assistance.

8. *Pose Questions to Answer Questions.* As with "Avoiding the Issue," this game is used to sidetrack real issues. Instead of answering a question, a worker or supervisor responds with another question. This behavior, of course, throws the responsibility for answering a question back to the person who asked it in the first place. For example, a worker might ask a supervisor, "Can I take Friday afternoon off?" The supervisor responds, "What would happen if I let the whole unit off on Fridays? Who would be around to serve clients?" This response avoids giving an answer. Instead, it places the responsibility for finding an answer on the worker.

block out things we don't want to hear. Many people read the paper and watch television simultaneously. It is likely that they are not paying close attention to what's on television until they hear a word or phrase that triggers their attention. We even have a phrase for this, "tuning out."

Another common communication problem, discussed earlier in the chapter, is that words and phrases do not always mean the same thing to both sender and receiver. This occurs frequently in the supervisory relationship.

Consider a supervisor who summarizes his evaluation of a worker's performance by writing, "Rajiv does a pretty good job of completing his work on time." The supervisor intends this description to reflect very positively on Rajiv's performance. Rajiv, however, feels the term "pretty good" is negative and detracts substantially from a positive evaluation. Clearly, each person interprets the same words in a totally different way.

Many of us hear only what we want to hear. Children, for instance, often hear the parental "maybe" as a more definite "yes." Another child-related example of a phenomenon called *selective listening* comes to mind. I was showing my father some pictures of a recent exotic vacation to the Costa Rican jungle while my nieces, ages 3 and 5, and nephew, 7, had their eyes glued to the television screen watching the latest *Spider-Man* DVD. The three totally ignored what I had to say until my father asked, "What's that?" I replied, "Oh, that's a horde of army ants devouring a tarantula." Spontaneously, all three children jumped up and dashed over to view a picture of the huge spider's remains. After a quick glance, all three returned to the TV.

Selective listening can also occur during the supervisory process. Supervisors can be equivocal. That is, they can make confusing statements subject to various interpretations. Workers then may interpret these remarks either as encouraging or discouraging, depending upon what the workers want or expect to hear. The only way to eliminate this problem is to listen actively and then verify that your understanding of the message is accurate.

Supervisors Who Take Credit for Your Achievements

At times a supervisor might not give you the credit you think you deserve for your work or may take credit for what *you* have done. At such times, you may choose to use the suggestions for confrontation and assertiveness described earlier in the chapter to work toward a fair conclusion. However, some supervisors in some situations will take the credit for your work regardless of what you do or how tactfully assertive you are. This is unethical, but it can happen. Scenario A in Highlight 2.7 presents such a situation.

So what do you do? Given the nature of the supervisor/supervisee relationship, your supervisor will probably have more power than you have—that is, unless your mother owns the agency. You might first decide how important it is for you to get the credit that is due to you. Was it more important that something was accomplished than that *you* accomplished it? In Scenario A of Highlight 2.7, an important community program was ready for implementation. How important is it, really, that the worker responsible get the credit (even if the worker is you)?

If you, as the worker, do feel that receiving credit is very important, what would you do? Would you go to an administrator above your supervisor for help and risk your supervisor's wrath? Would you learn a lesson from the experience and keep the information from your supervisor the next time? Would you try to put it out of your mind and go on with your daily business? Would you start looking for another job? There really is no perfect answer. It would be your responsibility to identify your various options, weigh the pros and cons of each, and decide what to do.

HIGHLIGHT 2.7

What Would You Do?

The following scenarios are taken from actual supervisory experiences. Each involves real problems that could theoretically happen to you. In each case, think about how you would use the recommendations we have just discussed to pursue some type of resolution with each supervisor.

Scenario A: Taking Your Credit

You are a school social worker in a large, urban high school. Your primary role is "to help students, families, teachers, and educational administrators deal with a range of problems that affect students" including "truancy, depression, withdrawal, aggressive or violent behavior, rebelliousness, and the effects of physical or emotional problems" (Gibelman, 1995, p. 175). In essence, you work with students to combat truancy, enhance academic performance, encourage responsible decision making, and prevent disasters such as student shootings. This allows numerous possibilities for development and implementation of creative projects.

You come up with what you consider a brilliant idea. What about starting a program where interested high school teens would provide tutoring, craft project supervision, and recreational activities for children living at a local homeless shelter?[a] This would not only furnish a needed community service, but also provide opportunities for youth to learn empathy, feel useful, and responsibly help others.

You briefly mention the idea to your supervisor, Harmony, for her approval. Without hesitation she gives you the go-ahead. You meet with personnel from the shelter, parents of some of the homeless children who may be involved, potential student participants, members of the Parent/Teacher Association at your school, and school administrators. You contact people from other communities that have similar programs and put in a significant amount of work writing up the proposal. Finally, you submit it to Harmony for her endorsement. She states, "I'll take it from here. Higher administration supports this."

You don't quite believe your ears. Does she really mean she's taking it over after all the work you put into it? That can't be. You reply, "Just say okay, and I'll start implementation. One of the first things will be to solicit student volunteers."

She responds, "No, you've got lots of other things to do. I'll take over now." You emphasize how the whole thing was your idea, how hard you've worked, and how you are *really* committed to carry out the plan. You hear yourself pleading with her. You suggest working on the project together.

"No," she confirms, "I'll do it. Don't worry about it anymore." You are devastated. Worse yet three days later, you see a big write-up about the project in the local newspaper giving Harmony all the credit. Your name isn't even mentioned.

What would you do?

Scenario B: The Communication Gap

You are a newly hired social worker for a unit of boys, ages 11 to 13, at a residential treatment center for youth with serious behavioral and emotional problems. Your responsibilities include counseling, group work, case management, some family counseling, and consultation with unit counseling staff concerning your unit's behavioral programming. Two of the dozen boys in the unit have been causing you particular trouble. They are late for your weekly counseling sessions, sometimes skipping them altogether. When you talk to them, they don't respond to your questions. Rather, they walk around the room, talk about how you don't know what you're doing, use pencils to pick holes in the furniture, and call you vulgar names.

You are at a loss regarding what to do with these two clients. You go into your weekly one-hour supervisory sessions and explain the situation to your supervisor. He makes a number of vague suggestions, such as recording some of your sessions, making home visits, and talking about the boys' behavior with them. By the end of your supervisory session, you feel you've gotten nowhere. You couldn't pin down any specific suggestions and still do not understand what you should do. You have difficulty understanding what your supervisor is saying. You can't "read" him. Sometimes when he makes a statement you don't know whether he expects you to laugh in response or to take him seriously and say, "Oh, gee, that's too bad."

What would you do?

Scenario C: The Angry Response

You are a social worker at a health care center (nursing home) with various clients who have been diagnosed as having a mental illness. Every six months, a treatment conference is held at which social workers, nurses, therapists (speech, occupational, physical), physicians, psychologists, and psychiatrists summarize clients' progress and make recommendations. It is your job to run the meeting and write the summary.

You are new at your job and are not familiar with how things are run at this agency. You find that during the meeting, the psychiatrist is very verbal. You would even describe him as "pushy." You feel intimidated and uncomfortable asserting your own opinions, which are somewhat opposed to his. His advanced education, status, and self-confident demeanor make you feel that his points are probably more important and valid than yours.

After the meeting, your supervisor, who was also in attendance, takes you aside. His face is red and his voice has a deadly, steel-like calm in it. He berates you for letting the psychiatrist take over the meeting. He surprises and upsets you so that you do not hear many of the specific things he says. You just know that he is furious with you and that he has implied or stated that you are incompetent. He walks off in a huff.

What would you do?

Scenario D: Gender Discrimination

You have the strong feeling that your supervisor, who is heterosexual and of the same gender as you, gives opposite-gender supervisees preferential treatment. For instance, the supervisor acts friendlier and more casual with them, directs more comments and questions to them during meetings, and seems to give them preference for their vacation choices. You have also heard they're getting higher raises when you feel your own work performance is at least as good as theirs, if not better.

What would you do?

Scenario E: Problems with Delegation

You are a caseworker for a social services agency in a rural county. Your job includes a wide range of social work practice, from investigating child abuse charges to working with families of truants to providing supplementary services to older adults so that they can remain in their own homes. You have a heavy caseload but feel very useful. In general, you really like your job.

The problem is that your supervisor insists on reading every letter and report you write before it goes out. You think this is a terribly time-consuming waste of effort. In many instances, it also delays your provision of service. Finally, you feel it's condescending and implies a lack of confidence in your professional abilities.

What would you do?

Scenario F: No Action

You are a social worker in a large urban community center serving multiple community needs. Services include counseling for emotional and behavior problems, provision of contraception, recreational activities for adults and youth, day care for children of working parents, meals for senior citizens, some health care, and various other services. Your job focuses primarily on counseling the center's clients, who are referred to you for this purpose. You enjoy your job and are proud of being a professional social worker.

The problem is another social worker who has his office next door. He has a similar job, but is assigned a different caseload and a slightly different range of responsibilities. The bottom line is that you seriously question his professional competence. You've observed him doing what you'd describe as "comic book therapy" with the children and adolescents on his caseload. In other words, his clients come in and select comic books from his vast collection instead of receiving any real form of counseling. He has boasted on several occasions that he went into social work only because somehow he was offered a scholarship.

One day you walk up to greet one of your clients, whom you unexpectedly see reading something in the center's waiting room. Your client, a fairly bright articulate boy of 13, places his hand over a portion of a picture in the book. You think to yourself how odd that is, because his hand is placed over the rear of a horse. He does look surprised to see you. He remarks that the horse's long white mane is pretty. You observe that the mane reaches the ground and extends along another foot. This also strikes you as peculiar. Finally, you ask him what the book is about. He sheepishly shows it to you. The picture depicts a castrated horse (hence, the elongated mane and tail due to hormonal changes). The book is titled *Washington Death Trips*. Among other items included in the book are pictures of dead babies in caskets, people who have butchered over five hundred chickens by hand for no reason, and various infamous murderers. You learn that your colleague loaned your client this book.

You are furious. Not only does this colleague offend your professionalism and your professional ethics, he has also had the gall to interfere with your client. You immediately go to your supervisor, who is also his supervisor, and complain about the incident. Your supervisor, a well-liked, easygoing, but knowledgeable and helpful person, hems and haws. You believe that your supervisor is afraid to confront your colleague.

What would you do?

Note

a. The idea for the program described in this vignette was adapted from one proposed by J. P. Kretzmann and J. L. McKnight in *Building Communities from the Inside Out* (Chicago: ACTA Publications, 1993, p. 41).

Supervisory Incompetence

Some supervisors are simply incompetent. The Peter Principle states that employees tend to rise in an administrative hierarchy until they reach their level of incompetence. Theoretically and ideally, you should be able to go to your supervisor for help. What if you get a supervisor who does not have the necessary skills to do the job? The old saying that you can't squeeze blood out of a turnip comes to mind. If a supervisor does not have the expertise, he can't share it with you. Scenario B in Highlight 2.7 hints at this problem.

One suggestion for coping in this situation is to find others in the agency who can help you when you need it. This must be done tactfully, however. You should avoid threatening an incompetent supervisor by openly exposing his incompetence unless you want to suffer hostile retributions. You can seek support from his other supervisees and begin documenting his incompetence. However, this also places you in jeopardy if he should find out. It can be very difficult to win in such cases, because power (and usually administration) is on your supervisor's side. You might just accept the situation and go on with your own business.

Laziness

Laziness on a supervisor's part is similar to incompetence, in that either way you probably will not get the help you need. Laziness can be dealt with as you would deal with incompetence. You can try to talk assertively to your supervisor, seek other sources of help and information, form coalitions with other supervisory victims, ignore the issue, or quit. There may be more potential for improvement if the supervisor has the necessary competence but just does not want to work hard. Incompetence and laziness can, of course, both exist in the same supervisor. Administrators over the lazy supervisor's head need to know about the situation. Therefore, think carefully before enabling the supervisor by doing his work for him or reminding him of agency deadlines.

Problems with Delegation

A primary administrative task for supervisors is mastering the art of delegation. *Delegation* means assigning responsibility or authority to others. Sometimes supervisors have trouble delegating tasks to employees and operate under dynamics opposite to those of the lazy supervisor. Lazy supervisors try to avoid work. Non-delegating supervisors are often workaholics whose problem is that they don't trust anyone, including their own supervisees, to do the work well enough. Scenario E in Highlight 2.7 illustrates a delegation problem, in that the supervisor insists upon reading every single word the worker writes. In this case, the worker's options include assertively confronting the supervisor about the problem, emphasizing the unnecessary costs in time and efficiency, learning to live with the situation, or getting another job. This particular scenario actually happened. According to the worker, the supervisor was driving him crazy. He couldn't take it anymore and got another job.

Inability to Deal with Conflict

We have already addressed the issue of conflict and shown how difficult it is for many people to deal with. This can also be true for supervisors. Highlight 2.7, Scenario F, describes a situation in which a supervisor feels uncomfortable about confronting a supervisee, so he simply does not do so. If you cannot depend on help from your supervisor, you may have to address the conflict yourself by following the suggestions provided earlier. Another alternative, as always, is to ignore the issue and work on learning to live with it.

A Final Note

In summary, life with supervisors will not always be ideal. We have mentioned only a few of the many issues that can arise in the supervisor/supervisee relationship. When a problem occurs, all you can do is use your communication skills to your best advantage, identify the alternatives available to you, weigh the pros and cons of each, and decide on the course of action you feel will be most advantageous for you.

On the other hand, you may also have supervisors who will serve as primary mentors to you. A *mentor* is someone who encourages you to do your best, exposes you to new knowledge and ideas, and provides you with exciting opportunities to develop your skills and competence. Just as there are bad supervisors, there are truly excellent ones.

Chapter Summary

The following summarizes this chapter's content as it relates to the learning objectives presented at the beginning of the chapter. Chapter content prepares social workers to:

A. *Use empathy and other interpersonal skills to work effectively within organizations and communities.*

Both verbal and nonverbal behavior can provide important venues of communication within macro settings. Nonverbal behavior entails eye contact, attentive listening, facial expressions, and body positioning. Multicultural sensitivity to variations in nonverbal communication is vital. Warmth, empathy, and genuineness are important relationship-enhancing traits. Warmth involves conveying a feeling of interest, concern, well-being, and liking to another individual. Empathy is the conveyance to people both verbally and nonverbally that you understand how they feel. Genuineness is the "sharing of self by relating in a natural, sincere, spontaneous, open and genuine manner" (Hepworth et al., 2010, p. 107).

B. *Recognize how diversity shapes life experiences and employ some approaches for improving communication with people who have physical disabilities.*

Verbal and nonverbal behavior should be modified to empower persons with disabilities and improve your relationship with them. Awareness of vocal tone and provision of spatial information to people with visual impairment may be appropriate. It is important to maintain eye contact with people who have hearing impairments and to communicate in whatever manner is most effective for them. It is essential to focus on the person with physical disabilities, not the disability.

C. *Describe a variety of interviewing techniques and apply them to macro practice situations.*

Verbal responses include simple encouragement, sensitivity to cultural differences, paraphrasing, reflective responding, clarification, interpretation, providing information, emphasizing other people's strengths, summarization, and eliciting information. Verbal techniques may overlap. Exercise caution when using the word "why."

D. *Examine assertiveness and propose means for its application in macro contexts.*

Assertive communication includes verbal and nonverbal behavior that permits a speaker to get points across clearly and straightforwardly, maintaining high regard for both self and the communication receiver. Nonassertive communication occurs when a speaker devalues herself completely, holding the communication receiver in much higher regard than herself. Aggressive communication engenders bold and dominating verbal and nonverbal behavior whereby a speaker presses her point of view as taking precedence above all other perspectives.

Each individual has assertive rights. There are advantages to being assertive within the macro environment. People can enhance their assertiveness skills by following a number of steps.

E. *Utilize critical thinking skills to investigate the pros and cons of conflict and propose procedures for conflict resolution.*

Conflict has various pros and cons. Pros of conflict include the potential for gaining new information and resolving problems. Cons may entail wasting energy and harming relationships. People may adopt various styles of addressing conflict. Conflict resolution involves seven steps: the confrontation; establishing common ground; emphasizing the importance of communication; emphasizing willingness to cooperate; empathizing with the opponent's perspective; evaluating the motivations of both sides involved; and coming to a mutually satisfactory agreement.

F. *Examine the supervisory relationship, some of its inherent problems, and the concept of consultation.*

Supervisors serve administrative and educational functions in addition to others. Supervisees expect supervisors to help them in their work and empower them.

Problematic situations in supervision may involve a supervisor taking credit for your achievements, supervisory incompetence, laziness, problems with delegation, and inability to deal with conflict, among others.

Consultation is the provision of help by a knowledgeable person to another seeking assistance concerning a work-related goal or issue.

G. *Formulate suggestions for using supervision, improving supervisory relationships, and enhancing the communication process.*

Using supervision effectively involves using your communication skills with your supervisor, keeping records up-to-date, planning supervisory agendas ahead of time, empathizing with your supervisor, displaying an openness to learning, demonstrating a liking for your work, working cooperatively with colleagues, providing feedback to your supervisor, warning your supervisor about potential problems, and learning your supervisor's evaluation system.

Competency Notes

The following identifies where Educational Policy (EP) competencies and practice behaviors are discussed in the chapter.

EP 2.1.1b Practice personal reflection and self-correction to assure continual professional development. *(P. 61):* Development of appropriate assertiveness allows practitioners to practice personal reflection and improve their interactions with others in macro contexts. Subsequent sections provide opportunities to appraise scenarios and demonstrate appropriate responses, in addition to suggesting an approach to assertiveness training.

EP 2.1.1f Use supervision and consultation. *(P. 75):* Effective work within an organizational structure involves using supervision. *(P. 77):* Effective work within an organizational structure involves using consultation when appropriate.

EP 2.1.3c Demonstrate effective oral and written communication in working with individuals, families, groups, organizations, communities, and colleagues. *(P. 55):* Effective oral communication is important when working in and with organizations and communities, and with colleagues. *(P. 71):* Effective communication is crucial for successful conflict resolution when working with individuals, groups, organizations, communities, and colleagues.

EP 2.1.4 Engage diversity and difference in practice. *(P. 53):* Physical disabilities reflect a dimension of diversity that practitioners must understand.

EP 2.1.10b Use empathy and other interpersonal skills. *(P. 46):* Interpersonal skills are vitally important to practice in and with organizations and communities. *(P. 52):* Practitioners should use empathy when practicing in and with organizations and communities. *(P. 56):* Highlight 2.2 provides an opportunity to demonstrate empathic responses in macro practice contexts.

EP 2.1.10g Select appropriate intervention strategies. *(P. 68):* Conflict resolution can be an effective strategy to address arguments and controversies encountered when working in and with organizations and communities.

On the Internet

Visit the *Generalist Practice with Organizations and Communities* Web site at *www.cengage.com/social_work/ kirst-ashman* for learning tools such as PowerPoint® slides, tutorial quizzing, Web links, and final exams.

CHAPTER 3

Group Skills for Organizational and Community Change

"Sure, I owe you one," said Gray Mfume to Jack Christiansen. Gray had just agreed to attend a community meeting on child abuse in Jack's place. Jack, who had announced his move to a new job in another community, had done many favors for Gray over the years and both were interested in the child welfare field. Jack had helped organize a community meeting to discuss what further steps might be taken to prevent child abuse, a topic of increasing concern in the city of Eagle Bluff following a series of shocking child abuse cases.

Jack had supervised the child welfare intake unit responsible for all initial investigations of child abuse in the county. His sudden departure would leave a void in Eagle Bluff. Additionally, Gray would really miss his friend and colleague.

The community meeting was to be held at the Morgan Neighborhood Center. It would involve representatives of various private and public agencies such as Lutheran Social Services, the local Department of Social Welfare, and interested citizens representing service clubs, such as Kiwanis. Gray wasn't particularly worried about his role in the meeting because he was not responsible for organizing it. He would attend as a favor to Jack but, given that Gray's job as a staff member at a home health-care agency carried no responsibility for child abuse intervention, he felt somewhat removed from the subject.

When the meeting ended, however, Gray had agreed to help establish a Parents Anonymous chapter in Eagle Bluff. (Parents Anonymous is a private organization dedicated to helping child abusers help themselves. It is run by volunteers and uses group work principles to help members learn more effective parenting and coping skills.) At the time, he knew very little about what would be involved in this activity–planning meetings, networking among professionals, managing conflict, and eventually serving as a member of the Parents

Anonymous advisory board. (The advisory board would help set policies, raise funds, and support the activities of the Parents Anonymous group.) The process of intervening in the community to establish a new service such as Parents Anonymous would require many skills for dealing with both task and treatment groups. (Task groups include such things as advisory boards, boards of directors, and committees. Treatment groups include support groups, such as Parents Anonymous, and therapy groups.) Addressing such a significant community problem with other interested, motivated community members would test Gray's skills both as a leader and as a facilitator.

Introduction

As Gray was to learn, creating change at the community level requires several group skills, because much of what gets accomplished at the macro level is done by groups or teams. Thus, being successful at changing organizations and communities requires understanding how teams and task groups work. It also requires a number of skills for participating in and leading groups and teams.

This chapter begins with a discussion of leadership skills essential for working with groups. It will also define networking and describe how the knowledge and skills required for networking can support macro level interventions. Because teams and task groups implement much of the change that occurs at the organizational and community levels, it will then discuss the skills needed for working in and with teams.

Achieving goals in most groups requires a certain level of systematic organization. Planning and conducting meetings, essential tasks for achieving large system change, are group skills. Anyone who has ever watched a committee or large group meeting may have been struck by the terminology used to get business accomplished. Motions, minutes, seconds, tabling, and amendments are all concepts drawn from parliamentary procedure, which allows group tasks to be accomplished and decisions recorded in an efficient and effective manner. Because of their significance, skills to help groups make decisions using parliamentary procedure will be thoroughly explained.

Finally, the last portion of the chapter will cover the perennial problem of conflict. Managing conflict, particularly in groups, organizations, and communities, is an important skill. Understanding the principles involved enhances your own potential for effective conflict management.

Learning Objectives

This chapter will provide content regarding how social workers:

A. *Demonstrate leadership skills needed to promote sustainable changes in service delivery and practice to improve the quality of social work services.*

B. *Engage in networking to analyze, formulate, and advocate for policies that advance social well-being.*

C. *Utilize teamwork and collaboration with colleagues and clients for improving agency services and social policies.*

D. *Utilize professional skills in planning and conducting meetings within groups, organizations, and communities.*

E. *Employ conflict management to help resolve organizational and community problems.*

Leadership and Leadership Skills

Leaders combine two attributes. First, they are headed in a particular direction and, second, they are able to persuade others to go with them. Both attributes require skills that social workers possess because of their preparation for practice. Leading involves working with other systems, whether individuals, families, groups, organizations, or communities. The goal of leadership is to help promote sustainable changes in service delivery and practice that improve the quality of social work services (CSWE, 2008, EP 2.1.9b). In this chapter we are particularly interested in the capacity to

EP 2.1.9b

exercise leadership in the latter two systems. Various writers have summarized the different skills needed to be effective as a leader. Each is addressed in the following sections.

Identifying Targets for Change

Social workers are often the first to identify situations where policies, procedures, or programs are ripe for change. This may occur because of their relative ineffectiveness, or because they are counterproductive. Identifying and giving voice to these shortcomings is a characteristic shared by most leaders. It is this target that provides a direction for not only the leader but the followers as well.

Capacity to Inspire

One of the ways in which social workers inspire others is through providing both a vision of what is possible and a means for achieving the vision. Both are necessary since a vision by itself is often limited by the obstacles to its achievement, and change without a vision can be directionless. For example, visions of what improved client services would look like or how a neighborhood might be transformed have the capacity to inspire others to participate in the change process. The capacity to inspire can be influenced by expertise in a given area that is recognized by others. The ability to influence others, a form of power, is sufficiently important that it is addressed in both Chapters 4 and 8.

Assertiveness

It is difficult, if not impossible, to lead others without a reasonable level of assertiveness. For example, the ability to voice concerns about problematic aspects of organizations or communities requires assertiveness. Assertiveness is addressed in both Chapters 2 and 11 because of its importance in bringing about large system change.

Communication Skills

Ideas or visions about the future are of little use if the leader cannot explain them to potential followers. Too often, great ideas are not acted upon because they were not articulated with sufficient clarity or were simply not feasible in a given situation. The leader must be able to explain not only what the vision is, but how it is appropriate and achievable within a given setting. With a clear description of the change sought, it is much easier for others to join in the efforts. People who are confused by a proposal will almost always refuse to participate.

Leaders must also recognize, acknowledge, and value the aspirations, ideas, and contributions of others involved in the change process. They are collaborative, share credit easily, and keep others fully informed about the change effort. Listening skills are, as always, a component of communication, and leaders must hear what others are saying. Building coalitions and consensus requires carefully considering how the ideas of others can be incorporated in the change process and increase commitment and involvement of these stakeholders. Leaders must "share power and responsibility with others" (Zachary, 2000, p. 75). By doing so, leaders are building ownership of the change effort.

Communication skills also involve using writing and speaking to convey information (CSWE, 2008, EP 2.1.3c). The ability to write letters, news releases, and similar documents is discussed in much greater detail in Chapter 14.

EP 2.1.3c

Leading by Example

Sheafor and Horejsi (2008) explain that leaders lead by their example. They are willing to perform the same activities they expect of others. They also demonstrate the capacity for hard work and, by their modeling, encourage others to participate. Leaders are also skilled in critically evaluating ideas and helping followers do the same. Effective leaders take responsibility for their own actions and model this for followers. They also mentor potential leaders (Homan, 2008). Ultimately, as followers recognize their own contributions to the process, they begin to demonstrate leadership skills that can be employed to further the group's work. Brueggemann (2006) describes the leader as pursuing a joint enterprise in which all members have the opportunity to share their expertise. This style of leadership is based upon premises that differ vastly from more traditional models in which the leader is considered to be the expert who must coerce or otherwise persuade people to take actions they otherwise might not take. We will explore some of these traditional models in Chapter 4 along with a critique of each.

Bringing New Perspectives

Several writers have identified the importance of leaders bringing new knowledge and skills to their work (Lauffer, 1981). This can be strategies drawn from business, education, or other professions that help broaden the perspectives and options available to the leader and potential followers. McNutt (2000) identifies technological skills and information that can be brought to bear on organizational and community problems. These run the gamut from using e-mail for online organizing, fundraising, and communication, accessing databases, and recruiting members. The effectiveness of using the computer for fundraising has been repeatedly demonstrated in recent national political campaigns. Also useful are skills in using mapping software and geographic information systems. The use of computers is discussed in more detail in Chapter 14.

Use of Self

EP 2.1.1b

Use of self involves at least three skills: self-awareness, self-disclosure, and purposefulness. Leaders require self-awareness of their own ideas and the capacity to modify them as needed. They need to recognize and examine their own motivations and actions and continually monitor themselves throughout the process (CSWE, 2008, EP 2.1.1b). At the same time, leaders self-disclose by appropriately sharing their thoughts, feelings, and observations with others, particularly individuals whom they hope to lead. In some cases, self-disclosure takes the form of openness and admitting vulnerability (Johnson, 1998a). A third component is purposefulness or the capacity to engage in goal-seeking behaviors. Purposefulness is deliberate, not random. The leader engages in actions that involve both direct and indirect means. An example is Salvadore, who consciously decides to have another member of his group present a proposal to the city council in order to expand the member's skill in public speaking and his self-confidence. Here Salvadore is directly using his knowledge of the other member. He expresses confidence in the member's capability and encourages him. Indirectly, Salvadore is also helping to meet the group's need to have multiple members who can engage in public speaking.

Understanding the Media

The capacity to understand and work with the media is a critical leadership skill. Because of the importance of this topic, it will be addressed in much greater detail in Chapter 14.

Task Group Leadership Skills

Leading task groups is an essential component of working for organizational and community change. Included

here are the capacity to develop and maintain the task group's work schedule and attend to the socioemotional aspects of the group. This topic will be addressed later in this chapter.

Managing Conflict

Knowing how to defuse conflictual situations and help individuals and other systems resolve differences is a critical leadership skill (Rose, 1999). Finding a middle ground that satisfactorily meets the needs of multiple parties is a challenging but necessary ability. As in other areas of social work, leadership requires partnering with others to ensure that social work goals are achieved (Brueggemann, 2006). We will address this topic later in this chapter.

Leadership and Administration

It is important to note that leadership in general is not synonymous with administration, which is often more concerned with issues of consistency and ensuring that rules are followed. It is possible to be a leader without holding an administrative position or title. At the same time, many administrators lack the leadership skills required for their respective positions. In addition, leadership may sometimes conflict with the interests of administrators, such as the social worker leading a group attempting to get a city to spend precious resources on a homeless shelter instead of an additional park. Administrators, with their own sets of constraints, often seek to maintain the status quo while social work leaders often seek vastly different goals. Don't confuse leadership and administration.

Leadership and Power

Leaders must have the capacity to exercise power, but power is not the central theme of leadership. It is certainly true that most administrative titles or positions are roles often associated with an expectation of leadership and power. However, focusing too much attention on power as a component of leadership can be problematic, as Meenaghan and Gibbons (2000) note. They point out the importance of being a servant-leader who is devoted to serving others. As a servant-leader, the social worker may both lead and follow, depending upon what the situation requires. This willingness to play both roles engenders trust and conveys the leader's recognition that others have much to contribute to the group's goals. It is also essential among some cultural groups that the leader generate a high level of trust before the group will accept the practitioner in the leadership role. Not using power when it is available can be an important contributor to leadership. This is not to say that power is unimportant, just that it must be employed judiciously. Chapter 8 will identify some of the different kinds of power that may be available to leaders.

Networking

Networks can be defined as a number of individuals or organizations that are interconnected to accomplish a goal that each feels is worthwhile. Networks can be established formally with the members working together all the time (in this case, the network can be viewed more clearly as a system) or can be an ad hoc arrangement that functions as a network only to achieve a particular goal. Membership in such networks is informal, and members may come and go according to their commitment to the goal and their capacity to make a contribution. (National Clearinghouse, 2004)

As a social worker you will often hear the term "networking" and may be confused, because networking really has two related but different meanings. One definition is that networking occurs when social workers attempt to strengthen or develop linkages among people, groups, or other organizations. In this definition, networking helps connect clients to others who can help them. For example, reconnecting a homeless person with her family may help her begin a new life. Thus, networking can be an important means of helping individual clients.

However, professionals also use networking to describe relationships they develop with colleagues for the purpose of improving services from social agencies and organizations. These linkages may be between different professionals or between professionals and groups such as paraprofessionals, citizens, and others. Networks create a synergistic (or multiplying) effect by using the power inherent in multiple agencies or people to help with a social work intervention. In networking, the worker helps connect these individuals, groups, or organizations and combine their efforts to achieve ends not possible by any of the organizations or people working alone. For example, the case that started this chapter was an example of networking: Jack helped bring together all those concerned with the issue of child abuse to consider alternative methods for dealing with this problem. The follow-up work by Gray built upon this networking, as seen in Highlight 3.1.

Kissman (1991) considers networking a basic tenet of feminist social work with its focus on connecting people to one another and enhancing the self-help potential of individuals to cope with problems arising from sex discrimination. This approach is viewed as very empowering to certain groups of clients, including single-parent families headed by women.

Importance of Networking

The following sections will describe five reasons why networking is important to social workers.

Clients Benefit from Informal Helping Networks

First, research has shown that clients benefit from being part of informal helping networks (Brody, 2006; Kissman, 1991). Few individuals or organizations can exist without working with others. We are interdependent, and we network to ensure that our needs can be met (Maguire, 1991). Networks help make individuals

HIGHLIGHT 3.1

Networking in Action

Gray used his networking skills to help implement a Parents Anonymous group in Eagle Bluff. Although his own agency was not involved in child-abuse-related services, his contacts in the community were quite extensive. The contacts he made on behalf of the Parents Anonymous (PA) group included the following:

1. Soliciting referrals from the local protective services division of the Department of Social Welfare.
2. Persuading a church to provide a meeting location for the group.

3. Soliciting donations from private donors and church groups.
4. Obtaining television coverage of the formation of PA through a local station.
5. Persuading a local private college to print advertising materials about the group.

Only through the combined efforts of public agencies, private organizations, and individuals was the success of this project assured. Networking enhances the problem-solving ability of individual workers.

feel more confident of their ability to weather a personal storm and help reduce stress. Additionally, networks can usually act/react much more quickly than can formal agencies.

Clients may also benefit indirectly from networking. For example, the Ontario Prevention Clearinghouse (Stroke Prevention Initiative) uses networking to improve efforts to prevent health problems in the province. By connecting with other organizations and agencies, the clearinghouse helps ensure that information is shared among service providers and those dedicated to primary prevention. Ultimately, individuals and groups of clients benefit from this sharing of information. Similarly, through the development of support service resource books, the clearinghouse helps agencies keep abreast of programs serving particular groups of clients.

Networks Reach Out to Clients

Second, networks can reach clients who would otherwise not seek out services. Sometimes clients have concerns about being labeled crazy or sick or being otherwise stigmatized.

Networks appear to be important in various other countries, such as Sweden (Duner & Nordstrom, 2007) and among age groups that range from children to the elderly (Gaugler & Kane, 2001). Balgopal (1995) suggests that they can provide help in a culturally sensitive way, essential when working in cross-cultural situations. New immigrants, for example, can often overcome cultural barriers and reduce marginalization by connecting with others from their homeland who arrived earlier and have already settled in. A Hmong mutual assistance association may provide services to Hmong refugees (immigrants from Laos) without causing them the embarrassment that might be associated with other mainstream agencies. Carefully used, networks can sometimes reach clients who would not normally seek or receive services from formal agencies. Similarly, working through tribal organizations can be a more effective way to reach underserved Native American populations.

Lewis and Suarez (1995) and Bentelspacher et al. (2006) note that it is typical for many African Americans to seek help for personal problems from their informal networks, which may be composed of people known in churches, gangs, or friendship groups. Some social networks may operate in social clubs, neighborhood associations, fraternal associations, and lodges, whereas others are formed on street corners, in parks, and on porch steps. Both Malcolm X (1965)

and Claude Brown (1965) describe in their autobiographies how these informal networks helped them cope with oppression and hostility by providing support and encouragement. Thompson and Peebles-Wilkins (1992) also note that ethnic networks help alleviate stress attributable to minority status, encourage minority clients to use available health care resources, and augment mental health services provided by formal agencies.

It is especially important to be aware of the networking roles played by churches, because they are more frequently offering direct services. Specific services may include support groups for single individuals and adolescents, counseling, and renewal groups for married couples.

Networks are very important for certain classes of clients. People experiencing chronic mental illness often have a very small group of people in their network. Because of the nature of the illness, most of the client's friends and family members cease to be ready resources. Some will drift away from the client; others may be estranged because of the difficulty of interacting with the client. Expanding the size of their networks is crucial to helping this population manage their lives.

Likewise, parents who neglect their children often have poor or nonexistent informal networks upon which they can rely. Without such assistance, these parents are more likely to rely on nonsupportive relatives and friends who may exhibit the same kinds of neglectful attitudes and behaviors. They typically receive little emotional support and cannot depend upon others for assistance with parenting. Moreover, they are likely to have fewer social skills needed to develop new social networks.

In rural areas, fewer formal resources and services are available because of the lack of funding and/or because there are not enough clients with a specific problem to justify services. Networking is critical in these areas and often requires the worker to learn the names and identities of those providing various forms of care. Care resources might include pastors or other lay religious leaders, public health departments, welfare department employees, school teachers or principals, Red Cross officials, and others who work in the social service arena. Knowing local resource people is important because the vicinity often lacks a central agency to which clients can be referred. Ideally, a social worker will know what kinds of services or resources are provided, by whom, for how long, what significance this help has for the recipient, and how the recipient perceives the help provided. You can expand your networking capabilities in rural areas by asking those you already know to introduce you to some of their friends and associates. This is a useful way to build interest and involvement while expanding your own capacity as a networker.

Networks Augment Formal Resources

Third, the more formal resources provided by you, your agency, or other social service organizations are supplemented by informal networks that offer advice, information, support, feedback, and sometimes concrete resources such as money, clothes, or other tangibles. Of course, not all the people in our networks are helpful. Some people actually create stress in others, some are not available when we need them, and some are helpful only in certain kinds of situations. Think of all the people who might surround you in a time of emotional crisis. Are there some individuals who would make matters worse? Perhaps there are others who cannot provide emotional support but would gladly lend you money or a car if you needed it. Many clients have similar networks of informal helpers and resources whom they can turn to in times of difficulty. Other clients may need help to review their own networks of friends. Helping them in this process assists clients to recognize their own sources of strength.

Networks Help Navigate Formal Systems

Fourth, networks may speed up action through a social system to help clients get services to which they are entitled. Too often, bureaucracies and red tape prevent clients from getting what they need in a timely fashion. (Bureaucracies and red tape will be discussed much more thoroughly in Chapter 4.)

Social workers have multiple opportunities to develop relationships with other social workers and with myriad professionals from various disciplines and agencies. Your ability to build and maintain those relationships may be the key to helping your clients negotiate the system and meet their goals. For example, a phone call to the right person, a recommendation to the appropriate individual, or an instruction to the client to be sure to mention your name to the other professional may prove to be all that is needed in some situations.

Network building usually occurs on a personal basis as you meet individual workers and professionals in other agencies. More formal efforts occur when agency administrators or staff deliberately set about contacting each other to facilitate service delivery. For example,

agency administrators commonly worry about duplication of some services, coupled with gaps in other services. Through networking with administrators from different agencies, one agency decided to end its home health care services when other agencies expanded their efforts in this area. (Home health care agencies provide a variety of medical and follow-up care for clients, many of whom would otherwise need to be hospitalized or placed in nursing homes.) This decision allowed the agency to refocus on unmet needs and use its scarce resources more wisely. Regular meetings among agency representatives also can lead to macro change efforts to close service gaps, change problematic laws and regulations (policies), or lobby for additional funding. An example of the use of networking to fill a service gap appears in Highlight 3.2.

Formal meetings, such as the one in Highlight 3.2, are only one way to encourage and facilitate networking among social agencies. *Service fairs* provide opportunities for various agencies to set up tables with brochures and information about the agency's services. For example, all agencies serving the elderly might participate in an elder care fair open to both professionals and the public. Possible participants include the local area agency on aging (which is part of a national network of agencies serving the elderly), nursing homes, home health care agencies, hospice agencies, hospitals, and organizations such as the American Association of Retired Persons (AARP) and the Retired Senior Volunteer Program. Yet another method of networking is through periodic meetings of a community welfare council, where representatives of all community social agencies meet over lunch. At the meeting, new programs are summarized, new staff are introduced, and ideas are suggested for dealing with common problems. For example, several agencies dealing with an influx of gang activities in the community might decide that they could be more effective by sharing information. Cooperative endeavors can emerge out of this networking, and the method has proven successful in the United States, Great Britain, and Canada, among others.

Clearly, social workers must understand the importance of networks and networking both for clients and for their own effectiveness as helpers and change agents. The absence of effective networking in a community can be embarrassing, waste resources, and hurt clients. For example, Biegel and Naparstek (1982) found that priests providing counseling services in the same area were not aware of each other's roles as counselors. In addition, mental health clinic administrators

HIGHLIGHT 3.2

Networking for Latchkey Kids

Grady Wray is a social worker at the Child Advocacy Council, a private social service dedicated to better serving the needs of poor children in Spring Harbor. She worries about the number of children who have no parental supervision after school and are at risk of becoming involved in drugs. These latchkey children care for themselves after school because their parents are still at work. Grady convenes a meeting of representatives of several organizations in the community, all of whom have a stake in services to children. All of the individuals invited are colleagues whom Grady considers to be within her own network of resources. Agencies represented include the YWCA, the Parent Teachers Association, the Girl and Boy Scouts, and the Department of Human Services. The participants decide that although each has some knowledge of the problem from the perspective of his or her own agency, they are not sufficiently clear about the scope of the problem they face. The group decides to undertake a needs assessment with a sample of elementary schools in Spring Harbor. (A needs assessment is a formal effort to identify specific problems and to define services not being provided in a community.) The needs assessment shows that a serious problem does exist: Literally hundreds of elementary school children are without supervision from the time school gets out until their parents get home from work.

Armed with this data, Grady's original network expands to include school administrators with an interest in addressing this problem. This larger group then begins to discuss options. Because of the cost of beginning a full-scale program and their lack of knowledge about what should be done, the administrators agree to try a limited-time project. Beginning the following fall semester, the school system will provide before- and after-school recreational child care at four strategically located schools. A year later, the success of the program encourages the system to expand

the child care facilities to all Spring Harbor schools. Eventually, more than 2,000 children participate. The program, offered at modest cost includes recreational activities, snack time, and small-group discussion sessions.

Latchkey children must care for themselves until their parents return from work.

located less than one-half mile apart had never met, though they served the same neighborhood. Similarly, lay helpers were often unaware of other such helpers living nearby. Obviously, not knowing who else is providing services to your clients reduces your ability to be of assistance. You simply don't have all the information you need about the resources your clients could use.

By getting to know other agencies in your community, you can become a resource for your own agency about other available community services.

Networks Help Workers Cope

A fifth value of networking, cited by Sheafor and Horejsi (2008), stresses the importance of networks in helping workers cope with their own professional stresses and strains. Your network of friends and professional colleagues can share your frustrations and discuss with you the difficult challenges all social workers face. Thus, networks can be used not only to satisfy client needs but also to keep workers functioning better. In addition, networks for professionals can help us reality-test and recognize problems in our own agencies. Too often we get so accustomed to the routine in our agencies that we lose sight of better ways of doing things. Talking with colleagues from outside our agencies can help us recognize a larger reality of possibilities and potentials.

We often develop our own networks when we contact other agencies for clients. The individual workers with whom we collaborate can become a resource for us in our own lives. Of course, networks also allow us to develop referral sources and potential places for referring clients. They allow us to learn from others, adapting their new ideas to our situations and agencies. Joint programs may emerge from such sharing.

Networks: Mutual Aid

Networks are not necessarily constant: Memberships in networks may change as needs dictate. Most important, however, networks are mutual. In other words, aided members must expect to help others in a similar fashion. This is one of the principles behind most self-help groups such as Alcoholics Anonymous. When working with clients in groups, we can help group members learn to rely on one another in times of need and to think about how they might expand their own networks outside the group. Members of a group might meet at each other's homes or call each other periodically, thus serving as resources for one another. For example, members of a Parents Anonymous group offered to help each other out by babysitting when one member or another felt particularly stressed and in danger of losing control. Networks survive and thrive when such mutuality is observed.

Types of Networks

Networks may be classified into categories based upon the *type of relationship* among members, the *degree of intimacy* members share, the *difficulty level* of the help needed, and the *size* of the network. For example, close, intimate relationships among members of a network are likely to provide different sorts of resources than those without such closeness. In these situations, people are so close to us and so important that they offer help with no expectation of reciprocity. Members of less-intimate networks are more likely to expect a

quid pro quo (literally, "something for something," or getting something in return for one's help).

Sometimes the difficulty or duration of the help needed makes a difference. Asking to borrow a friend's car to drive to the store is much less an imposition than asking for that same friend's car for a five-week trip to Alaska.

Networks may be composed of individuals, small groups of people, self-help groups, or self-help organizations. *Self-help organizations* are formal or semi-formal associations designed to provide mutual assistance and aid to participants facing similar problems or challenges. Examples include Alcoholics Anonymous, Parents Anonymous, and Parents Without Partners. Maguire (1984) notes that networking is the basis for self-help organizations because of the reliance on relationships to provide various resources in times of need.

Yet another kind of network springs up only from time to time as need arises. Members of a community may join together to raise funds for a family experiencing a major problem. Examples include loss of a home through fire, major medical expenses, or similar catastrophic events.

Inherently, networks are based on interpersonal relationships. Consequently, they are idiosyncratic (unique to the person) and flexible. As mentioned earlier, they change as needed. Also, network members must be willing to play the same role with others if the mutuality is to survive. Interpersonal relationships help keep networks going during difficult times. You cannot underestimate the role of personal liking and good working relationships in helping a network prosper and survive (Maguire, 1984).

For example, Veronica was the program assistant (formerly called a secretary) for the Foreign Adoptions Unit of a large private adoption agency. Ja Dawn and Moustafa also worked in the unit, along with about a dozen other staff. Veronica was part of an informal information network comprising a number of other program assistants in the agency. She also had an exceptionally good relationship with Ja Dawn, whom Veronica brought into this informal network.

Many times, Veronica would hear about major changes planned for the agency through her informal network or fellow program assistants. She often learned this information before it reached her own supervisor through the agency's formal communication system. The informal communication channels in Veronica's network were much quicker than the more formal channels. (Formal channels will be discussed more thoroughly in Chapter 4.)

Social worker preparing an agenda for a group meeting.

EP 2.1.9b

The quality and significance of personal relationships are crucial in the networking process: Veronica and Ja Dawn had a good relationship. Thus, whenever Veronica heard some news, she would immediately share it with Ja Dawn. Of course the relationship was reciprocal in that Ja Dawn would also help Veronica whenever possible. This included sharing information and assisting Veronica when things got too hectic in the agency. Other staff, such as Moustafa, never became part of the network, because his actions toward Ja Dawn were less helpful and more insensitive. His tendency to try to read the mail on Ja Dawn's desk and the fact that he treated her like a servant precluded his ever being invited into the network.

Problems with Networks

At least six problems can occur in networking. The first source of difficulty arises when professionals do not value the contributions of informal networks. Rather than encourage their existence, they ignore or otherwise devalue these networks. The risk that professionals will downplay the contributions of others is always present. Although an informal network composed of a client's friends and family may lack the professional training and community sanction governing the social work role, their contributions more than match those of the formal systems in duration, intensity, and quantity.

It is much more appropriate for the social worker to view the client's network as an ally in the helping process and perhaps to recruit network members to become part of the helping effort. The Dial family is a good example. When Mr. Dial died suddenly, family members turned to Mr. Dial's son-in-law for help in handling funeral arrangements, dealing with the estate, and providing emotional support. Alicia Hurt, the hospital social worker who initially helped Mrs. Dial, noted that John Dial, the couple's own son, was never mentioned as a possible source of assistance, despite the fact that he lived nearby. Alicia encouraged Mrs. Dial to call her son and involve him in some of the many decisions needed at this most difficult time. By reaching out to broaden Mrs. Dial's network, Alicia gave the client an additional resource and reduced her need to rely solely on the son-in-law, who lived in another city. It also helped build Mrs. Dial's confidence in her own son and strengthened their relationship.

A second problem is when a worker takes such an active leadership role with a client's informal network that the client feels incompetent, alienated, or left out. The social work role should be to help marshal the resources needed by the client, with the client taking the lead whenever possible. This is not an easy task and is especially hard for professionals who don't yet have the maturity to allow others to lead or who are threatened by nonprofessionals.

A third potential problem may occur within formal networks themselves. Negative or dysfunctional relationships can reduce the network's effectiveness. For example, some agencies or workers may see themselves as having higher status than others. In a recent natural disaster, some social workers declined to help because the assistance that the clients needed, which included locating housing, food, and clothing, was "beneath them." These workers, who saw themselves as therapists, were willing to offer individual and family therapy, but did not feel they should simply help someone find a place to sleep.

A fourth problem is failure to share information with other network members. Mike Clover, a social work educator, was asked to testify at a legislative hearing on a proposed social work licensing law. The law would require licensing of both BSWs and MSWs and was supported by a large network of social workers in the state. Mike did not inform key members of the network that he did not support licensing BSWs. In the middle of his testimony he responded to a question from a legislator by saying, "Well, if that's a problem, why not license only MSWs?" His failure to share information (namely, his position on licensing BSWs) caught the licensing network members off guard and threatened their progress in getting social workers licensed in the state.

Fifth, networks composed of representatives of different agencies can disintegrate when those agencies no longer support the network's activities. The State Division on Aging refused to send a representative to the meetings of a coalition (another type of network) trying to get additional funding for a foster grandparent program. The foster grandparent program was designed to get the elderly involved as substitute grandparents for children who had no grandparents of their own. The Division on Aging did not consider this program to have a high enough priority and refused to allow its workers to participate in the coalition. Overcoming these obstacles requires consistent effort over time.

Sixth, some professionals question whether the informal network can maintain an adequate level of confidentiality about the client's situation (Sheafor & Horejsi, 2006). Recall that the right of confidentiality belongs to clients and they can, and often do, share personal information with family and friends. Obtaining the client's permission to share otherwise confidential information is an appropriate means of addressing this concern.

There are two ways of overcoming difficulties in networking. Johnson and Yanca (2007) suggest it is important to recognize and acknowledge the mutual interests of different agencies and resources. A good first step, for example, might be to point out that five different agencies in one community are all interested in helping the homeless. This can help them recognize their similar goals and values. In the fifth example, even though a private agency would have operated the foster grandparent program, the program was designed to help the elderly. Assisting the elderly was also the goal of the Division on Aging. Keeping their mutual goals in mind could have resulted in a more effective effort to get additional funding for the foster grandparent program.

Another way to help a network survive is to provide various avenues of communication (e.g., face-to-face talks, newsletters, memoranda) to bridge the communication gaps. When cooperative opportunities present themselves, serving as a cheerleader and booster for the activity may help ensure equal commitment from others. This is not always easy. Recent flood threats in the Midwest and floods in the South have brought people and organizations together to help those most affected by the disasters. Cooperative efforts were encouraged by celebrities and coordinated by existing agencies. They involved thousands of volunteers and staff from many different agencies. On a more local level, efforts to hold fundraisers for victims of medical emergencies, fires, and similar calamities show the capacity for a community to cooperate in seeking specific benefits. The potential synergy available when professionals and informal networks collaborate is enormous.

Worker Roles in Networking

EP 2.1.1c

As noted, social workers may be involved with networks from many different angles. We may serve as a "clearinghouse" (Maguire, 1984, p. 203) for self-help organizations. Knowing what services each organization provides to which groups is essential for making effective referrals or for finding common ground from which to approach larger macro issues. Social workers may also help start a network (as did Gray Mfume in the vignette at the beginning of this chapter). Maguire's (1984, 1991) list of possible roles for a worker in a self-help network appears in Highlight 3.3 (CSWE, 2008, EP 2.1.1c).

Networking is an important mezzo level skill because it both ensures that clients receive needed assistance and provides a means to address larger problems in the community. It is a bridge skill useful in working with individual clients (e.g., by referring them to a self-help group), addressing needs of groups of clients (e.g., helping existing networks flourish and grow), and meeting needs at the community level (e.g., establishing new groups and networks). It is also important in helping us survive as social workers, improve the quality of the services we provide, and expand the repertoire of services available to those we serve.

Social workers can do a number of things to strengthen client networks. This includes working with a family's support network in a number of capacities. This might include educating members about the client's needs; mediating in areas where there are disputes; teaching problem-solving and social and communication skills; and reframing the perceptions of network members and the client. It is also possible to connect clients with volunteer resources in the community, such as respite care. Clients may need assistance learning how to make and keep friends and where to locate informal neighborhood or community helpers. If, in the past, they have had ties to religious organizations, there may be an opportunity to help the client reconnect to this potential resource.

Although we have stressed the role of working with groups, remember that micro level interventions are important to networking. For example, strong interpersonal relationships can help networks avoid rough spots, just as happens in couples and families. The knowledge gained from tending and maintaining networks also can prove useful at the macro level. When major opportunities for positive changes appear (or when crises threaten existing programs), it is easiest to assemble those with a vested stake in the outcome. Given your knowledge of the community and its agencies, you will be in a stronger position to help in this process. Knowing that five agencies in the community serve the homeless will make your job much easier if you are asked to coordinate services for this population. If you were unaware of the existence of these agencies, you might miss an excellent opportunity to improve services to the homeless.

Working in and with Teams

As a social worker you will have multiple opportunities to participate as a member of a team—in fact, many settings require that social workers practice routinely as team members (CSWE, 2008 EP 2.1.8b). *Interdisciplinary teams*

EP 2.1.8b

HIGHLIGHT 3.3

Worker Roles in Self-Help Groups

Maguire (1991) suggests several ways that a social worker might help a network self-help group. These include:

- Providing a place to meet
- Contributing or arranging for funds
- Providing information to members
- Training members as leaders
- Referring people to the group
- Publicizing group activities

- Accepting referrals from the group
- Providing credibility in the larger community
- Providing credibility in the professional community
- Serving as a buffer between the group and other agencies/organizations
- Providing social and emotional support for group leaders
- Consulting with group leaders

are common when service to the client requires the expertise of multiple disciplines (for example, psychology, social work, and nursing). This is often the case in hospitals and residential treatment facilities. In other situations, the team includes only social workers, each worker being responsible for overseeing some aspect of the client's case plan. A county social service department might assign some social workers to work with children in foster care, while others provide services to the children's parents.

In other macro situations, you will be invited to serve as a team member grappling with larger issues. For example, you may serve on an agency board of directors or an intra-agency committee. You may be part of an inter-agency team or task force charged with managing the problems caused when a large employer shuts down its factory in your community. These offer you excellent opportunities to have an impact on the larger environment.

Despite the various factors that can affect teams (membership, size, tasks), certain common elements characterize effectively functioning teams. For instance, teams exist to work on identified problems—perhaps gang violence, drug dealing in a community, or improving services to the elderly. To be effective in solving the problem, all teams require clear roles and accountability for the work of each member. They also need an effective communication system. Finally, all teams will benefit from an emphasis on fact-based judgments. This means that the team's decisions rest on facts, not on the whims or desires of individual members (Larson & LaFasto, 1989). Although these features are important for all teams, the most effective teams exhibit still other characteristics. These include clear goals, structure and membership tied to goals, commitment of all members, a collaborative climate, and standards of excellence. They also require external support and recognition and principled leadership. In this section we will expand on the characteristics of effective teams and try to identify some ways in which you can improve your competence as a team member.

Characteristics of Effective Teams

Larson and LaFasto (1989), Fatout and Rose (1995), and Wheelan (2005) have studied effective teams in various settings. Their research suggests that effective teams share at least nine common characteristics. These nine factors appear to operate whether the team functions in a human-service situation or in a business. Clearly, certain factors will be more important in some settings than in others.

1. Clear Goals

It has been said that if you don't know where you're going, you'll never know if you get there. This is certainly true of effective teams. All members of the group must understand the purpose and goals of the group. Clarity of goals, however, is not sufficient. The goals must be considered worthwhile. Each member must believe that what the team is attempting to do is desirable. This can help members confronting obstacles and rough times.

2. and 3. Structure and Membership Tied to Goals

Just as agencies organize in different ways depending upon their goals, so teams must be structured in ways that help goal achievement. Three types of team structures emerge. If the goal is to help a community solve a massive drug problem in its downtown area, a problem-solving team will probably be required. *Problem-solving teams* are composed of people who trust one another and can stay focused on the issues of importance.

Another structure is the *creative team,* whose task is to come up with a variety of possible products or ideas and who will need the autonomy to consider alternatives. Rigid systems may thwart rather than support creativity. These teams function best with a minimum of supervision and rules.

Creative teams also need members who are self-starters and don't have to rely on others for their ideas. If you can think of a friend who always seems to come up with interesting ideas, you probably know a prospective member of a creative team.

A third structure is the *tactical team* (Larson & LaFasto, 1989). Tactical teams are brought in to carry out a plan. For example, a tactical team might be brought in to help a community deal with a natural disaster. The team members might have expertise in areas such as helping trauma victims and developing community programs to cope with future disasters.

The importance of thinking clearly about team structure should be obvious when we consider the effect of having the wrong type of team on a job. Consider a team of social workers representing five different agencies assigned to find ways for their agencies to collaborate to provide better service to clients. All members were chosen because of their creativity and wealth of ideas. In their agencies, they often recommended changing this or that to make the organization function better. They also tended to be critical and likely to challenge accepted ways of doing things.

Each of these characteristics is helpful when the goal is to come up with new and creative ideas for agency-to-agency collaboration.

At the conclusion of their work, the team recommends a new joint system of providing service to multi-problem families. The new system would have a team approach whereby all members of the team would work collaboratively. The agency directors, believing that the new model could be very effective, decide to have the same team that designed the system implement the system.

By now you can see where this is leading. Because creative teams and tactical teams require different structures and people, assigning the same people to both types of teams is not likely to work. People who are highly creative and individualistic may not be as effective when the task is to operate a program on a regular basis. They may even find the highly directive nature of their new tasks at odds with their creative orientation or get bored with the system's implementation and see it as drudgery. Of course, creative teams may also come up with a plan that is difficult to operate because it is not practical. Therefore, a team comprising a combination of creative and tactical members may be most effective.

In short, it is important to think carefully about team goals and then select the structure that will best accomplish them. It is also important to choose people who have the technical competence and the necessary personal attributes to do the job. Some people work well with others and can submerge their individuality to reach group goals. Others are equally competent from a technical standpoint, but are more difficult to work with. Each has a place, but not necessarily on the same team.

4. Commitment of All Members

Effective teams are likely to have members who display a team spirit. This means they identify with the group and look forward to participating in team endeavors. Each member commits to the team, expects other members to be similarly committed, and contributes to the process in whatever ways are needed. Contrast this to a group whose members do not enjoy working with one another, avoid volunteering to do group tasks, and generally act as though they are the only ones on the team with good ideas.

5. Collaborative Climate

The collaborative climate in well-functioning teams is notable for the high degree of trust and mutual respect felt by individual members. Part of this trust rests upon consistent behavioral expectations. In other words, members usually know how the other members will act or think. This gives them confidence in the others because member behavior becomes predictable.

Members can be honest and open in their discussions with other members and will respect the contributions of other members. Ross (1995) stresses the importance of accepting and validating the abilities and competence of other members of the team. Collaboration often breaks down when social workers begin to believe that they are more effective than other team members. Attitudes such as "He's a nurse. What does he know about case management?" are going to cause problems.

Ross (1995) points out that collaboration can also be threatened by blurred roles or, conversely, overly rigid definitions of roles. Part of a collaborative environment is that all members recognize and accept their own skills and limitations. Collaboration is also threatened when members get territorial. Territorial members start by drawing an imaginary line in the sand and saying, "I do this, and no one on the team can handle this area except me." As you can imagine, all of these situations will lead to problems. It is easy to get into win-lose situations and hard to get out of them, so it is best to avoid them entirely. (Win-lose situations are those in which one party clearly wins and the other clearly loses, often causing anger and dissatisfaction in the losing party.) Believing that each member can make an important contribution is essential, as is mutual respect.

A collaborative climate is an essential element in globalization when working with others from different cultures. It has already proved critical in the business world, where employees in one country collaborate with those in another to produce better products, reduce costs, and enhance the work environment. The resolution of complex problems requires the talents of multiple individuals and organizations. Examples include groups who provide services to various populations around the world, such as Doctors without Borders. This organization must collaborate with local governmental agencies, other nonprofit social agencies, and indigenous leaders to provide medical and public health in emergencies. Likewise, Oxfam International, which has a focus on poverty and social justice, employs a collaborative climate as it confronts HIV and AIDS in Africa. Oxfam works with employers, national and local governments, and nongovernmental organizations to develop policies and procedures to deal with the spread of these challenges.

Of course, there are risks associated with some attempts to develop a collaborative climate, especially when it borders on what is known as *groupthink* (Ahlfinger & Esser, 2001; Janis, 1982). In groupthink situations, members do not do an effective job of problem solving or analyzing alternatives. Instead, they simply go along with what they perceive to be the sentiments of the majority. Groupthink occurs when too much emphasis rests on collaboration and conformity and not enough attention is given to thinking critically about alternatives. Members become too concerned with maintaining the "we" feeling and submerge their hesitations and concerns rather than risk disagreeing with their peers. To counter a tendency toward groupthink, it is permissible and even healthy to allow disagreements to surface because it is important to have as many people as possible support the final decision. Encouraging critical thinking is important, even while striving to maintain a climate of collaboration. Critical thinking involves challenging assumptions, verifying facts, questioning opinions not supported by data, and being willing to consider ideas that others have rejected. It emphasizes "clarity, accuracy, relevance, and completeness of information upon which to base decisions" (Gibbs & Gambrill, 1996).

EP 2.1.3

An example of uncritical thinking would be reading an account of an event in the local newspaper and believing that the account is completely factual. Using the Gibbs and Gambrill definition, we do not know, for example, whether the information provided is accurate or complete. We have the reporter's account, based either on witnessing the event or talking to those who did see it. Another example involves the reliance on eyewitness reports by crime victims. While the survivor of a crime is usually credible, there are limitations to this form of identification. Several recent cases involving the use of DNA evidence have freed individuals who were convicted based on eyewitness testimony. A third example can be drawn from the debates about health care reform in the United States. Without any evidence in any bill on the topic, some political figures began to say that "death squads" would be making decisions on the care of elderly patients. They suggested that these groups would have the power to refuse medical care to an elderly person against that person's wishes. This accusation made the rounds on the Internet, resulting in several hundred thousand entries, again without the slightest scintilla of evidence to support it. Believing an account on the Internet may be

more of a mistake than accepting an account in the newspaper. Critical thinking involves being cautious when examining evidence, relying on testimony from others, and accepting the opinions of others without some degree of verification (CSWE, 2008, EP 2.1.3).

6. Standards of Excellence

Most effective teams have agreed-upon standards of excellence for which they strive. A standard of excellence is a measure of the value or worth of an action. For example, an agency I once worked with always had workers who were outgoing, personable, and friendly. It did not seem to matter who was hired, because all members seemed committed to providing a warm, friendly atmosphere for clients. Not only did the agency recruit members who had these characteristics, but it also believed that reaching this standard was so important that the agency would exert various pressures to maintain it. The pressure might be exerted by individual members, the team leader, or the team as a whole. It could also include agreed-upon consequences for those who did not meet the standards.

Sometimes the team is subjected to outside pressure to maintain standards. For example, suppose an agency administrator questions why the interdisciplinary team is not responding as rapidly to case referrals as was typical in the past. The agency had always prided itself on responding to referrals within 24 hours of receiving them. Now the average time has become 72 hours. The standard of excellence has not been maintained.

7. Information-Based Decision Making

Effective teams make rational decisions grounded in analysis of available information. Ideally, information available would be complete, accurate, and timely. In reality, one or more of these elements is often lacking to some degree. Rarely, for example, do we have complete information about anything. Missing information is common in teams and other decision-making groups. Identifying gaps in information is important both to direct efforts to gain the missing information and to recognize the limits inherent in making a decision. Of course, sometimes teams have more information than they can use and must sift it to find salient elements that affect the decision.

Accurate information is easier to obtain to the extent that teams rely on multiple sources of information and cross-check data. For example, inconsistent data about such things as the percent of people living below poverty in a community or its demographic composition can be double-checked with official statistics.

Similarly, having up-to-date information is important, and teams should try to get the latest data available. Historical data may be helpful for showing trends or setting the context for a current decision, but timely information is essential (Fatout & Rose, 1995).

8. External Support and Recognition

We have seen that members of effective teams see themselves as a "team." In addition, many effective teams are perceived by people outside the team as somehow special. The team may be recognized for its special expertise and may receive external praise and support for its actions. For example, a community appoints a special team to work with employees who have lost their jobs because of plant closings. This team receives high praise from the news media and other groups in the community because it helps employees get other jobs or take college and vocational courses to develop new skills. The team's success in this endeavor is respected in the community. This external reward strengthens group cohesion and reinforces the special nature of the team.

9. Principled Leadership

Principled leadership gives a consistent message about the role of the team. It gives members the freedom to take risks in pursuit of the standard of excellence. Ideally, leaders can suppress their need to showcase their own personal accomplishments and focus instead on the accomplishments of other members.

In your career as a social worker, you will have many opportunities to work with various types of teams. Many will be effective and will share the characteristics Larson and LaFasto (1989) and Fatout and Rose (1995) describe. Others will be effective, but share only a portion of the features characterizing effective teams. Some teams will be ineffective just because they lack many or most of the characteristics described in this section. If you know what makes a team effective, your contributions have a better chance of helping the team reach its goals.

Planning and Conducting Meetings

You may assume from the prior discussions of networking and teamwork that social workers spend a fair amount of time in meetings. This is often the case. Social workers spend time in team meetings, group meetings, staff meetings, teleconferences, and community meetings. Some of this time is wasted because designated leaders run the meetings ineffectively. All of us have been in poorly run meetings that seemed to lack purpose, direction, or a sense of closure. They may have seemed to drag on forever. People talked about issues that were of no concern to anyone else and sometimes monopolized the discussion ad nauseam. Perhaps a handful of people dominated the discussion, or conflict got out of hand and became threateningly personal. However, meetings are a necessary part of the social work profession—and any meeting can be efficient and productive. Some helpful techniques to accomplish this are suggested next.

Plan Ahead

Preparation for meetings is critical. Before planning a meeting, you should always clarify its purpose in your own mind and identify objectives to be achieved in the meeting. Activities in the planning stages include identifying the participants, selecting a time and place for the meeting, providing participants with an agenda, and arranging the physical environment (setting up chairs, locating a microphone, or borrowing a flip chart or whiteboard, if needed). Think ahead about possible follow-up meetings and consider the need for formal reports (including their potential authors).

Clarify Purpose and Establish Objectives

The meeting's purpose should be clear both to you and to those you invite to participate. Is the purpose to plan a new service, carry out a project, or discuss common problems experienced by group members? **EP 2.1.10c** Meetings can have many ends. They can be used to organize people, share information, or resolve differences. Is this to be a single meeting or merely the first of several meetings occurring over the next few months? What are the meeting objectives? Do you hope to identify 12 new couples for possible inclusion in the new couples' communication course your agency is offering? Is the group expected to select from a list of candidates the person who will become the supervisor for the court services unit? Will you finish the meeting with a drafted set of policies and procedures for handling referrals from the intake to the ongoing services unit? Clarify and specify the meeting's desired objectives before the meeting begins (CSWE, 2008, EP 2.1.10c).

Select Participants

Sometimes you have little control over who attends a given meeting. If it is a meeting requiring agency representation, the agencies themselves will decide who represents them. Other times you will call a meeting and select people to participate. Try to include participants with a mixture of capabilities. Invite individuals who are knowledgeable about the topic under discussion. Ignorance rarely produces good outcomes. Likewise, include members committed to the outcome of the meeting and capable of carrying out their responsibilities. A good mix of vocal and reserved members is important in order to balance the two extremes: Some members may talk incessantly but not listen; others may be so quiet that you'll want to check for a pulse.

Depending upon the situation, you may need to consider whether attendees will need transportation, child care arrangements, or other services to assist them in their participation. This may restrict whom you invite, especially if you are unable to provide these necessary services. Before you can hold a successful meeting, you must have participants who show up.

Select a Time and Place

Always give some thought to the meeting's *date* and *time*. Otherwise, well-planned meetings can become flops. Don't hold the meeting on a religious holy day. Also consider participants' personal schedules: Early morning meetings are difficult for anyone responsible for getting children off to school or day care and for those who have to travel long distances.

Sometimes even your best efforts can go wrong. I once scheduled a meeting at a national professional social work conference, unaware that at exactly the same time the Pope was speaking across town. Not surprisingly, the Pope won this contest. Hardly anyone attended my meeting.

Whenever possible, preschedule regular meetings by setting your meeting times in advance so people can plan their schedules around them. This increases the likelihood that attendance will be high and lets people know you respect their time. Send a memo or notice to participants as early as possible, even weeks in advance, to assist group members in planning their own schedules.

Don't hold meetings and eat simultaneously. Trying to conduct meetings over meals is rarely productive. Most people find it difficult to concentrate on eating, talking, listening, and thinking all at once. Either eat first and get on with business, or schedule the meal to follow your work session. This may serve as a positive reinforcement for completing the work on time, because people will look forward to finishing the task and eating.

The meeting's setting is very important and should be considered carefully. Hold meetings in meeting rooms—not in your office. Will the meeting location offend or put off anyone who might like to come? For example, if you were planning a meeting of two rival street gangs, you would hold it at a neutral site rather than in the territory of either of the gangs.

Choose locations that simplify accomplishment of group business. Is adequate parking available? Is the location close to mass transit? Will people be readily able to find the meeting site? Did you include a map if needed? Is the room large enough to accommodate participants? Is ventilation adequate? Are the chairs comfortable and a table available? Do you need a microphone, whiteboard, flip chart, and so on?

Consider whether the meeting location is accessible to those with disabilities. This can be a critical factor in determining whether some people can attend the meeting. A colleague once planned a meeting in a restaurant with supper to follow the meeting. She visited the restaurant beforehand to determine if it was accessible to those with physical disabilities. She could see that the restaurant dining room was accessible and notified attendees of this. When the group arrived at 6:00 P.M., she discovered that the meeting room was in the basement of the restaurant, accessible only by stairs. She had not asked the restaurant directly about the meeting space and only assumed that the meeting rooms were on the same level as the main dining area. Four of us carried a meeting attendee and his motorized wheelchair down the stairs to ensure his participation in the meeting. To this day, I don't know what the wheelchair weighed, but my back still hurts when I think about it.

Additionally, consider the seating arrangements and overall room layout. Should people sit around a table, on chairs in a circle, or in theater style? The purpose of the meeting should determine the arrangements. For example, a round table facilitates discussion by all participants. Likewise, a lecture podium at the front of a room facing rows of chairs facilitates a lecture format in which one individual at a time speaks to the audience.

Prepare an Agenda

An *agenda* is a list of topics to be addressed at a meeting in some sort of prioritized order. The agenda lists the time and place of the meeting and, sometimes, those who are invited to participate. Retain extra copies of the agenda for those who forget or lose their own copy.

Highlight 3.4 shows a sample agenda. Note that the agenda's list of topics is brief. Lengthy explanations concerning how the topics will be addressed are inappropriate. The agenda simply lists general topics to be covered at the prescribed meeting. Other agendas may identify the nature of each topic—that is, whether it is an item for information only, for discussion, or for group action.

Distribute printed matter well before the meeting. Don't expect meeting participants to read and understand lengthy written material handed out at the start of a meeting. Consider the length and complexity and distribute the material accordingly. Send this material in advance with the agenda so attendees know in what order this material will be addressed (and, of course, have extra copies available at the meeting itself). The most important topics should appear earlier in the agenda, when people are most attentive, and the least important items at the end. The first portion of the agenda can be devoted to approval of minutes from the previous meeting and minor items that require little discussion. Sometimes it is possible to estimate the amount of time a discussion item will take in order to determine how many items the agenda should have.

EP 2.1.9b

Agenda items usually fall into the following categories: announcements (general information of interest to members), decision items (topics requiring the group to arrive at a decision), and discussion items (items requiring deliberation, but no action). It is often best to handle them in this order for several reasons. First, announcements may be relevant to discussion of items placed later on the agenda. Therefore, the members should hear this information early in the meeting. Decision items require much harder work in most groups and should be placed at the point when members have the most energy. Discussion items can be handled at the end because the group does not need to reach a decision. Agenda setting is an important leadership skill (CSWE, 2008, EP 2.1.9b).

Start Meetings on Time

Don't wait for stragglers. If you set the time for the meeting at 3:00 P.M., start promptly at 3:00 P.M. Doing this rewards those who are on time and teaches latecomers that you are serious about the schedule. Only the hardcore will continue to arrive late after they learn that your meetings start on time. If you are a member of a group instead of its leader, you can still suggest that the leader begin the meeting as scheduled. This can modify the latecomers' behavior to become more prompt as well. In some groups, names of late arrivals are noted in the minutes—an embarrassment they usually want to avoid. Sometimes there is merit in allowing a brief get-together time before the meeting, perhaps with coffee and cookies, so people can relax a bit. Either way, the meeting itself should begin as scheduled.

Introduce participants briefly (perhaps restricting introductions to name and agency), reexplain the purpose of the meeting, hand out any additional material, initiate the first topic on the agenda for discussion, and, if appropriate, offer encouragement to tackle the topic or take action.

State Ending Time at the Start

Right at the beginning of the meeting, let people know when it will end. Stick to that time. Don't allow

HIGHLIGHT 3.4

Example of an Agenda

- Agenda
- Community Welfare Council
- January 21, 2010
- Red Cross Building, Room 102
- 6:00 p.m.

1. Approval of minutes of December 20, 2009, meeting
2. Treasurer's report

3. Announcements
4. Preliminary discussion of social work month celebration (March)
5. Discussion/action on bylaw revisions
6. Approval of budget for 2010
7. Old business
8. New business
9. Adjournment

meetings to go on endlessly. Conversely, don't be afraid to end a meeting early if your work is done. Some of the most productive meetings dwindle off to oblivion and lack of conclusion because no one suggests ending them when the real business is concluded.

Let People Know How Much of Your Time They Can Have

If you are meeting with clients, colleagues, or others, let them know in advance what your schedule is. For example, specify that you have 20 minutes, 45 minutes, or even an hour and a half. This way they are more likely to stay on task. It also makes it easier when you must conclude the meeting because they know you have somewhere else to go.

Keep the Group on Target

Your role in a group may vary considerably. For the most part, we are assuming here that you play a leadership role. As the leader you must start the discussion and keep it going, clarify and summarize what others have said, and provide suggestions for new ways of thinking about or carrying out ideas.

Part of your task is to keep the group moving and on target—focused on goals and operating within time constraints (Toseland & Rivas, 2005). Encourage and allow all members to speak and ensure that quiet members are drawn out by making such comments as, "Don, we haven't heard your perspective on this. What do you think?" or "Ann, I know this issue has been especially problematic for your agency—any reactions to the suggestions we've heard so far?"

Promotion of harmony is important, but again not at the expense of thinking critically about the options. Some group leaders try to maintain harmony by stifling disagreements or differences of opinion. Often, it is better to hear all points of view and then discuss the best one instead of trying to create a false sense of harmony.

Another task of the leader is to test for agreement whenever compromises appear to be achieved. Don't assume that everyone understands the proposed compromise. You also can't assume that quiet members agree with the compromise simply because they have not expressed opposition. For example, you might say something like, "Bob, I know you have reservations about this plan. Are you comfortable enough with what is being suggested?" This gives Bob an opportunity either to show support for the plan or to voice hesitation and concerns.

Use humor to relax the group or to break the tension. Self-deprecating humor, which pokes fun at yourself, is often acceptable. Making fun of other members is not.

It is essential to avoid personal attacks and not let others engage in them. It is one thing to criticize or challenge an assumption or proposed solution. This is part of what critical thinking is all about. Making negative comments about other members or questioning their motives, however, only makes the situation worse. It invariably produces additional tension in the group. Generally speaking, we wish to keep tension low because we want an environment where people feel safe to participate (Sheafor & Horejsi, 2006).

Sometimes the leader may need to interrupt a meeting participant who talks too much. Those who hog the discussion can discourage others from participating. Long-winded speeches may be interrupted by a comment such as, "Mickie, I think we need to see if there are other points of view on this," or "We need to bring closure on this topic, Minnie, unless you're buying us all supper." Leaders also need to watch for silence, especially when it masks anger or other strong feelings. People who disagree wholeheartedly may be uncomfortable discussing it without the leader making it clear that differences of opinion are sought. At the same time, if an idea seems a bit off target, don't shoot it down immediately or let others do so. Creative ideas sometimes take getting used to. Give them a chance to be aired and considered. Also call on members with higher status last so that their opinions do not intimidate members with lower status who may disagree.

Staying on task and ensuring that all items get covered in sufficient depth are rare skills and worthy accomplishments. Sometimes you can structure this process by suggesting how members might handle certain topics, as follows:

- *You can identify items on which there is already unanimity and approve them together. This is sometimes called a* consent agenda.
- *Complex items, such as approval of a lengthy document, might be best done ad seriatim (item by item) rather than by letting people jump randomly from one section to another.*
- *Periodically summarize the areas of agreement and sum up when decisions have been made.*
- *Avoid discussing irrelevant topics or rehashing previous decisions.*
- *If new topics are brought up, it is often better to place them on future agendas. This practice avoids*

last-minute surprises or maneuvers and helps the group avoid discussion of a topic for which some members are unprepared.

- *If appropriate, a new business item can be referred to a committee. For example, a suggestion that the group hold a raffle might be referred to the finance committee rather than discussed in the larger group.*
- *Keep necessary reports brief. Longer reports should be submitted in written form and distributed to members in advance of the meeting.*
- *When oral reports are needed, ask for succinctness and place a time limit on each report. When you have set such a limit, stick to it assiduously.*

Sometimes members try to bring premature closure to a meeting to avoid dealing with a sensitive topic. In other situations, members rush to a decision without giving sufficient attention to an important item. In both situations, it is better to remind members that the topic needs their full involvement and discussion. It may also be necessary to encourage the group to consider other alternatives. For example, in a recent hiring situation, a search committee was about to recommend that two candidates be invited to come for interviews. Though the group appeared unanimous in selecting these two candidates, the group leader stated his concern that both the candidates were male and that the positions for which the applicants were applying had previously been held by two women. The group leader reminded the search committee that if both candidates were hired, the unit composition would have changed from 50 percent male and 50 percent female to 75 percent male and 25 percent female. After considering the implications of this decision, the search committee decided to invite additional women candidates who met the position qualifications.

Chairing a meeting is a tough job. Tropman, Johnson, and Tropman (1992) summarize the tasks by noting, "The chairperson must be able to lead and push, set limits, increase participation, and resolve differences. All these tasks must be accomplished in a dignified manner" so that the leader is always perceived as fair, impartial, and interested in all the members (p. 5).

End the Meeting on Time

We noted earlier that meetings should be concluded on time. However, there are times when a leader should suggest ending a meeting prior to its normal conclusion. Highlight 3.5 provides seven reasons for ending meetings.

Whenever possible, end a meeting on a high note. Summarize accomplishments, point to the good efforts of the group or of individual members, and discuss what steps will be taken to follow up on the group's decisions. Make sure that any action to occur between meetings is assigned to someone.

Plan for Follow-Up Meetings

You may have already planned for additional meetings. Perhaps you have set a schedule of meetings for the next few weeks or months. If so, the important task now is to get the minutes (official record of actions taken by the group) to the participants. Minutes should show when and where the meeting was held, who was present, and the name of the chairperson. The minutes should list the agenda items discussed, record decisions made, and list those who have tasks to do. State the meeting's ending time along with advance notice of the next meeting, if known. The minutes should be approved by the group at the start of the next meeting.

A major task following the meeting is to ensure that decisions made during the meeting are carried out. Ideally the responsible individuals have been identified, and the chair has noted who will accomplish which tasks. One potential problem in many groups is the failure to decide who will carry out the group's will. Since it is not possible to hold the entire group accountable, the chair should do whatever is needed to achieve the desired outcome. This may mean performing the task, appointing a group member to do so, or asking the group to identify the responsible person.

When one meeting is finished, the process of planning the next meeting then starts over, as just described. Of course, participants and meeting location may or may not remain the same. Highlight 3.6 provides a brief sample of minutes of a meeting.

Note that the minutes of this group do not describe who moved and seconded various motions. Some groups would record this information in the minutes.

Parliamentary Procedure

Minutes and agendas referred to in the previous section are part of *parliamentary procedure,* a highly structured technique used by groups of various sizes to make decisions and conduct business. It originated in the 14th century as a set of guides for the English parliament. The model of parliamentary procedure described in *Robert's Rules of Order* (Robert, 2000), first published in 1876, is the most commonly used set of procedures.

HIGHLIGHT 3.5

Ending Meetings

Meetings should be ended whenever any of the following is evident (Jay, 1984):

1. *More facts are required.* If a decision cannot be made without certain facts, the meeting should be ended or the group should move on to other agenda items that can be handled.
2. *The group needs the input of people not present.* This may occur when it becomes apparent that others not present will have significant roles to play in carrying out the group's plan. Sometimes the person was invited to the meeting but could not attend. Other times it becomes evident during the meeting that others should be asked to participate in the discussion.
3. *Members need more time to talk to others.* Some issues are so controversial that those present don't want to make a decision without consulting others. Agency representatives, for example, may wish to talk the matter over with their administrators or supervisors before making a decision.
4. *Events in the immediate future may change the issue's direction.* If a future event (such as a court decision, funding decision, or similar event) will significantly affect the decision the group is trying to reach, it may be best to end the discussion and wait for the event to occur. Alternately, the group can develop contingency plans to be implemented after the event occurs.
5. *There is not enough time to deal with the topic adequately.* Occasionally, we simply run out of time to discuss a subject in sufficient depth or to hear all opinions on a topic. It is better to end the meeting than to run overtime or to make a premature decision.
6. *A subgroup can handle this more easily than the entire group can.* An example of this is the decision by a board of directors to refer a discussion on the budget back to the budget committee and ask them to take another look at cutting costs. The difficulty of large groups handling certain complex topics is evident. Perhaps the issue is rewriting the bylaws of the organization. It is often difficult for a large group to write any document. Usually the task is better approached by a smaller group first. Sometimes the decision requires input from those with greater knowledge about a specific topic (like the budget committee).
7. *A decision has been reached.* Clearly, when the group reaches a decision, the meeting should be ended (or another agenda item addressed). Reaching a decision is the most common reason for ending a meeting. However, groups should not end a meeting to avoid dealing with controversial topics, because the decision is difficult or because the group's decision might be unpopular.

HIGHLIGHT 3.6

Minutes of a Meeting

- Minutes Community Welfare Council
- January 21, 2010

The meeting was convened at 6:00 P.M. by President Violet Flowers. Members in attendance included Janice Piles, Alice Yips, Nathaniel Washes, Sids Rancid, and Edward Leaks. Absent (excused) was Wrentam Magruder, who was attending a conspiracy conference in Dallas.

The minutes were approved as distributed. The treasurer's report was accepted. After a brief discussion about social work month, the matter was referred to the special affairs committee. They will report at the next meeting.

The bylaw revisions were approved by the required two-thirds majority. They will become effective after mailing to all members.

The budget was approved with one change. It was moved, seconded, and carried to move $1,000 from the contingency fund to the staff travel account.

There was no old business and no new business. The meeting adjourned at 7:30 P.M.

Respectfully submitted,
Alice Yips, Secretary

Groups generally agree in advance to use the rules to avoid last-minute disputes about how decisions will be made. Most deliberative bodies (legislatures), large task groups, and many smaller task groups use Robert's rules to facilitate their work. In fact, the bylaws and constitution (the rules by which most formal organizations operate) usually specify that the group's meetings will be conducted using *Robert's Rules of Order.*

Advantages and Disadvantages of Parliamentary Procedure

The foremost advantage to parliamentary procedure is perhaps that it allows minority elements of the group to be heard and their ideas to be considered. All group participants are allowed an opportunity to express their opinions. This helps protect those in the minority and allows them to state their concerns before the rest of the group. Parliamentary procedure is also a much faster means of resolving some issues. Attempting to reach consensus (general agreement among all members) may take much more time. Consensus requires convincing everybody present of the wisdom or acceptability of an idea. With parliamentary procedure, decisions can be reached as soon as a majority of those present is in agreement.

However, parliamentary procedure can be problematic. The nature of parliamentary procedure is that debate is heightened and encouraged, which may lead to win-lose or we-they confrontations. For example, the majority may win a vote on an issue over the strenuous objections of a minority. This can end up making the losers angry. Also, those who don't understand parliamentary procedure often find themselves being silent or unwilling to risk looking foolish. Thus, their views are not shared with the rest of the group.

Basic Parliamentary Concepts

In parliamentary procedure, the business of the group is presented in the form of *motions,* or proposed actions that the group is asked to support. Thus, a member of an agency board of directors may make a motion to approve accepting a donated vehicle from a local car distributor. The motion might be stated as follows: "I move we accept donation of the minivan from Larson Automotive and thank Mr. Larson for his most generous gift." A member who agrees with this proposal signals support by saying, "I second the motion." The motion or proposal is then open for debate or discussion by the members. After debate, the group may vote on the original motion or decide to postpone action.

A motion that is not seconded normally cannot be discussed by the group (it is the leader's responsibility to ask for a second before allowing discussion to begin). This prevents individuals from taking up the group's time by forcing discussions on topics no one else supports. Technically, motions generally fall into four categories: privileged, incidental, subsidiary, and main.

Privileged Motions

Privileged motions deal with the agenda itself but not with any particular business before the group. For example, motions to recess or adjourn are privileged motions because they affect the agenda. In the case of a motion to *recess,* the mover is asking to temporarily suspend deliberations of items on the agenda and to take a short break. A motion to *adjourn,* on the other hand, is appropriate when one wishes to end all deliberations until the next meeting. Because privileged motions can essentially end the group's deliberations entirely, they have the highest priority of the four categories. If you want the discussion to continue, it is appropriate to vote against such motions.

Incidental Motions

Procedural in nature, *incidental motions* relate to the business under discussion. Examples include *point of order* and *point of information.* These motions are used when the mover is concerned about some aspect of the way business is being transacted. For example, Sven, a member of the group, noticed that the discussion no longer related to the motion on the floor. A motion to approve purchase of a computer system evolved into a discussion about whether the offices for that agency are accessible to people with physical disabilities. At that point, Sven said, "Point of order." Sven's motion, which does not require a second, required the chairperson (or group leader) to call on Sven. (Other dimensions of the leader's role will be described later in this chapter.) Sven then said, "I believe the motion on the floor is to purchase a computer system. The discussion seems to have strayed off target." This motion is a good one for dealing with such lapses.

Point of information is a motion used when a participant is not clear about something occurring in the meeting. The chair may call for a vote on a motion when some people aren't clear about the intent of the motion. It is common then to say, "Point of information." (Getting the chairperson's attention in such a way is called being *recognized.*) Once the chair recognizes you, you might say, "If we vote in favor of this motion, does that mean that we can't change the budget until next year?" The chair would then clarify the intent of the motion and answer your question. Both motions are important but are used somewhat infrequently.

Subsidiary Motions

Subsidiary motions help deal with motions that are currently on the floor. These include motions to table, postpone, or amend the matter under debate. Each of these motions in some way handles an item on the group's agenda. For example, a motion to *table* or *postpone* essentially delays action on the proposed motion. A motion to *amend* is used when you wish to change the proposed motion in some way. Highlight 3.7 provides a more complete description of these and other motions.

Main Motions

Main motions introduce the primary issue before the group. Introducing a new proposal for debate, asking to reconsider a motion previously voted on, or requesting to remove an item previously tabled are examples of main motions. Ironically, given their title, main motions have the lowest priority because all other motions previously described can be used in some way to prevent or end debate on a main motion.

HIGHLIGHT 3.7

Common Parliamentary Definitions

Ad hoc committee: A special committee assigned one primary responsibility and then terminated.

Adjourn: To end a meeting officially.

Agenda: An official list of business to be discussed or decided at a meeting.

Amend: To add, delete, or substitute words or portions of a motion. Example: "I move to amend the motion on the floor by ..."

Bylaws: The major rules of an organization, usually more detailed than the constitution.

Call the question: A motion to stop debate and immediately vote on the matter before a group.

Committee: Any portion of the total group assigned a specific task. Examples are standing committees that always exist, ad hoc committees created as needed, and committees of the whole, in which the entire group acts as one giant committee.

Constitution: A document that describes the basic laws and governing procedures of an organization.

Debate: Discussion of topics a group is addressing.

Executive committee: A subgroup composed of the chief officers of an organization, often including one or more elected members. Responsibilities include transacting business between meetings of the entire group or organization.

Filibuster: Speaking for the primary purpose of taking up time and preventing a group from voting on a topic.

Majority vote: Greater than one half of the total of persons voting or ballots cast.

Minutes: The official record of decisions reached by a group.

Motion: A proposal, requiring action, submitted to a group. Example: "I move we donate $100 to the Community AIDS Project."

Nomination: A formal proposal for some office. Example: "I nominate Mary for treasurer."

Plurality: The receipt of more votes than any other person, but less than a majority. May occur when three persons are running for the same office.

Point of order: A statement to the presiding officer of a group that a mistake has occurred or a rule should be enforced. Example: "Point of order. I believe we already have a motion on the floor that requires a vote before we go on to other business."

Proxy: A signed statement giving another person the right to vote in one's place.

Quorum: The minimum number or proportion of members needed to legally transact business.

Recess: A short break in a meeting.

Refer to committee: A motion to delegate work on some specific matter to a smaller group.

Second: An indication of approval of a proposed motion. Example: "I second the motion."

Seriatim: A method of discussing and voting on a document by section.

Standing committee: Committee that continually exists and handles certain types of business. Example: Personnel, Finance, Nominations.

Table: A motion to indefinitely postpone action on a motion already on the floor. Example: "I move to table approval of the budget." This motion is not debatable.

Unanimous: Any vote on which there is no dissent. In other words, all members vote in favor of (or against) a proposition.

The primary principle established by parliamentary procedure is that each person has a right to be heard without interruption. The person who makes a motion speaks first on the topic. Afterward, all members have an opportunity to speak if they so wish. Debate must be related to the motion on the floor and cannot be on superfluous matters not before the group. It is not wise to allow a topic to be debated before an actual motion is on the floor. To do so encourages rambling and confusing discussions lacking focus. Once each person who wishes has had a chance to speak, the leader (chair) asks if there is any further debate. If there is none, the group then votes on the proposal. Sometimes a member of the group wishes to stop debate and bring a matter to a vote. This can be done by saying, "I call the question." This motion is not debatable. Once seconded, a motion to call the question requires an immediate vote. Because the right to discuss a motion is considered critical, stopping debate requires support from two-thirds of those voting. If the motion to call the question receives the two-thirds needed, the chair then calls for a vote on the main motion. This tactic is commonly used when debate becomes circular and nonproductive, positions are not changing, or members are eager to make decisions about the issue and get on to other items.

Ordinarily, all motions need a second. In Highlight 3.8, those in italics, however, do not need a second. Certain types of motions are debatable and others are not. In Highlight 3.8, those motions with an asterisk are debatable. Under most circumstances a simple majority of members is all that is needed to pass any given motion. However, a two-thirds majority must pass the following motions:

- *Object to consideration of a motion (this is done when an item is considered inappropriate or when the matter has already been decided at a previous meeting).*
- *Call to suspend the rules (this allows a group to operate outside Robert's Rules for a limited period of time).*
- *Call for an immediate vote (call the question—discussed previously).*
- *Limit or extend debate (may set a one-hour limit, for example, on discussion of an agenda item).*
- *Rescind a motion under consideration (does away with a motion currently being discussed).*

HIGHLIGHT 3.8

Classes of Motions

Privileged Motions

- Establishment of adjournment
- Call for adjournment
- Call for recess
- *Question of privilege*

Incidental Motions

- *Point of order*
- *Point of information*
- *Request for a revote*
- Appeal decision of the chair
- *Object to consideration of a motion*
- Request suspension of the rules
- Request to withdraw a motion previously made

Subsidiary Motions

- Table a motion
- Call for an immediate vote
- Extend or limit debate on a motion
- Postpone a motion
- Postpone a motion temporarily*
- Refer a motion to committee
- Amend a motion*
- Postpone a motion indefinitely*

Main Motions

- General main motions*
- Reconsider a motion previously voted on*
- Rescind a motion under consideration
- Resume consideration of a tabled motion

Note: Motions in *italic* do not need a second. An asterisk denotes motions that are debatable.

In point of order motions (discussed earlier), the chair's decision is final unless appealed to the group. A decision can be appealed to the group by saying, "I appeal the decision of the chair." The motion to appeal requires a second but cannot be debated. The chair will then ask, "Shall the decision of the chair be upheld? Those in favor say 'Aye'" (yes). Then the chair calls for "no" votes and announces the decision of the body.

When it is time to vote, the chair will say, "All those in favor of the motion, say 'Aye.'" It may be best to restate the motion to be voted on or to have the secretary read the motion. (The secretary is an elected member of the group, responsible for keeping the official record—minutes—of the organization's meetings.) At that point, all favoring the motion will respond, "Aye." Then the chair will call for "All opposed"—the "no" or "nay" votes—and all abstentions. The chair will decide which side prevailed based on this voice vote and announce the results. Sometimes members vote by raising their hands or by using paper ballots. This is especially true when the vote is close. Normally a simple majority must approve a motion. If a tie occurs in the voting, the motion does not pass. Sometimes the chair may vote to break a tie or to create a tie. Whether the chair is allowed to vote is often specified in the bylaws of an organization. A chairperson may choose not to vote to break a tie even when given that privilege by the bylaws.

As mentioned previously, a motion may be amended. This means it may be changed by a member proposing to add or delete something. For example, to amend a motion that authorizes purchase of a computer system, a member might say, "I move to amend the motion by placing a limit of $1,000 on the amount to be spent for each computer." This amendment also needs a second and would be voted on before the vote on the main motion. If approved, the amendment would then become a part of the original main motion. After consideration of all amendments, group members would vote on the main motion.

It should be clear in advance who is eligible to vote. Those who cannot vote should be identified. Some groups have classes of membership, some with voting privileges and some without. Sometimes visitors may be present who lack voting rights. If there is any possibility of confusion, calling for a show of hands rather than a voice vote allows you to count those entitled to vote.

Other rules governing parliamentary procedure include specification of a quorum (the minimum number of members who must be present to conduct business and make decisions) and use of an agenda. As mentioned earlier, most groups have a leader or chairperson responsible for helping the group conduct its business. A secretary keeps the minutes (the official record of a group's actions). Other officers may be needed, depending upon the type and size of the group, including a treasurer (who handles the group's dues and money) and perhaps a vice-chairperson (who replaces the chair when that person can't be present). Larger groups may create subgroups or committees to which certain business is sent for review. It is common, for example, to have both standing committees (permanent committees, such as a finance committee and a personnel committee) and special ad hoc committees (temporary committees established to address some specific issue). Committee members and the chairperson of each committee are usually appointed by the chair of the larger group. In less-formal groups, members may volunteer to serve on a committee.

The smaller the group, the less likely it is to use more formalized parliamentary procedures. Less formal procedures may allow a group to act quickly, especially if there is substantial agreement and no need for actual votes. In general, committees and subcommittees (smaller committees within larger committees) are likely to use less formal procedures. Committees and subcommittees often meet between meetings of the larger group and report their activities at regular meetings of the larger group. Committee membership may be as small as three members or as large as necessary to handle a given task.

Occasionally you will hear the term *steering committee*. A steering committee is sometimes created to help run an organization that does not want to become too formal. For example, a new neighborhood association may select a steering committee to help them get started. Once organized, the committee may select officers, set up bylaws, and the like. Such groups may reject formal titles such as chairperson or president. At the same time, the members of the steering committee are often the most political individuals in the group. In other words, they are the real movers and shakers.

A social worker skilled in the use of parliamentary procedure can be of enormous assistance to many groups. Knowing how to make motions, amend, and otherwise properly handle the group's business can make work go smoothly. Parliamentary procedure provides an orderly, predictable mechanism for handling a group's issues and decision making fairly. However, although parliamentary procedure provides a set of rules to guide groups in their deliberations, it was never meant to serve as an obstacle. Ultimately, the wishes of the group must prevail even if a violation of *Robert's Rules of Order* occurs. For example, whereas parliamentary procedural rules are clear and designed to help the group, they are not always followed closely. Sometimes the procedures called for in the rules become barriers to accomplishment of group goals. Smaller committees may decide to operate by consensus and dispense with voting on items when the group is in agreement. In addition, in legislative bodies, it is possible for a person to waste the body's time by endlessly speaking on a matter before the group. Often called *filibustering,* this method may stymie a body and prevent it from conducting its normal business. In these situations, groups may adopt other less cumbersome methods or decide to temporarily suspend some of the usual rules of parliamentary procedure.

Managing Conflict

Conflict is a fact of life—normal and, often, healthy. Disagreements over goals, methods, ideas, or almost any other topic can lead to conflict. For professionals, sources of conflict can include clients, coworkers, supervisors, or agency administrators. Conflict may occur between providers of services and consumers, between professionals with differing perspectives on service, between units or organizations seeking the same scarce resources, between organizations with sharply divergent goals and missions, or between management and workers, to name a few typical scenarios. Conflict may be based on affective (emotional) factors, such as personal animosity, or on substantive matters, such as how many workers are needed to serve child abuse victims. The latter category is more easily dealt with because these disputes often can be resolved through reasoning, acquiring additional data, and engaging in normal debate.

Conflict is common in groups and is a normal stage of development. Without it, the group often cannot move on to the next stage of problem solving. Realistically, you can't bring people with different experiences, needs, desires, and goals together without having some degree of conflict. Conflict can be positive and lead to new ideas and change. It can even get people excited about a topic and help generate alternative solutions (Fatout & Rose, 1995). When you select members of a group, choose people who have at least some degree of tolerance for conflict and acceptance of its inevitability.

Conflict is also a natural outcome of our efforts at advocating for others (CSWE, 2008, EP 2.1.5b). Those against whom the advocacy effort are aimed very likely will resent the confrontation and challenge to their ideas, decisions, and actions. In fact, the potential or actual conflict that underlies advocacy is what helps make this approach effective. For example, your level of comfort with conflictual situations may affect how successful your advocacy efforts will be. If the target of your advocacy efforts can tolerate conflict more than you, your effectiveness may well be diminished.

EP 2.1.5b

Organizations and groups must engage in conflict for a variety of purposes. Overcoming obstacles (such as staff's negative attitudes) to your agency's efforts to provide adequate services to gay and lesbian clients is a possible conflict you might face. Conflict sometimes achieves ends not otherwise attainable, such as when people are denied their basic rights and when collaborative approaches have not been successful in resolving the issue. Highlight 3.9 gives an example of how a social worker intern handled conflict in a hospital setting.

Conflict, however, can also be negative when it becomes an attack on the individual rather than on the person's ideas, gets enmeshed in a debate over values (instead of alternatives or ideas), or involves personalities. Personality conflicts are quite common and seem to reflect the inability of people to appreciate each other's strengths and good points. Personality conflicts are almost invariably negative for the two parties and, often, for those around them.

Conflict can be scary if in the past it has led to outbursts, fighting, and violence. People who associate differences of agreement with violence (perhaps occurring in their families, in other relationships, or in communities) are often very uncomfortable with conflict. Recognizing this is the first step toward meeting our goal—managing conflict.

Social workers may routinely encounter at least four forms of conflict: interpersonal conflict, conflicts over resources, representational conflicts, and intercessional conflict. Chapter 2 discusses such conflicts.

Interpersonal conflicts occur when disagreement over a concrete issue escalates to include personal attacks. The original issue could be an assessment, the best plan for a case, or who got promoted ahead of whom. The disagreement can rise to the level of conflict if both sides hold strongly to their views and are unwilling to compromise. As a result, a conflict over a

HIGHLIGHT 3.9

Conflict in the Hospital

Allison is in a dilemma. As a BSW student completing her field experience in a hospital, she is aware that the doctors make the primary decisions regarding patients. One hospital physician, Dr. Jones, has made it clear that Ms. Ortega will be discharged tomorrow. He will not prescribe a nursing home stay, though many elderly patients with similar injuries recuperate in such environments. Allison, who has talked to Ms. Ortega and her family, knows that the woman cannot take care of herself at home until her broken hip has healed.

Unfortunately, Dr. Jones finds Ms. Ortega a difficult patient. Because Ms. Ortega is Hispanic, the language barrier compounds the problem. He is adamant that she be discharged, though she really lacks a place to go. Allison cannot overturn the doctor's decision. There is little her supervisor could do about the case. Finally, Allison decides that her duty to the patient outweighs her duty to follow Dr. Jones's orders. She telephones Ms. Ortega's regular physician, Dr. O'Reilly, and explains the situation in detail. Dr. O'Reilly then orders a nursing home stay for Ms. Ortega.

Allison realized that only another doctor could overrule Dr. Jones and prescribe temporary nursing home care. Because Dr. O'Reilly is Ms. Ortega's regular doctor, his decisions carry more weight than that of a hospital staff physician. Allison has made certain that Ms. Ortega's needs are met. Dr. Jones never does find out about Allison's intercession.

---

specific area of disagreement can become personal, accompanied by a rise of attendant bad feelings.

Another form of conflict occurs over the use of, or access to, *scarce resources* such as money, time, attention, or power. One unit in an agency may receive a larger share of funds for new positions or may be suffering greater losses when the agency has to cut back on existing positions. Conflicts over resources are nearly inevitable, because we never have enough money, people, or other items to meet all the existing demands. Strom-Gottfried (1998) provides a telling example of resource conflict in the area of managed care: Managed care health insurance companies attempt to keep medical and mental health expenditures as low as possible, whereas providers such as social workers are primarily concerned with meeting the clients' needs for quality care. This difference in perspective can easily generate conflict.

Representational conflicts can occur when one person represents a group whose interests differ from those of other groups. Worker–management conflicts are of this nature. The person who is engaging in a conflictual approach is simply representing another group. Efforts to advocate for the interests of one group may be perceived as conflictual by opposing groups.

Sometimes you must intercede between two or more individuals or groups in conflict. These are *intercessional conflicts*. A family dispute that has pitted the parents against a specific child is an example. A variation of this occurs when the entire family is at war with one another and the worker, as counselor, is supposed to intercede. As you can see, conflict is a natural part of our work as social workers.

Once we recognize that conflict is almost inevitable, our goal becomes finding ways to manage or cope with it. Part of our role is to help people recognize conflict when it occurs and deal with it as straightforwardly as possible. Confirming differences of opinion and validating that people have a right to them is part of this process. Conflict should not usually be buried, but handled openly. Attaining positive outcomes in conflictual situations can be quite an achievement. Johnson and Yanca (2007) recommend discussing and negotiating the differences lying behind the conflict. By carefully listening to the points of view and reasons of both sides in a conflict, we find it easier to search for commonalities that link the conflicting parties. As part of this process, you must critically examine the logic behind a person's position and reexamine assumptions that underlie individual positions. They suggest some general steps (detailed in Highlight 3.10) for managing conflict.

Conflict in coalitions (alliances of different factions in a community) is also common. If groups have been at odds with each other in the past, it is not unusual for members to remain suspicious. Groups that have historically been oppressed often enter coalitions doubting the sincerity of other group members. They may doubt whether the other parties share their concerns or their level of commitment to change.

HIGHLIGHT 3.10

Steps in Managing Conflict

1. Seek clues to conflict—do not ignore it in anticipation that it will go away.
2. Define conflict as a group, not an individual, issue.
3. Listen to all points of view and recognize similarities and differences.
4. Employ active listening skills.
5. Clarify ideas and positions when they are unclear.
6. Avoid win-lose situations.
7. Work for cooperation, not competition.
8. Address both emotional and objective aspects of the conflict.
9. Always look for areas of agreement and common ground.
10. Focus on interests, not positions.

In coalitions where people represent a specific group, it is common for them to be torn between their responsibilities to the coalition and to their original organization. When you are part of a group working on getting a bill through the legislature, you may feel compelled to compromise your group's position in order to forge a working relationship with other coalition members. Compromise is often required to get bills passed. The coalition may push you to agree to a compromise even though it may not be as good for your group as you would have liked. This can be ameliorated somewhat if all parties recognize the greater good that brought them together in the first place. For example, a coalition of professional groups working for licensing of social workers and other human service providers found themselves often in conflict over issues such as the relative power of each group on the proposed licensing board and the wording of specific portions of the law. There were disagreements over what categories of professionals (for example, social workers, professional counselors, and marriage and family counselors) should have positions on the board. Eventually, by staying focused on the ultimate goal of getting all their groups licensed, the coalition learned to successfully manage major conflicts.

Bisno (1988) has helped our understanding of conflict by discussing both the types of conflict that you might encounter and various conflict management strategies. The following section draws heavily upon his insights.

Types of Conflict

Categorizing conflict helps us recognize that there are many types of conflict. As a result, our ways of managing conflict may change. Bisno (1988) and Strom-Gottfried (1998) highlight eight different types of conflict: interest/commitment conflict, induced conflict, misattributed conflict, data conflicts, structural conflict, illusionary conflict, displaced conflict, and expressive conflict.

Interest/Commitment Conflict

Interest/commitment conflicts are characterized by basic genuine clashes of opposing interests, values, or commitments. Disagreements over abortion clearly exemplify this. On the one hand, some people are strongly supportive of women's rights to control their bodies and believe that women must have reproductive freedom. On the other hand, some people are just as convinced that abortion is a form of murder and should be totally abolished.

Induced Conflict

Induced conflict is created to reach goals that could otherwise not be attained directly. It is created by individuals as a way of stirring up bad feelings among members of the group. An example of this is Ted, a social worker who is generally regarded as relatively ineffective in his agency because he has not participated in any continuing education efforts for the past 10 years. The agency administration is proposing a requirement that all workers attend a certain number of workshops or other learning experiences each year, a seemingly reasonable expectation.

Knowing that he does not have the power or support to prevent the adoption of such a requirement, Ted begins to stir up conflict. First, he warns people that the administration is usurping the social worker's professional prerogative by this rule. He suggests that as professionals, they should be the judge of whether they need additional training. Then he tells others that the agency is not going to provide any financial support for workers to attend these workshops. Finally, he emphasizes how the workers need to stand together against this arbitrary intrusion into their professional lives. By the time Ted is finished, several workers are viewing the situation from Ted's point of view and vowing to fight the proposal.

Ultimately, Ted has created a conflict out of thin air and placed the workers and administration in an adversarial position. By doing this he hopes to protect his own job and regain some of the influence he used to have in the agency.

Misattributed Conflict

Misattributed conflict is based on an honest mistake. It is conflict based upon incorrectly attributing behaviors or ideas to people or groups. It can be based on stereotyping or simply mistaken thinking about what someone said or did. It is important to recognize this is a real source of conflict, even though the source has been incorrectly identified. For example, Elwood Drab hung up the phone and turned to his assistant with a look of pure frustration. "That was Jim Boyles, our lobbyist at the capital. He says the bill to provide grant money for new drug abuse programs just got bottled up in the senate's public health committee. Jim thinks the committee got pressure from the public employees' union, who were afraid the bill would lead to shifting jobs from the state to private agencies. Set up a meeting with union president Tura Lye, and let's hit this thing head-on. There is no way that this bill threatens state jobs, and we need to convince her of that." With that, Elwood set off on a collision course with the union president. Unknown to Elwood (and to Jim), however, was the fact that the union did not oppose the bill. Rather, the source of the problem was a state senator who had heard that the grant program would teach students about drugs, an idea he vehemently opposed. Elwood was to discover his mistake too late. He had attributed the conflict to the wrong adversary. Moreover, he failed a basic premise of critical thinking, namely, that you base your actions on sound evidence. Because lobbyist Jim Boyles only "thought" the union was a problem, Elwood should have gotten his facts straight first.

Data Conflicts

Data conflicts occur when two sides have either inconsistent or inadequate data upon which to make decisions. Without accurate information, resolving such conflicts is difficult. At the same time, if both sides have access to the same data, resolution of the conflict is much more likely. A commitment to make decisions based upon accurate information is essential to ending conflicts of this nature.

Structural Conflict

Structural conflicts are disputes arising from differences in such factors as power, time, or physical or other environmental barriers (Strom-Gottfried, 1998). Power differentials are evident in Highlight 3.9, where the social worker clearly does not have the power to sway the doctor's decision about Ms. Ortega. Resolution of this dispute required that the power be equalized in some way, for example, through the use of an outside physician.

Time may contribute to a conflict when two parties do not see the same degree of urgency in a particular situation. A social worker may believe immediate action is needed, for example, in the case of a client requiring hospitalization to prevent a suicide. At the same time, a managed-care company, a supervisor, or other decision maker may feel that the client is only bluffing.

Physical and environmental barriers may produce conflict when two parties are not able to discuss differences face to face. Trying to communicate one's position through such mediums as writing, e-mail, voicemail, or in a telephone conversation does not always work, because the physical separation between parties precludes access to nonverbals such as facial expression, tone, or gestures. These nonverbal communication methods help us assess the truthfulness and sincerity of the people with whom we are talking. Absent these methods, we are left with much more limited information upon which to make our decisions—thus almost guaranteeing conflict.

Illusionary Conflict

Illusionary conflict is similar to misattributed conflict in that it rests on a mistake. Here, though, we are not dealing with something that actually happened but was blamed on the wrong person or group. In illusionary conflict, the disagreement rests on misperceptions or misunderstandings arising from confusion about, or lack of knowledge of, another party. In other words, there is no real conflict at all. An example may help explain this. Juan proposes the creation of a new unit in his agency to deal with perpetrators of domestic violence. The proposal is placed on the agenda of the board of directors for approval. At the last minute, Juan learns that Sally, the assistant director, has asked that the proposal be dropped from the agenda. Juan is furious, thinking that Sally is opposed to serving perpetrators because of her background working with victims of domestic violence. He goes to her office steaming, expecting a conflict over the proposal. When he gets there, Sally explains that she asked to have the proposal dropped because the board would not have time to consider the idea at this meeting because of other more pressing concerns. She promises Juan that it will be back on the next agenda with her full support.

Displaced Conflict

Displaced conflict is directed at people or concerns other than the real source of conflict. This arises when you get upset at work and take it out on others at home, or vice versa. You are really unhappy with a conflict in one area, but you vent the conflict in a totally unrelated area.

Expressive Conflict

Expressive conflict rests primarily on a wish to express hostility, aggression, or other strong feelings. In other words, conflict exists because someone is blowing off steam. Expressive conflict can occur when people who have not been responding assertively hold their feelings in over a long period of time and then finally explode over some minor issue.

Conflict arouses strong feelings and emotions in most people. Typically, social workers are no more fond of conflict than the rest of the population. We want to help people, to be liked and appreciated. Most important, unlike attorneys, we lack conflict training. Despite these hurdles, however, we can employ a variety of conflict management strategies when we are forced to deal with conflict. Johnson and Yanca (2007), Mayer (1995), and Strom-Gottfried (1998) have all suggested possible ways of resolving conflict, which appear in Highlight 3.10. These are relatively simple approaches that can be easily employed.

Advanced Conflict Management: Guidelines and Strategies

Methods listed in Highlight 3.10 for resolving and preventing conflict will not work in every situation. In addition, you may not wish to resolve the conflict but to use it to achieve professional goals. In such situations, you need advanced conflict management skills, addressed next.

Focusing on Power

Following are three general guidelines for using advanced conflict management strategies. All three address power issues.

1. *Always assess both your power and that of your adversary.* This is important because some conflict resolution strategies require you to use your available power. Knowing what power the adversary has will help you select the appropriate strategy. Sandra has lobbied hard with members of the city council to get them to approve funding for a new summer recreation program for children. Just one hour before the council is to meet, Henry Waddle, a local doctor, calls Sandra and tells her he is going to attend the meeting and speak in opposition to her proposal. Sandra explains why the program is important and says she welcomes his expression of reservations about the proposal.

   After talking with Dr. Waddle, Sandra quickly assesses her situation. Five of the seven council members have told her they will support her proposal. She knows that Dr. Waddle is considered something of a nuisance, because he is always speaking against spending money on social programs. Sandra correctly surmises that she has more power (in the form of pledges of support for the program) than does Dr. Waddle. She knows she can even afford to lose one of her supporters and still win by a four-to-three vote. Thus, she decides that she does not have to exert any more energy or effort to counter Dr. Waddle's influence.

2. *Avoid full disclosure of your power.* Never let the adversary know exactly how much power you have. This can be effective in two ways. First, the adversary may assume you have more power than you do. This works to your advantage. Second, because the adversary does not know the amount of power you have available, it makes it doubly difficult for him to respond. Think of it as a card game. If the opposing player does not know whether you have a good hand, she will have a hard time knowing what to do.

3. *Always use power sparingly.* Use only as much as needed to reach an objective. This avoids the possibility of overkill and still leaves your opponent in the dark about your strength. In the case just noted, Sandra could call others who might try to dissuade Dr. Waddle from coming to the meeting. Or she could tell Dr. Waddle how many votes she already has, thereby disclosing her own strength. Rather, Sandra plays it cool and never lets her opponent know how much support she has. Nor does she try to influence Dr. Waddle by having others call him. Such a tactic might lead him to think that the program has little support on the council and that his statement can change the outcome.

Other advanced strategies for conflict management are described next. In each we will indicate when the approach might be used and suggest some appropriate strategies and tactics to reach the goal of conflict management.

Forestalling or Sidestepping Conflict

It may be better to forestall or sidestep conflict when other approaches offer more promise, when the costs are too high, when conflict is inappropriate, or when the issues are not that important. Dinh Trong is in such a situation. Dinh is discussing with a fellow social worker how to handle a situation with their supervisor. The supervisor, Marvin, has just told Dinh that the agency plans to phase out its refugee mentor program when the grant expires next year. Dinh strongly supports the program but is a new worker in the agency. The colleague cautions that Dinh is still in a probationary period and thus is especially vulnerable to being fired. Engaging in a conflict with Marvin right now will probably cause more trouble than it's worth. Because the grant has another nine months to run and Dinh will be off probation in three months, the colleague suggests avoiding a conflict right now. Dinh follows the recommendation.

Of course, these strategies are characterized by avoidance and their use can prevent future problems. For one thing, you can identify potential areas of future conflict. Using this information, you can anticipate where problems are likely to occur later. Although Dinh decides not to act now, she recognizes Marvin as a potential adversary in efforts to keep the refugee mentor program.

Another way to avoid serious problems with conflict is to ensure that people feel free to criticize or raise questions about policies, procedures, or decisions. Some agencies seem to have an in-house critic who serves as a lightning rod for worker concerns. Instead of avoiding such people, managers and supervisors should listen to what they are saying. Often, they can provide advance warnings of problems or conflictual situations.

Of course, you also can avoid conflict by denying that any disagreement exists. This ignores the problem in hopes that it will go away. This "head-in-the-sand" approach is not very fruitful, because it does not lead to resolution of the conflict. Dinh can pretend that Marvin is in agreement, but this will not really be the case.

Another tactic is to leave the agency. This approach, of course, is drastic and should be used only in extreme situations. Dinh can quit over the issue of eliminating

the program but will also lose the ability to influence future events.

Finally, you can simply give in and agree that the opposing side is right. You might actually be convinced that the other side has a better argument or position, or you may not have the energy or ability to continue your opposition. Again, the tactic used depends on the amount of power at your disposal and the seriousness of the issue.

Homan (2004) warns that avoidance of conflict will be counterproductive within organizations. He recommends using other strategies whenever possible rather than simply ducking the issue. Conflict situations that are avoided can seem even larger and more problematic than they really are. Also, the conflict can erupt at almost any time and affect other areas of decision making and operations. Leaving it to fester is rarely wise.

Generating Conflict

Another approach to managing conflict is to create it. You can use this strategy when other nonconflictual approaches have failed or when you have sufficient power or influence to win on an issue. This approach also assumes that the cost of conflict is acceptable. The strategies include identifying potential conflicts and situations where conflict would be desirable. Then, conflict itself is created through a variety of tactics. Had Dinh been an experienced worker with strong support from her colleagues, she might have told Marvin that eliminating the refugee mentor program was dead wrong. She could have insisted on presenting her case to the agency director and brought in other workers who felt the same way. She could also have mobilized community support for the program. Again, this approach works best when you know you have enough power or influence to win the conflict.

Conflict can also be created through strategies such as consciousness-raising, whereby you attempt to get others who have been neutral to see the seriousness of the issues. This tactic has been useful in helping women recognize the many ways in which they are oppressed in a male-dominated society. Women's consciousness can be raised concerning self-esteem, assertiveness, and male–female communication issues.

Another tactic is exposing false consensus—or pointing out what no one else seems to want to talk about. This may be effective in situations in which there is an undercurrent of conflict that does not surface directly. For example, there were rumors that the director of an agency was looking for another position and might be leaving. She was well-respected and had successfully sought additional resources and better salaries for the workers. When the agency administration suggested setting up a committee to develop a new strategic plan, almost no one expressed any interest in participating. The workers were unwilling to work on a plan for the future when they did not know if they could count on the director to be there to help make it happen. It seemed like a waste of time to many of them.

Rather than leave supervisors with the impression that they were not interested in the agency's future, Rosanne decided to act. She quietly said what others were feeling—that many felt anxious about the future because of the possible loss of the director. Only when the group was able to discuss their concerns and fears about this uncertainty could they begin to think about the future.

Encouraging and articulating areas of disagreement (instead of accentuating commonalities) is another useful tactic to generate conflict. This helps to polarize issues and people. Then, if people see that others don't share their views, they can decide whether the issue is important enough to warrant further conflict.

Conflict Management by Covert Means

Conflict can also be managed by *covert means,* which are subtle ways of influencing issues. Because these methods are hidden, opponents may not recognize the power used against them. This approach is useful when the instigator can't cope with overt conflict, perhaps because his or her situation is too precarious. It might also be used when the costs of open conflict are too high for the conflict generator or when an opponent won't play by the rules to resolve the conflict. Perhaps the opponent is avoiding conflict by denying it exists and refusing to talk about it. Dinh could have quietly passed the word to the refugee community, their supporters, and others interested in the mentor program about Marvin's intention to end the program. Without getting drawn into the conflict herself, she could encourage others to mobilize their power to ensure that the program survived. This reduces the risk to Dinh, who is still a probationary worker. The risk of using covert means is that one treads awfully close to the edges of ethical behavior. It should be used only under the most compelling circumstances.

Other valuable strategies include passive resistance, concealment, and manipulation. *Passive resistance* means that you simply drag your feet in ways that create problems for the opponent. This might take the

form of turning in important forms late. It also could include operating strictly by the book. An example is an administrative assistant whose job description states she spends approximately 20 percent of her time typing. When she reaches the 20 percent mark each week, she simply refuses to do any more typing that week. Of course, this rankles her supervisor and those who depend upon her typing.

Concealment means exactly what it says. You do not let the other party know what you are doing. You hide your plan and your activity. This strategy works because the other party doesn't know what you're up to. This was the method employed by Allison in Highlight 3.9.

Manipulation means that you influence others without their being aware of it. This takes great skill and must be done in a way that does not compromise your ethical integrity. Alice leaves little anonymous reminders in her supervisor's mailbox about how rigid the supervisor can get. The reminders include a plaque that looks like a one-way street sign. It reads:

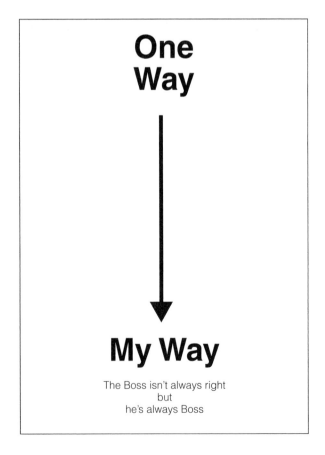

The boss gradually becomes more flexible, partly because of the manipulation used by the worker to suggest the need to change.

More Specific Tactics

The strategies just identified are broad approaches to conflict, but one can use other, more specific techniques or tactics. The six tactics that accompany these strategies can vary dramatically. They include negativism and noncompliance, stonewalling, deceit, seduction, emotional extortion, and divide and conquer.

Negativism and noncompliance with rules. Workers in a social service agency decide to deal covertly with a disputed agency policy specifying that they must exit by a certain door instead of the one closest to their parking lot and offices. The agency director is concerned about the security of employees using the closer door, but the approved door forces workers to walk an extra block to reach their cars. They consider this a nuisance because they are always in a hurry. Nearly every worker in the agency deliberately uses the parking lot exit as a show of noncompliance with the policy.

Stonewalling. This simply means refusing to act on a matter. It is a favorite tactic for dealing with policies that you find abhorrent. Operationally, it means that you refuse to enforce the policy, although you may not do this openly. Perhaps the policy requires workers to have their paperwork up-to-date before they can take time off. Supervisors who disagree with the policy might simply look the other way and refuse to enforce the rule.

Deceit or deception. This approach is not honest. Deception might be used to make others think you have more power than you really do. A community group convinces the county board to support a new program by arranging for each member of the board to receive multiple letters on the topic. Because few people take the time to write their elected representatives, a dozen letters on a single topic make it seem that there is widespread support for the new program. Actually, the group interested in the program numbered about a dozen.

Another related method is *seduction,* or the offering of inducements to convince neutral parties to join you or to convert opponents to your side. This method is routinely used in Congress and state legislatures. It works because one senator, for example, from the State of New York, wants the support of other senators to pass her bill providing new money for a subway system in New York City. To get the support of others, she offers to add to her bill a provision in which the State of Kentucky gets increased government subsidies for tobacco farmers. Of course, inducements such as this increase the cost of government.

Emotional extortion. One party with sufficient influence can induce another to change by withholding something valued by the other. The thing of value could be attention. Making others feel guilty about their behavior is another form of emotional extortion. Of course, these strategies are often at odds with ethical considerations.

Divide and conquer. This tactic reduces the influence of the adversary and neutralizes opposing players by approaching opponents individually or by bringing up subjects that produce a split within the opponent's ranks. One key member of a group might be offered a chance to achieve his own personal goals if he switches sides or remains neutral in a conflict. It is also possible to split a group's solidarity by getting it involved in a debate over which there is substantial disagreement. Those opposed to abortion, for example, are often divided about whether abortion is ever warranted. A bill to outlaw *all* abortions might be defeated because many abortion foes recognize its value in cases of rape, incest, or a threat to the life of the mother. Thus, the group's solidarity could be ruptured by an opponent who forces discussion of these divisive issues.

Conflict Management by Emergent Agreement

Managing conflict through *emergent agreement* works when one side convinces the other to change. Perhaps this follows the introduction of new evidence. For example, you might resolve differences by gathering data. Of course, both sides must be willing to look for new answers. Agreements resolved by the introduction of new data usually involve lower stakes and limited costs and risks. On the other hand, conflicts arising from differences in values do not yield easily to new data or information.

Conflict Management by Coactive Disputation

Another tactic to produce an agreement is called *coactive disputation,* wherein both parties are willing to consider joint problem solving, use facts to settle disputes, and remain open to persuasion. Thus, a group trying to pass a licensing law for mental health practitioners might sit down and try to resolve their differences so that they can jointly support a single bill. If they let their differences become a barrier, no one group will get what it wants. By working together to solve their disputes, they emerge a stronger force for change.

Conflict Management by Negotiated Agreement

EP 2.1.10k

Negotiated agreement occurs when both *sides* see negotiation as a logical way to end their disagreement. Negotiation is a process of bringing opposing parties together in order to arrive at a mutually satisfying agreement through discussion, compromise, bargaining, and other means (CSWE, 2008, EP 2.1.10k). It works when there are no large disparities in power between the two sides. Labor unions and businesses often reach negotiated agreements because both stand to lose substantially if they remain at an impasse. Employers cannot run their businesses without workers, and workers cannot live without their paychecks. Thus, both sides feel pressure to compromise.

Another tactic to manage conflict is to help all sides recognize and acknowledge the goals and interests of the other parties. This can be helpful, as all sides see that what the others want is not outlandish or ridiculous. It also can spur different sides to come up with creative outcomes or proposals that help others move toward or reach their goals. Sometimes, it also becomes clear that there is overlap in the goals and interests of different parties, suggesting that their differences are smaller than they appear.

Regular, patient communication and good listening skills can also help you arrive at an agreement. Messages need to be clear to reduce potential confusion. Confused people often say no to ideas they don't understand. Because the primary strategy here is negotiation, the tactics logically follow these steps: define the issues of disagreement, use objective criteria for settling the dispute, and seek mutually beneficial outcomes. An employer and a workers' union, for example, might agree to use an objective criterion—a specific index of inflation, for instance—as the basis for determining future raises.

Conflict Management by Indirect Means or Procedural Measures

This approach is employed in two situations—first, when both sides cannot or will not negotiate; second, when other management approaches are unpalatable. The typical solution is to submit the disagreement to a third party or *arbitrator* (a third party who both sides agree can help settle their differences). In some cases arbitration is required by law. Many public school districts and teachers' unions must by law submit their labor disputes to binding arbitration. In binding arbitration, the arbitrator's decision is binding on both parties. This way, they allow another party to settle things without having to resort to more drastic tactics such as striking.

Conflict Management by Exercise of Authority/Power

Exercising authority or power can simply overcome the opposition. Typically, the more powerful side uses it against the other less powerful faction when other methods either won't work or are unacceptable.

Tactics include rigidly enforcing rules, setting limits, going on strike, ordering the opponent to act a certain way, or firing the conflicting person(s). These more drastic approaches have many drawbacks. The fact that one side is clearly the loser in the conflict is a problem. Other approaches, such as negotiating, provide solutions from which each side can claim some satisfaction.

On a positive note, research has demonstrated that conflict management strategies can be taught to elementary school children with very good results for disputes involving peers and parents (Gentry & Benenson, 1993). Conflict resolution and mediation strategies are also being used to help eliminate problems in organizations of all sizes.

As we stated at the beginning of this section, conflict is natural and predictable. Anticipating that it will occur, learning about various types of conflict, and considering ahead of time the possible approaches to conflict management can only increase your effectiveness as a social worker.

In addition, understanding organizations (the subject of Chapter 4) and communities (Chapter 8) requires that you appreciate the role that conflict plays in both of these areas. The achievement of social work goals in these areas often demands that you use, resolve, or accept conflict.

Chapter Summary

The following summarizes this chapter's content as it relates to the learning objectives presented at the beginning of the chapter. Chapter content prepares social workers to:

A. *Demonstrate leadership skills needed to promote sustainable changes in service delivery and practice to improve the quality of social work services.*

Leadership skills include the ability to identify targets for change and to inspire others to undertake that change. It also includes skills of assertiveness, both written and oral communication skills, and the capacity to lead others by example. Effective leaders are capable of offering new perspectives on situations, using self (which includes self-awareness, self-disclosure, and purposefulness), and managing conflict.

B. *Engage in networking to analyze, formulate, and advocate for policies that advance social well-being.*

Networks are groups of individuals or organizations interconnected to accomplish a worthwhile goal. Networking is beneficial from a number of perspectives. It provides clients with informal assistance that augments what is available from formal resource systems. Networks can and do reach out to clients and help them navigate formal systems. Networking can also be a resource for helping workers cope with their own professional stesses and strains.

Networks differ depending upon such factors as the type of relationships among members, the degree of intimacy they share, the difficulty level of help members require, and the size of the network. Networks can be both enormously helpful but also challenging. These challenges can occur when professionals do not adequately value the networks or, conversely, take such an active leadership role as to diminish the contributions of other members of the network. In some cases, networks can be hurt by poor interpersonal relationships among members or by failing to share information with all members of the group. Another common challenge is maintaining confidentiality about a client's situation. Effective social work practice helps reduce these challenges through overt steps to value and acknowledge the contributions of all network members and to foster communication through such things as newsletters and face-to-face meetings.

C. *Utilize teamwork and collaboration with colleagues and clients for improving agency services and social policies.*

Opportunities to work with teams are common. These may be interdisciplinary teams with representatives of other professions or other task-oriented groups. Effective teams have clear goals, clearly delineated structure, and membership that is tied to the goals with commitment of all members. A collaborative climate, a set of standards used to make team decisions, and the practice of making decisions based upon information rather than feelings is another measure of an effective team. Finally, effective teams have external support and recognition for their work along with principled leadership that values the work of the team.

D. *Utilize professional skills in planning and conducting meetings within groups, organizations and communities.*

Meetings are a common occurrence in social work. Effective meetings involve the following characteristics. First, meetings are well planned in advance with clear purpose and objectives. Participants are selected based on the capabilities needed for the task at hand. The time and place must be communicated clearly along with an agenda of what will occur at the meeting. Starting and ending the meetings on time is important, as well as staying focused on both the tasks to be accomplished and the time available. Decisions reached at the meeting should be followed up either outside of the meeting or in subsequent meetings.

Depending upon the size and formality of the group that is meeting, it is important to be familiar with parliamentary procedures that can facilitate the business before the body. This includes understanding the advantages and disadvantages of parliamentary procedure, the use of motions to conduct business, common definitions used, and classes of motions.

E. *Employ conflict management to help resolve organizational and community problems.*

Conflict is a common factor in most areas of life and can occur among individuals, groups, and organizations, among others. Conflicts may be classified based on whether they revolve around different interests or commitments, structure, or disagreement over data. Sometimes conflicts are caused by members in order to create problems for a group or organization, while at other times simple confusion or misunderstandings may be at fault.

Managing conflict can involve a series of steps, including seeking to identify the source of the conflict, defining it as a group problem, employing active listening to all points of view, clarifying unclear ideas and positions, avoiding win-lose situations with a focus on cooperation, recognizing both emotional and objective aspects of the conflict, and seeking common ground based on shared interests.

Guidelines for conflict can also be employed when the conflict is necessary to achieve professional goals. These include focusing on both your power and that of your adversary, knowing when to forestall or sidestep conflict, generating conflict when it is needed, and managing it by both covert and overt methods. Covert methods include passive resistance, concealment, manipulation, negativism and noncompliance with rules, stonewalling, deception, inducements to convince others, emotional extortion, and divide-and-conquer approaches. However, it is important to point out that some of the covert approaches can be at odds with ethical considerations. Overt methods include conflict management by emergent agreement, coactive disputation, negotiated agreement, indirect means or procedural measures, and exercise of authority or power.

Competency Notes

The following identifies where Educational Policy (EP) competencies and practice behaviors are discussed in the chapter.

Educational Policy (EP) 2.1 Core Competencies:

Educational Policy (EP) 2.1.1b Practice personal reflection and self-correction to assure continual professional development. *(P 90):* It is critical that social workers recognize and examine their own motivations and actions and monitor themselves on a continuous basis.

Educational Policy (EP) 2.1.1c Attend to professional roles and boundaries. *(P 98):* Workers may play multiple roles in networks, including providing a place to meet, help in fundraising, sharing information, training leaders, making and accepting referrals, arranging publicity, adding credibility to the group, consulting, and providing various forms of social support.

Educational Policy (EP) 2.1.3: Apply critical thinking to inform and communicate professional judgment. *(P 101):* Critical thinking helps the social worker sort through information that may or may not be accurate or complete and to make informed judgments.

Educational Policy (EP) 2.1.3c Demonstrate effective oral and written communication in working with individuals, families, groups, organizations, communities, and colleagues. *(P 89):* Social workers must be effective communicators using both writing and speaking to convey information, ideas, and proposals.

Educational Policy (EP) 2.1.5b Advocate for human rights and social and economic justice. *(P 112):* Advocating for others often generates conflict, which the social worker must learn how to manage effectively.

Educational Policy (EP) 2.1.8b Collaborate with colleagues and clients for effective policy action. *(P 98):* Working with teams enhances opportunities to collaborate and increases the potential for effective policy action.

Educational Policy (EP) 2.1.9b Provide leadership in promoting sustainable changes in service delivery and practice to improve the quality of social services. *(P 88):* One goal of leadership is helping to promote changes in service delivery and practice that improve the quality of social services. *(P 96):* One skill of a leader is knowing how to prepare agendas for meetings. *(P 104):* The ordering of agenda items should consider which topics require discussion and those that are for informational purposes only.

Educational Policy (EP) 2.1.10c Develop a mutually agreed-on focus of work and desired outcomes. *(P 102):* Social workers must help clarify the purpose and objectives of meetings to avoid wasting time and encourage a focus on outcomes.

Educational Policy (EP) 2.1.10k Negotiate, mediate, and advocate for clients. *(P 120):* Negotiation is a process of bringing opposing parties together to arrive at a mutually satisfying agreement through discussion, compromise, bargaining, and other means.

On the Internet

Visit the *Generalist Practice with Organizations and Communities* Web site at *www.cengage.com/social_work/ kirst-ashman* for learning tools such as PowerPoint® slides, tutorial quizzing, Web links, and final exams.

CHAPTER 4

Understanding Organizations

Suppose you are a newly graduated social worker. All those years of grinding out papers and all-nighting it before exams have finally paid off. You have been looking at the Sunday want ads for "social workers," "counselors," "health care workers," "case managers," and any other titles you think might apply to you. You are finally going to be making money at a job instead of paying money out to get your education.

You're faced with a number of questions: What kind of social work do I want to do most? In what social work field am I most likely to get a job? How much money should I ask for? What might each job be like? What is the agency advertising the position like?

Additional questions you might ask yourself as you ponder entering the world of agency life might include the following:

- *Who will do the hiring?*
- *What will my supervisor be like?*
- *How much vacation will I get?*
- *What rules will the agency have?*
- *Will the agency dress standards be formal or informal? What exactly should I wear?*
- *What working hours will be required?*
- *How much freedom will I have in my work?*
- *What will my clients be like?*
- *How will my clients respond to me?*
- *What will the agency staff expect me to know already?*
- *How much training can I expect to get?*
- *What will my coworkers be like?*
- *How will I fit into a staff already used to working with each other?*

Introduction

This chapter will introduce you to work in organizations. We have established that an organization is a type of macro system. When you begin working in an organization, you become part of that larger system. In order to fit well, you'll need to understand how such large systems work. When the system is not working as well as it could, you may decide to try to change it—an action that will also require substantial understanding of how organizations are run.

Frequently, professionals just beginning their social work careers find the direct interaction and work with clients fascinating and exciting. Larger systems such as organizations and communities may hold less allure, but a solid foundation of knowledge and insight into how these large systems function is necessary for you to do your job effectively.

Learning Objectives

This chapter will provide content concerning how social workers:

A. *Examine organizations and their macro environments to enhance practice effectiveness.*

B. *Describe and analyze conceptual frameworks that empower or fail to empower organizations and staff as they provide services.*

C. *Assess organizational operations from a systems perspective.*

D. *Demonstrate ethical behavior when involved in agency politics.*

E. *Describe and analyze managed health care and assess its ethical implications.*

F. *Describe organizations that work with refugees and immigrants from a global perspective.*

G. *Identify and become involved in national and international social work organizations that exist to promote macro practice and the pursuit of social justice.*

H. *Recognize value discrepancies between social workers and traditional bureaucracies, and practice effectively within a bureaucracy.*

I. *Explain current trends in management.*

J. *Practice within settings employing two different management approaches—total quality management and service learning.*

K. *Demonstrate client empowerment on a macro level.*

Defining Organizations, Social Services, and Social Agencies

Before saying another thing about organizations and your social work practice within them, we need to clearly define the terms involved. These include *organization, agency,* and *social services.* A range of systems

concepts used in describing how macro systems operate will also be defined and discussed.

Organizations

Organizations are "(1) social entities that (2) are goal directed, (3) are designed as deliberately structured and coordinated activity systems, and (4) are linked to the external environment" (Daft, 2010b, p. 11). Each of the four numbered elements merits detailed discussion.

1. *Organizations are social entities.* Organizations are made up of people, with all their strengths and failings. Organizations may therefore exhibit similar positive attributes and weaknesses. Because organizations prescribe how people should behave and what responsibilities employees are to assume in their jobs, patterns of behavior develop in organizations just as patterns of behavior develop in people.

2. *Organizations are goal-directed.* They exist for a specified purpose. Social service organizations, for instance, are formed to provide services and resources to help people in some way. It is important to understand what an organization's goals are and to assess whether the organization's goals are really beneficial for clients. Finally, it is crucial to examine whether the organization is, in reality, attaining its goals for clients.

3. *Organizations are deliberately structured and coordinated activity systems.* Activity systems are clusters of work activities performed by designated units or departments within an organization. Such systems are guided by technology (the practical application of knowledge to achieve desired ends). An organization coordinates the functioning of various activity systems to enhance its own efficiency in attaining its goals. Organizations have structures that include policies for how the organization should be run, hierarchies of how personnel are supervised and by whom, and different units working in various ways to help the organization function.

   For example, an intake unit for a large county department of social services is an activity system. Workers under supervision process new cases by following established procedures, obtaining required information, and making referrals to the appropriate service providers.

   Another example is a family services organization that has a number of activity systems, including one staff unit providing marriage and family counseling, another providing family life educa-tion,[1] and still another focusing on community ac-tivities aimed at family advocacy, recreation, and support (Barker, 2003). Each unit pursues different functions in order to achieve the agency's general goal of providing family services.

All organizations have structures: For example, a toilet-seat factory might have one unit responsi-ble for designing seats, one for manufacturing them, and another for marketing them.

4. *Organizations are linked to the external environ-ment.* An organization is in constant interaction with other systems in the social environment, in-cluding individuals, groups, other organizations, and communities. Agencies providing social ser-vices interact dynamically with clients, funding sources, legislative and regulatory agencies, politi-cians, community leaders, and other social service agencies.

The term *organization,* then, is a broad concept. Organizations comprise groups of people, tools, and resources structured to accomplish any of a wide range of objectives. For instance, organizations include the Girl Scouts of America, Wal-Mart, the Pentagon, Enthronement of the Sacred Heart Archdiocesan Cen-ter, and the John Birch Society. The following sections will explore more thoroughly the specific types of or-ganizations in which social workers practice.

Social Services

This chapter focuses on organizations that provide so-cial services to clients. *Social services* include the tasks that social work practitioners and other helping profes-sionals perform for improving people's health, enhanc-ing their quality of life, increasing their self-sufficiency, supporting families, and helping people and larger sys-tems improve their functioning in the social environ-ment (Barker, 2003). That is quite a mouthful. In essence, social services include the wide range of activ-ities that social workers perform in their efforts to help people solve problems and improve their personal well-being. Social services may be *institutional,* that is, those provided by major public service systems that

---

1. *Family life education* is a group-learning program that focuses on addressing a wide range of life issues and crises (Barker, 2003; Har-ris, 2008). It is typically led by a social worker or other helping pro-fessional in any of a variety of settings, including health care centers, schools, churches, and community centers. Virtually any important life issue can be addressed, ranging from newborn care to child man-agement to preparation for retirement.

administer such benefits as financial assistance, hous-ing programs, health care, or education (Barker, 2003). They might also include *personal social services* that address more individualized needs involving interper-sonal relationships and people's ability to function within their immediate environments. Such services usually target specific groups (such as children or older adults) or particular problems (such as family planning or counseling) (Barker, 2003).

The terms "social services," "human services," and sometimes "social welfare" are often used interchange-ably when referring to organizations, agencies, and agency personnel. *Human services* are "programs and activities designed to enhance people's development and well-being" (Barker, 2003, p. 204). *Social welfare* is the "nation's system of programs, benefits, and ser-vices that help people meet those social, economic, educational, and health needs that are fundamental to the maintenance of society" (Barker, 2003, p. 408).

Social Agencies

A *social agency* or *social services agency* is an organiza-tion providing social services that typically employs a range of helping professionals, including social work-ers, office staff, paraprofessionals (persons trained to assist professionals), and, on occasion, volunteers (Barker, 2003). Social agencies generally serve some designated client population experiencing some defined need. Services are provided according to a prescribed set of policies.

Social agencies may be public or private. *Public* social agencies are run by a designated unit of govern-ment and are usually regulated by laws that directly affect policy. For example, a county board committee oversees a public welfare department and is responsible for establishing its major policies. (Of course, such a committee must follow rules set by any state or federal government that provides any of the money for the agency's programs.)

Private social agencies, on the other hand, are pri-vately owned and run by people not employed by a government. The services they provide include per-sonal social services. Note that sometimes services resemble those furnished by public social agencies such as corrections, protective services for children, and job preparation and training for public assistance recipients.

Private social agencies may be either nonprofit or proprietary. *Nonprofit* social agencies are run to ac-complish some service provision goal, not to make fi-nancial profit for private owners. Funding for services can range from tax money to private donations to grants to service fees. A board of directors presides over a private agency, formulating policy and making certain that agency staff run the agency appropriately.

Proprietary or *for-profit* social agencies provide designated social services, often quite similar to those provided by private social agencies. However, a major purpose of the proprietary social agency is to make money.

From our perspective, the terms "social services agency," "social services organization," and "social agency" mean essentially the same thing. Therefore, these three terms will be used interchangeably.

Organizational Theories and Conceptual Frameworks

EP 2.1.7a

In order to work within organizations, evaluate them, and sometimes strive to change them, you first need to understand the major theories regarding how organizations operate. *Organizational theories* and *conceptual frameworks* are ways to interpret and understand how organizations function by stressing specific concepts and explaining how these concepts relate to each other. This knowledge can be useful in determining how an organizational structure affects you as a worker and, in turn, your ability to serve clients effectively. Theories provide a lens through which to view the organizational environment and help you focus on what is most important in that environment for you to do your job.

Many organizational theories have been borrowed from business and management literature. Businesses and social service organizations have much in common. Both need resources, namely money, to function. Likewise, both produce results or products via some kind of process. For example, a business might manufacture the product of burglar alarms. A social services organization might furnish the product of improved family functioning.

There is a wide range of theories concerning how organizations work. Some of them directly contradict others, probably because there is such a vast array of organizational structures, functions, and goals. There are tremendous differences among social service organizations specifically, with even more variations among all types of businesses and organizations generally.

Two important concepts addressed by organizational theories are organizational behavior and management. *Organizational behavior* "is the study of human behavior in the workplace, of the interaction between people and the organization, and of the organization itself. The major goals of organizational behavior are to explain, predict, and control behavior" (DuBrin, 2007, p. 2). What components in the organizational environment are significant to those who work there? What issues do they face and how do they tend to react? "*Management* is the attainment of organizational goals in an effective and efficient manner through planning, organizing, leading, and controlling organizational resources" (Daft, 2010a, p. 5). Here, attention is focused on the interaction between managers, those in power, and workers, those who directly accomplish the organization's goals by doing various tasks. Later portions of this chapter will further explore the nature and macro context of organizations, in addition to some approaches to management.

Some organizational theories emphasize similar dimensions, such as expectations for how staff should be treated, the importance placed on profits, or the degree to which new ideas are encouraged. However, each theory about how organizations work stresses various concepts somewhat differently.

One means of considering the wide variety of organizational theories is to place them on one of two continuums (Burrell & Morgan, 1979; Netting & O'Connor, 2003). One scale is adherence to traditional rigid *structure,* on the one hand, versus seeking fundamental *change* for the better on the other. The second continuum involves a focus on *human well-being* and individuality on one side, and the objective, efficient completion of *tasks* on the other.

This chapter reviews the following theories of organization. Classical organizational theories developed early in the last century include scientific management, the administrative theory of management, and bureaucracy. They reflect rigid structure in addition to an emphasis on productivity and task completion. Neoclassical organizational theories portray a later shift in perspective to theory that is more oriented toward human relationships and motivation. Human relations theories and feminist theories stress the importance of the human component in organizational functioning. Feminist theories, of course, focus on the empowerment of women. The cultural perspective emphasizes the importance of expectations in the organizational environment and culture to maintain the organization's status quo. Political-economy theory emphasizes how organizations must adapt to their external environments, stressing the effects of resources and power. The institutional perspective also focuses on external pressures—not resources and power, but social institutions and their demands. Contingency theory stresses careful analysis of all variables to determine those that relate directly to an issue or problem (that could involve either "personal" or "situational factors") (Vecchio, 2006, p. 11). Culture-quality theories, characterizing the end of the last century, emphasize the importance of establishing a positive organizational culture that promotes worker motivation and improves the quality of their work. Finally, systems theories provide a perspective for understanding organizational functioning that fits well with social work. They provide a structured way of viewing organizations, yet focus on how change might occur. They can also involve both the importance of human well-being and the accomplishment of organizational tasks and goals.

Classical Organizational Theories

Classical management theories emphasize that specifically designed formal structure and a consistent, rigid organizational network of employees are most important in having an organization run well and achieve its goals (Griffin & Moorhead, 2010; Hodge, Anthony, & Gates, 2003). In general, these early theories view each employee as holding a clearly defined job and straightforwardly being told exactly how that job should be accomplished. These schools of thought call for minimal independent functioning on the part of employees. Supervisors closely scrutinize the latter's work. Efficiency is of utmost importance. Performance is quantified (that is, made very explicit regarding what is expected), regulated, and measured. How people feel about their jobs is insignificant. Administration avoids allowing employees to have any input regarding how organizational goals can best be reached. Rather, employees do their jobs as instructed and as quietly and efficiently as possible. Early proponents of these theories included Frederick W. Taylor, Henri Fayol, and Max Weber, each discussed in the following sections (Champoux, 2006; Netting & O'Connor, 2003).

Scientific Management

Frederick W. Taylor introduced the concept of *scientific management* (Champoux, 2006, p. 11). Developed in the early 20th century, it reflected a time when there was often great hostility between management and employees. Management pushed employees to work as hard as possible to maximize company profits. In response, employees worked as slowly and did as little as possible in order to protect themselves. They figured

that working faster and becoming more productive would endanger their and other workers' jobs if management could get more work out of fewer people. Management sought high profits and workers wanted high wages. Both were working against each other.

Four principles characterize Taylor's scientific management style (Champoux, 2006, p. 12):

1. Jobs and tasks should be studied scientifically to "develop" and "standardize" work procedures and expectations.
2. Workers should be chosen on a scientific basis to maximize their potential for being trained and turned into productive employees.
3. Management and employees should cooperate with each other and work together following standardized procedures.
4. Management should make "plans" and "task assignments," which workers should then "carry out" as instructed.

The Administrative Theory of Management

Also in the early 20th century, Henri Fayol proposed an *administrative theory of management* (Champoux, 2006). His ideas focused on the administrative side of management rather than the workers' performance. He proposed five basic functions that management should fulfill, including "planning, organizing, command, coordination, and control" (Champoux, 2006, p. 12). He concluded that all managers should abide by the following six basic principles, although he did indicate that they should use *discretion* (the opportunity to make independent judgments and decisions) concerning the intensity with which they pursued each principle (Champoux, 2006, p. 13):

1. *Division of labor.* Workers should be divided up into units so that they might perform specialized instead of more general tasks. He posed that specialization would lead to greater productivity.
2. *Authority and responsibility.* Management should have the authority to give orders to workers, oversee their activity, and make them comply with these orders. In response, workers would assume responsibility for completing their assigned work.
3. *Centralization.* Depending on what would maximize productivity, management should centralize authority (that is, place decision-making power and responsibility at the top of the organization's power hierarchy) or decentralize such authority (give power and responsibility to lower-level

managers and workers in the organization's power hierarchy).

4. *Delegation of authority.* Upper-level management has the responsibility of delegating responsibility and work assignments to managers and workers lower in the power hierarchy. Management should carefully analyze organizational processes and delegate authority as it sees fit.

5. *Unity of command.* Each worker should have one designated supervisor to whom he or she should report. This should avoid confusion and give consistent messages and orders to workers.

6. *Unity of direction.* Each unit in the organization (which is specialized under the division of labor) should have a single designated goal. This also should avoid confusion and inconsistency.

In essence, these principles should work together. High-level management should give power to lower-level management *(authority and responsibility)* as it sees fit *(centralization or decentralization; delegation of authority)*. Workers should be specialized *(division of labor)* and work in designated units. There should be a clear hierarchy of authority regarding who is responsible for each worker *(unity of command)* and each goal *(unity of direction)* to avoid confusion, enhance consistency, and maximize productivity.

Bureaucracy

Initiated by Max Weber in the early 20th century,

> bureaucracy *is an administrative structure with well-defined offices or functions and hierarchical relationships among the functions. The offices or functions have clearly defined duties, rights, and responsibilities. Each office or function is designed without regard for who will hold the office. Relationships within a bureaucracy are impersonal. Decisions are made according to existing rules, procedures, and policies. Bureaucracies attain goals with precision, reliability, and efficiency* [emphasis added] (Champoux, 2006, p. 14).

In summary, traditional bureaucracies emphasize the following (Griffin & Moorhead, 2010):

- *Highly specialized units performing clearly specified job tasks;*
- *Minimal discretion on the part of employees; and*
- *Numerous specific rules to maintain control.*

The Social Security Administration, the Detroit Department of Social Services, and the Federal Bureau of Investigation are examples of large bureaucracies. A later section of this chapter will address what it's like to work in an organization with a bureaucratic style of management.

Neoclassical Organizational Theories

Originating during the mid-20th century, neoclassical theories were reactions to classical management thought and "a transition in the theoretical movement from the overly simplistic, mechanistic perspectives of the classical theorists to more contemporary thinking about complex organizations" (Netting & O'Connor, 2003, p. 106). They addressed problems and omissions in classical theories. Criticisms of classical theories involved lack of attention to human needs and individuality, coordination of work and goals among various bureaucratic units, the importance of relationships among organizations in the larger macro environment, and the need to comprehend the decision-making processes in organizations (Netting & O'Connor, 2003, pp. 105–106).

Champoux (2006) describes the ideas expressed by one of the leaders of the neoclassical movement, Chester I. Barnard. Barnard defined an *organization* as a deliberately structured system of tasks and activities undertaken by two or more people. The implication is "that any system of two or more people with consciously coordinated activities is an organization. Organizations are based on cooperation and have a conscious, deliberate purpose" (p. 16). In order to achieve coordination and cooperation, organizations "offer inducements in exchange for contributions. *Inducements* include salary and fringe benefits. *Contributions* are things such as the work to be done. Barnard felt a person joined an organization when the inducements exceeded the contributions" (p. 16). Management's goal should be maintenance of this balance.

Barnard proposed that organizations functioned on the basis of two types of motivation—motivation to participate and motivation to perform (Champoux, 2006). "*Motivation to participate* is the motivation of an individual to join and stay with the organization and perform at a minimally acceptable level" (p. 16). Various organizations maintain different expectations regarding what is minimally acceptable performance. It is the responsibility of managers to balance inducements and contributions to retain staff and motivate them to complete their work. After management attends to workers' motivation to participate, they then should direct their attention to workers' motivation to perform. *Motivation to perform* involves inducements to produce contributions that are greater than minimal performance expectations (Champoux, 2006, p. 16).

Barnard's contributions changed how organizations were viewed in two major ways (Champoux, 2006). First, he emphasized deliberately coordinated tasks that required cooperation between two or more people. Thus, the theoretical focus was changing from production results to how people work together in an organizational environment. Second, he stressed the need to induce people by providing incentives (salary and benefits) to reinforce their contributions (work performance). This began to change the focus from controlling worker behavior and performance to motivating workers to perform. An emphasis on motivation reflected the beginning of a shift to consider workers as individuals with emotions, needs, and desires instead of mindless entities requiring control and direction. Think about your own future work scenarios. To what extent do you want to be treated as a mindless entity instead of a competent professional who needs administrative support?

Human Relations Theories

Human relations theories reflect the result of this shift to focus on "human relations" within the organizational environment. Vecchio (2006) explains:

> The human relations approach, which partially grew out of the field of psychology, emphasized the importance of motivation and attitudes in explaining worker behavior…. [T]he cornerstone of the human relations approach [is] … the belief that employees who are satisfied with their jobs will feel indebted to their employers and will show their appreciation by being more productive. This suggests a relationship between management and labor—that greater concern for improving the working conditions of employees will pay dividends to employers through greater productivity from happier and more appreciative employees. (p. 11)

Griffin and Moorhead (2010) explain that human relations theories assume

> that employees want to feel useful and important, that employees have strong social needs, and that these needs are more important than money in motivating employees. Advocates of the human relationship approach advised managers to make workers feel important and allow them a modicum of self-direction and self-control in carrying out routine

activities. The illusion of involvement and importance were expected to satisfy workers' basic social needs and result in higher motivation to perform. For example, a manager might allow a work group to participate in making a decision, even though he or she had already determined what the decision would be. The symbolic gesture of seeming to allow participation was expected to enhance motivation, even though no real participation took place. (p. 85)

Likewise, the immediate work group, a mezzo system, is critical in human relations theories. If workers were satisfied with their interpersonal relationships with their supervisors and in their work groups, they would become more productive; in this context, virtually all workers theoretically could become productive employees (DuBrin, 2007).

Theory X and Theory Y

The management styles of administrators and supervisors in organizations have considerable impact on the productivity and job satisfaction of employees. Douglas McGregor (1960) developed two theories of management style. He hypothesized that management thinking and behavior are based on two different sets of assumptions, which he labeled Theory X and Theory Y. Theory X reflects aspects of classical scientific management in its focus on hierarchical structure to provide a contrasting approach to the human relations Theory Y. These theories are addressed here because they emphasize the treatment of employees.

Theory X managers view employees as being incapable of much growth. Employees are perceived as having an inherent dislike for work, and it is presumed that they will attempt to evade work whenever possible. Therefore, X-type managers believe that they must control, direct, force, or threaten employees to make them work. Employees are also viewed as having relatively little ambition, wishing to avoid responsibilities, and preferring to be directed. X-type managers therefore spell out job responsibilities carefully, set work goals without employee input, use external rewards (such as money) to force employees to work, and punish employees who deviate from established rules. Because Theory X managers reduce responsibilities to a level where few mistakes can be made, work can become so structured that it is monotonous and distasteful. The assumptions of Theory X, of course, are inconsistent with what behavioral scientists assert are effective principles for directing, influencing, and motivating people.

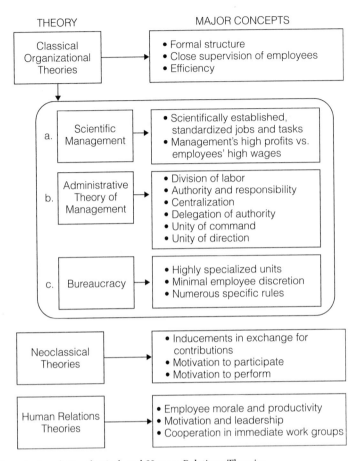

FIGURE 4.1 Classical Organizational, Neoclassical, and Human Relations Theories

In contrast, Theory Y managers view employees as wanting to grow and develop by exerting physical and mental effort to accomplish work objectives to which they are committed. Y-type managers believe that the promise of internal rewards, such as self-respect and personal improvement, are stronger motivators than external rewards (such as money) and punishment. A Y-type manager also believes that under proper conditions, employees will not only accept responsibility but seek it. Most employees are assumed to have significant ingenuity, creativity, and imagination for solving the organization's problems. Therefore, employees are given considerable responsibility in order to test the limits of their capabilities. Mistakes and errors are viewed as necessary phases of the learning process, and work is structured so that employees can have a sense of accomplishment and growth.

Theoretically, employees who work for Y-type managers are generally more creative and productive, experience greater work satisfaction, and are more highly motivated than employees who work for X-type managers. Under both management styles, expectations often become self-fulfilling prophecies.

Figure 4.1 summarizes the theoretical frameworks concerning organizations discussed thus far.

Feminist Theories and Organizations

Feminist theories involve

EP 2.1.4a

the liberation of women and girls from discrimination based on gender. The goal of feminist theory and practice is women's self-determination, [each individual's right to make his or her own decisions]. For some feminists this means securing equal rights for women within existing institutions—from marriage and the family to government policy and law. For others it means fundamentally changing these institutions (emphasis added) (Kirk & Okazawa-Rey, 2010, p. 4).

Many feminist theories

were developed in the context of women's organizing for change—for the abolition of slavery, for woman's suffrage, for labor rights, the civil rights of people of color, women's rights, and GLBT (gay, lesbian, bisexual, and transgender) rights. Feminist theories have been concerned with fundamental questions: Why are women in a subordinate position in our society and, indeed, worldwide? What are the origins of this subordination, and how is it perpetuated? (Kirk & Okazawa-Rey, 2007, pp. 14–15)

Note that a range of feminist theories exists with each perspective emphasizing various concepts (Kirk & Okazawa-Rey, 2007, pp. 15–17, 2010). The following are a few examples. *Liberal feminism* "grew out of one of the most significant strands of U.S. political thought, liberalism, a theory about individual rights, freedom, choice, and privacy" (p. 15). *Socialist feminism* "grew out of Marxist theories of the economy" and is "particularly concerned with the economic-class aspect of women's lives" (pp. 15–16). *Radical feminism* emphasizes how "male domination manifests itself in women's sexuality, gender roles, and family relationships, and it is carried over into the male-dominated world of work, government, religion, and law" (p. 16). *Postmodern feminism* stresses "the particularity of women's experiences in specific cultural and historical contexts and seeks to account for differences among women based on age, race, culture, national origin, ability, and other attributes" (Kirk & Okazawa-Rey, 2010, p.14). "*Womanist* views reflect African American experience and place race (as well as gender) in the forefront of feminist conceptualizations [emphasis added]" (Bricker-Jenkins & Netting, 2009, p. 278; Hyde, 2008).

For our purposes, we will arbitrarily select some of the major themes characterizing most feminist theories and apply them to organizational functioning. These include: using a gender filter; empowerment; "the personal is political"; the importance of process; and diversity as strength. Note that the implications of these themes often overlap.

Using a Gender Filter

Using a gender filter to view the plight of women in organizational environments establishes a new way of looking at the world by focusing on women and women's issues (Hyde, 2008). Such a filter assumes that sexism is relevant to the experiences of many women and is the basis for many of women's difficulties. Because sexism exists in organizational environments,

women's conditions, needs, and opportunities there should be stressed. Therefore, within organizational contexts, management and workers must be vigilant regarding the treatment of women in a fair, nondiscriminatory manner. Women should also have equal access with men to positions of responsibility and power.

Empowerment

We have established that *empowerment* is the "process of increasing personal, interpersonal, or political power so that individuals can take action to improve their life situations" (Gutierrez, 2001, p. 210). *Power* is the ability to move people on a chosen course to produce an effect or achieve some goal. Feminist conceptual frameworks stress that power should be distributed and equalized to whatever extent possible within an organization (Bricker-Jenkins & Lockett, 1995; Fisher & Burghardt, 2008; Hyde, 2008). This view would support a decentralized, democratic organizational structure that provides greater discretion on the part of workers throughout the organization (Hyde, 2008). In addition, organizations should empower women to be promoted and assume leadership positions.

Gutierrez and Lewis (1999) suggest that

attention should be paid to staff development," including "access to conferences, training workshops, and other educational opportunities ... Staff can also be supported through flex time and other policies that encourage flexibility and self-care. Similarly, providing opportunities for staff to develop programs and professional skills that match their own personal interests is an important part of the empowerment of staff within an agency (pp. 83–84).

The Personal Is Political

The phrase "the personal is political" means that women's conditions extend beyond personal situations (Bricker-Jenkins & Netting, 2009; Fisher & Burghardt, 2008; Hyde, 2008, p. 218). Feminist conceptual frameworks stress that "struggles over personal issues and relationships—personal choice, autonomy, commitment, and fulfillment—are inextricably tied to collective ones of the constituency group [women in general] and the larger society" (Fisher & Burghardt, 2008, p. 325). When we say that the personal is political, we mean "that many issues that historically have been deemed 'personal'—abortion, battery, unemployment, birth, death, and illness—are actually deeply political issues" (Thompson, 2010, p. 44). This concept promotes a way "to validate individual women's experiences as a starting point for recognizing and understanding discrimination against women as a group" (Kirk & Okazawa-Rey, 2010, p. 55)

Thus, a feminist perspective proposes that all woman are interconnected with each other. The issues affecting one affect women in general. Optimal health and well-being can only be attained through working together for positive change for all women (Bricker-Jenkins & Lockett, 1995).

The Importance of Process

Feminist theories emphasize that the process of *how* things get done is just as important as *what* gets done (Fisher & Burghardt, 2008; Hyde, 2008). The implication in an organizational context is that management should involve workers in decision making and planning to the greatest extent possible. The process of decision making should be based on equality and the participation of all. Workers should feel like important participants in the organizational environment. Important concepts include making certain all participants have the chance to speak and be heard, adhering to principles of ethical behavior, working toward agreement and consensus, and considering personal issues as important. Teamwork should be emphasized (Gutierrez & Lewis, 1999).

In contrast, a traditional patriarchal perspective that stresses male dominance often focuses on the significance of end results and goal achievement, paying much less heed to process. For example, consider a male administrator who ardently competes for a promotion to a higher administrative position. He uses tactics such as reporting information about other job candidates' weaknesses to decision makers. This serves to make other candidates look bad and make him look better by comparison. A traditional patriarchal perspective emphasizes the end result—namely, the importance of gaining the promotion. It does not necessarily focus on how the administrator got the job through his participation in a nasty mudslinging process.

Diversity as Strength

Feminist theories stress unity, harmony, and interdependence, on the one hand, and appreciation of diverse characteristics on the other (Bricker-Jenkins & Netting, 2009; Hyde, 2008). Gutierrez and Lewis (1999) explain that "efforts are made to bridge differences between women based on such factors as race, class, physical ability, and sexual orientation with the principle that diversity is strength" (p. 105). In order to remain unified, women should appreciate each other's differences

and work together for the benefit of all. Diversity (for example, gender, race, ethnicity, age, and sexual orientation) should not only be appreciated, but actively sought out and encouraged. New ideas to improve old ways of doing things should be promoted.

Powell and Graves (2003) recommend that all

organizations—large or small, public or private, profit or nonprofit—set the goals of being nondiscriminatory, diverse, and inclusive in their employment practices.... [Organizational] communications should convey the message that promoting nondiscrimination, diversity, and inclusion are important organizational goals. These communications may include speeches by top executives, with transcripts or videos available to internal and external groups, newsletters, status reports, recognition events, special awards, and publicity for employees who have done good work toward these goals. The mission statement *[a declaration of an organization's purpose and goals] of the organization should state that the organization regards achievement of these goals as critical to its success* [emphasis added] *(pp. 231–232).*

The Cultural Perspective

Organizational culture is "the set of values, norms, guiding beliefs, and understandings that is shared by members of an organization and taught to new members as the correct way to think, feel, and behave" (Daft, 2010b, p. 374). The cultural perspective on organizations assumes that each organization develops a unique mixture of values, standards, presumptions, and practices about how things should be done that eventually becomes habit (Daft, 2010b; Hellriegel & Slocum, 2009; Nelson & Quick, 2009).

Hellriegel and Slocum explain:

Organizational cultures evolve slowly over time.... [T]hey are not usually written down, but are the soul of an organization. A culture is a collection of unspoken rules and traditions that operate 24 hours a day. Culture plays a large part in determining the quality of organizational life.... Culture is rooted in the countless details of an organization's life and influences much of what happens to employees within an organization. The culture of an organization influences who gets promoted, how careers are either made or derailed, and how resources are allocated. (2009, p. 45)

Management and other personnel may not be consciously aware that such patterns and expectations have developed. They become ingrained in established means of accomplishing tasks and goals. If it worked before, it'll work again: "If it ain't broke, don't fix it." The result is the establishment of an ideological structure that frames how organizational members think about the organization and how it should work. This perspective not only guides people's view of current practices, but also shapes how they think about new issues. Employees tend to view new ideas by shaping them to conform to old, tried and true practices.

An advantage of the cultural perspective may be that performance becomes predictable, thus requiring less effort to develop new approaches. However, a disadvantage is that such an established view may squelch innovative ideas. There is pressure to retain the old way of thought.

For example, an energized worker in a social services organization might come to a staff meeting with a brilliant new treatment approach (in his opinion). The cultural perspective suggests that staff will tend not to evaluate the new approach fairly and impartially. Rather, they might nod pleasantly in feigned mild agreement and proceed to recycle the new approach into the same old routine.

It should be noted that the organization's culture might support "innovation" and "risk-taking" instead of the status quo (Johns, 1996, p. 289). If this were the case with the group discussed above, the staff would love the new treatment idea the worker presented. Personnel would shy away from old techniques and search for new ones. In this case, the advantages and disadvantages would be reversed. An advantage, then, would be the development of fresh, more effective intervention modalities. A disadvantage would be lack of stability and predictability.

Political-Economy Theory

Political-economy theory emphasizes how organizations must adapt to their external environments, stressing the effects of resources and power. Schmid (2009) explains political-economy theory as it applies to social services organizations:

> *Political-economy theory (Wamseley & Zald, 1976; Zald, 1970) recognizes that in order to survive and produce services, the organization must garner two fundamental types of resources: [1] legitimacy [having appropriate legal status and justification for existence] and power (i.e., political) and [2] production resources (i.e., economic). The underlying premise of this approach is the organization's dependence on resources controlled by agents and interest groups in the external environment. The greater the organization's*

> *dependence on these resources, the stronger the influence of external interest groups on processes within the organization. (p. 418)*

Hasenfeld (2009) notes that "the greater the resource dependency of the organization on an [any particular] element in the environment (e.g., governmental funding agency, regulatory organization, professional association, providers of clients), the greater the ability of the element to influence organizational policies and procedures" (p. 62).

Therefore, an organization is in a constant struggle to negotiate with resource providers and other controlling systems to gain as much control over its functioning as possible (Hasenfeld, 2009; Patti, 2008). An organization can do this in various ways (Patti, 2008). To gain power, an organization will strive to compete effectively with other agencies providing similar services. Or an organization might form *coalitions*, alliances of individuals, groups, and organizations with similar goals that become more influential and powerful when united (Mosley, 2009). Organizational leaders might bargain with external controlling elements to negotiate for more power and control in exchanges of services for resources.

Political-economy theory also characterizes the internal agency environment. Hasenfeld (2009) explains:

> *The internal dynamics of the organization will also reflect the power relations of different interest groups and individuals within the organization. Some of these groups (e.g., professional staff, executive[s] ...) derive their power from relations with important external organizations, others because they possess personal attributes, control internal resources (e.g., information and expertise), or carry out important functions (e.g., manage the budget) (p. 62)*

The Institutional Perspective

Like political-economy theory, the institutional perspective emphasizes the importance of external pressures on an organization. However, instead of focusing on power and resources, this perspective accentuates the pressures imposed by social institutions (Patti, 2008). *Social institutions* are established constellations of roles, expectations, values, groups, and organizations that are created to meet basic societal needs. Examples include "religion, the family, military structures, government, and the social welfare system" (Barker, 2003, p. 404). Social institutions are reinforced by various "social rules"; social rules govern society's expectations for behavior through laws, regulations, values, and assigned statuses (Hasenfeld, 2009, p. 65).

The institutional perspective assumes that "the more organizations adhere to the rules of these institutions—by embedding the rules in their structures—the greater will be their legitimacy and chances of survival" (Hasenfeld, 2009, p. 65). Schmid (2009) explains the application of an institutional perspective to social services agencies:

> For example, to ensure a steady flow of resources, human services organizations often adopt the espoused ideologies and goals of the government, which are not always attainable. These ideologies and goals can be expressed as "closing social gaps and reducing inequality between haves and have nots," "the need to redistribute power and transfer it to peripheral units," "integration of populations," and "changing attitudes toward minorities." Organizations that succeed in achieving those goals increase their legitimacy and, consequently, their prospects for survival, irrespective of the immediate efficacy of the required practices and procedures. (p. 421)

In other words, these ideals and social rules may sound good. However, for an organization actually to comply with them and achieve genuine results through service provision is often a difficult, and, perhaps, an impossible, task (Hasenfeld, 2009; Patti, 2008; Schmid, 2009). Thus, what often really happens is that organizations establish goals in concordance with social rules and receive the resulting legitimacy and support. However, such stated goals may have little to do with actual results achieved.

Contingency Theory

Contingency theory maintains that each element involved in an organization depends on other elements; therefore, there is no perfect way to accomplish tasks or goals (Daft, 2010b; Hasenfeld, 2009; Schmid, 2009). Each organization with its units or subsystems is unique. Thus, the best way to accomplish goals is to make individual determinations in view of the goal's context. The behavior of personnel is too varied and "complex to be explained by only a few simple and straightforward principles" (Vecchio, 2006, p. 11). Daft (2010b) clarifies:

> Contingency *means that one thing depends on other things, and for organizations to be effective, there must be a "goodness of fit" between their structure and the conditions in their external environment.*

> *What works in one setting may not work in another setting. There is not one best way. Contingency theory means "it depends." (p. 26)*

Therefore, different means are required to solve various problems depending on all of the variables involved. Daft (2010b) explains:

> *For example, some organizations experience a certain environment, use a routine technology, and desire efficiency. In this situation, a management approach that uses bureaucratic control procedures, a hierarchical structure, and formal communication would be appropriate. Likewise, free-flowing management processes [with few standardized routines and much worker discretion] work best in an uncertain environment with a nonroutine technology. The correct management approach is contingent on the organization's situation. (p. 26)*

A strength of this theory is its flexibility. It can be applied to any situation in any organization. However, a potential weakness is its lack of direction. The core idea suggests that all variables should be evaluated and any may be significant. Where does one start when evaluating a problem or planning a procedure? Staff? Input? Output? Process? It is difficult to determine.

Culture-Quality Theories

Theories stressing organizational culture and quality improvement characterized the final two decades of the 20th century and paved the way for future approaches (Vecchio, 2006). These views

> focused on how to build a strong set of shared positive values and norms within a corporation (that is, a strong corporate culture) while emphasizing quality, service, high performance, and flexibility. Simultaneously, Western industry developed an interest in designing an effective response to growing global competition. High quality was seen to be related to high employee commitment and loyalty, which were believed to result, partially, from greater employee involvement in decision making. In order to establish new mechanisms for employee involvement, changes were seen as being necessary in existing corporate cultures, and the establishment and maintenance of new cultures became the goal. Some organizations now seek to have employees openly discuss aspects of corporate culture and suggest techniques for achieving a culture that emphasizes greater teamwork and cooperation. (Vecchio, 2006, p. 12)

One application of culture-quality theories is total quality management, described later in the chapter.

Systems Theories

Systems theories emphasize how all parts of the organization *(subsystems)* are interrelated. These subsystems function together to take resources *(input)* and produce some kind of product or service *(output)* (Hutchison, 2008; Iglehart, 2009; Netting, 2008). An organization is more than the sum of its individual parts. It is an intricate mechanism where its parts work together to undertake the processing of a product or the provision of a service.

Systems theories also emphasize the environment and the effects of other systems upon the organization. In some ways, systems theories are more flexible than many other theories, because irrational, spontaneous interactions are expected rather than ignored. Systems theories emphasize constant assessment and adjustment.

Figure 4.2 summarizes the theoretical frameworks concerning organizations just described.

Which Organizational Theory Is Best?

No one really knows which organizational theory is best. As time passes, theoretical perspectives rise and fall in terms of their popularity. Daft (2010b) explains the reason for this uncertainty: "Today, almost all organizations operate in highly uncertain environments. Thus, we are involved in a significant period of transition, in which concepts of organization theory and design are changing as dramatically as they did with the dawning of the Industrial Revolution" (p. 26).

Most organizations probably reflect a mixture of concepts derived from various theories. It is beyond the scope of this text to explore organizational theory other than to provide a foundation to help you understand human behavior within the context of organizational macro systems.

Chapter 1 established that systems theories can serve as an umbrella approach for defining and understanding the functioning of macro systems, including organizations. Because of their flexibility and the complexities of working with real clients, this book will primarily view organizations from a systems perspective. As we have discussed, various organizational theories emphasize different aspects of organizations in terms of how you should view their functioning and what you should consider most significant. Regardless of the theory chosen, you can use a systems approach

to readily describe the processes involved in organizational life (Iglehart, 2009; Patti, 2008). Each management theory can be examined using concepts inherent in systems theories. Additionally, accreditation standards for social work programs emphasize how social work programs should provide content on "the range of social systems in which people live" (individual, family, group, organizational, and community) and "the ways social systems promote or deter people in maintaining or achieving health and well-being" (Council on Social Work Education [CSWE], 2008, EP 2.1.7). The following section will discuss social agencies as systems.

Social Agencies as Systems

We have established that systems theories provide a broad approach to understanding the world, and can be applied in many settings, among them social agencies. Following are definitions of terms that are extremely important to understanding systems theories and their relationship to social work practice. They include system, boundaries, subsystem, homeostasis, role, relationship, input, output, outcomes, positive and negative feedback, interface, differentiation, entropy, negative entropy, and equifinality

A *system* is a set of orderly and interrelated elements that form a functional whole. A large nation, a public social services department, and a newly married couple are all systems. For our purposes, we will refer primarily to social systems—that is, systems that are composed of people and affect people.

Boundaries are borders or margins that separate one entity (for example, a system) from another. They enclose the repeatedly occurring patterns that characterize the relationships within a system and give that system a particular identity, setting it apart from other systems. Boundaries establish how various units in a system relate to each other. An analogy to a boundary is your skin, which encloses you as a complex being and distinguishes you from the external social environment. A boundary may exist, for instance, between parents and their children. Parents maintain family leadership and provide support and nurturance to their children. A boundary may also exist between the protective services workers in a large county social service agency and those who work in financial assistance. Each orderly and interrelated group is set apart by specified boundaries in terms of its designated job responsibilities and the clients it serves. Yet, each group is part of the larger social services agency.

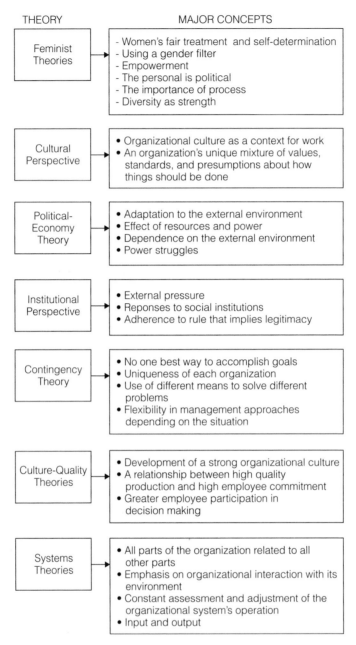

THEORY   MAJOR CONCEPTS

Feminist Theories
- Women's fair treatment and self-determination
- Using a gender filter
- Empowerment
- The personal is political
- The importance of process
- Diversity as strength

Cultural Perspective
- Organizational culture as a context for work
- An organization's unique mixture of values, standards, and presumptions about how things should be done

Political-Economy Theory
- Adaptation to the external environment
- Effect of resources and power
- Dependence on the external environment
- Power struggles

Institutional Perspective
- External pressure
- Reponses to social institutions
- Adherence to rule that implies legitimacy

Contingency Theory
- No one best way to accomplish goals
- Uniqueness of each organization
- Use of different means to solve different problems
- Flexibility in management approaches depending on the situation

Culture-Quality Theories
- Development of a strong organizational culture
- A relationship between high quality production and high employee commitment
- Greater employee participation in decision making

Systems Theories
- All parts of the organization related to all other parts
- Emphasis on organizational interaction with its environment
- Constant assessment and adjustment of the organizational system's operation
- Input and output

FIGURE 4.2 A Wide Range of Organizational Theories

A *subsystem* is a secondary or subordinate system, a smaller system within a larger system. Obvious examples of subsystems are the parental and sibling subsystems within a family. Likewise, a group of protective services workers in a large social services agency system forms one subsystem within the agency, and the financial assistance workers another. Both subsystems are set apart by designated boundaries, but they are still part of the larger, total agency system.

Homeostasis is the tendency for a system to maintain a relatively stable, constant state of balance. If something disturbs the balance, the system will readjust itself and regain stability. A homeostatic family system functions in such a way that it can survive and family members can stay together. Likewise, a homeostatic social services agency works to maintain its ongoing existence. However, neither the family nor the agency is necessarily functioning as well or effectively as possible. Homeostasis merely means maintaining the status quo. Sometimes that status quo can be ineffective, inefficient, or seriously problematic.

For example, families with alcohol- or other drug-dependent members often focus on maintaining whatever stability they have instead of working to solve the substance abuse problem. Homeostasis can be uncomfortable, painful, or distressing, but at least it's predictable. Likewise, a community may strive to maintain its homeostasis, despite the fact that its political leaders are excessively corrupt. Community members may hesitate to depose these leaders because potential replacements scare residents even more. At least the residents already know about the leaders they have. The unknown is scary—even though it might be better, it also might be worse.

A *role* is the culturally established social behavior and conduct expected of a person having a designated status in a particular group or society. In other words, each individual in a system assumes a role in that system. A person in the role of professional social worker is expected to behave in certain ways as defined by the professional code of ethics. Each of us probably fulfills numerous roles, because we are involved in multiple systems. Social workers may assume the roles of spouse and parent in their own family systems in addition to their professional role of BSW or MSW. Likewise, the same practitioner may assume the roles of dynamic executive director in a National Association of Social Workers' state chapter, humble volunteer at the local Humane Society, and enthusiastic organizer of golf foursomes.

A *relationship* is the dynamic interpersonal connection between two or more persons or systems that involves how they think about, feel about, and behave toward each other. For example, a social worker has a professional relationship with her agency supervisor. Ideally, they communicate and interact in order to maximize the worker's effectiveness. Relationships may exist among virtually any size systems. Workers in an agency may have relationships with each other, and one agency may have a relationship with another agency.

Input is the energy, information, or communication flow received from other systems. A parent may receive input from his child's teacher that the child is flunking physical education. Likewise, a public agency may receive input from the state in the form of funding.

Output, on the other hand, is what happens to input after it has been processed by some system. For instance, consider the circumstances involving a client

upon termination of the treatment process. A client with a heroin addiction[2] may be referred to an agency. This client receives treatment. The agency has taken its input (its own staff, funds, and other resources) and translated it into output, namely, treatment. When the treatment process or intervention is completed, the client's progress is evaluated. Whatever progress (or lack thereof) the client has made becomes part of the agency's *outcomes*.

Note that the term *output* is qualitatively different than *outcome*, a term frequently used in evaluating social work education. Output is a more general term for the result of a process. Outcomes are specified variables that are measured for the purpose of evaluation. Output is what is done, which may or may not have value. Outcomes measure positive or negative effects of a system's process. For example, an output of a social work education program is providing courses and teaching students. The output may or may not be effective. Measurable outcomes for that same program include variables such as the number of students passing certification exams, positive evaluation of the program by students, and positive evaluation of graduates by their social work employers. Similarly, the output of a neighborhood watch program for crime prevention is 40 neighborhood residents watching their streets, yards, and alleys for suspicious persons and events. This output may or may not be effective. The program's outcome is a decrease in burglaries and other neighborhood crimes.

This text—and most employers—will stress the importance of evaluating whether a system's output is worth its input. In other words, is the agency using its resources efficiently and effectively? Or can those resources be put to a better use by providing some other type of service?

Consider the above-mentioned client with the heroin problem. After receiving six weeks of treatment, he walks out of the agency, rushes home, and sticks a needle in his vein to administer a heroin injection. To what extent do you think the treatment was effective? Virtually any type of treatment is expensive. In this client's case, was the output worth the input, given the outcome? It certainly doesn't seem so. If the agency typically sees so little progress at the end of treatment for clients, you'd probably question the agency's

---

2. *Heroin* is "a strongly physiologically addictive narcotic … that is made by acetylation of [morphine] but is more potent than morphine and that is prohibited for medical use in the U.S. but is used illicitly for its euphoric effects" (Mish, 2008, p. 583).

usefulness. Should the agency's treatment process be changed to achieve better results (that is, outcomes)? Or should the agency be shut down totally so that resources (or input) could be better invested in some other agency or treatment system?

Feedback is a special form of input where a system receives information about that system's own performance. As a result *of negative feedback,* the system can choose to correct deviations or mistakes and return to a more homeostatic state. A supervisor may tell a social work supervisee that she has been filling out an important agency form incorrectly. This allows the worker to correct her behavior and begin to complete the form appropriately.

Positive feedback is also valuable. It occurs when a system receives information about what it is doing correctly in order to maintain itself and thrive. For example, receiving a significant raise as the result of an excellent job performance review provides feedback to a worker that she is doing a good job. Likewise, receiving a specific federal grant gives an agency feedback that it has developed a plan worthy of such funding.

An *interface* is the contact point between various systems, including individuals and organizations, where interaction and communication may take place. One interface is the written contract between a field instructor in an adoption agency and a student intern placed under her supervision. At the beginning of the semester, they discuss plans and goals for the semester. What tasks will the student be given, and what levels of performance will be expected? With the help of the student's field liaison (that is, the student's college professor), a written contract is established that clarifies these expectations. Contracts generally involve written, oral, or implied agreements between persons in some form of relationship concerning goals, procedures, time frames, and responsibilities assumed during their involvement.

At his midterm evaluation, the student receives a grade of D. Although he is devastated, he still has half of the semester to improve. Focusing on the interface between the field instructor and the field intern (in this case, the contract they established at the beginning of the semester) provides direction concerning what to do about the problem. By reviewing the terms specified in the contract, the instructor and student, with the university liaison's help, can elaborate on problems and expectations. Where did the student go wrong? Which of the student's expectations did the field instructor fail to fulfill? They then can establish a new contract governing the student's performance for the remainder of the semester.

It is still up to the student to "make or break" his field experience. However, the contract (or interface) provides a clearly designated means of approaching the problem. Having the field instructor and field liaison vaguely tell the student that he needs "to improve his performance" probably would not do much good. Rather, identifying and using the interface in the form of the student/instructor contract provides a specific means for attacking the problem. For example, the student's expectations might include observing a designated number of staff meetings, reading specified client records, and successfully completing goals established with two assigned clients.

Interfaces are not limited to those between individuals—they can characterize interactions among virtually any size systems. For example, an interface exists between the adoption agency providing the student placement mentioned above and the university social work program that places the student intern in that agency. This interface involves the specified agreements concerning the respective responsibilities and expectations of each of these two larger systems. Another interface is the contact between you and the fast food cashier at Harry's Hot Dog Heaven as you pay for your Double Dog Deluxe. Still another interface is a person's contact with the rabbi, priest, or minister and the other members of her synagogue or congregation as she attends weekly religious services.

Differentiation is a system's tendency to move from a more simplified to a more complex existence. In other words, relationships, situations, and interactions tend to get more complex, instead of more simplified, over time. For example, in the life of any particular family, each day adds new experiences. New information is gathered. New options are explored. The family's life naturally becomes more complex. Likewise, as a social services agency continues over time, it will likely develop more detailed policies, programs, and more connections with other agencies and with its surrounding community.

Entropy is the natural tendency of a system to progress toward disorganization, depletion, disintegration, and, in essence, death. The idea is that nothing lasts forever as a fully functioning, well-integrated system. Families of origin grow older and children leave to start their own independent lives or families. As history moves on, older agencies, systems, and cultures disintegrate and are eventually replaced by new ones.

Negative entropy is the progress of a system toward organization, growth, and development. In effect, it is the opposite of entropy. Individuals develop physically, intellectually, and emotionally as they grow. Social service agencies grow and develop new programs and clientele or improve their means of service delivery. For example, an agency might restructure "a department so that employees who were 'dead-ended,' unstimulated, unhappy, and unproductive interact with other units; the department's entropy would be replaced by new flows of energy in the form of new ideas, new alliances, and new challenges" (Anderson & Carter, 1999, p. 19).

Equifinality means that there are many different means to the same end. The philosophy behind its use suggests that one should not get locked into only one way of thinking. In any particular situation, alternatives do exist. Some may be better than others, but nonetheless, there are alternatives. Suppose that you are a hospital social worker. You discover that Herman, one of your clients who was hospitalized for acute appendicitis, is seriously depressed after the recent death of his wife. Upon discharge, you may refer him to any of seven community mental health agencies for either individual counseling or participation in a support group. He may reject such help and instead seek out spiritual support from his priest or pastor. Or his relatives may rally on his behalf, providing a surge of warmth and support. Any of these alternative means might help Herman battle his depression and improve his mental health.

Viewing Organizations from a Systems Perspective

EP 2.1.7a

As social workers, we want to serve our clients as best we can. To do this, we must maintain constant awareness of how well social service organizations are serving their clients. Because we will probably be working in social service organizations, we want those organizations to be as effective as possible. We also want other organizations with which our clients have transactions to be effective. Therefore, we must continuously assess the effectiveness of organizations. That is, we must ask ourselves to what extent each organization is attaining its designated goals.

Social service organizations can be compared to business organizations. Figure 4.3 illustrates this process and compares it to a business organization. The business (Fastbuck) manufactures doorstops; the agency (WINK) provides services to people suffering from sleep disorders.

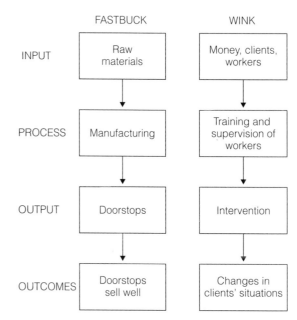

FIGURE 4.3 Fastbuck and WINK—Similar Processes

Resource Input

Both Fastbuck and WINK receive financial resources as part of their input.

Fastbuck gets its funds from stockholders, bank loans, and prior profits from selling Fastbuck doorstops. It uses the funds to purchase materials such as metals, chemicals, molds, and plastic to prepare for the production process and to hire staff to implement the process.

WINK's input may include money, clients, and workers. WINK secures its financial resources from public moneys (received from taxes) and a variety of private sources (such as donations, fees, and grants). Like the business organization, WINK hires staff to implement its processes. However, the social service agency's "raw material" is not metals or plastics, but clients.

Process through Organizational Technology

Both Fastbuck and WINK then process their "raw material."

Fastbuck relays its raw material through a manufacturing production process whereby materials are gradually reshaped, blended, and recombined to produce the desired product, namely, Fastbuck doorstops.

WINK, on the other hand, uses a completely different process on its "raw material." Instead of a manufacturing process, it provides other types of services: Workers will be trained to provide assistance, and are monitored, supervised, and evaluated so that the best output (intervention) is provided to clients. Clients will be screened (intake) for appropriateness (or eligibility) for agency services, oriented to the intervention process, and participate in the intervention.

Both Fastbuck and WINK use *organizational technology* to process and apply their resources. Organizational technology includes all the activities performed to complete the organization's tasks and achieve its goals—that is, to convert inputs into outputs. Fastbuck's organizational technology involves manufacturing and processing materials into doorstops. Likewise, WINK's organizational technology involves the types of intakes, assessments, interventions, evaluations, and follow-ups the agency undertakes in helping clients. One other example of organizational technology is your college classroom. The organizational technology includes the teaching process, the activities and discussions in which you participate, and the information you receive.

Output

Both Fastbuck and WINK produce output (that is, some finished product) at the end of their processes. Fastbuck produces complete new doorstops ready to be marketed against Chinese and Indian competition.

WINK, on the other hand, has provided output in the form of interventions: perhaps 20 hours of family counseling, a referral to another agency for specialized treatment, or the provision of financial assistance to a client.

Outcomes

For Fastbuck, the desired outcome is great sales of its doorstops.

The desired outcome for WINK is clients who sleep better following intervention. Such effects or outcomes may also include better mental health.

If the output of either organization does not achieve organizational goals, the process is deemed unsuccessful. A company whose doorstops do not sell—or an agency that continues to give service (output) without successful results (outcomes)—is doomed to failure.

The Nature of Organizations

Understanding how an organization functions is particularly important to you for at least three reasons.

First, you will most likely be employed by one. Your organization's policies, goals, and restrictions will directly affect what work you can and cannot do with clients. Second, the organization, not the client, will often be the source of the problem. (We will discuss this later in much greater depth.) Therefore, you will need to evaluate for yourself how well your organization is functioning in order to do your work effectively. Third, organizational analysis is critically important prior to undertaking any macro level changes. You must understand a number of dimensions inherent in organizations to comprehend and plan the implementation of macro changes. The ensuing discussion defines two types of agency settings and then covers organizational goals, culture, structure, power, and politics.

Agency Settings

Social workers usually work in one of two types of organizations: a predominantly social work setting or a host setting. Each has implications for effective practice and for the way you will experience your work environment.

Predominantly Social Work Settings

In these settings, social work is the main or primary profession employed. The administrators, supervisors, and most of the workers are social workers and carry social work titles. Other occupations or professions may be present (for example, homemakers or psychologists), but they represent a minority of the staff. An advantage here is that administrators and staff having similar educational and practice backgrounds tend to share similar professional values and perspectives. Workers' roles and purposes may be better understood by all agency personnel.

Note that sometimes, particularly in public social work settings, decision makers may not be professional social workers. Rather, they may be elected officials, lawyers, or political appointees to boards and commissions that interpret legislative policy and tell agency staff how to operate and what to do. In these cases, even in settings where social work prevails, practitioners may be at the mercy of decision makers with agendas other than practice effectiveness and client satisfaction. Power, cost efficiency, and personal values can motivate decision makers to achieve other ends. Social agencies don't operate in a vacuum, but are intricately intertwined with other systems in the environment.

Host Settings

In contrast to predominantly social work settings, host settings are characterized by the presence of a variety of professional staff. The main service provided by the agency is not social services. Typical examples are hospitals and schools. In hospitals, medical care of patients is the primary service, and medically trained personnel (e.g., nurses and physicians) constitute the largest segment of the professional staff. Most of the administrative staff and supervisors have medical backgrounds. Social work is just one of several ancillary professions contributing to the overall goal of providing medical care. Other professions include dietitians, pharmacists, and chaplains, to name a few.

The wealth of disciplines and professional perspectives can produce a challenging environment for social work. Typically, social workers must learn the language (for instance, medical terminology or relevant abbreviations) used by the other professions. Social workers' roles and purpose may not be understood by all personnel. Host settings like hospitals are likely to operate with a definite pecking order. Physicians are at the top of that hierarchy; social workers are not. This sometimes means that social work values and perspectives clash with those of the physicians and other medical personnel. The following example illustrates how this can work.

Laura, a hospital social worker, was working with Tom, a 61-year-old patient with Parkinson's disease, and his family. Parkinson's disease is "a chronic progressive nervous disease chiefly of later life that is … marked by tremor of resting muscles, rigidity, slowness of movement, impaired balance, and by a shuffling gait" (Mish, 2008, p. 901). Tom had been hospitalized for a kidney malfunction unrelated to his Parkinson's disease. However, nurses referred Tom to Laura after they observed him fall several times while walking from his bed to the bathroom. These nurses felt that Tom would need special equipment, such as a walker or a wheelchair. They indicated he might even require special placement instead of returning to his home.

Laura met with Tom. The Parkinson's disease seriously affected his ability to formulate words, but, with some difficulty, she was able to discuss his situation with him. He stated vehemently that he wanted to return home. He emphasized that the disease "wasn't that bad" and stressed that he would be all right now that the kidney problem had subsided, if he could just get home!

Laura also spoke alone with Tom's wife, Wendy, age 59. Wendy felt that Tom was denying the seriousness of his condition. She said that his muscular control and balance had deteriorated significantly in the past four months. Wendy told Laura that Tom had been a professor of engineering at a prestigious private college. She explained that it was very difficult for him to admit to his increasingly serious weakness. Wendy also expressed concern about her ability to care for him adequately at home. Tom was a large hulk of a man, and it was impossible for her to lift him if he fell. She believed that someone needed to be with him at all times, yet she hesitated to move him into a health care facility. She felt it might break his spirit and his heart.

Laura discussed with them a variety of possibilities, including supportive equipment, widening the doorways in their home, installing ramps in their home for wheelchair accessibility, and referring them to various other support services. Laura also began arranging for a visiting nurse to assist Wendy with Tom's care and to allow Wendy some respite time to herself.

Laura felt good about her work with Tom and Wendy. She believed she had helped them establish a viable plan that could maintain Tom in his own home until his increasing disability required more extensive treatment. Laura had already contacted the recommended services to establish their availability and viability in Tom's case. The next step was to finalize the plans and put them in place before Tom's upcoming discharge.

Laura came to work the next morning and was shocked as she read Tom's chart. It stated he was being moved that very day to a health care facility. What about the plans she had made with Tom and Wendy? What about Tom's adamant feelings about remaining at his own home? In disbelief she stared at the signature of Tom's attending physician, Dr. Strangelove. Dr. Strangelove had totally ignored all that she had written in the chart about Tom's discharge planning. How dare Dr. Strangelove do this? How dare he blatantly disregard his patient's wishes? How dare he act as if she did not even exist?

By the next morning she had simmered down a bit. After all, Tom and Wendy had the right to choose their own destinies. She was just there to help them if she could.

When she later talked to the head nurse about the matter, Laura was enlightened about what it means to work in a secondary setting. She found out that the physician's word rules in a medical facility. Apparently, Dr. Strangelove was a personal friend of their son Devin, who was also a physician. Dr. Strangelove and Devin both felt strongly that it was ridiculous for Tom to return home and far beyond Wendy's marital responsibility to "sacrifice" herself for Tom. They had apparently urged and eventually persuaded Wendy to place Tom in a residential facility. It was the head nurse's opinion that Tom was too weak to fight three people at once. So, defeated, he complied with their recommendations.

Laura was not convinced that the decision was the correct one for either Tom or Wendy. However, she understood that they had every right to make their own decisions regardless of the dynamics involved in the decision-making process. Laura also learned that she had significantly less status than a physician in this host setting.

We have established that both host settings, such as this hospital environment, and predominantly social work settings can characterize organizations. Other important concepts in understanding organizational environments involve organizational mission statements, goals, and objectives.

Organizational Mission Statements

Every social services agency should develop a *mission statement,* a brief declaration of the organization's purpose that "establishes broad and relatively permanent parameters within which goals are developed and specific programs designed" (Kettner, Moroney, & Martin, 2008, p. 121). It also includes what client populations are to be served and provides general guidance for what needs should be met.

For example, Lad Lake Inc., a private nonprofit social services agency, has a mission statement saying it "provides living and learning environments for at-risk youth and families in preparation for responsible living in our communities" (Lad Lake Inc., undated). This is a broad statement that encompasses a range of programs, including the following:

- *A residential treatment center for adolescents with severe behavioral and emotional problems.*
- *Special education programs and an alternative school in the community.*
- *Independent living services to support children transitioning out of the foster care system as they approach age 18.*
- *Outreach services offering "guidance, therapy, and even friendship" to young people and their families.*
- *An in-home therapy program.*
- *A mentoring program serving youth ages 7 to 21 "with a history of substance abuse, truancy, disorderly conduct, or an unstable family life".*

- *A "Brighter Future Initiative" program offering "intervention services" to youth "who have committed their first minor delinquent offense" and to their families.*
- *Parent training classes.*
- *A number of other creative initiatives. (Lad Lake, 2009)*

Kettner and his colleagues (2008) provide two other examples of mission statements. One concerns a family service agency whose mission is "to promote family strength and stability in a manner that allows each individual to achieve his or her potential while, at the same time, supporting strong and productive interrelationship among family members" (p. 122). Still another mission statement involves an agency offering services to alcohol and drug addicts. Its mission is "to promote and support the achievement of a positive and productive lifestyle, including steady employment and stable relationships, for those formerly addicted to chemical substances" (p. 122). The "key" to a mission statement is that it "should focus on what lies ahead for its clients or consumers if the agency is successful in addressing their problems and meeting their needs" (Kettner et al., 2008, p. 122).

Organizational Goals

Mission statements identify the organization's basic reason for existence. *Organizational goals* "are statements of expected outcomes dealing with the problem that the program is attempting to prevent, eradicate, or ameliorate. They are responsive to problems and needs, and represent an ideal or hoped-for outcome (Coley & Scheinberg, 2000). Goals need not be measurable or achievable. They tend to be more general and provide a sense of programmatic direction" (Kettner et al., 2008, p. 123). Goals, then, elaborate upon the mission statement of an organization.

EP 2.1.10h

Organizational goals serve at least three major purposes (Etzioni, 1964). First, they provide guidelines for the kinds of functions and activities organizational workers are supposed to pursue. Second, organizational goals "constitute a source of legitimacy which justifies the activities of an organization and, indeed, its very existence" (p. 5). Third, goals can "serve as standards by which members of an organization and outsiders can assess the success of the organization—i.e., its effectiveness and efficiency" (p. 5).

How does an organization establish its mission statement and goals? As services must be in line with current social welfare policy and legislation, so must the mission statement and official goals. Mission and goals will also reflect the organization's stance in terms of treatment modality and values.

Social service organizations and agencies, then, formulate goals in order to address any of a wide range of needs and problems concerning human well-being. Social service organizations are supposed to use their resources to address these needs and remedy problems. The establishment of goals directs this process.

One aspect of many private organizations that involves organizational goals concerns a spiritual dimension. Some social service organizations are faith-based—that is, sponsored by or affiliated with a religious or spiritual organization. Such organizations "may contain elements that are guided by the faith assumptions of the group or some form of spirituality," which are reflected in the organization's goals (Barker, 2003, p. 154). Highlight 4.1 discusses faith-based social service organizations.

Multiple Goals

Social service organizations are often complex entities that aim to accomplish multiple goals (Austin, 2002; Ginsberg, 1995). There are a number of reasons for this. First, agencies are accountable to legislative requirements and constraints. For instance, an organization providing group homes for children with developmental disabilities must conform to a range of state licensing rules that mandate minimum standards for service provision. These include the maximum number of clients in any particular residence, the amount of space required per child, the staff-to-client ratio, and even the requirement that toilet seats be open or split in the front instead of closed.

Multiple goals also are set because many social service agencies serve a range of client groups. For example, one organization may provide day care services, vocational training, adoption services, and foster care, all at the same time. Lad Lake Inc., described earlier, provides another example of an organization sponsoring a wide range of programs pursuing many goals under a broad mission statement. Each segment of the agency pursues more individualized goals in the context of the larger environment with its more encompassing organizational goals.

Additionally, organizations are accountable to various different segments of the public, each with its own demands. Such segments can include "other human service organizations, interest groups, legislative bodies, and professional associations" in addition to clients being served (Ginsberg, 1995; Hasenfeld, 1983, pp. 90–91).

For example, a child advocacy group may pressure a social services agency specializing in helping survivors of domestic violence to increase its standards for temporary shelter of mothers and their children. Likewise, professional organizations may require the same agency to provide minimum in-service training sessions for staff in various positions. Hence, the agency must pursue both of these goals in addition to many other goals established for numerous other reasons.

Both a mission statement and an organization's multiple goals provide that organization with general direction regarding its purpose. However, implementing goals involves breaking them down into a series of steps. Highlight 4.2 discusses how more specific organizational objectives can be used to achieve organizational goals.

Goal Displacement

In order to understand an organization's functioning, it is helpful to think in terms of "official" goals and "operative" goals (Perrow, 1961, p. 856). *Official* goals "are the general purposes of the organization as put forth in the mission statement, annual reports, public statements by key officials and other authoritative pronouncements"; *operative* goals, on the other hand, "designate the ends sought through the actual operating policies of the organization" (p. 856). Official goals entail what the organization publicly says it is *supposed to do*. Operative goals are what the organization *really does* in its day-to-day practice with clients.

Why must we make the distinction between official and operative goals? In terms of daily organizational behavior, official goals may have very little to do with an agency's actual operative goals.

One major problem encountered by workers in organizations is *goal displacement.* Goal displacement was originally defined as "substitution of a legitimate goal with another goal which the organization was not developed to address, for which resources were not allocated and which it is not known to serve" (Etzioni, 1964, p. 10). Goal displacement "occurs when an organization moves in different directions from its original purpose. For example, the leaders of an alternative agency could become so concerned over being able to survive financially that they might apply for any available funds [in the form of grants], even if receiving the grant will mean taking the agency in a different direction from its original cause or purpose" in order to comply with the grant's requirements (Netting & O'Connor, 2003, p. 51). Another example is an organization that begins pursuing its leaders' personal

HIGHLIGHT 4.1

Faith-Based Social Services

A common context in which social workers face up to issues in spirituality and religion involves faith-based organizations. *Spirituality* concerns people's "search for meaning, purpose, and value in life"; *religion* is "a set of beliefs and practices of an organized religious institution ... It is important to note that *religion* is one form of spirituality. The two concepts are not mutually exclusive" (Frame, 2003, pp. 3–4).

EP 2.1.4

Faith-based social services have gained much attention, support, and flexibility in recent years (Lupu & Tuttle, 2008). Because it is possible that you will either work in faith-based agencies or be working with them in some capacity, we will spend some time describing them here. Cnaan and Boddie (2002) explain the policy scene. The Personal Responsibility and Work Opportunity Reconciliation Act (PRWORA) of 1996 that structures the social welfare public assistance system in the United States includes a section known as "Charitable Choice." Before PRWORA was implemented,

> a faith-based organization contracting with the government had to remove all religious symbols from the room where service was provided; forego any religious ceremonies (such as prayers at meals); accept all clients-even those opposed to the beliefs of the providers; hire staff that reflected society at large and not the organization's spirit and belief system; adhere to government contract regulations; and incorporate separately as ... [a] nonprofit organization (p. 225).

The idea was clearly to maintain the separation between church and state. Charitable Choice, however, permits

> faith-based service providers [to] retain their religious autonomy... In addition, the government cannot curtail the religious expression or practice of faith-based services providers by requiring them to change their internal governance or remove from their property any "religious art, icons, scripture, or other symbols" (S104 (a)(2)) ... [The legislation also] allows faith-based organizations to have discretion in hiring only those people who share their religious beliefs or traditions and to terminate employees who do not exhibit behavior consistent with the religious practices of the organization. (p. 226)

Faith-based organizations may offer a broad assortment of services. These include "job-search, job-readiness, job-skills training programs; Literacy, General Education Development (GED) and English as a Second Language (ESL) programs; food, shelter, and clothing; social services and referral; child care and transportation; and counseling services, among others" (Texas Workforce Commission, 2004).

Tangenberg (2005) provides some examples of how diverse faith-based programs can be in terms of service programming, conceptualization of faith, and expression of spirituality:

> *The Daylight Shelter organization provides overnight shelter and meals to homeless individuals and families. Prayer occurs before meals, and evening worship services open to the public are offered five times each week. Engagement in religious activities is optional. Men and women also may choose to participate in 12-step recovery programs that are separated by gender and have a strong religious focus. Religious activities in the recovery programs are required and are discussed before participation so referrals to secular programs can be made if necessary.... Describing the program's spiritual base, the Director said:*
>
> *"Our program is Christ-centered.... [Program participants] have to go to church—hey pick their own churches—we do devotions every morning, we have Bible studies three times a week, we have Bible classes."...*
>
> *[In contrast,] [t]he Jackson Community Center is an organization with no religious references in its name or program activities, although it is closely affiliated with a large Protestant denomination. Primary services include adult basic education and employment preparation....*
>
> *Some board members must be members of the founding Christian denomination, and ties to the denomination are strong, although there are no expectations regarding the faith commitments of staff members. Values of dignity, care, and compassion are emphasized rather than a specific religious ideology, and financial and volunteer support is frequently sought from the religious community....*
>
> *[Yet another example involves] Peace House [which] is a drop-in center that provides meals and emergency services for homeless men and women and outreach to former center guests who are in jail or prison....*
>
> *Although it originated under Catholic auspices, Peace House includes staff from various faith traditions sharing spiritual values of compassion and service. No organized religious programs are available for guests, and no religious symbols are displayed, although staff meet daily for meditation and prayer and have a small weekly liturgy. (pp. 203–204)*

Many issues can surface when social workers enter the realm of spirituality in a faith-based setting. Questions can arise regarding how the worker's own sense of spirituality coincides or contrasts with the host agency's perspective. There are no easy answers to such questions. A worker may struggle with personal views that are at odds with the agency's. A practitioner must always address such issues in an ethical and professional manner. If views between the agency and the worker are too incongruent, leaving the agency may be an appropriate solution.

Derezotes (2006) reflects upon spiritually-oriented social workers:

> From a spiritual perspective, the common denominator of all religions should be kindness. The spiritually-oriented social worker respects the diversity of doctrines, rituals, and beliefs found in the religions of the world and she or he realizes that all religions can either foster and/or hinder spiritual development. The social worker never tries to change the religion of an individual or community, but may work to help make that religion more of a [supportive] Community of Spiritual and Universal Diversity. The social worker refuses to practice "religionism"; she or he does not evaluate a person or group based upon religion, but does evaluate the individual or group's unique expression of that religion ... [T]he worker also respects the client's spiritual faith system, and will ask the client ... if he [or she] wants to work toward his own spiritual growth and transformation. (pp. 260–261)

interests rather than achieving its official goals (Netting, Ketnner, & McMorty, 2008).

In other words, goal displacement occurs when an organization continues to function but no longer achieves the goals it's supposed to. Sometimes, it happens when the *process* of achieving goals takes precedence over the actual goal *attainment*. In social service organizations, it often means that the rules and following those rules become more important than providing services to clients. Highlight 4.3 provides an example of goal displacement.

Of course, goals can change in positive ways. A classic example is the March of Dimes, which began as an organization dedicated to raising money to eradicate polio, historically a major childhood disease. With the discovery of a polio vaccine, the disease ceased to be a major health problem. Instead of going out of business, however, the organization simply shifted its goal to raising money to combat birth defects. The new substitute goal had one advantage over the polio-related goal: Instead of focusing on a single disease, the organization now directed its attention to a broad category of problems. With such a broad scope, the organization will probably never run out of childhood health problems to combat, so it's unlikely that it will ever again face the dilemma of goal substitution.

This is not a criticism of the March of Dimes or any other organization. It is a fact of organizational life that agencies rarely go out of existence. Once a goal is achieved, most organizations do not disappear. Instead, they shift their attention to new goals. This process becomes a problem only when the means to the goals assume a life of their own. When this happens, agencies

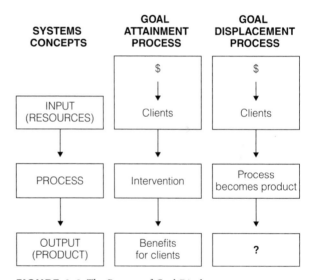

FIGURE 4.4 The Process of Goal Displacement

place greater emphasis on getting the files up-to-date than on providing effective services to clients.

Systems Theories, Organizations, and Goal Displacement

We have established that it is helpful to view social service organizations in terms of systems theories and that many of the concepts involved are similar to those we use to refer to business and industry. In industry, resources or input are processed by the organizational system, which turns out a product, or *output*. Figure 4.4 illustrates this sequence as "systems concepts."

When goal displacement occurs, however, the emphasis shifts to the process rather than the product.

HIGHLIGHT 4.2

Organizational Objectives Indicate How to Achieve Goals

Goals provide social services agencies with general direction concerning *what* should happen, but not with specific guidance regarding *how* it should be done. *Objectives* are smaller, behaviorally specific subgroups that serve as stepping-stones on the way to accomplishing the main goal. Brody (2005) explains:

EP 2.1.10h

> Typically, goals represent long-term endeavors, sometimes as long as three to five years, and may even be timeless. Examples of these goal statements would be "Improving access to health-care services for low-income persons" or "reducing racism in our community."...
>
> Objectives represent relevant, attainable, measurable, and time-limited ends to be achieved. They are relevant because they fit within the general mission and goals of the organization and because they relate to problems identified by the organization. They are attainable because they can be realized. They are measurable because achievement is based upon tangible, concrete, and usually quantifiable results. They are time limited (usually a year); this time frame helps the organization demonstrate concrete results within a specified period. (pp. 58–59)

Kettner and his colleagues (2008) recommend that the following questions be asked in order to establish a "clear, specific, measurable, time-limited, and realistic" goal that the agency is committed to achieve:

- *Is the objective clear? Does it mean the same thing to anyone who reads the statement? ...*
- *Does the objective specify results to be achieved, including numbers and changes in conditions? ...*
- *Is the objective written in such a way that it can be measured? Are measurement (numerical) criteria incorporated into the objective? ...*
- *Does the statement indicate a time limit within which clearly defined the objective will be achieved? ...*
- *Is the objective realistic given our technology and knowledge as well as available resources?" ...*
- *Does the objective identify who has responsibility for ensuring that the objective is achieved? (p. 125)*

Brody (2005) identifies four basic types of objectives used in social service agencies–impact *service, operational,* and *product* (p. 59):

Impact objectives *specify outcomes to be achieved as a result of program activities. They detail the return*

expected on the organization's investment of time, personnel, and resources. The following are examples:

- *To place 20 children in adoptive homes in one year.*
- *To secure jobs for 35 juvenile delinquents in 5 months.*
- *To increase the number of foster children reunited with their natural parents from 40 to 50 by June 30...*

Service objectives *are the organization's tally of activities provided or services rendered. Sometimes these are referred to as activity or process objectives. Examples include the following:*

- *To serve 300 clients in the program year.*
- *To conduct 680 interviews.*
- *To provide 17 neighborhood assemblies.*
- *To interview 20 children needing foster homes ...*

Operational objectives *convey the intent to improve the general operation of the organization. Examples include the following:*

- *To sponsor four in-service training workshops for 40 staff.*
- *To obtain a pilot project grant of $10,000 within six months.*
- *To increase the number of volunteers by 150.*
- *To reduce staff turnover from 20 percent to 10 percent annually.*

Operational objectives *are essential to enhance the way an organization functions. They are a means to the end for which the organization was established. By providing in-service training, for example, an organization improves the way it serves its target populations.*

Product objectives *are designed to provide a tangible outcome to benefit a target population or a community.... The following are examples of product objectives:*

- *To obtain passage of House Bill 41.*
- *To develop a neighborhood family support system.*
- *To review and critique a specific piece of legislation.*
- *To open four schools in the evening for recreation.*
- *To provide a media effort on teen pregnancy prevention...*
- *To sponsor a community-wide campaign on mental health. (pp. 59–60)*

HIGHLIGHT 4.3

Goal Displacement: Process Superseding Progress

A large county department of social services (or public welfare department) is located in the shell of an old department store with high ceilings and myriad small worker cubicles resembling a mammoth beehive. All outside windows have been sealed with bricks because of "heating and ventilation problems." No one really knows what that means. However, everyone inside the building knows that the interior is isolated from the outside world.

When entering the main door of the building, people have difficulty figuring out where to find a particular kind of service. This is true even of professional social workers, let alone clients entering the building for the first time. Consider what it would be like if you were a client applying for services from this agency. You probably have to stand in line for 15 to 20 minutes simply to find out where to go.

When you finally locate a waiting area for the services you need, you have to stand in line again for another 20 minutes or so to get the forms you must fill out for the services you need. You then receive 20 pages of complicated forms, which you must fill out meticulously, and take a seat. The chairs are made of hard plastic. There are large dust bunnies (sometimes referred to as "dust dinosaurs") rolling around your feet. It takes approximately an hour to fill out the forms, assuming you can read English well. You probably do not understand some of the questions, so you leave the spaces blank. You then take the forms to the desk, where they are placed in a pile. You wait your turn to see an intake worker (that is, someone who begins the process of providing services). You wait two or three hours.

Finally, your name is called and you are instructed to go to Cubicle 57 to see Ms. Simpson. You enter Cubicle 57 and see Ms. Simpson sitting at her desk, reading your forms. You begin a discussion with her about the additional information she needs to process your application. It seems, she indicates, that a number of critical elements of information are missing. You look at those blanks. She tells you to get the critical information before you continue the application process, but that critical information is somewhere at home. Well, that's all right. You'll just go home, get it, and start this whole process again tomorrow. At least you know where the waiting room is now.

In this example, the organization is supposed to provide services to people in need. However, the complicated process, commonly called *red tape,* has become more important to the workers than whether clients receive needed services or not.

People's access to resources has a major impact on the options available to them and, in effect on how they behave. Poverty and lack of resources are at the root of many of your client's problems. Therefore, it is crucial to understand how organizations affect resource provision and clients. Such a background can enable you to identify ways to change systems so that your clients really are served better.

Consider the example above. As a worker in that agency, you might target several things for change, including shortening the tedious forms, and informing community residents about what documentation and information to bring when applying for services. Simple things like putting up clearly visible signs in relevant languages instructing people where to go when they first enter the building might be helpful. Suggesting comfortable waiting room chairs might be useful.

The organizational system comes to see the process of providing services as its major function. The process, rather than its benefit to the client, becomes the organization's *product.*

Goal attainment refers to what is supposed to happen through the intervention process. An agency's goal attainment process is illustrated in the center of Figure 4.4: the input (in the form of resources) is used to benefit clients through the intervention process. Hence, "$" refers to resources with an arrow pointing to "Clients" in the top box. The result is supposed to be positive benefits for clients. Thus, an arrow points from the "$ to Clients" upper box to the middle box,

"Intervention." The intervention process is whatever treatment or technology the organization uses to help its clients. Finally, an arrow points from the "Intervention" box down to the "Benefits for clients" box.

Figure 4.4 also illustrates *goal displacement* on the far right. Here, input is used to maintain the *process* itself. In essence, the process becomes the *product.* Positive impacts on clients are forgotten as agency personnel focus on maintaining and completing the process. Figure 4.4 depicts this with arrows leading from the "$ to Clients" upper box to the "Process becomes product" middle box. The arrow leading from the latter box down to the "?" bottom box shows that the actual results for clients have become relatively unimportant and possibly unknown.

Organizational Culture

We have defined *organizational culture* as "the set of values, norms, guiding beliefs, and understandings that is shared by members of an organization and taught to new members as the correct way to think, feel, and behave" (Daft, 2010b, p. 374). Many aspects of culture entail unwritten rules, traditions, and practices that hold the organization together (Hellriegel & Slocum, 2009). Organizational culture can include expectations for level of performance, interpersonal communication and interaction, and management style. It can also "be understood through the visible manifestations of symbols, stories, heroes, slogans, and ceremonies" (Daft & Marcic, 2009, p. 64).

Organizational culture, then, involves many facets. For example, what kind of attire is considered appropriate within the organization's cultural environment—suits or jeans? A hospital social worker might choose to dress more formally because the environment is full of uniformed professionals and informal dress might appear "unprofessional." A residential treatment center for males with behavioral disorders, on the other hand, might manifest a very informal organizational culture, at least concerning dress. The latter culture might expect social workers and counselors to participate in informal group sessions in the living units, recreational activities, and administration of consequences for poor behavior. It makes sense to dress comfortably and informally in such an environment.

Another facet of organizational culture is the agency's "personality." Each agency has its own personality: It is more formal or informal, structured or unstructured, innovative or traditional than other agencies. From the first day of work within an agency, new employees should explore and begin understanding that agency's character. How much freedom do workers have in conducting daily professional activities? What tasks are considered the most important (for example, documentation of treatment effectiveness, other record-keeping, administrative conferences, or number of hours spent with clients)?

Organizational culture is a common concept in organization studies, regardless of the theoretical perspective assumed. The cultural theoretical perspective on organizations discussed earlier, of course, emphasizes culture as the primary dimension for understanding organizational functioning. Other theories give the concept of culture less emphasis in relationship to the numerous other dimensions involved in organizations.

Organizational Structure

Organizational structure is the "system of task, reporting, and authority relationships within which the work of the organization is done" (Griffin & Moorhead, 2010, p. 407). All large agencies (and most smaller ones) have a *formal structure*. Sometimes it is explicated in an organizational chart showing who reports to whom (Daft, 2010a; Griffin & Moorhead, 2010). Such charts depict lines of authority and communication within the agency. Frequently, the agency operates in accordance with this chart, at least with respect to some functions, such as how information is disseminated, either from the top down or bottom up.

Agencies also develop *informal* structures and lines of communication. For example, it is typical for an agency to structure its units so that all workers in the unit report to one supervisor. Consider the case of the Rocky County Foster Care Unit. Five workers and a supervisor work in this unit. When workers have questions or problems, they are supposed to bring them to Boris, the unit supervisor. Often, though, workers in the unit discuss their cases with other workers or with Natasha, the senior worker in another county agency. This means Boris may lack information—input or feedback from his supervisees—that might be important to his job.

Although confiding in Natasha may seem like a bad arrangement, it has some beneficial aspects. Workers who are sometimes uncomfortable talking with their supervisor can get help from other more experienced workers. Maybe Boris is not competent to provide answers or is too lazy or busy to take the time. Natasha might be an extremely knowledgeable, pleasant person who likes to help her colleagues. Sharing ideas and problems helps to produce a camaraderie among the workers. This decreases their stress levels and often leads to better job performance. Human relations theories stress the importance of such interpersonal communication and support in organizations.

The point here is not to praise or criticize informal structures and communication channels. Instead, it is to acknowledge that they do exist and are a reality in all organizations. In practice, being aware of both formal and informal avenues can strengthen your ability to do your job. Once you know all your options and alternatives, you can make more informed choices. This is, after all, a major goal of the planned change process.

Three concepts are especially significant when appraising an agency's formal and informal structures. These are lines of authority, channels of communication, and dimensions of power. The pros and cons of centralization versus decentralization will also be briefly addressed.

Lines of Authority

An agency's formal structure rests on *lines of authority* (Daft, 2010a; Griffin & Moorhead, 2010). For our purposes, authority is the specific administrative and supervisory responsibilities of supervisors to their supervisees. Who is designated to supervise whom? Agency policy usually specifies these lines of authority in writing.

We have established that an agency's formal structure is often explained in an organizational chart. Positions held by individual staff members are portrayed as icons (circles or squares) labeled with their respective job positions. Generally, job icons placed higher on the chart have greater authority than those placed lower. The hierarchy of authority in an organizational chart is depicted by vertical lines leading from supervisors down to supervisees (Daft, 2010a; Jansson, 2008). Jansson (2008) explains:

> Organizational charts [may] tell us a great deal about the players in a specific organization. ... [P]eople at high levels in the hierarchy ... usually have powers and prerogatives that enable them to shape decisions. They help make budgets; participate in hiring, firing, promoting, and supervising lower-level staff; obtain access to information about the personnel, programs, and budgets of the agency; and have access to information about the resources and institutions in the agency's external environment. (p. 143)

The formal organizational structure as demonstrated by an organizational chart, then, indicates how control and supervision are supposed to flow.

The chart in Figure 4.5 reflects the hierarchy of authority for Multihelp, an agency providing assessment and therapeutic treatment to children with multiple developmental and physical disabilities. Parents bring children with a wide range of physical and behavioral difficulties to the agency to assess the children's abilities in a variety of areas, plan treatment programs, and provide appropriate therapies.

The rectangles in Figure 4.5 designate those positions with some administrative responsibility in the agency system. The executive director has the most authority and is responsible for the overall performance of Multihelp. Below him are five agency directors, including the medical director (a physician), and those for accounting, maintenance engineering, food services for clients and staff, and transportation services for clients. Each director (except accounting) is, in turn, responsible for the supervision of other staff further down the hierarchy. The medical director is responsible for overseeing the entire clinical program, including the work of the various departmental supervisors. Departments include occupational therapy, physical therapy, speech therapy, psychology, and social work. Circles at the very bottom of the chart represent line staff who are providing services directly to or regarding clients.

If you examine this chart, it is painfully clear how this agency is run, right? If you look at the Social Work Department, there are two direct-service workers who report directly to their social work supervisor. It is obvious that these social workers go about their business of providing services to clients and look to their own supervisor for direction. The chain of command is so evident, you may believe that analyzing this chart is monotonous overkill.

The catch is that formal organizational charts depict lines of *formal* authority within agencies, showing how communication and power are supposed to flow. Sometimes, an agency's actual chain of command follows the formal chart fairly closely. Equally often, however, agencies develop *informal* channels of communication and power that are very different from those stated on paper. Let's explore Multihelp's informal channels of communication and dimensions of power.

Channels of Communication

All agencies have numerous ways in which information is conveyed or communicated. *Communication,* of course, is the process of imparting and exchanging information by using language, signs, symbols, or behavior. Communication, then, covers the many nuances of how information is conveyed, verbally and nonverbally. It entails subtle inflections, some comfort level between communicators, and multitudes of minute gestures.

Formal lines of authority imply that communication is supposed to flow harmoniously and synchronistically along these lines of authority. In other words, supervisees are *supposed* to communicate primarily with their identified supervisors for direction and feedback. Likewise, supervisors are supposed to communicate directly with their supervisees and the managers who supervise them. As we will see, in Multihelp, this is not the case.

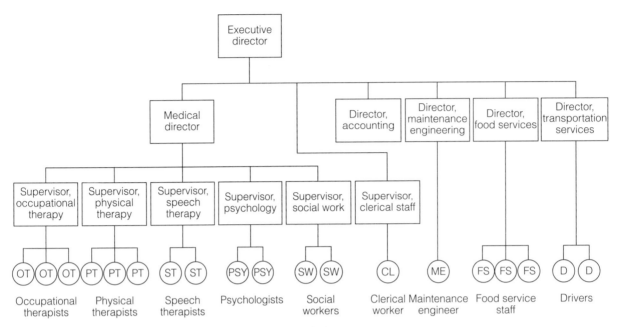

FIGURE 4.5 Multihelp—An Example of a Formal Organizational Chart

FIGURE 4.6 Contrasting Formal and Informal Structures in Agencies

Dimensions of Power in the Formal Structure

Power is the potential ability to move people on a chosen course to produce an effect or achieve some goal (Griffin & Moorhead, 2010; Homan, 2008). Like channels of communication, dimensions of power are supposed to follow the lines of authority. In the organizational chart, those in supervisory positions are supposed to have actual power (that is, clear-cut influence and control) over their employees. In real-life agency environments, this may not be the case. A later section of this chapter further discusses power and politics in organizational settings.

Informal Structure: Multihelp–An Example

Figure 4.6 shows one small portion of the formal organization chart depicted in Figure 4.5: the Social Work and Psychology Departments. Figure 4.6, however, shows both the *formal* and *informal* structures of these two agency departments. The real channels of communication and dimensions of power among supervisors and direct-service staff are very different from those illustrated in the formal organizational chart. The real relationships reflect the personalities and interactions of people, who have unique perspectives and identities, strengths and weaknesses, and problems and needs of their own.

The formal structure pictures Loraine, the Psychology Department's supervisor, as responsible for the administration and supervision of both Singh's and Shirley's job performance. Both Singh and Shirley have master's degrees in psychology. Likewise, the formal structure shows Keiko, the Social Work Department's supervisor, as having direct supervisory authority over both Sharon and Linda, each of whom has a master's degree in social work.

The right side portrays the real-life informal structure of these departments. Sharon, one of the social workers, has become good friends with Loraine, the Psychology Department's supervisor. Both single, they frequently socialize together and even vacation together. Their positive relationship is reflected by the bold line connecting them in Figure 4.6.

Sharon, on the other hand, does not get along with Keiko, her supervisor. Whatever "having a personality conflict" really means, it could describe Sharon and Keiko's relationship. They do not personally like each other. Additionally, Sharon views Keiko as incompetent, lazy, and interested in doing as little work as possible. On the other hand, Keiko perceives Sharon as an overly energetic, impulsive go-getter who acts "just like a bull in a china shop." They interact as little as possible with each other. Most communication between them takes place in memo form, with Keiko issuing Sharon direct commands regarding what should and should not be done. Figure 4.6 illustrates Keiko and Sharon's relationship by the arrow that curves up from Keiko and down again to Sharon. Communication and power consistently flow downward from Keiko to Sharon in a dictatorial, hierarchical fashion. Cross lines on the arrow indicate conflict.

Keiko, on the other hand, has much in common with Linda, the other social worker. They spend time together and frequently go out to lunch. Keiko views Linda as a calmly competent worker who communicates well and is enjoyable company. In effect, Keiko treats Linda like a friend and equal. Figure 4.6 illustrates this relationship with the bold line linking Keiko and Linda horizontally.

Now, let's investigate the informal relationships within the Psychology Department. Supervisor Loraine sees Singh, one of her supervisees, as a competent professional colleague. Hence, Figure 4.6 portrays Singh slightly below Loraine. The connecting arrow flows from Loraine down to Singh because Loraine maintains her supervisory and administrative status with respect to Singh. They essentially like each other on a professional basis, but neither considers the other a personal friend.

Loraine, on the other hand, perceives Shirley, her other supervisee, in a much different light. Loraine regrets hiring Shirley and has begun to document Shirley's performance difficulties in preparation for dismissing her from the agency. Thus, Shirley is positioned significantly below Loraine, the arrow connecting them running from Loraine down to Shirley. The chain of communication and power clearly positions Loraine in the more powerful, communication-controlling position and Shirley in an inferior, less powerful, communication-receiving status. Cross lines on the arrow again indicate conflict.

However, the plot is even more complicated. Sharon, who is substantially younger than Loraine, is about the same age as Shirley, who is also single. Sharon and Shirley have much in common and have established a firm friendship. They, too, occasionally spend time and socialize with each other. Thus, a vertical line connecting them indicates that they consider each other equals, friends, and colleagues, despite the fact that Loraine and Shirley's relationship is poor and quickly deteriorating.

Sharon is therefore in an uncomfortable and tenuous position. On the one hand, she values her friendship with Loraine and sees her as a professional ally within the agency who provides her with some leverage against Keiko. On the other hand, Sharon likes Shirley. Sharon understands that Loraine is not perfect (and that she herself isn't either). Thus, Sharon can listen to Shirley's complaints against Loraine and provide some sympathy. Sharon, however, must be extremely careful not to speak against either Loraine or Shirley to the other person. It is not easy to maintain such a balancing act.

Our point is to acknowledge that informal communication channels exist in any agency, including yours. Being aware of both formal and informal agency structures can provide you with information about where you can turn for help and support. It can also give you clues regarding who to treat with kid gloves or avoid altogether. Finally, it can help you decide how well you fit in and whether you should look for another job.

What eventually happened at Multihelp? Shirley left for another position in another state. Shirley and Sharon soon lost contact. Six months later, Sharon also left the agency for another social work position that more closely matched her energetic, enthusiastic style. She became a counselor for teens with serious behavioral and family problems. Sharon and Loraine continued to maintain their personal friendship for many years after Sharon left the agency. No one knows what happened to Keiko, Linda, or Singh.

Power and Politics in Organizations

We have established that *power* is the potential ability to move people on a chosen course to produce an effect or achieve some goal. As power is such an important concept regarding social service organizations, we will spend considerable time here discussing it and its implications for you at your job. Who has power and how it is used directly affects your ability to work effectively. Management has power over workers (including you when you get a job). However, we determined earlier that there are various types of power that don't necessarily coincide with the formal organizational chart. Therefore, a discussion of power in organizations is relevant to you for at least two reasons. First, management has the potential to empower you to do your job well. Second, as a worker you can think in terms of your own power and how you can strive to improve agency functioning. You may also develop tactics to influence people in power when advocating on clients' behalf or for improved service provision. For example, you might feel that agency hours should be extended to better accommodate clients' schedules. Or you might feel clients' needs are not being met adequately in some area (for example, counseling, transportation, financial support), and you decide to advocate on their behalf. Acquisition of a power base may also be useful when requesting benefits such as a raise or select vacation times.

Types of Power

There are (at least) the following five sources of power (Champoux, 2006; Daft & Marcic, 2009; Dumler & Skinner, 2008; Lussier, 2009):

1. *Legitimate power* (that attained because of one's position and vested authority);
2. *Reward power* (that held because of the ability to provide positive reinforcement and rewards to others);
3. *Coercive power* (the capability of dispensing punishments in order to influence others' behavior);
4. *Referent power* (that held as a result of other group members' respect and high esteem); and
5. *Expert power* (that based on established authority or expertise in a particular domain).

Supervisors and managers usually are given legitimate power. They also often have reward and coercive power. Anyone, including direct-service workers and supervisors or managers, can develop referent and expert power.

The concept of power is quite complex. For example, a supervisor has power by virtue of his or her position in the organizational structure. Yet, the extent of that power varies significantly depending on the supervisor's competence and interpersonal skills. Chapter 2 discussed some of the problems often apparent in supervisory relationships. An overbearing supervisor who is considered "too pushy" by supervisees may be met with considerable resistance by them. These subordinates may react by demonstrating passive-aggressive behavior, where they superficially appear cooperative, but covertly work against the supervisor as much as possible. Such supervisees also enjoy a certain amount of power themselves in that they can substantially affect the supervisor's effectiveness. The supervisor may then "look bad" to his or her own managerial superiors.

Determining who has power can be tricky. Sometimes, people with important titles or placement high in the organizational structure have little ability to influence subordinates' behavior in reality. "*Influence* is the effect a person's actions have on the attitudes, values, beliefs, or behavior of others. Whereas power is the *capacity* to cause a change in a person, influence may be thought of as the degree of *actual* change [some emphasis added]" (Daft, 2010a, p. 426).

Because people in power have the potential ability to influence your work behavior and how clients are served, it's important to know who has this power. Aldag and Kuzuhara (2005) explain:

> How can you tell who has power in an organization? Job titles may help; so may status symbols. Still, we know these things can be deceptive and that some people with a lot of power don't have fancy titles or big offices. Some other signs of managers' power include the abilities to do the following:
>
> - Intercede favorably on behalf of someone in trouble with the organization.
> - Get a good placement for a talented subordinate.
> - Gain approval for expenditures beyond the budget.
> - Obtain above-average salary increases for subordinates.
> - Place items on the agenda at policy meetings.
> - Get fast access to top decision makers.
> - Have regular, frequent access to top decision makers.
> - Obtain early information about decisions and policy shifts (Kanter, 1979; Rynecki, Smith, Shanley, & Wheat, 2003). (pp. 370–371)

Politics in Social Service Organizations

Aldag and Kuzuhara (2005) describe *organizational politics*:

> *When we hear someone speak of organizational politics, we probably think of such things as "passing the buck," "apple polishing," "backstabbing," and other "dirty tricks" we use to further our selfish interests. We use the term organizational politics more broadly to refer to activities that people perform to acquire, enhance, and use power and other resources to obtain their preferred outcomes in a situation where there is uncertainty or disagreement. Because the focus is on people's preferred outcomes, rather than organizational outcomes, this may or may not involve activities contrary to the best interests of the organization (Pfeffer, 1981). (p. 378)*

Don't automatically think that organizational politics are always evil and self-serving (Hellriegel & Slocum, 2009). Sometimes agency problems or needs should be addressed. A policy might not be working or a supervisor might not be performing all her responsibilities. You should be aware of organizational politics in order to improve problematic situations and implement positive changes. Most people prefer to be somewhat "political" by avoiding "criticizing your boss in public, losing control of your emotions during meetings, or challenging sacred beliefs or values of the organization. Therefore, being aware of politics may be important, if only to be alert for the political actions of others and to avoid personal embarrassment" (Aldag & Kuzuhara, 2005, p. 379). Highlight 4.4 describes some of the dynamics affecting people's political behavior in the agency context.

Using Agency Politics for Positive Change

We've indicated that as an agency worker, you may be in the position to advocate for positive change on the behalf of clients or agency personnel. The following are tactics to establish a power base within an agency setting so that you might have greater influence with decision makers.

First, conduct a *political diagnosis,* an assessment of "the location of power in an organization and the type of political behavior that is likely to happen. It identifies politically active individuals and coalitions in the organization, the amount of power they have, and the likely ways they will use their power" (Champoux, 2006, p. 367).

You can pursue several strategies to identify individuals who have power; start with "the organizational chart and a description of titles and duties" (Champoux, 2006, p. 367). Then interview people in various organizational units to determine how decisions are made, who has decision-making responsibility for distributing resources, how the identified people generally use their power or are likely to, and what their goals are for their performance and status within the organization.

HIGHLIGHT 4.4

Dynamics Contributing to Political Behavior in Agencies

There are at least two reasons why politics occur in organizations:

1. *Organizations are, by nature, political (Dubrin, 2007; Griffin & Moorhead, 2010).* They are made up of a range of units or departments, each striving to achieve its own goals and competing for resources. Competition is a fact of life when resources are limited or scarce. Power enhances the ability to compete.
2. *Some people are more power-oriented than others (Dubrin, 2007).* When power is limited, power-oriented workers, supervisors, or managers will often try to expand their influence. "Power-oriented managers [or supervisors] sometimes cope with the limited amount of power available by expanding their sphere of influence sideways. For example, the director of the food stamp program in a government agency might attempt to gain control over the housing assistance program, which is at the same level" (p. 270). (*Foodstamps* are credits distributed through a federal program to be used like cash to purchase primarily food, plants, and seeds [Barker, 2003]. *Housing assistance* often involves rental subsidies or vouchers by which government programs assist with rent mortgage payments, and low-rent public housing, or block grants to state and local governments for developing affordable housing [Dolgoff & Feldstein, 2003].) Some people who are extremely concerned with gaining power are characterized by "*Machiavellianism,* a tendency to manipulate others for personal gain" (DuBrin, 2007, p. 270). Such people thrive on gaining power for power's sake.

It is also important to identify any coalitions within the agency. "A *coalition* is an alliance of individuals who share a common goal. Coalitions are also interest groups that try to affect decisions in the organization. Coalitions can have members from widely scattered parts of the organization" (Champoux, 2006, p. 368). Assessing coalitions should involve the same strategies used in assessing the power of individuals within the organization. This should help establish the agency's *political network*, the system of "affiliations and alliances of individuals and coalitions" within the social service organization's environment (Champoux, 2006, p. 368).

A second tactic for enhancing power and influence involves developing contacts and relationships with people in power (DuBrin, 2007). Such people can provide you with support and information to help achieve your goals.

Third, to increase your power base, form coalitions yourself (Lussier, 2009; Vecchio, 2006). This may be as simple a thing as forming a coalition to have enough votes to get a proposal passed in a committee. Or it may involve a coalition approaching an administrator with a new idea to persuade him or her to adopt it. Involving more people tends to enhance your credibility and validity.

Fourth, get information about what's going on (Aldag & Kuzuhara, 2005; Dubrin, 2007). Keeping current helps you develop believable arguments on your behalf. Being knowledgeable inspires people's confidence in you.

Fifth, provide positive feedback where warranted (Aldag & Kuzuhara, 2005). Positive feedback can be given concerning others' statements, support, and performance; it should be "a straightforward and specific declaration of what the person did right" (DuBrin, 2007, p. 273). Positive feedback helps to strengthen interpersonal relationships. Persistent complainers tend to turn other people off. People with positive proposals who are known to be supportive are more easily heard.

Sixth, use assertive communication (DuBrin, 2009; Vecchio, 2006). "*Assertiveness* involves being able to state your thoughts, wants, and feelings straightforwardly and effectively, [taking] … both your needs and the needs of others into account" (Kirst-Ashman & Hull, 2009, pp. 164–165). Of course, being assertive does not mean that you should avoid tact. Always consider the communication receiver's feelings. Effective assertive communication means thinking about the best way to state your ideas at the most appropriate time.

Tactics Not to Use in Agency Politics: Problematic, Unethical Behavior

We've noted that inappropriate and unethical behavior can occur in organizations. Some political tactics are designed to hurt other people. Others are intended for selfish advancement. Some tactics can ruin your reputation or have very negative consequences in the future. The following six strategies should not be used when involved in agency politics.

EP 2.1.2

1. *Don't engage in "backstabbing"* (DuBrin, 2007, p. 274). Backstabbing "requires that you pretend to be nice but all the while plan someone's demise. A frequent form of backstabbing is to inform your rival's superior that he or she is faltering under the pressure of job responsibilities" (DuBrin, 2007, p. 274). People backstab to make themselves look better or, more important, to get ahead in competitive situations. Backstabbing is devious, self-serving, and unprofessional. It usually results in deterioration of interpersonal relationships and the ability to function as a team. "The recommended approach to dealing with a backstabber is to confront the person directly, ask for an explanation of his or her behavior, and demand that he or she stop" (DuBrin, 2007, p. 274).

2. *Don't set up a person for failure* (DuBrin, 2002, p. 247). "The object of the setup is to place a person in a position where he or she will either fail outright or look ineffective. For example, a supervisor who the agency head dislikes might be given responsibility for a troubled department. The newly appointed supervisor cannot improve productivity, is then reprimanded for poor performance, and the negative evaluation becomes part of the person's permanent record" (DuBrin, 2002, p. 247).

   At one point I was a newly promoted supervisor of a social work unit in a day treatment center for youth having serious emotional and behavioral problems. The center provided therapy and special education for troubled youth residing in the community. The program's two primary components were social services and therapy under my direction, and the school under its principal's direction. I was young and didn't know much about supervision or agency politics. For whatever reason, the school principal was not supportive of my promotion. The director informed the principal and me (who were equals on the organizational chart) that new recording requirements of clients' progress would require twice as much time and work as before. *None* of the staff—teachers, teaching assistants, or social workers—would be at all happy about that news. The principal asked me to make the announcement at an all-staff meeting. I foolishly did what he told me to and made the announcement both to my social work supervisees and to his teaching staff. Everyone immediately viewed me as the bringer of bad tidings and "the bad guy," an image that persisted for months. The principal benefited in at least two ways by setting me up for failure. First, he avoided being "the bad guy" himself. Second, he enhanced his power base by making me look worse than him.

3. *Don't "divide and conquer"* (Vecchio, 2006, p. 131). This strategy "usually involves creating a feud among two or more people so that they will be continually off balance and thus unable to mount an attack against you" (Vecchio, 2006, p. 131). They are essentially kept busy fighting with each other, allowing you to go about your business. Unfortunately, this tactic hurts interpersonal relationships. It also takes time and energy away from doing a good job.

   I once worked in a social work department supervised by Bob. Bob's approach to supervision was control by dividing and conquering. Two of the workers, Godfrey and Juanita, had been good friends for a long time. Bob told Godfrey that Juanita had been criticizing his work. Bob then told Juanita that Godfrey had been critical of her work. None of this was true. By disrupting Godfrey and Juanita's friendship, Bob broke up the coalition of support that they formed. In this way, Bob felt he had greater control of what went on in the department. It eventually backfired for Bob, however. A third worker, Cathy, talked both to Godfrey and Juanita who told her what Bob had been saying. Cathy subsequently told Godfrey and Juanita what each other had shared. The result was that they confronted each other and discovered that Bob had been lying. They confronted Bob, who consistently denied that he had said anything like that. Eventually, the entire department formed a coalition and sought help from the administration concerning Bob for this and many other behavioral problems. Bob was fired.

4. *Don't "exclude the opposition"* (Vecchio, 2006, p. 131). Another underhanded technique is to exclude a rival or adversary from participation in meetings, agency functions, or social events. One approach is to schedule an important decision-making meeting "when the opposition is out of town (on vacation …) or attending another meeting. With the opposition absent, it is possible to influence decision making or to take credit for a rival's efforts" (Vecchio, 2006, p. 131).

5. *Don't go over your supervisor's head without first exhausting all other options* (Vecchio, 2006). There are times when it might be necessary to go over your supervisor's head and complain to his or her supervisor. Some employees do this to complain about the supervisor's performance or how the supervisor is treating them. Consider the earlier example with Bob, Godfrey, and Juanita when the staff formed a coalition and sought help from administration. However, the staff first confronted Bob, who did not respond. The entire staff formed a coalition to address the issue the only way they knew how. Only then did they "air dirty laundry" about the department to higher levels of administration. Supervisors hate it when supervisees go over their heads and "narc" about their performance. It's much wiser to try to work out whatever the problem is internally before going outside of the department. Making an enemy of a supervisor by making him or her look bad can make your life miserable in the future. Additionally, administration will often side with the supervisor, as people in management tend to stick together. The result might be a decrease rather than an increase in your power and potential to influence.

6. *Don't throw temper tantrums* (Vecchio, 2006, p. 132). Emotional volatility may earn you the reputation of being overly emotional and overreactive. People tend to see the emotions and miss out on the content of what you're trying to communicate. You don't want to establish a reputation of being hard to work with. That will only encourage others to avoid you and not provide you with support when you need it.

Centralized versus Decentralized Organizations

Organizations can be placed on a continuum regarding their degree of centralization. On one side are extremely centralized organizations that are run according to classic scientific management theories. Their lines of authority are clearly established, a strict hierarchy is in place, and their units are clearly defined and cleanly separated. Workers have little discretion in making decisions on their own. Responsibilities are defined and policies implemented from above.

An example of centralization might be the Cauliflower County probation and parole department. Clients of any specific officer in any particular unit tend to have very similar characteristics. Procedures and treatment plans are relatively uniform. Clients and officers must abide by clearly defined rules and regulations. Little officer discretion is possible.

On the opposite side of the centralization continuum are extremely decentralized organizations, which offer and encourage great worker discretion. They likely have a wide variety of clients with vastly different problems, issues, and backgrounds. Workers in such organizations, thus, need discretion to make plans for viable solutions. For example, a community crisis intervention organization might be extremely decentralized. Clients coming in for help might have problems ranging from depression to illness to job loss to executive-level stress. Workers need a broad range of discretion to address a wide variety of problems.

The Macro Context of Organizations

To work effectively, social work practitioners must understand how their agencies function both internally and *externally* in the larger macro environment. This environment very much affects how well agencies can pursue and attain their goals and, in effect, what agency workers can do for clients. At least three environmental dimensions have impact on organizations: available resources, legitimation, and client sources (Schmid, 2009).

The Shifting Macro Environment and Shrinking Resources

Today's turbulent, shifting macro environment makes it increasingly difficult for social services agencies to thrive and grow. As the population expands worldwide, resources continue to shrink so that funding and financial support become increasingly difficult to get. It also means that competition becomes more intense. Social, political, and economic forces place social services agencies under intense pressure to reduce spending on the one hand, and prove their effectiveness and value on the other. Necessary resources (Alter, 2009; Holland & Petchers, 1987; Schmid, 2009), legitimation (Holland & Petchers, 1987; Schmid, 2009), and

adequate client sources (Holland & Petchers, 1987; Schmid, 2009) are all necessary for social service organizations to thrive. Managed health care, described in Highlight 4.5, provides an example of a major attempt at limiting health care spending while still providing services.

Necessary Resources

A social services agency must have the necessary resources or funding to function: to pay for staff salaries, rent and/or building maintenance, supplies, telephone, and innumerable other expenses. To determine whether macro change is possible in an agency, you need to assess whether potential resources are available. How much will your proposed macro level change cost the organization? This is true whether you want to implement a project, develop a whole new program, or amend some agency policy. (These macro interventions will be discussed much more thoroughly in Chapter 5 through Chapter 7.) What such a macro change will cost is often the deciding factor on whether you'll succeed or fail with your macro proposal.

Legitimation

Legitimation is the appropriate status or authorization to perform agency functions and pursue agency goals that is granted by external entities (e.g., local government). An agency must be legally viable. Once established, the agency must continue to abide by the rules upon which its existence is based. We have already briefly mentioned the importance of legislative requirements and constraints with respect to an agency's organizational goals.

But what if an agency does not follow the appropriate rules and regulations? For example, a health care center for older adults failed to follow the rules about maintenance of its bedridden patients, especially those with Alzheimer's disease. Clients' relatives visiting the center reported to the state's licensing agency that they had observed a number of seriously disturbing incidents during their visits, including clients wallowing in their own feces for a day or more, staff slapping clients in the face when the clients refused to cooperate, and employees depriving clients of food as punishment for undesirable behavior. Needless to say, once the health care center's practices were known and investigated, the agency was closed. It no longer possessed the legitimation and accountability needed to justify its existence.

Managed Care and Service Provision: Problems and Ethical Issues

A major social and economic force that affects many agencies' service provision is managed care. The concept serves as an umbrella for many different types of health agencies and health care. *Managed care* is "any medical insurance plan [privately or publicly administered] that controls costs through monitoring and controlling the decision of health care providers" (Mooney, Knox, & Schacht, 2009, p. 55). These include decisions "about medical procedures, diagnostic tests, and other services that should be provided to patients" (Kendall, 2007, p. 233). Kornblum and Julian (2007) explain that managed care involves

a wide range of health plans and practices that depart from the traditional model of private health insurance provided by one's employer. In the traditional model, insured patients chose their physician; physicians treated patients with absolute clinical autonomy; insurers generally paid physicians whatever they billed on a fee-for service basis; and employers paid premiums for their workers to private insurers, regardless of the cost. Managed care has altered all these arrangements by setting limits on individual medical visits or treatments—that is, by managing care. (p. 60)

Managed care has become an integral part of social work practice in numerous fields, including health care, mental health, work with older adults, public assistance, and child welfare (Corcoran, 1997). All people, including all clients, need health care to one extent or another. Gilbert and Terrell (2010) explain the significance of managed care:

Managed care is basically a form of human services organization ... that has become institutionalized in the health care economy, where about two thirds of Americans are now enrolled in networks of health care providers that contract with managed care organizations and abide by managed care rules. These rules have created an apparatus of incentives, procedures, and structures that revolutionized the nature of American health care, fundamentally altering relationships among doctors, hospitals, drug and insurance companies, and employers, and putting cost considerations front and center in the decision-making process. (pp. 184-185)

Managed care involves health insurance companies, hospitals, networks of physicians and other treatment providers, and *health maintenance organizations*

(HMOs). HMOs (one type of managed care that is quite common)

are prepaid group plans in which a person pays a monthly premium for comprehensive health care services. HMOs attempt to minimize hospitalization costs by emphasizing preventive health care. Preferred provider organizations (PPOs) *are health care organizations in which employers who purchase group health insurance agree to send their employees to certain health care providers or hospitals in return for cost discounts. In this arrangement health care providers obtain more patients but charge lower fees to buyers of group insurance* (Mooney et al., 2009, p. 55).

Managed care fundamentally altered traditional relationships between clients and social work practitioners. Historically, social workers in agency settings established treatment plans (that may address health and mental health concerns) in conjunction with clients, in addition to stressing informed consent and confidentiality to comply with ethical standards. Managed care takes these decisions out of workers' and clients' hands and puts them into the hands of removed third-party decision makers. A managed care representative, often a utilization reviewer or case manager, then reviews documentation and regulates "the services that clients receive, especially what specific services will be provided and at what cost" (Corcoran, 1997, p. 194). To some, managed care "represents the complete (and seemingly sudden) triumph of financial management concerns over virtually all other professional considerations" (Lohmann, 1997, p. 202).

Two primary principles promoted by managed care are *retention of quality and access* while *controlling cost*. That is, health and mental-health services should be of high quality and readily accessible to clients, on the one hand. Yet, they should be very cost-effective, on the other.

Managed Care's Means of Controlling Costs

Managed care employs several approaches to control costs. One method is the practice of *capitation*, "the provision of fixed payments made on a per-member per-month basis regardless of the use of services. In other words, the physician receives a fixed amount of money each month for every member of the [managed care plan]. ... Whether the member seeks care every day or never seeks care at all, the amount of money that the physician receives does not vary" (Kongstvedt, 2009, p. 69).

(continued)

HIGHLIGHT 4.5 *(continued)*

A second approach to controlling costs involves *gatekeeping,* the required authorization by a designated primary-care physician to make all decisions about "prescriptions, referrals to specialists, or hospital care" (Gilbert & Terrell, 2010, p. 185). This prevents patients from seeking out alternative care and care providers on their own.

A third cost-preventive mechanism is *utilization management,* where a health provider "often must apply to a utilization manager for approval to initiate a particular treatment regimen. This oversight by external cost-oriented monitors diminishes the degree of autonomy exercised by professionals and may also erode the professional's ability to maintain client confidentiality"; the managed care staff often have access to all of a patient's health information (even that not clearly related to the treatment request) in order to make a determination about treatment provision (Gilbert & Terrell, 2010, p. 185).

The Pros and Cons of Managed Care

Those supporting managed care state that it has decreased the cost of health care and emphasizes the importance of prevention (DiNitto, 2007; Karger & Stoesz, 2010). However, the research has been mixed regarding whether it really is less expensive and more efficient than traditional fee-for-service health insurance (Kornblum & Julian, 2007; Vandiver, 2008).

Physicians indicate that the quality of health care has decreased since the advent of managed care due to "limitations on diagnostic tests, length of hospital stay, and choice of specialists" (DiNitto, 2007; Karger & Stoesz, 2010; Mooney et al., 2009, p. 57). Karger and Stoesz (2010) explain further:

Managed care plans generally gate-keep the access to specialists for consumers. These plans do this by pressuring primary physicians not to refer or by limiting specialist care to one or two visits. Some managed care plans are reluctant to cover costly procedures or experimental treatments, especially those relating to cancer. Still other plans refuse to pay for medical care clients receive while out of state, even if it was required in an emergency. Other enrollees complain that managed care forces them to use only primary care physicians, hospitals, and specialists that are on an approved list, which restricts their freedom of choice.... Critics also note that the size of managed care operations has led to greater bureaucratization and impersonality. (p. 320)

Ethical Issues in Managed Care

Generalist practitioners must work within their employing agency setting. They are supposed to follow regulatory and other agency policy. However, they are also responsible for maintaining ethical practices and for making certain clients' needs are met. Several ethical issues may be raised concerning managed care.

The first involves the potential conflict between "the gatekeeping role of some managed care organizations and client self-determination" (Corcoran, 1997, p. 196). When subject to managed care, clients experience significantly decreased choices in their service providers. Rather, the managed care utilization reviewer can make this determination.

Similarly, managed care may conflict with the ethical principle of informed consent:

Informed consent requires that the client know in advance the clinical procedures, the risk of those procedures, and the available alternative procedures. Managed care may destroy informed consent by restricting the available procedures to a limited number. For example, a managed care company may determine the preferred practice and the preferred providers, with little consideration or disclosure of alternative procedures. (Corcoran, 1997, p. 196)

Managed care also has the potential to violate client confidentiality (Popple & Leighninger, 2008). Social workers are bound by the *Code of Ethics* that emphasizes how "social workers should respect clients' right to privacy" and "should not solicit private information from clients unless it is essential to providing service" (NASW, 2008, § 1.07a). However, if a managed care organization demands information before providing services, what should the worker do? What if the worker does not agree with the organization's expressed need for information and feels the regulations violate clients' right to privacy? Workers may be required to report confidential information, whether they feel it is ethical or not (Chapter 12 discusses the *Code of Ethics* in depth).

The point is not to get depressed about the managed care environment. Rather, practitioners must respond to the potential ethical dilemmas posed:

Perhaps the most important role for social workers will be as advocates for patients and families in dealing with managed care delivery systems. Patients and families will need to know what their entitlement benefits are and how to obtain proper services. Social workers will also need to continue to advocate for improving the health care system by serving on advisory committees and lobbying their legislators. (Edinburg & Cottler, 1995, p. 1641)

Managed Care and Advocacy in Social Work Practice

EP 2.1.5b

Popple and Leighninger (2008) emphasize the importance of advocating for "[l]aws protecting patients' rights in managed care." They explain:

Such legislation might include the right to information about a health plan's procedures and policies, the right of access to a medical specialist without approval of a primary care doctor, the right to an independent appeals process [for example, when patients disagree with gatekeepers' decisions], and the right to sue a health plan for damages when it improperly denies care. (p. 258)

At least five specific provisions could improve legislation to protect clients and their rights ("Managed Care," 1998); they could

- *guarantee patients the right to choose a doctor outside their health plans' networks if they agree to share the cost of services;*
- *ensure patients' access to detailed information about coverage, treatment options...;*
- *require companies to cover emergency care without prior authorization...;*
- *make health plans comply with state and federal laws that protect the confidentiality of ... health information; and*
- *require companies to set up procedures under which providers could appeal denials of coverage. (p. 1)*

Client Sources

An agency cannot last very long without enough clients to sustain it. This "array of client sources, which ranges from groups or programs that serve as client referral mechanisms to individuals who directly seek out services for themselves," is critical to an agency's existence and functioning (Holland & Petchers, 1987, p. 208; Schmid, 2009).

One agency provided special therapy services (including social work, occupational, speech, and physical) to schoolchildren in several rural counties. The counties did not initially have enough clients for each to hire its own full-time therapists, so each county purchased from the agency whatever therapists' time it needed—perhaps one or two days per week for a given social worker or therapist. Together, the counties provided enough work for the agency to maintain several full-time therapists in each discipline. However, new state requirements for providing adequate service to children were put into place. The counties also began to develop enhanced assessment techniques and procedures. As a result, a number of counties found that they could identify enough of their own clients to hire full-time therapists. Hence, the agency providing special services no longer had enough clients in enough counties. It simply had to shut down.

The importance of client sources characterizes a wide range of organizational contexts. Highlight 4.6 describes how organizations work with refugee and immigrant clients from a global perspective.

Social Work Organizations in National and International Contexts

Of special note are national and international social work organizations that exist to promote macro practice and the pursuit of social justice beyond that occurring in individual organizations and communities. Four of these organizations will be described briefly here.

EP 2.1.5

ACOSA

The Association for Community Organization and Social Administration (ACOSA) was formed in 1987 to provide a forum for enhancing macro practice theory research, and skills (http://www.acosa.org). Its membership consists of "community organizers, activists, nonprofit administrators, community builders, policy practitioners, students and educators" (http://www.acosa.org). Its specific goals include supporting an "annual symposium," facilitating networking both among educators and practitioners and with other professional organizations, and developing teaching materials and literature to promote macro practice; ACOSA also "sponsors the *Journal of Community Practice*, the leading peer reviewed journal in this field" (http://www.acosa.org/purposes.html; http://www.acosa.org).

HIGHLIGHT 4.6

Organizations in a Global Context: Helping Immigrants and Refugees

Casas (2001) relates his mother's description of his family's immigration from Mexico:

Your father, who was very well-read and could speak a little English, thought it was a good time to leave Mexico and go to another place that offered more opportunities and a better way of life ... It was extremely difficult for me to buy into this 100 percent; however, he had always taken good care of all of us and so we started to make our plans. It was hard to sell all our furniture and say goodbye to family and friends, never knowing if we would see them again. We packed several suitcases and came to the United States. We crossed the border at El Paso and continued on the train across New Mexico, Arizona, and then we found ourselves going through grove after grove of orange trees. The train went past San Bernardino and, while it did not stop there, your aunt Luz and your cousin Teresa were standing alongside the track to wave us through as we made our way north to Los Angeles. We stayed overnight in Los Angeles in a hotel that was not in the best part of town, thus we did not venture far from our room. The next day we continued to Crockett, California, where we were met by your aunt Maria and your uncle Jesus. Your father got a job the following day with ASARCO, the same [mining and ore processing] company that he had worked for in Mexico....

Your aunt and uncle lived in Tormey, a small town adjacent to Crockett, and had three rooms in their basement. These rooms became our home. As when I was a child, I was back to having nothing of a material nature, no furniture, no linens, no dishes, etc.... Tormey was also a company town, but much smaller and with less commodities than Avalos [our original home].... We started looking for a house to live in. There were very few available because the influx of people to California had been tremendous.... Not only was this a problem, we were Mexicans. No one wanted to rent to Mexicans because they said we were dirty people and did not know how to take care of homes. Eventually we found a landlord that took a chance on us. (pp. 81–82)

EP 2.1.4a

People who migrate from their country of origin to another often face momentous hurdles and stress. These may involve culture shock, language barriers, lack of money to meet basic needs, isolation from

critical support systems, and the need to "come to terms with the events that forced them from their homes" (Mayadas & Segal, 2000, p. 212). Internationally and nationally, organizations exist to meet the needs of immigrants and refugees and help them negotiate the migration process.

Potocky-Tripodi (2002) summarizes and discusses how organizations in a global context deliver services to refugees and immigrants of other national origin.[a] *National origin,* a dimension of diversity, involves individuals', their parents', or their ancestors' country of birth. "*Refugees* are those individuals who are forced to leave their country because of human rights violations and threats to safety"; *immigrants* are "individuals who depart their country or origin voluntarily in search of better economic and living arrangements" (Delgado, Jones, & Rohani, 2005, p. 5; Potocki, 2008). Potocky-Tripodi (2002) reflects that the global "network includes international, national, ... and local agencies, both public and private" and that "[i]t also includes professionals and paraprofessionals from a variety of disciplines" (p. 96).

International Organizations

International organizations often provide help before and during the migration process. "Most immigrants do not require assistance during these stages, and they make their departure and travel arrangements on their own. However, some immigrants and all refugees do require international assistance" (Potocky-Tripodi, 2002, p. 96). International organizations include both intergovernmental and private organizations. *Intergovernmental organizations* are those "such as the United Nations, which consist of member nations" (Potocky-Tripodi, 2002, p. 96). Often they provide help to immigrants and refugees, although this is not necessarily their primary function.

An example of an organization established for the sole purpose of assisting immigrants and refugees is the International Organization for Migration (IOM). Its established purpose is to "assist in meeting the operational challenges of migration; advance understanding of migration issues; encourage social and economic development through migration; and uphold the human dignity and well-being of migrants" (people moving from one country to another) (IOM, 2009). Premigration services include helping migrants get their documents in order, understand and follow required procedures, obtain necessary medical evaluations, and cope with cultural changes and conditions. During transmit IOM assists with transportation and evacuation plans.

An intergovernmental organization assisting only refugees is the United Nations High Commission for Refugees (UNHCR) (UNHCR, 2009). Its two primary purposes are to safeguard refugees and help them establish permanent residency, either in their country of origin or elsewhere.

Both IOM and UNHCR work closely with private (nongovernmental) voluntary organizations (PVOs) to provide assistance to refugees and immigrants. These are "funded by both government and private donations" and often "associated with religious organizations" (Potocky-Tripodi, 2002, p. 99; U.S Citizen and Immigration Services, 2009). Examples include CARE (targeting disaster relief), Catholic Relief Services, and the Salvation Army World Service Office. Whereas governments and international organizations usually finance help provision, PVOs provide the person power necessary to implement emergency help in the desperate circumstances plaguing refugees. Prior to migration, PVOs often maintain refugee camps, providing "food, shelter, and medical care" (Potocky-Tripodi, 2002, p. 99).

International organizations also exist whose major purpose is advocacy and the pursuit of social justice on the behalf of refugees and immigrants. Their main tasks include watching over human rights on a global basis, supplying information to the public, and applying pressure to improve national policies. Examples are Amnesty International and Human Rights Watch.

National Organizations

National organizations in the United States that aid immigrants and refugees are "concerned primarily with admissions, border control, deportation, and the resettlement stage of migration" (Potocky-Tripodi, 2002, p. 105). Similar to international organizations, they include both government and private organizations.

An example of a U.S. government organization is the Immigration and Naturalization Service (INS), a branch of the Justice Department. It is "responsible for enforcing the laws regulating the admission of aliens into the U.S., and for administering various immigration benefits, including naturalization" (being granted the rights and privileges of being a citizen) (Potocky-Tripodi, 2002, p. 105; U.S. Citizen and Immigration Services, 2009). Activities include monitoring border entry, finding and deporting people entering the country illegally, administering legal entry requirements, and overseeing work authorization for migrants.

Private U.S. organizations serving refugees and immigrants generally focus on the relocation and settlement process. "Since there is a comprehensive resettlement program for refugees but not for immigrants, most private agencies at the national level coordinate services to refugees" (Potocky-Tripodi, 2002, p. 108). Tasks include "meeting refugees at the arrival airport and covering all necessary expenses for the first 30 days. For the first 90 days, resettlement agencies arrange for food, housing, furnishings, clothing, employment medical care, counseling, English-language training, cultural orientation, orientation to the public transportation system, orientation to the U.S. monetary system, school enrollment for children, and any other necessary services" (Potocky-Tripodi, 2002, p. 108). Examples of private U.S. organizations include the Ethiopian Community Development Council and Church World Service.

Refugees may face any number of problems concerning significant cultural differences. For example,

> [t]he parents of an Iraqi family [recent refugees from Iraq to the United States] with their consent and in keeping with their traditions gave their two daughters, ages 12 and 13, in marriage to two adults of their community. The young men were charged with rape and the parents with child abuse. This is certainly an extreme, although not an isolated, case of cultural miscommunication. The result was that the INS denied asylum to refugees from the Jaffa area of Iraq. Issues such as these require understanding and sensitive handling of the situation, not penalization, as meted out in this case. (CBS, 1997; Mayadas & Segal, 2000, p. 202)

Like some international organizations, some U.S. organizations have advocacy and the pursuit of social justice as their primary purpose. They seek such goals as establishing friendly relationships between migrants and other citizens and lobbying for the just and compassionate treatment of migrants. An example of such an organization is the National Network for Immigrant and Refugee Rights (NNIRR) (NNIRR, 2009).

Local Organizations

Local organizations may be *mainstream,* those serving much broader populations than refugees and immigrants. Examples include county departments of social services, hospitals, schools, and counseling agencies. They may also be *ethnic,* those private agencies targeting the needs of refugees, immigrants, or other designated ethnic populations (Potocky-Tripodi, 2002, pp. 110–111).

Note also that many international and national organizations serving refugees and immigrants have local offices administering services.

(continued)

HIGHLIGHT 4.6 *(continued)*

Social Services for Immigrants and Refugees

Social workers and others can provide a wide range of services within the context of international, national, and local organizations. These include provision of information, referral to appropriate services, counseling, practical access to health services, vocational rehabilitation (including job counseling, training, and placement), services for youth or older adults, housing resources, legal aid, and other facets of resettlement (Potocky-Tripodi, 2002, p. 118).

Another example of some of the numerous issues and problems experienced by immigrants and refugees involved Phuc, age 15, an immigrant from Vietnam (cited in Lum, 2004; Matsuoka, 1990, pp. 344–345). Born and raised in Vietnam, he "excelled in math" there and dreamed of becoming an engineer. Phuc was very close to his extended family and "was often called upon to care for his grandparents and younger cousins." After his father died in a Vietnamese prison camp, his mother, "seeing little future for themselves in Vietnam," decided to leave. She risked everything to become a "boat person" and eventually relocated in the United States. Thus, at a very sensitive time in his adolescent development, Phuc was traumatized by being thrust into the vastly different U.S. culture.

A year later Phuc's mother remarried

another Vietnamese refugee, and they moved to a home in a middle-class community without a concentrated population of Vietnamese. Because of the lack of a Vietnamese community, reinforcement for appropriate Vietnamese behavior was unavailable beyond Phuc's family. The loss of reinforcement and role patterns that would ordinarily have given him a strong identity left him confused and depressed. In school, Phuc was having great difficulty understanding the lessons because he could not speak fluent English. Phuc felt inferior because he was doing poorly,

and soon he began skipping classes and spending time in the city with other Vietnamese youth who were involved in gang activity. Because he lived so far away, Phuc was regarded as a marginal gang member although he experimented with drugs and participated in some gang-related activity.

The school officials became concerned about his truancy and reported it to his parents. When his stepfather and mother discovered that their son had not been attending school, they became very angry, because back home he was an outstanding scholar. The stepfather felt that Phuc was lazy and disrespectful, so he physically punished him for his truancy at school. As a result, Phuc ran away from home. The police eventually picked him up, and because he refused to return home, he was placed in foster care. (cited in Lum, 2004, p. 292; Matsuoka, 1990, pp. 344–345)

Phuc's case was referred to a bilingual, bicultural social worker who proceeded to provide individual and family counseling while Phuc lived in foster care. Eventually, Phuc was able to express and deal with his anger and grief at the loss of his father and homeland. Through family counseling, his family learned how to give Phuc more attention through use of positive behaviors and to stop harsh physical punishment. They also learned to participate in more family activities, particularly ones involving the Vietnamese community. Finally, a bilingual tutor was found to assist Phuc with his schoolwork, so he could once again get on with his education and preparation for the future.

Note

Note that much of the content concerning the types of organizations providing services is taken from M. Potocky-Tripodi, *Best Practices with Refugees and Immigrants* (New York: Columbia, 2002), an excellent resource for more extensive information on these topics.

IASSW

The International Association of Schools of Social Work (IASSW), introduced in Chapter 1, was established in 1928 in Paris, France (http://www.iassw-aiets.org). Membership includes institutions of social work education around the world, organizations supporting social work education, and social work educators. "Its mission is:

To develop and promote excellence in social work education, research and scholarship globally in order to enhance human well-being.

1. *To create and maintain a dynamic community of social work educators and their programmes.*
2. *To support and facilitate participation in mutual exchanges of information and expertise.*
3. *To represent social work education at the international level.*" (http://www.iassw-aiets.org/index.php?option=com_content&task=blogcategory&id=25&Itemid=47)

In essence, "IASSW is committed to promoting peace, human rights, and social justice through social work education" (Dominelli, 2004, p. 11). Specific activities have included developing both an international definition of social work and, as indicated in Chapter 1, an international code of ethics for social workers. This was done in conjunction with another organization, the International Federation of Social Workers (IFSW) (introduced in Chapter 1 and described next). Additional pursuits include sponsoring a biennial conference of social work educators (the IASSW Congress), publishing a newsletter, and cosponsoring with IFSW and the International Council on Social Welfare (ICSW) (described in a following section) the journal *International Social Work*. One of the IASSW task forces "aims to bring schools of social work together so that they can undertake joint projects and exchange curriculum materials. The IASSW also funds small projects that enable social work educators to promote the ideas and practices of international social work…. IASSW also represents social work educators at the United Nations" where "it holds special consultative status" in shaping policies concerning children, women, older adults, and migrants (Dominelli, 2004, p. 4).

IFSW

The International Federation of Social Workers (IFSW) was established in 1956 as an international organization of national professional social work organizations in 78 countries (http://www.ifsw.org). Its goals are:

- *to promote the establishment of national organizations of social workers or professional unions for social workers*
- *to support Social Work Organizations in promoting the participation of social workers in social planning and the formulation of social policies, nationally, and internationally, the recognition of social work, the enhancement of social work training and the values and professional standards of social work. (http://www.ifsw.org/p38000046.html)*

Individuals and organizations may join the IFSW Friends program, from which they can receive information and discounts on publications and conferences. We have established that IFSW has worked with the IASSW to publish an international definition of social work and code of ethics and serves as a sponsor of the journal *International Social Work*. It publishes a newsletter, organizes periodic international conferences, and offers "means for discussion and the exchange of ideas and experience through meeting, study visits, research projects, exchanges, publications and other methods of communication" (http://www.ifsw.org/p38000062.

html). The IFSW also "has published [with the IASSW] a manual on Human Rights and Social Work in cooperation with the United Nations Centre for Human Rights," in addition to printing a training manual on children's rights and other books (http://www.ifsw.org/p38000062.html).

ICSW

The International Council on Social Welfare (ICSW) is "a global governmental organization which represents a wide range of national and international member organizations that seek to advance social welfare, social development and social justice. ICSW's basic mission is to promote forms of social and economic development which aim to reduce poverty, hardship and vulnerability throughout the world, especially amongst disadvantaged people. It strives for fundamental rights to food, education, health care and security" (http://www.icsw.org/intro/missione.htm; http://www.icsw.org). It thus works with governments, organizations, and individuals to advocate for and implement social and economic development. The ICSW publishes a monthly *Global Newsletter* and the *Global Policy Journal*, in addition to helping sponsor the publication *of International Social Work*. It offers biennial meetings and seminars and works with governments and other organizations to develop, advocate for, and put into action improved social policies.

Methods of Management

Another way of looking at how organizations function is by comparing management styles, which determine how employees are thought of and treated. We have defined *management* as "the attainment of organizational goals in an effective and efficient manner through planning, organizing, leading, and controlling organizational resources" (Daft, 2010a, p. 5). Management involves how employees are thought of and treated. Management style provides important clues for understanding people's behavior in the organizational environment. Often, an organization's management approach reflects some combination of the organizational theories described earlier in this chapter. Numerous bureaucracies continue to exist, with all their strengths and weaknesses, but alternative organizational perspectives and management styles are continuously being developed.

The following sections will address various aspects of management. First, traditional bureaucracy will be discussed. Subsequently, new methods of management will be described that are aimed at empowering workers to provide better services to clients. Finally, some problems workers frequently encounter in organizations will be reviewed.

Working in a Traditional Bureaucracy

The concept of bureaucracy, introduced earlier under classical organizational theories, reflects a traditional approach to management. Because it is such a commonly used concept, we will spend some time here addressing practice within bureaucracies. What words come to mind when you hear the term "bureaucracy"? Dullness? Tedium? Boredom? Repetitiveness? Red tape? Sludge?

For whatever reason, most of us have a terrible opinion of bureaucracies. *Webster's Dictionary* labels bureaucracy "a system of administration marked by officialism ('lack of flexibility and initiative combined with excessive adherence to regulations in the behavior of usually government officials'), red tape ('official routine or procedure marked by excessive complexity which results in delay or inaction'), and proliferation (rapid growth by 'production of new parts, cells, buds, or offspring')" (Mish, 2008, pp. 165, 861, 1044, 933). Even this definition is dull!

As classical organizational theories propose, bureaucratic management style emphasizes the importance of a specifically designed, formal structure and a consistent, rigid organizational network of employees in making an organization run well and achieve its goals (Daft & Marcic, 2009; Hellriegel & Slocum, 2009). Each employee has a clearly defined job and is told exactly how that job should be accomplished. This school of thought calls for minimal independent functioning on the part of employees. Supervisors closely scrutinize the latter's work. Efficiency is of utmost importance. How people feel about their jobs is insignificant. Administration should avoid allowing employees to have any input regarding how organizational goals can best be reached. Rather, employees should do their jobs as instructed, as quietly and efficiently as possible.

Traditional bureaucracies are made up of numerous highly specialized units that are supposed to perform specific job tasks. In the formal structure there is supposed to be little communication among horizontal units—that is, units of approximately equal status that perform different functions. Employees are supposed to

"stick to their own business" and get their own specifically defined jobs done within their own units. That's it. No discussion.

Traditional bureaucracies allow very little discretion on the part of workers. Policies and procedures for how to accomplish tasks are clearly specified. In other words, what any particular worker is supposed to do in any particular situation is designated ahead of time. Employees are allowed little, if any, ability and opportunity to be able to think for themselves and make their own decisions concerning their work. They are simply supposed to follow instructions.

The policies and procedures are infinitely complex and detailed. Regardless of what new situation might come up, workers should be able to consult the "rule book" regarding how they should deal with it.

Value Discrepancies between Workers and "The System"

Helping professionals (including social workers) have a value orientation that can clash with the traditional bureaucracy's reality (Knopf, 1979; Lewis, Packard, & Lewis, 2009). Expecting the values of a large bureaucracy to coincide with your own simply sets you up for disappointment.

EP 2.1.2a

Examples of discrepancies are many. For instance, helping professionals believe that the primary goal of bureaucracies should be to serve clients, while the actual goal of bureaucracies is to survive. Helping professionals believe bureaucracies should change to meet the emerging needs of clients, while bureaucracies resist change and run most smoothly when no one is "rocking the boat." Helping professionals believe bureaucracies should personalize services to each client and convey that "you count as a person," while bureaucracies are in fact highly depersonalized systems in which clients (and employees) do not count as persons but are only tiny components of a mammoth system. Highlight 4.7 lists additional conflicting orientations between helping professionals and bureaucratic systems (Knopf, 1979; Schriver, 2004).

Any of these differences in orientation can become an arena of conflict between helping professionals and the bureaucracies in which they work. Some helping professionals respond to these orientation conflicts by erroneously projecting a personality onto the bureaucracy. The bureaucracy is viewed as being "stodgy," "uncaring," "cruel," and "the enemy." A negative personality is also sometimes projected onto bureaucrats,

HIGHLIGHT 4.7

Orientation Conflicts between Helping Professionals and Bureaucracies

Orientation of Helping Professionals

The decision-making system is democratic.

Power is distributed equally among employees (organization has a horizontal structure).

Clients have considerable power in the system.

The system is flexible and changing.

Creativity and growth are emphasized.

Communication on a personalized level from person to person is encouraged.

Decision making and responsibility structure are shared.

Decisions are made by those having the most knowledge.

Clients' and employees' feelings are highly valued.

Orientation of Bureaucratic Systems

Most decisions are made autocratically.

Power is distributed unequally (organization has a vertical structure).

Power is held primarily by top executives.

System is rigid and stable.

Emphasis is on structure and the status quo.

Communication is from level to level.

A hierarchical decision-making structure and a hierarchical responsibility structure are characteristic.

Decisions are made according to the decision-making authority assigned each position in the hierarchy.

Procedures and processes are highly valued.

who may be viewed as "paper shufflers," "rigid," "deadwood," "inefficient," and "unproductive":

The HP (helping person) ... may deal with the impersonal nature of the system by projecting values onto it and thereby give the BS (Bureaucratic System) a "personality." [It is interesting that Knopf refers to a bureaucracy as BS.] In this way, we fool ourselves into thinking that we can deal with it in a personal way. Unfortunately, projection is almost always negative and reflects the dark or negative aspects of ourselves. The BS then becomes a screen onto which we vent our anger, sadness, or fright, and while a lot of energy is generated, very little is accomplished. Since the BS is amoral [that is, the BS can be neither moral nor immoral so the concept of morality does not apply to it], it is unproductive to place a personality on it. (Knopf, 1979, p. 25)

A bureaucratic system is neither good nor bad. It has no personality or value system of its own. It is simply a structure developed to carry out various tasks. However, practitioners may have strong emotional reactions to orientation conflicts between the helping professions and bureaucracies. Common reactions are anger at the system, self-blame ("It's all my fault"), sadness and depression ("Poor me. Nobody appreciates all I've done"), and fright and paranoia ("They're out to get me. If I mess up, I'm gone").

This description of bureaucratic systems highlights a number of the systems' negatives, particularly their

impersonal qualities. In fairness, Lewis and her colleagues (2007) stress that there are some positive aspects of bureaucracy, as it "provides a foundation for personnel practices that all workers appreciate"; these include "clear job roles and performance expectations, fair treatment, and due process" (p. 70). They continue, however, that it surely doesn't focus enough on the importance of interpersonal processes and the uniqueness of each individual. A later section of this chapter will address newer, more relationship-focused management approaches.

Also note that another advantage of being part of a large bureaucracy is the existing potential for changing a powerful system to clients' advantage. In small or nonbureaucratic systems, a social worker may have lots of freedom but little opportunity or power to influence large macro systems or mobilize extensive resources on behalf of clients.

How to Survive in a Bureaucracy

There are a number of tips on how a helping professional can best survive in a bureaucracy, including the following (Knopf, 1979):

1. Whenever your needs or the needs of your clients are not met by the bureaucracy, use the following problem-solving approach: (a) Precisely identify your needs (or the client's needs) that are in conflict with the bureaucracy, thereby defining the problem. (b) Generate a list of possible solutions. Be creative

in generating a wide range of solutions. (c) Evaluate the merits and shortcomings of the possible solutions. (d) Select a solution. (e) Implement the solution. (f) Evaluate the solution. This, of course, essentially follows the planned change approach you use in virtually any aspect of generalist practice.

2. Learn how your bureaucracy is structured and how it functions. Such knowledge will reduce your fear of the unknown, make the system more predictable, and help you identify rational ways to meet your needs and those of your clients. This includes knowledge of your agency's formal and informal structures. Recall that bureaucracies work to eliminate or minimize any informal communication or power structure, because informal relationships interfere with following the rules to the letter.

3. Remember that bureaucrats are people with feelings. Communication gaps are often most effectively reduced if you treat them with the respect and interest you offer clients. Many of the same techniques used in micro practice with clients also apply to working with agency colleagues and administrators (as discussed in Chapter 2).

4. If you are at war with the bureaucracy, declare a truce, or the system will find a way to eliminate you. With a truce, you can identify and use the strengths of the bureaucracy as allies, rather than have those strengths used against you. (Chapters 5 through Chapter 7 discuss how to evaluate your agency environment, regardless of management style, and pursue potential macro interventions.)

5. Know your work contract and job expectations. If the expectations are vague, seek clarity.

6. Continue to develop your knowledge and awareness of specific helping skills. Take advantage of continuing education opportunities (workshops, conferences, college courses). Among other advantages, your continued professional development will help you keep practicing with competence and skill and maintain mental freshness and stimulation. Try out new ideas and skills on old tasks and situations.

Mark Richards/PhotoEdit

Bureaucracies tend to emphasize their own survival rather than the comfort and needs of clients. Here, wearied people wait in line to see an official regarding services.

7. Identify your professional strengths and limitations. Knowing your limitations will increase your ability to avoid undertaking responsibilities beyond your competencies. (Chapter 5 more thoroughly discusses how to go about doing this.)

8. Be aware that you can't change everything, so stop trying. In a bureaucracy, focus your efforts on those aspects that most need change and that you have a fair chance of changing. Stop thinking and complaining about what you cannot change. It is irrational to complain about things that you cannot change or do not intend to try changing.

9. Learn how to control your emotions in your interactions with the bureaucracy. Counterproductive emotions (such as most angry outbursts) particularly need to be controlled. Learning how to respond to stress in your personal life will also prepare you to handle stress better at work.

10. Develop and use a sense of humor. Humor takes the edge off adverse conditions and reduces negative feelings.

11. Learn to accept your mistakes and perhaps even to laugh at some of them. No one is perfect.

12. Take time to enjoy and develop a support system with your colleagues. Use the informal structure of your agency as much as possible. Having others to go to for suggestions, support, and pats on the back is really helpful. Also, groups can be much more powerful and productive than an individual working alone.

13. Give in sometimes on minor matters. You may not always be right. Giving in on one issue may encourage other people to do the same at another time.

14. Keep yourself physically fit and mentally alert. Learn to use approaches that reduce stress and prevent burnout.

15. Leave your work at the office. Do not take all your burdens home with you. If you have urgent unfinished business, either do it before leaving work or make up your mind not to worry about it until tomorrow.

16. Occasionally, take your supervisor and other administrators to lunch. Socializing prevents isolation and facilitates your involvement with and understanding of the system. It also helps to enhance your position in the agency's informal structure.

17. Do not seek self-actualization or ego satisfaction from the bureaucracy. A depersonalized system is incapable of providing this. Only you can satisfy your ego and needs.

18. Make speeches to community groups that accentuate the positives about your agency. Afterward, do not hesitate to ask that a thank-you letter be sent to your supervisor or agency director.

19. No matter how high you rise in a hierarchy, maintain some direct-service contact. Direct contact keeps you abreast of changing client needs, prevents you from getting stale, and keeps you attuned to the concerns of employees in lower levels of the hierarchy.

20. Do not try to change everything in the system at once. Attacking too much will overextend you and lead to burnout. Start small and be selective and specific. Double-check your facts to make certain they accurately prove your position before confronting bureaucratic officials.

21. Identify your career goals and determine whether they can be met in this system. If the answer is no, then (a) change your goals, (b) change the bureaucracy, or (c) seek a position elsewhere in which your goals can be met.

Newer Approaches to Management and Worker Empowerment

In contrast to traditional bureaucracy, we will now describe some new management trends in social service and other organizations. Many new approaches have been developed to empower workers. The following four are discussed here: constructing a culture of caring, the learning organization, teamwork and team empowerment, and managing diversity. There are also dozens of specific methods of management. Two will subsequently be explained here—total quality management and servant leadership. Note that because all of these management trends and specific approaches focus on worker motivation, needs, and interpersonal dynamics, there's overlap in some of the concepts involved.

Constructing a Culture of Caring

We have defined *organizational culture* as "the set of values, norms, guiding beliefs, and understandings that is shared by members of an organization and taught to new members as the correct way to think, feel, and behave" (Daft, 2010b, p. 374). Organizational culture provides guidelines and establishes expectations for how people should behave while at work

(Brueggemann, 2006). Brody (2005) recommends developing a "culture of caring" in the social service agency setting. When staff feel connected with and supportive of each other, they can become a strong, cohesive force in achieving agency goals together.

Five core values characterize a caring organization (Brody, 2005). First, *job ownership* is the situation where workers feel that their job and their work performance is an important part of their identity (p. 152). They will strive hard to achieve goals and excellence in their work.

Organizations can promote job ownership by encouraging a second key value, *seeking a higher purpose* (p. 153). A caring culture encourages employees genuinely to feel that they're making a difference through their participation. It makes them feel like an integral, important part of a larger system. This can motivate them to work hard and learn new skills, not because management orders them to, but because they have a genuine desire to do so.

A third core value promoting a caring organizational culture is *emotional bonding* (p. 153). This means the organizational culture supports an environment where people truly care about and experience a vital feeling of connection with each other. This can be especially helpful in agencies where workers experience exceptional pressures to work with demanding clients.

The fourth core value is *trust,* the condition where people feel they can depend on each other to follow through on tasks and be supportive of one another (p. 153). They then don't have to waste energy on negative interpersonal interactions, conflicts, complaints, and criticisms.

Pride in one's work, the fifth core value, is the condition where workers have high self-esteem and great respect for their accomplishments at work (p. 153). Feeling good about yourself and being proud of the job you're doing motivates you to continue doing a good job.

The Learning Organization

EP 2.1.9a

A second management trend related to empowering workers is the concept of the learning organization. The *learning organization* is one "in which everyone is engaged in identifying and solving problems, enabling the organization to continuously experiment, change, and improve, thus increasing its capacity to grow, learn, and achieve its purpose" (Aldag & Kuzuhara, 2005; Daft, 2010a, p. 50).

Daft (2010a) further explains, "The essential idea is problem solving, in contrast to the traditional organization designed for efficiency. In the learning organization all employees look for problems, such as understanding special [client] ... needs. Employees also solve problems, which means putting things together in unique ways to meet a [client's] ... needs" (p. 50).

At least five primary concepts characterize the learning organization. First, power is redistributed from higher levels to lower levels in the organizational structure through increased worker participation (Daft, 2010a; Daft & Marcic, 2009; Jaskyte, 2008). Workers providing services directly to clients are given greater discretion to make their own decisions and plans. Power to provide input into and pursue organizational goals is distributed among all staff instead of being concentrated in management (Daft, 2010b).

> *Empowerment means unleashing the power and creativity of employees by giving them the freedom, resources, information, and skills to make decisions and perform effectively. Traditional management tries to limit employees while empowerment expands their behavior. Empowerment may be reflected in self-directed work teams, ... job enrichment, and employee participation groups as well as through decision-making authority, training, and information so that people can perform jobs without close supervision. In learning organizations, people are a manager's primary source of strength, not a cost to be minimized. (Daft & Marcic, 2009, p. 2)*

A second concept involves how learning organizations nurture the development of new ideas. Employees are encouraged to be creative and share their ideas with others (Daft & Marcic, 2009; Jaskyte, 2008). Risk taking on the behalf of improvement is encouraged (Hellriegel & Slocum, 2009; Lussier, 2009). Learning organizations "encourage employees to be creative without fear of punishment if they fail. Mistakes and failure are viewed as learning experiences" (Lussier, 2009, p. 208).

Third, learning organizations emphasize the *effectiveness* of service provision to clients instead of the *process* of service provision (Jaskyte, 2008). Clients' perceptions about services are sought out so that improvements in quality and effectiveness can be made.

Fourth, the use of teams is encouraged (Daft & Marcic, 2009; Jaskyte; 2008). Teams are encouraged to make recommendations and decisions that management takes seriously and implements. Teams are charged with regularly assessing processes and procedures in order to make improvements. In social service organizations, multidisciplinary teams (those including representatives from a variety of fields and with a range

HIGHLIGHT 4.8

"Learning Disabilities" Working against Learning Organizations

There are at least six "learning disabilities" that may occur in organizations and work against learning organization culture (Senge, 1990, pp. 18–25):

1. *I am my position.* This means that each worker has tunnel vision, focusing only on the tasks required in his or her position. Workers neither feel part of the greater whole nor feel that they have input into the organization's vision for the future.

2. *The enemy is out there.* It's not my fault. It's his. Or it's hers. Blaming others for the consequences of your own behavior works against the learning organization. People don't learn from their mistakes and improve their behavior. Blaming others only weakens interpersonal relationships.

3. *The illusion of taking charge.* Sometimes it appears that organizational leaders are taking charge of situations when they lash out at others while trying to solve problems. Superficially, they look like they're in control because they're calling attention to themselves. However, people who are really in charge don't react with emotional outbursts. Rather, they carefully think issues through, assess their own conduct, and make rational decisions.

4. *The parable of the boiled frog.* As unappealing as this analogy is, it paints a poignant picture. If you throw a frog into a pot of boiling water, it immediately reacts by jumping out. However, if you put a frog in cold water and gradually heat it to boiling, the frog will just stay put and come to an unfortunate end. That's because frogs have adapted to react to abrupt changes in temperature, not gradual ones. The analogy between this parable and organizational behavior is that management often reacts to a crisis or some other situation and shifts its focus on events as they occur. For example, an important, highly skilled employee quits. New legislation requires recording procedures radically different from the old ones. Huge funding cuts loom on the horizon. Senge (1990) would say that the major issues affecting organizations are ongoing, gradual developments. Of course, management must react to events, but managers should never lose sight of the long haul, ongoing processes, and longer-term, distant goals.

5. *The delusion of learning from experience.* Hopefully, each of us learns from our experiences so that we make better, wiser choices in the future. However, after a change is made in an organization (such as making a policy decision or implementing a new program), it often takes years to determine whether that change was effective or not. Thus, organizations don't necessarily learn from experience very quickly.

6. *The myth of the management team.* Some teams are made up of members with hidden agendas who engage in power struggles and attempted manipulation. Management should look beyond the external appearance of a team's functioning and carefully evaluate the team's accomplishments.

of backgrounds) can help improve insight into service provision. Thus, change occurs continuously. This contrasts strongly with traditional bureaucracies that usually work to maintain the status quo.

Fifth, "open information" is promoted; "a learning organization is flooded with information. To identify needs and solve problems, people have to be aware of what's going on. They must understand the whole organization as well as their part in it" (Daft & Marcic, 2009, p. 27).

Sixth, as in a caring organizational culture, a learning organization encourages individuals to "lead because they want to serve one another as well as a higher purpose" (Aldag & Kuzuhara, 2005, p. 588).

Their motivation focuses on the organization's greater good, rather than on their own personal power and gain. Servant leadership, discussed later in the chapter, reflects this type of approach.

Highlight 4.8 discusses six "learning disabilities" that serve to work against development of a learning organization (Senge, 1990, p. 18).

Teamwork and Team Empowerment

A *team* is a group of two or more people gathered together to work collaboratively and interdependently with each other to pursue a designated purpose. Teams can provide a useful means of empowerment in organizations by giving the responsibility for service provision to designated groups that work together (Daft, 2010a; Daft & Marcic, 2009; Lussier, 2009; Williams, 2009). In effect, it means giving power to teams of agency workers rather than individual managers or workers. Teams can identify problems and issues, discuss potential alternatives, make decisions about how to proceed, set goals, and evaluate progress.

Specific teams might consist of groups of staff members who either provide similar services or serve the same category of clients. Teams generally meet regularly and are expected to work cooperatively together on the clients' behalf. Ongoing resolution of any conflicts occurring among team members is emphasized. Negative internal staff conflict does not benefit clients. Therefore, it is not tolerated.

Teams are most effective and empowered when used under four circumstances (Williams, 2009). First, a "clear, engaging reason or purpose [should exist] for using them. ... Teams are much more likely to succeed if they know why they exist and what they are supposed to accomplish, and more likely to fail if they don't" (p. 354).

"Second, teams should be used when the job can't be done unless people work together. This typically means that teams are required when tasks are complex, require multiple perspectives, or require repeated interaction with others to complete" (p. 354). Tasks requiring specific skills that can be undertaken by a single worker don't necessarily require the multiple sources of energy and ideas generated by a team.

"Third, teams should be used when rewards can be provided for teamwork and team performance. Team rewards that depend on team performance, rather than individual performance, are the key to rewarding team behaviors and efforts" (p. 355). An agency might reward teamwork by giving the team's efforts and accomplishments public recognition in the form of praise, progress reports in an agency newsletter, or plaques that can be displayed in an office. Bonuses and raises also provide means of rewarding effective teamwork.

The fourth circumstance under which teams can function well is when they have clear authority to make recommendations or implement their decisions as a result of their efforts. Teams function most effectively when left to their own devices to determine their own processes and procedures (Williams, 2009).

Working as a team has several advantages to working as separate individuals (LSS, 1993). First, a team allows for the presentation and sharing of many ideas, perspectives, and experiences. Second, team members have a wider repertoire of skills than any one individual. Third, the entire team should "own" its conclusions, recommendations, and results. Fourth, members can teach each other skills in addition to sharing knowledge and information.

The *team* concept should be distinguished from that of a *group*. A team is virtually always a group, but a group might not be a team. Groups do not necessarily work cooperatively, individual roles may be unclear, participation of individual members may be hampered or discouraged, and, frequently, individual group members are seen as "stars" instead of cooperative co-participants (LSS, 1993, p. 18). The team perspective, on the other hand, should encourage performance of the team, allowing the entire team to gain recognition and respect within the agency environment.

Managing Diversity

"Diversity exists in an organization when there is a variety of demographic, cultural, and personal differences among the people who work there" and the clients who receive services there (Williams, 2010, p. 215). Lussier (2009) reflects:

EP 2.1.4

When we talk about diversity, we are referring to characteristics of individuals that shape their identities and their experiences in the workplace. Diversity refers to the degree of differences among members of a group or an organization. People are diverse in many ways. Within the workforce, people differ in their race/ethnicity, religion, gender, age, and ability. They also differ in their military status, sexual [orientation] ..., expectations and values, lifestyle, socioeconomic status, work style, and function and/or position within the organization. (p. 210)

In contrast to traditional approaches to management that stress conformity, current thought focuses on the appreciation of diversity. "*Valuing diversity* emphasizes training employees of different races and ethnicities, religions, genders, ages, and abilities to function together effectively. To be creative and innovative and to continuously improve [service delivery] ..., employees must work together ... in an atmosphere of dignity and trust" (Lussier, 2009, p. 211).

Daft (2007) concludes, "Diversity is a fact of life for today's organizations, and many are implementing new recruiting, mentoring, and promotion methods, diversity training programs, tough policies regarding sexual harassment and racial discrimination, and new benefit programs that respond to a more diverse workforce" (p. 421).

Specific Management Approaches

We've discussed some major themes in current management thought. Now we'll turn to two of the dozens of specific management approaches being used today that apply some of these themes—total quality management and servant leadership. Note that these two theoretical approaches simply provide examples of how management can be used to empower staff members in organizations.

Total Quality Management

The first of two specific approaches to management and leadership discussed here is *total quality management (TQM)*. Developed by W. Edward Deming (1982, 1986) and others (Crosby, 1980; Feigenbaum, 1983; Juran, 1989), "TQM is a philosophy or overall approach to management that is characterized by … customer focus and satisfaction, continuous improvement, and teamwork" that entails employee involvement and empowerment (Daft, 2010a; Williams, 2010, p. 673). It "focuses on managing the total organization to deliver quality to customers" (in the social services context—clients) (Daft, 2010a, p. 49). TQM involves both the application of systematic research and statistical analysis to determine what quality service involves, reflecting a scientific management approach, and an emphasis on human relations (Austin, 2002; Kronenberg & Loeffler, 1991; Martin, 1993).

"TQM means that the organization's culture is defined by and supports the constant attainment of customer satisfaction through an integrated system of tools, techniques, and training. This involves the continuous improvement of organization processes, resulting in high quality products and services" (Sashkin & Kiser, 1993, p. 39). Bedwell (1993) provides an even more straightforward description of TQM by stating, "The essence of total quality is simple: Ask your customers what they want; then give it to them!" (p. 29).

TQM is a management approach especially significant in social service agencies, because many of their administrators view TQM "as a preferred leadership model" (Baily & Uhly, 2008, p. 67). TQM is also often used as a means of organizational development in social services as a long-term approach to improve service delivery (Packard, 2009) and in organizational assessment (Poertner, 2008). To begin understanding how TQM is implemented and how it affects human behavior in a real agency, we will discuss a number of concepts. These include a focus on clients as customers, quality as the primary goal, employee empowerment and teamwork, TQM leadership, and continuous improvement.

A Focus on Clients as Customers

The central theme of TQM is the importance of the customer or client (Austin, 2002; Daft & Marcic, 2009). The quest for quality should be focused on what clients need and how effective and efficient they perceive service provision to be. Since staff who provide service directly to clients are central to client satisfaction, such staff are considered critical. TQM stresses that they should have high status and receive good, supportive treatment.

EP 2.1.10f

TQM maintains that *customer satisfaction,* the condition where an organization's "services meet or exceed customer expectations," is paramount (Williams, 2009, p. 673). Therefore, agencies must solicit information from customers in order to strive for greater effectiveness (Austin, 2002; Sluyter, 1998). This can be done in a variety of ways (Albrecht, 1988; Martin, 1993). For one thing, the agency can administer customer satisfaction surveys or community surveys that solicit information from customers or residents about agency services. Staff can also conduct extensive interviews with individual customers to identify and examine their feelings. Likewise, the agency can focus on customer complaints and undertake extensive investigations. Suggestion boxes for anonymous feedback can be placed in accessible places. Finally, the agency can assemble groups of customers (focus groups) to discuss services and to make suggestions for quality improvement.

It should be emphasized that not only is customer feedback regularly solicited, but that the agency *uses* this feedback to improve its service provision. There are many ways an agency might incorporate feedback: by prioritizing client and agency needs, planning new goals, and undertaking new projects and procedures.

Highlight 4.9 identifies seven interactions between workers and customers that should never occur in an organization championing total quality management.

Quality as the Primary Goal

In TQM, quality is the primary goal (Daft, 2010a; Williams, 2009). However, quality is a difficult term to define. There is "no universally accepted definition" (Martin, 1993, p. 27). Each organization must determine for itself what quality means in terms of its own service provision.

The Seven Sins of Service

Albrecht (1988) maintains the need to focus consistently on the quality of service provided to customers (or clients). He identifies "seven sins of service" that organizations commonly commit that work against maintenance and enhancement of service quality. They include "apathy," "brush-off," "coldness," "condescension," "robotism," "rule book," and "runaround" (pp. 14–16).

Of course, according to professional social work ethics, our clients or customers should always be our top priority. In an ideal world this would be so. In the real world, however, staff members are individuals with individual weaknesses and failings. These seven sins of service can and do occur. From an organizational perspective, of course, staff includes everyone from the agency director to various levels of administrative staff, to professional social workers and other helping professionals, to clerical staff, to maintenance staff. Regardless of job title and responsibilities, each is, in essence, a representative of the agency. Albrecht maintains that it is absolutely essential for all staff to avoid committing any of the seven sins described here.

Of course, as professional social workers, we are supposed to be warm, empathic, and genuine. We are to always treat the customer with respect. However, these values are more difficult to maintain when we have 23 customers waiting in line impatiently for service, or if we absolutely have to finish an eight-page report that we haven't started yet at 4:30 P.M. today, or if we have an excruciatingly painful migraine headache. During these times, Albrecht would say that it's especially important to be vigilant about not committing any of the seven sins. The following list describes each of the seven organizational sins:

1. *Apathy.* Albrecht describes this as the "DILLIGAD" syndrome, or "Do I Look Like I Give A Damn?" à la comic George Carlin (p. 15). In other words, it's easy for staff members to focus on getting their jobs over with so that they can go home and live their own lives. Apathy involves boredom with customer interactions and almost total lack of concern regarding the quality, usefulness, or effectiveness of the service provided.

2. *Brush-off.* This consists of getting rid of the customer if possible by passing the buck and doing the smallest amount of work feasible. For example, a staff member might tell a customer that he can't answer her questions accurately and send her off to another department probably on a wild goose chase.

3. *Coldness.* This "kind of chilly hostility, curtness, unfriendliness, inconsiderateness, or impatience" conveys to the customer "You're a nuisance; please go away" (p. 15). It is difficult to maintain a warm, interested interpersonal stance every minute of the day. Some customers may be hostile, feisty, or demanding, on the one hand. On the other, you as a worker may be tired, fed up, or disgusted.

4. *Condescension.* Treating customers with a disdainful, patronizing attitude implies you as the worker are more knowledgeable and, essentially, better than the customers are. When you condescend, you treat people as if they're not very bright. It might be characterized by the phrase, "Now don't you worry your stupid little head about it. I know best, and I'll take care of everything. Trust me."

5. *Robotism.* When you treat each customer identically, without changes in facial or verbal expression, or ask the same questions over and over to different customers, you are not responding to individual differences. Such differences don't concern you. Your main intent is to get the job done as fast and efficiently as possible while using as little brain power as possible.

6. *Rule book.* If you want to think as little as possible, use the rule book to give the organization's rules and regulations absolute precedence. "Go by the book" totally and completely without any hint of compromise. I once called a weight control clinic for information on exercising and maintaining my weight. A young woman answered the phone, obviously reading a boilerplate blurb about losing weight at the clinic. I asked her if the clinic also helped people *maintain* their current weight, not lose more. She answered by rereading the identical blurb she just had read to me. I asked her the same question two more times, after which she repeated the same blurb. Finally, exasperated, I said, "Can't you think for yourself or what?" and abruptly hung up.

Although this situation does not reflect a social work context, it does exemplify the sin of the rule book. The young woman answering the phone apparently was instructed to read her blurb and not say anything else. As a result, trying to get any help from her (in this case, information) was totally useless and frustrating.

7. *Runaround.* Stalling customers is a common sin. Workers tell a customer to call someone else for the information first, or to go to Window 217 and fill out the appropriate 27-page form. Runaround entails using as little of your own time as possible, on the one hand, and wasting the customer's time on the other.

For example, Lutheran Social Services of Wisconsin and Upper Michigan (LSS) defines six components of quality: accuracy, consistency, responsiveness, availability, perceived value, and service experience (LSS, 1993, p. 8):

- *Accuracy* measures the extent to which actual service provision matches customers' expectations. To what extent do customers feel they are getting the services they sought and hoped to receive?
- *Consistency* is "service accuracy over time" (LSS, 1993, p. 8). Are customers consistently getting the appropriate services, or is service provision inconsistent?
- *Responsiveness* refers to timeliness of service provision. How long do customers have to wait before they get the attention and services they need?
- *Availability* is the ease with which customers can obtain services. To what extent are the services actually delivered to customers who request and need them?
- *Perceived* value is the extent to which customers feel the service is worth it. To what extent are the services they received worth the expense, time, energy, and possible annoyance or frustration they experienced? To what extent is the service's value worth its total cost?
- *The service experience* sums up the total treatment experience with all of its nuances and subtleties. What is the customer's sum total evaluation of each word spoken with staff? How do customers perceive the agency, taking into account all their experiences with it? This covers each moment of interaction with the agency and each tiny aspect of the experience. For example, what was the time like that they spent sitting in a waiting room chair? How clean were those chairs, anyhow? Where they comfortable? How long were they forced to wait? How were the clients greeted when they finally met with their workers? What is their summary impression of their total treatment experience?

Employee Empowerment and Teamwork

We stress repeatedly that empowerment involves providing people with authority or power so that they might have greater control over what they do. A TQM approach means that workers must be "empowered" to make decisions about how to do their jobs; they "need to be encouraged constantly to develop pride in their work and their organization" (Dumler & Skinner, 2008, p. 359; LSS, 1993; Sluyter, 1998). Management places the major responsibility for effective service provision on direct-service workers. TQM not only emphasizes the importance of customers, but also employees in the agency units providing services directly to these customers. Likewise, other agency units providing input to direct-service units are considered important because of their support to the service providers. For example, supervisory input is considered important primarily because it should aid in the service provision process.

In some ways, you might envision TQM as an upside-down pyramid. In a typical bureaucratic organization, the power structure as reflected in a formal organizational chart is in the form of a triangle or pyramid. The agency director sits at the pinnacle. Below her might be assistant directors, beneath them managers, below them supervisors, and, finally, at the very bottom, the many workers. The pyramid's shape, of course, reflects the relative number of persons involved at each level. There is only one agency director. There are fewer supervisors than direct-service workers. Finally, there are fewer direct-service workers than there are clients. In TQM, because the client customers or consumers are given precedence, those providing service directly to them are considered, in a way, the most important. The agency's clients as customers thus form the top level of the inverted pyramid because they are considered the most significant. Right below them would be the direct-service workers, beneath them the supervisors, and so on in the reverse order of the bureaucratic pyramid. The agency director and, perhaps, the board of directors would be placed at the very bottom of the inverted pyramid.

TQM emphasizes each employee's importance. Matza (1990) describes empowerment as "getting employees—especially front line employees—to take care of the customer" (p. 21).

© David Young-Wolff/PhotoEdit

Total quality management emphasizes the use of teams and teamwork. Here, an enthusiastic worker shares a bright new idea for enhancing service provision.

TQM espouses not only empowerment of individual employees, but also "team empowerment" (Daft, 2010a; Ginsberg, 1995; LSS, 1993, Williams, 2009). As already discussed, this involves giving the responsibility for service provision to designated groups that work together. TQM emphasizes cooperation instead of competition (Martin, 1993; Muckian, 1994). Such teamwork also means that all organizational employees from top management to direct-service workers are "given the incentive to work together and the responsibility and authority to make improvements and solve problems" (Williams, 2009, p. 674).

Highlight 4.10 further explores empowerment of clients within the organizational environment.

A Total Quality Approach to Leadership

Strong support and leadership from top management is critical in implementing TQM (Dumler & Skinner, 2008; Martin, 1993; Sluyter, 1998). Dumler and Skinner (2008) explain:

Supervision has been widely practiced as a traditional method of keeping an eye on workers—that is, looking for mistakes [a method often practiced in traditional bureaucracies]. Some managers have even resorted to using information technologies to eavesdrop on employees. This type of practice has debilitating effects on performance and is ethically questionable....

The responsibility for quality control ultimately rests with management; however, managers must also promote worker self-management. To further employee self-management, managers must develop worker participation programs and policies. With knowledge of the [organization's] ... costs and goals, workers can practice control with minimal supervision. Management's job is to ensure that workers have the knowledge, the tools, and the power to prevent problems from arising. Managers must also encourage employee's suggestions ... by recognizing and implementing worker quality improvement decisions. And, if there are problems, management should give workers the first opportunity to solve them. (p. 358)

One task leaders must accomplish is the establishment of a "culture of quality" (Martin, 1993, p. 80). We've established that *organizational culture* is "the set of key values, beliefs, understandings, and norms

HIGHLIGHT 4.10

Empowerment of Clients on a Macro Level

We have defined *power* as the potential to move other people on a chosen course to produce an effect or achieve some goal, and *empowerment* as the "process of increasing personal, interpersonal, or political power so that individuals can take action to improve their life situations" (Gutierrez, 2001, p. 210). Chapter 1 established that a *client system* is any individual, family, group, organization, or community who will ultimately benefit from social work intervention. *Macro client systems* include communities, organizations, and larger groups of clientele with similar issues and problems. Despite typical organizational problems and wide variations in management style, social workers are responsible for client system empowerment.

By orienting their management approaches, organizations can serve as empowerment mechanisms for large groups of clients. A major goal of social work is to enhance clients' right of choice, participation in decision making concerning their own well-being, and the availability of resources for them. A "goal of effective practice is not coping or adaptation but an increase in the actual power of the client or community so that action can be taken to change and prevent the problems clients are facing" (Gutierrez, GlenMaye, & DeLois, 1995, p. 250). How, then, can organizational management as a mightier force than individual practitioners encourage the empowerment of large groups of clients and citizens?

Gutierrez and her colleagues (1995) identify a range of elements working for and against an agency's ability to empower large groups of clients. They selected six private social service organizations that oriented themselves to serving client "populations that have been associated with empowerment-based services" (p. 251). Empowerment-oriented intervention involves educating clients so that they understand their social environment helping them acquire "concrete skills for surviving and developing social power," emphasizing strengths upon which to build skills, and using democratic processes to involve clients in decision making (Gutierrez et al, 1995, p. 250).

Selected agencies included two focusing on women's services, two on people of color, one on young people, and one on older adults. The researchers interviewed both direct-service staff and administrators, using taped interviews with an established format, to identify environmental variables working for and against client empowerment. They identified four obstacles to empowerment—expectations of funding sources, the macro social environment, intrapersonal

issues, and interpersonal issues. Three positive supports for client empowerment included staff development, an enhanced collaborative approach, and appropriate administrative leadership and support.

Factors Working against Client Empowerment

The first barrier to empowerment is "*expectations of funding sources*" (Gutierrez et al., 1995, p. 252). Funding agencies do not necessarily give precedence to encouraging client participation. Involving clients in the decision-making and service provision process on a large scale takes more time and energy. More people are involved. More communication is necessary. Therefore, the empowerment process is time consuming. Funding sources must be sensitive to the significance of empowerment. They must consider it valuable enough to pursue despite increased costs in time and money.

The second impediment to empowerment is the "*social environment*," the macro context in which organizations function (p. 252). Other agencies not supportive of the empowerment concept may not encourage referrals to or from empowerment-based agencies. Likewise, competition among agencies works against client empowerment in that empowerment is best established when people and agencies work together.

Rivalry for people's time and participation in the community social environment also obstructs the client empowerment process. Community residents and practitioners have just so much time and energy. It becomes more difficult to involve people in the empowerment process who are also integrally involved in other organizations and processes. These might include neighborhood centers, advocacy groups, professional organizations (such as the National Association of Social Workers), or Parent/Teacher organizations.

"*Intrapersonal issues*" make up the third barrier to an organization's ability to seek client empowerment (Gutierrez, et al., 1995, p. 253). Sometimes the basic attributes of clients or workers interfere with the empowerment process. For example, to what extent can people with serious mental or physical disabilities participate in the empowerment process? Some practitioners express frustration at the time and energy involved in pursuing empowerment, especially when they find only limited success.

The fourth obstacle to organizational empowerment is "*interpersonal issues*" (p. 253). These involve the interactions and relationships between clients and practitioners. Some workers express serious concerns about

(continued)

HIGHLIGHT 4.10 *(continued)*

how difficult it is to let go of their own control and direction in the intervention process. This is especially so when empowered clients choose alternatives placing their own well-being at risk. For example, a client who is a survivor of domestic violence might *choose* to return to a destructive, abusive situation. It is difficult for some workers to accept their clients' right to choice when the workers feel the choice is inherently bad.

Organizational Conditions Enhancing Client Empowerment

In contrast to the obstacles, three supports are identified for client empowerment in organizations. The first key to client empowerment is "*administrative leadership and support*" (Gutierrez et al., 1995, p. 255). When administrators encourage the nurturance of client empowerment and practitioners feel this, "an atmosphere of empowerment" is established (p. 255).

A second support for client empowerment is "*staff development!*" (p. 254). This includes the in-service training and other educational activities the agency provides both to empower the staff and to teach staff members how to incorporate approaches for empowering clients. Management should develop means of soliciting and improving client input into service provision and teach these methods to the staff.

A third support for client empowerment is an "*enhanced collaborative approach*" (p. 254). This involves the importance of a teamwork perspective infiltrating the agency environment. Staff understand the concepts of input and shared decision making because they're living it. They, in turn, can use these concepts to involve and empower clients. Gutierrez and her colleagues (1995) conclude that "those organizations that empower workers by creating an employment setting that provides participatory management, the ability to make independent decisions about their work, communication and support from administrators, and opportunities for skill development will be more capable of empowering clients and communities" (p. 256).

---

shared by members of an organization" (Daft & Marcic, 2009, p. 63). A culture reflecting a total quality perspective is one "characterized by teamwork, cooperation, open communication, flexibility, autonomy and empowerment" (LSS, 1993, p. 74). "As all employees must be involved in the total quality approach, agency leaders must visibly demonstrate their commitment to TQM" (Brown, Hitchcock, & Willard, 1994, p. 3). Leaders are responsible for "changing the organizational culture from one that dwells on *status quo* to one that gets excited about change" (Bedwell, 1993, p. 30).

For example, one agency director whose private, nonprofit family services organization had adopted a TQM perspective illustrated her commitment in a very concrete way. Historically, staff would park in the best spots in the parking lot each workday morning because they always got there first. Clients (or customers, in TQM terminology), who regularly got there later, would get the parking spots furthest from the building—if there were any spots left at all. Traditionally, the agency director assumed "ownership" of the best parking spot right by the agency's main door. The assistant director (number 2 in the agency's hierarchy) then took the second-best spot, and so it went on down the line. The day-time janitor was assigned the very worst spot.

Reflecting the TQM philosophy, the director decided to demonstrate the importance of serving customers and giving them priority by ordering that customers should be left the very best parking spots. Staff were relegated to the worst. The director herself chose the spot in the farthest corner of the lot, next to an appallingly foul-smelling dumpster. She also rallied some of the agency's precious funds to purchase extra parking spaces for customers in a lot adjacent to the agency. She felt that clients should no longer suffer from parking scarcity problems.

Another example of how agency leaders can demonstrate their commitment to TQM principles involves a family services agency that had held its board of directors meetings at noon each Friday since 1946. The boardroom where their meetings were held was the only large meeting facility in the agency. Therefore, it was used for a variety of agency activities and business, including staff meetings, treatment conferences concerning individual cases, and educational activities for clients. When the agency adopted the TQM management philosophy, the board solicited and received feedback from clients. One recommendation was a stress management class that, ideally, would be held at (yes, you guessed it) noon on Fridays. Because TQM emphasizes clients' importance, the board changed its meeting time to another day and another time instead of noon on Friday. This was done despite some inconveniences for board members.

Note that the board of directors in a traditionally bureaucratic agency would likely assume the topmost status in an agency. In effect, the board function's as the agency director's boss. In traditional bureaucracies, top leaders usually receive top priority for access to agency resources such as prime meeting space.

Continuous Improvement

"*Continuous improvement* is an ongoing commitment to increase product and service quality by constantly assessing and improving the processes and procedures used to create those products and services" (Williams, 2010, p. 333). TQM is not a "quick fix" (Daft, 2010a, p. 49). Rather, it involves an ongoing commitment to the principles involved.

In the context of social services agencies, one indication that improvement is needed involves "variation" in service provision (Williams, 2010, p. 333). If service provision is uneven and unpredictable, then attention should be focused on improving the processes concerned to make them more consistently effective. Quality of effective service provision is the ongoing goal.

Servant Leadership

Another approach to the leadership aspect of management "that has gained increased popularity in recent years" (Northouse, 2010, p. 384) is *servant leadership,* developed by Robert Greenleaf (1970, 1977). Northouse (2010) explains:

> *Servant leadership emphasizes that leaders should be attentive to the concerns of their followers and empathize with them; they should take care of them and nurture them.*
>
> *Greenleaf (1970, 1977) argued that leadership was bestowed on a person who was by nature a servant. In fact, the way an individual emerges as a leader is by first becoming a servant. A servant leader focuses on the needs of followers and helps them to become more knowledgeable, more free, more autonomous, and more like servants themselves. They enrich others by their presence.*
>
> *In the Herman Hesse's (1956) novel* The Journey to the East, *there is an example of leadership that was the inspiration behind Greenleaf's formulation of servant leadership. The story is about a group of travelers on a mythical journey who are accompanied by a servant who does menial chores for the travelers but also sustains them with his spirits and song. The servant's presence has an extraordinary impact on the group. When the servant becomes lost and disappears from the group, the travelers fall into disarray*

> *and abandon the journey. Without the servant, they are unable to carry on. It was the servant who was leading the group. He emerged as a leader by caring for the travelers.*
>
> *In addition to serving, the servant leader has a social responsibility to be concerned with the have-nots and to recognize them as equal stakeholders in the life of the organization. Where inequalities and social injustices exist, a servant leader tries to remove them (Graham, 1991). In becoming a servant leader, a leader uses less institutional power and less control, while shifting authority to those who are being led. Servant leadership values everyone's involvement in community life because it is within a community that one fully experiences respect, trust, and individual strength. Greenleaf places a great deal of emphasis on listening, empathy, and unconditional acceptance of others. (pp. 384–385)*

Qualities of a Servant Leader

There are at least 11 characteristics that make one a good servant leader (Barbuto & Wheeler, 2005, A-15; Packard, 2009; Sipe & Frick, 2009). Some are inherent qualities that really can't be taught. Others are behaviors that can be learned and enhanced.

1. *Calling.* Becoming a servant leader is more than just choosing that course. You must have an innate desire to forgo your own needs. Instead, you must put the well-being of others in the organization and the organization itself before yourself. You must have a genuine desire to improve the lives and functioning of workers. Therefore, it's like a calling instead of a choice.

2. *Listening.* We've established that listening is a vital communication skill. Servant leaders are exceptional listeners (Dubrin, 2009). They seek out information from others in the organization and strive to understand what others are trying to say.

3. *Empathy.* Empathy involves not only *being in tune* with how others feel, but also *conveying to them* that you understand how they feel (Kirst-Ashman & Hull, 2009b).

4. *Healing.* Servant leaders encourage emotional healing. They are supportive people who are easy to talk to and trust. People are naturally drawn to them.

5. *Awareness.* Servant leaders have a keen awareness of what's going on around them. They look beyond superficial appearances and explore issues and situations in depth.

6. *Persuasion.* Servant leaders are experts at using persuasion. They avoid making commands, but rather explain their views carefully and help others see their point of view.

7. *Conceptualization.* Servant leaders look at the organization's total picture and have a vision about what the organization might become. They encourage others to be creative and dream of how things could or should be. Their conceptualization of the organization's operation and environment is clearly articulated to others.

8. *Foresight.* Servant leaders look ahead and prepare for what might happen in the future. Others look to them for guidance and depend on them to anticipate upcoming issues.

9. *Stewardship.* Stewardship is the condition and act of caring for the basic daily needs of others. It involves planning activities, managing processes, and helping to make other people's lives run smoothly. Stewardship involves a strong desire to serve and assist.

10. *Growth.* Servant leaders view others as being capable of growth and improvement. They maintain a positive perspective and encourage skill development and confidence building in others.

11. *Building Community.* A "*community* consists of a number of people with something in common that connects them in some way and that distinguishes them from others" (Homan, 2008, p. 8). Servant leaders encourage a sense of community among all the people who work in an organization. They urge others to work together as a part of something bigger and more important than any single individual could be.

Common Problems Encountered in Organizations

Here we will describe some common problems encountered by people who work in any organization, including social service agencies. These include impersonal behavior, rewards and recognition, agency policy and worker discretion, and traditions and unwritten rules.

Impersonal Behavior

The goals of accountability and efficiency can create difficulties for workers and clients. Sometimes agencies engage in behavior intended to be businesslike but are perceived by the workers as impersonal. For example, one agency director, in order to reduce postage costs and cut the time workers spent on clerical tasks, decided to eliminate the appointment letters that workers would type on their computers and send to clients who lacked phones or e-mail. The letters told the client when the worker was planning a visit and asked the client to let the worker know if this was not satisfactory.

No one quarreled with the wish to save money, but many workers were upset because they would be forced to go to clients' homes without giving the client prior notice. To many workers this seemed inappropriate and unprofessional behavior, even a violation of clients' rights. It could also be more time consuming. The director did not share these opinions and overruled the workers' objections. Finally, tired of arguing social work values against business values, one worker calculated the cost of driving across the county to see a client who wasn't home. The wasted mileage cost exceeded the cost of sending out the appointment letters. After some discussion and debate, the director canceled the policy and allowed the workers to send appointment postcards instead.

Lack of Rewards and Recognition

A second characteristic of most agencies is that they do not distribute rewards and recognition as well as most workers wish. In school, it is common to get periodic feedback on your performance. Papers are returned with comments and a grade. Exams are returned soon after they are given with the grade clearly displayed. After each grading period, instructors give grades in each course. Many people prefer this regular system of reinforcement and expect something like it to exist in the agencies where they work.

Unfortunately, much of the good work social workers do will never be recognized. It is simply not noticed in the busy life of the agency. Other good work will be noticed, but for many reasons no one will comment on it. Supervisors may come to take the good work for granted and not believe it needs regular reinforcement. Clients may appreciate our efforts, but are too involved in their own situations to show their gratitude. Sometimes supervisors like our performance, but clients do not. For example, workers who take child abuse cases to court are unlikely to hear the offending parent praise their efforts. Consequently, a good guiding principle is to learn to reinforce yourself. This means you must take pride in work you do well and accept that your work will not always be acknowledged.

Agency Policy and Worker Discretion

Agency policies can guide the behavior of workers and clients and provide direction in situations that are common in the agency. For example, an agency policy may require workers to sign out when they leave the building. This makes it easier for supervisors, administrators, and clients to know where workers are at any given moment. In effect, it is a form of accountability and makes sense to most workers.

Many new workers feel overwhelmed with all the policies, rules, regulations, and procedures they must learn and abide by. They may think that policies control or constrain their every action. In reality, workers have enormous discretion about how they do their jobs because policies, by their very nature, must be general enough to apply in many different situations. This means that no policy can foresee all the possible events, nuances, and complexities of any given case. Policies set general guidelines, but workers are responsible for using their discretion or judgment with specific cases. Thus, these policies do not present a real barrier to effective social work. Workers must be prepared to apply their professional knowledge and skills and realize that they cannot rely on agency policy to dictate decisions in the field.

For example, suppose you are a practitioner working for a family services agency that specializes in helping parents learn how to control their children's behavior. Agency policy might prescribe eight weeks to work with parents and demonstrate improvement in their children's behavior. However, you and the parents have relatively wide discretion in determining what specific behaviors to work on. Should you focus on the children's tantrums, their refusal to eat anything but pizza and Hostess Twinkies for supper, or their almost constant nagging for attention? The decision is a matter of discretion and realistic expectations of an eight-week treatment plan.

Traditions and Unwritten Rules

Like other systems, agencies have both written and unwritten rules. The written rules frequently appear in a regulation manual or personnel handbook. The unwritten rules are related to the organization's informal structure, reflecting who has power and who communicates with whom. As in families, the traditions and unwritten rules are often learned only through verbal exchanges with more experienced group members. Sometimes they are learned only when the novice worker inadvertently violates a rule of tradition.

A case in point arose when a new MSW graduate, Gary Hughes, took his first job at a huge state mental hospital. Each Wednesday afternoon at 2:00 P.M., all the social workers at the hospital gathered around a large conference table. The purpose of the meeting was to improve communication among the social work staff. The hospital's social services director and its formal policy encouraged social workers to feel free at these meeting to raise issues causing them problems or making their jobs more difficult. The social services director, Harvey Steinenfrank, who supervised four social work units, had offered Gary a job right out of graduate school. Gary had done his first field placement at the hospital and the director liked the quality of his work.

Gary's direct social work supervisor, Jannell Fesselfuff, seemed distant and acted as though she resented Gary's presence. Although she was always polite and professional, Gary felt Jannell did not really want him around. Finally, Gary decided to use the Wednesday afternoon meeting to discuss his feelings. All social work staff, supervisors, and Harvey attended these meetings.

At the meeting Gary shared his feelings with the assembled group. Jannell tactfully acknowledged that she felt as though Harvey, the social services director, had "dumped" Gary in her unit without talking to her about Gary's status beforehand. Jannell apologized for taking out her anger at Harvey on Gary. Harvey apologized to Jannell for not consulting her before assigning Gary to her unit. The air appeared to clear and Gary felt much better.

After the meeting, Jannell took Gary aside and told him she was extremely upset because he brought the topic up at the meeting. She stressed, "We never discuss anything important at these meetings. We just meet because Harvey likes us to get together. If you have a concern, please talk it over with me first and we'll work it out." Later, Gary learned from talking to other workers that Jannell was right. The group had an informal rule that they never discussed anything important at these meetings. To do so was to violate the workers' informal policy and expectations.

The importance of this example is that informal rules and traditions can affect our work. We learn best by observing others and asking privately about things that appear to be rules. Learning about informal rules by breaking them can be painful.

Looking Ahead

This chapter examined organizational theories, structure, and dynamics. It explored the internal and external environments of organizations to provide you with a better understanding of what it's like to work in an organizational setting.

Sometimes, problems surface in a social service agency, or service delivery needs improvement. You then might be in the position of trying to change "the system" to improve it. The next chapter introduces you to a process for assessing the potential for organizational change.

Chapter Summary

The following summarizes this chapter's content as it relates to the learning objectives presented at the beginning of the chapter. Chapter content prepares social workers to:

A. *Examine organizations and their macro environments to enhance practice effectiveness.*

Organizations are "(1) social entities that (2) are goal directed, (3) are designed as deliberately structured and coordinated activity systems, and (4) are linked to the external environment" (Daft, 2010b, p. 11). Social services include the tasks that social work practitioners and other helping professionals perform for improving people's health, enhancing their quality of life, increasing self-sufficiency, supporting families, and helping people and larger systems improve their functioning in the social environment (Barker, 2003). A social agency or social services agency is an organization providing social services that typically employs a range of helping professionals, including social workers, office staff, paraprofessionals, and, on occasion, volunteers (Barker, 2003).

Social agencies may reflect either a predominantly social work setting or a host setting in another discipline. Social agencies have mission statements describing their broad purpose and organizational goals that specify anticipated outcomes of service provision. Agencies most often have multiple goals. Organizational objectives indicate how to achieve goals. Sometimes, organizations experience goal displacement, in which alternative goals replace initial service goals. Faith-based social services reflect some degree of a spiritual or religious orientation.

Organizational culture is "the set of values, norms, guiding beliefs, and understandings that is shared by members of an organization"

and that guides expected behavior (Daft, 2010b, p. 374). Organizational structure is the "system of task, reporting, and authority relationships within which the work of the organization is done" (Griffin & Moorhead, 2010, p. 407). This involves lines of authority, channels of communication, and dimensions of power.

Organizations may be centralized or decentralized. Organizations are subject to the environmental dimensions of available resources, legitimation, and client sources. Common problems encountered in organizations include impersonal behavior, lack of rewards and recognition, agency policy that limits worker discretion, and traditions and unwritten rules.

B. *Describe and analyze conceptual frameworks that empower or fail to empower organizations and staff as they provide services.*

There is a wide range of conceptual frameworks describing organizations. Classical theories (scientific management, the administrative theory of management, and bureaucracy) emphasize formal organizational structure, close supervision of employees, and efficiency. Neoclassical organizational theories shifted their focus to employees' motivation to participate. Human relations theories emphasized employees' satisfaction. Feminist theories stressed women's self-determination, using a gender filter, empowerment, "the personal is political," the importance of process, and diversity as strength. The cultural perspective accentuates organizational norms and expectations that guide behavior (Daft, 2010b, p. 374). Political-economy theory stresses the importance of an organization adapting the effects of resources and power in the external environment. The institutional perspective focuses on the external pressures imposed on organizations by social institutions. Contingency theory maintains that each element involved in an organization depends on other elements; therefore, no one best way exists to accomplish organizational goals. Systems theories emphasize how all parts of the organization (subsystems) are interrelated, taking resources (input) and producing some kind of product or service (output).

C. *Assess organizational operations from a systems perspective.*

Social agencies can readily be viewed from a systems perspective. Concepts include system, boundaries, subsystem, homeostasis, role, relationship, input, output, outcomes, positive and negative feedback, interface, differentiation, entropy, negative entropy, and equifinality.

D. *Demonstrate ethical behavior when involved in agency politics.*

Sources of power in organizations include legitimate, reward, coercive, referent, and expert. Organizations are by nature political. Some people are more power-oriented than others. Agency politics can be used for positive change. Politics reflecting unethical behavior, such as backstabbing, should be avoided.

E. *Describe and analyze managed health care and assess its ethical implications.*

Managed care has become an integral part of social work practice in numerous fields. Managed care reflects "a wide range of health plans and practices" (Kornblum & Julian, 2007, p. 60), including health maintenance organizations and preferred provider organizations (Mooney et al., 2009, p. 55). Primary principles involved are retention of quality and access, while controlling costs. Methods for cost control include capitation, gatekeeping, and utilization management. Managed care has pros and cons. Ethical issues concern gatekeeping versus client self-determination, informed consent, and confidentiality.

F. *Describe organizations that work with refugees and immigrants from a global perspective.*

Various organizations serve refugees and immigrants on a global basis. These include intergovernmental organizations such as the United Nations and the International Organization for Migration. National organizations include both government and private organizations, the latter of which generally focus on the relocation and settlement process. Social workers can provide numerous services to refugees and immigrants in various macro contexts.

G. *Identify and become involved in national and international social work organizations that exist to promote macro practice and the pursuit of social justice.*

The Association for Community Organization and Social Administration (ACOSA) is a national

organization dedicated to the enhancement of macro practice. International social work and social welfare organizations include the International Association of Schools of Social Work, the International Federation of Social Workers, and the International Council on Social Welfare.

H. *Recognize value discrepancies between social workers and traditional bureaucracies, and practice effectively within a bureaucracy.*

Social work values stress democratic decision making, communication, and self-determination. Since traditional bureaucracy emphasizes autocratic decisions, a hierarchical power structure, and rigid control, value discrepancies between bureaucracies and social work are apparent. Social workers can survive in bureaucracies by following a number of suggestions.

I. *Explain current trends in management.*

Newer approaches in management include constructing a culture of caring, promoting a learning organization, using teamwork and empowerment, and managing diversity.

J. *Practice within settings employing two different management approaches—total quality management and service learning.*

Total quality management (TQM) emphasizes a focus on clients as customers, quality as the primary goal, employee empowerment and teamwork, TQM leadership, and continuous improvement. Servant leadership stresses the importance of leaders nurturing their employees by serving them. Leaders accomplish this through listening, empathy, healing, awareness, persuasion, conceptualization, foresight, stewardship, growth, and building community.

K. *Demonstrate client empowerment on a macro level.*

Factors working against client empowerment in organizations include 'expectations of funding sources,' the 'social environment,' 'intrapersonal skills,' and 'interpersonal issues' (Gutierrez et al., 1995, pp. 250–253). Organizational conditions that can ultimately enhance client empowerment include 'administrative leadership and support,' 'staff development,' and an 'enhanced collaborative approach' (Gutierrez et al., 1995, pp. 254–256).

Competency Notes

The following identifies where Educational Policy (EP) competencies and practice behaviors are discussed in the chapter.

EP 2.1.2 Apply social work ethical principles to guide professional practice. *(P. 156):* Social workers have an ethical obligation to conduct themselves ethically and to engage in ethical decision making.

EP 2.1.2a Recognize and manage personal values in a way that allows professional values to guide practice. *(P. 166):* Practitioners should recognize personal and professional values in order to function effectively in a bureaucracy.

EP 2.1.4 Engage diversity and difference in practice. *(P. 146):* Religion and spirituality are facets of diversity. Practitioners must understand how faith-based social services affect practice and service provision. *(P. 172):* Diversity can be valued and respected in organizations.

EP 2.1.4a Recognize the extent to which culture's structures and values may oppress, marginalize, alienate, or create or enhance privilege or power. *(P. 132):* Gender is one dimension of diversity. Feminist theories help one to recognize how an organization's structures and values concerning gender can affect work performance and the ability to undertake macro level change. *(P. 162):* Social workers should recognize how cultural structures and values affect immigrants and refugees.

EP 2.1.5 Advance human rights and social and economic justice. *(P. 161):* Social workers should recognize the global interconnections of oppression.

EP 2.1.5b Advocate for human rights and social and economic justice. *(P. 161):* Social workers should advocate for human rights and social and economic justice concerning managed care.

EP 2.1.7a Utilize conceptual frameworks to guide the processes of assessment, intervention, and evaluation. *(P. 128):* Various conceptual frameworks help in understanding organizational functioning, and guide the processes of assessment, intervention, and evaluation in macro practice with organizations. *(P. 141):* Systems theories provide a useful conceptual framework to guide the planned change process.

EP 2.1.9a Continuously discover, appraise, and attend to changing locales, populations, scientific and technological developments, and emerging societal trends to provide relevant services. *(P. 170):* A learning organization provides an environment that allows for continuous improvement and responsiveness to emerging trends and client needs.

EP 2.1.10f Develop mutually agreed-on intervention goals and objectives. *(P. 173):* Client input and participation are paramount in total quality management.

EP 2.1.10h Initiate actions to achieve organizational goals. *(P. 144):* Practitioners must understand what organizational goals are before initiating actions to achieve them. *(P. 148):* Establishing objectives helps to achieve organizational goals.

On the Internet

Visit the *Generalist Practice with Organizations and Communities* website at *www.cengage.com/social_work/ kirst-ashman* for learning tools such as PowerPoint® slides, tutorial quizzing, Web links, and final exams.

CHAPTER 5

PREPARE—Decision Making For Organizational Change

As the social worker at an elementary school, you notice an increasing number of children coming from turbulent homes. With each passing year, the truancy rates rise, children's grades deteriorate, and their illicit drug use soars. They need something, some kind of help. But what? Your job is to intervene individually with children suffering the most severe crises. You do some individual counseling, make some family visits, run a few support and treatment groups, and attend numerous assessment and planning meetings.

In a social work journal, you read about a new type of alternative programming for children who are at risk of developing the kinds of problems you're seeing. One idea in particular catches your eye: A school in Illinois has developed a "Friendship Program" for children at risk. Volunteers are solicited from social work students at a nearby university. The volunteers attend a dozen training sessions to learn how to work with these children. Each volunteer is then paired with an individual child and subsequently becomes the child's "special friend." The required commitment period is one year. Volunteers' responsibilities include spending time with their assigned child at least once a week, being available to talk when the child needs to, and providing a positive role model for the child.

In a way it reminds you of Big Brothers/Big Sisters programs, where volunteers, typically supervised by social workers, offer individualized support, guidance, and companionship to children missing a parent. However, in this Friendship Program, the child isn't necessarily from a single-parent home. The Friendship Program's only prerequisite for participating children is that school staff designate them as being at risk of problems, including truancy, deteriorating school performance, and drug use. School staff have substantial latitude regarding the criteria for identifying a child as "at risk"—normally a recent divorce in the family, extreme shyness and withdrawal, academic problems, or other social difficulties.

You think, "Wouldn't it be great if my school system had a program like that in operation?" How would you go about establishing such a program? It is not included in your job description. Is it possible for you to start something like that? Would it be worth your effort? Whom would you talk to about it? How might the school administration feel about starting up a program? What would it cost?

The previous situation illustrates a major thrust of this chapter: to propose and explain a seven-step decision-making process to use when deciding whether or not to pursue macro intervention within your agency environment.

Introduction

Historically in social work, the term "community organization" referred to an intervention approach in which social workers and other professionals worked with groups of people to collectively bring about some social change. Traditionally, social workers were trained primarily in skills oriented toward this kind of community organization instead of in skills working directly with individual clients, groups, and families. However, the social and political climate is very different today. Resources are scarce, and agencies engaged primarily in community organization are much less common.

Today, many beginning social workers get jobs that concentrate on helping individuals (micro systems) or families and other groups (mezzo systems). Consequently, if macro change efforts are going to be undertaken, they will most likely be generated by social workers employed in agencies providing primarily micro and mezzo services. These workers must be able to move the wheels of change from a job not intended for that purpose.

This chapter discusses the nuts and bolts of making macro changes, which are very different from those that agencies formally engage in. Usually, agency administrators implement changes as part of their administrative responsibility, or agency authority figures solicit help and advice from outside consultants (Lewis, Packard & Lewis, 2007). In both instances, formal authority figures (such as an agency director or board of directors) initiate and control the change process.

In an ideal agency, that would be the case. However, in the real world, administrators make decisions for a multitude of reasons, including regulations governing them outside of the agency; monetary restrictions on agency functioning; insufficient information about what is going on at the direct-service level (often caused by the administrative layers of bureaucracy that act to buffer, summarize, edit, and censor information before it can get from the bottom up to administrators); or even self-interest on the part of administrators.

In our context, organizational change results from the actions of practitioners with little or no administrative power (that is, those who usually work directly with clients or have lower-level supervisory status). Such practitioners can seek changes in agency policies, programs, or procedures so that the agency will serve clients more effectively (Kirst-Ashman & Hull, 2009; Hernandez, 2008). If, for whatever reason, agency administrators do not do what you think is right, necessary, or ethically responsible, it becomes your responsibility to identify problems and instigate change. Such organizational change has also been called "change from within" (Lewis et al., 2007; Resnick & Patti, 1980), "internal advocacy" (Patti, 1983), and "change from below" (Brager & Holloway, 1978; Lewis et al., 2007).

Four factors often characterize define this kind of organizational change (Gibelman & Furman, 2008; Holloway, 1987; Hernandez, 2008).

First, such change begins with staff who have lower levels of power and authority within the agency. These staff seek to influence administrators with significantly greater levels of power. Ideally, of course, agency administrators encourage constructive suggestions from staff. However, in real life, this is often not the case. Administrators may even discourage such communication for reasons such as the protection of their own egos or their concern for what they consider more global and important than staff input.

Second, lower-level or line staff express concerns about some problem or issue within the organization that transcends their own job descriptions and domains of responsibility.

Third, staff approaches go beyond those the organization has formally established. For example, the worker initiating the change might have to participate in special meetings out of his or her usual job experience. Indeed, the worker might have to confront superiors about issues involved. Confronting supervisors is not normally part of a worker's job description.

Fourth, the whole process is undertaken for the benefit of the organization's clients.

Initially, we will look at the types of organizational changes usually involved when you initiate change from within. Later, we will describe the decision-making process involved in pursuing organizational change.

Learning Objectives

This chapter will provide content concerning how social workers:

A. *Discern, appraise, and integrate multiple sources of knowledge in order to propose various forms of organizational change (including undertaking specific projects, initiating and developing programs, and changing agency policies).*

B. *Collect, organize, and interpret data in order to assess the potential for organizational change by employing a seven-step process entitled PREPARE.*

C. *Examine an extensive case example demonstrating the PREPARE process.*

D. *Practice personal reflection by assessing personal strengths and weaknesses with respect to the potential for macro change.*

E. *Appraise the potential for internal advocacy with the ultimate goal of improving client access to services.*

Change in Organizations

As a social work practitioner, you will likely encounter times when your agency is accomplishing tasks ineffectively, is not doing something it should do, or is simply doing the wrong thing. Holloway (1987) points out that some problems facing human services organizations are "profound," whereas others are very "subtle" (p. 731). Specific problems might include the following:

> *The agency does not reach out to potential clients, the agency is insensitive to clients' definitions of problems, it serves those for whom public sympathy is high and refuses to serve others, it makes referrals for its own rather than the client's convenience, or it offers one kind of service to meet all needs. (Holloway, 1987, p. 731)*

EP 2.1.10h

When such organizational problems exist, it is your responsibility to try to help your agency improve its service provision to clients. The National Association of Social Workers *Code of Ethics Preamble* (2008) states that it is your professional responsibility to "promote social justice and social change with and on behalf of clients." This involves striving "to end discrimination, oppression, poverty, and other forms of social injustice." Activities to achieve these ends include community organizing, advocacy, social and political action, policy development and implementation, and promoting the "responsiveness of organizations, communities, and other social institutions to individuals' needs and social problems." In other words, professional social workers are ethically responsible for pursuing macro level change when it is needed.

Macro changes within an agency are usually of two types. One involves changes made to improve the resources provided to clients. The other concerns changes made to enhance the agency's working environment so that personnel can perform more efficiently and effectively, thus improving service provision to clients. Such changes can involve undertaking projects, initiating and developing programs, and changing formal agency policies (Homan, 2008; Netting, Kettner, & McMurtry, 2008; Shaefor & Horejsi, 2009)—each of which are described next. Highlight 5.1 discusses a positive way to think about the changes you propose.

HIGHLIGHT 5.1

A Word about Innovations

One way to look at organizational change is to frame it as an *innovation,* that is, "any program, technique, or activity perceived as new by a population group or organization" (Brody, 2005; Rothman, Erlich, & Teresa, 1981, pp. 21–22). Thinking about macro change in organizations as innovations provides a bright, optimistic context for that change. Innovations imply freshness, creativity, and gusto. They can involve tried-and-true methods that are known well elsewhere but are totally exotic in your own agency. Or, innovations can be brilliant ideas you creatively think up yourself for how to improve the agency's functioning.

Once again, note that agency administrations may not recognize such brilliant innovations and ideas, let alone support them. Therefore, much of this and the next two chapters will address how to maximize your potential for success when resistance is likely.

Undertaking Specific Projects

The first type of potential macro change you are likely to encounter in your agency environment is the undertaking of some special *project*—that is, a time-limited, planned undertaking with specified goals and activities to accomplish a designated purpose, such as improving services to clients, training staff, or solving some agency or community problem. Projects are generally undertaken only for some designated period of time, usually no more than a year. Unlike program development or policy changes, projects are temporary.

Projects are usually specific regarding the client population they serve and the final goals they pursue. Projects also likely cost less than new programs and have fewer repercussions than major agency policy changes, a fact that makes them more appealing to administrators.

At least two broad categories of projects exist (Homan, 2008; Kettner, Datey, & Nichols, 1985, pp. 161–163). First, *service projects* address needs or issues requiring some new, innovative, or untried approach. For example, a worker at a residential treatment center for boys who have serious behavioral disorders may initiate a research project to determine the effectiveness of involving siblings along with parents in the family counseling that staff members provide. If the project is found effective, the worker might urge the agency to incorporate such treatment into its policies or develop an ongoing new program to continue this practice. The research project would be evaluated and then terminated, because projects are temporary. However, the worker and agency may then begin a new macro process of policy revision or program development.

Service projects may also address other short-term tasks. For example, workers may undertake the task of rewriting their old job descriptions to more accurately reflect what they are currently doing. Once the designated task is completed, the project is over.

The second type of project, the *support project,* involves short-term endeavors aimed at specific ends that support some other agency activity. Workers might organize a fundraising campaign for resources to build a new addition to their agency or they might develop an in-service training curriculum to enhance their skills.

Initiating and Developing Programs

The second type of macro change that might face you as a practitioner is the need to develop a new *program.* In the context of social services, a program (also referred to as a social program) is an ongoing configuration of services and service provision procedures intended to meet a designated group of clients' needs. A social program generally has identified goals to accomplish within an organizational or community environment. In contrast to a project, a program is more permanent.

Each social agency or organization can have any number of programs. For example, Lutheran Social Services, the organization of social agencies affiliated with the Lutheran church, has branches throughout the United States that host a number of programs, including adoption services, mental health services, services for people with developmental disabilities, services for older adults, and a variety of others.

Program development is not an aspect of most direct-service jobs. Why, then, might you consider trying to set up a whole new program? Because you see a major gap in the service delivery system that needs to be filled. You recognize clients' needs that are not being met.

For example, you might be a state probation officer. You notice a significant increase in your *caseload* (those client cases assigned to you and for which you're responsible) of men committing acts over and over again that in your state are considered misdemeanors. A *misdemeanor* is a minor crime, less serious than a felony, that normally results in incarceration for less than six months. Your clients are doing things such as speeding while driving under the influence or shoplifting CDs. As their probation officer, you see them doing thoughtless, "dumb" things that simply get them several-hundred-dollar fines and several-month jail sentences over and over again. You think this is senseless. There must be a better way to deal with this problem and help these men become responsible for their behavior.

At a conference, you hear about a deferred prosecution program being run in an adjoining state. This program provides people arrested for such misdemeanors with alternatives to fines and jail terms. They can opt to participate in a 12-week group run by two social workers. Group sessions focus on enhancing self-esteem, raising self-awareness, improving decision-making skills, developing better communication skills, and encouraging analysis of responsible versus irresponsible behavior. You hear that the program was initially funded by a grant (often referred to as "soft money," meaning temporary and limited funding). However, it was so successful that the state decided to implement and pay for it in several designated counties by using "hard money" (which means relatively permanent funding that becomes part of an organization's regular annual budget).

How does one begin the process of program development? At this day treatment center, a social worker helps adults who have cognitive disabilities participate in recreational activities. The worker feels that the center needs a new program to improve client care. She'll need to "learn the ropes" concerning how to get a new program off the ground.

At any rate, men who participated in the program were found to have a significantly reduced recidivism rate. (*Recidivism rates* refer to the proportion of criminals who repeat a crime. A recidivism rate of 25 percent means that out of 100 criminals, 25 committed another offense and 75 did not.) You think, "What a wonderful idea!" You begin to consider how to initiate such a program in your agency. This can be the beginning of program development.

Or, suppose you are a counselor at a large rural residential facility for adults with cognitive disabilities who are unable to live in the community by themselves. Your job involves teaching them basic daily living skills, such as how to dress oneself and make one's own bed. Additionally, you run socialization groups and activities for clients to teach them to relate to and get along with each other. Finally, you work with your clients' families to help them make visitation arrangements and address any other problems that may come up. Sometimes, for instance, parents have

difficulty controlling their adult child's behavior during the child's home visits.

The problem is that you are especially concerned about six of your clients. You feel they are not being stimulated enough to develop their full potential. You think that, with some special training and help, they would be capable of living either in a group home or in individual apartments with some supplementary support. This support might include teaching them how to cook, do laundry, pay bills, and possibly obtain employment. You feel they would be able to grow in such a setting, enhance their self-esteem, and become more productive members of society.

However, no such program exists in your area. There are neither group homes nor social workers assigned to provide supportive services to enhance the independence of clients like yours. Now what? How might you begin exploring the possible initiation of program development?

Changing Agency Policies

EP 2.1.8a

The third kind of macro change you may encounter is changing agency or organizational policies. Chapter 1 established that a *policy* is a rule or set of rules that tells us which actions among a multitude of options we may take and which we may not. It thus provides any macro system direction for its functioning and activities. Policies supply guidelines that govern how an agency operates. Policy dictates what should and should not be done in the agency setting. Policies may be formal or informal. *Formal policies* are written down and clearly specified, often in a policy manual. *Informal policies,* on the other hand, are not overtly stated, yet still guide and influence agency staff's behavior (Daft, 2010a; DuBrin, 2007).

The policy manual, by the way, may be the most important document in your agency. It compiles the rules and regulations that govern your responsibilities, rights, restrictions, and benefits. Policy manuals are excruciatingly dull when they don't apply to you, but tremendously interesting when you need them to answer your questions and find out about your rights. They are not written to stimulate the reader's interest. Rather, policy manuals usually consist of complex, legalistic language that is very difficult to understand clearly. Such manuals do, however, provide you with a statement of the agency's formal goals, procedures for working with clients, instructions for requesting vacation time, and grievance procedures to follow if you think you have been mistreated. Therefore, it is vitally important that you receive your own copy of the manual, have electronic access to it when you enter the agency, or have ready access to someone else's, such as your supervisor's.

Formal and informal policies formulate the core plan for what the agency does and how it does it. Policies involve both internal operations (process) and provision of services to clients (output). Internal operations include administrative arrangements and specific procedures for how the agency is run. For example, formal policies involving internal operations can address the lines of authority within the agency (who supervises whom), how many sick days and vacation days employees have available, and how such time is accumulated (a specific agency procedure).[1]

Examples of informal internal operating policies include who buys and signs birthday cards for fellow workers, how announcements are routed from one staff member to another, how supervisors and administrators expect to be treated, and how committee meetings are scheduled and run.

Formal or informal agency policies can also prescribe how services are provided to clients. They can specify the proper procedures for completing a family assessment, the forms to fill out as progress notes, what kinds of services will be provided to clients, and many other aspects of worker-client interactions.

Formal and informal agency policies usually represent long-established ways of doing things in the agency. As such, agency policies affect virtually all agency personnel and clients.

Practitioners entering the field might easily assume that agency administrators and supervisors are responsible for ensuring that the agency has "good" policies—effective and efficient policies that ensure that clients receive the services they need. They assume that is what administrators get paid for—keeping the agency running well so that workers providing direct services to clients can do their jobs. However, often this is not the case. For example, goal displacement may occur when the original goal of serving clients is gradually replaced with a new goal of maintaining the service process (as was discussed in Chapter 4).

Sometimes agency policy reinforces problems such as goal displacement. A formal policy might read that "crisis intervention workers in an agency must attend weekly staff meetings at regularly scheduled times," despite the fact that their clients may be experiencing extreme crises at these meeting times. Thus, agency policy that places higher priority on meetings than on addressing clients' crises has reinforced goal displacement.

Another example of a problematic formal policy is one that requires clients to fill out a 27-page admissions form before they can receive services. Perhaps a large percentage of the agency's clients are Hispanic and speak very little English. If the admissions form requires that potential clients be highly articulate in English, the agency essentially prohibits Hispanic clients from receiving services. Because of the language difference, the agency blocks clients from getting what they need.

Still another example of a problematic policy is an informal requirement that all members of a family must be present for the initial intake interview. If individual family members refuse to attend such interviews for any reason (such as employment during meeting times, lack of interest, or resentment about social

---

1. Often, sick time and vacation days are accumulated on the basis of time worked in the agency. For example, you might accrue one sick day for every month of completed work and two weeks of vacation for every year.

service involvement), the entire family would be denied access to treatment.

Our final example of a problematic agency policy concerns workload. Assume that agency policy requires you to make one home visit to each of the 100 families on your caseload every 40-hour work week. Including traveling time, it takes you approximately two hours to do each home visit. Therefore, in order to fulfill agency policy, you must make 200 hours worth of home visits in your 40-hour work week. Obviously, even if you omit eating lunch and using the restroom, this is impossible. Agency policies frequently create such dilemmas. Perhaps when the agency policy was instituted, caseloads averaged 12 families instead of 100. Established policies are often appropriate at their conception, but can become outdated. Over time, with increasingly stringent budgets, caseload numbers gradually creep up. For practical reasons, this agency policy needs to be changed: Perhaps caseloads could be cut drastically, the requirement that each family be visited weekly could be deleted, or some other fairly drastic policy change could be made in order to make the policy congruent with what is possible.

At times, you may feel that formal or informal agency policies interfere with, restrict, or even totally prevent you from doing the best possible job with clients. As a practitioner working directly with clients on a daily basis, you may be more in tune with "what's going on out there." It therefore makes sense for you to identify the impediments and difficulties confronting you every day. Even if it's not your designated job to change policy, it may be in your and your clients' best interests to do so.

Informal Agency Policies

Informal agency policies can be confusing. As we have indicated, they are implicit, unwritten rules about how the agency should operate. Often they are elusive and difficult to pin down. Many staff simply assume that "everybody knows about *that*." Unless an agency newcomer is psychic, he or she may behave inappropriately simply because he or she is ignorant of the unwritten rules. Sometimes these informal policies entail simple expectations for superficial actions. Other times they prescribe important rules of conduct whose violation is not to be taken lightly. Highlight 5.2 describes such a scenario.

Three types of informal agency policies involve practice procedures, agency goals, and personnel. Remember, however, that we will focus on them in the context of informal policies. Practice procedures, agency goals, and personnel are also covered by clearly established formal policies.

Informal Policies on Practice Procedures

Practice procedures refer to the techniques and approaches practitioners use to accomplish their goals with clients. Some practice procedures are formalized policies. For example, an agency might specify that goal attainment scaling, a specific method of evaluation, is used to monitor clients' progress.[2] (Chapter 10 discusses goal attainment scaling in greater detail.)

The way tasks are *actually* carried out in agencies (as opposed to how they are theoretically *supposed* to be carried out) directly affects clients' well-being, so knowledge and understanding of informal policies on practice procedures is infinitely important. Consider an agency where formal policy requires that cases be discussed and plans developed during periodic formal *treatment conferences* (groups that meet to establish, monitor, and coordinate service plans on behalf of a client) (Toseland & Rivas, 2009). Because of heavy caseloads and limited time, in reality most workers informally discuss clients' cases whenever they can snatch a few seconds of time. Sometimes they do so in hallways, other times while having a drink after work. These informal practices downgrade and sometimes even eliminate regular, responsible discussion of cases during staffings. Assuming a macro perspective, you might want to initiate and implement a change in the informal procedure so that case plans are once again discussed on a predictable basis. This might involve addressing the issue with other staff and administrators or initiating renewed formal case staffing procedures that are more efficient and doable.

Practice procedures within agencies vary widely and endlessly and therefore present many opportunities for improvement. Examples include counseling techniques, recordkeeping methods, and admissions processes. For instance, you might want to propose that progress notes be written using an established agency form, instead of just scribbled in the form of a note citing the date the client was seen and your impressions. You might suggest a procedure for decreasing each client's intake process from three steps (that is, initial phone contact, individual interview, and family interview) to two steps (namely, initial phone contact, when individual information is collected, and family interview).

---

2. *Goal attainment* scaling is an evaluation design used to monitor the progress of individual clients by establishing clearly defined goals and weighted scale categories to monitor progress over time. Data is then aggregated on a weekly, monthly, or annual basis to determine the extent to which specified goals have been achieved.

HIGHLIGHT 5.2

Case Example: "Hidden" Informal Policies

Suppose you're a new worker at a Veterans Affairs (VA) Hospital. You work in the vocational rehabilitation unit with clients who have mental or physical disabilities. Your main tasks are to assess your clients' abilities, refer them to the appropriate training facilities, and eventually help clients find jobs in the community. You have been on the job exactly six work days. You walk into your first multidisciplinary staff meeting. You are one of a number of staff members from various disciplines who are there to provide information and make decisions regarding treatment planning for a series of clients.

You feel you have done your homework and read through the ponderous section of the agency's policy manual that describes multidisciplinary staffing procedures. You are energetic, enthusiastic, and eager to make a good impression on your new supervisor and colleagues. You have worked with similar clients before and have taken special related courses in college. You feel confident and appropriately assertive.

During the meeting, you make six well-thought-out statements regarding your beliefs about the treatment of two clients. At the end of the meeting, you pat yourself on the back, thinking, "Wow, that was good. I must've made a good impression. Knowledgeable. Not too pushy. What more could they ask?"

After the meeting, several staff walk quickly past you without making eye contact. You think, "That's odd. What's up with them?"

A physical therapist sheepishly approaches you as you walk out the door. You have spoken to her several times informally and feel that you really hit it off. She says, "I don't mean to be rude, but perhaps someone should have told you some things about our staff meetings. The case manager [not you on this occasion] usually comes in with the treatment recommendations in pretty good shape. We all have an understanding that whoever is managing the case (including following up on recommendations, monitoring progress, and writing up reports) talks to those of us who are involved ahead of time for our input. If we started from scratch with every single case, we'd never get anything done."

How would you feel? In this case, two informal policies were unknown to you: First, staff meetings are held to finalize already-established plans, not to discuss or initiate loads of new ideas. Participants keep talking to a minimum in order to get through the process. The physical therapist did not refer to the second rule, which is that new staff are not supposed to talk much at meetings until they are at the agency at least three months. By this time, other staff have had time to get to know them and will give more credibility to their ideas.

How could one prevent such an "oops" experience? The fact that many policies are informal means that they probably will need to be learned informally. That is, talking to other staff about informal expectations, rules, and policies is probably a good plan. In this situation, prior to the staff meetings you might have talked to colleagues about how staff meetings are run, especially about how they differ from the description in the policy manual.

Another example of an informal policy about agency procedures causing problems is Ms. Winfrey's situation: She is a newly promoted supervisor of the large Supportive Services Unit (for older adults) in an urban social services agency with 2,000 employees. Unit staff members provide supportive services to senior residents in their own homes to help them remain as independent as possible. For instance, unit staff members help clients access services, pay bills, get food and medicine, and connect with required resources.

Ms. Winfrey's new job requires her to supervise five direct-service workers. The first day of work after returning from her two-week Rocky Mountain National Park summer vacation, Ms. Winfrey's administrative assistant, panicking, storms into her office. The assistant gives Ms. Winfrey a handwritten note from the agency's executive director, Mr. Sawyer. Ms. Winfrey is awestruck. She has seen the executive director only a few times and has never before received a handwritten note from him. This means serious business. What could possibly be wrong? She's only had her new job for a month. What could she have done? The note reads,

8/29/11
Ms. Winfrey,
Please submit the absence report forms for your staff
immediately. They are due the fifth of each month.
T. Sawyer

No one told Ms. Winfrey that absence report forms existed, let alone that they were due to someone on the fifth of each month. The policy was not contained in any document she knew of. Apparently, several administrative assistants in Mr. Sawyer's office tried to contact her during her vacation, but because of malfunctioning e-mail, the messages never got through. Finally, as a last resort, Mr. Sawyer took his very expensive time to address this superficially petty issue. Apparently, the agency loses major funding if timely absence reports are not religiously submitted to the powers-that-be.

Ms. Winfrey is flabbergasted. Evidently, the agency personnel expect new administrative staff to learn such procedures by osmosis or ESP. She had no idea how important this procedure was.

Eventually, Ms. Winfrey chalks the incident up as a mistake that was not really her fault. However, she *never* again forgets to submit the absence report when it is due.

Informal agency goals Informal agency goals often replace formally stated goals and thus become the real goals the agency strives to reach. Goal displacement is a good example, wherein the *process* of getting things done replaces the importance of actually getting things done (Etzioni, 1964). This is the case even though the formal goals still stress the importance of the output or services provided.

Informal personnel practices Agency treatment of personnel is integrally involved with formal and informal communication channels (discussed in Chapter 4). Conflicts can result in macro practice intervention. For example, staff might cooperatively organize to try to overthrow an administrator they intensely dislike (Dolgoff, 2005). There are no formal policies for doing that.

An administrator's significantly preferential treatment of staff in her unit, giving opportunities to a privileged few, may infuriate the unprivileged many. Another supervisor might use his power and discretion to give privileged staff better cases, first choice of limited vacation time, and more flexibility of hours. The unprivileged may then mobilize to develop and institute new formal policies to curb such unfair practices.

Be wary, however, about putting new policies in place to constrain the actions of one or two individuals. When those individuals leave, you will be stuck with the policy. One group of practitioners resented how their supervisor divided cases. One worker in the group, a personal friend of the supervisor, received the most interesting and least chaotic (therefore, least difficult

and time-consuming) cases. The remaining unit practitioners worked to develop, and urged administration to adopt, a policy that forced supervisors to divide cases equally and randomly. Passed through higher levels of administration, the supervisor lost most of his discretion regarding the assignment of cases.

Abruptly, both the supervisor and the friend left the agency for other positions. The remaining staff and the new supervisor were then burdened with the policy they had created. The staff would have preferred holding staff meetings, where clients could be assigned on the basis of each staff's expertise. They all preferred to have input into case assignments. However, this was not possible due to the rigid, newly adopted policy. The staff and the new supervisor were then faced with two choices: They could live with the new system, which severely restricted discretion and flexibility, or they could start a new macro change process, expending more time and energy to create a more flexible policy. By this time, the staff's other concern was their credibility with administration. They feared they would look as if they could not make up their minds and would simply be ignored. In effect, they were stuck.

Beginning the Change Process

Because macro interventions are often complex, practitioners usually must think about the problem and potential solutions in a general way before beginning any change process. There are a number of dimensions to consider. Macro change requires four critical elements, including "the change catalyst [we will use the term *change agent*], the action system, the innovation proposal, and the action plan" (Brody, 2005; Resnick, 1980a, p. 188; Rothman, 2001; Yankey & Vogelsang-Combs 2008). The *change agent* is the person who believes some change within the agency is needed (in our context, you). You, as the change agent, begin to think about a problem you believe requires change, and then you initiate the change process. The *action system* is the people and resources you will organize and employ to work toward the needed change (Packard, 2009). If you undertake the change yourself, you will be both the change agent and the action system. The *innovation proposal* is the idea you want to implement. Finally, the *action plan,* like any other plan in generalist social work practice, is a detailed blueprint for how to go about achieving the desired change (Rothman & Zald, 2008).

EP 2.1.9b

As a change agent—the practitioner who sees something wrong and is willing to expend effort to change it—you can either choose to initiate the process yourself or unite with others in your agency who have similar feelings about the problem (Gibelman & Furman, 2008; Resnick, 1980b). The latter approach is usually superior, because it gives you more power and influence. Either you alone or your coalition becomes the action system.

At this point, you have two major tasks to consider (Lewis et al., 2007; Resnick, 1980b; Yankey & Vogelsang-Coombs, 2008). First, you need to identify the action system's potential goal. What do you want to accomplish? Do you want to incorporate flexible hours into the agency's policy so that clients may be seen on evenings or weekends? Does your agency need to establish a crisis intervention line to respond to clients' needs more quickly? Do your adolescent clients need somewhere to congregate and participate in wholesome recreational activities as an alternative to gang membership? What is your final goal?

The second task involves thinking about the opposition you anticipate. Will agency administrators balk at greater costs or at changing established procedures? To what extent will coworkers and workers in other agency units either impede or support your ideas?

The Process of Organizational Change

We have established that the planned change process follows seven basic steps:

1. *Engagement*—the initial period where you as a practitioner orient yourself to the problem at hand and begin to establish communication and a relationship with others also addressing the problem.
2. *Assessment*—the investigation and determination of variables affecting an identified problem or issue and concentration on strengths, both as viewed from micro, mezzo, and macro perspectives, in preparation for formulating a plan of action to help a client system.
3. *Planning*—the use of empirically based practice to review potential alternatives, evaluate their pros and cons, and determine what course of action to pursue to promote the well-being of the client system, and pursue social and economic justice.
4. *Implementation*—the actual *doing* of the plan and monitoring of its progress.

5. *Evaluation*—determination of the effectiveness of the plan's implementation, including the attainment of goals at the micro, mezzo, and macro levels.
6. *Termination*—the ending of the professional social worker–client system relationship.
7. *Follow-up*—the reexamination of a client system's situation at some point after the intervention's completion in order to monitor the intervention's ongoing effects and to determine potential reassessment for further intervention.

We have established that such problems may involve individuals, families, groups, organizations, and/or communities. In effect, our generalist approach means that virtually any problem may be analyzed and addressed from a wide range of perspectives that could potentially involve any size system.

EP 2.1.10a

When you decide to assess the possibility of macro change, you switch into a new, more complicated mode. First, you must determine whether a macro change is a viable alternative. You might learn that no macro change is feasible and drop the whole idea. Second, you must choose the most desirable type of macro change. You can pursue changes in an organization, a social policy, or a community. (The latter two will be discussed much more thoroughly in Chapter 6 and Chapter 9.) Finally, you must select and follow your strategies for the change process you decide to use.

Macro level change is more intricate because so many more micro, mezzo, and macro systems are involved. It is also more extensive because it pursues goals outside your everyday job description. In addition, you assume greater risks. (We will discuss these risks under "Step 6" in this chapter.)

This chapter examines the seven-step PREPARE process to evaluate whether your goal is potentially worth a macro change effort within an organizational setting. You acknowledge a problem exists and judge whether you have the potential resources to pursue change. Figure 5.1 summarizes this process. For clarification, Highlight 5.5, located at the end of the chapter, outlines and reviews both PREPARE's steps and substeps. As Chapter 1 discussed, PREPARE represents the assessment and planning phases of planned change.

Note that many ways of approaching macro level change exist. PREPARE offers only one method of initial assessment. Additionally, you do not necessarily have to follow PREPARE's steps in the exact order in which they are presented. The important thing is to

1. **P**   Identify **Problems** to address.

2. **R**   Review your macro and personal **Reality**.

3. **E**   **Establish** primary goals.

4. **P**   Identify relevant **People** of influence.

5. **A**   **Assess** potential financial costs and benefits to clients and agency.

6. **R**   Review professional and personal **Risk**.

7. **E**   **Evaluate** the potential success of a macro change process.

FIGURE 5.1 PREPARE: An Assessment of Organizational or Community Change Potential

remember all of the variables involved. We use the acronym "PREPARE" to help in this process.

CASE EXAMPLE

Deciding to Go Macro

Social work students are usually eager to get into the field and work with clients of their own. It is often difficult for them to understand the demands of working in an organizational environment when they have not yet had the experience. They may also have difficulty comprehending the complex decision-making process necessary before initiating macro change. Agencies are full of individuals with distinct personalities. Each individual has strengths and weaknesses, personal opinions, and quirks. A macro change process involves many unique variables. Our intent is to make the decision-making process for pursuit of macro change more vivid and relevant to you. Therefore, we will follow a case example through each of the seven steps in the PREPARE process.

The Scenario

The setting is a Child Protective Services Unit in the Yalobusha County Department of Social Services in Plattsburgh, Wisconsin. The unit is composed of six workers and a supervisor. Farica, the unit's supervisor, is very worried about the significant increase in the workers' caseloads over the past year. It is becoming nearly impossible to handle even the crises on the workers' caseloads, let alone give adequate attention to each and every case assigned. State law requires that each reported case of child maltreatment (which includes physical or sexual abuse as well as neglect) be investigated within 24 hours after intake. In reality, a worker is lucky if he or she gets to it within four days. Farica's staff is being forced to violate the law.

The Personalities

Farica, a raven-haired, heavyset, intense person, is a motivated individual who works extremely hard to do a good job. She is very concerned about her clients' welfare. If anything, she takes her work too seriously.

Farica hates being the unit supervisor. She doesn't like her colleagues very much and abhors taking responsibility for their mistakes. She has a tendency to fly off the handle when angered. She accepted the supervisory position under duress when the prior supervisor left four months ago. At that time, one of the unit staffers had to take the job because a budget freeze prohibited any new hires. Other staff either didn't want the job (and all the headaches that came with it) or they were not interested in attending to administrative detail (an absolute requirement). Farica has been with the agency about 10 years.

Spiro, short, blonde, and ordinary-looking in appearance, has been in the unit for 25 years. He considers the unit a kind of home for him. He feels it is somehow *his* unit and is dedicated to its welfare. Spiro thinks of himself as a "great guy" and by far the most qualified and best worker in the unit. Spiro has anything but low self-esteem and thinks he is always right.

Spiro didn't want the supervisory position because he is much too busy earning a substantial income through his booming private practice. Spiro is highly motivated to achieve and is very responsible in his work. He typically likes to complete things two weeks before other workers even know they are due. He gets really annoyed when obstacles get in his way when he is performing his job.

Tina, an attractive, petite woman, is very articulate and concerned with her own performance. She wants to do a good job and get positive feedback from colleagues and her supervisor, but is not certain she really wants to be in social work. She has been with the agency five years. She is a bit paranoid about others criticizing her and her work. She takes offense relatively easily. She hesitates to become involved in any projects that are not directly related to her own job.

Arturo, a tall, thin individual, has been in the unit almost as long as Spiro. He feels he is tenured and is sitting back doing what he has to until he can retire in three years. He has a blustery manner and tends to be abrasive. People who don't know him are easily intimidated by his height and manner, which accounts for the fact that he frequently gets his way. He is very concerned about the welfare of his clients, however, and will expend substantial effort for those he thinks are "worth it." Arturo is terrible with details and spelling. He is not highly creative.

Dylan, a 320-pound giant of a man who considers himself quite intellectual, is more adept at thinking of global ideas than at completing day-to-day, mundane tasks such as paperwork. He's been with the unit approximately seven years. He has a laid-back approach to work and life. If things don't get done today, they will tomorrow or the next day. Or somebody else will eventually take care of them. He does the minimum work required to accomplish his job. However, he is also seriously concerned with children's welfare—the reason he sought this job—and so is willing to expend effort on their behalf.

Barney, of average height and weight, bald with a bushy dark brown mustache, is another laid-back individual who is not in a hurry to get anything done. It is very important to him that people consider him a nice guy. He also strongly believes that everyone must be treated equally, so he virtually never takes sides for or against his colleagues. He is very concerned about his clients and does most of his work. However, he has quite a difficult time making decisions and often seeks direction from colleagues, usually Spiro and Dylan. Barney spends a lot of time worrying about what he might have forgotten. He's been with the agency four years. Barney and Dylan are good friends, as they feel they have a lot in common. They can sit and talk together about global issues for two full hours and when they're finished, they can't summarize a thing they've said.

Samina, a relatively quiet yet assertive person, is very concerned about her clients and doing a good job. She is generally well-liked by colleagues because she is cooperative and easy to work with. She participates in group projects to some extent and generally carries her share of the work burden. However, she is very busy working part-time on her master's degree, which is distracting her. She has only been with the agency a year and a half. She likes her job and strives to have colleagues accept her.

Attending to the Problem

Spiro and Farica are the most acutely concerned about the enlarged caseload. Spiro is disturbed because he is the most committed to the unit and worries about failing to obey the law by meeting the time requirements. Farica is perturbed, too. She is worried about the clients' welfare in addition to her own ability to fulfill her

supervisory responsibilities, namely, seeing that her staff serve clients effectively. Other staff members are concerned about the problem, but not that much.

What should be done? Should a macro change be attempted? Or should they all just sit tight and see what happens?

Step 1: PREPARE—Identify Problems to Address

The first step is identifying the *problems* you feel are most significant. This often takes some time for you to clarify in your own mind specifically what needs to be addressed. Any macro environment, including an organization, is bound to contain a

EP 2.1.10d

multitude of imperfections and problems that vary drastically in their severity. What problem or problems are most severe and in need of attention? About which problems are you most seriously concerned? Can you ethically live with the problems despite inconveniences, or do you feel you must address them directly at the macro level? Finally, how can you most concisely identify the problem requiring macro level intervention?

This first step in the PREPARE process involves the following four substeps:

Substep 1: Decide to seriously evaluate the potential for macro level intervention.
Substep 2: Define and prioritize problems.
Substep 3: Translate problems into needs.
Substep 4: Determine which need(s) you will address.

The following sections discuss each substep in greater depth. Then, each will be applied to the Case Example involving Spiro, Farica, and the other child Protective Services Unit staff.

Substep 1: Decide to Seriously Evaluate the Potential for Macro Level Intervention

The first step entails thoughtfully considering the intervention's potential success. It requires exercising critical thinking skills to make decisions regarding how to pursue your professional practice. During this first step, address the following questions:

1. How heavily is the problem affecting clients' wellbeing?
2. Is the problem serious enough to merit macro change?

3. Are you willing to think through and appraise your actual potential to make a difference?

4. Are you certain that your clients would support such a macro change and that it is in their best interest?

If you sincerely feel and rationally determine that the pursuit of macro change is the *right* thing to do, then you should proceed to Substep 2.

CASE EXAMPLE

Identify Problems to Address

Substep 1: Decide to seriously evaluate the potential for macro level intervention.

Spiro is our identified change agent because he feels most strongly about the caseload problem. He thinks seriously about the questions posed in Substep 1. Yes, the problem *is* affecting clients' well-being. It *is* serious enough to merit the efforts that must be expended to cause a macro change. He himself is willing to pursue it. He feels certain that it *is* in his clients' best interests.

Certainly, society and the families involved would like to halt child maltreatment.

Substep 2: Define and Prioritize Problems

In this substep, you identify problems, prioritize them in order of their severity, and choose those that you will work on. At least three aspects of each problem merit attention (Brody, 2005; Rothman, 1984).

1. *Exactly what client population will be affected?* What are the demographic characteristics of the client population? Exactly who will benefit from the macro change?

2. *What type of problem is it?* Whom does the problem affect? Exactly how severe is it?

3. *What is the root of the problem?* How did the problem start? What variables serve to perpetuate it? How is the problem sustained by other systems in the environment? Such appraisal helps you think about the problem in various ways and understand it more fully.

CASE EXAMPLE

Identify Problems to Address

Substep 2: Define and prioritize problems.

1. *What is the client population for Farica's Child Protective Services Unit?* The clients are families whose children are being maltreated. Specifically, the

client population therefore includes all such cases referred to the agency.

2. *What type of problem is it? Who is affected by it? How severe is it?* The problem affects all the clients who are not being served. It also affects families that are receiving less attention than they need. Spiro estimates that possibly 50 families are currently affected. He determines that the problem is severe enough to warrant change.

3. *What is the root of the problem?* The foundation of the problem is that abusive families need attention and help to strengthen coping skills and minimize risk. Lack of staff time and attention prevents clients from receiving the help they need. Because there is only one designated problem, prioritizing does not apply in this case.

Frequently, problem identification may be more an emotional evolution than a rational statement of facts. Some issue begins to bother you. You may begin to feel something is unethical and wrong. You can begin by focusing on some organizational facet that either directly or indirectly interferes with effective service provision. The more you think about it, the more ideas you can generate about how to solve the problem. Later, you can talk to colleagues about the issues involved. You can test the waters to see what others think and who might be on your side. As you continue discussion, you can think about the problem in new and creative ways. Frequently, the problem's solution evolves over time as new ideas are integrated (Lewis et al., 2007; Resnick, 1980b; Yankey & Vogelsang-Coombs, 2008).

After defining problems, prioritize them, starting with the one that's most severe and requires the most immediate attention. Sometimes there is only one primary problem. Other times, there may be several. Decide which one or ones to target. See Figure 5.2, which shows Substep 2 of the problem identification process.

Substep 3: Translate Problems into Needs

Problems, of course, are any sources of perplexity or distress. Many times they arise from lack of resources.

FIGURE 5.2 Define and Prioritize Problems

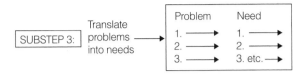

FIGURE 5.3 Translate Problems into Needs—Substep 3

Clients come to agencies because they have problems to solve. It is your and your agency's job to help them accomplish that.

Needs, on the other hand, are "physical, psychological, economic, cultural, and social requirements for survival, well-being, and fulfillment" (Barker, 2003, p. 291). The way to prepare for figuring out what an agency can do to better serve its clients is to translate agency and client problems into needs (see Figure 5.3).

Five phases characterize the process for clarifying and substantiating an unmet need in order to prepare for program development within your agency (Hasenfeld, 1987, pp. 454–455).

First, get background data and information to clarify exactly what the need is (Rothman & Zald, 2008). You can use substantiating data to prove that the need is significant enough to merit intervention. You can obtain facts from statistical reports kept by public agencies. Census data are often helpful. What are the characteristics of community residents? Public and private agencies often keep information on requests for services that cannot be met. Research studies sometimes document needs. Be creative. Think about what kinds of facts would help to prove the need. Who else might be interested in the problem and the need? Where might other interested parties make documentation available?

You might be a school social worker who identifies the *problem* that many of your clients are heavily involved in drug use. You determine that these clients *need* a drug education and treatment program in the school setting. Although drug involvement might be considered a community problem, you feel that the school system is the appropriate organization to address this need. Where can you find facts and statistics to establish the need in order to convince the school to address it?

One source might be police statistics. How many drug-related arrests have been made? Can the lack of treatment programs and referral sources be documented from police records? Another source might be specific local schools. What records are available regarding drug problems and seizures? Are research reports addressing similar adolescent populations available that might support the need for drug rehabilitation programs in general?

Second, recognize and specify other agencies or programs in the community that already address the need (Austin & Solomon, 2009; Brady, 2005). If the need is being met elsewhere, why start a new program? Return to the example of the adolescent drug problem. If a local hospital is already offering a treatment and rehabilitation program, further program development may be unnecessary. Rather, your intervention approach might then be to educate teens and parents about the problem and the hospital program. You could also facilitate their access to the existing program. On the other hand, establishing that *no* relevant programs exist strengthens your position that a program is needed.

You can find out about other services in various ways. First, consult the Internet. Second, consult supervisors and colleagues regarding their knowledge of other services. You can talk to anyone you think might have ideas. You can also consult your own records if you think they might be helpful.

Third, talk to other professionals serving similar clients. Find out how they perceive the problem and the need. They might enhance your understanding of what's involved and give you ideas about how to proceed.

Fourth, get clients involved (Austin & Solomon, 2009; Brady, 2005). You might talk with students and parents to find out how they perceive the problem and the need for intervention. You might also talk to community residents to test their feelings and potential support. Parent—teacher associations, church groups, and community businesspeople and professionals might provide further insight into and support for your plans.

Fifth, consider the value of a more formal needs assessment. A *needs assessment* is a formal effort to identify specific problems and to define services not being provided in an organization or community. First, one or more specific data-gathering tools (for example, surveys or information from small groups of clients or community residents) are used to determine the extent of need in a designated social arena (for example, mental health services or low-cost housing). Second, "judgment" is required "to assess the significance of the information gathered in order to determine priorities for program planning and service development" (Siegel, Attkisson, & Carson, 2001, p. 105). Data gathered in this way can be very convincing to decision makers.

CASE EXAMPLE

Identify Problems to Address

Substep 3: Translate problems into needs.

After identifying the problem clearly in his mind, Spiro goes through the steps to translate problems into needs.

1. *Getting background data.* Spiro goes to Farica, who keeps summary records of all cases referred to their unit. Together, they determine from the data that a current backlog of 12 cases needs immediate assessment attention and 42 cases require more extensive treatment. Analyzing the data, together they determine how many hours the typical case requires.

2. *Assessing services provided by other agencies.* Spiro already knows that his unit is the only agency providing this service in the area. His unit is the centralized resource receiving all referrals.

3. *Getting ideas.* Spiro talks with his colleagues to get their thoughts about the problem. He doesn't bother talking with Arturo, because he doesn't think Arturo has any ideas. (This is because of a strained relationship between the two: One day Arturo abruptly told Spiro that Spiro always steals his ideas. Spiro responded that he didn't think Arturo had any ideas to steal, and around it went. They no longer speak to each other.) With other staff members, Spiro considers various ways of looking at needs. Workers need more time to spend with clients. One way of getting this would be to decrease the number of clients. This alternative, of course, is not possible because all clients must be served.

   The other workers come to a consensus that more staff members are needed. The workers cannot do an adequate job of treatment without spending sufficient time with each family. However, they'll need more funding to add more positions. Neither Spiro (as a direct-service worker) nor Farica (as unit supervisor) has access to information about funding. They do know, however, that several months ago, when a prior supervisor left the agency, there was no funding to replace her.

4. *Involving clients.* One phase of treatment for families who are agency clients involves a support group for abusive parents. Tina is responsible for running the group and usually does not like any interference. Spiro asks her if he can speak to the group members at their next meeting. Tina feels somewhat threatened, but she reluctantly concedes. Spiro then attends the beginning of the next group meeting, explains the problem to the group, and solicits input from them regarding their feelings. The fact that these clients continue to be involved in a support group implies that they value the agency's services. Otherwise, they would not expend the effort to attend. As expected, they support Spiro's idea about the unit's needs.

5. *Considering a needs assessment.* Spiro determines that a formal needs assessment is not necessary. Not only does he review records with Farica, but they also prepare and administer a limited-term functional job analysis procedure. That is, over a two-week period, Farica monitors each unit staff person's time. Staff members are provided forms that divide their typical work activities into categories and are required to record the type of activity in which they are involved for each 15-minute period of work time. Categories of activities include face-to-face interviewing with clients, travel time, and time for keeping records. Farica and Spiro determine that staff are, indeed, working as efficiently as possible. Staff simply do not have enough time in a day to perform their jobs adequately. Spiro and Farica decide that further investigation using a formal needs assessment would be a waste of time.

Substep 4: Determine Which Need or Needs You Will Address

Even though many needs may appear critical, you must focus on one at a time. At any particular time in your work career, you will likely have many things on your mind. Even when you notice a problem in agency policies or programs, you should carefully assess what needs are most critical to address (this process was addressed in Substep 2). You cannot do everything. You have only so much time, energy, and general resources.

CASE EXAMPLE

Identify Problems to Address

Substep 4: Determine which need or needs you will address.

Spiro decides that clients need more of the workers' time. He thinks that the best way to address the defined need is to seek additional staff from the administration. Trying to get funding for more staff on his own is too awesome of a task. He has no access to any information about funding and no power to solicit resources himself. He and Farica have fortified their argument by analyzing the staff's workload and establishing that there is too much work for staff to complete effectively.

Step 2: PREPARE—Review Your Macro and Personal Reality

One major factor in deciding whether to pursue a macro level intervention is a serious appraisal of your *reality*. We define *macro reality* as the macro environment in which you work. It includes the numerous systems, subsystems, and other elements of your agency's internal operation and the agency's own macro environment. When considering macro intervention, ask yourself what your macro reality involves. What variables might work for or against you, either from within or from outside the organization, in your pursuit of macro intervention? How *realistic* is your chance of success in implementing this macro change?

Reality also refers to your own *personal reality,* the personal strengths and weaknesses that might affect your ability to undertake a macro intervention in the macro environment. Therefore, Step 2 of the PREPARE process has two substeps:

Substep 1: Evaluate organizational and other macro variables working for or against you in the macro change process.

Substep 2: Review your personal reality—the strengths and weaknesses that might act for or against successful change efforts.

Substep 1: Evaluate Macro Variables Working for or against You in the Macro Change Process

This evaluation—a method that organizes information so that major variables acting *for* or *against* macro change can be identified—is called a *force field analysis* or *environmental scanning.* Such variables appear in at least five arenas: (1) resources and funding, (2) constraining regulations or laws, (3) the political climate of the agency, (4) the external political climate, and (5) other factors (Austin & Solomon, 2009; Holloway, 1987; Lewis et al., 2007).

For each of the five variables involved in the evaluation of your macro reality, write a brief description of how you perceive the respective situations. Then evaluate the extent to which each variable works for or against your goals. Rate each from extremely positive to extremely negative and jot down a brief explanation. See Figure 5.4, which contains a chart to help complete Substep 1.

You may notice that because there is no central neutral category in the rating scheme, you are forced to decide whether each variable is positive or negative. This is because a neutral, wishy-washy position fails to help in your decision making.

Resources and Funding

First, how do you perceive the resources and funding available in your agency? Did the agency just receive a major grant or donation? Is the agency looking for ways to use these resources? Or is internal funding so tight that staff members are being laid off right and

SUBSTEP 1:

Evaluate organizational and other macro variables potentially working for or against you in the macro change process. These include:

VARIABLE	BRIEF DESCRIPTION	EXTREMELY POSITIVE	MILDLY POSITIVE	MILDLY NEGATIVE	EXTREMELY NEGATIVE
Resources and funding					
Constraining regulations or laws					
Internal political climate					
External political climate					
Other factors					

FIGURE 5.4 Evaluate Macro Variables—Substep 1

left? What types of resources do you think you'll need? Will the change be a minor project requiring only a few weeks of staff time? (Staff time is expensive.) If staff members are spending time on a macro project, how will their regular work get done? Who will take over or pay for the extra work? Will the necessary change require development of a whole new program costing half a million dollars or more?

Constraining Regulations or Laws

Second, are there any regulations or laws against your goals? For example, suppose your idea is to expand the capacity of 20 agency group homes for adults with cognitive disabilities from 6 male clients to 12 male and female clients. Your rationale is to provide greater opportunities for socialization and relationship-building. However, state licensing regulations mandate that such group homes may not have more than eight clients.[3] In this scenario, your idea for macro change would be doomed to failure because it did not follow the designated rules.

Internal Political Climate

Third, what is the political climate inside your agency? Does your administration urge employees to develop and try out new ideas? Or does your administration watch employees like private investigators and try to limit the time employees spend in the restroom? (Chapter 4 discussed different types of leadership and their consequences.) A large bureaucratic organization with a strict hierarchy of authority would probably be much less likely to support an innovative idea than a small, growing agency that actively responds to new concepts and quickly implements changes.

Factors against change. Three factors act against change in the agency environment (Resnick, 1980b): Therefore you need to address them when considering a macro change. First, an organization that has undergone a number of major external alterations and upheavals in recent months will probably be more resistant to change. Organizations as systems tend to seek homeostasis. Change generates anxiety and effort to address the unknown. It is logical that an organization would seek some peace and quiet in order to regain its equilibrium.

A second potential factor acting against organizational change exists if the agency is wedded to a specific philosophy or treatment modality (Brody, 2005). For example, a mental health agency espousing psychoanalysis would probably bristle at the idea of converting to a cognitive-behavioral approach.

The third variable working against agency change is the age of the agency and longevity of its staff. Consider an agency initially established 50 years ago. Its administration and staff, who have been around forever, are more likely to resist change than the administration and staff of a new agency with newer, younger staff.

External Political Climate

Fourth, what is the political climate *outside* your agency (Rothman & Zald, 2008)? Would the community and governmental structure be likely to support or obstruct your idea for macro change? For example, what if implementation of your idea would require a lot of money? What chance would you have if community residents were loudly protesting the tax increases they recently received?

Other Factors

Other factors could include a catastrophic natural disaster like a flood or hurricane, causing most attention and resources to focus on providing food and shelter to victims. It could be an economic upheaval, such as a major industry leaving or arriving in town, or a radical act of violence like a terrorist attack. Finally, it could be an event like a sexual harassment, racial discrimination, or fraud charge within the agency. Take into consideration anything that would distract administrators' and public attention from your macro change effort— virtually anything not included in the four categories just noted.

CASE EXAMPLE

Review Your Macro and Personal Reality

Substep 1: Evaluate macro variables working for or against you in the macro change process.

Spiro follows the suggestions for this substep as illustrated in Figure 5.4, which include evaluating the following variables:

1. Resources and funding

   Brief description: Resources are unknown. There have been rumors about funding crunches. However, other units have gotten minor staffing increases in the past three months.

   Evaluation: Mildly negative. (Spiro thinks funds might be available if the administration is

---

3. State licensing of facilities like group homes involves giving permission for such facilities to operate legally after checking that they comply with government rules and regulations for how they should operate.

convinced more staff is really necessary. Spiro knows that administrators have some funds available to distribute at their discretion. After all, some other units have gotten the staff they needed. Spiro feels that bringing his case to the administration's attention and making it strong enough will result in some positive action, namely, a staffing increase in his unit.)

2. Constraining regulations and laws

Brief description: Laws that require that staff respond within time limitations. Staff members can't possibly do so. Therefore, the staff is forced to break the law.

Evaluation: Extremely positive. (Spiro thinks that the agency is not in compliance with laws and regulations regarding what its staff is supposed to do. This is a persuasive factor for administrators. They want to comply with legal requirements to look good in the public's eye. When an agency does not look good, it may lose public funding or some administrators' heads may roll.)

3. Agency political climate

Brief description: Spiro characterizes the agency's internal political climate as "business as usual." Administration generally supports its units and their respective staffs as they do their jobs.

Evaluation: Mildly positive. (Spiro determines that the agency has not undergone any major upheavals recently. The agency's general philosophy is to attend to the public's basic needs. Actually, the agency's administration is pretty set in its ways. However, because Spiro can think of no clearly negative factors in the agency's climate, he decides it is mildly positive.)

4. External political climate

Brief description: The general public is supportive of providing services to combat child maltreatment (including physical, sexual, and emotional abuse in addition to neglect). However, funding appears to be tight.

Evaluation: Mildly positive. (Spiro decides that the external environment's potential influence is positive because of strong feelings about abuse. This positive influence is bolstered by the law requiring responsive attention to referrals. However, he determines this is only mildly positive because of the overall general lack of resources for programs. In other words, he feels his unit and its

work could compete fairly well with others for any funding that might be attainable.)

Substep 2: Review Your Personal Reality—Strengths and Weaknesses That May Act for or against Successful Change Efforts

The second substep targets your own personal qualities, including the strengths and weaknesses that may act for or against a successful change effort (Drucker, 2008). As in micro and mezzo practice, it is vitally important to assess your own personal traits before proceeding with a macro change proposal. Personal assets include your positive personal relationships with colleagues and administrators in the agency. Deficiencies or weaknesses include lack of sufficient knowledge about the problem and needs you want to address.

EP 2.1.1b

A number of specific personal factors exist that either facilitate or hinder your ability to work toward macro change within your agency (Burghardt, 2001; Rothman et al., 1981). You should evaluate each asset and weakness on a scale from very good to very bad, as Figure 5.5 suggests. Assets include positive interpersonal relationships with other staff members, the immediate supervisor, and various levels of administration; personal loyalty and dedication to the agency; your reputation within the agency; your understanding of client problems and needs; your ability to initiate macro change within the limitations of your own job role; and your own level of "self-confidence" (Rothman et al., 1981, p. 43). Limitations include lack of understanding of the community and how the agency fits into the community's total service delivery system; personal stress currently being experienced, such as a death in the family or a personal illness; debilitating exhaustion and fatigue; overinvolvement with your own job; and insufficient time. Rate each limitation from "serious problem" to "no problem." Figure 5.5 provides a format for beginning to evaluate your strengths, weaknesses, and potential for macro level change.

CASE EXAMPLE

Review Your Macro and Personal Reality

Substep 2: Review your personal reality—strengths and weaknesses that might act for or against successful change efforts.

   Strengths: Spiro sees himself as extremely competent and hardworking. He feels he

It is just as important to evaluate your own personal characteristics, strengths, and weaknesses in macro practice as it is in micro or mezzo practice. We have established that skill development in generalist practice evolves. First, you must know how to engage and interact with other individuals (micro practice skills). Next, you must expand your skills to working with groups of individuals (mezzo practice skills). Finally, you must acquire skills to work with and within agencies and communities (macro practice skills). Each level of skills builds and expands upon the earlier level(s).

It is important to assess your personal strengths and weaknesses that may act for or against a successful change effort. This is very similar to the process of self-awareness you underwent when developing your engagement and interviewing skills. You will use the same interpersonal skills working with people in macro practice as you do in other levels of practice. Your own behaviors, mannerisms, and characteristics will work for or against you in macro practice just as they do in micro or mezzo practice.

Picture yourself working with staff, administrators, and clients in the context of an agency. Answer the questions and follow the instructions below:

1. Complete the following four *who are you* statements. They can be adjectives, nouns, or longer statements. If you had to summarize who you are, what would you say?

I am _____ .

I am _____ .

I am _____ .

I am _____ .

2. What adjectives would you use to describe yourself? Circle all that apply. They are in no particular order or priority. They are just meant to stimulate your thinking about yourself.

HAPPY   SAD   HONEST   DISHONEST   SENSITIVE   INSENSITIVE   TRUSTWORTHY   UNTRUSTWORTHY   CARING

UNCARING   OUTGOING   SHY   WITHDRAWN   FRIENDLY   UNFRIENDLY   RELIGIOUS   NOT VERY RELIGIOUS

NERVOUS   CALM   FORMAL   INFORMAL   AGGRESSIVE   ASSERTIVE   TIMID   CONFIDENT

NOT VERY CONFIDENT   CAREFUL   CARELESS   CAPABLE   INCAPABLE   INDEPENDENT   DEPENDENT

AFFECTIONATE   COOL   WARY   BOLD   CHEERFUL   WITTY   UNASSUMING   THOROUGH   EASY-GOING

DETERMINED   CLEVER   RESPONSIVE   STRONG-MINDED   WEAK-WILLED (SOMETIMES)   RELAXED

INDUSTRIOUS   CONTROLLED   SPONTANEOUS   SERIOUS   FUNNY   TOUGH   PLEASANT

DARING   EAGER   EFFICIENT   NOT SO EFFICIENT   ARTISTIC   TACTFUL   INTOLERANT

VULNERABLE   LIKABLE   SMART   UNDERSTANDING   IMPATIENT   PATIENT   IMAGINATIVE   WORDY

CONCISE   OPEN-MINDED   FUNNY   ORGANIZED   SOMEWHAT DISORGANIZED   CONSCIENTIOUS   NEVER ON TIME

EMOTIONAL   UNEMOTIONAL   CONTROLLED   OPEN   CREATIVE   CURIOUS   SENSITIVE   SINCERE   PRECISE

RECKLESS   COOPERATIVE   PLEASANT   ETHICAL   BRAVE   MATURE   EAGER   SPUNKY

3. How would you rate yourself on the following?

	Very good	*Mildly good*	*Mildly bad*	*Very bad*
Relationships with other staff	_____	_____	_____	_____
Relationship with supervisor	_____	_____	_____	_____
Relationship with administration	_____	_____	_____	_____
Dedication to agency	_____	_____	_____	_____
Reputation within the agency	_____	_____	_____	_____
Understanding of clients	_____	_____	_____	_____
Ability for pursuing macro change within job role	_____	_____	_____	_____
Self-confidence	_____	_____	_____	_____

FIGURE 5.5 Evaluating Personal Characteristics for Macro Practice: Macro Practice Builds on Macro Practice Skills

4. How would you rate your level of concern on the following:

	Very serious	Moderately serious	Mildly serious	Not at all serious
Lack of understanding of community service system	_____	_____	_____	_____
Personal stress	_____	_____	_____	_____
Exhaustion and fatigue	_____	_____	_____	_____
Overinvolvement with job	_____	_____	_____	_____
Insufficient time to do work expected	_____	_____	_____	_____

5. Cite your four greatest strengths. They can be anything from personal qualities to talents to accomplishments. They don't have to be in any particular order or priority.

Strength A _____

Strength B _____

Strength C _____

Strength D _____

6. Cite your four greatest weaknesses. These don't have to be in any order of priority either.

Weakness A _____

Weakness B _____

Weakness C _____

Weakness D _____

7. How do you think your personal strengths will help you work with other staff, administrators, and clients in macro practice situations?

_____

_____

8. What weaknesses, if any, do you think you need to work on to improve your ability to work with staff, administrators, and clients in macro practice situations?

_____

_____

FIGURE 5.5 (continued)

has an excellent reputation within the agency. He is willing to expend the necessary energy to undertake macro change and is fairly confident of success.

Weaknesses: Unfortunately, Spiro is not very adept at evaluating his own weaknesses. He really sees himself as having none. In reality, his major weakness is his need to succeed and get his own way. The implication is that if he would acknowledge this weakness, he might better anticipate how people above him could resent his pushing them too hard.

Step 3: PREPARE—Establish Primary Goals

How can you fulfill your identified needs? What is your ultimate goal—that is, what will fulfill the need and solve the problem? What goals do you think you might be able to accomplish within the reality of your own macro environment? It is too early to establish goals with detailed action steps for how to achieve them. However, you should be able to set your sights on some distant target. *Establishing* a primary goal can provide you with general direction as you evaluate macro intervention potential and establish plans.

Goals generally have two characteristics (Resnick, 1980b). First, goals are derived from some identified *problem*. Second, the problem can be translated into some *specific need*, which suggests ideas about what the change should involve (we accomplished these tasks in Substep 3, Step 1). Resnick (1980b) describes goals as follows:

> Examples of goals may range from improving service provision by establishing regular meeting times for physicians, social workers, and nurses in a hospital to discuss cases, to the shifting of the program focus on a social work unit from individual services to a group or community service. A goal may be as minute as enhancing efficiency by designing a new face sheet on a case record or as major as improving administration-staff relationships by initiating an ongoing series of workshops. (p. 212)

Three concepts relevant to goal selection are potential for permanence, greater influence, and simplicity (Resnick, 1980b). First, give precedence to a goal that the agency is likely to integrate permanently. Don't waste effort on temporary remedies to permanent problems. Second, choose a goal that is likely to influence more agency units over a goal with more limited effects. The agency is more likely to maintain goals that will affect a greater number of units and personnel. Third, select goals that are simpler to manage over those that are more complex and require a lot of administrative effort. Administrators are usually busy and preoccupied with a wide range of concerns. They are thus more likely to accept and support goals requiring less of their energy.

CASE EXAMPLE

Establish Primary Goals

Spiro has already defined the problem: clients need more service time from workers. Translating this problem into a *specific need*, Spiro decides that his goal is to improve service provision by increasing the time workers within his unit can devote to it. He does not have enough details yet to decide exactly how he might go about this. His main idea is to increase the number of staff, which will allow each worker more time to serve clients.

When considering the concepts related to goal selection, Spiro foresees his goal as being relatively permanent—"relatively" permanent because funding cuts and changing regulations can often alter the fabric of agency life. Abrupt changes such as dismissal of staff

can result. Thus, Spiro considers his proposed goal to be as permanent as possible.

The second concept relevant to goal selection is deciding which goals have the greatest impact. Spiro's primary concern is for clients served by his own unit. Therefore, whether his goals have more widespread impact does not concern him.

The third concept relevant to goal selection is simplicity. Spiro feels his goal is as simple as he can propose, namely, improving services by adding more staff.

Step 4: PREPARE—Identify Relevant People of Influence

Whom do you know who might be available to help you make the changes you want to pursue? Potential action systems might include specific *people* or groups within the organization or the surrounding community. Most likely, people with access to influence or power within the agency are most significant. Are there any others you could go to for help? Do you have a former supervisor or professor who could help you develop a strategy?

You cannot yet make detailed plans for how to accomplish your goals. However, you can start thinking about your general purpose and potential plans. Identify individuals and groups within your agency and community who could potentially *help* or *hurt* your cause. Subjectively rank the support you anticipate from each on a scale from very good to very bad. You will be able to use this information later when you begin to work on expanding your base of influence and support. Figure 5.6 illustrates how you might identify relevant people of influence.

Note that decision makers have different leadership styles (described in Highlight 5.3) that can help or hinder your ability to pursue macro change.

CASE EXAMPLE

Identify Relevant People of Influence

Spiro first thinks about the agency administrators with the power to make financial and program-related decisions. Three administrators in the organizational chart have direct responsibility for the protective services unit. Pedro, the agency director, is a reasonable, caring person who likes Spiro. In the past, Spiro has volunteered for a number of projects that Pedro proposed. Spiro did a pretty nice job and Pedro appreciated his efforts. However, Pedro has much more to think about

POTENTIAL ACTION SYSTEMS	NAME	POTENTIAL SUPPORT			
		Very good	Mildly good	Mildly bad	Very bad
Individuals in the organization					
Groups in the organization					
Individuals in the community					
Groups in the community					
Others					

FIGURE 5.6 PREPARE—Identify Relevant People of Influence

as head of the entire agency than one relatively small unit. Spiro sees Pedro as a statesperson type of leader with some tendencies to be an advocate.

Harold, a stiff, unemotional person who is hard to read, is assistant director and second in command. Spiro sees him as a conserver. He is authoritarian in his approach to people below him. However, he is more involved in internal budgetary decisions than Pedro and wields substantial influence over how funds are spent. Spiro and Harold don't get along very well. Spiro gets along best with people who do what Spiro tells them to do. Spiro resents his lack of influence over Harold. One positive note, however, is Harold's concern for obeying the rules (such as the law regarding abuse cases). Spiro feels Harold may listen to an argument emphasizing the legal rationale.

Theresa, the general supervisor (directly above Farica as unit supervisor and below the assistant director) is unpredictable in her treatment of the child Protective Services Unit. She makes haphazard decisions and often attends to details the unit staff members feel are irrelevant rather than focusing on what staff members consider important. For example, she is very concerned about the exact mileage reported on mileage reimbursement sheets, but is totally disinterested in treatment plans or goals. Spiro views Theresa as a climber. She appears to have a very close relationship with Harold. In their interaction, Harold seems to listen to her suggestions, and in return she does whatever he tells her to do. Spiro does not get along at all well with Theresa. She has criticized his suggestions several times. Once again, Spiro does not get along well with

anyone who doesn't consistently let him have his own way.

Farica, as unit supervisor, has the most direct link with administration. She seems to get along fairly well with Theresa. However, Theresa is inconsistent in her treatment of Farica. Sometimes Theresa is supportive and sometimes not. Farica's relationships with Harold and Pedro appear cordial. She, too, has volunteered for some of Pedro's projects. He appears to respect her, although their relationship is not as close as Pedro's and Spiro's. Spiro feels his own relationship with Farica is relatively good. She generally cooperates with his suggestions. He believes, to some extent, he can manipulate her to support him.

Spiro feels that his immediate colleagues will support him. He envisions addressing the issue at an upcoming unit staff meeting. Barney, not a powerhouse of ideas himself, usually goes along with Spiro's suggestions. Dylan is easygoing enough to agree. He usually just wants to maintain collegial relationships with unit staff. Samina wants to avoid conflict at all costs and so will probably go along with Spiro. Arturo and Tina usually keep quiet and go along with the majority opinion. Despite Spiro's anticipated support of his unit staff, they have little real power to help. Spiro does want their support, however. Just in case the plan fails and anything negative results (for example, hostile reactions from administrators), he does not want to be the only one to blame. If he gets the entire unit to support him, any blame or bad feelings will be diffused.

Spiro decides that these agency administrators are the most relevant people of influence. There is also a

HIGHLIGHT 5.3

Leadership Styles of Decision Makers

EP 2.1.9b

Administrators have individual personalities, qualities, and flaws just like anyone else (Brody, 2005; Northouse, 2010). It is important to take these differences into consideration when thinking about the leaders who can be most helpful to you in the change process.

Personalities and priorities are related to leadership styles. There are five basic types of leadership styles, including "climber," "conserver," "zealot," "advocate," and "states-[person]" (Lauffer, Nybell, Overberger, Reed, & Zeff, 1977, pp. 13–15). These styles offer interesting food for thought. Keep in mind, however, that many people demonstrate a mixture of these distinctive styles.

The *climber* "tends to closely control subordinates to ensure nobody else is seen as a rising star" (Lauffer et al., 1977, p. 13). The climber may also be referred to as "the narcissist" (Brody, 2005, p. 7). These supervisors and administrators are very concerned about themselves and their own career moves. They tend to interpret any bright ideas on their subordinates' part as threatening to their own status. Therefore, they probably will not support a subordinate's proposal for macro change. They might even confiscate the idea and take it as their own. You can target a climber as a person to influence if you think he or she might latch on to the plan and exert pressure to have it adopted. However, don't expect to get any credit for the idea.

The *conserver* toils to preserve the homeostatic status quo. Like climbers, conservers are very concerned with and interested in themselves and their own work. Conservers are sometimes called "typical bureaucrats." They revel in filling out forms on a routine and timely basis. They tend to be strong proponents of goal displacement. Quality of service is not of much concern to them unless it involves their higher priority of following the rules. They generally abhor fresh and innovative ideas that might disrupt the steady flow of paperwork. Obviously, you would not get much support for macro change from a conserver.

The *zealot* is a go-getter who exudes energy and loves creative innovation. However, zealots are also very preoccupied with themselves. Zealots think they know best, regardless of others' opinions. They expect subordinates to be their faithful devotees. They may or may not listen to a macro change proposal, depending on how it fits into their view of the universe. You might approach a zealot with your innovation whether you think he'll agree with it or not. However, don't expect him to spend much time listening to your ideas. Zealots and climbers are more likely than conservers to support an innovation. A zealot is a little less likely than a climber to steal your idea.

The *advocate* is "a person who has exceptionally high commitment to the goals of the organization or unit of which she or he is a member, or to a client population serviced by the agency" (Lauffer et al., 1977, p. 14). Advocates are skilled administrators. They can protect their corner of the agency from such external threats as funding cuts and can mediate disputes among their own staff. Advocates are generally straightforward, primarily concerned about the well-being of both clients and agency. Advocates are probably the best administrators to approach with good, innovative ideas. They are the most likely to work toward the benefit of the agency and its clients. They are least likely to put their egos first or to steal your ideas. Because they tend to be assertive, they can be powerful allies.

The *statesperson* is "more concerned with the welfare of society as a whole than with the agency or a particular client population" (Lauffer et al., 1977, p. 14). A statesperson can be extremely helpful as a proponent of a new idea. One of her strengths lies in establishing excellent public relations with others. These are usually good people to target for potential positive influence. However, they are not good at attending to detail and carrying through on long-term proposals. They lose interest relatively quickly. Therefore, a statesperson might be very helpful at the beginning of the macro change process, but useless once the proposal has been adopted.

Community Advisory Committee made up of influential people in the community and of people who were clients in the past. The committee's purpose is to provide feedback and suggestions directly to Pedro and Harold. The committee's strength and influence generally depend on the energy and commitment of its current membership.

About 15 years ago, the child Protective Services Unit was in a similar predicament because of desperate understaffing. At that time, Spiro went to the Community Advisory Committee, explained the situation, and asked for help. At the time, he was unit supervisor. Spiro also went to the local newspapers and alerted them to the situation. Under this public pressure, the agency director (the one before Pedro) added two staff positions to the unit.

Finally, Spiro considers seeking funds outside the agency. The county supplies most of the funds. He could ask the county board to increase funding, but why would they listen to him? He is too low in the agency power hierarchy to matter. He knows that specified channels exist for making budget and funding requests.[4] The board would wonder why he didn't go through his agency channels. Seeking funds through grant writing or donations is also too uncertain. It takes too much time and effort to pursue these options with little hope of successful return.

In summary, Spiro feels that the potential of support from Pedro is mildly good, from Harold mildly bad, from Theresa very bad, and from Farica very good. Spiro also thinks the potential for using both the agency's Community Advisory Committee and the press is very good.

Rationales for Internal Advocacy

Internal advocacy involves a practitioner championing or defending the rights of clients when such advocacy is not necessarily part of the job description (Patti, 1983; Schneider et al., 2008). It is our professional and ethical responsibility as social workers to make certain that clients receive their due rights and services. There are at least four rationales or arguments for legitimacy that you can make to agency administrators on behalf of your quest for positive organizational change (Patti, 1983). Following are the four statements you might make about yourself:

1. *"I know a lot about the problems and issues involved."* In essence, because of your special knowledge, involvement, and skill, you can "assist the organization in coming to a more rational and effective solution than has heretofore been available to deal with the issue in question" (p. 220).
2. *"I'm on the agency's side."* You are simply trying to help the agency comply with its stated goals of providing effective services to clients.
3. *"My advocacy is necessary to supplement the agency's formal communication network."* Because it's hard to communicate information and ideas clearly through a number of administrative levels or individuals, administrators may be deprived "of

the data they need to assess accurately the effects of the agency's programs and procedures" (p. 220).
4. *"It's my right to express my feelings and ideas to improve both service delivery and my ability to do my job."* (This last argument is best used when supported by a group of staff.)

These arguments may help you establish your legitimacy as a change agent within the organization before beginning to implement the change. Even then, however, administrators can always just say no. You are then stuck with employing other tactics or halting your change attempt completely.

Step 5: PREPARE—Assess Potential Costs and Benefits to Clients and Agency

Any macro change requires some new input. Such input can be in the form of actual money spent, but also in how you might miss out on other good opportunities where your time would be better spent (Rubin & Rubin, 2008). This is often

EP 2.1.10e

referred to as *opportunity cost,* an important consideration in your *assessment* of potential costs and benefits. You could also lose political and social influence with those who disagree with your proposed change (Rubin & Rubin, 2008). For example, if you are constantly asking for extra funds for some project, administrators may get sick of you and ignore your requests. Then you would lose some of your potential power or influence. Colleagues might resent you for pushing your own agenda, and your social interaction with them might be affected.

It is very difficult to estimate potential costs in terms of actual money needed, but you do need to think about costs in a general way. Does your macro change require half a million dollars for new staff and office space when you really don't know that any funds are available? Might your macro proposal require a few hours a week of several staff members' time plus supplies and minor financing for publicity to advertise a new service?

Rubin and Rubin (2008, p. 412) suggest asking three questions before pursuing a new project. First, will the results be "worth the effort"? Second, might "alternative solutions produce more benefits at lower cost"? Third, "who gets the benefits and who pays the costs"?

---

4. It should be noted that funding channels for public agencies responsible to designated legislative bodies are very different than funding channels for private agencies, whose funding sources often vary widely.

CASE EXAMPLE

Assess Potential Costs and Benefits to Clients and Agency

What are potential costs?

Spiro does not have access to specific budgetary information. However, he does know that staff members are *occasionally* added to other units in the agency. He thus supposes that resources are available if he can develop a good enough argument for them.

Will the results be worth the effort?

Spiro strongly believes in the unit's work and goals, and he feels strongly that the potential results are worth the effort.

Might alternative solutions produce more benefits at less cost?

Spiro can't think of any viable alternative to pressing administration for additional staff. He and Farica have established that their unit is using its time as efficiently as possible.

Who gets the benefits and who pays the costs?

Spiro believes that clients will directly benefit and that the agency is responsible for paying the costs.

Step 6: PREPARE—Review Professional and Personal Risk

When agency policy and/or practice is wrong or ineffective, you will need to *review* and evaluate your own personal and professional risk if you engage in macro change, and weigh the severity of risk against the need and potential for positive macro change.

Ask yourself another set of three questions before seriously undertaking macro change in an organization to evaluate the potential *risks* to you, the initiator (Brody, 2005; Resnick & Patti, 1980; Rubin & Rubin, 2008). First, to what extent are you in danger of losing your job? Do you perceive no, some, moderate, or serious danger? Second, to what extent will such macro change efforts decrease your potential for upward mobility within the agency? Might you make enemies who could stand in the way of future promotions? Third, to what extent would your efforts for macro change seriously strain your interpersonal relationships at work? Figure 5.7 provides a chart to implement this step of the PREPARE process.

Could I Lose My Job?

At this point, you might be thinking, "What do you mean, lose my job?! Why would I do anything to endanger my job?" Often the problem with trying to change an agency's policies or practices is that you will have to "fight against the flow" of your agency's energies and established practices—and this could reduce your value to the agency.

Losing a job has a number of obvious consequences, including "inconvenience, possible embarrassment with friends and family, income loss, forced geographical mobility, and the burden of explaining negative job references" in addition to "loss of professional identity" (Patti, 1983, pp. 214–215).

There are at least two ways to deal with the threat of job loss (Patti, 1983). First, you can treat such a threat as a distraction from the real issue, namely, that some facet of the organization needs to be changed. Second, you can assume the perspective that job loss may be the price you have to pay in order to ethically fulfill your professional responsibility.

To what extent are you in danger of:	No danger	Some danger	Moderate danger	Serious danger
1. Losing your job?				
2. Decreasing your potential for upward mobility?				
3. Seriously straining work relationships?				

FIGURE 5.7 PREPARE—Review Professional and Personal Risk

Interpersonal relationships at work are critically important when trying to do your job and improve service provision. This supervisor is obviously annoyed at a supervisee's idea for an agency policy change. How supportive do you think he will be in implementing the change process?

Will My Career Path Be Affected?

"Making waves" by pressing for change can potentially derail a career path. Most newly graduated practitioners, especially those with little experience, are overjoyed to land their first job. However, within the larger scheme of things, you probably envision a longer-term career path for yourself. This perspective stretches far beyond a single job, let alone your first professional one. A career may involve different fields of practice and different client populations. It may also involve upward mobility—that is, gaining job positions of greater responsibility and authority within the agency's personnel structure. After working in an agency for a while, you may begin to target the positions you would ideally like to have.

Perhaps you begin seeing yourself in your supervisor's position. Or you might think even further than that and see another position higher in the formal hierarchy that appeals to you. You might like to have a job with more responsibility and a higher salary. You might even plan your progress through a series of jobs within the hierarchy. Where might you see yourself ending up in 5, 10, or even 20 years? Might you aspire to the executive director's spot, or would your own

supervisor's job be more appealing to you? Would you rather stay in direct contact with clients, as many practitioners choose to do?

At any rate, you need to undertake macro change very carefully and tactfully. If supervisors and administrators higher in the structure begin to see you as a troublemaker, your risk increases. They may not want to promote someone whom they see as difficult to work with or dissatisfied with agency authority and practice. Looking at macro situations from administrators' perspectives is helpful and interesting. Even in flexible, innovative agencies, the task of the administrators is to keep the agency running, and indeed, running smoothly. Therefore, when considering macro change, it is important to consider who in the agency might bristle at your suggestions and who might pat you on the back. All agency administrators should be considered and handled very carefully.

Will I Strain Interpersonal Relationships at Work?

The third risk to consider when pondering macro change is how your actions could affect your *relationships* with coworkers, supervisors, and other administrators.

Relationships with supervisors and other administrators are tied directly to the two potential consequences just discussed—keeping your job and pursuing upward mobility.

You should also consider how your actions will affect your relationships with your colleagues. Will some of them see you as a Dudley DoRight kind of character, looking to make yourself more visible to administration and thus more important? Will they be threatened by your suggestions because these suggestions may affect how they do their own jobs? Maybe they don't want to change. Remember, any change takes some degree of effort. People often resist expending extra effort.

You should carefully consider the extent to which you see others—including coworkers, supervisors, and administrators—supporting your macro change ideas. Getting together with an informal group of colleagues to discuss issues and muster support is a strongly recommended means of decreasing your own risk while increasing support for change. One other way to influence colleagues and decision makers is the potential use of "covert operations," described in Highlight 5.4.

A Strengths Perspective on Risk

Sometimes, involvement in macro activity will enhance your standing in an agency. It can demonstrate initiative and a sense of responsibility that others might highly respect. To a great extent, it depends on who is evaluating you and your change effort.

CASE EXAMPLE

Review Your Professional and Personal Risk

To what extent is Spiro in danger of losing his job?
The agency has a strong union. It's almost impossible to fire staff once they receive a positive two-year review. Therefore, Spiro feels that he is in no danger.

To what extent is Spiro in danger of decreasing his potential for upward mobility?
Spiro is quite satisfied staying in direct service and maintaining his clients in private counseling. If he were interested in becoming an agency administrator, he would probably evaluate himself as being in serious danger. Administrators don't promote "troublemakers." However, because he has no intention of going into administration, he decides the situation presents no danger to him.

To what extent is Spiro in danger of seriously straining work relationships?
Spiro is most concerned about relationships with colleagues he sees on a daily basis. He sees no danger in straining his relationship with Farica. He does see moderate danger, however, in straining relationships with higher-level administration, especially Theresa and Harold.

HIGHLIGHT 5.4

Consider "Covert Operations"

Covert operations might bring to mind military spies operating an intricate web of undercover activities in some foreign nation. However, in our context, covert operations to refer communication and actions designed to hide their true purpose. They are to manipulate the reactions of others without straightforwardly and honestly explaining your intent. Such tactics may involve treading near or over ethical lines.

Covert activities may include at least four scenarios:

1. Omitting presentation of some of the facts;
2. Emphasizing only those aspects of an argument that are in your favor;
3. Manipulating others by selecting what information to tell them and what to conceal; and
4. Doing anything else with generally sneaky undertones.

Sometimes a situation may be so severe or intolerable that you feel you must resort to covert activity because you can see no other way. However, covert activity in the field is generally considered to "violate the professional norm of openness" (Holloway, 1987, p. 735). Practitioners should carefully evaluate use of covert options before undertaking them. Covert activities should be used only when three conditions exist (Brager & Holloway, 1978): First, agency administrators are putting their own personal gains and interests before those of both clients and agency. Second, practitioners are provided no official, agency-sanctioned means of input into what goes on in the agency. Hence, covert activities would provide the only means of having such input. Third, you have already attempted to initiate macro change openly and were put down for it, or you know you would be put down for such change if you tried it.

Step 7: PREPARE—Evaluate the Potential Success of a Macro Change Process

This final step in the PREPARE process involves your *evaluation* and determination of whether to continue your change efforts or stop right here. It consists, essentially, of the following two substeps:

Substep 1: Review the prior PREPARE process and weigh the pros and cons of proceeding with the macro change process.

Substep 2: Identify possible macro approaches to use, roughly estimate their potential effectiveness, and select the most appropriate one.

Substep 1: Review the PREPARE Process and Weigh the Pros and Cons of Proceeding

Review the thoughts, facts, and perceptions identified in PREPARE's preceding six steps. Specifically, list the pros for taking action: Appraise client need (as established in Step 1 of the PREPARE process), positive organizational variables in your macro reality and your personal assets (Step 2), potential support from people of influence (Step 4), and potential benefits, including financial benefits (Step 5). (Note that Step 3—establishing primary goals—is not included in this process. We assume that your goals remain the same; this process helps you evaluate whether to pursue them.) Then list the cons against taking action. Weigh the negative organizational variables in your macro reality and your personal deficiencies (Step 2), potential resistance to change efforts from relevant people of influence (Step 4), potential costs (Step 5), and your own potential risk (Step 6). Figure 5.8 illustrates how you might evaluate the potential success of your proposed macro change effort.

At the end of this decision-making process, you must conclude one of three things. First, you might make a definite commitment to continue the change process. Second, you might determine that the time is not right. You could postpone the change process to another time. Third, you might decide that the potential for effective organizational change is too poor to continue your efforts. In the latter case, you would terminate the process, essentially forget about the idea, and go on with your ordinary work activities and responsibilities. In any case, at this point you must make a definite decision about what to do.

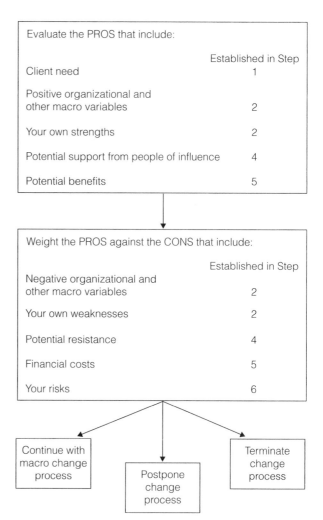

FIGURE 5.8 PREPARE—Evaluate the Potential Success of a Macro Change Process

CASE EXAMPLE

Evaluate the Potential Success of a Macro Change Process

Substep 1: Review the prior PREPARE process and weigh the pros and cons of proceeding with the macro change process.

Spiro determines that client need, the organizational and external macro environment, his own strengths, potential support, and the potential benefits far outweigh negative macro variables, personal weaknesses, potential resistance, financial costs, and his own risks. Therefore, he decides to proceed.

It is difficult to establish financial benefits in this case. What is the value of children being nurtured and taken care of rather than abused and neglected? Financial benefits are often difficult to establish when addressing issues involving service provision to needy people. When you can think of financial benefits, however, you will have a powerful argument when approaching decision makers.

Substep 2: Identify Possible Macro Approaches to Use, Estimate Their Effectiveness, and Select the Most Appropriate One

EP 2.1.10g

This substep is the transitional stage between *deciding* to pursue a macro change effort and actually *doing* it. At this point, you have committed yourself to pursuing some type of macro change. You have a pretty good idea about what type of macro approach you want to use. Approaches include those directed at changing agency policy, developing new programs, or undertaking some more limited project.

Chapter 6 will continue where this chapter leaves off in the macro change process. We will follow the choices and activities of Spiro, Farica, and the others involved in Spiro's macro intervention. Additionally, a number of other macro practice applications (for example, the establishment of a sexual harassment awareness program in a large public agency) will be studied.

CASE EXAMPLE

Evaluate the Potential Success of a Macro Change Process

Substep 2: Identify possible macro approaches to use, roughly estimate their effectiveness, and select the most appropriate one.

Spiro considers a variety of possible macro approaches. One is to go through administrative channels level by level, from Farica to Theresa to Harold to Pedro. He knows, however, that Farica has consulted Theresa informally in the past about needing staff. Theresa's response was vague and negative. Considering this and his own poor relationship with Theresa, he does not think talking to her is a viable approach.

We have already mentioned other options, such as going to the county board to request funding, writing grants, or asking for donations. The former idea is inappropriate because Spiro would be usurping agency administrators' roles and could look ridiculous. The latter two ideas are vague and time consuming, and are only temporary remedies anyway.

The macro method Spiro has been developing and clarifying in his mind involves the same approach he successfully used 15 years ago under another administration. Namely, he can use the agency's Community Advisory Committee to plead his cause, in addition to taking his pleas to the press. The current advisory committee is exceptionally active. Its chairperson, Waleeta, is extremely bright, dynamic, and committed to positive change.

In summary, Spiro chooses a strategy involving a personnel change. This falls within our category of changing agency policy. This type of change has both formal and informal dimensions. On the one hand, Spiro is essentially requesting a formal redistribution of funds to his agency unit. On the other hand, such a decision concerning expenditures involves the informal judgments of formally designated decision makers.

Highlight 5.5 summarizes and outlines the steps involved in the PREPARE process for determining whether or not to pursue macro change.

Looking Ahead

This chapter introduced macro practice organizational changes involving projects, program development, and agency policy. It described a detailed process (PREPARE) for *assessing* and beginning to *plan* organizational change potential and applied it to an extensive case example.

The next chapter will introduce you to a process (IMAGINE) for *implementing* and *evaluating* macro intervention within an agency setting and address the issue of changing agency policy. The case example from this chapter will be continued.

Chapter Summary

The following summarizes this chapter's content as it relates to the learning objectives presented at the beginning of the chapter. Chapter content prepares social workers to:

A. *Discern, appraise, and integrate multiple sources of knowledge in order to propose various forms of organizational change (including undertaking specific projects, initiating and developing programs, and changing agency policies).*

A project is a time-limited, planned undertaking with specified goals and activities to accomplish a designated purpose, such as improving

HIGHLIGHT 5.5

Summary Outline of the PREPARE Process

1. **P** Identify **Problems** to address.

   Substep 1: Decide to seriously evaluate the potential for macro level intervention.
   Substep 2: Define and prioritize problems.
   Substep 3: Translate problems into needs.
   Substep 4: Determine which need or needs you will address.

2. **R** Review your macro and personal **Reality**.

   Substep 1: Evaluate macro variables working for or against you in the macro change process. These variables include:
   - Resources and funding.
   - Constraining regulations or laws.
   - Internal political climate.
   - External political climate.
   - Other factors.

   Substep 2: Review your personal reality—strengths and weaknesses that may act for or against successful change efforts.

3. **E** **Establish** primary goals.

4. **P** Identify relevant **People** of influence.

5. **A** **Assess** potential costs and benefits to clients and agency.

6. **R** Review professional and personal **Risk**. Questions you might ask include:
   - Could I lose my job?
   - Will my career path be affected?
   - Will I strain interpersonal relationships at work?

7. **E** **Evaluate** the potential success of a macro change process.

   Substep 1: Review the PREPARE process and weigh the pros and cons of proceeding.

   Substep 2: Identify possible macro approaches to use, estimate their effectiveness, and select the most appropriate one.

services to clients, training staff, or solving some agency or community problem. A program or social program is an ongoing configuration of services and service provision procedures intended to meet a designated group of clients' needs. Agency policies, which may be formal or informal, are rules that tell us which

actions among a multitude of options we may take and which we may not.

B. *Collect, organize, and interpret data in order to assess the potential for organizational change by employing a seven-step process entitled PREPARE.*

The seven steps in PREPARE are: (1) identify problems to address; (2) review your macro and personal reality; (3) establish primary goals; (4) identify relevant people of influence; (5) assess potential financial costs and benefits to clients and agency; (6) review professional and personal risk; and (7) evaluate the potential success of a macro change process.

C. *Examine an extensive case example demonstrating the PREPARE process.*

The case example involved a Child Protective Services Unit that was experiencing a staffing shortage, negatively affecting service provision to clients.

D. *Practice personal reflection by assessing personal strengths and weaknesses with respect to the potential for macro change.*

Personal strengths and weaknesses include perceptions of self, attitudes toward colleagues and the agency, emotional and intellectual factors, skills, and other variables potentially affecting one's ability to proceed with macro change.

E. *Appraise the potential for internal advocacy with the ultimate goal of improving client access to services.*

Internal advocacy involves a practitioner championing or defending the rights of clients when such advocacy is not necessarily part of the job description. Rationales include being knowledgeable, promoting the agency's goals, supplementing informal communication channels, and assertively expressing one's right to advocate.

Competency Notes

The following identifies where Educational Policy (EP) competencies and practice behaviors are discussed in the chapter.

EP 2.1.1b Practice personal reflection and self-correction to assure continual professional development. *(P. 202):* Social workers should practice personal reflection regarding their ability to undertake successful macro level change efforts.

EP 2.1.8a Analyze, formulate, and advocate for policies that advance social well-being. *(P. 190):* Practitioners should analyze, formulate, and advocate for changes in agency policy that advance the well-being of clients.

EP 2.1.9b Provide leadership in promoting sustainable changes in service delivery and practice to improve the quality of social services. *(P. 193):* Social workers can serve as change agents to initiate change and improve service delivery. *(P. 207):* Practitioners must understand what leadership entails in order to become leaders themselves.

EP 2.1.10a Substantively and affectively prepare for action with individuals, families, groups, organizations, and communities. *(P. 194):* The PREPARE process prepares practitioners for action with organizations and communities.

EP 2.1.10d Collect, organize, and interpret client data. *(P. 196):* Identifying problems involves collecting, organizing, and interpreting client system data.

EP 2.1.10e Assess client strengths and limitations. *(P. 208):* In preparation for macro level change, practitioners should assess potential costs to clients and agency, which reflect limitations concerning the change process.

EP 2.1.10g Select appropriate intervention strategies. *(P. 213):* Selecting appropriate intervention strategies involves identifying potential macro approaches, estimating their effectiveness, and selecting the most appropriate one.

EP 2.1.10h Initiate actions to achieve organizational goals. *(P. 187):* Initiating change in organizations by undertaking specific projects, initiating and developing programs, and changing agency policies can help to achieve agency goals.

On the Internet

Visit the *Generalist Practice with Organizations and Communities* website at *www.cengage.com/social_work/ kirst-ashman* for learning tools such as PowerPoint® slides, tutorial quizzing, Web links, and final exams.

IMAGINE—How to Implement Macro Intervention: Changing Agency Policy

Recall the Case Example introduced on pages 195–196 in Chapter 5: The setting is the Child Protective Services Unit of the Yalobusha County Department of Social Services located in Plattsburgh, Wisconsin. The unit is composed of six workers and a supervisor. Farica the unit's supervisor, is very worried about the significant increase in the workers' caseloads over the past year. It is becoming nearly impossible to handle even the crises on the workers' caseloads, let alone give adequate attention to every case assigned. State law requires that each reported case must be investigated within 24 hours after intake. In reality, a worker is lucky to get to it four days later. Farika's staff is being forced to violate the law. It is physically impossible to do the job that the law requires of them.

Spiro, you recall, is one of Farica's supervisees. Arrogant and self-satisfied on the one hand, he is deeply committed to the agency and its service provision on the other. Hence, he becomes the change agent. He draws in Farika, his colleagues in the Child Protective Services Unit, and the Community Advisory Committee to become the action system. He has proceeded through the steps in the PREPARE process to determine whether to pursue macro intervention and has decided that, indeed, it is necessary. Now what?

Introduction

This chapter builds on the decision-making process covered in Chapter 5, which focused on whether to pursue some type of macro intervention. At this point, we assume this decision is positive. Macro intervention is the route of choice. This chapter, then, addresses how to proceed after the PREPARE process is completed. We will continue with the Case Example introduced in Chapter 5, following Spiro and Farica in their effort to increase their unit staff. How will they go about implementing a macro change concerning

agency policy? What steps should Spiro, Farica, and other action system members pursue in order to achieve their desired goals? This chapter will address these and other questions concerning macro change.

Learning Objectives

This chapter will provide content concerning how social workers:

A. *Distinguish, appraise, and integrate multiple sources of knowledge to apply the IMAGINE process involving macro intervention and evaluation.*

B. *Utilize a systems conceptual framework—including the macro client, change agent, target, and action systems—to initiate actions for achieving organizational goals.*

C. *Demonstrate effective written communication when using memos and e-mails.*

D. *Describe the application of mezzo concepts to macro practice when forming an action system.*

E. *Develop intervention goals, objectives, and action steps in order to initiate actions for achieving organizational goals.*

F. *Evaluate the use of collaborative and adversarial strategies to work together with colleagues, demonstrate effective communication with them, and neutralize opposition to the projected macro plan.*

G. *Propose ways to analyze, formulate, and advocate for policies that advance social well-being by changing agency goals, personnel practices, and practice procedures.*

H. *Initiate actions to achieve organizational goals by examining an extensive case example demonstrating the IMAGINE process.*

I. *Recognize the extent to which human diversity characterizes and shapes the human experience by assessing and enhancing cultural competence and empowerment in an agency setting.*

The Planned Change Process and Organizational Change

Given that the macro change perspective used here is that of a direct-service generalist practitioner with little or no administrative power, the change agent—you—will be required to extend your job description.

In macro generalist practice, you usually target a change that affects more than just your own work. Therefore, there are some differences between macro generalist practice on the one hand, and micro and mezzo generalist practice on the other.

Macro generalist practice does follow the basic planned change process of engagement, assessment, planning, implementation, evaluation, termination, and follow-up. However, two factors differentiate macro generalist practice from micro and mezzo. First, the change process involves many more people and systems than work with individual clients or groups of clients. Second, a major part of macro generalist practice

requires mustering support from colleagues and influencing decision makers to effect change at the macro level. Therefore, the macro planned change process is more complicated than that at the micro and mezzo levels.

EP 2.1.10

Chapter 5 introduced the three major arenas in which you are most likely to target agency change: undertaking some kind of project, developing a program, and changing an agency policy. Before pursuing any of these changes, you must determine the extent to which the change is necessary and worth the effort. Chapter 5 described the PREPARE process, which takes you through these assessment and planning aspects of change. Because of the extensiveness of macro level assessment, planning essentially becomes an extension of assessment.

The IMAGINE process follows the PREPARE process. You proceed through IMAGINE after you have decided to pursue a macro change, having completed PREPARE in order to make the decision that change is necessary.

Figure 6.1 depicts how the PREPARE process and the IMAGINE process relate to each other and to the steps in planned change. The PREPARE process deals with the decision whether to pursue a macro change or not. It assesses organizational change potential. Therefore, it addresses the *assessment* and *planning* steps of planned change. The IMAGINE process then follows PREPARE. It involves *implementing* the plan for macro level change and *evaluating* your success.

The final step in PREPARE is evaluating the potential success of a macro change process. If your decision is that you think change is possible, then you proceed and focus on the first step in IMAGINE. This step involves starting with the innovative idea inherent in your PREPARE assessment and planning. The remainder of this chapter will explore and discuss the IMAGINE process, beginning with a word about engagement in Highlight 6.1.

IMAGINE: A Process for Organizational Change

After completing the PREPARE assessment and planning process, we propose a paradigm (model) termed IMAGINE as a guide for initiating and pursuing macro change within organizations. The meaning of each letter in the acronym IMAGINE is illustrated in Figure 6.2. The IMAGINE change process can be applied to virtually any type of organizational change.

THE PLANNED CHANGE PROCESS:

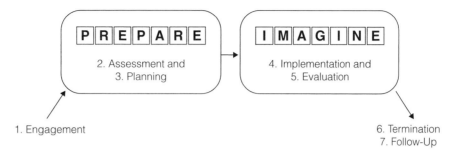

FIGURE 6.1 The Relationship between PREPARE and IMAGINE

HIGHLIGHT 6.1

A Word about Engagement

Engagement is the initial period during which you orient yourself to the problem at hand and begin to establish communication and a relationship with others also addressing the problem. It is important in micro, mezzo, and macro practice. As Chapter 2 discussed, engagement involves using relationship-building and positive interpersonal skills to initiate contacts, establish communication, and build trust.

During the macro change process, practitioners engage with each colleague, administrator, politician, or community leader with whom they come in contact.

Because of the more complicated dynamics in making macro changes, engagement is not the clearly defined first phase of intervention that it is with individual clients. Rather, engagement may occur often with different people as they become involved in the process. Likewise, engagement may occur over long periods of time, if practitioners interact with decision makers and others only rarely in the macro change process. It takes some time to get to know and trust others. Therefore, engagement in macro intervention is considered a potentially ongoing process instead of a distinct stage.

1. **I** Start with an innovative **Idea**.

2. **M** **Muster** support and formulate an action system.

3. **A** Identify **Assets**.

4. **G** Specify **Goals**, objectives, and action steps to attain them.

5. **I** **Implement** the plan.

6. **N** **Neutralize** opposition.

7. **E** **Evaluate** progress.

FIGURE 6.2 IMAGINE—A Process for Initiating and Implementing Macro Change

We will elaborate on each of IMAGINE's seven steps, then apply each to Spiro and Farica's organizational situation as described in the Case Example introduced in Chapter 5. As you may recall, they hope to reduce caseloads by adding staff to their agency.

*I*MAGINE: Start with an Innovative *Idea*

The first step in the IMAGINE process is to identify and start with an innovative *idea*. We assume that you have already spent time and effort thinking about the potential macro change, have progressed through the PREPARE assessment steps, and have

EP 2.1.9b

decided to proceed with a macro intervention. You have weighed strengths and weaknesses, risks and benefits. You have also determined whether to pursue a more limited project, more extensive development of some program, or a change in agency policy. This step is applied to Spiro and Farica's case illustration in the following Case Example.

CASE EXAMPLE

Start with an Innovative Idea

Spiro, one of Farica's staff members, is concerned about the staffing issue for a variety of reasons. (Spiro's and Farica's situation is reviewed at the very beginning of this chapter.) We have identified Spiro as our change agent. Using the PREPARE process (outlined in Chapter 5), he has considered a range of variables, including organizational resources and constraints, relevant people of influence, personal strengths, and risks involved. Spiro recalls that about 15 years ago, the child Protective Services Unit was in a similar predicament, desperately understaffed. At that time, Spiro went to the agency's Community Advisory Committee, explained the situation, and asked for help. He also went to local newspapers and alerted them to his unit's personnel shortage and the subsequent impact on clients. The result was the successful addition of two staff members. After deliberating over these past experiences, Spiro determines that the best way to solve the problem now at hand is to seek additional staff from administration.

IMAGINE: *Muster* Support and Formulate an Action System

EP 2.1.8b

The second step in the IMAGINE macro change process involves mustering support from others. We assume that your own job role has no agency-designated power to initiate macro change. Therefore, regardless of the type of macro change, you need help. You already have identified some relevant people of influence in Step 4 of the PREPARE process. When selecting a designated change strategy (that is, an agency policy change, project implementation, or program development), you will need to determine specifically whom you want to influence and how to do it most effectively.

Conceptualizing the Macro Practice Environment

As introduced in Chapter 1, four systems can help you picture the macro change process in your mind's eye (Compton, Galaway, & Cournoyer, 2005; Pincus & Minahan, 1973; Sheafor & Horejsi, 2009).

The macro client system. The *macro client system* includes those people who will ultimately benefit from the change process, usually some particular client population having similar characteristics and receiving similar agency services. For example, the macro client system might be all the clients with cognitive disabilities at a sheltered workshop in addition to these clients' families.[1] Note that a macro client system can also be an entire community or agency that benefits from the change.

Figure 6.3 depicts the macro client system. Two large circles are illustrated, one labeled "Agency System" and one "Macro Client System." "You the worker," are represented in bold by a small circle inside a slightly larger circle that illustrates your agency unit or division. Other small circles within the Agency System circle represent administration and other agency units. The Agency System circle arbitrarily depicts only four of the latter smaller circles—of course, the system could include any number of units.

The Macro Client System circle represents those clients receiving services and resources from your agency. Smaller circles within the Macro Client System circle illustrate that, in macro practice, many *individual client systems* make up the larger macro client system.

The arrow leading from the Agency System circle to the Macro Client System circle represents *service provision*. The agency system provides the macro client system (made up of all the agency's individual client systems) with services and resources.

Finally, note the arrow leading from the circle entitled "You the Worker" to the agency service system's provision arrow. This reflects your potentially direct role in influencing or implementing the macro change process to improve service provision to the macro client system.

The change agent system. In a macro practice perspective, the *change agent system* is the individual who initiates the macro change process. In our context, you, at least initially, are the change agent. Later on as you gain support and join coalitions with others who also believe in the proposed macro change, you as an individual change agent would become part of a larger action system dedicated to changing the status quo.

A note about the agency as a change agent system. Frequently in social work, the term *change agent system*

---

1. A *sheltered workshop* is an organization that provides a range of services to people who have physical or cognitive disabilities. Programs include job skill evaluation, job training, *sheltered employment* (a program involving work in a safe, closely supervised environment for people who have trouble functioning more independently), counseling, and help in finding employment (Barker, 2003).

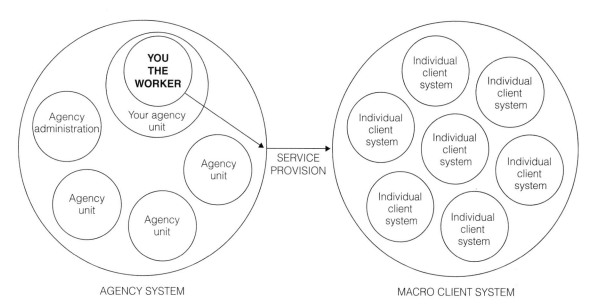

FIGURE 6.3 The Macro Client System in Macro Practice

refers to an agency involved in the implementation of some macro change. This book assumes the perspective that the vast majority of your opportunities to pursue macro intervention will be outside the context of your designated job with its formal job description. In reality, you will most often act as a catalyst to modify policies, implement projects, or develop programs within your own agency. It follows, then, that your agency or various units within it may not support or even agree with your proposed macro change. Your agency then becomes the target of your change efforts rather than a helper in the change process. This is true, at least initially, in the change process. Therefore, we will generally refer to the agency as the *agency system* instead of the change agent system.

The target system. The *target system* is the system that social workers must "change or influence in order to accomplish … [their] goals" (Pincus & Minahan, 1973, p. 78; Sheafor & Horejsi, 2009). Frequently our own agency or some subsystem within our agency becomes the target system.

As the macro change process continues, the target system may change. At first, it may be a specific group of decision makers somewhere in the agency that you target to influence. Later, this group of decision makers may join you in your quest. They may become part of the action system, working together with you to implement the proposed macro change. The target system may then become another influential unit within the agency system. Or you may even decide to target the top administrator.

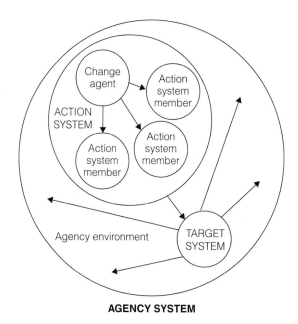

FIGURE 6.4 The Target System

Figure 6.4 illustrates the target system concept. The large circle represents the total agency system. The *action system* is illustrated as a circle within the large Agency System circle. You, as the *change agent,* are part of the Action System circle. Arrows run from you to three other circles labeled "Action system member" inside the Action System circle. These arrows illustrate that you as the change agent initiated the action system and developed its membership. Although only three circles are depicted, the action system can consist of any number of members, depending on the change agent's plan.

Another arrow runs from the Action System circle to another circle that is designated the *target system.* This target system is made up of some decision makers or people with power whom you feel you must influence in order to effect the proposed macro change. Several arrows run from the target system into the general *agency environment,* indicating that the target system could have an impact on other portions of the agency environment so that the agency is able to adopt the change.

In summary, Figure 6.4 depicts a three-stage process. First, you as the change agent initiate the macro change by formulating the action system. Second, the action system as a unit attempts to influence the target system to accept the validity of the proposed macro change. Third, the target system (hopefully) implements the proposed change within the agency environment so that the entire agency goes along with it.

The action system. The action system includes those people who agree and are committed to work together to attain the proposed macro change. As a change agent, you need to recruit supporters for your action system very carefully. It is best to muster support from staff who are well respected and competent (Homan, 2008). The administration is then more likely to have positive feelings about individual action system members and may react more positively to members' proposals and plans. Believable action system members lend credibility to the suggested change.

For example, you might work together with influential community residents such as local politicians, business-people, and clergy to initiate and develop an activity center for teens. Another example is working with colleagues and agency administrators to initiate and implement a crisis intervention program in your agency.

Figure 6.5 illustrates the relationships among the change agent, action, target, and macro client systems. As you know, this book assumes that you are the change agent system because you are the one who initiates the macro change idea. You are depicted in the circle labeled "You the worker" in bold at the top of the figure. It is eminently important to have the support and involvement of the macro client system before you initiate macro change: You must make certain you're working with this system and pursuing what the system's members want and need. An arrow points

from "You the worker" to a box labeled "Support and involvement of the macro client system," reflecting the latter's critical prominence throughout the macro change process. At this point, you may choose one of three options depicted in Figure 6.5. First, you might decide to pursue the macro intervention process by yourself. The leftmost arrow, pointing to you as the action system, portrays this scenario. Here you are both the change agent and the action system because you both initiate the change effort and plan to implement the change by yourself.

The second option is to join with others to implement the change process. Figure 6.5 depicts this with the center arrow, which points to a circle encompassing both you and other individuals and/or groups. This illustrates how you can be part of a larger action system. Although this circle arbitrarily portrays you in addition to three other individuals or groups, the action system could actually encompass any number of people or groups, including members of the macro client system.

The third scenario illustrated in Figure 6.5 indicates how you may initiate the idea but then hand it over to some other Action System to implement the changes. The rightmost arrow, pointing to an action system composed of other individuals, portrays this. You don't necessarily have to be part of the action system as long as the macro change process keeps going.

Arrows point from all of these action systems to the circle labeled "Target System," which represents the organization or community in need of change.

For example, state budget cuts abruptly ceased reimbursement for the special transportation of children with multiple physical and mental disabilities to and from a vital service provider. The children, most of whom were poverty-stricken, required transportation in specially equipped vans in order to accommodate wheelchairs and crutches. Accessible public transportation was not a viable option for most of them. An agency social worker whose job was to provide treatment decided that something must be done immediately. She called members of the County Board of Supervisors responsible for monitoring the county's budget and administering funds. She explained the vulnerability of these children and pleaded on their behalf. As a result, during its next bimonthly meeting, the board decided that the county would pay for the necessary transportation. The worker initiated the idea as the change agent system, but was unable to participate in its implementation. The board, then, became the

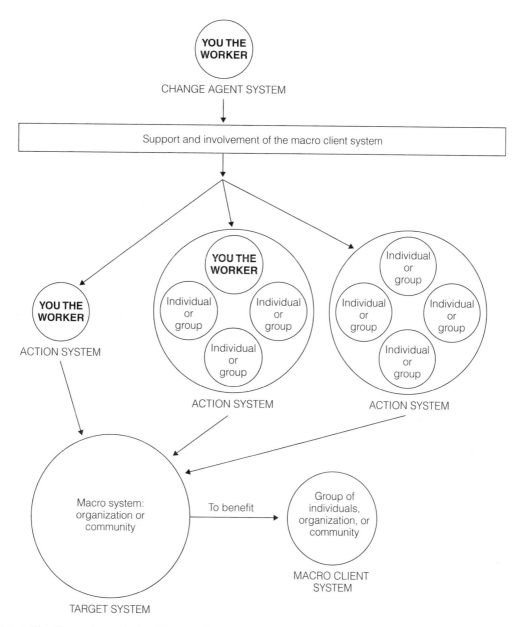

FIGURE 6.5 The Change Agent, Action, Target, and Macro Client Systems

action system. It implemented the necessary macro changes affecting hundreds of children with disabilities.

The final system illustrated in Figure 6.5 is the macro client system. After the action system energizes the target system into action, the intended beneficiary is the macro client system. Figure 6.5 depicts this with an arrow leading from the target system to the macro client system.

CASE EXAMPLE

Conceptualizing the Macro Practice Environment

As Spiro conceptualizes what he is trying to do, he defines the various systems he needs to work with. The *macro client system* consists of the clients his unit serves. He is initiating the macro change to benefit them and to fulfill the legal obligations designed to protect and help them (namely, for workers to abide by the 24-hour assessment requirement). The *target system* is upper-level administration, specifically Pedro, the agency director, and Harold, the assistant director. They are the agency decision makers ultimately responsible for acquisition and assignment of agency staff. Spiro himself is the *change agent,* as he is initiating the change. Finally, the *action system* includes Spiro, his supervisor and colleagues in the unit, and the agency's Community Advisory Committee.

Formulate an Action System: The Application of Mezzo Concepts to Macro Practice

Building an action system requires three major mezzo skills: "composition, understanding of and commitment to purpose, and group leadership and participation skills" (Resnick, 1980b, p. 211).

Composition of the Action System

Two aspects of composition—group size and characteristics of group members—are particularly relevant (Kraus, 2006; Resnick, 1980b; Toseland & Rivas, 2009).

The first aspect concerns how many members the group should have. If the group is too large, it is easy to get bogged down in interpersonal disagreements or multiple agendas. On the other hand, if the group is too small, it may be limited on creativity, information, and person power to complete the plan. A five-person action system is ideal in terms of limiting complexity and enhancing communication (Resnick, 1980b). As the implementation process proceeds, more members can be added when new tasks arise.

The second aspect of action system composition concerns the characteristics of individual group members. Several suggestions for selecting and approaching potential action system members include the following (Resnick, 1980b):

- *First, consider interpersonal variables. Select people who generally get along and communicate well with each other. Archenemies would probably carry old vendettas into the new macro proposal arena.*
- *Second, do not include people having vast differences in power within the organization. People with lower status may feel intimidated by those with more power. On the other hand, people with higher status may assume more control when working with group members of lower status.*

- *Third, do not automatically exclude potential members who can make only limited commitments. The effort they can afford to expend may be very useful. You cannot expect everyone else to have the same level of commitment and motivation that you do.*
- *Fourth, try to keep communication straightforward and aboveboard. Keeping secrets and criticizing other group members behind their backs erodes morale and detracts from the group's task.*

Understanding of and commitment to purpose. When forming an action system, make sure you clearly explain the major goals of the innovative idea. Also, describe how you perceive action system members' roles and how much time and effort you anticipate requiring of them. You need to make certain that members are committed to the purpose and goals of the macro change in order to avoid problems and misunderstandings later on.

Group leadership and participation skills. Any newly composed task group needs time to establish interactional and decision-making patterns. This is a significant process in itself, apart from trying to achieve the macro goals the group was established to accomplish. It is important, then, to pay attention to communication patterns. Before the group even begins, can you foresee a personality conflict between any members? For example, does one potential member perceive herself as a free-spirited, but devotedly committed free spirit and another as a staunchly regimented professional in a three-piece-gray-suit-world where changes should be made only after methodically, even tediously, thorough planning? Or can you predict that two or more individuals will vie for power in the group? Who would be the most effective leader? The idea that you may not be the best choice as leader could be a difficult thing for your ego to accept. As you can see, group composition has many nuances you will need to work with.

CASE EXAMPLE

Muster Support and Formulate an Action System

Spiro has already thought about the people both inside and outside his agency whom he might call upon for support. They include his unit supervisor and colleagues, the agency's Community Advisory Committee, and the local newspapers.

Spiro presents his idea formally at the next unit staff meeting. To his surprise, Farica, whom he expected to endorse the idea enthusiastically, is hesitant. She states that she knows the unit needs more staff, but she worries that such tactics may alienate the administration, especially Theresa, Farica's direct supervisor. This concerns Farica in particular because Theresa, as supervisor, is responsible for Farica's actions. Farica feels it is very important to maintain a good working relationship with her.

However, the other staff (including Tina, Arturo, Dylan, Barney, and Samina) are more supportive and appear to be happy someone has opted to take the lead. Surprisingly, Arturo, who usually stays out of these matters, voices spirited support. He is the only staff member in addition to Spiro who was around the last time the unit used this tactic 15 years ago. Eventually, the unit staff comes to a consensus that they have no choice but to pursue Spiro's idea.

The unit approves a motion asking Farica to send a memo to Theresa, with copies to Pedro and Harold, to alert them of the unit's needs. (See Highlight 6.2 for an explanation of how memos and e-mails are used professionally.) The memo is addressed to Theresa because it must go through the appropriate chain of command from bottom to top. Otherwise, higher levels in the agency's power hierarchy will most likely tell Farica to go through the proper channels (namely, Theresa) anyway. This would only delay the process. It is common practice to send copies of memos or e-mails to people higher up in the chain of command. This alerts them to issues without requiring a response. (A memo or e-mail requires a response only from the person to whom it is addressed.) Farica is aware that sending copies of the memo to Pedro and Harold places pressure on Theresa to respond appropriately. Because they are her direct supervisors, Theresa would probably want to please them.

During the unit meeting, Spiro suggests that the memo include the fact that the client support group encourages the unit's plea for help. Spiro wants the identification of need to be as strong as possible. Because the unit is sending a formal request, the administration cannot plead ignorance and say they were unaware of the unit's needs.

Later, Spiro meets with the agency's Community Advisory Committee. He explains the situation and pleads for their help. Waleeta, the chairperson, is taken with Spiro's self-confidence and charisma. She urges the other members' support. The advisory committee passes a motion in favor of Spiro's plan. They will await suggestions from Spiro concerning what specific strategies to pursue.

IMAGINE: Identify *Assets*

Regardless of the type of macro level change, you will need to determine what assets are available to implement the change. *Assets* are resources and advantages that will help you to undertake and complete your proposed change process. Assets can include readily available funding, personnel who are able and willing to devote their time to implementing the change, and office space where the change activities can occur.

EP 2.1.10e

HIGHLIGHT 6.2

Memos versus E-mails

Guffey (2010) explains the use of professional memos and e-mails:

> Paper-based interoffice memos [or memorandums] were once the chief form of internal communication [within organizations]. Today, employees use memos primarily to convey confidential information, emphasize ideas, deliver lengthy documents, or lend importance to a message. Memos are especially appropriate for explaining organizational procedures or policies that become permanent guidelines. ...
>
> E-mail involves the transmission of messages through computers and networks. ... E-mail is most appropriate for short messages that deliver routine requests and responses. It is inappropriate for sensitive, confidential, or lengthy documents. ... It is especially effective for messages to multiple receivers and messages that must be archived (saved). An e-mail is also appropriate as a cover document when sending longer attachments. E-mail, however, is not a substitute for face-to-face conversations, telephone calls, business letters, or memorandums. (pp. 99–100)

In our case example, Farica and the child Protective Services Unit staff feel that the staffing issue is of exceptional importance. Therefore, they decide to send a formal memo to stress its significance.

CASE EXAMPLE

Identify Assets

In his PREPARE assessment of macro change potential, Spiro identified a variety of strengths, including the constraining laws that unit staff are unable to follow; the agency's motivation to comply with regulatory laws; the public's concerns about the treatment of child abuse; Spiro's own competence and his reputation in the agency; Spiro's positive relationship with Pedro, the agency director; client support (as received from Tina's client support group); and the backing of the agency's Community Advisory Committee. Spiro will keep these strengths in mind throughout the macro change process and integrate them as thoroughly as possible into the intervention plan.

IMAGINE: Specify *Goals,* Objectives, and Action Steps to Attain Them

EP 2.1.10f

IMAGINE's fourth step concerns specifying *goals* and objectives and how to achieve them. A goal, according to *Webster's Dictionary,* is simply the ultimate "end toward which effort is directed" (Mish, 2008, p. 536). You have already identified your primary goals during Step 3 of the PREPARE process, and these goals provide you with direction regarding how to proceed with your macro intervention. What do you really want to accomplish? How can your clients' major needs be met through macro change? What are your primary and necessary end results?

Primary goals do not usually specify how they will be achieved. For example, you might want to improve conditions in the family-planning center where you work. Or you might want to increase clients' access to services by having the agency remain open for longer hours.

In order to reach goals, you must specify exactly how to achieve them. This involves breaking primary goals down into a series of *objectives,* which are smaller, behaviorally specific subgoals that serve as stepping-stones on the way to accomplishing the primary goal. For example, the goal of "improving conditions in a unit at a residential treatment center" is a broad goal that provides neither specificity nor a clear method of measuring success. Thus, the next step is to specify the improvements you wish to make. This is accomplished first by setting objectives that move you toward achieving your goal.

Appropriate objectives for the goal of "improving conditions" might include painting the walls in the

unit, implementing a new disciplinary system, and/or developing recreational groups. As you can see, this level of specificity provides clear direction for your efforts. Because objectives are more specific, they are often used as a measure of accountability. That is, painting the unit is an easily recognizable accomplishment: The unit gets painted or it does not. This is the ideal objective; you can easily tell when it has been achieved.

Let's assume our first objective is to paint the residential unit, and we plan to ask unit volunteers to do the job. Although this objective provides greater specificity, it doesn't describe each step that must be completed for the objective to be achieved.

Writing Clear Action Steps

EP 2.1.3c

Action steps are tasks one must complete (in the correct order and within the designated time frame) to achieve the desired objective—which, in turn, is designed to achieve your primary goal. The formula for creating an action step is to specify *who* will do *what* by *when:* "Who" is the individual who will accomplish the task; "what" is the task(s) assigned to that individual; and "when" is a time limit so the task is not delayed or forgotten.

Therefore, the objective of having the agency volunteers paint the unit contains the following action steps:

1. Bob *(who)* will meet with the volunteer coordinator to explain the painting project *(what)* by next Tuesday *(when).*
2. Noel *(who)* will prepare a purchasing requisition for the paint *(what)* by next Wednesday *(when).*
3. Reiko *(who)* will put masking tape on woodwork and place dropcloths over the carpet *(what)* by next Friday *(when).*
4. Chanette *(who)* will be at the unit 30 minutes before the volunteers arrive and will supervise them *(what)* on the following Monday *(when).*

As you can imagine, a single, apparently simple objective might have many action steps that must be achieved if the objective is to be accomplished. (Other action steps for this objective might include notifying the volunteers and unit administration, preparing "wet paint" signs, and arranging for removal and cleaning of equipment once the job is over. Each action step will require specifying who, what, and when.)

You can also imagine the consequences if steps are not carried out as assigned: If Noel does not requisition the paint, the volunteers can't work. If Reiko fails to protect the carpet, a costly mess could result. Should

A goal in the IMAGINE process might be to improve community conditions. Groups such as Habitat for Humanity involve volunteers to build new community residences for people in need.

Chanette sleep in on Monday, the volunteers may paint the computer, file cabinets, and anything else that doesn't move. Listing action steps alerts us to the critical activities necessary to reach an objective.

The following are more examples of well-written action steps:

Harry Carey *(who)* will notify all unit colleagues about the upcoming in-service *(what)* by noon on March 15 *(when)*.

I *(who)* will write a five-page paper describing the new treatment approach *(what)* by 9:00 A.M. on Friday, October 13 *(when)*.

Ms. Fidgety *(who)* will contact the designated community leaders for information about housing needs *(what)* by next Tuesday *(when)*.

You might now be asking yourself, "Why is it important to be so precise?" The answer is that if you aren't explicit regarding who has the responsibility for accomplishing the task, it's likely that the task won't get done.

For example, as a student you are probably very busy. You probably don't have much time to do anything but your required coursework. It would be nice to do a lot of in-depth reading on topics that interest you. However, you probably assign this a relatively low priority. You do what you have to do first. It's the same with generalist practitioners in the field. As a social worker, you will probably have an abundance of clients and will constantly strive to prioritize what needs to get done first. If it's not your specifically identified responsibility to complete a task by a certain deadline, it's easy to put it off ... and off ... and off. Such tasks rarely, if ever, get done.

It's interesting to note the phrase "get done." It is as if the task will magically do itself without any human intervention. In other words, this phrase is one to carefully scrutinize and, probably, to avoid.

In addition to being specific, your action steps should be measurable. That is, it is important to specify exactly what is required for an action step to be deemed completed. For example, if your action step is to contact five designated community leaders, you have not completed the step if you contacted only three of them. You need to contact all five.

CASE EXAMPLE

Specify Goals, Objectives, and Action Steps to Attain Them

Spiro's general *goal* is to improve service provision by pursuing the *objective* of increasing unit staff's time to address clients' needs. He has further refined this objective to increasing the number of unit staff members. In order to do that, he establishes an initial plan in the form of the following *action steps*:

1. Farica *(who)* will write the memo to Theresa, including recommendations made at the staff meeting *(what)*, by this Friday, Nov. 12 *(when)*.
2. Spiro *(who)* will meet with the agency's Community Advisory Committee to suggest to them that they draft a statement supporting the staffing increase *(what)* at their next meeting, at 7:00 P.M. on Tuesday, Nov. 16 *(when)*.
3. Spiro *(who)* will ask the advisory committee to have the statement completed and submitted to Agency Director Pedro *(what)* by Friday, Nov. 19 *(when)*.
4. Spiro *(who)* will check to make certain that action steps 1 and 3 are completed *(what)* by Monday, Nov. 22 *(when)* and then contact the two local newspapers *(what)*.
5. Spiro *(who)* will urge the two newspapers to print the stories as soon as possible *(what)*, hopefully by Monday, Nov. 29 *(when)*.

IMAG*I*NE: *Implement* the Plan

IMAGINE's fifth step is implementing the established plan. All macro changes need a plan to give them direction. Which decision makers need to be contacted as part of the target system? In what order should they be contacted? What should they be told? What recommendations should such decision makers be given? Implementation is the actual doing of the plan. The plan's goal is to establish the macro change.

Macro changes usually require regular communication and negotiation. Because some number of people are involved, the formula for change completion is usually both complex and fluctuating. Therefore, you will probably need to monitor the plan carefully to keep the change process on course as you continue working toward your goal.

CASE EXAMPLE

Implement the Plan

The advisory committee drafts and sends the formal memo to Pedro, as requested. Farica writes the memo and Spiro carries out his action steps as planned. The newspapers both print the stories—one on Saturday, November 27, and the other on Sunday, November 28. Spiro waits impatiently for the administration's response.

IMAG*I*NE: *Neutralize* Opposition

EP 2.1.10g

IMAGINE's sixth step is neutralizing (overcoming) any opposition to your macro plan. The macro change process is not usually a direct, unimpeded thrust whereby progress continues perfectly as planned. Rather, the process usually follows a twisting path full of surprises. Objectives, action steps, and plans often need modification in view of changes in the macro environment. People change their minds. New elements, such as funding cuts, enter the scene, seemingly out of nowhere. You may be assigned to a new supervisor. The larger the target of change and the agency environment, the more likely that new factors will develop to influence the change process.

As you encounter new issues and impediments, continued influence of decision makers remains important. Keep in mind the elements to consider before talking to administrators: anticipation of their logical reactions, the phases of resistance to expect, and the use of collaborative and adversarial strategies.

Communicating with Decision Makers

A critical point in the macro change process is when you present your plan to your target system. Think carefully about what information is needed to support your plan or argument. Too much detail will dilute your points. Too little information will weaken your ability to persuade. Make sure all information is accurate and back it up with facts as much as possible. Make time to complete three important tasks prior to your meeting with target system members: role determination, articulation of your formulated plan, and practice of your presentation before the meeting (Resnick, 1980b; Tropman & Morningstar, 2001).

Role determination means deciding in advance who will attend the meeting and who will say what. It is wise to choose action system members who you think will have the strongest positive impact on the target system (for example, decision-making administrators). You want to maximize your potential to influence those decision makers on your behalf.

Role determination also includes determining who will introduce the subject, who will present the rationale, who will respond to what types of questions, and so on. In essence, establish who will have the role of leader, who will assume the role of expert in the event specific facts are requested, and who will act as mediator if conflict arises between action and target systems.

Articulation of your formulated plan means you should perfect the way you will describe and present the issue, your concern, and your recommendations for change. This should be crystal clear in your mind. The action system members should also spend time identifying as many potential arguments as possible against the proposed plans. Your group can then think about and prepare responses to any queries or objections decision makers may raise. For example, administrators might say that the proposal's costs are too high or there are not enough staff members to complete the necessary tasks. In this event, how would you respond to defend and explain your proposal?

Practice your presentation by role-playing the meeting. Action system members who will actually meet with decision makers can play themselves. Other volunteers can play the decision makers and voice the decision makers' presumed concerns. This is a good way to further explore the issue and the plan. The better prepared you are to address concerns voiced by target system members, the more convincing your proposal will be.

Logical Administrative Reactions

If you examine and understand the concept of change from an administrative point of view, you better your chances of success. Often, outside agencies and systems control the resources available to an organization and wield influence over what the organization can and cannot do (Austin, 2002; Gibelman & Furman, 2008). The top administrator must view the agency and its needs as only one system within the mammoth external environment. Administrators may have constraints, such as licensing regulations or funding requirements, of which you as a practitioner are unaware. Of course, administrators retain their responsibility for providing effective services to clients. However, the more you

know about the agency and its interrelationships with other systems in the macro environment before implementing the macro change process, the better prepared you will be to utilize assets and anticipate problems.

Keep one other thing in mind concerning macro change in organizations: The size of the organization is probably inversely related to the ease with which macro change can be accomplished (Patti, 1983). It is often tremendously difficult to make significant changes in massive agencies, such as state departments of social services. Such organizations have multiple levels of administration. A dedicated red ant trying to move a huge mountain of brownish-gray sludge comes to mind. Each bureaucratic level provides new opportunities for information and ideas to become distorted, diluted, and forgotten. It is likely much easier to know and target influential decision makers in smaller agencies. Such agencies have smaller staffs and greater opportunities to know individual people's responsibilities and attitudes.

Phases of Resistance

Anticipate resistance to macro change (Holland & Ritvo, 2008). You might expect at least four stages of resistance as you try to muster support for your macro plan (Denhardt, Denhardt, & Aristigueta, 2002; Resnick, 1980b).

The first stage delivers a monumental dose of negativism. You might hear any of a wide range of negative responses. "That proposal simply can't work!" "How did you come up with such an irrational idea?" "My Uncle Olaf always used to say, 'if it ain't broke, don't fix it.'" Critics are usually outspoken, and potential supporters lie hidden in the woodwork. This is often a very frustrating stage.

In stage two of the resistance process, people have already mulled over the issues and thought about possibilities. Critics tend to die down a bit, and supporters slowly start to emerge. This phase may allow you to increase the strength of your action system as you identify potential supporters for your macro change proposal.

Stage three of the resistance process is characterized by conflict. Decision makers must decide whether to go ahead with the proposal. Once again, with good planning and perseverance, you have a chance of achieving your goal.

Stage four of the resistance process occurs after your proposal is already being implemented. Resistance may still be skulking in your internal agency environment. Overt conflict has probably gone undercover. Do not be deceived that all is perfectly well. People who do not believe in or like your proposed macro plan may work covertly against you. Beware of potential obstructions. You must continue to nurture and monitor your macro process in order for it to survive and thrive.

Collaborative and Adversarial Strategies

One way of looking at the broad range of potential strategies to pursue is by placing these strategies on a continuum, from collaborative (anticipating little resistance) to adversarial (anticipating significant resistance). The continuum reflects your perceptions of how much the target system is likely to go along with your proposed plan.

Patti and Resnick (1980) define and explain "collaborative" and "adversarial" strategies (pp. 224–225). Collaborative strategies are those used when you don't anticipate dogged or profound resistance from decision makers. Such strategies assume that it is better to work *with* than *against* the existing organizational system. Collaborative strategies also assume "that the target system is rational, open to new ideas, and acting in good faith" (Denhardt et al., 2002; Gibelman & Furman, 2008; Patti & Resnick, 1980, p. 224).

Adversarial strategies, on the other hand, are those used when you expect decision makers to express mildly significant to extremely vehement resistance to change. You may choose to use these strategies when you feel there is no potential for collaborative strategies or when collaborative approaches have failed. Therefore, adversarial strategies, which set the action system *against* the organizational structure, are preferable when those are the only approaches that might have a chance to work.

Collaboration and persuasion. Another way of looking at the continuum is in terms of persuading versus pressuring (Halley, Kopp, & Austin, 1998). When using collaborative strategies, your intent is to persuade decision makers to agree with your point of view by presenting a logical and convincing argument. There are four basic steps in persuading (Halley et al., 1998), as discussed next.

First, you initiate persuasion with any of three methods: (1) establishing something in common and starting from there, (2) straightforwardly sharing your honest feelings, and (3) "the blunt assault" (Halley et al., 1998, p. 226). Regardless of method used, you must articulate the problem clearly and succinctly.

1. Establishing something in common can be stating some aspect of the problem or proposed solution

with which you know both action and target systems will agree. For example, you might say, "I know that we all are seeking effective service delivery for our clients."

2. Sharing honest feelings may entail getting right to the point, even if the target system receives the point negatively. For instance, you might state, "I understand that you are opposed to a major change. However, I feel it is necessary to share my serious concerns with you."

3. The blunt assault takes sharing honest feelings much further. It should be used rarely because it falls much closer to pressuring on the continuum than the other two approaches. For example, you might say, "I have to be honest. I totally disagree with your position. I will be forced to fight you on this one. Let me explain to you why I feel this strongly. ..."

After initiating persuasion, the second step in persuading is allowing time to discuss, mull over, and answer decision makers' questions. Third, you state your macro change proposal (in essence, the solution to the problem) clearly and straightforwardly. Fourth, you summarize any progress you have made with the decision makers and any agreement regarding how to proceed.

There are eight additional strategies for using persuasion (Austin, Kopp, & Smith, 1986):

1. Educate the decision makers. Provide detailed, specific information. Help them understand the problem and see it more clearly from your point of view.

2. Discuss options. What potential solutions are there to your described problem? You can subsequently review with decision makers the potential advantages and disadvantages of your proposed plan.

3. Ask if a trial or partial policy, project, or program change is possible. Perhaps some partial proof can begin to establish your idea's validity.

4. Suggest that a committee be formed to discuss and consider the proposed plan. The committee could be composed of a range of staff, including representatives of both the decision-making target system and the action system.

5. Creatively identify how target and action system members could spend more time together to develop communication channels and become familiar with the issues from both sides. This might mean planning a special meeting or an in-service training session to present information to the target system about the problem you are addressing.

6. Appeal to the decision makers' sense of fairness, ethics, and right and wrong. What is the most ethical approach to service provision for clients? What goals are most important for the agency to pursue?

7. Develop a rational argument to support your proposed plan. Choose information that strongly supports your macro proposal. You might even write a summary for decision makers to review during the meeting and keep for later reference.

8. Specify to decision makers what the negative consequences of ignoring the identified problem might be. How will maintaining the status quo result in costs to them? Describe the seriousness of the costs. The greater the costs of stagnation, the greater the perceived benefits of change.

Highlight 6.3 discusses the adversarial end of the persuading–pressuring continuum.

CASE EXAMPLE

Neutralize Opposition

Theresa calls Farica at 7:45 A.M. on Monday, November 29, the first workday following the news article's publication. Theresa never calls anyone first thing on Monday morning unless it is urgent. Farica's secretary, Julie, tapes a written message to Farica's office doorknob to make sure Farica sees it first thing. Farica dreads seeing a note on her doorknob. It always means that, as Farica's mother would say, "Theresa's got a bug on her liver."

Theresa typically calls Farica when she is livid and probably raring for a fight. Farica thinks Theresa must be furious about the strategies for getting more staff. She has been worried about that ever since Spiro initiated the plan. On the one hand, Spiro's suggestions are best for the unit. She has supported Spiro, but not too visibly. On the other hand, Farica anticipated that going outside of the agency for help would infuriate the powers-that-be. She has desperately tried to remain on the fence and out of the line of fire. Now she feels as if she is looking down the barrel of an elephant gun.

Farica decides the time has come to face the music. As unit supervisor, she is supposed to manage and control her supervisees. She returns Theresa's call immediately. Theresa answers in a scathingly sharp tone of voice. She pointedly scolds Farica for allowing Spiro to speak with the Community Advisory Committee and asks if it was he who called the newspapers. Farica humbly responds that, yes, it was he. In reply, Theresa raises her voice and vehemently states that Farica and

Spiro are *never, never, never* to go outside the agency with agency business again. Furthermore, Theresa wants to meet with them both immediately. She abruptly hangs up.

Farica is disgusted. She feels as if Spiro has manipulated her into being the target of the administration's rage. This is why she hates being the supervisor. As such, she becomes ultimately responsible for everyone else's "mistakes."

Farica walks down the hall to Spiro's office. With his typical charming smile, Spiro says hello and asks her how it's "goin'." She responds that it's "goin'" terribly and tells him about her conversation with Theresa moments earlier. She also tells him that Theresa wants to meet with them "immediately!"

As the two walk to Theresa's office, they hypothesize that Pedro and Harold must also be furious. That must be why Theresa called Farica first thing in the morning. Higher administration probably put pressure on Theresa, as Farica's direct supervisor, to handle the situation pronto.

Farica and Spiro subsequently have a very unpleasant hour with Theresa chastising them for their major blunder, namely airing the agency's dirty laundry in public. Finally, Theresa instructs them to write a formal request to her for needed staff and include adequate documentation. Theresa emphasizes that decide what to do about any possible staffing needs. She also tells Farica and Spiro that she will make a record in their permanent personnel files regarding their poor judgment and behavior. She commands that this never happen again!

Farica and Spiro return to Farica's office. Spiro whines about how insensitive administration is and about Theresa's horrible personality. Together, they write a 10-page document requesting more staff. Farica submits it to Theresa that same day. The other unit staff members walk softly around the unit throughout the day, thankful they were not the targets of administrative wrath.

Both Spiro and Farica made some errors and misjudgments. Mistakes are common when instituting macro change. Such change is usually a difficult and complicated process. Spiro and Farica failed to understand the fiscal strain that Pedro and Harold were experiencing from the agency's funding sources. Making the problems public hurt rather than helped the agency's chances for receiving more resources. Psychologically, if people controlling funding sources thought the agency was not doing a good job and was suffering serious problems, these people would only put pressure on Pedro. They would indicate

HIGHLIGHT 6.3

Being an Adversary and Pressuring

Pressuring is a much "pushier" approach than persuading. Pressuring involves using more forceful and coercive tactics to achieve your goals and carries much higher potential risks than persuading. Decision makers are much more likely to react to this approach with bristling resistance and hostility.

Use pressuring only when three conditions are present (Halley et al., 1998): First, you have tried everything else, including persuading, and nothing has worked. Second, you feel very strongly that you must pursue the macro change. You can't just let it go. Third, you think you have a substantial chance of attaining your goals. If you think there is little or no chance, why bother wasting your energy and exposing yourself to risk?

One example of pressuring is the use of a formal grievance procedure. A *grievance* is the formal expression of a complaint by an employee feeling she has been wronged because of some inappropriate treatment, such as violation of agency regulations. Many agencies have a formal process to undertake if you think you have a valid grievance. The procedure usually designates a formal group whose task is to review your grievance and determine whether you were treated fairly.

The following are nine additional strategies you can pursue when pressuring for change (Austin et al., 1986; Rubin & Rubin, 2008):

1. Circulate a petition to gain collective support and submit it to the administration for consideration. A *petition* is a formal written request signed by any number of persons stating their support of the request.
2. Stage open confrontations regarding issues with decision makers during regular staff meetings. You might also initiate public forums and invite interested parties to come and hear both sides of the issue.
3. Inform sanctioning agencies from the external environment about the issue. For example, you could cite agency regulatory violations to regulatory agencies. You could tell funding sources

about problems that might lead these sources to withdraw resources. Please note, however, that administrations generally abhor this type of strategy. Administrators responsible for and committed to maintaining the agency's functioning and good standing understandably feel betrayed when anyone airs the agency's dirty laundry for all the world to see.

4. Go to the newspapers, television, and radio with information that will bring agency problems to public attention. As in point 3, however, be warned that agency administrations usually hate this type of tactic.
5. Encourage staff members or clients to interfere deliberately with service provision. This strategy halts the regular flow of agency activity and often interferes with funding and service.
Staff members might refuse to complete any record keeping until some specified problem is solved.
6. Initiate a strike. Strikes can obviously stop or seriously impede service provision. However, being on strike additionally means getting no paychecks. It may also mean getting fired.
7. Organize concerned personnel and others, including clients, to picket the agency. Once again, administrations are usually very annoyed with tactics that cause the public to view their agencies negatively.
8. Take the issue to the courts. Administrators also hate this strategy. It not only brings problems to public attention, but also costs a lot of money, both for the agency and probably for you.
9. Undertake formal bargaining. This would probably take place when employees are members of a union and have elected representatives to settle issues for them.

Remember that when choosing to pressure people in power, you increase your own risk. Risks may range from causing powerful people to hold negative opinions of you and label you a "troublemaker" to causing your supervisor to fire you.

that he had better solve the problems now and prove to them that he had done so. Pedro, in turn, would put pressure on Harold. Harold, subsequently, would pressure Theresa, and Theresa would lean on both

Farica and Spiro. Funding sources might also withhold resources until they were convinced that the agency was running smoothly and doing its job as it was supposed to.

Spiro and Farica had misjudged the situation. Farica, as unit supervisor, had not submitted a formal request for more staff to Theresa. Yes, Farica had approached Theresa informally on a number of occasions. However, one of the informal rules of agency life is that if a request isn't written down, it doesn't exist. Hence, Spiro and Farica perceived that they had already pursued it to its fullest. The first rule of using pressure in an adversarial situation is to make certain that you have already tried everything else, including every possible means of persuasion.

As it turns out, Farica must proceed to educate agency decision makers about the unit's staffing problems. Spiro and Farica have run into the typical first phase of administrative resistance, namely, a resounding "No, it is not possible under any circumstances!"

A week after the confrontation, Theresa writes Farica a form memo stating that, because of funding constraints, it is not possible to add new staff at this time. Farica and Spiro then decide that they need to get more information and suggest more specific, viable options. Farica sees Spiro as a strength in the further pursuit of their primary goal. He is motivated, knowledgeable, and hard-working, albeit rather aggressive and egotistical. She feels Spiro can provide her with much-needed assistance in the quest for additional staff.

Farica and Spiro proceed to talk with other agency units that have acquired additional staff. They learn about some other arguments that appear to be persuasive in the administration's eyes. For example, documenting that staff members are already expending more effort than is required is important. Farica documents that staff already work about 9½ hours instead of the required 8 hours per workday. She can thus diffuse the possible misconception that unit staffers are lazy and don't really need the requested help.

Another supervisor tells Farica about two retirements in units not nearly as pressed as Farica's. Perhaps Farica can suggest to administration that these positions, or portions of them (in the form of part-time instead of full-time staff) could be relocated to her own unit. Of course, Farica will present such suggestions in a constructive and thoughtful way, showing sensitivity to the administration's concern about controlling costs.

In subsequent communication involving both verbal and written contacts, Farica and Spiro emphasize that children are literally being hurt by the agency's lack of attention to their problems. In this way they try to respond to the decision makers' sense of fairness and ethics.

Farica calls other Child Protective Services Units in surrounding counties. She asks them about their caseloads and establishes that her staff-to-client ratio is indeed excessive in comparison. Her workers have significantly more clients than other similar units. This provides yet another persuasive argument to administration on behalf of getting additional staff.

Two months pass. Farica finally sends Theresa a formal memo. In it, Farica asks about and establishes an argument for the addition of two more staff members. In reality, Farica thinks that such a proportionately large increase in a relatively small unit is unrealistic. Adding two more to a staff of seven represents almost a 30 percent increase. However, Theresa does allocate to Farica four quarter-time positions.

You might ask, "Why four part-time positions instead of one whole person? Doesn't adding a bunch of part-timers only make things more confusing?"

The answer is that part-time staff usually cost the agency less. Such staff are paid less and don't receive the same benefits that full-time staff receive (for example, paid vacation and full health insurance).[2] They are also not as well protected by union rules. Remember that once an agency staff person receives "tenure" in Farica's and Spiro's agency, she essentially has a permanent job position. Within this particular agency, administration can pretty much hire and fire part-time staff at will. This allows administrators significantly more flexibility in how they allocate their resources.

You might also ask how ethical it is for administration to offer only part-time positions with poorer benefits to new staff. That is a good question. It poses an ethical dilemma. (An *ethical dilemma* is a situation in which it is impossible to comply with two or more ethical principles at the same time.) In this agency's case, the administration has a difficult choice. It must either offer less money and benefits to new staff or fail to serve clients in serious need. The administration, therefore, decides it's more important to provide benefits to clients than to staff.

IMAGIN*E: Evaluate* Progress

The final step in the IMAGINE macro change process involves *evaluating* the intervention's progress and effectiveness. All such processes need ongoing evaluation of progress made toward your goal. Are you progressing as **EP 2.1.10m**

---

2. It should be noted that, although part-time staff may appear to cost less on paper in terms of salary and benefits, such staff often cost the agency more in terms of administrative "workload" (i.e., supervisory time, staff meeting time, in-service training, etc.).

planned? Or are you "stopped dead in the water?" In the latter case, what can you do to get back on track?

Evaluation serves two major purposes: First, evaluation can monitor the ongoing operation and activities involved in achieving a macro level change. Second, evaluation can target the end results of your macro intervention. The monitoring and evaluation functions are complementary. Monitoring looks at the macro level change throughout the IMAGINE process; evaluating end results addresses the effectiveness of the process after it has been completed. How well have you achieved the goals you set out to achieve? (Chapter 10 discusses evaluation more extensively.)

CASE EXAMPLE

Evaluate Progress

Toward the end of the change process, Spiro and Farica form the primary action system because other action system members are no longer actively involved. In their pursuit of the designated macro change, namely, increasing staff, they were forced to seriously evaluate their change efforts. Because of total lack of administrative support and receipt of administrative chastisement, they determined that their original plan was ineffective. They needed to develop some completely new strategies.

At the completion of the macro change process, Farica and Spiro evaluate their overall effectiveness. What exactly were they able to accomplish? They gained the equivalent of an additional staff member for the unit, at least in terms of the time someone will be available to work in the unit. In effect, Farica and Spiro decide that their efforts have been successful.

Now or at some point in the future, Spiro or Farica may decide to undertake a new macro change effort. They can target either a similar or a very different need to enhance the unit's level of service provision and effectiveness.

Application of IMAGINE to Macro Intervention

The Child Protective Services Unit's situation, explored in the Chapters 5 and 6 Case Examples, shows how you can target agency policy for macro change. It offers only one example of the types of policy changes you may decide to target in your own agency. The particular policy they addressed was a staffing issue, which was part of agency policy (instead of other types of organizational change, such as project implementation or program development).

The remainder of this chapter will elaborate on changing agency policy. The PREPARE and IMAGINE processes will be applied to this dimension of macro change in some depth.

Changing Agency Policy

We have established that a *policy* is a rule or set of rules that tells us which actions among a multitude of options we may take and which we may not. It thus provides any macro system direction for its functioning and activities. Policy's purpose is to provide rational, predictable guidelines for a system's operation, especially with respect to how resources are distributed. Policy dictates what should and should not be done within the agency setting.

Policies differ from projects and programs in terms of breadth. Policies usually establish *general guidelines* for total agency functioning. Programs and projects, on the other hand, provide much more *specific detail* for what activities are performed within an agency.

Policies include both internal operation and provision of services to clients. Internal operation includes administrative arrangements and specific procedures for running the agency. These include lines of authority within the agency and types of benefits (for example, sick leave, vacation time, or health care) that employees receive. Formal and informal agency policies also concern how services are provided to clients. What specific services are available? Under what conditions do workers meet with clients? Are meetings held in workers' offices or in clients' homes? How long should such meetings take? What types of information must workers gather from clients? Agency policies concern these and any number of other questions about worker–client interaction and intervention.

Formal and Informal Agency Policies

The policies addressed in Farica and Spiro's Case Example have both formal and informal dimensions. Acquisition and distribution of personnel are formal, in that such actions require formal funding prerequisites and formal integration of staff into the agency's hierarchy of employees. Informal policies concern the everyday decision-making processes of people in power. Decision makers in Farica and Spiro's situation included Pedro, Harold, and Theresa, who have substantial informal discretion regarding how they allocate agency staff.

If, at any point in your role as an agency worker, you decide that some agency policy, either formal or informal, is unfair, outdated, or inappropriate, you should first review the decision-making steps illustrated in Chapter 5 to decide whether to pursue macro change. Next, follow the IMAGINE process to implement a policy change.

Types of Changes in Agency Policy

There are three major types of agency policy: organizational goals, personnel practices, and practice procedures. Each of these may involve both formal and informal agency policies.

Whenever a worker decides to pursue an agency policy change, she should first answer two questions related to PREPARE's Step 5: Will the change result in improved service delivery and resources to clients? And will the change result in improved working conditions for staff so that they will be better able to serve their clients in a more effective or efficient way? The bottom line is that, regardless of the type of policy change, the ultimate beneficiaries of that change should be your clients.

Note that one critical dimension worthy of careful consideration in any agency policy change is the agency's cultural competence, discussed in Highlight 6.4.

Changing Organizational Goals

We've established that *organizational goals* "are statements of expected outcomes dealing with the problem that the program is attempting to prevent, eradicate, or ameliorate" (Kettner et al., 2008, p. 123). Goals propose what an agency wants to accomplish. Rothman, Erlich, and Teresa (1981) reflect on the significance of goals:

> The collective welfare of practitioners' clients and constituents is profoundly affected by the organizational structures and goals of social agencies. Changing an organization's goals thus becomes a key task for many practitioners, and failure to accomplish this objective is frequently a great hindrance to effective practice. (p. 51)

Chapter 4 discussed organizational and agency goals in detail. Sometimes formal goals reflect an agency's real goals and sometimes they do not. Informal agency goals often replace formally stated goals. In these instances, the informal goals become the real goals the agency strives to reach. Goal displacement is a good example (discussed in Chapter 4).

In your role as agency worker, you may see that goals have become outdated. Over time, goals may become either too high or too low for the agency to accomplish effectively and efficiently. Agency goals may also become too complex or too numerous to accomplish realistically.

Changing agency goals can be significantly more difficult than changing other agency policies. Agency goals are broad and affect a wide range of agency personnel. Therefore, changing goals requires careful consideration, a broad support base, and the help of administrative decision makers. Targeting agency goals for change requires following the same basic PREPARE and IMAGINE processes you would use for other changes. However, you would proceed on the understanding that the accomplishment of change would probably be more difficult.

Changing Policies on Personnel Practices

Spiro and Farica's Case Example portrayed one type of policy change, that of increasing or reallocating personnel. Any number of other personnel policy changes will merit attention at some point in your agency life. These may include job position responsibilities, staff benefits (such as salary, health insurance, and vacation), methods of evaluating staff performance, and physical working conditions. At any point that you feel some agency condition affects the staff's ability to function optimally on behalf of their clients, you may target and pursue a policy change.

Changing Policies on Practice Procedures

Practice procedures are the means by which organizations and individuals working in them perform and conduct their work. These policies may be formal or informal.

Both formal and informal practice procedures vary endlessly from one agency to another. Examples include rules governing intervention approaches, recordkeeping methods, and staff evaluation criteria. Any aspect of worker–client intervention and interaction that you feel should be improved can be targeted for policy change.

Using IMAGINE to Change Agency Practice Procedures

To illustrate the application of IMAGINE to changing a policy on practice procedures, we will use a new example. You are a social worker in a small rural hospital. Your duties include assessments, provision of information, clarification of medical conditions, individual and family counseling, referral to

EP 2.1.8a

HIGHLIGHT 6.4

Using PREPARE and IMAGINE to Establish a Culturally Competent Empowering Organization

EP 2.1.4

One dimension of agency policy that may merit your attention in assessing possible macro change is *cultural competency*. Cultural competence in the organizational context is "a set of congruent behaviors, attitudes, policies, and structures, which come together in a system, an agency, or among professionals and enables that system, agency, or those professionals to work effectively in the context of cultural differences" (Bankhead & Ehrlich, 2005; Benjamin, 1994, p. 17; Cross, Bazron, Dennis, & Isaacs, 1989, p. 13). Nybell and Gray (2004) reflect:

> [C]ultural competence in social work organizations requires, at a minimum, that staffing, management, and leadership reflect the diversity of the client population. Achieving such a goal requires review of policies and practices related to hiring, development, promotion, and termination of personnel, as well as an assessment of the agency's standing in the communities of color served. It requires going further, to ask questions about the distribution of power in the agency. Who benefits from the current arrangements? Who is excluded or penalized? It requires a review of the allocation of resources between and among programs, with particular attention to the extent to which there is or is not equity for programs that disproportionately serve poor clients or clients of color. Where are the best-paid workers located? Where are the most workable caseloads assigned? Where does rapid turnover occur? It requires an assessment of space allocation, with an understanding that racial and cultural differences and inequalities are often built into that space, and, going further, explorations of the meanings assigned to this space by different interest groups. What is accessible and convenient and to whom? How do different interest groups perceive the arrangements of space? (p. 25)

So cultural competence is a multifocused, unifying thread connecting staff behaviors and attitudes, agency policies, and formal structure.

This intertwining theme should emphasize that every aspect of an agency's performance should be sensitive and responsive to the cultural diversity of its clientele and staff. How can the agency make clients from diverse cultural backgrounds feel as comfortable as possible in accessing agency services? How can

practitioners best communicate with clients from diverse cultures? How can staff be taught to maximize their own cultural competence? What agency policies, practices, and goals work for or against cultural competence?

You will be employed by some social services agency. Will that agency be culturally competent? You might assume, "Well, of course. It's the only ethical way to be," or "All social workers are trained to be sensitive to cultural diversity." In fact, agencies may be neither culturally competent nor particularly sensitive. Most agencies can improve on or expand their cultural competence. Agencies might need to provide continuing education for employees or expand the range of cultural competence to specific cultural groups. Some agencies may need to take a long, hard look at the entire concept of cultural competence and make major revisions in their mission statements and overall goals.

Cultural Incompetence: A Case Example

Isaacs-Shockley (1994) critiques the juvenile justice system with respect to its lack of cultural competence. She suggests that a six-point scale exists upon which agencies can be rated from extremely culturally incompetent to extremely culturally competent. She maintains that the operation of the juvenile justice system is located between "cultural destructiveness" and "cultural incapacity," the two least culturally competent points on the scale (Isaacs-Shockley, 1994, p. 19).

Culturally destructive agencies "exhibit attitudes, policies and practices that are destructive to cultures and consequently to members within the culture." She continues that in such organizations, "bigotry, coupled with vast power differentials, allows the dominant group to destroy the minority group and its culture" (Isaacs-Shockley, 1994, p. 19). In such agencies, some designated culture is considered superior to other cultures that should be subjugated, controlled, and perhaps eliminated. South Africa's now-repealed apartheid policy comes to mind.[a]

Agencies falling into the cultural incapacity category, the second-worst point on the cultural competency scale, "do not intentionally or consciously seek to be culturally destructive; rather, they lack the capacity to help persons or communities of color. The organization remains extremely biased, believes in the racial superiority of the dominant group, and assumes a paternal posture towards 'lesser' races and cultures" (Isaacs-Shockley, 1994, p. 19). Such agencies may overtly or covertly provide fewer resources to those whose culture is considered inferior, maintain racist policies, or reinforce negative stereotypes.

Isaacs-Shockley (1994) identified at least seven ways in which the juvenile justice system lies between the culturally destructive and culturally incapacitated points of the continuum (p. 20).[b] First, clients are likely to be "African American, male and poor" (p. 20; U.S. Census Bureau, 2008). Second, after entering the system, people are much less likely to reach higher educational levels or obtain better jobs than are those who are never involved in the system. Third, despite the fact that people entering the system are more likely to have "emotional disabilities, substance abuse, child abuse, and learning disabilities, they will most probably neither be assessed nor receive help for these problems" (p. 20; Stier, 2009). Fourth, many attitudes "the discretionary decision makers within the juvenile justice system hold about people of color (i.e., police officers, probation officers, prosecutors, etc.) are often based upon strong and deeply embedded racial biases and stereotypes" (p. 20). Fifth, families and communities of those youth involved in the system are allowed little input and participation. Sixth, there is a significant power imbalance in the system in terms of staff and administration, because most employees are from the dominant culture. Seventh, the system's focus is on punishment instead of treatment.

Assessing Cultural Competence

What, then, can be done to improve the juvenile justice system or any other system for the enhancement of its cultural competence? First, you as a practitioner should apply the PREPARE process to determine the viability of a macro change effort. Consider the extent of the change you are suggesting. On the one hand, you might consider making major changes in a larger organization's mission statement (which directs all of the organization's efforts). This would require significantly greater effort and resources than making a more minor but constructive change in agency in-service training policy (for example, requiring the incorporation of training sessions focusing on cultural competence).

After undertaking the PREPARE process, you might decide to pursue a macro level change. Then you would follow the IMAGINE procedure to make and implement your plans.

The following discussions regarding potential questions to raise and possible alternatives to pursue are not intended to conflict with PREPARE and IMAGINE. Rather, they are intended to enhance your ability to think about and examine the specific issue of cultural competence in your agency.

You might ask at least five fundamental examining questions aimed at assessing an organization's cultural competence:

1. *How responsible is the organization in responding effectively and efficiently to the needs of the culturally diverse people it serves* (Coggins & Fresquez, 2007; Hyde, 2003; Nybell & Gray, 2004)? Does the agency have a good grasp of the cultural diversity of its clientele? Must further research be performed to identify target clientele groups?

   To what extent does the agency create a "welcoming" climate for clients? One program director at an agency for women, called Recovery, Inc., commented on her organization's approach: "[W]e want the women who use our clinic to feel that this is a place that they can come and be comfortable, and also be involved. Our hours, the art on our walls, staff diversity, and the multilingual pamphlets and brochures are designed to make these women feel like this is their clinic" (Hyde, 2003, p. 51).

2. *In what ways is the agency empowering its staff so that staff may, in turn, empower clients from diverse backgrounds? Gutierrez and Lewis (1999) remark:*

   An empowering organization maximizes the power of its workers and constituents to participate fully in the governance of the organization. ... Organizations that empower workers to make independent decisions about their work through participatory management, communication and support from administrators, and opportunities for skill development can be more capable of empowering clients.... Access to conferences, training, workshops, and other educational opportunities is integral to the empowerment atmosphere of the organization. Staff can also be supported through flex time and other policies that encourage flexibility and self-care. Similarly, providing opportunities for staff to develop programs and professional skills that match their own personal interests is an important part of the empowerment of staff within the agency. (pp. 82-84)

   To what extent do agency staff members understand the needs, issues, and strengths of

(continued)

HIGHLIGHT 6.4 *(continued)*

their diverse client population? Does the agency recruit, support, and retain leadership and direct-service staff that reflect the client population's diversity? "[P]roviding promotions and salary increases" is one means of retaining a diverse staff (Gutierrez & Lewis, 1999, p. 84).

Hyde (2003) maintains that four values reflect agency cultural competence and empowerment. First, "[I]nclusivity means that diversity is broadly defined so that everyone belongs and 'owns' the effort" (p. 49). Everyone is included as an integral part of the agency. Second, building on strengths refers to the appreciation of diversity so that "differences are considered assets" (p. 49). A director of an agency entitled Job Training Services remarked, "What makes our agency so vital is that we believe in multiculturalism. We are a diverse staff and we all understand that it is a real benefit to have such different perspectives and experiences" (p. 49). Third, normalization "means that a multicultural perspective becomes fully ingrained in the organization"; cultural competence "is understood as a central component of agency functioning, and not a one-shot tangential, or sporadic intervention" (p. 50). Fourth, "challenging oppression ... means examining and confronting beliefs, actions, or practices that may be racist, sexist, homophobic, and so forth. This value also speaks to the need to question and, if necessary, dismantle the existing patterns of power and privilege within an agency" (p. 50). A clinic coordinator of an agency named AIDS Health Project reflected, "I believe that the heart of ... [a culturally competent organization] is taking on the hidden and not so hidden aspects of power in the agency. This means looking at who holds power and why. Is it only white men? Straight people? Professionals? This is the hard part of this work" (p. 50).

To what extent does the agency provide multicultural training to enhance "knowledge about different racial and ethnic groups" and conduct "culturally sensitive client assessments" (Hyde, 2003, p. 53)? A focus on communication skills involves "developing staff competency in direct service with clients," and teaching staff how "to listen and respond to clients, while respecting different cultural communication norms" (Hyde, 2003, p. 52).

3. *In what ways could services be administered differently in response to the needs of the agency's culturally diverse client population* (Coggins & Fresquez, 2007; Mason, 1994)? Are services being provided where they are readily accessible to culturally diverse client groups? If not, how might the agency make such services more accessible? Is the communication between agency staff and clients as effective as it could be? Should workers offer services in different languages? Can agency personnel solicit information from significant community leaders or from clients to identify and pursue better service provision?

4. *What is the "organizational vision" with respect to the culturally diverse community* (Gutierrez & Lewis, 1999, p. 83)? How might you best "envision the system as it should be and ... identify ways of funding such a system" (Mason, 1994, p. 5)? How could you maximize the involvement of people representing the diverse cultures your agency serves? How might you empower community residents? Can you and others helping you identify new potential resources for the community and the agency? Such resources might include "assisting with staff and board recruitment encouraging ... donations, identifying advocacy resources, and promoting parent or community education and support groups" (Mason, 1994, p. 5).

5. *How might you determine that the goal of cultural competence has been achieved* (Coggins & Fresquez, 2007; Mason, 1994)? What specific objectives and action steps might you identify to provide clear proof that your purpose has been actualized? What task groups might you and the agency establish to review progress, refine recommendations, and keep efforts on target?

Recommendations for Attaining Cultural Competence

After exploring the extent of your agency's cultural competence by answering questions such as those raised above, what can you do to improve the situation? Mason (1994) summarizes a number of suggestions regarding planning. One involves the identification of the client system. What aspects of cultural diversity are reflected by the client population? How would you most clearly define these client groups? Are you talking about one group or several?

Another planning suggestion entails an assessment of your agency's staff training needs to enhance cultural competence. To what extent is the agency "characterized by acceptance and respect for difference" (Lecca, Quervalu, Nunes, & Gonzales, 1998, p. 53)? What knowledge and skills do practitioners have? What do they really need to improve upon? What are their strengths and what are their deficits?

Figure out what obstacles stand in the way of your agency serving culturally diverse clients. Do they involve language differences, lack of administrative support, inadequate resources, or meager staff motivation? What problems should be your targets of change?

A further planning proposition concerns the development and achievement of goals and objectives. PRE-PARE focuses on the establishment of primary goals, and IMAGINE addresses goal-setting in a much more detailed and specific manner. The final planning suggestion entails establishing measurements to verify that objectives have indeed been attained. How can you prove that the agency has enhanced or attained its cultural competence?

Responding to the Juvenile Justice System Critique

A loose end remains in this discussion of cultural competence. What about the juvenile justice system? It is easy to complain about any system. Fixing it is more difficult. As with most problems in providing social services, financial resources are the bottom line. The trick is to figure out how to implement changes that will result in maximum benefits and minimal costs. What aspects of the huge problematic dilemmas reflected in the juvenile system would you attack first? Trying to resolve all of the issues at once would be a mammoth task. However, here we will attempt to break down some of the issues into smaller pieces, raise a few questions, and review some ideas and possibilities.

Several themes run through the criticisms presented in this highlight. One theme is punishment instead of treatment: People entering the juvenile justice system are more likely to have problems (such as substance abuse) and decreased chances for success in traditional society (that is, less chance for a good education and job). What ideas might you have to turn this around? Ideally, how would you try to increase the juvenile justice system's cultural competence?

A culturally competent agency responds effectively to the needs of the diverse population it serves.

Establishing policies that provide for treatment of problems such as substance abuse and emotional disability might empower clients. Such support might help them get to a point where further education and training, in addition to good jobs, are at least realistic possibilities for them to choose. Being addicted to crack neither allows for much learning and concentration, nor provides a very good impression when applying for a job. How might one get funding for such a treatment program? Might you write a grant application (addressed more thoroughly in Chapter 14, "Developing and Managing Agency Resources")? Could you convince politicians by proving that the total cost to society would be substantially less if young people leaving the system were healthy and capable?

What about emphasizing education and training within the system? This, too, costs money. However, what if you could establish policies that provided rewards for academic achievement? What if you could develop policies to emphasize development of self-esteem

(continued)

HIGHLIGHT 6.4 *(continued)*

and to aid in decision making concerning a future career path? Are there ways you could try to prove that these tactics would be cheaper for society in the long run and would humanely encourage people to lead productive, satisfying lives?

Another theme of the juvenile justice system critique focuses on unequal power. The argument is that decision makers in the system are biased against certain cultural groups, that most decision makers are not of these diverse cultures, and that the families of young people in the system have no input into what goes on in that system. Additionally, the point is made that impoverished African-American young men are significantly more likely to become involved in the juvenile justice system than are other groups.

What about biased decision makers? What types of policies could be developed to encourage or require training focused on cultural competence? Could citizens who support public politicians be educated regarding the importance of such a policy? Could they, in turn, put political pressure on these politicians to make far-reaching changes in how things are done in the juvenile justice system? What about recruiting more culturally diverse staff? How might that be done? Could potential

applicant populations be identified and targeted? What are the reasons that such recruitment is not successfully occurring already? Could communities and families of clients contribute ideas about how such policies might be changed?

The questions are endless. The problems are awesome. However, there may be ways in which you can start to make changes to enhance cultural competence, regardless of your agency work setting. Even tiny changes can begin the process of positive shifts in agency policy. Little by little, you might begin to work toward the goal of increased cultural competence for yourself and your agency.

Notes

a. *Apartheid* is "a policy of segregation and political and economic discrimination against non-European groups [formerly enforced] in the Republic of South Africa" (Mish, 1995, p. 53).

b. For research and statistics, see the Web site of the National Criminal Justice Reference Service at http://www.ncjrs.gov/.

necessary resources, discharge planning, and follow-up. You are concerned about the efficiency and effectiveness of a policy requiring the head nurse of each unit to verify each of your progress notes at the end of each day. The original intent was to double-check all written documents for accuracy. However, it turns out the head nurses don't have time to read the reports anyway. They typically initial each of a large volume of progress notes at the end of each day without reading a word of them. This process is inefficient and, in effect, demeaning. You feel that you and the two other hospital social workers are experienced and competent enough to complete progress notes without having them checked by unit head nurses. You already have a social work supervisor, and you resent the current policy, which gives the head nurses supervisory responsibility for your work.

IMAGINE: Start with an Innovative *Idea*

You begin with the innovative idea of changing the required reporting system in order to decrease wasted effort on the part of you and other hospital staff. You

go through the suggested steps for evaluating whether to pursue a macro change; in this case, a change in agency policy about practice procedures. You determine that the overall potential for positive change is good. You develop the following innovative idea: The hospital should abolish the practice of asking head nurses to review social workers' progress notes on a daily basis. Instead, the social work supervisor should spot-check the workers' notes periodically to maintain control of their quality.

IMAGINE: Muster Support and Formulate an Action System

You consider the agency's power structure and the potential for achieving a policy change. Your supervisor is a personable, competent woman, generally well liked among hospital staff. She gets along fairly well with the unit head nurses and with the hospital director. You believe your supervisor would provide substantial support for your ideas. She feels strongly that social workers should assume responsibility for completing their work in a professional, ethical, and conscientious way. Thus, she probably is not crazy about the head nurses' supervising social work productivity. Additionally, your supervisor spot-checks her supervisees' work anyway. Periodic review of daily progress reports would add little to her workload—an important consideration, because she probably doesn't want to make her job any more difficult or time consuming than it already is.

You also believe your two social work colleagues would support your idea. They feel as you do about having the unit head nurses check their work. They also find it inordinately unnecessary.

Your proposed action system, then, will consist of you, both of your colleagues, and your supervisor. This, of course, assumes that all three will agree to participate in the macro change process.

IMAGINE: Identify *Assets*

Your own assets include the facts that you have a good work record, you consistently complete your written work in a timely fashion, and you've formed excellent relationships with your two social work colleagues. You have a fairly good relationship with your supervisor, in addition to good relationships with most hospital staff members, including all but one of the unit head nurses. You do tend to butt heads with one head nurse who has an exceptionally condescending attitude toward you and other nonmedical staff. You swear that Ms. Hardhat eats nails for breakfast.

Another asset is your supervisor's good relationship with the hospital director and with most other hospital staff members—except for Ms. Hardhat. Still another asset is the fact that your intent is to increase efficiency without relinquishing quality of work. Your immediate supervisor will still monitor your work. Your guess is that the unit head nurses (except for Ms. Hardhat) will welcome discontinuing a bothersome, time-consuming, and meaningless task.

IMAGINE: Specify *Goals*, Objectives, and Action Steps to Attain Them

Your basic goal is to improve service efficiency by amending the policy stated earlier (an *objective),* which currently requires unit head nurses to check over and initial your daily patient progress reports. As a replacement for this practice policy, you recommend that the social worker supervisor periodically spot-check workers' daily progress notes to ensure their completion and quality.

Specific action steps leading to this objective include the following:

1. You will talk to each of your two social work colleagues by next Friday to solicit their support.
2. You will talk to your social work supervisor by two weeks from Friday to solicit her support.
3. You will determine with your supervisor the most effective strategy for implementing the policy change. For example, should she approach the unit head nurses or the hospital director about the proposed change? Should recommendations be made via a memo, an e-mail, or in person? Should the entire social work department or just the supervisor meet with decision makers?
4. You will specify further action steps for meeting your objective and achieving your goal after discussing them with your supervisor (e.g., meeting with your target system of decision makers to describe your proposed change).

IMAGINE: *Implement* the Plan

Implementing the plan, of course, simply means carrying out your action steps. Throughout this process, you can monitor your effectiveness. As it happens, things go fairly smoothly, except for some bristling on the part of Nurse Hardhat.

IMAGINE: *Neutralize* Opposition

Nurse Hardhat presents the primary opposition to your action system (the social work department). Your social work supervisor initiates a meeting with the daytime unit head nurses. At that time, Ms. Hardhat's expressed hesitations about the proposed changes are quickly dismissed. Other unit head nurses commend the change for allowing greater efficiency and creating less paperwork for them. They don't get along that well with Ms. Hardhat either, and they refuse to support her.

IMAGINE: *Evaluate* Progress

Two months after initiating the practice policy change and formulating the action system, you evaluate your progress. Your measurement of success is the fact that the new policy has been formalized, is included in the hospital's policy manual, and has become part of normal daily hospital operation. Further, there have been no problems experienced with the new system.

Looking Ahead

This chapter reviewed a process for proceeding with a macro intervention (IMAGINE). The process was then applied to the Case Example introduced in the last chapter concerning changing agency policy. The next chapter will apply the IMAGINE process to two other types of macro change—project implementation and program development within an agency setting.

Chapter Summary

The following summarizes this chapter's content as it relates to the learning objectives presented at the beginning of the chapter. Chapter content prepares social workers to:

A. *Distinguish, appraise, and integrate multiple sources of knowledge to apply the IMAGINE process involving macro intervention and evaluation.*

IMAGINE involves the following seven steps: (1) start with an innovative idea; (2) muster support and formulate an action system; (3) identify assets; (4) specify goals, objectives, and action steps to attain them; (5) implement the plan; (6) neutralize opposition; and (7) evaluate progress.

B. *Utilize a systems conceptual framework—including the macro client, change agent, target, and action systems—to initiate actions for achieving organizational goals.*

The macro client system includes those people who will ultimately benefit from the change process. The change agent system is the individual who initiates the macro change process. The target system is the system that social workers must "change or influence in order to accomplish ... [their] goals" (Pincus & Minahan, 1973, p. 78). The action system includes those people who agree with the proposal and are committed to work together to attain the proposed macro change.

C. *Demonstrate effective written communication when using memos and e-mails.*

Paper-based memos are generally used to communicate information or ideas determined to be exceptionally critical or important. E-mails involve electronic transmission of messages that are normally more informal. An e-mail may be used to send an attachment that is a memo.

D. *Describe the application of mezzo concepts to macro practice when forming an action system.*

Both group size and group member characteristics are important when composing an action system. Member commitment to purpose, leadership ability, and participation skills are significant aspects of the group process.

E. *Develop intervention goals, objectives, and action steps in order to initiate actions for achieving organizational goals.*

A goal is the ultimate "end toward which effort is directed" (Mish, 2008, p. 536). Objectives are smaller, behaviorally specific subgoals that serve as stepping stones on the way to accomplishing the primary goal. Action steps are tasks one must complete (in correct order and within the designated time frame) to achieve the desired objective—which, in turn, is designed to achieve the primary goal.

F. *Evaluate the use of collaborative and adversarial strategies to work together with colleagues, demonstrate effective communication with them, and neutralize opposition to the projected macro plan.*

Before communicating with decision makers, it's important to determine roles in advance, articulate the formulated plan, and practice the presentation ahead of time. It's also essential to anticipate decision makers' logical reactions, expect phases of resistance, and use collaborative and adversarial strategies. One should only use adversarial pressure when all else has been tried and failed, the pursuit of macro change is vitally important, and a good chance for success exists.

G. *Propose ways to analyze, formulate, and advocate for policies that advance social well-being by changing agency goals, personnel practices, and practice procedures.*

Changing agency policy may involve formal and informal aspects. Three types of agency policy that may be targeted for change are organizational goals, personnel practices, and practice procedures.

H. *Initiate actions to achieve organizational goals by examining an extensive case example demonstrating the IMAGINE process.*

The case example involved how Spiro, a staff member in a child Protective Services Unit, served as the change agent. He and other members of the action system followed the IMAGINE process and achieved some measure of success.

I. *Recognize the extent to which human diversity characterizes and shapes the human experience by assessing and enhancing cultural competence and empowerment in an agency setting.*

Cultural competence in the organizational context is "a set of congruent behaviors, attitudes, policies, and structures, which come together in a system, an agency, or among professionals and enables that system, agency, or those professionals to work effectively in the context of cultural differences" (Benjamin, 1994, p. 17). Questions were raised about the level of cultural competence apparent in the juvenile justice system. Questions assessing an organization's cultural competence include how effectively it: serves diverse clients; empowers its staff so that they, in turn, may empower their clients; considers alternative responses to diverse clients' needs; manifests an "organizational vision" that is culturally competent (Gutierrez & Lewis, 1999, p. 83); and evaluates its achievement of cultural competence goals.

Competency Notes

The following identifies where Educational Policy (EP) competencies and practice behaviors are discussed in the chapter.

EP 2.1.3c Demonstrate effective oral and written communication in working with individuals, families, groups, organizations, communities, and colleagues. *(P. 226):* Goals, objectives, and action steps should be clearly communicated.

EP 2.1.4 Engage diversity and difference in practice. *(P. 236):* It is critical that every aspect of an agency's performance should be sensitive and responsive to the cultural diversity of its clientele and staff. Social workers should advocate for changes that make their organization culturally competent.

EP 2.1.8a Analyze, formulate, and advocate for policies that advance social well-being. *(P. 235):* This Case Example illustrates how practitioners can analyze, formulate, and advocate for a policy that makes service provision more efficient and effective.

EP 2.1.8b Collaborate with colleagues and clients for effective policy action. *(P. 220):* Formulating an action system is an aspect of collaboration for effective policy action.

EP 2.1.9b Provide leadership in promoting sustainable changes in service delivery and practice to improve the quality of social services. *(P. 219):* Identifying and developing an innovative idea can demonstrate leadership.

EP 2.1.10 Engage, assess, intervene, and evaluate with individuals, families, groups, organizations, and communities. *(P. 218):* The PREPARE process, which emphasizes assessment and planning, provides the foundation for the IMAGINE approach (implementation [intervention] and evaluation), which concentrates on action with organizations and communities.

EP 2.1.10e Assess clients' strengths and limitations. *(P. 225):* Practitioners should assess the client system and other assets and strengths that may assist in the change process.

EP 2.1.10f Develop mutually agreed-on intervention goals and objectives. *(P. 226):* Practitioners should specify goals, objectives, and action steps to achieve them.

EP 2.1.10g Select appropriate intervention strategies. *(P. 228):* When appropriate, neutralizing opposition can provide an effective intervention strategy in macro practice.

EP 2.1.10m Critically analyze, monitor, and evaluate interventions. *(P. 233):* Evaluating the progress of a macro level intervention is a crucial step in the IMAGINE process.

On the Internet

Visit the *Generalist Practice with Organizations and Communities* website at *www.cengage.com/social_work/ kirst-ashman* for learning tools such as PowerPoint® slides, tutorial quizzing, Web links, and final exams.

CHAPTER 7

IMAGINE—Project Implementation and Program Development

The following are some positive reflections on macro practice:

- *How might you be able to make your job more interesting?*
- *If you could do anything you wanted to improve service provision conditions for your clients, what would you do?*
- *What kind of innovative program could your clients really use?*
- *What kind of project in your agency would you really like to sink your teeth into?*

The positive reflections stand in stark contrast to the following negative, rather depressing attitudes:

- *It's hopeless. There's nothing a plain old direct-service worker like me can do to change the system.*
- *The system's too big and impersonal. Why should I waste my time trying to fix it?*
- *I'm just an old cog in the wheel. I don't really matter in the big picture.*

Introduction

Macro practice can be an exciting, rewarding part of your professional life. Targeting large systems for change can result in momentous benefits to many clients. Chapter 6 introduced the IMAGINE process for macro change and applied it to an agency policy. This chapter will apply the IMAGINE process to two other types of macro level interventions: project implementation and program development.

Learning Objectives

This chapter will provide content concerning how social workers:

A. *Conceptualize, implement, and evaluate projects within agencies by using the IMAGINE process.*

B. *Examine and propose a number of macro practice projects.*

C. *Apply critical thinking to address macro practice dilemmas and advocate for human rights and social and economic justice.*

D. *Examine and evaluate the usefulness of Program Evaluation and Review Technique (PERT) to facilitate assessment, intervention, and evaluation in project implementation and program development.*

E. *Apply critical thinking to ethical issues concerning Temporary Assistance to Needy Families (TANF), examine the issues' implications, and propose solutions to advance human rights and social and economic justice.*

F. *Conceptualize, implement, and evaluate types of programs within agencies by utilizing the IMAGINE process.*

G. *Apply IMAGINE to the development of a sexual harassment awareness program that addresses oppression and discrimination.*

Initiating and Implementing a Project

EP 2.1.9b

Projects are directed at completing some time-limited and specific goal. This contrasts, of course, with developing a program (usually established as a permanent part of an agency's structure and service). Projects can involve testing some new treatment approach or technique, raising funds, completing a report about some aspect of agency functioning, or developing a curriculum outline for an in-service training program.

As a direct-service practitioner or lower-level supervisor, you will probably have more opportunities to plan and implement projects than to develop full-scale programs. It may also be easier to initiate a project than to change an agency policy. Workers undertaking projects usually have greater control over the tasks at hand because a project has a more limited scope. Sometimes, only the change catalyst's own work and time are affected if she is the only one working on the project. Resources, of course, are a major concern. If resources are available, along with permission and support from decision makers, then the potential for carrying out a project is probably pretty good.

Our example will assume that you, as the worker initiating a project, will remain integrally involved

throughout its implementation. This is in contrast to changing agency policy, which usually has much broader effects on numerous other staff members. Many staff members may be required to implement a policy change. Likewise, program development often requires a larger action system than does a project. Such action systems may be composed of several people, even a very large number of people. Therefore, you may remain significantly less involved in program development.

The IMAGINE process to initiate and implement a project for your agency is described next. Some aspects of planning and implementing an agency in-service training program within the IMAGINE framework will also be discussed.

We will assume that you have already completed the assessment of macro change potential described in Chapter 5. You have defined and prioritized problems and translated them into needs. You have decided which needs to address and identified your primary goals. You have also begun to assess variables working for and against your primary goals, influential people, your own risk level, and client need. Finally, you have decided that undertaking this project is the way to go at this point.

*I*MAGINE: Start with an Innovative *Idea*

Your innovative idea is becoming more and more clearly formulated in your head. Highlight 7.1 describes various types of projects you might propose in an agency setting.

IMAGINE: *Muster* Support

Determining from whom you will need to muster support for your project involves two variables. First, decide who else in the agency might be interested in helping you undertake the project. Who else feels strongly about the issue or would benefit from the project's success? Second, whom do you need to obtain permission from in order to undertake the project? Certainly, at least consider your immediate supervisor. Because a macro project is not within your own job description, you need administrative support from your supervisor and perhaps even from higher authorities in order to proceed.

Note that mustering support can be considered a form of engagement. *Engagement* is the initial period when a practitioner becomes oriented to the problem at hand and begins to establish communication and a relationship with any other individuals addressing the

HIGHLIGHT 7.1

Examples of Projects in Macro Practice

Projects, by definition, are relatively short-term, limited endeavors with specific measurable goals. There are no limits on the type of project you might dream up for your agency. Below are some examples of potential projects. It is up to you, as you work within your own agency setting, to establish what the agency's and clients' needs are. Then, only your own imagination will limit what type of project you would like to undertake. Of course, following the IMAGINE process helps to determine the project's feasibility. Nonetheless, personal creativity is key in project development. Examples of projects follow.

Meeting Clients' Special Needs

If your clients need clothing, a one-time clothing drive among community citizens would help. Or you might suggest a drive for Christmas gifts or food at Thanksgiving. One student organization conducts an annual project called "Pass-It-On," where members collect unwanted clothing and unused nonperishable foods (e.g., canned goods and dried packaged products) from students leaving the residence halls for the summer.[a] The organization then distributes these items to social service agencies in the community, such as homeless shelters and shelters for battered women, that can then dispense them to needy clients. In any of these cases, you establish a client need and plan how to meet it by initiating and implementing a project.

Fundraising Projects

Fundraising can be used for anything from research on a specific physical disability to building a new office building to sponsoring a student scholarship. It can involve projects such as bake sales, walk-a-thons (where participants solicit people to sponsor them financially for walking some designated distance), jump-rope marathons (similar to walk-a-thons, but involving jumping rope—speaking from experience, this requires considerably more stamina!), selling T-shirts or sweatshirts, or conducting raffles where winning ticketholders receive prizes. Such events often come under the auspices of a project because of their limited, short-term, goal-oriented nature. (Chapter 14 describes fundraising in greater depth.)

Evaluating Effects of Agency or Community Changes

Sometimes, changes implemented in the agency or surrounding community will affect your ability to serve clients. In such cases, you may determine that a project will be useful to evaluate the effects of the change. You might also decide that a project could help the agency or its clients adjust to the change.

Suppose your agency administration decides to change the crisis intervention services it provides to community residents. The administration determines that clients can receive a maximum of one month of crisis intervention services instead of the current three-month maximum.

You are horrified. You feel this change will seriously impede your agency's ability to provide adequate services to clients. You realize that it is essentially an administrative cost-saving measure. However, you think the administration will listen to you if you can prove that such a change will have serious negative consequences for clients. You plan a research project to evaluate the effectiveness of shortened intervention procedures.

Changes in the surrounding community can also affect an agency's ability to serve clients. Community decision makers may decide to build a superhighway through the middle of the community where most of your clients live. Your clients are outraged, but feel helpless and trapped. You have already tried to take an advocacy approach. You tried persuading decision makers to reroute the highway to another industrial area with less population. However, for various reasons, your attempts failed.

Now you consider ways to ease the transition of clients from one neighborhood to another. You begin planning a relocation project involving local realtors and landlords. You begin to think about establishing a centralized system aimed at pairing displaced homeowners and renters with new housing locations. An idea for a project is born.

Evaluation of New Intervention Approaches

You may become aware of new, more effective intervention approaches for clients. Perhaps it's a specific new technique that would be relatively easy to incorporate into agency practice, such as adopting a token "economy" for child-behavior management in a day care center.[b] A token economy (a behavior modification approach) involves the use of tokens ("reinforcers such as poker chips, coins, tickets, stars, points, or check marks" [Kazdin, 2001, p. 169]) that are earned by manifesting the

EP 2.1.6b

(continued)

HIGHLIGHT 7.1 *(continued)*

appropriate behavior and "then used to purchase ... [something desirable] such as food and other consumables, activities, and privileges" (Kazdin, 2001, pp. 169–170).

Schoolchildren participate in a clothing drive to help their community's homeless residents.

On the other hand, new intervention approaches may involve a radical change in theoretical orientation for agency practitioners. For example, after considering current research on evidence-based practice, you might determine that a shift from a psychodynamic to a cognitive treatment approach would enhance service provision and effectiveness.[c] In either of these cases, you might consider implementing a project to evaluate the effectiveness of the proposed intervention approach. Testing the approach or technique on a smaller scale can help determine whether a major agency adoption of the approach is worth the effort.

Suppose that you work in a state probation and parole department and watch scores of people age 16 or under pass through the revolving doors of "the system" again and again. You think about how senseless this is. You also note how expensive it is for the system. You

come up with an idea for providing additional intensive attention to first offenders to help keep them from returning in the future. You understand this has the potential to be a full-fledged program. However, at this point you know administrators would not buy such a radical idea without proof. How about a demonstration project, letting you implement a short-term intervention approach and then evaluating the results? If the results are positive, that is, effective and efficient, you might have a chance to develop an entirely new program.

You might be a protective services worker with an increasingly large caseload of families accused of some form of child maltreatment. Sometimes you feel that your periodic visits are like trying to plug a widening hole in a dike with your little finger. You have an idea about providing group parenting classes for some of your clients. Maybe this would be a way of offering more services to more clients in the time frame you have available. You also think about incorporating a self-help group for abusers under the umbrella of the project. Such a limited-term project might prove very effective.

Implementing Internal Agency Changes

You feel that your agency job description, written a decade ago, no longer really applies to what you do every day. You think it might be more helpful to you and your colleagues if you had a more accurate description to guide you in your day-to-day activities. You propose to your supervisor the short-term project of revising your job description.

Perhaps you work in a large hospital social services department. Your supervisor is responsible for overseeing dozens of staff members. As a result, you rarely have time to consult her about what to do with some of your most difficult cases. You come up with the idea that it would be helpful if you had access to a hospital staff psychologist for consultation purposes. The psychologist has not nearly the weighty responsibilities in this particular setting that your supervisor does. You talk to your colleagues and supervisor about your idea at the next group supervision meeting. You suggest undertaking a project in which a group of interested workers would examine the possibility of implementing this idea.

Providing Internal Services to Your Agency Staff

Some projects involve the development and provision of services to agency staff. For example, you begin to see a huge number of crystal-meth-addicted[d] clients added to your caseload. You talk to some of your colleagues and find that they're experiencing the same problem. You think that acquiring information about this problem and related treatment issues would be beneficial. You seek your supervisor's permission to use some of your work time to search the Internet for educational materials and to write a small grant to establish some agency library holdings concerning this issue.

Another example involves a group of adults who have cognitive disabilities. Many of them work in *supported competitive employment* settings overseen by another agency that provides the support. (Such settings provide work opportunities in ordinary work environments with necessary additional support such as job training, job coaching, interpersonal skill training, and transportation [Barker, 2003; Gargiulo, 2006, Hallahan & Kauffman, 2006]). You find that you have difficulty understanding exactly what your clients do at work. You think your colleagues working in other group homes run by your agency feel the same way. You propose a field trip to some of the work settings where you could observe clients' performance and talk to support staff. You feel this would provide you and your colleagues the opportunity to find out exactly what is going on in this major aspect of your clients' lives.

Notes

a. This program was developed by Michael Wallace, LCSW, an instructor at the University of Wisconsin–Whitewater.

b. *Day care* is the provision of daily caregiving and supervision for children by an individual, program, or facility when the children's guardians are unavailable to do so. In other contexts, day care may also be provided to others requiring special attention, such as people with physical or mental disabilities or older adults.

c. Psychodynamic approaches emphasize "the importance of inborn drives (particularly sexual) in determining later personality development," whereas cognitive approaches hold "[b]elief systems and thinking ... as important in determining and affecting behavior and feelings" (Sharf, 2000, pp. 6-8).

d. Crystal meth, technically *crystal methamphetamine,* is "a colorless, odorless form of d-methamphetamine, a powerful and highly addictive synthetic (man-made) stimulant. Crystal methamphetamine typically resembles small fragments of glass or shiny blue-white 'rock' of various sizes. Like powdered methamphetamine (another form of methamphetamine), crystal methamphetamine is abused because of the long-lasting euphoric effects it produces" (Frontline, 2006; National Drug Intelligence Center, 2003, p. 1). Because it is exceedingly addictive, extremely serious physical and mental effects typically result after repeated use.

Source: : Many of these projects are examples suggested by Kettner, Daley, and Nichols in *Initiating Change in Organizations and Communities* (Monterey, CA: Brooks/Cole, 1985).

problem. The practitioner, then, engages others by nurturing their interest in the change process.

IMAGINE: Identify *Assets*

EP 2.1.10e

Consider the four basic types of assets when initiating a project. The first is *time:* What is the anticipated duration of the project, and how much staff time will be necessary to complete it? Second, what *skills* are needed, and who has them? Are special therapeutic or accounting skills needed to pursue the project? Are the special skills of a consultant necessary? Third, what type *of staffing* is necessary to complete the project? How many staff members need to be involved? How much clerical help is needed? Fourth, what *financial resources* might be available to support the project? The opposite side of this coin involves the project's costs. For example, will the project require paper, postage, long-distance phone calls, or mileage reimbursement? Must you hire a consultant to help with a research

design or an expert to present a certain specialized type of in-service training?

IMAGINE: Specify *Goals,* Objectives, and Action Steps to Attain Them

EP 2.1.10f

Goals provide direction regarding how to proceed. As in other types of generalist intervention, project implementation should be broken down into measurable objectives and then into smaller action steps that are both behaviorally specific and measurable (that is, each action step specifies who, what, and when).

Suppose that you create a broad, primary goal of raising some money for a group of needy clients. The way you determine how to achieve this goal creates objectives that might include initiating fundraisers in the form of a bake sale and a telephone solicitation drive. These objectives then require a series of action steps. Who will contribute to the bake sale and set up tables? Who will organize the telephone crews, track pledges, and monitor results? How will money be funneled to people in need? Your own goal—and its objectives and action steps—will raise its own specific questions that need to be addressed.

IMAG/NE: *Implement* the Plan

EP 2.1.10g

Establishing goals, objectives, and action steps is an integral part of establishing a project strategy that maps out the entire project from beginning to end. One useful means of formulating and illustrating a plan is a PERT (Program Evaluation and Review Technique) chart (Federal Electric Corporation, 1963; NetMBA, 2007; Sheafor & Horejsi, 2009). A *PERT chart* is a flow chart or time chart that depicts a series of tasks or activities in the order that such tasks should be done to achieve project goals. Such a plan can guide the project planning and implementation process, and force action system members to anticipate and address potential problems.

The original PERT charts developed for industry were quite complicated and intricate. Today's charts include a variety of simpler formats adapted to individual and small group use. Therefore, we refer to the PERT formats illustrated in Figure 7.1 as being "amended" or revised.

You can depict PERT chart tasks horizontally or vertically. Necessary activities might be pictured in boxes connected by lines and plotted along a time line. Each sequence of activity boxes reflects the plan for how each goal should be achieved.

PERT charts assume a number of forms. In addition to having either a horizontal or vertical format, they illustrate individual tasks in various ways. For example, you can connect sequences of simple statements instead of specifying tasks. Likewise, in a complicated chart you can use a series of codes, such as numbers or letters, to indicate tasks or time frames instead of writing them out. You would then provide a key to explain the meaning of each number or letter.

It should be noted that for the purposes of simplicity and clarity, the PERT chart illustrated in Figure 7.1 displays only *one* objective accomplished by one person's series of action steps. In reality, multiple project objectives and tasks must often be accomplished simultaneously by different members of the action system.

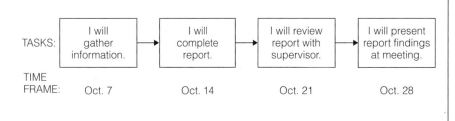

HORIZONTAL FORMAT WITH TIME LINE AT BOTTOM

As illustrated here, PERT charts can assume either a horizontal or a vertical format. Horizontal formats can depict a time line either at the bottom or at the top of the page. Vertical formats usually depict time lines on the left side of the page. It is important that the time frame for the completion of each task be very clear. It is also critical that tasks be illustrated in their correct sequence. Generally speaking, the completion of one task depends upon the completion of the task listed sequentially before it. Hence, you can clearly illustrate your plan for completion of some designated goal in a step-by-step sequence.

VERTICAL FORMAT WITH TIME LINE AT LEFT SIDE

FIGURE 7.1 Examples of Amended PERT Chart Formats

One or more of your tasks might depend upon others completing their tasks first. For example, another member of the action system may develop a list of resources for the in-service program, and your report depends upon having this data available. Thus, PERT charts can become more complex as tasks and participants increase in number.

PERT Charts Illustrate Objectives and Action Steps

PERT charts provide pictures of how the five elements involved in planning relate (Barker, 2003; NetMBA, 2007). The first element in planning entails the plan's goals, objectives, and action steps necessary to attain the goal(s). A PERT chart readily identifies a project's objectives and action steps. It's important that they all be both necessary and in the right order. The PERT charts in Figure 7.1 portray the objective of presenting informational findings at a designated agency meeting, the goals being to improve communication and share vital information with other staff. This is a pretty straightforward and simple objective.

PERT Charts Portray Specific Tasks

The second element in planning concerns the specific tasks and activities necessary for achieving each objective. Such tasks are the action steps you need to complete in order to accomplish your objectives and to attain your ultimate goal. Before presenting an informational report, you need to get the information. You probably also want to check it over with your supervisor for approval before sharing it with other agency staff members at an agency meeting. You need to have something in hand to show to your supervisor. Therefore, you need to write the report first.

PERT Charts Depict Task Sequence

The third important element in planning is specifying the necessary order in which action steps should take place, keeping three suggestions in mind (Rubin & Rubin, 2001). First, make sure that the sequence of tasks makes sense. For example, you would complete a report before submitting it to administration for approval. Second, make sure you note to yourself what activities should be given top priority. What tasks are absolutely necessary to achieve the most important objectives? You can use this to guide you when you are rushed and must make fast decisions about what you can and cannot do. Finally, think about the potential barriers and problems you might face when implementing the activities on the chart. Anticipating

problems before they occur can give you ideas about how to prevent or solve them.

Figure 7.1's PERT charts have the objective of presenting an informational report at a designated agency meeting. The end result or final activity in the sequence, then, is your presentation of the report at the actual meeting. However, before being able to accomplish that, you must gather the information you need. Second, you must pull the information into a form that makes sense. You must do this in preparation for presenting it for your supervisor's approval. Finally, you must sit down and review the completed report with your supervisor. All this must occur in the designated sequence so that you can present the report at the meeting, your final objective.

PERT Charts and Necessary Resources

The fourth element in planning involves the resources needed to complete the plan that PERT charts can compel you to think about. The charts illustrated in Figure 7.1 make a number of assumptions about resource availability, even though they do not mention specific resources as such. For one thing, they assume that whatever information you need for the report is available to you. The report might involve anything from an assessment of clients' needs to exploration of parking availability in your agency's lot. If the information you need to complete the report is not available, you will probably have to include additional steps in your PERT chart. For example, before the step identified as "I will gather the information," you might insert a new step, "I will identify information sources."

Another assumption in Figure 7.1's PERT chart is that you will have ready access to your supervisor to review findings with her. And it is also assumed that you will have the basic equipment (e.g., computer and accompanying apparatus) and office supplies with which to write the report.

PERT Charts Establish a Time Frame

The fifth element in planning is the time line for the plan's completion (Brody, 2005; NetMBA, 2007). How long will it take to complete each task and activity necessary for achieving objectives? How much time should you allow yourself to complete various aspects of the plan? How long should the entire plan take?

Both formats have a time line along one edge. The time lines in these particular charts illustrate weekly deadlines for achieving each of the four action steps. The intent is to complete each one and, eventually, reach the objective by the indicated target date. PERT formats in Figure 7.1 depict completion of the following tasks in the following order: (1) gathering information by October 7; (2) completing the report by October 14; (3) reviewing the report with your supervisor by October 21; and (4) presenting the report findings at a designated meeting by October 28.

Time lines on PERT charts can reflect virtually any units of time: days, months, or years, depending on the specified objectives. How do you establish the time frame for each activity in the sequence? Think about two issues. First, who will be responsible for accomplishing the activity? If more than one person is involved in implementing the project, the individual responsible for completing each task should be noted on the chart. Second, how long will it realistically take to complete each activity? This should be clearly noted on the chart. Each activity should be completed by the time indicated.

Advantages of PERT Charts

Advantages of PERT charts are numerous. They provide a general outlook on the entire project planning process. This allows you to coordinate a number of activity sequences at the same time in addition to foreseeing potential snares. Likewise, PERT charts establish time frames and deadlines for evaluating progress.

CASE EXAMPLE

A PERT Chart for Developing an In-Service Training Project

Suppose your primary goal is to improve service provision by enhancing workers' skills. You develop the bright idea that you and your colleagues could really use some input and training on a certain aspect of practice—resolving ethical dilemmas, dealing with hostile clients, or testifying in court. You determine that an in-service is a good objective to help achieve your goal. You also decide that it is worth your own effort to initiate the idea and try to implement it.

Figure 7.2 illustrates the PERT chart you might use for initiating and implementing your agency in-service training project. The following section applies PERT to your efforts.

In Figure 7.2, the time line on the PERT chart's left-hand side shows your intent to complete the planning process for the in-service training program during the month of February. Therefore, dates indicated include anticipated deadlines in February. As the lower left-hand side of Figure 7.2 indicates, dates for the actual

in-service programming are to be determined. This is because you cannot finalize these dates until you check with both administrators and speakers to establish convenient dates.

As you pursue your macro goal, your micro- and mezzo-level generalist practice skills will come into play again and again. You will use these skills as you communicate with, attempt to persuade, and possibly confront each individual or group of individuals within the macro system you are trying to persuade or change. All such staff members have individual personalities (it's tempting to use the word "peculiar" instead of "individual"). Thus, we will discuss this example of a PERT chart in the context of a specific agency with specific personnel.

You know that you need agency approval for expending staff members time. You might also need some monetary support to pay the person presenting the training sessions. Such payment, of course, depends on what speaker you get.

The first step in getting agency approval is checking out your idea with your direct supervisor. Your supervisor is a bright, straightforward person who loves the outdoors and has a gruff manner. You've often thought that he was probably a lumberjack in another life. Although he is forceful, he also has a very democratic style. You know that he typically encourages staff members to pursue innovative ideas with little interference. As you anticipate, your direct supervisor gives you a clear go-ahead.

By February 3, you will develop a staff interest survey that polls staff members regarding their interest in an in-service training session. Because you already have an idea about what you think is needed, you might ask them questions such as, "On a scale from 1 to 10, how interested are you in the proposed topic?" or "On a scale from 1 to 10, how likely are you to attend such an in-service?" You might also ask staff members for ideas about the most essential in-service topics. This last question may determine whether your proposed topic is indeed the one that staff members would support most heartily. It might also help gather ideas for future in-services. Be cautious, however, about the number of open-ended questions you include: Contrast a survey where staff members are asked merely to check the topics about which they would like additional training (close-ended) with one where respondents write their own choices (open-ended). The former survey results can be quickly summarized; the latter will take longer but will potentially provide you with a broader range of information.

FEBRUARY   EVENTS AND ACTIVITIES

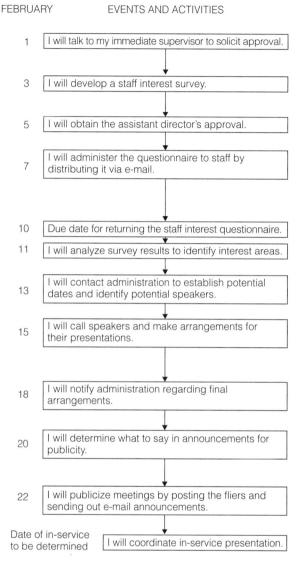

FIGURE 7.2 An Example of a PERT Chart for Developing an In-Service Training Project

The next person from whom you need permission in order to proceed is the agency's assistant director. You need to develop the questionnaire ahead of time because all documents distributed throughout the agency require her approval. Your plan is to make an appointment with her by February 5 to show her the questionnaire and discuss your in-service idea. You anticipate more resistance from this administrator than from your supervisor.

The assistant director is an intense person who seems to need excessive control over what goes on in the agency. She is hesitant to "rock the bureaucratic boat." She wants no uncontrolled changes to disrupt any of the agency's daily routines. She typically scrutinizes every tiny detail before providing support for any new project or proposal.

However, you feel that you can persuade her by emphasizing the need for continuing education hours (CEHs). These are given for training provided to professionals after they receive their formal degrees and are working in the field. State licensing boards for social workers of the require practitioners to complete a designated number of CEHs annually or biannually in order to continue in the profession. This is the case in your state. The fact that CEHs are required will fortify your argument to the assistant director that in-service training is necessary. You also plan to argue that providing such training in your own agency saves substantial staff time. Staff members who attend do not have to spend lengthy travel time to get to the training.

During the presentation, you note that this will be training that staff members clearly want and need. You emphasize the importance of the questionnaire in terms of verifying interest and need. Finally, you stress that you have some speakers in mind who would require little if any funding. (Local speakers usually receive reimbursement for mileage to and from the presentation and meals during the period they allocate to your agency. An honorarium may also be given in appreciation of their time and effort. This may be of any amount.) You ask her if any funding is available for expenses and honorariums for local speakers or to pay consultants or experts brought in from farther afield.

Predictably, the assistant director emphasizes that local speakers would be better. You think she really means that local speakers would be cheaper. However, you do have some good local people in mind, so you are willing to go along with her wishes.

With the assistant director's okay, you e-mail the questionnaire to the staff. You complete this process as planned by February 7. You state the due date for returning the questionnaire responses as February 10. You realize that some staff members will probably not return their questionnaire on time. As a matter of fact, because you've worked in the agency for quite a while, you can pretty much predict who will return their questionnaires as requested and who will drag their feet.

For example, consider Reid, whose desk and office are stuffed with stacks and stacks of papers gradually tipping over like crumbling skyscrapers and spilling onto the floor. Reid is renowned for losing anything sent to him. However, you have come to expect this. When he inevitably fails to respond, you believe he must take responsibility for his actions, so you usually proceed without his input. You decide to stick with your deadline of February 10, even with Reid.

To compensate for staff members who fail to return their input on time, you plan to talk briefly with some of the tardy types on February 10 and administer the brief questionnaire verbally. If enough staff members express their interest by promptly responding, those who do not respond will not matter that much.

On February 11, you will analyze and tabulate the results of the survey. This will allow you to exactly determine the areas of interest expressed by the staff. You may learn, for example, that the staff wants in-service training on working with chemical dependency clients or handling crisis situations. The staff's feedback may be even more varied, with expressed interest in five or six different needs. You will need to allow yourself enough time to review and summarize the findings—the amount of time will depend on the number and complexity of questionnaires responses returned.

By February 13, you contact the assistant director again to share the questionnaire results. During a phone conversation with her, you are able to report adequate support from the staff, identify potential dates when administration would allow staff to attend, and pinpoint potential speakers. You clarify with the assistant director that the staff will be encouraged to attend the in-service training during regular work hours, but will not be required to attend. You and the assistant director feel that getting some time away from their regular workload to participate in this activity will provide an adequate incentive.

It should be noted that when you first establish your project plan via a PERT chart, you assume that both administration and other staff members will ultimately support your project. If at any point they don't, you can either halt the planning process and forget the whole idea or revise your time line to add the necessary steps to overcome their resistance.

You anticipate a busy time between February 10 and 15. You must summarize the information gathered on the questionnaires and contact potential speakers. You have already established a series of possible in-service dates with the assistant director. You allow yourself an additional three days, from February 15 to 18, to contact potential speakers and allow them to check their schedules and get back to you. On February 18, you

notify both your direct supervisor and the agency's assistant director of your finalized plan: The agency will sponsor the first in-service on March 22. (Remember: Always keep administrators informed! Notify the administration regularly about where you are in the planning process.) Even though you have already solicited administrative support, you still need to maintain it.

By February 20, you write the announcements that will alert staff to the in-service's speakers and the event's date, which is March 22. You e-mail staff with the announcement by February 22. By then you also copy and post fliers throughout the agency with the information. For this you choose hot pink paper in order to get the staff's attention. You breathe a sigh of relief until March 22 approaches. At that time your responsibilities will resume as you oversee the in-service itself, introduce the speakers, and generally troubleshoot for any potential problems.

IMAGINE: *Neutralize* Opposition

After implementation, the sixth step in the IMAGINE process is neutralizing any opposition. Here it means removing any impediments that might obstruct your project's progress. In the case of the in-service training program, opposition might

EP 2.1.10g

assume the form of another agency supervisor complaining about the in-service as a waste of his staff's time. Or something unexpected might come up to interfere with the project. For example, your speaker might call you at 6:30 A.M. on the day of the in-service to tell you that she's got a horrible case of the flu and can't make it. Whatever potential problems develop, it will be your job to figure out solutions.

Murphy's Law states that "anything that can go wrong will go wrong" (Mish, 2008, p. 818). Corollaries to Murphy's Law include the following:

1. Nothing is as easy as it looks.
2. Everything takes longer than you think.
3. If there is a possibility of several things going wrong, the one that will cause the most damage will be the one to go wrong.
4. If you perceive that there are four possible ways in which a procedure can go wrong and circumvent these, then a fifth way will promptly develop.
5. Left to themselves, things tend to go from bad to worse.

6. Whenever you set out to do something, something else must be done first.

7. Every solution breeds new problems.

8. It is impossible to make anything foolproof because fools are so ingenious.

9. Nature always sides with the hidden flaw. (Bloch, 1977, p. 11)

One more corollary might be added to this list: Murphy was an optimist.

The effective social worker will not become totally depressed, throw in the towel, and forget the whole idea, but rather acknowledge that situations, and the variables in any particular situation, change constantly. It is the case in micro systems, and it is certainly the case in large, complex macro systems. It's important to remember that specific plans like PERT charts, however wonderful, must give way to unexpected changes, which can curtail the best-planned activities and cause projects to run amok. Always be vigilant and flexible. Plans can and often should be changed. You need to navigate your project through the entire implementation process, responding to new issues, needs, and problems as they arise.

Essentially, two major responsibilities characterize the neutralizing opposition step in the project implementation process. First, ongoing *coordination* is necessary to keep all participants involved in the implementation process working together and on schedule. The second responsibility involves regular *checking* that each designated activity sequence is completed in a timely and effective manner. Each completed step reflects progress toward the designated goal.

IMAGIN*E*: *Evaluate* Progress

EP 2.1.10m

You should state project objectives so clearly that it is readily apparent when each objective is met. When proposing objectives, keep in mind how they will be evaluated. Establishing specific, easily measurable objectives at the very beginning of the planning process will make evaluating their attainment easier.

Projects and Diversity

Projects can address any of a wide range of needs, including those of diverse ethnic, cultural, and racial groups. Highlight 7.2 provides an example of a project concerning substance abuse prevention for Puerto Rican adolescents.

Developing a Program

The second macro intervention approach this chapter addresses is program development. Along with initiating agency policy changes and implementing projects, you may well have the opportunity to set a whole new program in motion in your agency.

EP 2.1.9b

Chapter 5 established that, in the context of social services, a *program* (also referred to as a *social program*) is an ongoing configuration of services and service provision procedures intended to meet a designated group of clients' needs. Social programs provide the means for generalist practitioners to offer help and services to clients. When necessary social programs don't exist or when they are inadequate to meet clients' needs, you may determine that you should pursue program development. Highlight 7.3 presents a series of dilemmas illustrating why generalist practitioners need program development skills.

We propose a number of steps to follow in the program development process. We have arbitrarily designated their order, because sometimes in real practice you will not follow these steps in order. Your plan and process will depend on a wide range of variables, from agency environments to administrative personalities to designated job descriptions. However, these steps reflect the issues and activities you should consider when trying to develop a program. The steps are grouped according to the IMAGINE paradigm.

A case example later in this chapter follows the development of a sexual harassment awareness program in a large social service agency. This is only one of the many types of programs you might initiate within your own agency.

*I*MAGINE: Start with an Innovative *Idea*

As you know, the first step is developing an *idea*. You become aware of some deficit in available resources or some malfunction in service delivery. Two suggestions apply to this phase: Make certain you work with your client system and clearly articulate your program goals.

Work with Your Client System

This means that you must work closely with the people who will be receiving the services provided by the new program. In macro practice, it also entails working with other professionals, organizations, and agencies that

HIGHLIGHT 7.2

A Project Example: Substance Abuse Prevention for Puerto Rican Adolescents

We have emphasized that the types of projects you can initiate are endless. They can target any need or problem, deal with any staff or client population, and occur in any social services setting. It is of special importance to address the needs of diverse ethnic and cultural groups, who often are populations at risk of discrimination, economic deprivation, and oppression.

EP 2.1.4

Delgado (1998a, 1998b) describes a project conducted by Nuevo Puente (New Bridge), an agency established by a federal Center on Substance Abuse Prevention grant. The grant targeted *at-risk youth,* young people who, because of their life circumstances, are potentially susceptible to a range of social adjustment problems, including emotional or behavioral troubles, health difficulties, school failure, inadequate preparation for adult employment, or poverty (McWhirter, McWhirter, McWhirter, & McWhirter, 2007). "Latinas/os are the fastest growing racial/ethnic group in the United States"; they are vulnerable in that their high school drop out rates surpass those of any other group (Casas, Raley, & Vaszuez, 2008, p. 130). "Puerto Rican young people are thought to be the most vulnerable of all Latino groups to leaving school, being under- or unemployed, experimenting with 'hard' drugs, having poorer health status, and being involved with the criminal justice system" (Delgado, 1998b, p. 213).

To address the substance abuse problem, Nuevo Puente emphasized the importance of understanding three key concepts with respect to this population— "resilience," "self-esteem," and "coping strategies" (Delgado, 1998b, pp. 214–215; 2002). *Resilience* in this context is the strength and "ability to resist risk-taking behavior" (p. 214). *Self-esteem* is one's inner sense of one's own value. Lack of self-esteem can result in feelings of dislike for oneself and of lack of control over one's destiny. Nuevo Puente's philosophy reflected that "lack of pride in one's ethnic background" can directly relate to low self-esteem (Delgado, 1998b, p. 214). *Coping strategies* are behaviors and choices used to contend with and survive stress. Nuevo Puente's philosophy held that "youths are less likely to engage in problematic or risk-taking behavior as a means of coping if they have high self-esteem and a positive social network and are provided with opportunities to help themselves and their community" (Delgado, 1998b, p. 215).

EP 2.1.10i

Therefore, Nuevo Puente staff members viewed substance abuse as a much more complicated issue than appeal of or addiction to alcohol or drugs. Rather, they could see that increasing young people's resilience, theoretically, would *decrease* their substance abuse. Resilience is strengthened by increased self-esteem. Self-esteem, in turn, is fortified by enhanced cultural pride and confidence in one's own abilities.

The project had three primary facets. First a 72-hour training curriculum was used to enhance the youths' "cultural pride (Puerto Rican history, values, culture, arts, and traditions)"; "group leadership skills"; "self-sufficiency and self-determination; communication and relationship skills"; and tactics for addressing substance abuse (Delgado, 1998b, p. 217). Nuevo Puente's second dimension was a peer education and leadership program, where trained youth taught other adolescents about positive attitudes, facts about substance abuse and its consequences, and decision-making skills to attain positive outcomes.

Nuevo Puente's third facet helped adolescents involve themselves in a range of community activities. Such involvement can reinforce self-esteem and resilience, in addition to providing preventative information about substance abuse and preparing adolescents for future leadership roles. Activities included a number of teaching events such as a Three Kings' Day (a Puerto Rican holiday) celebration where participants performed Puerto Rican dances and presented skits about adolescents' encounters with substance abuse. Participating youths also prepared two videotapes aimed at community education that highlighted their Nuevo Puente experience and organized a car wash to finance a trip (where they solicited community businesses as sponsors). Finally, the adolescents conducted a *community assets assessment,* a systematic appraisal of the community's strengths that included individuals, associations, businesses, service providers, and institutions that contribute or could contribute to the community's well-being.

Upon evaluation, project results were quite positive (Delgado, 1998a, 1998b). Participants' school attendance improved dramatically. Qualitative interviews revealed how many youths felt "they developed greater pride in their heritage, learned the importance of group solidarity, discovered that their relationships with adults in authority positions revealed 'another side' to adults, and learned the importance of addressing all forms of substance abuse in the community" (Delgado, 1998b, p. 221).

can help you initiate and implement the new program. Other individuals and systems can help provide you with information about clients' needs and can assist you in the program development process. Working with the client system means that you remain open to feedback and strive to be responsive to the needs of others involved in the process.

Suppose your goal is to help homeless people by developing a program for them in an urban community. It is absolutely essential to involve homeless clients fully in the program development process. What good would it be to enthusiastically expend a great deal of energy developing a plan you think would be good for them if it is not something they want or believe they need? Perhaps converting an old department store into a series of apartments would be an utter turn-off to potential clients. They might be more interested in refurbishing deserted homes owned by the city because of the prior owners' failure to pay taxes. In this case, the homeless people who would benefit from the program would need a way to purchase the homes and the resource assistance necessary for fixing them up if they do all the work. Some cities support urban homestead programs where deserted homes are sold to people for $1 and materials for home refurbishment (paint, lumber, and plumbing and electrical supplies) are provided. People purchasing the homes agree to fix them up to abide by city codes (concerning electric wiring, heating, and water standards), live in the homes for some specified period of time (at least two or three years), and eventually pay back the city for the repair materials the city provided.

Articulate the Proposed Program's Purpose

EP 2.1.3c

The primary goals and objectives of the proposed program must be very clear in your own mind. You must be able to articulate them clearly and straightforwardly to others in order to solicit support. A program's purpose has three facets: defining the unmet need, identifying the clientele, and specifying the services to be provided. Following are examples of each.

Clearly define and document the unmet client needs. For example, you might be a social worker for a county department of social services. Your job involves helping clients who receive financial assistance. You provide counseling and assist these people in their job searches. You discover that most of your clients, primarily single mothers with one to four children, have tremendous difficulty finding reasonably priced and satisfactory day care facilities to care for children while they work. In order to develop either a day care program or a referral program for day care facilities, you would need to document clearly the need for such a program by performing a needs assessment. Needs assessments use procedures to measure a system's needs. Data is gathered and appraised to establish priorities for program planning and development. You might develop a questionnaire for public assistance recipients examining their day care needs. Or you might consult the state licensing agency that licenses day care facilities to find out how many facilities and what kinds are available in your area. You could call each facility and get information about costs, hours, and whether they accept infants.[1] If you can establish on paper real facts and statistics that the demand for day care significantly outweighs that which is available, then you have strengthened your argument for program development.

Identify the clientele who will receive services. Exactly whom will the program serve? In the day care program example, clients would include women receiving public assistance and their children. Essentially, anyone who applied for and received assistance could potentially apply for a job and, ultimately, use the day care services. Such participants would be included in the designated client population.

---

1. Day care facilities may not accept infants and children who are not toilet-trained because of the additional care and attention such children demand.

HIGHLIGHT 7.3

Why Program Development Is Relevant to You

EP 2.1.10g

Below are three vignettes illustrating how direct service workers can run into dilemmas that block them from providing needed services. What would you do if you, as a professional generalist practitioner, ran into similar glitches? Each dilemma could be solved through undertaking program development.

Dilemma A

You are a social worker in a Veterans Affairs (VA) hospital in East Los Angeles. The VA, a federal organization established in 1920, provides people who have served in the military with a wide range of services to enhance their overall health and welfare; services include those directed at physical and mental illness, vocational training, financial assistance, and a host of others. Specifically, you work in a unit that provides short-term housing and alcohol- and other drug-abuse (AODA) treatment for homeless veterans. You're finding that more and more of your clients come to you and tell you they simply can't find any full-time jobs, even for minimum wage. You find yourself thinking more frequently, "Even a full-time minimum wage job is pretty much a bummer in terms of taking care of yourself."

The issue, you believe, boils down to adequate job training. Why can't the VA provide educational and vocational training or finance the purchase of this training through some other agency? You have looked for resources to help your clients get back on their feet. They need work that is relatively permanent, provides an adequate standard of living, and enhances their self-esteem. What you and your clients really need is a job training program with a strong educational component. But there isn't one. Now what?

Dilemma B

You are an intake worker for the Sheboygan County Department of Social Services. The county is primarily rural, with a smattering of small towns. Your job is primarily to receive calls from people requesting services, gather initial information about them and their problems, provide them with some information about your county services, and make appropriate referrals to the agencies they need.

You are alarmed at the growing number of calls about older adults having difficulty maintaining themselves in their own homes. Most calls come from neighbors or relatives, some from older adults themselves. Examples of concerns include worries about falling and remaining stranded for days; forgetfulness, such as leaving the stove's gas burner on; lack of transportation to get to important appointments, for example, doctors' appointments; difficulties in understanding complicated health insurance and Medicare reimbursements; and depression caused by loneliness and isolation.

You typically refer such callers to the department's Protective Services for Older Adults unit. However, you know that all that unit can do is make an assessment home visit and either refer the older adult to a local nursing home or terminate the case. That's depressing. Many of those people only need company and supportive help to maintain their independent living conditions.

You have heard of programs providing such support elsewhere in the state. It would be great to have a program whose staff or volunteers could visit similar clients, help them with daily tasks, transport them to recreational or other activities, and generally provide friendly support. Such programs would help these older adults and allow them to remain in their own homes. There is no such program in your county. Is there anything you can do to initiate one?

Dilemma C

You are a school social worker in large, urban Warshawski High School. The pregnancy rate is soaring. An amazing 21 percent of all female students become pregnant by the time they graduate (or would have graduated, because many drop out because of pregnancy). A Planned Parenthood agency two miles away provides counseling about reproductive choices, contraception, and related health services such as pregnancy tests and physical examinations in preparation for using contraception. However, not many students are using its services.

The school requires all students to participate in a Family Life Education program (except for those students whose parents withhold permission). This program includes some content on human sexuality, including basic "plumbing" information (who has what sexual parts and what those sexual parts are called), with plenty of detail about fallopian tubes and epididymises. It also offers content on sexually transmitted infections. Other content stresses abstinence, focusing on the "Just Say NO!" approach to avoiding pregnancy. Both the school board and the school administration strongly forbid the discussion of contraception. They have openly stated that such content only encourages promiscuity by giving students permission for sexual experimentation.

You feel strongly that students need additional, accurate information on sexual issues, such as contraception and emotional relationships. They also require ready access both to contraceptives and to counseling on contraceptive use. Students are not getting this and, thus, suffer the consequences. You are aware of the research establishing that such programs have significantly decreased pregnancy rates and the transmission of sexually related infections in other high schools in similar settings. What can you do?

Commentary

Each dilemma represents the type of predicament that may well face you in practice. You may find yourself in a social work position with a fairly clear job description. (Job descriptions are just that. They describe the specific tasks and responsibilities you will be held accountable for while performing your job. Some job descriptions also include educational and certification requirements or types of experiences required in order to get the job to begin with and to continue to hold it. Generally, job descriptions summarize the tasks you get paid for doing.) However, in these dilemmas, the workers found that what their clients sorely needed was not available. There were gaps in the service delivery system. That is, significant numbers of people had needs that, to the worker's knowledge, no agency or program was addressing.

It was not really in any of the workers' job descriptions to do anything about these problematic client situations. However, each worker was forced to face each problem with increasing frequency. These problems, through no fault of the workers, were seriously impeding their ability to serve clients effectively.

We have established that one of the many reasons that macro practice is important for generalist practitioners is that many times "The System," whichever one it may be, is not doing the right thing. Usually, either the system is not serving clients the way it is supposed to (consider the discussion of goal displacement in Chapter 4), or, as in the previous dilemmas, the services clients need simply do not exist. Hence, we address the concept of *program development:* A program needs to be developed in order to meet clients' needs.

There will be times in a worker's career when resources desperately needed by clients will not exist. At these times, workers must determine whether it is possible, practical, and worth their effort to pursue the development of some new program. Often, workers will not be alone. There will be others—clients, administrators, colleagues, and persons in other agencies—who also support the establishment of badly needed services.

State the services the program would provide. In other words, clearly state the purpose of the program so that everyone involved understands what the proposed program would do. Continuing with the day care example, such a program might include provision of day care services by qualified providers. The plan might require potential day care providers to undergo some type of screening process before being hired. Daily day care services might be at a centralized location in the community and be open from 6:00 A.M. to 6:00 P.M. every day except Sunday. The agency might accept children of any age, including infants.

Highlight 7.4 provides another example concerning the importance of clearly articulating a program's purpose and the services it will provide.

IMAGINE: *Muster* Support

It is difficult, if not impossible, to initiate and establish a new program or service completely by yourself. You need support from a variety of other sources (Hasenfeld, 2001; Rubin & Rubin, 2008). As the change catalyst, you can solicit a steady source of support by establishing your action system. Such a group "then gathers resources and influence, actively representing the new program's objectives, and fights for its support in the community" (Hasenfeld, 2001, p. 461). Additionally, a group forming an action system can help you identify and articulate the primary goals for the proposed program; specify the client systems that will receive services; target potential financial resources for the programs; and share information about the program, its goals, and objectives with other groups, agencies, and organizations within the community such as the city council, the county government, and the mental health board (Hasenfeld, 2001; Kretzmann & McKnight, 1993).

Choose action system members very carefully. Chapter 3, which focused on using group skills for organizational and community change, examined task groups and their membership. You want motivated individuals who are seriously interested in the proposed program. You might also solicit support from

HIGHLIGHT 7.4

Ethical Questions and Critical Thinking about Public Assistance: Empowerment or Oppression for Women?

EP 2.1.8a

The example chosen here to illustrate the need to articulate a program's purpose when initiating program development is the current public assistance system described below. Instead of empowering people to support their families, the system inflicts constraints and rules on recipients, which are considered by many to be controlling and punitive. Issues include no provision for education and skill-building to get better jobs; insufficient limited health care; impositions on family structure (for example, encouraging marriage by providing financial incentives); and lack of adequate day care. When considering any kind of program development a worker must think about the many possible implications the program could have for clients.

In 1996, Congress passed the Personal Responsibility and Work Opportunity Reconciliation Act, which set up a new grant program. Temporary Assistance for Needy Families (TANF). This put a limit on federal funding given to states and gave states flexibility in administering the money to families (Popple & Leighninger, 2008). It essentially replaced Aid to Families with Dependent Children (AFDC), a program that provided financial assistance to eligible families in need for decades. "TANF was reauthorized in February 2006 under the Deficit Reduction Act of 2005" (Office of Family Assistance, 2007).

In contrast to AFDC, TANF establishes time limits for receipt of benefits (Popple & Leighninger, 2008). Clients must find work within two years of beginning the program and can receive no more than five years of benefits in their lifetime (Administration for Children and Families, 2006). This is a huge change from AFDC, where "people received assistance as long as they satisfied the program's eligibility rules, which were set by the individual states under federal guidelines" (Abramovitz, 1997, p. 312).

Programs and their policies can immensely affect the lives of people who receive benefits and services. The core of program development in the social services is to meet people's needs. Many questions can be raised regarding TANF, its effectiveness, and its rigidity.

TANF and Work

TANF requires recipients to work. Additionally, TANF "narrows the definition of work activities the government will fund, ruling out many of the skills-building and training options, including higher education" (Abramovitz, 1997, p. 312). TANF did cut welfare caseloads and increase employment among single mothers (Figueira-McDonough, 2007). In reality, however, wages of former TANF recipients are very low. The average monthly earned income of TANF recipients is $760.38 (Administration for Children and Families, 2008b). Figueira-McDonough (2007) explains:

> The average earnings of TANF recipients clearly cannot lead to self-sufficiency. Supporters of TANF insist that the intent of the program is not to erase poverty but to decrease dependence. The argument sounds far-fetched. The poverty standard is set [to provide] ... the minimum resources for survival, and those falling below that standard cannot be considered self-sufficient. From this perspective, the decline in the welfare caseload and the increase in the number of recipients working cannot be the only criteria of programmatic success.
>
> There is little evidence of self-sufficiency among welfare leavers. (p. 249).

Karger and Stoesz (2010) report some facts:

- "Most recipients leaving public assistance (50 to 60 percent) take jobs that pay just over minimum wage. Because of this, many low-income families continue to receive some form of public assistance, such as food stamps ...
- [One study found] ... that even though 54.5 percent of former TANF recipients were employed in 2000, by 2005 this had decreased to 39.3 percent ...
- Former TANF recipient families have not done well when it comes to average family income, with such income having decreased significantly over time. The average income in 2005 was $22,733, a decrease of $2,795 per annum from the average $25,528 in 2000" (pp. 284–285).

Note that the "number of years of schooling is significantly less for TANF recipients than for the general population. Over half (54 percent) of TANF recipients never completed high school, compared to only 14.5 percent of nonrecipients" (Popple & Leighninger, 2008, p.160).

Without significant training or education, what kind of jobs can people realistically get? How ethical is it to strongly encourage or force single mothers to work outside the home when they can earn only a meager, inadequate income anyway?

Given enough resources and policy changes, TANF could be significantly improved to help women attain brighter, more self-sufficient futures with acceptable income levels. Loomis and her colleagues (2003) studied Caroline Center, a career and learning resource center for women founded by the School Sisters of Notre Dame, which presents a potential model. Caroline Center's "mission is to provide the resources necessary to help women transition from poverty to self-sufficiency-poverty that may be from circumstances of unemployment or underemployment and self-sufficiency that is achieved by having a job that pays a living wage and includes benefits" (p. 32).

Caroline Center's program operates in three phases. "Phase I focuses on clarifying goals, determining career options, developing plans to reach identified goals, and providing basic job skill training, as well as offering personal and professional development workshops [e.g., guest speakers who are successful in their careers and provide positive role models]" (p. 34). Phase II is more individualized, "providing general job preparation and professional development workshops (e.g., mock job interviews, computer training, etc.)" (p. 34). Phase III involves "graduates" of the first two phases who become "employed at a living wage" and have "access to benefits (e.g., periodic meetings, mentoring, maintaining a social network with Caroline Center staff, and access to computers and services)" (p. 35). Career development activities provided throughout the program include "courses, electives, workshops, internships, job preparation exercises, ... specific job search training, ... [and] GED preparation courses" (p. 33). Other supportive services available include "counseling, housing assistance, medical care assistance, transportation, and professional attire" (p. 35).

Loomis et al. (2003) conclude that a number of variables, including the following, are related to programs that effectively, "enabled women to leave welfare and become self sufficient" (p. 28):

- Promoting interpersonal relationships in a context where virtually all aspects of life are addressed and participants are provided "membership, belonging, and identity" (p. 41).

- "Setting the tone for work and transitions by providing an appropriate physical environment" (p. 42).
- "Offering a career-focused curriculum with both in-class training and practical experiences" (p. 42).
- Providing resources to enhance social and emotional well-being and stability, and address "barriers to successes" (p. 42).
- "Creating a program culture" that emphasizes clear expectations, rules, and rewards (p. 42).
- "Recruiting staff and volunteers who share the mission and serve as mentors and role models" (p. 42).
- "Forging relationships with the local community, developing resources for volunteers and business partnerships" (p. 42).
- Setting a range of goals as women work through various stages of growth toward independence.
- "Caring about people and outcomes" (p. 42).

TANF and Health

In addition to the problems concerning lack of education and employment, a number of other questions emerge concerning TANF's policies. "Low-income families with children who meet certain eligibility requirements" in a state's public assistance plan as specified at the inception of TANF are automatically eligible for Medicaid.[a] Karger & Stoesz, 2010, p. 310). TANF provisions allow Medicaid to continue up to one year after the recipient leaves TANF and finds employment (Barusch, 2009). A problem is the limitation on Medicaid eligibility time. *Even after many public assistance recipients get jobs, how good are the benefits that most low-paying jobs offer? Do they provide any health-care benefits or paid sick leave at all?*

One study found that there "has been a decrease in the number of former recipients who have own-employer health insurance. In 2000, this was 26.3 percent; however, by 2005 only 21.8 percent had insurance, a decrease of 4.5 percent" (Karger & Stoesz, 2010, p. 285).

TANF and Family Structure

Family structure is defined as "the nuclear family as well as alternatives to nuclear family which are adopted by persons in committed relationships and the people they consider to be 'family'" *(Glossary to Educational Policy and Accreditation Standards,* 2002). This definition allows for a broad and open-minded interpretation of the various configurations of people who can work

(continued)

HIGHLIGHT 7.4 *(continued)*

together as a functioning, supportive family. In contrast TANF goals are "to provide assistance to needy families so that children can be cared for in their own homes; to reduce dependency by promoting job preparation, work and marriage; to prevent out-of-wedlock pregnancies; and to encourage the formation and maintenance of two-parent families" (ACF, 2008a). In effect, TANF intends to impose restrictions on how people structure their personal lives. For example, TANF permits states to refuse payment increases to women having more children while receiving assistance (Hagen & Lawrence,

2008; Karger & Stoecz, 2010). *How ethical is it for government "to regulate the childbearing behavior of poor women"* (Abramovitz, 1997, p. 314)?

Note

"*Medicaid* is a public assistance program funded by federal and state governments that pays for medical and hospital services for eligible people who are unable to pay for these services themselves and are determined to be in need. It was established in 1965 along with Medicare" (Kirst-Ashman, 2010, p. 227).

---

influential community professionals, religious leaders, and businesspeople—not only can they provide the credibility you will need to succeed, but community members likely consider such prestigious people important and will listen to their views. Therefore, influential community leaders' support lends the program greater credibility.

Finally, you might select action group members for their specific areas of expertise. For example, a certified alcohol- and drug-abuse counselor could provide valuable input as to how a drug rehabilitation program should be structured. Likewise, a lawyer whose practice targets juveniles or a police officer knowledgeable about youth could contribute relevant information regarding the legal aspects of working with juvenile drug abusers.

From members of this action group, you might establish a more formalized "board of directors, ... advisory council, or ... an internal task force within an existing agency" (Hasenfeld, 2001, p. 462). Such a formalized group can lend support, credibility, and community influence to your program.

Allocate Responsibilities to a Designated Task Group or Advisory Council

Much earlier (in Step 3 of PREPARE), as you were deciding whether to pursue such change, you identified relevant people of influence. Such people may be very useful as part of an advisory team or council. It is helpful to allocate responsibilities to a designated task group or advisory council (Hasenfeld, 2001). You can solicit such a group's help by asking them to discuss issues, make plans, and prepare objectives along with their respective action steps. Chapter 3 discusses task groups in detail.

Advisory councils or *advisory boards* are committees created outside of the organization's formal power structure that meet to provide information and feedback regarding the organization's functioning, propose changes and new developments, support fundraising, and educate the community about the organization (Sheafor & Horejsi, 2009). Such an advisory group functions much like a task group.

IMAGINE: Identify *Assets*

What variables will aid you in the program development process? Consider three approaches for identifying and maximizing assets: preparing the agency for change, conducting a feasibility study, and soliciting necessary financial resources.

EP 2.1.10e

Prepare the Agency for Change

Before actively pursuing program development, you must prepare the agency for the change process by addressing three major variables, all of which can increase your potential to achieve effective change (Brager & Holloway, 1983, p. 200).

First, you must enhance the *assets* in favor of the change (Homan, 2008). Assets, in this case, mean people who will help you. As part of formulating your action system, you can begin identifying people in the agency who would be most useful in helping you make the change. Who is in your target system?

Explore the informal communication network. Whom do you trust and respect in the agency, regardless of formal position? With whom do these people associate? Can you expand your support network indirectly through them? Might there be ways to influence the people at the top through others lower in the hierarchy? Whom does the executive director or top administrator trust?

The second variable is enhancing your own *legitimacy* (Brager & Holloway, 1983, p. 202; Brueggemann, 2006). We know it's important to understand your own strengths and weaknesses before pursuing any macro change (Burghardt, 2001). What personal and professional power can you muster? Often, you can increase your expertise regarding the proposed program. Ask yourself what would augment your position with administrators. What facts about the program and how it meets client needs might influence the target system in your favor?

The third variable is increasing the *stress level* or "sense of urgency" related to the need for program development; "[t]o bring about change, organization members need to demonstrate a great deal of cooperation and willingness to make sacrifices. To garner this cooperation, … [the change agent system] must convince organization members that there is a need—indeed, an urgency—to change" (Proehl, 2001, p. 88). Brager and Holloway (1983) comment that "unfortunately for change efforts, human service workers tend to perceive their function to be stress reduction. But change is unlikely to occur unless discomforting tension accompanies an attempt to change the status quo."

One useful method of escalating stress is by pointing out to others in the agency how the discrepancy between what the agency is doing (current policy or practice) and what it should be doing (proposed program) is significant and intolerable. This reinforces the argument in favor of the proposed program.

Note, however, that by increasing stress levels you put yourself at risk of being associated with that stress. Some of the stress's negativity may rub off on you. You are best off when you can position yourself as a concerned advocate for the agency instead of as an irritating complainer. Here, again, it is probably helpful to seek support and corroboration from other individuals and groups in the agency. When you are grouped with others on an issue, it is more difficult for opponents to single you out and point the finger of blame in your direction. Any blame or negativity becomes more dispersed and diffused.

Consider Implementing a Feasibility Study

To help identify your assets, consider implementing a *feasibility study,* a systematic evaluation of the resources necessary to achieve your program development goals

(Barker, 2003; Hasenfeld, 2001). In other words, you can explore how realistic your hopes of success are in developing this new program. How much will staffing and facilities cost? What kind of backing can you expect from the community housing the program and from other community agencies?

What other types of resources might be available? Hasenfeld suggests five potential sources: grants, assistance from local government, private donations by individuals and agencies, services and goods donated by other agencies, and volunteers.

One especially beneficial resource for many agencies is the United Way. This agency is a national alliance of local organizations formed to coordinate various fundraising efforts. It then determines how the resulting resources will be distributed to designated agencies providing any of a wide range of social services.

Ultimately, you need to decide whether you have enough resources to continue with your program development plan. If you can't possibly afford to implement the program, you might as well halt the process right here.

Solicit the Financial Resources You Need to Initiate the Program

You should have already identified possible funding sources. Now you need to transform the *potential* funding sources into *actual* funding sources (Hasenfeld, 1987, 2001). Where will your financial support actually come from? Who will make definite commitments to give you needed resources? In this process, you must convince people controlling targeted resources that your proposed program merits their attention, support, and whatever money you need. You may also want to instigate a fundraising crusade (a macro technique discussed more extensively in Chapter 14).

IMAGINE: Specify *Goals,* Objectives, and Action Steps to Attain Them

In this step, you formulate clear action steps leading to your prioritized objectives. You already identified specific problems and your primary goals during the initial phase of the macro intervention process; now you are developing a program. Your intent is to designate the order in which you'll address your specified problems. Your proposed program will begin to take shape according to the problems you determine are most important to solve.

EP 2.1.10f

We have consistently emphasized that objectives and action steps must be very clear. Specifying the performance expected, the conditions under which that performance is to occur, and the standards by which success is measured is just as necessary in macro practice as in micro practice.

For example, consider a possible *objective* of developing a program for adolescent drug abusers to pursue the more general *goal* of combatting drug abuse. Your objective might be to provide an inpatient, six-week treatment program (performance) for all identified drug-abusing teens in a specified geographic area (conditions), aimed at having at least 90 percent of clients remain drug-free for six months after leaving the program (standards). (Inpatient programs require clients in treatment to live in the facility day and night.)

Such an objective would also require its own *action steps* for successful completion. What steps are necessary to develop this program? *Who* would need to do *what* by *when?* Macro practice, of course, involves more individuals and groups—in addition to agencies, policies, and organizations—than does micro practice. Therefore, you might anticipate needing more action steps than you would, for example, when working with a single individual. Action steps for achieving macro change can require the cooperation of any number of individuals and groups before primary goals can be accomplished.

Consider Developing a PERT Chart

As we discussed earlier, a PERT chart is a tool for plotting your intervention plan in a linear manner. PERT charts can designate what participants are responsible for completing what tasks, and allow you to view the entire program development process from beginning to end. It also allows you to see how various phases of the process fit together by portraying a number of simultaneous activities. (Such a chart is illustrated later in Figure 7.3.)

Describe How the Program Will Provide Services

Before implementing the program, you must describe clearly how the program will actually provide services to accomplish its goals and objectives (Hasenfeld, 2001; Poertner, 2009). How will the program work in its day-to-day functioning? Suppose you initiate a drug rehabilitation program. What types of treatment techniques will the drug rehabilitation counselors be expected to use? What kind of training do they require? Will there be an outpatient program—where clients receive treatment without having to remain at the facility overnight or for long periods of time—in addition to the inpatient one? How will the inpatient units be run? What type of treatment will clients receive (group counseling, individual counseling, or job-seeking assistance)?

It is important to specify details that describe how the program will be run. What specific kinds of services will the program deliver to clients? Exactly how will the program achieve its specified goals?

IMAG*I*NE: *Implement* the Plan

Actual implementation begins with you presenting the macro change goal to the agency. At this point it is best to have as much influence as possible, which includes any assets favoring change—such as your own professional legitimacy and the existence of increased stress levels—that convince decision makers to pursue new solutions. To ensure this, you need to plan your presentation carefully.

You must carefully consider the identified target system's receptiveness to your idea. It is helpful to play out possible scenarios in your mind beforehand. Try to anticipate how the target system will react to your proposal. How might the proposal best be introduced to maximize its potential acceptance?

Ask yourself three questions about how to influence others who can provide support (Brager & Holloway, 1983). First, who should hear the initial proposal? What individual or group within the agency would be the most supportive and influential? It might be the top administrator, but it might not be. It might be an individual or group of individuals lower in the administrative hierarchy. Perhaps you can target persons who are potentially more supportive of your idea than the top administrator. You then can find out how much influence these others have with the top administrator (or other ultimate decision maker).

The more support you can muster for your idea, the greater your potential for success. Support from a broad and varied base (such as a number of disciplines or supervisory units) carries more weight than a narrow, homogeneous base (only one social worker or one small social services unit).

The second question is, who should present the proposal? We have discussed the importance of professional credibility. If at all possible, this individual should have strong influence with those hearing the proposal. Sometimes it is best for you to introduce the proposal as a member of a group. Other times, an especially credible, well-respected individual can be designated to present the idea. When appropriate, this may be you.

The third question is, how can you best present facts, issues, goals, and objectives to the target system? How can information about the proposed program be presented most positively to decision makers? Try to frame the proposed program to reflect or conform to various aspects of the decision maker's value system. For example, if you talk to a decision maker who feels agency accountability is a top priority, it is in your best interest to emphasize that your proposed program enhances accountability.

Get the Program Going

Getting the program off the ground involves a period between the agency's acceptance of the program development plan and the plan's actual operation. During this period or in the early days of running the program, you may need to focus on nurturing participating staff's support, considering a trial run, starting out small, and formalizing necessary contracts.

Nurture participating staff's support. The first matter to consider during implementation is the participating staff's support. You must encourage, gain, and maintain support from the employees who actually carry out the intervention. You might anticipate some hesitation and resistance on their part. All involved in implementation must understand why the proposed program is important. Strive to answer their questions, continue to seek their support, and thank them for their efforts. Continuously monitor any changes to make certain workers remain on track.

Sometimes the agency must hire new staff. These staff members also need to fully understand how the program is structured and operated. Explain all procedures as clearly as possible. Using a PERT chart can help, but make sure all involved staff members understand it.

How about a trial run? One possibility to consider when developing and beginning a new program is a trial run. Instead of plunging full speed ahead, try out the program with a few clients for a brief period of time to identify any flaws. Such flaws can be addressed and remedied more easily when programs start up. At this point, you have not established any precedents. It is very important that the new program be responsive to needed changes and improvements.

Consider starting out small. The "likelihood that an innovation will be adopted by a larger population is increased if the innovation is first utilized by a small group of opinion leaders. This small initiating group may be characterized as style setters, information disseminators, key communicators, spark plugs, or gatekeepers, among other descriptions" (Rothman, Erlich, & Teresa, 1981, p. 22). Your chances of having a program implemented significantly increase if you first try out one part of the proposed program or use a limited number of clients. This way you can showcase your innovation at lower cost and with much less risk. You also have an opportunity to demonstrate your idea's effectiveness before its total application as a program plan.

Formalize any contracts that might be needed. Contracts can be useful in program development on a variety of levels. They can solidify the agreements made in action groups or by a board of directors.

Purchase-of-service contracts from other agencies might provide services your program cannot offer. Service contracts are formal agreements between one or more organizations where one organization purchases some specified service within a designated time period from one or more other agencies. For instance, your agency might contract with another agency to furnish vocational rehabilitation or some other type of specialized counseling, instead of trying to provide it.

IMAGINE: *Neutralize* Opposition

Be wary of potential opposition throughout your change process. Two suggestions can assist this phase of the program development process: anticipation of a "honeymoon period" and the maintenance of ongoing administrative support.

Anticipate a "Honeymoon Period"

A "honeymoon period" often occurs when a new program starts out (Brager & Holloway 1983, p. 206). This period is often marked by high levels of enthusiasm and interest on the part of involved staff. Theoretically, as on a real honeymoon, life appears full of roses. Criticism is often suspended, and problems seem nonexistent.

However, after some time has passed, unanticipated problems may occur. This makes sense. You must begin implementing a new idea before you can possibly discover all the potential snags. Only after clear identification can you begin to work out the inevitable real-life problems. At any rate, staff interest and enthusiasm may wane as working on the new program becomes more humdrum. You can revitalize the program development process by giving it your continued attention and emphasizing the gains staff have made.

Maintain Administrative Support

Another relevant element in getting a new program going is maintaining the continued interest of the crucial decision makers. Sometimes these people are part of the original target system. Other times the target system changes over time as the action system implements its plan. Regardless, it is important for you to monitor and reassure whoever has responsibility for the program's ongoing existence and success. Once the initial excitement wears off, it is easy to be distracted by other new ideas, problems, or pressing agency needs. Providing decision makers with regular progress reports regarding accomplishments made and goals attained can solicit and maintain their interest and support.

IMAGINE: *Evaluate* Progress

EP 2.1.10m

As with any other type of generalist intervention, evaluation of your progress is critical. For program development this means monitoring daily progress, assessing the overall program's effectiveness, and establishing ongoing program services.

Monitor Daily Activities and Evaluate Program Impact

A bottom line for any program is that it has to work. Services provided must be effective and efficient if the program is to become a viable part of agency service provision. Two concepts are particularly important concerning evaluation programs: *Monitoring* is the day-to-day observance of the agency's performance, and *impact evaluation* is the measurement of the program's effectiveness (Rubin & Rubin, 2008, pp. 429–430).

Monitor your program. Monitoring daily program functioning is appraising how efficiently services are provided and learning how effectively clients are being served. *How* services are delivered to clients is just as important as *what* services are delivered. Clients should be able to depend on a service being provided in a timely, predictable fashion. Scheduling appointments and meetings should be done according to clearly defined procedures. Many questions need addressing. Is the target client population actually benefiting from the services? Do clients have ready access to what they need? Are the services provided the ones that clients want and need? Administering follow-up surveys may help answer these and other related questions.

Monitoring also includes checking the staff's work. Are personnel able to fulfill their job responsibilities adequately? Are they prioritizing and completing the most critical tasks before attending to minor details? Staff members should have straightforward, accurate job descriptions. They should all know exactly what tasks they are responsible for. Finally, billing (if needed) should be organized and predictable.

Monitoring also involves evaluating the program's costs and benefits (Rubin & Rubin, 2008). Are the benefits sufficient to justify the costs?

Rubin and Rubin (2008) make one other important point concerning program monitoring. The evaluator should distinguish between *effort* (that "measures the energy, time, or money spent by the organization to accomplish its goals") and *outcome* (that "measures the changes brought about by the program") (p. 432). Outcomes should be valuable and worth the effort. It is important to measure both effort and outcomes in order to get a clear picture of agency functioning.

Perform an impact evaluation. *Impact evaluation* investigates outcomes and determines whether program goals have been met. There are at least two types of measurements in impact evaluations (Rubin & Rubin, 2008). First, some outcomes are factual and can be readily observed. For example, you can count the number of homeless people placed in temporary shelter care. You can also count the monetary benefits indigent clients receive. The second kind of outcome is reflected in people's perceptions and opinions concerning the program's effectiveness. For example, you might develop and administer a questionnaire to solicit clients' feedback about the program.

Establish How Services Will Be Provided on an Ongoing Basis

The final step in IMAGINE's implementation phase establishes how services will be provided on an ongoing basis (Hasenfeld, 2001; Poertner, 2009). Stabilization of change or cementing change into the structure of the overall service provision system is a process that involves at least four major tasks. First, standardized procedures for continued implementation of the program should be clearly defined (Lewis et al., 2007). Ideally, these should become part of the ongoing agency policies and procedures manual.

Second, the new program should be linked as much as possible with other units and aspects of the organization (Lewis et al., 2007). This is important so that the unit does not become an isolated entity—isolated programs are easily hacked off. They have fewer connections and supporters when decisions are being made about agency priorities. Having more agency units support and rely on the program's services broadens the base of the program's support. Likewise, any decision makers trying to delete the program will run into stronger resistance.

Third, the program's importance should be established within the context of other programs and services in the community (Hasenfeld, 2001; Schmid, 2009). How does the program fit into the overall service provision picture? How might public relations techniques (such as press releases and communication with other agencies) be used to inform the public and other professionals about the program's usefulness? What services does the program provide that other organizations appreciate and need to complement their own services? How can the program work with other programs to fulfill people's needs? For instance, a child-care program "cannot in good conscience ignore the health needs of the children" and thus may structure regular visits from health care personnel at a community clinic to examine them (Hasenfeld, 2001, p. 470). Similarly, the staff of a program providing daily hot meals to older adults may work with outreach personnel from a mental health crisis line or the Visiting Nurses Association to identify and serve clients (Hasenfeld, 2001). Hasenfeld (2001) comments:

> *The success of the program in achieving viability is dependent on its ability to become a recognized "institution" in the community. Once the program is perceived by key elements in the community as desirable, indispensable, and an important contributor to the general welfare of the community, it has been "legitimated." Legitimacy implies that the community is willing to accept it as a viable and necessary component of the service structure. (p. 472)*

The fourth task involved in establishing a program on an ongoing basis is to develop a feedback system to monitor service provision, outcomes, resources, and efficiency (Poertner, 2009). A successful program develops means to evaluate its continuing effectiveness both internally and within the community service system.

To what extent does the program continue to meet its goals and objectives? How well does the program respond to external changes such as new legislation, other innovative programs with which it might compete, or alterations in funding sources?

Program Development: A Case Example

Programs can involve almost any type of service or event. Examples include those to help drug abusers, survivors of sexual abuse, single parents, children with physical disabilities, homeless people, or older adults residing in their own homes.

EP 2.1.10

It is impossible to give you a formula for developing a specific program for a designated agency setting. The variables are literally infinite. However, we do offer general guidelines you can follow and modify as needed in your program development. To illustrate program development, we will examine the development of a sexual harassment awareness program in a large public agency with special emphasis on the application of a PERT chart to facilitate the program development process. Highlight 7.5 describes two other ideas for program development.

IMAGINE: Start with an Innovative *Idea*

The innovative idea for our example case is the development of a sexual harassment awareness program for agency personnel. (See Highlight 7.6 on page x-ref. for a definition and discussion of sexual harassment.)

Sexual harassment has become an increasingly significant national issue. Surveys indicate that it is quite common in both work and educational settings (Carroll, 2010; Crooks & Baur, 2008). Lawsuits and publicity have raised public consciousness and escalated administrators' fears of legal liability, because administrators can be held legally responsible for inappropriate treatment of staff members in their own agencies. The NASW *Code of Ethics* states that "social workers should not sexually harass clients, supervisees, students, trainees, or colleagues" (NASW, 2008, 2.08).

So, if sexual harassment is illegal as a violation of civil rights and unethical according to professional standards, why don't victims stop it as soon as it occurs? In reality, the majority of sexually harassed women do not file a complaint (Carroll, 2010). Rathus,

HIGHLIGHT 7.5

Program Development Ideas Are Endless

The program development case example in this section is only one of an infinite number of possibilities for program development. The case example is extensive in order to illustrate each step in the program development process. Following are brief summaries of two other program development ideas.

Sanctuary for Young Homeless New Mothers

Schram (1997) describes a program designed to meet the needs of women under 21 with infants under one year old who have no family or partner with whom they can live. Additionally, participants must be alcohol- and drug-free at the time, "reasonably mentally and physically healthy," and plan to remain in the program for a year. Participants must also be committed to finishing their secondary education, finding a job, or entering post-secondary training or college. The name of the program is LIFT (Let Infants and Families Thrive). It is centered in a LIFT house that provides a home for participants.

Program participants are often homeless for many reasons, including health problems (such as substance abuse or disability), lack of family and social support, inadequate information about resources and their rights, difficulties in finding or keeping employment, lack of affordable child care or housing, emotional difficulties, or relationship problems with partners. Thus, young women were falling through the cracks in the service provision net. Schram (1997, p. 74) explains:

> Much of the homeless problem is hidden. For example, the young women might be living in dangerously overcrowded homes bunking with abusive mates or stressed family members. Many of them keep moving from one temporary shelter or a friend's couch to the next. Young mothers often do not admit that they are without a permanent home, because they fear that they will lose their children to the welfare establishment they are so dependent on but afraid of.

LIFT was developed as a private nonprofit organization with its own board of directors. It receives referrals from local social services agencies, hospitals, physicians, domestic violence shelters, and clergy. A full-time coordinator runs the program. Other staff members include a child care teacher, some part-time counselors, and numerous volunteers.

LIFT's goal "is to act as a bridge to independent living for each of the parents and as a solid launching pad for the infants" (Schram, 1997, p. 50). Essentially, LIFT functions as an artificial extended family providing critical support to isolated young mothers during the first vital years of their infants' lives. Participants can reside in the LIFT house for one year, after which they can opt to live in a small apartment within three blocks of the premises for the following two years. Meanwhile, they can continue to use and benefit from the program's services and resources.

Services include a day care center at the LIFT house, parenting classes, support groups, a GED (high school equivalency) tutoring program, and a mentoring program where LIFT participants are paired with appropriate community volunteers who help them develop a work or career path. Other issues addressed with program participants include improving self-esteem and self-confidence, acquiring job search and employment skills, and developing planning and decision-making abilities. The program's ultimate goal is for participants to establish a viable plan for their future in addition to developing good parenting skills.

Housing Development for Nonheterosexual Older Adults

Hamburger (1997) proposes and discusses the idea of special housing units for nonheterosexual older adults. The concept rests on two basic principles. First, home is extremely important not only to promote comfort and feelings of belonging, but also concerning accessibility to services, resources, and other people. Even the home's physical structure directly affects lifestyle and a person's potential for remaining in the home. For example, a four-story brownstone home in Manhattan would pose difficulties for people who can no longer climb steps easily. Similarly, a very small home with one bedroom would inhibit the possibility of having a live-in service provider to provide support or a boarder to increase income. In essence, the home directly affects an older adult's choices and quality of life.

The second principle behind nonheterosexual housing is "that sexual orientation is fundamental to one's being. Nonheterosexuals, like all minorities in a minority-phobic society, seek and form their own community with unique cultural norms" (Hamburger, 1997, p. 12). She continues that "the heterosexual assumption of the majority society and the asexual assumption ascribed to seniors encourage nonheterosexual cultural adaptations to be neglected and invalidated" (p. 12).

To explore this need. Hamburger (1997) surveyed 18 nonheterosexuals in the San Francisco Bay Area, most

Nonheterosexual older adults require a sense of community and belonging.

of whom were women. All had been actively involved in addressing issues concerning nonheterosexual senior services or housing advocacy. Most respondents indicated a preference for living "in a community where one's sexual ... [orientation] is irrelevant. Other responses suggest the desire for an environment in which the nonheterosexual culture is planned for, thus, housing should have appropriate units available for same-sex couples and be located near a larger gay/lesbian community, and related services should recognize the loss of a same-sex partner" (p. 15).

There are a number of impediments to the development of nonheterosexual senior housing. Finding adequate funding would be difficult. However, Hamburger (1997) remarks, "A housing development project supported by governmental funds could serve nonheterosexuals if marketed affirmatively and occupancy was made available to all seniors" (p. 22). Housing excluding heterosexuals might be labeled discriminatory. Private funding might provide another option.

If it is not feasible to develop housing projects, three other programmatic suggestions can still be implemented to improve the quality of life for nonheterosexual seniors (Hamburger, 1997). First, educational programs could be developed to educate both managers and residents of currently available senior housing regarding the special needs of nonheterosexual seniors. Second, a program could be formulated to work with the management of existing senior housing to identify and halt discrimination against nonheterosexuals. Third, a referral service could be created to assist nonheterosexual seniors in finding residences or roommates.

Nevid, and Fichner-Rathus (2008) explain some of the reasons for this lack of reporting:

Charges of sexual harassment are often ignored or trivialized by coworkers and employers. The victim may hear, "Why make a big deal out of it? It's not *like you were attacked in the street." Evidence shows, however, that persons subjected to sexual harassment do suffer from it. Some become physically ill (Rospenda et al., 2005). Others report anxiety, irritability, lowered self-esteem, and anger. Some find*

HIGHLIGHT 7.6

What Is Sexual Harassment?

Consider the following vignettes:

EP 2.1.5a

- A male worker enjoys "accidentally" bumping up against female colleagues and touching their private body parts.
- A coworker turns up the CD player he keeps in his office whenever he plays sexually explicit songs encouraging assaults against women.
- A female supervisor tells her male supervisee she will give him special preference for his vacation request if he will "have a drink" with her after work.
- A male supervisor tells his female supervisee that he could make her job easier if she would have sex with him.
- A newly hired male agency director commonly refers to women staff members as "bubble-heads" and states he will avoid giving them more important assignments. He is noticeably more likely to address questions and issues raised by his male workers than those raised by females.
- A male staff member thinks it's funny to send pictures of nude women involved in various sexual contortions as attachments to e-mails.

The preceding vignettes illustrate incidents of sexual harassment a serious form of sex discrimination that has gained considerable public attention. Not limited to business and industry, it also affects social service organizations and bureaucracies. One review of studies reveals that "between 26 percent and 38 percent of social workers have experienced unwanted sexual advances. Mirroring the results of research on sexual harassment outside of social work workplaces and educational settings" (Stout & McPhail, 1998, p. 201). Although sexual harassment can victimize either gender, more women than men have suffered its consequences (U.S. Equal Employment Opportunity Commission [EEOC], 2009). In 2008, the EEOC received 13,867 charges of sexual harassment, 84.1 percent of them filed by women (EEOC, 2009).

Sexual harassment is illegal. Title VII of the Civil Rights Act of 1964 covers discrimination on the basis of sex, along with discrimination on the basis of race. Title IX of the Higher Education Amendments of 1972 prohibits sex discrimination specifically on university campuses. The Civil Rights Act of 1991 permitted "compensatory and punitive damages to be awarded for the first time, although a $300,000 cap was put into place" (Stout & McPhail, 1998, p. 187).

Sexual harassment is defined as follows:

Unwelcome sexual advances, requests for sexual favors, and other verbal or physical conduct of a sexual nature constitutes sexual harassment when submission to or rejection of this conduct [1] explicitly or implicitly affects an individual's employment, [2] unreasonably interferes with an individual's work performance or [3] creates an intimidating, hostile or offensive work [or educational] environment. (EEOC, 2002)

There are two major dimensions to this definition. The first involves the concept of *quid pro quo,* a Latin term that means "this for that." In other words, "I'll scratch your back if you scratch mine" (Carroll, 2010; Hyde & Delamater, 2008). Sometimes, a victim is promised a reward for sexual cooperation. For instance, sexual harassment occurs when a female direct-services worker, seeking promotion to supervisor, is pressured to endure physical touching and kissing by her male agency director to maintain an ongoing, working relationship and receive a positive promotion decision. Other times, punishment may be threatened. A female worker may be pressured to submit sexually to her male supervisor in response to threats that resistance could result in her dismissal as part of announced cost-reduction efforts.

The second dimension, identified in condition three of the definition for sexual harassment focuses on the creation of a *hostile environment.* Here, offensive gender-related physical or verbal behavior interferes with people's ability to complete their work. Clear-cut rewards or punishments may not be directly related. Examples are sex-related comments about a particular woman's dress or unwanted physical touching where the perpetrator indicates he is just being "friendly."

Sexual harassment may entail a perpetrator becoming overly and inappropriately personal with the victim, either by sharing intimacies or by prying into the victim's personal life. A supervisor can overstep the boundaries of his role by questioning a supervisee about his or her love life. Such intrusion can threaten a person and interfere with the ability to concentrate on work.

Sexual harassment usually entails an element of unequal power and coercion (Bravo, 2008). However, it can also occur between equals or even be perpetrated by those in less-powerful positions. For example, it is possible for a male student to harass a female instructor.

Although women are most commonly victims of sexual harassment men are also victimized. In this respect it is a human rights issue. For example, a female supervisor in a position of power could pressure a male supervisee for dates or sexual favors. Or several male workers might make lewd comments to a male colleague about being gay.

harassment on the job so unbearable that they resign (Sims et al., 2005). College women's grades suffer (Huerta et al., 2006). College women have dropped courses and switched majors and even medical residency programs to avoid sexual harassment (Huerta et al., 2006; Stratton et al., 2005). (p. 608)

We will examine the development of a sexual harassment awareness program in the Ogalala County Department of Social Services. The change catalyst in our example is Cindy Cepsowicz, the supervisor of the agency's foster-care unit. She has always been a strong proponent of women's rights and is increasingly conscious of the sexual remarks and gestures she sees being made around the agency. She believes that there is a strong need to educate personnel regarding sexual harassment and to provide a means to help staff members who are victims. She formulates the goal of establishing a sexual harassment awareness program.

In this particular example, the potential client system includes the agency staff instead of the agency's clients. This is an internal agency issue that needs to be addressed so that staff can function more effectively on their clients' behalf. The staff also needs to develop their sensitivity to sexual harassment so they will treat each other and their clients appropriately.

IMAGINE: *Muster* Support

As the change catalyst, Cindy talks to other colleagues who she thinks have similar concerns and verifies that indeed they do. The colleagues she identifies for the initial action system include two of her supervisees, two other unit supervisors, a direct service worker from another unit, and the agency's personnel director. Each person in the action system is committed to the idea that sexual harassment is a serious problem that needs to be addressed within the agency environment. Each action system member is also willing to work on developing a plan of action and to address the issue with administration. The action system forms a task group.

Cindy, with her assertive leadership ability, organizational skills, and attention to detail, becomes the natural leader of the action system. The group's first step is the development of a clearly defined rationale for developing a sexual harassment awareness program.

IMAGINE: Identify *Assets*

Cindy has already identified other staff members as strong proponents of her idea and thus as assets. Support from staff is a major asset in the implementation of her plan. Cindy's close personal relationship with the agency's personnel director, whose influence could help Cindy's cause, is still another asset. By integrating supportive people into an action system, she has enhanced her own legitimacy. This strengthens her position that it is important for the agency to address the issue—both assets.

Another means of increasing Cindy's legitimacy is by strengthening her program development proposal with facts and specific suggestions. Cindy first educates herself about sexual harassment and the types of behavior it commonly involves. She researches recent court decisions in sexual harassment cases to clarify the issues facing her agency. She constructs a strong rationale to convince administrators to implement a program.

Developing a strong argument for Cindy's case can escalate administrative stress levels. Administrators must understand their responsibility to maintain a sexual harassment-free working environment. Worrying about legal problems they may face if they do not establish a program can cause administrators stress. This demonstrates that escalating stress can motivate decision makers to do something (in this case, develop a program) to alleviate the stress.

Cindy decides that no feasibility study is necessary. She feels her support and rationale for program development are strong enough to merit administrative attention. Her proposal for program development calls for some staff time, office space, and supplies. She believes the agency is large enough that these resources can be assigned to her proposed program with relatively minor shifting of internal funds. Cindy's specific plans are explained more thoroughly in the following section on developing objectives and planning action steps.

IMAGINE: Specify *Goals,* Objectives, and Action Steps to Attain Them

The action group's overall goal is to combat sexual harassment; their objective is to initiate and implement a program aimed at preventing and dealing with sexual harassment within their agency setting. To do this, the action group decides that the first action step is for Cindy and the personnel director to meet with the agency director within two weeks (this is the *who, what,* and *when* of a well-planned action step). The agency director, who is ultimately responsible for all agency business, becomes the target system. She is the decision maker whose support is necessary to get the program off the ground.

The three meet. The agency director is impressed with Cindy's organization and preparation. She gives the okay to establish a part-time position and initiate the program. The program's coordinator will provide education to the staff concerning sexual harassment, in addition to counseling and supporting victims. She will be available to address problems informally, thereby defusing potentially explosive situations.

The second action step is for Cindy and her action system to develop an extensive plan for the program's development. The third is to recruit within the agency for the part-time coordinator, and the fourth is to establish a PERT chart to direct and monitor program development. They share assignments and set deadlines for each action step.

It might be noted that Cindy herself chooses not to apply to be the program's coordinator. Although she firmly believes in the cause and the program, she feels her own job keeps her more than busy enough. She is happy with her role of getting the program off the ground and letting the new coordinator take over from there.

Establishing a Sexual Harassment Awareness Program for Employees (SHAPE)

EP 2.1.5c

To track the various phases of the development of the Sexual Harassment Awareness Program for Employees (SHAPE), Cindy's group produces a PERT chart like that shown in Figure 7.3. A similar program could be implemented in any of a variety of other organizational settings.

Description of SHAPE

SHAPE aims to educate staff members about sexual harassment issues and to provide counseling and support when complaints arise. In order to understand the intricacies delineated on the PERT chart, we will explore the proposed program and its goals in some depth.

SHAPE furnishes a viable alternative to confronting sexual harassment in a large organizational setting. By supplementing the existing formal complaint procedure (a vehicle to address any kind of complaint, including those involving sexual harassment), SHAPE offers an informal means of both preventing sexual harassment and of stopping it. Specific educational strategies targeting various units of the organization and the outside communities are utilized. Specific alternatives for victim counseling are defined and actively pursued.

Federal legislation supports SHAPE and its goals. For the purposes of this scenario, we assume that state law also provides strong support. We have already established that the agency's director backs development of SHAPE. Within this context, SHAPE prescribes a part-time coordinator who oversees program development and provides services. The coordinator will devote ten hours of her 40-hour work week to running the program. The portion of a position allotted to the coordinator's tasks is modifiable, depending on agency size. Larger organizations demand more time and attention than smaller agencies. The important thing is to adopt a well-defined policy on sexual harassment to support the program coordinator's position.

The SHAPE Coordinator's Role

Cindy's action group determines that the coordinator's role consists of five basic duties. Primary among them are (1) educational programming and (2) informal counseling/support. The coordinator will offer educational presentations about sexual harassment to as many agency personnel as possible. The coordinator will also (3) serve as a contact person for any informal sexual harassment complaints. Furthermore, counseling the offended individual regarding available alternatives and supporting preferred courses of action may be involved. The coordinator's approach will emphasize addressing the immediate problem and establishing a positive, supportive work environment.

The coordinator's other duties will include (4) monitoring existing formal procedures to ascertain their relevance and their responsiveness to sexual harassment complaints. Finally, the coordinator will (5) submit formal reports directly to the agency's director concerning progress, problems, and necessary program changes.

Cindy's action system selects a potential coordinator. It then solicits the agency director's concurrence and permission for this appointment. Subsequently, the action system and new coordinator create a PERT chart (illustrated in Figure 7.3) to direct program development and activity. The program goals they establish are explained next.

EP 2.1.10i

Educational programming. Educational programming is one of SHAPE'S foremost goals. Agency personnel need education about what sexual harassment is and what can be done about it. First, the agency's personnel structure must be analyzed and arbitrarily divided into units. Programming initially targets top-level administration, such as the agency director, assistant director, and unit division supervisors. The coordinator then arranges educational sessions for units from the administrative structure down to individual departments. The coordinator typically asks each unit to sponsor a presentation on sexual harassment issues during its regular unit meeting times.

The coordinator offers specific suggestions for stopping or averting sexual harassment to each unit she addresses. She tailors content to each unit's particular circumstances, using examples that unit staff members can understand and identify with. As part of her presentation, she encourages staff members to avoid using sexist terminology and references to anatomical gender differences when speaking to each other or to clients, and offers examples of phrases to avoid.

Educational presentations examine various forms of sexual harassment, the personal rights of victims, and how victims can take advantage of SHAPE. The coordinator suggests ways to discourage and stop sexual harassment. She strongly encourages staff members to contact SHAPE about any sexual harassment problems they encounter.

Providing support for victims. In addition to providing education, the coordinator can offer victims support in three major ways: counseling, assistance with formal complaint procedures, and taking informal, indirect action. Sometimes, a "no action" approach is appropriate.

Counseling. The coordinator can offer informal counseling and support to sexual harassment victims in various ways. First and most important, victims receive "empathy, validation, and empowerment" (Rogers & Henson, 2007; Stout & McPhail, 1998, p. 202). We have established that sexual harassment often results in serious psychological and physical, stress-related consequences (Rathus et al., 2008). For example, physical responses include "chronic neck and back pain, upset stomach, colitis and other gastrointestinal disorders, and eating and sleeping disorders"; psychological effects include irritability, nervousness, feelings of humiliation, and helplessness (Renzetti & Curran, 2003, p. 226). Often, victims alter their behavior patterns in response to the harassment (Rogers & Henson, 2007). For example, they will dress differently, act cool and detached, or actively seek to avoid any contact with the harasser. The coordinator can help a victim vent her feelings and validate them.

A second task for the coordinator is to help the victim understand the dynamics of sexual harassment. The victim must realize that the perpetrator is at fault and appreciate her right to work in a nonhostile environment.

The coordinator's third function is to help the victim determine a plan of action. This includes identifying available alternatives and evaluating the pros and cons of each.

One possibility is exploring how the victim can directly respond to the situation. Recommendations include telling the offender calmly and straightforwardly that the behavior is offensive and inappropriate, seeking emotional support from peers, looking for witnesses to corroborate complaints, and documenting informally and briefly specific details of the harassment.

Formal grievance procedure. At any point during the counseling process, it is the complainant's prerogative to initiate the formal complaint process. In this agency, a formal action for sexual harassment is pursued in the same way as any other complaint. If the complainant chooses to use the formal procedure, the coordinator may provide information about legal options, in addition to support and guidance during ensuing hearings. Victims frequently need assurance of their rights and information about each step in the formal complaint process.

Informal indirect action. One alternative available to the victim is that the coordinator indirectly provides feedback to the harasser through an educational presentation to the harasser's work unit or department. This option is available when the victim does not choose to pursue the formal grievance procedure and wants to remain anonymous.

During the educational presentation and subsequent discussion, the coordinator avoids making specific allegations. Rather, she provides examples to illustrate variations of sexual harassment that resemble, but are not identical to, those the complainant has reported.

No action. Some complaints may involve issues that do not constitute sexual harassment, but rather other issues. One example is a dispute between supervisory/administrative personnel and their supervisees that has no sexual or gender-related overtones; another is an affirmative action issue not related to gender. In these cases, the coordinator can fulfill several functions. First, she can educate the complainant regarding what sexual harassment is and help the latter identify and clarify the real problem. Second, the coordinator can help the complainant identify the courses of action that are appropriate to the situation: For instance, the coordinator might explain to the complainant the agency's policy for addressing affirmative action issues. Third, the coordinator can assist the complainant in identifying the preferred route and support her in her pursuit of that choice.

Occasionally, the coordinator takes a "no action" approach when an individual opts to withdraw a sexual harassment complaint. The complainant may decide that she or he misinterpreted the behavior in question or that it is not worth the effort to continue the process.

Planning the Program: Development of a PERT Chart

Now that you understand the proposed sexual harassment awareness program in substantial detail, we will show how a PERT chart can be used to implement the actual program. For the purposes of our discussion, we will assume that you have been chosen as the coordinator. The program's goals and activities have already been established, so you as the coordinator will follow and refine the PERT chart shown in Figure 7.3.

For our purposes, SHAPE has five major areas in which program objectives are set. These include initial planning, education, referral sources, counseling, and evaluation.

Figure 7.3 is set up vertically to fit a textbook page format. In real life, the format would as likely be horizontal; that is, reading from left to right. The time frame illustrated runs from February 2011 to March 2012. Establishing a new program often takes substantial amounts of time; in this case, over a year. Many details merit serious attention. Many wrinkles need ironing out.

As we begin to explore Figure 7.3's PERT chart, remember that we are operating under a number of assumptions in this example:

- The coordinator, theoretically you, has already been selected. The program has already been designed and its goals identified.
- The agency already has a firm grievance policy in place. (A *grievance* is an apparent act of unfair treatment or wrongdoing that is addressed through an official complaint.) Agencies typically are required to explain established grievance procedures in their policy manuals. You, of course, would need to be well aware of your role in helping complainants about sexual harassment pursue the designated grievance process.
- Finally, we will assume that the budget has already been developed. In addition to involving one-fourth of your own salary and benefits, the budget would probably include specific amounts for items such as supplies, computers and accompanying equipment, copying, educational resources and DVDs, secretarial help, travel and conferences, and publicity needs such as brochures. Figure 7.4 illustrates a simplified budget.

As program coordinator, you would follow and refine the established PERT chart with all of the above assumptions in mind.

Initial planning. In developing a program like SHAPE, the coordinator must first visualize how the program will fit into the agency's structure and functioning. For example, where will the office be located? Who will serve as the support secretarial staff? Who will answer the phone to receive complaints about sexual harassment? How will the program be publicized to agency personnel? Answering these and other questions will entail brainstorming with administration and other colleagues concerning the extent of the sexual harassment problem and their feelings about it. You would also seek to educate yourself more thoroughly about sexual harassment issues, especially with respect to legal

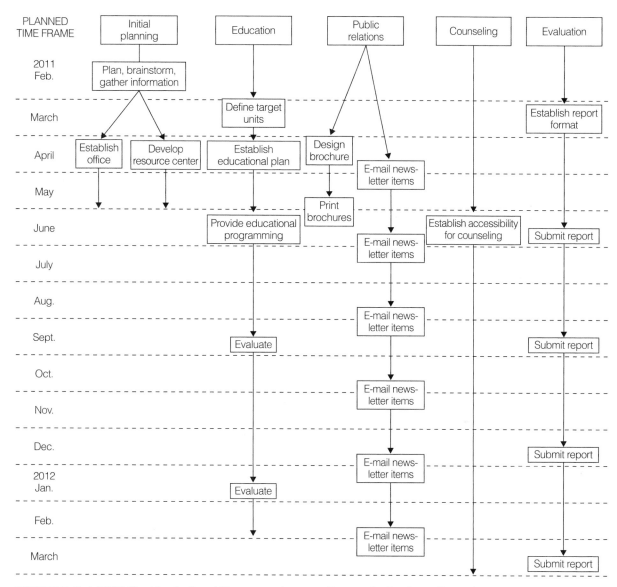

FIGURE 7.3 A PERT Chart for the Sexual Harassment Awareness Program for Employees (SHAPE)

aspects and the counseling of victims. The PERT chart indicates that you would begin this in early February (specifically, February 1, when your part-time position begins). You would continue through early April (specifically, April 7). (Due to space limitations, it was not possible to include days in the PERT chart. Therefore, we will specify the due dates here as we discuss the chart itself.)

You aim to set up SHAPE'S office from April 8 through May 31. This objective includes locating office space and getting administrative approval. You'll need a place where employees could come to you confidentially. They would need to feel comfortable talking with

Projected Needs	Cost
1. Supplies	$1,500
2. Copying	1,300
3. Computer equipment	5,000
4. Educational resources	3,000
5. Travel and conferences	3,000
6. Telephone	1,600
7. Brochures	1,700
8. Miscellaneous	1,300
Total	$18,400

FIGURE 7.4 A Budget Summary for SHAPE

you about such an intimately disturbing problem as sexual harassment. A preferred location would thus be out of the mainstream of agency traffic (not, therefore, an office right next to the reception area), yet one that could be easily found (not an office hidden in a corner of the agency's basement that could only be found after winding along a maze of heating ducts). Fearful or embarrassed victims may be reluctant to ask for directions.

You'll need to find an administrative assistant. Because this is only a part-time position, perhaps you could use an administrative assistant assigned to another agency unit by approaching the unit supervisor to discuss reconfiguring responsibilities to include answering the SHAPE phone and referring calls to the coordinator. Additional pay (built into the budget) for these extra duties might serve as an effective incentive for an administrative assistant to participate. Of course, you could always use voicemail for messages. However, because of the sensitive nature of the messages and fears about confidentiality, it's probably best to arrange for a human contact. It is important, however, not to coerce anyone to add to her own workload and do SHAPE'S work. This tactic would only cause your administrative assistant to resent SHAPE and you and resist doing the job. Perhaps you could suggest that administration increase her salary in view of her additional responsibilities or decrease some of her other workload. Otherwise, you might discover that every important document you give to her winds up hopelessly lost.

A second aspect of gathering information is the development of a resource center. The PERT chart indicates that you will pursue this goal concurrently with establishing the SHAPE office. You aim to complete the resource center by May 31. Since one of your goals is to educate the staff concerning sexual harassment, you need material. To this end, you could perform a library search or call other professionals involved in similar endeavors, such as the affirmative action offices of public agencies or the state office of Equal Employment Opportunity. Another goal is to start developing a reference library for your own professional education and for other staff members in need of this information. You could offer obtainable resources online and make hard copy materials available in the SHAPE office.

Education. As the agency's designated educator concerning sexual harassment issues, you would need a systematic plan for educating virtually all agency employees, from the agency's executive director to the nighttime custodial staff. You will have to determine how best to reach them. You consider conducting educational presentations in person.

You decide that it would be best for you to talk individually to each of the agency's units. How might you go about doing this? First, you examine an agency administrative chart that includes all staff, from top to bottom, in the agency's power structure, and shows how supervisory responsibility is structured. You could probably identify some obvious target units. For example, a Protective Services unit for older adults includes a supervisor and eight workers who meet for weekly group supervisory sessions. Perhaps you could speak to them on sexual harassment during a portion of one of their regular meetings. You develop a systematic plan for speaking to each agency unit. You could do it in any way that you choose, from alphabetical order to making random presentations according to how individual unit meetings fit into your own work schedule. You determine that you will define your target units by April 7 and finish such an educational plan by May 31 (both of which are illustrated on the PERT chart in Figure 7.3).

In summary, you first designate your target units. Second, you establish an educational presentation schedule. Finally, you follow your own proposed schedule and begin your educational programming.

Public relations. The third dimension of tasks illustrated in Figure 7.3's PERT chart involves the goal of establishing positive public relations. In order to come to you for help, people need to know that you exist. You might develop a descriptive program brochure that includes the definition of sexual harassment, a variety of brief examples, details of its illegal status, your own agency's policy, and maybe a clever cartoon to catch people's attention. You could distribute these during your educational sessions and give them to complainants coming to you for help. However, you will work on designing the brochure during the month of April, targeting May 15 for its completion date. You will have 200 copies printed by June 10, in time for your first series of presentations.

The second major way of notifying agency staff that you exist is by writing articles for the agency's bimonthly newsletter that is e-mailed to staff. (However, you are a little skeptical about this approach because you know how staff members love to delete newsletter e-mails without really reading them.) You could start with some basic definition of sexual harassment and progress to providing vignettes of sexual harassment that explore and highlight the problems involved. Additionally, you could discuss the legal basis for action against sexual harassment. Legal updates concerning other cases are another possibility. Figure 7.3's PERT chart indicates that you will submit your first item to the newsletter by May 1. You will then continue to submit items by the first of every other month (that is, July 1, September 1, November 1, January 1, and March 1). By then you will have gathered enough resources to have plenty of information to submit for newsletter publication.

Counseling. SHAPE'S fourth dimension of tasks involves the provision of counseling when needed. As indicated in the PERT chart, you anticipate making this service available by June 10. At that point you will also start your educational presentations. Staff members should begin to know who you are and where the office is. Set regular office hours that are clearly posted on the door. They can also be publicized in the agency newsletter. Your phone number should also be publicized and available, with an administrative assistant assigned to answer the phone during most office hours.

Evaluation of SHAPE functioning. SHAPE'S final dimension is evaluating the program's effectiveness. Any program needs some form of evaluation to determine whether it is worthwhile. As coordinator, you are directly responsible to the agency's director. Therefore, you need a means of being accountable to her. You decide to provide her with a record of your accomplishments. You will summarize for her the number of educational programs given, the names of staff members who participated, the number of complaints you handled, and your budgetary reports. You will submit these summaries to the director every three months. The PERT chart indicates that such reports are due on June 30, September 30, December 31, and March 31, respectively.

IMAGINE: *Implement* the Plan

The fifth step in the IMAGINE process involves implementing the plan. During this phase, you actually initiate the program and get it off the ground. You would follow action steps described in your PERT chart and monitor your progress. Such monitoring can entail the evaluation of whether you are completing your tasks and achieving your goals in a timely manner as planned or not.

Make sure you support your administrative assistant by doing such things as providing positive feedback

and listening carefully to her concerns, given that you are the primary staff person involved in the program. We have emphasized that maintaining good relationships with support staff is extremely important in any program.

You determine that a trial run is unnecessary because the program is relatively small. It involves only one-quarter of your job position time in addition to secretarial time. In essence, you are starting out small. You do not foresee any future need for expansion at this point. Because you will be providing the services, no formal contracts are needed concerning agreements with other agencies or consultants. Depending on the arrangement, you may need to amend your administrative assistant's contract to reflect new responsibilities and pay.

IMAGINE: *Neutralize* Opposition

IMAGINE's sixth step involves maintaining an ongoing wariness about potential opposition. We have established that, often, when a program is first initiated, there is a honeymoon period during which criticism may be muted. This interval is typically characterized by good (almost too-good-to-be-true) relationships with program participants and agency staff. As time passes, the honeymoon period passes, and problems may start to surface. Neutralizing opposition involves becoming aware of problems as they appear and dealing with them to the best of your ability.

IMAGINE: *Evaluate* Progress

Periodic evaluation is already built into SHAPE'S goals. You are to provide summaries of accomplishments to the agency's director every three months. This report makes you accountable for your activities. Summaries document the extent to which you prevent sexual harassment problems through educational programming, describe how you address any problems that do occur as they surface, and validate your usefulness by preventing major legal incidents. Additionally, the program structure is such that you can consult with the agency's director at any time to seek guidance and help.

Looking Ahead

This chapter reviewed the types of projects you might want to implement within your agency setting. The IMAGINE process was applied both to project implementation and to program development. An extensive example of program development regarding a sexual harassment awareness program was provided.

The next chapter will discuss the social worker's role in other macro settings—communities and neighborhoods. Community structure, politics, and power will be explored, setting the stage for you to understand and implement macro practice goals in a community setting.

Chapter Summary

The following summarizes this chapter's content as it relates to the learning objectives presented at the beginning of the chapter. Chapter content prepares social workers to:

A. *Conceptualize, implement, and evaluate projects within agencies by using the IMAGINE process.*

IMAGINE involves the following seven steps: (1) develop an innovative idea; (2) muster support; (3) identify assets; (4) specify goals, objectives, and action steps to attain them; (5) implement the plan; (6) neutralize opposition; and (7) evaluate progress. IMAGINE can be used to initiate and implement an in-service training program.

B. *Examine and propose a number of macro practice projects.*

Examples of projects in macro practice include food and clothing drives, fundraising projects, agency evaluation efforts, evaluation of new intervention methods, implementation of internal agency changes, and provision of internal services to agency staff. A specific example of a project is Nuevo Puente, a program targeting at-risk Puerto Rican youth.

C. *Apply critical thinking to address macro practice dilemmas and advocate for human rights and social and economic justice.*

Dilemmas addressed involve insufficient job training for clients at a Veterans Affairs hospital, inadequate attention to older adults living in their own homes and in need of support, and insufficient sex education at a high school.

D. *Examine and evaluate the usefulness of Program Evaluation and Review Technique (PERT) to facilitate assessment, intervention, and evaluation in project implementation and program development.*

PERT charts can facilitate implementation of a project or development of a program. Positive aspects include illustration of objectives and action steps, portrayal of specific tasks, depiction of task sequence, reference to necessary resources, and establishment of a time frame. PERT charts may be used for relatively simple projects such as preparing for a presentation to colleagues or for complex endeavors such as developing a multifaceted program.

E. *Apply critical thinking to ethical issues concerning Temporary Assistance to Needy Families (TANF), examine the issues' implications, and propose solutions to advance human rights and social and economic justice.*

Ethical issues involved in TANF include its implications for educational and economic advancement, long-term health insurance coverage, and impositions upon family structure. Questions can be raised concerning human rights, and social and economic justice addressing each issue.

F. *Conceptualize, implement, and evaluate types of programs within agencies by utilizing the IMAGINE process.*

When developing an innovative idea for program development, it's important to work with the client system and articulate the proposed program's purpose. Choosing an action system while mustering support should be executed very carefully. Identifying assets involves preparing the agency for change, considering a feasibility study, and soliciting financial resources. Specification of goals, objectives, and action steps may involve developing a PERT chart. A clear description of how the program will provide services is critical. Program implementation concerns nurturing participating staff, considering a trial run or starting out small, and formalizing necessary purchase-of-service contracts. While neutralizing opposition, a "honeymoon period" should be anticipated. Additionally, administrative support should be maintained. Evaluating progress involves monitoring daily activities, evaluating program impact, and establishing how services will be provided on an ongoing basis.

Examples of program development include a program for young homeless new mothers and housing development for nonheterosexual older adults.

G. *Apply IMAGINE to the development of a sexual harassment awareness program that addresses oppression and discrimination.*

"Unwelcome sexual advances, requests for sexual favors, and other verbal or physical conduct of a sexual nature constitutes sexual harassment when submission to or rejection of this conduct [1] explicitly or implicitly affects an individual's employment, [2] unreasonably interferes with an individual's work performance or [3] creates an intimidating, hostile or offensive work [or educational] environment" (EEOC, 2002).

IMAGINE is applied to the case example of SHAPE (Sexual Harassment Awareness Program for Employees) in a large public agency. Major programmatic elements include initial planning, provision of education to employees, public relations, counseling, and program evaluation. A PERT chart illustrates the program development, implementation, and evaluation process.

Competency Notes

The following identifies where Educational Policy (EP) competencies and practice behaviors are discussed in the chapter.

EP 2.1.3c Demonstrate effective oral and written communication in working with individuals, families, groups, organizations, communities, and colleagues. *(P. 257):* Practitioners must clearly communicate to others a proposed program's purpose, including client needs, service recipients, and services provided.

EP 2.1.4 Engage diversity and difference in practice. *(P. 256):* Color, culture, and ethnicity are dimensions of diversity. This project example involves understanding and working with Puerto Rican adolescents.

EP 2.1.5a Understand the forms and mechanisms of oppression and discrimination. *(P. 270):* Sexual harassment is a mechanism of oppression and discrimination.

EP 2.1.5c Engage in practices that advance social and economic justice. *(P. 272):* SHAPE encompasses a range of practices and services that aim to advance social and economic justice by combating sexual harassment.

EP 2.1.6b Use research evidence to inform practice. *(P. 247):* Social workers should evaluate and use new approaches and interventions that have been proven effective.

EP 2.1.8a Analyze, formulate, and advocate for policies that advance social well-being. *(P. 260):* Examination of TANF provides an opportunity to analyze the extent to which the policies and programs involved serve to advance social well-being.

EP 2.1.9b Provide leadership in promoting sustainable changes in service delivery and practice to improve the quality of social services. *(P. 246):* Social workers can provide leadership in initiating and implementing projects at the macro level. *(P. 255):* Practitioners can serve as leaders to improve the quality of service delivery through program development.

EP 2.1.10 Engage, assess, intervene, and evaluate with individuals, families, groups, organizations, and communities: *(P. 267):* Development of a sexual harassment awareness program provides an example of engagement, assessment, intervention, and evaluation occurring in an organizational program.

EP 2.1.10e Assess clients' strengths and limitations. *(P. 249):* When implementing a project, practitioners should identify and utilize client system strengths and assets. *(P. 262):* Identifying assets and strengths is a vital step in the IMAGINE process during program development.

EP 2.1.10f Develop mutually agreed-on intervention goals and objectives. *(P. 249):* After mustering support from others, practitioners who are implementing projects should work with the action system to specify goals, objectives, and action steps to attain them. *(P. 263):* In program development, specifying goals and objectives is a critical aspect of the IMAGINE process.

EP 2.1.10g Select appropriate intervention strategies. *(P. 250):* Appropriate intervention strategies should be selected when implementing a plan. *(P. 254):* Neutralizing opposition most often is an effective strategy when implementing a project in macro level intervention. *(P. 258):* Case scenarios provide opportunities to propose appropriate interventions involving program development.

EP 2.1.10i Implement prevention interventions that enhance client capacities. *(P. 256):* Nueve Puente's substance abuse prevention program for at-risk youth provides an example of prevention intervention. *(P. 273):* SHAPE's educational programming component aims to prevent sexual harassment from occurring, thus improving the organizational client system's ability to function effectively.

EP 2.1.10m Critically analyze, monitor, and evaluate interventions. *(P. 255):* Evaluating the progress of project implementation is a vital step in the IMAGINE process. *(P. 266):* Social workers should

evaluate program development by monitoring daily activities, analyzing program impact, and establishing how services should be provided on a daily basis.

On the Internet

Visit the *Generalist Practice with Organizations and Communities* Web site at www.cengage.com/social_work/kirst-ashman for learning tools such as PowerPoint® slides, tutorial quizzing, Web links, and final exams.

CHAPTER 8

Understanding Neighborhoods and Communities

Residents on South Sunrise Street were angry. Their quiet, residential neighborhood provided ample sidewalks for children to ride bikes and play. A nearby shallow creek paralleling their dead-end street even provided a place for kids to wade in the warm summers. Several years ago, the city informed residents that eventually the street would be widened. At that time, the city planned to add two more lanes of traffic to South Sunrise, but these would be built on the other side of the creek, away from their homes. Residents were unconcerned, because this plan did not affect their neighborhood.

Abruptly, the city changed its plans. One spring morning, residents received letters from the city announcing that rebuilding of South Sunrise Street would begin next month, and not on the other side of the stream as previously promised. As they read, residents envisioned mammoth bulldozers and steam shovels rumbling over the little creek. They envisioned barricades set up at the street's entrance, complete with threatening "ROAD CLOSED—RESIDENTS ONLY" signs. Residents were shocked and horrified. This plan would greatly widen the street, gobbling up front yards, sidewalks, and trees. The city's plans would shorten already-steep driveways to slopes difficult for mountain goats to master and prevent residents and guests from parking in front of their homes. The increased danger to children, the lack of involvement of street residents in the planning process, and the fear that this change would seriously diminish their quality of life spurred residents into action.

Residents pulled together and formed the South Sunrise Community Improvement Committee. They elected a president and also sought assistance from a social worker who lived on the street. Committee members met with city officials (including the neighborhood's city council representative and the director of public works, both of whom wielded power over city street planning), informed city council members of their plight, and seriously lobbied to halt what they considered a neighborhood disaster.

Finally, after strenuous effort, decision makers began to understand the plight of South Sunrise residents. After careful deliberation and consideration of alternative strategies, plans were changed. Instead of widening South Sunrise, the city chose a street two blocks over that proved to be a better target for change. The latter ran through a large plot of land occupied by several huge warehouses. No one lived there, so widening that street would have few effects on community residents.

As a result of their efforts, South Sunrise residents were able to maintain what they considered a good quality of life in their neighborhood. In addition, they opened a new channel of communication with city planners through their newly established Community Improvement Committee. Planners not only listened to residents on the street–widening issue, but also indicated a willingness to hear what residents had to say about other neighborhood concerns.

Introduction

Upon graduation, generalist social workers find themselves working in a wide range of social service agencies providing services to individuals, families, and groups. As workers provide services, they encounter problems that vary in seriousness and intensity. Take, for example, the case of Serge Menendez, an 18-year-old male high school graduate who is desperately yet unsuccessfully seeking work. Or consider Mike Gleason, who dropped out of high school and has even less potential for finding an adequately paying job. Finally, think about Debra Whitetail, 14, who just had a baby. She wants to finish high school, but has no one to help her care for her daughter. Debra's own mother died when Debra was four. Debra now lives with her grandmother, who works full-time and can't afford to quit to babysit Debra's daughter.

When dealing with individual clients, you may find it easy to lose sight of the broader social issues and problems that affect them. In reality, the problems extend far beyond the individual cases just mentioned. Each of these problems involves huge issues.

For instance, Serge is not alone. In poor school districts, as many as 50 percent of the students with high school diplomas lack the reading and writing skills needed for employment. Likewise, Mike is a student in a school district where dropout rates of 30 to 50 percent are not uncommon. Finally, Debra's lack of adequate child care is also part of a larger problem. Morrissey (2007), in a review of previous research on child care, found that high-quality child care is relatively rare, with some studies showing as few as 3 percent of children cared for in either high-quality centers or family care arrangements. While the rates of high-quality child care vary widely from state to state and study to study, there is evidence that many children are cared for in less-than-ideal arrangements. Some studies found that a third of caregivers infrequently or never played with the children in their care, and this is especially true for Latino and African American children. Morrissey notes that low-income families are more likely to be cared for in low-quality arrangements, simply because better child care costs more.

Debra's experience is shared by many other young women. She is just one of a million U.S teenagers who become pregnant each year. Although the United States has the highest rate of teenage pregnancy of any developed nation in the world, the problem of teen pregnancy is a global phenomenon. The risks associated with teenage pregnancy include more frequent illnesses and miscarriage, increased risk of poverty and reliance on welfare, higher rates of infant health and developmental problems, and high rates of child abuse. Other consequences include reduced rates of marriage and higher rates of unstable unions. Rates of teenage pregnancy vary from group to group, with Hispanic teenagers more than twice as likely as other teens to give birth (Ryan, Franzetta, & Manlove, 2005). Few teenage mothers receive any support from the father, eight out of ten do not finish high school, and 20 to 37 percent will have a second child within two years of the first child's birth (Raneri & Wiemann, 2007; Stephens, 1997).

Clearly, the welfare of individual social services clients is inextricably linked to policies and programs established by people in authority above you (CSWE, 2008, EP 2.1.8a).

It is also true that social workers must view individual clients' problems in the context of the complex larger environments in which these clients live. When one child drops out of school, it may be the

EP 2.1.8a

result of individual lack of motivation, lack of parental supervision, or any of a number of other factors unique to the child's particular family. However, when 30 percent of a school's enrollment fails to graduate, the explanation cannot rest solely on the individual dropouts or their families. Generalist practitioners must constantly keep this in mind.

The community and neighborhood exert significant influence upon individuals in most areas of the world, including the United States. Poor communities are often unable to provide high-quality schools and recreational facilities. Run-down neighborhoods may expose children to drug dealers, drive-by shootings, and gang violence. These particular problems—youth unemployment, school dropouts, and teen pregnancy—affect young people.

Of course, myriad other problems affect people of all ages and from all walks of life. Lisa Swanson, age two months, remains on life-support equipment. She was born to a cocaine-addicted mother almost three months early. Her chances of survival are still not considered very good. Vladimir Nurotuscki, who is living with AIDS, has great difficulty finding access to necessary health care. Norma Ray, 61, is homeless and suffers from increasingly serious Alzheimer's disease. She has no money and nowhere to go. Each of these individuals exemplifies a larger group of people suffering from similar problems. The generalist perspective requires us to confront macro problems and issues affecting many people as we address our individual clients' needs.

The importance of understanding the community cannot be overstated. Most people access resources at the community level, regardless of whether the program funding originates at the local, state, or national level. It is at the community level that government is potentially most responsive to individual citizens. Quality-of-life issues are most profoundly confronted at the local level. Being forced to live in substandard housing, being victimized by drug dealers and drive-by shootings, or having to choose between paying the rent and eating this week seriously diminish the quality of one's life. The absence of a day care program for Debra, the daily spectacle of homeless people sleeping in the doorways of closed downtown businesses, and the fact that almost one-third of Mike's peers will drop out of school and into a lifetime of poverty are cases in point.

The example of South Sunrise Street suggests that some of the larger problems confronting society can be addressed, at least in part, at the local level. Also, the responsiveness of local elected leaders to

community-level concerns makes it easier to address shared problems.

This chapter stresses the importance of understanding the communities and neighborhoods in which we live and work. The ability to understand these entities, comprehend clients' situations as existing within a context, and identify critical areas of need is essential. It is important not to lose sight of the forest (communities) when we are dealing with individual trees (our clients). Simultaneously, our responsibility as generalists is to intervene, when appropriate, to ensure that clients receive needed services, equitable treatment, and adequate resources. Remember that the generalist provides services to individuals, families, and groups in addition to *organizations* and *communities*.

Learning Objectives

This chapter will provide content concerning how social workers:

   A. *Identify the professional role of a social worker in neighborhoods and communities.*

   B. *Utilize conceptual frameworks to guide in understanding the functions and types of communities and neighborhoods.*

   C. *Employ a systems perspective to view the community as an ecological and social system.*

   D. *Identify key concepts needed to discover and appraise changes in neighborhoods and communities.*

   E. *Utilize community resource systems to assess and intervene with neighborhoods and communities.*

   F. *Identify how community factors such as social stratification, economic and political systems, and power may advance or impede human rights and social and economic justice.*

   G. *Describe the role that neighborhoods play as helping networks and how neighborhood organizations can serve as a resource for service delivery and sustainable change.*

   H. *Assess the ability of communities and neighborhoods to advance social well-being, and respond to the needs of their residents.*

The Role of Social Workers in Neighborhoods and Communities

As a social worker in a public or private human service agency, you may not initially see a role for yourself in neighborhoods or the larger community. After all, you were hired primarily to investigate child abuse and neglect cases, or to provide case management for clients with chronic mental illness, or to perform perhaps a hundred other professional tasks your agency expects. When you're immersed in case responsibilities, it may be easy to forget one of the things that makes social workers different from other professionals: social workers are concerned about the *social environment.* Generalist practitioners have an obligation that is drawn directly from the code of ethics of our profession. According to the National Association of Social Workers (NASW) *Code of Ethics* (NASW, 1999), each social worker is expected to

- *Enhance human well-being and help meet the basic needs of all people, with particular attention to the needs and empowerment of people who are vulnerable, oppressed, and living in poverty.*
- *[Attend] to the environmental forces that create, contribute to, and address problems in living.*
- *Promote social justice and social change with and on behalf of clients.*
- *[Be] sensitive to cultural and ethnic diversity and strive to end discrimination, oppression, poverty, and other forms of social injustice.*
- *Focus on individual well-being in a social context and the well-being of society. (P.1).*

EP 2.1.5b

Further, the profession expects social workers to engage in advocacy and social action and to promote social and economic justice (CSWE, 2008, EP 2.1.5b). This is an incredible array of expectations for our field.

This means that a responsible social worker has a much broader mandate than do other human-service practitioners, such as psychologists or marriage and family therapists. This is particularly so at the macro level. Sometimes you will become involved in a neighborhood or community because of a specific case (individual, family, or group) with which you are working. At other times, you will become involved because several agencies' representatives join together to address a problem extending beyond their individual walls, and they will invite you to participate. At still other times, you may volunteer to become involved (as did the social worker in the Sunrise Street neighborhood) because the need is there and you have the interest, knowledge, and skill to positively affect the outcome.

Social workers engage in a broad and colorful spectrum of activities when they intervene in neighborhoods and communities. Quality-of-life issues, such as those mentioned at the chapter opening, are critical to neighborhood and community residents. Issues like this are so significant and widespread that social workers have to choose what to target for action and what to ignore. Zoning and housing codes directly affect the quality of life of homeowners and renters alike. (Zoning and housing codes are a combination of city, state, and federal laws and regulations that cover everything from the safety of your plumbing, water, and electrical systems to the number of unrelated people who can live in a home or apartment. Housing codes usually require, for example, hot and cold running water, bathrooms, and heat in a house or rental unit.) Imagine what it would be like if there were no rules governing what a landlord could do to a tenant. Without these codes, landlords could turn off the heat and water supply simply because they disliked their tenants. Social workers sometimes work directly to get such codes adopted or to enforce codes already in place.

A social worker might lobby a city government to have abandoned, deteriorating homes in an urban ghetto sold cheaply to community applicants. The applicants would agree to repair and upgrade these homes themselves in return for ownership. Likewise, social workers might pressure a city planning council to require that a neighborhood developer set land aside for parks and recreational purposes. Or a social worker might find herself struggling in a neighborhood to overcome residents' opposition to a proposed group home for people with developmental disabilities. Residents there may be terrified by, and obsessed with, the many myths characterizing disabled people.

Social workers may also focus on issues or concerns that cut across multiple communities. For example, the United States clearly lags behind many other countries with respect to child well-being (UNICEF, 2007). A practitioner who is familiar with conditions in other developed countries might find it unacceptable that the United States ranks 20th out of 21 nations in areas such as poverty rates, health and safety, quality of education, and a host of other measures of child well-being. For example, the United States has a relatively high rate of infant mortality and low birth weight for children compared to most other wealthy nations. Impacting such disparities requires practitioner involvement at state and national levels to bring about changes in laws, policies, and regulations.

Likewise, social workers are in a position to recognize social and economic injustices that occur across various geographical and legal jurisdictions. For example, the U.S. government operates a guest worker program that brings more than 120,000 foreigners into the country each year to work in areas as disparate as landscaping, agriculture, and construction, among others. Despite the use of the term "guest worker," these individuals receive treatment that would not be tolerated by other citizens. Unable to change jobs, exploited and abused, these guest workers have few, if any, avenues of redress. According to a report by the Southern Poverty Law Center (2007), these workers are "routinely cheated out of wages, forced to mortgage their futures to obtain low-wage, temporary jobs, held virtually captive by employers and labor brokers who seize their documents, forced to live in squalid conditions, and denied medical benefits for on-the-job injuries" (p. 2). Such treatment of guest workers who are here legally is often repeated for undocumented workers who are here illegally. It should be clear that there is no shortage of problems that practitioners can target for change.

Generalist practitioners employ a vast array of skills to effect changes for clients. Vayda and Bogo (1991, p. 273) identify some additional typical activities requiring these skills:

1. *Assessing needs through use of interagency committees.* You may recall the interagency needs assessment in Highlight 3.2 in Chapter 3, which focused on the needs of latchkey children in a community.
2. *Identifying service gaps and recommending new programs.* You constantly confront the fact that young people have no social activities after school unless they are involved in sports. You suggest developing an after-school drop-in center with activities of interest to adolescents.
3. *Advocating for policy changes in response to needs identified by grassroots community organizations* (CSWE, 2008, EP 2.1.8a). You learn that children living in a homeless shelter with their families are not enrolled in school because school policies require children to have a permanent residence. Consequently, these children fall desperately far behind in school. The Community Homeless Coalition asks you, as a school social worker, to help change the school policy.

EP 2.1.8a

4. *Participating in professional association action groups.* You become involved with the local NASW chapter in lobbying for a new state law to prevent employers from firing gay and lesbian workers solely because of their sexual orientation.

Social workers can be particularly effective in macro areas because they are more likely to recognize and define social problems; they can help design appropriate programs to combat problems; and they can argue for new policies and programs to address these problems. As an agency worker, you are most likely to be acutely aware of how agency policies or state and federal regulations affect your clients. As you know, your involvement in these activities may develop either as part of your job or in addition to it.

Likewise, a neighborhood association (like that on Sunrise Street) may ask a social worker to represent it in efforts to dissuade the city from widening a street and cutting down all the mature-growth trees. As a social worker in the local neighborhood center, you are the logical person to turn to for assistance. In a recent case, a single dogged individual lobbied endlessly to convince the highway department to move a street design three feet off its proposed center to save 60 mature oak and maple trees. The highway department grudgingly agreed. The result was the loss of only a handful of minor scrawny saplings. Neighborhood property owners, all of whom were low- or fixed-income elderly residents, rejoiced.

Of course, social workers are also residents of their neighborhoods and citizens of their communities. In either capacity, you may end up in a leadership role helping fellow citizens address some issue. Social workers' ability to solve problems, to work with people in groups, and to understand systems help them in their roles as citizens.

Because we are most concerned about you as a generalist practitioner, we will focus most of our attention on this role. As a social worker, your primary functions are delivering existing services (such as case management or linking clients to services), helping to develop new resources (by lobbying for more funds or new programs in your agency), and modifying old services to benefit clients (such as identifying more effective ways of intervening with victims of sexual abuse). You are concerned about the individual, but always within the social environment. You will simultaneously view the community as the context of your practice as well as a potential target of change if clients are not getting the resources or services they need. You will ultimately need skills in advocacy, research, assessment, evaluation, engagement, and conscious use of self, as well as a commitment to social justice. Obviously, everyday agency demands for competence will require many of these skills. However, the social work profession requires still other skills for meeting professional expectations extending beyond the narrow window of agency practice.

Using these skills requires a great deal more knowledge about communities and neighborhoods.

Just as you cannot hope to work with people without understanding human growth and behavior, you cannot practice competently in the community without a similar knowledge of its growth and dynamics. The remainder of this chapter will help you understand communities and neighborhoods—the contexts for your macro practice.

Defining Community and Neighborhood

Definitions of the term "community" often fall into two categories, traditional and alternative (Schriver, 2004). Traditional communities are the primary focus of this chapter and book. They encompass places like cities, towns, and villages, identifiable geographical entities. These communities are characterized by residences, shared living space, and some array of businesses that serve the needs of those who live there.

A nontraditional definition of community incorporates what we have come to think of as nonplace (or nongeographic) communities. An example is the legal community or the social work community. These communities are also known as "identificational communities" (Schriver, 2004, p. 509). Members of these communities share common interests and may carry out some of the same functions as place communities. A professional community such as social work, for instance, may provide a sense of belonging, support, and validation of one's work, values, and ideas. As we shall see, these characteristics are also supplied to varying degrees by place communities.

Traditional definitions of community usually have several common components. The first is that a community occupies a *shared physical space.* In other words, it has defined boundaries. Thus, a community's boundaries might include all the area west of Peculiar Street, east of Banshee Avenue, south of the Sharptooth River, and north of Pineapple Boulevard. We can mark these boundaries on a map. They clearly separate one community from another.

A second component of the definition is *social interaction.* That is, community members interact with each other differently than they interact with people outside the community. Social interaction in communities can revolve around employment, recreation, church-going, or myriad other activities. Typically, the interactions occur frequently and face-to-face.

A community's third component is a *shared sense of identity.* Community members often form a strong affiliation and identity with their community. They will say with pride that they live in Chicago, Los Angeles, Tokyo, Oosberg, or Memphis.

Of course, for some residents, the sense of identity is stronger than for others. Newcomers often do not feel the same degree of identification with a community as those who have lived there all their lives. They may experience alienation and marginalization. Nor might the community readily accept newcomers. When running for city council (the city's elected governing board), the author remembers once being referred to as a "newcomer" in a newspaper article. That he had been a resident for eight years was irrelevant, given that others had lived in the community for decades. Being labeled a newcomer was almost equivalent to being called an ax murderer.

Combining the elements listed above, we conclude that a community occupies shared physical space where residents engage in social interaction and maintain a shared sense of identity. These definitions are helpful because they allow us to understand much of what goes on in a community. The intense attachment and sense of belonging and identity that long-time residents share helps explain, for example, why newcomers sometimes feel left out. It also explains why a smaller community might fight attempts by a larger adjoining city to annex (legally incorporate) its space.

Neighborhoods share some of the same features as communities. According to Martin, D.G. (2003). Enacting neighborhood. *Urban Geography* 24(5) 361–385, a convenient way of defining neighborhoods is to consider them geographical residential areas in which people share similar values, lifestyles, and housing types, and exhibit a sense of cohesion. Typically, a community is composed of many neighborhoods. In each, the degree of neighborhood identity is often even greater than the sense of identity found in the larger community. If you think about your home community, you may recall many recognizable neighborhoods. The standard of living is likely to be similar in a given neighborhood, whereas the community may have a wide variation in living standards. Housing prices or rental rates are similar within individual neighborhoods, further providing a sense of commonality.

We will discuss neighborhoods in more detail under "Neighborhoods."

Functions of Communities

What does a community do for people? Why do people cluster in neighborhoods and communities? Warren (1978) has identified five functions all communities serve:

1. *Socialization,* defined as the transmission of values, culture, beliefs, and norms to new community members. *Values* are those principles a group considers important. Loyalty is a value. *Culture* includes customs and ways of doing things. Some form of shaking hands when greeting strangers is a custom. *Beliefs* are ideas that members assume are true, but may not be verifiable, such as a belief in a supreme being or a belief that all police are biased. *Norms* are a community's expectations for how its members should act. For example, attending school is an expected behavior (norm) for most children.

   Socialization occurs through both formal and informal mechanisms. Formal mechanisms include laws, rules, and procedures adopted by a community's legal bodies. Informal mechanisms entail any informal transmission of such information; for example, through other community members' comments or reactions. A neighbor might casually note, "Yeah, look how much rain we've been having, and look how long your grass has grown." This neighbor really wants to convey that the lawn is in desperate need of mowing. Or a neighbor might say, "You got any offers for that '72 Chevy pickup truck parked in the front yard yet?"—suggesting that the pick-up truck makes the front yard look like a junkyard (and perhaps that's where the truck really belongs).

2. *The production, distribution, and consumption of goods and services.* All communities provide a variety of services and products consumed by residents. This includes housing, food, and perhaps banking and street maintenance. Communities encourage and regulate construction of homes, apartments, and commercial buildings. Some communities have a greater variety of goods and services available than others. Specific individuals may carry out these functions and provide the goods and services used by individuals and families, but the community is the context in which this exchange occurs.

3. *Social control,* which involves setting limits on behavior by creating and enforcing laws via police and other official bodies. In practice, social control is the enforcement of community norms and values. Such control ranges from enacting 25-mile-per-hour speed limits on city streets (when children are not present) to setting building codes and requirements for individual homes. The city may restrict the number of people allowed in any one dwelling unit and set standards for how large the yard must be for a new home. It may also restrict what you can do with your home. (City regulations might forbid using your apartment as a massage parlor, for example.)

   Social workers have been called "agents of social control" because in many positions, the practitioner's job involves enforcing community standards. The probation officer, for example, who helps ensure that the individual recently released from prison abides by certain restrictions, is enforcing community norms. The protective service worker investigating allegations of child abuse is also providing a control function. The sanction that social workers are given to carry out these types of activities arises from the community's wish to exert a degree of social control on its residents.

4. *Mutual support,* meaning that community members take care of one another. It ranges from informal action, such as giving directions to strangers, to formal actions, such as providing social services for identified groups of citizens. Examples of social services include child protective services for abused or neglected children, probation and parole services for criminals, and shelter for survivors of domestic violence, to name a few. Self-help groups and networks, as described in Highlight 3.3 in Chapter 3, also provide avenues of mutual support.

5. Providing for the *participation* of its residents. This means that residents have the opportunity to interact with others through recreation, talking, church-going, and other forms of socializing. Obviously, some members of a community participate more than others in these interactions. Shut-ins and institutionalized patients have much less opportunity to interact with others in the larger community. This social dimension of a community is often what people speak of when they praise a community's qualities. They may refer to a community as very open or friendly, or cold and "tight knit."

This reflects the commentator's sense of the community's quality and quantity of participation.

Whereas the definitions and functions just described apply primarily to communities, they apply almost equally well to neighborhoods. As we have seen, a neighborhood is "a region or locality in which inhabitants share certain characteristics, values, mutual interests, and styles of living" (Barker, 2003, p. 292). However, neighborhoods cannot offer the same breadth of services to residents (such as police forces supplying social control). Neighborhoods do carry out the other functions, however. Highlight 8.1 contrasts two communities of approximately equal size and their capacity to carry out common functions.

Types of Communities

Communities can be classified according to several dimensions, using size, economic health, or ethnic diversity as variables. We can also look at several very special types of communities that serve unique needs of inhabitants. These include reservation, bedroom, and institutional communities.

Perhaps the most common classification system is size. The largest type of community is the metropolis. *Metropolitan communities* are large cities that serve as the surrounding area's business and economic center. They may actually be composed of multiple cities located in close proximity to one another. Such multiple cities might include a large central city surrounded by suburban and satellite cities. (Suburban cities are small cities that adjoin another larger city, whereas satellite cities are located near, but not adjacent to, the central city.) For example, the metropolitan community of Madison, Wisconsin, comprises the city of Madison and the adjacent cities of Middleton, Sun Prairie, Verona, and many smaller towns that serve as bedroom communities for Madison. Such metropolitan communities may be thought of as a system with multiple subsystems of various sizes. They are a unified system in the sense that together they perform all the functions described earlier (Warren, 1978). Metropolitan communities vary in size from about 50,000 to several million residents.

There are also a variety of *nonmetropolitan communities*. Nonmetropolitan communities differ from metropolitan communities, again, mainly in terms of size. Johnson and Yanca (2001) discuss six different types of such communities:

1. *Small cities (15,000–50,000 population)*. Small cities are legally organized entities, usually with their own police department and several other city departments.

2. *Small towns (8,000–20,000 population)*. Smaller towns are usually not legally organized, or "chartered." The town may offer few, if any, services, relying on the county or parish to provide such basic services as police protection. (Larger towns may offer a variety of services.)

3. *Rural communities (under 10,000 population)*. Rural communities often consist of a very small town surrounded by townships. The community provides no services, and thus usually relies on the county or parish.

4. *Reservation communities*. Reservation communities are located on Native American reservations recognized by the federal government. They vary in size, depending on the number of residents in the particular reservation.

5. *Bedroom communities*. Bedroom communities are predominantly residential in nature, with little if any industry or business. Their residents work in nearby communities. That is, residents sleep and find recreation in their home communities, but work in nearby cities that offer more business and industrial opportunities.

6. *Institutional communities*. Institutional communities have one major employer that may overshadow the whole surrounding area. Therefore, sometimes they are called "company towns." The company or institution may own all or a large portion of the available housing stock, renting it to its employees. By virtue of this ownership and of their control of employment, these institutions often have enormous influence on community events. Residents have much less freedom when the employing organization literally controls the community through ownership of most property. Once a person leaves the employ of the company, the company maintains control of the property. A variation of the company town is the community dominated by a single large employer. Examples include college towns and communities with other large government facilities, such as prisons and mental hospitals. Although not as overwhelming in their impact as industrial company towns, these employers may still exert an enormous influence on life in the community. Likewise, in some communities a church may own most, if not all, of the property, renting homes to members of that religious organization. For example, in polygamous communities along the southern Utah/northern Arizona border

HIGHLIGHT 8.1

Examples of Two Communities

Hyerville is a community with a rich history. Founded by merchants hoping to serve farmers in the surrounding area, it quickly became a center for manufacturing of items the rural community needed. Early in its history, the community produced farm machinery, wagons, dairy equipment and tools. The town prospered quickly, growing in population and reputation. Townspeople helped found a local university, built many churches, and took a great deal of pride in their community.

Within 50 years of its founding, however, Hyerville was in trouble. Manufacturing companies shut down because of economic hard times and consumers' changing interests. Wagons were no longer needed when automobiles became available. The university, once a positive feature of the community, became a focus of its discontent.

The school's enormous growth brought too many students crowding into the old mansions along Main Street, parking their cars all over the residential areas near campus, and engaging in vandalism after weekend drinking bouts. Although several small manufacturing companies remain in town, the university is now the town's dominant employer, offering jobs mainly to well-educated outsiders. Local residents resent the institution "on the hill."

Despite this resentment, residents of Hyerville are generally very neighborly. Although it takes a while for them to accept newcomers, they find ways to welcome them. Block parties and invitations to join churches and social clubs are regularly offered. Residents generally know their neighbors' names, not to mention where they work, what kinds of cars they drive, and where they shop. Hyerville is a "neighborly" community in which to live.

Compare Hyerville to Spikeville, a city of approximately the same size. Unlike Hyerville, which has a downtown business district and a couple of discount stores, Spikeville has nothing. Built as a residential community to house railroad workers, it quickly followed the economic misfortunes of the railroad. Without businesses of its own, Spikeville has been forced to increase residential property taxes to pay for its school system.

To raise additional money, Spikeville encourages new home building by offering home sites at greatly reduced prices. Inexpensive housing has gone up quickly. However, residents who buy the new houses have no sense of attachment to the community like that in Hyerville. People do not know the names of their next-door neighbors, let alone what they do for a living. Without local business and industry, virtually everyone in Spikeville works outside the city. As a result, the city becomes largely a "bedroom community" to which people return after working somewhere else. This further reduces the sense of community identity.

Let's look briefly at how these two communities differ in terms of the functions they provide. Both communities provide socialization through their respective school systems. Other socialization mechanisms, such as participation in community activities, are much greater in Hyerville, where most residents spend their entire day in the community. As for the production of goods and services, Spikeville performs this function less well than Hyerville. Without a business sector, residents are forced to acquire goods and services outside the community. Hyerville, on the other hand, has an abundance of small shops, stores, and discount stores, as well as several other businesses and professional services.

Both communities provide social control through laws and local police departments. Both also have housing and health regulations and inspectors, but Spikeville seems less willing than Hyerville to enforce its rules. In addition, both communities provide certain kinds of support. However, Spikeville does so to a lesser extent. It has few social service agencies and makes few formal attempts to assist those in need. Finally, participation exists to a much higher degree in Hyerville. The availability of opportunities for people to spend time together is greater there because people both work and reside in the community.

It is clear that even cities of comparable size can be more or less effective in fulfilling their functions, depending on a variety of factors. Of the two cities, which one would you find more attractive as a place to live?

and in Texas, the Fundamentalist Church of Jesus Christ of Latter Day Saints (FLDS) owned almost all of the land and rented to members of its own congregation. When members fell from the good graces of church leaders, they were forced out of their homes, just as is the case with fired employees in company towns. (Note: FLDS is not part of LDS or the Mormon Church.)

As you can see, the first three communities differ from one another primarily by their size, whether they are legally chartered, and whether they provide services to residents. The reservation community is characterized not by size, but by the composition of its population (Native Americans) and the unique relationship of the community to the federal and state governments. Reservations are geographical areas set aside by the federal government to serve as communities for identified populations of Native Americans. Tribal governments have jurisdiction over some functions on the reservation, including law enforcement, and the federal government has a role in assisting the reservation communities by providing financial and medical services.

Bedroom and institutional communities differ from one another primarily in terms of the functions they perform for their residents.

Of course, any system of categorization of communities leaves gaps and involves overlaps. For instance,

some small towns of 10,000 people could also be referred to as rural areas because of the overlapping size definition. Thus, it is important to understand that one can define and describe communities by specific size rather than relying solely on such simple labels as "small town" or "rural community." In addition, some communities that rely largely on the recreational industry for their livelihood may have an official population as small as 10,000 but swell to many times that size during the "season." Examples are Branson, Missouri; Wisconsin Dells, Wisconsin; Gatlinburg, Tennessee; and Estes Park, Colorado. It is also important to note that different authors use different definitions in referring to various-size communities. The Census Bureau, for instance, updates its definitions of *urban* and *rural* from time to time to reflect different perspectives and changing demographics.

Communities may also be classified on the basis of ethnic composition or degree of homogeneity/heterogeneity. For example, a community may have a mixture of people of many nationalities or socio-economic classes or be dominated by a particular group. In some cases, although a diversity of ethnic groups is present, one group predominates. Miami, for example, has a very large population of Cubans. This has important implications for life in the community. Stores cater to specific population groups, and residents are often politically active to ensure that the needs of their group are considered.

Some communities are predominantly affluent and others are primarily working-class. Still other communities may be more diverse but have ethnic enclaves, such as Chinatown, Little Saigon, or Polish Hill. These factors are important in understanding what goes on in a community. For example, ethnic enclaves may offer special services to members of that minority group. Support groups and networks for Hmong residents (who migrated to the United States from Southeast Asia after the Vietnam War), for example, may be found in a particular area of the city. Language differences can complicate using community services such as education and human services. Similarly, a community's economic strengths and resources may allow new social services to be developed or may severely limit what is possible.

Clear community boundaries are not always easy to establish. Although the boundaries of cities are easily identified, community boundaries may be more diffuse. An ethnic community might be located primarily in one city but spill over into adjoining areas. The diversity of communities is compounded when one realizes

© Myrleen Ferguson Cate/PhotoEdit

Community murals provide a sense of identity for residents of ethnic enclaves.

there are almost 20,000 municipalities (cities) in the United States, about 17,000 townships (legally recognized geographical areas that may or may not have elected leaders), and more than 3,000 counties (U.S. Census Bureau, 2003, p. 276). Other communities share a common sense of identity but are not geographical entities like cities or towns.

What is most important, however, is that neighborhoods and communities serve a variety of purposes for residents, who also come in different sizes and compositions. The effective social worker, trying to understand a particular community's dynamics, would be wise to consider which of the community functions described earlier are being carried out and which are not. It would also be helpful to know what type of community is under scrutiny. For example, is this a rural community or a metropolitan one? Is it an ethnic community or a reservation community? This knowledge is helpful in assessing a community, but is not in itself sufficient to direct your efforts as a change agent.

In the following sections, we will consider the community as an ecological and social system and explain ways of understanding and assessing the community in a practice context.

Using the Systems Perspective

EP 2.1.7a

Generalist social workers use general systems theory to understand the relationships among various components of our society (CSWE, 2008, EP 2.1.7a). Systems theory posits that these elements relate to one another in an orderly, functional manner. For example, the human body is a system, in that all of the various internal systems (e.g., circulatory, nervous, respiratory) relate to one another in a specific and predictable manner. Likewise, a human being can be seen as one element in a system that includes the family, an employer, and a friendship group, and larger units such as a school, church, and community. Social systems may be viewed as a series of boxes nested one inside the other. Figure 8.1 illustrates this view.

Thus, if you think of yourself as the person in the center, you recognize that you are part of a much larger set of systems. First, you are part of a family system composed of your family's other members. Next, your family is a system within the community. Likewise, your community is a system within the state where you reside. You can carry this analysis further in both directions, considering either larger or smaller systems.

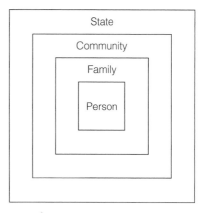

FIGURE 8.1 A Social Systems Model

For example, your state (e.g., Missouri or Wisconsin) is part of a larger system called the United States. Similarly, as the person in the center, you are composed of smaller units or internal systems (subsystems) such as the circulatory or nervous system.

As we grow up, we tend to see the community through our parents' and other family members' eyes. Of course, members of the community may view us as members of a particular family instead of as individuals. They might say, "He's a Johnson kid. What did you expect?" Or "Like father, like son."

In one sense, the diagrammatic model in Figure 8.1 is helpful because it may be seen as circumscribing (or limiting) one's behavior. If the environment (including the family or community) is unacceptably restricting the person's behavior, she or he may seek to change the environment somehow. For example, family members who place unrealistic expectations on a child may need help in recognizing and changing their demands. Helping the family change is an appropriate social-work role.

Similarly, if we want to understand individuals and families, we have to consider the influence of the community on both of these systems. Social workers must become more aware of the relationship between the individual and the environmental forces that impact on that individual. Unemployment affecting several families may have nothing to do with the personal inadequacies of the family members, but much to do with what is happening to jobs in the community. Social workers must look beyond the individual and focus on the larger social system to accurately assess client problems. In short, human behavior is a function of the interactions among the cultural, social, biological, and psychological aspects of our environment.

This perspective, and the recognition that we must identify and build upon client strengths, is the essence of generalist practice.

Various authors have described social work practice using a systems model (Compton, Galaway, & Cournoyer, 2005; Pinus & Minahan, 1973) in which at least four primary systems are identified: *change agent, target, client,* and *action* systems.

Typically a "problem" is reported to a worker or an agency that we refer to as the *change agent* system. This term is used because social workers are charged with responsibility for helping improve (change) circumstances and situations for their clients. The agency of which we are a part is thus a change agent system, because the entire agency's goal is to facilitate improvement for clients. You may have heard social workers called change agents. The concept comes from this model.

The *target* system includes those individuals, organizations, or community elements that need changing. We might, for example, want a member of the city council to change her vote on a housing project for the homeless. Perhaps we want the building inspector to enforce existing building codes so that poor clients do not have to put up with leaky plumbing and unsanitary conditions. Or maybe police officers tend to stop and question minority individuals on the street more often than nonminorities, and we want to ensure equal treatment. In each of these cases, the person or organization that we want to change is a target system.

The *client* system consists of those who will benefit directly or indirectly from the change. The client system may well initiate the change by bringing it to your attention. A client infected with AIDS who asks your help in getting health care when the local nursing home has refused him admission is an initiator. He is also the intended beneficiary or client system.

Action systems are those individuals, groups, or other entities that will carry out the effort to cause change. Sometimes this effort will be conducted by the social worker, sometimes by others. If we are trying to get the police department to treat oppressed groups more fairly, it might be best to have the city manager or city council manage the change. (The city manager is the chief administrative officer in some cities, and the council is the chief legislative body. Managers supervise all city staff, and the council supervises the city manager.) After all, they may be in the best position to put pressure on the police department and administration. Here the city manager or council would be the action system.

Any one of these systems may be responsible for bringing a problem to the forefront for action. Often, an individual client or group of clients, another professional, or an interested third party will identify a specific problem needing attention. An example is the social worker mentioned in Chapter 3 (Highlight 3.2), who raised concerns about the needs of latchkey children. She brought various groups together to discuss the problem. Another example is John Rogers, a social worker who helped form a neighborhood association. He pursued that course because it was a more effective way to address neighborhood problems than having individual residents try to handle things themselves.

As we have seen, one individual or group may play multiple roles. Thus, under the right set of circumstances, the social worker may be an action system and change agent system all in one. In other situations, the worker may play only a single role. Applying the idea illustrated in Figure 8.1 to the social worker's environment, we can place the worker in the center box within her agency (the next-larger box). Being a part of a larger system also means that agency rules, expectations, and traditions constrain the worker. Understanding these ideas should help the worker maintain perspective. For example, the worker must recognize that she is influenced by systems that include her employer and, as mentioned earlier, the social work profession itself.

The Community as an Ecological and Social System

Understanding several theoretical perspectives is necessary before you can assess and change systems. These perspectives include ecological, social systems, social structural, and human behavior theories.

Ecological Perspective

Ecosystems or *ecological theory* (Germain, 1991) emphasizes the importance of the transactions between systems within an environment (CSWE, 2008, EP 2.1.7a). For example, take the experience that many people of color have in their interactions (transactions) with police departments. The tendency of law-enforcement personnel to stop an African American driving through a predominantly white community definitely affects how the person of color views the police department. Thus, you can understand how

EP 2.1.7a

various groups in a community might have very different perspectives on such social institutions as law enforcement, schools, and employers. These transactions are the primary focus of ecological theory. When you try to understand human behavior within the social environment, remember that the community is part of that environment. How people experience their social environment has a major influence on their expectations about the future and their trust level in social institutions (including social workers). Intervening at the macro level requires a solid recognition of the community as an ecological system. Social workers must also focus on how two or more systems interact. Characteristics of the community—such as size, racial composition, age of residents, population density, and the existing social structure (e.g., who has power, resources, and influence)—are important aspects of every community. They will be particularly helpful as we figure out when and where to intervene.

Social Systems Perspective

In addition, every community can be viewed as a *social system* with all of the associated characteristics, including boundaries, homeostasis, Stressors, task and maintenance functions, and subsystems. Communities have *boundaries* (borders or dividing lines) that separate them from their environment. These may be political, physical, or psychological boundaries. Political boundaries are city or county limits or wards or precinct divisions. Physical boundaries might include rivers, roads, or other geological features. Psychological boundaries are psychic separations from others. Gay and lesbian communities have a sense of identity that creates a boundary between them and nongay and nonlesbian groups.

At the same time, all communities respond to change like any other system. That is, they tend to seek *homeostasis* or *equilibrium* (relative balance) and attempt to maintain the status quo when threatened by outside *Stressors*. Stressors are forces that disrupt the homeostasis of a system. Examples in people's everyday lives include getting married, losing a job, moving to a new community, divorce, illness, and various catastrophes. In the lives of communities, Stressors might include loss of a job or downsizing at a major employer, bankruptcy (this has affected several cities and, in the mid-1990s, Orange County, California), rapid growth or decline in population, scandals involving city government or officials, tragedies (such as the events of 9/11 and Hurricane Katrina), and even

pressure to change conditions in a community (such as attempts to pass legislation protecting the rights of gay and lesbian residents).

Communities perform both *task and maintenance functions* as they seek to maintain a range of services, attend to the needs of multiple audiences, and respond to special-interest groups. Task functions include such mundane activities as snowplowing, street maintenance, and police and fire protection. Maintenance functions, more social in nature, serve to maintain the identity and health of communities. They include activities that help make people feel positive about living in a community. Examples are Fourth of July fireworks, Christmas and holiday street lighting, and recreational facilities such as swimming pools and parks.

Although the community is often seen as providing assistance to its residents, the relationship between citizens and their community is hardly one-sided. Many *primary groups* (e.g., families) help the community function. Individuals, families, and groups use community services, thus helping to justify the existence of those services. In addition, many groups contribute their own services to augment those provided by the community itself. Self-help groups offer services not normally available from traditional agencies. Service clubs and similar organizations extend city services by contributing money, time, or personpower to projects that benefit the community. Thus, a Kiwanis Club may donate money and materials to build a park shelter. The Junior League may donate time to improve the appearance of a center for domestic violence survivors. College organizations and local businesses may volunteer to clean up city streets or highways as a way of helping communities.

In addition, each community may be viewed as a collection of *subsystems* (smaller, internal systems)—including economic, political, health, education, social welfare, and so forth—that often interact with and affect each other and other systems inside and outside the community (Fellin, 2001).

Social Structural Perspective

Social structural theory focuses on understanding how these various subsystems affect the individual and the group (CSWE, 2008, EP 2.1.7a). Attention is directed to how some social structures (systems) empower

EP 2.1.7a

clients and others alienate or oppress them. For example, a city hospital may treat poor patients so badly that they quit going there, despite their need for medical care. In contrast, a city job program may actually involve clients in the development of policies and procedures affecting them. The hospital oppresses clients; the job program empowers them. The latter gives clients a sense of importance and control over their lives whereas the former does not. Understanding how all of these social structures interact with each other and with community residents and groups can tell you a great deal about the health and desirability of a community.

Human Behavior Perspective

EP 2.1.7a

The final tool we use is *human behavior theory* (or *theories,* because several are commonly employed) (CSWE, 2008, EP 2.1.7a). These theories are more useful for understanding the behavior of individuals and families and less useful for larger systems. However, the roles of adaptation and stress (common to many human behavior theories) are useful in understanding how and why individuals behave in a certain manner when dealing with larger systems such as communities. For example, some groups, denied social or economic justice, lose any confidence in the willingness of larger systems (education, police, or social services) to help them. They adapt to injustices by becoming apathetic, angry, or both.

One human behavioral theory, which suggests that much of our current behavior is the consequence of past learning, may also help us understand why individuals in an organization or community act the way they do. Being victimized by drive-by shootings can cause an entire neighborhood to lock its doors, refuse to help neighbors, and keep its children constantly indoors. When this happens, the quality of life in the neighborhood is clearly affected.

Consider how the above two examples might influence individuals who have emigrated to the United States from some areas of the world that are in turmoil. Refugees from areas of Africa may have found that the larger systems (e.g., police, government) do not protect them from violence, and in fact may be the perpetrators of violence. Ethnic cleansing is a common occurrence in some regions of the world, where one ethnic group engages in systematic efforts to kill those who do not share their culture or religion. In such cases, trust in formal institutions may be completely absent and people may fear contacts with outsiders. Even well-meaning social workers may be seen as potential threats since we are often employed by governmental agencies.

Similarly, *rational theories,* which posit that actions and feelings arise from our thinking process, are also important. Suppose we wish to change the minds of members of a target system. If a decision maker believes that you have little community support for your ideas, she is not likely to give you what you seek. If she becomes convinced that you have great community support (whether you do or not, what she *thinks* is significant), she is more likely to accede to your request.

Through the use of multiple theories, you can become more effective in dealing with larger systems in the environment. If you understand why things are the way they are and have more insight into how systems work, you are in a much stronger position to change them. These theories can guide your practice, because they provide clues about what approaches to take to bring about change.

Additional Perspectives on the Community

Ideally, the most effective communities respond to the needs of all population segments. Often, however, certain portions of the community (such as the homeless) seem to be ignored—either because they lack power or because they are invisible, or both. Needs come to the attention of a community as a function of many factors. For example, when asked what constitutes a "good" community, residents will often identify both positives and the absence of negatives. The community's positive aspects may include that it's a safe place to raise kids, the cost of living is reasonable, parks and recreation services are excellent, and schools are good. Negative factors might include a high crime rate, air pollution, traffic problems, and inadequate school funding. Clearly, the list of qualities is highly individual. So how does a community focus on meeting a particular type of need? A need is often brought to community attention by people with a specific agenda. For example, wealthy and influential citizens concerned about public safety and crime convince the police force to crack down on drug dealers. In the process, the police department begins to stop every person of color they see on the streets on the grounds that they might be drug dealers. The needs of one group in this community have created problems for another group. In another city, the community responds to a vocal minority by undertaking efforts to preserve historic buildings, beautify city streets, and improve traffic flow on Main Street. In a third city, efforts focus primarily on economic development, bringing in new businesses and jobs, and combating job losses occasioned by local plant closings. In each case, cities are responding to needs expressed by only a portion of their residents.

It is important to recognize, then, that a community may choose to focus on some aspect of problem solving or resource utilization merely because of a strong interest group's lobbying. On the other hand, a community may expend resources and efforts based on a planned needs assessment or a comprehensive review of community problems. Such surveys are often, but not always, undertaken before launching new programs.

Again, ideally, given the enormous resources (financial, organizational, and human) available in a community, most citizen needs should be met. However, this is often not the case. The nature of the community as a system means that it is subject to numerous influences, including its subsystems (local groups, organizations, and residents) and its own larger environment (other communities, state and federal governments, and large economic entities).

EP 2.1.7b

The combination of pressures from its larger environment and its subunits can be seen in many ways. Key concepts, summarized in Highlight 8.2 and examined next, include competition, centralization, concentration, invasion, gentrification, and succession (CSWE, 2008, EP 2.1.7b).

Competition

To better understand how competition works, Fellin (2001) and Popple and Leighninger (2008) suggest looking at competition or conflict as one of the primary factors affecting any given community and its ability to meet community needs.

The first fact of life about communities is that they are often battlegrounds for groups and organizations competing for resources. *Competition* is the struggle within a community by various groups, all seeking to put their interests and needs ahead of any others. The competition may be waged over the best use of certain land or the most important items in a city budget. Various segments of communities compete for resources and attention. People who want better streets compete with those who want more police protection. Advocates for new schools compete with those who seek property tax reduction and limits on spending for education. The director of a city's parks and recreation program competes with the city streets department director for limited city funds. Will it be a new tennis court or new asphalt for Main Street? Should we spend money on bike trails or new sidewalks?

Competition is essentially a political activity in which many valid needs vie with other equally valid needs. Consequently, when you advocate for a particular program or need, you are always competing with others. It does not mean that the other needs are illegitimate, nor that your objectives are less worthy if they do not receive funding. All it means is that you are more (or less) successful in convincing those who control the resources that your own case has merit.

HIGHLIGHT 8.2

Key Concepts for Understanding Communities

Competition The struggle within a community by various groups, all seeking to have their interests and needs considered more important than others' needs.

Centralization The practice of clustering business services and institutions in one area of a city.

Concentration The tendency of certain groups (particularly ethnic groups) to cluster in a particular section or neighborhood of a community.

Gentrification A pattern whereby upper-middle-class families move back into downtown and

near-downtown residential areas, turning second floors of businesses into lofts and rehabilitating large older homes.

Invasion A tendency of each new group of in-migrants to force out or replace existing groups previously living in a neighborhood.

Succession The replacement of the original occupants or residents of a community or neighborhood by new groups.

The reality of competition is sometimes a surprise to new social workers who assume that a need, properly documented and presented, will usually (or even always) be met.

Centralization

Centralization is the practice of clustering business services and institutions in one area of the community (Knox & Marston, 2001). For example, most communities have a central business district, though this may no longer be the principal retail sector of the community because of the prevalence of shopping malls. Often the downtown shopping district has been replaced by another form of centralization—the urban mall. In another example of centralization, auto dealerships often locate adjacent to each other. Communities, through zoning and other land-use restrictions, frequently attempt to centralize certain businesses in specific areas. Perhaps it is an industrial park where all new commercial or manufacturing plants are encouraged to locate. Other communities have zoned districts so that adult book stores and strip clubs are centralized in a particular location. One community, in an effort to completely exclude "gentlemen's clubs," restricted them to a "brownfield," an area of the city where the ground was so polluted by chemical and manufacturing plants that it would cost millions to clean up the land. This restriction effectively prevented any such facilities from being built in the community. Zoning laws are a major means of ensuring that homeowners do not find an industrial corporation building suddenly popping up next door. It is also why subdivisions of expensive homes are approved and rules established excluding less-expensive homes.

Concentration

Another characteristic of communities, *concentration,* is the tendency of certain groups of people to cluster in a particular section or neighborhood. There are several reasons for this. Housing in this area may cost less, residents may seek to locate closer to family and friends, or discrimination in housing may force people to concentrate in certain areas. Recently a local newspaper undertook a study of landlords' reactions when Hmong refugees sought housing. When Hmong individuals called about apartments listed in the newspaper, landlords, recognizing the callers' accents, said the apartment was already rented. When a non-Hmong person called immediately afterward, landlords told them the apartment was available. Such blatant oppression and discrimination often result in housing segregation. New in-migrants (arrivals) may concentrate in the only community area where they do not experience such treatment, in neighborhoods populated with others of their nationality/ethnicity. Of course, the concentration of large, poor families in certain neighborhoods can cause other problems, such as overcrowding of available units.

Invasion

Another community characteristic, *invasion,* is the tendency of each new group of in-migrants to force existing groups out. Invasion primarily affects housing. Thus, African Americans living in a neighborhood may begin to leave as Asian Americans move in. They, in turn, will leave when some other group begins to move into (invade) the neighborhood. Eventually this can lead to older neighborhoods becoming more run-down, even though at one time they were very nice areas in which to live.

Gentrification

A corollary of invasion is the process known as *gentrification,* the tendency of upper-middle-class families to move back into downtown and near-downtown residential areas. This is discussed in detail later under "Demographic Development of Communities."

Another form of invasion occurs when certain types of land use begin to change. The conversion of large single-family homes into apartments may force the remaining single-family homeowners to sell rather than be surrounded by multifamily housing. When they do so, their homes will likely face the same fate, namely, conversion to multifamily homes. Of course, the converted multifamily housing provides shelter for more people than did the single-family homes. However, those forced out are often lower- or fixed-income older adults.

In a similar fashion, a predominantly retail downtown business district may lose its businesses as vacant storefronts are invaded by nonretail establishments, such as insurance offices, counseling centers, or law offices. These businesses produce less foot traffic than businesses such as department stores. Consequently, an office center may eventually replace the old business district.

Succession

Invasion is usually followed by *succession,* the replacement of the original occupants of a community or neighborhood by new groups. It is common to see a neighborhood that first housed Irish immigrants, then African Americans, now housing Hispanic Americans. Succession, of course, can continue indefinitely in some areas of a community, because it usually creates less expensive housing, which is attractive to low-income families and individuals.

Concepts Characterize Real Life

Centralization, concentration, invasion, and succession typically occur in most communities. Understanding each of them helps social workers better predict what will happen in their communities. Concentration helps us understand why large numbers of Hispanic-American clients are living in substandard housing, yet refuse to move. Similarly, gentrification becomes real when African-American clients are forced out of their near-downtown neighborhoods to make way for wealthy professionals bent on rehabilitating these buildings. Being able to pinpoint the factor responsible for the problem can help identify the best avenue for intervention. Gentrification of a former multifamily housing unit usually requires rezoning or permission to change the use of the property. Gentrification can be prevented by communities that refuse to permit this change of use or rezoning. Other kinds of invasion are more difficult to resist.

While we have highlighted the influence of the concepts of centralization, concentration, invasion, and succession with a focus on communities in the United States, the patterns are not limited to any single country. For example, the East End of London has experienced a long history of succession, with different ethnic groups locating there until they move elsewhere. Similarly, many French communities have seen this pattern occur, with the most recent example being high concentrations of economically depressed immigrants from Islamic countries. The result has been street protests, religious conflicts, marginalization, powerlessness, and other difficulties arising from a variety of factors, including poverty of the residents and challenges around assimilation into French culture, to name a couple. Cities in India have experienced similar changes over time, as have those in China, suggesting similarities in the development of communities.

Community Resource Systems

All communities have a variety of resource systems available to help residents. Three primary types include informal, formal, and societal. *Informal* (sometimes called "natural") resource systems include family members, coworkers, friends, neighbors, and others who provide emotional, social, or more tangible types of support.

A second type of resource system is the *formal,* or membership, organization. This system includes social or fraternal organizations (e.g., Elks, Kiwanis, Rotary, League of Women Voters, etc.) in which people hold memberships. Other examples include labor unions, professional associations (such as the NASW), scouting organizations, and churches. Churches may provide members spiritual support or more tangible benefits, such as emergency financial assistance. Too often, social workers neglect to explore the role of clients' religious and spiritual values and church affiliations, thereby excluding an important resource for many clients.

Societal resource systems are institutionalized organizations or services, such as private and public social service agencies, family service agencies, and libraries. These resource systems are established to provide specific kinds of assistance to community residents. Social workers employed in public and private agencies tend to think of these systems first when clients experience problems. Familiarity with these formal resource systems makes it easy to overlook other more informal systems.

An important lesson in understanding your community is that learning is a continuous process. Even experienced social workers may not be aware of the myriad resource systems available to help with any given problem. Consequently, we often operate with less than complete knowledge of our own communities.

Knowledge of a community's various resource systems is essential if you are to help individual clients or groups of clients with similar problems. If you know that the Church of Our Lady of Perpetual Misery provides low-cost meals to its shut-in members, your client (a member of the church) can receive help at little cost from people she already knows. This may be preferable to connecting her with a societal resource system she knows nothing about and with which she is not comfortable. Knowledge of resources is also important because you may wish to consult specific resource systems to learn more about community needs. For example, asking the local National Association for the Advancement of Colored People (NAACP) for assistance in pinpointing needs of that ethnic group may be more efficient and effective than talking to a multitude of individual African Americans.

Learning about a community often requires more than simply reading a community resource directory, however. Most communities have local gathering places where certain groups meet. In one case in the author's experience, a local restaurant served this function. Many influential formal and informal leaders in the community (e.g., business owners and city officials) gathered there for breakfast and discussed major community issues. Most mornings, you would see community residents greeting friends, moving from table to table to talk, and sharing opinions on various topics. Subjects discussed could include everything from the proposed new landfill to rumors about the city manager's car accident. (Was he drinking?) More could be learned about the community by listening and observing there than by reading an entire resource directory.

Figure 8.2 shows the vast variety of resource systems and organizations that may exist in a single city. Those listed here are only a very modest sample of the entire system. As you look at the figure, you can recognize two of the three types of resource systems, formal and societal. Governmental units, educational organizations, and social service agencies are examples of societal resource systems. Civic, spiritual/religious, consumer, business/trade, and professional groups are considered formal resource systems. Each of these groups, organizations, or services might benefit at least some of your clients at some point in their lives. Not knowing about these community resource systems reduces your ability to link individual clients and groups with needed services.

The existence of the array of resource systems illustrated in Figure 8.2 does not necessarily mean that most needy members of a community have access to them. In some communities, informal resource systems such as relationships among neighbors may be more

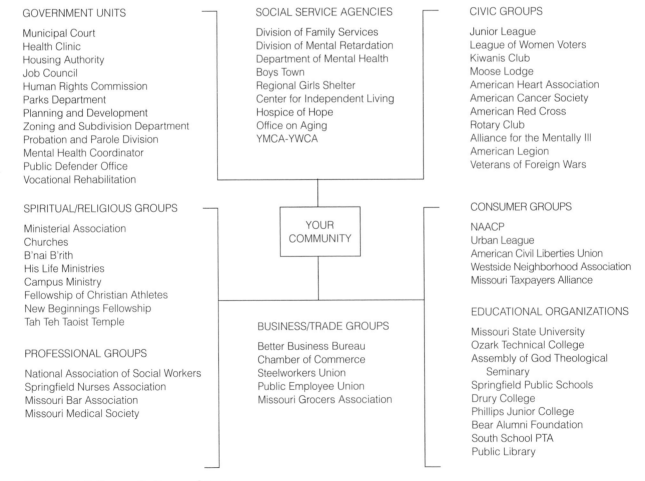

GOVERNMENT UNITS

Municipal Court
Health Clinic
Housing Authority
Job Council
Human Rights Commission
Parks Department
Planning and Development
Zoning and Subdivision Department
Probation and Parole Division
Mental Health Coordinator
Public Defender Office
Vocational Rehabilitation

SPIRITUAL/RELIGIOUS GROUPS

Ministerial Association
Churches
B'nai B'rith
His Life Ministries
Campus Ministry
Fellowship of Christian Athletes
New Beginnings Fellowship
Tah Teh Taoist Temple

PROFESSIONAL GROUPS

National Association of Social Workers
Springfield Nurses Association
Missouri Bar Association
Missouri Medical Society

SOCIAL SERVICE AGENCIES

Division of Family Services
Division of Mental Retardation
Department of Mental Health
Boys Town
Regional Girls Shelter
Center for Independent Living
Hospice of Hope
Office on Aging
YMCA-YWCA

YOUR COMMUNITY

BUSINESS/TRADE GROUPS

Better Business Bureau
Chamber of Commerce
Steelworkers Union
Public Employee Union
Missouri Grocers Association

CIVIC GROUPS

Junior League
League of Women Voters
Kiwanis Club
Moose Lodge
American Heart Association
American Cancer Society
American Red Cross
Rotary Club
Alliance for the Mentally Ill
American Legion
Veterans of Foreign Wars

CONSUMER GROUPS

NAACP
Urban League
American Civil Liberties Union
Westside Neighborhood Association
Missouri Taxpayers Alliance

EDUCATIONAL ORGANIZATIONS

Missouri State University
Ozark Technical College
Assembly of God Theological
　Seminary
Springfield Public Schools
Drury College
Phillips Junior College
Bear Alumni Foundation
South School PTA
Public Library

FIGURE 8.2 Community Resource Systems

significant for clients. Clients may rely on neighbors for help in times of need. In other communities there may be greater reliance on formal structures and societal institutions. New resources may need development when existing systems are either unresponsive to client needs or are simply not available. For example, the absence of a community shelter for battered women means that these individuals have nowhere to turn when they are in danger.

One major advantage of the systems and ecological perspectives is they permit us to step back and see a problem through a wider lens. We can view problems in the context of the larger systems in which those problems exist. We might realize, as we consider the problem and the array of community resources available, that the problem is simply bigger than the community. For example, community problems such as plant closings may have more to do with federal tax laws and foreign ownership of a local company than with the quality of the local workforce. Tax laws that encourage closing down a company and deducting the loss from one's corporate taxes can subtly encourage such shutdowns. This has virtually nothing to do with people living in the community. Similarly, new economic needs in the larger environment may cause changes in family structure. Changing economic factors may require both parents to work in order for the family to survive or may motivate all young adults to leave the community. Such factors permeate society and are not limited to just one community.

A community may lack the means, autonomy, or authority to do anything about a particular problem, such as changes in family structure. In addition, federal or state laws may limit the right of a community to raise money through taxation or to clean up a polluted industrial landfill. Often, solving these problems will require the resources and involvement of multiple levels of government.

Occasionally, community apathy or lack of citizen involvement amplifies community problems. In some communities, residents believe no one can do anything about the problem, so why try? In other cases, a lack of shared values prevents the community from taking concerted action. Residents in several communities battled over the need for additional schools and public facilities such as libraries. Such struggles may pit senior citizens on fixed incomes (who value low taxes) with little investment in the schools or libraries against parents and school officials (who value good schools). Unable to agree, they cannot join forces to address the community's education needs.

You cannot understand communities completely without looking at demographic development, the role of social stratification, and the impact of economic and political systems on a community's health. In the next four sections, we focus on each respectively.

Demographic Development of Communities

Understanding more about the economic, ethnic, social, and educational characteristics of a community. You may want to know how many people in your community fall below the poverty line (a subsistence level of income). Such information, called demographic data, describes a community in terms of such factors as race, gender, education level, and economic class. Thus, you could describe a given community as 40 percent African American, 30 percent Hispanic American, and 30 percent white. Normally, the best source of demographic data is the U.S. Bureau of the Census. The Census Bureau divides each community in the United States into census tracts based solely on numbers of people living in a given area. They serve as a handy way of dividing a community for study and analysis. Traditionally, population size has been used to distinguish between communities. We use terms such as *city, town, village,* and *metropolitan area* to designate communities of differing sizes. The definition of *urban,* for example, usually applies to a community with a population of more than 2,500 people that is incorporated (that is, legally chartered) with the state. Incorporated communities are permitted to do such things as levy taxes and can qualify for certain kinds of state financial aid. Being chartered or incorporated bestows the state's formal recognition upon a community. *Metropolitan areas,* similarly defined by size, are cities with a population of at least 50,000. The term *suburb* refers to incorporated areas adjacent to a larger central city. As mentioned under "Types of Communities" earlier in this chapter, metropolitan areas may include other smaller cities. We tend to use the term *rural* for everything that does not fit one of the above designations.

Urbanization and Suburbanization

Two primary trends, urbanization and suburbanization, have strong effects upon communities (CSWE, 2008, EP 2.1.9a). *Urbanization* is the trend in which multitudes of people move to large metropolitan areas and away

EP 2.1.9a

from rural, outlying areas. Urbanization has historically been a major factor in the growth of most large U.S. cities. The rate of urbanization is affected by transportation systems, communication systems, and employment opportunities. For example, the development of automobiles and trains made it possible for people to get into the cities more easily. In the early 1900s, the availability of factory jobs attracted millions of rural residents to larger cities, such as Chicago and New York. In the process, many social problems developed, including child labor, residential segregation, poor sanitation, and other offshoots of the rapid growth of cities. A modern equivalent of this trend is the large numbers of legal and illegal immigrants flocking to cities while better-educated professionals move away. The result is another example of succession, discussed earlier.

A second trend with major influence on American communities is *suburbanization*. Whereas movement in the early part of the last century was toward metropolitan areas (urbanization), the trend since 1940 has been toward suburbanization. In suburbanization, residents desert large cities and move to smaller communities nearby. This movement was encouraged by the development of the interstate highway system, suburban tract housing, mass transit systems, and tax advantages for home ownership. (By allowing deductions for interest on home mortgages, federal and state governments help support home ownership.) The desire for larger homes and more yard, changes in job location, lower property taxes, and fewer city problems combined to encourage suburbanization. Companies opening branch offices outside the central city also encouraged employees to live away from the city. Of course, those who benefit most from this trend are the most upwardly mobile members of our society, composed disproportionately of white, middle-class Americans. As a result, the phenomenon sometimes is called *white flight*. Increasingly, the large urban city has become the home of people of color, citizens with lower incomes, and others not able to take advantage of the trend. This process has been exacerbated by "blockbusting," a form of social and economic injustice in which realtors tamper with the natural buying and selling trends in a community or neighborhood. For example, an urban neighborhood that has undergone a transformation from completely or largely white to one that is becoming integrated is a potential target for blockbusting. A realtor, taking advantage of (or encouraging) white owners' fears about neighborhood changes, will offer to purchase (or list for sale) the

person's home. The owner, selling the home out of fear, often ends up with less than the actual value of the property. The realtor will then turn around and sell the property to people of color at higher prices. This manipulation of the housing market preys on the prejudices and worries of whites and gouges African-American and other ethnic groups seeking homes.

Gentrification

Although much recent movement has been away from the central cities, there is a notable exception—*gentrification*, the movement of upper-middle-class professionals and families back to the central city. Their purchase and renovation of older buildings result in increased value of buildings surrounding their properties (many of them currently rented to lower-income families). As these properties become more valuable, they are sold to other newcomers. Property values increase, and so do rents. This forces lower-income individuals and families to seek housing in less-expensive areas. For social workers, this can produce an ethical dilemma. On the one hand, rehabilitation of rundown buildings improves the quality of life in a community and prevents further deterioration. On the other hand, the process eventually hurts low-income families and individuals who may have few other housing choices. Do we encourage housing rehabilitation or focus on maintaining affordable housing for the poor? Are the choices mutually exclusive? These are difficult questions to answer. Innovative solutions are needed. For example, federal support for rebuilding dilapidated areas of cities (urban renewal) resulted in some communities redeveloping blighted business and residential neighborhoods. It also forced large numbers of the poor from their homes, because new housing rentals soared. The poor residents' flight resulted in further overcrowding of other parts of the city. Achieving the goals of rebuilding a community without hurting those displaced by the effort takes new and creative ideas.

Rural Communities

We have not said much about rural communities. Although many stereotype such communities as lacking sophistication and services, a trend to relocate to rural areas, particularly in the West, is growing. Migration from California places pressure on more rural states nearby, such as Nevada and Oregon, as newcomers seek a more relaxed, less expensive style of life.

There is a substantial body of literature on rural communities and on social work practice in rural areas.

One continuing theme in the literature is defining what we mean by the term *rural*. The term is defined differently by various units of state and federal government. Depending upon which agency is doing the defining, one rural area may be part of a larger metropolitan area or a stand-alone entity. Olaveson, Conway, and Shaver (2004) argue for a definition that takes into account such factors as population density, economics of an area, and proximity to densely populated areas. Traditional images of rural life involving family farms are no longer very useful for understanding rural areas. Relatively few individuals engage in farming, and the percentage of income from farming even among farm dwellers is less than 20 percent (Whitener, 2000).

Despite the differences in definition of *rural*, there is more agreement on both similarities and dissimilarities between rural and more urban environments. Some of the similarities are commonsense notions. For example, regardless of location, people have similar needs for food, water, housing, safety, and security, among others. The basic necessities of life don't vary a great deal regardless of where one lives. Scales and Streeter (2004) point out that rural communities often have many of the same problems that urban areas have. This includes the existence of poverty, drug abuse, family violence, mental illness, and other social problems.

At the same time, dissimilarities do exist between rural and urban environments. Human and other social services are likely to be less available in rural areas. Relatively few rural communities can afford the array of services available in larger population centers. Hospitals and medical facilities are much less prevalent in rural areas. Rural hospitals have largely disappeared over the past 50 years along with many local hospitals serving disadvantaged urban dwellers. At the same time, there has been a trend toward fewer but larger urban medical facilities often competing to offer similar specialized care. These facilities continue to expand in larger population centers.

Access to physicians is also greatly reduced in most rural areas. Physicians' choice of a living environment coupled with the trend toward fewer but larger hospitals has led to severe shortages of medical personnel in rural areas. The concentration of professionals and hospitals in urban areas might be less of a problem were it not for transportation issues. The lack of availability of public transportation in rural areas means that going to the doctor requires a major effort. Those rural dwellers without their own transportation are clearly disadvantaged not only in terms of access to medical care, but also to other social services routinely available to those who live in the city. This includes such things as aftercare resources, counselors for cases involving sexual abuse of children, and inadequate funding for rural health and social services.

Partly as a consequence of the lack of resources, rural areas are more likely to experience higher rates of death for both children and young adults (Olaveson et al., 2004), and poverty rates tend to be higher in rural areas, particularly in the southeast and southwest regions of the United States (Stuart, 2004).

Lack of heterogeneity among rural populations can also be a challenge. For example, those who are different by virtue of race, ethnicity, or political or sexual orientation may experience discrimination. In smaller communities, those who appear dissimilar to the rest of the population are more likely to face a degree of ostracism. The strong value systems in rural areas and the pressure to conform to longstanding traditions may make it more difficult for newcomers to fit in.

Value differences between rural and urban residents have been identified. Rural residents may have greater suspicion of outsiders, a slower work pace, different norms regarding mental health and education, and a higher emphasis on independence. There is a tendency to rely on themselves for problem solving, value higher levels of autonomy, and prefer informal to formal resource systems when help is needed. An example of this arose during the debate over health care in the first year of the Obama administration when many rural residents denounced the idea of a new federal program and voiced support for private charity providing health care for those without insurance coverage. While many opposed the role of the federal government in health care policy, there was not a concomitant rush to do away with either Medicare or Social Security, both of which are national policies upon which both rural and urban residents rely. Likewise, complaints about the fact that the U.S. Postal Service continues to run a deficit year after year exist side by side with demands that post offices serving small rural areas remain open despite the need to reduce postal service expenses.

Another major difference in rural areas is the relatively high incidence of religious and spiritual values compared to more urban areas. In times of crisis, rural dwellers are more likely to consult their spiritual advisor than a mental health professional (Furman, 1991; Watkins, 2004).

At the same time, the values of rural communities can be an asset. Rural residents are often more willing to help each other in times of need. When a neighbor's barn is damaged in a storm or a fence blows down,

HIGHLIGHT 8.3

Social Work in Rural Areas

Scales and Streeter (2004) and Gumpert, Saltman, and Sauer-Jones (1998) highlight some of the characteristics of social work practice in rural areas. Social workers new to a rural area may find themselves with relatively few colleagues, less supervision, and less personal privacy than would be the case in an urban area. Value conflicts with rural residents may also arise. For example, pressure on individual residents to conform to community norms may conflict with the social worker's belief in client self-determination. Similarly, a community belief in self-reliance may result in opposition to development of new societal resources. Residents may believe that people should be able to help themselves instead of relying on publicly supported programs.

The importance of religion and spirituality in rural communities can be an asset when the social worker is focused on a particular challenge. For example, a church group may agree to spearhead a fundraising project or gather items needed to furnish a domestic violence shelter. Alternately, several churches may pool their resources to assist in a community improvement effort. Using informal resources in a rural community requires a creative social worker who understands the multiple opportunities available outside of the urban environment.

Of particular value in rural community practice is the strengths perspective, which has two particular benefits. First, viewing the rural community as a place with multiple strengths helps overcome the tendency to focus on the negatives or shortcomings, such as lack of formal resources. Social workers who keep the strengths perspective in mind are more likely to overcome this anti-rural bias. Second, knowing that most systems have multiple strengths helps the worker to look for these assets when assessing community needs. In Chapter 9, we will further identify some of the many ways in which a social worker new to a rural area can gather information about the resources and assets of the community. Rural social workers often will benefit from making regular contact with ministers and pastors serving their practice venues. Social workers who are not sensitive to the importance of religion in the lives of many of these residents will quickly lose their rapport with such clients.

About one-third of social workers in rural areas tend to be engaged in advocacy, program development management, education, and training. Over one-half identify supervision as a primary job responsibility, along with provision of direct services. Rural social workers are very likely to know natural helpers in the community, who were sought out for their ability to assist others, and most of the social workers refer clients to these individuals and/or accept referrals from them. The social workers also emphasize the importance of observing rural cultural values in their own practice. They tend to use informal communication, adjust their pace of work to the environment, and carry out a variety of roles and tasks. Generalist practice, with its broad range of skills, is especially appropriate and practical for rural environments (Ginsberg, 2005; Hickman, 2004; Martinez Brawley, 1993).

---

other residents often show up to help. They may also be more willing to come together in informal resource systems that are stronger than those in urban settings. Rural areas are also more likely to have available "extended kinship systems, lodges, and churches" (Stuart, 2004). The church in rural areas can be a strong mechanism for integrating the individual into the community and a source of support when needs arise. Highlight 8.3 focuses on adjustments the rural social worker may face.

Where Is the Best Place to Live?

As you enter the job market, you may face the decision of where to live. How do you decide?

Over the years, there have been periodic analyses of the relative advantages of living in the city versus the suburbs versus rural areas. These comparisons, published in newspapers and popular magazines, do not always recognize that each location has its own advantages and disadvantages. Rather than relying on stereotypes of various communities, you should use the same nonjudgmental attitudes appropriate to working with diverse clients. In each community, you will need to learn the strengths and weaknesses of resource systems, the important values and norms of residents, and how to use those factors in improving the quality of life for clients.

Social Stratification

Social stratification, or the division of a society into categories (e.g., income or social class), is both a

EP 2.1.7b

conceptual tool and a fact of life (CSWE, 2008, EP 2.1.7b). On the one hand, you may find it useful to think of larger groups as composed of various subgroups. Depending upon your interests, you can stratify a community by race, gender, or age—all useful dimensions. For example, you may want to know about the types of jobs held by residents. Thus, you are likely to use a stratification system for types of employment (e.g., working class, blue collar, white collar, and so on). If you look at a community and discover, for example, that a disproportionate percentage of the population is women over age 65, this information may suggest the need for more social services, health care, or housing for this age and gender population. Similarly, stratifying the population by level of education may reveal a sizable population with little formal education. Armed with this information, you might delve further into this group's educational and training needs. A systematic needs assessment focused on this group might show that they need vocational training to prepare for jobs in local industries. This information can help you develop priorities. A needs assessment may be accomplished through surveying community residents, studying official government data such as census information, and reviewing agency files or other similar records. Needs may also be identified by inviting members of a target population to a meeting to discuss their needs or by asking relevant community officials (such as ministers, the mayor, or agency directors) to provide their views.

On the other hand, social stratification is a tool used to discriminate against groups who differ by gender, race, sexual orientation, or other characteristics. Any time we behave differently toward those with an identifiable characteristic, such as skin color, the negative side of social stratification is evident because we have used that characteristic as an excuse to deny group members' individuality.

In the United States we frequently find social class stratification, which divides people into categories based on socioeconomic factors such as income and education. The primary purpose of this information is to better understand our society and the vast disparities within it. Only when you understand the facts can you begin to target pieces of the system for change.

The number of actual categories in any stratification scheme is arbitrary. Thus, you may see references to lower class, middle class, and upper class, or perhaps lower- and upper-middle class. A more recent addition to the nomenclature is *underclass,* a term that refers to the poorest of the poor. This group is considered almost permanently trapped by social and economic factors such as discrimination, lack of education and marketable job skills, and personal factors such as chronic mental illness. It is composed disproportionately of people of color. Members of the underclass are among the most oppressed groups in our society and perhaps the most difficult to help. Despite the drawbacks of categorization, information on social stratification helps us recognize and understand the unique problems of such population segments. In other words, if you don't thoroughly understand the problem, you can't begin to solve it.

Community Economic Systems

Economic systems, whether at the national, state, or local level, are concerned with the "production, distribution, and consumption of goods and services" (Fellin, 2001, p. 245). This process of production, distribution, and consumption is one of the community's primary functions. The community is connected closely to our economic system. Everything from Steve's Supermarket to General Motors is involved in fulfilling this community function. Economic systems also include professionals (such as doctors, attorneys, and social workers) in addition to service companies (such as restaurants, laundries, and other service-giving businesses).

There is also an "underground" economic system (Fellin, 2001), consisting of off-the-books businesses (such as some enterprises providing child or lawn care), bartering, and even gambling. All of these exist without maintaining records, paying taxes, or otherwise participating in the above-ground, or legitimate, economy. Lower-income clients may well benefit from these underground activities at one level or another. For example, clients who provide babysitting for middle-class families may be paid in cash. No income taxes are deducted nor Social Security taxes paid. Because no records are kept, providers of service may not report this income to the Internal Revenue Service. Not abiding by the rules can save money but is illegal. Whereas clients may benefit by having more money in their pockets, they risk getting caught. Equally important, people who don't have Social Security deducted do not get credit for this work when they retire, nor receive Social Security disability/survivor's benefits.

In underground bartering, a dentist fixes the teeth of his plumber, who agrees to put in a new bathroom for the dentist. No money changes hands and no records are kept. The extent of the underground economy is unknown but is believed to be sizable. By understanding that it exists side by side with the money economy and why people participate in it, you will better grasp how your community's economic system operates.

We have established that the economic condition of a community is crucial to its health. For example, departure of businesses, closing of major employers, and other negative happenings can cause unemployment and personal stress for community residents. Such changes cause the community to lose tax revenues, thereby hampering its ability to maintain schools, pay social workers, or pave streets. A person who loses her job because of a deteriorating economic situation suffers personally by losing income, suffers decreased self-esteem, and may encounter forced relocation. Work provides not only income and benefits to residents, but also a sense of belonging and satisfaction with one's life. This satisfaction and sense of participation can enhance or detract from people's connection to the residential community where they live. People who derive great satisfaction and feelings of belonging from their jobs may feel less involved with the community where they live. Unemployed workers may be less likely to contribute to or participate in their communities. They are more likely to be concerned about their own situation. Communities need jobs and taxes to help fund basic services. Likewise, residents need employment to feel positive about themselves, provide an adequate lifestyle, and feel a part of their communities. Feeling alienated from one's community and hopeless about the future are common characteristics of some inner-city residents. We have referred to people experiencing these feelings as the underclass.

Like most other aspects of our lives, economic systems are affected by decisions made at all three levels of government: federal, state, and local. Federal and state taxing, local land use, and federal transportation policies may all have an impact on a company's decision to relocate in a community, expand operations, or move away. Ready access to highways, airlines, or railroads may make it easier for a company to ship its goods across the country or around the world. Local gifts of land or reduced taxes also help corporations decide to locate in a community. Lower state taxes may help some companies select a given state for expanding their operations. Other companies will consider such factors as quality schools and access to a strong labor pool as critical incentives.

One example of how economic conditions can affect a community is provided by Barbera (2007). She notes that many Mexicans lost their livelihood as a result of the North American Free Trade Agreement (NAFTA). NAFTA is an agreement between Canada, Mexico, and the United States that was designed to further trade among the three countries by eliminating quotas and tariffs charged on imports. Following implementation of NAFTA, the United States was able to sell large amounts of government–subsidized corn and other vegetables to Mexico at relatively low cost. This availability of low-cost vegetables meant that many Mexicans who made their living farming these crops were driven out of business. Faced with loss of their livelihood and few employment opportunities in Mexico, many of these individuals entered the United States in search of a more prosperous future, increasing an influx of undocumented workers seeking a better life.

The enormous emphasis communities place on recruiting new businesses is testimony to the importance of the economic system on the local level. Communities and states offer millions of dollars in tax breaks, loan forgiveness, and outright grants to attract and retain major employers. One community was so anxious to get a major employer into its new industrial park that leaders evicted a small cement company because the prospective new tenant considered it too messy.

In addition, there is often tension and competition in the community between the goals of a healthy economy and concerns about the environmental impact of new industries. Growing attention to environmental justice issues is surfacing across the United States. Concerns involve how poorer communities are becoming the target of industries that pollute more or produce potentially toxic by-products affecting workers and those living near the company. In all too many cases, economic decisions result in further damage to the urban environment. A recent incident illustrates the ability of community residents to pursue environmental justice. The U.S. Navy wanted to dispose of a large quantity of napalm, a gelled fuel used in the Vietnam War. Napalm was dropped from planes onto enemy forces, suspected hiding places, and other targets. It clings to whatever it comes in contact with and incinerates it. A company outside of Chicago entered into a contract with the Navy to burn up the napalm. Local residents engaged in a sustained drive to prevent the napalm from being shipped to and incinerated in their community, fearful of the potential effects on an already highly polluted environment. They argued that it was unjust to target a community struggling with pollution and other social problems for additional potentially dangerous pollution. The company, which had underestimated the strong community reaction, finally voided the agreement and informed the Navy that they would not be able to dispose of the weapon at this plant.

A related environmental justice issue is the tendency for urban growth to occur through development of farmland, green areas, and previously undeveloped rural areas, while ignoring deteriorating inner cities or neighborhoods where new jobs and housing rehabilitation are badly needed. Through this practice, the farmland is forever removed from its original use and green areas become large suburban neighborhoods. When nearby rural areas refuse to allow urban sprawl to infiltrate, the developers are forced to reconsider inner-city neighborhoods. This can mean that deteriorating cities and rural areas may find common ground in their wish to improve and maintain their respective qualities of life.

The crucial fact is that a healthy economic system supports the vast majority of the social programs and services in which social workers practice. In other words, taxes paid by corporations and wage earners pay directly or indirectly for most social services. Thus, you cannot overestimate the importance of the economic system. At the same time, failures of the economic system often directly affect clients and services. Although we may take pride in what the American economic system can produce, we must also recognize its limitations. Unemployment, plant closings, layoffs, and low-wage jobs are all part and parcel of our economic system. Understanding the community requires that we understand the role of the economic system in that community and the importance of human and social services to meet the needs of those affected by that system.

Community Political Systems

The term *political* has a negative ring for many people. It conjures up images of smoke-filled rooms and shady deals, decisions made for wrong and selfish reasons, and sometimes questionable actions by government officials. For our purposes, however, the political arena is where most decisions affecting social work practice are made. Funding for the programs that serve our clients, pay our salaries, and support our agencies comes largely from the federal, state, and local governments.

Government may support the development of programs benefiting the community, but this same government may also undercut and diminish those programs. This occurs when a governmental unit (federal, state, or local) decides to fund social service programs, refuses to fund them, or funds them insufficiently These decisions are so important to us and our clients that we cannot afford to avoid involvement.

Formal Organizations and Informal Political Processes

At the community level, the political system includes formal organizations such as city government (where funding decisions are made) and "informal political processes and activities" (Fellin, 2001, p. 283). Informal political processes are evident when certain people in the community exert significant power over decisions made by government officials. The processes are informal, because such people are not elected by citizens nor are they accountable to community residents. For example, a local banker may actually control or affect many of the decisions made by elected officials. Both the respect she engenders from others and her influence over financial resources may give her greater clout than an elected city council member.

The political system can encourage or discourage participation of community residents, especially minorities. Some communities, for example, have made it difficult to register voters by discouraging voter registration drives. Actions by federal and state political systems affect local matters in many areas such as housing, roads, and health. Highlight 8.4 provides a good summary of activities that characterize government involvement in the community (Rubin & Rubin, 2001, p. 260).

Three levels of government affect decisions within the community—federal, state, and local.

The *federal government* has multiple responsibilities. It funds many social programs, maintains the U.S. monetary system, oversees interstate commerce, and provides for the national defense. Finally, it protects the civil rights of U.S. citizens. Sometimes, the federal government acts in partnership with state government. An example is the recent federal welfare reform law, which established general rules allowing states to qualify for certain federal welfare funding. However, once those rules are met, states may develop their own policies with respect to specific programs.

State governments fund a significant portion of the health and mental health services provided by social workers and others. They also play a role in education,

HIGHLIGHT 8.4

Governmental Activities in the Community

Designing community programs Programs such as Neighborhood Watch, which involves neighborhood residents in crime prevention activities, is one example.

Allocating funds Monies for homeless shelters, general assistance, and playgrounds are examples.

Providing services for citizens Basic services such as police and fire protection are in this category.

Building projects This might include jails, county care centers for older adults, and community centers.

Awarding and supervising contracts Counties and cities often contract with private agencies to provide needed social services, such as domestic violence services.

Determining and enforcing laws This function is carried out by both the legislative branch (e.g., city council) and the administrative branch (e.g., police department).

Making and enforcing regulations Examples are housing, health, and sanitation ordinances.

Negotiating agreements Decisions about location of streets or highways are in this category.

Mediating disputes This may be done when city agencies are at odds with each other or with segments of the community. Some communities have contracted with agencies to provide mediation services to residents covering everything from child custody to landlord–tenant disputes.

Planning for the community Cities are usually solely responsible for planning local parks, streets, and sewer and water service.

---

providing financial support for local school districts and enforcing rules regarding how this financial support is spent.

Local governments (county or city) often provide health and social services. They also provide fire and police services. Clearly, there is much overlap—and sometimes tension and conflict—among levels of government. This is especially so when federal or state rules are unpopular at the local level. For example, states may set rules restricting the ability of a community to spend money on its school system. Often, however, there is effective cooperation.

Political decision making at the local level is different from that at the state or federal level. Debates at the upper levels often occur between parties (e.g., Democrats versus Republicans), but local politics are often more concerned with issues that cut across party lines: Snow removal, street maintenance, sidewalk repair, and good schools are issues that rarely involve political parties. A city council, for example, may consist of people from across the political spectrum (Democrat, Independent, Republican) who vote the same way on most major issues. To put it succinctly, there are no Republican sewer systems and no Democratic streets. Consequently, it is sometimes easier for local elected officials to reach compromises and agreements despite the fact that they may significantly disagree on national political issues. Of course, there are exceptions. Some community legislative bodies have adopted the same political party identifications found at the state and national level. The result can be seen in cities and towns where lack of cooperation stymies needed projects, such as sewer replacement and new schools. These communities may mirror congressional battles over conservative, moderate, and liberal ideologies and the proper role of government.

The formal structure of the community political system has several components. These include the official governance structure, consisting of elected officials (e.g., mayor, city council), the city bureaucracy, the staff who carry out the city functions described in Highlight 8.4, and appointed committees (such as the city planning commission or police and fire commissions) who advise the elected officials in their respective areas. The formal political structure also includes citizen participation. Formal citizen involvement can occur through organizations such as the Chamber of Commerce (an association of business owners). Informal involvement takes place both through the personal power and influence of individual community members and through the power structure. The power structure, usually outside the formal government structure, consists of business leaders and others with major influence over what goes on in a community. Power in a community has an impact on all aspects of community life. The influence of powerful people may determine whether or not a homeless shelter is built or a group home for emotionally troubled adolescents is allowed to locate in a given neighborhood. Although powerful people can play a large role in community decision making, this is not the only variable influencing the outcome. For example, the adequacy and accuracy of information upon which to base a decision are important factors. Sometimes a decision is made for political reasons in the face of clear evidence that another choice was more appropriate. At other times, inadequate or incorrect information forms the basis for a given decision. Community leaders may decide not to build a homeless shelter because they don't see the actual number of homeless living in their area. Relying on their own experience, city leaders may argue that the need is really small and can be accommodated by existing services. Or, they may ignore sound data that conflicts with their political or personal agendas. For instance, city leaders may object to funding a school program that provides information on family planning because they are opposed to government interference in what they believe is a family matter. Efforts to provide clean needles to addicts in order to help reduce the spread of AIDS have also been opposed. The next section will continue discussion of the community's power structure.

Power in the Community

The political system determines who makes decisions in a community. Because this is really a power issue, it is critical to understand how power operates within communities. This section will present a definition of power, consider types and sources of power, and explore the relationship between power and conflict.

Defining Power

Power is the ability to move people on a chosen course to provide an effort or achieve some goal (Homan, 2008). Highlight 8.5 provides an example of the influence of power.

From another perspective, power may also be seen as the ability to prevent someone from doing something he or she wants to do. Such negative power is more difficult to detect. Let's reconsider the situation described in Highlight 8.5. If Peter had wanted to adopt a pro-family policy for the shelter but had learned that the city manager wanted as many people served as possible, he might have dropped the idea altogether before ever proposing it. An exercise of power has occurred in both cases but is not as evident

---

HIGHLIGHT 8.5

Power at Work

Peter Kracker was an intense administrator with excellent skills for managing new organizations. As director of the new community shelter for the homeless, he was anxious to show he could run an efficient program. One of his first policies, borrowed from another similar shelter he had operated, was to institute a same-sex policy. This policy meant that the shelter would serve only clients of the same gender. The policy allowed Peter to house more homeless people, because he could create barracks-style physical arrangements with rows of beds for homeless men. Peter was quite proud of his accomplishment. His facility, originally designed to house 40 people per night, now held 65 each night.

At his third meeting with city officials (who were providing 75 percent of the shelter's funding), the city manager raised some concerns about the new policy. She had read that policies such as this, though common in homeless shelters, fueled the breakup of families by forcing family members to live apart. Often, they resulted in women and children being denied shelter entirely.

Peter defended his position and argued that he could serve more clients using his system. The discussion became quite heated until the city manager made it clear that she would not place the shelter in the budget next year unless Peter adopted a more pro-family policy.

Peter said that under the circumstances, he would revise the policy so that families could be housed at the shelter. If that action was needed to satisfy the funding source, he could hardly afford to act differently. Peter had just encountered an exercise of power. The city manager had the power to make or break Peter's program. If Peter wanted the program to survive, he had to comply with the city manager's desires.

in the second example, because there was no visible power struggle and others never knew the influence the city manager exerted.

Types of Power

We should also distinguish between potential and actual power. *Potential power* is power that has not yet been exercised. Potential power exists when we can influence others but have not done so. *Actual power* is the use of power to influence others. Sometimes potential power is not used because it would not be appropriate or because the payoff for using the power is questionable. A person might not exercise power because others might construe it as bullying or throwing one's weight around. Such overt use of power can make the more powerful person look bad. Sometimes people elect not to use power because they don't see how they will benefit from forcing a decision one way or another. People tend to use power only when it is in their interest to do so. When nothing important is at stake, there may be no motivation to use power.

Sources of Power

Sources of power vary. A financial asset is commonly recognized as a source of power. Other sources include business ownership; community status; possession of information; or links to other individuals, groups, or organizations with power. One person may have multiple sources of power or only a single source. A wealthy business owner has money, business ownership, and public acclaim as sources of power.

Power tends to be concentrated in a relatively small number of people. Because of this, it is important to know how to detect who has this power. One primary method, the *reputational* approach, involves simply asking others about who has power. Truly powerful people are likely to be mentioned most frequently. The *issues* approach is another means of detecting power. It assumes that there are always important community issues under consideration and that those who are influential in addressing these issues are powerful people. Identify the most important issues and then observe which persons are most influential. The people most involved in making decisions are likely to be the most powerful. Homan (2008) suggests that powerful community members can be spotted by looking at the membership lists of important community groups and organizations, noting whose names appear in the local media most often, and identifying those

who are sought out by others for their opinions. These techniques can be useful for both the reputational and issues approaches to power assessment.

A third method of detecting power is the *positional* approach. The positional approach assumes, reasonably enough, that those who hold various important positions in a community also have power. Thus, one would assume that the city manager, mayor, and president of the city council hold power. The same would be said of persons holding titles such as chairman of the board or executive director.

It is entirely possible, however, that those with official positions have relatively little power. In some situations, others with no official positions may actually be making decisions. The richest person in town may be directly involved in decisions affecting the local college, the county board, and the school board, despite holding no official position in any of these bodies. Community members listen to his ideas because he has money, prestige, or other sources of power. Therefore, it is better to use the positional approach in tandem with another method to avoid overemphasizing the importance of official positions.

Note also that some people are accorded power in one area but not in another. Thus, one may look to a person for leadership in business but not in civic or political matters. There is also evidence that power is not always static. That is, power may be fluid and shifting in some situations and remain constant and concentrated in others. This means that holding power depends upon the situation: An individual has power in one situation but not in others, but some people consistently wield power in all decisions.

Another source of power is that which comes when a number of people join together behind a cause or idea. Barbera (2007) describes how Mexican immigrants in Philadelphia were organized by community leaders to deal with multiple problems that included being victimized by violence, lacking fluency in English, and dealing with an unresponsive police department, among others. By joining together, Mexican immigrants in the community were able to secure benefits and acquire power that was not available to them as individuals.

Other factors may affect power. Those who own local businesses are more likely to have power than those who manage businesses that are part of a chain. Chain store managers move around every few years and put down relatively few roots in a community. Transitory community residents are less likely to hold power, so they usually have limited community influence.

Communities that have many (especially locally owned) businesses are also likely to have more people with power than are communities with only one or two major businesses. This occurs because there are more people with experience in leadership and with the resources to exert power.

Power and Conflict

Power becomes more visible in times of community conflict. Powerful people may be involved in a number of community issues, including disputes over road locations or sidewalk placement, labor strikes, locations of group homes, and similar matters. These situations upset the community's equilibrium and challenge the status quo. The issues may be significant, such as deciding whether to grant millions of dollars in tax breaks to lure an employer into town. They may also be relatively insignificant, such as determining the proper action to take when high school students are caught having sex in the school hallway. Note that what is considered significant or insignificant varies widely from one issue to another. The latter issue could split the community even more than such significant issues as the gain or loss of a major employer. During conflicts like this, you are most likely to observe those with power influencing the outcome. Learning who has power and where the real conflicts in a community lie is also important for your own benefit. At times, you will be involved in a community conflict (such as when you seek justice for those denied human services); at other times, you will need to walk the line between either side in a dispute. Knowing who the players are and the salient issues may help you remain neutral.

Conflict that impacts a community can also be seen at levels above the individual locale, including in the state, national, and international arenas. A good example is the debate about what the United States should do with respect to the millions of undocumented workers in the country. While many conservatives oppose any form of amnesty that would allow those who came here illegally to stay, business leaders want a supply of workers to meet their needs in industries as diverse as agriculture, service, and manufacturing. Industries that rely on workers who will do jobs that other Americans will not do, such as landscaping companies, hotels, and restaurants, want a relatively inexpensive source of labor. Liberals, concerned with the rights of immigrants and refugees as well as their general welfare, prefer laws that will be more sensitive to the individual and family needs of these workers (Hancock, 2007).

For the most part, our attention has been focused on communities, and we addressed neighborhoods only in passing. The following section will explain the functions of neighborhoods, their types, their role as social networks, and the importance of neighborhood organizations.

Neighborhoods

Neighborhoods exist throughout the world. All of us grow up in neighborhoods. Most of us have memories of our old neighborhoods. Neighborhoods are the contexts for primary and secondary groups (families and friends). They are also the place where our earliest interactions with others outside our family occur. The neighborhood's influence on residents can be considerable. When you hear the term "neighborhood," you might think of a place with dwellings and other buildings, such as schools. We also think of neighborhoods in terms of their physical characteristics—a "new neighborhood" or a "rundown neighborhood."

Defining a neighborhood as a geographical/residential area in which people share similar values, lifestyles, housing types, and exhibit a sense of cohesion captures the most significant aspects of this term. For most of us, neighborhoods refer to a geographical area, such as the third ward, Beacon Hill, or Marlborough Estates. For many people, the term "neighborhood" may also conjure up the social relationships or activities that occur among people in an area ("a friendly neighborhood"). Clearly, a neighborhood can be a place where significant social relationships occur among residents. This is perhaps the most important factor in what people consider their neighborhood. One's sense of belonging is part of this subjective social factor. Of course, we often try to foster this sense of belonging through zoning ordinances and covenants designed to maintain a certain sense and feel in a neighborhood. Zoning ordinances, you may recall, are local laws designed to ensure that all the properties in a neighborhood are compatible. Covenants are similar standards that can even govern what residents may or may not do on their own property. For example, your neighborhood covenant may state that you are not allowed to put up a clothesline or install a swimming pool.

Earlier we described all systems as having boundaries. Neighborhoods are no exceptions. All neighborhoods have some sort of boundaries that separate them from the larger system (or other subsystems and neighborhoods). Residents usually define and are clearly aware of such boundaries. Sometimes the boundaries are more psychological than physical. Often there are natural boundaries, however, such as major streets, rivers, railroad tracks, or other geographical features. Even ethnicity may divide one neighborhood from another.

Frequently, outsiders define the neighborhoods. School boards may decide where to establish the boundaries between one school and another. They require a certain neighborhood's children to attend a specific school. These decisions often provoke reactions from neighborhood residents who think of a particular school as theirs and don't want their children to go to another school.

The following sections will discuss the functions of neighborhoods.

Functions of Neighborhoods

EP 2.1.7a

Neighborhoods have many functions; the most typical are social, institutional, political, and economic (CSWE, 2008, EP 2.1.7a).

Social Functions

Social functions include providing friendships, status, socialization, mutual assistance, and informal helping networks. Residents may select a neighborhood because it provides status, comfort, or an opportunity to interact with neighbors. Although significant, the relationships one has with neighbors are often not the most important ones in a person's life. Rather, they represent resources in times of need. Neighborhoods are important to social workers for this same reason—they represent untapped resources for helping clients.

Neighborhoods may also contribute to one's sense of well-being or help at-risk populations, such as older adults, feel they have someone to turn to. Often, neighborhoods offer the kind of assistance that could not be acquired elsewhere. Neighbors may babysit for each other's children, borrow one another's vehicles, ask for help with projects, loan tools and equipment, serve as sounding boards for unhappiness about community issues, and provide emergency assistance. Most important, relying on one's neighbors does not carry the stigma of reliance on formal systems. You can ask for assistance from neighbors without being seen as bad or weak. Of course, not all neighbors are resources. Some inner-city neighborhoods are threatened by drug dealers, crack houses, and random violence. Although these neighborhoods' usefulness as a resource may be

reduced, residents still consider the area "their" neighborhood.

Institutional Functions

Neighborhoods may also carry out *institutional functions.* These include providing employment, connecting new residents to older residents, providing access to specific services, and otherwise helping neighborhood members integrate. Institutional functions are performed by neighborhood schools, local offices of larger community agencies, churches, and the like. Organizations that help this process include parent–teacher associations, fraternal organizations (e.g., the Elks), ethnic organizations, block clubs, and neighborhood centers.

Political Functions

Neighborhoods also serve a *political function,* allowing members to become involved in the political process to influence elected and appointed decision makers. One of the ways neighborhoods create a balance of power in the larger community is through the use of neighborhood organizations. Neighborhood organizations are groups formed to help the neighborhood achieve specific goals, such as renovation of older buildings. We will discuss neighborhood associations later in this chapter under "Neighborhood Organizations." Other types of political functions include activities such as encouraging people to vote, pushing the city to provide better police protection from drug dealers, or fining landlords who allow their buildings to deteriorate. Becoming involved in this sort of self-advocacy activity often increases residents' political sophistication, enhances their confidence, and allows them to become further involved in the political process, an example of empowerment. Residents may campaign for specific candidates, seek political action on issues they are concerned about, and otherwise lobby for their agenda.

Economic Functions

Economic functions of neighborhoods include provision of housing and places to shop. These are the functions most threatened by technology, changing demographics, and changes in the nature of businesses. For example, neighborhood shopping centers and markets are becoming much less common as large malls and superstores proliferate. Economic function is threatened by illegal practices, such as redlining, that further reduces the value of the housing in a neighborhood. Redlining is "the practice by certain financial

HIGHLIGHT 8.6

Goodbye to Geneva

When the Geneva steel plant closed its doors in 2000, hundreds of workers lost well-paying jobs and a good deal more. Follow-up studies of more than 600 workers painted a sad portrait for the former steelworkers. The results showed the following:

- Only 20 percent of the laid-off workers were employed in permanent full-time positions.
- The unemployment rate among former workers was six times as high as was the case for the rest of the region.
- Workers were seven times more likely to face major financial difficulties.

- Workers were four times as likely to have lost their homes because of nonpayment of mortgages.
- Workers were more than 13 times as likely to report needing prescription medicine, but were unable to purchase it because of financial problems.
- Those laid off were five times more likely to describe their marriage as worse than it had been.
- Those laid off were twice as likely to report symptoms of depression as other community residents. (Cornwall & Brown, 2003)

institutions of designating an area of a city as being too risky and unprofitable to lend money to those who want to rebuild or refurbish buildings there. The term came from the red line that various institutions drew on maps around ghetto areas to identify those locales that would not be funded" (Barker, 2003, p. 362).

As mentioned earlier, communities (and neighborhoods) are often devastated by economic shifts caused by mergers, acquisitions, downsizing of companies, and other economic factors. Although these are perhaps beneficial for the corporation, the impact on families and neighborhoods is usually detrimental. Some states have now passed laws requiring corporations to notify their communities when planning to leave the community. A portion of those thrown out of work may never find equivalent employment. Many are out of work for significant periods. Many, if not most, end up with a lower standard of living even after they find suitable employment. Some are forced to sell their homes and seek less expensive housing in other parts of the community, thus disrupting their neighborhood ties. Highlight 8.6 describes one such example.

In some communities, plant-closing task forces have been established to help residents cope with these catastrophes. Such task forces typically include representatives of social and human services, educational and vocational training institutions, and employment agencies. Some states have put in place efforts to help those affected. The kinds of services typically available to dislocated workers include testing, job counseling, assessment, training (including classroom, on-the-job, basic

skill, and literacy education), job development, and job search. Other support services sometimes provided include financial assistance for emergencies, transportation, child care, and health insurance, among others.

In contrast, a rapid influx of new companies, jobs, or residents may also prove disruptive to a neighborhood or community. A small bedroom community finds itself with more students in school, but lacks the economic tax base to provide adequate education to them all. This occurs because the corporations employing the children's parents are located in other tax jurisdictions.

Types of Neighborhoods

Neighborhoods are of several types. There are neighborhoods composed of highly mobile residents who will be there for only a short time. Despite this, a neighborhood may maintain a degree of solidarity and integration (organizing block parties or Neighborhood Watch programs). Another type consists of residents who have lived there all or most of their lives. Other neighborhoods are characterized by the lack of integrating mechanisms. They are almost disorganized in a social sense. People feel little sense of commonality with their neighbors and there are no neighborhood activities to help build this sense of community. Thus, we can define neighborhood type by looking at the degree of transiency and cohesion among residents. Transient neighborhoods with little cohesion are less likely to function as informal resource systems.

We also categorize (and stigmatize) certain neighborhoods by giving them different names. The term *ghetto,* for example, is used to describe a section in which a specific ethnic group or people of color must live. Other neighborhoods are called *slums,* indicating they are run-down, deteriorating, or otherwise blighted areas.

We also refer to ethnic neighborhoods when ethnic similarity among the residents is great. Most sizable cities and many smaller ones have defined ethnic neighborhoods: Frenchtown (Tallahassee), Chinatown (San Francisco), Clark Park (Detroit). The degree of residential segregation that occurs in these neighborhoods challenges the image of the melting pot. The melting pot, as you may recall, was an idea that everyone in America, regardless of country of origin, would somehow blend into the mix and become "an American." A more apt description of the mix of peoples found in America would be "a salad bowl."

Sometimes, entire communities move toward ethnic similarity. Sixty-three major cities with populations over 100,000 have people of color as their single largest group (U.S. Census Bureau, 2002). A good example of this is New Orleans, a city that was almost 70 percent black at the time Hurricane Katrina destroyed much of the city (Saenz, 2005). There has been a great deal of criticism of the federal government's response to this disaster, some blamed on racism because those most affected by Katrina were black and poor (Herring, 2006). Public opinion surveys conducted in the storm's aftermath found that the vast majority of white victims felt the government's response to the storm would have been the same whether the victims were white or black, contrasted with 75 percent of the black victims, who felt otherwise (Herring, 2006). Other surveys found that 57 percent of Americans blamed the victims of the storm itself for some of their misfortune (Huddy & Feldman, 2006). Those who remained in the city during the storm were criticized for their decision despite the fact that almost 60 percent of the lower-income black households lacked a vehicle to transport them to safety (Lieberman, 2006; Sherman & Shapiro, 2005).

Community residents campaign to end predatory lending that preys on low-income homeowners.

The development of ethnic neighborhoods can be traced to a variety of factors. Like the rest of the population, the most oppressed and poorest members of society seek housing they can afford. The somewhat lower costs of housing in certain areas act as a magnet to attract lower-income residents. Housing discrimination in other parts of a community may encourage this process. Minorities of color may find it difficult to get bank loans for purchasing a home or impossible to rent existing properties in more desirable neighborhoods. However, the ethnic neighborhood provides at least one advantage: the opportunity to live with others who share some cultural similarities. This combination of factors helps explain why ethnic neighborhoods have residents from a range of economic classes living together, a pattern not common in other residential neighborhoods.

Neighborhoods as Helping Networks

Neighbors can be part of an informal network of helpers; they can provide everything from day care to crime prevention. It is important to learn who are the natural helpers in the community. In one neighborhood, several neighbors relied on their neighbor, Horace, for help fixing anything and everything. When the water heater broke in the middle of the night, Horace was called first. When another neighbor needed help putting up a new mailbox or assembling a bunk bed for his kids, Horace helped out. When a nearby sorority house furnace went out one winter night, members of the sorority sought Horace's help again. Horace had become one of the natural helpers in the neighborhood.

Devore and Schlesinger (1996) summarize the importance of neighbors as a source of friendship and support in many ethnic neighborhoods as well. Neighbors can be a "source of caring and healing" (p. 314) for both physical and emotional problems. Neighbors can provide temporary or regular child care for each other, join in a Neighborhood Watch program, or simply listen to the concerns of their neighbors. They can help reduce feelings of marginalization and alienation.

Neighborhood Organizations

America has been called a nation of "joiners" because of our tendency to join organizations. We join churches as well as organizations for business, social, political, self-help, and service purposes. Young neighborhood residents may join gangs for some of the same reasons—social or economic benefits. Older residents may form or join neighborhood associations to address

common needs and concerns. These concerns might arise when properties in the area are neglected or crime frightens residents into action. By organizing, residents can exert greater pressure on city officials to take action. Depending on the problem, goals might include more frequent police patrols or demolition of dangerous buildings. Perhaps residents would like more people to buy older homes in the neighborhood and repair them. Another goal might be to prevent vacant homes from being used as crack houses.

Associations have many positive benefits for the community and neighborhood. They encourage cooperative efforts to address common difficulties faced by all residents. The efforts of individual residents also affect others. When one person becomes involved in an effort to improve the neighborhood, others may begin to feel that something can actually be accomplished, and they too may pitch in.

Associations may be formal organizations with bylaws, dues, and several membership categories or informal networks that meet in a resident's living room. Programs and goals can be as simple as getting a bad railroad crossing repaired or as complex as developing a grant program to help low-income residents buy their homes with little or no down payment. A social worker might play a number of roles in these types of associations. You might be involved in starting a neighborhood association when concerned residents bring a problem to your attention. You may also work with other associations as they grapple with the same problems you face: low-income clients living in inadequate, poorly maintained housing or gang violence running rampant in the neighborhood.

It is estimated that there are more than 100,000 neighborhood organizations in this country (Biegel, 1987). Some big cities have more than 500 such organizations (Reid, 1997). Denver alone has more than 200 registered neighborhood organizations (denvergov.org). Neighborhood organizations also exist in other countries, including Mexico (Rowland, 2006). The vast variety of organizations and the benefits they seek are staggering. They run the gamut from those interested in better police protection in their neighborhoods to those actually providing social services and advocacy for community interests. Neighborhood organizations may exist for single or multiple reasons. They may seek to improve housing conditions, enforce existing city laws, or prevent deleterious activities, such as drug dealing, from occurring in the neighborhood. Many associations begin in response to a crisis, such as burglaries in the neighborhood or the threat to

South Sunrise Street mentioned at the start of the chapter. They usually become sufficiently broad to continue their operation after the threat has been overcome (another example of goal displacement). The Neighborhood Watch program, in cooperation with local law enforcement, is one such effort. Most important, neighborhood associations help connect people to their neighborhoods and communities. They allow residents to get involved, to exert influence on the political process, to get help, and to help others. They also provide a resource that social workers can use.

Lenk, Toomey, Wagenaar, Bosma, and Vessey (2002) and her colleagues have identified the potential for neighborhood associations to become allies with other community activists pursuing such ends as better community health and other policy-related goals. They note, however, that the most politically effective associations typically were located in neighborhoods with lower median incomes and larger populations. Involvement of neighborhood associations in community coalitions also produced more politically active organizations.

Ohmer (2007), in a study of neighborhood organizations, discovered another benefit to such associations besides the potential to bring about change in the community. For example, she found that those active in such organizations had greater levels of self-efficacy with respect to knowledge, skill, and perceived effectiveness in influencing policy. Increased sense of community among active participants was also noted. Active members also were more likely to see their organization as having the ability to create community change. Empowerment of both members and their organizations is one definite outcome of such organizations.

In many communities, city government encourages and supports the existence of neighborhood organizations. Los Angeles, for example, promotes neighborhood councils designed to involve the public in city governance and decision making and to help residents access city services, identify their own priorities, and communicate these to elected and appointed officials. Los Angeles also provides a set of guidelines to facilitate development of such councils. Similar activities exist in cities across the country.

Often, community residents band together to achieve ends that could not be accomplished by individuals alone. For example, one community, worried about the lack of local health care, created an inexpensive health care system to serve the entire area. The community converted an abandoned potato warehouse into a health center, offering free services to low-income residents. Community residents talked local doctors into donating time each week to work in the health center. In addition, residents began an emergency health care fund for indigent residents who needed more serious medical care.

With input from fourth-year students from a nearby medical school, the community developed a health advocacy plan. Highlight 8.7 gives examples of two positive community organizations whose efforts resulted in significant positive community change.

Highlight 8.8 illustrates a list of neighborhood organizations in a small city with a population of about 150,000. The number and variety of organizations is fairly typical of many other communities. Each organization undertakes a variety of activities on behalf of residents of the neighborhood. Some focus on crime prevention, others on property maintenance. Some are concerned about ensuring an adequate supply of low-income housing; others worry more about parking problems caused by students at the local high school and college.

Local city newspapers may carry news of neighborhood organizations. New residents may be welcomed, meetings announced, and accomplishments of residents' children praised. Newspapers can help neighborhood associations in other ways. One newspaper prints weekly pictures of neighborhood properties that are eyesores. Besides spotlighting and potentially embarrassing the property owner (almost all of whom are absentee landlords), the newspaper interviews city officials responsible for enforcing ordinances requiring maintenance of buildings. This puts pressure on officials as well. The publicity helps force landlords to improve their properties and provide better living conditions for their low-income tenants.

Neighborhood associations are an excellent source of information for new residents. The large number of city offices that provide neighborhood services may be unknown to the resident, or the newcomer may find the long list overwhelming. Social workers new to a community might also find neighborhood organizations useful as they try to determine what to do about existing problems encountered by their clients. A list of potential neighborhood resources appears in Highlight 8.9.

Community and Neighborhood Resources

As you can see from the list in Highlight 8.9, cities often try to address a number of community and neighborhood problems. In addition, they engage in

HIGHLIGHT 8.7

Two Effective Neighborhood Associations

Case A

Brentwood was once an affluent neighborhood. Large Victorian homes lined the street for three blocks, though many had been converted into apartments over the years. The transition from single-family to multifamily housing had been difficult, but the mixed-use neighborhood was beginning to pull together. Now a new problem appeared on the horizon. The old Bailey estate (the house had burned to the ground two years ago) was for sale. A local auto repair shop had shown interest in buying the property and using it to store cars awaiting repair. Residents had visions of their children being crushed under wrecked cars, trapped in trunks, and generally having to live next to a junkyard.

The neighborhood association held raffles and bake sales and solicited donations to raise enough money to buy the property from the owner and convert it into a park. Using funds donated by a local civic club, they purchased playground equipment and turned ownership of the property over to the city.

Case B

The Altoona Betterment Association had already made a name for itself by aggressively asking owners to maintain their rundown properties. Writing to individual owners, the association pointed out what needed to be done (mainly, cleanup of debris and repair of rental properties). They also pressured the city to provide sufficient police protection so that drug dealers were forced out of the neighborhood.

A low-income housing project for senior citizens had been built in the area because of the efforts of the association. Now they were about to take a more important step, namely, attracting a physician to their neighborhood. The physician, new to the area, was planning to open a family-care office and build his practice. After repeated encouragement from the association and pledges of cooperation in fixing up and maintaining an old Victorian house, the doctor agreed to open his practice in the neighborhood.

HIGHLIGHT 8.8

Neighborhood Organizations

The following examples show the wide variety of neighborhood associations possible:

Roundtree Neighborhood Watch Group
Roundtree Urban Conservation District
Wellington Hills Homeowners Association
Cinnamon Square Property Owners Association
Citizens Association for the Betterment of
  Western Springs

Mid-Town Neighborhood Association
North Central Neighborhood
Roundtree Area Advisory Committee
Sherman Avenue Project Area Committee, Inc.
United Neighborhoods Organization, East
Walnut Street Historical Neighborhood Association
Woodland Heights Neighborhood Improvement
  Association

other endeavors less well known to residents. For example, cities actively seek new businesses and workers. Attracting workers and their families to a community is important in keeping a city progressive and alive. Recreation departments provide the usual park programs, golf courses, and swimming pools for neighborhoods, but are also active in creating tot-lots (programs for very small children), gang diversion activities, employment programs for teenagers, and drug abuse prevention programs. Social workers involve themselves in

many of these by providing services, helping to implement programs, or simply advising officials.

Fire departments provide fire prevention and fire safety programs; health departments wrestle with immunizations, AIDS, family violence, and infant mortality. Planning and zoning departments are instrumental in locating day care and child care facilities in a community, and police departments often work with other agencies to address family violence, gang activities, and community policing (a program of having police

---

HIGHLIGHT 8.9

Neighborhood Resources

Finding out where to turn for assistance for problems in one's neighborhood can often be frustrating. Many different city offices have multiple purposes. Titles of offices don't always help. The list below is from a medium-size city. As a social worker, you might wish to develop a database like this for your own use as you help clients confront problems they encounter in their neighborhoods.

    Abandoned or unsafe buildings: Building Regulation Dept.

    Overcrowded housing (more than three unrelated people): Building Regulation Dept.

    Housing rehabilitation loans: Planning and Development Dept.

    Illegal use of property (zoning code violations): Building Regulation Dept.

Zoning information: Planning and Development Dept.

Inoperable vehicles parked in yard: Health Dept.

Abandoned vehicles on street: Police Dept.

Tall weeds (over 12 inches): Health Dept.

Trash, appliances, auto parts left in yard: Health Dept.

Parking in front yard: Police Dept.

Noise disturbance: Police Dept.

Dangerous or stray animals: Health Dept.

Neighborhood planning: Planning and Development Dept.

Neighborhood Watch program: Police Dept.

Operation I.D. engraver: Police Dept.

Street lights: City Utilities Dept.

Carpool information: Community Development Dept.

Bus routes: City Utilities Dept.

---

walk their neighborhood beats, meeting residents in their homes and at neighborhood gatherings, and planning joint crime-prevention efforts). Libraries may serve as meeting places for support groups of various types. They also offer information and referral services.

Putting It All Together: Assessing Communities and Neighborhoods

EP 2.1.10d

Once you begin to understand the dynamics affecting communities and neighborhoods as systems, it becomes easier to assess a particular neighborhood or community (CSWE, 2008, EP 2.1.10d). It is important to understand the purposes of such an assessment. You could undertake an assessment to prepare for moving a new agency into a community. An assessment might help you respond to an identified community problem. Community assessment could help you orient yourself to a new environment as you begin a new social work position. Remember that your ethical obligation and role as a social worker is to go beyond the responsibilities of your official job description and work to improve conditions affecting society. To do

this, you will need to learn a great deal as you begin your first job.

In assessing a community, you can turn to many sources of information. These may include census records, planning agency documents, and business development plans. These are often available from city agencies, such as the planning department, regional planning agencies, Chamber of Commerce, or industrial park boards. Newspapers are often a good source of information on current issues, such as finding out how a particular problem developed. Many papers report on the background of a current community problem, trying to highlight (not always accurately, however) important dates and names. Other sources of data include libraries, books about the community's history, and information from the Internet.

Another useful source of information on community needs can come from the local United Way. This organization often undertakes community assessments to identify unmet needs in their catchment or service area. A good example is a recent assessment undertaken by the United Way of Salt Lake, Utah, that combined data gathered from key informants, a household survey, and a survey of service providers. This information was supplemented by a variety of other sources, including data from information and referral centers, private children's organizations, state government agency records, and local housing authorities, among others. The advantage of using existing data sources such as United Way reports is the wealth of information available. For instance, the United Way assessment identified problems as disparate as transportation and medical services for a growing population of older adults, health care, insurance, housing, substance abuse, medical care for mothers and newborns in ethnic populations, and respite care for caregivers and people with disabilities (United Way of Salt Lake, 2007).

If you work in a particular neighborhood—in a neighborhood center, homeless shelter, or similar facility—you might also wish to secure a map of the community or neighborhood. If you are focusing efforts on a neighborhood, consider enlarging your map to provide greater detail. You also may wish to locate a city directory that lists all residents on a street-by-street basis. This will tell you who lives on the streets in your neighborhood.

As you learn about a community, you can create and maintain a database of important officials and individuals simply by jotting down on note cards (or in a computer database if you have access to one) the names and titles of these people as their names emerge in the news. This way you will always know who the critical people are in your community and who might be a resource for a particular problem.

Depending upon need, it may be useful to focus on a certain segment of the total picture. You might augment information gained from reviewing official documents, such as census records, with data gathered by talking directly to decision makers and other key informants. Key informants are knowledgeable persons in the community with special expertise in your area of interest. The latchkey programs described in Chapter 3 (Highlight 3.2) used key informants to determine the extent of need for such programs. Typical key informants might include school principals, ministers, neighborhood association officers, ethnic group leaders, city officials, and business leaders. In this manner you can learn about interrelationships and connections of which you were not previously aware. A local minister may serve as administrator of a nursing home, be a senior member of a major civic organization, and sit on the board of directors of the local bank. Lobbying this individual in one context can also influence him in his other roles. The confluence (merging) of interests makes this individual very important in the local community and gives him significant actual and potential power. No single source of information could have disclosed this series of connections.

There are many models for assessing communities (Homan, 2004; Netting, Kettner, & McMurty, 2004; Sheafor & Horejsi, 2003). Most share similar components or suggest gathering information on specific topics. A typical assessment model appears in Highlight 8.10. It might be used for major projects such as development of a new agency, expansion of social services, or comprehensive planning to improve a community's human services.

Sometimes an assessment is limited in scope to one particular problem area being experienced by the community. Bowen, Martin, and Nelson (2002) discuss assessing a community's capacity to deal with a specific issue. Community capacity is "the link between the operation of formal and informal networks of social care in the community" (p. 554) and the actual results achieved by these networks. It is based on evaluating two factors, the first being the extent to which community residents, leaders, and agencies have a shared sense of responsibility for the welfare of the community's members. This part of the assessment looks at the actions of community members and organizations with respect to a given problem such as gang violence or poverty. Do members work together or otherwise engage in efforts to make the community a better place to live?

The second factor is the "collective competence" (Boren et al., 2002, p. 554) of the community in addressing the identified challenges, making the most of change opportunities, and attacking the problem. A competent community, by definition, will "identify community needs and assets, define common goals and objectives, set priorities, develop strategies for collective action, implement actions consistent with agreed-upon strategies and monitor results" (p. 554). Community capacity is an assessment not of the potential of a community to achieve, but rather what actual steps are taken in response to challenges. It is concerned with such things as the strength of bonds between and among individuals, networks, and organizations in the community and the connections that exist among the various stakeholders. High levels of community capacity are particularly needed when stressors are present, as might happen when a major employer leaves the area or when natural disasters strike. It is such events that require formal and informal networks, agencies, and community leaders to work closely together to deal with the threat. Absence of such shared bonds and commitment leaves a community vulnerable to whatever disasters and major problems happen to come along. Social workers need

HIGHLIGHT 8.10

A Model for Community Assessment

Name of neighborhood or community:

Location: including physical setting, location, boundaries, relationships to other communities, and so on

Population characteristics: including size, age and gender distribution, nationality, ethnicity, religion, and so on

Income: by subgroups (women, minorities, etc.), poverty rate

Community attractiveness: characteristics that attract and hold residents, such as climate, cost of living, amenities

Housing: types, conditions (e.g., unoccupied homes could be a sign of poor housing or something as innocent as cottages used only part of the year)

History: Why did people settle here? Where did early residents come from? What changes have occurred over time in population attitudes, beliefs, and values? Note important social, political, and economic events.

Geography: What characteristics have helped or hurt the community (for example, location on a major river often means business develops in a strip along the river and cheap electricity; it may also mean periodic flooding and affect street patterns and transportation)?

Other factors: mobility of residents, and so on

Education: educational characteristics of population by gender, school dropout rates, differences among subgroups (e.g., minorities), financing, buildings, student–teacher ratios, programs for children with special needs, extracurricular programs

Social/cultural systems: parks, cultural resources, recreational activities, social clubs, and civic organizations

Commerce and industry: major employers and industries, unemployment rates, local or absentee control of business, role of unions, future prospects, stability of industries, and so on

Religion and churches: role and influence in community

Governmental type: city manager, mayor, city council?

Political factors: role of political parties, voting patterns (who, what percentage), major issues, tax structure, elected versus appointed officials, financial stability, law enforcement and other city services

Social and health systems: number and type of hospitals and clinics, primary social service agencies, problems and limitations of each, responsiveness of services, informal helping systems, planning bodies

Sources of information: radio, TV, newspapers, prominent individuals who speak for population segments

Quality of education: programs of note, condition of facilities, special problems such as court–ordered integration, higher education availability

Power distribution: assess with reputational, positional, or issues methods

Miscellaneous: major community difficulties and steps being taken in response; gaps in services and facilities; concerns of the community, including who is concerned and why; what has been done in the past to deal with problem; conditions that led to this situation; strengths and limitations of the community for dealing with the problem

---

to be aware of a community's capacity to deal with new challenges and to identify ways to increase its ability to do so.

Understanding the community and its problems is essential to be effective in improving our clients' quality of life. Only then can we combat community-wide problems. In social work, we select interventions based upon our assessment of the problem. Although Highlight 8.10 presents a comprehensive model for assessing a community, other methods are available for more limited goals. A good example of this is evident

in Highlight 8.11. It depicts a community grappling with its children's needs. The community described in Highlight 8.11 used a survey of community children to focus on specific needs. It then used that data to plan and carry out a set of interventions.

The needs of a community should be the determining factor in how elaborate of an assessment approach is used. Undertaking a large, involved assessment of an entire community when we are interested in addressing only a narrow, specific problem is probably unwise and certainly more expensive. We may end up with

HIGHLIGHT 8.11

KidsPlace

The assessment that led to the development of Kids-Place began with a community survey of 6,700 children to find out their needs, interests, perspectives, and hopes. From their survey, city officials discovered a wide variety of needs, from steps at the aquarium so that younger children could see the exhibits to information about shelters for runaway children.

Several hundred volunteers (including social workers) helped draft a series of goals. They then carried them out with the combined support of private and public social service agencies and resources. These included creating bike routes for kids, expanding playground facilities, reducing bus fare so kids could ride at lower cost and developing an annual KidsDay

when admission to various recreational and cultural events is free. Stores posted window signs indicating that children could safely seek help—which could mean having a place to go to the bathroom or to call their parents—there. City budget development processes now weighed children's needs. More basic changes included zoning–law changes making family day care an allowable use for buildings. This was an important change, because city zoning laws can cause difficulty for anyone trying to open a day care center. The KidsPlace model of planning and services has proven successful enough to be replicated in several cities (Louv, 1994).

unnecessary data that are not helpful with the current problem. However, a comprehensive analysis of the community may show that problems in one area, such as unemployment, are clearly related to problems in other areas, such as child abuse or domestic violence. The size and scope of a community's problems must be carefully considered when deciding how much time, energy, and money should be expended on a community analysis.

Chapter Summary

The following summarizes this chapter's content as it relates to the learning objectives presented at the beginning of the chapter. Chapter content prepares social workers to:

A. *Identify the professional role of a social worker in neighborhoods and communities.*

Social worker roles in neighborhoods and communities include advocacy and social action, promotion of social and economic justice, identifying broad and systemic quality-of-life issues, lobbying, assessing needs, identifying service gaps, advocating for policy change, and participating in professional association action groups.

B. *Utilize conceptual frameworks to guide in understanding the functions and types of communities and neighborhoods.*

Traditional views of a community include a shared physical space with both social

interactions among residents and a shared sense of identity. Neighborhoods are characterized as geographical residential areas in which people share similar values, lifestyles, and housing types, and exhibit a sense of cohesion. Communities can also be understood by their functions, which include socialization, production, distribution, and consumption of goods and services, social control, mutual support, and provision of a means of participation by residents. The sizes of communities vary dramatically from small cities and towns to rural communities, reservation communities, bedroom communities, and institutional communities or company towns.

C. *Employ a systems perspective to view the community as an ecological and social system.*

Systems theory helps us understand the interrelated parts of the community as well as its context. The community may be seen as a change agent, target, client, or action system since it is both the focus and context for social work practice. The community can also be viewed from ecological and social system perspectives, and both perspectives help us understand the problems, challenges, and positives of any community. Likewise, we can employ social structural theory as well as human behavior theories to identify how and where problems arise. The latter include behavior theory and rational theory.

D. *Identify key concepts needed to discover and appraise changes in neighborhoods and communities.*

Among the key concepts needed to understand neighborhoods and communities are competition, centralization, concentration, gentrification, invasion, and succession. Most communities experience some or all of these changes.

E. *Utilize community resource systems to assess and intervene with neighborhoods and communities.*

Community resource systems include three primary types: informal, formal, and societal. Informal systems involve family members, coworkers, Mends, neighbors and others who provide various kinds of support. Formal or membership systems include social and fraternal organizations, labor unions, churches and professional groups such as NASW. Societal resource systems are both public and private social service agencies with an institutionalized mission to provide help to community members. Social workers need to become familiar with all of these resource systems.

F. *Identify how community factors such as social stratification, economic and political systems, and power may advance or impede human rights, and social and economic justice.*

Two primary trends have had strong influences on communities, urbanization and suburbanization. Another trend in some areas has been gentrification which has brought people back to the central city but not without generating some problems. In addition, social stratification is a concept that has helped social workers recognize discrimination against groups based on their ethnicity, gender, sexual orientation, or other factors. Social stratification can be seen in access to living environments, health care, and other social services.

A community can also be understood by looking at its economic system which involves the issues of production, distribution, and consumption of goods and services. A community's economic health plays a major influence on resources available to residents ranging from employment opportunities, income, health care, and societal resource systems.

The political system of a community is important to understand because it is often where decisions are made that affect most if not all residents. Both formal organizations (like city government) and informal political processes must be understood as playing different but important roles. The governmental activities in a community can include such things as planning, designing and implementing community programs, allocating funds, building community resources (jails, community centers), awarding and supervising contracts with private agencies, determining and enforcing laws and regulations, negotiating agreements, and mediating disputes.

Power in a community is the capacity to move people in a desired direction to accomplish some end or to prevent someone from doing something they otherwise want to do. Power can be either real or potential and the source of power may come from such things as resources, official positions, reputation, or size of the group. Who has power at a given time may depend upon the issue being considered. Social workers need to know who has power in those situations where change is needed.

G. *Describe the role that neighborhoods play as helping networks and how neighborhood organizations can serve as a resource for service delivery and sustainable change.*

Neighborhoods have multiple functions for residents. These include social, institutional, political, and economic. In this way they share some of the characteristics of a community since they are, after all, a system within the larger community. Neighborhoods may differ by type, with some consisting of highly mobile residents and others who remain there throughout much of their lives. Neighborhoods also may be characterized by their ethnic makeup (e.g., Chinatown) or wealth (Bankers Hill). One important role of neighborhoods is as helping networks providing informal resources to residents. This can include social support, financial assistance, child care, or physical assistance in emergencies. Some neighborhoods form organizations designed to achieve the goals of the residents, including access to community resources.

H. *Assess the ability of communities and neighborhoods to advance social well-being, and respond to the needs of their residents.*

There are many models for assessing the ability of communities and neighborhoods to meet the needs of residents. Factors that may be helpful include location, population characteristics, income level, attractiveness, housing, geography, history, educational opportunities, social/cultural systems in existence, commerce and industry, religion and churches, type of government, political factors, social and health systems, sources of information, and distribution of power, among others. Some may be of greater salience than others in understanding a particular neighborhood or community.

Competency Notes

The following identifies where Educational Policy (EP) competencies and practice behaviors are discussed in the chapter.

Educational Policy (EP) 2.1 Core Competencies

Educational Policy (EP) 2.1.5b Advocate for human rights and social and economic justice. *(P. 284):* The profession of social work expects practitioners to engage in advocacy and social action to promote social and economic justice.

Educational Policy (EP) 2.1.7a Utilize conceptual frameworks to guide the processes of assessment, intervention, and evaluation. *(P. 291):* A systems perspective provides a useful conceptual framework in all stages of the planned change process. *(P. 292):* Ecosystems or ecological theory helps social workers better understand the social environment of a community. *(P. 293):* Social structural theory is a commonly used framework for understanding how subsystems affect the individual and group. *(P. 294):* Human behavior theories help the social worker understand the behavior of individuals and families within their environment. *(P. 310):* Neighborhoods are more easily assessed when we are aware of the functions that they typically provide to residents.

Educational Policy (EP) 2.1.7b Critique and apply knowledge to understand person and environment. *(P. 295):* Among the key concepts important for understanding the community are competition, centralization, concentration, gentrification, invasion, and succession. *(P. 303):* Social stratification is a conceptual tool that can be useful for understanding larger systems but also can be used to discriminate against groups that differ by gender, race, sexual orientation, or other characteristics.

Educational Policy (EP) 2.1.8a Analyze, formulate, and advocate for policies that advance social well-being. *(P. 282):* Social workers need to understand the connection between policies and programs and the welfare of individual social service clients. *(P. 285):* Advocating for policy change in response to needs identified by grassroots community organizations is a social work responsibility.

Educational Policy (EP) 2.1.9a Continuously discover, appraise, and attend to changing locales, populations, scientific and technological developments, and emerging societal trends to provide relevant services. *(P. 299):* Among the trends that have an impact on communities are urbanization and suburbanization.

Educational Policy (EP) 2.1.10d Collect, organize and interpret client data. *(P. 316):* Assessing community and neighbors involves collecting data, organizing data, and making interpretations that help in the planning and intervention steps.

On the Internet

Visit the *Generalist Practice with Organizations and Communities* Web site at www.cengage.com/social_work/kirst-ashman for learning tools such as PowerPoint® slides, tutorial quizzing, Web links, and final exams.

CHAPTER 9

Macro Practice in Communities

"Officer needs assistance!" With his last breath, police officer John Bennett radioed for help and then collapsed. As he lay dying in the parking lot of the temporary domestic violence shelter on Byron Street, his assailant escaped into the dingy, rundown neighborhood. Although the location of the shelter was supposed to be a secret, the man had located his estranged wife and threatened to kill her. Officer Bennett, responding to a call from the shelter, was shot and killed. The man was later arrested, tried, and sentenced to prison. Ironically, the death of Officer Bennett helped spur efforts to protect victims of domestic violence and led to one of the most effective community organization efforts in the history of Richland City.

Just about everyone in the tiny community of Ozaukee showed up. The mayor and sheriff attended. So did the police chief, school officials, and church leaders. Also present were representatives of all the service clubs (Kiwanis, Rotary, etc.). The community meeting was in response to the death of Frank Vanet, a 17-year-old killed by a fellow student. Though his assailant had told many people before the killing that he was going to shoot Frank and had even showed them his gun, this did not change the tragic outcome. "How could this happen in our community? This isn't New York, where people don't care about one another," said the president of the Parent-Teachers Association. The apparently gang-related incident galvanized the people present. As a first step, they agreed to organize a huge town seminar focused on gangs and gang violence. Later steps would come out of that town meeting.

Central Springbok was close to becoming one of those neighborhoods where nobody will live. People were leery about the older homes needing repair. They preferred to settle in newer neighborhoods. Steve Odom was tired of hearing that nothing could be done to convince people to live there. As a member of the board of directors of Commercial Bank, his opinions were important in the community. At his last Rotary Club meeting he heard Annie Wentmeyer, a social worker from the Springbok Community Action Agency, describe how central Springbok was an example of a neighborhood on the edge. As he talked with her afterward,

Steve learned that other communities had successfully revitalized similar neighborhoods by making the purchase of homes there more attractive with low-interest loans and homesteading arrangements. In the latter, cities that had foreclosed on properties because the owner didn't pay the taxes offered the homes to families who agreed to fix them up and live there.

At the next meeting of the bank board, Steve presented his idea for encouraging low-income families to move into central Springbok. He suggested offering low-interest loans, with 3 percent down payments, and no closing costs. Following some discussion of its feasibility, the bank board directed its president to begin the program as soon as feasible.

Introduction

Sometimes it takes a tragedy to spur community action on a problem. The first two case examples illustrate that traumatic events can sometimes make a community face a problem head-on. Other times, a good idea produced at a propitious time can have similar impact and benefit. The last case example shows how sharing ideas can sometimes spur others to action. Each community described attended to a problem and initiated concrete steps to change things.

Social workers are often more aware of community problems than other professionals. After all, they work in the community, and are often in contact with the most oppressed populations. They make home visits to the poorest neighborhoods and confront myriad social problems daily. Social workers often witness the impact of unemployment, crime, drug use, health problems, gang violence, and educational troubles. Along with police officers, social workers are perhaps more likely than any other professionals to confront these social ills.

Sometimes, social workers are employed to deal directly with community problems. In one state, for example, the state Division of Alcohol and Drug Abuse employs community organizers to investigate neighborhood needs and implement programs to meet those needs. One neighborhood's need might be the creation of a neighborhood phone directory identifying resource persons such as babysitters and lawn caretakers. Another might involve holding a neighborhood block party or potluck dinner to bring residents together. The ultimate goal is always reduction of chemical-dependency risk factors, such as community disorganization and lack of attachment to one's neighborhood.

Unfortunately, except for the relatively few social workers employed by community organizations (like Annie Wentmeyer, mentioned previously), most of us are not hired to deal directly with these larger issues. As employees of various agencies, we provide specific services to those who experience these social problems. We often deal with the aftermath of community problems. In other words, we may deal with family problems (stress, child abuse, poverty, and so on) partly attributable to widespread unemployment resulting from the closing of a major shipyard. Does this mean we can avoid responsibility for trying to solve the larger societal and community problem? Can we stand by and let our clients and other citizens suffer injustice and lack of resources? The answer, of course, is no. Our professional obligations supersede our allegiance to our individual agencies. Our responsibilities to our profession and society dictate that we try to do something whenever possible.

Learning Objectives

This chapter will provide content concerning how social workers:

A. *Advance social and economic justice in their communities.*

B. *Utilize conceptual frameworks and strategies for empowering communities.*

C. *Apply the PREPARE model to engaging and assessing the potential for community change.*

D. *Employ the community asset mapping approach to identifying community resources.*

E. *Apply the IMAGINE model to intervening, and to evaluating change in a community.*

Change in Communities

Wanting to make your community and society a better place to live is a natural desire. Highlight 9.1 comments on the breadth of possible community change. Social workers have a unique opportunity to influence their communities, because social work is the only profession that mandates working with both people and their environments. Consequently, social workers are often active at the community level. Their involvement may take the form of signing petitions to support or protest some proposed action. It may also include involvement in political processes by voting, working for candidates, contributing time and money to political campaigns, and working with others to improve living conditions. Additionally, social workers can demonstrate on behalf of causes such as developing services for older adults or improving the quality of drinking water. Likewise, they can act against problematic practices such as destruction of neighborhoods through banks' refusing home loans. They can also target culturally insensitive planning, such as scheduling community-wide activities during periods in which certain groups celebrate their religious holidays. Highlight 9.2 describes an example of how social workers can work with others to improve the quality of life in a community.

To be an effective community change agent, you must master several techniques of, and approaches to, implementing change at the macro level. One of our biggest strengths as social workers is our ability to work with others and encourage changes affecting large numbers of people. People working together can usually make greater changes than individuals working alone. The individual and group skills you have learned will be equally useful at the macro level. (Chapters 2 and 3 provide a useful review of these skills.) Here, we will describe other macro approaches that should add to your repertoire of social work skills. Social workers use change strategies ranging from letter writing to legislative advocacy to concerted social action. *Social action* is a method of practice designed to place demands on a community in order to obtain needed resources, attain social and economic justice, enhance quality of life, and address social problems affecting disenfranchised and disadvantaged populations.

Philosophical Perspective on Macro Practice: Pursuit of Social and Economic Justice

Erlich, Rothman, and Teresa (1999) describe some of the important philosophical considerations that underpin community practice. They note that the decision to act in a given situation cannot be left solely to those who are the beneficiaries of a change effort. Although social work is committed to the principle of client self-determination, complex situations may suggest that social workers must act on their own. For example, clients may be uncertain about specific goals or ambivalent as to the best alternative. Groups and individuals may seek goals that are potentially very harmful to others. In addition, workers may encounter situations where they must assertively suggest a particular course of action. This does not excuse forcing others to do what we think should be done. Neither does this stance condone dishonesty or browbeating clients to accept our definition of the problem or solution. It does recognize our obligation as social workers to undertake changes in conditions that deny people social and economic justice. When we are working with

HIGHLIGHT 9.1

Community Change Activities

The community change activities described in this chapter are certainly not an exhaustive list of what is possible. Indeed, community change activities can involve grand as well as minor goals. They include programs to rehabilitate neighborhood housing, maintain pressure on slum landlords, and develop low-cost food cooperatives to help members reduce their food bills. Other programs focus on developing and maintaining small neighborhood parks, establishing a credit union for a low-income neighborhood, and patrolling neighborhoods to counter criminal behavior. Still other efforts aim at developing a community newspaper to cover local activities, creating self-help groups for widows, and providing medical care to the Chinese population to reduce the need for nursing-home placement. The programs addressed in this book are merely a subset of what is possible when we begin to address community needs.

Source: Homan (2004), Rubin and Rubin (2001).

HIGHLIGHT 9.2

Social Workers in the Community

Entwistle (1992) describes the collaborative activities of several social workers and others who formed a group to help a community solve some of its drug- and alcohol-related problems. Participants included representatives of the police department, members of Urban League (a community service agency), a social worker specializing in dealing with gangs, a substance abuse consultant and the director of a Hispanic social action agency. They divided into several action groups, one of which dealt with treatment and rehabilitation of chemically dependent persons.

Because low-income persons could not take advantage of costly inpatient treatment programs, the action group gathered leaders of local treatment programs and explained that free beds for the indigent were needed. As a result agency directors agreed to provide 14 free beds for low-income clients. Another group agreed to coordinate allocation of the beds.

A third action group focused on influencing the criminal justice system. Members met with judges to ask for more stringent jail terms for drug dealers. Another action group centered its efforts on holding absentee landlords responsible for drug dealing in their buildings. Yet another group lobbied the city council to ensure that no new liquor licenses were granted to facilities located near schools or existing liquor stores. All of these efforts made group members realize they could influence the system.

As an outgrowth of their attention to the community problems, the members discovered another critical need: lack of adequate health care and health insurance for low-income elementary school students. The action group then organized a group of pediatricians, general practitioners, and specialists to provide free emergency care to children who were hurt or became ill at school. Volunteers transported students to physicians' offices or clinics.

The program was eventually expanded to include mental health providers, dentists, pharmacists, and laboratory services. Churches, social clubs, and local industry donated money for X-rays, medications, and other medical items. More than 200 children received care in the first year, and volunteers handled such routine tasks as office work, transportation, and locating follow-up services. Eventually, the program expanded to almost all schools in the community. A five-year evaluation project accompanied the program to measure its impact and ensure that it continued to meet community needs.

---

specific community groups, we might expect that what we do must always relate directly to what beneficiaries of our efforts think is important, as long as that goal is legally and ethically defensible.

The question of what is legally and ethically defensible is always open to a degree of interpretation. While laws are often thought of as black and white, this is rarely the case. If it was, we would have no need for lawyers and courts to decipher what a law means. Similarly, what is ethically defensible can be open to question, which is another area where critical thinking is important. Before taking an action, the social worker needs to think about such things as:

- *Am I proposing to undertake this change to help my clients or to satisfy my own needs?*
- *What negative outcomes might occur if I pursue this project?*
- *Are the tactics that I propose to use consistent with values of the profession?*
- *In hindsight, will a reasonable person in the community agree that my actions were justified?*

- *Does the proposed action involve fraud, deception, or other forms of dishonesty?*
- *Do my proposed actions conflict with the policies of my own agency or organization?*

Some of the answers to the above questions may result in changes in tactics, while others may require additional consideration. Critical thinking about our practice is always necessary, especially in the case of legal and ethical issues.

Social workers must work and live within the boundaries of professional values (CSWE, 2008, EP 2.1.2). This requires that we avoid the trap of thinking the end justifies the means. *How* we achieve our goals is very important. More radical approaches to community change often do not recognize this limitation. There are still groups in society that believe the ends justify the means. Some abortion protesters burn medical clinics, assault and kill medical personnel, harass patients, and physically bar people trying to receive medical services.

EP 2.1.2

Their perspective is that the end justifies almost any means, a value orientation with potentially catastrophic consequences if adopted by the whole of society. It is essential not to leave our ethical standards behind when we work in the community. We should remember that, as social workers, we work in a political environment. Our actions directly affect how others perceive, respect, and treat us.

Philosophical Perspective on Macro Practice: Empowerment

Just as the pursuit of social and economic justice is a fundamental goal of practice in the community, the same may be said of empowering community members. "The goal of empowerment is to increase the abilities of individuals, families, and communities to get what they need; influence how others think, act, or believe; and influence how resources are distributed" (Everett, Homstead, & Drisko, 2007, p. 162). It involves helping others develop a sense of mastery or control over aspects of their environment, usually through increasing their competency and self-efficacy.

Historically, empowerment has been a tradition in American social work that draws its roots from both religious and secular sources (Simon, 1994). Leaders as diverse as Dorothea Dix, Jane Addams, Mahatma Gandhi, and Paolo Friere have embraced the empowerment concept as critical to bringing about change (Homan, 2004; Lin-horst, 2006; Simon, 1994). In addition, the NASW *Code of Ethics* Preamble speaks specifically about the goal of empowering vulnerable and oppressed populations. It is clearly an important aspect of practice with all sizes of systems, including the community (CSWE, 2008, EP 2.1.5c).

EP 2.1.5c

Bush (2004) has discussed the importance of empowerment in social work literature and identified five competencies needed to engage in effective empowerment. These include *informational, intellectual, intrapersonal, interpersonal,* and *interventional* competence.

The first, *informational* competence, includes the knowledge and awareness social workers possess regarding the groups with whom they are working. This knowledge might include styles of communication, worldview, behavioral patterns, and lifestyle. She points out that absence of this knowledge limits the ability of the social worker to engage in empowerment.

Intellectual competence for empowerment requires that the social worker consider how informational

knowledge can be used to work with the client system. It involves thinking about how best to approach a given group, anticipating potential challenges, and planning for them.

Intrapersonal competency for empowerment involves the social worker's "genuine affinity for the individual or community with whom he or she is working" (Bush, 2004, p. 51). In practice, this means honestly caring about the community and being committed to its empowerment, as well as an awareness of one's own values, biases, and worldview.

Interpersonal competency for empowerment is the ability "to communicate with genuineness and warmth" (Bush, 2004, p. 51). To do this, the worker must be able to respond to communication patterns that may be unique to the community being served. This might include slang or other communication devices used in a given community. It also requires engaging the community without violating its norms and respecting the uniqueness of each system.

The final competency is *interventional,* which requires that the social worker be able to utilize knowledge and various skills in pursuit of empowerment. Such skills include identifying an appropriate intervention plan, engaging community networks and other resources in the change effort, and monitoring and evaluating the process and outcome.

As you can see, empowerment is a multiparty process. Unlike such fantasy figures as Batman and Superman, social workers cannot bring about permanent change in social conditions without the help of those most affected by those conditions. Ultimately, it is the members of a community who must develop the knowledge and skills to create and maintain change in the community. Moreover, not engaging the community members in the change effort is a form of paternalism. Empowerment, therefore, is a critical goal of community practice as it is in other realms of social work. By empowering community members, we are engaging in at least two activities: drawing out abilities that are already present in members, and teaching and modeling new abilities.

Drawing out innate abilities can occur through several mechanisms. First, social workers must help community members assess and recognize inherent knowledge and skills. This is more likely to occur when the social worker makes an effort to get to know members of the community. One way it can occur is when the worker lists the kinds of tasks and activities that are needed to achieve a particular goal. This might include preparing news releases, letters to the editor, or fliers related to a specific goal, going door to door to inform other residents and solicit additional support, or hosting a meeting of similarly concerned citizens, among many others. The process of identifying tasks needing accomplishment will bring out some members who have such skills. It may also produce suggestions about others who might be asked to help. In each case, the social worker should make a point of showing appreciation for the offer to help and demonstrate confidence that the member is capable of achieving the task. Another approach is offering to help on a task if individuals say they aren't sure they can do it by themselves. This helps recruit members and gives the worker the opportunity to encourage, praise, and otherwise support the individual. You might respond to a member who voices doubt about his or her own ability to pursue a task by saying "Would you be willing to help me on this task?" Knowing that one is not alone in the task and that the worker will take a leading role builds confidence.

Additionally, there will be other areas in which members can come to recognize their own capabilities. Perhaps they have contacts or individuals that may be of assistance in the process of creating change. These may be friends, coworkers, or others in the community who share the same interests as the member.

Identifying those beliefs, attitudes, and behaviors that inhibit people's ability to accomplish their goals is another method for empowering community members. Past failed attempts to change things may be dampening enthusiasm about future change. Fatalistic attitudes that nothing one does will change anything can also be challenged by the worker. Once individuals and groups realize that they are being controlled by such ideas, it is easier to help them take steps to bring about change. Sometimes the barriers are not inherent in the community members, but in policies, rules, or procedures imposed by others. For example, a city council may have set a limit of 10 minutes for public comment on any proposed ordinance, a length of time that is insufficient for adequate discussion of a complex topic. Helping members recognize that this limitation is not engraved in stone, but rather a decision taken by council members, makes it less threatening. Such decisions can be challenged and changed with sufficient community interest.

Even the process by which community members come to recognize they are not alone in their desire for change is empowering (Homan, 2004). Feeling like you are the only one who is concerned about a particular problem is disempowering. Knowing that others share your concerns empowers individual members by giving them the confidence that their ideas are sound. It also helps move an issue from an individual concern to a social problem, which means that it affects multiple members of the community, not you alone.

Teaching and modeling new abilities occurs each time the social worker takes an action that furthers the community goals. Deconstructing complex activities by explaining exactly what you did or what needs to be done helps members recognize that creating change is not magical, but consists of readily identifiable concrete steps that others can use. Another teaching modality is to help members anticipate what will occur in the future. You can do this by helping members consider possible outcomes, evaluate the likelihood of each, and decide how they will respond to these eventualities. By doing this, the social worker is helping develop cognitive skills and increasing members' confidence in their ability to deal with the future. Homan (2004) suggests asking questions and seeking input from members to demonstrate valuing their ideas and to help them build confidence in their own judgment. Likewise, involving as many as possible in decision-making and task activities helps develop skill in these areas. As members increase their ability to create change, the worker will use every opportunity to recognize and praise these individuals and their skills.

Once community members develop skill in achieving their collective goals, the worker can further empower them by gradually taking a back seat and allowing members to lead the change effort. Developing confidence in their own ability to create change is not only empowering, but also consistent with the social work value of self-determination.

Any large-scale change activity is bound to encounter setbacks. Homan (2004) points out the importance of preparing members for these setbacks by acknowledging when failure occurs and talking about your own lack of successes. By doing so, members come to recognize that a specific lack of success in one area need not prevent the group from accomplishing its goals. Failures are learning opportunities that can lead to greater creativity and better problem solving in the future.

Finally, celebrate successes by publicly recognizing both group and individual achievements. This helps balance out areas where success has not been achieved, helps empower both members and the group as a whole, and paves the way for future success.

Highlight 9.3 suggests further options for social workers to empower clients.

HIGHLIGHT 9.3

Empowering Clients' Participation in Decision Making

Linhorst Eckert and Hamilton (2005) suggest ways in which clients with severe mental illness can be empowered in relation to social agencies that provide needed services. Their suggestions easily apply to other client groups and include the following points:

- Develop multiple formal structures and processes that provide ongoing opportunities for clients to participate in agency decision making. Options might include such things as actively seeking input from clients and placing client representatives on boards, committees, and other decision-making bodies.

- Help clients develop decision-making skills of their own by employing such interventions as assertiveness training and communication skills training.
- Train agency staff, committee members, and board members on how best to work with clients in decision-making activities.
- Clarify the extent of client decision-making power when they participate in agency or organizational boards and committees. Power in most formal organizations tends to rest in administrative personnel such as agency directors and boards, and clients must be helped to understand this dynamic.

Perspectives on the Community

EP 2.1.7

The community can be viewed from at least three different perspectives (CSWE, 2008, EP 2.1.7). First, the community is the *context* in which we practice. Whether we are direct-service workers, supervisors, planners, or community change agents, we all practice in a community of some sort. The community, as the place where we work, significantly influences what services we provide and what problems we address (or ignore). It also determines what change efforts are feasible. Economically poor communities, for example, often lack the resources to meet human needs as readily as wealthier areas. An example of a community as context is the City of Midvale. Midvale had a number of residents, including many older adults, who were not aware of the services routinely available in the community. In order to address this problem, the Neighbor-to-Neighbor program was created, using neighborhood residents as Community Health Outreach Workers (CHOWs). The CHOWs went door to door in their neighborhoods explaining the types and kinds of resources offered in Midvale. Because many of the residents spoke Spanish, the CHOWs also spoke Spanish as they talked with neighborhood residents. The goals of the program were to empower Midvale residents by informing them about community services, and to develop a supportive community in which neighbors knew one another and could serve as a resource in times of need. In the case of

Midvale, there was not a need to develop new programs, challenge the status quo, or engage in social action. The community need of greatest importance was to help residents learn how to use those services that already existed.

Second, the community is the *target* of our change efforts. In other words, the community is the thing we are seeking to change. If a community remains unresponsive to the needs of a significant segment of its population, then that community must change. Macro change is required when communities or institutions constrain individuals by limiting their opportunities (social or personal).

When we target the community for change, our efforts are directed at causing that change. We may accomplish this through creating new services, improving the delivery of existing services, or replacing the political leadership. Consider the problem of gang violence that plagues many cities. Many communities respond to gang violence by hiring more police, but others approach the problem more creatively. A Streetworkers program in one large city targets actual and potential gang members. This program is designed to end the gang violence destroying the quality of inner-city life. Streetworkers act as mediators between police and gang members to reduce the occurrence of violent incidents. Mediators seek compromise and suggest alternatives to settling problems by resorting to violence. Preventing a problem is a more positive approach than simply increasing the number of police who are available to pick up the pieces after the damage is done.

Third, the community is the *mechanism* for change. That is, the community can actually solve its own problems by drawing upon the talents and mutual interests of community members. Consider Ozaukee, mentioned at the start of this chapter. That community is trying to prevent gang-related values and violence from undercutting residents' concern for fellow citizens. A broad cross section of the community is working to ensure that others do not suffer the fate of Frank Vanet, the murdered teenager.

Another example is a housing program operating in a small, rural community. Sponsored by a nonprofit housing corporation much like Habitat for Humanity, the program is designed to empower low-income individuals to own their own homes. It works by having eight or so families working together to build homes for each family. Each family helps the others build their homes, and all homes must be completed before a family can move into their own unit. This co-op arrangement allows each family to contribute sweat equity to their home while also taking turns providing related services such as child care for the children. The result is that each family has about $25,000 of equity in their homes when they move in, which eliminates the need to come up with a down payment. In addition, each participant is able to develop a sense of confidence and achievement by employing skills they may have never utilized before.

Approaches to Community Change

There are at least three separate orientations from which we can tackle community problems. One orientation emphasizes working with the power structure in a consensual, gradual way that focuses on service delivery. Social workers have historically been involved in organizations sponsored by the traditional establishment, including social settlement houses, neighborhood and community centers, and the United Way. The United Way is a "national federation of local organizations established to systematize and coordinate voluntary fund raising efforts. The money raised … is used to fund social agencies; nonprofit human services organizations, and some health, education, and recreation programs in local communities" (Barker, 2003, p. 449).

A second orientation focuses on conflict, mediation, and challenges to the power structure. The goal is to obtain or maintain power and develop alternate institutions to meet existing needs. Examples include tenant organizations and community reform movements. This approach finds the current system of services inadequate, unresponsive, and unwilling or unable to change. We will talk about this more when we look at conflict tactics.

The third orientation is neighborhood maintenance, which combines a consensual, peer-pressure system with legal action and political lobbying to improve property values, maintain neighborhoods, and deliver services. Neighborhood associations (described in Chapter 8), civic clubs, and property owner organizations are typical mechanisms used in this approach. They all serve to improve and maintain neighborhoods. Smaller-scale examples of specific activities are organizing bike-safety programs for local children and holding self-defense classes for neighborhood women.

As social workers, you may operate from any or all of these orientations during your career, depending on several variables, such as the nature of your job, the amount and type of sanction from your agency, your personal time, and the type of community problems you encounter. This chapter will offer examples illustrating each of these approaches.

Beginning the Change Process

As you know, steps in the planned change process are engagement, assessment, planning, intervention, evaluation, termination, and follow-up. We will follow these steps as we consider a variety of community problems.

Engagement in the Community

Engagement is the point at which you and the client system make initial contact, get to know each other, and make a decision about whether you and/or your agency can be of help (CSWE, EP 2.1.10). It is also the point **EP 2.1.10** where the client is oriented to the helping process and you explain further steps that you and the client will follow. In the community setting, engagement involves some of these same purposes. For example, your recognition that a community problem exists often follows a period of observation; it subsequently results in a clearer understanding of the history, experiences, and complexities of the community (Landon, 1999). The problem may have been brought to your attention by a single client, a community group, or you may have discovered it by yourself. In the first two cases, the engagement phase involves a period during which the client or group develops a comfort level with you as the worker.

During this period, you will also make contact with others involved in the problem or change opportunity. You will build relationships with each client system using a variety of micro level skills discussed in

Chapter 2. You will also begin using the social work principle *professional use of self*. In other words, "you are using your knowledge, experience, and perceptions in the professional worker/client relationship in a planful manner" for several purposes (Kirst-Ashman & Hull, 2006, p. 63). For example, you will employ your knowledge of neighborhoods and communities to help understand the social environment with which the client is interacting. You will also share your understanding and perspectives with the client system to ensure that you both are on the same page when it comes to assessing and planning for action. In addition, you will use both micro and mezzo level skills to further the goal of the macro intervention. Every action, decision, and communication should be guided by your professional knowledge, skills, and values.

You may wonder how long the engagement phase should last. Unfortunately, there are no cookbook answers to this question—the answer is similar to the response faculty often give when students ask "How long should this paper be?" The phase should last as long as it takes to accomplish the tasks of this portion of the planned change process.

PREPARE: Assessing Potential for Community Change

Because the PREPARE and IMAGINE models provide a detailed breakdown for most of the planned change process, we will use these models in this chapter. (Figure 9.1 repeats the PREPARE model introduced in Chapter 5 [Figure 5.1].)

Step 1 : *PREPARE*—Identify *Problems* to Address

Identifying problems in the community is usually not difficult. Problems have a way of making themselves known without much effort on our part. In the cases that began this chapter, three communities learned of problems in various ways. Regardless of how a problem comes to light, several substeps are needed to identify the problem you are going to address. These were discussed in Chapter 5 and will be reviewed here. First, you must seriously evaluate the potential for macro level intervention. Second, you must define and prioritize the problems. Third, you must translate the problem into needs. The final step is to determine what needs you will address (since it may not be feasible to tackle all that you have identified).

1. **P** Identify **Problems** to address.

2. **R** Review your macro **Reality**.

3. **E** **Establish** primary goals.

4. **P** Identify **People** of influence.

5. **A** **Assess** potential financial costs and benefits to clients and agency.

6. **R** Review professional and personal **Risk**.

7. **E** **Evaluate** the potential success of a macro change process.

FIGURE 9.1 PREPARE—An Assessment of Community Change Potential

The next section describes some of the more common ways that community problems come to our attention, using case examples for illustration.

Identification by News Media Reports

Sometimes, the news media reports a sensational event that underscores the existence of a community problem. One community learned of a gang infiltration problem when the news media reported police attempts to apprehend those responsible for gang "artwork." This case is explained in Highlight 9.4.

Another example comes from the publication of governmental reports relative to a particular problem. A report from the U.S. Department of Health and Human Services entitled *More Choices, Better Coverage: Health Insurance Reform and Rural America* (2009) was highlighted in papers across the country. The study brought to the public's attention several problems being experienced by residents in rural areas of the nation. The study found that rural areas "have higher rates of poverty, chronic disease, and uninsurance, and millions of rural Americans have limited access to a primary health care provider" (p. 1). "People in rural areas are also more likely to have chronic health conditions such as heart disease and diabetes," and "one out of every five farmers is in medical debt" (p. 2), according to the report. Unlike many news media accounts, the report also identified several recommendations for addressing the high rates of poverty, uninsurance, and chronic diseases, and increasing rural

HIGHLIGHT 9.4

Gang Graffiti

The city of Thistle is a booming community of 150,000 residents. Lately, gangs and gang "wannabes" have begun to appear in the community. This initially becomes evident through the graffiti gangs use to mark their territories and provoke other gangs. The local newspaper reports a series of violent incidents apparently related to territorial issues.

In response, a citizen's committee composed of representatives of several civic and social service organizations is formed. The committee evaluates the situation and decides that an intervention is needed. By doing so, they carry out substep 1 in the PREPARE problem-identification process (introduced in Chapter 5). In sub-step 2, they prepare to deal with the media-defined problem of gang graffiti and identify as their first priority the removal of the markings. This will destroy the gangs' territorial markers, remove the provocation for other gangs, and eliminate an eyesore.

By translating the problem into a need—graffiti removal—the committee completes substeps 3 and 4 (translating problems into needs and determining which needs to address). Operation Paint Out is launched to beat the gangs at their own game. Volunteers are recruited to paint over gang graffiti. Soon, almost every display of graffiti has been painted over by members of the volunteer Paint Out Corps. A defaced wall is repainted in 15 minutes by a group of teenagers, at least one of whom had once considered joining a gang. The experience helps convince him and other youngsters that gangs are destructive to their community. The gang concept is not so romantic, after all. This paint-out effort is only one of several steps the community pursues to take back the city from gangs.

Note that whereas gang graffiti was easily recognized as a problem in Thistle, all such "public artwork" cannot be considered graffiti. For example, Delgado (2000) highlights the importance of murals in the Latino community. The creation of murals in public or free spaces is a common practice and reflects a group or community effort. Often the murals depict ethnic pride, religious values, social justice concerns, or other symbolic events and themes. Rather than a weakness, this form of public art represents a strength of the Latino community.

---

residents' access to health care providers. The recommendations, while directed at rural problems, also applied to many urban areas as well. They included providing affordable health insurance coverage, eliminating preexisting conditions and health status issues that are used to deny coverage, and increasing preventive services, among others.

Identification by Social Service Providers

Still other problems are identified by those who provide social services. In one state, leaders of four social welfare departments (mental health, elementary and secondary education, social services, and health) met over breakfast to discuss their collective unhappiness with problems their individual agencies couldn't seem to handle. Although their combined budgets equaled several billion dollars, the money did not seem to help. Their primary concerns included keeping children in school as long as possible, helping them remain safely in their homes, and keeping them out of prison.

The group formed what they called "The Sustaining Program," designed to find ways to deal with neighborhoods and school districts beset with frequent homicides, drug dealing, armed children, high incidence of child abuse, and rising high school dropout rates. The program included individual counseling to students, latchkey programs for children lacking adult supervision after school, and assistance with the children's homework. Program counselors made home visits and encouraged parents' participation in school affairs, further helping to connect parents with the school system.

In another agency, the annual budget development process involves consultation among supervisors, social workers, and other staff to identify community conditions that require intervention. A policy established by the agency board of directors requires seeking regular feedback on community needs to ensure continuation of appropriate services. Because most new programs and projects have financial consequences, this method allows the agency to reallocate resources on a timely basis.

Sometimes, a single agency identifies a problem and undertakes a solution. For example, a local organization dedicated to improving the supply of low-income housing pointed out that nearly 6,000 people in the community were living in cars, shacks, or other substandard housing. They organized a community meeting featuring local entertainers to raise money for their next project. The organization, which builds homes for low-income families, requires these families to pay 1 percent of the cost of the building, maintain payments on a no-interest loan, take living skills classes, and donate time to help build homes for others. To involve the community in the process, the organization asked residents to sign up to buy nails, lumber, paint, and other materials. Because supply costs varied, almost anyone could help. One person could purchase a box of nails for $5 and another an appliance for $300.

Finn and Checkoway (1998) note that the Youth Action Program of East Harlem, New York, began as a mutual effort of teachers and students to identify needed changes in their community. The focus initially was on homeless youth. Today, the program trains dozens of low-income young people to rehabilitate buildings to provide housing. The program also provides personal counseling and a variety of other social and educational services. Similar youth-fostered programs exist in Washington, DC, Indianapolis, Indiana, and Selma, Alabama, among 40 other locations. The focus varies by location. For example, in Albuquerque the emphasis is on cultural awareness, racism, and environmental concerns, as well as the safety and health of children.

Identification by Beneficiaries

Frequently, those most directly affected by a problem bring it to our attention. For example, a neighborhood association became concerned when absentee landlords began to violate city laws limiting the number of unrelated persons living in the same residence. The overcrowding in some homes and apartments contributed to maintenance problems, health and sanitation difficulties, and generally increased neighborhood deterioration. The association approached the city council to strengthen relevant laws and to urge that landlords be fined or jailed for law violations.

Describe Problems Clearly

Of course, it is not sufficient merely to identify a problem. You must describe problems with sufficient clarity that others can understand what needs to be done. The case example involving the death of Officer Bennett (which started this chapter) may clarify how to identify a problem.

Geri was the newly appointed director of an agency operating a domestic violence shelter. A BSW, she was a committed social worker who cared deeply about her community's residents and her clients. She knew that John Bennett's death and the community's concern were good starting points for a discussion of domestic violence and the needs of its survivors. At least people were now aware of the "battered wife" problem and of the violence inflicted on women and others. Yet the problem needed further definition. Geri subsequently clarified the problem as described in the following paragraphs.

Survivors of domestic violence had no safe place to stay for periods of 30 days or more. The lack of a permanent, secure shelter for battered women and their children was the primary problem. In the long run, such a facility would eliminate the periodic need to find a new home for the shelter, which had been the pattern for several years. In previous years, Geri's organization simply found a person or a group to lend them a house for a short period of time. When the owner wanted the house back, the board had to locate a new shelter. Because the houses belonged to other organizations, it was impossible to provide enough security to prevent entry by angry husbands.

National rates of domestic violence and local police reports made it possible for Geri to estimate the number of women and children physically victimized in Richland City each day, week, and month. This information, reported to the shelter's board of directors and then publicized in various media, helped convey the seriousness of the problem. Largely because of increased media attention following Officer Bennett's death, the time was right for change.

Recognize that only the most pressing problems are likely to get media attention when so many things are happening simultaneously in a community. This increases the importance of gathering adequate data about a community problem. For example, a problem affecting a thousand people is easier to address for change than one that concerns only a hundred.

Research the Problem Carefully

No matter how the problem comes to your attention, research it very carefully to ensure that you have all the needed data (CSWE, 2008, EP 2.1.6). How serious is the problem? How many people are affected? Describe the problem as carefully as possible.

EP 2.1.6

Is this an unrecognized problem not yet acknowledged by others? Is it necessary to spend time educating people about the seriousness of the problem? Is there just one problem, or is there a series of problems that must be prioritized? Is this a long-standing problem that has been ignored, or one for which previous solutions have failed? What factors cause or contribute to the problem? Keep in mind that what appears to be a cause might actually be a coincidence. For example, an increase in gang activity in a community may coincide with an increase in arrests for selling drugs. The two events may or may not be related. Both may reflect major problems in the community caused by lack of legitimate employment and recreational opportunities, absence of appropriate community services, or a decision by the police to target gangs and drug sales. But that doesn't mean one has caused the other.

Causes might be seen differently by different groups. Cultural experiences and values can dramatically affect how people view the same set of events (Homan, 2004). Consider seven family members living in a two-bedroom house. Some people might consider this evidence that residents just don't know how to live "normally." Still others may blame greedy landlords for trying to stuff as many people as possible into any

available living space. Yet others may believe that such crowding results from lack of available housing for large, low-income families. Others think crowding is caused by lending institutions that refuse loans to low-income families, thereby forcing them to live in inadequate housing.

Potential sources of data include census records, previous needs assessments, agency reports of services delivered, or media accounts of problems. Any of these may help assess the extent of community need. Local or regional planning agencies, university or college research centers, or other bodies may have gathered useful information. Some of this information may also be found on the Internet.

In rural areas where data may be less readily available, Haulotte and Oliver (2004) suggest contacting the County Extension Agent, as well as consulting local newspapers and regional publications and local bulletin boards. The latter often contain a great deal of information about what is happening in the rural area. Grocery stores may give a clue to such things as ethnic

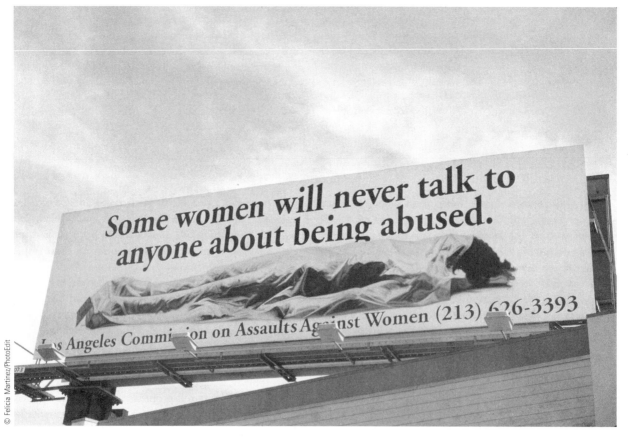

This billboard reflects a community public awareness program.

or religious composition of the community, while restaurants and cafés may serve as gathering places for local residents to share news. They also mention that funeral home directors may have information on the culture, values, and traditions of the rural community and may be a good source of information.

Sometimes the absence of local data is a problem. However, it may be possible to extrapolate from national, state, or county data and relate it to your community. You could use state data to estimate the number of births to unmarried teenagers occurring in a community. Such information would be useful if you were trying to highlight the need for family planning services for this age group. This extrapolation would be appropriate if there were few demographic differences between the state and the community. However, an urban community in a predominantly rural state may not find state figures very useful. The circumstances in urban and rural communities may be radically different.

Sometimes data is available to show changes in a community over time. One study surveyed the sexual experiences of teenagers at 10-year intervals. It found that, despite fears to the contrary, teens were not much more sexually active than their parents had been 20 years earlier. This information helped lower anxiety about widespread teenage sexual behavior.

At other times, you might want to compare your situation to some sort of average. One community discovered that, compared with other cities of similar size, it had significantly fewer school social workers serving children. Sometimes it is possible to compare your situation with a national standard.

You might discover that you have only a fraction of the number of police officers you need when compared with a national standard. This standard might recommend 2 police officers for each 1,000 city residents, and you only have 1. Your community's citizens thus are less protected. It follows that they may be at significantly greater risk of theft, property damage, and assault.

Completion of the problem-definition stage should enable you to determine, with some degree of assurance, who is affected by the problem, to what extent, and what sort of remedy might be appropriate. You should also have at least an elementary grasp of what will happen if you intervene and of who the participants in the change process should be. This includes clients affected by the problem, change agents, action systems, and target systems. Recall that the change agent system includes the organizations or agencies

that sanction the worker. The action system is "the people and resources in the community with which the social worker deals to achieve desired change" (Barker, 2003, p. 5). The target system represents those you will seek to influence in order to achieve your goals.

Community Capacity Building

You will note that the first step in the PREPARE model uses a problem-based approach to community change. However, this is not the only mechanism that can be employed. For example, community asset mapping (described in Step 2) and community capacity building are alternative methods of beginning the change process (CSWE, 2008, EP 2.1.10a). Community building is a neighborhood-based approach to improving conditions in an area. Consistent with the strength approach, it emphasizes the value of identifying characteristics of the community that can be used to bring about change and involve members directly in the process. It also is based on the premise that neighborhood residents should establish the priorities that will be pursued. In order to build a community, it is important to identify activities and events that can be used to bring residents together. These might include such things as neighborhood parties and walk-about evenings, in which residents walk their neighborhood, stopping at various houses along the way for treats and refreshments. Such measures tend to give residents a sense of community with their neighborhoods and can be used as a springboard for other activities and purposes.

EP 2.1.10a

"Community building's central theme is to obliterate feelings of dependency and to replace them with attitudes of self-reliance, self-confidence, and responsibility. It gives high priority to establishing and reinforcing sound values. And these are not ideas being imposed from the outside—they are what the leaders of distressed neighborhoods across the nation themselves are saying they want to see accomplished" (Gibson, Kingsley, & McNeely, 1997, p. 3). According to these authors, the characteristics of community building include efforts that are

- "Focused around specific improvement initiatives in a manner that reinforces values and builds social and human capital.
- Community-driven with broad resident involvement.

- *Comprehensive, strategic and entrepreneurial.*
- *Asset-based.*
- *Tailored to neighborhood scale and conditions.*
- *Collaboratively linked to the broader society to strengthen community institutions and enhance outside opportunities for residents.*
- *Consciously changing institutional barriers and racism"* (pp. 6–8).

The efforts lead to building upon what already exists in a neighborhood or community, maximizing resident input, focusing on specific concrete improvements, building the capacity of residents to achieve future change, and linking to the larger community. In this process, community building intends to remove the barriers of racism and oppression that prevent people from being able to meet their own needs. In the past, community building has led to elimination of drug sellers from specific neighborhoods, revitalization of urban areas, increase in the number of low-income students going on to college, reductions in child abuse, and creation of a development corporation that would bring much-needed business and services to a community (Gibson et al., 1997). Moreover, the community-capacity-building approach has proven successful in other areas, including India, Brazil, the Philippines, Colombia, South Africa, Bangladesh, Zimbabwe, and Spain (National Center for Economic and Security Alternatives, 2007). The emphasis on recognizing existing assets and strengthening the capacities of communities and their residents appears to be a promising approach to community change.

Step 2: PREPARE—Assess Your Macro and Personal *Reality*

Your macro reality includes those organizational and other variables that can work for or against you in the macro change process. Your personal reality, you will recall, comprises your own strengths and weaknesses and their potential impact on the change effort.

What variables work for and against efforts to respond to the identified community problem? Are people invested in the status quo? Who benefits from the current situation? You will need some sense of how likely the system is to change. How might individuals and leaders in that system respond? Also, knowledge of the available resources would be helpful. Of course, costs must be figured two ways: What are the costs of acting, and what are the costs of not acting? Can you anticipate help from others? How about opposition?

Who might be on each side of the fence? Who might straddle the fence and try not to take a position? What you are undertaking is a *force field analysis,* a review of the barriers to accomplishing your goal and the factors likely to help you achieve it.

Typical barriers include lack of resources (money, people, laws, rules, and so on). They also include individuals or groups who benefit from the status quo. A company that hires only part-time workers at minimum wage avoids paying fringe benefits such as health insurance or retirement. This company benefits from the status quo. Those who work for the company, disproportionately women, might be considered an oppressed population. Their belief that nothing can be done is a barrier to changing the situation.

Positive factors include the availability of money, people, and other resources; motivated individuals, groups, and organizations; the skills of participants; the influence of individuals; the size of your group; and any other force that supports change (Erlich et al., 1999; Homan, 2004). A large group of influential community citizens is in a very powerful position to bring about change.

Community Asset Mapping

One method of assessing the macro reality is to identify all of the community resources that may be relevant to the current situation. *Community asset mapping (CAM)* looks at potential resources, whether they are human, financial, or material, in an attempt to accurately predict the likelihood of a successful change effort. "Asset mapping involves documenting the tangible and intangible resources of a community, viewing it as a place with assets to be preserved and enhanced, not deficits to be remedied" (Kerka, 2003, p. 1). Asset mapping has proven successful in both rural and urban communities and forms a foundation for mobilization around identified strengths (Fuller, Guy, & Pletsch, 2002). The process of identifying community assets is based on the premise that "all local residents, regardless of age, gender, race, ethnic background, place of residence or other characteristics, can plan an effective role in addressing important local matters" (Beaulieu, 2002, p. 4). Three characteristics describe this approach to community change (Kretzmann & McKnight, 1993). First, the process is asset-based because it focuses on what already exists in a community. Second, it is internally focused within the community and does not rely on external experts to determine community needs. Third, it is relationship driven in that "local people, informal organizations and institutions work hard to connect with one another in order to be sure they are working as a team, and not against one another. This means that good communication is essential" (Beaulieu, 2002, p. 5).

Benefits of asset mapping. Identifying these assets is a process of applying the strengths perspective to communities just as we do with individual clients, families, and groups. CAM involves "an inventory of all good things about your community and ranking the most valued aspects of your community" (Fuller et al., 2002, p. 3). It helps determine the wealth of a community that might be brought to bear on a particular challenge. Ultimately, it is a community building approach rather than a community development approach, which tends to use outside experts to do a needs assessment and then undertake community change. By their nature, needs assessments focus on what is wrong with a community rather than its effectiveness or strengths. Asset mapping helps residents think about their own communities and develop a shared sense of what makes them a good place to live. It is a device that tends to unite residents with a common vision.

Community asset categories. Community assets might be as diverse as abilities and gifts possessed by individual community members, other community organizations, and both formal and informal resources. Also included are relationships among relevant individuals and among individuals and community organizations. Thus, resources might include people or tangible items such as a wheelbarrow. Fuller and colleagues (2002) list five broad categories of assets into which skills can be divided. These include *built assets* such as physical structures (e.g., a community center or meeting place) or public areas such as a community swimming pool. A second category is *natural assets,* which might include a community's environment (i.e., quality-of-life features that make the community an attractive place to live). *Social assets* are the third grouping and include factors such as the friendliness of residents and resources that bring people together (e.g., church or neighborhood parties). The fourth category is *economic assets* that might include the availability of jobs, economic conditions in the community, and similar items. The final category is *service assets.* These include health, educational, and welfare services available to community members. Other categories can be established and employed. For example, Kretzmann and McKnight (1993) break gifts down into the categories of local institutions, citizens associations, and gifts of individuals. The system of categories that is used can

be selected based upon the characteristics of the community and the needs of community members.

Sources of information. Potential sources of information about a community's assets might include family members and friends; community members or beneficiaries of a change effort; public resources such as telephone books, community resource handbooks, and official records; and media such as newspapers or television programs that maintain Web sites of public service announcements. Inviting a cross section of community members to participate is recommended to ensure diverse perspectives. The number of people invited to participate in any single session might range from 15 to 30, depending upon the size of a community. The goal is to "get to know the assets within communities, share an appreciation for the value of these assets [and] understand how we can build and/or sustain these assets" (Fuller et al., 2002, p. 9).

Types of resources. Types of resources vary depending upon whether we are talking about an individual, an organization, or some other entity. With individuals, we may focus on the skills or assets that they bring to the process. For example, one person may have skills in carpentry and building, another in the use of technology such as a computer, and someone else might be a great cook. Others may have leadership skills, ability as an artist, or skill at raising money. Some people's assets are that they know others with resources. For example, a friend may own a moving van or a truck that can be used for transporting goods. Another resident may know someone who can operate construction equipment, a skill that might prove beneficial in a community project. If we are to be successful in our change effort, we should locate every skill that might reasonably be employed. Again, these skills may be found among those involved in the change process or among others known to them.

Resources might also lie in organizations to which community residents have access. These can range from service clubs to religious and cultural organizations. Other examples might include associations such as SCORE (Senior Core of Retired Executives) or a local parent–teacher organization. As you can imagine, by tapping these organizations, we dramatically expand the resources at our disposal.

Besides individual and organizational resources, institutions may be valuable in some way. These might include medical facilities, colleges or universities, schools, and social service agencies. These bodies may be able to provide research assistance, meeting locales, free or low-cost services, or other benefits. Some law firms encourage their lawyers to do pro bono work on behalf of the community, and one might be valuable as an advisor on legal issues. Other agencies may encourage their employees to engage in community service projects, such as donating time to a child care agency or doing yard work for older adult clients no longer able to carry out these responsibilities.

The final resource types are those that are external to the community. These might include state agencies or organizations, governmental units, foundations, and others that might be able to help on a short-term basis.

In a given situation, it may not be desirable or practical to identify assets of larger communities, and it might be necessary to focus on a neighborhood or district within a community. Obviously, the larger the community, the more resources available, but also the more difficult it is in terms of time and effort to gather this information.

Cataloging skills. One step in organizing the process of identifying community assets begins with individual members. We can do this by giving all members of the group an inventory list of possible skills/resources and allowing them to check off those that they believe they possess. This establishes a capacity inventory of individual members. It could also include a line after each to identify others that they believe have this skill or asset. An abbreviated example of one such checklist is shown in Figure 9.2. Once members have identified their skills, these are placed in each of the five categories just described. Members then discuss and

Child Care

Caring for infants under 1 year _____
Caring for pre-school children (1-5) _____
Caring for children ages 7-12 _____

Transportation

Have a driver's license _____
Have a car available _____
Have a commercial license to drive a bus _____
Have skill in operating construction equipment _____
Have skill operating farm machinery _____

Community Skills

Have organized scouting activities _____
Have organized parent-teacher activities _____
Have conducted tag or garage sales _____
Have organized block parties _____

FIGURE 9.2 Individual Capacity Inventory

prioritize the top assets in each category. Similar inventories can be produced of local informal institutions and organizations that are relevant to the community.

Once the information has been gathered, it can be placed in a pictorial format. Figure 9.3 shows such a community asset map that includes members of a neighborhood association and their skills and connections (CSWE, 2008, EP 2.1.10e).

EP 2.1.10e

Potential barriers to community asset mapping. Identifying the assets of a community empowers it to move forward with a change effort, but barriers may be encountered that interfere with the process. For example, there may be no one who wants to or is capable of assuming a leadership role in the change effort. Another barrier is lack of time to conduct the mapping and resistance from formal agencies and other professionals. Finally, the groups who may benefit most by community asset mapping may be afraid to participate (Kerka, 2003).

Pursuing community change. Once an inventory of assets is completed, the next step is to invite members to develop a shared vision of the community's future. This involves discussions by all stakeholders about the priorities to be achieved. This step is followed by the creation of a team that can build upon the assets identified and locate additional resources that can be brought to bear. The focus remains on using as many community assets as possible and relying less on external sources, except when these can be focused on community priorities. External resources should not be used if they end up dictating what things should be accomplished or how best to achieve a priority.

Assessing Target Systems

You must also be concerned about the target system (CSWE, 2008, EP 2.1.10). If you are trying to get local banks to stop discriminating against people of color when making home loans, you must assess the banking system. Among the factors to consider is the

EP 2.1.10

power of the target group. Do members of the target group have money, information, media and political influence, or other assets that need to be addressed? For example, bankers are usually influential in a community.

To what extent does the target system share your aspirations, values, and goals? The more you have in

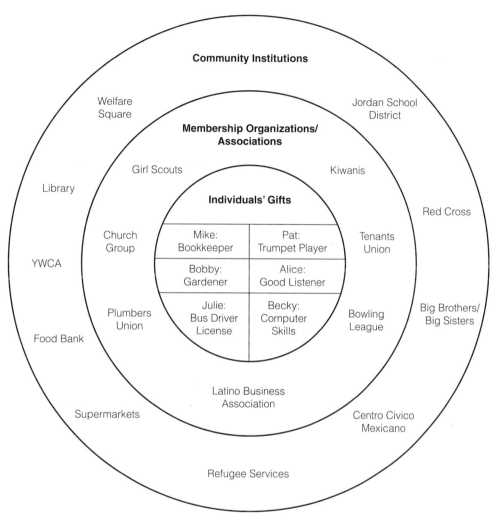

Community Institutions

Welfare Square

Jordan School District

Membership Organizations/ Associations

Girl Scouts

Kiwanis

Library

Red Cross

Individuals' Gifts

Mike: Bookkeeper	Pat: Trumpet Player
Bobby: Gardener	Alice: Good Listener
Julie: Bus Driver License	Becky: Computer Skills

Church Group

Tenants Union

YWCA

Plumbers Union

Bowling League

Big Brothers/ Big Sisters

Food Bank

Latino Business Association

Supermarkets

Centro Civico Mexicano

Refugee Services

FIGURE 9.3 Community Asset Map

common with the target system, the more you can employ collaborative tactics rather than conflictual approaches. A human service agency dedicated to providing service to the poor is likely to share your values and goals; a company that exploits workers in order to make money for its owners is less likely to share your values. Consequently, the lack of shared values or goals is an impediment.

What are the consequences for the target system if it changes? Are the consequences welcome or unwelcome? The more unwelcome, the greater the likelihood that conflictual approaches will be necessary. Giving workers a raise may make the company's widgets too expensive and cause loss of jobs. This is a very negative consequence. A change in policy that can be explained

and achieved so as to bring public praise to the agency or company has positive consequences.

What are the *general characteristics of the target*? Is it a public organization responsive to public opinion or voters? Is it a private company influenced by its board of directors or stockholders? Is it well organized or poorly managed? Knowledge of these characteristics may help you decide how difficult it will be to change the target system and what tactics you should employ to cause that change. Organizations not responsive to public opinion or voters are more difficult to change. A poorly managed or badly coordinated organization can be criticized on these accounts and is therefore more vulnerable than an efficient organization. Finally, how is the target system likely to react to your attempts to produce change (Homan, 2004)? Some target systems react in such a way that the reaction actually helps your cause. A target that blindly attacks your group might actually turn fence-sitters into allies for your efforts. Personal attacks on you or your group can do the same thing. Perhaps the best indicator of how the target will react to your change effort is to study its previous responses to such attempts. The sum of this information about your target is also part of your force field analysis.

For Geri, the force field analysis was easy. Few in the community would automatically oppose a permanent shelter for battered women. The transient nature of the facility made it hard for police and other agencies to remember where the shelter was located from month to month. In addition, security was always a problem. Because the agency did not own the building, it could not make physical changes to the property to protect its residents. Geri knew that police officers would appreciate a stable place to refer the abused women they encountered. Other social service agencies would also benefit and, ultimately, so would clients. Geri's job as program director was to meet the needs of her clients, so her board of directors was likely to support her.

Though relatively new to the community, Geri was full of enthusiasm for the project and possessed a "can-do" attitude, a real asset in a social worker. Yet she knew that the effort to find a permanent home would involve many people and require strong community support. Geri summarized the opposing forces as lack of money, her own and the board's inexperience in tackling major projects, and the fact that she had only a small staff. On the positive side, Geri recognized that the community had often donated money to the shelter (partly in response to media attention), and the fact that now the need for the shelter was greater. It was often necessary to turn people away because of lack of space. Besides, Geri's review of state and national statistics suggested that the incidence of domestic violence was increasing. The increase had prompted the state to provide grant money to help communities cope with domestic violence. Geri also knew that the cost of purchasing a building would be modest compared with previous local fundraising campaigns that sought to raise hundreds of thousands of dollars. Highlight 9.5 illustrates the results of her force field analysis.

Geri did not view the opposing forces as extremely negative. The supporting forces ranged from mildly to extremely positive, with items 2, 3, and 5 being most positive. Geri knew she could not accomplish this project by herself and would need to involve others from her board. At the same time, she was new to the organization and this was an opportune time to bring about change. This change in the leadership of the agency (referred to as "bureaucratic succession" in Chapter 5) provided an ideal chance to move in a different direction. The board and Geri were in something of a honeymoon period (also discussed in Chapter 5). Geri and the board were getting comfortable with each other, and each felt very positive about the other. This meant the board was willing to try things it might later find too threatening. Geri assessed the situation as an excellent opportunity to meet a community need. She decided she could not waste her chance to implement such a macro change.

Step 3: PREPARE—*Establish* Primary Goals

Establishing a primary goal flows easily from a problem you have clearly defined. In this case, Geri found it easy to establish a primary goal. Because it was no longer

---

HIGHLIGHT 9.5

Geri's Force Field Analysis

Opposing Forces
1. Lack of money
2. Geri's inexperience
3. Board's inexperience with major projects
4. Shortage of staff

Supporting Forces
1. Past community support and interest

2. Board support
3. Demonstrated need for shelter
4. State grant money for domestic violence
5. Geri's enthusiasm and attitude
6. Relatively inexpensive goal
7. Increased public interest in domestic violence

feasible to keep using temporary locations and loaned buildings, the community needed a permanent shelter for battered women. She would subsequently direct all her efforts toward this primary goal. In other situations, you could have several goals, so you would have to decide which one was of greatest importance. Geri knew that the potential impact of this goal was high and that achieving it would definitely influence the ability of her organization to meet the future needs of domestic violence survivors.

A goal should generate interest in a given problem so that board members and other influential citizens are motivated to help solve it. Unless you can frame a goal so that it is easily understood and clearly responds to a significant problem, important people are not likely to get involved. This is critical in the next step, identifying influential people.

Step 4: PRE*PARE*—Identify Relevant *People* of Influence

EP 2.1.10e

Identifying relevant people of influence is sometimes a challenge. As discussed in Chapter 5, they are individuals and groups within your agency and community who could potentially help or hurt your cause. Who are the people of influence in your own community? Are there groups whose assistance you might count on? Are there any persons in your organization whom you can ask for help? You want people who bring certain characteristics to the

activity. Highlight 9.6 discusses such characteristics (CSWE, 2008, EP 2.1.10e).

Geri, you may recall, had a very limited circle of influential contacts and friends. New to the community, she did not know many people. However, her board of directors included persons from many different agencies and organizations. In addition, many board members were members of other groups. Doctors, for example, often serve on boards of other organizations (such as local medical associations). Lawyers serve on many boards and often belong to local civic clubs. If Geri could persuade board members to tap their own circles of resources and influential friends, the possibilities of success could expand dramatically.

Sitting down with the board, Geri helped them identify individuals and organizations they could contact for support of their goal. These included the news media, service organizations, and local philanthropic foundations. Geri also knew about grants that could be applied for and had learned who controlled these funds. As director of the agency, she was frequently asked to address local groups. In fact, both the Junior League and Kiwanis had asked how they might help the shelter. Geri counted those groups as possible sources of support. After talking further with the board, Geri concluded that they had a reasonably sized network of influential people whom they could approach for help in securing a permanent site for the shelter. This network included a local TV reporter, a newspaper editor, three local service clubs, the local bar association president, and 17 other community and business leaders. Another example is shown in Highlight 9.7.

HIGHLIGHT 9.6

Identifying People of Influence

Homan (2004) has suggested getting people who meet the following criteria:

1. *People who get things done.* This includes those with a reputation of providing leadership and accomplishing goals. Past leaders of major fundraising drives might be in this category.
2. *People to whom others look for guidance.* Among these are leaders others turn to for advice and help. They are often successful and respected senior members of the community.
3. *People who will become leaders in your organization.* Included here are younger staff members

whose enthusiasm and drive are recognized by others.

4. *People who can motivate their peers.* This group includes not only those who are obvious leaders, but also those colleagues who work behind the scenes to get others involved in projects.
5. *People who have connections with other important people or resources.* Among this group would be those who have friendships and business relationships with influential people.
6. *People who have particular skills.* Examples might include those with public speaking ability, writing skills, and mediation skills.

HIGHLIGHT 9.7

Gathering People of Influence

Cherrytown had a serious problem that affected its older adult population. Many frail senior citizens could not receive routine medical care because they had no way of getting to the doctor or hospital. Although emergency service was available through the local ambulance company, there was no such arrangement possible for routine office visits. The result was that many older adult residents simply gave up going to the doctor. The problem was especially acute for residents with physical disabilities who needed specially equipped vans to get from their homes to medical services. Transportation for routine medical needs was not covered by Medicaid or Medicare, the two primary governmental health care programs for older adults.

A recent community needs assessment identified this problem, although it had existed for over 10 years. Francine Bodes-Well, social worker for the Council of Churches Elder Service program, thought the time was right to try to do something.

She listed all the influential people in town who had an interest in ensuring that frail older adults received medical care. In all, she listed 22 agency representatives, including the Visiting Nurses Association, the Council of Churches, the Medic-Transport Service, the City of Cherrytown, and the Mental Health Association.

Calling them together to discuss the problem and possible solutions led to the creation of the Eldercare Coalition. A *coalition* is a temporary alliance of various parties or groups in a society designed to pursue joint action toward a goal. Creation of the coalition allowed its members to contribute to solving the problem. A cooperative arrangement allowed the coalition to borrow a bus from the adult day care center. The coalition then formed an Eldercare Transit Service. Each bus would be assigned a driver and a certified nurse's aide. The service would provide nonemergency medical transportation with fees determined on a sliding scale. Service would not be denied for lack of money, however. Funding for the service came from fees paid by users, contributions from several agencies, and a small start-up grant.

A four-month evaluation of the service found that rider-ship had risen so dramatically that a second bus would be needed months earlier than projected. Older adults used the van at a rate that doubled every couple of months, rising from 18 passengers in the first month to 84 at the end of the fourth month. The general level of satisfaction was high, as evidenced by client satisfaction surveys and a survey of agencies whose clients used the service.

Sometimes, the influence you need is not located in individuals alone. For example, White and Featherston (2005) and Torres and Margolin (2003) highlight the potential value of interorganization collaboration among nonprofit agencies. Although agencies sometimes compete with one another for particular clients, there is ample room for cooperative efforts. In fact, funding agencies may require such collaboration as a condition of receiving grant monies. If other agencies serve the same target, consider their potential as allies. An interagency team may turn out to be an effective means to harness the resources not available to you or your agency alone.

Step 5: PREPARE—*Assess* Potential Financial Costs and Benefits

Assessing potential costs and benefits to clients and the community is often easy. For Geri, the benefits of a permanent home for the shelter would be enormous.

She believed the community would be better served by having the shelter in one place and not having to move periodically to some new location. Permanency would enhance board members' sense of identification with the facility, staff, and other agency personnel. Geri's agency could allocate money to make the shelter more secure, thereby providing greater safety for residents. This was especially important, because privacy and security are critical for domestic violence shelters. The agency could make its physical environment more attractive to clients and staff. Money spent fixing up the building would produce longer-term benefits, because the building would belong to the agency. Physical improvements to the building would increase the value of the property.

Benefits to the clients are usually clear when we formulate a goal. We begin a change process in response to problems affecting clients, and our goals reflect our desire to help. However, it is possible to overlook some aspects of this benefit-to-cost consideration. Efforts to achieve a goal often subtract from efforts expended for other goals or services. Opportunity costs (defined in Chapter 5) apply in most situations. Geri and her board's effort to secure a permanent shelter could easily take time from their efforts to meet current clients' needs. Money spent for a building could also have been spent hiring a social worker to help residents of the temporary shelter or giving raises to the small staff already providing services.

It is essential that you weigh the costs of using specific tactics to achieve a designated goal. Be aware of how the tactics you are considering affect the political climate you are facing. If the political mood in a community is strongly against new taxes, a campaign to build a new school is likely to fail. Can you move quickly and decisively, or must you progress more slowly with less grand objectives? If your ideas are too unrealistic in a given political climate, you may fail, and failure can be costly. It discourages supporters and makes it harder to get their involvement in future projects.

Some costs are more difficult to calculate. Any time you undertake a macro level change effort, you risk making someone unhappy. How is this possible? Change is often resisted because it exposes people to the unknown. What will the future be like if you succeed in your macro change effort? Even if you agree that a new shelter is a good idea, how will it affect the neighborhood surrounding the shelter? Will you have to contend with neighbors who object to a group facility in their neighborhood? This often happens when establishment of group homes or low-income housing units is proposed. Residents may fear this will make their neighborhood less attractive and their property of less value. How much time and energy will it take to overcome this potential barrier? It is safe to say that everything has a cost. You always need to think about such expenses before launching any community project.

Step 6: PREPARE—Review Professional and Personal *Risk*

Chapter 5 identified three types of risks you can incur as a change agent—losing your job, reducing your potential for upward mobility, and straining work relationships. These risks increase when you undertake community-level change, for several reasons. First, trying to change an element of a community often requires tackling large-scale problems that are resistant to change. The resistance you encounter may require

more drastic action on your part. Remember that someone always benefits from the status quo, and selling change to those who are happy with the ways things are is tough. Those who hold power seldom relinquish it readily. Second, your efforts to change the situation may cause you to be seen as a troublemaker. Sometimes changing the status quo can be seen as too daunting. Undertaking schemes that seem too grandiose can lead others to believe that nothing can be done.

A third problem is that adopting conflictual strategies can brand you as "unprofessional. " After all, you are supposed to be a social worker helping people, not a rabble-rouser trying to run the community. Fourth, attacking problems that your agency does not view as within your job purview may leave you unsupported. Perhaps neither your colleagues nor your supervisors will accept your new role.

All of these examples can be scary to the individual social worker. Even with the sanction of your profession and its values, you always assume some risk. Realistically, however, few social workers lose their jobs for trying to make the communities better places to live. Some, however, lose the support from colleagues who do not feel the same level of intensity about the problem or simply do not consider the goal that important.

Generally, though, the benefits of large-scale change efforts are easily identified, and your colleagues can understand why you have undertaken the effort. In addition, they might become part of the group that is helping you bring change. In one community, a social worker concerned about the lack of low-income housing helped convince the city and a private company to relocate houses rather than tear them down. Previous plans called for the two entities to raze the properties to make way for other projects. After moving the homes to a new location (a relatively inexpensive alternative to building new houses), the city and the company could donate them or sell them inexpensively to low-income families who would fix them up. In addition, the company would likely receive a tax benefit for donating the homes. The creative nature of this endeavor attracted the admiration of other social workers, who wished they had thought of such a novel idea.

In the case of the new home for the shelter, Geri really ran few risks. She would certainly not lose her job, because her board of directors supported her efforts. As agency director, she was expected to lead and be involved in community activities. It is doubtful the

EP 2.1.1b

board of directors had this in mind when they hired her; nevertheless, Geri felt there was little chance she would be seen as acting outside her mandate or without sanction. Her one big risk was failure. If she undertook the project and could not make it work, she might lose credibility with her board, which might then hesitate or even refuse to support her future ideas. Also, if she did succeed and the permanent home became an expensive problem for the agency, she might incur the anger of her employer—the board. How would the board react if the house got termites, or if the furnace and water heater broke in the first year of operation? These were all risks she was willing to take (CSWE, 2008, EP 2.1.1b).

Step 7: PREPAR*E—Evaluate* the Potential Success of a Macro Change Process

After considering the pros and cons of undertaking a community change effort, you ultimately decide whether or not to go ahead. This involves evaluating the potential benefits and success of the change effort coupled with an assessment of the most effective tactics to achieve your goal. Some tactics carry a higher risk than others. Conflict or contest tactics that include bargaining, negotiating, demonstrating, civil disobedience, and lawsuits are perhaps the most risky, because some people perceive such tactics as radical or unprofessional. Others may be afraid that the tactics themselves will cause problems. Yet, conflict tactics may be the only way to achieve your goal. Bargaining and negotiating are the least offensive conflict tactics, because they are based on the premise that both sides can discuss the problem and arrive at an acceptable solution. Demonstrations, including picketing and public displays of disagreement, are more problematic. They may engender public ridicule from those who don't support your ideas, and they may embarrass the targets so much that they refuse to change their position. Civil disobedience, including refusing to obey the law or other rules, often brings condemnation from law-abiding citizens and allows others to criticize your tactics as too radical. Finally, lawsuits are an expensive and risky proposition, because you may not prevail in court. Court decisions against your side can end up costing you financially. Moreover, judges and juries may decide cases based on very narrow grounds, and you can lose on a technicality even though your position is ethically and morally sound.

Collaborative approaches carry much less risk, but they may not be as effective in getting you where you

want to go. Remember, the tactics you adopt must be consistent with your value system. Ends don't justify the means, and your chosen strategy must mesh with the NASW *Code of Ethics*.

At this point in the PREPARE process, you will be faced with the same three alternatives described in Chapter 5: You may elect to (1) pursue the community change effort, (2) postpone it indefinitely, or (3) terminate the process. In Geri's case, she had already decided that the potential benefits were many and the risks few. Highlight 9.8 presents a review of Geri's evaluation. Geri reasoned that the proposed tactics were unlikely to produce either conflict or bad feelings. On the other hand, had Geri decided not to go forward, others probably would not have thought badly of her, nor would a decision to postpone have earned disapproval. In this situation Geri was as close to a win-win situation as possible. No matter what she did, she was likely to be praised for her decision. However, the benefits of obtaining a permanent community shelter for battered women made the choice clear—she had to go for it.

Once you make the decision to seek some improvement in your community or its service delivery system, you are still not at the halfway point. Though the planning process is critical, actual achievement of a goal is often the toughest task, because there are always unforeseen obstacles to impede your progress. You may face unexpected financial costs or opposition. In addition, the planning process in the PREPARE paradigm is largely cognitive or "on paper." Achievement of your own goals requires that you actually do something. This brings us to the IMAGINE model of implementation, which incorporates the intervention, evaluation, termination, and follow-up steps in the planned change process.

IMAGINE: A Process for Community Change

Chapters 6 and 7 introduced the IMAGINE model for guiding you through the implementation of a macro system change effort. The seven steps of IMAGINE are applicable to most, if not all, community change situations. To illustrate this process, we will continue with our example of Geri and the shelter for battered women (see Figure 9.4).

*I*MAGINE: Start with an Innovative *Idea*

The innovative idea you will begin with is the plan you identified for effecting change. By now, you have carefully

HIGHLIGHT 9.8

Evaluating Potential Success

PROS

FACTOR	EVALUATION
Client need	High client need
Organizational variables	Neutral to positive
Own strengths	Good to excellent
Potential support	Good to excellent
Financial benefits	Unclear

CONS

FACTOR	EVALUATION
Organizational variables	No perceived negatives
Own weaknesses	Minor (mostly inexperience)
Potential resistance	Minor, perhaps none
Financial costs	Cost estimates unclear
Geri's risks	Relatively minor

considered your options and made a decision about the approach most likely to succeed. This approach represents your best assessment, your innovative idea about how to handle the problematic situation confronting you. In Geri's case, her plan was to find a permanent building to house the shelter for battered women. Highlight 9.9 describes yet another innovative idea.

1. **I** — Start with an innovative **Idea**.

2. **M** — **Muster** support and formulate an action system.

3. **A** — Identify **Assets**.

4. **G** — Specify **Goals**, objectives, and action steps to attain them.

5. **I** — **Implement** the plan.

6. **N** — **Neutralize** opposition.

7. **E** — **Evaluate** progress.

FIGURE 9.4 A Process for Initiating and Implementing Macro Change

IMAGINE: *Muster* Support and Formulate an Action System

Mustering support and forming an action system are essential steps in the process, because rarely can we accomplish a major project without enlisting the help of others (CSWE, 2008, EP 2.1.8b). Recall that the action system includes people and resources you begin to organize and employ to help you work toward the needed change (see Chapters 6

EP 2.1.8b

and 7). Even Geri, as an agency director, could not achieve her goal without assistance. As a starting point, you have identified relevant people of influence who might be helpful. Geri, for example, identified members of her board of directors and local citizens who could help her in her project. Homan (2004) suggests a useful technique for recognizing the relevant people to whom your action system has access. He recommends asking each person in the action system to list two to three community leaders he or she would be willing to ask for a favor connected with your project. This is also a sound way of assessing whether your action system is well connected. If the action system comes up with a sizable number of names, you have a potentially powerful group. If the names are few in number or appear to be relatively unimportant in the community, you have a big problem.

HIGHLIGHT 9.9

An Innovative Idea

April Showers, director of the Mountain City Food Harvest knew there had to be a better way. Although 30 agencies in Mountain City served more than 5,000 meals per day to the needy, tons of food were thrown away by area restaurants, bakeries, and other food establishments. What if there were a way to get the two together—those who need food and those who have it and must get rid of it? What if, say, leftover chicken from Kentucky Fried Chicken could be given to the Mountain City Kitchen, an agency serving the homeless?

April hit upon an idea. She could contact each eating establishment and ask to bring in pans for the vast quantities of leftover food they have each day. These pans could be picked up in refrigerated vans for transportation to local group homes, shelters for the homeless, and kitchens serving low-income clients. In a matter of less than two years, April's vans plied the city streets for 35 hours each week, reaching more than three dozen businesses. The result was a yearly delivery of 18 tons of food. To help encourage restaurants to cooperate, April provides receipts for the amount of food donated, which is tax-deductible for the contributing businesses. The result is a win-win situation in which all participants benefit in some way.

Geri could start with her board of directors, several of whom are very influential members of the community. At a special meeting of the board, she outlined the goal of getting a permanent home for the shelter. Geri had already spoken privately to several board members, including the chairperson, about her idea. She had also notified the board that she would bring the idea before them for their approval after she did some more groundwork. Geri then outlined some suggestions about how they might proceed and described the steps she and the board members might take to ensure the success of their mission. She suggested the news media could be asked to highlight the effort. She identified several possible sources of help, including local service clubs with whom she had prior contact. She also raised the possibility of seeking a state grant to help defray some of the costs of the project. She answered questions and anticipated some concerns board members might have. Reviewing the possible advantages and disadvantages of the proposal, Geri proved that she had thought carefully about this plan. Board members were impressed. "Yes, we made the right decision when we hired her!" one member thought to himself as he heard her discuss the plan. One by one, most board members agreed the goal was attainable. Even doubters recognized that the goal was desirable, though they retained their reservations about whether the plan would work.

As an action system, the board was responsible for helping implement the plan. Through their contacts, the board members could probably influence a large segment of the population. Because board members were influential, others in the community would be more likely to take a positive view of the goal than if Geri had undertaken the change by herself.

In this situation, the board was a "naturally occurring" group. (That is, it was not formed for the specific purpose of carrying out this plan.) In other circumstances, you would need to follow the recommendations described in Chapters 6 and 7 to create your action system. However, the board of directors was an experienced action system. Like any action system, it consisted of people with varying degrees of commitment to the goal. Ultimately, how much time and energy each would contribute varied from member to member. Some members, committed activists who had helped begin the first services to battered women, were behind the project 150 percent. They would devote as much time to this as possible, given their own responsibilities as employees and family members. Other board members were community professionals (lawyers, social workers, physicians, pharmacists) who were somewhat less committed to an all-out push to achieve the goal. However, despite their other commitments, these individuals had a wide array of contacts in the community. Their influential help would compensate for their own lack of time to expend on the project.

Geri also knew that board members sometimes have short memories. She checked carefully with the board secretary to ensure that decisions to support this project were described clearly in the official minutes of the meeting. She also verified that the actual steps each member would take were clearly recorded. This record of *who* was going to do *what* by *when* was important for keeping the process on track. (Had Geri known about doing PERT charts, described in Chapter 7, she could have devised a written plan to guide the board/action system as it went about its business.)

IMAGINE: Identify *Assets*

Remember that assets are any resources or advantages that aid you in undertaking and completing your change process. Assets include money, people, time, energy, facilities/office space, and so on. Geri had many assets. First, she had an influential action system with a variety of community contacts. For the most part, the action system was solidly behind the project. Geri's office in the temporary shelter gave her a place to operate as she carried out her tasks. As always, money was scarce, but the potential for getting some grant money and other types of contributions was great.

Although new in the community, Geri was an effective problem solver and, as a BSW, she was prepared to tackle a variety of tasks. She knew the goal of attaining a permanent home for the shelter would excite some people. She felt that hardly anyone would be against the idea. Thus, her assets included herself, the contacts and enthusiasm of her action system, and the attractiveness of the goal to other community members.

IMAGINE: Specify *Goals,* Objectives, and Action Steps to Attain Them

Normally, the primary goal would already be identified in general terms in the PREPARE process. At this point, you need to be even more specific about what you actually want to accomplish and how you will get there. We refer to these subgoals as *objectives*. We call the actual activities needed to achieve your objectives *action steps*. For example, one of the steps in establishing a permanent shelter for Geri's agency might be to designate either herself or some board members to investigate various properties. Before the agency can relocate, the action system must know *where* it can go.

EP 2.1.10f

Although the terms may get confusing, major projects benefit from being broken down into manageable pieces with clear indications of what needs to be done, when, and by whom. Using the terms introduced in Chapter 6, we identify three possible levels of specificity in goals and objectives. These appear in Highlight 9.10. Writing down each allows you to see whether all pieces of the puzzle are in place. You thus can tell if each step in the process has been followed as planned (CSWE, 2008, EP 2.1.10f).

In Highlight 9.10 it is easy to see that any objective might consist of a series of action steps. You might even break each action step down further. Action Step 5, for example, could be further specified as "Ramon Morales and Natasha Sharif will speak to Chief Frisbie on April 20 to request help in establishing a Neighborhood Watch program." Keep in mind that there are often many tasks to accomplish, and someone has to do each of them. Unassigned tasks will not be completed. Tasks without deadlines will probably not

HIGHLIGHT 9.10

Goal, Objectives, and Action Steps: Reducing Gang Activity

Primary Goal:	Reduce gang and drug activity in Third Ward.
Objective 1:	Develop Neighborhood Watch program in Third Ward.
Action Step 1:	Mrs. Watermolen and social worker Framo Phlegm will call meeting of Third Ward residents at St. John's Church for April 15.
Action Step 2:	Mr. Newt and Ms. Wart will prepare fliers to be distributed to neighbors and at local grocery by March 25.
Action Step 3:	Mrs. Watermolen and Framo Phlegm will develop agenda for meeting and Mrs. Watermolen will lead meeting (April 15).
Action Step 4:	Mr. Newt and Ms. Wart will distribute fliers, and Pastor Danish will arrange refreshments for meeting (April 10–15).
Action Step 5:	Representatives selected at meeting will contact the police department to help neighborhood set up watch program (April 25).
Objective 2:	Increase police department patrols of Third Ward
Objective 3:	Eliminate vacant house at end of block as haven for gangs.

be done when they should be. (See Highlight 9.11 for a list of typical tasks.)

Let's return to our social worker. Geri had a clear goal, getting a permanent home for the shelter. To get there, however, would take many steps. An outline of one objective and its respective action steps appears in Highlight 9.12 on page 349.

As it turned out, Geri and the board chairperson discovered a variety of buildings they could bring to the board for approval and action. One building's owner would finance the sale with a small down payment from the agency. The other building would require bank financing, but the price was very reasonable. In addition, at least one local service group was willing to cosign a loan for the building if the agency needed this assistance.

Once the board selected what they believed was the best option, Geri and the board would carry out their plan. This is the beginning of the implementation phase of the IMAGINE process.

IMAG*INE*: *Implement* the Plan

At this stage, it is important to recognize the strengths of everyone involved in the implementation process. Some members are good public speakers and others are well organized. You must know your own strong points and those of the people helping you carry out the plan. Some people are more process-oriented and others are more task-oriented. This means that some members of the

EP 2.1.10g

HIGHLIGHT 9.11

Getting Things Done

Homan (2004), Tropman and Morningstar (1995), and Burghardt (1982) provide excellent guidelines for some of the tasks with which you may become involved when undertaking a community change effort.

Holding Meetings

1. Arrange for the location—try to make it accessible for everyone.
2. Advertise the meeting as widely as possible.
3. Set up the chairs, tables, and microphone where you want them before the meeting.
4. Arrange for refreshments.
5. Prepare an agenda of topics to be covered.
6. Arrange for child care, if possible.
7. Be ready to accept donations.

Mass Mailings

Mass mailings are letters, brochures, or other materials sent to large numbers of people informing them of events or soliciting their support.

1. Schedule work sessions for mailings (when can volunteers get together to stuff envelopes?) at least three weeks before mailings.
2. Make the experience enjoyable by providing food or music.
3. Have a sponge available to moisten envelope flaps.
4. Try to get a bulk mailing permit allowing mail to be sent for a fraction of the normal cost.

Churches and nonprofit organizations often have bulk mailing permits already and may let you use theirs. Permits can be purchased at the post office.

Leafleting

Leaflets are brochures or other handouts. They might describe your organization's views on a topic or announce meetings and other events.

1. Hand out leaflets where they will do the most good. Consider a person handing out information on a constitutional amendment to roll back taxes and cut government spending. He sets up his table in front of a state office building housing the Department of Health and Human Services. For the most part, the people using the building are clients who benefit from the services and government employees whose jobs are based on those services—hardly persons interested in cutting off their own resources.
2. Use two-person teams to hand out leaflets. This ensures that one is available to talk to those who wish to learn more, while the other continues to distribute information. They also keep each other company when things are slow.
3. Be ready to write down the name, address, and telephone number of anyone supporting your cause.

HIGHLIGHT 9.12

Goal, Objective, and Action Steps: Obtaining a Permanent Shelter

Goal: Obtain permanent home for shelter for battered women.

Objective	Locate building that will adequately house the shelter and its program (by June 1).
Action Step 1:	Geri will look at real estate ads in newspapers and contact local realtors (by May 1).
Action Step 2:	Banker Smith will learn whether his bank or any other bank in town has foreclosed on (taken back ownership of) a suitable building (by May 1).
Action Step 3:	Board will review available buildings at the May 3 meeting, narrowing list to five possibilities.
Action Step 4:	Geri and board chairperson will visit each building and discuss possible financing of property with sellers (by May 15).
Action Step 5:	Geri will explore available grant sources to purchase or remodel building(s) for shelter (by May 15).
Action Step 6:	Geri and board chairperson will report to board about options and give their recommendation (by May 22).
Action Step 7:	Board will act on recommendation and begin process of acquiring building(s) (by May 22).

action system may move at different speeds. Task-oriented people prefer to get right to the point, complete a task, and move on. Process-oriented helpers want to spend more time talking about how things can best be done, considering every possibility. Recognize that different tasks depend on different skills. Try to match needs with skills. If some people are better at letter writing, use them for that. Others can work on grants or participate on a subcommittee. Break your activities into smaller tasks so that each action system member has a role (CSWE, 2008, EP 2.1.10g).

Holding meetings is one of the most frequent activities in the implementation phase. You will be running meetings and using the mezzo skills discussed in Chapter 3. Little gets done without the combined efforts of many people, and meetings are often helpful in bringing that combination of people together. As a group leader, you will use skills such as familiarity with *Robert's Rules of Order* to move business along.

It is also important that you involve people as quickly as possible in *doing* things. This keeps them feeling part of the group and gives them a sense of accomplishment. Stay on task and do the follow-up work, make phone calls, and arrange meetings. A general guideline for your practice is: Do not procrastinate—do it *now*.

Let's turn again to Geri and the shelter for battered women. Carrying out the plan to get the shelter typifies

the challenges you face when trying to carry out a community-level plan. There are always twists and turns that you do not expect, complicating your choices and actions. As Geri and the board chairperson pursued their goals through the series of action steps, it became clear that this was just the start of the process. The decision to purchase a building would lead to even more objectives and action steps. In that sense, you often carry out a plan and revise it simultaneously. Highlight 9.13 on page 350 further describes some activities that characterize the implementation phase of this process.

As you can see, several objectives and appropriate action steps are incorporated in Geri's example. The objective of purchasing a building required action steps related to arranging funding (bank loan). Rehabilitating the property (another objective) required action steps to identify needed remodeling, estimate costs of such remodeling, and write a grant application to cover the costs. This pattern is repeated in almost all macro implementation activities.

IMAGINE: *Neutralize* Opposition

Neutralizing opposition may be either a large or a small task, depending upon how controversial your change effort is. Trying to get the city to drop its plan to run a highway through a low-income neighborhood is

HIGHLIGHT 9.13

Implementing the Plan

Geri and her board of directors agreed to purchase a dilapidated two-story home near a college campus. Once a fine old home, the building was for sale for about 80 percent of its actual value because the owner wanted to sell it quickly. To Geri, however, this meant that there was already 20 percent equity built into the property. (This meant that whoever bought the property already acquired 20 percent of the home's value for free.) Using this information, Geri persuaded the board to seek a bank loan to buy the property, using the 20 percent equity in lieu of a down payment. Board members were excited about the possibility of having a permanent home but were also more than a little skeptical. "It will happen," Geri kept telling them.

Geri learned that a state fund had been established to help support community responses to domestic violence. She wrote a grant application and received a $40,000 grant to rehabilitate the property. Now real progress was possible.

With the grant in hand, board members began to tap other community resources. Geri contacted local church and civic groups and asked for their help. Some "adopted" a room, buying furnishings and paying for needed repairs. The Lions Club agreed to hold a raffle to support the new Bennett Refuge House, which was named for Officer Bennett, the police officer whose death in a domestic violence incident opened this chapter. Although the amount of money the Lions Club raised was not large, the involvement of this respected

service organization encouraged other organizations and individuals to help.

Donations of kitchen cabinets were received. Geri traded an unused garage door opener (the garage was converted to a group-therapy room) for a toilet. Influential board members used their business contacts to gain additional help. A lawyer on the board asked his law firm to contribute funds to fix up a staff office. Another law firm did all the paperwork gratis. The criminal justice system also found a way to help: Juveniles and adults sentenced to perform community service for their criminal conduct were given the opportunity to work off their obligation at the shelter.

Geri contacted a youth conservation organization (sponsored by the state) that worked on several public construction projects in the community. They agreed to build a fence around the shelter and to turn the basement into office space. The social work department of the nearby university provided students as both volunteers and field interns, allowing further expansion of services.

The board of directors of the Bennett Refuge House decided to become more diversified in membership. Members were added representing many different new perspectives: the probation department, the university social work department, news media, civic groups, additional local businesses, and active volunteers. All new members brought with them a variety of contacts and membership in other groups.

likely to encounter major opposition. City officials, road planners, businesses, and other groups may benefit from this road. Because of their potential gain, they are likely to fight on their own behalf. Overcoming their opposition or changing their minds could be difficult.

On the other hand, a plan that initially had no obvious opposition may incur some along the way. This was the case in the situation described in Highlight 9.14 on page 351. In Geri's case, a board member might change her mind about the value of a permanent shelter during the discussions about purchasing a building. She might conclude that the project is too expensive. Neighbors could have raised concerns about the location of the shelter in their neighborhood. Had the latter happened, efforts would be required to deal with such opposition. Opposition can be handled through

collaborative strategies or through adversarial approaches. Collaboration in Geri's case might involve persuasion, communicating ideas to others, educating opponents, listening to opponents' concerns and responding accordingly, and rational argument, to name a few. Had only a few vocal neighbors caused a problem, Geri and her action system could have asked other residents to sign a petition in support of the shelter. The action system could have sent letters to the news media emphasizing the desirability of the shelter and the weakness of opposing arguments.

Social Action: Confrontation and Conflict Approaches

Social action involves efforts by groups of individuals to create change in an organization or community. Social action activities need not necessarily involve

HIGHLIGHT 9.14

Confronting a Bad Idea

Golden Lake Park is the spiritual home of much of Grand Rapids' African-American community. Every fall for the past quarter century, the park has played host to more than 4,000 people of color with ties to the city of Grand Rapids. This group wants to maintain the park as it has been for the past 25 years. When the city park board announced that it was going to build a million-dollar community center in the park, the battle lines were drawn.

Opponents of the idea formed the Community Coalition and enlisted the help of diverse elements of the community. African-American residents felt the move would destroy the park's heritage. The Community Coalition collected more than 300 signatures on petitions from homeowners living near the park. Next, they arranged for crowds of people to attend meetings of the city council and speak against the move. More than 50 people turned out to oppose the idea at one meeting, and 70 showed up in opposition at another public meeting.

The coalition also put pressure on the state Department of Natural Resources, which had previously given a grant to help develop Golden Lake Park. The terms of that grant permanently restricted the use of the park to public outdoor recreation, which was not compatible with the building of a community center there. At the coalition's initiation, the state agency told the city that it would be violating the terms of its agreement with the Department of Natural Resources. If the city wanted to go ahead with its plan, the state agency ruled that the city council would have to buy park land equal in value to that which they were using to build a multipurpose community center. Caught between confrontation with the African-American community and the cost of trying to find new park land, the city gave up. A new site for the community center would be sought. The African-American community had successfully overcome or neutralized opposition to its desire to keep Golden Lake Park unchanged.

confrontation and conflict. However, the effort required to cause significant changes in the status quo within large systems often requires different approaches. We have said previously that it is best to start with nonconflictual approaches whenever possible. They can save energy used up in conflict and avoid resultant bad feelings. Conflictual tactics will likely have repercussions. Moreover, you should not use confrontational approaches on behalf of any client group without first obtaining the group's agreement. Be sure to fully inform clients about possible risks associated with such approaches. Realistically, however, more confrontational and adversarial social action approaches are sometimes needed.

Social action may take the form of a group lobbying its legislators or a decision maker, or writing letters to newspapers or elected officials. (Chapter 10 addresses these skills more thoroughly.) More drastic examples of social action and conflict approaches include such things as strikes, rallies, boycotts, marches, demonstrations, informational picketing, and court action. This type of social action has a rich history, from women's marches for the right to vote in the early 1900s to current marches protesting violence against lesbian and gay people. Likewise, the civil rights and antiwar movements of the 1960s and 2000s have used

marches and demonstrations to call attention to their concerns.

Similarly, boycotts of products have been used to oppose mistreatment of farm workers and to force lettuce and grape growers to negotiate with their workers. Workers commonly employ labor strikes to force employers to bargain with them.

More intrusive and controversial approaches to social action include sit-ins, civil disobedience (for example, lying in front of a bulldozer to prevent it from entering a neighborhood), and fasts or hunger strikes. The intensive nature of these tactics can lead to burnout. They must be used carefully.

Specht's (1969) classic article categorized more conflictual approaches into the following three groups, each increasing respectively in severity.

1. *Clashes of position.* This approach includes actions such as "debate, legal disputes, written statements of intent, or public speeches" (p. 10). To this list we would add bargaining. Because bargaining and negotiating are such commonly used approaches to social change, Highlight 9.15 on page 352 describes some guidelines for their use. Also in this category are rallies that mobilize and inform supporters (Brueggeman, 2006).

HIGHLIGHT 9.15

Bargaining and Negotiating

Bargaining/negotiating (considered identical for practical purposes) is a process whereby two or more parties reach a mutually acceptable decision. It is a common approach to use when engaging in community interventions. Bargaining works best when the decision maker's image is consistent with your goal. Assume you are working with a group of neighborhood parents who seek more supervised recreational opportunities for their children. City officials who believe they have an interest in helping inner-city children are more likely to bargain if their image (their reputation for concern) and your goal (providing recreational opportunities for children) are consistent. Pointing out to city officials that closing a city park at 5:00 P.M. means these children have no place to play and will probably remain unsupervised on the street is going to be persuasive. After all, both of you want a better community and opportunities for these children.

Contrast this with Taxpayers for No Property Tax, a group whose sole concern is cutting city taxes. The willingness of city officials to bargain with them is reduced, because the group's values and image are narrowly focused on tax reduction. They can't bargain as effectively because their goal—reduction of property tax—clashes with city officials' obligation to meet the needs of citizens for multiple city services.

A disadvantage of bargaining is that it takes time to arrive at an agreement. Those who can afford the time, can tolerate the stress of prolonged discussion, and have the stamina for bargaining have the advantage.

Those who have both a capacity for and an interest in protracted negotiations are likely to have more success. As a result it is typical for negotiators to act as though they don't mind waiting or to pretend that they are willing to fight against your proposal. In essence, they are bluffing, so it is probably in your best interest to act as if you too have plenty of time, even if you don't. Your adversary probably has time constraints too.

Simultaneously, recognize that threatening to take an action if the other side does not agree carries some risks. If the threat is credible—that is, if the other side believes you can carry out the threat—your position is stronger. At the same time, it is important that the threatened action be proportionate to the goal. A threat to boycott all city services if the park hours are not extended is out of proportion to the solution you seek. Generally, if the threatened action does not seem credible or is out of proportion to the goal, your effectiveness is lessened. Realize that all of these tactics exist for the purpose of convincing the other side that you will expend as much energy as necessary to achieve your goal.

Bargainers often put forward positions or requests that neither side thinks are reasonable. This is a time-worn tactic in labor negotiations, but not necessary in all bargaining situations. In some situations the tactic of making absurd demands may backfire, making the other side see you as totally unreasonable. If you sense that you and the other party are not that far apart on key issues, try adopting a more reasonable goal instead of "asking for the moon."

2. *Violations of normative behavior.* Specht defines this category as such activities as "marches, demonstrations, boycotts, protests, vigils (extended demonstrations), rent strikes, dropping out (of an organization), haunting (following one's opponent for long periods), renouncing honors, … fasts, and interjection (having large masses of people congregate in an area" (p. 10). That is, they are not illegal activities but are considered outside the norm. They carry greater risk than clashes of position. In fact, today haunting might be considered stalking and could violate state or local laws.

Burghardt (1982) points out that although marches and demonstrations can be attention-getting, they can also take on a life of their own. They can attract vocal opponents, resulting in escalating problems. Marches require preparation for water supply, medical care, leadership, and signs. You have to coordinate contacts with and request support from other groups who will participate.

March organizers must develop lists of definitely committed participants to make certain they have enough people for an effective march. Six people walking down the street makes little impact. Organizers want to ensure that participants arrive on time and have backup plans if anyone on their list decides not to come. Timing for marches and demonstrations is also important. Noon and quitting time during the week are considered very effective because of the likelihood that a large number of people will witness the event.

If you are marching to raise awareness of a problem, pick specific start and stop points in advance. A length of about one-and-a-half miles is typical (Burghardt, 1982).

Maintaining security during a march or demonstration is also important. March security includes keeping people in line, leading chanting, identifying leaders, and deciding who will carry the medical equipment in case of emergency.

Before the demonstration or march, it is important to coordinate placing of signs, distributing fliers, and preparing press releases. Distribute the press releases about a week before the gathering and follow up with an invitation to the media personnel you hope will attend. Press releases should be brief, containing specifics of the march (what, when, where, why, who). Provide the name and number of a contact person. Remember that the media like new information, new angles, and/or important people. Often it is wise to schedule a press conference together with a rally (Burghardt, 1982). A rally is simply a gathering of people, usually with several speakers exhorting the audience to support a specific goal. Combining a rally with a march gets both the public and the media involved and, if successful, is a capstone for your group.

Rallies should begin or end the march. In either case, arrange rally speakers and sound systems in advance. Each speaker should emphasize something different. One might discuss why the march is taking place, another might describe the problem, and a third might suggest solutions. The event should end with encouragement for future action and should identify specific steps that will be taken on behalf of the goals and objectives (Burghardt, 1982). Rallies help energize people and recruit others interested in the goal.

3. *Violations of legal norms.* The approaches with the highest risk include "civil disobedience and noncooperation, tax refusal, sit-ins, … and other violations of law" (Specht, 1969, p. 11). We emphasize that such methods are potentially harmful to the members of your action system and to yourself. Because they are outside legal limits, possible consequences can include arrest, conviction for a crime, and loss of support from colleagues who feel you have gone too far. The recent abortion protest controversy is a good example of this. For many professionals, getting convicted of a crime means loss of a license to practice. It can also result

in loss of one's job. At the same time, these methods have historically been used effectively to change community and institutional behavior, laws, and government policies.

It is important to reemphasize that these approaches are not ends in themselves. You should not undertake them simply for the sake of doing them. Your goals must be very clear. You must view clashes of position, violations of normative behavior, and violations of legal norms as action steps to obtain goals and objectives, not the goals and objectives themselves. Rather, they are used to generate publicity, boost morale, or help locate similarly minded people and groups. To be most effective, social action needs "a clear assessment of its real and potential resources, a focused target, and a program designed to attract as large a group as possible" (Burghardt, 1982, p. 73).

Choose Goals Wisely

Resources needed for social action include the people expected to help carry out the various activities envisioned. Getting too grandiose in your goals can disappoint people and reduce their future involvement. Predicting that 500 people will show up for a protest rally at city hall and having only 50 come is a real letdown. We recommend selection of manageable goals and objectives. If you need to change direction after you discover that more is possible—great! It's better to expand your horizons than to have to cut back drastically because your initial planning was unrealistic. The latter makes it look as if you are not a strong group and reduces your credibility. One of the goals of social action is to choose an issue that is likely to get others excited and involved and that will ultimately succeed. This is more effective because it gives participants a sense of purpose and accomplishment.

IMAGINE: *Evaluate* Progress

EP 2.1.10m

Evaluating progress is much easier if you clearly specify your objectives and action steps in measurable terms (CSWE, 2008, EP 2.1.10m). Suppose, for example, that you were supposed to contact your state senator by September 14 to ask his support of a bill licensing BSWs in your state. It is now September 21, and you have not gotten around to doing this. Having a written list of objectives and action steps is a reminder that you have unfinished business. The process of verifying that the steps are being carried out is called *monitoring the ongoing operation.*

More important. however, you will be concerned about the results of your process. We will discuss evaluation in more detail in Chapter 10. Because we have taken you so far through the case of the shelter for battered women, we'll let you see how it turned out. A brief evaluation appears in Highlight 9.16.

The purpose of the evaluation phase is primarily to learn whether the identified objectives were achieved. A secondary purpose includes deciding what additional effort, if any, is needed to stabilize the change. For example, without a plan for paying the mortgage on the property, the future of the permanent shelter would be precarious at best. The multiple sources of funds available to the shelter help ensure that it will continue to exist for some time. In addition, broadening membership of the board of directors provides a wider base of support than previously existed. In macro terminology, we often refer to this as *stabilizing change,* because it allows our accomplishments to continue indefinitely.

In this stage, you might also look for any negative consequences of the implementation. Sometimes unexpected (iatrogenic) and problematic results appear. Perhaps the original old house that became the permanent shelter was built over a sinkhole or has a leaking underground fuel storage tank that no one knew about. Perhaps the heavy traffic in and out of the shelter causes parking problems in the neighborhood. Negative consequences may be overcome or adjusted to, or may force you to abandon the project. You always hope there will be no negative outcomes, but expect that some may appear.

Termination and Follow-Up

Terminate a change effort when it has proven successful, is unsuccessful and can't be fixed, or is too costly to continue. For example, you may have underestimated the obstacles and forces against the project arising from community indifference. Maybe conditions have changed, and the goal is no longer as important to your client group. You may terminate the project if unintended consequences are sufficiently negative. If you have to give up on a worthy goal, find out what, if anything, can be salvaged from the effort. Sometimes the failure of one project leads a group to take on another goal that is more attainable.

Community members organize a campaign to raise the minimum wage in Florida.

HIGHLIGHT 9.16

Evaluating Progress and a Follow-Up

The board of directors purchased the home. Geri and many others helped it become a major player in the human service community. The Junior League continued to support the house by decorating and refurnishing several rooms. The local medical association contributed money for remodeling projects. Church groups and private individuals donated clothes so that residents of the shelter, who often left their homes with few belongings, would have clean, serviceable wearing apparel. Although the progress was sometimes slow, neither Geri nor the board lost sight of the purpose of the agency: to protect women and children suffering from domestic violence.

Seven years after Officer Bennett's death, the community finally had a full-fledged shelter for battered women offering individual and group counseling, children's groups, and job training. The shelter also owned and operated a transition house, where women and their children could live once they were ready to leave the shelter. Later, the shelter acquired a community meeting building where the board and other community groups could hold regular meetings. Funding for projects and operations came from donations, grants, fees for service, contracts with various social service organizations, and United Way contributions. Officer Bennett would have been proud.

Do follow-up when needed to ensure that agreed-upon tasks and action steps were actually carried out. Perhaps the city agreed to build a new community center but then dragged its feet about allocating the money. This requires follow-up to see that promises are kept. Follow-up is important because too often people and organizations revert to their old ways when "the heat is off" them. Keeping the pressure and heat on them won't produce a diamond, but it will help ensure that they keep their promises.

Chapter Summary

The following summarizes this chapter's content as it relates to the learning objectives presented at the beginning of the chapter. Chapter content prepares social workers to:

A. *Advance social and economic justice in their communities.*

The pursuit of social and economic justice by social workers is part of the responsibility of the profession. At the same time, social workers must work within the boundaries of the profession's values. This means that our actions must be ethically and legally defensible.

B. *Utilize conceptual frameworks and strategies for empowering communities.*

The goal of empowerment is to help community members get what they need. It also involves influencing others to help meet those identified needs. Empowering communities requires five competencies: informational, intellectual, intrapersonal, interpersonal, and interventional. Using these competencies, the social worker draws out existing abilities of community members while teaching and modeling new abilities. This helps ensure that community members are active participants in change efforts, recognizing their own power. Social workers can also help members take increasing responsibility for the change effort, build self-confidence, and overcome obstacles and setbacks.

The community may be viewed as the context in which social workers practice, the target of our change efforts, or the mechanism for change. In some cases, all three perspectives may be applicable. Depending upon the perspective, social workers may elect to work within the community's power structure, employing a gradual consensus model focusing on enhancing service delivery. Examples include the United Way, social settlement houses, and neighborhood or community centers, among others. Another approach is conflictual in nature, focusing on mediation and challenges to the power structure. Tenant organizations and community reform movements are examples of this approach. The last alternative is neighborhood maintenance, which uses consensus, peer pressure, legal action, and political lobbying to improve property values, maintain neighborhoods, and provide services. Examples include neighborhood associations, civic clubs, and property owner organizations.

C. *Apply the PREPARE model to engaging and assessing the potential for community change.*

Social workers employ professional use of self in the process of engaging and building relationships with both community members and other professionals. The engagement process leads into the PREPARE model of assessing the potential for community change. The PREPARE model focuses the social worker's attention on several steps that must be completed before moving to the IMAGINE stage. These steps include identifying the ***problem*** to address, assessing your macro and personal ***reality, establishing*** primary goals, identifying relevant ***people*** of influence in the community, ***assessing*** potential financial costs and benefits, reviewing both professional and personal ***risk,*** and ***evaluating*** the potential success of a macro change process.

D. *Employ the community asset mapping approach to identifying community resources.*

The community asset mapping approach is used to identify all of the community resources that may be relevant to the situation at hand. Assets may be human, financial, or material. This model is based on the strengths of the community rather than focusing on its deficits or shortcomings. It has the benefit of being able to unite residents in pursuit of a common vision for the future. Among human assets are such things as relationships among people, skills of members, organizational memberships, and knowledge of other formal and informal community resources.

E. *Apply the IMAGINE model to intervening, and to evaluating change in a community.*

The IMAGINE model is focused on the implementation phase of a community change effort. Like the PREPARE model, it involves a series of steps: Start with an innovative ***idea;*** ***muster*** support and formulate an action plan; identify ***assets;*** specify ***goals,*** objectives, and action ***steps; implement*** the plan; ***neutralize*** opposition; and ***evaluate*** progress. Each of the steps in the IMAGINE model involves additional activities that are essential to successful implementation of a community change process.

Competency Notes

The following identifies where Educational Policy (EP) competencies and practice behaviors are discussed in the chapter.

Educational Policy (EP) 2.1 Core Competencies

Educational Policy (EP) 2.1.1b Practice personal reflection and self-correction to assure continual professional development. *(P. 343):* As part of the PREPARE model, social workers are expected to consider the professional and personal risks involved in undertaking a community change effort.

Educational Policy (EP) 2.1.2 Apply social work ethical principles to guide professional practice. *(P. 326):* Social workers must operate within the boundaries of professional values and the ethics of the profession when practicing in the community.

Educational Policy (EP) 2.1.5c Engage in practices that advance social and economic justice. *(P. 327):* Empowering vulnerable and oppressed populations is one practice that can advance social and economic justice. Empowerment involves five competencies: informational, intellectual, intrapersonal, interpersonal, and interventional.

Educational Policy (EP) 2.1.6 Engage in research-informed practice and practice-informed research. *(P. 333):* It is important to research a community problem carefully to determine the nature and seriousness of the problem, gather data, and identify causes.

Educational Policy (EP) 2.1.7 Apply knowledge of human behavior and the social environment. *(P. 329):* Social workers must employ multiple perspectives to understand any community. The community may be the context in which social workers practice, the target of change efforts, or the mechanism for change.

Educational Policy (EP) 2.1.8b Collaborate with colleagues and clients for effective policy action. *(P. 345):* Mustering support and formulating an action plan in the IMAGINE model is one way of collaborating with colleagues and clients to bring about changes in the community.

Educational Policy (EP) 2.1.10 Engage, assess, intervene, and evaluate with individuals, families, groups, organizations, and communities. *(P. 330):* Engagement in the community is the first part of the planned change process. *(P. 338):* Assessing the target system is one step to be employed when affecting change in the community.

Educational Policy (EP) 2.1.10a Substantively and affectively prepare for action with individuals, families, groups, organizations, and communities. *(P. 335):* Among the approaches that can be considered when working in the community are community asset mapping and community capacity building.

Educational Policy (EP) 2.1.10e Assess client strengths and limitations. *(P. 338):* Cataloging skills in the community asset mapping approach is one means of assessing client strengths and limitations. *(P. 341):* Identifying relevant people of influence as part of the PREPARE model is one way of identifying client system strengths and limitations.

Educational Policy (EP) 2.1.10f Develop mutually agreed-on intervention goals and objectives. *(P. 347):* Part of the IMAGINE model involves working with others to specify goals, objectives, and action steps needed to bring about change.

Educational Policy (EP) 2.1.10g Select appropriate intervention strategies. *(P. 348):* Implementing the plan is the fifth step in the IMAGINE model of planned change.

Educational Policy (EP) 2.1.10m Critically analyze, monitor, and evaluate interventions. *(P. 353):* Evaluating progress is much easier if objectives and action steps have been clearly specified earlier in the IMAGINE process.

On the Internet

Visit the *Generalist Practice with Organizations and Communities* Web site at www.cengage.com/social_work/kirst-ashman for learning tools such as PowerPoint® slides, tutorial quizzing, Web links, and final exams.

CHAPTER 10
Evaluating Macro Practice

Angie Ahmed, usually an enthusiastic, effervescent individual, felt overwhelmed and defeated. The youth services program she nurtured and supervised for her agency had operated smoothly for the past six years. Until now, no one had ever challenged her on the program's success. Suddenly, the local United Way office was requesting definitive proof that her program had been successful in meeting its goals. Angie quickly gathered her staff of social workers and activity specialists to discuss the problem. The youth services program had originally been set up as one of many programs operated by her agency. Angie, hired just two years ago, supervised seven staff members. The program offered after-school recreational activities and educational programs to a number of adolescents. Her agency's basement was outfitted with pool tables, foosball tables, and video games. Every day, as many as 10 to 15 kids spent time there, playing and having a wonderful time. Of course her program was successful—who could doubt it, looking at the many kids who took advantage of and enjoyed the program?

As Angie and her group talked, however, some serious problems began to surface. First, the agency kept very few records on the youth who used the services. Worse, there were no specific records on the actual number of adolescents who had participated in the recreational program over the past few years. Moreover, Angie discovered that staff members were in disagreement over the program's purpose. Some felt the goal was to divert kids from delinquent activities. Others felt the program was primarily designed to help adolescents develop social skills with their peers. Still others argued that the goal was to keep the kids in school and help reduce the dropout rate.

Unfortunately, when it came right down to it, there were no adequate records to document that any of these goals had been achieved. The United Way's request could not be met. The agency received no funding that year to help pay for staff. When Angie left a month later to take another job, the agency decided it could no longer afford the youth services program and simply closed it down.

Rosalee Mercado was director of the First Offenders Diversion Project in a city of about 50,000 people. The project, supported by the county government, *offered first-time offenders an opportunity to avoid getting a criminal record by participating in an eight-week, group-based program. Individuals arrested for the first time for such crimes as shoplifting, domestic violence, and similar offenses, after being screened for appropriateness, were referred to the diversion program.*

It was time again for Rosalee to make her annual budget request to the county board (an elected board responsible for governing the county). The board had requested that each program provide information on its effectiveness in terms of reaching intended goals. Rosalee had anticipated this need several years earlier and had been carefully gathering data. In a few short hours, she pulled together proof that individuals who completed the entire eight-week program were rarely arrested for further criminal activity. First offenders in the county who chose not to participate when offered the opportunity were three times as likely to be re-arrested within the following year. The county's average cost for bringing these offenders to trial and paying for their care in the city jail was five times as high as the cost of paying for the diversion program. Of course, this calculation did not include the effects on the offenders' victims, for whom the loss of property or personal injury was much more costly. Rosalee appeared before the county board with detailed data displaying her program's success. Happily, she again received funding for the next year. Board members could brag to their constituents about how well this program was doing and stress that county tax monies were extremely well spent supporting this program.

Introduction

EP 2.1.6

The differences between the two chapter-opening cases show one of the principal reasons for evaluation in macro practice: A program must prove a certain degree of success to receive continued support, whether the money comes from private or public sources. This is what we mean by research-informed or evidence-based practice (CSWE, 2008, EP 2.1.6). Although advocates may support some programs for a short time on faith alone, eventually they will ask for hard data and facts to prove that programs are working. Records must be maintained to show evaluators what is actually happening, thereby justifying the program's continued existence. Rosalee understood this principle; Angie did not. Rosalee and her staff clearly realized the sole purpose of her program was to help divert first-time offenders from the criminal justice system and thereby

reduce their chances of re-arrest. Angie and her staff, on the other hand, were not certain about their program's goals, nor had they collected sufficient data to verify its success. Hence, the program folded. In summary, program evaluation is necessary to ensure continued services to our clients and employment for ourselves.

Learning Objectives

This chapter will provide content concerning how social workers:

A. *Recognize the context of program evaluation.*

B. *Utilize concepts important in the evaluation process.*

C. *Use program evaluation research to inform practice.*

D. *Identify barriers to and problems in completing evaluations.*

E. *Describe and analyze different models of evaluation.*

F. *Utilize the stages and steps in performing an evaluation.*

G. *Demonstrate effective professional communication in presenting evaluation data.*

H. *Make ethical decisions in evaluation that are based upon the values and ethics of the NASW Code of Ethics.*

Overview of Evaluation

Evaluation is a process of determining whether a given change effort was worthwhile. This means that evaluation measures a number of aspects of a program, including money; time; actual efforts, such as hours expended providing services; and numbers of clients served (output). It also measures changes in the quality of life for those served. Evaluation requires information on how a program is being run and what it has achieved. The essential questions to ask about all of our interventions (micro through macro) are, "Do they work? How do we know?"

Evaluation research has a rich history at the macro level. Cox, Erlich, Rothman, and Tropman (1987) note that in the early 1900s people undertook to measure whether literacy rates were improving for—and employment skills being acquired by—participants in many community programs. Program evaluation research continued during the 1920s and 1930s, focusing on ways to improve the productivity of employees. The New Deal era of the 1930s and 1940s saw repeated attempts to determine whether changing the living conditions of people subsequently changed their behavior. Efforts to measure the success of delinquency prevention programs, treatment of mental disorders, and community change outcomes (such as reductions in crime and gang activity) are more recent. Although evaluation is fraught with potential barriers and problems, it is important both for professional reasons and for financial accountability to make the attempt. Our ethical responsibility to our clients and to the organizations we serve requires us to ensure not only that our efforts do not hurt clients, but also that they achieve our intended ends. Moreover, if we don't expend the effort to measure success, others assuredly will, and they might cut off program funding. If we can't prove our effectiveness, we are at the mercy of others. Another intent of evaluation is to accurately measure what we are doing. We often work with professionals from other fields who are well ahead of social work in assessing effectiveness. Evaluation of effectiveness helps us maintain credibility as competent practitioners in a legitimate profession. The ability to demonstrate the efficacy of our change efforts is fundamental to becoming an evidence-based profession. Evaluating our programs and practices using appropriate research tools helps create a knowledge base that can be used by others as they undertake similar changes. Basing our interventions on evidence rather than opinion or testimonials elevates both our practice and our profession.

Evaluation of macro practice can be viewed from two perspectives. For example, assume that your regular job is to provide protective services for children. As a practitioner, you are interested in knowing not only whether your own efforts to protect children are effective, but also whether the entire program in which you work is producing desired results. Thus, determining effectiveness of specific programs (program evaluation) is an important macro practice activity.

On another level, you may be involved in efforts to create a local children's advocacy center where abused children can be interviewed in a nonthreatening environment. Or you may be developing a community education program to encourage reporting of suspected child abuse and neglect. In both cases, you will be interested in evaluating your own success as a macro level change agent.

As you can see, evaluation of macro practice can encompass two distinct levels. This chapter will look at evaluation of macro practice from both of these perspectives.

We may also be interested in learning whether the program is serving the numbers of clients we originally envisioned. A successful program that reaches only a very small percentage of the intended population may not be worth its cost. In evaluation, we can't operate on the principle that "If it saves just one child, it's worth it."

Evaluation can also focus on explaining how the outcome we achieved actually came about. This type of evaluation is concerned more with the process than with the outcome.

Evaluation can be defined many ways, but always comes down to making judgments about what we are doing. The judgments may concern effectiveness, cost, relationships between events, or numerous other factors.

Purposes of Program Evaluation: A Summary

Program evaluations

- *Help us save time and money or avoid wasting precious resources on approaches that either don't work or don't work very well.*
- *Allow us to spend our resources on unmet needs as we discover gaps among those being served.*
- *Allow us to change our programs to make them more effective, identifying areas of strength and weakness.*
- *Assure us that planned programs provide the services we intended.*
- *Build support for continuing effective programs.*
- *Distinguish which services produce the more favorable outcomes.*
- *Identify side effects that were not intended or planned for.*
- *Help us gain personal satisfaction from knowing that our programs work and work well. (Posavac & Carey, 1997)*

Because evaluation can be done for multiple purposes, we must think carefully about what it is we want to know before we begin an evaluation. Failing to consider the purpose may cause us to select an evaluation design that does not give us the results we seek.

Key Concepts in Evaluation

EP 2.1.6

Of course, like any other specialized endeavor, evaluation has its own terminology and concepts that we have to master to be effective as evaluators. All are defined next (CSWE, 2008, EP 2.1.6).

Control Group

Ideally, one way to know whether your work is effective is to compare your program's success with clients to the success of a similar group of clients not involved in your program. For example, Rosalee's First Offenders Diversion Project compared the rearrest rate of group members with the rate of those who had committed similar crimes but did not participate in the group. The group used for comparison purposes that is not receiving the intervention is called a *control group*. Although we could say that our treated group did very well because fewer than 20 percent were ever

re-arrested, it would be less significant if the untreated control group showed an even lower re-arrest rate. This has actually happened—well-intentioned interventions do not always work as planned.

Experimental Group

The group that receives an intervention is called the *experimental group*, because an intervention is essentially an experiment. In an experiment we test a hypothesis (proposal) that a certain intervention will produce a certain desired outcome.

Dependent Variable

A *dependent variable* is that which we are most interested in understanding, measuring, or predicting. In other words, it's whatever we are trying to measure or achieve during a program's intervention process. What variable are you trying to study and evaluate? This is the dependent variable. If you try to reduce a neighborhood school's dropout rate by implementing a peer counseling program, the school's dropout rate is the dependent variable. We use the variable to measure whether our intervention is working.

Independent Variable

An *independent variable* is that which we believe is likely to influence, cause, or contribute to a particular phenomenon. In other words, an independent variable explains changes in the dependent variable. In a group program aimed at reducing delinquency among adolescent males, the program itself is the independent variable. It is the "treatment" variable being evaluated.

Sampling

In many large programs, it is nearly impossible to interview or follow up on every person who participates in an experimental group or control group. In addition, it can become prohibitively expensive to do so. As a consequence, we often use a sample or subset of the total group rather than the entire group. There are many ways to select a subset of a population, and this text cannot cover all the methods currently in use. However, one of the most important kinds of sample is called a *random sample*.

Random Sample

A random sample is one in which every member of a population has an equal chance of being selected for inclusion in the sample. If you simply survey people you run into at the supermarket, it will not be a random sample. Only those community members who happen to be in the store at a particular time would have a chance of being selected. You would miss all the people who could not be in the store at that time (all school-children, for instance), and your sample would therefore be *biased.* It would not accurately reflect the total population. Random sampling is especially important when we want to show that our sample represents the general population. We can't say this when the sample is not random. Under ideal conditions, you might assign people randomly to experimental and control groups to make it less likely that factors other than the intervention caused any differences in outcome between the groups. Random selection of a sample brings a higher degree of rigor to our attempts to assess a program's effectiveness. It also allows us to use more sophisticated evaluation techniques.

Experimental Design

Perhaps the most elaborate method for evaluating a program's efficacy is to use an *experimental design,* which generally involves attempts to manipulate the intervention to determine whether change occurs in a target group. If you want to know whether your community's antidrug program is effective, an experimental design might add to, discontinue, or modify your program to determine whether it affects the use of drugs in the area. These designs often use control groups, experimental groups, and random assignment of subjects to the two groups.

Unfortunately, experimental designs often cannot be followed in practice because we are not able to randomly assign clients to groups (that is, it would be unethical to withhold treatment from a control group just to test the effects of doing so). As a consequence, we must use less rigorous research designs. Among those frequently used is the quasi-experimental design.

Quasi-Experimental Designs

Quasi-experimental designs use some, but not all, of the elements found in the typical experimental design. Thus, a quasi-experimental design might use a control group and an experimental group, but not random assignment of clients to the two groups. These designs meet at least some of the standards for experimental designs, so we call them quasi-experimental. Social workers must often employ this type of design because we cannot randomly select who participates in our programs.

Baseline

Deciding whether something has changed over time (such as the frequency of domestic violence) requires that we know the original amount or frequency of occurrence of that phenomenon. Measuring that amount or frequency of domestic violence in a community produces a *baseline,* which tells us how often a problem or behavior occurred either at a specific point in time or during a specified period. A child welfare agency has received an average of 15 reports of child abuse per week for the past two years. The agency implemented a campaign to educate local citizens about child abuse and the importance of reporting child abuse. Then the agency uses the original average of 15 reports per week as a baseline to determine whether reports of child abuse have increased or decreased. An increase might indicate the educational program's success.

Sometimes we simply don't have data about something because no records were kept. This leaves us with two possibilities. First, we can create a *retrospective baseline* composed of data collected after the fact from people's memories. Neighborhood residents might not have kept written records of how often in the past they were victims of various crimes, such as theft or vandalism. However, if asked, they can probably recall how often they were victimized in the past year (Nurius & Hudson, 1993).

A second way of gathering data for a baseline when no records have been kept is a future-oriented approach. We gather data between the point of initial contact and the beginning of the intervention. For example, we might begin gathering data when the client initially requests our help in dealing with the neighborhood crime problem. Thus, we are seeking data while helping the neighborhood develop a Neighborhood Watch program. This model of data gathering, simultaneous with our intervention, is called a *concurrent baseline* (Nurius & Hudson, 1993).

Whereas baselines are often helpful in assessing whether change has occurred, they are not always available or necessary to evaluate the effectiveness of an intervention. Let's take a new program that provides food to homebound people: Meals-on-Wheels. Because no such program existed previously, the effectiveness of the program during its first year might be evaluated by using the actual number of meals delivered to older adults. Of course, in subsequent years, we would use the actual number of meals served in the first year as a baseline.

Mean

The *mean* is an arithmetical average derived from adding all the entries and dividing by the number of entries. To find out the mean age of neighborhood residents, we add up all their ages and divide by the total number of people in the neighborhood. Let's figure the mean for the five members of a family. Currently, family members are 51, 47, 27, 25, and 48. The sum of those five numbers is 198. Dividing 198 by 5 gives us a mean of 39.6 years. Calculating the mean age for a neighborhood might reveal that most of the people in the neighborhood are older adults. Such a finding has implications for what services might be important in that neighborhood.

Sometimes we compare the mean of the experimental group with that of the control group to learn whether there is a difference between the two. The First Offenders Diversion Project documented that the mean number of post-intervention arrests for its "graduates" was lower than the rate for those who did not participate in the program.

Sometimes the mean or arithmetical average is not useful because it provides skewed data. For example,

consider the family we just discussed when its 104-year-old grandmother was still alive. When her age was added to the 198 years the total was 302. Dividing this by the six family members gives the family a mean age of just over 50 years. This suggests a somewhat unrealistic picture of this family. Thus, the problem with using a mean is that it can mislead you when extremes distort the collected data. To eliminate this problem and provide a more useful figure, we often use the median.

Median

The *median* is the centermost figure in a distribution of figures listed from highest to lowest or vice versa. For certain kinds of data, medians provide a more useful basis for comparison. We often compare median incomes of groups or community residents. We do this by taking the annual income figures for each individual, arranging them from lowest to highest, and selecting the figure that appears in the middle of the distribution. The median can be calculated for any set of numbers. Consider the five-member family just described. Their ages were 51, 47, 27, 25, and 48.

The Meals-on-Wheels program helps many older adults remain in their own homes and prevents premature placement in a nursing home.

To calculate the median age we must reorder them as follows: 25, 27, 47, 48, and 51. Because 47 falls in the middle of this distribution, that is the median. If we added the 104-year old grandmother to the group, the median would fall between 47 and 48—a relatively small shift and still a reasonable representation of the family's age. This illustrates the value of a median value versus a mean value.

Mode

The *mode* is the most frequently observed score in a group of scores. Thus, we might find that the modal number of credits carried by full-time college students is 15 per semester. This means that, out of the various numbers of credits students can carry (typically from 12 to 18), most students are carrying 15.

Standard Deviation

A *standard deviation* is a measure of the amount of variability of observations around a mean. Standard deviations are easily calculated using a computer or programmable calculator. Suppose you examine a community's distribution of wealth. You discover (from looking at income figures) that the mean annual family income is $50,000 with a standard deviation of only $2,000. This suggests that most people in the community have incomes somewhere between $48,000 and $52,000. If the standard deviation were $10,000, it would suggest a wider variation among family incomes (that is, more families with incomes well above or well below $50,000).

Reliability

Reliability is the likelihood that a measurement will yield the same results at subsequent times. If you are trying to find out whether your assertiveness groups are helping to make domestic violence survivors more assertive, you might look for an instrument to measure assertiveness levels. That instrument should also be reliable. That is, a person who receives a low assertiveness score should receive about the same score no matter when the instrument is given. The score should change only if the person receives assertiveness training between the first and second measurements. Evaluators usually measure and report reliability so as to reveal whether it is high or low for a given statistic. Thus, you may report that your assertiveness group was effective 75 percent of the time, and that the method of measurement is about 90 percent reliable (indicating high reliability) or only 50 percent reliable (reflecting relatively low reliability).

Validity

Validity is the ability of an instrument to measure what it is supposed to measure. A written test used to judge whether a person can ride a bicycle would not be a valid test of bicycle-riding ability. Similarly, a test measuring self-esteem should deal directly with matters of self-esteem. Several different kinds of validity are possible. They involve different ways of determining the validity of a given instrument.

Face validity means that a commonsense view of the instrument suggests that it measures what it's supposed to measure. A test composed of questions regarding historical events from 1945 to the present has face validity as a measure of post–World War II historical knowledge. It really does measure acquisition of historical knowledge about that time period. Thus, the test measures what it is supposed to measure.

Predictive validity, on the other hand, is a measure of validity based upon the ability of an instrument to predict future performance. If social work exams could accurately tell us which test takers will become good social workers following graduation, such tests would have predictive validity. That is, they could predict future behavior (in this case, competent social work practice). Whenever possible, evaluators use measurements that have high validity and different kinds of validity (such as face, predictive, and so on). The combination has more value and the results are much more respected.

Descriptive Statistics

Statistics that describe a phenomenon (such as a community) are called *descriptive statistics*. A mean (referred to earlier) might be used to describe the average age of a population. We might learn that a community has only a 2 percent minority population. This statistic might be helpful in understanding why community residents fear an influx of low-income housing. Their lack of contact with different cultures may be causing their anxieties.

Inferential Statistics

Any set of statistics used to make an inference (or draw a conclusion) about a population based upon a sample of that population is called *inferential statistics*. Not knowing the average income in a community, we might survey a sample of residents. Based upon the income information they provide, we would infer the income level of the entire community from that sample.

Outcome

An *outcome* is a quality-of-life change resulting from social work interventions. A program that reduces the incidence of burglary or drug selling in a neighborhood produces a definite change in the neighborhood residents' quality of life. Another program that helps domestic violence survivors avoid further injury and encourages them to develop new friendships and resources enhances their quality of life. These changes are outcomes. Of course, unanticipated consequences or outcomes are also common, so we must always be aware that they may occur. For example, graduates of an assertiveness training group may test out their new-found skills with an employer who promptly fires them for insubordination. Being fired for being assertive is an example of an unintended consequence.

Outcome Measures

An *outcome measure* is the means by which we determine the actual outcome of an intervention. There are *practice outcomes* and *functional outcomes,* as well as *process of care outcomes. Practice outcomes* are those that can be observed by either the client system or the social worker. An example would include a valid and reliable instrument that can measure the agreed-upon outcome. If we were measuring the success of a program designed to address depression in veterans, we might employ one of the readily available depression inventories with all clients. Scores on the depression instrument would be a useful outcome measure. Likewise, if we are evaluating a program designed to help clients deal with stress in their lives, we would use an instrument that measures this variable. On the other hand, if the evaluation is of a job-finding service for unemployed clients, the outcome measure would consider such things as the following:

- *Did the client find employment?*
- *Does the employment provide adequate income?*
- *Does the employment provide benefits such as health insurance?*

Functional outcomes focus on changes in the client's quality of life. They are concerned with those factors that are significant or important to the client. Consider for a minute the program mentioned previously. Is it sufficient that the client was successful in obtaining employment if the job is really awful? If the client hates the job, this increases the likelihood that she will quit

sooner or later. Thus, we might want to know other aspects of the outcome, such as:

- *How does the client evaluate the job in terms of suitability?*
- *Does the job utilize training or education that the client has achieved?*
- *How are the working conditions of the job perceived by the client?*

Process of care outcomes are those that relate directly to how a service was provided. These outcomes are usually measured via one of two methods: opinions of those receiving social work services, or comparisons to a set of standards. The former outcome measures utilize such things as client satisfaction surveys, which will be discussed later in the chapter. The latter uses an objective standard for a particular service. For example, a standard set by a professional group for recordkeeping could be used to compare actual recordkeeping done by social workers. This will be discussed in more detail when we address quality assurance reviews.

Outcome measures can be completed by the social worker providing service, the client, or significant others, depending upon the service provided and the nature of client challenges. For example, social workers providing services to survivors of domestic violence might complete a form that asks about the following client behaviors:

- *Did the client follow through on contacting a referral agency if such a referral was made?*
- *Has the client developed a plan for the immediate future?*
- *Is the client making appropriate decisions regarding her life?*
- *Has the client demonstrated awareness regarding the dynamics of domestic abuse?*

Forms like this are often part of the recording expected of social workers and have been used in agencies providing services such as crisis intervention, sexual assault survivor assistance, and educational programs. Similar instruments may be completed by clients who rate such things as knowledge gained from a particular program or quality of services provided by the agency, among others.

Outcome measures are also used in community organization efforts and other macro practice undertakings. For example, the Federation of Congregations United to Serve, a faith-based organization in Orange

County, Florida, sought to increase health care funding for children in the face of a budget-cutting legislature. They lobbied the governor, legislators, and other decision makers about the need for health insurance for children. The outcome measure was legislative approval of money for an additional 5,000 children in the state's KidCare program.

Statistical Significance

Statistical significance is a measure of the risk that exists when we generalize from a sample to the population. Ideally, your sample and the population from which it was drawn are identical. Practically, however, it is likely that any sample deviates slightly from the original population. This deviation can be calculated and reported. If you surveyed a sample of people from a community to learn their views on their most pressing problems, you would hope to get results from the sample that you could apply to the entire community. We usually try to limit the risk of error in this process to small percentages, such as 5 percent. To say this differently, we want to be wrong about our belief only 5 times out of 100. Often, statistical significance will be shown in the form of a figure such as $p = .05$ or $p = .01$. This means that there is a 95 percent or 99 percent probability (p), respectively, that the sample accurately represents the population.

Chi-Square Test

The *chi-square test* is a statistical procedure to compare the expected frequencies in a study to observed frequencies. Expected frequencies are the outcomes that are expected to occur. Sometimes this expected frequency is based on the probability that something will occur. When flipping a coin, you would expect to get a head one time and a tail the next. Thus, for every 10 flips of the coin, you would expect to get five heads. Similarly, if you were looking at a sample from a population that the U.S. Census Bureau says contains 10 percent people of color, you would expect your sample to have the same percentage; namely, 10 percent. Observed frequencies are the actual results you get from your coin toss—say, eight heads and two tails—or the real percentage of people of color in your sample (perhaps 25 percent).

The importance of the chi-square test and similar procedures is that they can tell you whether your outcome could have occurred by chance. If you are comparing high school dropout rates and find that the

average dropout rate for a school is 7 percent, that is the expected frequency. If you find that the dropout rate for people of color in that school is 34 percent, this is well above the expected frequency. The chi-square test can help you determine whether this is a fluke or indicates that people of color are more likely to drop out of this school.

A chi-square test is also useful in evaluative studies to determine whether the sample being evaluated resembles the total population. If you wanted to know whether your sample differed from the population, you could compare, for example, the age, ethnic, or gender breakdown in the sample (observed frequency) with the expected frequencies based upon what exists in the population. A population consisting of 24 percent Native Americans and 60 percent women would lead one to expect similar frequencies in the sample. If the sample did not differ from the population on these dimensions, we could say with greater assurance that the sample was representative of the population.

Problems and Barriers in Program Evaluation

Trying to evaluate a social work program or project can be quite complicated. Multiple problems and barriers can interfere with undertaking the evaluation, interpreting results, and **EP 2.1.10m** using the results to improve programs. The following section identifies six common problems and barriers discussed by Yegidis and Weinbach (2002), Posavac and Carey (1997), Dudley (2009), and others. They include failure to plan for evaluation, lack of program stability, relationships between evaluators and practitioners, unclear evaluation results, evaluation results that are not accepted, and evaluations that are not worth the effort (CSWE, 2008, EP 2.1.10m).

Failure to Plan for Evaluation

Too often, the decision to evaluate a program comes well after the program has been in operation. Without a built-in plan for evaluation, including decisions on what information to gather and for what purposes, evaluators are at a loss for ways to proceed. In the case of Angie Ahmed and the youth services program that opened the chapter, the program originators never really considered the need to evaluate what they did. When they were eventually asked to prove the effectiveness of their program, they lacked the data and even the means for gathering data. When an agency considers an evaluation plan at the start of the program's operation, it is much easier to gather baseline information, establish management information systems (including forms, computer databases, and the like), and create a time line for evaluation. If the agency waits until the program has already begun, or worse, waits for several years, critical data may be unrecoverable.

Lack of Program Stability

A common evaluation problem is that no program is static. That is, programs typically change over the course of their operation. Staff members may learn to do some things better. Clients or the community may change. More or less money may become available. The composition of the staff itself may drastically change. Philosophies and support for the program may wax and wane. Finally, staff turnover may result in goals different from those pursued by the originators of the program. Thus, it is likely that the program you started evaluating several years ago is not quite the same program now. The longer the evaluation process proceeds, the more changes are likely to occur.

This leaves evaluators in a bind, because they may not know what has changed. It may not be possible to modify the evaluation design in midstream to accommodate the changes. Or there may be no appropriate way to measure the new "thing" that has emerged. Of course, in reality you can't keep anything in a steady state for long. One option is to test only small parts or components of a program to see if they work, without trying to tackle too large a project at a time. Rather than try to evaluate an entire program, you might decide to focus only on the intake operation. It may be best to test programs over short periods to avoid problems associated with longer time frames. You might decide, for example, to evaluate for only the first year of operation or only the fourth year.

Other options include using periodic measures rather than waiting until the end to assess progress. Likewise, holding changes to a minimum for short periods of time may reduce the factors that could confound or confuse the evaluation.

Relationships between Evaluators and Practitioners

Relationships between those who carry out a program and those who evaluate it can be problematic. Personality differences, which can always arise, are exacerbated by role-related problems. Practitioners are usually concerned primarily with *delivering a service*. Evaluators, on the other hand, are interested in *measuring the effectiveness of that service*. These two roles need not be conflictual, but they can be. When you evaluate a worker's effectiveness, it is easy for that worker to feel threatened. Practitioners may feel like their worth is under examination, a potentially painful situation. In addition, an evaluation is likely to uncover things that need improvement. Such findings are frequently threatening or at the very least uncomfortable.

Evaluators' standards may be more rigorous than those of practitioners. Evaluators are likely to be more interested in the specifics of data collection and encourage random assignment of clients to control and experimental groups. Practitioners, on the other hand, are more concerned with providing service, preferring to do the paperwork later when they have time. Evaluators usually feel that completing required paperwork, which includes keeping records and documenting good content, is extremely important. Practitioners sometimes think such paperwork is a waste of time compared to actually doing their jobs with clients. Practitioners are appalled to think that a client would be denied service because that client had been randomly assigned to some control group. Evaluators might want to know precisely how many incidents of gang-related activity occurred after a Streetworker program was initiated. Involved practitioners, on the other hand, may see no need to keep precise records of each specific event because they know from discussions with neighbors that things are "getting better."

This problem is manageable if administrators support the evaluation effort, involve practitioners in designing the evaluation, use measures that don't place undue recordkeeping burdens on staff, and reduce disruptions in service. If evaluators take these steps, practitioners will feel that they have a bigger stake in the evaluating effort. They will also be less weighed down with paperwork and better able to do their usual work with clients.

Sometimes it is possible to present an evaluation as focused on the theory underlying a particular intervention instead of on the intervention itself. This can make the evaluation process seem less threatening. If an evaluation focuses on the theory behind a particular type of delinquency prevention program (such as after-school recreation), it will appear less of a threat to the workers. After all, if the theory behind an intervention is flawed, the workers cannot be blamed for unsatisfactory outcomes.

Finally, it is important to give practitioners feedback during the process so that they see the importance of the evaluation to their practice. This feedback helps practitioners improve services and feel that they are more a part of the evaluation process.

When Evaluation Results Are Unclear

Sometimes even a well-planned evaluation produces equivocal or unclear results. Perhaps we can't really establish that our new Neighborhood Watch program reduced crime in the neighborhood. Maybe only a modest drop in burglaries occurred. Further, perhaps the police added another officer to the neighborhood patrol at the same time that we began our program. Maybe *this* was responsible for the small reduction in the crime rate. We can't tell for sure whether the watch program or the added patrol caused the reduction. Often it is difficult to say with any degree of certainty that the goal was achieved because of our efforts. Perhaps the most logical solution to this predicament is to conduct multiple evaluations so that no one explanation can rule out all your findings. It may also be possible to use various statistical techniques to rule out the effects of unexpected changes. These techniques, however, are beyond the scope of this text.

When Evaluation Results Are Not Accepted

Sometimes evaluations demonstrate things that the people involved do not or cannot accept. For example, a program may prove successful but not be continued because it is not politically popular. An evaluation might threaten a favored program or cast doubts on its efficacy. Yet the program is continued and the evaluation ignored.

Recent discussions about the Drug Abuse Resistance Education (DARE) program are a good example. Extremely popular with police and school officials, the program sends police officers into schools to provide a drug abuse prevention course. Anecdotal reports from police participants are very positive. They make comments such as, "The kids tell you a lot of their problems," or "The children are now much more friendly toward the police." Other comments suggest that "kids are friendly toward one another and feel good about themselves." Yet studies designed to assess whether participation in DARE stops adolescents from using drugs and drinking alcohol found that no significant differences exist between participants and nonparticipants. Other studies, summarizing research involving thousands of children, raise similar questions. Despite these questions, the DARE program continues to be praised as effective because it is politically popular.

Another example involved a social worker testifying before a legislative committee. The committee was interested in knowing whether the state would benefit by privatizing some aspects of the criminal and juvenile justice systems. A few legislators wanted to turn some functions (such as prisons and juvenile detention facilities) over to private organizations with the hope that they could deliver similar outcomes at a lower cost. When the social worker told them that the research on the effectiveness and efficiency of privatized functions was not definitive, the committee was not happy. They wanted clear recommendations to move in one direction or another, and the evaluation results could not provide such assistance.

When Evaluation Is Not Worth the Effort

Some evaluation efforts are simply not worth pursuing. A special event that occurs only once does not necessarily merit evaluation. The women's club that donates labor and materials to refurbish the domestic violence shelter is an example of a one-shot project. The neighborhood association that contributes its expertise to repair the roof of one of its older adult members does not merit an evaluation effort. Rubin and Rubin (1986) suggest that you undertake an evaluation effort under only three conditions: First, perform an evaluation only when you are certain that the information gained will actually be used. Second, evaluate only when the cost is low compared to the potential value of knowing whether the program is successful. Third, consider an evaluation only when the result is likely to improve social work practice.

Evaluations may not be worth the effort because of a variety of factors. Dudley (2009) notes that the outcome measures chosen for evaluations must meet certain standards. If, for example, the measures available for the evaluation effort are not useful to stakeholders, it is probably inadvisable to proceed. Useful outcome measures will assist boards of directors, agency staff, and those providing funding to make decisions about eliminating, continuing, or expanding a given program.

Likewise, serious problems with the validity or reliability of the measures will compromise the evaluation effort. For example, an agency that develops its own instrument for measuring changes in clients' behavior without ensuring that the instrument is valid and reliable is asking for trouble. Not only do we not know whether the instrument can measure what it is supposed to, we don't know whether it is sensitive enough to measure the changes in the client's behavior. Unfortunately, an agency that elects to purchase instruments that have been tested for validity, reliability, and sensitivity to change may encounter yet another challenge: Many standardized instruments are available but may be too expensive to purchase for a cash-strapped social service organization.

As you can see, many potential problems can affect evaluation efforts. Sometimes you can overcome these barriers with careful planning, sensitivity to the concerns of those involved in the process, and a willingness to be flexible. The next sections will look at some evaluation designs you might use to assess the effectiveness of your macro practice interventions.

Kinds of Evaluations

EP 2.1.6

Generally speaking, evaluations can be classified as either formative (i.e., monitoring) evaluations or summative (i.e., impact) evaluations. In addition, evaluations may be classified as to whether they are concerned with determining the effectiveness of an intervention or its efficiency. The kind of evaluation we choose is usually driven by the program we are trying to evaluate. This is consistent with the idea of practice-informed research in that the program (practice) influences the kinds of research we pursue and the research tools we use. In the following sections, we will discuss the importance of selecting the evaluation approach that best judges our practice (program) (CSWE, 2008, EP 2.1.6).

Formative (or Monitoring) Evaluations

Formative evaluations focus more on the *process* than on the outcome of an intervention. Formative evaluations occur during the implementation stage and are designed to improve the change effort (Royse, 2004). They may gather information on the provision of a service (such as the number of hours of counseling, number of phone calls to the crisis line, or the number of people served per month). They may also focus on more subjective measures, such as clients' or workers' judgments of change efforts. Thus, a formative or

monitoring evaluation will reveal whether the program is serving as many clients as initially expected. It will also tell us whether, in the social workers' and clients' opinions, the program achieves its goals.

Formative evaluations do not address whether the effort is worthwhile, or even whether it is more worthwhile than other programs. They focus on describing what the program does and what is happening during the service delivery process. To help in this process, formative evaluations can compare what actually happens in a program to a set of model standards that represent an ideal to which the program can be compared (Royse, 2004). Various national organizations such as the NASW or the Child Welfare League of America produce sets of standards covering a wide range of areas, including standards for staff qualifications and case management services.

Sometimes consultants are invited to review a program and provide input as to whether the program is operating by accepted practices. Research on effective past programs can also provide helpful guidelines to use in monitoring a program.

Monitoring can be used to assess whether the program is actually serving its intended population. Basic data collected for monitoring purposes might include such things as demographic data on each client (name, age, sex), the problems for which they sought help (emergency shelter, food), the service actually provided by the agency (voucher for food, transportation), and the outcomes achieved (job obtained, no future police contact). During the beginning planning stages of program development, workers must carefully consider what kinds of information might be helpful to monitoring, because once a program is launched it is unpleasant to discover that needed information has not been collected. If no records are kept on actual services provided, an agency cannot document what it did to help clients. If no follow-up is done, it can mean that the agency is unable to prove that it services helped clients in the long run.

Data to assist with monitoring is usually available through such avenues as treatment manuals, minutes of board or committee meetings, monthly and annual reports, and case records, to name just a few. Additional data can be gleaned by interviewing staff, clients, referring agencies, and other stakeholders. Comparisons can be done using national standards, data drawn from governmental agencies (such as census information), and needs assessments, among others.

Summative (or Impact) Evaluations

Summative evaluations measure the consequences of services provided. They are normally conducted following an intervention and focus on changes occurring in the target population. Is a program actually doing what it says it intends to do? Is it achieving its goals? A summative evaluation might focus on whether a Neighborhood Watch program reduced the number of area burglaries, increased residents' sense of security and peace of mind, or contributed to a greater sense of community among residents. Most program evaluations are summative. A simple example of a summative evaluation is given by Bembry (1996), who evaluated the success of a program designed to increase the number of volunteers providing help to a variety of agencies in Maryland. He tracked the number of volunteers at 28 different sites over a two-year period. A 40 percent increase occurred after the hiring of a volunteer coordinator.

Funding sources such as county boards, boards of directors, and legislatures are concerned about whether the program's intended outcomes are achieved. Consider a program aimed at reducing drug-related crimes in an inner-city area. Has this happened? Was the incidence of such crimes actually reduced? Were first-time offenders in the diversion program diverted from future criminal behavior (or at least future arrests)? Did another program successfully rehabilitate 25 rundown homes in its first year of operation, as predicted in the grant application? These types of issues are most important in summative evaluations. Ultimately, they are also the issues most likely to determine whether a program is continued or abandoned.

Effectiveness and Efficiency Evaluations

Evaluations are also distinguished by whether they concern effectiveness or efficiency. To be effective, an intervention should produce a desirable end product. This might be a lower incidence of elder abuse, better school attendance for at-risk children, or fewer incidents of gang violence in a target neighborhood. Most of our evaluations are, in fact, designed to assess whether the intended product was achieved. These are effectiveness evaluations.

Efficiency evaluations, on the other hand, are concerned with whether a program achieves outcomes in

The DARE program is popular with police officers, yet shows little success in preventing drug use by youth.

the least expensive manner. For instance, an extraordinarily expensive drug treatment program would be considered less efficient than one that achieved the same goals at a lower cost. Similarly, a program that achieved its goals in inappropriate ways (such as through unethical treatment of clients) would not be considered efficient, even if its goals were accomplished.

Both types of evaluations (effectiveness and efficiency) are important and useful, depending upon our needs. We are always concerned about determining whether we are effective. We should also concern ourselves about whether our programs are efficiently run.

Evaluation Approaches

EP 2.1.7a

Planning evaluations for judging the effectiveness or efficiency of a program, whether formative or summative in nature, requires familiarity with some of the most useful methods and designs used in social work practice. There are many evaluation approaches to use, depending upon needs and circumstances. The following sections will address two methods, quantitative and qualitative, and several common designs, including one-group post-test designs, pretest/post-test designs, client satisfaction surveys, goal attainment scaling, target problem scaling, case studies, group comparisons, and quality assurance reviews (CSWE, 2008, EP 2.1.7a).

Quantitative Methods

Quantitative methods use objective (numerical) criteria (such as scores on a test, number of arrests, or frequency of temper tantrums) to learn whether change has taken place following an intervention. Using baselines, these methods compare change over time in designated target behaviors. Quantitative methods require specificity in identifying the problem, selecting observable indicators of the problems, deciding how measurement will take place (including who will do it), gathering data, and analyzing data.

One advantage of quantitative methods is that you can sometimes aggregate data from many studies in a technique called *meta-analysis,* the combining of the results of several smaller studies (for example, single-subject designs), and statistically analyze the overall findings. This synthesis and analysis yields more useful results than would be possible with only a handful of cases. Meta-analyses might calculate the average change between clients' scores on baseline data and their scores on the same dimension following intervention. This

change is called *effect size* because it shows the effect of our interventions. The use of meta-analysis is becoming more common in social work literature. It is described in more detail in Yegidis and Weinbach (2006).

Qualitative Methods

Qualitative methods are designed to learn the experiences of a particular group of people. In the process, the researcher gains a better understanding of the human condition. Qualitative research methods examine a program without using quantitative measures as just described. They typically involve an in-depth review of a small number of cases, and their goal is to describe or explore the experiences of clients or others involved in the process. Qualitative methods aim at understanding what made a program work for specific clients or what participants would do differently if they could do it over again. Qualitative methods include interviews, reviews of logs or journals, and similar approaches.

Qualitative research tends to focus on the human experience and to provide a substantial amount of information that is then categorized, sorted, and analyzed to determine patterns. As a consequence, this research methodology may lead to new understandings or theories that can be tested later. When combined with quantitative methods, the result is a significantly broader and deeper understanding of an organization.

One-Group Post-Test Designs

One-group post-test designs are, as indicated by the title, evaluations that look at a single target group, focusing only on changes that have occurred following intervention (post-test). These designs are used when we lack baseline data that would allow us to compare the change from time A (before an intervention) to time B (after an intervention). The ability to compare pre- and post-test results (sometimes called A-B designs) is more useful to the evaluator. However, the evaluator is often unable to gather baseline data to allow such a comparison. An agency might launch a program to keep kids from becoming involved in delinquent behavior without knowing how much delinquent activity the kids are already involved in. All agency staff members can do is look at the youngsters who complete the program and say that 75 percent of them have had no contact with the juvenile justice system. They cannot prove, however, that their program was the reason for the 75 percent nondelinquency rate. Perhaps 75 percent of participants were not involved in delinquent activity before the program even started.

Without a baseline, no one can prove that the program is responsible for deterring delinquent behavior.

Pre-Test/Post-Test Designs

Sometimes we have an opportunity to compare a situation after intervention with the situation before intervention. These designs (sometimes called A-B) are more useful than post-test-only designs because they allow us to show changes over time. Compare arrests for drug dealing in a neighborhood before and after an intensive neighborhood association effort to report all suspicious persons to the police. Although arrests might increase briefly when the program begins, they decline quickly as dealers recognize that the neighborhood is inhospitable. These designs require the existence or creation of a baseline against which comparisons can be made following the intervention. Later in the chapter, Highlight 10.2 will describe these designs and others more thoroughly.

Client Satisfaction Surveys

Client or consumer satisfaction inventories or surveys measure general satisfaction with a service or achievement of specific goals. They can be used to keep a record of complaints received or problems encountered in providing a service. They can also be used to tally positive comments from clients or service users. Ideally, client satisfaction surveys include questions that cover such variables as staff behavior, accessibility of service, fairness of agency policies, and other factors. Client satisfaction data, besides being fairly easy to obtain, is a valid source of certain kinds of information. For example, such data may help explain why clients drop out of a particular program at an unusually high rate or determine which agency services are most well-received. However, client satisfaction surveys are not useful in other situations. A delinquency prevention program should not be considered a success simply because the participants (at-risk adolescents) enjoy the program or recommend it to their friends. The critical variable is whether the delinquency rate drops following group members' participation in the program. Figure 10.1 shows a survey used by a hospice program.

One of the major drawbacks to client satisfaction surveys is that the results are almost invariably positive, regardless of the client population, services provided, or other variables. Reasons for this positive bias may rest with the qualities of the questionnaires themselves, such as lack of reliability and validity, the fact that many clients often have little or no choice about where

they receive service, or may doubt the anonymity of the survey and wish to avoid any risk associated with a negative response. Despite this drawback, client satisfaction surveys are used frequently and often provide clients with the ability to comment about specific aspects of their experience.

Goal Attainment Scaling

Goal attainment scaling (GAS) is a design used to monitor the progress of individual clients and then to aggregate the data on a weekly, monthly, or yearly basis. At the first step in the process, workers and clients jointly set goals that both believe are reasonable, desirable, and attainable. Goal attainment scaling is flexible and helps staff and clients monitor progress. The ability to see actual progress in a case can be very reinforcing. When you try to evaluate whether your agency is effective, it is helpful to have individual case records showing the types and percentages of goals achieved. You are then able to summarize the results of individual worker–client interactions and apply the results to the entire agency. For example, a community agency may provide services designed to allow older adults to live in their own homes as long as possible. The kinds of services available from the agency include lawn mowing, snow removal, interior and exterior painting, cleaning, household repairs, and replacement of vital equipment such as furnaces and water heaters. With each referral, the agency social worker meets with the client to identify unmet needs and goals. The workers then follow the following steps:

- *Select a problem and list the goals associated with the problem. Typical goals might include (1) painting a house and (2) replacing a water heater. Both goals are clear and easily measured.*
- *Establish a scale for each goal that ranges from –2 to +2, representing the two extremes of possible outcomes. Figure 10.2 shows how this scaling might look.*
- *Monitor the outcome and the points associated with the level of achievement. In this case, a local painter volunteered to paint the house for free (Goal 1 outcome level [+1]) and a plumber offered to install the water heater for free (Goal 2 outcome level [+2]).*
- *Calculate the average outcome level for all goals. In this case the mean score is +1.5 (the average of +1 and +2), which means a better-than-expected outcome overall. GAS can be used to evaluate programs to the extent that a similar system is in use*

Mary Rose Hospice
Bereavement Services Survey

Mary Rose Hospice strives to continually evaluate and enhance our services. We would like to request your assistance in completing this questionnaire. Please let us know if you utilized any of our support services and, if so, how helpful these services were to you. Please return your completed survey in the enclosed envelope.

1) The Bereavement Program was adequately explained to me.   Yes ____   No ____
   If no, what can we do to improve the explanation of our program? _____
   _____
   _____

2) Bereavement Services helped me better understand my grief.
   Very Helpful _____   Helpful _____   Not Helpful _____

3) The mailings I received were informative and encouraging.
   Very Helpful _____   Helpful _____   Not Helpful _____

4) Phone contacts from Mary Rose Hospice following the death of my loved one were appreciated.
   Very Helpful _____   Helpful _____   Not Helpful _____

5) I was aware that I could call on Mary Rose Hospice for support in dealing with grief.
   Very Aware _____   Aware, but hesitant _____   Not Aware _____

   Do you have any other comments or suggestions? _____
   _____
   _____
   _____
   _____

                    Name (optional) _____

Thank you very much for your feedback. Your assistance will enable us to better serve future families.

FIGURE 10.1 Client Satisfaction Survey

LEVEL OF OUTCOME	GOAL 1	GOAL 2
Much worse than expected (−2)	House remains unpainted.	No funds available for water heater installation.
Somewhat worse than expected (−1)	Painter located but cost is too high.	Water heater donated, but no one can install it.
Expected outcome (0)	House is painted at minimal cost.	Water heater donated with client paying for installation.
Somewhat better than expected (+1)	House is painted at no cost.	Water heater installed at token cost to client.
Much better than expected (+2)	House is painted by volunteer at no cost.	Water heater installed at no cost to client.

FIGURE 10.2 Goal Attainment Scaling

by multiple social workers, allowing an overall score to be calculated for all clients served.

Goal attainment scaling is often, but not always, a qualitative design and is very flexible. It generally has good face validity and usually does not interfere with the intervention. Its reliability is considered good. GAS can be combined with other measures, such as client satisfaction surveys. For example, evaluation of an after-school, latchkey children's program could measure the level of satisfaction of parents and children as well as the number of children enrolled in the program.

Target Problem Scaling

Target problem scaling is a method of monitoring changes in a client's behavior. It is primarily a qualitative design used in simple evaluations (Figure 10.3 illustrates an effort to quantify this method). Its premise is that one identifies a problem, carries out an intervention, and repeatedly measures whether the problem has been reduced, modified, or eliminated. These measures are considered generally reliable, even though the degree of validity is unknown (Alter & Evens, 1990, p. 64). That is, because the client or worker monitoring the behavior may tend to interpret the changes in

TARGET PROBLEM Name of rater: _____ Alice _____	TARGET PROBLEM RATING— SEVERITY SCALE[a]			TARGET PROBLEM RATING— DEGREE OF CHANGE[b]		GLOBAL IMPROVEMENT RATING
	Start	Time 1	Time 2	Termination	Follow-up	
Afraid to walk in neighborhood	ES	S	NP	4	4	
Children have no place to play	ES	ES	NVS	3	5	4

a. Degree of Severity Scale: NP (no problem), NVS (not very severe), VS (very severe), ES (extremely severe)
b. Improvement Scale: 1 (Worse), 2 (No change), 3 (A little better), 4 (Somewhat better), 5 (A lot better)

Instructions: This form is to be completed by both the client and the social worker. It may be used at repeated intervals throughout and following the intervention. It can be used for formative and summative evaluations. Each problem should be listed. Global improvement is the mean of the change ratings for all problems.

FIGURE 10.3 Target Problem Change Scale

behavior in the same way over the length of the intervention, it is likely to be reliable. On the other hand, because the changes are measured by individual interpretation and judgment, validity may be open to question. Asking clients whether they feel less suicidal this week than they did last week (as might be done in a program aimed at helping at-risk teens) will not necessarily yield a valid response.

The form in Figure 10.3 illustrates two concerns expressed by neighborhood residents: fear of walking in their own neighborhood and lack of a place for their children to play. These problems are rated as equally severe (extremely severe, or "ES") at the start. As a result of the neighborhood intervention, both problems diminish in severity. People are no longer afraid to walk in their neighborhoods, and the issue of a place for kids to play is no longer so severe. The degree of change in each problem area is also assessed at termination and a year later. Improvement has been substantial with respect to both problems (ratings of 4 and 5). A global or average rating helps give a composite picture of all the problems being addressed. The advantage of such a scale is twofold: First, you can use it to assess changes in a macro-level problem in a single area or neighborhood. You could also combine it with ratings from other neighborhoods to provide a more comprehensive view of residents' opinions. In the latter case, a survey might yield findings about the success of a particular type of intervention (program, policy, or project).

Case Studies

Case studies are qualitative measurement designs allowing the use of a single case or a small group of cases. They allow us to study a problem in some depth to identify the factors that led to a certain outcome. For instance, interviews with neighborhood members can reveal which factors were most responsible for their increased sense of safety over the past six months. Once we have identified what factors produced what results, we are in a better position to form a hypothesis about our interventions. Ideally, however, results of case studies should be replicated several times before we attempt to generalize about an intervention's success and apply our findings to other programs.

Case studies allow us to use unstructured interviews and ask whatever questions are needed to help understand a situation. For example, you might wish to ask neighborhood residents what issues they consider most important. Because each resident may select different issues, it is not always possible to anticipate what they will say. Follow-up questions may be needed to elicit further information. As you can see, this creates a very unstructured interview, but it can yield excellent information that might be missed if you simply asked residents to choose from a list of the five issues you think are most important.

Group Comparisons

Group comparisons, as the name suggests, compare outcomes between two or more groups—one of which is the treatment group and the other the control group. The control group may receive no treatment, or it may be exposed to some type of intervention (but not the same type as used with the treatment group). Because we can't usually do random assignment to control and experimental groups as required in true experimental designs, we often use quasi-experimental designs.

Quasi-experimental designs use comparison rather than control groups. In comparison groups, we try to match the two groups on important variables such as gender, age, ethnicity, income, or social class, and any other variable that might affect the outcome. We might compare two neighborhoods whose residents are of similar ages, gender breakdown, and income. Although we cannot randomly assign people to live in a particular neighborhood, we can try to find a neighborhood similar to the one in which we are working. The variables, of course, depend on what you are trying to find out in the study. Typical group comparisons are pretest/post-test designs or post-test only designs. Much of what we attempt to measure in group comparisons can be considered status change. Changes in a client's status include such things as employment, attending school, or taking any specific actions (such as getting a job, moving to an independent living situation, or completing a GED). Such concrete outcomes make it much easier to compare across groups.

Of course, we can also compare the groups on other dimensions, such as behavioral checklists (used by clients or significant others to monitor changes in behavior) or tests of knowledge (such as knowledge about sex and birth control). The limitation of quasi-experimental designs such as group comparisons is that other factors—such as maturation, preexisting skills, and so on—might have caused the change. Each factor is a potential threat to validity. We cannot be sure (because we did not randomly assign people to guarantee close similarity between the intervention and nonintervention groups) that observed changes were—or weren't—caused by factors other than our intervention. For example, we might be quite pleased to find that 90 percent of the at-risk teens in the target group finished high school compared with only 50 percent of the teens in the comparison group. However, it is possible that the target group teens had higher intelligence to begin with or had parents who were more motivated to help their children complete high school. Only random assignment of cases can rule out alternative explanations of outcomes.

Quality Assurance Reviews

A quality assurance review involves determining compliance with an established set of standards and using the findings to correct shortcomings or deficiencies. The standards may be established by government regulations, an accrediting agency or other professional organization, or by the agency itself. It may be an ongoing effort or be conducted primarily when problems are perceived in an agency's service delivery. Quality assurance reviews can be done by reviewing case files, records of complaints, and letters from clients and/or others receiving service. Quality assurance focuses on finding defects in service and enhancing uniform quality of service. Conducting a quality assurance review requires that an agency have some accepted standard of performance. Perhaps all workers are required to prepare monthly written file summaries of their work with clients. Or maybe every client must have an agreed-upon treatment plan in the file. A quality assurance review might focus on whether these standards of performance have been achieved. To do this, you might review every file in the agency or just a subset of files. You might also review agency records to decide whether client-identified problems were resolved and whether adequate records were kept that would allow other types of evaluations. Similarly, if we knew that agency policy requires all reports of suspected child abuse to be investigated within 48 hours, we can review records to see whether this level of service was attained. The purpose of quality assurance reviews is to ensure that the agency or program is meeting its own standards of quality. Figure 10.4 shows a typical quality assurance review.

Summary of Evaluation Designs

Each design can be used to gather information useful for monitoring or evaluating interventions. Some are clearly more useful than others, depending upon the questions we want answered. Those focused on process will tell us little about the outcome of the intervention; outcome-focused designs won't tell us how we got the results we observed. To do an effective evaluation, we must consider our purpose before selecting a design. In the following section we will discuss the stages in evaluation and provide examples of useful instruments and tests.

Stages in Evaluation

Following the steps in an evaluation of a macro intervention is important to the success of your evaluation. Without a blueprint to follow and careful advance planning, it is easy to discover that no assessment of

EP 2.1.10m

QUALITY ASSURANCE CASE REVIEWS 7/1/04 TO 6/30/10						
ITEM	7/1/04 TO 6/30/05 MET	7/1/05 TO 6/30/06 MET	7/1/06 TO 6/30/07 MET	7/1/07 TO 6/30/08 MET	7/1/08 TO 6/30/09 MET	7/1/09 TO 6/30/10 MET
1. Required forms are completed on a timely basis.	73%	75%	85%	88%	93%	90%
2. Diagnosis is supported by clinical data.	100%	99%	99%	100%	100%	97%
3. Initial treatment plan case disposition is appropriate.	100%	99%	98%	100%	94%	93%
4. Ongoing treatment plan is appropriate.	85%	95%	97%	100%	99%	97%
5. Progress notes document implementation of treatment plan.	91%	96%	98%	97%	99%	96%
6. Consultation is obtained if appropriate.	92%	95%	98%	97%	100%	96%
7. Collateral and other providers are involved if appropriate.	96%	100%	100%	99%	100%	100%
8. Adequate follow-up is documented.	89%	95%	100%	100%	99%	97%
9. Adequate assessment of suicide or violence potential is documented.	95%	97%	97%	100%	99%	100%
10. Vocational rehabilitation needs are adequately assessed.	89%	94%	97%	91%	94%	94%
11. Discharge plans are documented.	91%	94%	98%	99%	100%	99%
AVERAGE	**90%**	**97%**	**97%**	**97%**	**98%**	**96%**

FIGURE 10.4 Quality Assurance Review

progress can be made. If you do not consider in advance what sort of records and data to collect, you may discover that you don't have the information needed to prove program effectiveness. The following sections will describe the steps to be followed in evaluating a macro intervention. These include (1) conceptualization and goal setting, (2) measurement, (3) sampling, (4) design,

(5) data gathering, (6) data analysis, and (7) data presentation (CSWE, 2008, EP 2.1.10m).

Stage 1: Conceptualization and Goal Setting

The conceptualization stage begins with agreement upon the goals to be achieved and the indicators of goal achievement to be employed (Rubin & Rubin, 1992). A goal is a "statement of observable effects that are expected from a set of actions" (Love, 1991, p. 87). If the goal is to deliver a minimum of 35 meals per week to older adult shut-ins living in Center City, the goal could be made even more specific by indicating that it must be reached by the end of the first year of operation. Normally, we prefer to start with a clear description of where we are and where we want to go. The "where we want to go" is the goal sought through our intervention. Measuring goal achievement is a process of comparing actual accomplishment to intended goals. Those goals may be quantitative (that is, measurable by some specific amount), such as providing shelter to 100 homeless persons in the first year, or qualitative (that is, without a set numerical target), such as increasing client satisfaction with services provided by the discharge planning unit. Goals may be set for individuals, units, or entire agencies. Likewise, goals may extend over any time period.

Establishing goals is not always easy. Sometimes the goal initially seems too hard to quantify or measure. A vague goal of increasing happiness or reducing stress is too general. Professional social work requires us to think more clearly about what we hope to accomplish. One common problem involves goals that are so poorly defined they cannot be measured. An agency's goal could be to improve the quality of life of community residents, but "quality of life" is undefined and can involve many different aspects. It is easy to see how evaluators might throw up their hands in disgust. Sometimes goals are unrelated to the actual service being delivered. Some youth agencies operate personal challenge programs, such as rock climbing, rappelling, and wilderness camping. These programs are typically provided to emotionally disturbed adolescents and delinquent youth. The goal in the latter case is to deter the youth from further delinquency, yet the service provided does not necessarily relate to this goal. Sometimes goals are never explicitly stated, only implied. A program might be based on an implicit belief that providing after-school recreational activities for adolescents can keep them from using drugs. Yet this goal is never actually articulated. Because measuring achievement of implied goals is very difficult, it is best to err on the side of explicitness. That is, try your best to state your goals clearly and unambiguously.

Feedback Systems

A *feedback system* is any method employed to help us know whether goals were achieved. We should be able to assess how we are doing in relation to either the starting point or the desired end point. The starting point might be established by using a baseline. The desired end point might be our stated goal. We need to establish a system for periodically gathering data to assess progress toward goals. Weekly or monthly reports on clients seen, problems encountered, services given, and outcomes achieved are typical feedback mechanisms. Evaluations often use benchmarks (short-term indicators of progress) that show how things are going. Feedback systems allow you to monitor your progress and avoid waiting until the last minute to decide whether you are moving in the right direction. You might expect that, by the end of the first quarter of the year, you would have served about 25 percent of the total number of clients you hoped to serve during the entire year. Comparing quarterly reports to this benchmark helps you know how you are doing and perhaps make needed changes.

All of these considerations lead to some general rules for planning an evaluation. These appear in Highlight 10.1.

Stage 2: Measurement

In the measurement stage, you refine the measures you will use to learn whether the stated goals have been accomplished. If you decide to evaluate a program to help people out of poverty, the poverty rate is one logical indicator. However, you will still need to determine which poverty rate to use and how the rate will be computed. If the goal is neighborhood improvement, you might use such measures as numbers of trees planted or neighborhood residents' perceptions about how the community looks.

The amount of time and effort staff members expend to implement a program is probably more difficult to measure than objective results, such as the number of trees planted in a neighborhood. By definition, objective measures are clear and easily interpreted. The more objective the measures, the higher the agreement rate about what they mean.

Of course, if the chosen indicators show no change over time, the intervention may have been unsuccessful—or you may have selected the wrong indicator. Using results of a client satisfaction survey to measure the effectiveness of an elder abuse program would be senseless—measuring changes in the frequency of abusive incidents would be much more meaningful. The author once asked employers to evaluate graduates of a particular social work program, only to find out that

HIGHLIGHT 10.1

Guidelines for Planning an Evaluation

Rule 1 :	Build in the plan for evaluation when developing the program.
Rule 2:	State program objectives clearly—avoid remarks like "to meet the needs of teenagers in Hooten" or "to improve the well-being of older adult residents." What does meeting the needs of teenagers mean? Which needs? How will you meet them? When will you be able to say you've achieved your goal and met the need? Likewise, how can you improve the well-being of older adult residents? What does well-being mean? Which older adult residents? How will you know when you have met your goal? A better example is "to reduce by 50 percent the number of truancies per month for children in the program." Fifty percent is a clearly established percentage. Similarly, you should be able to identify those teens involved in the program. You will have accomplished your goal when you achieve a 50 percent reduction in truancies, not 49 percent nor even 49.9 percent. Your stated goal here is very clear.
	Still another example of a well-written goal is "to increase by 33 percent the number of applications received from prospective foster parents." Once again, your numbers and expectations are very clear. You can very easily measure progress toward your goal.
Rule 3:	Select the indicators you will use to determine whether the objectives have been met. School attendance records would be good indicators for a truancy reduction program.
Rule 4:	Choose and use the correct tools and procedures—that is, focus on actual outcomes and people's perceptions rather than on other factors that won't tell you whether things have changed. Rely on official court records rather than on vague recollections of teachers or parents.
Rule 5:	Interpret the findings. First list the facts in a logical order. Second, list the questions that remain unanswered. Third, list your interpretations of the data. Fourth, provide recommendations with options showing the strengths and limitations of each option. Your findings should then point you in the right direction to continue improving your program.

the employers rated all the graduates in the upper 25 percent of social workers known to the employers. In fact, employers rated most graduates in the upper 10 percent. In this case, the indicator used was not sophisticated or sensitive enough to gauge accurately what we were trying to measure. Figure 10.5 lists problems or programs and possible outcome measures to assess achievement of objectives.

Quantitative evaluations offer certain kinds of information, but you might also consider using qualitative measures to gather other information. For example, your collection of data from police records indicates that 75 percent of the residents who completed their stay in a halfway house for convicted felons were not re-arrested. This would be useful quantitative data. However, if you wanted to learn why people dropped out of the program or what factors led some people to remain to the end, you would likely use a qualitative design. Such designs might involve interviewing each dropout or all participants to identify themes or factors characteristic of those who stayed and of those who dropped out.

Sometimes it is important to know whether the changes we observe are temporary or permanent. Because many programs produce temporary changes in behavior but no permanent modification (somewhat like our driving speed after we spot a police car behind us), they are considered less effective. We may also be concerned about unexpected consequences of our programs. Were people hurt by participating, or were problems exacerbated? Unanticipated consequences have been well documented in research and can have a very negative impact on clients.

Stage 3: Sampling

Sampling is the stage where we decide whether to gather data from all participants (recall that we refer to this group as "the population") or sample part of the population. Often, the costs of gathering data for an entire population are prohibitive. Frequently, it is unnecessary to gather data from everyone, because a well-selected sample can achieve the same results as gathering data from the entire population.

Problem or Program	Potential Outcome Measures
Child abuse	Recurrence of abuse within 12 months
Truancy from school	School attendance records
Inadequate minimum wage	Increase in state/federal minimum wage
Foster children separated from siblings	Percent of siblings placed together
Drug awareness program	Pre- or post-test of knowledge on drugs

FIGURE 10.5 Possible Outcome Measures

Good sampling follows rules and procedures that meet certain criteria. For example, the size of sample you will need is generally a function of population size, diversity of the population, and desired error level (small samples increase the possibility of error in the results). Experts often disagree on the optimum sample size, but there are formulas to use. Though some of the formulas are complicated, Austin, Cox, Gottlieb, Hawkins, Kruzich, and Rauch (1982) say a sample size of one-tenth of the population is sufficient to eliminate most sampling errors. Yet other authors argue that a sample size of 50 percent or larger is required to rule out error. Mailed surveys (used frequently to gather opinions and data) often get return rates well below this level. An effective means of deciding appropriate sample size involves using the software package SPSS (Statistical Package for the Social Sciences).

A particular type of sampling, random sampling (discussed earlier in this chapter), is commonly used in evaluation. Two additional types are worthy of mention: systematic and stratified sampling.

Systematic Random Sampling

This method simply divides the population by the desired sample size. For a population of 500 families served by your agency, you decide to survey a sample of 100. You compute that 500 divided by 100, of course, is 5—so you will select every fifth person from the population for inclusion in the sample. Some bias could creep in if there were something characteristic about every fifth person that was not true of the rest of the population. That risk, however, is relatively small, and you would still retain some of the advantages of a random sample.

Stratified Random Sampling

Stratified random sampling is used in special situations. For example, you might want to explore the worker–client experiences of the clients your agency serves.

However, your agency serves only a very small percentage of minority clients, and you are especially interested in their views. A simple random sample might leave you with no minority clients because they compose such a small percentage of the total client population. To avoid this, you might want to ensure that minority clients are proportionately represented in your sample. To do this you can assign numbers to both minority and nonminority clients and, using a table of random numbers (located in most statistics texts), select a proportionate number of minority clients. (A table of random numbers is a list of numbers produced by a computer and is used for selection of random sample members.) If your agency serves 1,000 and only 100 (10 percent) are minorities, then 10 percent of your sample should also be minority. This will help ensure that the sample is representative of the entire population.

As mentioned earlier, random samples allow us to say within a given range of accuracy whether the results we observed in the sample are typical for the entire population. Systematic random sampling and stratified random sampling are just two of the random sampling approaches available.

Stage 4: Design

The design stage is concerned with selecting an appropriate design and eliminating other possible explanations for the observed outcomes (Rubin & Rubin, 1992). As we have seen, many different designs are available to help us evaluate the effectiveness of our programs. Each design has strengths and limitations. Some are easier to use than others, but the others may produce more valid and reliable results. You need to rule out certain other explanations for changes that occur. A drug treatment program that selects only the most promising candidates is likely to be *creaming,* or selecting the "cream of the crop." When this happens, its results may reflect the characteristics of this group of people rather than substantiating the success of the program. As a result, one cannot say with assurance that the program will work on other populations.

Similarly, *maturation* may explain certain outcomes. Maturation is an internal process in which time itself affects the client. A group of children who become less hyperactive as they grow older may simply be maturing. Hyperactive behavior may decrease just because they're aging. Their behavioral changes have little to do with the program in which they are participating and much more to do with their developmental stage. A variety of factors besides creaming and maturation affect outcomes, although these are perhaps the two most common.

You can sometimes rule out these extraneous factors more easily by using control or comparison groups. Likewise, you can randomly select those who are involved in your interventions. Frequently, however, you must accept the possibility that other factors may account for the changes observed.

Several designs help control for alternative explanations; others do not. We identified some of these designs earlier. The list in Highlight 10.2 provides additional information on these and other common designs, discussing their respective strengths and limitations.

Stage 5: Data Gathering

Data gathered for evaluating whether goals are achieved or not can come from several sources. Data may include direct observation by the worker, written surveys sent to clients, interviews with clients or others, and reviews of existing data sources (such as census figures). Some data focus on the program's individual participants, and some collect more global types of information (such as official government records). At the individual level, a worker can review case notes or other official records to learn whether expected outcomes were achieved. If a program was designed to help unemployed workers find adequately paying jobs, agency records may show whether clients reached this goal. Reviewing case records one by one may be an adequate source of data for this evaluation.

Other data sources are family, friends, and others who have the necessary knowledge about the clients. You may ask their opinions, ratings, or observations of clients. For example, consider an agency program focused on anger control for teens. Parents may be the best source of data regarding whether the program is successfully changing their children's behavior.

Workers can also detect changes themselves by observing clients in their natural settings. Observations of schoolchildren on the playground or in the classroom may help a school social worker learn whether group activities are resulting in improved peer interactions. Finally, the actual measurement of identified variables is a source of data. Exam scores, changes shown on instruments or scales, and similar measures allow the identification of changes taking place over a given time period.

Data sources are largely aimed at determining whether changes have taken place in individual program participants. There are, of course, other useful sources of data for gauging broader changes. Such sources are described in Figure 10.6.

Data from all of the sources just listed may allow us to decide whether broad changes are occurring in a community or larger area. You might want to find out whether a community-wide program to immunize children against a specific disease is working. You could compare incidence of the disease before and after the immunization program was carried out. Another example involves efforts to thwart criminals targeting urban older adults. You can assess such efforts by reviewing law enforcement records of crimes reported to the police before and after the anticrime program was initiated (CSWE, 2008, EP 2.1.3a).

EP 2.1.3a

Instruments, Tests, and Scales

Evaluating a program's effectiveness is often facilitated when the agency already uses standardized instruments for the quantitative analysis of clients' progress. These instruments can measure specific variables. There are instruments that measure critical thinking and such intangibles as knowledge, attitudes, and behavior. The latter focus mostly on changes in individuals. A community program aimed at preventing or reducing suicidal behavior by teenagers might utilize an instrument to measure changes in suicidal thoughts or depression. Environmental change measures, such as the Oregon Quality of Life Scale (Bigelow, Brodesky, Steward, & Olson, 1982), assess whether living conditions and other quality-of-life issues for the client have improved. Such environmental change measures are focused not on the individual's thoughts and feelings, but on tangible changes in such things as quality of housing and access to resources.

Locating measurement instruments can be easy or difficult, depending upon what you are trying to measure.

HIGHLIGHT 10.2

Six Common Evaluation Designs

Pre-Experimental Designs

1. *One-Group Post-Test-Only Design.*

    By definition, a one-group post-test design involves a single group in which progress is measured only at the end of the intervention. You could use such a design to evaluate the effects of a community drug abuse prevention program. Program participants are adolescents considered at-risk because of their home situations. Asking "graduates" of the program to complete an anonymous survey describing their drug use following participation in the program could be the post-test. If reported drug use was low or nonexistent (and participants were honest), we might conclude that the program was effective.

    The lack of a control group and of long-term follow-up are potential problems, however. Other factors may be responsible for the absence of drug use. Because no baseline of prior drug use existed, participants may never have been into drugs. Moreover, the lack of drug use might turn out to be very temporary.

    With some post-test-only designs, we don't really know whether the clients changed, because we have no information on them prior to the intervention. A test of knowledge about illegal drugs given to a group of adolescents following a training program does not prove that their knowledge improved, because group leaders don't know the level of their knowledge before they participated in the training program.

2. *Post-Test-Only Design with Nonequivalent Groups.*

    This design employs a comparison group that we hope will be similar to our experimental group. Of course, the two groups may not be similar on the variables that matter. Consider a treatment group for adolescent delinquents. You might include in the comparison group others of the same age, gender, or life experiences (such as a history of delinquent behavior). The second group allows you to compare results in the experimental group (which received an intervention) with those in the comparison group (which did not). If the experimental group improves (such as by engaging in fewer incidents of school truancy or gang-related behavior), you might claim the intervention program was responsible for the changes.

3. *One-Group Pre-Test/Post-Test Design.*

    This model assesses change overtime using the same test or a variation of the same test at two points. It works best when you can measure something such as knowledge, attitudes, and so on with a specific instrument. Again, it is difficult to know what caused the change over time. Unlike the post-test-only design, however, we have greater reason to believe the intervention produced the change.

Quasi-Experimental Designs

Several types of quasi-experimental designs may be employed in evaluating outcomes. These include non-equivalent control-group designs, time-series designs, and multiple time-series designs.

1. *Nonequivalent control group designs* use two groups, both of which are given pre-tests and post-tests. The groups are similar on important variables (such as gender and age), but there is no random assignment. This method allows us to rule out some alternative explanations for outcomes because we have tried to control for such things as creaming, maturation, and so on.

2. *Time-series designs* use a series of observations before and after an intervention to gather longitudinal data to help spot patterns occurring overtime. This model works when real control groups cannot be used or are not available.

3. *Multiple time-series designs* are essentially the time-series design with an added control group. They are best for ruling out alternative explanations for observed changes, because differences between the untreated control group and the experimental group are more likely the result of the intervention received by the latter.

Experimental Designs

An ideal model, experimental designs are most difficult to use in actual practice. Such designs require both random assignment of subjects and a control group that receives no (or different) treatment to compare with the treatment group.

SOURCE: Royse (2004).

TYPE OF DATA	TYPE OF AGENCY
Census data	U.S. Department of Commerce
Housing data	U.S. Department of Housing and Urban Development
	Local housing authority
Local employment situations and community needs and plans	Regional planning council
Disease incidence prevalence	State/local health departments
	Centers for Disease Control and Prevention
Local needs assessment and community goals	The United Way
	Regional planning council
Archives and public records	Public libraries

FIGURE 10.6 Sources of Data

Sometimes a professional journal article will mention an instrument and direct you to where you can find information about it. Other times you might need to consult some of the excellent resources referred to in Figure 10.7 that describe and explain many appropriate instruments.

We will not begin to describe the host of difficulties involved in constructing your own instruments and questionnaires. It is a much more efficient use of your time (and increases the validity and reliability of the instrument) to use existing instruments whenever possible. Factors important in instrument selection are

Corcoran, K., & Fischer, J. (2007). *Measures for clinical practice and research* (4th ed.). New York: Oxford University Press.

Fayers, P. M., & Machin, D. (2000). *Quality of life: Assessment, analysis and interpretation.* New York: John Wiley.

Goldman, B. A., & Mitchell, D. F. (2002). *Directory of unpublished experimental mental measures,* Volume 8. Washington, DC: American Psychological Association.

Jordan, C., & Franklin, C. (2003). *Clinical assessment for social workers* (2nd ed.). Chicago: Lyceum.

Maddox, T. (2008). *Tests: A comprehensive reference for assessments, in psychology, education, and business* (6th ed.). Austin, TX: Pro-Ed.

McDowell, I. (2006). *Measuring health: A guide to rating scales and questionnaires* (3rd ed.). New York: Oxford University Press.

Touliatos, J., Perlmutter, B. F., & Straus, M. A. (2001). *Handbook of family measurement techniques.* Newbury Park, CA: Sage.

FIGURE 10.7 Sources of Measurement Instruments and Tests

validity, reliability, the sensitivity of the instrument to any changes caused by the intervention, length of the instrument, difficulty level for the client, and ease of use. We have already discussed the importance of reliability and validity with respect to research. It is equally important that the instrument actually reflect changes that took place following your intervention. An instrument not sensitive enough to assess changes in assertiveness following an assertiveness training program would not help evaluate that program. Logically, you would seek an instrument that was not too long (people refuse to fill out very long instruments) or too difficult. If an instrument uses language and grammar appropriate for college graduates, it might be inappropriate for those without this education. Ease of use is important because complicated or difficult instruments are less likely to be completed by the respondent.

Finally, instruments should not themselves cause changes by leading a client to respond in a certain way (Royse, 2004). Most good instruments ask questions in a neutral manner and give no clues as to the "right" answers. Most scales and instruments are copyrighted and have some restrictions on their use. Consequently, you must seek permission to use them. Figures 10.8 and 10.9 show two scales that are not copyrighted.

The CES-D Scale was developed to help measure depression and its symptoms. The instrument asks respondents to react to 20 statements concerning behavior related to depression. Respondents are asked to indicate one of the following: "rarely or none of the time"; "some or a little of the time"; "occasionally or a moderate amount of time"; or "most or all of the time." Past evaluations of the instrument have found acceptable levels of validity and reliability (Royse, 2004).

As you might expect, responses to this instrument have different weights. A 0 (zero) is given for any response of "rarely or none of the time." A "most of the time" response receives 3 points. The statements numbered 4, 8, 12, and 16 are given reverse scores (in other words, 0 points for "most of the time" and 3 for "rarely"). These statements are positive-sounding items (unlike the others), and scoring must be reversed to maintain consistency with the negative items in the instrument. Total scores on the instrument may range from a low of 0 to a high of 60. Obviously, the higher the score, the more likely the person is to have symptoms of depression. If you were evaluating a program that provided intervention to clients experiencing symptoms associated with depression, an instrument like this might serve as a pre-test and post-test to determine changes following the intervention.

Circle the number for each statement that best describes how often you felt or behaved this way during the past week.

	RARELY OR NONE OF THE TIME (Less than 1 day)	SOME OR A LITTLE OF THE TIME (1–2 days)	OCCASIONALLY OR A MODERATE AMOUNT OF THE TIME (3–4 days)	MOST OR ALL OF THE TIME (5–7 days)
DURING THE PAST WEEK:				
1. I was bothered by things that usually don't bother me.				
2. I did not feel like eating; my appetite was poor.				
3. I felt that I could not shake off the blues even with help from my family or friends.				
4. I felt that I was just as good as other people.				
5. I had trouble keeping my mind on what I was doing.				
6. I felt depressed.				
7. I felt that everything that I did was an effort.				
8. I felt hopeful about the future.				
9. I thought my life had been a failure.				
10. I felt fearful.				
11. My sleep was restless.				
12. I was happy.				
13. I talked less than usual.				
14. I felt lonely.				
15. People were unfriendly.				
16. I enjoyed life.				
17. I had crying spells.				
18. I felt sad.				
19. I felt that people disliked me.				
20. I could not "get going."				

SOURCE: Royse (2004).

FIGURE 10.8 CES-D Scale

Another noncopyrighted scale is the Rosenberg Self-Esteem Scale illustrated in Figure 10.9. This is a normed instrument that allows comparisons of those who complete it with a broader population. Normed instruments have been given to normal or typical populations and give us a measure of how the average person responds. This instrument asks respondents to indicate strong agreement, agreement, disagreement, or strong disagreement in reaction to 10 statements involving self-esteem. Scores on this instrument range from 1 to 4. The statements 1, 3, 4, 7, and 10 are scored in reverse by giving a response of 4 for "strongly agree" and 1 for "strongly disagree." Scores range from 10 to 40 points, with higher scores reflecting greater self-esteem. This instrument has good validity and reliability scores.

Instructions: Below is a list of statements dealing with your general feelings about yourself. If you agree with the statement, circle A. If you strongly agree, circle SA. If you disagree, circle D. If you strongly disagree, circle SD.

	AGREE	STRONGLY AGREE	DISAGREE	STRONGLY DISAGREE
1. On the whole, I am satisfied with myself.	A	SA	D	SD
2. At times I think I am no good at all.	A	SA	D	SD
3. I feel that I have a number of good qualities.	A	SA	D	SD
4. I am able to do things as well as most other people.	A	SA	D	SD
5. I feel I do not have much to be proud of.	A	SA	D	SD
6. I certainly feel useless at times.	A	SA	D	SD
7. I feel that I'm a person of worth, at least on an equal plane with others.	A	SA	D	SD
8. I wish I could have more respect for myself.	A	SA	D	SD
9. All in all, I am inclined to think that I am a failure.	A	SA	D	SD
10. I take a positive attitude toward myself.	A	SA	D	SD

SOURCE: Royse (2004).

FIGURE 10.9 Rosenberg Self-Esteem Scale

Stage 6: Data Analysis

Data analysis is the actual process of assessing the nature and significance of the results obtained. Some types of analysis are relatively simple and straightforward. You may only be interested in explaining single variables *(univariate analysis)* and descriptive statistics (mean, median). Thus, your analysis may concern the mean number of homeless people a program serves per day and the median age of shelter residents. This level of data analysis requires relatively little skill and no sophisticated computers. You can simply count the people the program serves and calculate the median of shelter residents' ages. You might not even need your calculator.

A higher level of analysis is *bivariate analysis,* which determines the degree of association between two variables. You might explore the potential relationship between the number of times a social worker sees a client and the success the client has in finding a job. Here we are looking at two variables (number of service hours provided to the client and client's job-seeking success). We might discover that there is a close positive relationship between these two variables: The more frequently workers see individual clients, the more likely these clients are to successfully find employment. You could also find that there was no relationship between number of meetings and job-finding outcome. You might even find a negative relationship between the two variables—the more contact clients have with workers, the less successful they are in finding jobs. This relationship would not appear in a univariate analysis, because univariate analysis explores only one variable. You can use bivariate analysis without the aid of computers, but the availability of software packages such as SPSS and SASS (Statistical Analysis for the Social Sciences) makes computations much easier.

A third level, *multivariate analysis,* examines three or more variables in relation to one another. A common multivariate technique is *regression analysis,* a statistical procedure to determine how much of a change is due to the event under your control (independent variables) and how much to other factors. If the income of people in the job training program increases 10 percent following six months of training, it appears that the program is successful. Assume, however, that the income level of people in the comparison group also goes up, but this change is simply due to inflation. Regression analysis would help determine the actual amount of the increase attributable to the job training program and the amount attributable to inflation. Multivariate analysis generally requires use of a computer and statistical software (such as SPSS or SASS) designed specifically for this level of analysis.

Stage 7: Data Presentation

The presentation of data must clearly communicate the evaluation's results to your intended audience. Written reports should contain a brief single-page (if possible) "Executive Summary" that highlights the evaluation's most significant findings. Conclusions should flow from the findings. Be prepared for reactions from those who are unhappy with the findings. There is often a tendency for workers to be defensive about our programs, especially when they are viewed unfavorably by others. The final evaluation report will likely contain six sections (Royse, 2004): (1) introduction,

(2) literature review, (3) methodology, (4) results, (5) discussion, and (6) references and appendices. Each section is described next.

Part 1: Introduction

The introductory section reviews the situation that prompted the evaluation in the first place. Here you describe the research questions you want answered. "Did the community education program on child abuse increase the number of reports of suspected abuse and neglect filed with the Department of Human Services in the two months following introduction of the program?" Or "Does an eight-week, self-esteem group for at-risk 13-year-olds reduce the number of times these adolescents are referred to the school social worker for disruptive classroom behavior?" Or "Did the implementation of a neighborhood watch program in the Jabberwocky School area reduce the number of burglaries and thefts reported in this neighborhood?"

Part 2: Literature Review

The literature review should provide a thorough summary of existing research on the topic under consideration. The purpose of the literature review is to ensure that you are familiar with previous research related to your intervention. For example, if previous research shows that a particular approach or program has not been effective, this information should be described in the literature review. At the same time, prior studies that indicate effectiveness of the same program you are evaluating should be reported.

Because of the potential wealth of material available through electronic sources and databases, CD-ROM-based documents, and full-text retrieval through the Internet, you may well have to be very specific about what ends up in your literature review. In some cases you will need to focus carefully on the specific program in use (e.g., self-esteem groups for teens) rather than group interventions for teens. If relatively little information is available on a topic, that point should be included in your literature review. The lack of prior research on an intervention approach can underscore the importance of doing your own evaluation.

Part 3: Methodology

The methodology section describes the evaluation design and the data collection methods used. If pre- and post-tests without a control group were used, this should be stated. If you gathered data using a self-report form completed by program participants, report this. Likewise, if you used agency records as your primary data source, indicate that. Also state whether you sampled the population or used the entire population for data collection. Explain what sampling system you used. Identify any instruments, scales, or surveys you used and describe to the readers the study's subjects. Finally, discuss the data analysis system selected (univariate, bivariate, multivariate).

Part 4: Results

The results component describes your findings with appropriate graphics (charts, graphs) and reports on the findings' importance. Data may be displayed using line graphs, bar charts, three-dimensional bar charts, and pie charts. Figure 10.10 depicts a pair of pie charts comparing the expected and actual demographic breakdowns of homeless shelter residents. The shelter expected the resident population to consist of 58 percent single males, 25 percent single females, and 17 percent families with children. The actual population consisted of 50 percent families with children, 34 percent single females, and 16 percent single males. Imagine the implications for the program of these findings. How would a client population of primarily women and children require different attention and services than one made up primarily of single men?

Figure 10.11 shows a line graph and a three-dimensional bar chart, each depicting the same information. Charts and graphs can be varied to clearly show the results achieved. A bar chart can be used to visually compare changes in the shelter's population across two or more years. A line graph can easily show trends. Generally speaking, you will choose the type of chart that most clearly communicates your data to the reader. Your goal is always clarity.

Part 5: Discussion

The discussion section briefly summarizes your findings, describes any unexpected findings, and describes any practice implications. Your findings might suggest that the program you are evaluating is not serving the originally intended population. Unexpected findings might include such things as the fact that agency policies are actually making the situation worse and forcing clients to seek help elsewhere. Practice implications might include information such as which intervention worked best with a certain group of clients.

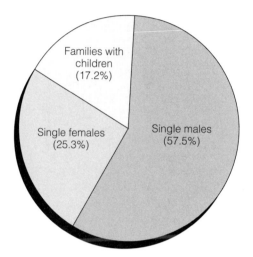

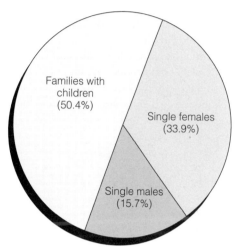

FIGURE 10.10 Pie Charts

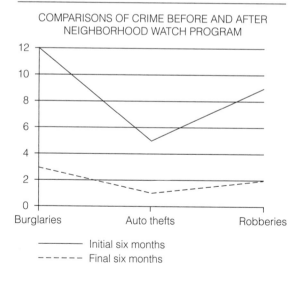

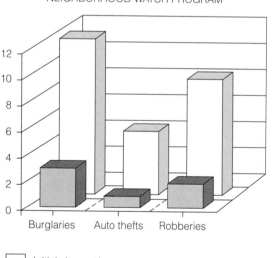

FIGURE 10.11 Line Graph and Three-Dimensional Bar Chart

Finally, describe any limitations of the research. One limitation might be that because subjects were not selected randomly, the results cannot be generalized to any other group. Another limitation might be that the size of the sample was too small.

Part 6: References and Appendices

References include any sources (books, journal articles, and similar items) you consulted in preparing and conducting your evaluation. Perhaps you consulted a statistics book to look up an explanation or definition for a particular method or test. References also include all the literature sources cited at the beginning of the study and any works you quote within the study.

Appendices might include any documents too large to fit into the study itself. For example, a copy of a questionnaire might appear in the appendix. Related reports might also be included in an appendix. So also might letters sent to accompany surveys or to inform clients about a program, and any details too involved for inclusion in the basic report.

Summary of Data Presentation

EP 2.1.3c

Always present data as clearly as possible. Think carefully about what to say and how to say it. Use your common sense. If the report is to be read by people with little background in the field (perhaps members of the board of directors), consider how to make the information as easily understood as possible. Trying to impress the readers may end up confusing them. Most people will ignore unclear results. Any tables used in the report should be numbered and titled. Columns of data need headings to tell readers what is presented below. Similarly, rows in a chart should have headings providing helpful information. Again, recognize that different audiences may require different presentations. For example, decision makers may want a brief summary rather than a 457-page report. Public presentation of data requires more use of graphics than might be required for a written report. For example, you might wish to use overhead slides or handouts summarizing data, because reading data from a report can be excruciatingly boring—to you and to your audience (CSWE, 2008, EP 2.1.3c).

Ethics and Values in Evaluation

Royse (2004) provides some excellent guidelines for maintaining ethical standards while doing evaluations. He stresses that, whenever you contemplate using subjects as part of the evaluation (such as when interviewing or testing), those subjects must be volunteers. Any person volunteering should know the risks (if any) associated with participation. Of course, no one should be harmed because of participating in the evaluation. The privacy of participants should be zealously protected. There have been many examples in the popular press and in various governmental reports of well-meaning practitioners failing to inform clients

adequately of the risks to which they were being exposed. In some cases, evaluators have deliberately concealed information from participants. Our ethical obligation to clients must guide our interventions and our evaluations.

The NASW *Code of Ethics* informs our research efforts in several ways. First, it is a social worker's obligation to stay current with relevant research and ensure that clients receive the most effective assistance possible. We also have an obligation to contribute to the development of knowledge in our field. When we are considering engaging in research or evaluation projects, we must protect clients. Today, all major organizations require a careful consideration of the potential harm that might come to people by virtue of their participation in our research. Human subject committees or Institutional Review Boards now routinely review research proposals that may expose people to emotional or physical danger. Social workers must be prepared to meet with such committees and to always consider ways to ensure that no one is hurt either by participating or refusing to participate in a research project. Of course, clients usually have the right to refuse services. Each client must understand the purpose of the service being provided, any risks involved, their right to refuse now or later, and their right to question what is happening to them. When clients are not capable of making these decisions, it is our responsibility to seek a third party who can act in the clients' best interest. Although some situations give clients little in the way of options (for example, involuntary services), the client should still know the consequences of refusing to participate.

Clients also must give permission before audio or videotaping contact with them or before letting a third party observe sessions. Any written record that reflects contact with clients should be protected. This prevents unauthorized access, even for benign purposes such as evaluating service effectiveness. Client confidentiality is equally important in the evaluation process. The NASW *Code of Ethics* standards in this area may sound stringent, but they are designed to prevent serious harm to clients and to end the misuse of research participants that has occurred over the years.

Ethical standards are not the only area affecting research; our values play a role. Sometimes values can become a barrier to effective action following an evaluation. This can happen, for example, when we refuse to recognize that cost factors do enter into the decision-making process. If it costs too much to help individual clients deal with their problems, we should consider abandoning the program and spending the money on a program that has a payoff. Although sentiments such as "If it helps one person, I'm satisfied" may show your heart is in the right place, this is not an acceptable response when it comes time to measure results. Few funding agencies will continue supporting programs of dubious effectiveness or efficiency when more promising approaches are available.

EP 2.1.2

Perhaps the most important ethical consideration for doing an evaluation is our obligation to clients. We have a duty to ensure that clients are given the most effective interventions possible and that programs are based on solid research, not on hunches, feelings, or other gut-level reactions. We also can learn from our evaluations. For example, a program or intervention that proves successful in one setting might prove effective in another situation. Program evaluation data can help us identify programs that are likely to be applicable to different groups in the same setting or to similar groups in different settings. This is consistent with our professional obligation to continue enhancing the knowledge base of social work practice (CSWE, 2008, EP 2.1.2).

Chapter Summary

The following summarizes this chapter's content as it relates to the learning objectives presented at the beginning of the chapter. Chapter content prepares social workers to:

A. *Recognize the context of program evaluation.*

Evaluation of programs is designed to determine whether the change effort was worthwhile. It helps answer questions such as "Does this program work?" It is an ethical obligation of each social worker to engage in evaluation of his or her own effectiveness and participate in the agency's efforts to determine efficacy. Absent proof that a program works, funding agencies are likely to turn their attention and resources to other activities that can prove their effectiveness. In addition, evaluation enhances social work's credibility vis-a-vis other professionals with whom we work.

B. *Utilize concepts important in the evaluation process.*

Key concepts in the evaluation process include experimental and control groups, dependent and independent variables, sampling, experimental and quasi-experimental designs, and baseline. It is also important to understand the meaning of concepts such as mean, median, and mode and standard deviation. Reliability and validity are important terms when using instruments and other measures that are designed to determine whether changes have taken place. Social workers also employ descriptive statistics such as the average age of a population, and inferential statistics are used to draw a conclusion or inference about a population.

Other terms important for social workers to know include outcomes (quality-of-life changes) and outcome measures. The latter is simply the means by which we determine the actual outcome of an intervention. One outcome measure in an employment agency might be successful attainment of employment lasting at least six months. Finally, we need to understand two other concepts, statistical significance and the chi-square test. The former is a measure of the risk that exists when we generalize from a sample to the population. We often refer to an evaluation finding as being statistically significant, meaning that it is unlikely that the results we obtained occurred by chance. The chi-square test is simply a statistical procedure that we use to compare the expected frequencies in a study to the actual observed frequencies. It is an important tool in knowing whether the results we obtained are similar to those found in the general population.

C. *Use program evaluation research to inform practice.*

Social workers use evaluation research to inform practice because as we learn what works and what does not work, we change our programs and methods to reflect these findings. Social workers who fail to utilize the results of research on program effectiveness are doing a disservice to their clients and agencies and are in violation of their ethical responsibilities. It is our responsibility as social workers to keep current with new literature in our field, inform our supervisors and others of our findings, and work to ensure that our practices and programs are the best they can be.

D. *Identify barriers to and problems in completing evaluations.*

Many barriers and problems can occur in the process of program evaluation. We may fail to plan adequately for an evaluation and be left without the tools needed to conduct the assessment. We may also be attempting to evaluate a program that has become a moving target. A lack of program stability can result in our measuring a hodge-podge of interventions, as staff and methods of interventions have changed over time.

Another barrier is the tension that sometimes develops between practitioners and evaluators, whose primary roles are different. This is lessened when it is the practitioner who conducts the evaluation since the same person is doing both jobs. Reducing this tension is possible through a variety of techniques.

Sometimes an evaluation produces results that are equivocal or unclear. This is a problem because we always hope for clear outcomes that show what we are doing is effective. It can also produce bad feelings when the organization that sponsored the evaluation ends up with results that don't help stakeholders in their decision making.

In some situations the results obtained are simply not acceptable. Many stakeholders hold strong beliefs and opinions about the worth of a particular program, and results that challenge these are not welcomed. A legislator, for example, might be upset that the research did not show that privatizing the state prison system was a good idea. Since this clashed with his political agenda, the study results and the research are both rejected.

Some evaluations are not worth doing. This may occur because the intervention was a one-time event, or will not produce useful data. The absence of adequate records may make any attempt at evaluation a waste of time and money.

E. *Describe and analyze different models of evaluation.*

Social workers may be involved in different kinds and models of evaluation. These include formative or monitoring evaluations that focus on the process rather than the outcome of an evaluation. The intent may be to see whether the process has occurred in the way it was supposed to. Summative or impact evaluations are focused on measuring the consequences or outcomes of services provided. These evaluations want to answer the question of effectiveness—did it work?

Two other types of evaluation exist, effectiveness and efficiency. The former is designed to learn whether an intervention was effective, while the other is interested in whether the outcomes were achieved at a reasonable cost.

Evaluations may involve quantitative or qualitative methods or both. The first uses objective (numerical) criteria such as test scores to measures changes over time. The second is focused on the experience of a particular group such as clients. Using smaller numbers of cases and going into greater depth, qualitative research can be used to better understand how a program effected those it was designed to help. In many cases, both methods are used in evaluation.

The designs we select for an evaluation may be of several kinds. We may use one-group post-test designs that look at a single target group and how they have fared following intervention. A better approach is to use a pre-test/post-test design that compares data from before the intervention to changes following it. An example might be to compare crime incidents in a particular neighborhood before and after implementing a community policing program.

If our particular goal is to learn the degree to which our clients or community members are pleased with an intervention, one method available is a client satisfaction survey. It is not an effective measure of whether an intervention worked, but it does get the opinions of stakeholders about the intervention.

Other methods employed for evaluating programs include goal attainment scaling, target problem scaling, case studies, group comparisons, and quality assurance reviews. Each focuses on measuring different aspects of an intervention and can often be used both in program and practice evaluation activities.

F. *Utilize the stages and steps in performing an evaluation.*

The stages in evaluation include the following: conceptualization and goal setting, measurement, sampling, design, data gathering, data analysis, and data presentation. Each step is essential if the results are to be of greatest value to the stakeholders. For example, poor conceptualization or sloppy data gathering can ruin an evaluation. A poor job of presenting the data can be demoralizing to stakeholders and undermine an otherwise sound evaluation.

G. *Demonstrate effective professional communication in presenting evaluation data.*

Accurately communicating data results is expected of anyone charged with responsibility for this stage in an evaluation. A professional–quality report should include an introduction, a review of the literature, a description of methodology, the results obtained, and a discussion. It should be followed by appropriate references and appendices. Each section except the first should naturally follow from the previous section so that the results or findings lead naturally into the discussion. Data must be presented as clearly as possible with due consideration of the audience. Jargon should be eliminated where possible, and public presentation of data will likely require greater use of graphics than a written report.

H. *Make ethical decisions in evaluation that are based upon the values and ethics of the NASW Code of Ethics.*

Ethical decision making by evaluators involves attention to several items. This includes the individual's right to choose to participate, clear explanation of any risks inherent in participating in the research, protection of participant rights through use of human subject review panels, avoidance of harm to those who do participate, and security measures designed to protect client-identifiable information from unauthorized individuals or groups. In the final analysis, clients should expect that we will always have their best interests foremost in our minds. This includes our participation in research designed to learn whether our interventions and programs are as effective as they can be.

Competency Notes

The following identifies where Educational Policy (EP) competencies and practice behaviors are discussed in the chapter.

Educational Policy (EP) 2.1 Core Competencies

Educational Policy (EP) 2.1.2 Apply social work ethical principles to guide professional practice. *(P. 389):* Ethics and values play a crucial role in how social workers design and carry out evaluations and the ways in which they communicate their findings.

Educational Policy (EP) 2.1.3a Distinguish, appraise, and integrate multiple sources of knowledge, including research-based knowledge and practice wisdom. *(P. 381):* Social workers gathering data in an evaluation must carefully consider the appropriateness and utility of the various sources of information available to them.

Educational Policy (EP) 2.1.3c Demonstrate effective oral and written communication in working with individuals, families, groups, organizations, communities, and colleagues. *(P. 388):* Presentation of data and evaluation results must be of professional quality and be communicated appropriately to different audiences.

Educational Policy (EP) 2.1.6 Engage in research-informed practice and practice-informed research. *(P. 360):* Careful evaluation requires both the use of appropriate research tools as well as designing programs in a way that facilitates evaluation. *(P. 362):* Key concepts from the research field that are applicable to evaluation of programs include control group, experimental group, dependent and independent variables, sampling, random sample, experimental and quasi-experimental design, baseline, mean, median, mode, standard deviation, reliability, validity, descriptive and inferential statistics, outcome and outcome measures, statistical significance, and chi-square test. *(P. 370):* The kinds of evaluations we undertake are usually influenced by the program we are trying to evaluate.

Educational Policy (EP) 2.1.7a Utilize conceptual frameworks to guide the processes of assessment, intervention, and evaluation. *(P. 372):* Among the conceptual models that are available for evaluating practice and social programs are qualitative and quantitative evaluations, as well as various designs that include one-group post-test, pre-test/post-test, client satisfaction surveys, goal attainment scaling, target problem scaling, case studies, group comparisons, and quality assurance reviews.

Educational Policy (EP) 2.1.10m Critically analyze, monitor, and evaluate interventions. *(P. 367):* It is important to think critically about the potential problems and barriers that may be encountered when considering evaluation of a program or service. Not all programs can be evaluated effectively and sometimes evaluation would be a waste of time. *(P. 376):* Evaluating interventions often incorporates the steps of conceptualization and goal setting, measurement, sampling, design, data gathering, data analysis, and data presentation.

On the Internet

Visit the *Generalist Practice with Organizations and Communities* Web site at www.cengage.com/social_work/kirst-ashman for learning tools such as PowerPoint® slides, tutorial quizzing, Web links, and final exams.

CHAPTER 11

Advocacy and Social Action with Populations-at-Risk

Andrea Munoz was beside herself. After working for years providing shelter and food to the homeless at the downtown complex called The Pantry, she had gotten used to handling problems. She had built The Pantry into the main supplier of shelter and food to the homeless in Orange Harbor using a variety of techniques. Indeed, The Pantry was a remarkable social agency with a wonderful history of working with businesses in the neighborhood and with other social service agencies. Her success at raising funds and acquiring other resources for the shelter was legendary.

Now the very success of The Pantry was causing a problem. Many of the homeless people who learned of The Pantry arrived in old vehicles that they parked on the street and in the nearby municipal lot. Some slept in their vehicles when there was no room in the old hotel Andrea used for sheltering the homeless. Herein lay the problem.

The neighborhood in which The Pantry was located was a mixture of small businesses and older homes. Locals called the area Parkside because it was adjacent to a large city park. The Parkside Integrity Group (PIG) was a neighborhood association begun several years earlier to deal with a variety of local problems. As PIG became more effective, it successfully produced many changes in the neighborhood. These included better street lighting, more police patrols, and a decrease in drug use and dealing in the area. Now PIG decided that its next project was to reduce the number of homeless people sleeping in their cars in the neighborhood. Well-organized and vocal, the association approached the city council with a petition requesting an ordinance prohibiting overnight parking without a permit. They claimed that sleeping in cars overnight was a common occurrence among homeless people congregating near the central city's two largest shelters and food kitchens. By discouraging this, the neighborhood association hoped to improve the quality of life in its low-income neighborhood. At the same time, The Pantry wanted to give the homeless the same rights due all the community's citizens, namely, worth and dignity. Unfortunately, PIG—an organization that had helped the neighborhood address such problems as reducing crime, drug abuse, and residential deterioration—ended up targeting the homeless population. The homeless clearly became an oppressed group in the community of Orange Harbor. In essence, PIG was trying to evict them from the community.

The city council weighed the needs of two competing groups and voted to ban overnight parking without a permit. This effectively prevented the homeless from using perhaps their last resource, their vehicles. Andrea had lost this battle to the NIMBY Syndrome—Not in My Back Yard. NIMBY is the strange malady in which people support group homes and similar facilities in principle as long as they are not located in their own neighborhoods. The Pantry clients' and other homeless people's lack of political power made the city council's ruling a foregone conclusion. In a struggle between taxpayers, homeowners, and the homeless, the latter almost always lose. In other words, those with the power are almost always able to oppress or subjugate those without power. The homeless have no power.

Introduction

Longres (1995) has argued that social workers cannot afford to blame victims for their situation; neither can they blame the environment or society. A more rational approach is to assess the interaction between the environment and the individual to determine where the problems lie. This process is at the heart of generalist social work practice.

At the same time, social workers must recognize that certain population groups are at greater risk of being disadvantaged or harmed by actions of other individuals, groups, organizations, or communities. The homeless described in this case are a typical example. Such groups call for a variety of different macro approaches from social workers, including advocacy, social action, and empowerment.

Learning Objectives

This chapter will provide content concerning how social workers:

A. *Utilize key concepts involved with macro practice.*
B. *Utilize advocacy, social action, and empowerment activities with populations-at-risk.*
C. *Identify factors that place a population at risk for social and economic injustice.*
D. *Utilize the professional role of the social worker in advocating for human rights and social and economic justice.*
E. *Analyze and critique the use, value, and limitations of advocacy, opportunities for macro level advocacy, and principles guiding advocacy.*
F. *Engage in the professional role of legislative advocacy and political activity that advances social and economic justice and social well-being.*
G. *Analyze and critique conceptual models of social action while recognizing the ambiguity inherent in resolving ethical concepts.*
H. *Critique controversial forms of macro practice in relation to the knowledge, skills, and values of generalist social work.*
I. *Describe participatory action research that uses practice experience to inform scientific inquiry and research evidence to inform practice.*

Defining Advocacy, Social Action, Empowerment, and Populations-at-Risk

In order to discuss the role of social workers in advocacy, we must consider social action, empowerment, and populations-at-risk. Each concept is briefly defined and discussed in the following sections, followed by a more detailed description later in this chapter. Highlight 11.1 summarizes these and other key concepts involved in advocacy (CSWE, 2008, EP 2.1.7a).

EP 2.1.7a

HIGHLIGHT 11.1

Key Terms

Advocacy is representing, championing, or defending the rights of others.

Case advocacy is work on behalf of individuals and families.

Cause advocacy is work on behalf of groups of people.

Discrimination is negative treatment of individuals, often based upon their membership in some group (such as women) or upon some characteristic they share with others (such as a disability).

Empowerment is ensuring that others have the right to power, ability, and authority to achieve self-determination.

Oppressed populations refers to groups that experience serious limitations because others in power exploit them.

Populations-at-risk are those groups in society most likely to suffer the consequences of, or be at risk for, discrimination, economic hardship, and oppression.

Social action is a coordinated effort to achieve institutional change to meet a need, solve a social problem, correct an injustice, or enhance the quality of human life.

Social and economic justice exists when every individual has opportunities, rights, and responsibilities equal to those of all other members of a society. This includes the opportunity to obtain gainful employment, adequate housing, food, and medical care without experiencing discrimination or other forms of oppression.

Defining Advocacy

EP 2.1.10k

Advocacy is representing, championing, or defending the rights of others. All generalist social workers engage in advocacy at some level as part of their responsibility to clients (CSWE, 2008, EP 2.1.10k). Macro practice, in particular, often involves *cause advocacy,* which is work on behalf of groups of people who lack the ability (resources, talent, or skill) to advocate for themselves. Cause advocacy should be distinguished from *case advocacy,* in which the worker advocates for individual cases or clients. You are likely to pursue case advocacy in micro and mezzo practice with individuals and families. At the same time, however, cause advocacy may well grow out of case advocacy. This occurs when multiple individuals or groups experience essentially the same problems.

It is not unusual for a generalist social worker to discern a pattern when working with multiple clients. Perhaps it becomes clear that many clients are experiencing similar problems with a particular agency whose policies discourage them from seeking help. In other circumstances, you might learn that certain resources such as day care centers for low-income working parents are not available in your community. The result is that many parents leave their children in less-than-adequate situations with very poor supervision. Awareness of this situation may well set the stage for cause advocacy. Highlight 11.2 provides such an example.

Social workers have a rich history of cause advocacy. This includes working for civil rights legislation and fighting for the rights of people with physical and emotional disabilities and for other populations-at-risk. Advocacy can take the form of merely persuading others to accept your definition of the problem and your suggested solutions, or it can assume a more conflictual approach. As you begin to document the existence of a macro level problem, you are taking one of the first steps to change the situation. Macro level interventions may well involve you in a range of actions from consensus to confrontation as you seek to empower underserved people and make systems more responsive to their needs.

Defining Social Action

Chapter 9 defined social action as a method of practice designed to place demands on a community to obtain needed resources, attain social and economic justice, enhance quality of life, and address social problems affecting disenfranchised and disadvantaged populations. Of course, social workers are not the only ones who pursue social action. It may be undertaken by other professionals, agencies, organizations, churches,

HIGHLIGHT 11.2

Advocacy Produces System Change

Mrs. Ackerman and her two daughters, Nadia and Fadia, arrived at the Division of Family Services (DFS) office at 9:00 A.M. to turn in their welfare application. They spent four hours in the agency waiting room before getting any help. When Mrs. Ackerman later mentioned this to Genevieve Moran, her social worker at Catholic Charities, Ms. Moran was appalled. "I don't know why they can't do a better job of serving their clients," Genevieve said. "I just think this is unacceptable."

With that, she picked up the phone and called DFS. "This is Ms. Moran at Catholic Charities. Is Bob Evans available?" With that call, Genevieve took the first of a series of steps. First, she met with Bob to discuss what she perceived to be a common problem: very slow service to clients at DFS. Bob set up a meeting with the secretary/receptionist, financial aid supervisor, and financial aid worker. They decided to adopt a pro-client policy that would provide the following:

1. Each client would receive a set appointment time.
2. Any delays over five minutes would be communicated to the client, and no clients would be left to wonder why they were not being waited on.
3. A client satisfaction survey would be used two weeks after the client had been seen to assess clients' attitudes toward the service they had received.
4. Staff training would emphasize the importance of responding to clients in a timely fashion, showing courtesy to clients, and demonstrating respect for the client's time.

Client satisfaction survey results indicated general contentment with the new efforts to treat clients better. Although a single client had brought the situation to Genevieve's attention, her advocacy ultimately benefited all clients served by DFS.

HIGHLIGHT 11.3

Coordinated Social Action Efforts

Mount Holland is a small community housing a medium-sized state university. Most students at the university are people of color, and many are from relatively poor families. Local landlords in the community have turned many older homes into student housing units, crowding more residents into each apartment than the law allows. In addition, these apartments are poorly maintained. A piece of linoleum nailed to the walls of a small closet is presented to students as a "shower stall." Vermin and unsanitary conditions are commonplace.

Although students do not like the situation, as a group they are relatively powerless. Complaints to the landlords are largely ignored, and efforts to strengthen

housing maintenance regulations have been stymied by apartment owners. Progress occurs only when the University Student Housing Association and Citizens for a Better Mount Holland (both organizations focused on the needs of their members) combine efforts. The student group is committed to ensuring students decent living conditions. The citizens group is concerned with making the community a safer, more attractive place to live. By lobbying the city council and the Mount Holland Planning Commission and by mounting a letter-writing campaign, they succeed in achieving enactment of a property maintenance code for the City of Mount Holland.

cities, or anyone affected by a particular problem. It is important to coordinate social action efforts because rarely is there only one group concerned about the issue or problem. Often there are many, although they may be unaware of each other's interest. Coordinated efforts can also bring more influence to bear than can single individuals or groups. Highlight 11.3 gives an example of the benefits of coordinated efforts.

The example in Highlight 11.3 demonstrates a relatively "gentle" form of social action, persuasion through lobbying. Often, however, social action implies a more confrontational approach to planned change, because more consensual approaches have not proven successful. (Chapter 9 addresses this issue.) This chapter will discuss whether social workers' social action skills used in the past are still relevant today.

Defining Empowerment

Empowerment is the use of strategies that increase the personal, interpersonal, or political power of people so that they can improve their own life situations. Power, as you may recall, is the ability to move people on a chosen course to achieve some goal (Homan, 2008). Believing that people have both the right and capacity to achieve their goals is consistent with social work values, particularly self-determination. Empowerment is a frequent description of social work's goal with people of color and other oppressed groups. This reflects our recognition that oppressed populations benefit most when our efforts (1) enhance their power to help themselves, (2) reduce the negative influences of social and agency policies, and (3) build new helping models that acknowledge the very real problems these groups experience. Highlight 11.4 emphasizes the need for sensitivity when addressing empowerment.

Defining Populations-at-Risk

Populations-at-risk are those groups in society most likely to experience and suffer the consequences of discrimination, economic hardship, and oppression. Historically, among the groups most frequently experiencing these societal influences are women, lesbian and gay people, and persons of color. Persons of color include African Americans, Hispanic Americans, Native Americans, Asian Americans, and Pacific Islanders, to name a few. Examples of what places these groups at risk will be covered under the next section, "Populations-at-Risk." Other groups are also at risk, including older adults with physical, emotional, or developmental disabilities, and those holding religious views significantly different from those of the rest of society. This is not an exhaustive list of populations that may be at risk. Any marginalized group (i.e., those with less power and viewed as less important in society) is potentially a population-at-risk. Likewise, any group that other groups in our society believe to be "different" can be victimized. Those differences can be based on skin color, intellectual ability, belief systems, gender, age, sexual orientation, culture, political ideology or class. It is important to keep in mind that it is not the population-at-risk that produces the risk, but rather the actions and reactions of the rest of society. For example, a gay person is not at risk because he is gay, but because of how others in society think and feel about his sexual orientation. Similarly, women are not at risk because of their own characteristics, but because others in society benefit from oppressing women in a variety of ways. Focusing too closely on the population-at-risk can segue into blaming the victim rather than recognizing that others' actions produce the risk.

HIGHLIGHT 11.4

Caveats in Empowerment

Empowering client groups requires that we understand their situations and life experiences, especially when these differ significantly from our own. Lacking personal experience with these groups, we tend to rely on the literature in social work and related disciplines to understand their situation. This can produce disastrous results.

Marla Moodie is a new social worker, working with refugees from Southeast Asia. She is very interested in understanding their culture and providing the help they need. She is aware that immigrants often have little power and less access to resources and are more likely to experience social and economic oppression.

To better understand this important group of clients, Marla seeks articles and books on Asian culture. Although she ultimately reads several well-documented articles about Asians, she is still unwittingly operating on a database of limited value. As Fong and Mokuau (1994) point out, social work literature tends to lump Asian groups together without appropriate differentiation. The result is that the literature generally ignores huge variations between and within groups, which significantly limits understanding of specific groups. Empowerment can't take place when we apply inaccurate stereotypes, make assumptions based on limited samples, and try to make a single model fit all members of a diverse group. This is true whether the group we are working with consists of women, people of color, the homeless, or gay and lesbian people.

Marla's efforts result in a fine understanding of Asian lifestyles and values as a whole. Unfortunately, she still knows little about the experiences, values, and aspirations of the Southeast Asian refugees with whom she is working.

Populations-at-Risk

This section will consider three major aspects of populations-at-risk: (1) factors that can contribute to putting a population at risk, (2) some examples of populations-at-risk, and (3) the role of social workers in helping these groups.

Factors Contributing to Putting Populations at Risk

EP 2.1.4a

Several primary factors can help place a population at risk, including physical differences (such as skin color) and values and beliefs (including religious beliefs) that differ from those of the dominant or more powerful segment of a society. It can also result from preconceptions about the ability or competence of members of a group (such as women). Finally, populations may be at risk as a result of our economic system. Each of these factors will be discussed next (CSWE, 2008, EP 2.1.4a).

Being different from other, more powerful groups in society often places a group at risk. Some may consider it human nature to be uncomfortable around those who are different from us. Because we often lack common experiences with people whose characteristics are different from ours, we may avoid them. However, experience has shown that such discomfort can be ameliorated over time by learning more about the group. We may also discover that we have more in common with those individuals than we thought. Our commonality is enormous and our differences become minuscule. Initially, however, our lack of familiarity and resulting discomfort with a population may place them at risk. We may avoid them, hurt them through ignorance, or deliberately engage in actions that will penalize them. A business owner may refuse to hire a person of color because he wears his hair in dreadlocks and has several earrings. Cab drivers may refuse to pick up young Hispanic-American males at night for fear of being robbed or assaulted.

Of course, our discomfort with others may be derived from values and beliefs they hold that are widely divergent from our own. Some religious values define homosexuality as sinful, thereby subjecting gay and lesbian people to discrimination. The logic goes something like this: "What these people are doing is bad, so they deserve mistreatment." This is not to suggest that all religions condone discrimination against gay and lesbian people. Several religions do not believe that homosexuality is a sin. Even religions that do consider it as such may still value the individual as a human being, another of God's creatures. The periodic debates over preventing homosexual individuals from marrying often reflect these varied and often contradictory values.

Values are often behind other instances of discrimination and oppression. In countries as disparate as Sudan, Bosnia, Rwanda, Ethiopia, and Macedonia, among others, ethnic divisions and religious differences contribute to genocide and *ethnic cleansing,* a term used to describe the efforts of one group to eradicate opposing groups by such activities as murder, rape, destruction of homes and buildings, and elimination of public documents, such as birth records. Those being eliminated are considered by their oppressors to be subhuman and therefore deserving of maltreatment.

Sometimes a group is at risk because others in society define it as economically or socially insignificant. Consider our own government's sad treatment of various peoples of color. First Nations Peoples were herded off their land and systematically exterminated, partly for economic reasons (whites wanted their land) but also because they were defined as barbarians. African Americans were first enslaved for economic reasons and later were considered so insignificant that they were not allowed to vote. Women, too, were denied the vote until 1920. Asian Americans were prevented from owning land by the state of California, and the federal government attempted to prevent further immigration of Asians. Most people of color have experienced deliberate governmental efforts to exterminate, subjugate, or otherwise limit their rights to "life, liberty and the pursuit of happiness." This malevolent behavior was condoned by belief systems that reduced minorities of color to subhuman status or defined them as economically insignificant. The current argument advanced by some segments of the population about the supposed intellectual inferiority of African Americans is an example of efforts to reduce the value of these groups.

We have briefly suggested the role economics may play in placing a population at risk. Economic justice has often been denied to certain groups in society. Sometimes the argument is made that this treatment is inherent in our economic structure (CSWE, 2008, EP 2.1.5a). The nature of a capitalist economic system is to deliver a product at the lowest cost possible, which may mean keeping salaries and benefits as low as

EP 2.1.5a

possible. Companies' common practice of hiring part-time workers (particularly women) to avoid paying benefits (e.g., health insurance and retirement) normally given to full-time employees is one example of a cost-cutting practice. The economic injustice that arises from such practices is justified by views such as "Women don't need these benefits, because their husbands have full-time jobs," or "If they were really unhappy with the situation, they wouldn't have accepted the job." The fact that this practice unfairly affects certain groups is ignored. Employers believe it is an effective way to make a bigger profit.

Another example of economic injustice placing groups at risk is evident when businesses decide to move away from communities where wages are considered "too high." Two groups are affected by these decisions: First, company employees and the community now housing the business are often victimized by what is considered a purely economic decision. Workers lose their livelihoods, homes, and sense of identity. Communities suffer loss of taxes, which may mean they cannot afford to provide city services. An entire community can become a population-at-risk when it is heavily dependent on a major employer that relocates.

Second, the community that attracts the business is also a population-at-risk. The company will pay workers significantly less than their former employees were getting, a practice that exploits the new hires. Again, this series of decisions is considered good business, because it is designed to maximize profits and minimize the cost of producing a product or service. It is a guiding principle behind our economic system.

Examples of Populations-at-Risk

As we have seen, many factors contribute to a population being at risk in our society. Some groups are inherently at higher risk than others for certain negative outcomes. Several of these groups are described in the following sections. However, it is important to recognize that many at-risk populations experience intersectionality by virtue of being members of multiple groups. For example, a person may be simultaneously a woman, a person of color, and a lesbian. Another may be an immigrant with a disability currently receiving public assistance. These factors can increase the risk of social and economic injustice, powerlessness, and alienation for such individuals.

African Americans

We have already described some of the historic discrimination and oppression experienced by African Americans. However, this group continues to be a population at great risk on several fronts (Lum, 2007; Wells, Merritt, & Briggs, 2009). They are almost three times as likely to live below the poverty line as non-Hispanic whites. Almost 20 percent have no health insurance (U.S. Census Bureau, 2005). Infant mortality rates for African Americans are almost 80 percent higher than for whites. Black women are almost twice as likely to use abortion services as are whites. Black males are more than seven times more likely to die from homicides than are white males; when we specify black males between 25 and 34 years of age, the rate difference (versus white males) increases to 10 times more likely. Similarly, African Americans are less likely to survive physical illnesses such as cancer and more likely to suffer from hypertension and strokes. Black males are incarcerated at 6.6 times the rate of white males (U.S. Bureau of Justice Statistics, 2009). These factors help explain why African Americans are considered a major population-at-risk.

Hispanic Americans

Another ethnic group at risk is Hispanic Americans (or Latinos, as some prefer to be called). They represented 31.5 percent of all federal prisoners in 2000. Moreover, the percentage of Hispanic-American juveniles incarcerated is increasing faster than that of other groups. Hispanic Americans are also more likely to drop out of school and less likely to have completed four or more years of college than either blacks or whites. Almost one-third lack health insurance (U.S. Census Bureau, 2005). In the trend toward one-parent families, Hispanic Americans are experiencing a rate increase almost three times that of the rest of the U.S. population (U.S. Census Bureau, 1998). Current debates in the United States focus on reducing the ability of Hispanic and other immigrant groups to benefit from social, health, and economic services routinely available to whites.

First Nations Peoples (Native Americans)

First Nations Peoples experience many serious health and social problems (U.S. Census Bureau, 2007). In all categories of causes of death, from cancer to accidents, they have a rate higher than that of the rest of the U.S. population. For some causes of death (for example, alcoholism and tuberculosis), the rate is five to seven times higher. The suicide rate is highest of all U.S. ethnic groups (Suicide Reference Library, 2004). Twenty-nine percent have no health insurance (U.S. Census Bureau, 2005). Attempts by tribal groups to improve their economic situations through the institution of casino gambling on tribal lands are often met with opposition from whites and from groups opposed to gambling on religious grounds. The continuation of traditional First Nations Peoples activities, such as spear fishing (even when guaranteed by treaties), is also met by antagonism and resistance from majority-group people.

Asian Americans and Pacific Islanders

Asian Americans and Pacific Islanders, particularly refugees from Southeast Asia who emigrated to the United States after the Vietnam War, experience a host of problems that place them at risk. Given low proficiencies in the English language and agrarian and rural backgrounds, many have had great difficulty making the transition to an urban lifestyle. Traditional customs and norms often clash with those of whites in America. Reliance on family and clan for support often places them outside the usual formal networks of social service providers available to nonimmigrants. In addition, the enormous diversity within these groups is often ignored by white Americans, who assume that all Asian Americans have similar experiences, values, and behaviors.

Women

Women have constituted a population-at-risk for generations. From an unwillingness to grant women the vote to more recent manifestations, such as lower pay for the same jobs, women remain an at-risk group. They are more likely to be subjected to sexual harassment in the workplace and maltreatment after surviving a sexual assault. Denial of a woman's right to control her own body also arises during the debate on abortion. The willingness of some men to subjugate women in the workplace and in the home increases the risk to this population.

Lesbian and Gay Persons

One of the population groups most at risk in the United States is lesbian and gay persons. Lacking the traditional civil rights protection accorded women and people of color, this group often experiences discrimination. This includes the refusal to hire gay or lesbian persons for teaching or other jobs involving children. Based upon a homophobic and irrational fear that members of this group are more likely to cause harm to children, this discrimination is often supported by current laws.

Partners of gays or lesbians are denied the rights accorded to other next of kin, such as child custody and access to the partner's health insurance. Even the U.S. military, one of the first employers to end racial discrimination, carries on discrimination against gay and lesbian people by discharging anyone who openly discusses being homosexual or who engages in any homosexual act. Needless to say, these restrictions are not placed on heterosexuals in the military. Like many abortion opponents who believe their religion's tenets allow them to limit the rights of women to control their own destiny, those denying rights to gays and lesbians often couch their opposition in religious terms. In the end, both groups are trying to force their religious views on the rest of the population.

Immigrants and Refugees

Immigrants (both documented and undocumented) and refugees arriving in the United States constitute a population-at-risk. The tensions and recent political attention focused on immigrants underscores their vulnerability. In many states, undocumented immigrants are denied public services and access to public assistance, and are considered unwanted. At the same time, businesses that depend on a plentiful supply of cheap labor—including the hospitality industry, landscaping companies, and others—are able to take advantage of their employees without regard for fair labor standards. Exploitation and discrimination are common because businesses know that an employee in the United States illegally is not likely to complain about such things as pay levels, working conditions, or risks associated with the job. A Southern Poverty Law Center study found "Latinos are routinely cheated out of wages by employers and denied basic health and safety protections. They are racially profiled by overzealous law enforcement agents and victimized by criminals who know they are reluctant to report crime to these same authorities. Even legal residents and U.S. citizens of Latino descent said racial profiling, bigotry and other forms of discrimination are staples of their daily lives" (Southern Poverty Law Center, 2009, p. 1).

Refugees from countries that have been wracked with war and genocide need access to mental health services after experiencing rape, murder of family members, mutilation, and other forms of violence. Even residents from Middle Eastern or other Muslim nations who are here legally are subject to hostility and discrimination because of fears they might be terrorists. The latter problem is not limited to the United States, as several nations have imposed barriers to the inclusion of Muslims and other refugees or have pursued discriminatory policies against these groups. Examples include the United Kingdom, Kuwait, Indonesia, Bangladesh, and Mexico, among others. Being discriminated against because of their status as immigrants and refugees is a common problem that has been documented in numerous countries as diverse as New Zealand, France, Botswanna, Australia (D1TSHWANELO, 2006; Evans & Kelley, 1986; Spoonley, 2006–2007). Clearly, such discrimination is a global phenomenon.

Clients Receiving Public Assistance

Historically, people receiving welfare benefits (AFDC, TANF, General Relief, Food Stamps, etc.) have been at risk in America. Benefit levels have typically been so low as to prevent recipients from moving above the poverty line. Eligibility requirements have been onerous and confusing, and recipients have experienced a stigma for "taking handouts." Discussions around welfare reform suggest that efforts to change the system are being driven by dislike of the poor, punitive attitudes toward recipients, and expectations uninformed by the realities of the real world. For example, welfare clients are given a relatively short time to get off assistance or may lose their benefits. Yet, training for jobs or an occupation is severely limited. Recipients capable of earning a college degree are not allowed to pursue this option but are relegated to short-term training with much lower income-producing potential.

Another punitive feature of welfare reform is a cap on family benefits, supposedly designed to prevent recipients from having additional children. The fact that such family caps do not affect recipients' decision to have children was used by New York social workers advocating changes in that state's welfare program. They also were successful in persuading the state to allow recipients to retain a significant portion of their earnings before they lose their assistance. Such advocacy can mean the difference between remaining below the poverty line and getting off public assistance.

Similarly, welfare reform efforts have been improved by the activity of social workers who lobbied for increased transportation and child care provisions, without which recipients cannot hope to find and hold employment. Advocacy for this population-at-risk is essential if public assistance clients are to achieve a significant degree of self-sufficiency.

Other At-Risk Populations

Other groups in our society can be at risk in numerous ways. The homeless risk not benefiting from a community's school system. The transient nature of the homeless population often means that school systems will not accept homeless children because they lack a permanent residence. Trying to reach this population-at-risk takes extra effort. Some communities are using tutors to work with homeless children and adolescents. Tutors also help adults get their high school equivalency degrees, give advice about finding jobs, and teach parenting skills. Programs of this type reach a segment of a population-at-risk normally excluded from social and educational programming. It often takes an advocate for the homeless to supply the special programs they need.

Another group at risk in our society are those with physical and mental disabilities. Although protected in some ways through the Americans with Disabilities Act (ADA), they remain among the poorest and least educated, not only in the United States, but across the globe. It is estimated that worldwide, 98 percent of children with disabilities are not attending school (Inclusion International, 2004). Despite the benefits of the law, many continue to suffer discrimination in everything from transportation to employment. Even human service professionals may hold stereotypes about them, such as their being sick or incompetent (Mackelprang & Salsgiver, 1999).

A newer population-at-risk is made up of teenagers who have no plans for college. They remain at risk of a marginal economic existence without further training or some other employment-enhancing education. Vocational opportunities are essential, although some school systems are oriented primarily to students planning to attend college.

Another group of teens at risk are those who have planned, unplanned, or unwanted pregnancies. Besides the physical health risk to the mother, both parents have a high risk of poverty, dependence on welfare, and involvement in various other social problems. Advocacy efforts for this group may include increased funding for family planning, opposition to efforts to cut funds for this purpose, and establishment of programs that advocate abstinence, birth control, and parenting education. Both conservatives and liberals can agree on such goals, which promise long-term benefits for the individuals and for society.

The Role of Social Workers with Populations-at-Risk

Social workers are in an excellent position to help prevent populations from being placed at risk. The profession is often keenly aware of the needs of certain segments of the population who bear the brunt of economic decisions affecting a community. Social workers see the long-term poverty that comes from child-rearing burdens placed prematurely on teenaged girls. We are also trained to recognize the negative impact of discrimination on people of color and other groups, such as lesbian and gay people.

Social workers must also be vigilant regarding how their agencies and other societal institutions interact with high-risk populations. We need to review agency policies to see if they work to the disadvantage of any groups. Do we, for example, serve minority populations with the same frequency as other agencies? Or do our practices (lack of minority workers, daytime-only office hours, or other factors) discourage some populations from using our services? Do our hiring practices discourage applicants of color from applying for positions in the agency?

Likewise, social workers must alert themselves to the community's treatment of populations-at-risk. Do the community's decisions reflect an interest in all segments of the population? Does the city seem to ignore the problems in Hispanic-American neighborhoods but rush to provide police services to upscale areas? Are the parks in African-American neighborhoods maintained with the same care as other parks in the city? Are the public hospitals in the community providing a comparable level of treatment for poor patients as for their well-to-do clientele?

Do all the positions of influence in the community seem to go to men, with women rarely offered status or important roles? Does the city allow landlords to discriminate against gay and lesbian people who apply for housing? Does the community really enforce laws protecting the rights and needs of schoolchildren with physical and mental disabilities?

In each of these situations, social workers can work to prevent groups from becoming at risk. Be alert to what goes on in your community and take an active part in its operation. You can also decide to try to change policies, practices, and procedures that negatively affect at-risk populations. Finally, you can work for systems designed to alleviate the problems experienced by populations-at-risk. One of the most effective methods for achieving these goals—advocacy—is discussed in the next section.

When working to assist populations-at-risk, social workers will face some practical and ethical considerations: First, even those at risk have the right to choose their own destiny. Clients have the general right to self-determination, even if the choice made places them at

risk. As social workers we can develop needed services, offer them to populations-at-risk, and encourage those in need to use the services. Ultimately, this may be the limit of our ability to intervene. One example of this is the teen who elects to become pregnant despite the risks to her health and welfare. Similarly, a homeless person with a chronic mental illness may prefer staying on the street to entering a shelter. The fact that we know a person is at risk does not automatically mean we can do anything about it. Clients have the right to fail as well as to succeed. Sometimes the decision is very logical to the client: The teen may see having a child as a means of acquiring independence or as a means to escape a more unsatisfactory life with her sexually abusive father. The options open to the individual may make this level of risk seem less than continuing in his or her present situation.

Advocacy

Advocacy has been used by social workers for a very long time. This section describes the values and limitations of advocacy, discusses agency commitment to advocacy, and considers opportunities for advocacy. It will suggest some typical concerns about advocacy. Finally, it will provide some principles and guidelines for macro level advocacy and review some advocacy tactics.

The Values and Limitations of Advocacy

The ethical codes of the National Association of Social Workers (NASW) and the Canadian Association of Social Workers (CASW) make it a worker's duty to engage in advocacy. This obligation arises from our heritage of respect for the worth and dignity of every person and the rights (both moral and legal) that are ours as a part of this society. Advocacy is consistent with the values of the social work profession. We have seen that the groups for which advocacy works change over time—from civil rights for people of color in the 1960s to legislation for people with physical disabilities in the 1990s. In each case, these macro level efforts profoundly changed the quality of life and opportunities of both groups.

A major benefit of macro level advocacy is that it can attack core problems rather than merely treat crisis situations. It can help workers feel a sense of participation when they are actively involved in solving a problem, rather than merely putting Band-Aids on it. It can also empower clients to tackle their own issues, thereby helping them develop personal skills and a sense of efficacy.

One factor limiting the effectiveness of advocacy is that, by their nature, human and societal problems often do not lend themselves to massive change. Sometimes all we can do is tackle one piece at a time or take the first steps in the process. Look at the advocacy efforts undertaken to ensure that women (and, 50 years later, African Americans) had the right to vote in this country. Although this right was ensured by constitutional amendment, it did not guarantee that people would vote. The next step was encouraging people to exercise the right. Getting people to register to vote is still necessary today, and getting them out to vote is yet another major step, given that less than half of the population votes in presidential elections. These are incremental steps in the process of getting people to participate in the electoral system.

At the same time, some tasks cannot be accomplished now, because the climate and conditions for change just aren't there. For example, it is difficult to successfully advocate for bold, new programs when the entire political process is focused on cutting taxes and reducing government spending.

EP 2.1.1b

One significant limitation to advocacy is our own lack of courage and knowledge about how to tackle the problem (CSWE, 2008, EP 2.1.1b). Apathy is perhaps the most dangerous threat to progress in combating oppression and pursuing social and economic justice. Some of this apathy stems from lack of faith that one can have much impact on major societal or community problems. In other cases, doubt over how to begin contributes to a sense of incompetence. Fortunately, advocacy utilizes the same process of planned change described in Chapters 5 through 7. Although the problem may be much larger than we are used to dealing with, the process for tackling major macro problems is essentially the same for all generalist interventions.

Agency Commitment to Advocacy

The degree of interest in advocacy on behalf of populations-at-risk varies from agency to agency. Some agencies have a strong advocacy mission inherent in their service giving. Most shelters for survivors of domestic violence are committed to the enactment and enforcement of strong laws against spousal abuse and development of new programs that help women become self-supporting. Other agencies actively pursue outreach efforts to ensure that their services are available to populations-at-risk and groups underserved by existing agencies. Still other organizations are devoted almost exclusively to advocacy, and, for the most part, their goals are consistent with those of the social work profession. Following is a list of some of these organizations and their interest areas.

Unfortunately, some agencies do not see advocacy as an important part of their mission. The degree to which one's agency is committed to advocacy tends to affect the worker's sense of commitment to pursuing large system change. If your agency does not believe that advocacy is important for social workers, it is less likely that you will pursue it. Only your commitment to the profession and your professional obligation to clients are available to motivate and sanction your efforts.

Opportunities for Macro Level Advocacy

We have identified by example some of the types of advocacy in which generalist social workers may engage. Highlight 11.5 describes the importance of thinking broadly about macro issues. However, we have touched on only a few of the available opportunities. Recall that advocacy can help people take control of their own lives and problems, so it can be considered a form of self-help or empowerment. Advocacy activities might include forming groups of people with similar interests or problems who can work in concert to achieve goals they could not achieve as individuals. We can also give clients a role in running agencies by placing them on the board of directors or hiring them for certain staff roles.

Advocacy might include efforts to change policies and laws at the institutional, community, or other level. It can also involve planning for new services or modifying the way agencies allocate resources for specific programs.

Another set of advocacy activities can be undertaken with gay and lesbian clients, who constitute a population-at-risk. Homophobia (irrational fear and loathing of homosexuals), even among social workers, can result in our failure to address the topic of sexuality with gay and lesbian adolescents. Often this group faces a range of problems and discrimination: They often lack support from their families; are at higher risk of substance abuse, suicide, and violence; and suffer from negative stereotypes about sexual orientation held by their peers (Barret & Logan, 2002). Sometimes these stereotypes grow out of deeply held religious beliefs.

FIGURE 11.1 Advocacy Organizations

Name of Organization	Web Site	Purpose
American Civil Liberties Union	www.aclu.org	Dedicated to protecting the rights of all Americans, focusing on first Amendment issues, rights to privacy, due process, and equal protection under the law.
Child Welfare League of America	www.cwla.org	Active in lobbying and humanitarian projects in United States.
Children's Rights, Inc.	www.childrensrights.org	Dedicated to reforming government child welfare services across the United States.
Children's Defense Fund	www.childrensdefense.org	Advocacy for U.S. children, particularly poor and minority children and those with disabilities.
Clean Water Action	www.cleanwateraction.org	A national organization of diverse people and groups working together for clean water, pollution prevention, and an environmentally sustainable economy.
Community Organizations International	www.acorninternational.org	A global organization of groups committed to social, economic, and environmental justice.
Disabled Peoples' International	www.dpi.org	A grassroots, cross-disability network with member organizations in over 110 countries, including the developing world.
National Center for Youth Law	www.youthlaw.org	Protects abused and neglected children, increases youths' access to health care and other public benefits, and ensures the fair treatment of youth in the justice system.
National Alliance on Mental Illness	www.nami.org	Grassroots mental health advocacy organization providing support, education, policy advocacy, and research.
Parents, Families and Friends of Lesbians and Gays (PFLAG)	www.pflag.org	Located in and representing communities nationwide, promotes the health and well-being of gay, lesbian, bisexual, and transgendered persons, their families, and friends through support, education, and advocacy.

Other times they result from irrational fears that simply talking about gay and lesbian lifestyles will make people become lesbian or gay, though this is contrary to all evidence (Barret & Logan, 2002). An advocacy role for social workers might include providing information to parents and supporting them as they struggle to accept their own children.

We might also advocate for special programs to meet the needs of gay and lesbian adolescents. Developing socialization activities focusing on dating, AIDS, and talking to one's parents might be appropriate. We can also advocate for support groups and school programs aimed at teachers.

Advocacy may involve efforts to change laws that actively discriminate against gay and lesbian individuals. Laws, policies, and practices that prohibit gays in the military, prevent gay parents from gaining custody of their children, or fail to recognize the emotional and economic importance of same-sex unions are appropriate for advocacy. In most states the partner of a dying homosexual has no rights to make medical decisions about the ill person, as legally married spouses may be permitted to do. Advocating for changes in the law to recognize the emotional and legal relationships between gay and lesbian partners is an appropriate activity for social workers.

HIGHLIGHT 11.5

Advocacy for Change–Thinking Big about Child Care

Advocating for change can also be done in ways most social workers might not think about. A few cases illustrate that stepping back and thinking on a larger scale can produce benefits no amount of individual effort can create. For example, San Francisco identified a lack of adequate low-cost day care as a community-wide problem. To help remedy the problem, the city imposed requirements on developers of new office projects. Any building project over a specified size was required either to set aside free space for child care or to contribute to a fund providing affordable child care to low- and moderate-income families (Young, 1987). Other cities have adopted similar proposals, and social workers have been and can be involved in such advocacy efforts.

Likewise, to meet the child care needs of students and school staff, some school systems have added in-school and after-school child care. For those without sufficient income to pay the full cost of child care, other communities establish a sliding scale fee, ensuring that no one is denied care because of income level. In still other communities, the city provides funds to help low-income parents pay for child care in reputable facilities. Facilities not meeting city standards may apply for grants to bring them up to appropriate service levels.

These examples of advocacy have occurred at the city level, but it is also possible to achieve many of the same goals on a more local basis, such as the neighborhood. A neighborhood center could be an ideal site for a child care center. Or perhaps a church with unused space could be converted to meet the need for low-income child care.

The important lesson is that social workers must be prepared to intervene at many levels in order to achieve social work goals. It also means we must be concerned about decisions made at every level—local, county, state, and national—because each has the capacity to influence our clients, programs, and goals as social workers.

We also need to maintain a broad perspective about who benefits from our advocacy efforts. We should recognize that child care is not a concern only for people with children. Lack of affordable and dependable child care affects others, including coworkers, employers, and those who depend upon the worker. Thus, the issue transcends family status. Low-income parents with inadequate child care are at risk of entering the welfare system or leaving their children in situations that do not guarantee their safety and health. Thinking big is a useful habit to develop in macro level practice.

SOURCE: Young (1987).

We also know that gay and lesbian individuals experience a higher degree of violence, discrimination, harassment, and isolation because of other people's reaction to their sexual orientation (Schriver, 2004; Swim, Johnston, & Pearson, 2009). Similarly, recent studies have found gay and lesbian youth at higher risk of suicide than their peers (Barret & Logan, 2002). This discrimination, the lack of understanding and support, and the acceptance problems experienced by these adolescents contribute to this higher suicide rate. However, once we recognize that groups are at risk, social workers can more effectively advocate for appropriate programs to help reduce or eliminate the risk. Many schools provide literature on lesbian and gay lifestyles that do not portray them in a negative or derogatory way. In some communities, programs exist aimed at giving gay and lesbian adolescents a place to gather and socialize, a function that the "gay bar" serves for many adults.

At the same time, schools and communities that demonstrate a sensitivity to the needs of lesbian and

gay persons are under attack by conservative groups who oppose any positive references to homosexuality. Advocacy can take the form of opposing efforts by these groups to determine what is "normal" and fighting their attempts to impose their religious values on others. It can also involve supporting and voting for political candidates who truly believe in the worth and dignity of all persons, not just those whose sexual orientation matches theirs.

Concerns about the Use of Advocacy

Advocacy is a longstanding tradition in social work, but practitioners often are reluctant to pursue this avenue. Workers may be afraid of controversy, which is a natural consequence of advocating for an oppressed group or population-at-risk. Some view advocacy as too confrontational and worry about how others may perceive their efforts. For example, an agency director may be averse to having her workers engage in advocacy, because board members or other funding groups may be offended by what they perceive as challenges to the status quo.

Being unable to determine the outcomes of advocacy is another problem. Some potential advocates fear being considered troublemakers who place the agency at risk. Still other workers honestly believe they cannot produce any change in the system, no matter what they do. This lack of a sense of efficacy is a real barrier for new social workers who lack confidence in their own power. Finally, change produced by advocacy and other means is often scary. Social workers may fear what will happen if they advocate for a change and the change actually occurs.

Principles of Macro Level Advocacy

As should be clear by now, advocacy may be directed toward individuals, groups, or organizations; elected or appointed officials; public and private human service agencies; legislative bodies; court systems; and/or governmental entities (such as the Housing Authority). We include this wide array of possibilities because any of them can prevent groups from gaining access to service or can treat them inhumanely. Undertaking advocacy efforts, however, requires that we consider several principles that should inform our efforts.

First, *we should work to increase accessibility of social services to clients.* It is not sufficient simply to offer a service without learning whether the groups we seek to serve are actually being helped. Clients for whom English is a second language will have difficulty completing lengthy forms written in English. If they can't complete the forms, they may not receive the services. We must advocate for our agencies to find ways to serve all those who need help, not just those for whom our service is convenient.

Sometimes the services themselves are satisfactory, but other problems prevent clients from using them. For example, services may be available only during the day when clients are at work. Or there may be long waiting periods before services can be received. Another problem entails service locations that are inaccessible to clients, such as when a building is not accessible to the disabled or when services are offered only at sites far from clients' homes.

A second principle for social work advocates is that *we must promote service delivery that does not detract from the dignity of the groups we serve.* In other words, clients should not be put in humiliating or embarrassing situations in order to receive services. Consider a situation that requires clients to wait in a filthy, crowded waiting room for hours in order to receive

public assistance. It is appropriate to advocate for a change in such conditions, because they are an affront to clients' dignity.

Sometimes services are provided in a fashion that is demeaning to clients. One large county social services agency located workers' desks in a giant facility resembling a remodeled warehouse. There were no walls or partitions between the desks, so anyone within sight or hearing of the workers would know what the client and the worker were talking about. Privacy was almost nonexistent for clients coming to the agency for help.

A third principle is that *advocates should work to ensure equal access to all who are eligible.* Services might be more accessible to white clients than to African-American or Hispanic-American clients because of the location of the agency or organization, lack of public transportation, or the cost of services provided. This kind of service delivery is unacceptable and needs to be changed if we are to provide equal access.

Guidelines for Macro Level Advocacy

Although all of these suggestions for action are reasonable, they do not provide sufficient guidance for many advocacy situations. Following are general guidelines for advocacy implementation.

Be Reasonable in What You Undertake

When you advocate to change an organization, you are really struggling to change the values, beliefs, and assumptions of the people who make up the organization. Advocacy may be the only reasonable alternative when an organization performs its functions poorly or actually hurts its clientele. Nevertheless, it is difficult to bring about change in some organizations and agencies, especially when there appear to be many changes needed. Obviously, it makes sense to tackle only those things that are reasonably achievable and not try to change everything at once. Remember that people have investments in the status quo. It is easier to get them to change a few things than to undertake wholesale change that threatens their survival. A social worker who wants his agency to hire some bilingual workers to help Spanish-speaking clients is more likely to achieve success than a colleague who advocates that supervisors and administrators all take pay cuts to finance service expansion. One goal is manageable and requires only that future hiring be directed toward recruitment of Spanish-speaking social workers. The other goal is an affront to administrative staff and would affect them and the agency in a major way.

Teamwork Often Produces Better Outcomes

EP 2.1.8b

Whereas a person working alone can often achieve great ends, teams make it much easier to achieve major outcomes. Macro level advocacy works best when many people are giving the same message. Joining with others increases your power and influence. Several workers in a county human services agency found that they were unable to help clients needing certain services because there was no resource manual available for the county. (Resource manuals contain lists of agencies that offer various services in a geographical area. They are often organized alphabetically and by the kinds of service provided. Sometimes they are available on the Internet.) By working with a nearby college, they were able to put together a county-wide resource manual. Individually and collectively, they lobbied the agency director until she agreed to pay for the printing costs and the expense of mailing the manual to all agencies in the county. An individual worker might have been able to accomplish this goal, but the combined teamwork of the social workers made it much easier to achieve (CSWE, 2008, EP 2.1.8b).

Being an Advocate Often Requires Being Assertive

Keep in mind that you can't always be the nice person. Consistently being nice means sometimes ignoring very real grievances and injustices. Trying to change things will cause you to make some enemies from time to time. Remember that today's enemies are tomorrow's allies. The agency director who is upset with you today because you pointed out that he was not providing services to female clients despite his pledge to do so will welcome your support next year when he requests additional funding to expand these services. Being assertive can be an asset when seeking change in systems.

Flexibility Is a Strength, Not a Weakness

Be flexible—sometimes an approach may call for being bullheaded and difficult to deal with. Other times you need to be more flexible, warm, and friendly. You must be able to select the appropriate behavior depending upon the need. Mary Andrews is a case in point. She is one of the most gentle, warm, and easygoing workers in the Frunk County Department of Human Services. Everyone likes her. However, when her agency began to propose budget cuts that would significantly reduce services to single teenage mothers, she became the strongest possible advocate. She confronted the agency's administrative council (consisting of supervisors and administrators) with the needs of this group and the potential consequences of ending services to them. She pointed out that proposed cutbacks were contrary to the agency's mission of helping the most vulnerable groups in society. She spoke with passion, marshaled facts, and challenged her superiors to do the right thing. Some of the supervisors were upset at her actions, but her arguments won over the majority. Mary had taken the risk of upsetting people because unmarried teenage mothers had no other advocate in the system.

Accept That Sometimes You Win, and Sometimes You Lose

Sometimes your advocacy efforts will not achieve your goals, but you may be able to block your opponents from achieving theirs. Or at least you may force your opponents to take your ideas into account. You may not be successful getting the city to create a new homeless shelter, but you may be able to stop the closing of an existing shelter. You might also force the city to relocate a proposed highway that threatens an intact, but poor, neighborhood and would create additional homelessness.

Be Prepared to Use a Variety of Strategies

We are not suggesting that advocacy must be a confrontational or win-lose experience. In fact, we have stressed that collaborative strategies should probably be tried first. Taking a matter to court, for example, is a confrontational act that can lead to costly appeals, no matter who wins. Any situation that continually results in a win-lose outcome is likely to frustrate the losers. Win-win approaches are more likely to work. Disputes may be resolved through negotiation, arbitration, or mediation.

Advocacy Tactics

A variety of advocacy tactics can be employed, and most of them are part of the educational preparation of the generalist social worker. These include persuasion, fair hearings, embarrassment of the target, political pressure, and petitioning. We will address each of these in the following sections.

Persuasion

Persuasion can take the form of providing the target system (the one we wish to change) with additional information that may allow the target to make a different decision. There are many useful ways to persuade others. One method, *questioning,* simply means asking the target system a series of questions designed to make its members think about their original conclusion. If you believe that someone has made a decision based upon faulty information, you can ask him or her whether that information is available in public records. A follow-up question might be whether anyone has double-checked to see whether the information provided verbally is consistent with the published information. If you are trying to develop a juvenile detention facility in the community (because juveniles who are now detained end up in the city jail with adult felons), the mayor might state that she sees no need for a juvenile detention facility in the community. You can challenge her with questions such as, "Can you indicate the number of juveniles who were incarcerated in the city jail last year because there was no detention facility? How does that number compare to the average for a city our size?" (Changing-Minds.org, 2007).

A second approach to persuasion is objectivity or *providing arguments on both sides of an issue.* This involves stating not only your opinions and facts, but also acknowledging the opinions, concerns, and facts of the other side. The advantage of this is that it lets the other side know you understand their arguments but still think your position makes the most sense. It also surprises people used to hearing only one side of the argument. Perhaps you are trying to get a program started to provide needles and bleach (for sterilizing needles) for drug users to help prevent the spread of AIDS. You know the research shows that this is an effective method for slowing the AIDS epidemic. At the same time, you must be able to articulate all of the arguments against your idea and have responses for each.

Persistence is the third strong persuasion method. Most people give up when they meet resistance. The target system may expect you to give in, too. A social worker who perseveres is determined but not abrasive, and will win points. Suppose you are a part of a group trying to develop a recreation center for barrio children. You have found an abandoned building, and a civic group has promised to provide funds to renovate it. The city manager has promised to check into having the city take ownership of the building, because the taxes on it have not been paid in years. Unless the city owns the building, the project can't go forward. Despite the promises, however, the mayor has taken no action. A patient, repetitive request for a progress report every week or so may turn out to be very effective. The mayor may decide it is easier to do what you want than to have you come around and check on him every week. It's worth a try. Highlight 11.6 provides another example of persuasion.

Voting is a key form of legislative advocacy.

HIGHLIGHT 11.6

Advocacy in Action

Mendel Hawkins knew that his support group for parents at risk for abusing their children maintained a tentative existence. Attendance was often spotty. Members could elect not to attend, because participation was completely voluntary. However, Mendel did not think lack of interest was the barrier. It was true that parents often gave various reasons for their poor attendance, which made it difficult to identify the problem. Mendel's agency thought the group was important enough to assign him to lead it, but he wasn't sure whether they would continue to support it with its poor attendance. Although Mendel and Annie, his supervisor, discussed the situation from time to time, they still couldn't figure out the root of the problem.

Mendel proposed asking group members to help him problem solve. Annie, however, did not think it wise to ask clients for their ideas. "I doubt they can provide much insight," she said. "Most of them don't have experience solving their own problems. How do you expect them to solve ours?" Pushing the idea a bit, Mendel decided on his own to ask the parent group members about their attendance. It soon became clear that two factors were limiting attendance. First, most parents in the group were low income and had limited resources. They usually lacked reliable transportation and, if they owned a car, it was not in good shape. Frequent breakdowns made it impossible to plan for anything until they went out to see if the car would start.

In addition, there was the problem of inertia, of just getting up and moving. Members of the parents' group said they would come regularly if they had transportation, especially if they knew someone was coming to get them. From this discussion was born the idea of having a group member provide rides, with the agency reimbursing the driver for gas. At least two of the group members said they would be willing to drive others to the group, picking them up on the way. However, they could not afford the cost of serving as a carpool. Mendel doubted the agency would like this idea, but elected to test the suggestion on his supervisor. Annie laughed when Mendel made the suggestion. "Why don't we just send a chauffeured limousine for them?" she asked, only half-kidding.

"Look," said Mendel, "we have the chance to try a new idea at relatively little cost to reach a population this agency says it wants to reach. We told the United Way that we serve parents at risk of abuse and that we are truly interested in outreach. Well, here we have the chance to put our money where our mouths are and get some real results. Take the idea to Jamal [the deputy director]. Tell him we're only asking for an average of $10 per meeting to reimburse one driver for gas. That works out to about $2 per person and reliably doubles the number of members who attend each week. We might even be able to use this idea, especially if it works, to convince the county board that we are an innovative agency and should get money for a purchase-of-service contract for doing something the public agency should be doing."

"Right, and horses can fly," replied Annie. Nevertheless, she proposed the idea to Jamal, who thought it was a marvelous and inexpensive way to get to a hard-to-reach client group. "Tell Mendel I'll allocate $500 to the project, but I want an evaluation. How many clients attended each meeting before and after we started to provide transportation? What was the average cost per client? And ask Mendel to take more time with his group to see if there are other things we can be doing that are low cost and creative. I'm going to approach the Aloysious Lutheran Church Women's Auxiliary about funding this idea on a continuing basis if it pays off. I don't think Mendel is realistic about the county picking up the tab, but I think the auxiliary is looking for an innovative way to help in the area of child abuse. That's their focus this year. I think we can get some help on this one. Now get out of here and let me eat my lunch."

With that, Annie bounced out of her chair and headed for the door. "Thanks, Boss," she called as she headed back to her office. Once again, Mendel's advocacy for clients had paid off.

Fair Hearings, Grievances, and Complaints

Fair hearings, grievances, and complaints are administrative procedures designed to ensure that clients or client groups who have been denied benefits or rights to which they are entitled get equitable treatment. In fair hearings, clients notify the agency that they wish to have a fair hearing concerning the decision maker's actions. This means that an outside person (usually a state employee) is appointed to hear both sides of the argument. If the fair hearing examiner finds that the decision maker has violated state or federal policies, the examiner will direct the individual or agency to comply with the rules and award the client his or her rightful benefits. This approach makes sense when a public agency has been denying benefits to a group or clearly violating rules it is required to follow.

Grievances and complaints are also mechanisms for dealing with a decision maker who has violated policy. Grievance procedures are usually a part of an agency's own policies. For unionized workers, they are often part of the union agreement between employees and the employer. For example, the agency director decided that agency staff would no longer be permitted to take their 15-minute afternoon break. The director's goal was to increase the daily productivity of each staff member by 15 minutes. However, the social workers filed a grievance under their union contract and won. The agency director was required to pay each employee for 15 minutes worth of work each day for the entire period his silly policy was in place. The result, following the effective use of a grievance procedure, was an expensive embarrassment for the agency.

Complaints are similar to grievances but are provided for in certain laws. Recently, a large restaurant chain was treating African-American customers with disrespect. Workers provided poor service and generally discouraged the customers from eating there. A group of customers filed a civil rights complaint against the firm and forced the company to change its practices.

Similarly, people with disabilities must be granted reasonable accommodation by employers if that will enable the person to do a given job. Some employers, however, routinely refuse to hire people with disabilities. Complaints can be filed with the state and federal governments under the Americans with Disabilities Act (ADA) to force compliance with the law.

Sometimes, just the threat of using the formal grievance or complaint process is enough to change an adverse decision. Other times, if the agency has no policy for a fair hearing or appeal, other confrontational tactics can be employed. It is often possible to seek advice and assistance from an attorney. Not infrequently, an attorney's letter suggesting the possibility of legal action is sufficient to cause adversaries to change their position. (Pursuing legal action is a major endeavor and is addressed under the "Social Action" heading on page 395.) It is important to keep in mind that tactics and approaches such as fair hearings, complaints, and grievances, which are often used in case advocacy, can be used just as effectively for cause advocacy.

Embarrassing the Target of Change

Most of us like to think of ourselves as decent individuals who treat others with a reasonable degree of fairness. Consequently, it is upsetting when others point out that we are not what we hold ourselves out to be. This is also true of organizations and people in them that purport to be sensitive to their clients' needs. When opponents use the media to call attention to failings, the result, predictably, can be embarrassment. This can either persuade the target to change in the desired direction or result in even greater resistance. Thus, embarrassing the target carries a degree of risk. Highlight 11.7 provides an example of embarrassing the target.

HIGHLIGHT 11.7

Embarrassing the Target

A residential treatment center serving predominantly Hispanic-American children was run by a director who encouraged the staff to use corporal punishment, ignored needs of the residents, and generally did not provide effective training for the staff. The emotional problems experienced by many boys were ignored and led to several attempted suicides, frequent runaways, and other problems.

After approaching the director and failing to convince her to make improvements, the staff decided to undertake a series of actions. One such step was informing the news media of the conditions at the center. Once the local television station and newspapers picked up the story, the situation was too embarrassing for the director and her superiors to sweep under the rug. The director was forced to step down, and new policies were adopted at the center that recognized the physical and emotional needs of the residents. The decision to involve the media was difficult, but there was no other way of protecting the needs of a vulnerable population-at-risk.

Letters to the local newspaper may focus attention on a target, especially if enough people write. Picketing an organization or handing out fliers pointing out what the agency is not doing is another way of embarrassing the target. Sit-ins and demonstrations are also tactics designed to embarrass (and inconvenience) the target. Both involve "massing or marching together in highly visible settings or picketing the entrances of buildings where the behavior that the demonstrators find objectionable is believed to be taking place" (Barker, 2003, p. 114). In the case of sit-ins, you physically occupy the offices or hallways of the organization you are attempting to embarrass.

Political Pressure

Political pressure is the application of political power to force changes that would not otherwise occur. Not all agencies, organizations, or situations are susceptible to political pressure. Public (tax-supported) organizations are more likely to be sensitive to the concerns of political figures who control them. Elected officials may be contacted by constituents and asked to look into a matter that falls under their jurisdiction. Consider a neighborhood composed of many First Nations Peoples. The streets in the area are in terrible condition, and the city never seems to repair them. In addition, the streets are rarely plowed during the winter, so many residents are stranded in their homes. How do you deal with the failure of the city to perform the same functions for this neighborhood and these residents that it does for others? You might contact a city council member and ask her or him to look into the situation. The council member could inquire why the public works department does not schedule repairs in this part of town. She or he might also ask for city records showing the snowplowing routes during the winter. Just having a political figure ask these questions may be sufficient to bring about a change.

At the state level, a social worker can contact a member of the legislature about a persistent problem involving funding for people with mental illness, clearly a population-at-risk. The legislator may ask the head of the state division of mental health why clients with chronic mental illness are not being provided services mandated by state law. This usually will bring some action or response from the agency or its staff. Publicly funded agencies do not enjoy having legislators looking over their shoulders, especially when they are not doing things they should be doing. At the same time, political figures must respond to constituent concerns in order to get re-elected.

Petitioning

Petitioning is the act of collecting signatures on a piece of paper that asks an organization or agency to act in a specified manner. A social worker might help a neighborhood petition the city for better police protection to deal with drug use and gang violence. Gathering petitions can be done by going door to door asking each resident to sign or by setting up a table in a central location where large numbers of people normally congregate. Thus, a local beauty parlor, bar, barbershop, or shopping area may be appropriate. Although petition signatures are relatively easy to collect, this is also one of their limitations. Because they are easy to gather, petitions may not have the desired impact on the target system. The target system might conclude that the people who signed the petition don't really feel very strongly about the matter.

It is perhaps most helpful to present petitions in a public forum. Thus, you might present the petitions to the city council at its regular meeting. Presenting them at a time when others can see what you are doing helps make your efforts a matter of public record. In the case that opened the chapter, the neighborhood association used petitions to support its case that there should be no overnight parking allowed in their area. Highlight 11.8 presents a possible petition form.

Blank petition forms are usually photocopied so that several people can collect petitions at the same time. Extra copies of the petition can also be placed at appropriate locations.

Legislative Advocacy[1]

EP 2.1.8

Legislative advocacy is similar to cause advocacy in that the social worker is working for a broad category of clients or citizens. Legislative advocacy, a macro level intervention like other types of cause advocacy, specifically involves efforts to change legislation to benefit some category of clients. At its most basic, it involves urging lawmakers to pass the laws you want. For simplicity, we will use the term "legislators" to refer to both state and federal lawmakers (CSWE, 2008, EP 2.1.8).

Legislative advocacy may also include efforts to defeat bills considered harmful in some way. A proposed

1. Material in this section is adapted from *Understanding Generalist Practice* (6th ed.) by Karen Kirst-Ashman and Grafton H. Hull, Jr. Used with permission of Brooks/Cole Cengage Learning.

HIGHLIGHT 11.8

A Petition Form

As residents of neighborhoods along Bush Creek, we are outraged by the City of Paris's failure to stop the pollution in this waterway. Raw sewage wastes, including fecal matter, are being discharged into Bush Creek, endangering the health of our children and ourselves. Waterford Park, the only playground in our area, is closed because the creek runs right through the middle of the park. We, the undersigned, demand that the City Council bring an immediate end to the sewage discharge, clean up the existing pollution in Bush Creek, and reopen Waterford Park.

NAME	ADDRESS	NAME	ADDRESS

reduction in funding for the Head Start program would mean limiting or cutting off Head Start services previously available to clients. Head Start is a federal preschool program for children from disadvantaged families that provides education designed to improve their school readiness before they reach elementary school.

Another example of harmful legislation is a proposed state bill to restrict access to reproductive health services, such as Planned Parenthood. This agency provides information, contraception, counseling, and physical examinations, all directed at helping people (usually women) gain control over their own reproduction. Services are usually provided on a sliding fee scale, which means that fees are based on how much people can pay. Poorer people pay less. Richer people pay more.

Legislation limiting access to such services might incorporate requirements such as forcing girls under age 18 to provide written parental permission before they can receive any services. This type of legislation has been introduced at both state and federal levels. Another inhibiting proposal might involve denying the agency any state or federal funding if the staff discusses abortion as a possible alternative to unwanted pregnancy. Both of these examples limit available

services. The first places restrictions on the basis of age. The second limits the potential for informing clients of the options available to them.

Responsibility for legislative advocacy is part of being a social worker because so many decisions affecting social work programs, social workers, and clients are made in the legislative arena. Thus, it is impossible *not* to be concerned about and involved in legislative advocacy. Some workers may feel a bit awed at the prospect of trying to get laws passed and programs funded. Fortunately, legislative advocacy has one unique feature that makes this less difficult: The primary rule of legislative advocacy is that getting elected and re-elected tends to be very important to most legislators (Haynes & Mickelson, 2010). This means that most legislators want to know what their constituents want and are therefore susceptible to their constituents' influence.

In addition, most legislators must make decisions about many proposed bills based on very limited information. Bills are often complex. This increases the likelihood that a legislator will depend on others for information. As a consequence, legislators may very well be influenced by a small number of advocates or by a particularly persuasive argument about a given bill. In other words, you are encouraged to tell your state and federal senators and representatives what you think should be done about bills and issues. You can also mobilize other workers or clients to write or call in what they think. This is one means of gaining some power over what laws are passed or defeated in the political process.

Simultaneously, realistic barriers reduce the likelihood of getting new legislation passed. First, there is the fact that the majority of bills will not become law. Although thousands of bills are introduced at both federal and state levels each year, only a very small proportion is ever passed and subsequently signed into law by the executive (president or governor). There are many reasons for this outcome. For example, most legislative sessions are somewhat short, lasting only a matter of months. Lawmakers might not even get to the bill you're interested in. This means that desired legislation may have to be reintroduced the next year. Often, this involves starting the whole process of influence over from scratch.

Additionally, legislative bodies are unpredictable. Turnover in membership from session to session after elections, changes in control (from Republican to Democratic leadership or vice versa), and economic news (lower-than-expected tax revenues resulting in less available money) make the entire legislative process more complicated. People in power also make unpredictable decisions that affect legislation. In one race for president, the successful candidate pledged, "No new taxes." However, within a short time, he approved new taxes sought by the opposing party. His change in position became an issue when he ran for re-election. The unpredictability of the legislative process and the importance of compromise in the political environment also mean that a candidate's past positions are no guarantee of future actions. Social workers must be clear about this.

Complicating matters further is the fact that even bills that seem to benefit everyone may not become law. Even documented evidence strongly supporting a bill will not guarantee passage (Jansson, 2003). A number of factors can kill a potentially good bill. These include economic conditions and political positions taken by the lawmaker or a political party. In addition, the values and personal experiences of legislators can derail a bill. For example, the effort by the NASW to achieve licensure for social workers in one state was stymied for years because the speaker of the house was personally opposed to social workers. The point is that many factors may override logic and compelling arguments and defeat a bill.

To make matters more complex, even a legislator's agreement to support a bill may prove meaningless. Pet projects of legislators can end up buried or defeated in a committee. Legislative committees are smaller groups of legislators who evaluate the merits of each bill and decide whether to recommend it to the entire legislature. If a committee does send a bill to the floor of the legislature, it may still be defeated or returned to the committee for further work. Finally, governors and presidents can, and often do, veto bills for their own reasons.

Factors Affecting Legislative Advocacy

Success as a legislative advocate requires an understanding of the factors influencing the legislative process. The financial or fiscal implications of a bill are perhaps most important to its chances for success. Put simply, bills that cost a lot of money are less likely to be approved.

A bill's popularity is also a significant factor. The more people (whether the general public or legislators) who support a bill, the more likely it is to pass. In addition, a bill is more likely to pass if it targets a group or issue that is seen as a problem by the rest of society. Bills to increase the length of prison terms for certain types of crimes or to require mandatory sentences for drug pushers tend to pass more easily. At the same time, a bill to provide more money for drug-related education in the schools is less likely to be passed because it will cost more money.

Steps in Legislative Advocacy

State and federal legislatures follow a similar series of steps in the process of turning ideas into laws. These steps are also appropriate intervention points for social workers seeking input in the legislative arena. The steps for legislative advocacy include the following:

1. Developing a draft of the bill.
2. Figuring out who else will help you support the bill.
3. Getting specific legislators to sponsor the bill.
4. Asking your legislative sponsors to introduce the bill.
5. Working with various interest groups to broaden support for the bill.
6. Educating the general public about the bill's value.
7. Trying to influence positively any legislative subcommittee members responsible for decision making about the bills.
8. Trying to influence other legislators to vote for the bill's passage.

HIGHLIGHT 11.9

Steps in the Legislative Process

1. Introduction of a bill in House/Senate
2. Referral to committee
3. Committee report to House/Senate
4. Action by House/Senate
5. Bill sent to other chamber
6. Committee reports to the chamber
7. Debate and action by the chamber
8. Bill referred back to original chamber
9. Signing of bill by both chambers
10. Bill referred to president/governor for signing

Step 1: Developing and Revising the Draft Bill

Formulating an original piece of legislation may sound formidable. It requires both legal knowledge and a familiarity with existing laws, related policies, and programs related to the proposed bill. Consequently, most ideas for laws are sent to an already established unit (sometimes called a legislative reference bureau) that is responsible for writing the first draft of a bill. Reference bureau staff members develop a synopsis of the bill to help legislators understand its intent. Once in draft form, the bill needs further refinement, including clarifications and changes to make the bill reflect its supporters' intentions. If your bill would fund day care centers for children of low-income parents, you want to be sure the bill defines what "low-income" means.

Because legislative reference bureaus work for the legislative body, it is difficult for social workers to have much direct impact on their work. As a result, a bill can languish for a time before the reference bureau staff gives it the needed attention. One state bill strongly sought by social workers was buried in the reference bureau for 11 months and was released about a week before the legislative session ended. As a result, the bill died without ever coming before the lawmakers.

Influencing the reference bureau to develop, revise, and complete work on a law can often be more effectively done by a member of the legislature. Thus, it may be appropriate to seek a legislator's assistance if a bill seems to be stuck in the bureaucracy.

In the process of pursuing a macro intervention in the legislative arena, you will have to become something of an expert on the bill(s) in which you have an interest. Haynes and Mickelson (2003) make several recommendations to ensure you have the expertise needed to become an effective lobbyist. You should know the issue thoroughly. For example, you must clearly understand a bill's history and its fiscal and social implications. It is best to also know what other bills or existing laws are affected by the proposed legislation.

Gaining this type of knowledge constitutes an important step in the assessment process conducted by every social worker. Steps in the legislative process are summarized in Highlight 11.9.

Step 2: Identifying, Obtaining, and Maintaining the Bill's Supporters

Every bill has some natural supporters. These are individuals or groups that are naturally interested in the bill's topic or will obviously benefit from the bill. Make a list of those individuals and groups. They are potential allies.

It is equally important to predict who will be neutral or opposed to a bill. If you hope to see this bill become law, you need to know who will work against it. Those who are initially neutral are potential supporters. Later, you may be able to persuade them to support the bill. Lists of supporters and opponents will include legislators, legislative staffs, external groups (e.g., the National Association of Social Workers [NASW]), governmental agencies (e.g., the Department of Health and Social Services), social service providers, and those who will benefit from the bill.

Once you have identified potential supporters, it is essential to iron out any differences between groups that support the bill. It is not uncommon for people to support bills for vastly different reasons. As a result, each group may have ideas for improving the bill. One group may dislike a particular section or wording. These differing perspectives must be reconciled if at all possible. Modifying a bill to suit other groups is just one cost of keeping these supporters on board.

In many cases it is wise to meet with both supporters and opponents and go over actual copies of the draft bill. This permits all parties to detail their positions and gives you the opportunity to develop further allies. This process usually results in changes in the bill to appease and gain the support of neutral or opposing groups.

Whenever possible, it is wise to seek support from the governor or president as well as from federal or state agencies affected by the bill. A bill providing increased funding for education for prison inmates will be of great interest to the state bureau of corrections. Another bill outlawing employment and housing discrimination against lesbian and gay persons will be of interest to the departments of justice and labor.

State and federal agencies are more likely to be successful in getting bills they support approved. At the same time, an agency's opposition can be fatal to a bill because state and federal agencies administer bills passed by legislatures and Congress. This gives them status as experts on legislation affecting their respective areas of responsibility.

Step 3: Arranging for Sponsorship of the Bill

It is essential to identify legislators willing to introduce and work for passage of a bill. It is also important to seek the help of legislative or congressional staff members. Often, these individuals have great influence with the legislators. Modifying a bill to gain their support can be a wise move.

To get some idea about whether given legislators will support your proposed law, look at their track records. Determine whether they supported similar bills in the past. Have they taken any public positions on this topic?

Another factor of importance is the "safety" of the legislator's seat. Legislators who easily win election (or re-election) can often take riskier positions than those who worry that they may lose the next election. "Safe" legislators may be more inclined to support a bill if they know it won't cost them their jobs. It is great to have the support of a legislator, but an individual who refuses to compromise is a potential danger. Compromise is the currency of politics, and those unable or unwilling to understand this are likely to be risky allies.

Whenever feasible, seek support from legislators in the majority party. The fact that they control the legislative process makes them important. It is even better to have bipartisan support. Obviously, it is also important to get as many sponsors for a bill as you can. Multiple sponsorships increase the likelihood that the bill will pass.

Step 4: Introducing the Bill

Once you have identified legislative sponsors for your bill, ask them to introduce it before the legislative session or as early in the session as possible. Early bills give you more opportunity for lobbying and, if necessary, amending the bill to attract supporters. Bills introduced too late in a session usually end up in the wastebasket and must be reintroduced in the next session. Lobbying involves attempts to political decisions and public policy through a variety of means.

Any attempt to influence legislators regarding a bill is an example of lobbying. Lobbying is an effort to persuade someone else to accept your interpretation of events, facts, and evidence. Lobbying is consistent with social workers' responsibility to pursue such goals as social and economic justice for populations-at-risk. Calling or writing to a legislator asking for support is a form of lobbying. So is testifying before a legislative committee. Our status as amateurs may actually help us, because we are not paid lobbyists. Our conviction and values tend to drive our efforts. This is a relatively novel idea in a world where the paid lobbyists may outnumber the legislators several times over.

Step 5: Working with Interest Groups to Broaden Support for a Bill

Because every bill has many possible supporters, it is important to determine which groups and individuals have an interest in your bill. Sometimes potential supporters are not aware that a bill has been introduced. Other supporters may lack confidence in their ability to influence the outcome even though they are very interested. Your goal is to reach as many of these supporters as you can. You will need all the help you can find. One benefit of involving people in your effort to get a bill passed is that they may become future players in the political process.

Step 6: Educating the Public

Although many bills are of little interest to the general public, there are times when public education can be helpful. Repeated polls have shown that most people do not favor stringent barriers to abortion. Yet state legislatures continue to pass bills (many of them vetoed) setting up various hurdles for women seeking abortion-related services. Public education can be used to rouse opposition to bills not favored by a legislator's constituency. This opposition may force a change in that person's vote. Public education can also take the form of writing letters to the newspaper, holding public forums on a topic, and going door to door with leaflets that explain a bill.

Step 7: Influencing Legislative Committee Consideration

The specific committees that consider given bills are another potential focus of lobbying efforts. If, for example, all health-related bills are sent to the Health and Human Services Committee, this group can be a lobbying target. Committees are the bodies responsible for reviewing, modifying, and recommending action on a bill. Committee appointments are important sources of power for legislators—the leadership of the House or Senate usually makes these appointments.

Note that committees often appoint subcommittees to deal with individual bills. An education committee might have subcommittees dealing with elementary and secondary education as well as with colleges and universities.

Because each bill must go through one or more committees or subcommittees, these bodies have a great deal of power. They can refuse to act on a bill or vote against sending it to the full body. The power of committees and their members makes them a logical target for lobbying. Obviously, a bill must have the support of enough committee members to get reported out to the entire House or Senate. Because getting committee members' support is a critical goal for social workers seeking a bill's passage, it is important to evaluate the composition of the committee, noting each member's political party, identifying the committee leadership, and recognizing potential supporters and opponents on the committee.

Committees often hold public hearings on a bill. These hearings allow a broad range of people to express opinions. The hearings can be a forum for social workers and their allies to present arguments for or against a proposed law. Both expert testimony and the opinions of ordinary citizens are welcome at these hearings.

Kirst-Ashman and Hull (2012) provide suggestions for presenting testimony at public hearings, including identifying those who will speak, in what order, and what they will say. People who testify should provide a written copy of any testimony to the committee members before speaking. The written statement should be able to stand on its own (that is, it should not need any additional verbal clarification). Additionally, it should be worded so that it is clear, straightforward, and reads well. Jargon should be omitted. Don't use professional terms that only those in your field will understand. The statement should say specifically why this law is important and what particular benefits it will have. Argue the case on its merits. Certainly, do not preach. Use factual material and cite its source (for example, census data, specific government studies, or publications).

It is also permissible to use case examples to illustrate the impact of a specific bill. If you are lobbying for a bill that prohibits housing discrimination against gay and lesbian persons, give examples of how the absence of such a law has affected various people.

Use humor very carefully. It's important to be perceived as a serious, professional person. What you think is funny may be seen as insulting, juvenile, or inappropriate by someone else.

Avoid hostility and focus your testimony on the proposed legislation. Be brief, show respect for committee members, and be ready to answer questions, including hostile ones. Be ready to admit you don't have an answer rather than try to bluff your way through.

It is always best to prepare yourself in advance by practicing what you will say. Dressing professionally is expected, and you should address members of the committee appropriately. Always maintain your demeanor. Remember, the way you present yourself can be just as important as what you have to say. Finally, afterward, thank the committee for the opportunity to speak. If you need to do any follow-up, such as sending additional data, do so immediately.

Thinking about testifying before a legislative committee may be very scary. However, having the ability to get up in front of a group, describe a problem, propose a solution, and ask others to support the position is an important skill for macro practitioners. At one level, this is not much more involved than participating in a multidisciplinary team staffing within an agency. There, one must present information, answer questions, and sometimes defend one's assessment. In legislative hearings, a judicious combination of hard data and case examples can be helpful in communicating the impact of existing or proposed policies. Of course, the social worker is not the only one who can testify on macro issues—clients can as well. In fact, their perspective may be more useful than one provided by the professional relating someone else's story.

Step 8: Influencing Action on the Floor

Most bills are modified by legislators once they reach the floor of the House or Senate. You should expect this to happen and be willing to compromise by accepting amendments to the bill. Of course, you must also be willing to work outside the House or Senate by lobbying neutral legislators. This is an opportunity to educate them so that when they have a chance to speak or vote on the bill, they will do so with full knowledge of the facts. You can also seek media coverage of the bill and call legislators to remind them of your wishes just before a vote is taken. Remember that legislators on both sides of the issue can be lobbied, not just those supporting your position.

If at all possible, you and your supporters should be present for the debate on a bill. This is helpful in recognizing opponents' positions. It also can lay the groundwork for changes that may bring these lawmakers around.

Do not become discouraged when a bill is amended. Amended bills are much more likely to be approved than those in which changes have not been made.

Once a bill has received favorable action in one house of a legislature, a similar process occurs in the other chamber. Generally, a bill may be introduced in either house first, although some constitutions require that certain types of bills originate in one house or the other. The legislative process ends, hopefully, when the chief executive (president or governor) signs the bill.

Other Ways to Get Involved

Macro interventions in the legislative arena are not limited to legislative advocacy. It is often much easier to work with legislators who share our values. Therefore, an appropriate macro level intervention is working for the election of candidates favorable to social work positions and issues. Working in a political campaign can be a very positive experience. Social workers, given their various professional skills, can play many roles in political campaigns. Everything from door-to-door campaigning, distribution of campaign materials, phone contacts with likely voters, fundraising, locating and placement of yard signs, and office work are helpful activities. Those who receive your help during their campaigns are likely to remember you when you seek their support later.

Another way to become involved at the macro level is by joining Political Action for Candidate Election (PACE), which was established by the NASW to work for candidates who support social work values and ideals. Both state and national PACE activities occur each year and include providing financial support and other assistance to candidates.

Lists of your elected representatives can be acquired from the public library or by contacting your city hall. In addition, some states publish very detailed books listing all state officials. These may be found in your public library and can often be obtained for free from your state legislator.

Writing to lawmakers is relatively easy. Highlight 11.10 gives examples of forms of address

HIGHLIGHT 11.10

Communicating with Elected Officials

When writing to elected officials, use the correct form of address for such letters. Some common addresses and the accompanying salutation appear below.

Letters to the president:
The President
The White House
1600 Pennsylvania Ave. NW
Washington, DC 20500

Salutation: Dear Mr./Ms. President:

Letters to U.S. Senators:
The Honorable (full name)
United States Senate
Washington, DC 20510

Salutation: Dear Senator (last name):

Letters to members of the House of Representatives:
The Honorable (full name)
U.S. House of Representatives
Washington, DC 20515

Salutation: Dear Representative (last name):

Letters to Cabinet Members:
The Honorable (insert full name)
Secretary of (insert name of department)
Washington, DC (correct zip code)

Salutation: Dear Secretary (last name):

Addresses for state and local officials are usually available at your public library or city hall. You may also choose to contact your elected representatives using e-mail and the Internet. For example, the national site for the Democratic Party is www.democrats.org and for the Republican National Committee is www.rnc.org. Contacting state office holders is generally easy. Each state maintains a Web site or page with links to elected officials, state agencies, and related organizations and individuals. Indiana's Web site, for example, has information on the governor, lieutenant-governor, other constitutional officers, the general assembly, courts, state agencies, and boards and commissions, along with links to state and local associations, telephone directories, calendars of events, and public records.

and methods of contacting your representatives. Your letter should be succinct and should clearly state your position. It should identify the bill or issue of interest and inform the legislator of the need or problem being addressed. The return address should be included on the letter so that the recipient can respond to your letter. Whenever possible, point to the results of evaluations of programs or policies that support your point of view.

Haynes and Mickelson (2006) believe that social workers are especially well suited to grasp the impact of social policy on clients and services. After all, you are the ones most aware of what happens to clients as a result of a particular social policy. Yet, macro practice has assumed a decreasing role in social work practice, if recent surveys are to be believed. Fortunately, several social workers are using their social work skills in the political arena. U.S. Senator Barbara Mikulski began as a member of the Baltimore city council and eventually became the first social worker in the Senate. At the local level as a council member, she worked on issues of concern to neighborhoods, such as potholes, education, and transportation.

Some of the skills that social workers already possess, such as the ability to compromise and bargain, are particularly useful in the political arena. The art of politics is the art of compromise, because it is very rare that anything gets into law in its original form. A hard lesson for many social workers is that the political process does not operate on the same principles as other areas of social work. All political decisions are based on values (Haynes & Mickelson, 2006). We must often present arguments for particular positions without providing the alternative perspective. Our normal tendency to present both sides of the argument is not usually effective in convincing political figures to take specific stands in favor of our legislation or policies. The tactic of using cases to illustrate need can have strong emotional appeal. It is an effective way to show decision makers the impact of their previous actions or to point out how change would benefit a particular segment of the population.

Deciding whether to become involved in the political process also requires that you consider where a particular problem arises. Is it rooted in the legislative arena (such as absence of a law or existence of a poorly written law) or in the judicial area (as happens when judges misinterpret or narrowly interpret the law)?

One judge continually sentenced sexual offenders to relatively minor prison terms and seemed to ignore the impact the offense had on the victim. A group of victim advocates organized a court watch program to ensure that at least one court watcher would be present in every court case involving a sexual offense. Court watchers were usually identified by an arm band or other insignia. The goal of this program was to communicate to the judge that his actions were under scrutiny. Because judges must stand for election periodically, they are sometimes susceptible to the same political pressures as other elected officials. Later, the same tactic was used with a district attorney who was considered too willing to plea-bargain sexual offense cases or to request modest sentences for convicted offenders.

Another potential source of a problem could be in the administrative area, where rules are promulgated. Both governmental bodies and individual agencies develop rules to implement laws that have been enacted and to facilitate ongoing enforcement of those laws. Perhaps proposed regulations (or those already in place) are having very negative effects on a particular group of clients. A regulation or rule that discourages clients from seeking help until they are in a financial crisis may make the situation much worse than if clients could apply for assistance before they had used up their very last dollar.

Of course, sometimes the problem is rooted in the ideologies of political figures themselves. In this case the solution may be to replace the individual at the earliest opportunity. A local district attorney advocated that any victim of rape should put up the greatest possible amount of physical resistance, even if that resulted in her being seriously injured. He argued that such actions gave him a better case to take to court. Of course, he ignored how his philosophy might lead to the injury or death of the victim. Despite attempts by various groups to present their concerns about this dangerous approach, the district attorney refused to change his mind. Because he already had a poor reputation for sensitivity to issues involving women, he was targeted for replacement in the next election. Social workers, women's organizations, and others concerned about rights of the victims worked to ensure that he was not re-elected.

Awareness of macro level problems does not ensure that any action will be taken to address the problems. Often, we must document the problem in terms that are understandable to others. This means we need information on many things. We need to know how many people are affected, how serious the problem is, and how the problem came about. This means we must analyze the problem to know whether it occurs in the legislative, political, judicial, or administrative realm.

Senator (and MSW) Debbie Stabenow (D-Mich.) with Read to Achieve students.

Other Political Activities

Legislative advocacy is just one way of participating in the political process. The generalist social worker can do many things to influence macro level change. You can, for example, get involved in registering voters. Our clients are one of the groups with the poorest record of political participation. Yet voting is a basic way for clients to express their views. Clients can't do that, however, unless they are registered. Registering to vote is becoming increasingly easy and can be done in conjunction with registering a motor vehicle. In addition, social workers have been active in registering clients at their agencies.

At certain times of the year (usually just before elections), one can register in local shopping malls, on college campuses, and in other public locations. Registration is encouraged, and many registration sites are established. In some states, it may be possible to have a colleague certified as a voter registrant. That person can then register others in accordance with whatever policies and procedures have been set by the state. Consider, for example, a recent referendum over a hotly contested state constitutional amendment that

would have seriously damaged education, social welfare, and similar programs. University student government leaders were certified as registrants, set up a registration table on campus, and registered hundreds of new voters just in time for the election. The proposed amendment went down to defeat.

Bernstein (2004), summarizing the impact of the George W. Bush administration, noted that several factors were working against the well-being of a large segment of the population. For example, the U.S. Census Bureau reports that 1.7 million additional people fell below the poverty level during Bush's administration, raising the total of the poor to 35.9 million. Middle-class workers experienced a drop in real income over the period 2002–2004, and African-American workers had a severe decline in income over this period. At the same time, states that might be expected to help support the safety net for their poorest citizens are in the middle of a fiscal crisis, unknown since the Great Depression of the 1930s. State Children's Health Insurance Programs (SCHIP) are also in trouble because of insufficient federal support and weak state resources. The Economic Policy Institute (2003) notes that significant losses in well-paying manufacturing jobs have been replaced by low-paying jobs in the service industry. Some labor organizations fear that the combination of record-high government deficits, coupled with insufficient funds in job training programs, will mean a permanently high level of unemployment for the foreseeable future (Labor Research Association, 2004). An absence of adequate government oversight and unchecked individual and corporate greed contributed to the collapse of several companies, including Enron, in which employees lost nearly all of their life savings, and Worldcom, whose executives borrowed millions of dollars at the same time they were falsifying company financial figures.

At the end of the Bush administration in 2008 and the beginning of the Obama administration in 2009, the government sought to prevent a repeat of the Great Depression by injecting over a trillion dollars into the economy, primarily through loans and grants to banks, insurance companies, the automotive industry, state and local governments, and many other entities. At the time of this writing, the results of these efforts are still unclear. Unemployment is almost 10 percent for the first time since 1982, and many analysts argue that it will remain high for several years. Others see improvements in such things as housing sales, industrial productivity, and the early repayment of government loans by some recipients (mainly banks). At the same time, the Obama administration and Congress approved a badly needed major transformation of health care in the United States. If successful, the changes will occur over a period of years, with the eventual costs still unknown. The next few years appear to be characterized by a high degree of uncertainty, with many social problems continuing to need attention.

These experiences and others suggest some of the reasons why social workers must become politically active. First, the very profession is at risk. Many conservatives see no role for social workers and resent the profession's identification with the poor, with oppressed groups, and with others traditionally at risk. In addition, most of the programs to provide economic resources and meet social and economic justice needs are funded by federal and state tax revenues. The social work "industry" of helping those damaged by the effects of a capitalist economic system is threatened by our failure to become involved in the political process.

Logical roles for social workers include running for nonpartisan political office (city council, school board) and seeking appointment to boards and commissions in their area of interest. Both state and local boards exist, and many times openings in these bodies are announced in the newspapers. Licensing boards for social work and social service advisory boards are typical of such bodies. Citizen advisory boards often exist to help communities better meet the needs of the physically disabled. In addition, social workers can seek seats on police and fire commissions, park boards, and building commissions.

They can also become involved in local, state, and national campaigns, as long as their activities take place outside the workplace. Possible activities include distributing campaign materials, driving voters to the polls, speaking on behalf of a candidate, and putting up yard signs. The Hatch Act, which prohibits some types of political activity on the part of government employees, rarely presents a real threat to social workers. However, in isolated cases, workers have been criticized for confusing their official position and their off-duty roles. This can occur when a social worker writes letters to the editor, endorses a candidate, or otherwise participates in a political process while *simultaneously* identifying him- or herself as an employee of an agency. Most agency policies and common sense dictate that such actions would be confusing to the general public and should be avoided. Whenever possible, you should avoid even the appearance of using your professional position to push for your personal goals. It is always wise to check your agency policies to see if they contain any other restrictions.

Legislative advocacy is an important activity for the generalist practitioner concerned about laws and policies that affect social work clients and agencies. Another significant activity that can be employed on behalf of vulnerable populations is social action, discussed next.

Social Action

Social action usually involves more complex, complicated, and confrontational approaches to achieving goals than your day-to-day work entails. As a consequence, the use of some social action tactics raises difficult questions and produces differences of opinion about social work's obligation to use this approach.

Alinsky's Social Action Approach

Saul Alinsky (1971), a strong advocate of militant social action activities on behalf of the poor, offers some key perspectives on social action that still have great relevance more than 40 years after they were articulated.

First, according to Alinsky, *power* is essential to change the status quo. Those individuals and organizations with power can control their environment much more easily than those with little or no power. Power may come in the form of human or financial resources. When you lack money, you need people to overcome that deficit. When enough people are involved and concerned about something, even those with money can't stop progress. The civil rights movement in the United States involved so many people that it helped bring an end to laws discriminating against African Americans and other persons of color.

Second, power is not the sum of what you actually have, but rather the sum of the *appearance* of what you have. To phrase it differently, it matters less how much power you actually have than how much power others *think* you have. Social workers in many states were successful in achieving licensing for their profession, despite the fact that the actual number of social workers was relatively small. Lawmakers assumed that a sizable group was interested in the legislation because they were hearing from so many people.

Third, power is not given to you. Rather, you acquire power by taking it from those who have it. Thus, the very act of acquiring power is potentially confrontational.

Fourth, use methods familiar to you (or the action system) and unfamiliar to the target system. It is easier to be successful when your opponents are caught off guard by your methods. Consider the refusal of a city public works committee to recommend paving gravel roads in a low-income neighborhood. The committee of seven individuals meets in a small room at city hall that has seats for an audience of 15 people. Having all 150 members of your neighborhood group attend a public works committee meeting will undoubtedly catch the committee off guard. The methods you use must also be consistent with the interests, wishes, and needs of the group with whom you are working.

Fifth, Alinsky believes that all organizations have rules that they say they live by. The rules may be policies, laws, or other regulations that the organization must follow. By making them abide by announced policies and rules, you are asking nothing more than what they say they normally do. Because those rules are generally based on a set of high moral standards, by living within its own rules, an organization often becomes much fairer in dealing with others. An organization that refuses to hire people with disabilities despite laws prohibiting such discrimination can be forced to obey the rules.

Sixth, people should be organized around issues that are vital to them. For example, if gay or lesbian teachers are being denied employment in the school system because of their sexual orientation, this is a significant issue. It makes more sense to use employment discrimination as the focal point rather than to highlight a concern with less impact on the group members. Stated differently, you will have much less success getting people involved in issues about which they don't care.

Seventh, remember that most people in power respond to political pressure. Whether this is right or wrong is immaterial. If you know what buttons to push, push them.

Eighth, and most controversial, remember that successfully attacking a target requires a clear demarcation between good and evil, or haves and have-nots. It is much easier for people on the sidelines to take action if the differences between the groups are clear. This requires, however, that you paint your opponent as bad and yourself as good. Take the situation of an employer who refuses to hire women because the job involves exposure to chemicals that can cause birth defects. It is easy to portray the employer as sexist, guilty of gender discrimination, and a law violator. At the same time, you can paint yourself as concerned about sex discrimination and equal rights for women. This is the good-bad characterization of which Alinsky speaks.

Extreme positions like this can backfire, however, when others do not view your opponent in the same light. In this example, some may think the employer is really concerned about women and does not want them exposed to substances that produce birth defects. Others may believe the employer is taking a reasonable approach to reducing his liabilities, because he could be sued for placing workers in an environment where they could be hurt.

Ninth, turn negatives into positives. Alinsky says you must expect to lose some fights, so you must always be prepared to salvage whatever is possible. This way you can learn from the negatives and can perhaps figure out a more effective strategy next time. It is common for the losing party in a dispute to say that its real goal was to have its grievances heard or to draw attention to a particular problem. This is an attempt to turn a negative (losing) into a positive (spotlighting a problem). In political jargon, this is called *spin*.

Tenth, prepare yourself to propose an alternative. Ripping away at the enemy is fine until the time comes to propose a different solution. Be ready with that solution. Otherwise, you become identified as a crank or chronic complainer. If the city says it cannot provide sufficient additional police to patrol an area wracked by burglaries and assaults, perhaps you can propose that the police help organize a citizen patrol and Neighborhood Watch program to help reduce crime.

Concerns about Social Action

Zippay (1994) and Brueggemann (2006) argue that some of Alinsky's principles are less useful today than when he first articulated them. For example, they note that enemies are harder to identify and that the high-tech world of today makes the role of the media much more influential in affecting ideas, perceptions, and actions. In addition, the tactic of mobilizing one group to attack another typically polarizes people, whereas other approaches may accomplish the same end without the same side effects.

Zippay also argues that we need to connect people to existing sources of power both inside and outside the community. She emphasizes the role of external resources in solving community problems. The nature of many community problems precludes solution without outside funds, according to her perspective. By themselves, cities don't have enough money to solve such major problems as drug abuse and unemployment. She urges practitioners to work with business, civic, and community leaders to achieve goals instead of creating an us-against-them approach. The skills she believes are most important for neighborhood leaders include understanding bureaucracies and political systems, fundraising, legislative advocacy and lobbying, and working with local boards, business leaders, and committees. For the most part, these are much more collaborative approaches than what Alinsky advocates.

Brueggemann (2006) also supports the use of collaboration and coalitions to bring about change. He points out the dangers of reactive approaches that respond to problems but do little to prevent them from occurring in the first place. This method does not change fundamental or underlying conditions, nor does it challenge the basis on which decisions are made. For example, when governmental institutions and administrations argue that what is good for the wealthy is also good for the poor, social workers must reject this simplistic and anachronistic perspective. When a corporate executive's salary is hundreds of times higher than the salaries of the workers who produce a product, it is fair to question why this is. Accepting the argument that "only by paying executives exorbitant salaries can the corporation prosper" ignores reality and perpetuates economic injustice.

At the same time, Gelman (1997) argues that social workers who violate rules and regulations end up putting themselves, their clients, and their profession at risk. The debate about what strategies and tactics to use is likely to continue, because both arguments have merit and both have proven effective in different situations. Perhaps the most important lesson from this debate is that, to be effective generalists, social workers must be flexible. The need for flexibility is evident in Highlight 11.11, which looks at social action considerations on behalf of the homeless.

Legal Action

Legal action has been used for many years to force changes that would otherwise not have occurred. Women's right to an abortion was not recognized until the 1973 decision in *Roe v. Wade*. More recently, the courts have prevented states from placing severe restrictions on the right to an abortion.

The longstanding practice of having "separate but equal" school systems for African Americans and whites (which produced greatly inferior facilities and teaching materials for the former) was struck down in 1954 in a court case (*Brown v. Board of Education*). More recently, courts have been used to end practices that allow one school district to spend substantial amounts on each student while another poorer district spends a fraction of the amount overall. By doing so, the courts have acted to prevent some districts from continuing funding practices that discriminate against the poor.

Yet another example of using the courts involves First Nations Peoples. Many tribes suffered major losses in the 1800s, when tribal lands were stolen or acquired through exploitation or government action. Court decisions have returned lands or required restitution to the plaintiff tribes. In these instances, the courts have been able to resolve disputes that had existed for a century.

Courts have also been a resource for powerless people to force organizations and institutions to abide by existing laws. The Americans with Disabilities Act has provided a means for courts to force an end to discrimination against people with disabilities. Legal action has also been used to achieve new interpretations of old laws.

Legal action is used when it appears that one party has not been abiding by generally accepted rules. Perhaps your adversary has broken the law. Maybe the

HIGHLIGHT 11.11

Social Action on Behalf of the Homeless: Some Considerations

Social action strategies designed to help the homeless must recognize that the homeless are not a homogeneous group. Thus, the strategies for help may have to be different depending upon the needs of a particular subgroup. For example, North and Smith (1994) found that homelessness among nonwhite people was most often caused by socioeconomic problems (lower income, welfare system inadequacy) whereas whites were more likely to have problems caused by drug abuse or psychiatric illness. There were also major differences within each group. Would these observed differences between the two groups suggest different types of programs?

Substantial evidence suggests that many homeless people are being sheltered by family and friends. Yet we have no policies or programs to assist these caregivers, who are clearly helping the oppressed. Is this an appropriate goal for social action?

Homeless children are more likely to lack immunizations and are at greater risk of failing in school,

according to Ziesemer, Marcoux, and Marwell (1994). Which of these problems is the most pressing? Why?

Meeting the needs of the homeless may entail such varied strategies as stress management for problems associated with poverty; reducing the number of Stressors affecting people; reducing stress by having homeless shelters remain open all day, by allowing older siblings and fathers to remain with their families, by providing day care and preschool programs, by providing supportive services during and after a shelter stay, and by allowing choice and control over daily living. Schools can reduce stress by removing barriers to enrollment, easing access to various programs, and "providing transportation, parent-student orientation, free breakfast and lunch, school supplies, and a safe place for possessions" (Ziesemer et al., 1994, p. 667). Depending upon the barriers to achieving these goals, appropriate strategies might range from advocacy to social action.

agency or organization has not operated in accordance with its own policies and procedures. Sometimes rights granted by the U.S. Constitution, such as due process, are not followed. Due process requires that organizations and agencies abide by policies, procedures, regulations, and other rules before they deprive someone of liberty, property, or life. Thus, if a public agency cancels a benefit to a client without providing an opportunity to appeal the decision, the agency has not given the individual the due process to which he or she is constitutionally entitled. Other nations have adopted similar laws in order to ensure that governmental decisions are reached in a fair and impartial manner and that the individual is not deprived of rights without due process.

Taking legal action is definitely a form of confrontation. It is designed to threaten, embarrass, or otherwise coerce your opponents into doing something they would not otherwise do. Legal action may be taken against individuals, groups, agencies, organizations, companies, and governments. It can be taken on behalf of an individual person or organization, or on behalf of a class of individuals. Such *class action suits* argue that an entire group has been hurt and

needs the courts' help to remedy the problem. Class action suits have been used on behalf of people who have certain things in common, such as race or gender. A suit could be filed on behalf of men denied employment at a restaurant that has historically hired only women. Although a single plaintiff may start the process, it is common for such suits to become class action suits because all members of the group are affected.

Of course, you do not always have to use the more drastic step of going to court. Sometimes, the suggestion that one is ready and able to seek redress through legal action accomplishes the same purpose. Most people prefer to avoid lawsuits because of the cost, bad publicity, and time involved. Indicating to adversaries that you are seriously considering suing them can get their attention. Logically, lawsuits are more effective threats against those who do not have their own attorneys. Agencies or organizations that have attorneys on staff have an advantage. They can simply assign that individual to deal with your case and it costs them little or nothing extra. Thus, the threat of a suit may be more effective against those who must acquire outside legal assistance. Even thinking about having to hire an attorney and go to court may be sufficient reason to reconsider one's position.

Using legal action to achieve your group's goals carries other benefits. As Homan (2008) has indicated, finding that the courts will help you is an empowering experience for those long used to having no power. Moreover, lawsuits are a way of working through channels and using the system to accomplish your goals.

Another benefit is that courts tend to be more immune to the political process, so there is less likelihood that the judge will be swayed by contributions, letters, phone calls, or other tactics used in other circumstances. This can be to your advantage.

On the other hand, lawsuits can seemingly take forever to run their course, leaving you and your group waiting. The process of accepting delays, dealing with postponements, and the like can sap the strength of everyone involved in the process. Delays tend to favor those with the most resources and the most to lose when the case is settled. Thus, this party to the suit normally seeks delays. The tendency for things to be delayed can also work in your favor. Projects that are tied up in court may be abandoned as costs mount or deals fall through. Court delays can also lead to other tactics for changing the situation. A court delay might allow time for a change in the law to become effective. It might even allow you enough time to get a law changed or enacted. Delays may also encourage the other party to compromise rather than have the threat of the court decision hanging over them. Thus, delays should not necessarily be considered an evil. They can work to your benefit.

The attorney who will represent you in a court case should be consulted to determine typical concerns such as costs, how long it is likely to take before the case is resolved, and the probability of succeeding with your suit. Attorneys can also explain some of the formal procedures and terminology you will encounter in the court system. The very act of filing a lawsuit can give you information about your opponents that was not previously available. A legal step entitled "discovery" allows each side to see documents in the possession of the other. Let's say that a social agency is proposing to sell the homeless shelter it owns to a developer who will tear it down to build an office building. You might learn through discovery that this sale violates the terms of the agreement under which a donor gave the agency the building to begin with.

When you decide to use legal action to pursue your claim, others may brand you as a troublemaker. Accept the label as a cost of dealing with people whose own behaviors are the real problem. If you are put off by being labeled, you will lose some of your ability to succeed. The other side counts on your wishing to be seen in a favorable light. They hope that by attacking you or your group, they can dissuade you from your lawsuit. Remind your critic that what you are doing is equivalent to calling the police to stop someone from committing a robbery. If the policies or actions of others were not violating the rights of your clients, the lawsuit would be unnecessary.

Courts are also a good place to deal with certain types of situations. Court injunctions, for example, are sought when immediate steps are needed to stop an impending action that, if allowed to proceed, could not be undone. Let's take the example of a university that plans to tear down houses in a low-income neighborhood adjacent to its campus in order to build a performing arts center. The residents have long maintained that the university is insensitive to the neighborhood's needs. Now the university wishes to further destroy their neighborhood. Filing a suit over the proposed destruction would take too long, and the university would go ahead with its plans while the suit was underway. But neighborhood residents can ask the court for an injunction to stop the university from any action that would destroy the neighborhood. If granted, the injunction allows the neighbors time to file a suit challenging the university's action, because the injunction prevents the university from doing anything until the suit is resolved in court.

Legal action can be used for other purposes. Perhaps a law is so confusing that it is not being enforced or its enforcement is uneven. Courts can interpret a law to ensure a consistent perspective on its intent. Sometimes the court will rule that a law is simply unworkable because it is too broad or is poorly worded. Court suits can force people to do things they promised to do. Suing an agency for specific performance means that you want them to follow agreements into which they entered. Sometimes money can be sought from those whose actions have hurt others. Money damages might be demanded from an organization that wrongfully discharged minority workers or discriminated against women in the hiring process.

As you have seen, legal action can be employed for a great many purposes. Moreover, even the threat of legal action can be effective. Legal action can force organizations to follow the laws or their own rules, or to make them live up to their promises. Successful lawsuits can help empower a group. At the same time, legal action is expensive, time consuming, and may ultimately be unsuccessful. Like other methods, legal action should be pursued when it is the most appropriate way to resolve a problem.

Participatory Action Research

EP 2.1.6b

Participatory action research (PAR) is a method of involving people affected by a problem in efforts to study the issue, identify and carry out appropriate interventions, and evaluate the success of the effort. As such, its focus is on social action to bring about societal change. It is participatory in that it carefully ensures that those most directly experiencing a situation are involved at all steps in the change process. The use of the term *action* reflects the emphasis on members taking concrete steps to study, act, and evaluate. They are working together on real problems. Research is an inherent part of the process, since only by studying a social problem or challenge can we better understand what needs to be done. The study itself is guided by scientific principles that include objectivity and careful analysis of findings, and the interventions are based upon proven theories or other evidence-based outcomes (CSWE, 2008, EP 2.1.6b).

PAR is also a method that has found widespread acceptance in many countries, including England, Canada, the United States, Caribbean countries, the Netherlands, and a number of developing countries. It has been used for changing aspects of an organization as well as tackling large-scale problems in a community. Participants have ranged from youth dealing with neighborhood and community issues to professionals seeking more effective ways of involving stakeholders in problem solving. Participatory action research has several real benefits for those who carry out the research. First, they are the ones most acutely aware of and affected by the problem. Thus, their views and experiences matter and are central to the research. They are the beneficiaries of the change effort. Second, the experience of working with others on one project builds confidence in their ability to tackle others. Involving those directly affected by a condition in the process is empowering. Third, it also gives the individual a sense of participation with others and hope that changes will occur.

EP 2.1.1c

The social worker in PAR can play many roles that include facilitator, reporter, teacher, planner, and synthesizer, among others (CSWE, 2008, EP 2.1.1c). The worker is responsible for helping to ensure that

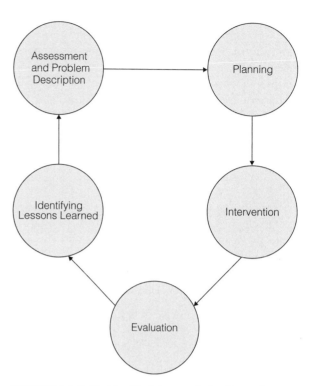

FIGURE 11.2 Model of Participatory Action Research

all relevant individuals and groups are involved in the activities. This means encouraging all who want to participate, listening to input, soliciting suggestions, and summarizing decisions. It also includes educating stakeholders in how to access and assess information.

The process of PAR is similar to the steps in any planned change project. Figure 11.2 shows how PAR evolves. We begin by identifying and describing the problem, a process of assessment. Once the problem is formulated, the next step is to consider what steps will be needed to ameliorate or eliminate the problem. Like planning in the planned change process, we determine the risks and rewards associated with various interventions and select the one(s) that are most likely to produce success. In the intervention phase, we carry out the actions we had identified in the planning step. We then move to the evaluation phase, which involves determining what worked and what did not and why. This leads to a recognition of what we have learned and paves the way for the process to either continue or be abandoned. This may involve a reassessment of the original problem, which has not been resolved, or using our new knowledge to tackle another problem.

Empowerment

Inherent in both social and legal action is a commitment to the principle of empowerment. As described earlier, empowerment suggests that people have "the right to power, ability, and authority to achieve self-determination" (Hartman, 1993, p. 365). Social workers generally observe the principle that clients have the right to self-determination. However, as Hartman notes, "self-determination was a hollow promise sharply limited by lack of access to resources, to opportunity, to power" (p. 365). Oppression, exploitation, and the absence of alternatives all lower the opportunity to self-determine and can result in social and economic injustice. Populations-at-risk require the power to change their situations, and empowerment is focused on this goal.

One source of power that can be shared with clients is that power inherent in the social worker–client relationship. Though social workers might like to believe otherwise, power is unequal in the client–worker relationship—clients have less, we have more. Some of this power is vested in the agency through its resources. Hartman suggests that sharing power with clients may mean giving clients more of a role in deciding how agency resources are spent, organizing clients of the agency as a collective and dealing with them as a group, or creating alternative programs.

Other sources of power can inhibit client empowerment. For example, your expert knowledge is a form of power that can further distance you from clients. You also gain power over clients by your ability to persuade them. This power grows out of interpersonal skills, such as empathy and your rapport with clients. When you say or do things that confuse clients, you reduce their power. When you use your power to make something happen to benefit the client, you are also increasing the power imbalance.

Demystifying what you do can empower clients. Rather than telling a client group, "I talked to a friend of mine at city hall, and he has agreed to meet your group to talk about what can be done," suggest that the group leader contact the official directly.

Another source of power is the legitimate authority vested in you by the state. Social workers who work for public agencies, such as protective services or probation and parole, have social control roles that can conflict with the profession's commitment to empowering people. Because of your role, client groups may tell you what they want you to hear rather than share their true feelings. Thus, this power can get in the way of

client groups being honest and able to discuss their problems freely.

EP 2.1.10e

The strengths perspective, so important to generalist practice (Saleebey, 2009), assumes that power resides in people, and we should seek it through such things as refusing to label clients, avoiding paternalistic treatment of clients, and trusting clients to make appropriate decisions (CSWE, 2008, EP 2.1.10e). Group work tends to be empowering because it emphasizes collaboration and collective planned change. Macro practice that involves the use of client groups to achieve identified goals extends this empowerment.

In summary, empowerment of oppressed groups and of those experiencing social and economic injustice is a legitimate goal for generalist social workers. It is consistent with our commitment to improve social conditions, assist populations-at-risk, and restore the capacity of people to solve their own problems.

Chapter Summary

The following summarizes this chapter's content as it relates to the learning objectives presented at the beginning of the chapter. Chapter content prepares social workers to:

A. *Utilize key concepts involved with macro practice.*

Key concepts in macro practice include advocacy (including both case and cause advocacy), discrimination, empowerment, power, oppressed populations, populations-at-risk, social action, and social and economic justice.

B. *Utilize advocacy, social action, and empowerment activities with populations-at-risk.*

Social workers engage in many activities to help populations-at-risk. These include recognizing the indicators of risk, noting differences in treatment across groups, and deciding what strategies are most effective in dealing with the problem. Possible strategies include advocacy, social action, and empowerment.

C. *Identify factors that place a population at risk for social and economic injustice.*

Many factors can place a population at risk, including any difference (physical, values, beliefs, power, etc.) from the majority population. Common populations-at-risk can include people of color, women, lesbian and gay persons, welfare recipients, homeless individuals and families, those with disabilities, immigrants and refugees, and other groups. At-risk populations can be subject to both overt and covert discrimination.

D. *Utilize the professional role of the social worker in advocating for human rights and social and economic justice.*

A potential role for social workers is to advocate for changes that advance human rights and social and economic justice. Advocacy can include working on behalf of a single group (e.g., women) or to support a specific cause (such as antidiscrimination laws for gay and lesbian people). Advocacy strives to increase accessibility of social services to clients, promote service delivery that maintains the dignity of the groups served, and ensure equal access to all who are eligible for a service.

E. *Analyze and critique the use, value, and limitations of advocacy, opportunities for macro level advocacy, and principles guiding advocacy.*

Serving as an advocate involves both professional values and ethical limitations. It is also helpful if one's agency is a supportive environment for advocacy since this gives the social worker a sense of support when trying to bring about change. Advocacy without considering professional values and ethics, the rights of and risks to clients, or potential consequences of the strategy can be problematic. Advocates should be reasonable in what they undertake and employ teamwork whenever possible to better marshal resources. Other skills needed include assertiveness, flexibility, and persuasiveness, the latter of which involve a willingness to ask questions, ability to see both sides of an issue, and persistence. Advocates may employ fair hearings, grievances, and complaints when needed to make organizations abide by their own policies, regulations, or applicable laws. They can also engage in acts designed to embarrass the change target, pursue political pressure, and petitioning.

F. *Engage in the professional role of legislative advocacy and political activity that advances social and economic justice and social well-being.*

Legislative advocacy is another approach to advocacy that focuses on changing laws, regulations, or other legislative-derived issues. It can include both pushing for new laws and opposing others. The effectiveness of legislative advocacy can be influenced by such factors as the popularity of the idea inherent in a bill, its cost, and others which may or may not be beyond the control of the social worker. To use legislative advocacy, the social worker must know how to draft legislation, identifying potential supporters, lobbying legislators to support a bill, attracting support from other interest groups, educating the general public, and influencing legislative subcommittees considering the bill and other legislators who will ultimately vote on the bill.

Social workers can also engage in other forms of political activity on behalf of social work interests and values. They can do this by voting, registering other voters, running for office, supporting the candidacy of candidates who are sympathetic to social work concerns, and seeking appointments to boards and commissions that make decisions and interpret rules, among others.

G. *Analyze and critique conceptual models of social action while recognizing the ambiguity inherent in resolving ethical concepts.*

Social action is a broad term that has encompassed everything from more militant activities such as sit-ins, demonstrations, and picketing to educational and lobbying decision makers. It can include actions such as dumping sewage from a polluted stream on the steps of city hall or holding a teach-in designed to explain to the public why a change is needed in the way and organization does business. The civil rights marches and activities of the past were examples of social action as are the current efforts to protect gay and lesbian people from discrimination. Since all social action involves considerations of professional ethics, social workers need to balance their goals with the expectations of their profession. Sometimes this involves making difficult decisions and considering whether one's ends justify the means to be employed, especially when using more aggressive methods of social action.

H. *Critique controversial forms of macro practice in relation to the knowledge, skills, and values of generalist social work.*

The Alinsky approach to social action is a more militant model that was used in the 1960s and sporadically since. It involved a series of principles that include acquiring and using power, making it appear as though you have more power than you do, the need to take power from those who have it, using methods that are familiar to you but not your opponents, forcing organizations to live up to their own rules, organizing around issues that are vital to the members, using political pressure whenever needed, painting your group as good and the other as bad or evil, salvaging what you can from defeats, turning negatives into positives, and preparing to propose an alternative rather than just tearing up your enemies' positions.

Some concerns about this model have been discussed in the social work literature. They include a feeling that at least some principles of the model may no longer be applicable, for example, painting your opponent as bad or evil. Working with rather than against opponents is offered as an alternative since it emphasizes collaboration and the use of coalitions. Others have pointed out that some activities may place the worker, client, and profession at risk. It is a debate that will likely go on for the foreseeable future.

I. *Describe participatory action research that uses practice experience to inform scientific inquiry and research evidence to inform practice.*

Participatory action research is a method of involving people who are affected by a problem in efforts to study the issue, undertake efforts to combat the problem, and evaluate the outcomes. It is a model with global utility that has been employed in many countries, with applications from small projects to large-scale change efforts. The PAR model is similar to the steps in any planned change project, beginning with assessing the problem, identifying logical implementation steps, and then evaluating whether the intervention achieved the intended goals.

Competency Notes

The following identifies where Educational Policy (EP) competencies and practice behaviors are discussed in the chapter.

Educational Policy (EP) 2.1 Core Competencies

Educational Policy (EP) 2.1.1b Practice personal reflection and self-correction to assure continual professional development. *(P. 403):* Advocating for others requires that we examine our own lack of

courage and whether we have the ability to tackle a problem.

Educational Policy (EP) 2.1.1c Attend to professional roles and boundaries. *(P. 425):* Social workers using participatory action research may engage in many roles, including facilitator, reporter, planner, and synthesizer, among others.

Educational Policy (EP) 2.1.4a Recognize the extent to which a culture's structures and values may oppress, marginalize, alienate, or create/enhance privilege. *(P. 398):* Among the factors that may help place a population at-risk are such things as our economic system, values and beliefs, and preconceptions held by others in society.

Educational Policy (EP) 2.1.5a Understand the forms and mechanisms of oppression and discrimination. *(P. 398):* Economic justice has been denied certain groups as a result of an economic system that values delivering a product at the lowest possible cost, which can result in low wages, few benefits, and part-time employment for those who produce the product.

Educational Policy (EP) 2.1.6b Use research experience to inform practice. *(P. 425):* Participatory action research uses scientific principles to ensure that interventions employed are supported by evidence whenever possible.

Educational Policy (EP) 2.1.7a Utilize conceptual frameworks to guide the processes of assessment, intervention, and evaluation. *(P. 394):* Understanding concepts such as advocacy, social action, empowerment, and populations-at-risk is essential for social workers working to bring about change in the macro environment.

Educational Policy (EP) 2.1.8 Engage in policy practice to advance social and economic well-being and to deliver effective social work services. *(P. 411):* Legislative advocacy is a form of policy practice designed to enact or change legislation in order to benefit some category of clients. It may also involve efforts to defeat bills that create economic or social injustice.

Educational Policy (EP) 2.1.8b Collaborate with colleagues and clients for effective policy action. *(P. 407):* Teamwork makes it easier to accomplish a goal because of the combined abilities and competence of those who comprise the team. Accomplishing some goals requires the joint efforts of several individuals or groups.

Educational Policy (EP) 2.1.10e Assess client strengths and limitations. *(P. 426):* Empowering clients begins with the strengths perspective, which holds that power resides in people.

Educational Policy (EP) 2.1.10k Negotiate, mediate, and advocate for clients. *(P. 395):* Advocacy is a part of a generalist social worker's responsibility to clients.

On the Internet

Visit the *Generalist Practice with Organizations and Communities* Web site at www.cengage.com/social_work/kirst-ashman for learning tools such as PowerPoint® slides, tutorial quizzing, Web links, and final exams.

CHAPTER **12**

Ethics and Ethical Dilemmas in Macro Practice

The family services agency where you work has suffered significant budget cuts. It appears that the agency must totally eliminate some of its services in order to stay afloat. Potentially targeted programs include day care for working parents, sex education and contraception counseling for area teens, a treatment program for domestic violence perpetrators, and the thriving but expensive foreign adoptions program. Your community has depended on your agency's provision of all these services for many years. Thus, adequate alternate services to meet these respective needs do not exist. What is the ethical thing for you and your agency to do? From an ethical viewpoint, what services or programs should be abolished?

A major influenza pandemic is ominously anticipated by the next winter (Barsky, 2010). Because of the nature of the flu virus and inadequate preparation time, it is predicted that insufficient amounts of vaccine will be available to inoculate the entire population. Public spokespeople have announced the rationing and dissemination schedule for vaccinations. In your state it appears that wealthier suburban communities have been allocated many more dosages of the vaccine than poorer urban neighborhoods, including those in which many of your clients live. Is this fair? Is this ethical? What could you do about this inequity?

The private social service agency you work for does not have a formalized affirmative action policy. You have observed the agency director making racist remarks and jokes. You cannot believe that he has gotten away with it. You have worked for the agency for only three months of your six-month probationary period, so you could easily be dismissed. The agency has no people of color on staff, despite having numerous such clients. You feel that recruiting staff of color is essential to the agency's ability to perform the way it's supposed to. What should you do? Should you simply look away and pretend you don't know anything about the problem? Should you charge into the director's office like a bull in a china shop and complain? How about talking to other staff to see what they think? Or should you call the press or a regulating agency and blow the whistle? Should you quit your job? How do you determine the most ethical thing to do?

The community in which you live and work provides no services for homeless people, despite the fact that their numbers are escalating. Every day on your way to and from work, you pass at least a half-dozen people roaming the urban streets. Many times you see children with them, dirty, probably hungry, and obviously not in school. Most people at your agency don't really want to talk about it. You get the feeling that your colleagues think they have enough to do trying to accomplish their own jobs. Work demands continue to increase while funding resources shrink. Should you ignore these homeless community residents, or should you try to implement some macro change to provide them with desperately needed services? What is the ethical thing to do?

Introduction

Even though this book is oriented toward practitioners who work primarily in micro and mezzo settings, you will always be working within the macro contexts of your organization and the community. Therefore, the surrounding macro environment will invariably affect decisions you make concerning what to do, what not to do, what is right, and what is wrong. Public laws and agency policies will regulate what you do and how you do it. That is all well and good. However, what about those times when what you consider the right thing to do seriously conflicts with these laws and policies? What about when the existing laws and policies ignore or don't allow for services your clients need? What happens when you see colleagues, administrators, or community leaders doing things you consider unethical? This chapter deals with making ethical decisions within macro contexts. It focuses on those decisions you must make when there is no absolutely clear *right* thing to do.

Learning Objectives

This chapter will provide content concerning how social workers:

A. *Examine and apply the NASW Code of Ethics.*
B. *Relate how spiritual diversity characterizes the human experience and apply ethical boundaries when addressing spirituality.*
C. *Make ethical decisions by applying standards of the International Federation of Social Workers (IFSW)/International Association of Schools of Social Work (IASSW) Ethics in Social Work, Statement of Principles.*
D. *Recognize and manage personal values, including those concerning stereotypes and prejudices, so that professional values can guide practice.*
E. *Apply a strategy of ethical reasoning to arrive at principled decisions.*
F. *Review two strategies for ranking ethical principles.*
G. *Appraise a range of ethical dilemmas occurring in macro contexts, tolerate the ambiguity involved in decision making, and propose viable options to address the dilemmas.*
H. *Recognize and communicate the importance of appreciating cultural differences in ethical practice.*

Professional Values and Ethics in Macro Contexts

Along with knowledge and skills, professional values comprise the third support for the foundation of generalist social work practice. *Values* are what you consider "*good* or *desirable*" (Dolgoff, Loewenberg, & Harrington, 2009, p. 21). They underlie your judgments or decisions about relative worth—that is, what is more valuable and what is less valuable. For example, the *NASW Code of Ethics* (2008) identifies six core values of the profession: (1) service, (2) social justice, (3) dignity and worth of the person, (4) the importance of human relationships, (5) integrity, and (6) competence. These values frame the perspective with which social workers view their work with people and were discussed briefly in Chapter 1. However, whereas social workers are committed to each of these values in the abstract, these six concepts do not necessarily provide guidance about what to do in particular situations. A further refinement is necessary, and professional ethics provide that.

EP 2.1.2

In contrast to values that indicate what is "*good and desirable*," *ethics* designate "what is *right* and *correct*"; ethics, then, are sets of principles that guide the behavior of professionals (Dolgoff et al., 2009, p. 2). They are based upon the values of the profession and represent ideals that social workers should endeavor to reach. As such, they further direct our actions in our capacity as social work practitioners. In effect, they provide suggestions about how we apply the values of the profession. The importance of ethics has been underscored by Cournoyer (2008), who notes that ethical responsibilities take precedence over "theoretical knowledge, research findings, practice wisdom [insight gained from life experience and service to clients], agency policies, and, of course, your own personal values, preferences, and beliefs" (p. 90). This is a significant statement requiring careful consideration. It means that an ethical decision on your part supersedes all other aspects of your practice.

Cournoyer (2008) identifies at least five dimensions of ethical decision making that merit your attention:

First, you need to understand those legal duties that apply to all professional helpers. Second, you must be familiar with the state, local, and federal laws and regulations that affect the profession and practice of social work in your locale. Third, you should thoroughly comprehend the core social work values and be extremely familiar with the social work code of ethics. Fourth, you must be able to identify those ethical principles and legal duties that pertain to specific social work practice situations. Fifth, when several competing obligations apply, you need to be able to decide which take precedence. This represents the greatest challenge and involves the most advanced critical thinking skills. When there is no conflict among the ethical and legal responsibilities relevant to a particular situation, you should easily be able to make a decision and take appropriate action. You merely conform to the appropriate legal and ethical obligations. In other words, you simply "do the right thing." Frequently, however, the applicable principles and duties conflict with one another so that adherence to one obligation means violating another. Deciding which obligation takes precedence is the most complex and challenging aspect of ethical decision making. (pp. 90–91)

© A. Ramey/Photo Edit

This social worker and nurse discuss with an older adult the ethical care of her mother (whose image is reflected in the mirror) in a community hospice. One ethical question is the patient's right to make decisions about her care versus her daughter's and the hospice staff's.

One of the ethical dilemmas that may confront a social worker involves what to do when a client reveals that she is going to commit a crime. How does the social worker balance a client's right to confidentiality with the potential harm to another person or to society?

Another similar challenge involves a client who has revealed that he has contracted HIV (Reamer, 1987). He has just been given the diagnosis. Although access to expensive drugs and treatment can significantly prolong life, this condition is almost certainly fatal in the long run. The social worker knows that the client has been having unprotected sexual relations with several people over the past months. During their meetings, the client has revealed these people's identities. After discussing options, the client refuses to tell his sexual partners about his diagnosis. Additionally, for various reasons, the social worker doubts that the client will begin to use precautions against spreading the disease in the near future. Agency policy mandates that social workers not violate clients' confidentiality. This means that, according to policy, the social worker may not tell anyone about the HIV diagnosis without the client's clearly expressed written permission. But the worker worries that if the prior sexual partners are not told about the HIV diagnosis and their potential exposure, they (as well as the client) may continue to spread the disease. Which ethical concept is more important—the worker's commitments to her employing organization and its policy, or her ethical responsibility to the general welfare of society and the well-being of other people? What if the social worker discovers more and more clients in similar situations? Can the social worker ignore a policy that negatively (and critically) affects scores of people? Should the social worker assess possible initiation of a macro change process? Does she have time and energy to do this in view of her other job responsibilities? There is no easy answer.

There are numerous other ethical dilemmas. A law might dictate a lengthy procedure for removing the perpetrators from the home in cases of alleged sexual abuse. What about the immediate, critical need of the victims to be kept safe? Or suppose you work at a public assistance agency that requires applicants for resources to maintain residency for a specified time period before they become eligible for help. You know of several single parents who have come to your agency pleading that their children are starving. They are desperate for help, but have not lived in the area long enough to satisfy the residency requirement.

You can think of nowhere else in the community that these families can turn for help. What should you do? Should you let a family starve? Is it your ethical responsibility to pursue some macro change efforts on these families' behalf so that they can get the resources they need to survive?

Professional values and ethics do provide some basic guidelines, but many times, a social worker has to make hard choices about what is the more ethical action.

The NASW Code of Ethics

EP 2.1.2b

In addition to our own professional values, there is one more reason to understand and abide by the NASW *Code of Ethics*: legal liability. We are in an increasingly litigious society, and many social workers have found themselves defendants in lawsuits alleging that they have harmed a client or family in some way. A common accusation is that the defendant engaged in substandard practice and behaved improperly. Because the NASW *Code of Ethics* represents the official ethical standards of the social work profession, it is the most likely yardstick to be used in judging whether your actions were appropriate. This is true regardless of whether you are actually a member of the NASW. Although one can never eliminate the possibility of being sued, conducting your practice in accordance with the accepted ethics of your profession can significantly reduce your chances of being found guilty of malfeasance. Cournoyer (2008) notes that keeping "professional quality records about your ethical decision making process as well as other aspects of your service to clients" can function as a helpful safeguard (p. 91).

Because of the code's significance, we will examine it section by section. Note that reference numbers are provided in the forthcoming subtitles so that you might more easily locate each section when referring to the code itself. The code is available on the Web at www.naswdc.org/pubs/code/default.asp. The NASW *Code of Ethics* provides ethical guidelines for how to make decisions and practice social work in six general areas.

These six areas include the social worker's ethical responsibilities to clients, to colleagues, in practice settings, as professionals, to the social work profession, and to broader society (NASW, 2008). Highlight 12.1 features a summary of the codes. The following sections discuss the code item by item.

HIGHLIGHT 12.1

A Summary of the Ethical Standards in the NASW Code of Ethics

1. Social workers' ethical responsibilities to clients

   1.01 Commitment to clients
   1.02 Self-determination
   1.03 Informed consent
   1.04 Competence
   1.05 Cultural competence and social diversity
   1.06 Conflicts of interest
   1.07 Privacy and confidentiality
   1.08 Access to records
   1.09 Sexual relationships
   1.10 Physical contact
   1.11 Sexual harassment
   1.12 Derogatory language
   1.13 Payment for services
   1.14 Clients who lack decision-making capacity
   1.15 Interruption of services
   1.16 Termination of services

2. Social workers' ethical responsibilities to colleagues

   2.01 Respect
   2.02 Confidentiality
   2.03 Interdisciplinary collaboration
   2.04 Disputes involving colleagues
   2.05 Consultation
   2.06 Referral for services
   2.07 Sexual relationships
   2.08 Sexual harassment
   2.09 Impairment of colleagues
   2.10 Incompetence of colleagues
   2.11 Unethical conduct of colleagues

3. Social workers' ethical responsibilities in practice settings

   3.01 Supervision and consultation
   3.02 Education and training

   3.03 Performance evaluation
   3.04 Client records
   3.05 Billing
   3.06 Client transfer
   3.07 Administration
   3.08 Continuing education and staff development
   3.09 Commitments to employers
   3.10 Labor–management disputes

4. Social workers' ethical responsibilities as professionals

   4.01 Competence
   4.02 Discrimination
   4.03 Private conduct
   4.04 Dishonesty, fraud, and deception
   4.05 Impairment
   4.06 Misrepresentation
   4.07 Solicitations
   4.08 Acknowledging credit

5. Social workers' ethical responsibilities to the social work profession

   5.01 Integrity of the profession
   5.02 Evaluation and research

6. Social workers' ethical responsibilities to the broader society

   6.01 Social welfare
   6.02 Public participation
   6.03 Public emergencies
   6.04 Social and political action

SOURCE: National Association of Social Workers, Inc. Copyright 1999 National Association of Social Workers, Inc. Reprinted with permission.

Social Workers' Ethical Responsibilities to Clients

The first section of the NASW *Code of Ethics* is divided into 16 specific categories that delineate the social worker's obligations to clients. These responsibilities involve decisions workers make in micro practice, and they concern agency policies and procedures about how clients should be treated. They also involve public laws under which practitioners function. Thus, ethical responsibilities to clients are both micro and macro concerns.

1.01 Commitment to Clients

The first principle is simple and straightforward: The client should come first. Exceptions may occur when legal responsibilities (such as mandatory reporting of child abuse) of the worker conflict with commitment to the client. Whenever possible, clients should be made aware of this conflicting obligation. Clients should expect to be treated with respect and dedication and to receive the social worker's best efforts on their behalf.

1.02 Self-Determination

Social workers are obligated to respect and encourage clients' rights to make their own decisions, identify their own needs, and choose the most appropriate option when faced with possible courses of action. Exercising self-determination requires that clients know what the resources and choices are and the consequences of selecting any of them. At times, social workers may encounter situations where a client's actual or intended course of action poses a clear and present risk to themselves or others (such as a client choosing suicide over medication). In these rare instances, social workers may use their professional judgment to prevent a client from exercising self-determination.

1.03 Informed Consent

Informed consent means that clients know the risks of social work services or other interventions, limitations imposed by managed care, costs of service, alternatives that are available, and their right to refuse to participate. If clients have diminished capacity to make an informed decision, a third party should be consulted. Examples would be a client under the influence of alcohol or drugs who is temporarily incapable of making a wise decision, or a person with an IQ level too low to comprehend what is being proposed. Often, social workers work with involuntary clients who are forced by the court or by law to receive services. Even in these cases, the client should be informed about the length and type of services being provided, the limits on a client's right to refuse the service, and the consequences of a refusal. For example, clients in a first-offenders criminal justice diversion program may choose not to participate. One of the consequences of this refusal will be notification to the court and a trial for the original offense. Although this may not look like much of an option, it is still the client who has the right to choose. As a colleague observed many years ago, clients have the right to fail.

Once you have begun to work with a client, other opportunities for informed consent may surface. For example, clients have the right to refuse visual or audio recording of their sessions with social workers.

They also have the right to refuse the presence of or observations by third parties, such as students, other workers, or supervisors.

1.04 Competence

It should come as no surprise that clients have the right to a competent social worker. In practice, this means that you must use interventions for which you have appropriate training or education. It also means that you must represent yourself as having only those skills and credentials you actually possess. Inferring or suggesting to clients that you have capabilities or experience beyond your actual level is unethical. One social worker, wanting badly to provide clinical services, got a friend to verify that she had provided the necessary hours to become certified as a mental-health provider. Following certification, the social worker began to see clients in a mental health setting. Clients of the social worker clearly were not getting the level of competence they assumed.

Learning new skills or approaches (as you will continually have to do) requires that you use supervision and consultation appropriately. The person providing supervision or consultation should have competence in the new skill or approach. When confronted with situations or problems beyond your level of competence, you must seek supervision or consultation and, when needed, refer clients to others with requisite skills.

Many states now mandate a certain number of continuing education hours prior to relicensing social workers. This is a recognition by the legislature or licensing body that one is never through learning and that clients deserve practitioners who are

EP 2.1.1e

well informed. Sometimes these requirements specify the content (such as a course on ethics), but mostly the choice of topics is up to you. If you need divorce-mediation or child-management skills, use this opportunity to increase your competence while meeting your relicensing requirements. Take advantage of college and university courses as well as special programs sponsored by the NASW and other groups.

1.05 Cultural Competence and Social Diversity

Social workers should strive to identify and appreciate the strengths inherent in any particular culture and recognize differences among cultures. Practitioners should "obtain education about and seek to understand the nature of social diversity and oppression with respect to race, ethnicity, national origin, color, sex, sexual orientation, gender identity or expression, age, marital status, political belief, religion, immigration status, and mental or physical disability" (NASW, 2008, 1.05). Highlight 12.2 discusses the importance of addressing religion and spirituality in social work practice.

1.06 Conflicts of Interest

Conflicts of interest are situations where the client's benefit is actually or potentially compromised by an action of the social worker. They can arise in any number of situations. For instance, it is unethical for social workers to exploit others for their own personal benefit. Consider an agency administrator who awards a bid for new agency furniture to a company that promises to provide him a new couch and recliner for his home. His obligation to get the best deal for his agency has fallen prey to his personal interests, namely, decorating his den.

Dual or multiple relationships are also an ethical trap. Corey, Corey, and Callanan (2007) explain:

Dual or multiple relationships … *occur when professionals assume two or more roles at the same time or sequentially with a client [emphasis added]. This may involve assuming more than one professional role (such as instructor and … [counselor]) or blending a professional and nonprofessional relationship (such as counselor and friend or counselor and business partner). Dual relationships also include providing [counseling] … to a relative or a friend's relative, socializing with clients, becoming emotionally or sexually involved with a client or former client, combining the roles of supervisor and [counselor,] … having a business relationship with a client, borrowing money from a client, or loaning money to a client. … [Helping] professionals must learn how to effectively and ethically manage multiple relationships, including dealing with the power differential that is a basic part of most professional relationships, managing boundary issues, and striving to avoid the misuse of power. (p. 262)*

According to Syme (2003), dual relationships

are not necessarily harmful, or unavoidable [e.g., when a worker belongs to the same church or health club as a client], but there is always the potential for a conflict of interest and of exploitation of the person seeking help. This makes it critical that whenever

there is a possibility of a dual relationship the … [practitioner], who is the person who knows the difficulties that could arise in such relationships, must think about and perhaps discuss with a supervisor the potential conflicts of interest and exploitation before entering into such a relationship. (p. 8)

One example of a multiple relationship is an agency supervisor who accepted a student into field placement without informing the university that the student had previously received therapy from the supervisor. Nor did she inform the agency or school that she was paying the student to clean her house on a weekly basis. In this case the student knew about the multiple roles and still sought out the placement. However, the field instructor's obligation to the client, agency, and school were clearly in conflict, and her services as a field instructor were terminated for this breach of ethics.

One of the more problematic areas of dual relationships is when a social worker is providing services to multiple people who have relationships with each other—such as family members, friends, or neighbors. It is then the social worker's professional responsibility to maintain her distinct role with each client, carefully adhere to other ethical standards such as privacy and confidentiality, and inform clients about these role expectations.

1.07 Privacy and Confidentiality

The social worker has a primary obligation to respect a client's right to *privacy* (people's right to be free from other people's intrusion in their personal affairs) in at least two ways. First, information a social worker seeks should be clearly related to providing service, not information sought out of pure curiosity. Second, information learned from a client must be maintained in confidence. *Confidentiality* is the ethical principle that workers should not share information provided by or about a client unless that worker has the client's explicit permission to do so. This confidentiality is not absolute, of course. Agency records, worker's notes, and the worker may be subpoenaed into court in many states. Additionally, laws may require reporting of certain information such as the commitment of a felony.

Of important note is a controversial change in the code implemented in August 1999 by the NASW Delegate Assembly (an elected group of members from all state chapters that meets every three years and serves as the NASW's highest decision-making

HIGHLIGHT 12.2

Ethical Boundaries and Spirituality

Religion and spirituality reflect yet another aspect of human diversity. *Religion* involves people's spiritual beliefs concerning the origin, character, and reason for being, usually based on the existence of some higher power or powers. These beliefs often include designated rituals and provide direction for what is considered moral or right. *Spirituality,* a related concept, is "the individual search for meaning, purpose, and values" that typically rises above everyday physical limitations and connects one to something greater than oneself (O'Neill, 1999, p. 3). Religion implies membership in a spiritual organization with customs, traditions, and structure. Spirituality may involve religion, or it may reflect a personal, internalized view of existence.

Gotterer (2001) explains the significance of spirituality and religion for social work practice:

> Social workers, typically involved with vulnerable people in situations of pain or crisis, need a greater awareness of spiritual and religious issues. Tragedies such as the untimely death of a loved one force a person to confront the inexplicable. People nearing death often wonder whether there is an afterlife. Trying times may cause a person to question the meaning and purpose of life. Those subjected to serious disease or long-term oppression need some way to make sense of their experience. Spiritual concerns such as hope, meaning, inner strength, and doubt are relevant in many clients' lives. (p. 187)

A client's spirituality may be a great source of strength. However, workers must be exceedingly careful not to impose their own religious and spiritual views upon clients. The overriding principle of self-determination clearly affirms that "social workers should never try to impose their own beliefs on clients" (Canda & Furman, 2010; O'Neill, 1999, p. 3). It is very important for social workers to fully understand their own spiritual and religious convictions in order to maintain clear boundaries between their beliefs and those of their clients (Mattison, Jayaratne, & Croxton, 2000).

In 2008, Canda and Furman (2010) surveyed a random sample of NASW members who provided service directly to clients about spirituality and religion with respect to practice. They conclude:

> Most social workers in our study believed that it is appropriate to raise the topic of spirituality in a non-sectarian manner [not involving any particular religious affiliation or group] with clients on every issue we explored, but especially regarding terminal illness, bereavement, substance abuse, and suffering effects of natural disaster ... Most respondents also believed that it is appropriate to raise the topic of religion in cases of terminal illness, bereavement, adoptive and foster parenting, substance abuse, and suffering the effects of a natural disaster. ... Unfortunately, ... nearly 65% of respondents did not receive content on spirituality or religion in their social work education. ... A majority of ... responders agreed that social workers should become more knowledgeable about spiritual matters ... and religious matters. ... Nearly 25%, however, agreed that workers do not have the skill to assist clients in religious and spiritual matters. (pp. 6–9)

On the one hand, social workers should not seek to convert clients to their ways of thinking. On the other hand, "it is also problematic to ignore or fail to adequately address clients' religious and spiritual needs because they are viewed as unimportant or irrelevant" (Mattison et al., 2000, p. 54). Therefore, it is best to learn about clients' religious and spiritual beliefs from various sources including religious readings, spiritual leaders, or the clients themselves. "Social workers must develop sensitivity and competence in dealing with spiritual diversity, just as in dealing with cultural diversity" (Canda, 1997, p. 304; Carroll, 1997). This means that a social worker with Muslim beliefs who is working with Christian clients should help these clients focus on the strengths they can draw from their Christian faith. Likewise, a Christian worker should help Muslim clients utilize the strengths inherent in their Muslim faith. Frame (2003), however, warns that "[i]f clients are not open to religious or spiritual aspects of their difficulties, it is inappropriate to bring ... [these issues] into counseling or to employ methods that are particularly based in religious or spiritual beliefs or practices" (p. 184).

Mattison and her colleagues (2000) call for two macro level changes to provide guidance for social workers in the spirituality arena. First, the NASW *Code of Ethics* should be made more specific regarding how these issues should be handled. They explain that the "profession needs to explore issues of whether or not assessment of religion and spirituality need to be areas of routine client assessment. Standards regarding both assessments and interventions need to be established, as well as whether or not the practitioner should initiate these discussions or wait for clients to raise them" (p. 55). Second, social work should "address the question of to what degree the profession should incorporate religion and spirituality into professional training" so that practitioners are more competent in this area (p. 55). To what extent should social work programs incorporate this content in their curricula? Accreditation standards require that competency involving "knowledge, values, and skills" concerning *religion* as a dimension of diversity should be achieved (CSWE, 2008, EP 2.1, 2.1.4). To what extent should agencies establish clear policies regarding practice procedures and spirituality? Guidelines could help practitioners make more informed decisions about what to do. Finally, to what extent should agencies provide staff with formal training to enhance their competence in this area?

body). The change involved the deletion of the phrase originally included in the 1996 code, marked in bold-face below (NASW, 2008, 1.07c):

> *The general expectation that social workers will keep information confidential does not apply when disclosure is necessary to prevent serious, foreseeable, and imminent harm to a client or other identifiable person **or when laws or regulations require disclosure without a client's consent.***

The NASW's national committees on ethnic diversity; women's issues; and lesbian, gay, and bisexual rights feared that the old language "could be interpreted as a requirement, or at least an encouragement, to report on clients whenever there were laws or regulations mandating reporting, regardless of social work values" ("Ethics and Reporting," 1999, p. 5). Of special concern were issues regarding immigration status, HIV status, and sexual orientation. At that time, many delegate participants believed there was national pressure for states to pass restrictive and punitive legislation concerning these groups.

Note that the code still includes references concerning how clients should be reported under certain circumstances, such as the following:

> *However, social workers' responsibility to the larger society or specific legal obligations may on limited occasions supersede the loyalty owed clients, and clients should be so advised. (Examples include when a social worker is required by law to report that a client has abused a child or has threatened to harm self or others.) (NASW, 2008, 1.01)*

Whenever possible, clients should know about the limits to their privacy and the confidentiality of worker records. Agency records may be routinely available to supervisors and administrators. Cases are usually discussed with supervisors. Clients should know these exceptions, along with any legal agency policy mandates.

Confidentiality also becomes a potential problem in groups or when working with a family as a group.

Clients should agree to maintain, in confidence, information they learn during group or family sessions as a mutual obligation to one another. At the same time, confidentiality cannot be guaranteed in such situations where nonprofessionals hear patients' disclosures.

Information that must be shared with others should be as limited as possible, and client consent should be obtained beforehand. This includes data provided to managed-care companies or consultants and information disclosed when teaching or in other situations. Identifying information should never be disclosed without client consent.

The use of computers for maintaining records has opened up other possibilities for breaching confidentiality. Lax attention to computer records can mean others get access to information for which they are not authorized. Turning a computer off and using a password, for example, helps prevent unauthorized access to files. Similarly, e-mail and fax messages can go astray, be read by people other than the client, and leave a worker in a vulnerable situation. Even leaving a voicemail message on a client's home phone is not secure, because others in the home often have access to the voicemail. Technology can make our job easier, but it also offers opportunities to violate a client's rights and our ethical obligations.

Pay close attention to when and where you disclose confidential information. Talking in a public setting about a case can result in unintended disclosure of information. Two social workers discussing a client over a meal at a local restaurant mentioned the client's name several times. A waitress overheard the conversation and reported the information back to the client (a friend of hers), who informed agency administration. Needless to say, both social workers were embarrassed, and both received letters of reprimand from their agency.

Finally, workers have an obligation to ensure confidentiality and privacy of client records when making referrals, terminating a case, or in the event of the worker's death. Agency policy may already provide for such situations, but you are advised to check on it.

1.08 Access to Records

Clients should have reasonable access to records that concern them. If they need help interpreting information in the files, you should provide this. Only severe harm to the client justifies withholding records, and this should be documented in the client files. Of course, no information on other individuals should be shared with a client.

1.09 Sexual Relationships

Although it should be obvious that any sexual relationship between a worker and client is unethical, the number of social workers censored by the NASW for this very behavior is evidence that the message is not always getting through. The NASW *Code of Ethics* explicitly prohibits sexual activities or contact between current or former clients and workers, regardless of whether it is consensual. The prohibition extends to clients' relatives or others with whom the client has a close relationship. The potential harm to the client is substantial and makes it nearly impossible for the practitioner to maintain appropriate professional boundaries.

Similarly, it is inappropriate to provide professional services to a client with whom one has had a prior sexual relationship. Responsibility for violations of these prohibitions rests solely on the social worker, not the client, regardless of whether the latter initiated, agreed to, or willingly participated in the activity.

These ethical guidelines may seem superficially simple and straightforward. However, real life and human failings may complicate matters. For example, a 22-year-old student in her internship called this author about her temptation. She was working at a halfway house for young men on parole who also had substance abuse problems. She said she was totally enamored with one of her clients. She confessed that she had difficulty controlling her emotions. We talked about what effects inappropriate and unethical behavior could have on her reputation, her career, and her client. She had only four more weeks of placement at the agency. The agency had an established policy that no staff, including staff who left the agency, should enter into romantic involvement with clients for at least six months following the client's termination. This student knew that involvement with the client was wrong. We didn't even get into the other potential problems of entering into a relationship with a person who had been in jail and who was substance addicted. The student was struggling. As she didn't call again, we don't know what she chose to do. Sexual temptation is not an uncommon kind of situation.

1.10 Physical Contact

Physical contact between clients and workers is prohibited if it may produce psychological harm to the client. Appropriate, "culturally sensitive" physical contact is permitted as long as the worker sets clear boundaries for such contact (NASW, 2008, 1.10).

1.11 Sexual Harassment

Sexual harassment is explicitly prohibited and includes such actions as solicitation for sexual favors, verbal or physical sexually tinged contact, and advances (as discussed in Chapter 7). In addition to the ethical prohibition, sexual harassment is also punishable under various state and federal laws and regulations.

1.12 Derogatory Language

Social workers are not to use derogatory language in any of the their communication about or with clients. Showing respect for clients demands that the worker use precise language and avoid terminology that would be objectionable. Derogatory language includes belittling statements, demeaning comments, or words that demonstrate a low opinion of the client or others.

1.13 Payment for Services

Social workers are responsible for establishing fair and reasonable fees that reflect accurately the services provided. The client's ability to pay should also be taken into consideration. Nonmoney transactions, such as bartering or accepting goods or services in exchange for professional services, should be avoided. Also, you should never expect clients to pay for a service when they have a right to that service free of charge through your employer or agency.

1.14 Clients Who Lack Decision-Making Capacity

The client's decision-making capacity may affect a social worker's ethical responsibility. It is not uncommon for a client to have diminished capacity for making decisions. When you must act on behalf of these clients, it is critical that you take all reasonable actions to protect the clients' interests.

1.15 Interruption of Services

Continuity of service is an obligation of the worker that requires that appropriate efforts be made to ensure clients get services they need. This may involve referring clients to others when you are incapacitated or when you leave your job.

1.16 Termination of Services

EP 2.1.10L

Termination of services should occur when the professional relationship is no longer necessary or when it no longer is beneficial. Termination should be discussed in advance and clients should be informed about available options. Withdrawing services abruptly is likely to be harmful to clients and should be avoided. When this is not possible, any harm to the client should be minimized. Clients may be terminated (usually by a supervisor) for failing to pay an overdue balance when this possibility has been made clear to the client and discussed with the worker. In no case should a client be terminated when doing so places the client or others in immediate danger. Likewise, you should never terminate with a client in order to further your own relationship with a client, whether sexual, financial, or otherwise.

Social Workers' Ethical Responsibilities to Colleagues

Although it may seem unusual, social workers have an ethical obligation to their colleagues. This obligation includes professional treatment of colleagues, dispute resolution, relationships with colleagues, and handling of the impairment of another worker.

2.01 Respect

Social workers are required to treat colleagues with respect and never to misrepresent the competence and views of their coworkers. Unwarranted negative criticism is frowned upon and should never include references to a person's race, color, gender, sexual orientation, or other personal characteristics. Collaboration and cooperation with other social workers and with professionals from different disciplines is encouraged whenever it benefits the client.

If you take another professional's place after he or she leaves, continue treating that person with respect. It is easy to criticize someone who has left for not doing a very good job or leaving you with some disorganized mess to clean up. Avoid such overt criticism. Likewise, do not criticize someone who has assumed one of your old positions.

Don't talk behind colleagues' backs or purposely try to make them look bad. Don't deceitfully manipulate conflicting situations to your advantage. Address issues openly and honestly.

For example, Charley is a social worker who does not treat colleagues ethically. He is interested in his own personal image and in having power within his agency unit. Typically, if he has a criticism of a colleague, he does not confront that colleague openly. Charley hates open confrontations because he can't always control them. Instead, he goes to Bob, the person who supervises them both, and complains about the colleague in question behind closed doors. Concurrently, he emphasizes how well Bob usually solves such problems. One colloquial term for this latter behavior is "brownnosing." From Charley's perspective, he can achieve three goals from this action. First, flattering the supervisor can gain Charley greater power by strengthening his alliance with Bob who, because of his supervisory position, has greater power. Second, Charley makes himself look better by comparison when he criticizes his colleague. Third, Charley can solve an identified problem without doing anything about it himself. He can avoid uncomfortable confrontation. Unfortunately, Bob is not quite sharp enough to catch on. He inevitably follows Charley's suggestions, thereby reinforcing and perpetuating Charley's unethical behavior, despite the fact that most of Charley's colleagues have lost respect for him because of such actions.

2.02 Confidentiality (Among Colleagues)

You are obligated to maintain in confidence information provided by colleagues in their professional capacity. Colleagues should also be informed when confidentiality is not possible.

2.03 Interdisciplinary Collaboration

The well-being of clients is the primary basis for collaboration among professionals on an interdisciplinary team. Responsibilities of all parties should be clarified, as well as any ethical obligations. You should attempt to resolve any ethical issues through discussion among team members and use appropriate channels to handle unresolved disagreements.

2.04 Disputes Involving Colleagues

Social workers should neither take advantage of a dispute involving colleagues and their employer for their own interests nor exploit clients in disputes with colleagues. Clients are not to be drawn into conflicts among or between social workers and their colleagues.

For example, one school social worker was angry with his school's administration because he felt supervisors had treated him unfairly. He called students' parents and the local television station to complain about the agency's "ineptness," resulting in significant and inappropriate damage to the school system's reputation.

2.05 Consultation

Seeking consultation from colleagues is recommended whenever the client's interests can be better served. *Consultation,* the act of seeking help from someone with expertise in a subject to devise a plan or solve a problem, should involve only a colleague, administrator, or another person who has the appropriate competence or experience. It is your obligation to know whether the individual has the expertise to assist you. It is also your responsibility to share as little about the client as needed to conduct the consultation. Clients' privacy must be maintained.

2.06 Referral for Services

Clients must often be referred for services, especially when the worker lacks the expertise to help the client or when the goals of the intervention are not being achieved. Referrals require that the worker take steps to ensure an effective referral, including, with clients' permission, providing all appropriate information. At no point may you seek, give, or receive payment for making a referral. It is permissible, of course, to bill a client for other professional services you have rendered.

2.07 Sexual Relationships

Sexual activities between supervisors and supervisees is prohibited, as are such activities between students and field supervisors or in any other situation where one worker exercises authority over another. Sexual relationships between colleagues in other situations that may create a conflict of interest should be avoided.

2.08 Sexual Harassment

As with clients, workers are not to engage in sexual harassment of supervisees, students, or colleagues.

2.09 Impairment or 2.10 Unethical Conduct of Colleagues

If you are aware of a colleague's impairment or incompetence, you must consult with that individual (if possible) and help the person seek assistance. Impairments include mental health problems and substance abuse. If a colleague fails to address the problem, you should take appropriate action through employers, licensing bodies, or professional organizations such as the NASW.

2.10 Unethical Conduct of Colleagues

Whenever possible, you are obligated to prevent, expose, or otherwise discourage the unethical behavior of colleagues. You should be aware of agency and professional avenues for handling such situations and should employ them after talking with the colleague. The code does not require you to discuss a problem with a colleague when this is unlikely to be productive. The code does require you to defend and help colleagues who have been wrongly accused of unethical actions.

Social Workers' Ethical Responsibilities in Practice Settings

You have seen that social workers have an ethical responsibility toward their clients and their colleagues. It should therefore not be surprising that there is a corresponding obligation to the settings in which we practice. These responsibilities cover such topics as the use of supervision and consultation, education and training, performance evaluations, billing and client records, and commitment to one's employer, among others.

3.01 Supervision and Consultation

Supervision and consultation have been major components of social work practice for decades, and their importance is recognized by the *Code of Ethics.* No one should purport to provide either without the requisite **EP 2.1.1f** knowledge and skill, and both consultants and supervisors should operate only within their specific areas of knowledge and competence. Both supervisors and consultants must establish appropriate boundaries and avoid dual or multiple relationships with those they supervise or help if there is risk or potential harm to the supervisee. As described in Chapter 2, note two major differences between consultation and supervision: First, consultation is usually time-limited and addresses a specific matter, whereas supervision is ongoing and deals with various issues. Second, supervision involves designated authority over supervisees, whereas consultation may entail no such authority. Of course, any evaluation performed by a supervisor must be conducted fairly and maintain respect for the supervisee.

3.02 Education and Training

Just as social workers and supervisors in practice must operate within their areas of competence, so must those performing roles as teachers, trainers, and field instructors. Educators are required to base their instruction on the most up-to-date information available. They are also obligated to fairly evaluate those they teach and to avoid dual or multiple relationships that may place the student at risk. Maintenance of clear boundaries is also required. In field settings, the field instructor and educator are responsible for notifying clients when services are being performed by students. In many agencies, for example, identification badges note that the student is an intern or practicum student. Although not required to do so by the code of ethics, field students should also take on this responsibility rather than leave clients uninformed.

3.03 Performance Evaluation

Performance evaluation is a frequent obligation of those in supervisory and administrative roles. The code obliges evaluators to conduct their evaluations in a fair manner, based upon clear performance criteria, and in a way that is considerate of the person being evaluated.

3.04 Client Records

Each social worker is duty-bound to ensure that documentation in records is accurate and clearly identifies the services given. Documentation should be kept up to date to help ensure delivery of services to the client. A client's privacy should be protected to the maximum extent, and only information relevant to service should be included in the record. Client records should be stored after services have been terminated. The length of time records must be maintained may be governed by state law or contract.

3.05 Billing

Billing practices of social workers should ensure accurate representation of the type and extent of services provided and clearly identify the service provider.

3.06 Client Transfer

Prior to accepting a client for service, the social worker should determine whether the client has an ongoing professional relationship with another service provider. Through discussions with the client, the worker should review the benefits and risks of beginning service with a new provider. Client needs should be the primary determinant of whether the social worker accepts the client for service. In each case where a client is accepted for service, the worker and client should discuss the appropriateness of consultation with the prior service provider.

3.07 Administration

It is the responsibility of social work administrators to advocate for sufficient resources to meet client needs. Similarly, any social worker should advocate for open and fair allocation procedures that do not discriminate against clients and that reflect clear and consistent criteria. Social work administrators are also required to ensure adequate staff supervision and that the employing environment supports compliance with the code. It is also administrators' responsibility to work to eliminate any conditions that undermine compliance with the code.

3.08 Continuing Education and Staff Development

EP 2.1.1e

Both administrators and supervisors are responsible for providing or arranging continuing education and staff development for those they supervise. Training and education provided should reflect the latest developments in the field.

3.09 Commitment to Employers

Just as social workers have obligations to clients and colleagues, they also have responsibilities to employers and the organizations that employ them. This obligation requires that we adhere to commitments to our employing organizations and to do our best to improve agency policies, procedures, and services provided to clients. This expectation is particularly related to the topic of this text: the importance of changing organization policy and evaluating the effectiveness of programs and services.

Social workers must also help make employers aware of our obligations under the *Code of Ethics* and of the code's impact on social work practice. Agency policies, procedures, and regulations should not be allowed to interfere with the ethical practice of social work. When there is a conflict between policies and the code, the worker is obliged to seek changes in the former.

One example is a social services agency that provides services (such as financial planning and debt management) and financial resources to clients who satisfy a means test. A *means test* involves the evaluation of a client's total income and assets to determine whether the client complies with the criteria for receiving agency services and resources by falling below a designated amount of "means." Despite the fact that the client is very poor and is struggling with significant debt, he does not qualify. He has too many assets. He is not poor enough. He really needs the agency's help, yet the agency can't help him. To what extent might the agency's policy be changed or the means test be revised to improve the agency's ability to meet this and other clients' real needs?

Another example is an agency policy that says only clients with a semipermanent residence and a phone number where they can be contacted may receive help. The agency says it needs to establish client residency that qualifies community residents for services and resources. Homeless people, by definition, have neither an address nor a phone number. Yet they are residents of the community. This is an example of a policy that you might target for change to fulfill your ethical obligation to work for better policies.

It is also the social worker's responsibility to prevent or end discrimination in employment practices or work assignments. Social workers should neither accept employment nor place students in field agencies that lack fair personnel policies. Each issue of the *NASW News* lists individuals and organizations that have been sanctioned for failing to live up to the *Code of Ethics.* At a minimum, it would be prudent to check this list prior to seeking employment or other professional associations.

Finally, the social worker is expected to make appropriate use of agency resources, conserve funds when possible, and never to employ funds for unintended purposes. The employer has a reasonable expectation that employees will not misuse goods or services intended for the benefit of those served by the agency.

3.10 Labor–Management Disputes

The *Code of Ethics* specifically allows social workers to participate in labor unions to improve both services to clients and working conditions. If the union goes on strike or engages in other disputes with management, the worker is expected to be guided by the principles of the code. The impact on clients of any strike or job action should be considered by the social worker prior to pursuing a particular course of action.

Social Workers' Ethical Responsibilities as Professionals

EP 2.1.1

As professionals, social workers have obligations that extend beyond those of others in society. The obligations govern our public and private conduct and require honesty and integrity in our actions.

4.01 Competence

It is imperative that we accept employment or professional responsibilities only when we have the ability to perform those duties satisfactorily. In some situations,

it may be appropriate to accept employment with the intent of acquiring the competence to do the job. An example might be agreeing to undertake specialized training required by an employer or agreeing to pursue a graduate degree in social work as a condition of employment.

At the same time, you must make every effort to maintain your skills and knowledge through professional literature, continuing education, and similar means. One of the simplest ways of assimilating new knowledge is through reading professional journals. NASW members automatically receive *Social Work,* the field's most widely circulated journal. Additionally, practitioners often subscribe to journals more specifically directed at their own clientele or arena of practice. *Social Work in Mental Health, Affilia: Journal of Women and Social Work, Journal of Baccalaureate Social Work, Child Welfare, Journal of Community Practice,* and *Social Work with Groups* are among the many journals available. Books, of course, are another knowledge source. Your practice should always be based upon recognized knowledge that reflects the ethics of the social work profession. If you later find that you cannot perform the tasks required of your position even with continuing education, the ethical thing to do is to look for another job. The key here is thoughtful consideration and honesty.

4.02 Discrimination

Social workers are expressly forbidden to engage in any form of discrimination based upon "race, ethnicity, national origin, color, sex, sexual orientation, gender identity or expression, age, marital status, political belief, religion, immigration status, or mental or physical ability" (NASW, 2008, 4.02). This is consistent with similar prohibitions included in other parts of the code. Although none of us is perfect and most of us are affected by stereotypes and prejudice, we can at least continue striving to identify and eliminate them. We can work to avoid acting on them. Highlight 12.3 poses some suggestions for addressing your own stereotypes and prejudices.

4.03 Private Conduct

Social workers must not allow their private conduct to interfere with their professional responsibilities. An example is a social worker who placed an anti-abortion bumper sticker on her car (normally an acceptable display of private opinion) and then made home visits to pregnant teenagers struggling with what to do about their pregnancy.

HIGHLIGHT 12.3

Combating Your Own Stereotypes and Prejudices

EP 2.1.2a

Combating your own stereotypes about and prejudices against various groups of people is an ongoing process. For whatever reasons, we all develop them, even if we hate that fact. The important thing is to continue working to identify them and obliterate as many as we can. One problem is that we may think we have one taken care of and another one pops up.

For example, Danielle, 42, is a white social worker in a very white rural county in a midwestern state. She is married to Gerhard, 45, also white and an engineer. Danielle engages in constant warfare with her own stereotypes and prejudices. She hates the fact that she *has* them. She knows she's not supposed to have any. She really doesn't want to have any. It is a constant struggle for her to identify them.

Gerhard's boss, Steve, invites both of them to a Christmas dinner party with Steve's other supervisees and their spouses. Danielle thinks about the upcoming Christmas dinner. She pictures Steve, an African American, in her mind. She has never met him. She knows a few African-American people, but none are among her close personal friends. She'd never even met an African-American until she went to college. She has done substantial reading about African-American culture out of genuine interest. In her living room she displays an entire wall of African masks and figures that were bought by a friend, at Danielle's request, when that friend visited central Africa.

Danielle and Gerhard attend the dinner. By chance, they sit at the same table with Steve and his wife, Sue, also an African-American. Whatever stereotypes and prejudices Danielle had harbored (and fought to get rid of) about Steve and Sue as African-Americans soon dissipated, much to Danielle's relief. Steve and Sue were both from central Manhattan. They spoke concisely and fast, having what Danielle considered strong "New York accents." What Danielle had studied about African-American culture had nothing to do with her interpersonal interactions that particular evening. Sue, as a matter of fact, had just spent two weeks participating in a dig in central France (anthropology was one of her primary interests). Danielle found Sue a fascinating, good-humored individual and liked her very much.

So what exactly was the problem? Danielle found herself switching gears from fighting any remnants of

prejudices and stereotypes about African-Americans to identifying and combating her prejudices and stereotypes about New Yorkers. She thought to herself that if it's not one thing, it's another. She had a lot more attitudinal changes to work on.

A major difficulty in combating stereotypes and prejudices is that you're not supposed to have any in the first place, which makes it very difficult to identify them. If you admit that you sustain some stereotype or prejudice, you admit to a serious failure. However, before you can work to eliminate a stereotype or prejudice, you must be clearly aware that it exists. This is a catch-22 situation.

Following these steps is one means of beginning to combat personal prejudices:

1. *Carefully observe and monitor your thoughts when interacting with anyone belonging to a group with characteristics significantly different from your own.* Part of this involves acknowledging that you notice a difference. Are you especially aware that this person has Asian facial characteristics, red hair, speaks with an Italian accent, walks with a limp, or comes from western Tasmania? Does the awareness of the characteristic stand out in your mind? Are you making prejudgments to yourself about this person on the basis of this characteristic? True, it is important to recognize people's characteristics in general, to have good observational skills. However, the fact that you are paying special attention to some specific characteristic, some difference between you and the other person, may alert you to a potential prejudice.

2. *Identify exactly how you treat this person differently.* Are you monitoring the words you say? If so, in what manner? Do you treat this person differently? If so, in what ways? Begin to measure the difference between the way you treat this person because he or she belongs to some particular group against the way you treat people who are not very different from yourself.

3. *Gradually change your behavior toward the identified person, bringing it more in line with your behavior toward "nondifferent people.* Of course, always be vigilant regarding cultural differences. That is, be sensitive to other people's potential cultural expectations. Respect cultural differences, but identify the differences in

(continued)

HIGHLIGHT 12.3 *(continued)*

behavior that are based on your own prejudices. In effect you can *normalize* your behavior toward this "different-group" person.

4. *Monitor your progress in combating your stereotypes and prejudices.* To what extent have you managed to amend your behavior to the "different" person so that you now treat that person as "nondifferent"? To what extent do you no longer have to expend any effort to do this? When you no longer notice any difference when interacting with the person in question, you have probably made substantial gains in demolishing your stereotype or prejudice—at least insofar as this individual is concerned.

5. *Maintain a perspective that appreciates and respects both individual and cultural differences.* Being fair, open minded, and impartial on the one hand, and sensitive, perceptive, and appreciative of differences on the other, is far from easy. It requires an ongoing vigilance over your own personal perceptions and actions. You do not want to prejudge others on the basis of their membership in some group. You want to interact and communicate with each client, colleague, or administrator as an individual. Yet you also want to be sensitive and respectful to the cultural differences that do exist.

Of course, your private behavior can impinge on your role as a professional in other ways. Streaking your hair in rainbow hues or undergoing multiple body piercings is certainly your right. However, in the event that it turns off your clients, colleagues, and administration, you may wish to forgo such bits of self-expression. Be aware that personal choices, like personal values, can have a potential impact on those with whom we work. Professional obligations must come first.

4.04 Dishonesty, Fraud, and Deception

Dishonesty, fraud, and deception have no place in the practice of social work. This is another guideline that may appear absurdly simple. However, once again, people are imperfect and sometimes exercise poor judgment. They may rationalize to themselves that they have a good reason for their behavior. Dishonesty and deception can characterize any number of scenarios, ranging from forging case notes to exaggerating mileage reimbursement for extra cash to calling in sick when you're not.

4.05 Impairment

Although social workers are not expected to be free from personal, legal, or mental health problems, they must not let these difficulties interfere with their professional performance or harm those to whom they have a professional obligation. Social workers with these impairments are obligated to seek appropriate help, such as reduce their workload, terminate their practice, and take any other steps needed to protect clients and colleagues. An example of this is a practitioner whose own mental health

difficulties escalated to the point where he began to use disparaging terms toward other members of his interdisciplinary team. This resulted in the colleagues refusing to work with him because of the personal insults and other behavior. Because the agency expected practitioners to work together in teams, the worker's personal impairment was deemed to be interfering with his professional obligations. When the practitioner refused to seek assistance with his problems, the agency took administrative action to remove him from his position.

Social workers are, of course, not free from the same kinds of difficulties that beset the general population. In fact, Rompf and Royse (1994) found "social work students more likely than a comparison group to report having grown up in families where there was psychosocial trauma," including alcohol or drug addiction and child maltreatment (p. 169). What do we as professionals do with our dysfunctions, especially when they become serious? Once again, the answer is to try to maintain awareness of your own mental health and performance and to be honest about it. If you honestly feel that your own problems are interfering with your work, then do something about it. Get professional help. If the problems are so severe that you cannot function adequately, then get into an inpatient treatment program, take a leave of absence, or quit and seek another job. Your professional work and your clients' interests come first.

4.06 Misrepresentation

Social workers must be careful to not allow their statements or actions as private citizens to be misconstrued as representing the social work profession or one's employing agency. If you speak on behalf of any organization, you should have received authorization to do so, and what you say should reflect the views of that body.

Similarly, accuracy is required when communicating one's qualifications and credentials to clients, agencies, and the public. If others misrepresent our qualifications, it is our duty to rectify the inaccuracy and to always indicate the actual nature and outcomes of services we provide.

An example of a violation of this standard involves a scenario where Indihar, a unit supervisor, discovered that Joanne had applied for the state's Licensed Clinical Social Worker certification. This was the highest level of practice licensed in that particular state. Among other things, requirements included an MSW degree and at least two years of supervised post-MSW clinical experience. Indihar knew that Joanne did not have the required two years of supervised clinical experience. Joanne had taken time off to raise her children after receiving her degree and assumed a professional social work position only six months ago for the first time since graduation. Joanne had asked Jared, another social work colleague of hers, to indicate that he had been her supervisor for the required two years. He signed the required form to verify this "fact," even though he had never supervised Joanne in his life. Now, is this beginning to strike you as being a bit unethical?

At any rate, Indihar contacted the state licensing office and informed staff there of the situation. They investigated and found out that Indihar was correct. Joanne was denied that licensure. Indihar put a letter of reprimand in Joanne's personnel file. For whatever reason, Jared never suffered any consequences for his behavior. Two months later, Indihar left the agency for what she considered an even better job in another city. Joanne immediately applied for Licensed Clinical Social Worker again and, shortly thereafter, received her license. The new supervisor who took over Indihar's old position never found out about the whole thing. Somehow, the letter of reprimand had mysteriously disappeared from Joanne's personnel file.

Other ethical questions can be raised concerning these incidents. Should Indihar have pursued the fact that Jared essentially perjured himself? Should the new supervisor have double-checked Joanne's credentials when Joanne applied for certification, or should she have respected Joanne's supposed integrity? Should Indihar have made certain that Joanne's new supervisor was informed of the situation, even after Indihar had left and was intricately involved in her new job? What do you think?

4.07 Solicitations

Social workers should not solicit clients in any way that takes advantage of their vulnerability, nor should we ask clients to provide testimonials of our service to them. In advertising our services, the burden is on the social worker to ensure that we do not take advantage of a client's vulnerability.

4.08 Acknowledging Credit

Claiming credit for work that you have not done or submitting work done by others as your own is a violation of the code. This is plagiarism.

Social Workers' Ethical Responsibility to the Social Work Profession

Each social worker has a responsibility to the profession as a whole that ensures its integrity and encourages the improvement of programs and services. The quality of services provided by each of us has an impact on the reputation of the profession we serve.

EP 2.1.1

5.01 Integrity of the Profession

Our responsibility to the profession requires that we seek to promote and maintain the highest practice standards. This includes advancing the ethical standards, knowledge, skills, and competence of the profession. Avenues for achieving these ends include doing research, teaching, providing consultation and professional services, testifying before policy-making bodies, public presentations, and participation in the NASW and other professional organizations. To the greatest extent possible, we should also help develop the knowledge base of the profession and share practice information with colleagues by such means as presenting papers at conferences, submitting journal articles, and speaking up at meetings. We should also prevent the unauthorized or unqualified practice of social work by others.

5.02 Evaluation and Research

Our obligation as social workers extends to our involvement in evaluating the programs of which we are a part and the services we provide. It also requires that we recognize that evaluation and research contribute to the development of professional knowledge. To the greatest extent possible, we should ensure that our own practice reflects the best research-informed practices of our profession.

Social workers who engage in evaluation and research must be cognizant of the possible consequences of such activity and adhere to guidelines that protect participants. Review boards should be consulted as appropriate. Informed consent (in writing) should be obtained from participants without any penalty for refusing to participate. Neither should participants be given undue inducement to participate. Participants should be told the extent, duration, and type of involvement expected of them as well as any benefits or risks entailed.

In the event that participants cannot themselves give informed consent, the social worker should seek this from a proxy authorized to act on the participants' behalf. Only in rare instances should we participate in any research or evaluation without consent from participants. When participants do consent, they must be notified that they may withdraw at any point without penalty. Appropriate services should be made available to participants who continue as well as to those who withdraw from involvement in the research. Protection of clients from mental or physical harm, danger, or deprivation should be ensured.

Results of evaluation and research activities should be shared only with those with a legitimate need to know. The identity of participants should be protected unless written consent has been obtained. Presentation of findings throughout must be accurate. Errors that are discovered later must be corrected. Prohibitions against dual or multiple relationships also apply, as do conflicts of interest. At all times, participants' interests must have primary emphasis. It is also the social worker's obligation to remain current on appropriate research strategies and approaches.

Social Workers' Ethical Responsibilities to the Broader Society

Social workers also have obligations that extend to the broader society of which we are a part. These responsibilities deal with the general welfare of society, our participation in public activities and emergencies, and social and political action.

6.01 Social Welfare

Social workers are expected to act to benefit the general welfare of society at all levels. This includes pushing for living conditions that promote meeting people's basic needs and pursuing social and economic justice for all. This advocacy may be directed at societal institutions as well as at the values of society.

6.02 Public Participation

Social workers should encourage the public's involvement in the development and improvement of public policy. This might include voting, participating in efforts to get others registered, and providing public forums where critical social policies are discussed.

6.03 Public Emergencies

In the event of public emergencies, social workers should offer their professional services to the extent possible and with consideration of the needs of the public. Recent examples of this include local social workers and social work programs that volunteered their services to assist people victimized by natural disasters and terrorism. Flooding of New Orleans and the Gulf Coast and the September 11, 2001, terrorist attacks on the Twin Towers of the World Trade Center in Manhattan and the Pentagon in Washington, D.C., are such public emergencies in which social workers have become involved.

6.04 Social and Political Action

EP 2.1.8

The goals of providing people equal access to all critical societal resources requires that social workers pursue appropriate political and social action. It also requires that we be keenly aware of the impact of decisions in the political arena on social work practice and services. Supporting the efforts of the NASW's PACE (Political Action for Candidate Election) is one means of becoming politically active. The organization is devoted to raising funds and providing support for political candidates who are sympathetic to social work issues.

Another method is to become involved in election campaigns of political candidates. Even writing legislators to offer your opinion on a range of issues important to social work and our clients can have a substantial impact on social policy development. You might even participate in an organized network of social workers, already established in some states, who contact each other when political pressure is needed to sway elected officials' votes and decisions.

It is also our obligation to work to expand choice for all persons and to promote conditions that reflect respect for cultural and social diversity throughout the world.

One aspect of responsibility to the broader society concerns ethical responsibility on a global basis. It is our obligation to work to expand choice for all persons and to promote conditions that reflect respect for cultural and social diversity throughout the world. Social workers are responsible for assuming a "global perspective" and for recognizing "global interconnections of oppression" (CSWE, 2008, p. 1, EP 2.1.5). The next section discusses international social work ethical principles.

International Ethical Principles

EP 2.1.2b

Chapters 1 and 4 introduced the International Federation of Social Workers (IFSW) and the International Association of Schools of Social Work (IASSW). The IFSW (2009) is an organization of social workers affirming that "professional social workers are dedicated to service for the welfare and self-fulfillment of human beings"; it aims "to promote social work as a profession through international co-operation" (IASSW, 2009). The IASSW is an association of schools of social work, social work educators, and supportive organizations; its purpose is "to develop and promote excellence in social work education, research and scholarship globally in order to enhance human well-being" (IASSW, 2009).[1] Together, the IFSW and the IASSW developed an Ethics in Social Work, Statement of Principles (IASSW, 2004).[2]

The Statement of Principles is divided into five sections: "Preface," "Definition of Social Work," "International Conventions" (international documents and declarations that are "particularly relevant to social work practice and action"), "Principles," and "Professional Conduct" (IASSW, 2004).

The NASW *Code of Ethics* calls upon social workers to "promote the general welfare of society, from local to global levels" (NASW, 2008, 6.01). Practitioners are also expected to apply standards proposed in the international Statement of Principles "as applicable" regarding their practice and ethical concerns on a global level (CSWE, 2008, p. 4). Although it is beyond the scope of this book to review the Statement of Principles in detail, we will address the two primary and related principles the statement stresses—"human rights" and "social justice" (IASSW, 2004).

Human Rights and Social Justice

Social workers are responsible for extending their "social justice values within the context of global human rights" (NASW, 2009, p. 204). *Human rights* involve the premise that all people, regardless of race, culture, or national origin, are entitled to basic rights and treatment. We have established that *social justice* is "an ideal condition" in which all members of society have "the same basic rights, protection, opportunities, obligations, and social benefits" (Barker, 2003, pp. 404–405). Human rights are entitlements to which people should automatically have access. Social justice involves the protection and preservation of human rights politically and legally.

In response to the atrocities of World War II, the General Assembly of the United Nations adopted a Universal Declaration of Human Rights (UNDR) in December 1948 (United Nations [UN], 1948). Mapp (2008) elaborates:

> Within the UNDR, there are three areas of rights: [1] political and civil rights, [2] social, economic, and cultural rights, and [3] collective rights. Political and civil rights are often referred to as "negative freedoms" as they require a government to refrain from an overuse of its power against individuals. Included in this are rights such as freedom of speech and the right to a fair trial. The second groups of rights—social, economic, and cultural rights—are referred to as "positive freedoms" as they require a government to take action for them to be realized for individuals. They include such rights as medical care, the right to an education, and the right to a fair wage. The last group, collective rights, are rights for groups of people and include the rights to religion, peace, and development. (pp. 17–18)

NASW policy statements maintain that the struggle for human rights continues; this is demonstrated by "events such as wars, genocide, and ethnic cleansing; discrimination and social exclusion based on race, ethnicity, caste, or religious identity; gender inequality, battering, rape, and the sale of women; child abuse; sweatshops, child labor, and slavery" (NASW, 2009, p. 204). The NASW calls for social workers to advocate for human rights on a global basis; for example, practitioners should "work for the eradication of modern-day slavery and growing incidence of human trafficking" and "advocate for the elimination of the practice of torture" (NASW, 2009, p. 206).

---

1. The IFSW's and the IASSW's Web site are www.ifsw.org/f38000041.html and www.iassw-aiets.org/, respectively.

2. The Ethics in Social Work, Statement of Principles can be accessed at www.iassw-aiets.org/index.php?option=com_content&task=blogcategory&id=27&Itemid=50.

What Can You Do?

There are a number of things you might choose to do on behalf of global human rights. You might consider the following suggestions:[3]

- *Think about seeking an international job or position addressing international issues. Many potential sources exist. One example is the American Refugee Committee (ARC), which "works with refugees, displaced persons, and those at risk of being displaced to help them survive crises and rebuild lives of dignity, health, security, and self-sufficiency" (Mapp, 2008, pp. 175–176).[4] Another example is CARE, "an international organization dedicated to eradicating global poverty" (Mapp, 2008, p. 176).[5] Still another example concerns work with one of the many agencies involved in international adoptions.*
- *Donate to organizations such as those just mentioned that serve people on an international basis, advocate for human rights, or pursue social justice.*
- *Get an international internship.*
- *Volunteer at agencies that help people on an international basis. They may need and appreciate your help at local agencies, so you don't necessarily have to leave the country or even your neighborhood in order to serve. You can also volunteer to help them during their fundraising drives.*
- *Join organizations that advocate for human rights.*
- *"Educate others about the [human rights] problem. Break the ignorance" (Mapp, 2008, p. 48). Whenever an opportunity arises, advocate on the behalf of human rights issues and social justice.*
- *Support and vote for legislators who address human rights and social justice issues. You might also help educate legislators regarding the magnitude of these somber concerns.*

Personal Values

EP 2.1.2a

Our values are our beliefs about what is good, appropriate, or correct (Dolgoff et al., 2009). We all have a right to our personal values and to ideas about how we personally feel

things should be. We have opinions about whether public finances should be used to build a new baseball stadium or to establish an ongoing jobs training program for women on public assistance. We have personal values and beliefs about religion, state and federal tax rates, and whether people should change their last names when they marry.

At this point in your social work education, you should have addressed the concept of personal values and how they must stand apart from professional values. You have probably done this within the micro and mezzo contexts. For example, how do you avoid imposing your personal values on your clients? How do you hold your own values in check when helping a family reach a decision? As you run a group, how do you prevent your own values from interfering with the values of group members?

It is just as important to separate your personal values from professional, objective judgments in the macro context. When addressing macro issues, such as potential agency policy change or development of a community resource, it is critical to work on behalf of the client system's needs and beliefs, not your own.

Tropman (1995, p. 68) proposes several questions about which you may hold strong personal opinions:

- *How much should the government do for people?*
- *Does the government owe everyone an adequate income?*
- *Should people be allowed to work for as long as they want?*
- *How much responsibility should the family take in caring for its older members?*

When confronted with any macro situation, you must carefully identify your personal values and distinguish them from what is in your client system's best interest from that system's own perspective. What if the social service agency you work for implements a new policy that requires family members to care for senior members in order for the family to receive any benefits? To what extent might your personal values and opinions differ from what is best for these older adult clients and their families? What would you do? Would you respond, "Okay, I'll go along with the policy?" Or would you try to inhibit or stop the policy's implementation? What would your professional values encourage you to do?

The answers to such situations are not easy. If a perfect answer existed, you would not even be contemplating the problem—it would already have been solved. We will discuss a wide range of ethical dilemmas and

---

3. *Human Rights and Social Justice in a Global Perspective: An Introduction to International Social Work* by Susan C. Mapp (Chicago: Lyceum, 2008) provides an excellent resource for ideas to pursue involvement and advocacy concerning global issues.

4. The ARC's Web site is www.arcrelief.org.

5. CARE's Web site is www.care.org.

how you might address them under "Ethical Dilemmas in Macro Contexts" in a subsequent section of the chapter.

Types of Ethical Issues Confronting Agency Practitioners

The six core values identified in the NASW *Code of Ethics* are all primary areas where ethical issues may confront social workers. The issues addressed in this section reflect a combination of these areas. As we have established, ethical issues in direct practice do not occur in a vacuum. Rather, they occur within organizational and community macro contexts. Social welfare policies and programs impose both responsibilities and constraints on your direct practice. Thus, they provide structures within which you must solve any ethical dilemmas confronting you. Finally, ethical issues arising among colleagues are different from those occurring with client systems, regardless of whether the system involves an individual, family, or group. Dealing with collegial and even administrative ethical issues requires a broader macro focus.

The following examples will assume a generalist approach, but acknowledge that an ethical dilemma can involve two or three practice perspectives at once. We will emphasize ethical dilemmas within the macro context.

Ethical Absolutism versus Ethical Relativism

Two basic approaches exist for determining what is the right thing to do in any given practice situation (Dolgoff et al., 2009; Reamer, 1990). One theoretical approach is that *of ethical absolutism,* which assumes that moral laws exist to govern ethical decision making in virtually any situation. In essence, decision making is not necessary, because the answer should be clear to you. The assumption is that there is only one correct way of doing things. Perhaps you know people who espouse this view in other aspects of their lives. Their way is the only way—not only the right way, but the only way—to approach a task or consider an issue.

Consider the view that there is only one way of stacking and arranging the dishes in a dishwasher. Any other way is totally wrong, inexcusable, and even reprehensible. Or that the right time to wash dishes is

immediately after a meal. And they must be done by hand. People who use dishwashers are lazy and will never get anywhere in life. Dishwashers waste water and soap. They don't clean well enough. People taking an ethical absolutism approach assume a black-or-white, right-or-wrong perspective on an issue. Other people's views are wrong. There is no flexibility.

Reamer (1999, pp. 146–149) cites a further example that relates directly to social work practice.[6] He describes a Refugee Resettlement Center that provides a wide range of services to immigrants to the United States, including "housing referrals, financial and job counseling, language tutoring, and concrete help with federal immigration officials" (p. 147). The U.S. Immigration and Naturalization Service (INS) begins exerting substantial pressure upon the center's director, Hernando Juarez, to report any illegal aliens coming to the center's attention. In actuality, a significant number of illegal aliens come to the center for help on a regular basis. Historically, the center's administration and staff have maintained that the agency's aspiration was to serve all immigrants in need, whether they were "legal" or not.

Hernandez approaches the staff during an agency meeting and asks them to reconsider their informal policy of not "snitching on" (the term used by many agency staff) illegal aliens who are desperately in need of help. Hernando raises two issues. First, the center is acting illegally by not reporting known illegal aliens. He fears the INS might initiate reprisals and even legal action against the center. Second, Hernando questions whether adherence to the nonreporting policy prevents center staff from reporting information about the illegal aliens for other purposes. What if center staff were aware of other reportable problems involving illegal aliens, such as child abuse or felonies? What if you were a social worker on staff at the center? What do you think the center should do—maintain its present nonreporting policy or not?

Ethical absolutism would dictate one of two clear-cut responses. First, an ethical absolutist could say that the law must be obeyed, no matter what. Therefore, the nonreporting policy must be rescinded. Center staff must report any illegal aliens who come to their attention. That is the law. There is no other choice.

Other ethical absolutists might assume the opposite position. They might declare that, of course, staff members must adhere to the informal nonreporting policy.

---

6. The example as Reamer presents it is modified to comply with content employed here.

That is part of the center's mission and its moral philosophy. Therefore, that is the only way to go.

What do you notice about the last two paragraphs? What do they have in common? They both assume an absolute approach and adhere to a principle unilaterally, giving no thought to appraising the issue from other perspectives.

The second approach to making ethical decisions is that of *ethical relativism* (Dolgoff et al., 2009). Here an ethical decision is based on the context in which the decision is made. Ethical relativism requires the evaluation of any particular action on the basis of its potential consequences. In other words, this perspective assumes that there are always a number of alternative choices in any situation involving ethics. It is up to you to determine the best course of action. Which alternative will result in the most good and the least bad consequences? The emphasis is on *results* rather than on *principles*.

An ethical relativism approach in the case of the Refugee Resettlement Center would require giving careful thought to the situation and examining the problem from many angles. What action would produce the most desirable results? An ethical relativist might consider the arguments proposed for and against each alternative. On the one hand, changing the policy and requiring the reporting of all illegal aliens would comply with INS regulations and keep the center out of any potential trouble with the INS. It would also prevent U.S. citizens from subsidizing illegal noncitizens. The center receives its funding from a range of sources, several of them publicly financed.

On the other hand, changing the policy to report illegal aliens would deprive many people of services they gravely need and would directly oppose part of the agency's mission to serve any immigrants in need. To what extent would the INS really pursue this issue with the center? The INS has never done anything in the past. Both agencies value their positive relationship.

Reamer (1999) continues evaluating the situation, raising several points. If the agency begins reporting illegal aliens to the INS, what will happen to its reputation? How likely will other immigrants be to utilize the agency services when they hear about the center's violations of confidentiality? Potential clients might question whether the center would violate their own confidentiality and privacy.

One final point on the pros and cons of changing the policy deals with the difference between not reporting illegal aliens in general and not reporting illegal aliens who commit serious crimes. In the latter case, the center could implement a reporting policy without requiring universal reporting of illegal aliens to the INS.

The prior discussion, rather than giving you an absolute answer, demonstrates two evaluative thought processes by which a conclusion could be reached. Ethical absolutism maintains that there is always one correct answer. Ethical relativism requires thoughtful review of the many variables involved in a given situation to determine the most advantageous result. From the preceding discussion, what is your own opinion regarding the center's best course of action? Would maintaining the current nonreporting policy or changing it to a reporting policy produce the best results?

Social work is not simple. Any profession involving such intensive work with people and their problems is complex, to say the least. Thus, we propose a blend of ethical absolutism and ethical relativism. Ethical relativism espouses no definite guidelines for addressing any situation involving ethical decisions. Each situation is unique, with a unique conglomeration of people and variables. Therefore, there are no consistently established values or rules to follow. Social work, however, does have recognized values inherent in its code of ethics upon which to base decisions. You might consider this a form of ethical absolutism. Yet, as social workers, you must look at many variables in order to come to a decision. You might think of this as ethical relativism. In summary, social work requires a blend of absolutism and relativism to arrive at an ethical decision.

For example, what does the NASW *Code of Ethics* (2008) have to say about situations such as the Refugee Relocation Center? The code is clear in specifying that the social worker's primary responsibility is to the client, but also recognizes that our legal obligations or responsibilities to society in general may, in some circumstances, supersede our loyalty to clients. It also requires that we not ask clients for information that is not absolutely necessary in order to provide service. Perhaps the question of a client's "legal" status can be avoided if it is not essential to providing service.

Certainly, the social worker is obligated to participate in the setting of agency policies to ensure that they do not discriminate against people—and the code does not discuss the client's legal status. The code also says we should not engage in dishonesty, fraud, or deception—and providing services to undocumented immigrants in violation of the law is a potential problem. At the same time, the Preamble to the code notes that it is the primary mission of the profession to help meet basic human needs of all people, especially those who are vulnerable or oppressed, an apt description of clients served by the Refugee Relocation Center. Taking these items into consideration, what would be your solution to the situation?

Ethical Dilemmas

EP 2.1.2c

Ethical dilemmas are problematic situations whose possible solutions all offer imperfect and unsatisfactory answers. In other words, your ethical guidelines conflict with each other. There is no one outcome that can conform to all the ethical principles in the professional code. You are stuck with deciding what to do.

When we reconsider, however, this is not really true. First of all, in social work we have professional values. *Ethical dilemmas* always involve values. Rarely does an ethical dilemma present us with equally bad alternatives. Rather, we can use values to carefully examine and weigh alternatives to determine the best one.

Consider the case of Simone Bullior. Simone is a foster care worker responsible for finding homes for children. She has a set of three siblings—Mary, Jamal, and Jarel Jones, ages four through seven—badly in need of a foster home. She has no homes available that will take three children. The one foster family that could take three children already has a 12-year-old boy, Nathan. Simone's supervisor suggests moving Nathan to another foster home to make room for the three children. Simone knows that it is very important to keep the three Jones children together, given their closeness and past life experiences. She also knows that Nathan has really adapted well to the foster home and is making real progress. She is faced with an ethical dilemma. Does she consider the welfare of three children ahead of that of a single individual? Does she consider the wishes of the foster parents, who would prefer to keep Nathan? After all, foster parents are supposed to be involved in planning placements and care of the children. What are the values involved in this situation?

In an ethical dilemma, then, we are faced with a situation in which a decision must be made under circumstances that set two or more ethical principles in conflict. As another example, perhaps you cannot abide by both the social work ethic of confidentiality and the obligation to save a suicidal person's life. However, because we have professional values, we can formulate some guidelines for making tough choices. We can

establish a hierarchy to decide what aspect of any particular ethical dilemma is more important than another.

Facing an Ethical Dilemma: Decision-Making Steps

EP 2.1.2d

The first step in determining what to do about an ethical dilemma is to establish the fact that you actually have one. A series of variables can help you conceptualize the potential problem. This decision-making process uses the eight steps illustrated in Figure 12.1.

Step 1: Recognize the Problem

The first step in confronting a potential ethical dilemma is to recognize the problem (Corey, Corey, & Callanan, 2007). The seed might be a gut reaction, an unarticulated feeling that something is not right. Something does not fit or make sense. You must determine that an ethical dilemma exists before going any further.

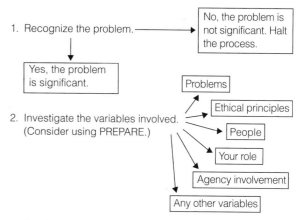

3. Get feedback from others.
4. Appraise values that apply to the dilemma.
5. Evaluate the dilemma on the basis of established ethical principles.
6. Identify and think about possible alternatives to pursue.

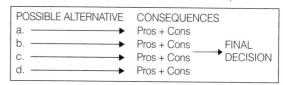

7. Weigh the pros and cons of each alternative.
8. Make your decision about what to do.

FIGURE 12.1

Step 2: Investigate the Variables Involved

The second step is investigating the complex matrix of variables that encompass the dilemma (Corey et al., 2007; Dolgoff et al., 2009). Which ethical principles are in conflict? What problems are involved? What people are involved? How are you yourself involved? What is your agency's involvement? How might your agency be affected by resolution or lack of resolution of this dilemma? Roll the dilemma around in your mind. Think deeply about what it is and why it exists. What other variables might provide you with clues to a workable solution? You might follow the PREPARE process described in Chapter 5 to stimulate your ideas.

Step 3: Get Feedback from Others

If at all possible, talk to other people about your concerns (Corey et al., 2007). Bounce your ideas off them to more firmly establish your objectivity. Brainstorm with them different ways of viewing and eventually handling the dilemma. A trusted supervisor or colleagues familiar with the dilemma's context could be helpful.

Step 4: Appraise the Values That Apply to the Dilemma

Assess and choose the values and ethical guidelines that best apply to the dilemma (Corey et al., 2007; Dolgoff et al., 2009). You may discover that there is no ethical dilemma, only a more straightforward ethical problem. A problem can have a clear solution. A dilemma by definition has competing, imperfect solutions. If the code provides you with a clear answer, use the code's directives to follow steps toward the problem's resolution.

Step 5: Evaluate the Dilemma

Make conscious decisions about what values are more important than others. You can establish a hierarchy of principles, based on values, that can guide you through the process of confronting an ethical dilemma. Remember that ethical dilemmas always involve situations in which you cannot do all the right things. Each dilemma presents some conflict among ethical principles so that you cannot abide by them all. You might determine that staying alive is more important than telling the truth. Telling the truth is the ethical thing to do, but what if you are in a situation where it is impossible to both tell the truth and keep someone (perhaps yourself) alive at the same time? Your best course of action might then be not to tell the truth. Under "Ranking Ethical Principles," we will review two approaches to evaluating ethical principles and use them to elaborate on a wide range of potential ethical dilemmas that could confront you in practice.

Step 6: Identify and Think about Possible Alternatives

What can you do in your job to solve the dilemma? What creative ideas can you come up with? Finding a solution could employ the IMAGINE process (described in Chapters 6 and 7) to change a policy, initiate a project, or even develop a program.

Step 7: Weigh the Pros and Cons of Each Alternative

Weighing the pros and cons of each alternative is a common practice in social work and is useful in resolving ethical dilemmas (Corey et al., 2007). What course of action is best for the client? What alternative is most likely to succeed? How might you best proceed?

Step 8: Make Your Decision

Finally, make a decision about what is the best route for you to take. The IMAGINE process might apply here, depending on the alternative you choose. The main thing about confronting an ethical dilemma is to do some serious thinking about it before taking action.

Ranking Ethical Principles

The following sections will review two ways to address Steps 4 and 5 in the ethical decision-making process. One approach pairs and ranks identified values against each other (Reamer, 1999): One value supersedes the other, so you know which **EP 2.1.2d** one to choose in any conflict between the two. The second approach also proposes a hierarchy of principles whereby those higher in the hierarchy consistently supersede those lower in the hierarchy (Dolgoff et al., 2009).

Reamer's Guide to Ethical Decision Making

Reamer (1999) suggests examining an ethical dilemma on the basis of six ethical guidelines that rank one ethical principle against another. Each guideline can aid decision making in ethical dilemmas involving the principles.

1. Rules about Basic Survival Supersede Rules Governing Lesser Actions

Reamer poses that "rules against basic harms" or evils should supersede those against lesser harms. Thus, rules that ensure "health, food, shelter, [and] mental equilibrium" should supersede lesser rules concerning confidentiality, lying, or protection of goods or property (Reamer, 1999, p. 72). In other words, the most important rules protect people's right to survive. They reinforce people's ability to get what they need to continue living. Additionally, this principle justifies "spending a disproportionate percentage of government funds on the most vulnerable" over other desirable but less at-risk groups (Reamer, 1999, p. 72). Thus, ethical principles apply to interventions in micro, mezzo, and macro practice as well as in policy.

2. One Person's Right to Well-Being Supersedes Another Person's Right to Self-Determination

"Individuals have a right to self-determination and to act as they wish ... unless the actions threaten the welfare of others" (Reamer, 1999, p. 73). This principle once again emphasizes the importance of survival. It also ranks one person's survival and well-being above another person's personal freedom.

If a client tells his social worker that he committed an armed robbery for which another person has been incarcerated, the social worker, according to this principle, should report the confession despite breaking confidentiality with her client. The well-being of the person who is unjustly sitting in jail is more important than the client's right to privacy.

3. One Person's Right to Self-Determination Supersedes That Same Person's Right to Well-Being

This guideline emphasizes the individual's right to make her or his own decisions, regardless of whether such decisions are in that individual's best interest. Thus, a person has the right to participate in behavior that is harmful to her- or himself, such as drug use, smoking, and even, potentially, suicide. We must stress, however, that this principle applies only if "the individual is making an informed, voluntary decision with knowledge of relevant circumstances and that the consequences of the decision will not threaten the well-being of others" (Reamer, 1999, p. 73). The individual making the decision must be of sound mind and totally aware of the potential consequences of the behavior.

Therefore, for example, a man with a physical disability who is eating poorly, suffering health problems, and living in squalor has the right to do so if he is, indeed, capable of making informed, independent, conscious decisions. This assumes, of course, that he is hurting no one but himself. On the other hand, if he has a dependent living with him, something will have to be done—in accordance with Guideline 2, which indicates that one individual's (the dependent's) right to well-being takes precedence over another individual's right to be free (to choose to live in squalor).

4. Obeying Rules You Have Agreed to Support Supersedes the Right to Freely Break These Rules

Obeying rules, laws, and regulations takes precedence over the personal right to break them. Reamer (1999) specifically refers to those rules that you have already agreed to obey, such as the policies of the agency for which you work.

Another example involves NASW members and the NASW *Code of Ethics*. As an NASW member, you have agreed to follow the NASW's rules and directives, and the NASW can censure members who do not obey those rules. The code of ethics forbids engaging in sexual relationships with clients. This ethical rule takes precedence over your personal right to enter into such an intimate relationship.

5. People's Right to Well-Being Supersedes Adherence to Rules You Have Agreed to Support

Once again, the individual's right to survival and well-being assumes precedence, this time over the rules you have agreed to support. This guideline indicates that the basic right to survival is more important than adherence to rules and regulations to which you have voluntarily agreed. If your agency adopts a policy denying services to people who are deemed illiterate because they are unable to complete the necessary application forms, these people's well-being is more important than the agency rule. This guideline directs you to provide people with the services they need rather than follow the unethical agency rule.

6. Preventing Harm and Fulfilling Basic Needs Supersedes Withholding Your Own Property

This guideline indicates that people have the right not to suffer major harm, such as starvation, and to have basic needs met, such as housing and education, even if that requires others to sacrifice property (Reamer, 1999). This guideline relates specifically to the government's right to levy taxes to provide the general populace with what they need. In other words, poor people have the right to have basic needs met, even at the expense of wealthier people. Children, even if they are poverty stricken, have the right to food, clothing, and lodging. It follows that the state has the right to tax wealthier people in order to accomplish this.

How does this particular principle relate to the thousands of impoverished homeless people wandering our streets? Does the taxation and social service structure as it now exists abide by this ethical principle? If so, why are the homeless women, children, families, and single individuals still out there? If this principle does not apply, why doesn't it?

Postscript

You may or may not personally agree with Reamer's proposed ethical guidelines. They provide one example of an ethical guide to decision making in practice. They are solidly founded on the NASW *Code of Ethics*. Regardless of what ethical guidelines you use in practice, you will continue to be responsible for your own behavior and decisions.

Dolgoff, Loewenberg, and Harrington's "Ethical Principles Screen"

Dolgoff and his colleagues (2009) propose a hierarchy of ethical principles with which to evaluate the potential courses of action in any ethical dilemma. A hierarchy is a ranked order in which a principle takes precedence over the principles below it. In other words, it is more important to abide by the first principle than by principles two through seven, by the second principle than by principles three through six, and so on. Thus, the "Ethical Principles Screen" is a prioritized list of seven ethical principles summarized in Figure 12.2 (Dolgoff et al, 2009, p. 66). The acronym "ETHICS for U" is used to assist in remembering the principles' order. The following section discusses these principles more thoroughly. Reamer's guidelines, on the other hand, contrast pairs of principles, and no pair has a clearly established relationship with any other pair.

Principle 1: People Have the Right to Exist with Their Basic Needs Met (Life)

This principle stresses that people have the right to live. As a social worker, you should put this before any other ethical principle. When an ethical dilemma involves a life-or-death variable, you choose an action to save the life, even if this means breaking confidentiality with a client or suppressing the rights of others. Sustaining life takes precedence. You might note that

PRINCIPLE	ETHICAL RIGHT– PEOPLE HAVE THE RIGHT TO:	BASIC CONCEPT– RIGHT TO:
1. **E**	**Exist** with their basic needs met.	(Life)
2. **T**	**Treatment** that is fair and equal.	(Equality)
3. **H**	**Have** free choice and freedom.	(Autonomy)
4. **I**	**Injury** that is minimal or nonexistent.	(Least harm)
5. **C**	**Cultivate** a good quality of life.	(Quality of life)
6. **S**	**Secure** their privacy and confidentiality.	(Privacy)
7. **for U**	**Understand** the truth and receive available information.	(Truthfulness)

FIGURE 12.2 A Hierarchy of Ethical Rights: ETHICS for U

people's right to survival also characterizes the most important consideration in Reamer's ethical principles.

Principle 2: People Have the Right to Treatment That Is Fair and Equal (Equality)

This principle guarantees fair and equal treatment. As a social worker, you should make decisions to abide by this principle except when life or death is involved. Ethical Principle 1 is the only condition that takes precedence.

Principle 3: People Have the Right to Have Free Choice and Freedom (Autonomy)

We all know the value that social work places on self-determination. It is a person's basic right to make his or her own decisions. The ethical principles screen indicates that only people's right to survival or their right to equal treatment takes precedence over their authority.

Principle 4: People Have the Right to Injury That Is Minimal or Nonexistent (Least Harm)

This principle states that people have the right to be protected from injury. In the event of potential injury, people have the right to experience the least injury possible, the least lasting harm or injury, and finally, "the most easily reversible harm" (Dolgoff et al., 2009, pp. 67–68).

Principle 5: People Have the Right to Cultivate a Good Quality of Life (Quality of Life)

People have the right to seek and attain a "better quality of life" than they currently have (Dolgoff et al., 2009, p. 68). This applies to individuals, groups, neighborhoods, communities, states, and nations. Only Principles 1 through 4 take precedence over this right.

Principle 6: People Have the Right to Secure Their Privacy and Confidentiality (Privacy)

People have the right not to have their private information made public. Such information might include people's names, what they say, professional beliefs and findings about them, and anything written about them.

It is interesting that confidentiality is so strongly stressed in social work practice. Why, then, is it number six of seven on the ethical principles screen list? The section "Ethical Dilemmas in Macro Contexts" will focus on ethical dilemmas and discuss this issue more thoroughly.

Principle 7: People Have the Right to Understand the Truth and Receive Available Information (Truthfulness)

People not only have the right to know the truth, but they also have the right to accurate information. It would be nice to have the truth and nothing but the truth unveiled to you all of the time. When it is possible, this is an important axiom for social workers to follow. However, what if you are legally forbidden to disclose information to clients? Should you be forced to tell them everything you think, even when your thoughts and ideas are negative? Must you always show people all your notes about them and the issues concerning them?

The use of ethical screens or similar devices to resolve dilemmas is a critical skill for social workers. Dealing with clients in an ethical manner is a clear expectation for all practitioners. At the same time, various studies have demonstrated that social workers often observe such client rights as self-determination more in the abstract than in practice (Manning, 1997). Such lapses result when workers choose to put expediency or cost factors above clients' rights. The strengths model referred to in earlier chapters assumes that clients have been fully informed about their rights, options, and opportunities. It is essentially impossible to use this model without the worker adhering to this critical value and remaining alert to dilemmas that threaten our commitment to ethical practice.

Ethical Dilemmas in Macro Contexts

The following sections will discuss a few of the many dilemmas you may encounter, including distribution of limited resources, community support (or the lack thereof) for service provision, relationships with colleagues, engaging in sexual activities

EP 2.1.2c

with clients, neglecting child maltreatment, incompetence due to personal problems, conforming to agency policy, breaching confidentiality, co-optation versus co-operation, conflict of interest, potential harm to participants, and stigmatization tactics.

Distribution of Limited Resources

Resources not only are consistently limited but also appear to be continuously shrinking. Hard decisions must frequently be made regarding what is more and less necessary. Consider your own education. You pay tuition. Tuition, along with state and other funds, helps to pay for your educational process. There is a limited amount of funding to pay for potentially unlimited educational services. Suppose educational costs continue to rise and expenses increase. If you had control over the budget at your educational institution and you had to make some hard spending choices, which of the following options would you choose to reduce spending?

1. Turn your classroom heat far down in winter (if you live in a cold northern state) or raise the air-conditioning temperature in fall and spring (if you live in a warm southern state).
2. Increase tuition by 22 percent.
3. Increase typical class size by 100 percent.
4. Increase parking costs by 300 percent.
5. Employ teaching assistants (not necessarily highly qualified), instead of full-time faculty, as instructors.

If you had to choose one of these, none would be very appealing. Each involves giving something up. This is always the case with limited resources. You can't have everything you want or even need.

Reamer (1999) describes four variables to consider when trying to make the right distribution of scarce resources: the principles of equality, need, compensation, and contribution (p. 131). The principle of *equality* might seem simple at first. True equality means that all people eligible for services, resources, and opportunities should have equal access to them. Everyone should have equal access to resources, right? However, does the system really work that way?

Next, what about *need?* Needs are "physical, psychological, economic, cultural, and social requirements for survival, well-being, and fulfillment" (Barker, 2003, p. 291). Shouldn't people who have greater needs have better access to scarce resources? Why should people who need resources less than others still get these resources?

Compensation refers to the provision of resources or treatment to pay for expenditures of effort or to make up for poor prior treatment. Should people of color, who have often been discriminated against in hiring, be given some compensation in the form of, for example, preferential treatment? Should people who work hard be paid more than those who don't work hard or at all? Would you personally work for nothing? Would you work harder for more money? Would you work less enthusiastically for less money?

The principle of *contribution* asks whether people who contribute more to a resource delivery system get more from that system than people who contribute less. Retirement funds are a good example. People who contribute more to their retirement fund by working longer and/or contributing a larger chunk of their paychecks get more at retirement than do those who work for shorter periods and contribute less. People who contribute nothing to a retirement fund get nothing from a fund. Is this fair? Is this ethical? The issues all these questions address are complicated. There are no easy answers.

Many times in practice you will be confronted by the need to make decisions about limited resources. Who will get the services and sustenance they need? Who will have to go without? The following examples show how the decision-making process shown in Figure 12.1 can be applied to various cases.

Imagine a woman placed in a nursing home (Reamer, 1990): By age 79, Hillary Krist had lived in the same nursing home for 12 years. Supported by government funds, she had some difficulties with her sight and hearing. She also had severe arthritis. However, she was able to get around fairly well and care for herself.

A legislative committee was assigned to evaluate the state's overall costs for nursing home care. The committee assessed residents' needs across the state, the level of assistance older adults required, and the extent of services various nursing homes provided. The committee then performed a massive healthcare evaluation on all nursing home residents, giving them scores for the amount of assistance they needed in their daily living care. The result for Hillary was not advantageous. The committee determined that she was living in a home that provided too high a level of support for her needs. Higher levels of support meant more expense. Hillary abruptly received a notice in the mail saying that she would have to move to another designated nursing home in two weeks. Hillary was totally distraught. How could she leave her friends and the only home she had known for over a decade?

Hillary's nursing home social worker, Hannah Hefner, was seriously concerned about Hillary's well-being. Older adults often adjust poorly to such major changes in life circumstances. Hannah was a direct-service practitioner who focused on micro-oriented activities with individuals and families. However, a decision made on a macro level high above her and without her input now directly obstructed her ability to practice ethically and effectively.

Hannah *recognized the problem.* Her second task was to *investigate the variables involved in the case* (Steps 1 and 2). She called the committee and requested details about how decisions were being made. She *sought feedback from others* (Step 3) by talking to her supervisor. She also called other nursing home social workers she knew to discuss the situation with them and see if they were experiencing similar problems.

Next, Hannah *appraised the values applying to the dilemma* and *evaluated the dilemma on the basis of the hierarchy of ethical principles involved* (Steps 4 and 5). She could not be certain whether Principle 1 could be applied to the dilemma. Hannah was not certain how the move would affect Hillary emotionally and physically. She concluded that Hillary would probably survive the move. Concerning Principle 2, Hillary was being treated equally with other clients in similar situations. Hannah anticipated that many other clients would experience serious upsets as a result of the state committee's decision. Principles 3 (the right to self-determination), 4 (the right to experience the least harm), and 5 (the right to a decent quality of life) all indicated that it was unethical—that is, not in Hillary's best interests—to move her. Principle 6 (the right to privacy and confidentiality) did not apply in this case. Principle 7 (the right to be told the truth and be privy to all relevant information) implies that Hillary should have been notified much earlier regarding the decisions that were being made about her and how they were being made.

Hannah *identified and seriously considered possible alternatives to pursue* (Step 6). She *weighed the pros and cons of each* (Step 7). First, Hannah pleaded with state committee representatives on Hillary's behalf. This could have resulted in macro change affecting a large group of older adult citizens. If committee members had listened, they might have been enlightened regarding their decision's possible affects on many people. However, the committee members remained firm in their decision. It was fiscally inefficient to allow Hillary to remain in a facility that, at that time, provided inappropriately expensive care. Ethical Principle 2 (the right to equality) supports the stance that the state should treat all of its clients in the nursing home system equally. It was not justifiable to deny other clients the more intensive care they needed just because Hillary would be upset about being transferred.

Hannah determined that there was nothing she could do about the inevitable conclusion, that Hillary would have to be moved. However, Hannah did *decide what she could do* for Hillary (Step 8). She could ease Hillary's transition as much as possible (Reamer, 1990). Acting on Ethical Principle 7, Hannah made certain that Hillary understood the reasons for the decision. Hillary could comprehend both the need to be fair to all citizens and the rationale of fiscal exigency. Hannah also investigated the new home and described it to Hillary. Because of the short time frame, Hannah was unable to take Hillary there for a visit. This would have allowed Hillary to adjust to the whole idea more slowly.

Hannah thought that the committee could have followed several procedures that would have aided residents' transitions to new homes (Reamer, 1990). It could have given both Hannah and Hillary much more notice so that they could have been better prepared for the adjustment. The committee could also have explained the process and rationale more clearly to residents, giving them some choices about where they wanted to go instead of assigning them specific homes. Finally, the committee could have implemented an appeals process so that residents in truly dire straits would have somewhere to turn. But, alas, Hannah thought, it was too late to do much for Hillary. The only thing Hannah could do at that point was make Hillary's transition as comfortable and predictable as possible.

Yet Hannah might have decided that the ethical thing for her to do was to pursue this issue on others' behalf. Hannah could have resolved to assess the potential for a positive macro level change that would affect many people in positions similar to Hillary's. Hannah might have worked to improve the planning for, involvement of, and treatment of such people.

Hence, Hannah could have become a change catalyst system and begun to form an action system. The action system might then have decided what alternatives to follow. This might have involved the solicitation of voters' support for recommended changes by walking from house to house and encouraging them to sign a petition. Likewise, the chosen alternative might have been to undertake a major newspaper campaign focused on alerting the public to the fate of people like Hillary and on improving the quality of their treatment.

Community Support (or the Lack Thereof) for Service Provision

What if a service is useful and needed, but the community simply does not want it? This is one potentially serious dilemma in macro practice (Reamer, 1999). For example, Sara Newheart works for a private social service organization that runs a number of group homes for people with cognitive disabilities. Each home is supervised on a full-time basis. Sara is in the process of preparing six people to move into a duplex. These clients have been housed in a large institution for many years. Sara and other involved professionals have determined that these clients will fare and progress much better if they are mainstreamed into the community.[7] They have been unable to maximize their potential in this dull, sterile setting.

Suddenly, the agency receives a letter from the Neighborhood Organization stating that community residents are vehemently against this plan. They do not want a facility harboring "that type of people" in their neighborhood! Sara suddenly *recognizes that she has a problem* (Step 1).

Social workers are committed to public participation in decisions that shape social policies and institutions, and they are supposed to be sensitive to cultural differences. Sara has always prided herself on her concerns in these areas. She is also committed to helping her clients move to the least restrictive environment so that the quality of their lives can improve. She realizes that the Neighborhood Organization members have a right to want a good quality of life for themselves. She realizes that they have not had an opportunity to have

---

7. *Mainstreaming* involves taking people with exceptional characteristics and placing them in environments where people without such exceptional characteristics live, work, and learn (Barker, 2003). The intent is usually to provide these exceptional people with the same or similar experiences and opportunities that are available to everybody else.

input into the creation of a new institution (group home) in their own neighborhood. At this point, she and her supervisor face an ethical dilemma between social work's obligation to the broader society and her duty to her clients. The community's vehement resistance to opening the facility is preventing Sara from doing her job and helping her clients. Sara has a direct-service position, but she is confronted with an ethical dilemma at the community level.

The next thing to do is to think more extensively about the situation and *investigate the variables involved* (Step 2). What factors are involved? What variables should be investigated? What clients' needs are at stake? What is the ethical thing to do?

One variable is the process of *deinstitutionalization,* the principle that people should be able to live in the least restrictive environment and do so as independently as possible. Deinstitutionalization is designed to achieve two goals: The first goal is to prevent people from being inappropriately placed in institutions; the second goal is to develop alternatives in the community so that those who are already institutionalized can be given the opportunity to live as independently as possible. This latter goal often requires providing services, education, training, and housing to ensure that clients are able to live as normal a life as possible.

Sara firmly believes that her clients will be much better able to function normally in a community than in an institutional setting. She foresees involving them in nearby sheltered employment. She thinks about teaching them how to travel on the city's transportation system. She sees the community facility as much better for her clients' overall well-being than the institution. Therefore, Sara strongly feels it is in the best interest of her clients to enter the group home.

Sara *gets feedback from and consults with other relevant people concerning the issue* (Step 3). She also consults with her immediate supervisor who, in turn, works with higher-level administration concerning this matter. Additionally, she talks to colleagues at other group homes to see what they have done to address similar issues.

How does the hierarchy of ethical principles apply to this situation (Steps 4 and 5)? The ethical codes do not supply a simple answer to her dilemma. Sara, thus, must consider the ethical principles, one by one. Principle 1 is really not involved—life, the right to live and have basic needs met, is not at stake. Principle 2 applies, in that people with cognitive disabilities should have equal access to community living and the rights involved, as anyone else in the community does. This takes precedence over Principle 3, which might apply to the community members' right to make their own decisions.

Consider the community's perspective. Community residents don't know much about cognitive disabilities. The unknown breeds fear and suspicion. People have unjust and untrue stereotypes about and prejudices toward people with cognitive disabilities. One common myth is that people with cognitive disabilities can't control their behavior. Perhaps another stereotype is that such people are violent. Sara needs to think about and empathize with the community residents' perspective.

Principle 2 also supersedes Principle 4. The latter could relate to the community residents' right to protection from any injury or harm caused by the group home's residents. Principle 5 emphasizes the importance of pursuing a decent quality of life. This is so, both for Sara's clients and for community residents. Principle 6, concerning privacy and confidentiality, does not clearly relate to this situation. However, Principle 7, which addresses the right to be told the truth, can be related to the community's need for education. Community residents need to understand what Sara's clients are like and that they can become an integral part of the community.

In summary, Principle 2, receiving fair and equal treatment, appears to take precedence over other concerns. Thus, Sara can work to resolve the dilemma with this principle in mind.

The group home's administration made the mistake of not educating and involving the community before initiating a new facility. What can Sara and the agency do now to remedy this? First, Sara *must identify and think about possible alternatives* to pursue (Step 6). Then, she must *weigh the pros and cons of each alternative* (Step 7). Finally, she must *come to a final decision concerning what to do* about the problem (Step 8).

Sara works with her supervisor to develop a plan to educate the community and involve it in running the new facility. She develops a presentation and asks the Neighborhood Organization if she can come and speak to them at their next meeting. She brings a PowerPoint presentation with her to show the types of activities, projects, and accomplishments other clients have pursued in other agency group homes. (Of course, she does this only after getting these clients' informed consent and that of their guardians.) She emphasizes how valuable the community experience is to these human beings. She answers questions, confronts myths and stereotypes, and allays fears.

Additionally, Sara discusses the possibility of inviting neighborhood residents to sit on the agency's board of directors. Agency administration thinks this is a great idea. The Neighborhood Organization is invited to recommend potential board members. In this way the agency can include the community in its program development process. The Neighborhood Organization, delighted by the offer, accepts and suggests specific potential board members. Understanding the issues involved and feeling that it has input into the program, the Neighborhood Organization no longer stands in the way of the program's development.

It would be nice if everyone lived happily ever after, never to confront an ethical dilemma again. However, this is not the case. After the agency opens the group home, one of the residents runs away and breaks into a neighbor's garage. He causes some minor damage that makes the neighbor and the Neighborhood Organization members irate. Meanwhile, organization officers demand to review residents' files. This, of course, creates another dilemma concerning confidentiality. And so it goes. Both the ethical decision-making process and the hierarchy of ethical principles posed here can be used to address each dilemma as it occurs.

Relationships with Colleagues

What if you find out one of your colleagues is doing something unethical? Maybe that colleague is skirting major responsibilities. Perhaps the colleague is even doing something you feel is actively harming clients. What if that colleague happens to be a pretty good friend of yours? Ethical dilemmas concerning colleagues are often very challenging to deal with. They may pose some of the greatest obstacles to your work within the macro environment.

The NASW *Code of Ethics* dictates that professional social workers "should treat colleagues with respect," but it also emphasizes that the worker's primary responsibility is to clients (NASW, 2008). So what do you do when these two principles conflict?

Dolgoff and colleagues (2009) indicate that you have six choices when dealing with colleagues' unethical behavior.

1. You can simply ignore the behavior, the "out of sight, out of mind" attitude. If you don't think about the issue, it will cease to exist.
2. You can approach the colleague yourself and share your concerns with him or her informally. This is an especially attractive alternative if you believe the colleague is inexperienced or ignorant about the

scope and ramifications of the behavior, or if the problem is relatively minor.
3. You can inform your supervisor about the situation. There may even be established agency procedures for dealing with such violations of agency policy.
4. In the event that the colleague is an NASW member, you can bring the unethical behavior to the attention of the local NASW chapter for censure. In this case, you must have definite proof that the behavior has occurred and be willing to testify about it.
5. You can bring it to the attention of the state licensing board for professional social workers. In this case, as when reporting to the NASW, you must have clear evidence to support your accusation.
6. Consider whistle-blowing—that is, bringing the issue to the public's attention.

Highlight 12.4 addresses the issue of whistle-blowing.

If, indeed, you choose to make a colleague's unethical behavior known by following any of alternatives two through six, a number of possible consequences may occur (Dolgoff et al., 2009; Loewenberg, 1987). First, your colleague may decide or be forced to discontinue the unethical behavior. Second, your colleague may suffer punitive repercussions for his behavior. Third, your colleague may be publicly embarrassed for his behavior, thereby losing clients to more reputable peers. Fourth, your colleague may be cautioned not to continue such behavior in the future and threatened with some form of punishment. Fifth, the agency or an organization responsible for maintaining professional ethics and behavior may denounce such behavior publicly.

Negative consequences can also result from raising an issue outside your own agency by choosing alternatives three through six (Sinclair, 1993). These include "humiliation to the alleged violator; embarrassment to professionals associated with the agency; a diminishing of the stature of the agency within the community and a resultant compromise of the agency's effectiveness; [and] a reduction in its funding" (p. 390). Thus, taking issues outside the agency should be considered very seriously.

We will address three examples of potential issues with colleagues, including having sexual relationships with clients, failing to report child maltreatment, and allowing personal problems, such as alcohol addiction, to seriously impede professional performance (Congress, 1999; Dolgoff et al., 2009; Reamer, 1990).

HIGHLIGHT 12.4

Whistle-Blowing

EP 2.1.10g

Whistle-blowing is the act of informing on another or making public an individual's, group's, or organization's corrupt, wrong, illegal, inefficient or hazardous behavior. In other words, whistle-blowing means taking the problem outside the organization and making it known to others, possibly the entire public arena.

Some organizations, such as the federal government, provide established means for whistle-blowing that maintain the anonymity of the person reporting the problem. Likewise, laws exist to protect the whistle-blower from retaliation by supervisory and administrative personnel whose positions are threatened by the whistle-blower's revelations.

However, despite the fact that there is some protection, whistle-blowing is usually a risky business—and the degree of risk varies in direct proportion to the seriousness of the allegations. This makes sense. Airing "dirty laundry" outside an agency can be very threatening to people who run the agency. All agencies have problems of one sort or another, just as all individual people have problems. However, people responsible for agency activity do not like the negative aspects of their activity to be displayed for all to see. Such exposure reflects badly on those who run the agency because the implication, perhaps rightly, is that the administration is at fault. As a result, whistle-blowers may be fired, reassigned to insignificant responsibilities at remote locations, or harassed into quitting. In short, administrators and other people in power can make a whistle-blower's life extremely miserable.

Whistle-blowing's consequences can affect the whistle-blower directly. The organizational administration or others who resent the whistle-blower's allegations can attack him or her personally. Others can seek to pinpoint and emphasize the whistle-blower's faults. We know that *everyone* has faults.

Colleagues may ostracize the whistle-blower, so whistle-blowers often feel tremendously isolated. They may receive threats to themselves or loved ones. They may even lose their jobs. Perhaps worse yet, they may be blacklisted as troublemakers in the professional community and find it virtually impossible to obtain new employment unless they undertake a major relocation.

Yet, sometimes whistle-blowing is necessary, especially after other less extreme measures (such as working through the agency administration) have been tried and have failed. Sometimes, whistle-blowing is an ethical imperative when violations of policy or law directly threaten the welfare of others. Several movies have focused on this subject, including *Erin Brockovich* and *The Insider*. In most such cases, an employee blows the whistle on unsafe practices after complaints to administration have been ignored.

The choice of whether to blow the whistle should be based upon the seriousness and the harm involved, the quality of the evidence of wrongdoing, the impact on both the agency and the perpetrator, the motivation of the whistle-blower, and other options available (Reamer, 1999). Whistle-blowing may not be justified, but may be necessary.

Most cases involving potential whistle-blowing are ambiguous; there is frequently a fine line between *breaking* the rules and only *bending* them (Reamer, 1990). Therefore, we continue to stress that the decision to act is a very serious one. Before blowing the whistle on agency or colleagues, consider four questions (Reamer, 1990).

First, how great is the threat to the potential victims? Is it life-or-death? Or is it only a minor infraction of the rules? Is it worth the time, energy, and risk it takes?

The second question involves what type and quality of proof you have available that the wrongdoing has occurred or is going on. How solid is your evidence? Do you have written documentation? Do you have witnesses? Or do you have some ideas based on informal observations and hearsay?

The third question concerns whether less severe alternative measures might remedy the problem. Are there established agency channels through which you can work? How difficult would it be to navigate through these channels? How much resistance do you anticipate encountering? Can you confront your suspect personally before trying other more severe measures? Can you solicit support from colleagues? Will your supervisor help?

The final question addresses whether you can assume the burden of risk. How much do you really have to lose? Is it worth it? Is whistle-blowing really the only way to attack the ethical problem? Or are there other, less risky alternatives you can pursue?

Frederica, a public assistance worker facing an ethical dilemma over a newly promoted supervisor, wonders whether to blow the whistle on this supervisor (Reamer, 1990). Frederica has been working for the agency for almost two years and is becoming increasingly frustrated by the attitudes and work habits of a number of her immediate colleagues. She sees that they spend as little time with clients as possible, even denying them needed and rightful assistance if the workers do not have time to complete all the necessary paperwork. At other times, workers bend the rules to give clients benefits to which they are not entitled. For example, workers might not report all the clients' income. Many clients work as domestic help, receiving cash from employers so no record of earnings exists. Workers make decisions solely on their own discretion. Additionally, Frederica notes that workers consistently pad the travel expense accounts that reimburse them for home visits. Frederica is appalled.

Although she doesn't like the thought of "making waves," she finally confides her concerns to her friend and colleague Zenda. Zenda dismisses Frederica's concerns almost condescendingly, indicating that such violations are simply a means of bending rules that aren't very good to begin with. She explains that such worker discretion is really an informal agency policy and adds that padding travel expense accounts is universally accepted as a means of increasing workers' relatively meager salaries. Zenda tries to soothe Frederica and allay her concerns.

It doesn't work. Frederica decides to keep her concerns to herself until she can figure out what to do about them. Suddenly, Frederica learns that Zenda has been promoted to unit supervisor. Frederica is stunned. How can Zenda maintain order and help supervisees follow agency and other regulations when she herself regularly violates them?

What can Frederica do? Should she ignore the whole situation? Should she confront colleagues about their behavior? Would such criticism cause her colleagues to ostracize her? Should she confront Zenda again, even though it did no good the first time? Should she report her concerns to someone higher in the administration? How will that make Zenda feel toward her? If Zenda considers Frederica a traitor, how miserable can Zenda make Frederica's life as an employee? Should Frederica report the problem to the NASW or the state licensing board? Should she blow the whistle to the public? How long does she think she will keep her job if she takes the problem outside established agency channels?

There is no easy answer to Frederica's situation. How would you apply the hierarchy of ethical principles to her decision-making process? What would you do if you were she?

The decision to blow the whistle, whether to higher levels of administration or to someone outside the agency, is a tough one. It requires weighing the numerous pros and cons of your own individual situation. If the ethical dilemma literally concerns life and death, you must attack the problem in some way. However, what way? Many courses of action are available to you. Whistle-blowing is usually only one of them.

If you are considering blowing the whistle because you see no other choice, several recommendations are useful:

First, be certain that you clearly define the variables and issues involved. What, specifically, is the problem? What documentation can you offer as proof of your allegations? What ethical standards or rules are being violated? In what ways are these standards and rules being breached?

Second, know what your rights are. Do you work for a public agency whose policy sanctions employees' right to free speech? How easy is it for your agency to fire you? Do you belong to a union on which you could depend for help? Is the union strong or relatively weak?

Third, be prepared for the consequences. What is the worst thing that could happen to you? Could your supervisor put a note of reprimand in your permanent file, barring you from future promotions? Would such a note work against your request for a positive letter of recommendation? Could you be fired as a result of your actions? Could your actions ruin your reputation in the professional community, branding you as a troublemaker no other agency wants to hire? If the worst does happen to you, what are you prepared to do?

Fourth, follow the chain of command. Going over your supervisor's head almost always puts you at risk of his resentment and wrath. After all, you appear to have negated his authority and competence. This is usually very threatening to supervisors. In fact, it probably would be threatening to you, if you were in their position. At any rate, if at all possible, try to follow the agency's predetermined and sanctioned chain of command. If that doesn't work, then consider more extreme options such as whistle-blowing.

Fifth, establish a clearly defined plan of action. Whom do you plan to tell about the problem? In what order will you tell people? What will you do if they react positively? How will you proceed if they respond negatively? Whom can you solicit as allies? Are other workers and administrators willing to support you? Are there external organizations, such as the NASW or licensing bodies, that would aid you or even advocate for your cause? Can you ask experts to support your case? What are your specific goals? What is your time frame for achieving them?

In summary, consider the whistle-blowing alternative very carefully. Weigh potential gains against risks and negative consequences. There is no crystal ball. All you can do is act as your conscience dictates and do the best you can.

Engaging in Sexual Activities with Clients

What if you know of a colleague who is doing this? The NASW *Code of Ethics* straightforwardly states that engaging in sexual activities with clients is forbidden. Such behavior should occur "under no circumstances" (NASW, 2008). However, you happen to be out with a friend at a local hotel bar and see your colleague checking into a room with a person you know is his client. You have always respected this colleague as a knowledgeable, competent, responsible practitioner.

What do you do? You have already *recognized the problem*. The next step is to *investigate the variables involved* (Steps 1 and 2). The fact is that this colleague is checking into a hotel room with a woman you know is his client. Agency policy and professional ethics clearly indicate that this is taboo. You respect this colleague but seriously question his judgment in this situation. If he is engaging in such behavior with this client, has he done so with others? Is he establishing relationships with other clients right now? Given that you have seen him, have other people seen him too? How will this affect the agency's and the profession's reputation?

The next step is *getting feedback from others* (Step 3). You have a good relationship with your supervisor. You trust her and feel she might be good to talk with about the situation, but, should you talk to her—or even to other colleagues—before confronting the colleague who appears to have gone astray? If you do directly confront him, will that necessarily change his behavior? In this situation, you determine to reconsider feedback from others later in your decision-making process.

You proceed to *appraise the values that apply to the dilemma* and *evaluate the dilemma on the basis of established ethical principles* (Steps 4 and 5). Does this behavior violate ethical Principle 1, the right to sustain life and have basic needs met? No. What about ethical Principle 2? Does the action involve the right to equal treatment? No, again. However, Principles 3 (having autonomy) and 4 (exposure to least harm) raise serious concerns. The reasons for the code's strong statement about sexual relationships is that such relationships often cause serious harm to clients.

The situation also exhibits an unequal distribution of power. The social worker as the professional, in effect, has influence and perhaps even decision-making power over the client. This may impede the client's autonomy and right to have free choice.

So which of the alternatives mentioned earlier will you pursue? You *identify your various alternatives* and *weigh the pros and cons of each* (Steps 6 and 7). You

decide that this is serious enough that you must do something. You cannot simply ignore your colleague's behavior. You determine that reporting your colleague to the NASW or the state licensing board for censure or whistle-blowing to the public are too severe. You decide to deal with the issue closer to home, either by confronting your colleague directly or by talking it over with your supervisor. This is a difficult call. It would be easier to tell your supervisor and let her deal with the situation than to confront and scold your colleague. However, it might be more fair and effective to talk to your colleague first, find out all the facts, and observe his reaction. You *decide to confront him as soon as possible* and get it off your chest (Step 8). Depending on how he responds, you can tell your supervisor at a later time. You also decide that a series of in-services on proper professional conduct are in order. You will suggest this to your supervisor tomorrow. You can always share your specific reasons for your suggestion with her at some later time.

Neglecting Child Maltreatment

What if a professional colleague makes a misjudgment that has serious repercussions for clients? Consider a case of child maltreatment proposed by Dolgoff and his colleagues (2009). Jimmy Beam, age five, is raced to the emergency room of Clemency Hospital at 2:00 A.M. He has suffered serious head injuries, a compound fracture of his left arm, and several crushed bones in both hands. Jimmy's parents say their only child had been running and had fallen down three flights of stairs. He is bleeding profusely from numerous abrasions. Clem Zendt, the hospital social worker, is notified of Jimmy's arrival and called to his bedside the next morning. Physicians attending to Jimmy immediately suggest the possibility of child abuse. It makes no sense that Jimmy was brought into the hospital at that time in the morning after running and falling down flights of stairs. They ask Clem to talk to the family to gather more information before reporting suspected child maltreatment.

When he attempts to talk to the Beams, they refuse to discuss the matter. They say they already have a caseworker at County Social Services, Fred Slintfone, who is providing them with family counseling. They say Clem should talk to him.

Clem contacts Fred immediately. Fred says he was seeing the family for a number of problems, including wife battering and alcoholism. He strongly suspected that child maltreatment was occurring in the Beam home, but had said nothing about it. Fred feels that reporting them for suspected child abuse would ruin his relationship with the family and his ability to help them gain control of their problems.

In Clem's mind there is absolutely no question that Fred should have reported to Child Protective Services that he strongly suspected child maltreatment in the Beams' home. State law mandates that social workers and other professionals report any *suspected* child maltreatment. Clem learns that Jimmy has suffered serious and irreversible brain damage. He will live, but will have to be institutionalized because of the extensive care he will require.

How should Clem proceed? This is a difficult decision. There is no absolutely correct answer. He has already *identified the problem*. He proceeds to *investigate the variables involved*. Clem feels that Fred made a serious mistake, essentially ruining Jimmy's life. Fred didn't do it intentionally, but the result is disastrous. However, what good will it do to report it? Jimmy is no longer in danger, because he will no longer be living with his parents. The damage has already been done. But what about Fred's grim mistake? If he's not held responsible, will he ever make a similar mistake again?

Clem *appraises the values that apply to this dilemma* and *evaluates the dilemma* on the basis of our proposed hierarchy of ethical principles. How do each of the seven ethical principles apply to this case? Which of the six alternatives for dealing with unethical behavior on the part of colleagues should Clem pursue? *What alternatives* does Clem have and *what are the pros and cons of each*? Should he ignore the dilemma and classify it as a non-issue? Should he sit down and have a serious talk with Fred? He works for an entirely different agency. What right does he have to intervene? What effect will his feedback have, anyway? Should he tell someone else, such as his own supervisor, the state branch of the NASW, or the state licensing board? Is this case sad and extreme enough to blow the whistle on Fred and his agency? *What would you decide to do if you were in Clem's place?* Highlight 12.5 looks at the issue of not taking any action.

Incompetence Due to Personal Problems

What if a colleague is inadvertently doing harm to or at least not working as she should with clients? What if her personal problems are keeping her from performing adequately? Once again, what if this colleague is a personal friend of yours?

Consider the following case that involves alcohol problems (Reamer, 1990). Irma LaDouce is a social worker at a residential center for children who have

been diagnosed with both mental retardation and behavioral problems. She is responsible for her caseload's behavioral programming, consultation with child care workers and teachers to implement the programming, and family counseling. Irma is good friends with Farrah Froemming, a colleague who has the same job description and supervisor. As a matter of fact, Farrah was initially responsible for getting Irma her job three years ago. It was Farrah's strong recommendation of Irma that convinced the hiring supervisor to give Irma the job. Irma owes Farrah a lot. Irma loves this job.

The problem is that Farrah is going through a really rough divorce. Irma, as her good friend, is trying to be as supportive as possible. She likes Farrah, appreciates all Farrah has done for her, and respects Farrah's competence. During these hard times, Irma makes a point of meeting Farrah after work for a drink and dinner. Irma notices that Farrah has increased her number of before-dinner cocktails from one mild highball to three double scotches on the rocks. Irma notices that more and more frequently Farrah slurs her words when Irma calls her at home. Finally, Irma notices that Farrah has liquor on her breath when coming to work two days in a row. At other times, Irma notices an overpoweringly strong aroma of mouthwash or powerful breath mints. Irma suspects that Farrah is taking a few nips on the side from a bottle of vodka she keeps in one of her desk drawers. Farrah's office door is closed now much more than it used to be.

Social workers impaired by substance abuse are ethically bound to seek help.

© Getty Images

HIGHLIGHT 12.5

Negative Responsibility

This might be a good time to introduce the concept of *negative responsibility* (Reamer, 1990, p. 183). Positive responsibility is responsibility for your own behavior. Whatever you choose to do, you are responsible for your actions and their consequences. Negative responsibility means that you are also responsible for those actions you choose *not* to take. In other words, you assume some of the responsibility for any harm done because you knew about a problem and chose not to do anything about it.

Consider, for example, the woman whom a group of men raped and beat in an inner-city neighborhood several years ago. Dozens of tenants looked on silently from the windows of their apartment buildings high above the scene. No one raised a hand to help the woman. They just watched. These watchers weren't hurting her. They had nothing to do with the whole thing. How much were they to blame? What was their negative responsibility for the woman's death?

When a major portion of the San Francisco freeway buckled and collapsed during the 1989 Loma Prieta earthquake, dozens of vehicles were crushed and people were trapped. Without hesitation, onlookers and community residents rushed to the earthquake victims' assistance, despite that fact that these people lived in a very poor urban neighborhood and had serious

problems of their own to face on a daily basis. Nonetheless, these helpers cared. They turned their negative responsibility into positive action. Instead of standing on the sidelines watching the appalling scene, they jumped right in to help.

Reamer (1990) notes that issues of negative responsibility are relative. You can't rush into battle on every single issue every single time, especially at your own expense. You must weigh the pros and cons of your actions. He makes three suggestions:

First, think seriously about the degree of impending harm to the people involved (in many cases, clients). Our hierarchy of ethical decision-making principles takes a clear stand on life-or-death issues as a number-one priority for ethical action.

Second, assess the extent to which the potential victims can help themselves. To what extent is the problem their own responsibility? If the victims are children, they probably have little ability to help themselves without assistance. They probably need your help even more than adults do.

Third, consider the extent to which your involvement endangers your own welfare. Is it a good plan to jump into a raging river to save a drowning person when you can barely swim?

The worst thing is that Irma sees Farrah handling one of her clients too roughly, in Irma's opinion, on two separate occasions. Another incident involves one of the child care staff who casually mentions that Farrah slapped a child one day.

Irma *recognized and defined the problem* as Farrah's difficulty in dealing with personal situations that affect her ability to perform her work effectively. Regarding *investigation of the variables involved,* Irma already knows much about the situation from her many discussions with and observations of Farrah. Irma *considers getting feedback from others,* especially her supervisor. However, in this instance, she first needs to decide whether she will approach Farrah before going any further with the issue.

Irma *appraises the values that apply to this dilemma.* Irma is faced with a conflict between respecting a colleague and treating her in good faith and maintaining the primacy of clients' interests. According to the hierarchy of ethical principles, clients have the right to be

free from injury (Principle 4) and to have a decent quality of life (Principle 5). Farrah is failing to deliver on both of these principles. Treating the children with inordinate roughness and even slapping them is illegal as well as unethical. Failing to perform her job adequately deprives clients of the best possible quality of life in this setting.

As a result, *after evaluating the dilemma on the basis of established ethical principles,* Irma determines that primacy of clients' rights supersedes Farrah's right to make her own decisions. Irma *considers the six alternatives*: ignore the behavior, talk to Farrah about her concern, talk to their supervisor about the issue, report the problem to the NASW or to the state licensing board, or blow the whistle to the public.

Irma *weighs the pros and cons of each alternative.* She decides she cannot ethically ignore the issue in view of the harm done to clients. Nor does she seriously consider contacting the state NASW chapter, reporting to the state licensing board, or blowing the whistle to the public. These would make the whole agency look bad. Additionally, she knows it is almost always best to try to work through the appropriate internal agency channels before going outside the agency. Otherwise, agency personnel might blame her for not following proper and potentially more effective channels to remedy the situation and help Farrah cope unobtrusively with her alcohol and personal problems. It is important to work within your own agency system whenever possible instead of fighting against it.

Irma *makes her decision* regarding what she will do. Because Farrah is her friend, Irma decides to confront her first. She will encourage Farrah to seek help and tell Farrah she is more than willing to help her do so. Depending on Farrah's response and actions over the next few days, Irma decides to hold off briefly on sharing her concerns with their supervisor. Irma hopes that Farrah will seek help, possibly by admitting herself to the inpatient substance abuse program that their agency's health insurance will pay for. If Farrah fails to respond appropriately, Irma will talk to their supervisor. It will then be up to the supervisor to take action.

Irma knows that her decision might endanger her friendship with Farrah and that she might regret her decision. However, she evaluates the potential benefits and risks and determines her best course of action.

It must be emphasized that there is often no best or easy solution to an ethical dilemma. You must weigh each dilemma on the basis of the circumstances, issues, and values involved. This and other examples of resolutions to ethical dilemmas are only that—examples. In your future practice experience, you will have to take into account each unique situation involving an ethical dilemma and assess it independently.

Conforming to Agency Policy

A primary aspect of the macro environment in which generalist practitioners work is the agency policies that regulate their actions. The NASW *Code of Ethics* asserts that professional employees "generally should adhere to commitments made to employees and employing organizations" (NASW, 2008, 3.09a). Superficially, it might seem obvious that workers are supposed to abide by agency policies. Some policies are almost inviolable on an ethical basis. For example, workers should use the agency's resources only for purposes intended by the agency and not to meet their own personal needs (NASW, 2008).

Thus, workers are paid for doing what the employing agency assigns them to do, right? The problem is that often an organization's goals are not totally consistent with professional values and ethics (Corey et al., 2007; Dolgoff et al., 2009). Chapter 4 discussed common problems in agencies—especially large bureaucracies—such as goal displacement. A common form of goal displacement occurs when the agency places more importance on the process of getting things done (for example, completing paperwork on time) than on the effectiveness of results achieved. Thus, you as a worker may find yourself in an ethical quandary regarding whether to be loyal to your agency and its policies or to provide your clients with what they need most.

Another example involves a private, nonprofit, faith-based organization called Positive Youth Mentors and its policy against having gay men serve as Youth Mentors for male youth. Long Chow, a worker for the Youth Mentors organization, recruited and oversaw several dozen volunteer Youth Mentors and their clients over extended periods of time. Axel, age 29, had been a Youth Mentor to Joe, age 10, for almost eight months. Long believed Axel was exceptionally good at this volunteer job. Joe, who a year ago had been a shy, passive, almost lifeless boy, was now coming out of his shell. It was exhilarating to see a wide grin spread over Joe's face sometimes when he and Axel participated in games and activities. Axel usually spent one evening a week and a few hours during the weekend with Joe, taking him to movies, playing ball or miniature golf, or jogging in the park. Long felt that the two had established a very positive relationship. Axel was an excellent male role model and a partial support system for Joe. Also, Joe's mother liked and respected Axel. She felt he was a godsend to Joe at a very difficult time in Joe's life.

The problem was that Axel sat down with Long and, in a concerned tone of voice, told Long that he was gay. Axel believed that it was not right to deceive Long. He had known about the policy from the beginning of his involvement with Youth Mentors, but felt that his sexual orientation had nothing to do with his relationships with children. Axel was in a secure, long-term relationship with his partner. He had absolutely no sexual interest in children. Indeed, Axel loved children and regretted that he would have none of his own. Therefore, he had volunteered to be a Youth Mentor. He believed that he could provide worthwhile experiences for a young boy and, at the same time, enjoy doing it. Subsequently, Axel was assigned to Joe.

Long suffered an ethical dilemma. It was clearly against agency policy to allow gay men to be Youth

Mentors. The policy had originated several years earlier when a boy accused a Youth Mentor, who happened to be gay, of sexually abusing him. Long believed that Axel was truly good for Joe. He understood that sexual orientation and sexual abuse were unrelated issues. Breaking Joe and Axel up would tear Joe apart, and Joe had already suffered too many other losses in his life.

Long had *identified the issue.* He had *investigated the variables involved* by talking extensively with Axel, researching the history of agency policy, and becoming knowledgeable about the lack of relationship between sexual orientation and sexual abuse. Long consulted the agency director, his direct supervisor, to *get feedback from others.* The director, busy with many aspects of agency life, emphasized the importance of adhering to policy and offered no better solutions. Sometimes trying to get helpful feedback from others does not work. Long also evaluated the legal status of the policy, which turned out to be ambiguous in his particular state. In other words, he could get no definite answer regarding whether it was legal or illegal to discriminate against gay people in this manner.

Long *appraised the values that applied to the dilemma* and *evaluated the dilemma on the basis of established ethical principles.* This situation didn't seem to fit very well. Principle 1 in the hierarchy of ethical principles (the right to live and have basic needs met) really did not apply. Principle 2 (the right to equality) applied to Axel, but not to Joe. Through no fault of his own, Axel was not being treated equally with other volunteers upon which the agency depended. However, Axel was a volunteer, not a client. Principle 3 (the right to autonomy) might also be applied to Axel. His sexual orientation was his own business. He should have the right to free choice concerning his own behavior when it harmed no one else. Although the policy implied a violation of Principle 4 (the right to experience the least harm) in terms of protecting clients from sexual abuse, Long knew the assumption (that gay men sexually abuse children) upon which it was based was wrong. In actuality, removing Axel from the picture would probably harm Joe emotionally. Did Joe have the right to be protected from intentional harm according to ethical Principle 4?

Long *thought about the alternatives available* to him. Long could ignore the situation and purposely disobey agency policy. However, he had voluntarily joined the organization and had agreed to abide by its policies, including this one against inclusion of gay men. Therefore, Long would be held liable and censurable for not heeding this policy (Reamer, 1999).

Talking to his supervisor, also the agency director, did not help. There was really no one else higher in the agency structure to whom he could turn. Reporting to someone outside the agency made no sense. By doing so, he would break confidentiality with Axel. Thus, Long could see no solution to be derived from that tactic. Long didn't want to quit his job. What good would that do? He loved his work, and it wouldn't help solve the problem at hand.

One alternative was to attempt changing agency policy and establish better screening procedures for all Youth Mentor candidates, gay or straight (Reamer, 1990). Long felt that this might be the answer. He *made his decision* and began planning a strategy for accomplishing such a policy change. In effect, Long decided to assess his potential as a change catalyst system to address a macro (organizational) issue. If Long was successful, then the dilemma confronting Axel would disappear.

If one accepts the argument that helping the organization modify discriminatory policies is an ethical responsibility of social workers, then Long made an appropriate choice. He would attempt going through agency channels before undertaking more drastic measures. At any point in the future, he could revert to one of the other alternatives or tactics. All of this would depend on his evaluation of the situation, its context, and the relative significance of ethical principles at the time. How do you think this scenario turned out?

Examples of conflicts between workers' professional ethics and agency policies exist everywhere. Organizations might cut corners and deprive or even harm clients by cutting services under budgetary pressure (Dolgoff et al., 2009).

Workers might even discover agencies undertaking clearly unethical practices in the name of greater efficiency. Consider a nursing home that supports the policy of drugging clients to keep them minimally active. If clients just lie in bed all day doing nothing, it costs the agency much less in terms of staffing for supervision and other activities.

What would you do if you were a social worker at such an agency? You know that it is obviously not in the clients' best interest to be drugged senseless until they literally die. These practices obviously violate at least ethical Principles 2 (the right to equality and equal treatment), 3 (the right to autonomy), 4 (the right to least harm), and certainly 5 (the right to a decent quality of life). There are also questions regarding whether the agency is in violation of Principle 1 (the right to life). In this severe case of an agency's unethical behavior, what alternatives are available? What choices would you make? What would your plan entail? Once again, there are no easy answers to ethical dilemmas.

A related issue regarding conforming to agency policy is the extent to which policy supports a multi-cultural context for service provision. Highlight 12.6 addresses this matter.

Breaching Confidentiality in a Macro Context

Confidential information is any information a client communicates to an agency for purposes of receiving services. It includes everything from the client's name, address, age, gender, and sexual orientation to the nature of problems or concerns for which help is being sought. It also includes other items in a client record, such as psychosocial evaluations, the results of psychological tests, and anything else that pertains directly to the client. Clients have a right to expect that this information will be protected and not shared without explicit permission. Although confidentiality is not absolute, as we have described earlier, it should be protected with due diligence. This is the expectation of the NASW *Code of Ethics* and is a common tenet in the ethical standards of other helping professions.

Essentially, a professional practitioner is not supposed to divulge information about a client unless that client gives him or her explicit permission to do so. The maintenance of confidentiality is of major importance to the social work profession. However, the code allows the social worker to share such information when "there is a compelling need for such disclosure" (NASW, 2008, 1.07q). The code thus places the burden upon the worker to prove that any breach of confidentiality is indeed *compelling*. Several possible reasons are provided.

Absolute confidentiality means that the clients' confidence will not be broken no matter what. *Relative confidentiality,* on the other hand—what the code refers to—means that professional practitioners may have to break confidentiality under compelling circumstances. Ethical dilemmas involve relative confidentiality. The hierarchy of ethical principles clearly emphasizes that there are numerous instances when confidentiality must be broken.

There are at least eight common reasons for breaking confidentiality (Corey et al., 2007; Huber & Baruth, 1987; Reamer, 2006; Sinclair, 1993):

1. When a court appoints a social worker to evaluate a person, that worker is obligated to provide the court with information about the client.

2. In the event that a worker determines that a client is a potential suicide risk, that worker should inform the appropriate helping body.

3. When a client sues a social worker, such as for malpractice, the worker may have to share information about the client.

4. When a client introduces "mental condition" as a claim or defense in a court action, the worker may be forced to respond to this claim.

5. Workers must report confidential information in the event that a minor is being maltreated.

6. A worker must report information and get help for a client who the worker suspects has such a severe mental condition that he or she requires hospitalization.

7. When otherwise confidential information is made an issue in court, a worker must respond.

8. Social workers must report to the appropriate authorities when a client reveals that he or she is going to harm someone else.

Chapter 13 discusses confidentiality within the legal context.

Confidentiality issues in a macro agency setting can be much more complicated than an individual practitioner's adherence to privacy principles. Dolgoff and his colleagues (2009) emphasize this complexity by citing several contexts in which confidentiality becomes exceptionally difficult to maintain. These include communications with other professionals, administrative recordkeeping requirements and access to information, relationships with insurance companies, and police needs. Each context can present problems either for the individual practitioner or for general agency policy.

Communication with Other Professionals

To what extent is it the agency's formal or informal policy to talk to other professionals about your clients, their problems, and their issues? Are all clients alerted to the fact that you may discuss their cases with others, including supervisors and interdisciplinary team members? What about multiproblem clients involved with a range of other services and resources? Must you inform your client about every other professional, even from other agencies, to whom you talk about that client? Isn't sharing information critical in many instances to coordinate services and provide the most efficient and effective intervention possible?

Administrative Recordkeeping

Then there are recording requirements. To what extent do your agency superiors have access to information

HIGHLIGHT 12.6

Agency Policy and Ethics in a Multicultural Context

EP 2.1.4

Highlight 12.3 established the importance of identifying and combating your own stereotypes in the process of developing appreciation for individual and cultural differences. This is only one step (albeit a critically important one) in the attainment of cultural competence in practice (Corey et al., 2007). Questions can be raised regarding the extent to which ethical codes of the helping professions in general and social work in particular have fully explored how principles should be applied in multicultural contexts (Pack-Brown & Williams, 2003).

For example, Pack-Brown and Williams (2003) cite the following scenario:

Suppose Maria, a client of color from a collectivistic culture [that emphasizes the importance of involvement and connections with family and community], begins to think of you as "family" and asks you to attend her graduation and family celebration afterward. The question comes unexpectedly. Your mind races for a reply that, on the one hand, conforms to ethical sanctions against dual relationships and, on the other hand, is responsible to your client's genuine valuing of her relationship with you as an esteemed "mentor." You search for a way to balance these factors with your knowledge that the client's cultural context embraces multiplicity in relationship roles. Western counseling norms of strict relationship boundaries are not emphasized in your client's culture. (p. 136)

Pack-Brown and Williams (2003) make three general recommendations regarding how to respond to such issues. First, "anticipate potential conflict" (p. 138). This involves becoming as knowledgeable as possible about your clients' cultures by consulting with experts, reading, attending conferences and seminars, and cultivating friendships with those of other cultures. It also concerns developing an "[o]ngoing self-examination" of your attitudes about people with backgrounds different from your own (p. 139).

The second suggestion for applying ethical principles in multicultural contexts is to assess the "cultural sensitivity" of your ethical code (p. 139). Although attending Maria's graduation would technically constitute a dual relationship, the NASW *Code of Ethics* states that "[s]ocial workers should not engage in dual or multiple relationships with clients or former clients in which there is a risk of exploitation or potential harm to the

client. In instances when dual or multiple relationships are unavoidable, social workers should take steps to protect clients and are responsible for setting clear, appropriate, and culturally sensitive boundaries" (NASW, 2008, 1.06c). It continues that sometimes "dual or multiple relationships can occur simultaneously or consecutively."

The code does not forbid dual or multiple relationships outright. Rather, critical thinking should be used to identify alternatives, seek help from others such as supervisors or peers, and make a decision about what to do (Pack-Brown & Williams, 2003). In such a case as Maria's, you might ask yourself the following questions:

Is there a risk of harm or exploitation if I attend Maria's events?

Do I risk harming Maria if I do not attend?

What decision, attending or not attending, would best respect Maria's dignity?

How can I respond in a way that reflects Maria's worth as an individual and as a client about whom I care? (Pack-Brown & Williams, 2003, p. 140)

The third suggestion for applying ethical principles in multicultural contexts is to "balance culture" and the ethical code (p. 140). There are several ways to respond to Maria's request (Pack-Brown & Williams, 2003). You could decline the invitation by explaining that you can't ethically attend clients' personal events. Although this response gets you off the proverbial hook, it fails to balance the issue of cultural sensitivity to Maria's needs and values. Another alternative involves asking Maria "why it would be important to her for you to attend," another relatively insensitive question that avoids the issue. Accepting the invitation immediately without giving it adequate thought fails to address the professional ethics aspect. A final possibility is, as Pack-Brown and Williams (2003) suggest, that you "[t]ell Maria you feel honored to be asked but that her invitation presents a dilemma to you" (p. 141). This is a straightforward approach that shares your reality with Maria. You might then thank her for the invitation and, finally, ask her "to share with you how it would feel to her if you did or did not attend" (p. 141).

A dangerous threat to multicultural competency in organizations is *cultural encapsulation,* the perspective characterized by defining reality "according to one set of cultural assumptions," insensitivity to cultural variations, irrational adherence to one's own beliefs as being the only right ones, and an overly simplified view of both reality and problem resolution (Pedersen, 2008, p. 7;

Sue, 2006). The following 10 conditions tend to characterize cultural encapsulation in agencies and their staffs:

1. All persons are measured according to the same hypothetical "normal" standards of behavior, irrespective of their culturally different contexts.
2. Individualism is presumed to be more appropriate in all settings than a collectivist perspective.
3. Professional boundaries are narrowly defined, and interdisciplinary cooperation is discouraged.
4. Psychological health is described primarily ... [using technical jargon and vague labels, with little or no attention to how people effectively function in their unique cultural context....]
5. Dependency [on others, including family or community members] is always considered to be an undesirable or even neurotic condition.
6. The person's support system is not normally considered relevant in analyzing the person's psychological health.
7. Only linear-based, "cause-effect" thinking is accepted as scientific and appropriate.
8. The individual is expected to adjust to fit the system even when the system is wrong.
9. The historical roots of a person's background are disregarded or minimalized.
10. The [social worker] ... presumes herself or himself to be already free of racism and cultural bias. (Pedersen, 2008, p. 8)

Agencies can combat cultural encapsulation and support a multicultural context for ethical practice in a number of ways (Pack-Brown & Williams, 2003). First, agencies can provide or support formal training to staff concerning cultural sensitivity to diverse client populations and consciousness-raising about the various expressions of cultural encapsulation. Second, agencies can also assist practitioners' informal, "ongoing development of multicultural skills" by encouraging that staff "stay ... abreast of multicultural research, seek ... consultation, and participat[e] ... in informal supervision groups with other practitioners" (p. 133). "[S]ocial work ethics committees also are sources of guidance," with "functions [that] include educating members and answering inquiries about ethical courses of action in specific circumstances" (p. 135).

about your clients? Virtually every agency requires recordkeeping for the sake of accountability. However, who exactly will have access to this information? Who will know about your client's intimate problems? In what kind of detail will others be able to investigate your clients and their lives? What about funding agencies? What client information should they have access to? Should you be certain to tell your clients about each and every person who will have potential access to their records? Should you get their signed consent for revealing this information? How does your agency's policy help or hinder you in trying to answer these questions?

The records issue is becoming increasingly complex because of extensive electronic recordkeeping. Who exactly might have potential access to information about clients? One state automatically tests all blood donors for HIV. The blood donation centers forward the identities and demographic data of individuals who test positive to a centralized data bank. The blood centers also inform the designated individuals of their positive HIV status. However, they do not inform these people that their names will be added to the HIV-positive data bank. Nor do the blood centers inform donors that they will be tested for HIV in the first place. Who, then, has access to the names of people testing HIV-positive? Do administrative assistants or other employees working with and around the computers have opportunities to look at the list of names? If so, whom might they tell? Can insurance companies readily check this data bank for the purpose of denying people coverage if they have preexisting HIV-positive status?

Insurance Company Requirements

What about insurance companies who reimburse for services provided to clients? Should social workers always be totally honest and open concerning their records and services? What if you determine that an insurance policy is unfair? What if an insurance company will reimburse for six weeks of inpatient treatment for alcoholism only if the referring worker deems the problem "very serious"? What if the worker feels the problem is only "mildly serious"? This latter diagnosis will allow the client only four outpatient treatment sessions, which the worker knows will be insufficient to help the client. Should the worker report the problem as "very serious" in order to give the client a chance at solving her problem?

Again, significant privacy issues arise from the extensive presence of computers. Access to client files can always lead to breaches of confidentiality, either inadvertent or deliberate. The following incidents suggest some of the possibilities: Quittner (1997) relates the experience of a child sexual abuser who used his job as a technician at a major hospital to search computerized records seeking possible victims. Other examples include a banker serving on a state health commission who accessed a list of cancer patients, checked it against a list of bank customers with outstanding loans, and then revoked the loans of customers who had cancer. Similarly, a major company planned to cooperate with a health care system to identify workers experiencing poor work performance who might benefit from antidepressants. These examples should raise the concerns of social workers about the extent to which electronic recordkeeping can diminish a client's right to privacy and confidentiality.

Police Concerns

Finally, police often have the right to know about clients' problems, regardless of whether such problems are shared with workers confidentially. Some states require social workers to inform the authorities whenever the workers become aware of a felony or threatened felony. What if revealing such information will annihilate your relationship with your client? What if you hear about the supposed felony fourth-hand and from a relatively unreliable source? As you can see, the concept of confidentiality is fertile ground for ethical dilemmas.

Co-optation versus Cooperation

Co-optation refers to eliminating opposition to a cause, plan, or organization by assimilating opponents into the group favoring the cause, plan, or organization. Co-opting enemies makes former enemies look foolish if they disagree too much with the cause, plan, or organization because they are now members of the co-opting group. In other words, co-optation absorbs the opposition.

Cooperation, on the other hand, involves different factions working together to achieve some mutually agreed-upon goal without either faction losing its own identity. The factions remain separate groups.

Frequently, a direct-service social worker trying to implement a change in an organization or community lacks adequate power and experience to do so. Higher-level administrators or people with greater experience are much more accustomed to wielding power and to making changes or stopping them from occurring. It is relatively easy for people in power to "seduce" a worker into co-optation. Hence, people with more power often find it useful to co-opt, rather than cooperate with, a worker seeking some kind of organizational or community change.

Co-optation can assume several forms. Those with power may appear to befriend a worker by offering personal camaraderie or other social opportunities that the worker might not otherwise experience. Being invited to gatherings of important executives, community leaders, and other big names can begin to create a "we" feeling in the worker. She may begin to lose steam over what she had hoped to change or implement. It may become easier for her to believe what the people in power are telling her. After all, she might think, they do have greater experience and wisdom, not to mention money. Co-optation can serve to awe an inexperienced, relatively powerless worker into agreeing with the status quo.

Another means of co-optation concerns how decision makers appeal to a worker's sense of reason. They may suggest that the worker simply—and naïvely—does not understand how difficult things are or how impossible it would be to accede to the worker's requests and goals. Again, people in power can co-opt by establishing a "we" feeling of solidarity and safety with the worker.

In the event that co-optation tactics are effective, the worker may find himself losing his perspective. He may also lose effectiveness in representing his clients' interests and weaken in his advocacy efforts. He may even be viewed by others, including clients who support positive change, as "selling out to the enemy" (the people in power).

Conflict of Interest

A *conflict of interest* is a situation in which personal gain conflicts with professional objectivity. Often, it involves playing two conflicting roles that have conflicting goals. For example, Vita is a member of the Citizen's Disability Board, an advisory board charged with advocating for the needs of city residents who have disabilities. An *advisory board* is a group or committee that meets to supply data and information, expertise, and suggestions for achieving an organization's goals. The city's mayor appointed Vita and the other four board members. The board had been trying to persuade the city to adopt a comprehensive ordinance requiring the city's rental apartment owners to make all units accessible to individuals with physical disabilities. As a social worker, Vita is acutely aware of the needs of the city's residents with disabilities. However, Vita is also part-owner of an old apartment building that would be horrifically expensive to modify to accommodate residents with physical disabilities. When Vita's board debates this issue, what should she do? She holds two conflicting roles at the same time. Voting for what she thinks is right—making the entire city accessible—would affect her personally and financially in a very negative manner. Perhaps the best thing would be to remove herself from the board, and thus from this conflict of interest.

Another example of conflict of interest involves Leticia, who is running for a seat on the city council. She is also a member of the city's Police and Fire Commission and has been very active in pushing both the police and fire departments to hire more women. Her community, however, is very conservative. Potential voters have little or no interest in recruiting more women or minorities for the police and fire departments. If anything, most voters are generally against this strategy. This community context sets the stage for a conflict of interest on Leticia's part.

After she declares her candidacy for a seat on the council, she becomes much less vocal in her support of hiring women and minorities. She wants to get elected, and therefore feels she must go along with what her voting constituency wants. By being silent on the issues, she is implying that the city needs the very best officers it can recruit, regardless of gender or race. She no longer appears to support hiring women and minorities. Has Leticia "sold out" her fellow police and fire commissioners in order to get elected to the city council? Has the possibility of getting elected made her agree with and become part of a constituency with little interest in expanding opportunities for female and minority personnel?

Another example is an agency director who accepts a free turkey for his own family from a vendor who supplies food to the agency's summer lunch program for homeless children. This director runs a serious risk of having his judgment, or lack thereof, called into question on the grounds of showing partiality to this particular vendor.

Potential Harm to Participants

What if doing the "right" thing causes more harm than good? Any attempt to bring about large-scale organizational or community change poses the risk of some negative consequences. A public assistance worker might nag a landlord (or "slumlord," as his tenants call him) to improve his dilapidated rental properties in order to bring them up to code. The landlord might decide that such upgrading is not worth it financially and abandons the property rather than fixing it up. The clients then may face the serious problem of finding another place to live that is within their meager means.

Stigmatization Tactics

Stigmatization means identifying or describing someone or something in disgraceful, contemptuous, or reproachful terms. In a confrontational situation, such as when trying to implement macro change, painting your opponent as bad or evil may permanently alienate that opponent. It is easy to criticize or stigmatize an opponent, especially in the heat of pursuing some marvelous cause. However, by doing so, you can make a permanent enemy on whom you can never again depend for help. Therefore, it is best to avoid a we/they or good-guy/bad-guy dichotomy.

It is probably in your interest to recognize realistically that there are few permanent friends, allies, or enemies in a professional context. Some issues, such as the right to adequate housing or ready access to quality education, may be permanent, but the perspective each participant assumes toward these issues is not. It depends on each person's own interests in a particular macro scenario (agency or community). The cantankerous landlord today may become a member of the city council or of your own agency's board of directors tomorrow. In summary, be careful. Stigmatizing the "enemy" may backfire later when you badly need his or her support.

Furthering Ethical Practice in Agency Settings

In addition to maintaining awareness of ethical dilemmas that occur in various settings and resolving them effectively, there are other things that you can do to further ethical practice. For example, you can ensure that your agency keeps clients informed about policies and procedures that affect them. This might include such information as an explanation of and orientation to services offered by the agency, payment arrangements, and a list of the professionals representing the agency. Because clients may not understand such terms as "treatment plans" or know how to arrange services, this information should be routinely provided. Clients should be informed about confidentiality and the limits to this right as well as about other rights and responsibilities. Encouraging the agency to put together a brochure that contains such information (in several languages) is one way of helping to achieve this goal.

Similarly, creating an appeal or grievance procedure for clients is a means to help maintain ethical standards. You may also encourage your agency to engage in continuous quality improvement and evaluation of outcomes to help safeguard clients' rights to effective practice. This information could also be included in an information packet or brochure.

You might consider proposing that the agency adopt a code of ethics for employees. This could be an existing code such as the NASW's or one specific to the particular agency.

Looking Ahead

This chapter reviewed the NASW *Code of Ethics* and proposed approaches for conceptualizing an ethical dilemma and ranking ethical principles. Finally, it explored a wide range of ethical issues and dilemmas that can occur in macro practice settings. The next chapter will explore another macro context social work practitioners may face—working with the courts.

Chapter Summary

The following summarizes this chapter's content as it relates to the learning objectives presented at the beginning of the chapter. Chapter content prepares social workers to:

A. *Examine and apply the NASW* Code of Ethics.

The NASW *Code of Ethics* addresses social workers' ethical responsibilities to clients, to colleagues, in practice settings, as professionals, to the social work profession, and to the broader society. Each dimension includes subcategories.

B. *Relate how spiritual diversity characterizes the human experience and apply ethical boundaries when addressing spirituality.*

A client's spirituality may be a source of strength to be explored. Social workers should not impose their personal spiritual values on clients. The NASW *Code of Ethics* could be more specific regarding how practitioners address spirituality. Social work education should consider the extent to which a focus on client spirituality should be incorporated into curricula.

C. *Make ethical decisions by applying standards of the International Federation of Social Workers (IFSW)/International Association of Schools of Social Work (IASSW) Ethics in Social Work, Statement of Principles.*

The IFSW/IASSW Ethics in Social Work, Statement of Principles consists of five sections.

Social workers may need to apply these standards depending on the situation. The statement stresses two principles—human rights and social justice.

NASW policy statements maintain that the struggle for human rights continues. Numerous suggestions are made regarding how social workers can advocate for human rights and social justice. Suggestions include getting international jobs or internships, making donations to or joining international organizations, volunteering, and educating others—including decision makers—concerning the magnitude of human rights issues.

D. *Recognize and manage personal values, including those concerning stereotypes and prejudices so that professional values can guide practice.*

Values are what one considers "good or desirable," while ethics designate "what is right and correct" (Dolgoff et al., 2009, p. 21). Social workers should monitor their values and follow steps to change inappropriate ones, including stereotypes and prejudices.

E. *Apply a strategy of ethical reasoning to arrive at principled decisions.*

Decision-making steps when facing an ethical dilemma include: (1) recognize the problem; (2) investigate the variables; (3) get feedback from others; (4) appraise the values that apply to the dilemma; (5) evaluate the dilemma; (6) identify and think about possible alternatives; (7) weigh the pros and cons of each alternative; and (8) make your decision.

F. *Review two strategies for ranking ethical principles.*

Reamer (1999) proposes six ethical guidelines, each of which ranks one ethical principle against a second principle. Dolgoff and colleagues (2009, p. 66) employ an ethical principles screen, the acronym for which we propose is Ethics for U.

G. *Appraise a range of ethical dilemmas occurring in macro contexts, tolerate the ambiguity involved in decision making, and propose viable options to address the dilemmas.*

Ethical dilemmas in macro practice may concern distribution of limited resources, community support (or the lack thereof) for service provision, relationships with colleagues, engaging in sexual activities with clients, neglecting child maltreatment, incompetence due to personal problems, conforming to agency policy, breaching confidentiality, co-optation versus cooperation, conflict of interest, potential harm to participants, and stigmatization tactics. Examples, options, and/or subsequent questions are proposed for each type of dilemma.

Whistle-blowing should be undertaken only very carefully. Negative responsibility concerns the potential repercussions for opting not to address an ethical problem.

H. *Recognize and communicate the importance of appreciating cultural differences in ethical practice.*

Ethical principles should be applied within the context of people's cultural values and expectations. Social workers should avoid "cultural encapsulation," where reality is viewed narrowly from one's own cultural perspective (Pedersen, 2008, p. 7).

Competency Notes

The following identifies where Educational Policy (EP) competencies and practice behaviors are discussed in the chapter.

EP 2.1.1 Identify as a professional social worker and conduct oneself accordingly. *(P. 444):* Social workers have ethical responsibilities as professionals. *(P. 447):* Social workers have ethical responsibilities to the social work profession.

EP 2.1.1e Engage in career-long learning. *(P. 436):* Social workers should engage in competent practice based on up-to-date treatment approaches. Maintaining and enhancing competence is a lifelong endeavor. States often require continuing education to maintain credentials. *(P. 443):* Agency administrators should provide continuing education and staff development.

EP 2.1.1f Use supervision and consultation. *(P. 442):* Social workers should use supervision and consultation in an appropriate and ethical manner.

EP 2.1.2 Apply social work ethical principles to guide professional practice. *(P. 432):* This entire chapter addresses professional values and ethical principles to guide practice.

EP 2.1.2a Recognize and manage personal values in a way that allows professional values to guide practice. *(P. 445):* Practitioners should strive to recognize and

combat their stereotypes and prejudices. *(P. 450):* Practitioners should identify personal values and prevent them from interfering in professional practice.

EP 2.1.2b Make ethical decisions by applying standards of the NASW *Code of Ethics* and, as applicable, of the International Federation of Social Workers [IFSW]/International Association of Schools of Social Work [IASSW] Ethics in Social Work, Statement of Principles. *(P. 434):* This and the following sections review the NASW *Code of Ethics*. *(P. 449):* Practitioners should employ ethical principles established by the IFSW and the IASSW as appropriate.

EP 2.1.2c Tolerate ambiguity in resolving ethical conflicts. *(P. 453):* Practitioners must learn to tolerate and deal with ambiguity as they address any of the ethical dilemmas potentially encountered in macro practice. *(P. 457):* Numerous ethical dilemmas may confront social workers as they practice in macro settings.

EP 2.1.2d Apply strategies of ethical reasoning to arrive at principled decisions. *(P. 453):* One approach to ethical decision making is examined. *(P. 454):* Two means of ranking ethical principles are discussed.

EP 2.1.4 Engage diversity and difference in practice. *(P. 470):* Social workers must demonstrate cultural sensitivity when practicing in multicultural settings.

EP 2.1.8 Engage in policy practice to advance social and economic well-being and to deliver effective social work services. *(P. 448):* Social workers have the ethical responsibility to engage in social and political action to enhance people's general welfare.

EP 2.1.10g Select appropriate intervention strategies. *(P. 462):* Sometimes whistle-blowing may be the most effective ethical intervention strategy.

EP 2.1.10l Facilitate transitions and endings. *(P. 441):* Practitioners should terminate services to clients in an ethical manner.

On the Internet

Visit the *Generalist Practice with Organizations and Communities* Web site at www.cengage.com/social_work/kirst-ashman for learning tools such as PowerPoint® slides, tutorial quizzing, Web links, and final exams.

Working with the Courts

Social worker Rita Moro is about to appear in court to testify regarding the possible need for protective guardianship of her client, Alfred Garcia, age 87. Mr. Garcia has Alzheimer's disease and, according to his family, cannot function well alone. Following an assessment process, it is Ms. Moro's[1] opinion that this client is unable to care for himself or make realistic decisions about his own care. The presiding judge asks the worker to identify the "least restrictive" alternative or option available to the client. In order to function as a professional social worker, Ms. Moro must know the legal definition of "least restrictive care," assess the available options meeting the criteria in the community, and respond to the judge during a court hearing.

Archer Daniels, a child protective services social worker, has been subpoenaed into court, along with his client's agency records, regarding an alleged physical abuse incident. In his case notes, Mr. Daniels has written that the mother appeared "depressed." Upon cross-examination, the defense attorney asks Mr. Daniels to give a clinical definition of depression. He is unable to do so, which significantly reduces his credibility in the eyes of the judge. By failing to define the term adequately and to cite specific examples of depressed behavior or appearance in the record, Mr. Daniels looks as if he does not know what he is talking about. He is unable to help his client as effectively as possible.

During cross-examination at a dispositional hearing, Mary Clark testifies regarding her experience in providing individual and family counseling to the defendant. The defendant has been found guilty of having sexual intercourse with a minor. The prosecuting attorney looks Ms. Clark directly in the eye and poses his final question: "Can you promise me, Ms. Clark, that the defendant

---

The authors wish to thank Pat Christopherson for her many contributions to this chapter. Patricia M. Christopherson, ACSW, ICSW, is a Professor Emeritus in the Department of Social Work at the University of Wisconsin–Eau Claire. She wishes to acknowledge the help of numerous social workers and attorneys who suggested examples and topics for this chapter.

1. Unlike most other chapters in this book, in this chapter surnames are used intentionally and consistently to reflect the formality of the courtroom process.

will never have sexual contact with minors again?" Ms. Clark recognizes that no one can assure the future behavior of another person. Confounded, Ms. Clark is at a total loss for how to respond to the question. She has no idea how to answer yes or no without being able to offer further explanation.

Introduction

The significance of the legal system for social work practice cannot be overestimated. We consider the court system one of the primary macro arenas for generalist practice. Some of the most important progress in providing social services to vulnerable populations has resulted from legal decisions. Judges have expanded the rights of people with developmental disabilities and forced national, state, and local governments to confront discrimination in the school systems. Social workers and others serving as advocates for those denied social and economic justice have repeatedly asked the court system to intervene. Courts frequently force governments, organizations, and agencies to abide by their own rules, adhere to the U.S. Constitution, and honor the intent of legislation. For these reasons alone, it is important for social workers to understand the legal system, particularly those components most likely to be experienced by the generalist practitioner.

Moreover, various states and communities in the United States have created drug courts and mental health courts for the purpose of handling the specialized needs of defendants in such cases. Both drug and mental health courts are venues in which social workers may find themselves practicing. The focus of these courts is to "reduce the number of incarcerated people with substance abuse disorders and mental illness" (Tyuse & Linhorst, 2005, p. 233). Such courts rely on less adversarial approaches and are designed to pursue treatment and problem-solving models. Services provided include linkage to community resources, inpatient or outpatient programs, vocational training, and others designed to prevent relapse. Not only can social workers provide services in conjunction with drug and mental health courts, but they can advocate for the creation of such courts in their local communities. The availability of such programs means that those caught up in the criminal justice system have another option to incarceration.

Additionally, social workers may speak before legislative bodies or testify in administrative or civil hearings. In each case, the social worker is playing a role at the macro level in policy and program implementation. The process of presentation in such instances of macro practice is similar to testimony in a court of law.

The United States is becoming a more litigious society. To an increasing extent, citizens are asking the legal system to address moral, health, and social issues in addition to those in the traditional areas of criminal justice. For example, courts are now routinely asked to determine what medically constitutes the term "life." That is, society is asking the courts to decide if "life" is defined as heartbeat, brain activity, or meaningful interaction with the environment (consciousness). Another issue before the courts in some states is the question of gay marriages. Values are becoming more diverse, and knowledge about human growth and development is expanding. It is arguable, then, that the courts will be asked to address increasingly complicated questions of fact and judgment.

EP 2.1.1e

Social workers have joined members of other helping professions to work more directly and frequently with the legal system. The exchange between the social welfare and legal systems often produces situations in which social workers feel ill prepared. They may feel unable to serve the needs of clients, agencies, or the larger society. Additionally, they may feel unable to present themselves in the most professional manner. A national study of the educational backgrounds and work experiences of child welfare personnel indicated that although practitioners with baccalaureate social work degrees perceived their education as better preparation for child welfare work than other baccalaureate degrees, a significant number did not think they were adequately trained in "preparing/giving testimony in court" (Lieberman, Hornby, & Russell, 1988) (CSWE, 2008, EP 2.1.1e). This chapter will provide basic background information about the legal system and those legal circumstances in which social workers will need further help in their efforts to benefit clients within this macro context.

Seven areas have been identified as basic to all social work practice and its relationship to the legal system: confidentiality; clients' consent to intervention; legal rights of clients; documentation of evidence in the case record; legal authority for practice; testimony in court; and legal duties implicit in professional practice (Saltzman & Furman, 1999).

This chapter will focus on practical and general preparation for court and actual testimony, regardless of practice area (for example, child welfare or working with older adults). Social workers need to be educated about courtroom protocols and procedures to serve clients more effectively. The courtroom is also open to public scrutiny in most cases, except those involving minor children. As such, it provides an arena for visibility and accountability that may seem unfamiliar and exposing to a social worker whose day-to-day practice is conducted under less scrutiny.

Many laws governing social work practice and the possible resultant grounds for testimony are legislated and regulated on the state level. It is therefore advisable for generalist practitioners to recognize that differences between states are likely. Workers need to educate themselves about appropriate state statutes governing their areas of practice. Likewise, it behooves any social worker facing courtroom testimony to learn what protection, if any, is available to him or her by statute. Does the state where you practice offer privileged communication with clients—that is, do state statutes protect from public disclosure any information shared between the client and another party? Many states do not recognize the confidentiality of communication between clients and social workers. In such circumstances, workers must be prepared to face contempt-of-court charges if they refuse to divulge information garnered during sessions when they assumed their privacy was protected.

Learning Objectives

This chapter will provide content concerning how social workers:

    A. *Utilize concepts related to courtroom processes.*
    B. *Differentiate between social work practice and courtroom protocol.*
    C. *Demonstrate professional demeanor in behavior, appearance, and communication in the courtroom.*
    D. *Practice within the phases of the adjudication process.*

    E. *Analyze and attend to various strategies used in cross-examination.*
    F. *Apply concepts to a child welfare protective services case.*

Functions of Professional Terminology

Every profession utilizes words and expressions that are unique in usage or meaning. One function of such terminology is to shorten communication and ensure shared meaning. A doctor and a pharmacist can talk comfortably with each other about medicinal dosages and chemical equations. Each knows that the other has the necessary background to interpret similar meanings of the terms they use. Therefore, they can expect to understand each other.

A second function of professional terminology is to establish boundaries between users of such terms, such as the designated professional, and those who do not belong to these professions. In other words, the role of medical, legal, or social service provider becomes more clearly separated from the role of service user because of this different use and understanding of terminology. The words clients or patients use are probably much more general than those used by professionals. Members of any profession must often be very specific in word choice and usage because of complex and/or adversarial situations they encounter.

Once a social worker consults with an attorney or steps into a courtroom to testify, he or she may recognize both of these functions of legal terminology. When interaction with the legal system occurs, the social worker must learn to recognize and use key terms according to their legal definitions. This ensures shared meanings and allows social workers to interact comfortably as full participants in the legal process.

Important Legal Terms and Concepts

Following are definitions of some of the most relevant legal terms and concepts for social workers: laws, criminal law, civil law, violations, jurisdiction, allegation, court process, due process, stipulation, burden of proof, standards of proof, evidence, witnesses, guardian *ad litem,* confidentiality, privileged communication,

EP 2.1.7a

and subpoenas. Highlight 13.1 elaborates upon the significance of using legal terminology in whatever your area of practice may be (CSWE, 2008, EP 2.1.7a).

Laws

Laws are "those standards, principles, processes, and rules … that are adopted, administered, and enforced by a governmental authority and that regulate behavior by setting forth what people may and may not do and how they may do what they can do." Put more simply, the law consists of "those guides to social conduct which are created and enforced by public officials" (Saltzman & Furman, 1999, p. 6). Laws may govern not only behavior but also the procedures that are to be used "in investigating, presenting, managing, and deciding legal cases" (Alexander, 2003).

Criminal Law

Laws can usually be classified in one of two categories: *criminal law* and *civil law.* Criminal laws are those that govern the operation of state and federal criminal justice systems. Individuals or organizations who break these laws can be sanctioned or punished by the government. While a citizen might witness someone breaking a criminal law (for example, committing a crime), only the government is authorized to prosecute and punish the law breaker.

Civil Law

Like criminal law, civil laws govern the behavior of individuals or organizations. However, they are materially different from criminal law in that it is usually private citizens who exercise the power to punish the person who has broken a civil law. It is not uncommon for a given behavior to involve both criminal law and civil law. For instance, if an individual assaults another person, that individual may face a criminal charge enforced by the government while simultaneously being sued by the injured party. Because of the difference in definitions and standards used by criminal and civil courts, it is possible for a trial in each court to result in a different outcome. Thus, the alleged assaulter could be found not guilty in a criminal court but still be made to pay damages in a civil court.

Violations

Violations are offenses that involve the breaking of a law or rule. Generally, the terms "violation" and "offense" can be used interchangeably. Violations of the law can occur in three different ways. First,

HIGHLIGHT 13.1

Legal Terminology in Your Area of Practice

Mastery of legal terminology is important both to specify meaning clearly and to relate to other professionals. As a generalist practitioner you will need to know all professional terms in your area of practice. Most often, the specific definitions of terms and their relevance to your practice are defined and governed by state or federal statute. Legal definitions are not only important to know for testifying in court. A social worker must know the appropriate statute to ensure compliance with client and interdisciplinary professional interactions.

In some instances, the legal definition might not be similar to the commonsense definition or the one most frequently used in practice. Confidentiality between a professional and a client may or may not be protected by law. Social workers may have to break confidentiality to report child abuse, because this is legally mandated. In other words, reporting suspected child abuse takes precedence over confidentiality. Depending upon your area of practice, you may need to know the legal definitions of child abuse, child neglect, least restrictive care, restitution, diversion, permanency planning, or family-based services.

You are well advised to consult with supervisors or your agency's policy manual for the appropriate definitions at the beginning of employment. Such definitions are the basis for professional decision making of all sorts. A social worker would need to know the various levels of sexual assault to make an accurate referral of a client to law enforcement officials.

On the witness stand, you should be able to document your authority and expertise by citing legal definitions. Your professional credibility will be greatly diminished if you cannot adequately define terms relevant to a case.

The legal terms listed and defined in this chapter are common to most social work practice, regardless of problem area. Familiarity with all of these terms assures increased comfort with the legal process generally and with testifying in particular.

criminal violations are offenses penalized by fine and/or imprisonment or probation. Usually, criminal offenses are deemed the most serious and are familiar to most members of a society.

Criminal violations are divided into felonies and misdemeanors. In most states, *felonies* are crimes considered serious enough to be punishable by imprisonment for a term of one or more years. Murder, kidnapping, and first-degree sexual assault are typical felonies. *Misdemeanors* are less serious crimes punishable by confinement in a city or county jail for a period of less than one year. Misdemeanor violations might include battery (bodily harm to another with intent and without consent), negligent operation of a vehicle, or carrying a concealed weapon without a permit.

The second type of violation is *civil offenses*, for which the sole penalty is forfeiture of money or goods. Violations of state fish and game laws, malpractice suits, or product liability cases are examples. If found guilty of a civil violation, the defending hunter, professional, or company often has to make restitution and/or pay a fine.

The third type of violation involves *ordinance offenses*. Ordinances are civil (noncriminal) laws enacted by a local unit of municipal government. Conviction for a noncriminal offense can draw a fine but not incarceration of the offender. For example, local governments establish zoning regulations, require registration of bicycles, or limit ownership of animals.

Jurisdiction

Jurisdiction means authority to act. A court can proceed and its findings be binding only if it is authorized by law to handle the case before it. Jurisdiction may be challenged based on age (adult versus juvenile court) or location (site of the offense versus place of arrest).

In all states, juvenile court has jurisdiction over most illegal acts committed by people under age 18. However, there are exceptions. In some states, adult courts have exclusive jurisdiction over boating and vehicle regulation violations committed by those 16 years of age and above. Therefore, 16- and 17-year-olds, although technically children, are prosecuted in adult court instead of juvenile court when they commit such violations. In other instances, often dependent upon the nature of the offense and the age of the alleged offender, adolescents can be waived into adult court. There, they face the stiffer consequences adult courts are authorized to impose. Some state legislatures have changed the legal definition of childhood to

include an automatic waiver into adult court depending on the nature of the alleged crime.

Juvenile courts typically have jurisdiction over youths judged to be (1) delinquent, (2) in need of services, or (3) referred to as dependent, neglected, or abused. Many baccalaureate social workers will first interact with the legal system with clients in one of these three areas. "Delinquency" definitions vary state by state, but factors included in the jurisdiction typically include age and the identified behavior, often defined as a behavior that would be a law violation if committed by an adult. "Children in need of services" is often defined using incorporation of status offenses: These are children who have committed acts that, if committed by an adult, would not be illegal. Examples include truancy or curfew violations. When the courts get involved in protecting a child, it is in direct response to complaints alleging violation of a particular state's statutes. Most states will have provisions within their codes for the following circumstances, including when a child has been:

Without a parent or guardian.

Abandoned by a parent or guardian.

Physically or sexually abused by non-accidental means.

Referred by a parent or guardian when he or she is unable to care for or control the child.

Placed for care or adoption in violation of the law.

Habitually truant, with little or no successful parental involvement.

Habitually truant from home, and courts are asked by the parent or guardian to intervene.

Neglected during a period when the parent is incarcerated or hospitalized.

Neglected by a parent or guardian regarding food, clothing, medical care, and so forth, under conditions other than poverty.

Refused for medical or AODA (alcohol and other drug abuse) treatment by the parent or guardian.

Alleged to have performed a delinquent act but is under 10 years of age.

Immunized inadequately or not at all.

Determined to be not responsible for a delinquent act by reason of mental disease or defect.

Such a wide range of conditions necessitates excellent assessment and recording skills by the intake worker and case manager. A social worker might be asked questions regarding any of these three areas pertinent to interviewing, social history, referral, treatment, management, and follow-up. A worker might be testifying in only a limited area, but such testimony would be governed by state statute, state administrative law, and agency policy.

Initially established in the early 1900s as "family courts," such legal arrangements were organized and run on a more informal, often paternalistic model, where there was no legal recourse to appeal or rights similar to those of an adult. Family courts often had jurisdiction over divorce, paternity, child support, adoption, and other intrafamily misdemeanors.

Social welfare agency personnel may, at times, have to ascertain geographic jurisdiction before proceeding legally. State or federal statute and/or case law precedent may determine jurisdiction where residence of the alleged offender and location of the alleged violation are different. In such cases, a determination of jurisdiction is necessary before determination of guilt or innocence begins. A social worker may be involved in the apprehension of a juvenile legally residing in one state who is alleged to have committed an illegal act in another state. Different circumstances and appropriate state statutes may dictate how the legal system would proceed. For example, attorneys and judges would consult the law to determine jurisdiction over a juvenile arrested for delinquent behavior outside the state of his legal residence. The alleged offender may be extradited (surrendered) to another authority for prosecution.

Social workers involved in jurisdictional disputes over procedures are well advised to consult with their supervisors or corporation counsel (that is, the attorney hired by the agency for legal services). Jurisdiction may not be straightforward and may require the advice of those with advanced legal training for interpretation of the appropriate statutes.

In addition to such consultation, the district attorney may be called upon to help determine jurisdiction. The district attorney (sometimes called the state or prosecuting attorney) is an elected or appointed officer who acts as attorney for the people or government within a specified district, such as a city or county.

Allegation

A term heard frequently when violations are discussed, an *allegation* is the assertion of one side in a lawsuit setting out what that party expects to prove at the trial. More specifically, its use is based on the protection and legal right of a defendant to be assumed innocent until determined guilty. Hence, in written and oral communication, the defendant is referred to as the "alleged"

perpetrator of a crime. Until a determination of guilt has been legally obtained, the defendant has only been accused of committing a crime. Thus, social workers should develop the habit of calling the defendant in a legal case an "alleged" offender until guilt has been legally determined.

Court Process

There are two phases of the court process. During the *adjudication phase,* facts are presented, and the charge is determined by a judge or a jury. This phase is quite familiar to the average citizen. Both sides present testimony to the individual (judge) or group (jury) who bears responsibility for making the decision as to guilt or innocence. The second phase, *disposition,* occurs after adjudication and refers to the sentence determination. In many child welfare or adult criminal cases, the social worker may be asked by the judge to write a lengthy, detailed, pre-sentence dispositional report that includes suggestions and options for the judge. In most cases, laws provide a specified range of sentence for a given crime.

Often, the adjudication and disposition phases are separated by time. The judge may order a pre-sentence investigation report or consult case precedents (that is, decisions made about similar cases decided earlier by other judges) before disposition. The judge is limited by law and precedent regarding the degree and nature of the punishment. In some cases, adjudication and disposition may occur sequentially on the same day.

Due Process

The Fourteenth Amendment to the U.S. Constitution mandates that courts must provide *due process* during the conduct of business. Specifically, law in its regular course of administration must document that it guarantees the protection of a fair trial. Specific procedures must be followed. Often, the expression "due process rights" is used to refer to safeguards protecting the accused person. The bottom line is that each individual is innocent until proven guilty.

Since 1967, due process rights have protected juveniles as well as adults (*In re Gault,* 1967). Juvenile codes (that is, state statutes applying to persons under age 18) vary by state in the degree that due process rights are recognized and protected. In some states, social work practice is likely to be governed by the concept of "best interest of the child" (that is, decision making by any authority figure should reflect the adult's judgment as to the best alternative *for the child*) in conjunction with due process safeguards. For example, a social worker may recommend in a court report that the mother, instead of the father, get custody of their children in a divorce dispute. Such a recommendation would be based on the "best interests" of the children according to the assigned social worker's investigation and judgment.

Stipulation

Attorneys representing both parties can agree to *stipulate* to any matter pertaining to the proceedings or trial. By so doing, they are, in effect, agreeing on the point of information or fact. In a murder trial, the attorneys could stipulate that the defendant had, in fact, shot the victim. The disagreement then might focus on whether the defendant was legally sane at the time of the incident. Usually, "sanity" in legal terms means the ability to recognize the implications of one's behavior and to assist in one's own defense. The defendant's social worker could testify at the trial about information pertinent to the client's sanity.

Burden of Proof

In the United States, the *burden of proof* rests on the prosecution or plaintiff (that is, the party making the complaint). It is the responsibility of that party to prove the allegations set out in the petition filed before the court. The defendant is the person against whom a claim or accusation has been brought in court.

Standards of Proof

Standards of proof pertain to the *level or degree of certainty* needed to prove an allegation in court. There are generally three different levels: beyond a reasonable doubt, clear and convincing evidence, and preponderance of the evidence.

Beyond a reasonable doubt is used in criminal or delinquency cases (*In re Winship,* 1970). It necessitates evidence that is entirely convincing to a moral certainty (sometimes referred to as 90 percent sure).

Clear and convincing evidence refers to approximately a 70 percent degree of certainty. Such a degree of certainty may, for example, be used in cases of child abuse or neglect. In other words, a social worker might be asked to state how certain he is that the abuse or neglect actually occurred.

Preponderance of the evidence (51 percent minimum certainty) is the standard of proof applied in civil (as opposed to criminal) cases; some states also use this

standard for child abuse and neglect cases. In some agencies, the standard of proof used by social workers and supervisors in a child abuse case investigation is preponderance of the evidence. In other words, the social worker would want to establish at least 51 percent certainty that the abuse occurred before taking some remedial action. Generally, the more severe the charge, the higher the standard of proof required for a conviction.

Evidence

Evidence may take several forms: real, documentary, or testimonial. *Real evidence* consists of tangible objects, such as weapons or photographs. *Documentary evidence* pertains to certified documents, usually identified and authenticated by proper authorities. For example, X-rays or medical records are documentary evidence, and the authenticity of either would be stipulated to or testified about by an employee of the department responsible for such records. *Testimony,* of course, refers to the actual interviewing of a witness by the district attorney or the defendant's attorney.

Hearsay Evidence

The type of testimony typically most questioned by counsel during the court session is hearsay evidence. *Hearsay* refers to testimony about a statement made outside the courtroom.

A social worker who is given information about an alleged child abuse incident by a neighbor during the course of that worker's investigation cannot testify in court about the neighbor's story. If the case goes to court, the hearsay restriction limits the testimony the social worker can give about the incident learned from the neighbor. Instead, the neighbor might be subpoenaed to testify about his or her own observations.

In most instances, hearsay testimony is not admissible for several reasons. First, there is no opportunity to cross-examine the person making the original statement. Second, the original statement was not made under oath. Third, there is a problem of accuracy in repeating a statement made by someone else. A demonstration of such a problem is the game "Telephone," wherein a group of people sit in a row and each whispers to the person on one side what was just whispered by the companion on the other side. At the end of the line, the final person states out loud what he or she heard. Typically, significant distortion has occurred as information was perceived and passed along by the various people. The courts acknowledge the possibility of distortion; hence, hearsay information is generally not allowed.

The fourth problem with hearsay testimony is that there is no opportunity for the finder of fact (judge or jury) to observe the demeanor of the person making the original statement. To what extent does the witness's nonverbal behavior coincide with and support what the witness is saying verbally?

There are numerous exceptions to the hearsay rule too detailed or specific for presentation in this chapter. For further information you are advised to consult Barsky and Gould (2002).

Quality of Evidence

To be admissible, usually all forms of evidence must have three qualities. First, the source must be *competent,* that is, qualified to make the observation. For example, a witness must not have been legally intoxicated at the time of the event. Second, information must be *relevant,* meaning that it must bear on the proceeding at hand. Finally, information must be *material* and thus have important consequences for the case.

Witnesses

Courts of law define two distinct types of witnesses: lay (that is, factual) and expert. The term *lay witness* refers to one who is limited in testimony to what she or he saw, heard, smelled, or touched. In addition, a lay witness can give her or his opinion about a perception, typically involving such factors as speed, intoxication, or insanity. Opinions on other topics by lay witnesses might also be requested and given, assuming there is no objection from opposing counsel.

In many states, social workers testifying about an investigation of child neglect might be limited to this type of restriction. That is, they might be considered lay witnesses who could provide only testimony as identified above.

An *expert witness,* on the other hand, is rendered "qualified" by the judge to give opinions in a particular area of expertise. Expert witnesses typically have advanced degrees, training, credentials, continuing education, practice experience, and the like, cited in court to document their expert status. The status of expert is conferred only for the length of any one particular trial. In other words, it is possible for a social worker with a particular background to be judged an expert by one judge and not by another. The expert status is not transferable from one court case to another. A judge could determine that an individual developmental psychologist is an expert in a specific neglect case. As such, she could testify about normal child development and its pertinence to the particular case before the court—but perhaps not in other neglect cases.

Judges vary greatly in admissibility of social workers as expert witnesses, and they have the authority to determine who will be admitted as an expert for the case before the court. In any case, the generalist practitioner must be prepared to defend his or her qualifications for the status of expert. Lengthy and detailed questions might be asked about the social worker's education and experience by either side's attorney to support or challenge the request for expert designation.

Guardian *Ad Litem*

The United Nations Convention on the Rights of the Child and the laws of many states provide that a child's interests must be considered in various court-related situations. Adults judged incompetent by a court (or who are in court for that to be determined) are provided similar protection. In the United States, this protection has historically been provided by a *guardian ad litem* who is appointed by the court to represent the individual's "best interest." It should be noted that best interests are to be determined by the guardian *ad litem,* and not by what the client might identify as his or her preferences. This fact, common to English-speaking countries, raises serious ethical questions. Bilson and White (2005) have argued that this neglect of the client's point of view suggests that children should be provided an advocate in place of or in addition to a guardian *ad litem.* The advocate would ensure greater representation of the child's interests and increase children's participation in various legal proceedings while the guardian *ad litem* would protect the client's legal rights.

Guardians *ad litem* are required in some states and countries in divorce proceedings. This is the case in Florida and Switzerland, among many other places. While the term "guardian *ad litem*" is common in the United States, other countries use different terms to describe the individual providing this service.

In some states, the guardian is mandated by law to be an attorney. In others, it can be any member of the community in good standing, including a family member, a professional, or any other citizen. Bilson and White (2005), based on a review of several studies, suggest that volunteers serving as guardians are equally or more effective in this role than lawyers.

In the capacity of guardian *ad litem,* the appointed party may question witnesses on the stand on behalf of the client. In general, this party represents a viewpoint distinct from those of either the plaintiff or the defendant and their respective counsels.

Confidentiality and Privileged Communication

Both of these concepts involve the degree of protected disclosure of communication between professionals and their clients.

To many social workers, confidentiality is the more known and recognized term of professional responsibility. *Confidentiality* refers to the principle that information shared between the client and social worker is intended to be kept private. However, social workers must be aware of how state statutes and agency policies define confidentiality between client and helper. Of course, true confidentiality occurs rarely in a professional setting given that secretaries, transcriptionists, filing clerks, supervisors, and, to a certain degree, colleagues in the same or contracting agencies have access to information. Such information is often shared orally or, more frequently, in writing via charts, social histories, progress notes, and so on.

Although many clients are aware of these policies regarding shared knowledge about agency records, it is advisable to inform clients during the first meeting about what information would or would not be held in confidence. Furthermore, the generalist practitioner needs to be aware of ethical obligations to report certain types of information—such as child abuse, mandated of all professionals identified in state law. It is also advisable that disclosure rules, legal requirements, and agency policies be shared at the very first meeting with clients and victims. When there are multiple clients, disclosure can be even more complicated, because one person can sign a release but the spouse, for instance, may refuse.

Confidentiality, as both a professional and a legal term, is seldom as pure as inexperienced social workers or clients might expect. The social worker must be aware of any and all restrictions that determine the limits of a "confidential" relationship. Confidentiality has always been an issue in matters important to the well-being of the general public. A physician is mandated to report births, deaths, gunshot wounds, or sexually transmitted diseases in many states. True confidentiality would prohibit such reporting.

Another example concerns confidentiality among professionals. Doctors or hospitals may limit access to specific information (such as an AIDS diagnosis) for other health care providers based on a need-to-know criterion. In other words, to protect the patient, only those health care providers in jeopardy of contracting AIDS themselves from a particular patient "need to know" the diagnosis. The argument to limit disclosure of HIV status rests on the premise that among health care professionals, precautionary procedures regarding transmission of deadly diseases should be standard operating procedure in all medical situations. Thus, there is no overriding "need to know" in any particular instance. This type of confidentiality restriction and discussion is relatively recent. Historically, professionals working in agencies under a binding contract and with the same client may have disclosed information to each other using a more general rule. A full description of all the variables affecting confidentiality and privileged communication is beyond the scope of this chapter. For a more complete discussion of confidentiality, see Stein (2004) and Barsky and Gould (2002).

Privileged communication refers to information shared between the client and another party that is protected by statute. Usually, the other party is a professional, spouse, or member of the clergy. In such instances, the professional is protected from disclosing information learned in the course of regular duties in a court of law. Only the client or patient (and not the professional) can claim privileged communication. This is a very important distinction. In other words, a professional is not exempted from divulging confidential information in the courtroom if the client has not claimed privileged communication. Likewise, if the client does claim privileged communication, the professional is barred from disclosing the information, regardless of the professional's preference. Additionally, it is important to note that the court protects the professional in privileged communication.

Privileged communication coverage by profession varies by state. In most states, physicians, lawyers, spouses, and religious personnel are covered. Social workers may be covered if engaged in clinical social work since all states protect psychotherapists from having to divulge confidential client information (Alexander, 1997). However, this is not necessarily the case for social workers engaged in other roles. Social workers can be subpoenaed in other situations and required to testify about knowledge on a topic. In such circumstances, refusal by such an unprotected professional to share information would result in being held in contempt of court. *Contempt of court* refers to willful disobedience to or open disrespect for the rules of the court. Accordingly, the involved judge may punish with a fine or jail term. Generalist social work practitioners must be fully informed of the definitions, coverage, and case law regarding confidentiality and privileged communication in the state where they practice. It is important to note that in 1996, the U.S. Supreme Court extended privilege to social workers testifying in federal cases. The case, *Jaffee v. Redmond*, 518 U.S. 1 (1996), recognized that, like psychologists and psychiatrists, communications between clients and social workers should remain confidential and that this is essential to psychiatric treatment.

Subpoenas

EP 2.1.2b

Many social workers, in the course of their professional careers, will be *subpoenaed* to appear in court to testify regarding a client. Often, the subpoena requires that the professional bring any and all paperwork, files, reports, and informal notes as well. Because the exchange between the client system and the social worker is "owned" by the client, if he or she signs a waiver or release of information, the social worker is then legally free to share the information. The NASW's *Code of Ethics* notes, however, that the professional maintains client confidences "except for compelling professional reasons." Authors of any social history, progress note, and so forth need to ask themselves at every opportunity whether there is a compelling reason that anyone would "need to know" the information in written format—because once it is part of the record, even if not pertinent to a particular testimony, such documents can be included in the information shared in court. In the face of a subpoena, social workers do have options. While a subpoena cannot be ignored, the social worker should determine whether the client has given written permission to release his or her information. If not, the social worker should respond to the subpoena by writing the attorney a letter immediately. The letter should not confirm nor deny that the social worker is providing services, reference both state law and the profession's *Code of Ethics* regarding confidentiality, and offer to respond to the subpoena either by having the client grant written permission or through a court order (Fulton, 2003). The attorney then must either provide the client's permission or ask the court to compel your testimony. Ultimately, it is up to the judge to decide what to do, and the social worker can request that the court withdraw the order to testify (CSWE, 2008, EP 2.1.2b).

Once subpoenaed, the social worker should keep a detailed note on what steps were taken to ensure compliance with the order but still protect the client as much as possible. For example, the social worker may want to get written permission from the client to discuss file contents with the client's own attorney. The area of subpoenaed documents often creates a potential conflict between legal requirements and professional ethics. An attorney familiar with the laws of the case being tried or the corporation counsel should be consulted, and the discussion noted in writing.

Differences between Courtroom Protocol and Social Work Practice

Fundamental differences exist between social work and legal systems. The following section addresses the common differences between standard social work practice and courtroom proceedings. Figure 13.1 introduces and summarizes the major points.

Adversarial versus Conjoint Problem Solving

Court proceedings in this country are based on one model of human problem solving, which proposes that truth and justice are more likely to be served if each side in a case presents information either beneficial to its own cause or detrimental to its opponent's. For the duration of the proceedings, plaintiff and defendant become adversaries. They single-mindedly pursue the presentation of fact and innuendo favorable to their respective cases. The finder of fact, be it judge, jury, or hearing examiner, can then make a reasonable decision. Decision makers assume that each side has presented its most convincing information and argument.

Courtroom process appears to be game-like in comparison to typical social work interactions. In court, each attorney presents a line of reasoning that might best persuade decision makers. It is interesting to note that each attorney could just as easily present the opposing viewpoint using a contrasting line of reasoning. Interactions in court appear fixed and ritualistic. They are prescribed by conventions unfamiliar to the daily communications, activities, and routines of social workers. Highlight 13.2 explains how, in some ways, court is like a stage performance.

Social work practice is much more likely to be based on a model of planned change that stresses a conjoint solution. Such solutions emphasize the different parties' similarities, negotiations, and compromises.

SOCIAL WORK PRACTICE

PROCESS: Conjoint problem solving

INFORMAL ATMOSPHERE
1. Dress: casual
2. Name usage: first name
3. Deadlines: flexible; some dictated by law or administration
4. Space: managed by nonverbals, furniture, culture
5. Language: open; inconclusive (e.g., "It seems . . .")
6. Nonverbals: congruent with internal state

CLIENT RIGHTS
1. Confidentiality
2. Self-determination
3. Consent to treatment

OUTCOME: Stoppage of abuse/Rehabilitation/Strengthening of family/Placement/Services

COURTROOM PROTOCOL

PROCESS: Adversarial/game-like; ritualistic

FORMAL ATMOSPHERE
1. Dress: formal
2. Name usage: "Your Honor"; last name with title
3. Deadlines: rigid; defined by law
4. Space: managed by judge, furniture, protocols
5. Language: definitive, precise
6. Nonverbals: may be incongruent with internal state

DUE PROCESS RIGHTS OF THE DEFENDANT PROCEDURALLY
1. Right to be notified of charges and face accuser
2. Right to legal counsel
3. Right to cross-examine witnesses
4. Privilege against self-incrimination

OUTCOME: Determination of charge/Disposition

FIGURE 13.1 Social Work Practice versus Courtroom Protocol

HIGHLIGHT 13.2

Court Is Like a Stage

It is important for a social worker to remember that unlike much social work practice, there is an element of drama or theater in the courtroom. Players move in assigned parts toward a specialized outcome that hopefully, includes both truth and justice. The social work role often assumes a secondary or supporting nature. That is, the professional has no primary responsibility for formulating arguments or making final decisions.

A court is the turf of other professionals. Social worker participation is circumscribed by the dictates of the other key roles and the players in these roles. Typically, single pieces of information or testimony do not by themselves lead to a specific conclusion. Instead, it is how lawyers put the pieces together that establishes a theme. It is the accumulation of evidence that builds a case.

Attempts are made to reduce blaming and not to picture any given party as the sole culprit. The helping professional often tries to foster a sense of goodwill and common good among the differing parties.

When members of the social work profession, therefore, are subpoenaed to testify in court, they are entering a very different arena from the one in which they typically conduct day-to-day business. The setting and the rules of procedure are vastly different. Generalist social workers may feel vaguely uncomfortable because of those differences. Consider a situation in which one of the attorneys has been hired, in part, to make the social worker's testimony less consequential and

credible. Most social workers do not operate in a daily arena where it is someone else's job to discredit the perception of their professional competence. It is easy to feel threatened under such adversarial conditions.

Formal versus Informal Atmosphere

A court of law is conducted according to historical precedents that dictate the setting, appearance of the participants (such as the judge's robes and attorneys' business attire), and rules of conduct. The space within the courtroom is managed by the arrangement of furniture and the physical proximity of the various players. Formal attire, including long robes for the judges, attests to the seriousness and significance of the proceedings. Language is circumscribed by law and age-old protocols. Judges, for example, are addressed as "Your Honor." Likewise, a witness must take a formal oath in a specific physical posture attesting to the truth of future statements.

Aspects of court procedure, such as deadlines for document submission, filing of petitions, presentation of pre-sentence investigations, and appearance for testimony are to be taken seriously. One's cause can be compromised severely if such deadlines are not met.

The practice of social work is typically more informal. Often, dress is casual and first names are used. Deadlines exist, but may not be rigidly enforced. Consequences for missing deadlines are usually much less severe than those courts may impose. Space in an agency is not mandated by strong external or historical precedents. Each worker is free to arrange furniture and decorate as desired within restraints imposed by space and considerations for colleagues' needs and well-being. Generally, there is more latitude in interpersonal interactions. Common courtesy dictates friendly or informal day-today discourse. Social workers may or may not rise when greeting a client, for example.

The social worker coming from the social welfare environment will note the strong contrast with the atmosphere in a court of law. Social workers may feel they are on unfamiliar ground and present themselves much less comfortably as a result.

Practitioners are advised to prepare themselves for the differences in formality and to dress much more formally than usual for a court appearance. The clothes one should wear to court—a somber, serious suit and conservative jewelry for women, a conservative suit with inconspicuous tie for men, and business dress shoes for both—contrast sharply with the casual slacks, sweaters, and shoes worn for an average day in the office. When dressed for court, expect office colleagues to ask whether you're planning to attend a funeral.

Both the social worker and clients can become more comfortable with the proceedings by reviewing the physical layout of the courtroom. Many social workers stress to their clients the differences in formality between court and almost any other familiar setting. As a social worker, you might take future witnesses to an empty courtroom to educate them on-site regarding layout, participants, procedures, terminology, and other details.

Legal Due Process versus Client Rights

In both a court of law and in the social work profession, rights and responsibilities of the defendant/client and the attorney/social worker are protected by historical precedent and by case law. Over time and based on the results of specific cases, certain roles of attorney and social worker in relationship to their respective clients have been defined and protected. For example, confidentiality has been honored both professionally and legally.

In a court of law in this country, the defendant is assumed to be the one most in need of safeguards protecting his or her rights. Potentially, defendants have the most to lose. Thus, defendants have a number of procedural rights, including the right to be notified of all charges against them, the right to legal counsel, the right to cross-examine all witnesses, and the privilege against self-incrimination. This last privilege assures defendants that they do not have to participate in any procedures that could suggest guilt. The *Gault* decision in 1967 assured these same rights to juveniles. All of these safeguards are measures to prevent the government from arbitrarily usurping individual freedoms.

Client rights in professional relationships have evolved through time as both individual professionals and the profession as a whole have monitored compliance with recognized values and ethics. At other times, the rights of clients have been defined or protected by legal or legislative decisions. Many states now have statutes outlawing contact of a sexual nature between a client and a member of certain professions.

Common client rights include foreknowledge of confidentiality and its constraints, self-determination, and informed consent for treatment. Earlier, this chapter discussed confidentiality and its limitations. Basically, a client who shares information has the right to know if the professional is legally and ethically required to report any of this information (for example, child abuse). Likewise, if a client's social worker or other helping professional is called to testify in court about the client, the client has the right to invoke privileged communication. This limits what the professional can disclose. A client also has the right to select alternatives from the choices available to him or her (self-determination) without undue pressure from the helper. Last, a client has the right to be informed about the choices for treatment and the known consequences of every treatment. The client can, thereby, select and consent to one choice, any combination of choices, or none at all.

Outcome: Determination of the Charge versus Rehabilitation

The ritualistic procedures of courtroom protocol result in a decision of guilt or innocence (adjudication phase). This is followed by the disposition phase (or sentence), which is usually determined by the judge. The end result is clear and unambiguous. The time frame is relatively short, and all efforts are directed to a specific conclusion.

In contrast, social work practice is much more ambiguous in process and, often, in outcome. Usually, client or system change is the goal. However, a case can be open for an indeterminate period, depending on the circumstances and what the agency dictates. Social workers often work "for the best interests of the child" or for the "preservation of the family." Yet, such goals are open to varied interpretations and final results will vary. Social workers need to be aware of the difference in focus between their regular, daily practice and formal courtroom protocol in order to be more relaxed and effective courtroom participants.

Presentation in Court

This section focuses on how social workers can best present their testimony in courts of law. Highlight 13.3 elaborates upon a social worker's role in court.

Preparation for Testimony

A number of issues are involved in preparing for court testimony. They include appropriate documentation, review of other documents, establishment of expert witness status, review of testimony with the attorney, and preparation of witnesses. In essence, once you as a social worker receive a subpoena, your first task is to review your own case record and then reread other applicable documents.

Documentation

As a generalist practitioner prepares for an upcoming court date, the payoff of good documentation becomes obvious (CSWE, 2008, EP 2.1.1d). Some experts argue that the best preparation for testimony lies in the assessment and case note documentation of the social worker's opinions or observations (Barsky & Gould, 2002). Often, the credibility or believability of testimony is directly related to the amount and accuracy of detail the worker has put into the case record. If opinions and facts are not well documented in a case, the benefit of the doubt will often go the way of not taking any action. This means that whatever change was recommended by the social worker, such as removal of children from a neglectful or abusive home, will not occur because there was not enough documented evidence to support such a radical decision.

EP 2.1.1d

Documentation that is adequate for courtroom testimony typically includes acknowledgment of all contacts the worker has had with the client and others involved in the case. Contact dates, including the year, should always be noted. (It is amazing how fast years fly by and how difficult it is to remember in what year you wrote what note.) It can also be important to cite "no-shows" or cancellations of appointments, which may demonstrate a client's lack of commitment and inability to assume responsibility.

HIGHLIGHT 13.3

Summary: Your Role in Court

Overall, it is important to remember that the primary mission of a professional social worker testifying in court is to *inform* or *educate* the finder of fact. Social workers are generally advised to present themselves as "friends of the court." As such, the generalist practitioner does not have an overinvestment in the outcome of the legal process.

As part of the educational effort, you need to refresh your own memory regarding the details of the case. Learn as much as possible about the policies and state statutes governing such cases. Review your own professional credentials and be able to articulate them clearly. Finally, meet with the attorneys involved to learn of any information that can increase your credibility and comfort on the witness stand. Additionally, defendants need to be advised regarding the importance of their appearance and demeanor in court. It is arguable that the more serious the charge, the more important it is that defendants be aware of how they present themselves.

In your documentation, avoid value-laden terms such as "egocentric," "callous," or "obnoxious." More neutral terms, plus one or two behaviorally specific descriptions, enhance the record's and the worker's credibility. A parent might be described as "inattentive" if his toddler were sitting nearby sticking a paper clip into an electrical outlet. It should be emphasized that any observation needs the support of such specific examples.

Positive as well as negative observations should be included in the record. Such impartiality in the record establishes that the worker is objective and has good observational skills. Last, subjective professional impressions should be clearly separated from behavioral observations and facts. Impressions should be clearly labeled as such. For example, you might state, "It is my impression that…," "My impression is …," or "My opinion is.…" If you can provide documentation of a statement made by a client or another person, you might indicate that in the record as well.

Following these suggestions will likely improve the credibility of your testimony should you be called into court. It is not unusual for practitioners to be summoned into court years after terminating with a client and closing the case record. Specific and detailed case notes may be your only link with the information necessary for a credible performance (Barsky & Gould, 2002).

Review of Other Documents

After reviewing the record, the social worker may want to review several additional documents. These include the agency policy and procedures manual, relevant state statutes for key definitions or outlines of procedures, and pertinent case law (if applicable).

An *agency policy manual* may document that the social worker was following recognized procedures in the investigation of the elder abuse case before the court. Or, while testifying in court, the professional may be asked to provide definitions of client populations from an agency manual. As a professional practitioner, you will appear much more knowledgeable if you can either recite from memory or readily find in the manual the section under discussion.

Appropriate state statutes can help substantiate the choice of out-of-home, independent, supervised apartment living as "the least restrictive" alternative in an adult protective placement hearing. In such cases, the worker has to demonstrate in court that some limitation on an older adult client's mobility, housing, or finances necessitated intervention for her safety. As a worker on the witness stand in this instance, you might

be asked to define "least restrictive" and describe how your choice of supervised housing fits the criteria of the definition. Credibility on the witness stand will be greatly enhanced if you can cite definitions, procedures, or exceptions from the governing statutes.

Perhaps a recent legal decision confirms the appropriateness of an intervention chosen by a worker in a particular case. Application of law in one state may have implications for care nationwide. Standards of care may be cited as an ethical obligation, substantiated by another state's laws. The well-informed social worker can strengthen his or her testimony by knowing and citing other states' standards or precedents. In other words, it pays to be as well informed as possible about the context of the case before the court. Relating the details of any specific case to the context of agency procedures, current professional literature, or recent case law can only strengthen anyone's testimony, including yours.

Establishment of Expert Witness Status

Once on the witness stand, you may be asked several questions relevant to your professional and personal history. An attorney might raise such questions in order to build a case for expert witness status or to increase the credibility of your future testimony. If you anticipate being called to the stand, it is a good idea to refresh your memory regarding your educational background, previous professional experience, continuing education, published works, professional memberships, and the number of similar cases you have handled in the agency.

Review of Testimony with Attorney

Prior to the court date, you should meet with the attorney regarding your role in the court presentation (CSWE, 2008, EP 2.1.10a). The attorney may have developed a theme or orientation to the case that necessitates specific information from you to complete the argument. For example, your testimony regarding a series of abuse reports over several years in a family with several children would strengthen the prosecuting attorney's theme of chronically poor and risky parenting skills.

EP 2.1.10a

One of the specific areas where you should focus your attention is on the petition to be presented to the court. A *petition* is essentially a complaint that specifies the reasons for a case being brought to court and usually identifies a remedy sought by the petitioner

(Saltzman & Furman, 1999). The petition is a legal document generally prepared by the district or state attorney. For example, a petition in a child welfare case might describe the instances of abuse suffered by a child, detail information provided by witnesses and others, and cite the specific laws that are applicable. Finally, it might recommend that custody of the children be removed from the parent because she could not protect them from harm (such as the abuser). Because the petition represents a detailing of the basis for the action sought by the petitioner, it is critical that it be factually correct. It is also important that the social worker know what the petition alleges and the direction the prosecutor intends to take the case. Figures 13.2 through 13.5 later in this chapter show the stages in a typical petition. Highlight 13.4 depicts an actual court petition.

You may want to discuss the strengths and weaknesses that you see in the case as it would be presented in court. Additionally, you and the attorney may want to develop strategies for its presentation. You might want to suggest a specific line of questioning to document certain background information. You should also share with the attorney any documents or information he or she is unaware of. It is also appropriate to discuss the opposing counsel and the judge in terms of known personal preferences, prejudices, or prior decisions. Some judges and attorneys develop reputations for specific questions, attitudes, or behavior in the courtroom. You may have to press the lawyer for such a pretrial meeting. However, it is usually well worth the effort. Such prior planning can enhance your professional credibility and provide for a much more coordinated effort.

Preparation of Witnesses

It is very important for any future witnesses to address their own verbal and nonverbal presentations of themselves. Remember the formality of court versus the informality of the social work agency! As a future witness, you may decide to consult the attorney on a wide range of issues including appropriate dress, eye contact, and the language you should use.

In preparation for a court appearance, you may also want to discuss these same issues with your client. In particular, you may need to educate clients about the importance of nonverbal communication during testimony. The witness stand is not an appropriate place for chewing gum or wearing sunglasses. It is well documented that nonverbal behavior can be very persuasive, either positively or negatively. All parties involved

in the courtroom drama need to be aware of self-presentation as credible presenters of fact or opinion.

Phases in the Adjudication Process

Major phases in the adjudication process involve direct examination of witnesses and subsequent cross-examination. Redirect and re-cross-examinations are also possible. The following section will discuss specific techniques for effectively responding to questions in both major phases. Approaches and tactics frequently employed by opposing counsel during cross-examination will be explored as well.

Direct Examination of Witnesses

The purpose of direct testimony is to communicate as persuasively as possible the facts pertinent to a case. The plaintiff's attorney or the district attorney's staff uses direct examination to get to the facts of the case. At this point, the attorney questioning the plaintiff is likely to be on the plaintiff's side in the adversarial process. Thus, questions will most likely be relatively benign and straightforward.

The social worker as a witness is allowed to use notes during testimony. Using notes is especially recommended when there is a large amount of specific data relevant to the case. Likewise, notes are useful when a social worker suspects that anxiety may hamper recall.

Memorizing data is not recommended because it sounds robotic and less persuasive. Additionally, the witness may block on memorized information and appear evasive or unnecessarily rattled. If there is a possibility that you will be called upon to consult the case file, it is advisable to review the file prior to testifying. In this way, you can more easily locate relevant information. It can be disconcerting to have a roomful of people waiting quietly while one is shuffling through a large volume of papers looking for one specific fact.

Testimony is recorded by a court reporter, who transcribes the comments of all parties as they occur. It is thus important that all questions be answered clearly in words. Nonverbal behaviors such as hand or head gestures are inappropriate. Word choice and usage should reflect awareness of the audience, including the judge, jury, attorneys, and observers. The finder of fact, especially a jury, may be unfamiliar with professional jargon. If, for example, you describe a child to a jury as "acting out," you must be prepared to elaborate upon the behaviors and attitudes reflective of the

HIGHLIGHT 13.4

A Court Petition

Following is an actual court petition to remove a child from her mother's home. Details of names, locations, and dates have been changed.

State of   Case No: _____
Circuit Court Branch   Merriweather County
Children's Division

PETITION FOR DETERMINATION OF
STATUS-PROTECTION/SERVICES

IN THE INTEREST OF: Samantha Doe   DOB: 5/28/09
                     4857 Seaside   Sex: F
                     Vintage City, ST 12345

Father:

Mother: Jane Doe, same

Guardian, Legal Custodian: Mother

Is the child in temporary physical custody? No   Date/Time of Custody:

Where:

TO THE CIRCUIT COURT, CHILDREN'S DIVISION: Lois Lane, your petitioner, states on information and belief that the above-named child is in need of protection or services in that pursuant to State Statutes 48.13(10) her parents are unable to provide the necessary care including adequate supervision and medical care so as to seriously endanger the physical health of Samantha Doe, d.o.b. 5/28/09.

Samantha Doe was admitted to Morning Glory Hospital on February 8, 2010, with a large contusion over the left side of the face and ear with bruising and petechiae. The left tympanic membrane was significant for blood. The right tympanic membrane was clear. The left eye was red and bruised. The child sustained a basilar skull fracture. Jane Doe, mother of the minor child, said her boyfriend Brutus Brown, d.o.b. 5/19/83, was home during the day babysitting the child, and in an oral statement to Deputy Sheriffs, he stated that he took the child's mother to work at Major Industries at approximately 7:40 A.M. on the morning of February 8, 2010. Brutus Brown indicated that he left Geraldine and Frieda, older sisters of Samantha, at home with her while he took the children's mother to work. The older girls are 11 and 8 years old, respectively. Brutus Brown

states that he arrived back home at around 8 A.M. and got the two older girls off to school on the bus at 8:20 A.M. "Brutus Brown stated two different things during the interview, 'She jumped up when he checked on her. The other, she rolled over.'" Brutus Brown stated he went into the kitchen with Samantha, got her a bottle, and asked her if she was tired. She stated yes so he put her back down in the crib. Samantha is 20 months old and is small for her age, according to Lane. Brutus Brown stated he could tell that she was still tired. Brutus Brown said he was going to go back and lie down but went into the kitchen and poured a bowl of cereal. Brutus Brown stated he then heard her crib side slide down and heard a thud. Brutus Brown stated she started crying. Brutus Brown stated when he entered the room that Samantha was lying on a small child's chair that was near the corner of the crib. Brutus Brown picked up Samantha and she stopped crying. Brutus Brown stated that he then kicked the chair because he "was pissed." Deputy Fife asked why he was pissed. Brutus Brown hesitated and told Deputy Fife that he was pissed because the other kid had left the chair there and if it had not been there then this would have not happened. There are two girls that sleep in this bedroom. Brutus Brown then put cold packs on the injury. Brutus Brown told Deputy Fife that her face was black and blue around 0900 hours and he thought he should take her to the doctor. Brutus Brown stated that he was injured at work and had a hospital flier on what to watch for in head injuries. Brutus Brown stated she was not bleeding or vomiting and he checked her pupils. Brutus Brown stated that if she was bleeding he would have taken her to the doctor. Brutus Brown did not leave the house. Around 3:30 P.M. he was shaving and gave Samantha a bath and noticed that her face was "black turned purple with little purple dots." [A copy of Brutus Brown's written statement would be attached to this petition as "Exhibit A."]

The child was subsequently admitted to Morning Glory Hospital on February 8, 2010, with Hypothermia (body temperature of 88.8 degrees F); and a transverse fracture of both the tibia and fibula of the left leg with a mild apex lateral angulation without displacement; a 5 centimeter by 3 centimeter yellowish bruise on her lower back; a bruise on her ear; and a scrape on her upper lip. Jane Doe told investigators she believed the injury to her daughter occurred on Monday 2/7/10. She stated she worked in the morning until 1500 hours and arrived home at approximately 1507 hours. Between 1507 hours and 1530 hours Jane Doe was at the residence with her daughter Samantha and boyfriend Brutus Brown. They were in the kitchen area and noticed Samantha was having problems walking and running around. She was wearing some slick footed pajamas and on two or three occasions slipped and fell on the linoleum floor of the kitchen. Jane Doe said at least two, possibly three falls occurred. During these falls, Samantha would pick herself up and run around with no apparent trouble. Jane Doe explained that Brutus Brown told her he put Samantha down for a nap about 1300 hours and she awoke shortly before Jane's arrival home. Jane Doe continued to state that approximately a half-hour after falling in the kitchen Samantha suddenly had problems walking and difficulty standing on one leg. Jane Doe thought Samantha had twisted her ankle. There were no signs of bruising or swelling until about a half-hour later when slight swelling was noted. At that time, because Jane Doe believed Samantha had twisted her leg, she took a cool pop container, wrapped it around Samantha's leg, and used it in an attempt to make the swelling go down. During that time Samantha never cried and showed no indications of pain. After icing the leg for approximately one hour Brutus Brown told Jane Doe he noticed the leg was becoming tender. Samantha could not walk on the leg and was eventually

put to bed. On the following morning, Tuesday, Jane Doe stated she again worked in the morning. Her observation of Samantha showed the leg appeared fine except she could not walk on it. Jane Doe described how Samantha would point to her injured foot and how she could not put weight on it. When asked where her "owie" was, Samantha would point to both her right and left legs. Jane Doe stated she got home from work shortly after 1430 hours. At that time Brutus Brown had just finished giving Samantha a bath and had put her to bed. After about ten minutes Jane Doe noticed that Samantha was crying. When she checked on Samantha, she noticed her legs were blue and she appeared ice cold. They then wrapped her in a blanket. They noticed both legs were purple and red and she was extremely cold to the touch. An ice pack, which had been placed on her, was taken off and blankets wrapped around Samantha in an attempt to warm her. Jane Doe and Brutus Brown then took Samantha and the other daughters from the Robindale schools to the Group Health Cooperative Clinic in Vintage. Upon arrival at the clinic Samantha was suspected of having a broken leg and was suffering from extreme hypothermia. Her body temperature was found to be 88 degrees. She was cyanotic and was immediately given oxygen and intravenous fluids. An attempt was made to warm Samantha and she was transported by ambulance to Morning Glory Hospital. Jane Doe was asked about the specifics of the time of the injury occurring on Monday. Jane Doe explained how Samantha was running and trotting back and forth between the living room and kitchen and how she fell in the middle of the kitchen and did not hit anything. On one occasion Jane Doe stated Samantha fell harder than normal. However, she got back up without crying or whimpering.

Brutus Brown stated to Det. Sgt. Steven Dziwig that on Monday, February 7, 2010, he was babysitting for Samantha at the couple's home at 4857 Seaside, Vintage City. Jane Doe went to work around 0700 hours and he was left alone babysitting for Samantha after the other kids went to school. Jane Doe was supposed to work until approximately 1430 to 1500 hours. During the day, Brutus Brown stated he was home alone with Samantha and never left the house. He was working on fish tanks all day long. During the bulk of the time, Samantha was playing in the living room with a school play set she has. At about 1530 hours, shortly after Jane Doe returned home from work, Brutus Brown described several incidents of Samantha slipping and falling on the floor. Brutus Brown blamed the incidents on the slippery pajama bottoms Samantha was wearing, along

(continued)

HIGHLIGHT 13.4 *(continued)*

with the linoleum floor. Brutus Brown believes Samantha fell three times on the floor. Most of those occurred in a situation where Samantha was half running across the floor, slipped, and fell. Brutus Brown did not see the actual falls although he was in the area. He stated Samantha never cried and both Jane and he were present to witness Samantha getting right back up and going again. Brutus Brown described the incidents of her falling as just having her feet come out from underneath her and falling down with her body hitting the floor. Brutus Brown noted Samantha has probably fallen like that on a hundred occasions, and he believes it was slight enough where she would not have gotten injured. Brutus Brown stated he never saw any bruises after the initial fall although he was concerned enough to inspect her. Brutus Brown put Samantha in her crib for a nap shortly afterward and gave her a bottle. She slept for a half-hour to 45 minutes. When Samantha awoke and was brought into the living room, it was noted she appeared to have difficulty standing on her leg. This was noted when Jane Doe asked Samantha to come to her. Brutus Brown said he then looked at the leg and saw no bruises. He thought the leg may have possibly fallen asleep so he rubbed it in an attempt to make the circulation come back. About a half-hour later Brutus Brown said he rechecked Samantha's leg. Again he noted she was having difficulty walking and determined maybe she had twisted an ankle. There was no indication of pain or crying but the ankle did feel swollen. No bruise was present. Brutus Brown decided to put ice on the leg in an attempt to reduce the swelling. He took an ice gel from the refrigerator and wrapped it around her leg. At that time, Brutus Brown stated he considered taking Samantha to the doctor but did not. Brutus Brown said he did not realize the extent of Samantha's injuries. He thought the ankle was only twisted and was nervous about taking her to see a physician because of previous child abuse allegations. Brutus Brown explained at that point that he was resentful toward the doctors for the previous treatment of Samantha. He stated he did not like the way the doctors had interviewed him and talked down to both himself and Jane. He explained how he would check on Samantha nightly and was more responsible for checking on her than her mother was. Brutus Brown noted how Samantha goes with him everywhere and how easily she stays with him. It was noted at that time that Brutus Brown was holding Samantha. She was sleeping and appeared very comfortable with him. Brutus Brown continued stating he placed the ice pack on Samantha's leg, decided to leave the injury alone, and put her to bed. The next day when Jane Doe left for work, she placed Samantha in the bed with Brutus Brown. After getting the kids off to school, Brutus Brown and Samantha remained and watched cartoons. During the day Samantha continued to have problems walking and standing on the leg. Brutus Brown tried to make her crawl on the leg rather than walking on it. He did note on several occasions she managed to stand with little difficulty but had some problems walking. Shortly after lunch, approximately 1130 hours, Brutus Brown gave Samantha a bath. He described the bath as a lukewarm bath in the bathtub of the family bathroom. He stated it had four to five inches of water in the tub and it was lukewarm to the touch. He stated Samantha spent quite a while (half hour to 40 minutes) in the bathtub, and upon taking her out and getting her dressed, he noticed her clothes were dirty. Brutus Brown remembered he was to take the clothes which had been washed and put them in the dryer, which he had forgotten. Instead Brutus Brown dressed Samantha in a diaper. He wrapped the ice pack around the lower portion of her leg and put a sock over it. Brutus Brown then wrapped Samantha in a blanket or two to keep her warm and placed her in her bed. She remained in bed until approximately 1430 to 1435 when Jane Doe returned home. Approximately 10 to 15 minutes after Jane returned home, Samantha was crying in a very distressed fashion. Brutus Brown stated he ran in and picked her up. At that time her legs were blue and she seemed incoherent and sluggish. She was also very cold. At that time the ice pack was taken off Samantha, she was wrapped in a blanket and placed in the family car. Brutus Brown, Jane Doe, and Samantha then stopped at the two schools, picked up the other daughters, and went to the clinic where Samantha received emergency treatment.

Regarding the broken leg, Dr. Herman P. Smith stated it could not have occurred from a fall in the way described. Dr. Smith says he is unable to determine exactly how the injury occurred. Both bones in the leg were broken. Dr. Smith said it could have occurred from a snapping-type injury or being stepped on or kicked. Dr. Smith considers this type and severity of injuries abuse. Dr. Smith then discussed the low body temperature Samantha had when she was brought in. Dr. Smith stated it was 88 degrees and that was so low hypothermia had occurred and Samantha had actually stopped shivering. He explained how she immediately needed oxygen because of the problem and the situation was life threatening. Dr. Smith considers this situation extreme neglect. He told investigators this low body temperature could not have occurred in the manner, way, or time factor Jane Doe and Brutus Brown described it as occurring. Dr. Smith stated he believed the child could have been given an ice-cold bath by Brutus Brown and no other scenario makes sense. Dr. Smith also completely discounted the theory as to how the injury occurred on Samantha's back. He explained the human body was not so fragile that bruising could occur under those circumstances. He stated the injury could not have occurred that way and expected some other means was responsible. Regarding the injury to the ear, he again stated that could have occurred during a fall or as a result of being struck. Dr. Smith believes that also strengthens the child abuse theory. Other bruises and scratches and scrapes, especially those to the face area, could have been explainable according to Dr. Smith. Dr. Smith was very adamant in this case about the fact child abuse and neglect had occurred.

The mother has failed to provide adequate supervision and care for her daughter, resulting in injuries and the lowering of the child's body temperature, placing the child in serious physical danger.

Count 2—The child is further in danger under Section 48.13(10) in that the mother is unable, for reasons other than poverty, to provide necessary care and supervision and that the mother and her boyfriend, Brutus Brown, reside together at 4857 Seaside, Vintage City, along with Samantha and her two older sisters. Brutus Brown has been charged with the delivery of cocaine from the residence where the children reside and did reside at the time of the sale. [A copy of the criminal complaint would be attached as Exhibit "B."]

The mother states that the drug paraphernalia and other drugs that were kept in the bedroom shared by her and Brutus Brown were not hers but Brutus Brown's. Exhibits "C" and "D" are the materials that were removed during a voluntary consent to search the premises executed by the East Central Drug Enforcement Group in February of 2010.

The mother, Jane Doe, has not been charged or arrested with the incident.

However, the physical safety of the children are at risk due to the nature of the illegal drug sales and the children being present when law enforcement officers arrested Brutus Brown. Because of information given by Brutus Brown to East Central Drug Enforcement Officers regarding at least one other participant in the drug sale, those around him as well as Brown may be at risk for retaliation. Based on all the aforementioned facts, the mother is not able to provide a safe, appropriate living situation for the children and in fact the children are in danger where they presently reside with Brutus Brown.

Signature of Prosecutor	Signature of Petitioner
Carl Z. Batterman	Lois Lane
Name of Prosecutor (typed) State Bar No. 1004726	Name of Petitioner (typed)
March 11, 2010	March 11, 2010
Date	Date

---

term in lay language (that is, language that can be clearly understood by nonprofessionals).

When asked a question while on the stand, the witness should answer the question and only the question. Try to stay away from the hypothetical and the passive voice. In other words, try to talk directly about the person or situation being discussed and avoid conjecturing about possible causation or explanation. Furthermore, language is more lively and forceful if the *active voice* is used ("John *pointed* the gun at Tim," not "The gun *was pointed* at Tim by John").

If counsel asks, "Do you have an opinion on whether Mr. Smith can manage his own money?", simply reply "Yes" or "No." Do not elaborate on your opinion of Mr. Smith's financial management abilities. Instead, wait for the next question. The attorney might then ask, "What is your opinion of Mr. Smith's ability to manage his own money?" Subsequently, limit your answer to address only Mr. Smith's ability to manage finances. Do not elaborate on any other topics such as his work performance or personal relationships.

© Heide Benser/Corbis

The formal atmosphere in a courtroom may intimidate clients and even new social workers.

If necessary, ask to have a question repeated or reworded. If the question is still not understandable, it is appropriate to say so. Credibility is not seriously hurt if you simply do not know the answer to one or even several questions. If the answer is an estimate, indicate this. Do not allow an attorney to force you to give a more exact, but possibly inaccurate, figure.

Witnesses may refresh their memories, too, by consulting exhibits or personal notes. *Exhibits* are tangible articles, such as weapons or copies of documents, that have been collected, identified, and made available to the court for a particular case. While still on the witness stand, you may correct information in previously given testimony. However, it is more advisable to limit such clarifications and to speak accurately the first time.

Remember that you can say, "I don't know." All courts recognize that there are limits to a professional's knowledge or experience.

At times a question may be quite complicated. Then it is entirely appropriate to pause and think about a response before proceeding. Obviously, the practitioner does not want to appear to be manufacturing an answer on the spot. However, such pauses allow time

for contemplation and increase the social worker's control of how questions are *paced*. It is recommended that the witness maintain control of the question-and-answer process. Otherwise, the attorney can rush and possibly confuse the respondent.

We have already stressed the importance of a pretrial conference with one's attorney. At that time, it may be wise to establish some nonverbal sign language; in this way, the attorney will know when you wish to follow up on previous testimony, consult data not immediately available, or even take a break.

Witnesses are totally responsible for their own answers while on the stand. Witnesses must answer all questions directed at them to which the opposing counsel does not object. Always address answers to the finder of fact, usually the jury or the judge. There is no need to establish eye contact with opposing counsel or the defendant, especially if that is uncomfortable. Most often, the witness should stop instantly, in mid-sentence, if the judge interrupts or the opposing counsel objects. At other times, it might be advisable to finish a sentence if one's attorney has decided that sharing such information is pivotal to the case.

Direct examination offers the opportunity for the district attorney or the plaintiff's attorney to present evidence supporting a decision of "guilty." The evidence is accumulated incrementally with testimony, depositions, and exhibits. All of this substantiates the presentation of fact as the plaintiff knows it. Your testimony as a social worker—for the prosecution or for the defense—is one piece of a jigsaw puzzle. There will be opportunities for you to provide information in the case-building process. Typically, you are given enough time to answer every question. Each question will usually build upon one of its predecessors. Highlight 13.5 provides examples of questions that might be asked during direct examination for the case described in Highlight 13.4.

HIGHLIGHT 13.5

Questions for Direct Examination

Questions for direct examination on the case presented in Highlight 13.4 would typically include:

1. What is your name?
2. By whom are you employed?
3. What position do you hold? How long have you been in this position?
4. What are the current job duties of that position?
5. What is your post–high school education?
6. What degrees do you hold?
7. What professional licenses or certifications do you hold?
8. Are you a member of any national or state organizations in your field of work? If so, what are they and how long have you been a member?
9. How many years of experience do you have as a social worker?
10. Are you responsible for investigating child abuse?
11. Does your agency have a written manual or a written set of procedures on how to conduct a child abuse investigation?
12. Did you comply with those procedures? If not, why not?
13. When were you assigned this case?
14. What was the first thing you did when you were assigned this case?
15. What law enforcement officers worked with you on this case?
16. Did those law enforcement officers generate a written report? If so, do you have a copy?
17. Did you generate a written report? If so, do you have a copy?
18. Did you take any written notes or tape-record any interviews in this case? If so, do you have them with you? If you do not have them with you, why not?
19. Is the *complete* file that the agency has on this incident with you? If not where are the rest of the materials?
20. After you received the child abuse referral from your supervisor, how did you proceed?
21. Did you interview the mother? What did she say about the incident in question? Who else was present during that interview? Where did the interview take place? When? What did you say to the mother before the interview? How did you explain your presence there?
22. Did you interview the boyfriend? What did he say about the incident in question? Who else was present during that interview? Where did the interview take place? When? What did you say to the boyfriend before the interview? How did you explain your presence there?
23. Did you interview the child, the subject of the report? What did the child say about the incident in question? Who else was present during that interview? Where did the interview take place? When? What did you say to the child before the interview? How did you explain your presence there?
24. Did you interview any of the child's siblings? What did they say about the incident in question? Who else was present during that interview? Where did the interview take place? When? What did you say to them before the interview? How did you explain your presence there?
25. Were there any other witnesses to the incident? Were they interviewed? If not, why not?
26. Did you interview Dr. Smith? What did the doctor say about the incident in question? Who else was present during that interview? Where did the interview take place? When? What did you say to the doctor before the interview? How did you explain your presence there? What information did Dr. Smith have that you provided him prior to your interview? What was Dr. Smith's conclusion? What treatment was prescribed for the child, including medications?
27. Do you recommend that the child be temporarily removed from her home? Why? If so, for how long?

Cross-Examination of Witnesses

Cross-examination is the step in the courtroom process that is most likely to show the adversarial nature of the proceedings. The goal of cross-examination is to decrease the likelihood that the finder of fact will believe the information provided during direct examination. The goal of cross-examination is not usually to seek objective information. In other words, cross-examination is that portion of the courtroom drama wherein the witnesses' personal and/or professional credibility is most often challenged.

Defense attorneys are expected to advocate for their clients' positions. To do so, they need to weaken testimony that is harmful to their clients. The idea is that this process serves truth and increases the likelihood of a just outcome. First, the plaintiff and counsel attempt to build a strong case for themselves. Then, the defense follows with a more critical, or even hostile, cross-examination of the same person.

Often, this process feels foreign to social workers on the witness stand. It is easy to take the probing questions of the opposing attorney personally. In reality, these questions have nothing to do with an attack on you personally. They are simply a means for opposing lawyers to strengthen their respective cases.

Attorneys conducting cross-examinations adhere to several general principles. First, a cardinal rule of opposing counsel is never to ask questions to which they do not already know the answer. Cross-examination is not the time to accidentally discover new information pertinent to the case. Thus, often, cross-examination is designed to trick the witness into saying what the attorney wants to hear. Examples of such leading questions include

"Does it not seem likely that…?"
"Wouldn't you agree that…?"
"Is it not the case that…?"

Many of these questions are phrased in the negative or worded so that agreement with them provides answers opposite to those that the witness intended to give. One could be asked, "Does Mr. Smith still beat his wife?" Any direct answer indicates agreement with the fact that Mr. Smith does, or once did, indeed physically assault her. Opposing counsels listen very closely to the respondent's answers. They look for any additional information that the social worker might accidentally volunteer that could provide a lead for further questioning or raise a doubt about the testimony given thus far.

Another tactic employed by cross-examining attorneys is to prohibit witnesses from repeating their direct testimony. The more frequently finders of fact hear the same testimony, the more likely they are to believe it. Questions asked during cross-examination are often limiting. The opposing counsel may not want to permit a witness to explain or elaborate.

A final ploy used by opposing attorneys is "saving" their ultimate point for the closing question. This deprives witnesses of opportunities to soften the impact of their responses. Remember the disposition hearing described at the beginning of the chapter? A social worker was asked whether a man found guilty of sexual assault would ever sexually assault again if the opportunity arose. By asking the worker, "Can you promise me, Ms. Clark, that the defendant will never have sexual contact with minors again?" the attorney attempts to limit Ms. Clark's response. The obvious reply is, "No, I cannot promise that." The opposing counsel would then close the questioning. This would prevent Ms. Clark from elaborating. A more effective response might be, "I cannot speak in terms of promises. That is outside the boundaries of certainty recognized by anyone in the mental health field." Another strategy for a witness might be to say, "I can't answer that with a simple yes or no." Highlight 13.6 elaborates further on cross-examination.

Strategies in Cross-Examination

There are four strategies of attack in the cross-examination of a witness, all involving confrontation: confrontation of direct testimony, of the credentials of the witness, of the person him- or herself, and of the profession represented (McGoverns & Peters, 1985). Attacking a profession indicates more desperation on the part of the opposing counsel than attacking any of the other three.

Attacking Direct Examination Testimony

Common attacks of direct testimony focus on several issues. First, opposing counsel will address any discrepancies between records and testimony. Second, any discrepancies between direct and cross-examination on the part of any witness will be further examined. Any such differences will likely be addressed if the result looks advantageous to the opposing counsel.

Counsel may attempt to show that the social worker disliked the plaintiff and is therefore biased. This ploy can succeed if indeed the worker made a comment to

HIGHLIGHT 13.6

Cross-Examination

Cross-examination would focus on any real or "perceived" weaknesses in the direct examination. Depending on the answers supplied, such questions might include

1. How many cases of this nature have you investigated? Testified about?
2. Have you attended any special courses, training, or seminars in child protective services?

Notice that the above cross-examination questions focus on qualifications of the investigating social worker. If this were the only focus of the attorney, the social worker's direct testimony about this particular case would be judged unassailable. The student should review the written record and ascertain potentially vulnerable points of information. Consider, for example, that in the case of Samantha Doe in Highlight 13.4, a possible vulnerable point is the lack of follow-up by the worker from the first reported incident until the second emergency room admission.

Another potential area of inquiry on cross-examination would be the relationship between Brutus Brown's arrest record and the abusive incidents; Brown's criminal case occurred first. The social worker could be asked why she did not intervene sooner because one of the reasons given for the child's removal is Brown's arrest record. Another area of inquiry might be whether the social worker made her role in investigating the case and any possible court action clear to the mother and Brown during the interview and then *documented* such information for the record. The cross-examining attorney may ask a series of relatively straightforward questions laying a foundation to bring out how *soon* after the investigation the social worker recorded the information. The social worker should anticipate the direction of cross-examination if at all possible. For example, in this case, the social worker needs to anticipate her actions or lack thereof between the two incidents one month apart, as this will be questioned.

that effect and was overheard. However, this can be deflected by indicating that personal reactions were not a part of the professional exchange between the social worker and the defendant.

Counsel may attempt to show that the social worker is inexperienced or that real assistance was not offered as mandated by the law. Questions may address whether the social worker made out-of-court statements inconsistent with statements made in court.

Last, the worker's accuracy of observation or even memory might be questioned. Opposing counsel may also solicit contradictory evidence not heretofore in the record.

Questions that weaken or impeach previous statements made during direct examination provide the opposing counsel's strongest opportunity to help the finder of fact doubt the witness's testimony. Thus, it behooves all witnesses to review direct examination statements and be prepared for questions on any obviously unclear or ambivalent statements.

Attacking Credentials

Attacking credentials includes posing questions regarding a worker's professional qualifications. This might involve the worker's formal education, continuing education, training, or virtually any other element that could help counsel build a case. There could be questions regarding specific coursework, membership in professional organizations, and other credentials.

New social workers are often self-conscious about their perceived lack of experience. However, it is generally accepted that members of any profession were novices at some point in their careers. Simple acknowledgment of length of employment or type of professional experience is appropriate. Such straightforward truthfulness is usually not to your disadvantage. You need not be defensive. As a professional, you may be quizzed about previous testimony. This would include whether you had ever been paid to testify or whether you had testified for either side in similar cases.

If you have been established as an expert witness, you should be prepared to answer all questions involving your areas of expertise. Otherwise, your credibility will be seriously eroded before the court.

Attacking You as a Person

Resorting to personal attacks indicates that the examiner thinks neither your testimony nor your credentials is vulnerable. Questions involving personal attacks include:

"Do you believe in corporal punishment?"
"Wouldn't you personally like to see Mr. Davis get custody of the children?"
"How clean do you keep your house?"
"How many children do you have?"

The intent of these questions is to demonstrate that the professional's personal beliefs or experiences bias his or her work with the client involved in the court case. Such ploys are common among those familiar with courtroom proceedings. If an attorney asks you such questions while you are on the witness stand, you must decide either to answer or to dispute their relevance to the current situation. Again, a non-defensive stance is recommended.

Attacking the Profession

Attacks on the witness's profession reflect last-resort efforts to discredit damaging testimony. Questions might include:

"Is social work a licensed profession?"
"Can just anyone be a social worker?"
"How many continuing education credits are mandated yearly for social workers?"

The intent of such questions is to eat away at the profession's value and credibility. You need not be defensive about the profession of social work. The courts recognize its body of knowledge and professional expertise.

Other Confrontational Tactics

Other tactics used by opposing counsel usually relate to three variables. The first concerns the type of question asked. Attorneys may demand "yes or no" answers. Or they may reverse word order to confuse the witness.

A second confrontational tactic involves the general pacing of questioning. Attorneys may fire questions at the witness in rapid succession, or a set of questions answered in the affirmative may be followed suddenly by a question that the worker, with forethought, would answer in the negative.

A third manipulative tactic involves the attitude opposing counsel projects during cross-examination. A condescending attitude may be used to make the witness appear inept. A friendly attitude may be an attempt to lull the witness into a false sense of security and well-being. In general, it is best for a witness to project a calm and competent exterior. Answer questions in a pleasant and firm voice. The display of any emotional reaction may feed into the attorney's game plan and/or reduce your air of professional objectivity.

Suggestions for Cross-Examination Testimony

Cross-examination can address any information covered earlier in the trial. Thus, all information is open for review and reversal during this portion of a trial. The social worker should prepare for possible questions in any area cited. As the questioning begins, the professional needs to focus carefully on the content of previous direct testimony. Many social workers with much courtroom experience also keep in mind weaknesses in previous testimony. In preparation, they try to formulate the strongest responses possible. To repeat, the witness should make every attempt to control the pacing of the questions. This can be done by using pauses, asking for clarification, or repeating the question silently to oneself before responding.

It is generally advisable not to answer ambiguous or unclear questions. Such ambiguity may be purposeful and might reflect an attempt to elicit additional information helpful to the opposition.

Use Listening Skills

Social workers have excellent training in listening skills. Cross-examination is an opportunity to practice listening with immediate and practical results. It is advisable to listen carefully and to answer completely and honestly. **EP 2.1.10b** Speculation, admitting errors, and admitting you cannot totally remember generally do not cause problems unless such answers are repeated frequently (CSWE, 2008, EP 2.1.10b).

Listen carefully to any objections from the attorney representing the side for which you are testifying. Such objections may provide clues about how to answer. If the objection is overruled, answer the question to the best of your ability. Have it repeated if necessary. During the process, be polite at all times.

If you are distracted by your own emotional response to the attorneys or to the questioning, the attorneys have taken control of the process. They are then more likely to successfully challenge your direct testimony. Be aware of personal styles or gimmicks used by attorneys to make a witness anxious or distracted.

After cross-examination, a witness may be called back or asked to remain on the stand for redirect examination or re-cross-examination. In such cases, you can assume that your testimony plays a pivotal role in the outcome of the case. Further clarification, damage control, and additional information are often discussed at this point. For example, the attorney may want the jury to hear again some specific detail of the witness's testimony in light of cross-examination. A social worker may also be recalled to clarify timing of interventions.

Stages in the Juvenile Court Process

Social workers in protective services interact with the legal system regularly. Not all such interactions, of course, end up in court. Vestiges of the more formal "family" model of interactions when children are deemed in need of protection remain in the system. The formal and informal steps concerning child welfare in these instances do vary by state. However, to help the student understand a general model of the steps involved in the investigation of a report of child abuse or neglect, an example of the four stages follows. Note, for example, in the *temporary custody stage* (Figure 13.2) how powerful the implications of the initial assessment of the social worker are; the social worker is authorized and has the power to take the child into custody and remove him from the home! Beginning with the *jurisdictional stage* (Figure 13.3), the social welfare and the legal systems interact more frequently. Figure 13.4 describes the steps in the *dispositional stage* of a juvenile court hearing. By the *post-dispositional stage* (Figure 13.5), a child has been placed out of the home, his status and record are reviewed every six months, and permanent plans are made to place the child for adoption or return him home. The responsibilities in the decision-making process have lifelong implications for the child, and the social worker must have documented and defended these actions several times.

Developing Issues in Social Work and the Law

EP 2.1.9a

As any entry-level social worker or agency supervisor knows, legislative and administrative guidelines have emerged as the basis of social work practice at an increasing rate (CSWE, 2008, EP 2.1.9a). Although this has been acknowledged for some time in child and adult protective services, it is becoming equally explicit in other areas of practice. For example, social workers in hospitals and nursing homes must have a working knowledge of patient rights, advance medical directives, and legal guidelines regarding the appointment of and interactions with guardians and protective payees. Group-home workers must know state codes regarding physical restraints, mental health commitments, and the referral process to another type of agency or facility. Increasingly, legal mandates and ethical applications together define and lead practice; unfortunately, the two may not be in full agreement with each other. The discrepancy may leave the professional with conflicting legal and client obligations.

Confidentiality and privacy of client information and the type of storage of documents relating to any given case are new and developing issues. As more and more social welfare offices utilize cell phones, laptop computers, e-mail, and network servers accessible to interdisciplinary teams, the inadvertent but potential

Juvenile court is one arena where a social worker's input and testimony may be required.

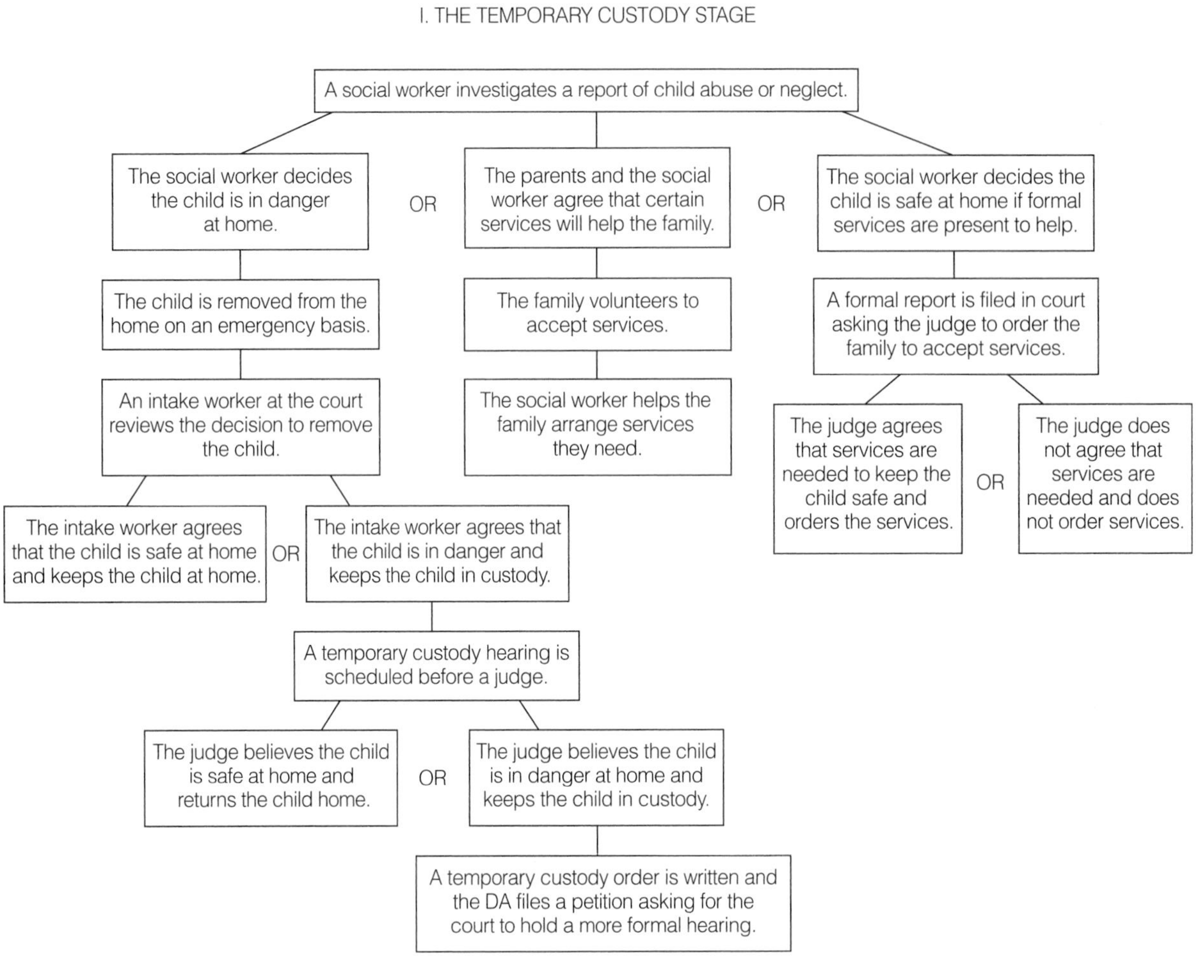

I. THE TEMPORARY CUSTODY STAGE

A social worker investigates a report of child abuse or neglect.

The social worker decides the child is in danger at home.

OR

The parents and the social worker agree that certain services will help the family.

OR

The social worker decides the child is safe at home if formal services are present to help.

The child is removed from the home on an emergency basis.

The family volunteers to accept services.

A formal report is filed in court asking the judge to order the family to accept services.

An intake worker at the court reviews the decision to remove the child.

The social worker helps the family arrange services they need.

The judge agrees that services are needed to keep the child safe and orders the services.

OR

The judge does not agree that services are needed and does not order services.

The intake worker agrees that the child is safe at home and keeps the child at home.

OR

The intake worker agrees that the child is in danger and keeps the child in custody.

A temporary custody hearing is scheduled before a judge.

The judge believes the child is safe at home and returns the child home.

OR

The judge believes the child is in danger at home and keeps the child in custody.

A temporary custody order is written and the DA files a petition asking for the court to hold a more formal hearing.

FIGURE 13.2 Temporary Custody Stage of the Juvenile Court Process

release of information with corresponding liability is exponential in its implications. For example, patient information located on computer pages accessible to multiple parties can sometimes allow unauthorized persons to change data on the record. A hard-copy record would be much more difficult to change, and yet, often, computer screens seem less "real" and thus inviolable to the user. Added problems are cross-disciplinary usage, terminology, "need-to-know" restrictions, and access to other professionals' case notes—all have tremendous implications for ethical mistreatment and the resultant liability (Dickson, 1998, pp. 124–131).

Traditionally, juvenile or family courts have had jurisdiction over several areas of child welfare, including delinquency, children in need of services or supervision, and neglect and abuse issues. In the area of delinquency, there has always been an attempt, not always successful, to balance the "nurturing" and the

"punishment" aspects of cases. In recent years, many states, in an attempt to deal with an increase in the seriousness of juvenile crimes, have lowered the age at which a juvenile is automatically transferred into adult court. This change in jurisdiction has had far-reaching implications for the youths involved and the correctional system generally. The trend appears to be continuing: More serious crimes committed by children of any age will enter a courtroom process much more similar to the adult "adversarial" model (Sickmund, 2003).

Forensic social work will continue to expand as society asks the courts to decide complicated moral and ethical issues. Social work has moved toward a mental health and humanistic perspective since the 1930s, but the swing now appears to be moving back toward more application of law with its resultant liability. More and more social workers will be actively

II. THE JURISDICTIONAL STAGE

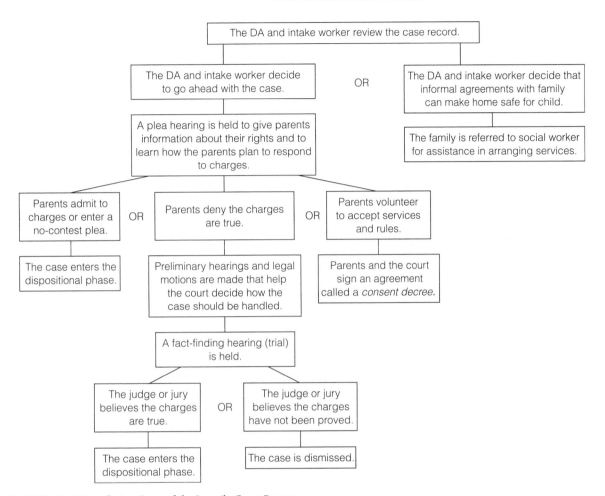

FIGURE 13.3 Jurisdiction Stage of the Juvenile Court Process

participating in forensic activities (Maschi, Bradley, & Ward, 2009). The malpractice implications for agencies and personnel are likewise increased. Corporation counsels will be consulted with more frequency, and legal issues will be included in more and more continuing education seminars and workshops.

In specific fields within the social work profession, more legislation will define illegal activity and the resultant change in job descriptions for social workers. For example, in child abuse and neglect cases, an emerging issue is "fetal abuse": drug use by the mother and the resultant damage to the fetus. Social workers in mental health may be subpoenaed in court to testify in such cases or even to actively supervise medical treatment for the pregnant woman abusing chemicals. The legal and ethical implications of such instances shake the traditional role of confidentiality and client self-determination.

There are also additional areas of forensic social work that continue to emerge. For example, social workers are also working alone and with others in doing life history research for capital cases. Capital cases are those in which the death penalty may be imposed on the person found guilty of a crime. Social workers may gather evidence about the client's past life experiences as well as about social and psychological aspects of the individual's life. Data to be gathered can include prior criminal acts, educational attainment, health and mental health issues, and economic status. This information may be used to help identify mitigating factors that could lead to a less severe sentence such as life imprisonment (Schroeder, Guin, Pogue, & Bordelon, 2006).

III. THE DISPOSITIONAL STAGE

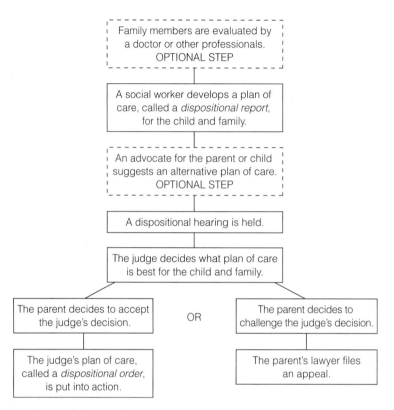

FIGURE 13.4 Dispositional Stage of the Juvenile Court Process

IV. THE POST-DISPOSITIONAL STAGE

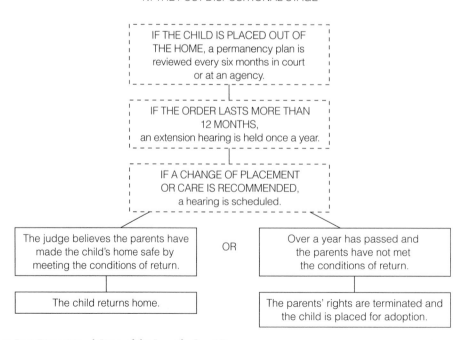

FIGURE 13.5 Post-Dispositional Stage of the Juvenile Court Process

The area of forensic social work may see social workers in such varied roles as helping the defense attorney in jury selection and educating counsel about the potential value of social work knowledge and skills in helping understand the client, jurors, witnesses, and other stakeholders in the legal process. It can also include intervening with defendants with respect to such things as "pretrial demeanor and trial behavior" (Schroeder et al., 2006, p. 359) and helping clients understand how both their verbal and nonverbal behavior can influence jurors.

One measure of the growth of forensic social work is the existence of a national organization (the National Organization of Forensic Social Work). Another is the number of books devoted to this area of practice. For readers wanting additional information, resources include, *Understanding Legal Concepts* (Alexander, 2003) and *Forensic Social Work* (Maschi et al., 2009).

Chapter Summary

The following summarizes this chapter's content as it relates to the learning objectives presented at the beginning of the chapter. Chapter content prepares social workers to:

A. *Utilize concepts related to courtroom processes.*

The social work arena is substantially different from the legal system that many social workers will encounter in their work. In particular, a variety of concepts unique to the justice system must be learned. These include such terms as law (both criminal and civil), violations, jurisdiction, allegation, court process, due process, and stipulation. Other important legal concepts are burden of proof, standards of proof, evidence (real, documentary, and hearsay), quality of evidence, witnesses, guardian *ad litem,* confidentiality and privileged communication, and subpoenas.

B. *Differentiate between social work practice and courtroom protocol.*

Some of the major differences between social work practice and courtroom protocol include the process itself, the atmosphere, and the outcome. The social work process is focused on problem solving, while the courtroom is more adversarial and ritualistic. The social work atmosphere tends to be more casual, with people on a first-name basis. Language is more focused on impressions and is less definitive than in the courtroom, where dress is formal, last names and titles are employed, and language is definitive and precise. The courtroom atmosphere is controlled by the judge and established protocols. The outcomes in courts and social work practice are also very different. Courts focus on a determination of charges and disposition, while social work practice is focused on rehabilitation, strengthening families, stopping abuse, and provision of services, including placement.

Similarities between courtrooms and social work practice include rights of the client or defendant and the rights and responsibilities of attorneys and social workers. Both are guided by historical precedent, legislative decisions, case law, and by a set of professional standards.

C. *Demonstrate professional demeanor in behavior, appearance, and communication in the courtroom.*

Courtroom demeanor requires social workers to dress professionally, prepare for their court testimony, provide documentation of all contacts between client and social worker, avoid value-laden language, and employ behaviorally specific terminology in both records and testimony. Social workers must be prepared to reference documents such as an agency policy manual, state statutes related to the case, and other factual and relevant information. Review your prospective testimony with the attorney ahead of time and familiarize yourself with the petition in cases involving juveniles. Meeting with one's client prior to the court data is also recommended.

D. *Practice within the phases of the adjudication process.*

The adjudication process in court involves several phases. These include direct examination and cross-examination of witnesses. Direct examination is designed to communicate the facts in a case and questions are posed to the witness by either the district attorney's staff or by a plaintiff's attorney. Notes may be used during direct examination and memorizing data is not recommended. Answer only the question you were asked and don't offer more information. If asked whether you have an opinion, state yes or no, but don't offer it unless asked. Saying "I don't know" is permitted. It is generally advised to stop speaking if either the judge speaks or an opposing attorney objects to a particular question.

Cross-examination is typically the locus of adversarial behavior in the courtroom. It is conducted to challenge the credibility (personal and/or professional) of the witness. Cross-examination employs confrontation of the direct testimony, credentials of the witness, personal credibility of the witness or the profession represented.

E. *Analyze and attend to various strategies used in cross-examination.*

Attorneys will attack discrepancies between records and testimony and between information given in direct testimony and that provided under cross-examination. As a social worker you must anticipate this type of challenging of your credibility and that of your profession. The social worker is in a position to control the pacing of questions by using pauses, asking for clarification, and avoiding answering unclear or ambiguous questions. Employing listening skills is important in cross-examination. Answer honestly and completely and maintain professional politeness at all times. Be alert to behaviors of the attorney designed to intimidate, distract, or cause anxiety in the witness.

F. *Apply concepts to a child welfare protective service case.*

Child protective service workers often are called upon to participate in the legal system. Some will end up in court and others will not, depending upon the nature of the case. Within the juvenile courts, some processes will differ from those in adult court. In the juvenile courts, the first stage is the temporary custody phase in which the social worker investigates a report of child maltreatment. The worker must decide whether the child is in danger at home and whether removal of the child is required. If the child is removed, a temporary custody hearing is scheduled and the judge makes a final decision. If the child is safe at home but the family requires and agrees to services, the case will go nor further at this time. Services will be provided to the family with the goal of keeping the child safe. If, on the other hand, the family is not receptive to accepting services, the social worker can formally ask the court to require the parents to accept services in order to keep the child safe. Again, the judge has the final word in the decision.

If a family challenges the worker's assessment and recommendations and wishes to refute the recommendation for temporary custody, the jurisdictional stage of juvenile court begins. Here the district attorney or intake worker reviews the case and makes a decision of whether to proceed further. If the decision is made to go ahead, a plea hearing will be held to inform parents of their rights and give them a chance to respond to the charges. Parents can still agree to accept services during the jurisdictional stage either voluntarily or by signing a consent decree with the court. If neither option is accepted, there will be a fact-finding hearing or trial, after which the judge or jury believes the charges are true or have not been proven. In the former situation, the dispositional phase begins. In the latter, the case is dismissed.

The dispositional stage involves an evaluation of family members (optional), or the social worker develops a plan of care (dispositional report). This report will go to the judge, who will hold a dispositional hearing and decide what plan of care is best for the child and family. Once the judge makes a decision, the parents can either accept the judge's finding or appeal the decision.

In cases where the child is placed out of the home (such as foster or group home care), a post-dispositional stage begins. This requires the worker to prepare a permanency plan that will be reviewed periodically within the agency or by the judge. After a year of such placement, the court will hold an annual extension hearing. Another hearing will be held at such time as the plan of care or placement changes. If the judge believes the child can return home, it is so ordered. If not, parental rights will be terminated and the child will be placed for adoption.

In each phase of the juvenile court proceedings, social workers must be familiar with the activities occurring and the decisions that can be reached. They must also be prepared to defend their recommendations regarding the child and family.

Competency Notes

The following identifies where Educational Policy (EP) competencies and practice behaviors are discussed in the chapter.

Educational Policy (EP) 2.1 Core Competencies

Educational Policy (EP) 2.1.1d Demonstrate professional demeanor in behavior, appearance, and communication. *(P. 489):* In a court setting the importance of good documentation and other communication skills becomes evident.

Educational Policy 2.1.1e Engage in career-long learning. *(P. 478):* One area where many generalist social workers felt they needed additional training or education was in preparing and giving courtroom testimony. Social workers must continually upgrade their knowledge and skills to reflect the needs of their clients and agencies.

Educational Policy (EP) 2.1.2b Make ethical decisions by applying standards of the NASW *Code of Ethics* and, as applicable, of the International Federation of Social Workers/International Association of Schools of Social Work Ethics in Social Work, Statement of Principles. *(P. 486):* In responding to a subpoena, the social worker should reference both state law and the profession's code of ethics regarding confidentiality.

Educational Policy (EP) 2.1.7a Utilize conceptual frameworks to guide the processes of assessment, intervention, and evaluation. *(P. 479):* Social workers must understand court-related concepts such as laws (criminal and civil), violations, jurisdiction, allegation,

court process, due process, stipulation, burden of proof, standards of proof, evidence (real, documentary, testimony), quality of evidence, witnesses, and guardian *ad litem*. Other useful concepts include confidentiality, privileged communication, and subpoenas.

Educational Policy (EP) 2.1.9a Continuously discover, appraise, and attend to changing locales, populations, scientific and technological developments, and emerging societal trends to provide relevant services. *(P. 501):* Social workers must be continually aware of changes in legislative and administrative guidelines and alert to new interpretations of legal and ethical principles.

Educational Policy (EP) 2.1.10a Substantively and affectively prepare for action with individuals, families, groups, organizations, and communities. *(P. 490):* It is important to prepare yourself before going to court. This may involve meeting with the attorney regarding your role and reviewing any applicable documents.

Educational Policy (EP) (2.1.10b) Use empathy and other interpersonal skills. *(P. 500):* It is important to use listening skills when in court, particularly when being cross-examined by opposing counsel.

On the Internet

Visit the *Generalist Practice with Organizations and Communities* Web site at www.cengage.com/social_work/ kirst-ashman for learning tools such as PowerPoint® slides, tutorial quizzing, Web links, and final exams.

CHAPTER 14

Developing and Managing Agency Resources

"But where will we get the money?" asked Heather Jones, a social worker in the regional office on aging. Heather and two of her social work friends, Tina Lax and Wolf Jackson, were discussing the plight of family members caring for Alzheimer's disease patients. Few of these family members had any time off from the stress of caring for loved ones suffering from this dreaded brain disorder that can leave its (primarily older adult) victims confused and with significant memory loss. Eventually it produces dementia, and victims may require help with such simple tasks as eating or going to the bathroom. Unable to remember who or where they are, and often unable to manage the simplest self-care tasks, Alzheimer's sufferers place a fantastic burden on the family members who take care of them. The three friends had been sorting out ideas and had hit upon a possible solution. "Look," said Tina, a social worker for a local agency serving Alzheimer's patients, "what we need is a place for caretakers to bring their family members for a few hours each week so they can get some time off from such onerous responsibility."

"Well, you know the senior centers in each county rarely have anybody there in the afternoon after lunch," said Wolf Jackson, a social work instructor at a local college. "What if we could use the centers to provide respite care for people with Alzheimer's or related disorders?" (Respite care is "the temporary assumption of responsibilities of a person who provides for the home care of another.") "The goal is to give the caretaker a break from the responsibilities so that tensions are minimized, the caretaker can have some other interests or take care of personal crises, and the client can stay out of institutional care" (Barker, 2003, p. 370). Wolf had learned about the unused centers while evaluating the effectiveness of some local aging programs.

Soon the three were spinning out related ideas. "What if we could get a social worker to direct the program along with a licensed practical nurse (LPN) and perhaps an activity director at each location? We could provide a great service and give these caregivers a rest," said Tina.

"Yeah!" chimed in Wolf. "We could offer respite care for enough hours each week that caregivers could reserve a set time for their family member. We might even be able to coordinate this care with other community services, like blood pressure screening and glaucoma testing."

Heather's question about financial resources slowed them down only temporarily. "What about the county or state picking up the cost?" asked Wolf.

"Nope," said Heather. "They already told me they will be short of funds for existing programs. But the governor has promised more money for programs for the elderly in the next budget." "That's too long to wait," said Tina. "We have people ending up in nursing homes because their caregivers can't get a break each week. That's a terrible waste of money and devastating to many of these families."

"The latest issue of the Alzheimer's Newsletter *[a monthly publication about the disease] had a notice about possible grants from a national foundation. They're particularly interested in funding innovative ideas for serving the elderly in rural areas," Heather enthusiastically suggested.*

"Do you still have the newsletter?" asked Wolf.

"Yes, if I can remember where I left it," replied Heather. When Heather tracked down the missing newsletter (under the couch pillow where her golden retriever, Prince, sleeps), the three friends plotted their course of action.

"Let's try for one of these grants," said Tina. "We have nothing to lose and a lot to gain if we can pull it off."

Introduction

Most social workers and administrators would agree that the single most important resource of any social agency is its staff. Recruiting, training, promoting, supervising, and managing the agency's human resources is an ongoing responsibility primarily undertaken by administrators. Baccalaureate social workers and new master's degree workers are usually not thrust into this responsibility immediately upon graduation. Yet they too must have some basic understanding of such issues as effective supervision and management of staff. (Chapter 2 described various functions of supervisors and provided suggestions for using supervision effectively. Chapter 4 provided basic information about the workings of organizations, including the various theoretical approaches used by administrators and supervisors. The chapter also described common problems encountered by workers in social service organizations.)

This chapter will discuss creating and maintaining various nonstaff agency resources, including the agency's reputation and use of technology.

The agency's reputation is important because both agencies and services require good public relations to keep the support of taxpayers and contributors. Specifically, we will look carefully at the topic of working with the media to help ensure that your agency receives the most fair and positive treatment possible from the news media serving your community. Technology can be used to manage resources and assist in an organization's operation. Technology, particularly computers, has become an everyday reality in most social service agencies.

In the last two sections we will introduce several important aspects of resource development, with a specific focus on fundraising, grants, and contracts. Fundraising is a primary concern for all nonprofit and many public agencies. Learning how to raise money to pay for existing services, to develop new ones, or to test creative ideas is an important skill for social workers. This chapter will look at several fundraising ideas that have proven effective for a variety of agencies and organizations.

Because most agencies and social workers are involved with grants or contracts at some point, the last portion of the chapter will discuss these topics in great detail. Most private nonprofit agencies receive grants or contracts to provide services, and many public agencies do as well. In addition, many public agencies contract with private agencies to provide services the former cannot or choose not to offer. Thus, it is difficult to function in the field of social work without some familiarity with grants and contracts.

Learning Objectives

This chapter will provide content concerning how social workers:

A. *Work with the media to advance social well-being and social and economic justice.*

B. *Utilize professional communication strategies with the media.*

C. *Use technology for managing resources, facilitating service delivery, and evaluating the effectiveness of agency practices.*

D. *Utilize fundraising, with a particular focus on grants and contracts.*

Working with the Media

"The media" refers to television, radio, and newspapers that deliver news and information to the public. Obviously, the purpose of the media is not just to paint you or your agency in a favorable light. Yet, the potential value of the media to your agency or organization is substantial. There are at least four ways in which the media can be beneficial to an agency.

First, skillful use of the media can make the public aware of your organization. This is important because public awareness creates a potential source of new clients, alerts potential donors to your existence, and can create a favorable impression of your organization and the services it provides.

Second, the media can be helpful in fundraising. Individual fundraising activities (such as a pancake breakfast or raffle) can be highlighted in the media. The need for specific items or services can also be announced. Equally important, the media can encourage the public to contribute much-needed money to your agency.

Third, an effective media-relations effort can prevent minor problems from becoming more serious. Concerns or problems that arise and become known to the public can be countered more easily when the public has a positive perception of your agency.

Fourth, the media can also be helpful in publicizing problems and influencing decision makers. Media attention can focus the public's awareness on a problem such as lack of service to a particular group. It can help expose unfair treatment by government officials or other individuals. Highlight 14.1 provides an example of using the media.

General Guidelines for Using the Media

Several authors (Homan, 2004; Sheafor & Horejsi, 2006) provide general guidelines for working with the news media.

First, *make it your policy to maintain ongoing relationships with media personnel.* Your contacts with the media should begin as early as possible. Don't wait until a problem arises before contacting the media. Having an ongoing relationship with members of the media makes it much easier to work with them when you require their assistance. Remember, the media exist to provide news and information to the public. That means the material provided to the media should be of interest to others. Reporters appreciate people who help them by providing possible story ideas. Is there a critical service that does not exist because there is no money? Are children or older adults being hurt because of the actions of a particular agency or government department? Is there a particularly successful program serving the needs of chemically dependent individuals? Has your agency decided to provide services to an underserved population, such as displaced workers? Generally speaking, if an item interests you and you alone, the media won't touch it with a 10-foot pole.

Second, *nurture a variety of contacts within the media.* All of the various media can and should be viewed as potential resources for your agency. Too often, social

HIGHLIGHT 14.1

The Media's Influence

The Child Advocacy Institute had been in operation for several years, providing services for the County Protective Services Department and local law enforcement agencies. The institute, a not-for-profit advocacy center for children, maintained a specific focus on interviewing victims and documenting the existence of physical and sexual child abuse. Most of its funding came from a contract provided by the county and from grants and donations. The agency director, who lacked any recognized educational credentials for the job, generally was regarded as an effective fundraiser for the institute. The agency operated under the control of a board of directors, who were slowly becoming concerned about the director's leadership. The director, in a move to deflect the board's concerns, decided to quit and create a new agency with the same function and a similar name as the predecessor. The potential confusion and disruptions of leadership and funding would have devastated the original institute. Her new agency would, she believed, continue to receive county funds, and she anticipated taking the contract for services with her. These actions might have gone unnoticed by the general public had the local newspaper not taken an interest in the story.

In a series of articles, the paper noted that the Child Advocacy Institute had been denied national accreditation for a number of reasons, including the alleged videotaping of children in the nude and the director's misrepresentation of her credentials. The accrediting body had even suggested that the institute should change its name because it was casting a shadow over child advocacy efforts of other agencies with similar names.

The newspaper also raised questions about the institute's financial strength, the future of another spin-off agency provided by the institute, and the for-profit status of the new agency the director was attempting to create. The controversy resulted in several agencies refusing to use the services of the institute. The director continued to argue the merits of her case with public officials, but the relentless media attention eventually took its toll. Elected county officials decided to take control of the institute and place it under the sheriff's jurisdiction, effectively ending the director's efforts to stay in her position or to start a new agency supported by public funds.

The media focus on the institute pushed elected officials to act. This illustrates the media's effectiveness in bringing issues to public attention.

---

workers rely on a single individual (one reporter) or one medium (a newspaper) rather than using all of the media available. Any agency benefits from a variety of resources to which it can turn when in need. Consider the media among those resources.

Third, *if you happen to be a local expert on a subject, let the media know this.* Your expert perspectives on health care might be sought by local media when the national media focus on this subject. Once you have developed a relationship with media personnel, maintain regular contact with them.

Fourth, *make sure you have sanction, or permission, to speak for your agency.* Agency administrators don't like to see their workers quoted as speaking for the agency when administrators have not authorized such action.

Fifth, *make it easy for the media representatives to contact you.* Providing home and office numbers and addresses is helpful. Also give them the names of others they can talk to about your agency or issue if you can't be reached.

Sixth, *learn the media's time schedules.* All the media have deadlines for their reports and stories. Learn these time frames and give media representatives timely notice of newsworthy events. If you miss the deadline for tonight's local TV broadcast, your story may get lost tomorrow. Even if you are on schedule, however, some big news item such as a major fire, earthquake, or other sensational event may dwarf your particular news.

Seventh, *avoid playing favorites among the news media.* Don't give a press release to one media representative without also providing it to the others. The only exception to this guideline is the exclusive interview, wherein you give a single reporter a story and this person is the only one who has the information until it appears in the media.

Eighth, *recognize that the media can and do make mistakes.* When they do, be careful how you react. If a serious error requires correction, handle this diplomatically. Tactfully explain the reasons for your request and ask for a correction. Don't waste time asking for corrections of minor errors. On the other hand, praise reporters who produced a good story. Giving praise and support works just as well with media representatives as it does with the public. Most of us like to know others think we do a good job. Never be afraid to compliment a reporter on an exceptional article or report.

Ninth, *don't be disappointed if a story you hoped would appear does not.* This is the nature of the news business. Perhaps your story got cut to provide room for a train wreck or the arrest of a local drive-by shooter. That's life in the big city, as they say. Recognize that reporters are not any happier about this than you are, because they like to see their names in print (or be on camera). If your news item happens to disappear, thank the reporter anyway and say you look forward to future opportunities to work together.

Tenth, *remember that anything you say to the media can, and often does, end up in print* (Homan, 2004). Even specifying that something is "off the record" does not guarantee that it will not become part of a story. In theory, off-the-record comments are intended to help reporters better understand a story or point of view and are not intended to show up in their report. However, reporters are interested in news items, and the off-the-record comment may be truly newsworthy to them. Their sense of obligation to their employers and the public may supersede your wish for something to remain off the record.

Contacts with the Media

Media contacts can come about in a variety of ways. First, the media may contact you. If media personnel have heard about you or think there is a news story in something with which you're connected, they may make the first move. Second, you can call the media yourself and explain that you have what you believe is a newsworthy item. If it shows promise, the media representative will probably set up an appointment to meet you. Third, you may contact the media through a news release. This is a written announcement of some event that you believe is of interest to the public. Highlight 14.2 offers an example of a news release.

Media Interviews

EP 2.1.10a

If you are going to be interviewed by the news media, prepare well in advance (CSWE, 2008, EP 2.1.10a). This means thinking carefully about what is most important to get across. Newspaper reporters usually spend several minutes to an hour on an interview. They try to allow time for you to expand on an idea. On the other hand, television interviews often last only a minute or two, which allows you little time to come up with your answers. Watch the local news programs to observe how little time on the air any story actually gets. Time the taped interviews to get an idea of what can be said in a minute or two.

Practice going over the important "sound bytes" that carry your primary message. Sound bytes are the short passages that people tend to remember from an interview. For example, Diane might have a lot she would like to say, but the important message is: "The city is putting our children in danger. No child should be at risk of getting shot just walking to school. A mayor and police chief who won't do their jobs should be replaced. We have tried to meet with Mayor Doublespeak and Chief Nightstick and they refuse. We are tired of the runaround and sick of hearing rescue squad sirens in our neighborhood. The association has no choice but to ask the court to intervene." Amazingly, just this little statement takes almost 30 seconds to say. This suggests how little information really appears in television interviews. Prepare yourself for this strict time limitation.

EP 2.1.3c

Respond to questions clearly and candidly. Don't take offense if reporters ask probing or difficult questions. That is their job. Offer to answer any other questions they have that may come up later. If you don't have information they need immediately, try to get it quickly. Remember, the media work under tight deadlines. If you are seen as a credible, cooperative, and helpful interviewee, media representatives will value your contribution to their work and jobs (CSWE, 2008, EP 2.1.3c).

Letters to the Editor and Editorials

We have spoken mainly about dealing with the media through interviews and news releases. Obviously, these are not the only ways in which we can work with the media. For example, every newspaper has a "Letters to the Editor" section, where interested readers share their views on various topics. Such sections provide ample opportunity to have your say, along with the other respondents. Note that most papers limit the length of what they will print and expect you to identify yourself, including your name and address. Some papers will withhold your name and address if desired. However,

HIGHLIGHT 14.2

Example of a News Release

Fremont Street Neighborhood Association
1234 Fremont Street
South Swampland, Missouri 65803
417-863-1000

For Immediate Release
Neighborhood Association Pushes City for Action
South Swampland, MO—August 1, 2008

The Fremont Street Neighborhood Association has threatened to sue the city of South Swampland for failing to adequately protect children walking to school along East Doyle Avenue. Association President Diane Chambers said that two children were hurt in drive-by shootings during the past four weeks, and the city does nothing about the problem. The Neighborhood Association Board of Directors voted yesterday to sue in Circuit Court, charging the mayor and police chief with discrimination against the predominantly African-American neighborhood along Fremont Street. The association is calling for increased police patrols and arrests of the gang members who frequent the area, brandishing weapons and selling drugs to children. They also demand the city close the south end of Fremont Street to prevent drivers from racing down the street. "If the city fails to take action to alleviate the problem, we will take them to court," said Chambers. "We are also considering filing a discrimination complaint with the state Office of Civil Rights," she said. Chambers said a rally is scheduled for 10:00 A.M. Monday. Former Fremont Street resident and professional ballplayer Sam Malone, along with association officers, will hold a news conference.

For further information, contact Diane Chambers at 863-1000 or 883-5060.

###

Note: A news release should be typed double-spaced, with margins of at least 1.5 inches all around.

all newspapers want this information to prevent anonymous misuse of the media. Because anonymous letters cannot be traced to anyone, they are always suspect.

Expect editing or shortening of your letter if it is too long. Don't get excited if it doesn't appear at all. This can happen from time to time. Newspapers may receive lots of letters and often can't print them all.

Letters to the editor should not contain libelous (defaming) statements that can get you and perhaps the paper sued. Of course, the best defense against the accusation that you have said something damaging about another is that the statement was true.

When you write to the paper, reference something that was in the paper recently. This orients both the paper and its readers to why your item is relevant. After all, the purpose of the letter section is to let the

readers have their say about things that appear in the paper, not to tell everybody that your neighbor has an obnoxious, constantly barking pit bull.

Sometimes you can entice the newspaper editors to write an editorial on a particular topic. Editorials are the newspaper editor's views on issues of concern in your community. Editorials can cover everything from the editor's position on local elections to concerns about problems in city government.

You will probably need to meet directly with editorial staff and ask if they would consider an editorial about your cause or agency. Be prepared to give them background information and facts that they will need to support their position. Homan (2004) suggests that you emphasize the logical relationship between your issue and their past stand on similar matters. Highlight 14.3 presents a typical newspaper editorial.

HIGHLIGHT 14.3

Example of a Newspaper Editorial

County Needs New Juvenile Facility

The proposed county juvenile detention facility will be discussed by the board of supervisors at its meeting tonight. The number of juveniles detained for a week or longer in the county has increased threefold in the past two years.

Keeping juveniles in the county jail, even when the jail is not busy, is, in our opinion, a poor practice.

Depending upon their situation, juveniles housed in the county jail need various amounts of supervision. Few require the same level of security as adult inmates. We see no way that keeping adult criminals with juveniles (many of whom aren't even charged with a crime) can benefit anyone. We strongly urge the board to consider funding a separate facility for our community's juveniles who need temporary detention.

Using Technology in Your Agency

EP 2.1.9a

Few, if any, social agencies operate without extensive use of various forms of technology, most commonly computers. Computers have joined various other technologies (telephones, dictation equipment, fax machines, photocopiers, and voicemail/answering machines) as indispensable facets of our professional lives. Computers now make it possible to produce sophisticated presentations (PowerPoint), develop in-house publications (brochures, posters), facilitate planning through creation of charts and diagrams, access a vast library of information through the Internet, and allow practitioners to talk across wide distances through e-mail and videoconferencing. Essentially, all are tools helping us to do our jobs better. In this section we will describe some typical uses you and your agency will have for computers (CSWE, 2008, EP 2.1.9a).

Understanding Computer Hardware

Large agencies have used computers for decades to perform certain functions, such as printing payroll checks for workers, client public assistance checks, and checks to pay agency bills. Before the arrival of personal computers in the early 1980s, outside companies performed this work for a fee. Often, the computers used for printing checks were what are known as mainframes or mini-computers. In those days, computer use required a high degree of training and substantial knowledge of computer systems. Some agencies operated their own computer systems. However, the closest many agencies came to modern technology was the use of typewriters with memory for printing out form letters.

With the beginning of the age of personal computers, a major transformation occurred. Personal computers became commonplace in most agencies, first with secretaries and administrative personnel and later with other staff members. This did not mean the end of larger computer systems. Many agencies still use these for a variety of purposes, especially when large volumes of data must be maintained. It does mean, however, that most agency technological functions can be performed by nonexperts with boxes on their desks and the right computer software. Most software available today can be used by anyone willing to take the time to learn the operating rules. Specialized training may not be needed.

Laptop computers are used in some agencies, allowing workers to take their units with them as needed. These computers often come with wireless connections, making it possible to communicate over short distances with computers in the office. It is common to have computers in an office networked together so that they can easily communicate with each other, use centralized software such as a database, and provide security backup in the event that an individual computer fails.

Computers continue to go through a series of metamorphoses in sophistication, speed, and capabilities. It is the nature of this technology that whatever hardware and software are in use today will be replaced, upgraded, or otherwise improved in a very short time.

Understanding the Software

"Software" describes the various specialized programs that produce the results we want. Most of us are familiar with word processing programs, which are made by many companies and allow the computer to operate as a typewriter. We can type data that appear on the screen, revise the data in numerous ways, print the data using our printer, and/or save the data for later retrieval. Agencies use word processing software to enter data in client files, keep worker records of client contact, send letters, and the like.

Software may be designed for a single purpose, such as word processing, or be "integrated," allowing several functions to be accessed within a single program. An integrated system might allow you to type a letter to a client, look in a database to find the client's home address and your last contact with the client, and then use a calendar program to schedule an appointment on your first open date next month. If you were using single-purpose software, you would have had to exit or minimize one program before going into another.

Software exists for an infinite variety of purposes. *Database software* allows us to maintain extensive records and retrieve that data quickly. We might like to know which of our clients we have not seen in the past month. We can easily get a list of those clients and their addresses (sorted by client name or by date if we prefer). If we want to know for which clients a report to the court is due this month, the database will tell us. Just about any piece of information can be entered into a database system. Figure 14.1 shows the way information might be displayed in a database.

Of course, much more information can be contained in a database than what is represented here. We could list the presenting problem, names of family members, and any other data. At the same time, databases are useful for purposes other than maintaining client records. We could, for example, use a database to keep membership records for a community association or organization, to maintain a record of contributors to a political campaign, or to save a list of social workers and their agencies, phone numbers, and other information. You can also have the database reorganize information into reports. You might want a report on all members of your organization who have not paid their dues. As you can see, a database can be a useful piece of software, whether you are working with macro, mezzo, or micro problems.

Spreadsheets are software packages that allow us to calculate and maintain various kinds of financial or numerical information. Spreadsheets are essentially electronic accounting ledgers into which we type the same type of information we would write into an accountant's ledger. All software spreadsheets allow us to keep track of what we spend on various projects, and changes in a figure can be automatically reflected in the changed total. Figure 14.2 displays a typical spreadsheet.

A real spreadsheet could have many more columns and rows, depending on the financial information you were recording. Spreadsheets allow you to build formulas and automatically recalculate totals. This way, as the number of purchases you make increases, the total spent at the bottom changes along with it. Thus, the $700.22 shown in Figure 14.2 would keep changing as new items were entered into the spreadsheet. You can also calculate what a 5 percent increase in your

NAME	STREET ADDRESS	CITY, STATE, ZIP	TELEPHONE	LAST APPT.
Abbot, Lois	1234 Hollywood Dr.	Los Angeles, CA 19876	835-4578	2-12-04
Costello, Bud	4321 Mudslide Rd.	Los Angeles, CA 19876	835-8754	3-24-04
Hardy, Stanley	3454 Bonk Circle	Huntington Beach, CA 19874	458-2345	3-12-04
Laurel, Olivia	987 W. Hartburn La.	Huntington Beach, CA 19874	458-9345	3-18-04
Mangreen, Newt	1776 Idea St.	Los Angeles, CA 19876	777-6666	7-4-05
Peru, Rosina	1890 Money Blvd.	Los Angeles, CA 19876	345-1945	11-3-04

FIGURE 14.1 Information in a Database

DATE	ITEM	COST	CATEGORY
1-3-08	Postage	14.56	O1
1-5-08	Desk	456.00	E3
1-5-08	Chair	134.00	E3
1-7-08	Paper	95.66	S2
Total		700.22	

FIGURE 14.2 A Spreadsheet

organization's income would do in various categories such as operating expenses, equipment, supplies, and personnel. The codes 01, E3, and S2 in Figure 14.2 are a means of categorizing items as *operating expenses, equipment,* or *supplies* respectively (and the spreadsheet could sort all entries by these codes if you wish). Users tend to develop their own systems of categorization based upon the needs of their agency.

There are many other types of software in use: Agencies use financial packages to do payroll, pay bills, and update financial records. Some larger agencies may even have special programs written to perform tasks unique to the agency or reflecting the agency's specialized needs.

Agency Software Usage

Computer software usage varies by agency. Besides the general types of software packages just referred to, many agencies will use software specifically designed to meet social workers' needs. Specialized software packages now exist for many social work purposes. These include maintaining client records, creating a log of worker notes, word processing, evaluating client progress, tabulating categories of client problems and worker responses, using computerized assessment instruments, accessing Internet resources, communicating via e-mail, and developing PowerPoint presentations for communicating with the public and decision makers, to name just a few. It can also be used for locating information to assist with referrals to other appropriate service providers and match children needing out-of-home placement with likely services such as foster care, group homes, and other facilities.

Other agencies have become almost completely paperless operations as social workers do such things as case notes, billing, appointments, and work schedules on a computer. The use of computers means that data do not have to be repeatedly reentered. For example,

the computer can use the social worker's appointment schedule to do billing, saving separate entries for the two activities. Specialized software packages exist for helping social workers complete intake interviews and assessments, as well as discharge planning and measurement of outcomes. Eggertsen (2006) reports on the use of a geographic information system (GIS) to study multiple placements for children in out-of-home care in Utah. The software allows agencies to produce maps showing areas where services are nonexistent or where transportation problems prevent clients from using available services. The availability of this type of program can forecast the demand for future services, study the demographic characteristics of neighborhoods, suggest where new offices should be located, and map health and other social problems in the community. GIS has been used in rural South Africa, India, and England to study issues such as access to health care and AIDS prevention (Antonyappan, 2003; Lovett, Hagnes, Sunnenberg, & Gale, 2002; Tanser, Gijsbertsen, & Herbert, 2006).

Social workers can also use communication software to fax a document from their computer and send a file electronically. E-mail allows you to leave a detailed message that the reader can respond to later. E-mail is also used in task groups to communicate between meetings and to get feedback about ideas prior to a face-to-face meeting. Of course, e-mail can be a mixed blessing because of security and confidentiality issues. It is often difficult to use humor with e-mail because it is hard to know how the recipient will respond. It is also easy to get sloppy and careless when e-mailing. Errors in spelling, punctuation, or grammar and other problems can detract just as much from your electronic letters as from your hard-copy documents. Remember that this medium is just another way people can judge your competence and strengths.

The thought of making an assessment based upon symptoms typed into a computer is challenging. However, the software already exists to do this with relative ease. The ability to refer a client to an appropriate service can be enhanced if a list of available agencies and resources exists in a database. One can enter, say, a problem such as lack of transportation for medical care and get a listing from the databases of all agencies and organizations that might provide this service.

Of course, the potential to determine eligibility for various financial assistance programs is obvious. If client data is entered into a software program, you can easily determine whether the person meets the guidelines for a given program.

Client data entered into case records are part of agencies' *management information systems (MISs)*, methods for gathering, analyzing, and evaluating data in an agency or organization. The data collected on a client through the use of application forms and other agency records are also part of the MIS. Other facets of the MIS could be data on employees, their training, level of experience, and agency assignments. Most of this information is now computerized, allowing administrators to better manage their agencies. An agency administrator can use such data to analyze and understand what kinds of problems clients experience and what types of services are provided by the agency. This information becomes invaluable when deciding which programs should receive additional funding or where improvements are needed in service to clients. An analysis of agency workload might reveal that the unit providing child neglect and abuse services is getting twice as many referrals as in the past, although the staffing has not changed. This might justify adding staff to the unit, especially if another unit was underutilized. Highlight 14.4 gives an example of how management information might be used.

Management information systems also help agencies identify problems not being met by existing resources. Perhaps many clients are in need of emergency housing, but the agency does not provide this service. Or perhaps the agency offers specific services that no one is using. Such a situation might suggest that agency resources be redeployed where they are most needed.

Evaluation of outcomes can be enhanced by an effective MIS. Outcomes, you will recall, are quality-of-life changes resulting from social work interventions. It should be relatively easy to see what percentage of clients report satisfaction with the services they receive. It should also be possible to see how many cases are closed and whether client goals have been achieved. (Chapter 10 described some of these scenarios.)

The sharing potential of computers can mean that the secretary typing a letter to a client, the billing department preparing a monthly statement, and you may simultaneously get information from the client's record. It also means you can leave a message for your supervisor on her computer such as "I'm taking a six-month vacation in Fiji. See you in May. Please hold my calls."

We have talked mainly about the use of computers in agencies, but there is no limit to how this technology can be used in other environments. For example, computers are being employed more and more in political campaigns for public office, including the election of 2008, which saw Barack Obama use social networking and YouTube in his successful run for the presidency. Campaigns commonly use common software packages such as spreadsheets and databases to keep records of donations and expenditures, identify likely voters, prepare reports, and analyze voting trends. They have also proved useful in allowing a candidate or candidate's staff to maintain e-mail contact with enormous lists of supporters. Computers assist with "robocalls," in

Management Information Systems

Chris Vlahoulis was new at his job as deputy director of the Millennium Service Agency. Millennium provided a variety of outpatient mental health services to clients, ranging from marital counseling to children's groups. The agency director had asked Chris to prepare a report on clients seen in the previous 12 months. Chris knew quite a bit about computers, but little about the system of data gathering employed in his agency. He quickly discovered that all client data were entered into a database that allowed him to ask specific questions about the information contained therein.

Chris asked the database to list all presenting problems reported by clients in the past year. The computer gave him a list that showed how many people had what diagnoses. Interestingly, Chris discovered that many clients presented problems with substance abuse. What was most interesting, however, is that no workers in the agency had any certification as substance abuse service providers. Only a couple had any specialized education for working with this client group. Chris could use the data to show the number of client problems and also to recommend that workers receive additional training in helping chemically dependent clients.

which candidates record a message that is then sent to thousands of confirmed and potential supporters. Recent campaigns have seen the use of computers for discussion groups, fundraising, position statements, and surveys to gather data on potential supporters. After an election, an elected official can use the computer to hold online meetings with constituents or to schedule phone-in meetings with voters. In this regard, the Internet has had a major impact on how political campaigns are managed and operated.

Many communities are using databases of crime reports to identify neighborhoods with high crime rates. Citizen patrols and police are then concentrated in those neighborhoods, thus helping to reduce criminal behavior. The computer's ability to aggregate data like this can be very helpful in revealing common problems that otherwise might appear to be isolated. A computerized database of problems might show that a neighborhood school has expelled twice as many students this year as last. One might then look at possible explanations for such a dramatic increase in punitive actions taken by the school principal or school board.

Computers can also be used to publish newsletters and other public-access documents, such as brochures describing agency services. These can be done on regular word processing software or, with greater ease, on desktop publishing software. This type of software was developed to help lay out pages of documents, move pictures around, and perform the kinds of tasks that were once done only by professional compositors and print shops. The availability of this software can reduce the cost of producing a document. Because it is tailored specifically to developing such items, it also makes the task easier than using a regular word processor.

Technology is also being used in creative ways to deliver health services, including social work services to remote locations. Using computers, videoconferencing, and other tools, social workers are providing services that include online counseling, referral, assessment, follow-up in home health settings, distance education, and supervision, among others. While there remain practical, legal, and ethical issues in the delivery of social work services through the use of technology, there is growing evidence that this trend is increasing (McCarty & Clancy, 2002).

Computers are being employed to serve as a support for foster, adoptive, and kinship parents in Pennsylvania through www.taplink.org. They are also used to help social service agencies map client data by location and even determine the most efficient routes to drive from one client's location to another. These capabilities are inherent in what is known as Geographic Information Systems (GISs).

Using the Internet

Increasingly, social workers are using the Internet for many purposes. This includes doing research, accessing national and state databases, communicating through e-mail, accessing groups and organizations with interests that may be of benefit to clients, and carrying out discussions with colleagues around the world. A worker interested in gathering data from the U.S. Census Bureau, for example, can simply type in www.census.gov and have access to the enormous wealth of information gathered by this branch of the federal government. Similarly, www.naswdc.org will reach the national office of the National Association of Social Workers. Most major organizations maintain a Web page that contains information you might find useful as well as a means to contact them. Interested in advocacy for children? So is the Children's Defense Fund—and it can be reached at www.childrensdefense.org. Do you want to reach Community Organizations International? They're at www.acorninternational.org. Would information on the homeless be useful? If so, you might access the Directory of Homeless and Housing Advocacy Coalitions at www.nation-alhomeless.org/Factsheets/index.html.

Other Internet resources include such things as the social welfare blog (socialwelfarespot.blogspot.com), social networking applications, and podcasting, among others. Social workers can create their own communities of practice or similar networks with colleagues who share specific interests. One example is found at www.socialworkcafe.net. Another source of useful information for social work practitioners is www.nyu.edu/socialwork/ip, which includes news items and articles dealing with subjects from around the world. Examples include articles dealing with social welfare topics in the United Kingdom, China, New Zealand, Canada, India, and the Philippines. The breadth of topics is wide, including such diverse items as designing sustainable communities, violence in mental health facilities, the history of urban centers in the United States, alcohol abuse prevention, prison overcrowding, dyslexia, and gay and lesbian issues. The Internet allows social workers to learn about interventions, problems, and challenges facing practitioners across the world as well as to obtain access to several online journals. It can also assist in locating what is known as fugitive or grey literature that includes articles and publications that did not appear in mainstream journals.

EP 2.1.3

As you can see, the Internet provides a wealth of resources for macro practice as well as for other levels of practice. It can also be a source of incredibly useless, incorrect, and biased data and information. It is important to maintain a critical perspective when accessing information on Web sites. Because anyone or any organization (including those opposed to the basic purposes of social work) can establish a Web site, the viewer must carefully analyze any information found on the Web. Fortunately, books devoted solely to social work and the Internet have become available to assist in using this important resource (Schiller, 2005; Vernon & Lynch, 2000). We recommend consulting one of these sources for more details. Other good sources for evaluating Web-based information can be found at several university sites, including: www.lib.berkeley.edu/TeachingLib/Guides/Internet/Evaluate.html, www.library.cornell.edu/olinuris/ref/webcrit.html, and http://lib.nmsu.edu/instruction/evalcrit.html See Figure 14.3 for other online sources (CSWE, 2008, EP 2.1.3).

General Observations about Computers

Like any tool, computers can be misused. Sometimes people use data in computer files without authority, thereby endangering confidentiality.

Computer mistakes can be annoying, damaging, and difficult to correct. Whether for good or evil, computers generally do exactly what we tell them to

World Wide Web resources for social workers
www.nyu.edu/socialwork/wwwrsw

Data from U.S. Census Bureau
www.census.gov

The nonprofit lobbying guide
www.wkkf.org/advocacyhandbook/index.html

Official federal government information
www.gpoaccess.gov

Web-based toolkit to end violence against women
toolkit.ncjrs.org

International/Federation of social workers
www.ifsw.org

Comparative global information
www.nationmaster.com

FIGURE 14.3 Other Potential Online Resources

do. If we err and tell a computer to enter data into the file of John R. Smith when we really meant John T. Smith, the computer does what we tell it to do. It doesn't know that we made a typing error and meant to hit an adjoining key. Similarly, if we say we saw the client first on 8–15–09 but typed 8–15–08, the machine does not know what we meant, only what we told it to do. A careless mistake in an e-mail address can send information to the wrong person—or to your entire agency, proving embarrassing or worse. In one large agency, a staff member sent an e-mail containing risqué jokes to a friend. She accidentally sent it to the entire staff of 250 people, thereby earning the anger of her boss and a large dose of embarrassment.

Like any new skill, computer use requires learning time. Sometimes it seems as if the learning curve for computers goes straight up before it levels off and we feel some degree of comfort. Initially at least, it may take us longer to enter data using the computer than it did the old-fashioned way. This phase passes, however, and we all get better and faster at entering information. Increasingly, there is evidence that social workers and their clients can use computers very effectively for many purposes, from recordkeeping to evaluation.

Learning different software packages for different purposes (for example, for word processing or establishing a database) requires mastering different commands and keystrokes. Most computer software

EP 2.1.1e

comes with sufficient information to learn the basics very rapidly. Some more sophisticated programs are difficult to learn. Classes may be available at nearby colleges or technical schools to help those desiring formal instruction. In addition, books are available for most major programs to help you learn your new software. Many software programs come with detailed workbooks and online help menus to teach the user how to implement the software (CSWE, 2008, EP 2.1.1e).

One of the nicest things about using a personal computer is that you are the boss. If you make mistakes, you can usually correct them easily. If you get frustrated with your progress, you can turn the darn thing off and start another time. Once mastered, computer skills will enhance your effectiveness as a generalist practitioner.

Other Macro Uses of Technology

Access to technology is playing a large role in countries across the globe. Cell phones are being used by individuals and groups to communicate in totalitarian states, organize demonstrations, and access information. Photos and videos captured on cell phones have been used to show incidents of brutality carried out by police, the military, or paramilitary bodies. In many cases, these recordings are the only record of events because some governments seek to prevent new media from reporting on antigovernment demonstrations. Likewise, access to television has been encouraged by the availability of satellite dishes when governments have shut down local TV stations. Information is much more available across national boundaries than has been the case in the past.

EP 2.1.9a

Newer technology such as Facebook has been employed to launch protests in Croatia, and computer-savvy individuals have created blogs in counties such as Fiji, Malaysia, Egypt, and Iran to protest government laws, policies, and practices. Messages and photos have been posted on YouTube and Twitter, calling attention to events that have not been covered by mainstream media. The use of technology has allowed groups with limited or no power to organize and demand changes in organizations, communities, and countries and has provided yet another tool for social workers pursuing societal change (CSWE, 2008, EP 2.1.9a).

Fundraising

Few social workers begin their careers with the clear goal of becoming fundraisers. The frequently expressed motivation for a career in social work—"I want to help people"—does not often extend to raising money. A failure to mention fundraising as a goal is not particularly surprising. First, raising money is not seen by the novice as a social work task. Second, many of us lack confidence in our ability to raise money. Finally, compounding these two factors is the absence of much education or preparation to be a fundraiser. Yet, all social agencies require financial resources to operate.

The typical agency today receives funding from a number of different sources, including fees for services charged to agency clients. For example, a mental health agency may charge all clients on a sliding fee basis for counseling provided by agency staff. Additional funds may come from insurance companies that provide mental health coverage for clients. Sometimes referred to as third-party reimbursement, this source of revenue enhances the agency's revenue stream. The advent of managed care in the health insurance industry has placed restrictions on what the agency can charge the insurer, under what conditions payment will be made, and the length of time services may be provided to the client. A local Catholic Family Services agency received Title IV-B funds for counseling, a federal grant to promote teen abstinence, and housing funds from the Federal Emergency Management Agency, along with fees for service, United Way contributions, and donated money, goods, and services from another Catholic agency.

As noted below, some agencies also seek contracts with other agencies to provide specific services or to work with certain groups of clients. For example, a private agency may approach the local welfare agency with a proposal to help TANF[1] clients develop the job skills to move off the welfare rolls. The private agency might propose to work with 50 clients, teaching them work and interviewing skills, along with providing support groups. They may propose charging a flat amount for working with these clients or provide service on a per-case basis. The Catholic Family Services agency just described had contracts with several businesses to provide employee assistance programs,[2] a common type of service contract.

Some agencies will look for ways to collaborate with other community agencies to meet a shared need or reduce unnecessary competition. This collaboration may also be important when either or both of the agencies seek grant funds, because it demonstrates commitment to using resources efficiently. Managing agency resources today involves considering all potential funding sources to help support agency operation.

However, raising the funds to run an agency can be a daunting task. Although public agencies often receive most of their funds from tax money, nonprofit (or not-for-profit) organizations use a combination of public funding and private donations to help meet the need. As a result, the division between nonprofit and public agencies has blurred substantially over the years

---

1. TANF is an acronym for Temporary Assistance for Needy Families, the primary public assistance program that replaced Aid to Families with Dependent Children (AFDC). Its goal is to get recipients off assistance as soon as possible by emphasizing job seeking and training and by limiting the length of time a client can receive money.

2. *Employee assistance programs* are designed by companies and other organizations to help their employees cope with problems that can interfere with job performance. Services provided can range from marital and financial counseling to help with substance abuse and dependent care problems.

because both need to raise funds. Most private non-profit agencies receive grants or contracts from public sources (that is, tax money). A private agency might receive a contract or grant from a public agency to offer a service the public agency cannot afford or does not wish to offer. Similarly, many public agencies accept donations and grants from private individuals, foundations, and organizations. Later in this chapter, we will examine the use of grants and contracts, two common methods of raising money for program operations.

Often, however, neither grants nor contracts by themselves are sufficient to fund agency programs. Perhaps no grant or contract is available for what an agency wants to do. Even if one is, the amount of money available is often insufficient. Grants are generally used for one-time projects and rarely given on a continuing basis. Raising money, even for causes we deem worthy (such as social programs), is not an easy task.

Many of us find asking for money very difficult. Perhaps this is because we have little or no preparation for fundraising. Perhaps it is because we don't feel comfortable asking others to help us. After all, as social workers we are usually the ones giving help. Whatever the reason, fear of fundraising is a hurdle to overcome.

Not only is money needed to operate basic programs, but funds are needed to support new civic and political causes (including political candidates). Money is also necessary for campaigns to convince voters to support bond issues, tax increases, or help for disaster victims. Highlight 14.5 gives an example of fundraising to help an individual deal with a calamity.

Sources of Funds

Social workers are frequently asked to help raise funds for a variety of causes, ranging from ongoing operation of an agency to political campaigns. Thus, we must be aware of the potential sources of fundraising—fortunately, there are many. Rubin and Rubin (2008) and Homan (2008) identify several alternate sources of funds, including individual donors, benefits and their variations, direct solicitation, foundations, and membership dues. In addition, church organizations and service clubs often provide funding if the area to be supported falls within their sphere of interest. The following sections address each of these sources. Under "Finding Out about Grants and Contracts," we will discuss foundation and corporate sources.

Individual Donors

Individual donors are people who dig into their own pockets for money to help a project or activity. These people have many motivations for giving: Some people give because they are getting something they value in

---

HIGHLIGHT 14.5

Fundraising

Fortuitous Crunk didn't know how many friends she had until disaster struck. Her house, on the edge of the inner city, was a bit run-down, but provided shelter for her family of four children. One of these children was a foster child with severe developmental disabilities. One frosty fall evening. Fortuitous awoke to hear the neighbor's dog barking. It turned out to be a lucky break. When she awoke, she smelled smoke and managed to get all her children out of the house before it was completely engulfed in smoke and flames.

Because of her poverty. Fortuitous had never carried fire insurance on her property. Thus, when her house burned down, she faced the possibility of joining the other homeless persons living in the public park six blocks away. Her neighbors, however, would not let this happen. They immediately began to raise money to repair her home. First they alerted the news media to the neighborhood's efforts to help one of their own.

Such public interest stories often appeared in the "Friends and Neighbors" section of the local paper. The neighbors also held a series of fundraising events, including a pancake and sausage breakfast at a neighborhood church. This event not only raised funds through people buying their breakfasts, but also brought in donations. A local builder offered to assign a crew of carpenters and plumbers for one day to help with the rebuilding. A large lumberyard in town donated lumber, nails, and sheetrock for walls and ceilings in the badly damaged structure. Finally, the neighbors picked a weekend to pitch in and put the finishing touches on the house. They had successfully raised $6,000, not including the value of donated materials and labor. The money purchased furniture to replace what was destroyed in the fire. The entire process from the night of the fire until Fortuitous was back in her home took exactly 39 days.

return. People who buy raffle tickets hope to win a red Ferrari 458 with leather cockpit and a top speed of 202 mph or even a free hamburger at McDonald's. Likewise, those who buy a ticket to a concert or church-sponsored chicken dinner are getting something concrete in return for their contribution. Others give from a sense of personal or civic obligation based on their own values. Some give because they devotedly believe in your cause, project, or activity. Still others contribute expecting recognition for their goodwill. In fact, most people probably give for a combination of reasons. You likely will be more successful in your fundraising efforts if you can provide potential donors with multiple reasons to support the cause or activity. Consider some of the different ways of raising money from individual donors, including benefits and direct solicitation.

Benefits

The pancake and sausage breakfast her neighbors used to raise funds to repair Fortuitous's home (see Highlight 14.5) is one example of a *benefit.* Benefits are activities and events held to raise money for a worthy cause. Examples include concerts, dinners, and sporting events. Musicians holding a concert and giving proceeds to charity is a benefit. Every year some sporting events (for example, professional football and baseball games) are held to benefit specific charities. Of course, benefits can be much more modest—say, a giant neighborhood garage sale with the funds going to pay for a neighbor's child's liver transplant.

There are several challenges in raising funds by holding benefits. First, a great deal of work is often required to plan and carry out a benefit. Look back at Fortuitous's situation and think of the things needed to get a pancake breakfast off the ground. Fortuitous's neighbors had to agree on a location and date. They had to acquire sufficient food (purchased or donated) to meet the anticipated need. (They didn't want to run out too early or to have too much left at the end.) Fortuitous's neighbors needed to ensure that cooking facilities for a large group as well as adequate supplies of plates, utensils, cups, and glasses were available. In addition, servers were needed to prepare and serve food and to clean up the breakfast's aftermath. Still other help was required to advertise the breakfast and prepare posters, tickets, and news releases. Planning and arranging all of this took time.

Whether a group gets items donated for a benefit or pays for them, the task is formidable. You also need people to sell tickets to the event. Tickets sold in advance are generally more profitable to a benefit than

those sold at the event itself, because many people buy tickets to events but don't plan to attend. Sometimes organizations and businesses buy blocks of tickets that they distribute to employees or customers. Again, not all those who receive tickets will necessarily attend. This actually works out quite well: If you don't have to make 500 pancakes but someone paid you for that many, you come out ahead. Therefore, benefit sponsors profit from unused tickets, because food is paid for but not actually consumed.

It is important to encourage media attention to your event by showcasing those who contributed their time and money to make it happen. This is also a way of saying thanks to those who helped and giving donor businesses free publicity. Additionally, you should announce the event to other community organizations and groups. Send notices to service clubs, such as Lions and Rotary clubs, and to groups such as Parents Without Partners.

Of course, benefits work best when people find the event attractive and want to come. You can do this in a variety of ways. Perhaps the cost-to-benefit ratio is quite good (that is, donors are getting a very good deal—all you can eat for $8 or a chance to meet a famous person for only $15). Perhaps this event is the place to be (because all the important people in town are likely to come). Maybe the benefit is attractive because participants really want to support the cause. Ideally, events should have several of the aforementioned characteristics. Held every year, benefits can become very successful. They can even develop into ongoing sources of funding.

Some churches and other organizations have adopted an interesting variation on the benefit: They solicit donations from their members or the public to avoid holding a benefit. Because the work involved in benefits and activities can be great, members are often enticed into contributing cash rather than having to work the event. There's always an angle if you really want to raise money.

Benefit Variations

Another variation on the benefit idea is joining forces with another organization, such as a business. Each year some businesses donate part of their proceeds or a day's receipts to a community charity. This charity or cause could be yours. Perhaps Shady Sam's Shine Shop could make a donation for every car washed. Each person who had a car washed last Saturday represented a donation of $4 to your organization. Such events and activities benefit both you and the business. Because of the extra publicity and goodwill, more people may patronize the business on that special day.

Finally, consider other variations on the benefit theme. Rather than hold specific events, such as breakfasts, fundraisers can sell a product or service—car washes, candy, Christmas cards, and cookie sales (remember the Girl Scouts!). Perhaps most people who make these purchases are parents or relatives of those selling the goodies, but that doesn't matter to those receiving the funds.

The primary limitation to benefits and other such activities is the relatively limited amount of money that can be raised. If your needs are small (under $10,000), these events can be quite useful. Unfortunately, they do not produce the tens of thousands of dollars needed each year to pay for major services. Except for annual events that evolve into major community activities, benefits don't usually provide substantial ongoing sources of money.

Direct Solicitation

Direct solicitation of gifts means asking others to contribute. Instead of selling raffle tickets, chicken dinners, or rock concerts, we say straight out, "We need your money." Of course, we can't do this without paying attention to some basics. It makes no sense to ask people to give more than they can afford. Individual requests for money must be based on the gift-giving potential of donors and their possible motivations (discussed previously) for giving to your cause. Assessing how much someone can give is not always easy. It helps if you know what this person has contributed to other activities. If you don't know, make an educated guess. Unless you are asking hundreds of people each to give $10, you might wish to focus on those individuals who are capable of larger gifts. Asking 200 people to give you $10 each could net you $2,000. Asking four people with sufficient incomes to give you $500 each seems like a simpler task. Of course, asking one person to give you the entire $2,000 is not out of the question. Many individuals regularly contribute this much and more.

Some gifts are reported publicly, so it is possible to anticipate a donor's potential contribution. People running political campaigns must identify donors and contribution amounts. This information is often published in the newspapers. Additionally, newspapers publish a wide range of other articles describing contributions for various causes. Recently, a paper credited a donor who gave $13,000 to build a new animal shelter. Another paper named an individual who contributed $20,000

to a campaign opposing the building of an urban entertainment park. Local universities publish lists of donors, often with the actual amounts or the general category of contributions. Other civic organizations, such as the theater or symphony, list major contributors in their programs for attendees. It is possible to cull these various lists to identify individuals who have the potential for larger donations. If your responsibilities routinely involve fundraising, you should develop your own personal list of possible donors and of the range of their contributions.

Once you have done your homework, you are ready to ask for the contribution. Make an appointment with the designated donor, carefully rehearse what you are going to say, show up on time, and make a pitch **EP 2.1.3c** that you have carefully developed. What you say depends upon what you and the donor have in common. Do you both have ideas about what is good for your community? If so, share this in your pitch or proposal. Are your opinions the same on political issues? Then include that fact. Are you both concerned about a particular problem that this donation can help resolve? Then emphasize that point. If you can identify any commonality with a donor, at the very least you can clearly articulate the value of your project and how the donor's contribution can help the cause (CSWE, 2008, EP 2.1.3c).

Some fundraisers recommend asking for a specific amount from a donor; others suggest the donor should make that determination. If you ask for too little, donors might think you didn't believe they had the potential to give much—a possible insult. If you ask for too much, you might flatter them by implying that they're wealthier than they are. In that case, they might give a bit more than they normally would to avoid looking stingy. The final decision about whether to ask for a specific amount is yours.

When the donor offers an amount, it is best to solicit the donation at once. Donations promised for later sometimes don't appear. If you can't get the money immediately, ask for a specific time you can return for it. Remember the old adage "A bird in the hand is worth two in the bush." It's still true.

Foundations—Seeking Group Giving

Every community is filled with dozens (sometimes hundreds) of groups, organizations, and associations with potential for contributing to any given cause. Every social or fraternal organization (Rotary, Elks,

Working with the media is an important skill for community organizers.

Kiwanis, Junior League) gives substantial amounts to their respective communities. They exist, at least ostensibly, for this very purpose. Thus, you will be missing a beat if you ignore these organizations.

Finding a list of these organizations is usually easy. Check the local library, the Yellow Pages, or the chamber of commerce for a list of all civic organizations. Normally, you will be given a list (often slightly out of date) that will include each organization's name along with that of its president or chairperson. If you don't know whether the organization supports your kind of project, try to talk with a member or even the president about your idea. Find out how other causes solicit gifts. Typically, you must provide a written request. Many organizations also expect a presentation. Perhaps you can get on one of the organization's agendas. Most such groups have a planned speaker or program at each meeting. This is a wonderful opportunity to get your ideas across to the membership and to drum up enthusiasm for your project.

The organization's board of directors or steering committee may make the actual decision about whether or not to make a donation. Thus, you should write a proposal describing the need and the amount you would like the organization to contribute. Sometimes it is best to ask for specific items, such as a computer and software package for a group home or playground equipment for a day care center. Perhaps you would like the group to underwrite the cost of sending a child to summer camp. Generally, such organizations will give to causes that are consistent with their own purposes and history. For example, Lions clubs are often very interested in issues dealing with vision and eyesight. The Kiwanis are interested in children.

Although financial contributions are always welcome, perhaps the organization can help you in some other way. Some organizations undertake projects that combine donations of money with donated efforts from their members. One women's organization donated money to buy furniture and draperies for a group home, and then contributed members' time to paint and decorate the home. A Kiwanis club contributed both money and labor to build a park shelter. Both kinds of help—money and volunteer effort—are welcome.

Membership Dues—Creating Your Own Organization

Another way to raise funds is to ask people to join an organization and pay dues. The membership dues are then available for various projects. Civic organizations often raise funds for their own projects in this way. Belonging to a group and paying dues helps raise one's sense of commitment to the organization. Many of us belong to organizations whose purposes we support to varying degrees. One individual might belong to a civic club, a church group, a parent–teacher association, two or more professional associations, a neighborhood association, and a recreational organization. Of these, the neighborhood association was started specifically to help generate funds for improving the neighborhood.

Each of these organizations collects membership dues and uses them for various purposes. Some organizations, in turn, donate the money to other worthy causes. Others use the funds purely to operate their organization. If you think about the membership organizations you know of (or belong to), you can get an idea of the potential money these groups can raise.

Of course, the decision to start a membership group must be well thought out. The reason for starting a membership group should be clear. It is sometimes easier to ask people to join a group than to contribute money. By joining, they get something in return for their money. Belonging to a group is a way for a person to feel connected. Many social work students join student organizations for this very purpose.

Potential members include everyone with the slightest interest in the group's purpose. If dues are low enough, as Homan (2008) recommends, it is easy to ask people to join. Develop a membership application that is short and easy to complete. Typical information on the application should include name, address, e-mail address, and telephone numbers for home and work. You may decide to request other information, such as name of employer or of other organizations to which the prospective member belongs. Whenever you come across people with an interest in your cause, invite them to join. Subsequently, provide members with benefits. These include membership cards and periodic newsletters that inform members about the organization and issues of concern to them. Most organizations also make regular (at least annual) requests for additional contributions to support special projects.

One well-known way of raising money is to sell a product or a service. The annual Girl Scout cookie sale is a particularly successful example of this fundraising method.

One benefit of membership as a source of revenue is that dues are generally free of the restrictions associated with other kinds of donations. Because the total amount of dues you can collect depends upon the membership, the size of the member pool becomes important. Membership dues provide continuous funds (although usually not nearly the amount available from other sources, such as grants and contracts).

Other Fundraising Techniques

You can raise money in various other ways besides those previously described. Homan (2008) points out that telephone and mail solicitations are sometimes used to raise money. Both methods work best if you target individuals with proven track records of supporting your cause or causes similar to yours. Cold calls, in which you simply dial a number and hope for a favorable response, are very unproductive in terms of dollars generated. Although they can eventually result in a list of potential contributors, much money and time must be spent on the effort. If your organization happens to be famous or everyone automatically knows why you are calling, the task is easier. When Girl Scouts go door-to-door selling cookies, they are essentially making cold calls, but this is rarely a problem. Almost everybody knows why they are there, knows about the product they get in return for their "donation," and feels good about contributing.

Whether you are using the phone or the mail to raise money, develop your plan very clearly. Your approach should indicate who you are, why you're calling (or writing), and why the targeted donor should support your organization. If you are phoning, do so from a location where you won't be disturbed. Often, it helps to have multiple phones available and have several people calling at once. This can even be fun (you might serve pizza during the session to make it a social event for participants). You can also send a mail solicitation and follow up with a phone call. This alerts people to your cause and gives them time to think about it before they pledge an actual donation.

If you are telephoning your solicitation, rehearse what you will say and perhaps write out your "spiel" in advance. Role-play some typical responses you might encounter. And, as the Boy Scouts say, "Be prepared."

Raising money using the mail alone often expends much effort for very little money. Preparing envelopes and stuffing and stamping them can be boring tasks. One alternative is to make the mailing activity festive by having food or music so that people can chat and relax while they are working. Another alternative is to hire people to do such tedious tasks for you. However, given that we assume you don't have much money to start with, we suggest you use volunteer help whenever possible.

No matter what method you use, keep focused on a professionally produced product. Your mailed materials should be of good quality and present a very positive image of you and your cause. Proofread everything and then have someone else do it again.

EP 2.1.3c

For example, a campus women's programming committee chaired by a social work professor once undertook a fundraiser to enhance opportunities for student education about date rape. The idea was to solicit funds to bring in outside speakers who were experts on the subject. A graduate student (in counseling and guidance) and member of the women's programming committee assumed leadership of the project. This student developed a mailing that described the fundraiser and solicited donations. She subsequently sent it to almost every student, faculty member, staff member, and administrator on campus. So far, all of this sounds good. However, the graduate student spearheading the event spelled the word "assault" as "asault" on the flier *nine times.* Worse yet, the student sent the flier out on university letterhead. Needless to say, the social work professor chairing the committee that sponsored the fundraiser received calls from the chancellor, the vice chancellor, almost all division heads, and, it seemed, every other administrator on campus, all complaining about the flier and how ignorant and foolish it made the entire university look. The social work professor was mortified. She would never again allow anything to do with her to be circulated unless she had carefully scrutinized, proofread, and edited it (CSWE, 2008, EP 2.1.3c). Additionally, she never again assumed that graduate students could spell. The sad thing is that the student had volunteered her time and effort. She had only the best of intentions, but a simple mistake ruined the entire project.

Grants and Contracts

Social work programs are almost always in need of additional resources, and macro change efforts often require funds not already in any agency budget. Geri's agency (the domestic violence shelter mentioned in Chapter 7) had no money to renovate its building. It also received no support from other agencies for the services it provided to survivors of domestic violence. Each of these problems was resolved, one as a result of a state grant and the other through a contract with a public human services agency.

Most social workers will deal with grants and contracts at some time in their work experience. Indeed, many of you are already familiar with grants. Pell Grants and other grants are often part of the financial aid package provided to students attending colleges and universities. According to Barker (2003), a grant is "a transfer of funds or assets from one government, organization, or individual to another for fulfilling some broadly specified function or purpose" (p. 183). Contracts are agreements between two organizations or bodies that specify that one will provide certain services in exchange for payments from the other. In other words, one organization is buying the services of another.

In social work parlance, grants and contracts are nothing more than the moving of resources from one entity to another. Typically, grants and contracts are given for specific purposes, such as providing services to a certain target group. A family service organization might receive a grant from the United Way, a local fundraising body, to provide special services for survivors of sexual abuse. A contract agreement might be arranged between the county Department of Social Services and a private inpatient drug treatment program, whereby the county agency agrees to pay the other program a set amount for each client served.

Grants may fund a new service in total, or they may be combined with other funds (other grants, contracts, fees for service, and tax revenues). They may provide funds to operate a single program or a series of programs. The granting agency or organization provides the grant because it believes in and supports the cause or purpose for which funds are sought.

Normally, the agency seeking a grant or contract prepares a written proposal for the organization that has the money to give. That proposal describes what the agency will do with the money if the grant or contract is approved. The funding body reviews the proposal and may (1) accept the proposal and fully fund it, (2) accept the proposal and partially fund it, (3) request that the proposal be modified in some way, or (4) reject the proposal. Because the funding organization is under no obligation to give anyone the money in the first place, it often has the right to reject an application without explanation. Frequently, however, granting agencies offer information about why a proposal was not funded. They may also suggest changes in the

proposal that would increase the likelihood of future funding.

The rest of this chapter covers various sources of grants and contracts, describes the contract and grant application process, and provides tips on writing good proposals.

Finding Out about Grants and Contracts: Where Are They?

Several major sources of grants and contracts exist in the United States. One source is government agencies at the federal, state, and local levels. Various divisions of the federal Department of Health and Human Services provide grants to fund experiments with promising new approaches to solving specific human problems. They might provide money to a program seeking to prevent drug abuse among rural adolescents. Geri's agency received a state grant to rehabilitate its new building.

A second major source of grants includes foundations, which are private organizations set up explicitly for gift giving. Generally, the money given by the foundation comes from a business or commercial activity. The Ford Foundation is one example.

The third major source of funds is businesses and corporations. Rather than funneling the money through a foundation, a corporation will provide the grant or contract directly. Annually, grants and contracts from each of these sources total billions of dollars. Each granting or contracting source has specific advantages and disadvantages for those receiving funds. Government grants and contracts are often restrictive in nature, limiting funding to only those purposes approved by the particular legislative body (Congress or a state legislature). This might mean, for example, that money can only be spent on drug treatment services for people who fall below the poverty line. Private foundations and corporate sources are often more flexible in what and when they may fund. Consequently, they might be more willing to support creative new programs or to respond quickly to a funding request. Private foundations and corporate sources may more readily give money to an untested, but promising, program aimed at stopping gang violence in urban neighborhoods.

Gathering information on sources of grants and contracts is not difficult. Public and university libraries usually have material on granting sources. Libraries typically have reference books, such as the *Foundation*

Directory, that describe private foundations. The directory contains information about each foundation, including the type of programs or purposes for which it provides support. The directory is available online for a fee (fdncenter.org). The *Annual Register of Grant Support* is another source that is updated annually. It is more comprehensive because it lists not only foundation grants but also those provided by governmental and business organizations.

These resources typically provide enough information about the granting agency to allow the reader to decide whether a specific grantor is an appropriate organization to approach for funding. They usually indicate deadlines for submitting proposals and provide mailing addresses.

It is very important to accurately establish the granting agency's title and address before sending in an application. A faculty colleague who was not renowned for her attention to detail once applied for a research grant, but she somehow lost the accurate title and address of the granting agency. She wrote up a grant proposal anyway and, believing that she remembered part of the agency's title, she combined the words she thought she remembered and sent the proposal. She could not remember the agency's exact address either, but she thought she remembered part of it. She addressed the package, combining the parts of the address she thought would direct her proposal to the Washington, DC, governmental department she thought was funding the grant. Worse yet, she rushed to make the posting deadline and missed it by three days. She was so late she had "no time" to make a copy of the material. So she sent the only copy of the proposal to someone she wasn't sure of to a place she wasn't sure of. Needless to say, she neither received the grant nor heard from the intended agency.

The lessons from this example are threefold: First, verify the name and address of the agency. Second, make a copy of the document for your own records. You never know when a document requiring dozens of hours of labor will get lost in the Twilight Zone. Third, meet the deadline specified in the agency's announcement of grant availability. Getting a proposal in late can be the same as not sending it at all.

EP 2.1.3a

Other resources available in the library are publications such as the *Chronicle of Higher Education, Foundation News, The Foundation Directory, Foundation Grants to Individuals, National Directory of Corporate Giving,* and the *Foundation Center Information Quarterly.*

These publications include information on sources of grants, describe recent grant recipients, and generally give current information about grant giving in the United States (CSWE, 2008, EP 2.1.3a).

Other possible sources of information about granting agencies include research and grant offices operated by universities and large nonprofit organizations such as the NASW. In addition, there are subscription services (providing periodic reports on specific types of grants) and workshops on grants. Both colleges and private agencies may offer grant-writing workshops that help the novice grant writer put together a convincing proposal.

The Internet is also a potential source of information about possible grants. Sites include the *Chronicle of Philanthropy* (www.philanthropy.com), the Foundation Center (http://fdncenter.org), the Grantsmanship Center (www.tgci.com), and the *Catalog of Federal Domestic Assistance* (www.cfda.gov). Other sources include a monthly newsletter, *The Internet Prospector* (www.internet-prospector.org), the *Council on Foundations* (www.cof.org), and *Independent Sector* (www.independentsector.org). Each site contains information to help you find potential funding sources. These sites may lead you to the Web pages of the funding agencies themselves. Some of these sites will even have the application forms available online. A handy resource for the inexperienced grant writer is the Charity Channel (www.charitychannel.com/), which provides a wealth of information about grant writing, helpful articles, and classes.

Finally, you can learn of grant opportunities by talking to other social workers about their respective experiences and ideas. Often, talking with successful grant writers offers insight into both potential sources of grants and tips for writing better proposals. The goal in this process of reviewing possible funding sources is to eliminate those unlikely to fund your proposal and to focus your efforts on the likely ones. In addition, discussions with experienced grant writers at a college or university may lead to a collaborative grant. Such a grant would involve both your agency and the academic institution, combining the expertise of social work faculty with that of agency personnel. A grant might be available to help reduce substance abuse among homeless adolescents. Your agency might be interested in receiving a grant to help homeless adolescents in your community. The university social work faculty might help with the grant and take responsibility for evaluating the success of your proposed program.

Government Grants

Certainly the largest source of grant funds in the United States is the federal government. Federal programs are listed in the *Federal Register* and the *Catalog of Federal Domestic Assistance.* State programs are often announced in the *State Contract Register.* Such sources describe hundreds of programs covering such divergent areas as space and energy or health and education. Granting agencies include the National Institute for Mental Health, the National Institute on Aging, and many other federal units of various sizes.

Typically, these agencies announce the availability of grants and send out requests for proposals (RFPs) These RFPs describe the type of program that the agency expects to fund and the dollar amount available. They contain the deadline for submission and other information useful to the prospective grant writer. Many RFPs ask you to send for a grant application packet, which is to be completed and returned. Again, it is important to read the RFP carefully. Everything you need to know about the grant is likely to be in there.

Sometimes a government grantor will hold a meeting, called a *bidder's conference,* where grantors provide more information to interested parties. These conferences help you understand the grantor's needs and, in turn, allow grantors to learn about you and others who are applying for grants. Highlight 14.6 discusses one government grant application.

Foundation Grants

Foundations range in size from those with assets in the billions of dollars to those with extremely modest endowments of less than one million dollars. Although some foundations carry famous names (e.g., Rockefeller, Ford, Carnegie, and Kellogg), many are named for individuals or families with only local reputations. All foundations are governed by boards of directors that often decide which grant applications to fund. Larger foundations usually have professional staff members, whereas many smaller ones operate very informally. In the latter foundations, a single staff member may have responsibility for reviewing the grant, deciding whether to fund the request, and determining the amount of money to be provided. An example of one small foundation with which the author is familiar was established by a local family to help address various community

HIGHLIGHT 14.6

My First Grant

On my first day on the job with a county human services agency, the deputy director dropped a folder on my desk and said she wanted me to finish writing a grant that had been started by my predecessor in the job. Not wishing to appear completely ignorant I stifled my initial inclination to say, "What's a grant?" Looking through the folder, I quickly discovered the grant proposal was designed to solicit money from a state criminal justice agency. The purpose of the grant was to create a group home for delinquent boys. Well, at least now I knew what the deputy director wanted me to do and why.

I quickly saw why my predecessor had not completed the grant application. Under the section on "Need for the Grant" he had provided three case examples designed to illustrate the type of kids for whom the group home would be designed. These examples were certainly interesting, but would not offer a compelling argument for a public granting agency. The application was long on stories but very short on specifics. There was, for example, no indication of how many adolescent males might need this type of facility. The number of "beds" in the facility had

never been considered. Nor was there any comparison of costs to show that this proposal would reduce costs to the county by allowing youths to be treated and reside in their home community.

After I looked through the forms and information provided by the granting agency, I had a much better sense of what needed to be done. In about a week, I had the proposal in draft form for review by agency administrators. A modified copy was provided to the county social services board (a body that oversaw operations of the human services agency), which agreed to continue funding the group home after the grant ran out providing that the project proved successful.

Three weeks later, I explained and advocated for the proposal before the regional criminal justice board, which subsequently approved sending it through to the state board. Within the month the state board approved the proposal, and we were able to open our group home. My success with this project would later give me the confidence to prepare other grant proposals. Unfortunately, I could never again claim a 100 percent success rate for my grant applications.

needs. They provide small amounts for worthy causes, for example, an annual dinner honoring foster parents for working with neglected and abused children.

Most foundations have identified specific areas where they concentrate their grant giving. They may focus on grants for social service activities, for community betterment, or for beautification. Other foundations give only to specific geographical locations such as certain cities, counties, or states. Some will fund capital improvements (buildings); others will not. Finally, some will provide money for beginning programs, but not for continuing them.

Getting accurate information about foundations is not particularly easy. Unlike government grants, for which information may be available in libraries and through public announcements, many foundations do not advertise their existence or suggest what types of grants are available. They typically do not issue RFPs. The Foundation Center is a most helpful source of information about private foundations. The center maintains offices in New York and Washington, DC, under its own name, and in Chicago, where it is called Donors' Forum. Many states also maintain reference centers where information about foundation grants is readily available. Usually, there is no charge for using the reference center, although customized computer searches for information may carry a fee.

Fortunately, assistance in locating information about foundations is available. The *Foundation Directory,* often available in public libraries, lists the largest foundations to help readers locate appropriate grantors. Unfortunately, this resource does not provide information on smaller foundations. Sometimes foundation resource books are available for specific states (such as California, Maine, or Michigan). These listings contain information on each foundation, including its purpose and its grant-giving record for the previous year. Most listings show restrictions foundations have placed on their giving and the grants they have available.

For those whose activities include frequent grant writing, several organizations provide periodic listings of granting agencies. To receive such listings, you must pay for a subscription, so these are normally useful only for larger organizations that can afford the cost. They are typically expensive and cover only the largest foundations. Examples include the Foundation Research Service and the Taft Information System.

It is best to check with a foundation to see if it is willing to accept unsolicited proposals. Unsolicited proposals are ones in which the foundation has not previously indicated an interest. The grant writer has simply put forward an idea and asked the foundation to consider it. Sending a letter showing the intent of your proposal before preparing the full document is also wise. This makes sense because you don't want to put a great deal of work into a proposal that simply does not fit the granting organization's interests. Larger foundations with a sufficient staff may discuss your ideas with you to help you learn whether your proposal is fundable. Most smaller foundations have no such staff, making it very difficult to get significant amounts of information from them.

Business and Corporate Grants

Many large businesses have established charitable arms or divisions (often called foundations) to dispense funds for various purposes. Usually these granting bodies give money to nonprofit agencies or organizations. *Nonprofit organizations* are those that do not intend to produce revenue over their costs of operation (the Child Welfare League of America and the NASW are both nonprofit organizations). Grantors typically evaluate both the proposal and the organization to ensure that the money will be used as intended. Corporate foundations usually specify the purposes for which they will donate funds. Typically, it is possible to discuss an idea with the corporate foundation representative before submitting an application. We recommend this step whenever possible. To get initial information, you might turn to the community relations departments of corporations in your communities to learn whether they have grants available. Building relationships by meeting and talking with the staff of these departments and other employees in these corporations is a recommended method for strengthening your proposal.

Many business foundations exist to support research in areas that indirectly benefit the corporation. Still others fund areas not at all related to the needs of the particular company. Unlike other sources of grants, there are no universally helpful resources identifying the purposes and grant-making history of corporate foundations. This information is best gleaned from talking with others who have successful track records in obtaining corporate grants. Corporations may find proposals that cast them in a favorable light very attractive, especially when the proposals' intent merges with a corporate image or interest. A corporation that sells medical equipment used for older adult patients may be very interested in a proposal for serving seniors through a new adult day care center named after the company.

Unlike most government granting agencies, private foundations and corporations may make a site visit to your agency. They will talk with the staff, examine your physical facility, and study your programs. Although this step may seem bothersome, it is wise to recognize that many of these organizations do not require a lengthy proposal. On-site visitation replaces endless writing. Fewer than 10 pages may be required, compared with a government grant proposal, which may run to dozens of pages.

How to Apply for a Grant

Getting grants is neither mysterious nor particularly difficult. Being successful requires the same kind of preparation and care you would give to other important projects. The project can be divided into three steps—the pre-application phase, the application phase, and the post-application phase (see Figure 14.4). Figure 14.5 lists potential grant information sources.

PRE-APPLICATION PHASE

- Identify potential grant sources.
- Contact potential sources.

APPLICATION PHASE

- Develop draft proposal.
- Consult with potential grantor.

POST-APPLICATION PHASE

- Review grant proposal.
- Revise grant if requested.
- Plan for ending of grant.

FIGURE 14.4 Steps in Applying for a Grant

Not-for-profit fund-raising and grant writing
mapnp.nonprofitoffice.com

Federal Register grant opportunities
fr.cos.com

Edutopia
www.edutopia.org/grantinfo

FIGURE 14.5 Potential Grant Information Sources

Pre-Application Phase

In the first stage, you must identify potential grant sources. The resources described previously should help you in this part of the project. Your list of potential sources should focus on those that sponsor activities like yours. Exclude those that have shown no interest in your particular field, do not grant funds for projects in your locale, or have other unacceptable limitations.

In this stage, you will also make preliminary contacts with likely grantors to identify deadlines and discuss their organization's interest in proposals such as yours. You probably should write to grantors for further information about their goals and purposes. When you have received the necessary information, the first rule is to read everything with great care. For example, there may be length or budget limits to the application that, if not observed, will doom your proposal to the circular file.

Application Phase

Next, develop a draft of the proposed grant. This should describe what you intend to do, why it is worthy of funding, and the approximate cost of the project. Your draft should state who will do what and what goals or objectives are to be achieved. Don't forget to include the project director's or applicant's résumé.

Generally speaking, most granting agencies don't give funds to individuals. Thus, any proposal is more likely to be funded if an organization rather than an individual applies. This means that you should fully discuss any plans to apply for a grant with your administration and board of directors, assuming that your organization will receive the funds. Topics that must be decided include who will administer the grant, what facilities or staff will be required to carry out the purposes of the grant, and what services the organization must provide (e.g., clerical, janitorial, or equipment). What expenses or costs will the organization incur? Are there any special precautions that must be taken to protect human subjects or keep project records safe for an extended period? Highlight 14.7 describes these items in more detail.

It should be noted that your grant application may well require approval by, and a signature from, your agency's board of directors or administration. Many grantors want this to ensure that the proposal is fully supported by your organization. Grantors typically expect that your application will include data justifying

HIGHLIGHT 14.7

Critical Topics Regarding Grant Applications

Who will administer the grant?
Someone in the agency will need to take overall
responsibility for ensuring that deadlines are met,
goals are achieved, and financial records are maintained. Previous experience in administering grants
is helpful.

What facilities or staff will be required?
Decide what staff and space will be needed to
achieve the purpose of the grant. Identify specifically the individuals and physical areas to be used.
If people will be hired to carry out the project,
identify the qualifications of those individuals.

What services must the organization provide?
Decide what clerical support, bookkeeping, and related services your organization will provide. Both
the types of activities and the costs of providing
them are important. If your organization will contribute equipment, computer analysis of data, or
other items or services, these should be described.

What expenses or costs will the organization incur?
Identify the nongrant money to be spent by your
agency to carry out the grant. Describe any other
expenses for personnel, equipment and/or services
that the agency will pay for.

*What precautions are needed for recordkeeping or
protecting human subjects?*
In some situations involving sensitive information
about clients, the records must be kept under lock
and key. Sometimes a granting agency will require
that records be kept for a specific period of time,
such as 5 or 10 years. In addition, you must describe any special precautions needed to protect
clients served by the grant from possible harm. This
is not a major concern in most grants to provide
human services, because clients are not exposed to
experimental methods that may endanger their
lives or health. However, clients should be informed
about any possible risk.

the need for this grant, including, in some cases, letters
of support from others in the community. These letters
of support may reaffirm the need for the grant or
pledge cooperation with your agency if it receives the
grant. Each grant source has its own set of requirements, which may range from very specific to quite
general. One common expectation, however, is that
your application will include provisions for an impact
evaluation demonstrating how the quality of life improved as a result of your grant-supported project.

Spending the necessary time at this stage to "work
the bugs out" will bring greater benefits once the grant
is received. You do not want to be in the position of
receiving a grant and then having to spend weeks figuring out who will do what. This sort of catch-up planning after receipt of a grant often means your program
can't be carried out as quickly as possible. This delay
often comes at the expense of clients who should be
receiving services.

Writing a Grant Proposal

Before writing a grant proposal, consider the different
kinds of proposals you could write and what goes into
a good grant proposal. The following items must be
addressed in most, if not all, grants.

Description of a grant proposal. Any successful grant
proposal will start with the most important ingredient:
a good idea. Ultimately, it is the soundness of your idea
that influences granting agencies to fund a particular
proposal.

Talking with a granting agency representative before
submission of a proposal can strengthen your proposal.
Applications received early might allow feedback from
the grantor agency's staff requesting modification before final submission. Funding bodies tend to be more
supportive of proposals that are innovative, yet have
strong potential for success. They also support fiscally
sound proposals. The extent to which an agency is perceived as hardworking and dedicated can also be an
asset.

Many, but not all, granting agencies have a specific
format for applicants to follow. Be sure to follow the
application instructions carefully. There may be required forms, especially budget forms.

Whatever the format, however, a good proposal has
certain characteristics:

1. *The proposed activity must relate to the interests or
   purposes of the funding agency.* For example, a proposal to provide services to help women escape
   prostitution should not be sent to a foundation

interested in funding medical research. It makes no sense (and wastes everybody's time) to prepare proposals that do not meet the funding body's objectives.

2. *The proposed activity will, in some way, promote a desirable end.* The proposal might allow service to a previously unserved population or test a new method of preventing recidivism among delinquents. Perhaps it promises to develop a more efficient system of linking the services provided by multiple agencies. In short, the idea itself should sound promising.

3. It shows that *the proposer knows the territory.* That is, the applicant is already familiar with the literature in this field and knows what has previously been tried and found effective. Grant proposals incorporating approaches that previous research have proven ineffective are likely to meet with failure.

4. *The people carrying out the project are competent to do so.* They have experience in this area and the credentials to achieve the proposal's objectives. Résumés detailing this information should be included with the project application.

5. *The expected results justify the costs involved.* Grant applications involve both time and money. The granting agency must be convinced that the outcomes are sufficiently important to warrant expending the necessary time and money.

EP 2.1.3c

The length of a good proposal varies tremendously. Some grant applications are only a few pages long; others may run to hundreds of pages. A lengthy proposal is not necessarily a good one. You must convince the application's reviewers that you have a good idea. A clear explanation of your idea is much more important than the length of your proposal (CSWE, 2008, EP 2.1.3c).

Problems with proposals. Rejection of a proposal can occur for a variety of reasons (Gordon, 1997; Hohmann, n.d.; Rhein, 1996; Sheafor & Horejsi, 2006). These include the following:

1. *The proposal was poorly written.* Proposals with misspellings, grammar errors, or typos are likely to be rejected. If it looks as if you did not put effort into doing a good job now, granting agencies may not believe you will carry out the grant project, either.

2. *The competence of those who would carry out the proposal was not clearly documented.* A track record or other evidence that you can do what you propose is important. Granting agencies don't like to think they're giving the money to people who can't do the job.

3. *Inadequate planning was evident in the application.* A proposal that does not include critical information or leaves out important activities (such as evaluation) is less likely to be funded.

4. *The application itself was not carefully prepared.* Missing deadlines or not addressing parts of the application required by the grantor indicates you did not prepare the application with diligence.

5. *The proposal was good but needed revisions, and there was insufficient time to modify it.* Grant applications often seem to be done at the last minute. If you have a good idea but not enough time to revise your proposal to meet the grantor's wishes, you may find your proposal rejected.

6. *The problem being addressed is not significant.* A problem may not be significant from at least two perspectives. First, the problem may be of no interest to the granting agency because it falls outside the area for which it usually provides grants. A problem may also be insignificant because it proposes to help a very limited number of people or because the problem upon which it is focused is relatively unimportant. Asking for $175,000 to help six people overcome their fear of bats would likely be a loser on two counts: Too few people are being helped, and being afraid of bats is rather trivial compared with the needs of homeless populations, crack babies, and AIDS victims.

7. *The proposal does not make clear how funds will be used.* Unclear details about how you intend to spend the grantor's money is a serious problem. You should indicate clearly what the money will be used for, such as hiring staff, renting office space, or providing transportation for clients.

8. *The means proposed for dealing with a problem don't make sense.* The grantor expects that the solution you propose is logical and related to the problem at hand. Offering family therapy to homeless people may not be seriously considered in light of the more pressing needs of this population.

9. *Objectives cannot be adequately assessed.* Objectives that are not measurable or are too vague are likely to cause the grantor to turn down your proposal. A proposal to offer services to the homeless without specifying what those services will be, how many people will be helped, and in what time frame the help will be delivered is not likely to be viewed favorably.

10. *The grant seeker has no past record of dealing with the proposed problem.* Granting agencies must have

faith that you can do what you propose to do. If you don't seem to have experience with the services you propose to offer or the problem you seek to solve, the proposal is not likely to be successful.

11. *Human subject concerns have not been addressed.* Grantors want to know that you have the approval of your agency's human subjects review board before you undertake a new program. If your proposal potentially places people at risk of any kind, you should seek approval before asking the granting agency for money. Such approval guarantees to the grantor that any risks to people have been anticipated and minimized.

12. *The budget was unrealistic.* The amount requested may have been out of proportion to the size of grants the funder provides. Also, it may have been considered too small or too large for the problem the proposal hoped to address. The funder may have recognized that the money you asked for was unreasonably large without adequate explanation for the amount requested. Alternately, a request for a small amount might be judged insufficient given your description of the problem.

It is easy to become discouraged when a grant proposal is rejected, but there are steps you can take to learn from this experience. First, contact the agency or organization that rejected your proposal and ask if a representative would be willing to meet with you to discuss how you can improve your proposal. If the agency is willing to do so, use the opportunity either to resubmit the revised proposal to the same agency or to another funder. Second, ask if you could see the reviewers' comments on your proposal. Some funders will allow this while others will not—either way, it does not hurt to ask. Third, reapply. Many funders reject proposals the first time they are received and welcome reapplications since it tends to show determination on your part. Depending upon the funding agency, it may accept a new proposal only once per year or more frequently. Take advantage of the opportunity to build a relationship with the funder. Show your appreciation regardless of outcome by sending a thank-you letter to the organization.

If the proposal was to a federal agency, it may be possible to contact your legislator to help you get information. Since these types of funders are required to meet certain standards, you may have a shot at meeting some special criteria. For example, if your proposal would fund services in a rural area and the grant went to services in an urban area, you could argue that the granting agency did not take into account the importance of serving a rural population. At the least, your legislator may be able to learn more about why your proposal was turned down, and this can be helpful as you work to improve it for the next submission.

Kinds of Grants and Contract Proposals

Grant and contract proposals frequently fall into several categories. They include the following:

1. *Program proposals* are designed to provide a particular service to a particular size of system—individual, family, group, organization, or community. A shelter for battered women applied for and received a grant to open a transition facility for women who were moving out of abusive relationships. The facility, a multi-unit apartment building, was designed to provide low-cost housing for shelter residents needing a place of their own. The transition facility represented an extension of services already provided by the domestic abuse shelter.

2. *Research proposals* typically involve studying a particular problem or testing a specific intervention approach. They can be used to evaluate new programs or approaches. They can also be used to gather information leading to new programs or services. A proposal might be developed to study the needs of homeless children or adolescents. The findings could then suggest appropriate services to offer these groups.

3. *Training proposals,* as the name implies, are requests for funds to train or educate a specific group. This might be agency staff, volunteers, laypersons, or others. A training grant could be written to provide workshops on a new juvenile code for county agencies that must administer the new law. Training funds could also be used to educate staff on how to work more effectively with AIDS patients or other clients.

4. *Planning proposals* are designed to allow an organization or agency to plan for a new program. Planning proposals are often the first step to setting up a program. Thus, you might request funds to begin planning a new juvenile shelter facility and later apply for funds to operate the shelter during its first year.

5. *Technical assistance proposals* provide for specialized help, allowing organizations or individuals to carry out a program. You might apply for a technical assistance grant to hire experts who would design a program to rehabilitate a block of historic buildings into low-income apartments. Usually, such funds are used to hire people with special

skills who would not normally be available to the agency or organization.

6. *Contract for services* is simply an agreement between two agencies or organizations for one to provide services to be paid for by the other. Public agencies often engage in contracting for services instead of providing services themselves. Sometimes this is called *privatization of services.* The services may be required by law, so they must be provided. However, the agency may find that it can purchase services from another organization for less than it would cost the agency itself to provide the service. *Contracts for service* generally involve an agreement to provide designated services in exchange for a specified dollar amount. Sometimes these proposals call for a per-person charge, such as $3,000 for each person served by an agency. A public agency might pay another agency to provide outpatient treatment for substance abuse. At other times, an agency agrees to provide services for anyone who wants them. A shelter for battered women might agree to take any women needing its services without limiting the number of clients it would accept per night or per year.

Parts of a Grant Proposal

Applications include the following specific sections: cover page, table of contents, abstract or summary, narrative section, budget section, staff credentials, certifications of compliance, cost-sharing description, and agency or institutional endorsements. In shorter applications, some of these items are combined.

Cover page. A cover page or letter should accompany the proposal. Often the granting agency provides such a sheet, possibly requiring specific signatures. The cover page should include information about the agency and persons who are applying for the grant (names, addresses, e-mail addresses, and phone numbers). It should detail the subject of the proposal ("A group home for delinquents"). The document should state the starting and ending times for the project and the amount of money requested. Finally, the date of application should be included. Highlight 14.8 shows a sample cover page.

HIGHLIGHT 14.8

Example of a Cover Page

Application for Training Grant

Grantor:	Waterman Foundation 1234 Left Bank Road West Pavilion, Georgia 33333
Applicant:	Waterworld Family Planning, Inc. 2372 S. Suprema Boulevard Springfield, Missouri 65807
Principal Investigator:	Mary Hadalamb, ACSW 417-883-5060
Subject:	Training of social workers to provide family planning information and service to low-income clients living in Waterworld County.
Dates:	July 1, 2009–June 30, 2010
Amount:	$95,005

_____
Signature of Principal Investigator   Date

_____
Signature of Agency Director   Date

Table of contents. The table of contents will be a separate page identifying each distinct section of the proposal. It should include page numbers so that readers can locate information quickly.

Abstract or summary. A 200- to 300-word summary makes it easier for the reader to get a quick overview of your proposal. Complete this portion only after the rest of the document has been finished so that it captures exactly what the full proposal says. Abstracts include a short narrative highlighting the objectives, methods, results, and value of the proposal. Write the abstract carefully, because some agencies may use this portion alone for evaluating your proposal. Highlight 14.9 shows an example of a summary.

Narrative section. Next, include a narrative section describing the problem and what you will do about it. Provide more detail in this section. If the agency specifies a length limitation for the narrative section, follow these instructions. Topics to be addressed include a statement of the problem, goals and objectives to be achieved, methods to be employed, and evaluation. Provide separate headings for each of these sections.

1. *Statement of the problem.* This should not only summarize the issue being addressed, but also identify causative factors and past efforts to solve the identified difficulty. This shows the grantor that you understand the problem and are aware of prior attempts to alleviate the situation.

   Include appropriate data and documentation on the problem area. Provide specific statistics on the number of people affected by the problem or the number of communities dealing with the difficulty. Describe the age, gender, or other demographic information about the proposal's beneficiaries that may be useful in clarifying the problem. Provide citations and references for your data. Sources of data have been addressed in previous chapters. It is important that your data presentation show a thorough understanding of the problem. Beyond

HIGHLIGHT 14.9

Example of a Summary or Abstract

Summary

The devastating effects of Alzheimer's disease and related disorders (ARD) on the victim and caregiver are now part of the public consciousness. The burden of caring for a loved one who has ARD can be awesome. The number of support groups for caregivers has continued to expand around the country, along with the rise in number of people with the disease. Support groups are essential for the physical and mental health of caregivers; however, support groups are not enough. As noted by the Alzheimer's Disease and Related Disorders Association, the most-needed service to enhance the quality of life of ARD victims and their caregivers and prevent early nursing-home placement is available, low-cost, effective respite care.

As pressing as the need for respite care is in urban areas, the need for respite care in rural areas is desperate. Every aspect of the health care system in rural areas is in short supply: physicians, home care, homemaking services. Add to this the reality of the long distances that must be traveled for the most basic necessities and the isolation of people with ARD, and you can begin to appreciate their caregivers.

The purpose of this project is to enhance the quality of life for people with ARD and their caregivers living in the rural areas of southwest Missouri. In order to accomplish this goal, a partnership will be established between the local area agency on aging, the Alzheimer's Association, and the regional university to provide scheduled, low-cost effective respite care.

Specifically, this project will employ existing but underutilized senior centers in six rural southwest Missouri communities as sites for respite care for people with ARD. Under the general direction of a social worker, an LPN, and an activity director at each location, respite care will be provided to approximately 10 people a day, three days a week at each center—a total of 37,440 hours of respite care hours per year. This will be an extraordinary addition to the service base in the rural areas of the state.

Caregivers will be able to reserve a time each week for their family members. The centers will offer these services in conjunction with existing community resources such as churches, schools, and other health care systems.

In short, this respite care program for people with ARD and their caregivers in rural areas will fill a gap in service. In so doing, it will reduce the tremendous burden of this terribly debilitating condition for all family members.

hard data such as statistics, it is also permissible to include qualitative information, such as opinions of community leaders and case examples to illustrate typical problems. You might also provide a description of current services addressing the problem. You should indicate who is providing what services with what results.

Highlight 14.10 below displays an example of the statement of the problem in a successful grant. The problem statement describes the number of individuals affected by the problem (e.g., Alzheimer's disease) and the location (e.g., rural areas of the state). It also describes the general purpose of the project.

2. *Goals and objectives.* These are the end products of your grant project. They should be worth pursuing and should be limited in number and scope. Objectives that seem of little importance to the granting agency will probably eliminate your proposal from consideration. At the same time, trying to do too much or failing to establish measurable goals are equally bad. Goals are generally stated broadly and cannot be directly measured. Your objectives, on the other hand, should be as specific as possible. Highlight 14.11 on page 540 gives an example of both goals and objectives. If you plan to provide prenatal care to 200 low-income women in the first year of operation, state this as an objective.

HIGHLIGHT 14.10

Example of a Problem Statement of a Grant Application

Responding to Caregivers of People with Alzheimer's Disease: Respite Care in Rural Areas

Problem Statement/Needs Assessment

The awesome burden of caring for a loved one with Alzheimer's disease is well documented (Mace & Rabins, 1991; Motenko, 1989; Pruchno & Resch, 1989). Nevertheless, in America today, it is estimated that more than one million people are full-time caregivers to family members who have this degenerative, consuming condition. Demographic projections suggest the caregiving population will increase dramatically in the next 25 years, and the need to provide care to a loved one will become the norm.

Often, caregivers themselves are elderly, sometimes frail, and always overwhelmed. Yet they continue to provide the necessary intimate care of feeding, bathing, toileting, and dressing in the home rather than institutionalize their loved one. Unfortunately, caregivers who perform these tasks for many years also lose their identity, their sense of personhood, and their will.

Statistics augmenting these general statements are telling. Working women caring for elderly family members have a typical work week of 70 to 80 hours. In some cases, these responsibilities are equivalent to three full-time jobs. Most caregivers provide care for one to four years, including 60 percent who provide full-time care for at least three years. Most caregivers have few, if any, resources to help with their responsibilities. One-third of families with an Alzheimer's victim live below the poverty line.

The effects of this unrelenting burden on caregivers are predictable: poor emotional and physical health. Family caregivers suffer more stress-related illness resulting from exhaustion, lowered immune functions, and injuries than the general population. One-third of caregivers self-report their health as fair or poor, a much higher percentage than others in their age cohort. Caregiver depression is reported at 43 to 46 percent, about three times the national average. These factors are exacerbated by the fact that 36 percent of the caregivers are at least 65 years old. Alarmingly, 12 percent of caregivers for people with Alzheimer's report becoming physically ill or injured as a direct result of caregiving.

To cope with this tremendous burden, caregivers need assistance with caregiving responsibilities. Unfortunately, the kinds of services helpful in caring for a person with Alzheimer's are either too expensive or nonexistent.

For many people, the single most frequently expressed need is the opportunity to reduce their burden for short periods of time. It is the constancy and ubiquitousness of caregiving that is so oppressive, not the caregiving itself. They voice a uniform desire to have some time away from their caregiving.

Respite care, a time-out from caregiving, has become a universal response to the burdens of these people in need. Respite care can be offered in a variety of forms and models, but in whatever form, it makes a difference in the lives of caregivers. Over the past four years, the Alzheimer's Association has operated a National Respite Care Demonstration Program to establish and evaluate model respite care programs. In 1990, some 50 local Alzheimer's chapters provided respite care services to an estimated 3,000 families in 20 states, through programs as varied as the families they serve. Although the outcomes of this and other demonstration respite care programs are not quantitatively definitive, caregivers' needs for respite at home are predictable. It is also predictable that all of the problems experienced by caregivers are amplified for those in rural areas. It is often assumed that in rural areas an informal helping network of friends, neighbors, and volunteers assists family members in need (Collins & Pancoast, 1976). However, research on caregivers living in rural areas (Wolk, Pray, Kalkbrenner, & Propp, 1986) indicates that the nature of Alzheimer's disease is so oppressive and foreign that informal networks are insufficient to meet their needs. Still, the harsher existence related to care-giving in rural areas remains. Basic health care, including the presence of physicians, is often unavailable, necessitating long distance travel for routine health care. In the case of caregivers, this problem is complicated because of their own health needs, as well as those of the person with Alzheimer's.

Beyond basic health care, many ancillary health services in rural areas are in short supply. Support groups, in-or out-of-home respite care, mental health services, and hot meal programs are limited or absent. Transportation problems, higher poverty levels, and the general under-funding of human services by federal agencies is a prescription for isolation and frustration.

Southwest Missouri, a catchment area encompassing 27 counties, is by any accepted definition of the term predominantly rural. Problems encountered in this part of the state are comparable to rural problems everywhere. Moreover, the rate of Alzheimer's disease for the 27 counties is high because the population is older than the national and state averages.

For this project, four counties in southwest Missouri are targeted for services: Lawrence, Polk, Barry, and Wright. The Missouri Division of Aging uses a formula that estimates that 11 percent of people between the ages of 65 and 84, and 50 percent of people age 85 and over, have Alzheimer's disease or related disorders. Applying this formula to the 65-and-over population in the four counties produces these estimates of people with Alzheimer's disease: Lawrence—795; Polk—594; Barry—661 ; Wright—434; total—2,484.

Most of these people live several miles from town. In previous research, a high percentage of rural caregivers had little or no respite from their responsibilities for months or even years (Wolk et al, 1986).

In southwest Missouri, a number of agencies have responsibility for providing services to the people in these counties. Specifically, the Alzheimer's Association of southwest Missouri offers support and education in this region of the state. However, the office is staffed with only an executive director and volunteers. Realistically, the capacity to provide extensive support and education in so broad an area is limited. Regardless, the association is engaged in providing the following services: support group development advocacy, fund-raising, community awareness, and volunteer training.

Another organization serving this geographic area and the elderly population is the Southwest Missouri Office on Aging, a designated Area Agency on Aging. This agency receives most of its funding from the Older Americans Act and Social Service Block Grant Funds. The Southwest Missouri Office on Aging is centrally administered, but each of the 17 counties in its catchment area operates a senior center. These centers offer a range of services from providing a meeting place and serving congregate meals to the full complement of services to the elderly. Several centers operate in-home companion programs intended to reduce the burden of caregivers caring for frail elderly, though not for elderly with any sort of dementia.

Some counties have augmented the funding for services by passing a county sales tax. Some have additional transportation dollars from the local city government to help people get to the center. Although the centers remain open throughout the afternoon, not all have scheduled events or active participation after lunch. For the most part, none of the centers are readily accessible to or staffed to accommodate people with Alzheimer's disease or their caregivers.

It is now common knowledge among specialists in the field of aging that when a family member cares for a loved one with a chronic physical or mental condition—and in particular, Alzheimer's disease—two lives are altered. The burden of caregiving, without sufficient support services, becomes oppressive. Clearly, caregivers in the rural areas of southwest Missouri want to keep their family members in the home and out of institutions as long as feasible. However, as they toil to accomplish this goal, the caregivers become entangled emotionally and physically in this debilitating disease. Caregivers need periodic and predictable relief from their responsibilities.

The primary purpose of this project is to assist in the reduction of the burden on caregivers of people with Alzheimer's disease and related disorders (ARD) in rural areas of southwest Missouri. A significant aspect of this proposal will be the cooperation of several community agencies employing existing but underutilized resources to accomplish its primary purpose.

SOURCE: Grant application adapted with permission from James Wolk, June Huff, and Lou Ann Trent.

HIGHLIGHT 14.11

Examples of Goals and Objectives

Goals and Objectives

Goal 1—To reduce the physical, emotional, and financial burden on caregivers of people with Alzheimer's disease living in five rural areas of southwest Missouri.

> Objective 1—By the end of the first year, participant caregivers will experience a 25 percent reduction in their use of stress-related medication.
>
> Objective 2—By the end of the first year, participant caregivers will experience a 25 percent reduction in their level of stress.
>
> Objective 3—By the end of the first year, participant caregivers will reduce their number of physician's visits by 25 percent.
>
> Objective 4—By the end of the first year, there will be a 50 percent increase in the number of caregivers involved in support groups.

Goal 2—To improve the quality of life of people with Alzheimer's disease living in rural areas of southwest Missouri.

> Objective 1—Within three months, participating people with Alzheimer's will increase their social interactions by 25 percent.
>
> Objective 2—During the first year, progression of the disease will be 25 percent slower compared with a matched group of people with Alzheimer's.

Goal 3—To increase rural community awareness, knowledge, and interdependence regarding Alzheimer's disease.

> Objective 1—By the end of the first year, 50 percent of the caregivers of people with Alzheimer's disease and related disorders will have knowledge of the support services available.
>
> Objective 2—By the end of the first year, 80 percent of the health care providers will have referred at least one person to supportive services.
>
> Objective 3—By the end of the first year, at least one school in each community will be participating in services provided to people with Alzheimer's and their caregivers.

Reducing by one-half the incidence of repeat delinquent acts by juveniles living in the Orange County Housing Authority is another measurable objective. Objectives should show a time frame by which changes are to occur.

Grant proposal objectives include two types: outcome and process (Coley & Scheinberg, 2008). *Outcome objectives* show what the result will be of our change efforts. A useful outcome objective might be providing immunizations to all children over the age of three living in the Woodland Park neighborhood. This type of objective says specifically what you will do—give kids immunizations. You may also, however, want to include *process objectives* that describe the steps you will take to accomplish the outcome objectives. A process objective might be conducting a door-to-door neighborhood education campaign focused on encouraging parents to immunize their children. In other words, it is a step in the process of getting all kids in the neighborhood immunized. Keep objectives as brief and clearly stated as possible, whether they are outcome- or process-oriented goals.

3. *Methods.* These are the activities you will use to accomplish your objectives. Ideally, you would like to describe the broad tasks you will complete before and after the funds are provided. You might wish to describe the staff to be hired, space to be acquired, equipment to be purchased, and services to be provided.

Then discuss details about your organization and how it is/will be organized to carry out your proposal. Will this project be carried out by an existing unit, or will a new structure be established? Will you need to create a new unit to house your project? What staffing needs exist? What duties and tasks will those involved in the project perform? You might include a job description in the appendix to provide greater detail or to support the narrative. Highlight 14.12 describes the method used in the Alzheimer's grant.

4. *Evaluation.* The evaluation section requires that you think carefully about your ultimate goals and exactly how you will prove that you have been successful. Make certain that your identified objectives are measurable. Generally speaking, if your

HIGHLIGHT 14.12

Example of a Description of the Method

Description of the Method

Caregivers of people with Alzheimer's disease and related disorders (ARD) in rural areas of southwest Missouri experience profound burdens in order to keep loved ones in the family home. The dearth of available support services for caregivers in those rural areas of the state is clear. Moreover, the informal networks in those rural areas are insufficient to meet the expressed need. Therefore, what is needed in the rural areas of southwest Missouri is some type of formal agency service to help reduce the burden of caregivers and improve the quality of life for people with this disease.

In order to accomplish the stated goals and objectives of this proposal, several conditions seem paramount. First, any response to these complex problems and to the unmet needs extant in rural areas should be an inter-agency effort and not a unilateral organizational activity. An interagency effort will maximize the strengths of the existing formal and informal networks. Second, any response should capitalize on existing but possibly underutilized resources in these rural communities. Third, there should be centrally located administration and professional support, but the services should be decentralized, incorporating the strengths of existing resources. Fourth, the model of service should be replicable in other rural areas of the state and nation.

The goals and objectives of this project and the conditions for service delivery can most effectively be met through a model of respite care provided at several locations throughout the southwest Missouri area. This model is consistent with the stated conditions for service delivery to achieve the outlined goals and objectives.

Under the general auspices of the Southwest Missouri Office on Aging, coordinated with the Alzheimer's Association of Southwest Missouri and Missouri State University, weekly respite care will be provided to people with ARD in rural counties. Specifically, six communities located in four counties in rural southwest Missouri operate senior centers under the administration of the Southwest Agency on Aging: Monett, Cassville, Aurora, Mount Vernon, Bolivar, and Mountain Grove. These centers operate Monday through Friday, but usually end their activities after the congregate lunch is completed. For the rest of the afternoon, numbers of participants at centers are limited.

It is planned that each of these six centers will be available for respite care to people with Alzheimer's three afternoons a week each. The days of the week will be staggered in order to allow central administration to be on-site when necessary. Operating hours will be 2:00 to 6:00 P.M. Each center will be able to serve up to 10 participants per shift. Caregivers would be able to schedule a fixed time each week that their family member can be brought to the center for respite care. Once the program is fully operational, 180 people with ARD will be served, with caregivers receiving a total of 720 hours of respite care per week. Moreover, the center will provide support groups for the caregivers. The structure of the respite care will provide an accessible opportunity for caregivers living in rural areas to participate in these groups. Also, every effort will be made to bring indigenous resources to the center. The local schools, churches, and senior center participants will be organized to contribute to the services for people with ARD and their caregivers. Finally, it is generally acknowledged that caregivers often need assistance beyond respite. Professional help in acquiring important and necessary services will integrate with the provision of respite care. On-site assistance will be available to help caregivers access services for themselves or their family member.

To deliver the services of this rural respite care program, staffing must be professional in nature. The six sites will be coordinated by a person with a Bachelor's degree in Social Work housed at the Southwest Missouri Office on Aging, Springfield, Missouri. A social worker has skill in working with individuals as well as communities. Moreover, the social worker will travel to each center on a regular basis to meet with caregivers about their social services needs.

Each respite care program will be managed by a licensed professional nurse. It is believed that medical skills will be necessary in working with this client group. Even though these centers will be in rural areas, it is believed that recruitment of LPNs will be possible. It is planned that the pay will be higher than current home health hourly wages and that predictable part-time work will be a desirable option. The LPNs will be responsible for implementing the program, controlling admissions, collecting fees, supervising other staff and volunteers, and coordinating activities with the senior center directors. It is expected that the person will be employed twenty (20) hours per week. This schedule will permit approximately eight (8) hours per week for community coordination and administration without clients.

(continued)

HIGHLIGHT 14.12 *(continued)*

Because the days of the week will be staggered by the center, it is assumed that the various respite managers will provide temporary coverage for each other.

In addition, each center will have a 20-hour-a-week activity director. This person will have experience in developing level-appropriate activities and exercises for people with Alzheimer's disease. They will have primary responsibility for carrying out the activities.

The nature of Alzheimer's disease requires ongoing training. The Alzheimer's Association of Southwest Missouri will provide this training for staff as well as volunteers.

It will also be necessary to cultivate relationships in the communities with a number of people who will assist in encouraging family members to participate in the respite care program. In particular, physicians who treat people with Alzheimer's disease and clergy who minister to families will be invaluable sources of support and strength for caregivers who may be reluctant to abdicate total control over their loved one. The social worker as well as the LPNs will be networking with these important community resources.

In addition, contacts will be maintained with the existing senior center participants to encourage them to volunteer in the respite care. Moreover, they will be called upon to assist in helping the caregiver become involved with the senior center or other appropriate community services in preparation for the time when their family member cannot be cared for in the home.

Also, the staff will capitalize on existing transportation services available in some of the counties. Where no transportation is available, "good neighbor" programs will be developed that reimburse people who provide needed transportation. Finally, the respite care staff will attempt to develop positive working relationships with the local schools. The students can provide a resource and a perspective that will add to the community nature of the program.

In summary, the respite care program will be offered at six rural sites in existing senior centers. Each program will be staffed by an LPN and an activity director with the entire program coordinated by a BSW. Each center will be open three days a week for four hours a day, and care-givers will have scheduled time each week. As much as feasible, community resources will be integrated into the program, and the caregivers will be provided services as needed, beyond the respite care, in the form of support group and social work services.

During the first year of the program, it is the intent to provide this service for free or at low cost. However, it is also recognized that if this service proves valuable, it will need to be funded on a continual basis. To that end, there will be a minimal fee scale developed for the families. Prior to beginning the second year, all aspects of this revenue collection effort will be analyzed to determine its feasibility as a significant future revenue source.

---

objectives (which are really more definitive and specific parts of the goal) are achieved, you have probably reached your goal, too. Address the question, "How am I going to evaluate whether my objective has been achieved?" An objective of providing family planning services to 100 adolescent girls is fairly clear-cut. You either provided service to at least 100 girls or you did not. Service provision to 99 girls indicates that you have not met your stated objective.

You might also wish to know which of two service methods worked the best. If some girls received individual service and others were given group counseling, which method was most effective? Did the group method result in more or fewer of the adolescents avoiding pregnancy?

In addition, process evaluation may be important. It focuses on the process of giving service and should not be confused with outcome evaluation.

Process evaluation is concerned with such factors as whether the staff provided the service intended, whether the cost of the service provided was reasonable, and whether clients were satisfied with the service provided. It is entirely possible that the staff provided the service indicated, clients were satisfied or happy with what occurred, but the results (outcomes) of the project were not satisfactory. Perhaps all of the girls who received the family planning service praised their workers and thought the cost of service was fair, but 90 percent had unplanned pregnancies anyway. Here the process was carried out well, but the outcome objective was not achieved. You need to decide what data are important to your evaluation. Obviously, you want basic demographic information such as age, gender, race, and other similar items. In other kinds of programs, you may discover that the outcomes were different for men and women, or that younger children were affected differently by the project. The number of hours of service provided to each client may be an important variable, so you may wish to gather this information. Numbers of clients served and data from workers and clients may be useful.

EP 2.1.6

Coley and Scheinberg (2008) suggest you incorporate several steps into your evaluation plan. First, they suggest specifying the purpose of the evaluation, describing the design to be employed, and detailing what will be measured (CSWE, 2008, EP 2.1.6). They also recommend that you detail the data that need to be collected and decide whether your evaluation uses a sample of the population or the entire population of persons served. (The differences between "population" and "sample" were discussed in Chapter 10. For our purposes, we refer to all of the participants for whom we provided service as the population. A sample would simply be a subset of the population.)

The timetable for data collection should be specified along with a description of how the data will be analyzed and reported. In some situations, the evaluation component is performed by someone or an organization hired specifically for this purpose. If the evaluation is going to involve significant costs (which might be the case if it is done by an outside group), a budget for evaluation should accompany the proposal. Highlight 14.13 describes the evaluation component of the respite care grant.

This section also includes what happens when the grant period is over and the money is gone. What plans are there for carrying out the project after this point? Many funding agencies want some assurance that a good idea developed through a grant project will continue when the grant expires. Often the grant writer will need written assurances from agency executives or board chairpersons that the project will be continued if it proves successful.

5. *Bibliography.* Of course, like the papers you do for class, your grant proposal should include a bibliography. This should list the references to which you referred in your proposal. Highlight 14.14 illustrates the bibliography used for the Alzheimer's grant.

As you can see, the narrative section must address several areas and is extremely important. You must include sufficient detail so that reviewers do not become confused about your purpose or doubt your ability to carry out the project.

Budget section. A budget section with explicit detail is essential. The most common type of budget for proposals is a *line-item budget,* which identifies personnel

HIGHLIGHT 14.13

Example of an Evaluation Section

Evaluation

An outcome evaluation will be conducted by the Center for Social Research at Missouri State University. In order to evaluate the objectives under the first goal, an extensive social history of each caregiver will be completed upon admission of a family member. This history will include information related to the physical and mental health of the caregiver. At the end of the first year, a follow-up interview will be completed to ascertain the changes that have occurred in those aspects of the caregiver's life. Also, a 10 percent random sample of caregivers will be personally interviewed in-depth to ascertain a more subjective understanding of goal completion. Finally, the Burden Scale developed by Zarit et al. (1986) to determine the stress experienced by caregivers will be administered on a pre- and post-test basis.

In order to evaluate the objectives under the second goal, all participants in the respite care program will be administered the mini-mental scale that assesses their level in the progressive nature of Alzheimer's disease. The scale will be readministered every three months. Participant scores will be compared against a control group of people with ARD who are not participating in the respite care program.

In order to evaluate the objectives under the third goal, a series of interviews with key actors in the community will be conducted regarding their knowledge and behaviors related to ARD. A follow-up set of interviews will be conducted at the end of the grant year to ascertain changes. Additionally, a 10 percent random sample of known people with ARD and caregivers will be surveyed by questionnaire at the onset of the project and then again at the end of the first year.

HIGHLIGHT 14.14

Example of a Bibliography

Bibliography

Gitlin, L. N., Winter, L., Earland, T. V., Herge, E. A., Chernett, N. L., Pierson, C. V., & Burke, J. P. (2009). The Tailored Activity Program to reduce behavioral symptoms in individuals with dementia: Feasibility, acceptability, and replication potential. *The Gerontologist, 49*(3), 428–439.

Keith, P. M., Wacker, R., & Collins, S. M. (2009). Family influence on caregiver resistance, efficacy, and use of services in family elder care. *Journal of Gerontological Social Work, 52*(4), 377–400.

McDonald, A., & Heath, B. (2008). Developing services for people with dementia: Findings from research in a rural area. *Quality in Ageing—Policy, Practice and Research, 9*(4), 9–18.

Ornstein, K., Smith, K. L & Boal, J. (2009). Understanding and improving the burden and unmet needs of informal caregivers of homebound patients enrolled in a home-based primary care program. *The Journal of Applied Gerontology, 28*(4), 482–503.

Sussman, T. (2009). The influence of service factors on spousal caregivers' perceptions of community services. *Journal of Gerontological Social Work, 52*(4), 406–422.

Thorpe, J. M., Van Houlven, C. H., & Sleath, B. L. (2009). Barriers to outpatient care in community-dwelling elderly with dementia. *The Journal of Applied Gerontology, 28*(4) 436–460.

costs, operating costs (such as supplies or rental of equipment), travel, and capital costs (such as building costs or the cost of purchasing equipment). Such budgets tell the reviewer specifically what the grant covers. However, they do not separate individual portions of a program or, for that matter, specific programs. Highlight 14.15 shows a typical line-item budget taken from the Alzheimer's grant. Many programs or functions might be included in a budget such as this.

In contrast to line-item budgets, *functional (or program) budgets* depict costs based upon specific proposed program elements or functions. Thus, a proposal for training peer counselors and creating a drug education program in a high school would be separately budgeted. This means the cost for each of the two components would be shown individually rather than lumped together as in line-item budgets. Highlight 14.16 shows a functional or program budget.

Both line-item and functional budgets require similar attention to detail. You should include both salaries and fringe benefits (such as health insurance, Social Security, and retirement) when calculating personnel costs. You must also decide how much of each person's time will go into performing the functions associated with the proposal and what proportion of time is allocated to work unrelated to the grant proposal. If your grant proposes using 100 percent of two people's time, you would simply include both person's total salaries along with fringe benefits. However, if your grant proposal funds only 15 percent of one person's time, 25 percent of another's time, and 65 percent of a third person's time, the calculations become more complicated. You need to multiply the various percentages for each person times their annual salaries and benefits to arrive at the costs to be charged to the proposal. (A perfect task for a spreadsheet.)

The same is true for use of space. If you are renting or using an entire building, it is easy to calculate the cost. However, if you are using only 25 percent of the space for your grant project, you can request funds for the value of only 25 percent of the space. Highlight 14.17 shows an example of these calculations. As you can see, we are using a portion of four people's time and a corresponding portion of their assigned office space.

If you are going to be operating several programs in your agency (most agencies offer a variety of services and programs), you will also need to estimate how much total space each program will require. For example, if the total space needs of the peer counselor program is 500 square feet and the drug education program requires 250 square feet of office space, you will require a total of 750 square feet. If the agency has a total of 7,500 square feet of space available, it is clear your two programs will use 10 percent of the available space in your building (.10 x 7,500 square feet = 750 square feet). This generally means that 10 percent of

HIGHLIGHT 14.15

Example of a Line-Item Budget

Budget

Expenses

Personnel Salaries

Baccalaureate Social Worker @ 100%	$ 35,000
Six LPNs @ $12.00/hr x 20 hrs/wk	74,880
Six Activity Directors @ $8.00 x 12 hrs/wk	29,952
Executive Director Alzheimer's Association @ 5%	2,000
Project Director Area Aging Agency @ 5%	2,000
Benefits @ 15% of employees' salaries	21,575
Subtotal	$165,407

Operating Expenses

Telephone (one line @ $90/month)	$ 1,000
Supplies ($100/month)	1,200
Employee Travel ($.35/m x 5,000 m)	1,750
Public Awareness Material	1,000
Office Equipment	1,000
Copying and Postage	2,000
Good Neighbor Travel ($.35/m x 8,000 m)	2,800
Subtotal	$ 10,750

Evaluation

Contract/Outside Evaluator	Subtotal	$ 5,000

Indirect Costs

5% of personnel costs	Subtotal	$ 8,270
	Total	$189,427

Revenue

37,440 hrs Respite/Year @ 50% billable hrs x $5.00/hr	$ 93,600
Total grant funds requested	$ 95,827

HIGHLIGHT 14.16

Example of a Functional or Program Budget from a Peer Counselor and Drug Education Program

Category	Peer Counselors	Public Education
Personnel	$50,000	$20,000
Operating expenses	15,000	6,000
Equipment	1,500	3,500
Total	$66,500	$29,500
Grand total $96,000		

HIGHLIGHT 14.17

Example of Allocating Time and Space Costs

Individual	Percent Assigned to Project	Salary ($)	Project Cost ($)
Nadia Bleefme	15	20,000	3,000
Sarah Ranrap	25	28,000	7,000
Marcus Mucous	65	35,000	22,750
Bob Burann	100	37,250	37,250

Four offices @ 100 square feet per office = 400 square feet total

Office space used: (15% + 25% + 65% + 100%)/400 = 200 square feet

Office space rent is $40 per square foot per month

Office space cost of project: $8,000.00 ($40 × 200)

the rent and utilities will be charged to the grant, because these are also expenses of offering the program. If the building is rented for $65,000 per year, this means that the grant will pay for 10 percent of that amount, or $6,500. In other words, if a grant proposal indicates it needs 10 percent of an agency's space, then you need to include in the grant budget 10 percent of other agency costs across the board.

Describe operating costs such as travel with an explanation of how much is allowed per mile as well as costs of other individual items, such as hotel and meal expenses. This helps show that the amounts budgeted are reasonable and appropriate. Similarly, personnel costs should be broken down to show how much each person or group is being paid.

Make budgets realistic. Sometimes, applicants minimize the costs of certain elements, hoping that a lower dollar amount will increase their funding chances. However, unrealistically low budgets may flag a proposal as poorly conceptualized.

Similarly, bloated budgets with unnecessarily high estimates are suspect. Of course, it is always difficult to forecast costs for one-year periods, let alone multi-year periods. It is sometimes helpful to show a budget to others to see if you have missed anything or whether your estimates appear reasonable. In fact, acknowledge that you will usually forget something and plan for this eventuality with the agency that will receive the grant. Sometimes this means building in a slight overestimate of costs or asking the agency to set aside a contingency fund for costs not covered by the grant.

Items that might appear unusual or questionable to others should be discussed in an accompanying budget narrative. Here you should justify and explain the costs within the context of the proposal. Large-cost items should be clearly explained. Highlight 14.18 provides an example of a budget narrative for the Alzheimer's grant.

Credentials of staff. One section should describe the credentials of staff members carrying out the activities proposed in the grant. Its purpose is to strengthen your credibility; you want to emphasize that your staff members are capable of accomplishing what your grant proposes to do. Generally, a one-page summary of each person's work experience and education is sufficient. Résumés that clearly illustrate each person's qualifications should be appended.

Certifications of compliance. If required, add a section to the proposal discussing compliance with civil rights laws and protections for human subjects. Most governmental grants require specific assurances that people will not be hurt by your project and that your agency obeys federal, state, and local laws and regulations. Federal law protects human beings from being subjected to treatment that endangers their physical or mental health. Activities that expose people to stress or that are deceptive will probably not be funded. If the proposal uses research respondents, address subjects' confidentiality. Explain how you will gather

EP 2.1.2b

HIGHLIGHT 14.18

Example of a Budget Narrative

Budget Narrative

The salary for the BSW director is consistent with salaries of experienced social workers in the area with administrative responsibilities.

The hourly wage for the LPN is higher than the prevailing rate. However, in rural areas, especially for part-time work, the salary must be competitive with home health agencies in order to attract competent personnel.

The hourly wage for the activity directors is about the rate for personnel of this training in the area.

The 5 percent buyout of administrative time from the Alzheimer's Association and the Southwest Missouri Office on Aging is necessary to augment the work these agencies will be performing in support of the respite care program.

The outside evaluation will be conducted by the Center for Social Research at Missouri State University. The center has considerable experience with process and outcome evaluations. The figure of approximately 5 percent of the total grant costs is consistent with other center contracts.

First, as noted in the description of services section and the budget the project plans to collect in fees

$56,160 during the first year of operation. Although the project will always allow participation of people who are unable to pay, it is believed that the projected amount is modest and can be increased in the future.

Second, several of the communities have passed mill taxes to pay for certain types of human services. A project such as the respite care program fits well with the intended purposes of that type of tax.

Third, the state of Missouri has in the past made resources available through block grant funding for innovative programs. The success of this project especially given that it demonstrates networking with other institutions in the community (such as schools and churches) will be highly regarded.

Fourth, the participating agencies in the initial grant, as well as other agencies, might increase their in-kind contributions. Specifically, as needs change within the human service field for the elderly, positions could be reallocated to meet more pressing issues.

Plans for Continued Support

Though none of the following funding possibilities are absolute, taken together they provide a package of financial options for future support.

---

information in such a way as to maintain subject confidentiality. Additionally, describe how you will obtain subjects' informed consent. Generally, projects that carry low risk to human beings are easier to justify. Recent revelations indicate that researchers in some medical studies subjected participants to risks including crippling disease and death. These incidents have made it more important than ever to guarantee protections; funding agencies will not want to get involved in something that carries risk to the subjects (CSWE, 2008, EP 2.1.2b).

Cost sharing, matching funds, and indirect costs. Another important budgetary concept is that the total amount of funding needed for a proposed project may come from different sources. Cost sharing is an arrangement whereby both the agency receiving the grant and the organization dispensing the grant contribute to the proposed project. Cost-sharing methods include indirect costs and matching funds.

Indirect costs are often referred to as "overhead." If you glance back at Highlight 14.15, you will see a line

item labeled "Indirect Costs." Indirect costs are so named because they are only indirectly related to the grant proposal. Indirect costs compensate your agency for its expenses in operating the grant activity. An agency seeking a grant of $500,000 to operate a homeless shelter for two years needs that money for direct expenses such as personnel, rent, utilities, and equipment. However, the agency will do the bookkeeping, pay salaries, and supervise the staff of the shelter. These activities and their related expenses represent indirect costs. These costs are usually included in the grant application and listed in the budget. The Alzheimer's grant listed an indirect amount equal to 5 percent of personnel costs. Among the expenses that might be charged to indirect costs are such things as clerical support for projects, operation and maintenance of a facility, and administrative costs. Many organizations charge a set amount to cover these "overhead or indirect costs." This amount is usually figured as a percentage of the total grant and may equal 20, 30, or 40 percent or more. Thus, a grant to provide a new program costing $100,000 might have additional indirect costs of 30 percent. The granting agency would then be asked to pay $130,000 ($100,000 plus the $30,000 overhead).

To keep expenses as low as possible, some granting agencies do not allow indirect costs to be charged to their grants. Instead, they expect the agency receiving the grant to absorb the indirect costs. Some granting agencies accept indirect costs but limit the amount you may charge to the grant. However, if a granting agency does allow indirect costs to be charged to a grant, this money goes directly to your agency. You might consider it a bonus for the agency.

Matching funds or cost-sharing grants assume that the receiving organization will contribute part of the total project costs. The principle behind cost sharing is that an organization contributing some of its own resources to a project is more likely to operate efficiently and effectively. Grantors that do not let your agency charge indirect costs to the grant are forcing your agency to share the costs of the project.

Matching of funds or cost sharing may be handled in one of two ways. First, some agencies are expected to contribute actual cash to the grant project, often referred to as a *hard match*. If a grant requires an agency to provide a 10 percent cash match, a grant project costing $100,000 would be financed by $90,000 (90 percent) from the grantor and $10,000 (10 percent) from your agency. Generally speaking, agencies do not like to apply for grants when cash matching is required. Agencies simply do not have unallocated money available for such projects.

The second method of matching (a *soft match)* allows an agency to provide its share of the costs through contributed services or activities. An agency might contribute the cost of space (as in our example of 10 percent of the total agency space being allocated to a grant project). If the space is already being paid for by the agency, it is an easy contribution for the agency to make. Figure 14.6 gives an example of how such a calculation might be made.

Because it is much easier for agencies to contribute services instead of cash, most prefer the soft match arrangement—sometimes referred to as *in-kind contributions*. In-kind contributions are expenses that the organization will incur whether the grant is received or not, such as overhead. In some situations, the grant-seeking agency may seek to increase the amount of its in-kind contribution. A local business might be asked to donate a van to the senior center, and the value of the van would be used as a match to help

Total cost of operating child abuse prevention program		$40,000
Grantor will provide up to 80% of program costs (.80 × $40,000)		$32,000
Grantor requires 20% match for all grants (.20 × $40,000)		$8,000

Agency will provide its "match" of $8,000 through contributed services as follows:

a. 10% of one supervisor's time (annual salary of $40,000 × 10%)	=	$ 4,000
b. 10% of supervisor's office space (annual cost of $2,000 × 10%)	=	$ 200
c. 100% of new worker's office space (annual cost of $1,500 × 100%)	=	$ 1,500
d. 15% of secretarial staff's time (annual salary of $15,333 × 15%)	=	$ 2,300
Total		$ 8,000

FIGURE 14.6 Calculating a Soft Match

the senior center obtain a grant for outreach services to older adult citizens in the community.

Agency or institutional endorsements. The last portion of the grant application should include a signature page for executives of the receiving agency. Relevant signatures might include those of the agency director, chief elected official, or others who will accept ultimate responsibility for administering grant funds. These signatures reflect the agency's support for the grant's proposed project. Both administrators and involved staff members commit themselves to the grant via their signatures. Ironically, as the grant writer you may not be required to sign the grant, although you did all the work of preparing it.

In addition, this section may include letters of support or endorsements from other agencies or individuals. Requesting these endorsements is especially important if several agencies are expected to work together on a project. The juvenile court judge may be asked to provide a letter requesting grant money for a juvenile detention center. If it is important that the supporting letters contain specific information, you may actually draft the letters. You then send the draft to the endorsing agency where administrators will modify or adapt it and return it to you. These letters indicate that other organizations support your proposal (Coley & Scheinberg, 2008).

Post-Application Phase

Many grant sponsors require that the grant application be received or mailed by a specific date. Proposals not received by this date are very likely to be ignored or returned to the sender. It is often wise to mail materials so that you are notified of their receipt. This prevents problems when a proposal gets lost.

Once received, grants are reviewed. The reviewers vary, depending upon the type of organization. In private foundations, either a single individual or a committee may review proposals. With government grants a committee is more likely to function as reviewer. Committee members will then give points for various portions of the proposal, such as budget and statement of problem. Those proposals receiving the highest points are usually funded. The number of proposals funded depends on the amount of money available. Sometimes, although a proposal receives fewer points, the agency believes it has merit. In some of these cases, the grantors will ask for revisions in order to address their concerns. The grant writer can then resubmit the revised proposal for reconsideration.

When the grantor is a foundation, there may be additional considerations. Coley and Scheinberg's research (2008, pp. 13–14) suggests that the following positive factors are important in determining whether an agency receives grant funds or not. Ideally, the agency:

1. *Shows a cost-effective operation.* This means the cost of the intervention is reasonable, given the expected outcome.
2. *Supports other organizations in the community.* Cooperative endeavors and collaborative activities tend to be more highly rated.
3. *Reflects cultural sensitivity and diversity.* Services provided should be sensitive to client differences especially in relation to culturally diverse populations.
4. *Focuses on primary prevention of the problem.* Prevention of a problem tends to be more effective than intervening after the problem has already arisen.
5. *Has a proven track record.* Foundations like to go with winners who have demonstrated they can do the job. A record of past grants received can be helpful.
6. *Establishes new, innovative programs.* Foundations prefer to encourage the development of new approaches rather than replicate something tried elsewhere.

7. *Receives funding from other sources.* Funding from other sources indicates wider support for a proposal and enhances its chance of being funded.
8. *Has a previous relationship with the foundation.* A past record of dealing with a foundation is helpful.
9. *Has a reputation that is not too radical.* Foundations can be somewhat conservative and may not be willing to have their names linked with radical proposals.
10. *Demonstrates a positive and measurable impact on those being served.* Agencies must show positive outcomes that clearly benefit their target populations.
11. *Has a competent and professionally trained staff.* Competence of the people who will carry out the grant project is important. It is risky to give money to people who don't have the experience or education for the task.

When Funding Is Less Than Requested

Frequently, grants will be funded, but at a lower amount than originally requested. This generally requires major rethinking about whether the project is workable with the smaller amount. Don't assume that it is easy to "just cut corners a bit" and still serve the same number of people or operate on the same scale. A realistic conclusion is that less money means less program.

When the Grant/Contract Runs Out

Almost all grants run for a specified period, typically a year or two. After that time, the grant money will be gone. You must plan either to continue the program by finding other sources of funds or to terminate it. It is easy not to think clearly about this eventuality and neglect to plan for the post-grant period. Some granting agencies will require that you address this matter in your grant application. Highlight 14.18, the budget narrative example, includes a section on funding the project after the grant is over. The purpose of this requirement is not to commit the agency to continue a poor or ineffective program. Instead, it is to ensure that sound programs meriting continuation have some chance of surviving after the grant money runs out. Preparing for this period is part of the responsibility for good planning that any grant application project demands.

Chapter Summary

The following summarizes this chapter's content as it relates to the learning objectives presented at the beginning of the chapter. Chapter content prepares social workers to:

A. *Work with the media to advance social well-being and social and economic justice.*

The term *media* refers to television, radio, and newspapers that deliver news and information to the public. Skilled use of the media can benefit your organization. Working with the media involves several guidelines. These include maintaining ongoing relationships with media personnel, nurturing a variety of contacts within the media, informing the media if you are an expert on a topic, and making sure you have sanction from your agency to speak to the media.

B. *Utilize professional communication strategies with the media.*

Communication strategies for use with media include making it easy for media to contact you, staying familiar with media time schedules, and avoiding favoritism among news media. It also includes expecting that some media reports will contain errors and that even a lengthy interview with the media and a interested reporter will not guarantee that your story will appear. A final strategy is to remember that anything said to the media can end up in print.

Contact with the media can occur by their contacting you, you contacting them directly, or through a news release designed to interest the media. Working with the media can include doing interviews for radio, television, newspapers, and special community newsletters and writing letters to the editors of the media. It can also involve persuading editors to write editorials on a topic that you think is important.

C. *Use technology for managing resources, facilitating service delivery, and evaluating the effectiveness of agency practices.*

Using technology for a variety of purposes requires that social workers be fairly competent in the use of both computer hardware and software. Familiarity with word processing software, databases, and spreadsheet programs is an asset: and social workers will need to learn the unique software that their agencies employ. These might include the software just mentioned as well as geographic information systems, the scheduling programs, management information systems, and publishing software. Ability to use the Internet to locate valid and reliable information is essential in order to maintain currency in one's field.

D. *Utilize fundraising, with a particular focus on grants and contracts.*

Fundraising is an expected component of some social work positions. To be effective as a fundraiser it is helpful to understand the different sources of fund—individual donors, benefits, direct solicitation, foundations, and membership dues. Both telephone and mail (and e-mail) solicitations are common, though the amounts raised can vary dramatically.

Another major source of funds is through grants and contracts. Grants are essentially gifts designed to support a particular project or program, while contracts generally involve agreements between one agency providing a service and another agency paying for the service. There are multiple sources for grants and contracts that include governmental agencies, private agencies, business and corporations, and foundations. The steps in applying for a grant include a pre-phase application, an application phase, and a post-application phase. Writing a grant involves putting together a document that has the following characteristics: relates to the interests or purposes of the funding agency, promotes a desirable end, demonstrates familiarity with the literature in the field, has competent staff to carry out the project, and expected results justify the costs involved. Unsuccessful grants often experience problems with one or more of the above characteristics as well as being poorly written, inadequately documented, unclear, and unrealistic.

Different kinds of grants and contract proposals exist. These include proposals intended to provide a program, engage in research, train staff, engage in planning, fund technical assistance, or contract for services. Typical components of a grant include a cover page, table of contents, abstract or summary, narrative section, budget, staff credentials, and certification of compliance with applicable laws and human subjects protections.

Competency Notes

The following identifies where Educational Policy (EP) competencies and practice behaviors are discussed in the chapter.

Educational Polio (EP) 2.1 Core Competencies

Educational Policy 2.1.1e Engage in career-long learning. *(P. 520)*: Because of the increasing use of computers and other technology, the social worker will need to continually upgrade his or her skills by reading or taking classes. This will help ensure the worker remains current with the latest software.

Educational Policy (EP) 2.1.2b Make ethical decisions by applying standards of the NASW *Code of Ethics* and, as applicable, of the International Federation of Social Workers/International Association of Schools of Social Work Ethics in Social Work, Statement of Principles. *(P. 546)*: Certificates of compliance required by many granting agencies are generally consistent with the values and ethics of the profession of social work because both require that the client's confidentiality be maintained, risk of harm to a client is small or nonexistent, and informed consent is obtained before any intervention is carried out.

Educational Policy (EP) 2.1.3 Apply critical thinking to inform and communicate professional judgment. *(P. 520)*: While the Internet can be a valuable source of information, social workers must maintain a critical perspective to recognize unless, incorrect, or biased data and information.

Educational Policy (EP) 2.1.3a Distinguish, appraise, and integrate multiple sources of knowledge, including research-based knowledge, and practice wisdom. *(P. 529)*: There are many resources for grants, and social workers should be judicious in deciding which grantors' interests match their needs and how best to approach them.

Educational Policy (EP) 2.1.3c Demonstrate effective oral and written communication in working with individuals, families, groups, organizations, communities, and colleagues. *(P. 513)*: Whether one is dealing with print media or broadcast media, it is important to respond to questions clearly and candidly, recognize the particular needs of different types of media, and be helpful in communicating information. *(P. 524)*: Fundraising also requires that the social worker be an effective communicator, whether in person or through the use of written communication. *(P. 527)*: Remember to carefully proofread anything that you send out in order to ensure that errors and mistakes are eliminated.

(P. 534): A good grant proposal clearly communicates how the proposed activity relates to the interests of the funding agency, promotes a desirable end, shows the applicant knows the territory and is competent to carry out the project, and demonstrates that the costs are justified by the expected results.

Educational Policy (EP) 2.1.6 Engage in research-informed practice and practice-informed research. *(P. 543)*: The evaluation section of a grant application must demonstrate appropriate use of research skills and tools and a valid attempt to measure whether the grant accomplished its purpose.

Educational Policy (EP) 2.1.9a Continuously discover, appraise, and attend to changing locales, populations, scientific and technological developments, and emerging societal trends to provide relevant services. *(P. 515)*: Most social agencies use various forms of technology, particularly computers, and the social worker will need to learn new software and become familiar with other things such as use of the Internet. *(P. 521)*: Technology is being used across the world to organize for change, document violations of law, and augment information provided by mainstream media.

Educational Policy (EP) 2.1.10a Substantively and affectively prepare for action with individuals, families, groups, organizations, and communities. *(P. 513)*: Prepare well in advance for an interview with the media, including thinking carefully about what is most important to communicate.

On the Internet

Visit the *Generalist Practice with Organizations and Communities* Web site at www.cengage.com/social-work/krist-ashman for learning tools such as PowerPoint® slides, tutorial quizzing, Web links, and final exams.

CHAPTER 15

Stress and Time Management

Consider this scenario: You are a social work practitioner for a county department of social services. It is now 8:00 A.M. By 4:30 P.M. today, you are supposed to accomplish the following tasks:

- *Meet with your supervisor for your weekly supervisory rendezvous.*
- *Complete appointments established with six clients as noted on your weekly calendar.*
- *Call to schedule a dentist's appointment as soon as possible. You cracked a molar and it hurts like all get out.*
- *Return phone calls to the following clients about crisis issues: Ms. Hermanez, Ms. White, Mr. Scissorhands, Ms. Cheatum, Mr. Beauregard, Ms. Leinenkugal, Ms. Doohee, Mr. Howe.*
- *Find the homeless Shaver family a place to stay.*
- *Enroll Tina Tuna in an alcohol treatment program.*
- *Decide what to get your mother for her birthday (it's tomorrow, and you already forgot to send her a card on time).*
- *Try to stop thinking about your fight with your significant other this morning.*
- *Have lunch.*
- *Use the restroom—probably twice.*
- *Prepare an agenda for tomorrow's 8:00 A.M. staff meeting.*
- *Help Ms. Loophole place her critically ill father in a hospice.*
- *Drop your car off to get your leaky tire fixed.*
- *Complete your two weeks' worth of progress notes before your supervisory meeting.*
- *Call Irma about riding together to the state social work conference next Thursday.*
- *Talk to your colleague Horatio about the minor conflict you had yesterday.*
- *Make appointments with eight clients for next week.*
- *Drive the Hanratti family to the doctor.*
- *Take your client Pauline Prudo to Planned Parenthood for contraception counseling.*
- *Check up on your client Merhan Birmquach, who you believe is seriously depressed and potentially suicidal.*

• *Work on that grant application that's due in two weeks.*

What would you do?

a. Cry.
b. Take a sick day.
c. Punch a hole in the wall.
d. Use good time-management skills.
e. Update your résumé.

What do you do when you have scores of tasks to complete right now? How can you handle the stress from the demands of clients who you feel desperately need your help? How can you keep your own personal concerns from interfering with your ability to accomplish your work? How can you keep from going absolutely crazy with all the pressure?

Two practical means of coping with professional and personal stress are recognizing and using established stress- and time-management techniques. You can't necessarily get rid of all the pressure in your life, but you can begin to control it.

Introduction

Two variables are critically important to conducting your professional life effectively and efficiently. They are stress and time. Both can and will affect your ability to do your job. They exist whether you like it or not, and they are related. Failure to manage time well can become a major stress producer. However, you can begin to get control of these. Stressors and time-management techniques allow you to maximize your time both professionally and personally.

Stress and time are also two critical facets of your macro environment. They are integrally involved in everything you will be doing. In order to fulfill your job responsibilities with clients, comply with supervisory directives, and make decisions concerning your macro objectives, you will need to get control of both your time and stress level.

Learning Objectives

This chapter will provide content concerning how social workers:

A. Conceptualize the dynamics of stress and explain the General Adaptation Syndrome.

B. Practice personal reflection regarding stress levels, identify potential stressors in agency settings, and propose means to address stress in order to improve practice effectiveness.

C. Conceptualize how poor time management can cause stress and affect performance.

D. Practice personal reflection and propose means of adopting time-management techniques to improve practice effectiveness.

E. Assess the dynamics of procrastination and suggest means for combating it to improve practice efficiency and effectiveness.

Stress and Stress Management

Stress is the comprehensive process by which external pressures affect individuals emotionally and physically, producing some internal tension (Kottler & Chen, 2008; Olpin & Hesson, 2007). Kottler and Chen (2008) describe some potential reactions of stress:

EP 2.1.1b

Stress is the feeling you experience when you can't seem to sit still, when your thoughts are racing and you feel out of control. Your body feels tense, as if tied into a knot. You feel revved up but you can't figure out where to direct your energy. Time pressures weigh on you. Concentration seems difficult.

Inside your body you feel intense pressure in your neck, in your back, in your belly. You notice your jaw muscles are clenched. There is, perhaps, a throbbing in your head. Your heart rate has increased, and your hands feel clammy. (p. 8)

Each individual may experience a potentially stressful situation differently, although most of us recognize that certain situations cause unusual stress. For example, abruptly losing your job or hearing of a significant other's catastrophic death will always cause stress.

Even positive events can be stressful. They, too, can force you to deal with new circumstances and expend energy pursuing unfamiliar or different activities. Getting married or receiving a promotion, desirable events for most people, still cause stress.

Environmental situations can also create stress. For example, expending time and effort to change an agency policy may add to the pressure you already feel from fulfilling your everyday responsibilities to clients. Or the abrupt shutdown of a major industry in the town where you work may leave thousands of people unemployed. Your client caseload soars. You see the need to develop a range of new services, from job retraining to relocation planning to food pantries for hungry, newly unemployed workers and their families.

Likewise, personal characteristics, such as perfectionism, can magnify stress. Most of us, however, can withstand significant amounts of stress and survive. When we are exhausted, we go to sleep. When memories are too painful, we forget. In effect, we have developed coping mechanisms to keep our stress levels under some control.

Certain factors are associated with stress. Rigid, authoritarian attitudes and so-called "Type A" personalities appear to be more prone to stress (Daft, 2010a). The Type A personality frequently fights the clock to squeeze more work into smaller and smaller time frames. Likewise, irrational thinking can cause stress. Believing that your intimate other can satisfy all of your needs—which, of course, is impossible—can produce stress.

General Adaptation Syndrome

Your body appears to respond to both negative or positive stress in the same way. Selye (1956), one of the initial authorities on stress, found that the body reacts to all stressors in the same way, regardless of the source of stress. This means that the body reacts to positive stressors (a romantic kiss) in the same way it reacts to negative stressors (an electric shock). The body has a three-phase reaction to stress: (1) the alarm phase, (2) the resistance phase, and (3) the exhaustion phase. This stress response process is known as the General Adaptation Syndrome (GAS) (Kottler & Chen, 2008; Olpin & Hesson, 2007; Selye, 1956). Following is a brief outline of how this syndrome works.

In the *alarm phase,* the body recognizes the stressor and responds by preparing for fight or flight. A stressor can be any stimulus that causes stress. The body's reactions to a range of stressors are numerous and complex: The body sends messages from the hypothalamus (a section of the brain that regulates a range of physiological functions) to the pituitary gland to release its hormones. These hormones trigger the adrenal glands to release adrenaline.

The release of adrenaline and other hormones results in

- *Increased breathing and heartbeat rate.*
- *A rise in blood pressure.*
- *Increased coagulation of blood to minimize potential loss of blood in case of physical injury.*
- *Diversion of blood from the skin to the brain, the heart, and contracting muscles.*
- *A rise in serum cholesterol and blood fat.*
- *Gastrointestinal tract problems.*
- *Dilation of the pupils.*

This range of changes results in a massive burst of energy, better vision and hearing, and increased muscular strength—all changes that increase our capacities to fight or to flee. A major problem of the fight-or-flight reaction in modern times is that we often cannot deal with a threat by fighting or by fleeing, especially in agency life. In our civilized society, fighting or fleeing—helpful to primitive humans—is generally considered unacceptable behavior.

In the *resistance or repair phase,* bodily processes seek to return to homeostasis. The body strives during this phase to repair any damage caused by the stressors. The body can adapt itself to hard physical labor, a serious stressor. In handling most stressors, the body generally goes through only the two phases of alarm and repair. Over a lifetime, a person goes through these two phases hundreds of thousands of times.

The third phase, *exhaustion,* occurs only when the body remains in a state of high stress for an extended period of time. If such stress continues to affect the body, the body is unable to repair the damage. If exhaustion continues, a person is apt to develop a stress-related illness or even to die.

© 2010 Commstock/Jupiterimages Corporation

In a work environment, pressures to perform and high expectations for perfection can produce stress.

Macro Context for Stress

Social workers often consider themselves, their profession, and their agency work environment to be highly stressful. Certainly, dealing with the complicated needs of multiple clients, confronting the huge amounts of paperwork and documentation required for accountability, and operating within bureaucratic systems can produce significant stress.

A great concern in social work practice is *burnout*, "a state of physical, emotional, and mental exhaustion that results from constant or repeated emotional pressure associated with an intense, long-term involvement with people. It is characterized by feelings of helplessness and hopelessness, and by a negative view of self, and negative attitudes toward work, life, and other people" (Corey & Corey, 2011, p. 316). Burnout can occur when you have too much work and feel that you have too little control over getting it all done. Obviously, social work usually addresses problems. Constant confrontation with problems is also stressful.

On the other hand, Simpson and Simpson (1992) explain: "Words cannot convey the satisfaction of having successfully intervened in someone's life. It is a good feeling to know that you have made a difference. And although the work can be grueling, it is rarely dull because people are rarely dull. Only the paperwork is tedious, and you will find that the case in every profession" (p. 18).

To avoid burnout and enhance your usefulness, good stress- and time-management skills are essential. The following sections will explore stress-related problems and techniques for changing your perception about, and managing, stress. Because time management is so critical for effective control of stress, we will extensively explore the issues concerning time and techniques recommended to manage it.

Perceptions of Stress

Stress becomes a problem only when the stressors are so great that your adaptive system is overwhelmed.

This can happen either from too much stress in a short time or from the cumulative effects of stress over an extended period. It is typically the chronic or long-term stress that causes us the greatest concern. Because of the prolonged time involved, you can develop both physiological and psychological problems. Interestingly, it is often not a single major event that triggers stress-related problems. Rather, it is many sometimes trivial occurrences and factors that add up.

Stressors can be better understood if we recognize that they differ in quality, duration, and quantity (Kottler & Chen, 2008; Olpin & Hesson, 2007). That is, some stressors are harmful because of their importance (seriousness). Others are detrimental because of the length of time they work on us or because of the large number of stressors occurring at one time. What one person considers stressful, another may not. Individual judgment defines just how stressful an experience is. Individual judgment also determines how effective we perceive our coping mechanisms to be.

Thus, both the type of problems encountered and your perception of how well you can cope with them affect the stress-related problems you experience. Feeling you simply cannot cope with a particular problem, no matter what, can lead to increased anxiety. The anxiety increases stress and starts a snowball effect. The consequences of stress, thus, can include physiological, psychological, or behavioral problems.

Physiological Stress-Related Problems

Often the first recommendation for coping with stress is to recognize its existence and magnitude. *Physiological* problems of stress include headaches, stomach upset (such as colitis), and skin rashes or hives. They also can include high blood pressure, which, of course, can be life-threatening. Although most of us have some of these symptoms from time to time, you should recognize that chronic, long-lasting symptoms are warning signs that your stress level is out of control.

Psychological Stress-Related Problems

Psychological difficulties from chronic stress include anxiety and depression. *Anxiety* is "a mood state wherein the person anticipates future danger or misfortune with apprehension. This response causes a markedly negative effect consisting primarily of tension and [other physical features. People who are anxious frequently experience] … a vague feeling of apprehension manifested as worry, unease, or dread" (Gray & Zide, 2008, p. 118). *Depression,* technically referred to as *depressive disorder,* is a psychiatric condition characterized by disheartened mood; unhappiness; lack of interest in daily activities; inability to experience pleasure; pessimism; significant weight loss not related to dieting, or weight gain; insomnia; an extremely low energy level; feelings of hopelessness and worthlessness; decreased capacity to focus and make decisions; and preoccupation with thoughts about suicide and one's own death (American Psychiatric Association, 2000).

Attempts to cope with psychological stress vary. Some people turn to excessive intake of alcohol, drugs, or food. Others smoke or even consider suicide.

Behavioral Stress-Related Problems

Behavioral correlates of stress include any behaviors resulting directly from excess stress. A father might hit his five-year-old daughter when he's had a hard day at work. Or a woman might argue incessantly with her significant other when she's under extreme duress. Other people withdraw inwardly and isolate themselves.

Figure 15.1 illustrates an example of the stress process in a macro context, reacting to pressures at work. First, a stressor occurs. In this case, the problem stressor is too much paperwork. Second, a person's perception of the problem shapes that individual's reactions to stress. Figure 15.1 illustrates that the person, depending on his or her individual make-up and perception, may experience physical symptoms such as stomachaches, headaches, or hives; psychological symptoms such as anxiety or depression; or behavioral symptoms such as angry emotional outbursts. Depending on the individual, the environmental context, the problem, and the person's perception of the problem, each individual will react differently to stressors.

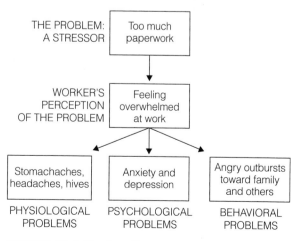

FIGURE 15.1 The Stress Process

Confronting Stress: Flight or Fight

People react to stress in highly individualized ways. We have mentioned that some people react to extensive stress by *fleeing* it, or pursuing activities to avoid confronting the stress. We have already mentioned that they might drink to excess, use drugs, overeat, or smoke.

Other people react to serious stress by *fighting* and attempting to manage it. Positive ways to handle stress include the various stress-management techniques we will discuss next.

Managing Your Stress

Managing stress often means reducing it or finding ways to keep it under control. Fighting stress to control it is more effective in the long run than fleeing from it. The latter only can result in physiological, psychological, or behavioral problems.

There are three primary approaches to stress management. This is true both in your work setting and in your personal life. First, you can change the way you think about the stressful event. Second, you can try to change the stressful event itself. Third, you can adopt specific strategies and techniques to help control your stress level.

Changing Your Thinking about the Stressful Event

The ABCDE theory of irrational thinking, developed by Albert Ellis, conceptualizes how your thinking can affect your stress level (Ellis, 2005; Kottler & Chen, 2008; Olpin & Hesson, 2007).

The ABCDE approach includes the following steps:

A = Activating event (identify the stressor)
B = Belief system (identify rational and irrational beliefs)
C = Consequences (mental, physical, behavioral)
D = Dispute irrational beliefs
E = Effect (change consequences) (emphasis added) (Olpin & Hesson, 2007, p. 101)

Corey and Corey (2011) offer the following explanation:

This theory explains the relationship among events, beliefs, and feelings. According to Ellis, your interpretations of events are frequently more important than what occurs in reality. He calls A an Activating event, B one's Belief system, and C the emotional [or physical or behavioral] Consequence. Consider the situation of [applying for a new job and] going through an interview. Let's imagine the worst outcome: The director of

the agency interviewed you and said that you lack the necessary experience for a placement in this agency. You do not get the job you badly wanted. The activating event (A) in this case is the situation of being rejected. The emotional consequences (C) you experience may include feeling depressed, hurt, and even devastated. Chances are that you hold what Ellis would term "irrational beliefs" about not having been accepted. Ellis would say that your beliefs (B) about this rejection might be some combination of the following thoughts: "It is absolutely horrible that I didn't get this job, and it surely proves that I'm incompetent." "I should have gotten this job, and this rejection is unbearable." "I must succeed at every important endeavor, or I'm really worthless." "This rejection means I'm a failure...."

[Such irrational belief systems and thinking can also affect our work as social workers. We as practitioners] often incorporate a wide range of dysfunctional beliefs that impair our capacity to function effectively when people seek our assistance. At times we may distort the processing of information, which can easily lead to faulty assumptions and misconceptions. As a helper, you can complicate your life by telling yourself that you must be all-knowing and perfect. If you feel depressed or agitated about the job you are doing, it is essential that you examine your basic assumptions and beliefs to determine how they are influencing what you are doing and how you are feeling. As you become more aware of your faulty thinking, you are in a position to change these patterns. (pp. 308–309)

The following five themes often characterize an irrational belief system that results in stress and its symptoms: "(1) Life isn't fair; (2) It's awful; (3) I can't stand it; (4) I must get what I want; and (5) I'm incompetent" (Kottler & Chen, 2008, p. 145). The D in the ABCDE theory involves *disputing* such irrational beliefs. Kottler and Chen (2008) explain how such disputation might work:

Basically what you are trying to do is to force yourself to look logically, rationally, and systematically at your situation. Imagine that the events were recorded and you were watching the reenactment on a screen. What would you observe? What would the recorder capture in objective, accurate images?

There are three major questions to ask yourself when disputing your irrational beliefs:

1. ***Where is the evidence that what you are experiencing is true?*** *We don't mean to invalidate the*

legitimacy of whatever you are thinking and feeling—you are perfectly entitled to any beliefs you want. But assuming that you don't like the way you are feeling and want to do something about it, then it is time to consider things more objectively. Ask yourself what a camera would record about this scene. Are things indeed as dire and disastrous as you think they are? Is this really the worst thing that ever happened to you? Is it true that you can't stand what is happening, that you will die as a result?

2. *Who says that things must be the way you think they are?* *YOU do. You are the one who is demanding that things be a particular way. Examine your "shoulds" and "musts" that signify your rigidity and your imposing of your standards and values on the rest of the world. Look at your tendency toward perfectionism, holding expectations for yourself and others.*

3. *Does your response seem logical and reasonable, given the situation?* *Return to the task of watching yourself. How are you exaggerating things? How are you making invalid assumptions? How are you overgeneralizing based on limited cases? How are you overpersonalizing? (pp. 145–146)*

Olpin and Hesson (2007) provide some additional examples of how an *activating* event results in a stressful *consequence* as a result of a person's irrational *belief* system; they also explain how *disputing* (D) irrational beliefs can result in positive psychological *effects* (E):

A person performs poorly on a test. That event is A, what actually happened. This fact might activate the belief system that sounds something like, "I really did poorly on that test. That is just horrible! I always do that. I'm really incompetent at everything I do. I'll never succeed. I'm worthless." The emotional result of thinking this way might include anxiety, loss of self-esteem, and even depression. We sometimes call this type of negative, irrational thinking awfulizing… This person is overreacting to the facts of the situation.

Consider another example in which a normal college student asks a girl out for a date and she turns him down (A). Irrational thinking based on a faulty belief system might sound like this: "I must not be good enough for her. Girls always turn me down. I'm such a loser." The emotional feelings (C) this person will experience may include anxiety, depression, and low self-esteem. This way of thinking might even lead to a vicious circle of additional events that reinforce this student's negative belief system (B) about

his inability to have a comfortable situation with the opposite sex. As a result, he may avoid asking another person out on a date or avoid social situations altogether.

This irrational way of thinking, however, can be fixed by learning to successfully dispute (D) the irrational thought. In rational thinking, the student who did poorly on the test could change her way of thinking to a more accurate series of thoughts, which sound something like this: "Boy, that test was rough! Everybody struggles occasionally on tests. The important thing is that I learn from today's experience. How can I improve my performance on the next test?" With these thoughts running through her head, she will feel powerful, assertive, and ready to continue pursuing her academic activities.

The young man who is turned down for the date might more accurately say these things to himself: "She must have a lot going on in her life. There are a lot of other girls who would be happy to spend some time with me. Everyone gets turned down occasionally. It's no big deal." He will be confident enough to find another person to go on a date and will feel much better about himself. He will feel more courageous, confident, and self-assured with these thoughts foremost in his mind.

Once we dispute (D) the irrational belief, we are free to enjoy the positive psychological effects (E) of the more rational belief. By reinforcing realistic, self-benefiting beliefs, you can eliminate your emotional and behavioral problems in the present and avoid future problems of that sort. In the process, you'll experience far less stress. (pp. 101–102)

Figure 15.2 depicts the ABCDE process using the case example of having difficulty achieving a goal established with a client.

The following are some additional suggestions to consider for changing your thinking about a stressful event:

1. *Accept that some stress cannot be avoided.* Do you have to worry about every stressor? Or can you accept the fact that some stressors will exist regardless and put them out of your mind as much as possible?

2. *Realize that the primary changeable element in your life is you.* Appreciate the fact that you can control your thinking and your behavior.

3. *Separate insoluble problems from others.* If you can't solve the problem, can you put it out of your mind and stop worrying about it?

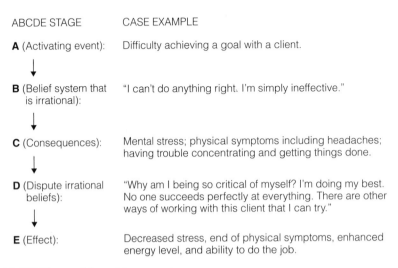

ABCDE STAGE | CASE EXAMPLE

A (Activating event): Difficulty achieving a goal with a client.

B (Belief system that is irrational): "I can't do anything right. I'm simply ineffective."

C (Consequences): Mental stress; physical symptoms including headaches; having trouble concentrating and getting things done.

D (Dispute irrational beliefs): "Why am I being so critical of myself? I'm doing my best. No one succeeds perfectly at everything. There are other ways of working with this client that I can try."

E (Effect): Decreased stress, end of physical symptoms, enhanced energy level, and ability to do the job.

FIGURE 15.2 The ABCDE Theory of Stress Management

4. *Examine your expectations.* Put plainly, dump the unrealistic ones. Both positive thinking (reframing a negative event to make it more positive) and talking to others about your expectations can be helpful. Recognize that some things are not worth getting upset about.

5. *Avoid should/should not thinking.* This limits your options. Are you wasting time worrying about what you should be doing while you're not doing it? Either do it or don't, but don't waste time worrying about it. Thinking differently really can reduce your stress level.

6. *Analyze your needs.* What do you really need? How much does the stressful event really affect you? To what extent should you let it bother you? Are you wasting your time and energy thinking about it?

7. *Emphasize your strengths—physical, emotional, and spiritual.* Could your time be better spent placing greater emphasis on positive aspects of your life instead of dwelling on stress-producing negatives?

Changing the Stressful Event

At least seven problem areas in a work context can cause you undue stress: inadequate or distressing work settings, frequent urgent deadlines, too much work to accomplish in the time allocated, distractions to accomplishing work (such as frequent interruptions), problematic relationships with other staff members, role ambiguity, and poor matches between staff and job. Sometimes you can change such stressful events. Other times you can't. The following will explore the possibility of implementing changes to control each type of stressful event.

Inadequate or distressing work setting (Corey & Corey, 2011; Dolgoff, 2005; Gibelman & Furman, 2008). Is your work environment helpful for getting your work done? Do you have sufficient privacy? Or do you have to work in a tiny cubicle separated only by paper-thin partitions of shoulder height?

A social worker we know once held a job as a counselor at a mental health center where she was supposed to do counseling in an office located in a large room with paper-thin dividing walls. It was virtually impossible to maintain confidentiality or to avoid distractions from other therapists going about their jobs. The answer was the purchase of a "white-noise" machine for each therapist. These machines blurred noise in the external environment so that other workers could not understand what was being said outside their office cubicle. This minor change in work environment— acquisition of the white-noise machines—made all the difference in the world in the worker's ability to do her job.

There are other ways to evaluate and improve your immediate work environment. Can you make your office more pleasant? Can you put up pictures that appeal to you? Can you paint your office some tantalizing color? Or would music help? Does music relax you and thereby assist you in getting work done? (Don't forget to use earphones so as not to disturb others around you.) These are only a few of the many questions you might ask yourself about improving your work environment.

Frequent urgent deadlines (Corey & Corey, 2011; Daft, 2010a). Do you feel that you can never catch up, no matter what you do? Paperwork is an ongoing problem for many workers. You have to complete your paperwork for the sake of accountability, but it's often excessively demanding and time-consuming.

How might you assume greater control of deadlines and paperwork? Is there any way you can decrease the urgency of deadlines? Can you decrease the amount of paperwork you must do? Can you record less? Are you incorporating too much detail? Are there ways you could be more efficient in completing your paperwork?

Is there any way that you can gain more lead time for accomplishing tasks and goals? Is there any way you can better manage your time? (Time management is discussed more thoroughly later in this chapter.)

Do you clearly understand your job, or are you trying to accomplish too much? You might discuss with your supervisor the appropriate expectations of your role.

Too much work and too little time (Brody, 2005; Corey & Corey, 2011). The problem of an overly heavy workload is related to the discussion of urgent deadlines. Do you clearly understand your job role? Are you spending your time on the tasks that are most significant? Are you wasting time on tasks that should not have priority?

As suggested, you might discuss your role with your supervisor. She might be able to help you better define your responsibilities and prioritize your job tasks. Are you wasting time trying to accomplish repetitive tasks? Can you better manage your time? Can you develop a form or procedure for accomplishing repetitive tasks to decrease the amount of time you have to spend on them? You might also examine your expectations for your performance. (We have discussed this in more depth under "Changing Your Thinking about the Stressful Event," the first approach to stress management.)

Note that having too little to do can also produce stress (Brody, 2005). Staff members may be bored or feel they have no purpose. Inequitable workloads can cause resentment among staff members that can also result in stress.

Distractions to accomplishing work. Are people constantly popping into your office? Does the phone ring incessantly? Do you feel you never have an opportunity to think? How can you get better control of your time? (Once again, this refers to time-management techniques to be discussed under "Managing Your Time.") Can you shut your door during certain times of the day? Can you put a "Please do not disturb" sign on your office door? Can you possibly set aside some predetermined time to finish your paperwork? Can you have an administrative assistant or secretary hold your calls and take messages or record them on your answering machine or voicemail so that you're not constantly distracted?

Problematic interpersonal relationships (Corey & Corey, 2011; Daft, 2010a; Daft & Marcic, 2009). Often, problematic interpersonal relationships at work involve one of two scenarios: First, you have a colleague, supervisor, or administrator who has poorly developed interpersonal skills. Such people have difficulties effectively interacting and communicating with others. Second, you alone have a "personality clash," for whatever reason, with a specific individual. If so, examine whether it is possible to resolve the conflict. In the case of the person with generally poor social skills, can you and other colleagues talk to your supervisor about the problematic staff member? Can this person's own supervisor help him improve his interpersonal skills? Can the agency send him to receive some training to improve social and communication skills?

If you have a personality conflict with someone else, can you approach this person and straightforwardly try to resolve the conflict? Can you ask your supervisor to function as a mediator? (Chapter 2 discussed some specific techniques for dealing with conflict, enhancing assertiveness, and gaining help from supervisors.) If you don't think resolution is realistically possible, can you minimize your involvement or interaction with the individual without interfering with your own ability to do your job?

Role ambiguity (Brody, 2005; Daft, 2010a; Dolgoff, 2005). When job descriptions, worker expectations, or administrative policies are unclear, it's difficult to know the right thing to do. This can cause anxiety and stress.

Agencies having an extremely laid-back atmosphere may contribute to such ambiguity. Consider an outpatient counseling center for adolescents (Brody & Nair, 2003). Because the agency administration desires to encourage a warm, informal atmosphere, rules and agency activities are extremely relaxed. Staff members take two-hour lunches, spend hours talking with clients in unstructured sessions, and receive no formal supervision. As a result, goals are rarely set and even less frequently attained. There are few if any helpful policies, such as what to do when a client threatens suicide. Ironically, staff members feel overworked because the lack of structure results in inefficient use of time where little work gets done. They find themselves regularly working overtime, yet spinning their wheels.

Contradictory expectations for worker performance can add to role ambiguity and create stress (Brody, 2005; Daft, 2010a). For example, an agency's administration might tell workers they're supposed to help poor people, but then impose massive restrictions regarding service eligibility and provision (Brody & Nair, 2003).

Poor match between staff and job (Brody, 2005). Stress can result when workers are given responsibilities for which they aren't qualified. It can be amazingly frustrating to practitioners when they don't have a clue about what to do. Stress can also occur when required work is way below a person's ability level. Social work interns may experience this kind of stress when their internship expectations primarily (and inappropriately) involve filing records and licking envelopes.

Adopt Stress-Management Strategies

The third way to manage stress is by adopting specific strategies and techniques to help subdue your stress level. There are at least four types of stress-management strategies: relaxation approaches, exercise, reinforcing activities, and social support.

Relaxation approaches. These five techniques—deep breathing relaxation, imagery relaxation, progressive muscle relaxation, meditation, and biofeedback—are effective techniques for reducing stress and inducing the relaxation response (becoming relaxed). Making yourself comfortable and at ease, avoiding distractions, and closing your eyes are helpful for each of these approaches.

Deep breathing relaxation helps you stop thinking about day-to-day concerns and concentrate on your breathing process. For 5 to 10 minutes, slowly and gradually inhale deeply and then exhale. Meanwhile, tell yourself something like, "I am relaxing, breathing more smoothly. This is soothing, and I'm feeling calmer, renewed, and refreshed." Regular practice of this technique will enable you to become more relaxed whenever you're in some tense situation—such as prior to giving a presentation or running a meeting.

Imagery relaxation involves switching your focus (for 10 to 15 minutes) from your daily concerns to your ideal relaxation place. It might be lying on a beach by a scenic lake in the warm sun. It might be soaking in a frothing hot tub while relishing your favorite magazine. It might be looking down on a vast wilderness landscape from the top of some picturesque mountain.

Regardless, savor all the pleasure, the peacefulness. Focus on everything that you find calming, soothing, and relaxing. Sense your whole body becoming refreshed, revived, and rejuvenated.

Progressive muscle relaxation is based on the principle that people cannot remain anxious if their muscles are relaxed (Olpin & Hesson, 2007). You can learn the technique by tightening and relaxing muscles, set by set. When relaxing each set of muscles, you should concentrate on the relaxed feeling and the fact that your muscles are becoming less tense. Schafer (1998) describes the technique:

1. *Find a quiet place where you can recline or sit comfortably.*
2. *Begin with a 6-second quieting response. [This is an exercise where you push out your stomach and inhale a deep breath, hold your breath for a few seconds, breathe out gradually and entirely, allow your shoulders and chin to drop, and experience the flow of relaxation run down from your neck down your torso to the tips of your fingers.]*
3. *Squeeze each of the following, hold for 10 seconds, then release and draw a deep breath. When finished at one location, move on to another.*

   - *Right fist*
   - *Right forearm*
   - *Right upper arm*
   - *Left fist*
   - *Left forearm*
   - *Left upper arm*
   - *Shoulders and neck*
   - *Head and face*

   If you wish, move to your feet and legs, then to your abdomen.
4. *As you proceed, be aware of the contrast between tension and calm. Be aware of the pleasant sensation of relaxation. Most of all, be aware of your power to produce deep quiet. (pp. 394, 406–407)*

Various *meditative approaches* are also being used today to decrease stress and tension. (Deep breathing relaxation and imagery relaxation are two forms of meditation.) There are at least four basic components common to meditative approaches that induce the relaxation response: (1) being in a quiet environment free from external distractions; (2) being in a comfortable position; (3) having an object to dwell on, such as a word, sound, phrase, or image; and (4) having a passive attitude so that you stop thinking about day-to-day concerns (Schafer, 1998).

Biofeedback equipment provides mechanical feedback to people about their stress levels (Kottler & Chen, 2008). Such equipment can inform people about increasing stress levels of which they may be unaware until markedly high levels are reached. A person's hand temperature can vary 10 to 12 degrees in an hour's time, with an increase in temperature indicating an increase in relaxation. Similarly, biofeedback equipment can measure the functioning of numerous physiological processes. These include blood pressure, hand temperature, muscle tension, heartbeat rate, and brainwave activity. In biofeedback training, a person is first taught to recognize high levels of anxiety or tenseness. Then the person is instructed on how to reduce such high levels by either closing the eyes and adopting a passive "letting-go" attitude or by thinking about something pleasant or calming. Often, relaxation approaches are combined with biofeedback to elicit the relaxation response. In summary, biofeedback equipment provides a person with immediate feedback about the kind of thinking that is effective in reducing stress. Information concerning biofeedback equipment and other methods of professionally supervised stress management may be found in a large city's Yellow Pages under "biofeedback equipment and systems" or "stress-management services."

Exercise. Exercise has multiple benefits. Because the alarm phase of the General Adaptation Syndrome (GAS) automatically prepares us for large muscle activity, it makes sense to exercise. Through exercising, we use up fuel in the blood, reduce blood pressure and heart rate, and reverse the other physiological changes set off during GAS's alarm stage. Exercising helps keep us physically fit so we have more physical strength to handle crises. Exercising also reduces stress and relieves tension, partly by switching our thinking from our daily concerns to the exercise we are involved in. For these reasons, everyone should have an exercise program. A key to making yourself exercise daily is selecting a program you enjoy. Various exercises are available, including walking, jogging, isometric exercises,[1] jumping rope, swimming, lifting weights, and so on.

Reinforcing activities. These activities are pleasurable experiences and are key to what we might call *personal therapies.* They relieve stress, change our pace of living,

Exercise such as aerobics provides an excellent stress-management technique. It relieves tension and helps take your mind off everyday pressures.

© Stephen Simpson/Workbook Stock/Getty Images

are enjoyable, and make us feel good. What is a reinforcer (pleasurable experience) to one person may not be to another. Common examples are listening to music, going shopping, hugging or being hugged, taking a bath, going to a movie, having a glass of wine, taking part in family and religious get-togethers, taking a vacation, going to a party, singing, and so on. Such activities add spice to life and remind us that we have value. Personal pleasures can also be used as payoffs to ourselves for jobs well done. Most of us would not seek to short-change others for doing well; we ought not to short-change ourselves. Such rewards make us feel good and motivate us to move on to new challenges.

Enjoyable activities outside our work and family responsibilities also relieve stress. Such involvement switches negative thinking from daily concerns to positive thoughts about the enjoyable activities. Therefore, it is stress-reducing to become involved in activities we enjoy. Such activities may include golf, tennis,

---

1. *Isometric exercises* involve those in which "opposing muscles are so contracted that there is little shortening but great increase in tone of muscle fibers involved" (Mish, 2008, p. 664).

swimming, scuba diving, taking flying lessons, traveling, and a host of others.

Social support. The importance of *social support* in reducing stress should not be overlooked (Corey & Corey, 2011; Dolgoff, 2005). Sharing feelings and frustrations with colleagues, supervisors, family, friends, and even professional counselors can help alleviate internal tension and develop coping strategies.

Managing Your Time

EP 2.1.1b

"I can't do it, I just can't! Oh, if only I had more time." How often have you thought something like this or heard others complain this way? So often it seems that there is simply never enough time to finish everything you absolutely must get done. If you don't have three exams to study for, you have four papers due next week. If you don't have papers due next week, then you have to work at your part-time job for 35 hours, do the laundry, clean the apartment for friends coming over next weekend, have the car fixed, and keep up with your regular homework.

People who are disorganized with their time usually feel that they're living on the brink of catastrophe. The key is that they feel out of control. They are swept this way and that by the torrents of time demands. Time-management techniques can help people acquire a sense of control over their lives. As a social worker, you will be faced with the need to juggle many responsibilities. Your macro environment is saturated with demands and potential stressors. Learning specific ways to use your time more effectively and efficiently will help you manage your workload better. This section will identify various techniques to help you manage your professional (and personal) time. Highlight 15.1 describes some typical time "troublers and controllers" (Mackenzie, 1972).

How Poor Time Management Causes Stress

If you are not managing your time efficiently, then you are probably not being nearly as effective as you could be. There are at least five reasons why insufficient or total lack of time management results in stress: "preoccupation" with the myriad tasks you're supposed to accomplish, poor task "pacing," "stimulus overload," stimulus underload, and "anxiety" (Curtis & Detert, 1981, pp. 190–191; Schafer, 1998).

Preoccupation

Have you ever had so much on your mind that you felt totally overwhelmed? Perhaps it seemed you had so much to do that you couldn't possibly finish it all anyway, so why even try? Did you end up paralyzed? Maybe the problem was that you were worrying about all the things you needed to do instead of paying attention to the task at hand. If you don't keep your mind on what you're doing, how can you expect to do a good job? Preoccupation with a huge throng of tasks is overwhelming and distracting. It adds to your overall level of stress.

Poor Task Pacing

It's interesting that academia, in some ways, is so very different from the real work world. Specifically, academia is based on a series of escalating peaks of stress. At the beginning of a term, the workload is probably not too bad for a while, but soon enough, midterm exams come up. Then you have three exams on one day or two 20-page papers due in the same week. During these periods, pressure escalates, and you probably feel some degree of stress. Then, finally, there's semester break when you have almost total respite from the seemingly unending flow of assignments, exams, research papers, and other academic responsibilities. Finally, you may have a summer break, when you probably have to work, but not in school.

Hence, school creates an environment where stress levels escalate to a pinnacle, then abruptly fall away. In your working environment you should ideally try to maintain more even stress levels, avoiding such drastic, upsetting variations. In other words, it is important to pace yourself on a more regular basis so that you can both accomplish your tasks and control your blood pressure.

Stimulus Overload

Stimulus overload is having too much to do. No matter how you utilize management skills, you cannot possibly complete all of your assigned tasks. Stimulus overload is similar to preoccupation, in that both can lead to stress and dissatisfaction with your work. It seems there is no possible way for you to do a good job.

Stimulus Underload

Stimulus underload is the opposite of stimulus overload. It occurs when you don't have enough to do to maintain your interest. Either there are not enough tasks or the tasks are numbingly dull. Have you ever spoken to someone who retired or quit working outside

HIGHLIGHT 15.1

Time "Troublers" and Controllers

Several habits cause you and just about everyone else to waste time. Review the time "troublers," likely reasons, and possible options listed below. Then answer the questions.

Time Troubler	Likely Reasons	Possible Options
What a mess	Confusion, disorder	Throw out, reorganize, file
Hurry, hurry	Doing too much too fast, too little attention to detail	Undertake less, allow more time, just say "No"
I just can't decide	Terror at making mistakes, cowering at responsibility, can't prioritize and set goals	Use decision-making, problem-solving, and goal-setting skills
Oops! Forgot to plan	Just didn't think, things happened too fast	Take time to think things through ahead of time, allow time for thought
There's just too much to do	Unable to say no, too much pressure to perform, can't prioritize	Prioritize goals, just say "No," evaluate what is possible to accomplish
I'll do it later	Overwhelmed, don't feel like it, it's too hard	Prioritize tasks, plan how to accomplish the most significant
There's that phone again	Can't resist answering, too nonassertive to not answer or to speak briefly, can't control yourself	Talk briefly, stick to the main points, offer to return call later
Unwanted guests	Just can't say no, talking is fun, allows you to avoid work	Limit easy access and availability, be assertive

Now answer the following questions:

1. What is your number-one time troubler? _____

   What are the likely reasons for this troubler? _____

   What are your potential options for controlling this troubler? _____

2. What is your number-two time troubler? _____

   What are the likely reasons for this troubler? _____

   What are your potential options for controlling this troubler? _____

SOURCE: Adapted from Mackenzie (1972).

the home who comments that he can't get anything done, despite having significantly more time than he had before? An old cliché comes to mind: "Work expands to fill the time available." With fewer or not enough things to do, it is easy to become lethargic, to move slowly and sometimes pointlessly. Stimulus underload can cause stress if you can't finish the tasks you feel you should. Time-management skills can reduce stress by helping you analyze how you spend your time and plan to spend the time you have more productively.

Anxiety

We have established that *anxiety* is "a mood state wherein the person anticipates future danger or misfortune with apprehension" often involving "worry, unease, or dread" (Gray & Zide, 2008, p. 118). Anxious people may appear nervous, skittish, and edgy. They may have difficulty both controlling useless movement (pacing back and forth or tapping their fingers annoyingly on the table) and redirecting their energy and attention to completing tasks at hand. Anxiety can result in lack of attention to time management. The probable consequence is stress.

Anxiety can result from any number of causes. These include personal problems, such as not being able to pay your full phone bill this month or a fear that your significant other is being unfaithful. Anxiety can result from worries about work or school. It can arise from subjective feelings of failure or low self-esteem. Whatever its causes, anxiety detracts from your ability to perform any task, thus resulting in stress. As we will see, good time-management skills can help you control both your anxiety and your time. (Note, however, that chronic, long-lasting anxiety that cannot be controlled may signal the need for professional help.)

Styles of Dealing with Time

Different people have divergent approaches to dealing with time. There are at least five styles, or ways people view and handle their time (Filley, 1978). First, there are people who are just bored. They are bored with work. Actually, they are lazy and don't like to expend any energy. They are bored with leisure time, too. They are critical of everything and complain a lot. Many are whiners. You probably don't like these people very much.

Second, there are people who are happy-go-lucky. They love their leisure time and would just as soon spend all of their time playing and relaxing. They probably should be extremely wealthy, because they don't like to work. They usually do work when they have to, but feel it is a waste of their precious leisure time. They are the people the boss frequently has to tap on the shoulder and ask not to read the newspaper for the first 45 minutes of their workday.

The third type of people are the "nose to the grindstone" type (Filley, 1978, p. 117). They work, work, work to get ahead, ahead, ahead. They hate having fun because they don't really know how to. Sometimes other people refer to them as drudges or workaholics.

In the fourth style, people perceive time as invaluable. Such an individual sees time "as a precious commodity, and feels guilty if it is wasted. Such people seem to be active and productive, both in their work and their leisure" (Filley, 1978, p. 117). These people differ from the "nose-to-the-grindstone" type in that they place value

on *time* rather than on *work*. They place equal emphasis on leisure time. They usually can't sit still. They can often drive other people crazy.

Finally, the fifth style is that of people who look at time as something they can choose to manage. They think in terms of priorities and goals. They make conscious choices concerning how to spend both their work and leisure time. In essence, they control time rather than letting time control them. These people are time managers. The following sections discuss the skills time managers use.

Time-Management Approaches

There are at least three approaches to time management that involve expending some amount of effort to learn new approaches to handling time and changing old behavior patterns. They include planning, controlling your own behavior, and dealing with procrastination (Alamo Colleges, 2009; Dartmouth College Academic Skills Center, 2009; MayoClinic.com, 2009).

Planning Your Time

Planning your time involves four primary steps. First, figure out how you currently spend your time. You can't make changes until you know what you need to change. Second, establish goals for yourself. How would you ideally like to spend your time? What would you really like to get done? Third, prioritize your goals. What goals are the most important? What do you need to accomplish first, second, and so on? Fourth, specify the tasks you must accomplish in order to attain each prioritized goal.

Step 1: Figure out where the time goes. Are you spending too much time on some activities and not enough on others? Are you avoiding unappealing tasks you know you should be doing? Do you dawdle? Do you spend more time than you think you should watching your favorite soap opera?

Your first task in time management is to figure out how much time you spend pursuing or not pursuing various activities. Figure 15.3 illustrates one method for achieving this. First, draw a circle representing a typical 24-hour workday. Estimate exactly how you spend your time during that day and mark off appropriately sized sections. How much time do you usually spend sleeping? Studying? Working? Lying around doing nothing? Circle A in Figure 15.3 shows how one individual illustrated approximate time spent on various activities (or lack of activities).

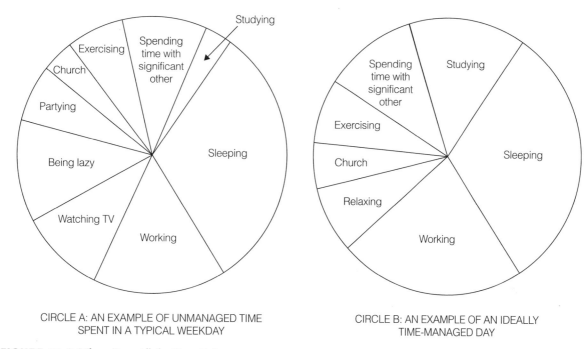

CIRCLE A: AN EXAMPLE OF UNMANAGED TIME
SPENT IN A TYPICAL WEEKDAY

CIRCLE B: AN EXAMPLE OF AN IDEALLY
TIME-MANAGED DAY

FIGURE 15.3 Where Does All the Time Go?
Source: Kirst-Ashman, K., & Zastrow, C. *Student Manual of Classroom Exercises and Study Guide for Understanding Human Behavior and the Social Environment,* 2nd ed. (Chicago: Nelson-Hall, 1990), pp. 133–135.

After completing your visual depiction of how you actually spend a day, draw another circle of the same size. Divide this circle to illustrate how you would ideally like to spend your day. Would you like to spend more time studying and working? Would you prefer to decrease your lazy time? Circle B in Figure 15.3 demonstrates how the same individual would ideally prefer to spend his time. He deletes being lazy and watching television. Instead, he increases studying and working time and adds a shorter relaxing category. In a similar manner, your own circle should provide a rough idea of how you spend your time and how you would like to. You should be able to identify both how you waste your time and how you ideally want to spend it.

Another more detailed and time-consuming technique for analyzing how you spend your time is *time-mapping,* that is, keeping an hourly, half-hour, or 15-minute record of how you spend your time (Schafer, 1998). Keeping such a log (as many professionals, such as lawyers, typically do) allows you to determine how you really spend your time (Kottler & Chen, 2008). You can get a realistic grasp of how long each activity takes. You might choose to track your time for only one day or for several days. Highlight 15.2 shows how to begin tracking 15-minute blocks. You would

then continue this process to cover a 24-hour period. You probably would simply block out whatever period or periods of time you spend sleeping. In any event, this approach should provide you with a fairly accurate picture of how you spend your time. It should pinpoint for you those periods when you waste time. Subsequently, this information can be a guide to those time periods over which you want to gain greater control.

We assume here that you are a student. Therefore, your time-tracking will be substantially different than if you were working in a full-time professional social work position. However, many of the methods used to gain control over your time at this period of your life are identical to those you can use to gain control over your agency work time.

Step 2: Establish goals for yourself. One reason that people fail to use time wisely is that they simply do not set goals for themselves. They drift in time from day to day, maybe getting things done and maybe not. Therefore, one of the primary steps in time management is to establish goals.

You have already begun to explore how you actually spend your time. You should also have begun to think about how you might improve your time management.

HIGHLIGHT 15.2

Time-Tracking

Day: _____

Time Segment	How Time Was Spent
6:00 A.M.	_____
6:15 A.M.	_____
6:30 A.M.	_____
6:45 A.M.	_____
7:00 A.M.	_____
7:15 A.M.	_____
7:30 A.M.	_____
7:45 A.M.	_____

(Continue this process in a similar manner to account for your time during a full 24-hour period.)

At this point it is helpful to establish specific goals for how you would like to spend your time.

Arbitrarily, we will divide time up into daily units. The point is for you to get a perspective on what you would like to accomplish on a short-term basis. Of course, you can use the same technique to establish longer-term goals of a week, a month, three months, a year, two years, or whatever. You can set goals for virtually any period of time. The intent of this exercise is to teach you the goal-setting and decision-making procedure. Highlight 15.3 gives you a format for doing this. Identify your goals using this format. Earlier chapters have emphasized the importance of establishing measurable goals. This is true when establishing any type of goal, ranging from your own personal time-management to major macro goals. For example, a goal stating "improve my personality" is pretty difficult to measure, but a goal to "give a genuine compliment to two colleagues today" is easier to monitor.

Note that your goals as a student will be different than your goals as a full-time professional social worker. However, once again, you can use these same procedures to manage your work time and workload in the future. Highlight 15.3 lists spaces for 10 possible goals. The number of goals is arbitrary. You could list 2, 10, or whatever number you wish.

Step 3: Prioritize your goals. You may become overwhelmed and immobilized when confronted with a cluster of goals all at one time. Therefore, after identifying goals, prioritize them according to their importance. One common method of prioritizing is the ABC method (Olpin & Hesson, 2007; Schafer, 1998), wherein you assign a value A, B, or C to each goal you cite. "A" goals are those you absolutely want to get done no matter what. These are top-priority goals.

"C" goals, on the other hand, are unimportant goals. They might be things that you would like to accomplish, but in all likelihood never will. You might want to write the first 40 pages of the great American novel today. Or you think it would be nice to call your four best friends from high school by tonight. If you don't really think a "nice" goal is important or don't really think you'll get around to it today, drop it. Don't waste precious time

HIGHLIGHT 15.3

Planning Time-Management Goals

Identify up to 10 things you would like to accomplish today. (Remember that goals don't have to be set up on a daily basis. They can be for weeks, months, or years, depending on the unit of time over which you wish to gain control.)

1. _____   6. _____

2. _____   7. _____

3. _____   8. _____

4. _____   9. _____

5. _____   10. _____

worrying about things that you cannot or will not do. "C" goals often get relegated to the circular file.

"B" goals lie between "A" and "C" goals. You think you do need to get them done pretty soon, but you really do not think you'll have time to do them today. Frequently, today's "B" goal becomes tomorrow's "A" goal. This happens as a deadline approaches or your anxiety increases. If you can't decide whether a goal should be "A" or "B," automatically assign it a "B." If you're not certain that it's critical enough to be an "A" goal, it probably isn't.

Now, further prioritize each category of goals. Among the "A" goals that you absolutely feel you must get done, determine which one is the most critical life-or-death goal to attain today. Make this goal "A1." Continue through your "A" goals, numbering them in order of priority. When finished, do the same thing first with your "B" goals and ultimately with your "C" goals. This should provide you with a clearly prioritized plan for how to go about your day. First, pursue goal "A1," then "A2," and so on down the line. Highlight 15.4 illustrates one person's goal planning for one day.

Note that you can prioritize goals in diverse areas of your life, including your personal life involving family, friends, and recreation, in addition to work. You can do this either separately or on one prioritized list. Highlight 15.4 includes goals in various areas. Priorities depend on the individual's value system. The goals specified here would probably significantly differ from those you would formulate for yourself. But then again, maybe not.

Highlight 15.5 illustrates a potential prioritized goal list for a professional social worker working in a health care center for older adults. As we discussed, you can establish goals for virtually any area of your life.

Step 4: Specify tasks for each goal. After prioritizing your goals, it is helpful to list the specific tasks needed to accomplish each goal. A hospital social worker might identify the goal of arranging Ms. Jones's transfer from the hospital to a nursing home. She arbitrarily labels this goal "A1." Specific tasks to accomplish this particular goal might include notifying Ms. Jones's son and daughter, locating an appropriate nursing home, arranging transportation, working out financial arrangements, and notifying the nursing staff that arrangements are complete.

Obviously, these tasks need to be accomplished in a particular order. For example, you arrange transportation only after you know the nursing home in which the client will be placed. Thus, it is probably wise to assign numerical priority to each task to guide your progress from one task to the next.

It is also important to leave sufficient time to complete each step. Think ahead and try to estimate how much time each step will most likely take. Do not allow 30 minutes to transport Ms. Jones to the nursing home if the hospital is 45 minutes from the home—45 minutes, that is, when there is no summer road construction and you aren't traveling during rush hour. In this case, it would be better to allow an hour and a half for the task.

HIGHLIGHT 15.4

Prioritized Plan for "A Day in My Life"

The following is an example of one individual's daily goals, listed in an unprioritized order. They are followed by their designated "ABC" and numerical assignments.

Day: Monday

1. Finish Statistics assignment due Tuesday for class A3

2. Take Harry to the doctor A1

3. Go to aerobics class B5

4. Talk to Professor Tuffgrade regarding research project B1

5. Work at Walmart for four hours A4

6. E-mail Kristen C3

7. Play poker B3

8. Clean the bathroom B4

9. Clean the refrigerator C2

10. Go to class A2

11. Buy beer for poker game B2

12. Watch *The Young and the Restless* C1

13. Call Mom B6

HIGHLIGHT 15.5

Prioritized Plan for a Professional Workday

The numbered items to the left below make up a nursing home social worker's unprioritized goal list for one workday. The arbitrarily prioritized "ABC" and numerical standings are depicted to the right of each goal below.

Day: Monday

1. Finish last week's progress notes C1

2. Call Sybil about Ms. Sicperson A1

3. Meet with supervisor B1

4. Get resources for Mr. Ed B2

5. Take Ms. Harrington to her daughter-in-law's A2

6. Complete resource file C2

7. Attend two-hour in-service B3

8. Run social support group A3

Get Control of Your Own Behavior

What do we mean by controlling your own behavior? Doesn't everyone automatically control what he or she does every day? The answer is no.

Time management involves more than planning daily goals. It requires following a number of principles that guide your choices for goal planning. These principles include committing yourself to the time-management process, evaluating your actual job requirements, clustering similar activities together, using a calendar, attending to each document or handling each sheet of paper only once, delegating any tasks you can, avoiding doing other people's work, bringing order to your desk, planning time for contemplation, designating leisure time, managing meetings effectively, managing your correspondence appropriately, using e-mail and the phone efficiently, and reviewing your weekly progress.

Look at yourself. Develop a time-management perspective. Instead of falling prey to the various stresses discussed earlier, look yourself right in the eye and commit to time management. Don't make excuses that you're too busy to spend time to get control of your time. Busy people aren't necessarily productive or efficient people. The purpose of time management is to become more effective and efficient in the use of your time. In the long run, time management saves you time.

Understand your job. If you have a job, of course, you understand it, right? Not necessarily. We have established that most positions typically have job descriptions indicating what you are paid to do. However, many social work jobs are complicated. They involve not only your micro and mezzo obligations to clients, but also your macro responsibilities to your agency and community. They require a lot of discretion regarding what you should do and how. Discuss with your supervisor what your job description really is: What are your specific responsibilities? Allow her or him to help you make decisions regarding how to prioritize goals and the respective tasks necessary to achieve them.

Bunch similar activities together. Sometimes, it is helpful to block portions of time for completing similar types of tasks (Schafer, 1998). Some social workers set aside a specific day for doing paperwork. Others identify a portion of each day for tasks such as returning all phone calls. Concentrating on completing a cluster of similar tasks often saves the mental energy of switching from one orientation to another. It would probably be inefficient for you to spend every other 15 minutes switching from studying policy to studying research. Focusing on one until you have completed your assignment and then moving on to the other is probably a much more coherent approach.

Use a calendar. Using a calendar does not mean just recording your appointments. Employing a calendar means establishing a whole new perspective on time. Instead of trying to keep everything in your head, look at your calendar and let it guide you. It can tell you whether you have time to assume additional responsibilities. When someone asks if you can do something, consult your calendar to see if you have sufficient time to undertake whatever tasks the new responsibility involves. Consider such factors as the time it will take to go from one responsibility to another. Agreeing to do something for which you do not have sufficient time results in over-scheduling, a source of stress for many people.

Calendars come in many formats, including daily, weekly, or monthly; electronic or paper. It doesn't matter which you choose. Select whatever format best suits your needs and preferences. Use your calendar as a record of your work. Check off appointments that have been kept. Jot down mileage to and from appointments. Insert notes that will save you time, such as the room number of a hospitalized patient or the directions to your client's house.

The goal is to make your calendar an indispensable tool for managing your time. The calendar should go with you everywhere, along with an address book. In emergencies, you will have at your disposal both a means to reach people and your calendar. If you find yourself running behind, take a minute to call and notify your next appointment. If you do this, you will feel less pressure to race to your next stop. Both clients and colleagues will appreciate knowing your reasons for being late.

Attend to each document or handle each sheet of paper only once. What do you mean only once? Many people might respond to this suggestion in a similar manner. However, think about it. How much time can you waste reading an electronic document or a sheet of paper, putting it in a folder or on your desk somewhere, losing it, thinking about it again, finding it, reading it again, and so on? Generally, if you don't have time to focus your attention on that document right now, wait until another period in your day when you will have time to address it. You probably should take some time as soon as possible, because the information might be important. It might be a deadline notification from your supervisor or possibly a termination notice. Who knows? Making time for such activities highlights the importance of planning time for thinking about and responding to relevant correspondence.

An example of a colleague comes to mind: Sam is an avoider. If he is forced to take notes, they are typically brief and vague. Sam feels it's too difficult to both take notes and pay attention to what's going on. In one particular situation, he was recording the recommendations made at an important staff meeting. It was his turn. All other participants had already assumed similar responsibilities at other meetings. After the meeting, Sam got up, said he would finish the notes later, and left for his office. Days passed. Weeks dragged by. Finally, after several other staff members reminded Sam about his task, he finished the notes. He complained energetically about how difficult this task was. He whined about how hard it was to remember what occurred weeks ago. Sam's minutes were vague and did not capture the sense of the meeting. Sam wrote down what he thought he remembered from the meeting. The record was so bad that staff had to hold the same meeting all over again. This time, participants did not ask Sam to assume any note-taking responsibility.

Sam is also a procrastinator. A later portion of this chapter, "Procrastination," discusses this behavior and what to do about it.

Delegate. Too often, it is easy to feel that in order to get something done right you have to do it yourself. Instead, if at all possible, delegate (Dartmouth College, 2009; Olpin & Hesson, 2007; Schafer, 1998). *Delegating* simply means assigning responsibilities to someone else. We have discussed delegation in the context of supervision, as a critical supervisory skill. Although it is probably easier for a supervisor to "assign" tasks to someone else, you can still watch for your own opportunities to do so. Is there some repetitive task that your administrative assistant might be able to do as part of her or his job? Are there volunteers or students available to help you?

Delegating, of course, requires defining what needs to be done with sufficient clarity that another person can complete the job. Next, leave the initiative with the delegatee. If you tell people exactly how to do a job, you limit their creativity and further involve yourself in details that should be left to others. Don't forget to thank people and reward them for helping you and for doing the job right. Like you, most people appreciate praise, acknowledgment, and other forms of recognition.

Don't do other people's work. In time management, the flip side of delegating is making certain you do your work and your work only, not that of other people (Sheafor & Horejsi, 2009). Consider Sam, the procrastinator mentioned earlier. People who regularly fail, do a poor job, or never really learn how to complete a task can be very manipulative. Others learn that they are not dependable. Therefore, they get out of a lot of work. Colleagues no longer ask Sam to take notes at meetings because he inevitably "screws it up." Thus, he does less work, and his colleagues take up the slack and do more.

If you tend to have high expectations for the quality of work, be vigilant that you do not end up doing other people's work because you do it better or more effectively than they do. Think in terms of each individual being responsible for her or his own tasks and failings.

Bring order to your desk. Remember the adage "A messy desk reflects a messy mind." No one knows if this is really true. However, organizing items on your desk so you can find them easily is a time saver (Sheafor & Horejsi, 2009). Additionally, if you follow the prior suggestion of handling each document or sheet of paper only once, organizing your desk will be easier. Instead of allowing documents to drift amid an ocean of paper, you will deal with each paper once and put it in its resting place.

Another aspect of bringing order to your desk is making sure the information you use frequently is readily at your disposal (Olpin & Hesson, 2007). Keep contact information, forms, files, or manuals you use often somewhere that's readily available and easy to find. Saving time involves wasting as little as possible on useless activities, such as looking for lost or hard-to-find information.

Leave time for contemplation. Even with an ever-so-busy schedule, allow yourself some "downtime" each workday (Kottler & Chen, 2008; Schafer, 1998). You need time to organize your thoughts and evaluate your progress toward your designated goals. If you are constantly harried and distracted, you can't focus as well on the tasks and goals at hand.

Designate leisure time for yourself. Workaholics often burn out and have heart attacks at a young age. Incorporate some leisure time into your schedule on a regular basis. What happens when you don't do this? Have you ever forced yourself to complete task after task after task with no relief in sight? Did you, perhaps, finally find yourself saying, "To heck with it" and end up doing nothing at all?

It is important to gain a realistic perspective on your time. Time with friends, family, and yourself alone are all important facets of life. If you control this and use such good time to reward yourself for work, you may find yourself working much more eagerly and effectively.

For example, we knew a student who would study like crazy virtually all day—in addition to going to class, of course—from about 9:00 A.M. to 9:00 P.M. However, unless she had an exam the following day, at 9:00 P.M. she would abruptly stop whatever she was doing and go off either to play sheepshead (a card game unique to Wisconsin and Minnesota) or to do something else with friends until about midnight. She made a point of not feeling guilty about having fun, because she already had put her work time in. She felt she deserved some reward and relief.

Manage meetings effectively. Most social workers have many chances to arrange, conduct, and participate in meetings, which occur any time two or more people come together for some designated purpose, usually to pursue some type of goal. We have established that meetings involving social workers can range from staffings (where particular clients' progress is discussed), to task groups (where a variety of professionals get together to do something, such as propose amendments to social work certification requirements), to large political meetings (where political tactics are discussed). Chapter 3 discussed a number of ways to manage meetings more efficiently and effectively, including planning ahead, clarifying meeting purposes and objectives, carefully selecting participants, specifying a time and place, preparing an agenda, starting on time, stating the ending time at the meeting's beginning, periodically alerting participants to how much time remains, keeping the group on target, ending the meeting on time, and planning for follow-up meetings.

Manage your correspondence. Because correspondence (e-mails, letters, memos, announcements, and advertising) can consume a major portion of our busy time, it is appropriate to consider ways to manage this efficiently.

Write brief replies by e-mail or by hand as quickly as possible to correspondence you receive. Remember that it's time-efficient to handle paper or address an e-mail message only once. If you answer immediately, you save the time required to re-read old messages.

Always keep a copy of what you send, even if doing so somewhat delays your response. Otherwise, especially if you have a deluge of paper and e-mail, you may not remember what you said, or worse yet, whether you responded to the correspondence at all.

If possible, use established formats to structure your correspondence instead of "reinventing the wheel" and writing a totally new response each time. This is especially true if you routinely receive requests for similar information or need to send many people the same message. Of course, you can easily send the same response to a large group via e-mail. Tailoring each response to the individual recipient is also viable. You might keep examples of exceptionally well-written letters you receive or have sent to give you ideas about how to phrase things effectively.

Open second- and third-class mail, including the "junk mail" we get both at home and at the office, once a week near a recycling bin. It is probably not important enough to make a real claim on our time. You should either immediately throw it out without opening it or bunch it together and save it until you have a small block of slow time. Such slow time might include lunch if you're having it at your desk, time waiting for an appointment to appear, or time at the end of the day when you are simply too "bushed" to do anything more difficult and productive. The same is true about getting rid of "junk" e-mail.

If you doubt the efficacy of these suggestions, try this experiment. Save all your junk mail in a box or junk e-mail in a folder for a week or two. When you open it, count the items you think are important. How many of them affected your day-to-day work as a social worker? How many of them had any importance in your personal life? The chances are good that most, if not all, of this material is of limited or no value.

Use the phone efficiently. Consider using conference calls instead of holding meetings. Conference calls are especially effective if the main reason for the meeting is to consult or to give information. Meetings take travel time, and much time is wasted getting started. Conference calls can be set up and managed at much less cost than many meetings.

Outline your phone calls before dialing. Think about what you want to say and note the most important points on a piece of paper. This will help you use your phone time efficiently and ensure that you cover everything you had planned to.

Review your weekly progress. At each week's end, review the extent to which you actually achieved your time-management goals. Were you on target? Or did you overestimate (or underestimate) what you could accomplish for the week? How did this past week and the progress you made relate to your longer-term goals? Should your goals for next week be higher, lower, or about the same?

To get a perspective on time management for life, it is sometimes helpful to stop and ask yourself, "Is this the very best way I can be spending my time right now?" Periodically addressing this issue can help orient you to your life's broader picture. You might find yourself working two hours overtime to get those rotten progress notes done while you are missing your 81-year-old grandmother's birthday dinner. At such times, what really is most important to you? Does your quest for effective time management overshadow something else you might be doing that means more to you?

A related question to ask yourself occasionally is, "If I were faced with death this very moment, what would I regret?" Is there someone close to you whom you haven't contacted for too long a time? Have you managed to avoid making your will? Whatever your concerns might be, confronting yourself like this can help you manage major life priorities. Perhaps you haven't had enough time for your family. The old cliché is that time passes too quickly. Small children soon grow up and move away. Older adults get yet older and die. Is there time you should be spending with someone now—or soon—before it's too late?

Postscript. Following these suggestions will help you use time more effectively. Because we can't manufacture time, we have to ensure that we use it as efficiently as possible. The multiple responsibilities of social workers require that we adopt strategies to help us do our jobs better. Time management is just one of those strategies.

Procrastination

The third major time-management dimension is fighting the tendency to procrastinate. *Procrastination* is the "tendency to put off doing something until a future time because it is perceived as being too onerous, unpleasant, or unappealing" (Schafer, 1998, p. 498). Most of us—perhaps all of us—put off what we're supposed to do at some time or another. No one is totally faultless. However, when procrastination interferes with your ability to accomplish your goals in a significant or ongoing manner, then you are no longer in control. To gain control of your time, you can implement a number of techniques for fighting procrastination.

Reasons for procrastination. The first reason is the quest for flawlessness. Some people cannot tolerate being anything but 100 percent perfect. Given that no one is that perfect, this sets people up for failure. If you can't do it perfectly, why do it at all? Such an attitude prevents people from accomplishing their goals. Another aspect of the quest for flawlessness is putting the task off until another time. Perhaps you know that you will have to complete the task sometime. However, you are so averse to it right now (because you want to do it flawlessly) that it's easier to worry about the whole thing later.

A second reason is worry that you will only fail at doing the task well anyway, so it's best to avoid it altogether (Kottler & Chen, 2008; Olpin & Hesson, 2007). It is no news flash that our society places extremely high value on success. We generally do not want to fail, no matter what. If you feel that you may fail to accomplish a task, it can be easier to avoid the task altogether.

A third reason is feeling overwhelmed. If you perceive a task as awesomely difficult and perhaps even scary, it may be easier for you to avoid it altogether than to do it and get it over with.

A fourth reason is nonassertive overacceptance of responsibilities. People who just can't say no to requests can easily overextend themselves. Trying to get too much done can distract you from getting anything done at all. We have discussed how easy it is to become overwhelmed, unable to focus on anything adequately, and immobilized.

The fifth reason is idling away your time with useless busyness. You can avoid completing a task by doing something else and keeping busy. Busyness can provide you with an excuse for not doing what you're supposed to. For example, you might have to complete a research paper for one of your classes, and you hate doing research papers. You can avoid the actual writing of the paper by spending scores of hours researching articles on the topic or by washing your car. Highlight 15.6 helps identify personal reasons for procrastination.

The cons of procrastination. Sometimes it seems that procrastination is your best choice. It allows you to avoid some unpleasant work. However, there are at least four reasons why procrastination is unappealing (Lakein, 1973). First, it's probably best that you complete your own task rather than passing it on to someone else. Shirking responsibility is irritating to people. Others may not do the task the way you want it done or know it should be done. Additionally, you can get a

HIGHLIGHT 15.6

Self-Analysis of Procrastination

1. What tasks do you procrastinate over?
2. What are your reasons for procrastinating over them? Why do you find them aversive?

3. What tactics can you use to control your procrastinating behavior?
4. When will you begin implementing these tactics?

bad reputation as someone who cannot effectively complete assigned work.

Second, unappealing tasks probably won't go away. They usually remain wedged in your consciousness, nagging you to get at them. Doing the task and getting it over with stops this bothersome nagging. Third, unappealing tasks rarely get any easier. If anything, the longer you put off a task, the harder it gets. Maybe you will forget some of the details. Possibly, the task will increase in complexity as time goes on. Fourth, and perhaps worst, is that the longer you put something off, the more aversive it becomes. If it seems like it's bad to start out with, it will only get worse.

Battling procrastination. Procrastination plagues most of us at some time or another. So, what exactly do you do about it? Following are several suggested techniques:

1. *Break up a large, threatening task into a number of smaller, more manageable tasks.* Even if you start doing a task for only five minutes, you are still combating procrastination and getting greater control over your time.

   Suppose you have to write a 20-page term paper. Thinking in terms of the entire gigantic paper—including all the research, thinking, and typing involved—can be paralyzing. Instead, divide the process into smaller, more doable pieces. First, start researching sources. Second, take notes from these sources. Third, make an outline of topics as the skeleton of your paper. Fourth, arrange your notes in the order that you think you will use them. Fifth, sit down and type a rough draft. Sixth, edit that draft. Seventh, type your final draft. When thinking about these seven smaller tasks, don't envision yourself doing them all at once. Picture yourself doing them on different days at various times. As you complete each task, you will gain the satisfaction that task completion can give you. At the same time, you will be chipping away at completion of the final project.

2. *Do the worst job first.* Often, anticipating a tough job keeps you from ever getting it done. Doing the job immediately means that other, less unappealing tasks will look better and easier in comparison. The other advantage of doing tough jobs first is that it ensures sufficient time to see the job through to completion. Saving the hard jobs until the end of the day often means that they don't get done.

3. *Complete whatever it is you start.* Coming back to an old project or task requires taking the time to get oriented to it again. You will probably need to waste precious time rethinking what you have already done. If you start reading an article, finish reading it. If you stop reading and begin again later, you will probably have to reread the beginning to get yourself oriented again. If you begin working on a letter or social history, finish it before turning your attention to other tasks. If you don't establish the habit of doing this, you will find your desk full of half-finished projects, most of which are probably overdue. Be persistent, even dogged, about finishing a task.

4. *Do it right now.* How many times have you heard friends say that they're going to quit smoking, lose 20 pounds, stop drinking, or study harder—someday? What have you noticed about these comments and these people's plans? Well, for one thing, when they say they're going to do something, they obviously have not done it yet. Framing plans in the *going to* perspective is a good way to procrastinate.

   We have a friend who is going to write a novel someday. She barely writes letters, but she is going to write that important novel. She's been going to write it for about 15 years now. One minor related problem is that she can't spell very well and needs a lot of help with her grammar. A suggestion for becoming a good writer is to write—write a lot. Write right now. It need only be a page or two a day, but do it. Forcing yourself to do whatever your task is right now can save you a lot of wasted energy and worry.

An Ending Thought

This chapter emphasized the importance of stress- and time-management techniques for leading an effective work and personal life. In view of the often stressful macro environment, the suggested approaches can make life much more enjoyable and manageable.

Chapter Summary

The following summarizes this chapter's content as it relates to the learning objectives presented at the beginning of the chapter. Chapter content prepares social workers to:

A. *Conceptualize the dynamics of stress and explain the General Adaptation Syndrome.*

"Stress is the feeling you experience when you can't seem to sit still, when your thoughts are racing, and you feel out of control" (Kottler & Chen, 2008). The General Adaptation Syndrome includes the three phases of alarm, resistance, and exhaustion. Stress can result in physiological, psychological, and behavioral problems. Confronting stress often involves either fleeing it or fighting it.

B. *Practice personal reflection regarding stress levels, identify potential stressors in agency settings, and propose means to address stress in order to improve practice effectiveness.*

Practitioners can cope with stress by changing their thinking about a stressful event, changing the event itself, or adopting stress-management strategies. Albert Ellis proposed an ABCDE approach to changing how one thinks about stressful events. There are facets of agency life that may cause stress that may be attended to and changed. These include inadequate or distressing work setting, frequent urgent deadlines, too much work and too little time, distractions, problematic interpersonal relationships, role ambiguity, and a poor match between worker ability and job requirements. Stress-management strategies may involve relaxation approaches, exercise, reinforcing activities, and social support.

C. *Conceptualize how poor time management can cause stress and affect performance.*

Reasons for poor time management include preoccupation, poor task pacing, stimulus overload, stimulus underload, and anxiety. Any of these factors can cause stresss, resulting in ineffectiveness. People adopt different styles of managing time.

D. *Practice personal reflection and propose means of adopting time-management techniques to improve practice effectiveness.*

Time management approaches include improved planning of time. This involves assessing how time is spent and planning improvements through goal setting, prioritizing, and specifying tasks to achieve goals. Another time-management approach entails getting control of one's own behavior. This can be done through looking at yourself, understanding your job, bunching similar activities together, using a calendar, attending to each document or paper only once, delegating, avoiding doing others' work, bringing order to your desk, leaving time for contemplating, designating leisure time, managing meetings effectively, managing your correspondence, using the phone efficiently, and reviewing weekly progress.

E. *Assess the dynamics of procrastination and suggest means for combating it to improve practice efficiency and effectiveness.*

Procrastination is the "tendency to put off doing something until a future time because it is perceived as being too onerous, unpleasant, or unappealing" (Schafer, 1998, p. 498). Reasons for procrastination include the quest for flawlessness, fear of failure, being overwhelmed, overacceptance of responsibilities, and useless busyness. Battling procrastination includes breaking up large, threatening tasks into smaller, more manageable ones, doing the worst jobs first, completing whatever you start, and getting things done immediately.

Competency Notes

The following identifies where Educational Policy (EP) competencies and practice behaviors are discussed in the chapter:

EP 2.1.1b Practice personal reflection and self-correction to assure continual professional development. *(P. 554):* Excessive stress may interfere with work performance. Stress management requires personal reflection and self-correction to assure continual professional effectiveness. Means of analyzing stress levels are discussed, and various approaches to stress management are suggested.

(P. 564): Time management requires personal reflection and self-correction to assure continual professional effectiveness. The relationship between poor time management and stress is explained, and various approaches to time management are proposed.

On the Internet

Visit the *Generalist Practice with Organizations and Communities* Web site at www.cengage.com/social_ work/kirst-ashman for learning tools such as Power-Point® slides, tutorial quizzing, Web links, and final exams.

References

Abramovitz, M. (1995). Aid to families with dependent children. In R. L. Edwards (Editor-in-Chief), *Encyclopedia of social work* (19th ed., Vol. 1, pp. 183–194). Washington, DC: NASW Press.

Abramovitz, M. (2007). Ideological perspectives and conflicts. In J. Blau (with M. Abramovitz) (Ed.), *The dynamics of social welfare policy* (2nd ed., pp. 126–183). New York: Oxford.

Administration for Children and Families (ACF). (2006). Welfare reform reauthorized. Retrieved from http://www.acf.hhs.gov/opa/spotlight/welfarereauthorized.htm.

Administration for Children and Families (ACF). (2008a). Major provisions of the Personal Responsibility and Work Opportunity Reconciliation Act of 1996 (P.L. 104-193). Retrieved from http://www.acf.hhs.gov/programs/ofa/law-reg/finalrule/aspesum.htm.

Administration for Children and Families (ACF). (2008b). TANF adult recipients with income by type of non-TANF income October 2006–September 2007. Retrieved from http://www.acf.hhs.gov/programs/ofa/character/FY2007/tab44.htm.

Ahlfinger, N. R., & Esser, J. K. (2001). Testing the groupthink model: Effects of promotional leadership and conformity predisposition. *Social Behavior and Personality, 29*(1), 31–42.

Alamo Colleges. (2009). Strategies for success: Time management. Retrieved from http://www.alamo.edu/sac/history/keller/ACCDitg/SSTM.htm.

Alberti, R., & Emmons, M. (2008). *Your perfect right* (9th ed.). Atascadero, CA: Impact.

Albrecht, K. (1988). *At America's service.* New York: Warner Books.

Aldag, R. J., & Kuzuhara, L. W. (2005). *Mastering management skills.* Mason, OH: South-Western.

Alexander, R. (1997). Social workers and privileged communication in the federal legal system. *Social Work, 42*(4), 387–391.

Alexander, R., Jr. (2003). *Understanding legal concepts.* Pacific Grove, CA: Brooks/Cole.

Alinsky, S. (1971). *Rules for radicals.* New York: Vintage Books.

Alter, C. F. (2009). Building community partnerships and networks. In R. J. Patti (Ed.), *The handbook of human services management* (2nd ed., pp. 435–454). Thousand Oaks, CA: Sage.

Alter, C., & Evens, W. (1990). *Evaluating your practice: A guide to self-assessment.* New York: Springer.

American Psychiatric Association. (2000). *Diagnostic and statistical manual of mental disorders: Text revision DSM-IV-TR* (4th ed.). Washington, DC: Author.

Anderson, R. E., & Carter, I. (1999). *Human behavior in the social environment: A social systems approach* (5th ed.). New York: Aldine de Gruyter.

Antonyappan, J. M. (2003). Preventing HIV/AIDS among women and children in India. *Development, 46*(2), 90–95.

Apgar, K., & Callaghan, B. N. (1980). *Four one-day workshops.* Boston: Resource Communications Inc. and Family Service Association of Greater Boston.

Asbell, B., & Wynn, K. (1991). *Touching.* New York: Random House.

Austin, D. M. (2002). *Human services management: Organizational leadership in social work practice.* New York: Columbia.

Austin, M. J., Cox, G., Gottlieb, J., Hawkins, J. S., Kruzich, J. M., & Rauch, R. (1982). *Evaluating your agency's programs.* Newbury Park, CA: Sage.

Austin, M. J., Kopp, J., & Smith, P. L. (1986). *Delivering human services: A self-instructional approach* (2nd ed.). New York: Longman.

Austin, M. J., & Solomon, J. R. (2009). Managing the planning process. In R. J. Patti (Ed.), *The handbook of human services management* (2nd ed., pp. 321–337). Thousand Oaks, CA: Sage.

Axinn, J., & Stern, M. J. (2005). *Social welfare: A history of the American response to need* (6th ed.). Boston: Allyn & Bacon.

Bailey, D., & Uhly, K. M. (2008). Leadership. In T. Mizrahi & L. E. Davis (Editors-in-Chief), *Encyclopedia of social work* (20th ed., Vol. 1, pp. 153–160). Washington, DC: NASW Press.

Balgopal, P. (1995). Asian Indians. In R. L. Edwards (Editor-in-Chief), *Encyclopedia of social work* (19th ed., Vol. 1, pp. 256–260). Washington, DC: NASW Press.

Bankhead, T., & Erlich, J. L. (2005). Diverse populations and community practice. In M. Weil (Ed.), *The handbook of community practice* (pp. 59–83). Thousand Oaks, CA: Sage.

Barbera, R. A. (2007). Juntos working for human rights in Philadelphia. *BPD Update Online* (Winter 2007).

Barbuto, Jr., J. E., & Wheeler, D. W. (2005). *Becoming a servant leader: Do you have what it takes?* Lincoln, NE: University of Nebraska-Lincoln Extension, Institute of Agriculture and Natural Resources, A-15 General.

Barker, R. L. (2003). *The social work dictionary* (5th ed.). Washington, DC: National Association of Social Workers.

Barret, B., & Logan, C. (2002). *Counseling gay men and lesbians.* Pacific Grove, CA: Brooks/Cole.

Barsky, A. E. (2010). *Ethics and values in social work: An integrated approach for a comprehensive curriculum.* New York: Oxford.

Barsky, A. E., & Gould, J. W. (2002). *Clinicians in court.* New York: Guilford.

Bartlett, H. (1970). *The common base of social work practice.* New York: National Association of Social Workers.

Barusch, A. S. (2009). *Foundations of social policy: Social justice in human perspective* (3rd ed.). Belmont, CA: Brooks/Cole.

Beaulieu, L. (2002). Mapping the assets of your community: A key component for building local capacity. SRDC Series #227. Retrieved from http://srdc.msstate.edu/publications/227/227_asset_mapping.pdf.

Bedwell, R. T., Jr. (1993). Total quality management: Making the decision. *Nonprofit World, 2*(3), 29–31.

Bembry, J. X. (1996). The impact of volunteer coordinators on volunteer programs: An evaluation of Volunteer Maryland! *The Journal of Volunteer Administration, 15,* 14–20.

Benjamin, M. P. (1994). Research frontiers in building a culturally competent organization. *Focal Point, 8*(2), 1719.

Bentelspacher, C. E., Duncan, E., Collins, B., Scandell, D. J., & Regulus, T. (2006). African American informal support networks: A transactional, reciprocal exchange analysis. *Social Work in Mental Health 4*(3), 23–43.

Bernstein, D. (2004). The politics of poverty. Retrieved from http://www.bostonphoenix.com/boston/news_features/top/documents/03218337.asp.

Biegel, D. E. (1987). Neighborhoods. In A. Minahan (Editor-in-Chief), *Encyclopedia of social work* (18th ed., Vol. 2, pp. 182–196). Silver Spring, MD: National Association of Social Workers.

Biegel, D. E., & Naparstek, A. J. (Eds.). (1982). *Community support systems and mental health: Practice, policy and research.* New York: Springer.

Bigelow, D. A., Brodesky, G., Steward, L., & Olson, M. (1982). The concept and measurement of quality of life as a dependent variable in evaluation of mental health services. In G. J. Stohler & W. R. Tash (Eds.), *Innovative approaches to mental health education* (pp. 345–366). New York: Academic Press.

Bilson, A., & White, S. (2005). Representing children's views and best interests in court: An international comparison. *Child Abuse Review, 14,* 220–239.

Bisno, H. (1988). *Managing conflict.* Newbury Park, CA: Sage.

Bloom, L. Z., Coburn, K., & Perlman, J. (1976). *The new assertive woman.* New York: Dell.

Blythe, B., & Reithoffer, A. (2000). Assessment and measurement issues in direct practice in social work. In P. Allen-Meares & C. Garvin (Eds.), *The handbook of social work practice* (pp. 551–564). Thousand Oaks, CA: Sage.

Boehm, W. W. (1959). *Objectives of the social work curriculum of the future.* New York: Council on Social Work Education.

Bowen, G. L., Martin, J. A., & Nelson, J. P. (2002). A community capacity response to family violence in the military. In A. R. Roberts and G. J. Greene, *Social workers' desk reference.* New York: Oxford University Press.

Brager, G., & Holloway, S. (1978). *Changing human service organizations: Politics and practice.* New York: Free Press.

Brager, G., & Holloway, S. (1983). A process model for changing organizations from within. In R. M. Kramer & H. Specht (Eds.), *Readings in community organization practice* (3rd ed., pp. 198–208). Englewood Cliffs, NJ: Prentice-Hall.

Bravo, E. (2008). Sexual harassment. In A. Kesselman, L. D. McNair, & N. Schniedewind (Eds.), *Women: Images and realities* (4th ed., pp. 202–204). Boston: McGraw-Hill.

Bricker-Jenkins, M., & Lockett, P. W. (1995). Women: Direct practice. In R. L. Edwards (Editor-in-Chief), *Encyclopedia of social work* (19th ed., Vol. 3, pp. 2529–2539). Washington, DC: NASW Press.

Bricker-Jenkins, M., & Netting, F. E. (2009). Feminist issues and practices in social work. In A. R. Roberts (Editor-in-Chief), *Social workers' desk reference* (2nd ed., pp. 277–283). New York: Oxford.

Brieland, D. (1995). Social work practice: History and evolution. In R. L. Edwards (Editor-in-Chief), *Encyclopedia of social work* (19th ed., Vol. 3, pp. 2247–2258). Washington, DC: NASW Press.

Brill, N. I. (2005). *Working with people: The helping process* (8th ed.). Boston: Allyn & Bacon.

Brody, J. G. (2006). Informal social networks: Possibilities and limitations for their usefulness in social policy. *Journal of Community Psychology, 13*(4), 338–349.

Brody, R. (2005). *Effectively managing human service organizations* (3rd ed.). Thousand Oaks, CA: Sage.

Brody, R., & Nair, M. D. (2003). *Macro practice: A generalist approach* (6th ed.). Wheaton, IL: Gregory.

Brown, C. (1965). *Manchild in the promised land.* New York: American Library.

Brown, M. G., Hitchcock, D. E., & Willard, M. L. (1994). Why TQM fails and what to do about it. *Soundview Executive Book Summaries, 16*(5), 1–8.

Brueggemann, W. G. (2006). *The practice of macro social work* (3rd ed.). Pacific Grove, CA: Brooks/Cole.

Burghardt, S. (1982). *Organizing for community action.* Beverly Hills: Sage.

Burghardt, S. (2001). Know yourself: A key to better organizing. In J. E. Tropman, J. L. Erlich, & J. Rothman (Eds.), *Tactics & techniques of community intervention* (4th ed., pp. 150–156). Itasca, IL: Peacock.

Burrell, G., & Morgan, G. (1979). *Sociological paradigms and organizational analysis.* London: Heinemann.

Bush, I. R. (2004). An examination of five essential competencies for empowerment practice. *Journal of Baccalaureate Social Work, 9*(2), 47–62.

Canda, E. R. (1997). Spirituality. In R. L. Edwards (Ed.), *Encyclopedia of social work, 19th edition supplement* (pp. 299–309). Washington, DC: National Association of Social Workers.

Canda, E. R., & Furman, L. D. (2010). *Spiritual diversity in social work practice: The heart of helping* (2nd ed.). New York: Oxford.

Carroll, J. L. (2010). *Sexuality now: Embracing diversity* (3rd ed.). Belmont, CA: Wadsworth.

Carroll, M. M. (1997). Spirituality and clinical social work: Implications of past and current perspectives. *Arete, 22*(1), 25–34.

Casas, J. M. (2001). I didn't know where I was going but I got here anyway. In J. G. Ponterotto, J. M. Casas, L. A. Suzuki, & C. M. Alexander (Eds.), *Handbook of multicultural counseling* (2nd ed., pp. 78–95). Thousand Oaks, CA: Sage.

Cases, J. M., Raley, J. D., & Vasquez, M. J. T. (2008). ¡Adelante! Counseling the Latina/o from guiding theory to practice. In P. B. Pedersen, J. G. Draguns, W. J. Lonner, & J. E. Trimble (Eds.), *Counseling across cultures* (6th ed., pp. 129–146). Thousand Oaks, CA: Sage.

Cassidy, C., & Kreitner, R. (2010). *Supervision: Setting people up for success.* Mason, OH: South-Western.

CBS. (1997, April 20). *60 minutes.*

Champoux, J. E. (2006). *Organizational behavior: Integrating individuals, groups and organizations* (3rd ed.). Mason, OH: South-Western.

ChangingMinds.org. (2007). Using questions. Retrieved from http://changingminds.org/techniques/language/syntax/questions.htm.

Cnaan, R. A., & Boddie, S. C. (2002). Charitable choice and faith-based welfare: A call for social work. *Social Work, 47*(3), 224–235.

Cnaan, R. A., & Rothman, J. (2001). Locality development and the building of community. In Coggins, K., & Fresquez, J. E. (2007). *Working with clients in correctional settings* (Rev. ed.). Peosta, IA: Eddie Bowers.

Cohen, M. I. (1987). Youth employment. In J. E. Kyle (Ed.), *Children, families and cities: Programs that work at the local level* (pp. 69–108). Washington, DC: National League of Cities.

Coley, S., & Scheinberg, C. (2000). *Proposal writing* (2nd ed.). Thousand Oaks, CA: Sage.

Coley, S. M., & Scheinberg, C. A. (2008). *Proposal writing* (3rd ed.). Newbury Park, CA: Sage.

Collins, A. H., & Pancoast, D. L. (1976). *Natural helping networks.* Washington, DC: National Association of Social Workers.

Compton, B. R., Galaway, B., & Cournoyer, B. R. (2005). *Social work processes* (7th ed.). Belmont, CA: Brooks/Cole.

Congress, E. P. (1999). *Social work values and ethics.* Chicago: Nelson-Hall.

Cooper, G. L. (1981). *The stress check.* Englewood Cliffs, NJ: Prentice-Hall.

Corcoran, K. (1997). Managed care: Implications for social work practice. In *Encyclopedia of social work 1997 supplement* (19th ed., pp. 191–200). Washington, DC: NASW Press.

Corey, G., Corey, M. W., & Callanan, P. (2007). *Issues and ethics in the helping professions* (7th ed.). Belmont, CA: Brooks/Cole.

Corey, M. S., & Corey, G. (2011). *Becoming a helper* (6th ed.). Belmont, CA: Brooks/Cole.

Cornwall, M., & Brown, R. (2003). *Geneva results.* Provo, UT: Dept. of Sociology, Brigham Young University.

Council on Social Work Education (CSWE). (2008). *Educational policy and accreditation standards.* Alexandria, VA: Author.

Cournoyer, B. R. (2008). *The social work skills workbook* (5th ed.). Belmont, CA: Brooks/Cole.

Cowger, C. D., & Snively, C. A. (2002). Assessing client strengths: Individual, family, and community empowerment. In D. Saleebey (Ed.), *The strengths perspective in social work practice* (3rd ed., pp. 106–123). Boston: Allyn & Bacon.

Cox, F. M., Erlich, J. L., Rothman, J., & Tropman, J. E. (1987). *Strategies of community organization.* Itasca, IL: Peacock.

Crooks, R., & Baur, K. (2008). *Our sexuality* (10th ed.). Belmont, CA: Wadsworth.

Crosby, P. (1980). *Quality is free.* New York: Mentor.

Cross, T., Bazron, B., Dennis, K., & Isaacs, M. (1989). *Towards a culturally competent system of care: A monograph on effective service for minority children who are severely emotionally disturbed* (Vol. 1). Washington, DC: CASSP Technical Assistance Center, Georgetown University Child Development Center.

Curtis, J. D., & Detert, R. A. (1981). *How to relax: A holistic approach to stress management.* Palo Alto, CA: Mayfield.

Daft, R. L. (2004). *Organization theory and design* (8th ed.). Cincinnati, OH: South-Western.

Daft, R. L. (2007). *Organization theory and design* (9th ed.). Mason, OH: South-Western.

Daft, R. L. (2010a). *Management* (9th ed.). Mason, OH: South-Western.

Daft, R. L. (2010b). *Organization theory and design* (10th ed.). Mason, OH: South-Western.

Daft, R. L., & Marcic, D. (2009). *Understanding management* (6th ed.). Mason, OH: South-Western.

Dartmouth College Academic Skills Center. (2009). Managing your time. Retrieved from http://www.dartmouth.edu/~acskills/success/time.html.

Day, P. J. (2006). *A new history of social welfare* (5th ed.). Boston: Allyn & Bacon.

Delgado, M. (1998a). Community assessments by Latino youth. In P. L. Ewalt, E. M. Freeman, & Delgado, M. (1998b). Strengths-based practice with Puerto Rican adolescents: Lessons from a substance abuse prevention project. In P. L. Ewalt, E. M. Freeman, & D. L. Poole (Eds.), *Community building: Renewal, well-being, and shared responsibility* (pp. 213–223). Washington, DC: NASW Press.

Delgado, M. (2000). *Community social work practice in an urban context.* New York: Oxford University Press.

Delgado, M., Jones, K., & Rohani, M. (2005). *Social work practice with refugee and immigrant youth in the United States.* Boston: Allyn & Bacon.

Deming, W. E. (1982). *Quality, productivity, and competitive position.* Cambridge, MA: MIT Center for Advanced Engineering Study.

Deming, W. E. (1986). *Out of the crisis.* Cambridge, MA: MIT Center for Advanced Engineering Study.

Denhardt, R. B., Denhardt, J. V., & Aristigueta, M. P. (2002). *Managing human behavior in public & nonprofit organizations.* Thousand Oaks, CA: Sage.

Derezotes, D. S. (2006). *Spiritually oriented social work practice.* Boston: Allyn & Bacon.

Devore, W., & Schlesinger, E. G. (1996). *Ethnic-sensitive social work practice* (3rd ed.). Columbus, OH: Merrill.

Dickson, D. T. (1998). *Confidentiality and privacy in social work.* New York: Free Press.

DiNitto, D. M. (2007). *Social welfare: Politics and public policy* (6th ed.). Boston: Allyn & Bacon.

DITSHWANELO—The Botswana Centre for Human Rights. (2006). Shadow report to the United Nations Committee on the Elimination of Racial Discrimination. Retrieved from http://www.fidh.org/IMG/pdf/bw032006a.pdf.

Dolgoff, R. (2005). *An introduction to supervisory practice in human services.* Boston: Allyn & Bacon.

Dolgoff, R., & Feldstein, D. (2003). *Understanding social welfare* (6th ed.). Boston: Allyn & Bacon.

Dolgoff, R., Loewenberg, F. M., & Harrington, D. (2009). *Ethical decisions for social work practice* (8th ed.). Belmont, CA: Brooks/Cole.

Dominelli, L. (2004). International social work in a globalizing world. *Social Work Education Reporter, 52*(2), 4, 11.

Drucker, P. M. (2008). Managing oneself. In J. Rothman, J. L. Erlich, & J. E. Tropman (Eds.), *Strategies of community intervention* (7th ed., pp. 411–424). Peosta, IA: Eddie Bowers.

DuBrin, A. J. (2002). *Fundamentals of organizational behavior* (2nd ed.) Mason, OH: South-Western.

DuBrin, A. J. (2007). *Fundamentals of organizational behavior* (4th ed.). Mason, OH: South-Western.

DuBrin, A. J. (2009). *Essentials of management* (8th ed.). Mason, OH: South-Western.

Dudley, J. R. (2009). *Social work evaluation.* Chicago: Lyceum.

Dumler, M. P., & Skinner, S. J. (2008). *A primer for management* (2nd ed.). Mason, OH: South-Western.

Duner, A., & Nordstrom, M. (2007). The roles and functions of the informal support networks of older people who receive formal support: A Swedish qualitative study. *Aging & Society 27,* 67–85.

Economic Policy Institute. (2003). Retrieved from http://www.epinet.org/newsroom/releases/03/12/031219statejobwatch.pdf; http://www.epinet.org/stmt/2003/statement_signed.pdf.

Edinburg, G. M., & Cottler, J. M. (1995). Managed care. In R. L. Edwards (Editor-in-Chief), *Encyclopedia of social work* (19th ed., Vol. 2, pp. 1635–1642). Washington, DC: NASW Press.

Egan, G. (2010). *The skilled helper: A problem-management and opportunity-development approach to helping* (9th ed.). Belmont, CA: Brooks/Cole.

Eggertsen, L. (2006). Primary factors related to multiple placements for children in out-of-home care in Utah. *Dissertation Abstracts International, 67*(5), 1916.

Ellis, A. (2005). Rational emotive behavior therapy. In R. Corsini & D. Wedding (Eds.), *Current psychotherapies* (7th ed., pp. 166–201). Belmont, CA: Brooks/Cole.

Elze, D. E. (2006). Oppression, prejudice, and discrimination. In D. F. Morrow & L. Messenger (Eds.), *Sexual orientation & gender expression in social work practice: Working with gay, lesbian, bisexual, & transgender people* (pp. 43–77). New York: Columbia.

Entwistle, B. (1992). *Making cities work.* Pasadena, CA: Hope.

Equal Employment Opportunity Commission, U.S. Department of Justice Civil Rights Division. (1997, May). *The Americans with Disabilities Act: Questions and answers.* Washington, DC: Author.

Erlich, J. L., Rothman, J., & Teresa, J. G. (1999). *Taking action in organizations and communities.* Dubuque, IA: Eddie Bowers.

Ethics and reporting eyed after assembly. (1999, November). *NASW News, 44*(10), 5.

Etzioni, A. (1964). *Modern organizations.* Englewood Cliffs, NJ: Prentice-Hall.

Evans, M. D. R, & Kelley, J. (1986). Immigrants' work: Equality and discrimination in the Australian labour market. *Journal of Sociology, 22*(2), 187–207.

Everett, J. E., Homstead, K., & Drisko, J. (2007). Frontline worker perceptions of the empowerment process in community-based agencies. *Social Work, 52*(2), 161–170.

Fatout, M., & Rose, S. R. (1995). *Task groups in the social services.* Thousand Oaks, CA: Sage.

Federal Electric Corporation. (1963). *A programmed introduction to PERT.* New York: Wiley.

Feigenbaum, A. (1983). *Total quality control* (3rd ed.). New York: McGraw-Hill.

Fellin, P. (2001). *The community and the social worker.* Itasca, IL: Peacock.

Figueira-McDonough, J. (2007). *The welfare state and social work: Pursuing social justice.* Thousand Oaks, CA: Sage.

Filley, A. C. (1978). *The complete manager: What works when.* Champaign, IL: Research Press.

Finn, J. L., & Checkoway, B. (1998). Young people as competent community builders: A challenge to social work. *Social Work, 43*(4), 335–345.

Fisher, R., & Burghardt, S. (2008). Social advocacy: The persistence and prospects of social action. In J. Rothman, J. L. Erlich, & J. E. Tropman (Eds.), *Strategies of community intervention* (7th ed., pp. 315–332). Peosta, IA: Eddie Bowers.

Fong, R., & Mokuau, N. (1994). Not simply "Asian Americans": Periodical literature review on Asians and Pacific Islanders. *Social Work, 39,* 298–305.

Frame, M. W. (2003). *Integrating religion and spirituality into counseling: A comprehensive approach.* Belmont, CA: Brooks/Cole.

Frontline. (2006). How meth destroys the body. Retrieved from http:// www.pbs.org/wgbh/pages/frontline/meth/body.

Fuller, T., Guy, D., & Pletsch, C. (2002). *Asset mapping: A handbook.* Ottawa, Canada: Canadian Rural Partnership.

Fulton, B. (2003). Subpoena: Devil or the deep blue see (sic). *NASW News,* Winter, 3 & 6.

Furman, L. E. (1991). The impact of the rural crisis on two-generational farm families. *Family Practice Quarterly Journal, 17*(1), 26. University of North Dakota: Department of Family Medicine. Grand Forks.

Gambrill, E. (2005). *Critical thinking in clinical practice: Improving the quality of judgments and decisions* (2nd ed.). Hoboken, NJ: Wiley.

Gambrill, E., & Gibbs, L. (2009). *Critical thinking for helping professionals* (3rd ed.). New York: Oxford.

Gargiulo, R. M. (2006). *Special education in contemporary society* (2nd ed.). Belmont, CA: Wadsworth.

Garvin, C. D., & Cox, F. M. (1995). A history of community organizing since the Civil War with special reference to oppressed communities. In J. Rothman, J. L. Erlich, & J. E. Tropman (Eds.), *Strategies of community intervention* (pp. 64–99). Itasca, IL: Peacock.

Gaugler, J. E., & Kane, R. A. (2001). Informal help in the assisted living setting: A 1-year analysis. *Family Relations 50*(4), 335–347.

Gelman, S. R. (1997). Advocacy or unethical practice: "On do the right thing." *Reflections, 2*(3), 23–24.

Gentry, D. B., & Benenson, W. A. (1993). School-to-home transfer of conflict management skills among school-age children. *Families in society, 74*(2), 67–73.

Germain, C. (1991). *Human behavior in the social environment: An ecological perspective.* New York: Columbia University Press.

Gibbs, L., & Gambrill, E. (1996). *Critical thinking for social workers: A workbook.* Thousand Oaks, CA: Pine Forge/Sage.

Gibbs, L., & Gambrill, E. (1999). *Critical thinking for social workers: Exercises for the helping profession* (Revised ed.). Thousand Oaks, CA: Pine Forge.

Gibelman, M. (1995). *What social workers do.* Washington, DC: NASW Press.

Gibelman, M., & Furman, R. (2008). *Navigating human service organizations* (2nd ed.). Chicago: Lyceum.

Gibson, J. O., Kingsley, G. T., & McNeely, J. B. (1997). *Community building: Coming of age.* Washington, DC: Urban Institute.

Gilbert, M. J. (2008). Transgender people. In T. Mizrahi & L. E. Davis (Editors-in-Chief), *Encyclopedia of social work* (20th ed., Vol. 4, pp. 238–241). Washington, DC: NASW Press.

Gilbert, N., & Terrell, P. (2010). *Dimensions of social welfare policy* (7th ed.). Boston: Allyn & Bacon.

Ginsberg, L. (1995). Opening remarks: 20th annual institute on social work in rural areas. *Human Services in the Rural Environment, 18/19,* 19–20.

Ginsberg, L. H. (2005). *Social work in rural communities* (4th ed.). Alexandria, VA: CSWE.

GlenMaye, L. (1998). Empowerment of women. In L. M. Gutierrez, R. J. Parsons, & E. O. Cox (Eds.), *Empowerment in social work practice: A sourcebook* (pp. 25–51). Belmont, CA: Brooks/Cole.

Glicken, M. D. (2006). *Learning from resilient people: Lessons we can apply to counseling and psychotherapy.* Thousand Oaks, CA: Sage.

Glossary to educational policy and accreditation standards. (2002). Developed by Commission of the Council on Social Work Education. Alexandria, VA: Council on Social Work Education.

Gordon, M. (1997). *Writing a grant proposal.* (National Institute of Mental Health technical assistance paper). Rockville, MD: Author.

Gotterer, R. (2001). The spiritual dimension in clinical social work practice: A client perspective. *Families in Society, 82*(2), 187–193.

Graham, J. W. (1991). Servant-leadership in organizations: Inspirational and moral. *Leadership Quarterly, 2*(2), 105–119.

Gray, S. W., & Zide, M. R. (2008). *Psychopathology* (2nd ed.). Belmont, CA: Brooks/Cole.

Greene, R. R., & Livingston, N. C. (2002). A social construct. In R. R. Green (Ed.), *Resiliency: An integrated approach to practice, policy, and research* (pp. 63–93). Washington, DC: NASW Press.

Greenleaf, R. K. (1970). *The servant as leader.* Newton Centre, MA: Robert K. Greenleaf Center.

Greenleaf, R. K. (1977). *Servant leadership: A journey into the nature of legitimate power and greatness.* New York: Paulist.

Griffin, R. W., & Moorhead, G. (2010). *Organizational behavior: Managing people and organizations* (9th ed.). Mason, OH: South-Western.

Guffey, M. E. (2010). *Essentials of business communication* (8th ed.). Mason, OH: South-Western.

Gumpert, J., Saltman, J. E., & Sauer-Jones, D. (1998). Toward identifying the unique characteristics of social work practice in rural areas: From the voices of practitioners. Paper presented at the 44th Annual Program Meeting, Council on Social Work Education, Orlando, FL.

Gutierrez, L., GlenMaye, L., & DeLois, K. (1995). The organizational context for empowerment practice: Implications for social work administration. *Social Work, 40*(2), 249–258.

Gutierrez, L. M. (2001). Working with women of color: An empowerment perspective. In J. Rothman, J. L. Erlich, & J. E. Tropman (Eds.), *Strategies of community intervention* (6th ed., pp. 209–217). Itasca, IL: Peacock.

Gutierrez, L. M., & Lewis, E. A. (1998). *Empowering women of color.* New York: Columbia.

Hagen, J. L., & Lawrence, C. K. (2008). Temporary assistance to needy families. In T. Mizrahi & L. E. Davis (Editors-in-Chief), *Encyclopedia of social work* (20th ed., Vol. 4, pp. 225–229). Washington, DC: NASW Press.

Hall, E. (1969). *The hidden dimension.* Garden City, NY: Doubleday.

Hallahan, D. P., & Kauffman, J. M. (2006). *Exceptional learners: An introduction to special education* (10th ed.). Boston: Allyn & Bacon.

Halley, A. A., Kopp, J., & Austin, M. J. (1998). *Delivering human services: A learning approach to practice* (4th ed.). New York: Longman.

Hamburger, L. J. (1997). The wisdom of non-heterosexually based senior housing and related services. *Journal of Gay and Lesbian Studies, 6*(1), 11–25.

Hancock, T. (2007). Combating the fear: Fulfilling social work's edthical obligation to undocumented immigrants. BPD Update Online, Winter.

Hardcastle, D. A., & Powers, P. R. (2004). *Community practice: Theories and skills for social workers* (2nd ed.). New York: Oxford.

Harkness, D. (2008). *Consultation.* In T. Mizrahi & L. E. Davis (Editors-in-Chief), *Encyclopedia of social work* (20th ed., Vol. 1, pp. 420–423). Washington, DC: NASW Press.

Harris, M. B. (2008). *Family life education.* In T. Mizrahi & L. E. Davis (Editors-in-Chief), *Encyclopedia of social work* (20th ed., Vol. 2, pp. 197–200). Washington, DC: NASW Press.

Hartman, A. (1993). The professional is political. *Social Work, 38*(4), 365–366.

Hasenfeld, Y. (1983). *Human service organizations.* Englewood Cliffs, NJ: Prentice-Hall.

Hasenfeld, Y. (1984). Analyzing the human service agency. In F. M. Cox, J. L. Erlich, J. Rothman, & E. Tropman (Eds.), *Tactics and techniques of community practice* (2nd ed., pp. 14–26). Itasca, IL: Peacock.

Hasenfeld, Y. (1987). Program development. In J. Rothman, J. L. Erlich, & J. E. Tropman (Eds.), *Strategies of community organization* (4th ed., pp. 450–473). Itasca, IL: Peacock.

Hasenfeld, Y. (2001). Program development. In J. Rothman, J. L. Erlich, & J. E. Tropman, *Strategies of community intervention* (6th ed., pp. 456–477). Itasca, IL: Peacock.

Hasenfeld, Y. (2009). Human services administration and organizational theory. In R. J. Patti (Ed.), *The handbook of human services management* (2nd ed., pp. 53–80). Thousand Oaks, CA: Sage.

Haulotte, S. M., & Oliver, S. (2004). A strategy for uncovering, accessing, and maximizing assets and strengths in rural area social services. In T. L. Scales & C. L. Streeter (Eds.), *Rural social work: Building and sustaining community assets* (pp. 108–117). Belmont, CA: Brooks/Cole.

Haynes, K. S., & Mickelson, J. S. (2003). *Affecting Change* (5th ed.). Boston: Allyn & Bacon.

Haynes, K. S., & Mickelson, J. S. (2006). *Affecting Change* (6th ed.). Boston: Allyn & Bacon.

Haynes, K. S., & Mickelson, J. S. (2010). *Affecting change* (7th ed.). Boston: Allyn & Bacon.

Hellriegel, D., Jackson, S. E., & Slocum, Jr., J. W. (2002). *Management: A competency-based approach* (9th ed.). Cincinnati, OH: South-Western.

Hellriegel, D., & Slocum, J. W., Jr. (2009). *Organizational behavior* (12th ed.). Mason, OH: South-Western.

Hepworth, D. H., Rooney, R. H., Rooney, G. D., Strom-Gottfried, & Larsen, J. (2010). *Direct social work practice: Theory and skills* (8th ed.). Belmont, CA: Brooks/Cole.

Hernandez, V. R. (2008). Generalist and advanced generalist practice. In T. Mizrahi & L. E. Davis (Editors-in-Chief), *Encyclopedia of social work* (20th ed., Vol. 2, pp. 260–268). Washington, DC: NASW Press.

Herring, C. (2006). Hurricane Katrina and the racial gulf. *Du Bois Review, 3*(1), 129–144.

Hesse, H. (1956). *The journey to the East.* London: P. Owen.

Hickman, S. A. (2004). Rural is real. In T. L. Scales & C. L. Streeter, *Rural social work* (pp. 65–75). Belmont, CA: Thomson Brooks/Cole.

Hodge, B. J., Anthony, W. P., & Gales, L. M. (2003). *Organization theory: A strategic approach* (6th ed.). Upper Saddle River, NJ: Prentice-Hall.

Hohmann, A. A. (n. d.). *Tips on developing an NIMH grant application.* (National Institute of Mental Health Publication.) Rockville, MD: Author.

Holland, T. P., & Petchers, M. K. (1987). Organizations: Context for social service delivery. In A. Minahan (Editor-in-Chief), *Encyclopedia of social work* (18th ed., Vol. 2, pp. 204–217). Silver Spring, MD: National Association of Social Workers.

Holland, T. P., & Ritvo, R. A. (2008). *Nonprofit organizations: Principles and practices.* New York: Columbia.

Holloway, S. M. (1987). Staff-initiated change. In A. Minahan (Editor-in-Chief), *Encyclopedia of social work* (18th ed., Vol. 2, pp. 729–736). Silver Spring, MD: National Association of Social Workers.

Homan, M. S. (2004). *Promoting community change: Making it happen in the real world* (3rd ed.). Pacific Grove, CA: Brooks/Cole.

Homan, M. S. (2008). *Promoting community change: Making it happen in the real world* (4th ed.). Belmont, CA: Brooks/Cole.

Hopps, J. G., & Lowe, T. B. (2008). Social work profession: Overview. In T. Mizrahi & L. E. Davis (Editors-in-Chief), *Encyclopedia of social work* (20th ed., Vol. 4, pp. 238–241). Washington, DC: NASW Press.

Huber, C. H., & Baruth, L. G. (1987). *Ethical, legal and professional issues in the practice of marriage and family therapy.* Columbus, OH: Merrill.

Huddy, L., & Feldman, S. (2006). Worlds apart. *Du Bois Review, 3*(1), 97–113.

Huerta, M., Cortina, L. M., Pang, J. S., Torges, C. M., & Magley, V. J. (2006). Sex and power in the academy: Modeling sexual harassment in the lives of college women. *Personality and Social Psychology Bulletin, 32*(5), 616–628.

Hutchison, E. D. (2008). Social work education: Human behavior and the social environment. In T. Mizrahi & L. E. Davis (Editors-in-Chief), *Encyclopedia of social work* (20th ed., Vol. 4, pp. 124–128). Washington, DC: NASW Press.

Hyde, C. A. (2003). Multicultural organizational development in nonprofit human service agencies: Views from the field. *Journal of Community Practice, 11*(1), 39–59.

Hyde, C. A. (2008). Feminist social work practice. In T. Mizrahi & L. E. Davis (Editors-in-Chief), *Encyclopedia of social work* (20th ed., Vol. 2, pp. 216–221). Washington, DC: NASW Press.

Hyde, J. S., & DeLamater, J. D. (2008). *Understanding human sexuality* (10th ed.). Boston: McGraw-Hill.

Inclusion International. (2004). *"Education for all" cannot be realized while 98% of children with disabilities remain out of school.* Toronto: Author.

In re Gault, 387 U.S. 1428 (1967).

In re Winship, 397 U.S. 358 (1970).

Iglehart, A. P. (2009). Managing for diversity and empowerment in human services agencies. In R. J. Patti (Ed.), *The handbook of human services management* (2nd ed., pp. 295–318). Thousand Oaks, CA: Sage.

International Association of Schools of Social Work (IASSW). (2004). Ethics in social work, statement of principles. Retrieved from http://www.iassw-aiets.org/index.php?option=com_content&task=blogcategory&id=27&Itemid=50.

International Association of Schools of Social Work (IASSW). (2009). Welcome to IASSW. Retrieved from http://www.iassw-aiets.org/.

International Federation of Social Workers (IFSW). (2009). Welcome to IFSW. Retrieved from http://www.ifsw.org/f38000041.html.

International Organization for Migration (IOM). (2009, December 2). Mission. Retrieved from http://www.iom.int/jahia/Jahia/about-iom/mission/lang/en.

Isaacs-Shockley, M. (1994). Cultural competence and the juvenile system: Irreconcilable differences. *Focal Point, 8*(2), 19–20.

Ivey, A. E., & Ivey, M. B. (2007). *Intentional interviewing and counseling: Facilitating client development in a multicultural society* (6th ed.). Belmont, CA: Brooks/Cole.

Ivey, A. E., & Ivey, M. B. (2008). *Essentials of intentional interviewing: Counseling in a multicultural world.* Belmont, CA: Brooks/Cole.

Ivey, A. E., Ivey, M. B., & Zalaquett, C. P. (2010). *Intentional interviewing & counseling: Facilitating client development in a multicultural society* (7th ed.). Belmont, CA: Brooks/Cole.

Jaffee v. Redmond, 518 U.S. 1 (1996).

Jandt, F. E. (2007). *An introduction to intercultural communication: Identities in a global community* (5th ed.). Thousand Oaks, CA: Sage.

Janis, I. (1982). Groupthink: Psychological Studies of Policy Decisions and Fiascoes. (2nd ed.). New York: Houghton Mifflin

Jansson, B. S. (2003). *Becoming an effective policy advocate* (4th ed.). Pacific Grove, CA: Brooks/Cole.

Jansson, B. S. (2008). *Becoming an effective policy advocate: From policy practice to social justice* (5th ed.). Belmont, CA: Brooks/Cole.

Jansson, B. S. (2011). *Becoming an effective policy advocate: From policy practice to social justice* (6th ed.). Belmont, CA: Brooks/Cole.

Jaskyte, K. (2008). Management: Practice interventions. In T. Mizrahi & L. E. Davis (Editors-in-Chief), *Encyclopedia of social work* (20th ed., Vol. 3, pp. 158–163). Washington, DC: NASW Press.

Jay, A. (1984). How to run a meeting. In F. M. Cox, J. Erlich, J. Rothman, & J. E. Tropman (Eds.), *Tactics and techniques of community practice* (2nd ed.). Itasca, IL: Peacock.

Johns, G. (1996). *Organizational behavior: Understanding and managing life at work* (4th ed.). New York: HarperCollins.

Johnson, A. K. (1998). The revitalization of community practice: Characteristics, competencies, and curricula for community-based services. *Journal of Community Practice, 5*(3), 37–62.

Johnson, D. W. (2009). *Reaching out: Interpersonal effectiveness and self-actualization* (10th ed.). Upper Saddle River, NJ: Pearson.

Johnson, L. C., & Yanca, S. J. (2001). *Social work practice* (7th ed.). Boston: Allyn & Bacon.

Johnson, L. C., & Yanca, S. J. (2007). *Social work practice: A generalist approach* (9th ed.). Boston: Allyn & Bacon.

Juran, J. (1989). *Juran on leadership for quality: An executive handbook* (4th ed.). New York: McGraw-Hill.

Kadushin, A. (1995). Interviewing. In R. L. Edwards (Editor-in-Chief), *Encyclopedia of social work* (19th ed., Vol. 2, pp. 1527–1537). Washington, DC: NASW Press.

Kadushin, A., & Harkness, D. (2002). *Supervision in social work.* New York: Columbia.

Kadushin, A., & Kadushin, G. (1997). *The social work interview: A guide for human service professionals.* New York: Columbia University Press.

Kanter, R. M. (1979, July–August). Power failure in management circuits. *Harvard Business Review,* 31–54.

Karger, H. J., & Stoesz, D. (2006). *American social welfare policy: A pluralist approach* (5th ed.). Boston: Allyn & Bacon.

Karger, H. J., & Stoesz, D. (2010). *American social welfare policy: A pluralist approach* (6th ed.). Boston: Allyn & Bacon.

Kazdin, A. E. (2001). *Behavior modification in applied settings* (6th ed.). Belmont, CA: Wadsworth.

Kendall, D. (2007). *Social problems in a diverse society* (4th ed.). Boston: Pearson.

Kerka, S. (2003). *Community asset mapping: Trends and issues alert #47.* Columbus, OH: Ohio State University.

Kettner, P. M., Daley, J. M., & Nichols, A. W. (1985). *Initiating change in organizations and communities: A macro practice model.* Monterey, CA: Brooks/Cole.

Kettner, P. M., Moroney, R. M., & Martin, L. L. (2008). *Designing and managing programs: An effectiveness-based approach* (3rd ed.). Thousand Oaks, CA: Sage.

Kirk, G., & Okazawa-Rey, M. (2007). *Women's lives: Multicultural perspectives* (4th ed.). New York: McGraw-Hill.

Kirk, G., & Okazawa-Rey, M. (2010). *Women's lives: Multicultural perspectives* (5th ed.). Boston: McGraw-Hill.

Kirst-Ashman, K. K. (2010). *Introduction to social work and social welfare: Critical thinking perspectives* (3rd ed.). Belmont, CA: Brooks/Cole.

Kirst-Ashman, K. K., & Hull, G. H., Jr. (1993). *Understanding generalist practice.* Chicago: Nelson-Hall.

Kirst-Ashman, K. K., & Hull, Jr. G. H. (1999). *Understanding generalist practice* (2nd ed.). Chicago: Nelson-Hall.

Kirst-Ashman, K. K., & Hull, Jr. G. H. (2002). *Understanding generalist practice* (3rd ed.). Pacific Grove, CA: Brooks/Cole.

Kirst-Ashman, K. K., & Hull, Jr., G. H. (2006). *Understanding generalist practice* (4th ed.). Belmont, CA: Brooks/Cole.

Kirst-Ashman, K. K., & Hull, Jr., G. H. (2009). *Understanding generalist practice* (5th ed.). Pacific Grove, CA: Brooks/Cole.

Kirst-Ashman, K. K., & Hull, Jr. G. H. (2010). *Understanding generalist practice* (6th ed.). Belmont, CA: Brooks/Cole.

Kissman, K. (1991). Feminist-based social work with single-parent families. *Families in Society, 72*(1), 23–28.

Knopf, R. (1979). *Surviving the BS (bureaucratic system).* Wilmington, NC: Mandala Press.

Knox, P. & Marston, S. (2001) *Human geography: Places and regions in global context* (2nd ed.). Englewood Cliffs, NJ: Prentice-Hall.

Kongstvedt, P. R. (2009). *Managed care: What it is and how it works* (3rd ed.). Sudbury, MA: Jones & Bartlett.

Kornblum, W., & Julian, J. (2007). *Social problems* (12th ed.). Upper Saddle River, NJ: Prentice Hall.

Kottler, J. A., & Chen, D. (2008). *Stress management and prevention: Applications to daily life.* Belmont, CA: Wadsworth.

Kraus, K. L. (2006). Task/work groups. In D. Capuzzi, D. R. Gross, & M. D. Stauffer (Eds.), *Introduction to group work* (4th ed., pp. 241–268). Denver, CO: Love.

Kretzmann, J. P., & McKnight, J. L. (1993). *Building communities from the inside out.* Chicago: ACTA Publications.

Kronenberg, P., & Loeffler, R. (1991). Quality management theory: Historical context and future prospect. *Journal of Management Science & Policy Analysis, 8,* 203–221.

Labor Research Association. (2004). *Bush policies guarantee long-term high unemployment.* New York: Author.

Lad Lake. (2009). The programs. Retrieved from http://www.ladlake.org/programs/index.php.

Lad Lake, Inc. (Undated). *Mission statement.* Dousman, WI: Author.

Lakein, A. (1973). *How to get control of your time and your life.* New York: Signet.

Landon, P. S. (1995). Generalist and advanced generalist practice. In R. L. Edwards (Editor-in-Chief), *Encyclopedia of social work* (19th ed., Vol. 2, pp. 1101–1108). Washington, DC: NASW Press.

Landon, P. S. (1999). *Generalist social work practice.* Dubuque, IA: Eddie Bowers.

Larson, C. E., & LaFasto, F. M. (1989). *Teamwork.* Newbury Park, CA: Sage.

Lauffer, A. (1981). Reorganizing community organization: Notes on changes in practice and needed changes in the graduate social work curriculum. *Social Development Issues, 5*(2–3), 166–179.

Lauffer, A., Nybell, L., Overberger, C., Reed, B., & Zeff, L. (1977). *Understanding your social agency.* Beverly Hills: Sage.

Lecca, P. J., Quervalu, I., Nunes, J. V., & Gonzales, H. F. (1998). *Cultural competency in health, social, and human services: Directions for the twenty-first century.* New York: Garland.

Lenk, K. M., Toomey, T. L., Wagenaar, A. C., Bosma, L. M., & Vessey, J. (2002). Can neighborhood associations be allies in health policy efforts? Political activity among neighborhood associations. *Journal of Community Psychology, 30*(1), 57–68.

Leonard, E. C., Jr. (2010). *Supervision: Concepts and practices of management* (11th ed.). Mason, OH: South-Western.

Lewis, E. A., & Suarez, Z. E. (1995). Natural helping networks. In R. L. Edwards (Editor-in-Chief), *Encyclopedia of social work* (19th ed., Vol. 2, pp. 1765–1772). Washington, DC: NASW Press.

Lewis, J. A., Lewis, M. D., Packard, T. & Souflee, Jr., F. (2001). *Management of human service programs* (3rd ed.). Pacific Grove, CA: Brooks/Cole.

Lewis, J. A., Packard, T. R., & Lewis, M. D. (2007). *Management of human service programs* (4th ed.). Belmont, CA: Brooks/Cole.

Lieberman, A. A., Hornby, H., & Russell, M. (1988). Analyzing the educational backgrounds and work experiences of child welfare personnel: A national study. *Social Work, 33*(6), 485–489.

Lieberman, R. C. (2006). The storm didn't discriminate. *Du Bois Review, 3*(1), 7–22.

Linhorst, D. M. (2006). *Empowering people with severe mental illness.* New York: Oxford University Press.

Linhorst, D. M., Eckert, A., & Hamilton, G. (2005). Promoting participation in organizational decision making by clients with severe mental illness. *Social Work, 50*(1), 21–30.

Loewenberg, F. M. (1987). *Fundamentals of social intervention* (2nd ed.). New York: Columbia University Press.

Lohmann, R. A. (1997). Managed care: A review of recent research. In *Encyclopedia of social work 1997 supplement* (19th ed., pp. 200–213). Washington, DC: NASW Press.

Longres, J. (1995). *Human behavior in the social environment.* Itasca, IL: F. E. Peacock.

Loomis, C., Brodsky, A. E., Arteaga, S. S., Benhorin, R., Rogers-Senuta, K., Marx, C. M., & McLaughlin, P. (2003). What works in adult educational and employment training? Case study of a community-based program for women. *Journal of Community Practice, 11*(2), 27–45.

Louv, R. (1994). *101 things you can do for our children's future.* New York: Random House.

Love, A. J. (1991). *Internal Evaluation.* Newbury Park, CA: Sage.

Lovett, A., Haynes, R., Sunnenberg, G., & Gale, S. (2002). Car travel time and accessibility by bus to general practitioner services: A study using patient registers and GIS. *Social Science and Medicine, 55*(1), 97–111.

Lum, D. (2004). *Social work practice with people of color: A process-stage approach* (5th ed.). Pacific Grove, CA: Brooks/Cole.

Lum, D. (Ed.) (2007). *Culturally competent practice* (3rd ed.). Pacific Grove, CA: Brooks/Cole.

Lupu, I. C., & Tuttle, R. W. (2008). *The state of the law 2008: A cumulative report on legal developments affecting government partnerships with faith-based organizations.* Retrieved from http://www.religion andsocialpolicy.org

Lussier, R. N. (2009). *Management fundamentals* (4th ed.). Mason, OH: South-Western.

Lutheran Social Services of Wisconsin and Upper Michigan (LSS). (1993). *Getting started. TQS at LSS: A workbook on total quality service for employees.* Milwaukee, WI: Author.

Mace, N. L., & Rabins, P. V. (1991). *The 36-hour day: A family guide to caring for persons with Alzheimer's disease, related dementing illness, and memory loss in later life.* Baltimore, MD: Johns Hopkins University Press.

Macionis, J. J. (2008). *Social problems* (3rd ed.). Upper Saddle River, NJ: Pearson Prentice-Hall.

Mackelprang, R., & Salsgiver, R. (1999). *Disability: A diversity model approach in human service practice.* Pacific Grove, CA: Brooks/Cole.

Mackelprang, R. W., & Salsgiver, R. O. (2009). *Disability: A diversity model approach in human service practice* (2nd ed.). Chicago: Lyceum.

Mackenzie, R. A. (1972). *The time trap: Managing your way out.* New York: AMACON.

Maguire, L. (1984). Networking for self-help: An empirically based guideline. In F. M. Cox, J. L. Erlich, J. Rothman, & J. E. Tropman (Eds.), *Tactics and techniques of community practice* (2nd ed., pp. 198–208). Itasca, IL: Peacock.

Maguire, L. (1991). *Social support systems in practice.* Washington, DC: NASW Press.

Managed care. (1998, January). *NASW News,* p. 1.

Manning, S. S. (1997). The social worker as moral citizen: Ethics in action. *Social Work, 42*(3), 223–229.

Mapp, S. (2008). *Human rights and social justice in a global perspective: An introduction to international social work.* New York: Oxford.

Martin, D. G. (2003). Enacting neighborhoods. *Urban Geography, 24*(5), 361–385.

Martin, L. L. (1993). *Total quality management in human service organizations.* Newbury Park, CA: Sage.

Martinez-Brawley, E. E. (1998). Community-oriented practice in rural social work. In L. Ginsberg (Ed.), *Social work in rural communities* (2nd ed., pp. 67–81). Alexandria, Va: Council on Social Work Education.

Maschi, T., Bradley, C., & Ward, K. (2009). *Forensic social work.* New York: Springer.

Mason, J. L. (1994). Developing culturally competent organizations. *Focal Point, 8*(2), 1–8.

Matsuoka, J. K. (1990). Differential acculturation among Vietnamese refugees. *Social Work, 35*(4), 341–345.

Mattison, D., Jayaratne, S., & Croxton, T. (2000, Spring). Social workers' religiosity and its impact on religious practice behaviors. *Advances in Social Work, 1*(1), 43–59.

Matza, B. R. (1990). Empowerment: The key management skill of the 90s. *Retail Control, 58*(11), 20–23.

Mayadas, N. S., & Segal, U. A. (2000). Refugees in the 1990s: A U.S. perspective. In P. R. Balgopal (Ed.), *Social work practice with immigrants and refugees* (pp. 198–227). New York: Columbia.

Mayer, B. S. (1995). Conflict resolution. In R. L. Edwards (Editor-in-Chief), *Encyclopedia of social work* (19th ed., Vol. 1, pp. 613–622). Washington, DC: NASW Press.

MayoClinic.com. (2009). Time management: Tips to reduce stress and improve productivity. Retrieved from http://www.mayoclinic.com/health/time-management/WL00048.

McCammon, S., & Knox, D. (2007). *Choices in sexuality* (3rd ed.). Mason, OH: Thomson.

McCarty, D., & Clancy, C. (2002). Telehealth: Implications for social work practice. *Social Work, 47*(2), 153–161.

McGoverns, J., & Peters, K. (1985). *Courtroom survival for expert witnesses* (tapes 1 and 2: L172–5 A and B). Seattle: Author.

McGregor, D. (1960). *The human side of enterprise.* New York: McGraw-Hill.

McNutt, J. (2000). Organizing cyberspace: Strategies for teaching about community practice and technology. *Journal of Community Practice 7*(1), 95–109.

McWhirter, J. J., McWhirter, B. T., McWhirter, E. H., & McWhirter, R. J. (2007). *At-risk youth: A comprehensive response.* Belmont, CA: Brooks/Cole.

Meenaghan, T. M., & Gibbons, W. E. (2000). *Generalist practice in larger settings.* Chicago: Lyceum.

Mish, F. (Editor-in-chief). (1995). *Merriam-Webster's collegiate dictionary* (10th ed.). Springfield, MA: Merriam-Webster.

Mish, F. C. (Editor-in-chief). (2008). *Merriam-Webster's collegiate dictionary* (11th ed.). Springfield, MA: Merriam-Webster.

Mooney, L. A., Knox, D., & Schacht, C. (2009). *Understanding social problems* (6th ed.). Belmont, CA: Wadsworth.

Morrissey, T. W. (2007). Family child care in the United States. *Child Care and Early Education Research Connections.* Retrieved from http://www.researchconnections.org.

Morrow, C. A. (1987). Child and family homelessness. In J. E. Kyle (Ed.), *Children, families & cities: Programs that work at the local level* (pp. 109–156). Washington, DC: National League of Cities.

Mosely, J. E. (2009). Policy advocacy and lobbying in human services organizations. In R. J. Patti (Ed.), *The handbook of human services management* (2nd ed., pp. 455–470). Thousand Oaks, CA: Sage.

Motenko, A. K. (1989). The frustrations, gratifications, and well-being of dementia caregivers. *Gerontologist, 29*(2), 166–172.

Muckian, M. (1994). TQM bumps and bruises. *Business* (June), 20–35, 39.

Murphy, B. C., & Dillon, C. (2008). *Interviewing in action in a multicultural world* (3rd ed.). Belmont, CA: Brooks/Cole.

National Association of Social Workers. (1999). *NASW Code of Ethics* (amended). Washington, DC: Author.

National Association of Social Workers. (2008). *Code of Ethics.* Washington, DC: Author.

National Association of Social Workers. (2009). *Social work speaks: National Association of Social Workers policy statements 2009–2012* (8th ed.). Washington, DC: NASW Press.

National Center for Economic and Security Alternatives. (2007). Models and innovations: International community-building models. Retrieved from http://www.ncesa.org/html/intermodels.html.

National Clearinghouse on Child Abuse and Neglect Information. (2004). *Systems, networks, and teams.* Washington, DC: Author. Available online at http://nccanch.acf.hhs.gov/pubs/usermanuals/subscare/systems.cfm#networks.

National Drug Intelligence Center. (2003). Crystal methamphetamine fast facts. Retrieved from http://www.usdoj.gov/ndic/pubs5/5049/index.htm.

National Network for Immigrant and Refugee Rights (NNIRR). (2009, December 2). Home page. Retrieved from http://www.nnirr.org.

Nelson, D. L., & Quick, J. C. (2009). *ORGB.* Mason, OH: South-Western.

NetMBA. (2007). PERT. Retrieved from http://www.netmba.com/operations/project/pert.

Netting, F. E. (2008). Macro social work practice. In T. Mizrahi & L. E. Davis (Editors-in-Chief), *Encyclopedia of social work* (20th ed., Vol. 3, pp. 139–144). Washington, DC: NASW Press.

Netting, F. E., Kettner, P. M., & McMurtry, S. L. (2004). *Social work macro practice* (3rd ed.). Boston: Allyn & Bacon.

Netting, F. E., Kettner, P. M., & McMurtry, S. (2008). *Social work macro practice* (4th ed.). Boston: Allyn & Bacon.

Netting, F. E., & O'Connor, M. K. (2003). *Organization practice: A social worker's guide to understanding human services.* Boston: Allyn & Bacon.

Nichols, W. R. (Ed.). (1999). *Random House Webster's college dictionary.* New York: Random House.

Norman, E. (2000). Introduction: The strengths perspective and resiliency enhancement—A natural partnership. In E. Norman (Ed.), *Resiliency enhancement: Putting the strengths perspective into social work practice* (pp. 1–16). New York: Columbia.

North, C. S., & Smith, E. M. (1994). Comparison of white and nonwhite homeless men and women. *Social Work, 39*(6), 639–647.

Northouse, P. G. (2010). *Leadership: Theory and practice* (5th ed.). Thousand Oaks, CA: Sage.

Nugent, W. R. (2001). Mediation techniques for persons in disputes. In H. E. Briggs & K. Corcoran (Eds.), *Social work practice: Treating common client problems* (pp. 303–323). Chicago: Lyceum.

Nunnally, E., & Moy, C. (1989). *Communication basics for human service professionals.* Newbury Park, CA: Sage.

Nurius, P. S., & Hudson, W. W. (1993). *Human services practice, evaluation, and computers.* Pacific Grove, CA: Brooks/Cole.

Nybell, L. M., & Gray, S. S. (2004, January). Race, place, space: Meanings of cultural competence in three child welfare agencies. *Social Work, 49*(1), 17–26.

Office of Family Assistance. (2007). Welcome to the Office of Family Assistance. Retrieved from http://www.acf.hhs.gov/programs/ofa.

Ohmer, M. (2007). Citizen participation in neighborhood organizations and its relationship to volunteers' self and collective efficacy and sense of community. *Social Work Research, 31*(2), 109–120.

Olaveson, J., Conway, P., & Shaver, C. (2004). Defining rural for social work practice and research. In T. L. Scales & C. L. Streeter (Eds.), *Rural social work: Building and sustaining community assets* (pp. 9–20). Belmont, CA: Brooks/Cole.

Olpin, M., & Hesson, M. (2007). *Stress management for life: A research-based experiential approach.* Belmont, CA: Wadsworth.

O'Neill, J. W. (1999, September). Social work turns back to the spiritual. *NASW News,* p. 3.

Oxfam International. (2007). *A good practice of Oxfam International collaboration.* The Hague, Netherlands: Author.

Packard, T. (2009). Leadership and performance in human services organizations. In R. J. Patti (Ed.), *The handbook of human services management* (2nd ed., pp. 143–164). Thousand Oaks, CA: Sage.

Pack-Brown, S. P., & Williams, C. B. (2003). *Ethics in a multicultural context.* Thousand Oaks, CA: Sage.

Patti, R. J. (1983). Limitations and prospects of internal advocacy. In H. Weissman, I. Epstein, & A. Savage (Eds.), *Agency-based social work* (pp. 214–223). Philadelphia: Temple University Press.

Patti, R. J. (2008). Management: Overview. In T. Mizrahi & L. E. Davis (Editors-in-Chief), *Encyclopedia of social work* (20th ed., Vol. 3, pp. 148–158). Washington, DC: NASW Press.

Patti, R. J., & Resnick, H. (1980). Changing the agency from within. In H. Resnick & R. J. Patti (Eds.), *Change from within: Humanizing social welfare organizations* (pp. 217–230). Philadelphia: Temple University Press.

Pederson, P. B. (2008). Ethics, competence, and professional issues in cross-cultural counseling. In P. B. Pedersen, J. G. Draguns, W. J. Lonner, & J. E. Trimble (Eds.), *Counseling across cultures* (6th ed., pp. 5–20). Thousand Oaks, CA: Sage.

Perrow, C. A. (1961). The analysis of goals in complex organizations. *American Sociological Review, 26*(6), 856–866.

Pfeffer, J. (1981). *Power in organizations.* Marshfield, MA: Pitman.

Pincus, A., & Minahan, A. (1973). *Social work practice: Model and method.* Itasca, IL: Peacock.

Pittman, K. J., Adams-Taylor, S., & Morich, M. (1987). Adolescent pregnancy prevention. In J. E. Kyle (Ed.), *Children, families & cities: Programs that work at the local level* (pp. 157–194). Washington, DC: National League of Cities.

Poertner, J. (2008). Management: Quality assurance. In T. Mizrahi & L. E. Davis (Editors-in-Chief), *Encyclopedia of social work* (20th ed., Vol. 3, pp. 180–183). Washington, DC: NASW Press.

Poertner, J. (2009). Managing for service outcomes: The critical role of information. In R. J. Patti (Ed.), *The handbook of human services management* (2nd ed., pp. 165–181). Thousand Oaks, CA: Sage.

Popple, P. R. (1995). The social work profession: History. In R. L. Edwards (Editor-in-Chief), *Encyclopedia of social work* (19th ed., Vol. 3, pp. 2282–2292). Washington, DC: NASW Press.

Popple, P. R., & Leighninger, L. (2008). *The policy-based profession: An introduction to social welfare policy analysis for social workers* (4th ed.). Boston: Allyn & Bacon.

Posavac, E. J., & Carey, R. G. (1997). *Program evaluation* (5th ed.). Upper Saddle River, NJ: Prentice-Hall.

Potocky, M. (2008). Immigrants and refugees. In T. Mizrahi & L. E. Davis (Editors-in-Chief), *Encyclopedia of Social Work, Vol. 2* (pp. 441–445). Washington, DC: NASW Press.

Potocky-Tripodi, M. (2002). *Best practices for social work with refugees & immigrants.* New York: Columbia.

Powell, G. N., & Graves, L. M. (2003). *Women and men in management* (3rd ed.). Thousand Oaks, CA: Sage.

Proehl, R. A. (2001). *Organizational change in the human services.* Thousand Oaks, CA: Sage.

Pruchno, R. A., & Resch, N. L. (1989). Husbands and wives as caregivers: Antecedents of depression and burden. *Gerontologist, 29*(2), 159–165.

Quittner, J. (1997). Invasion of privacy. *Time,* August 25, pp. 29–35.

Raneri, L. G., & Wiemann, C. M. (2007). Social ecological predictors of repeat adolescent pregnancy. *Perspectives on Sexual & Reproductive Health, 39*(1), 39–47.

Rathus, S. A., Nevid, J. S., & Fichner-Rathus, L. (2008). *Human sexuality in a world of diversity* (7th ed.). Boston: Allyn & Bacon.

Reamer, F. G. (1987). Values and ethics. In A. Minahan (Editor-in-Chief), *Encyclopedia of social work* (18th ed., Vol. 2, pp. 801–809). Silver Spring, MD: National Association of Social Workers.

Reamer, F. G. (1990). *Ethical dilemmas in social service* (2nd ed.). New York: Columbia University Press.

Reamer, F. G. (1999). *Social work values and ethics* (2nd ed.). New York: Columbia.

Reamer, F. G. (2006). *Ethical standards in social work: A review of the NASW Code of Ethics* (2nd ed.). Washington, DC: NASW Press.

Reid, B. (1997, July 25). Neighbors find unity powerful. *The Arizona Republic,* Community pp. 1–2.

Renzetti, C. M., & Curran, D. J. (2003). *Women, men, and society* (5th ed.). Boston: Allyn & Bacon.

Resnick, H. (1980a). Effecting internal change in human service organizations. In H. Resnick & R. J. Patti (Eds.), *Change from within: Humanizing social welfare organizations* (pp. 187–199). Philadelphia: Temple University Press.

Resnick, H. (1980b). Tasks in changing the organization from within. In H. Resnick & R. J. Patti (Eds.), *Change from within: Humanizing social welfare organizations* (pp. 200–216). Philadelphia: Temple University Press.

Resnick, H., & Patti, R. J. (Eds.). (1980). *Change from within: Humanizing social welfare institutions.* Philadelphia: Temple University Press.

Rhein, R. (1996). Dollars and grants. *The Journal of NIH Research, 8,* 229–230.

Robert, H. M. (2000). *Robert's Rules of Order revised* (10th ed.). Cambridge, MA: Perseus.

Rogers, J. K., & Henson, K. D. (2007). "Hey, why don't you wear a shorter skirt?" In S. M. Shaw & J. Lee, *Women's voices, feminist visions: Classic and contemporary readings* (3rd ed., pp. 486–497). Boston: McGraw-Hill.

Rompf, E. L., & Royse, D. (1994). Choice of social work as a career: Possible influences. *Journal of Social Work Education, 30*(2), 163–171.

Rose, S. J. (1999). Social workers as municipal legislators: Potholes, garbage, and social activism. *Journal of Community Practice, 6*(4), 1–16.

Rospenda, K. M., Richman, J. A., Ehmke, J. L. Z., & Zlatoper, K. W. (2005). Is workplace harassment hazardous to your health? *Journal of Business and Psychology, 20*(1), 95–110.

Ross, J. W. (1995). Hospital social work. In R. L. Edwards (Editor-in-Chief), *Encyclopedia of social work* (19th ed., Vol. 2, pp. 1365–1377). Washington, DC: NASW Press.

Rothman, J. (1984). Introduction. In F. M. Cox, J. L. Erlich, J. Rothman, & J. E. Tropman (Eds.), *Tactics and techniques of community practice* (2nd ed.). Itasca, IL: Peacock.

Rothman, J. (2001). Approaches to community intervention. In J. Rothman, J. L. Erlich, & J. E. Tropman (Eds.), *Strategies of community intervention* (6th ed., pp. 27–64). Itasca, IL: F. E. Peacock.

Rothman, J. (2007). Multi modes of intervention at the macro level. *Journal of Community Practice, 15*(4), 11–40.

Rothman, J., Erlich, J. L., & Teresa, J. G. (1981). *Changing organizations and community programs.* Beverly Hills: Sage.

Rothman, J., & Tropman, J. (1987). Models of community organization and macro practice perspectives: Their mixing and phasing. In F. M. Cox, J. O. Erlich, J. Rothman, & J. Tropman (Eds.), *Strategies of community organization* (6th ed., pp. 3–26). Itasca, IL: Peacock.

Rothman, J., & Zald, M. N. (2001). Planning and policy practice. In J. Rothman, J. L. Erlich, & J. E. Tropman, *Strategies of community intervention* (6th ed., pp. 298–311). Itasca, IL: Peacock.

Rothman, J., & Zald, M. N. (2008). Planning and policy practice. In J. Rothman, J. L. Erlich, & J. E. Tropman (Eds.), *Strategies of community intervention* (7th ed., pp. 171–186). Peosta, IA: Eddie Bowers.

Rowland, A. M. (2006). Neighborhood organizations, local accountability and the rule of law in two Mexican municipalities. *Working Paper Series, Issue Number 8.* San Diego: UCSD Center for US-Mexican Studies and USD Trans-Border Institute.

Royse, D. (2004). *Research methods in social work* (4th ed.). Pacific Grove, CA: Brooks/Cole.

Rubin, A., & Babbie, E. (2010). *Essential research methods for social work* (2nd ed.). Belmont, CA: Brooks/Cole.

Rubin, H. J., & Rubin, I. S. (1986). *Community organizing and development.* Columbus, OH: Merrill.

Rubin, H. J., & Rubin, I. S. (1992). *Community organizing and development* (2nd ed.). Columbus, OH: Merrill.

Rubin, H. J., & Rubin, I. S. (2001). *Community organizing and development* (3rd ed.). Boston: Allyn & Bacon.

Rubin, H. J., & Rubin, I. S. (2008). *Community organizing and development* (4th ed.). Boston: Allyn & Bacon.

Ryan, S., Franzetta, K., & Manlove, J. (2005). Hispanic teen pregnancy and birth rates: Looking behind the numbers. *Child Trends Research Brief.* Washington, DC: Child Trends.

Rynecki, D., Smith, T., Shanley, M., & Wheat, A. (2003, August 11). Field guide to power. *Fortune,* 126–127.

Saenz, R. (2005). *Beyond New Orleans: The social and economic isolation of urban African Americans.*

Population Reference Bureau Report. Washington, DC: Population Reference Bureau.

Saleebey, D. (2009). *The strengths perspective in social work practice* (5th ed.). Boston: Allyn & Bacon.

Saltzman, A., & Furman, D. M. (1999). *Law in Social Work Practice* (2nd ed.). Chicago: Nelson-Hall.

Sashkin, M., & Kiser, K. J. (1993). *Putting total quality management to work: What TQM means, how to use it and how to sustain it over the long run.* San Francisco: Berrett-Koehler.

Scales, T. L., & Streeter, C. L. (Eds.). (2004). *Rural social work.* Belmont, CA: Brooks/Cole.

Schafer, W. (1998). *Stress management for wellness* (4th ed.). Belmont, CA: Wadsworth.

Schiller, P. (2005). *Information technology for social work.* Boston: Allyn & Bacon.

Schmid, H. (2009). Agency-environment relations. In R. J. Patti (Ed.), *The handbook of human services management* (2nd ed., pp. 411–433). Thousand Oaks, CA: Sage.

Schneider, R. L., Lester, L., & Ochieng, J. (2008). Advocacy. In T. Mizrahi & L. E. Davis (Editors-in-Chief), *Encyclopedia of Social Work, Vol. 1* (pp. 59–65). Washington, DC: NASW Press.

Schram, B. (1997). *Creating small scale social programs: Planning, implementation, and evaluation.* Thousand Oaks, CA: Sage.

Schriver, J. M. (2004). *Human behavior and the social environment* (4th ed.). Boston: Allyn & Bacon.

Schroeder, J., Guin, C. C., Pogue, R., & Bordelon, D. (2006). Mitigating circumstances in death penalty decisions: Using evidence-based research to inform social work practice in capital trials. *Social Work, 51*(4), 355–364.

Schwartz, W. (1961). The social worker in the group. In W. Schwartz (Ed.), *New perspectives on services to groups: Theory, organization, practice* (pp. 104–111). New York: National Association of Social Workers.

Selye, H. (1956). *The stress of life.* New York: McGraw-Hill.

Senge, P. (1990). *The fifth discipline: The art and practice of learning organizations.* New York: Doubleday/Currency.

Sharf, R. S. (2000). *Theories of psychotherapy & counseling: Concepts and cases* (2nd ed.). Pacific Grove, CA: Brooks/Cole.

Sheafor, B. W., & Horejsi, C. R. (2003). *Techniques and guidelines for social work practice* (6th ed.). Boston: Allyn & Bacon.

Sheafor, B. W., & Horejsi, C. R. (2006). *Techniques and guidelines for social work practice* (7th ed.). Boston: Allyn & Bacon.

Sheafor, B. W., & Horejsi, C. R. (2008). *Techniques and guidelines for social work practice* (8th ed.). Boston: Allyn & Bacon.

Shebib, B. (2003). *Choices: Counseling skills for social workers and other professionals.* Boston: Allyn & Bacon.

Sherman, A., & Shapiro, I. (2005). *Essential facts about the victims of Hurricane Katrina.* Washington, DC: Center for Budget and Policy Priorities.

Sickmund, M. (2003). Juveniles in court. *Juvenile offenders and victims: National Report Series Bulletin,* 1. Washington, DC: Office of Juvenile Justice and Delinquency Prevention.

Siegel, L. M., Attkisson, C. C., & Carson, L. G. (2001). Need identification and program planning in the community context. In J. E. Tropman, J. L. Erlich, & J. Rothman (Eds.), *Tactics & techniques of community intervention* (4th ed., pp. 105–129). Itasca, IL: Peacock.

Simon, B. L. (1994). *The empowerment tradition in American social work.* New York: Columbia University Press.

Simpson, C., & Simpson, D. (1992). *Exploring careers in social work.* New York: Rosen Publishing Group.

Sims, C. S., Drasgow, F., & Fitgerals, L. F. (2005). The effects of sexual harassment on turnover in the military: Time-dependent modeling. *Journal of Applied Psychology, 90*(6), 1141–1152.

Sinclair, L. (1993). Making ethical decisions. In K. K. Kirst-Ashman & G. H. Hull, Jr. (Eds.), *Understanding generalist practice* (pp. 372–397). Chicago: Nelson-Hall.

Sipe, J. W., & Frick, D. M. (2009). *Seven pillars of servant leadership: Practicing the wisdom of leading by serving.* New York: Paulist Press.

Siporin, M. (1975). *Introduction to social work practice.* New York: Macmillan.

Sluyter, G. V. (1998). *Improving organizational performance: A practical guidebook for the human services field.* Thousand Oaks, CA: Sage.

Smith, R. F. (1995). Settlements and neighborhood centers. In R. L. Edwards (Editor-in-Chief), *Encyclopedia of social work* (19th ed., Vol. 3, pp. 2129–2135). Washington, DC: NASW Press.

Smith, T. W. (1987). *Public attitudes toward cities and urban problems.* Washington, DC: National League of Cities.

Southern Poverty Law Center. (2007). Close to slavery: Guestworker programs in the United States. Montgomery, AL: Author.

Southern Poverty Law Center. (2009). Under siege: Life for low-income Latinos in the South. Retrieved from http://www.splcenter.org/news/item.jsp?aid=375.

Specht, H. (1969). Disruptive tactics. *Social Work, 14*(2), 5–15.

Spoonley, P. (2006/2007, March/April). Immigrants face employment discrimination. *Human Resources Magazine, 7.*

Stein, T. J. (2004). *The role of law in social work practice and administration.* New York: Columbia University Press.

Stephens, G. (1997, March/April). Youth at risk: Saving the world's most precious resource. *The Futurist,* 1–7.

Stier, K. (2009, March 24). Getting the juvenile-justice system to grow up. Retrieved from http://www.time.com/time/nation/article/0,8599,1887182,00.html.

Stout, K. D., & McPhail, B. (1998). *Confronting sexism and violence against women: A challenge for social work.* New York: Longman.

Stratton, T. D., McLaughlin, M. A., Witte, F. M., Fosson, S. E., & Nora, L. M. (2005). Does students' exposure to gender discrimination and sexual harassment in medical school affect specialty choice and residency program selection? *Academic Medicine, 80*(4), 400–408.

Strom-Gottfried, K. (1998). Applying a conflict resolution framework to disputes in managed care. *Social Work, 43*(5), 393–401.

Stuart, P. (2004). Social welfare and rural people. In T. L. Scales & C. L. Streeter (Eds.), *Rural social work: Building and sustaining community assets* (pp. 21–33). Belmont, CA: Brooks/Cole.

Stuart, P. (2008). Social work profession: History. In T. Mizrahi & L. E. Davis (Editors-in-Chief), *Encyclopedia of social work* (20th ed., Vol. 4, pp. 156–164). Washington, DC: NASW Press.

Sue, D. W. (2006). *Multicultural social work practice.* Hoboken, NJ: Wiley.

Suicide Reference Library. (2004). Friends of Indians–health fact sheet. Retrieved from http://www.suicidereferencelibrary.com/test4~id~596.php: Suicide Awareness, Support, and Education.

Swim, J. K., Johnston, K., & Pearson, N. B. (2009). Daily experiences with heterosexism: Relations between heterosexist hassles and psychological well-being. *Journal of Social and Clinical Psychology, 28*(5), 597–629.

Syme, G. (2003). *Dual relationships in counseling & psychotherapy.* Thousand Oaks, CA: Sage.

Tangenberg, K. M. (2005). Faith-based human services initiatives: Considerations for social work practice and theory. *Social Work, 50*(3), 197–206.

Tanser, F., Gijsbertsen, B., & Herbst, K. (2006). Modeling and understanding primary health care accessibility and utilization rural South Africa: An exploration using a geographical information system. *Social Science & Medicine, 63*(3), 691–705.

Texas Workforce Commission. (2004, May 10). Charitable choice bulletin board: Frequently asked questions. Retrieved from http://www.twc.state.tx.us/svcs/charchoice/ccfaq.html.

Thompson, B. (2010). Multiracial feminism. In G. Kirk & M. Okazawa-Rey (Eds.), *Women's lives: Multicultural perspectives* (5th ed., pp. 38–49). Boston: McGraw-Hill.

Thompson, M. S., & Peebles-Wilkins, W. (1992). The impact of formal, informal and societal support networks on the psychological well-being of black adolescent mothers. *Social Work, 37,* 322–329.

Tice, C. J., & Perkins, K. (2002). *The faces of social policy: A strengths perspective.* Pacific Grove, CA: Brooks/Cole.

Ting-Toomey, S., & Chung, L. C. (2005). *Understanding intercultural communication.* Los Angeles: Roxbury.

Torres, G. W., & Margolin, F. S. (2003). *The collaboration primer.* Chicago: Health, Research and Education Trust.

Toseland, R. W., & Rivas, R. F. (2005). *An introduction to group work practice* (5th ed.). Boston: Allyn & Bacon.

Toseland, R. W., & Rivas, R. F. (2009). *An introduction to group work practice* (6th ed.). Boston: Allyn & Bacon.

Tripodi, T., & Lalayants, M. (2008). Research: Overview. In T. Mizrahi & L. E. Davis (Editors-in-Chief), *Encyclopedia of social work* (20th ed., Vol. 3, pp. 512–520). Washington, DC: NASW Press.

Tropman, J. E., Johnson, H. R., & Tropman, E. J. (1992). *Committee management in human services* (2nd ed.). Chicago: Nelson-Hall.

Tropman, J. E., & Morningstar, G. (1995). The effective meeting: How to achieve high-quality decisions. In J. E. Tropman, J. L. Erlich, & J. Rothman (Eds.) *Tactics and Techniques of Community Intervention* (3rd ed., pp. 412–426). Itasca, IL: Peacock.

Tropman, J. E., & Morningstar, G. (2001). The effective meeting: How to achieve high-quality decisions. In J. E. Tropman, J. L. Erlich, & J. Rothman (Eds.), *Tactics and techniques of community intervention* (4th ed., pp. 183–197). Itasca, IL: Peacock.

Tully, C. T. (2000). *Lesbians, gays, & the empowerment perspective.* New York: Columbia.

Tyuse, S. W., & Linhorst, D. M. (2005). Drug courts and mental health courts: Implications for social work. *Health & Social Work, 30*(3), 233–240.

UNICEF. (2007). *Child poverty in perspective: An overview of child well-being in rich countries.* Florence, Italy: Author.

United Nations (UN). (1948). *Universal declaration of human rights.* Adopted December 10, 1948. GA Res. 217 AIII (UN Doc. A/810). Retrieved on May 26, 2009 from http://www.un.org/Overview/rights.html

United Nations High Commissioner for Refugees (UNHCR). (2009, December 2). What we do. Retrieved from http://www.unhcr.org/pages/49c3646cbf.html

United Way of Salt Lake. (2007). *Community assessment 2007.* Salt Lake City, UT: Author.

U.S. Bureau of Justice Statistics. (2009). *Prison inmates at midyear 2008—statistical tables.* Washington, DC: U.S. Department of Justice.

U.S. Census Bureau. (1998). *Statistical abstract of the United States, 1997.* Washington, DC: Author.

U.S. Census Bureau. (2002). *Census 2000, summary file 1.* Washington, DC: Author.

U.S. Census Bureau. (2003). *Statistical abstract of the United States: 2003* (123rd ed.). Washington, DC: Author.

U.S. Census Bureau. (2005, August 30). *U.S. Census Bureau news.* Washington, DC: Author

U.S. Census Bureau. (2007). *The American community: American Indians and Alaska Natives: 2004.* Washington, DC: Author.

U.S. Census Bureau. (2008). *Statistical abstract of the United States: 2009* (128th ed.). Washington, DC: U.S. Department of Commerce.

U.S. Citizenship and Information Services (USCIS). (2009, December 2). Home page. Retrieved from http://www.uscis.gov/portal/site/uscis

U.S. Department of Health and Human Services. (2009). *More choices, better coverage: Health insurance reform and rural America.* Washington, DC: Author.

U.S. Equal Employment Opportunity Commission (EEOC). (2002). Facts about sexual harassment. Retrieved from http://www.eeoc.gov/facts/fs-sex.html.

U.S. Equal Employment Opportunity Commission (EEOC). (2009). Sexual harassment charges EEOC and FEPAs combined: FY 1997-FY 2008. Retrieved from http://www1.eeoc.gov//eeoc/statistics/enforcement/sexual_harassment.cfm?renderforprint=1.

Vandiver, V. L., (2008). Managed care. In T. Mizrahi & L. E. Davis (Editors-in-Chief), *Encyclopedia of Social Work, Vol. 3* (pp. 144–148). Washington, DC: NASW Press.

Vayda, E., & Bogo, M. (1991). A teaching model to unite classroom and field. *Journal of Social Work Education, 27*(3), 271–278.

Vecchio, R. P. (2006). *Organizational behavior* (6th ed.). Mason, OH: South-Western.

Vernon, R., & Lynch, D. (2000). *Social work and the web.* Pacific Grove, CA: Brooks/Cole.

Wallace, H. R., & Masters, L. A. (2006). *Personal development for life & work* (9th ed.). Mason, OH: South-Western.

Wamseley, G. L., & Zald, M. N. (1976). *The political economy of public organizations.* Lexington, MA: Heath.

Warren, R. (1978). *The community in America* (3rd. ed.). Chicago: Rand McNally.

Watkins, T. R. (2004). Natural helping networks: Assets for rural communities. In T. L. Scales & Wells, S. J., Merritt, L. M., & Briggs, H. E. (2009). Bias, racism and evidence-based practice: The case for more focused development of the child welfare evidence base. *Children and Youth Services Review, 31*(12), 1215–1356.

Wells, S. J., Merritt, L. M., & Briggs, H. E. (2009). Bias, racism and evidence-based practice: The case for more focused development of the child welfare evidence base. *Children and Youth Services Review, 31*(12), 1215–1356.

Wheelan, S. A. (2005). *Creating effective teams: A guide for members and leaders.* Thousand Oaks, CA: Sage.

White, S., & Featherston, B. (2005). Communicating misunderstandings: Multi-agency work as social practice. *Child and Family Social Work, 10,* 207–216.

Whitener, L. A. (2000). Developing a safety net for farm households. *Rural America, 15*(3), 32–43.

Williams, C. (2009). *Management* (5th ed.). Mason, OH: South-Western.

Williams, C. (2010). *MGMT* (2nd ed.). Mason, OH: South-Western.

Wolk, J. L., Pray, J. E., Kalkbrenner, L., & Propp, J. (1986). Alzheimer's disease in rural areas: Can informal networks meet the needs? *Human Services in the Rural Environment, 10*(3), 8–13.

X, Malcolm. (1965). *The autobiography of Malcolm X.* New York: Grove.

Yanke, J. A., & Vogelsand-Coombs, V. (2008). Strategic planning. In T. Mizrahi & L. E. Davis (Editors-in-Chief), *Encyclopedia of social work* (20th ed., Vol. 4, pp. 169–173). Washington, DC: NASW Press.

Yaskyte, K. (2008). Management: Practice interventions. In T. Mizrahi & L. E. Davis (Editors-in-Chief), *Encyclopedia of Social Work, Vol. 3* (pp. 158–163). Washington, DC: NASW Press.

Yegidis, B. L., & Weinbach, R. W. (2002). *Research methods for social workers* (4th ed.). Boston: Allyn & Bacon.

Yegidis, B. L., & Weinbach, R. W. (2006). *Research methods for social workers* (5th ed.). Boston: Allyn & Bacon.

Yessian, M. R., & Broskowski, A. (1983). Generalists in human service systems: Their problems and prospects. In R. M. Kramer & H. Specht (Eds.), *Readings in community organization practice* (pp. 180–198). Englewood Cliffs, NJ: Prentice-Hall.

Young, B. (1987). Comprehensive child care program. In J. E. Kyle (Ed.), *Children, families & cities: Programs that work at the local level* (pp. 45–49). Washington, DC: National League of Cities.

Zachary, E. (2000). Grassroots leadership training: A case study of an effort to integrate theory and method. *Journal of Community Practice, 7*(1), 71–94.

Zald, M. N. (1970). Political economy: A framework of comparative analysis. In M. N. Zald (Ed.), *Power in organizations* (pp. 221–261). Nashville, TN: The Vanderbilt University Press.

Zarot. S. H., Todd, P. A., & Zarit, J. M. (1986). Subjective burden of husbands and wives as caregivers: A longitudinal study. *Gerontologist, 26*, 260–266.

Ziesemer, C., Marcoux, L., & Marwell, B. E. (1994). Homeless children: Are they different from other low-income children? *Social Work, 39*(6), 658–668.

Zippay, A. (1994). Should today's community organizer use the tactics handed down from earlier generations? No. In M. J. Austin & J. I. Lowe (Eds.), *Controversial issues in communities and organizations* (pp. 119–124). Needham Heights, MA: Allyn & Bacon.

Name Index

Subject Index